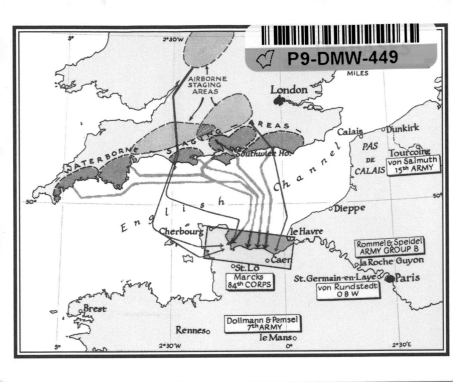

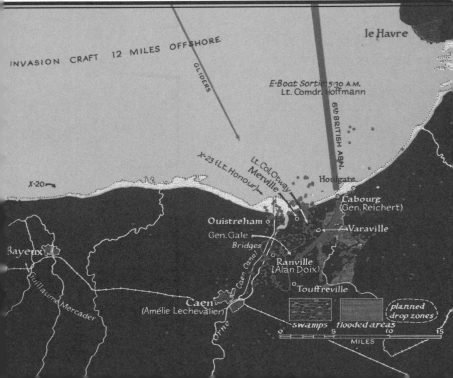

Library of America, a nonprofit organization,
champions our nation's cultural heritage
by publishing America's greatest writing in
authoritative new editions and providing resources
for readers to explore this rich, living legacy.

CORNELIUS RYAN

CORNELIUS RYAN

THE LONGEST DAY
A BRIDGE TOO FAR
OTHER WORLD WAR II WRITINGS

Rick Atkinson, *editor*

THE LIBRARY OF AMERICA

Cornelius Ryan:
The Longest Day, A Bridge Too Far
is published with support from

THE FLORENCE GOULD FOUNDATION

and

MALCOLM O'HAGAN

Contents

Introduction

CORNELIUS RYAN hoped to be buried among the American war dead in the military cemetery near Normandy's Omaha Beach, a place he called "my spiritual home," although he was neither a combatant nor an American when the invasion he later chronicled occurred on June 6, 1944. That hope was not to be; only members of the U.S. armed forces, and American civilians serving with the armed forces, who died during World War II can be buried there. Instead Ryan would find a more prosaic grave in suburban Connecticut, his adopted home as an Irish émigré, beneath a headstone with a one-word epitaph of his own choosing: "Reporter."

He chose well. Relentless, innovative reporting was key to Ryan's success as a nonfiction storyteller. There were a dozen or more correspondents in World War II as good or better than he was as a journalist, including A. J. Liebling, William L. Shirer, Ernie Pyle, John Hersey, Martha Gellhorn, and Alan Moorehead, a prolific Australian writer.[1] Several combatants and journalists published memoirs, meditations, or postwar accounts as evocative as anything Ryan ever wrote, among them E. B. Sledge, Bert Stiles, George MacDonald Fraser, and Chester Wilmot. Yet few modern writers on war have been more enduring, and none had greater commercial success, selling millions of books in two dozen languages with titles that became part of the vocabulary of the Second World War, notably *The Longest Day* and *A Bridge Too Far*.

His friend Herb Caen, a prominent newspaper columnist in San Francisco, called Ryan "the man who invented D-Day," and the British critic Malcolm Muggeridge considered him "perhaps the most brilliant reporter in the world." Certainly his meticulous research and taut narrative revived public interest in one of the most extraordinary events of the twentieth century. Like Bruce Catton and Barbara Tuchman, Ryan demonstrated that creditable, rigorous history could be written by

---

[1]To that list I might add Robert Sherrod, W. C. Heinz, Eric Sevareid, Don Whitehead, and Janet Flanner.

nonacademic historians for a wide audience. His battle books harnessed the skills he had learned as a journalist, particularly as an interviewer and a collator of information, while using techniques often associated with fiction—dialogue, interior monologue, the accretion of minute detail, and rapid, cinematic cutting from scene to scene. He foreshadowed literary journalists like Tom Wolfe, Joan Didion, and even Truman Capote, who claimed to have invented the nonfiction novel with *In Cold Blood* in 1966.

Ryan was a master of suspense, even when writing about events once known to every seventh-grader. All those pointillist brushstrokes of detail empower the reader's imagination, putting him or her in a combat glider over Normandy or on a muddy Dutch canal bank during an artillery barrage. His characters rarely have great depth, in part because there are so many of them; they tend to display a few elemental characteristics and a few primal emotions, anxiety and fear being preeminent. The battle books rely heavily, though by no means exclusively, on interviews, with all the perils inherent in human memory: selective amnesia, vainglory, and recollection distorted by time, shame, or the influence of other accounts. Ryan often quotes extended dialogue, no doubt the approximate recollection of witnesses rather than a precise transcription. As a narrator he remains offstage, rarely intruding with commentary or judgment. Events speak for themselves, and behavior reveals character.

"I am not actually writing about war. I use it only as a framework," he once declared. "I am writing about the human spirit in the midst of war—incredible courage, loyalty, hope, despair, and, all too often, ineptitude and bad management." Indeed, his great theme is the struggle for courage before and during battle, yet he never suggests that valor is commonplace. If he occasionally romanticizes certain aspects of the war, as in his zeal for the French Resistance, he does not write victors' history. Allied soldiers die from the folly and miscalculation of their leaders as well as from German bullets.

The veteran reporter never took a reader's indulgence for granted. "I need a cracklingly crisp first sentence that makes the reader want to go on to the next one," he explained. "And by the end of the first paragraph I've got to hook my reader or I am lost, and worse, I will have lost him." Ryan intended to write a pentalogy, five volumes about the European theater in 1944–1945. Although he only lived long enough to complete three of those books, he still succeeded in writing about history's most terrible bloodletting in a way that attracted a following as vast as the armies he helped to immortalize.

*   *   *

He was born in Dublin in 1920, and educated by the Christian Brothers on Synge Street. While studying violin at the Irish Academy of Music he also learned to tap dance and later formed his own dance band, the Hi-Lo Orchestra, to play at country inns and tennis clubs. At seventeen, by his own account "a particularly obnoxious—and I suppose insufferable —know-it-all," Ryan wrote two sonatas, two plays, four short stories, and a one-hour radio documentary intended for the BBC. In 1940 he moved to London, working as a management trainee in a Battersea biscuit factory and helping to feed thousands who took refuge every night in air raid shelters during the Blitz.

The Reuters news agency hired Ryan as a copyboy, but he soon moved to the *Daily Telegraph* as a reporter covering the U.S. Eighth and Ninth Air Forces, which flew missions from Britain against targets on the Continent. On D-Day, a day after turning twenty-four, he twice flew with B-26 bombers supporting the Allied invasion. The first flight aborted with mechanical problems five miles short of the French coast; returning to England, Ryan boarded another plane that attacked enemy targets just beyond the Normandy beaches. In subsequent weeks, he flew several times with squadrons trying to prevent German panzer reinforcements from reaching the beachhead. After one harrowing sortie through heavy flak, he described for his newspaper readers "a harsh grating noise and the sound of metal against metal. A piece of shrapnel had gone right through the blade of one of our propellers."

As Allied forces finally battered their way out of Normandy to race east across France, Ryan joined the ground troops, covering the U.S. First Army and then Lieutenant General George S. Patton's Third Army. His reporting made no pretense of neutrality, referring to "our troops," and writing of the enemy, "There is no escape for them. Our advance is too rapid." Some dispatches were ordinary or awkward. The stress of combat violence, rough living in the field, and simply getting a censored dispatch from the front to the home office on deadline rarely encouraged lyricism even when Ryan captured the immediacy of a liberated Frenchman waving a large tricolor or farmers continuing to work their fields despite the boom of nearby mortar and artillery shells.

Yet as the war edged east into Germany, his dispatches grew sharper in focus and in tone. In a Rhineland village, he reported that surrendering German civilians "will invariably tell you that they hate Hitler and that it was all a terrible mistake." At the liberated concentration camp in Ohrdruf he described murdered inmates "sprinkled with quicklime" and recounted how they "have been flogged to death, shot, tortured, and maltreated." As Patton's legions barreled into Czechoslovakia, Ryan wrote of a German general who shot himself in the head after signing a surrender document in Pilsen, "His wife stepped forward and wiped the blood from the General's face."

After the end of the war in Europe in May 1945, Ryan made his way to the Pacific, arriving in Japan shortly after the final capitulation and reporting on the aftermath of the atomic bombing of Hiroshima. Perhaps his finest dispatch, and among the war's most vivid, came after he accompanied American officers in Tokyo on September 11, 1945, as they arrested Tojo Hideki, Japan's bellicose prime minister from 1941 to 1944. Ryan was standing a few feet from Tojo when he shot himself in the chest but missed his heart. In a story datelined "by Tojo's bedside," he wrote, "Blood seeped across his shirt to his breeches. It seeped through the upholstery of the chair in which he was slumped and was gathering underneath in a large, spreading pool." Spangled with detail, the account described Tojo's costume—"white shirt, grey-blue military riding breeches and brown riding-boots"; his cigarette brand, Hope, with "finest Virginian" printed on the label; and various melodramatic utterances, including "Let MacArthur have my corpse . . . I wait for the righteous judgment of history." Periodically checking Tojo's pulse, Ryan scribbled notes in the room for nearly three hours until an American ambulance finally hauled the bleeding man to a hospital.[2] The *Daily Telegraph* proudly

---

[2]Ryan's Tojo story is printed in this volume on pp. 859–67.

noted that Ryan's dispatch had cost more than £250 ($1,000) to cable to London at "urgent" rates, making it "probably the most expensive newspaper message of the war." As for Tojo, he recovered from his wounds to be hanged as a war criminal in December 1948.

By then Ryan was long gone. The *Daily Telegraph* sent him to Jerusalem in 1946 to cover the conflict in Palestine between British troops and the Jewish underground. He moved to New York in 1947, writing for *Time*, *Life*, and later for *Newsweek*. In 1950 he married Kathryn Ann Morgan, an Iowa-born editor for Condé Nast Publications, and became an American citizen. Later that year *Collier's* magazine hired him to write long, expository pieces on subjects as varied as nuclear war and auto racing. "Remember that stupidity is your greatest asset," he later told aspiring journalists. "Don't be afraid to say that 'I don't understand.'" In composing a first draft, he also advised, "Start off with these two words: 'Dear Mother,' as though you are writing a letter home. It's amazing how it works." At times his enthusiasms got the better of him, as in his vigorous promotion of the spaceflight ambitions of Wernher von Braun, a former SS officer, Nazi Party member, and aerospace engineer whose V-2 rockets had killed thousands of civilians on behalf of the Third Reich. (A movie based on von Braun's life, *I Aim at the Stars*, inspired one wit to propose a caustic subtitle, "But Sometimes I Hit London.") As the German expatriate became a central figure in the American space program, Ryan served as his ghostwriter and, by Ryan's account, von Braun's "right arm, bag carrier, and above all, friend."

But the bigger canvas of long-form narrative also permitted his growth as a writer. If some pieces for *Collier's* were banal —"I Rode the World's Fastest Sub"—others were gripping and emotionally trenchant. "The Major of St. Lô" recounted how American troops had honored an officer killed in action in July 1944 by placing his flag-draped body on a rubble mound outside a battered Norman cathedral.[3] After the collision of two ocean liners off Nantucket in July 1956, which caused the sinking of the S.S. *Andrea Doria*, Ryan visited the lost vessel's sister ship for a precise sense of place, leading him to assert, for

---

[3]"The Major of St. Lô" is printed on pp. 868–75 of this volume.

example, that sixty-five steps led from the promenade deck to the bridge, three levels up. He interviewed survivors, amassed a 150,000-word research file, constructed a detailed chronology of the fatal voyage, then booked a room in the Waldorf Astoria hotel and in five days wrote a narrative focused on cabin number 56, where a doomed passenger on the *Andrea Doria* had been trapped by debris. *Collier's* reportedly sold nearly a million extra copies of that issue. His approach certainly owed something to Walter Lord's *A Night to Remember*, a 1955 best seller about the sinking of R.M.S. *Titanic*, but the writer Theodore H. White would observe that Ryan was experimenting with "a different style of narrative, the episode-by-episode recreation of large events."

He experimented further later that year with "One Minute to Ditch!," a fine-grained account of a Pan American airliner forced to make a water landing between Hawaii and California after two engines failed. That story would fill the cover of *Collier's* December 21, 1956, issue just as the magazine, hopelessly in debt, abruptly folded. Ryan took assignments for *McCall's*, *Sports Illustrated*, the *Saturday Evening Post*, and other publications, while confessing, "I loathe the insecurity of freelancing."

* * *

Since making a brief, nostalgic visit to Normandy in 1949, Ryan had contemplated writing about the first twenty-four hours of the invasion. "I see this as a carefully documented human narrative concerned only with ordinary people caught up in fear and crisis," he wrote. Kathryn agreed to support him and their two children as he began to research D-Day. He sought veterans by placing advertisements in magazines, newspapers, and even army camp bulletins. "Were You There on 6 June 1944?" one query asked. To those who replied he sent three pages of detailed questions, including, "Were you wounded?" and "In times of great crisis, people generally show great ingenuity or self-reliance; others do incredibly stupid things. Do you remember any examples of either?" To question number 3—"Where did you arrive in Normandy, and at what time?" —Wayne Patterson Bengel, a former paratrooper in the 101st Airborne Division, answered, "Jumped from C47 at 1:15 Am. in the morning, June 6, 1944. Sure of this time because my shockproof watch stopped upon the opening shock of the parachute." In the margin Ryan scribbled in pencil, "good."

As he accumulated more than a thousand questionnaires, Ryan and his assistants interviewed several hundred respondents and other witnesses in the United States, Canada, Britain, Germany, and France. On twelve hundred index cards, he constructed a chronology of the Allied landings, hour by hour and minute by minute. General Maxwell D. Taylor, a combat commander in Normandy who had become the U.S. Army's chief of staff, authorized his use of previously classified German war diaries, as well as Allied after-action reports down to company level. *Reader's Digest* agreed to underwrite his research in exchange for serial rights, but at times he despaired at the jumbled heap of information collected. "I do not know how I'm going to do this right now," he told Kathryn. To an editor at Simon & Schuster, which contracted to publish his book, he wrote, "I'm doing my best to abide by a single rule of thumb: accuracy . . . the men who died on both sides on D-Day deserve that much."

As a war correspondent he had helped compose the first rough draft of history; now, as a military historian, he lengthened and widened his lens to write a more enduring account. Fifteen years had passed since D-Day, allowing enough perspective to be comprehensive and veracious, telling the story from all sides, like a cyclorama, while also shifting his vantage from high to low, from headquarters war rooms to landing craft under fire. All those questionnaires and reports could hardly scratch the surface of the stupendous documentation accumulated during the war; by one estimate, the U.S. Army's records alone weighed seventeen thousand tons. Moreover, Ryan would write each of his battle books before the greatest secret of the war became public in 1974 with the disclosure of Ultra, the extraordinary British ability to intercept and decode many secret German military messages.

He confessed to "cold fear when the research for a book was finished. The subject material has always seemed greater than my ability to handle it." That diffidence notwithstanding, *The Longest Day* in less than three hundred pages told a story both panoramic and intimate. "Never had there been a dawn like this," he wrote of June 6, and never had there been a World War II history quite like this, a book that opened and

closed with the reader at the elbow of the senior German commander in Normandy, Field Marshal Erwin Rommel. Between
appearances by Rommel, General Dwight D. Eisenhower, and
a few other senior officers, the invasion was seen through the
previously anonymous soldiers and civilians whom Ryan called
his "kings." "Bash on! Bash on!" a British sergeant off Sword
Beach roars at his driver, but perhaps also at Ryan. The narrative pace is headlong, with some chapters as short as three
paragraphs and the final few pages shifting scenes more than a
dozen times.

Published in 1959, the book proved an enormous success.
Translations appeared in twenty-three languages, including Af-
rikaans, Hungarian, and Turkish. Not everyone was charmed;
Drew Middleton, military affairs correspondent for *The New
York Times*, called it "the Fifi-Dupont-was-washing-her-drawers-
when-the-American-tanks-arrived style of military history," in
which trifling details obscured larger themes. Nonetheless Ryan
estimated that he eventually received at least twenty thousand
fan letters from readers, including one from the daughter of a
D-Day casualty: "I am 27, and I never knew my father. He was
killed on Omaha Beach." Reading *The Longest Day*, she added,
dispelled the resentment she felt at his absence. "I cried because I love him, and he might have loved me. I cried, too, because his life was over before mine ever really began, yet he gave
me my life. Thank you for giving me my father after all these
years."

Time reported that at John F. Kennedy's inauguration on
January 20, 1961, the new president found common ground
with Eisenhower, his predecessor, in an animated, private discussion of *The Longest Day*. Ryan also wrote the screenplay for
the 1962 film version, a three-hour movie produced by Darryl
F. Zanuck—"one of the last of the great vulgarians," the author
complained—and starring John Wayne, Henry Fonda, Robert
Mitchum, Richard Burton, and other prominent stars. When
the film premiered in Paris, fifty French army tanks rolled past
the theater, fireworks erupted near the Eiffel Tower, and the
chanteuse Edith Piaf sang in celebration.

With help from Kennedy, his fellow Irish American, Ryan
soon began working on his next book. Rather than advance
chronologically through the campaigns of Western Europe,

he jumped to the end and the battle for Berlin in 1945, after
Kennedy asked Soviet authorities to let him conduct research
in Moscow. Again supported by *Reader's Digest*, Ryan interviewed top Red Army commanders and reviewed military archives to confirm mass rapes by marauding Soviet troops in
Germany. He compiled a "best anecdotes list" for each Berlin
neighborhood, recounting how Red Army rubes unscrewed
German lightbulbs to take home "under the impression that
they contained light and could be made to work anywhere.
Water faucets were yanked out of walls for the same reason."
He quoted Hitler's chauffeur about how after the Führer and
his mistress, Eva Braun, committed suicide, ventilation fans
above their Berlin bunker "picked up the smell of the burning
bodies and sucked it into the rooms. 'We could not get away
from it. It smelled like burning bacon.'"

   The Last Battle asserted that Eisenhower's political naiveté
prevented Anglo-American forces from capturing Berlin before the Soviets in the spring of 1945. That was a fatuous thesis,
unsupported by battlefield realities; it also ignored the political
agreement, reached by the Allied powers in 1944, to divide
conquered Germany and Berlin into postwar occupation zones
regardless of troop dispositions when victory came. The allegation wronged Eisenhower, whose political acumen was a primary reason for his appointment as Allied commander-in-chief
and a distinguishing characteristic in his success as a victorious
general. After the book's publication in 1966, Eisenhower, by
then a former two-term president, reportedly commented,
"How silly can a writer be?"[4] Still *The Last Battle* became a
best seller and would be translated into Arabic, Icelandic, and
twenty-one other languages. "A popular history at the top of

---

[4]Stephen E. Ambrose wrote a scathing review that ignited a bitter feud between the two popular historians: "Refighting the Last Battle: The Pitfalls
of Popular History," *Wisconsin Magazine of History*, vol. 49, no. 4 (Summer
1966). In a September 10, 1970, letter to S.L.A. Marshall, Ryan called Ambrose "opinionated and graceless." See also Mark Lewis, "Dueling D-Day
Authors: Ryan Versus Ambrose," *Forbes*, January 29, 2002, and Timothy D.
Rives, deputy director of the Dwight D. Eisenhower Presidential Library,
"Stephen Ambrose: A Rebuttal," July 19, 2010, blog post, "In the Service of
Clio," http://sarantakes.blogspot.com/2010/07/i-am-deputy-director-and
-supervisory.html (accessed November 5, 2018).

the form," *Kirkus Review* advised. "Be prepared. *The Longest Day* has sold 4,000,000 and this is even better."[5]

Ryan considered writing about Vietnam, the Kennedy assassination, the Irish uprising of 1916, and the Office of Strategic Services, wartime predecessor to the Central Intelligence Agency. Instead he took on his most ambitious battle project yet: the story of a star-crossed Allied attempt in September 1944 to outflank German defenses on the Rhine by capturing Arnhem, a Dutch riverine town, with both an overland assault from Belgium and the largest airborne operation of World War II. By now the war had Ryan in an iron grip. "I have no less than 7,000 books on every aspect of World War II," he told Herb Caen. "My maps alone could wallpaper at least two houses . . . You may think this is all a kind of a madness, an obsession." For the new book, provisionally titled *The Big Drop*, he again placed advertisements, collected questionnaires, interviewed hundreds of participants, and constructed a chronology of Operation Market Garden so granular that it filled, by his reckoning, "7 or 8 file cabinets."

Yet months passed, and then years with little progress on the manuscript. Ryan let himself be distracted, with speeches, lectures, screenplays, interviews, and a surprise fiftieth birthday party in June 1970 attended by journalist luminaries like Walter Cronkite and Art Buchwald, as well as General Omar N. Bradley. He admitted making "two hundred false starts" on his book, and by August 1971 had written only forty-seven pages.

In truth he was sick, mortally, with metastatic prostate cancer diagnosed shortly after that birthday extravaganza. Between fitful work on the book, now retitled *A Bridge Too Far*, he shuttled between oncologists in search of a cure, or at least palliative treatment. "The last three years have been very, very tough," he wrote Caen in June 1973. "My working hours have been cut down to almost two or three a day . . . I am three years late with it and the publishers are screaming, the advances have been spent and we are trying to keep our heads above water." In a plaintive postscript he added, "Summing it all up, Herb, I've always had the guts to fight back and I'm

---

[5]A memo to Ryan from his agent on October 3, 1968, noted that Simon & Schuster reported sales to date of 1,239,441 for *The Last Battle*.

continuing to do so, but between you and me your old pal is scared shitless."

In a display of fortitude worthy of his "kings," Ryan wrote the final 356 pages in five months, more than he had written in the previous three years. By that time cancer had spread to his shoulder, hip, and knee. Published in September 1974, the book would spend nineteen weeks on The New York Times Best Sellers list, and was translated into nineteen languages; a subsequent movie, directed by Richard Attenborough, featured James Caan, Michael Caine, Sean Connery, and Laurence Olivier. The gutful valor of combatants is fully acknowledged, yet *A Bridge Too Far* also evinces a certain bitterness, at the blameworthy planning behind Market Garden, at war's waste, and, perhaps, at his own encroaching mortality. Ryan cited one historical assessment—"the Allies had won a 50-mile salient— leading nowhere"[6]—as if wondering where the salient of the writing life had led.

"I suppose being only human I am hoping to get a Pulitzer with this book, or at least be cited for the three books," he confessed. In this he would have been disappointed—that year's Pulitzer Prize for history went to Dumas Malone for *Jefferson and His Time*, Vols. I–V—but Ryan lived long enough to accept the Legion of Honor from the French government and other accolades. Henry Steele Commager, among the most prolific and celebrated American intellectuals, described Ryan as "one of the great amateur historians. That doesn't mean he's not professional in his skills and techniques. [He is] amateur in the sense that he has not been taken in by the academy."

After his death, on November 23, 1974, Kathryn discovered that for more than four years her husband had secretly kept a detailed chronicle of his illness and the effort to finish his last work. She combined that material with her own extensive diary to write *A Private Battle*, a searing account of their joint struggle.

Veterans from the 82nd Airborne Division formed an honor guard at Ryan's funeral. Mourners included retired Lieutenant General James M. Gavin, who as a young officer had

---

[6]The assessment is from John C. Warren, *Airborne Operations in World War II, European Theater*, USAF Historical Division, 1956, p. 146.

parachuted into Normandy on June 6 and into Holland on September 17. Another veteran paratrooper recited the division's burial service for a fallen comrade. Cronkite read from *The Longest Day*, and a boys' choir sang "The Battle Hymn of the Republic." The man who to the end had "never seen myself as a writer but only as a journalist," was lowered into his reporter's grave.

Osmar White, an Australian journalist who had also covered the Third Army in Europe, wrote, "The living have the cause of the dead in trust."[7] So long as he lived, Ryan kept that trust. He keeps it still.

Rick Atkinson

[7]Osmar White, *Conqueror's Road*, p. ix (Cambridge University Press, 2003).

THE LONGEST DAY:

JUNE 6, 1944

For All the Men of D Day

CONTENTS

"Believe me, Lang, the first twenty-four hours of the invasion will be decisive . . . the fate of Germany depends on the outcome . . . for the Allies, as well as Germany, it will be the longest day."

—Field Marshal Erwin Rommel
to his aide, April 22, 1944

FOREWORD

D Day, Tuesday, June 6, 1944

OPERATION OVERLORD, *the Allied invasion of Europe, began at precisely fifteen minutes after midnight on June 6, 1944—in the first hour of a day that would be forever known as D Day. At that moment a few specially chosen men of the American 101st and 82nd airborne divisions stepped out of their planes into the moonlit night over Normandy. Five minutes later and fifty miles away a small group of men from the British 6th Airborne Division plunged out of their planes. These were the pathfinders, the men who were to light the dropping zones for the paratroopers and glider-borne infantry that were soon to follow.*

The Allied airborne armies clearly marked the extreme limits of the Normandy battlefield. Between them and along the French coastline lay five invasion beaches: Utah, Omaha, Gold, Juno and Sword. Through the predawn hours as paratroopers fought in the dark hedgerows of Normandy, the greatest armada the world had ever known began to assemble off those beaches—almost five thousand ships carrying more than two hundred thousand soldiers, sailors and coastguardmen. Beginning at 6:30 A.M. and preceded by a massive naval and air bombardment, a few thousand of these men waded ashore in the first wave of the invasion.

What follows is not a military history. It is the story of people: the men of the Allied forces, the enemy they fought and the civilians who were caught up in the bloody confusion of D Day—the day the battle began that ended Hitler's insane gamble to dominate the world.

5

PART ONE

THE WAIT

I

THE VILLAGE was silent in the damp June morning. Its name was La Roche-Guyon and it had sat undisturbed for nearly twelve centuries in a great lazy loop of the Seine roughly midway between Paris and Normandy. For years it had been just a place that people passed through on their way to somewhere else. Its only distinction was its castle, the seat of the Dukes de La Rochefoucauld. It was this castle jutting out from the backdrop of hills behind the village that had brought an end to the peace of La Roche-Guyon.

On this gray morning the castle loomed up over everything, its massive stones glistening with dampness. It was almost 6 A.M., but nothing stirred in the two great cobbled courtyards. Outside the gates the main road stretched broad and empty, and in the village the windows of the red-roofed houses were still shuttered. La Roche-Guyon was very quiet—so quiet that it appeared to be deserted. But the silence was deceptive. Behind the shuttered windows people waited for a bell to ring.

At 6 A.M. the bell in the fifteenth-century Church of St. Samson next to the castle would sound the Angelus. In more peaceful days it had had a simple meaning—in La Roche-Guyon the villagers would cross themselves and pause for a moment of prayer. But now the Angelus meant much more than a moment of meditation. This morning when the bell rang it would mark the end of the night's curfew and the beginning of the 1,451st day of German occupation.

Everywhere in La Roche-Guyon there were sentries. Huddled in their camouflage capes, they stood inside both gates of the castle, at road blocks at each end of the village, in pillboxes built flush into the chalk outcroppings of the foothills and in the crumbling ruins of an old tower on the highest hill above the castle. From up there machine gunners could see everything that moved in this, the most occupied village in all of occupied France.

Behind its pastoral front La Roche-Guyon was really a prison; for every one of the 543 villagers, in and around the area there were more than three German soldiers. One of these soldiers was Field Marshal Erwin Rommel, commander in chief of

Army Group B, the most powerful force in the German west. His headquarters was in the castle of La Roche-Guyon.

From here in this crucial fifth year of World War II, a tense, determined Rommel prepared to fight the most desperate battle of his career. Under his command more than half a million men manned defenses along a tremendous length of coastline —stretching almost eight hundred miles, from the dikes of Holland to the Atlantic-washed shores of the Brittany peninsula. His main strength, the Fifteenth Army, was concentrated about the Pas-de-Calais, at the narrowest point of the Channel between France and England.

Night after night, Allied bombers hit this area. Bomb-weary veterans of the Fifteenth Army bitterly joked that the place for a rest cure was in the zone of the Seventh Army in Normandy. Hardly a bomb had fallen there.

For months, behind a fantastic jungle of beach obstacles and mine fields, Rommel's troops had waited in their concrete coastal fortifications. But the blue-gray English Channel had remained empty of ships. Nothing had happened. From La Roche-Guyon, on this gloomy and peaceful Sunday morning, there was still no sign of the Allied invasion. It was June 4, 1944.

2

IN THE ground-floor room he used as an office, Rommel was alone. He sat behind a massive Renaissance desk, working by the light of a single desk lamp. The room was large and high-ceilinged. Along one wall stretched a faded Gobelin tapestry. On another the haughty face of Duke François de La Rochefoucauld—a seventeenth-century writer of maxims and an ancestor of the present Duke—looked down out of a heavy gold frame. There were a few chairs casually placed on the highly polished parquet floor and thick draperies at the windows, but little else.

In particular, there was nothing of Rommel in this room but himself. There were no photographs of his wife Lucie-Maria or his fifteen-year-old son Manfred. There were no mementos of his great victories in the North African deserts in the early days of the war—not even the garish field marshal's baton which

Hitler had so exuberantly bestowed upon him in 1942. (Only once had Rommel carried the eighteen-inch, three-pound gold baton with its red velvet covering studded with gold eagles and black swastikas: that was the day he got it.) There wasn't even a map showing the dispositions of his troops. The legendary "Desert Fox" remained as elusive and shadowy as ever; he could have walked out of that room without leaving a trace.

Although the fifty-one-year-old Rommel looked older than his years, he remained as tireless as ever. Nobody at Army Group B could remember a single night when he had slept longer than five hours. This morning, as usual, he had been up since before four. Now he too waited impatiently for six o'clock. At that time he would breakfast with his staff—and then depart for Germany.

This would be Rommel's first leave at home in months. He would go by car; Hitler had made it almost impossible for senior officers to fly by insisting that they use "three-engined aircraft . . . and always with a fighter escort." Rommel disliked flying anyway; he would make the eight-hour journey home, to Herrlingen, Ulm, in his big black convertible Horch.

He was looking forward to the trip, but the decision to go had not been an easy one to make. On Rommel's shoulders lay the enormous responsibility of repulsing the Allied assault the moment it began. Hitler's Third Reich was reeling from one disaster after another; day and night thousands of Allied bombers pounded Germany, Russia's massive forces had driven into Poland, Allied troops were at the gates of Rome—everywhere the great armies of the Wehrmacht were being driven back and destroyed. Germany was still far from beaten, but the Allied invasion would be the decisive battle. Nothing less than the future of Germany was at stake, and no one knew it better than Rommel.

Yet this morning Rommel was going home. For months he had hoped to spend a few days in Germany the first part of June. There were many reasons why he now believed he could leave, and although he would never have admitted it, he desperately needed rest. Just a few days earlier he had telephoned his superior, the aged Field Marshal Gerd von Rundstedt, Commander in Chief West, requesting permission to make the trip; the request had been immediately granted. Next he had made a courtesy call to Von Rundstedt's headquarters at St.-Germain-en-Laye, outside of Paris, to take his leave formally. Both Von Rundstedt and his chief of staff, Major General Günther Blumentritt, had been shocked at Rommel's haggard appearance. Blumentritt would always remember that Rommel looked "tired and tense . . . a man who needed to be home for a few days with his family."

Rommel *was* tense and edgy. From the very day he arrived in France toward the end of 1943, the problems of where and how to meet the Allied attack had imposed on him an almost intolerable burden. Like everybody else along the invasion front, he had been living through a nightmare of suspense. Hanging over him always was the need to outthink the Allies as to their probable intentions—how they would launch the attack, where they would attempt to land and, above all, when.

Only one person really knew the strain that Rommel was under. To his wife, Lucie-Maria, he confided everything. In less than four months he had written her more than forty letters and in almost every other letter he had made a new prediction about the Allied assault.

On March 30 he wrote: "Now that March is nearing its end and without the Anglo-Americans having started their attack . . . I'm beginning to believe they have lost confidence in their cause."

On April 6: "Here the tension is growing from day to day . . . It will probably be only weeks that separate us from the decisive events . . ."

On April 26: "In England morale is bad . . . there is one strike after another and the cries of 'Down with Churchill and the Jews' and for peace are getting louder . . . these are bad omens for such a risky offensive."

On April 27: "It appears now that the British and Americans are not going to be so accommodating as to come in the immediate future."

On May 6: "Still no signs of the British and Americans . . . Every day, every week . . . we get stronger. . . . I am looking forward to the battle with confidence . . . perhaps it will come on May 15, perhaps at the end of the month."

On May 15: "I can't take many more big [inspection] trips . . . because one never knows when the invasion will begin. I believe only a few more weeks remain until things begin here in the west."

On May 19: "I hope I can get ahead with my plans faster than before . . . [but] I am wondering if I can spare a few days in June to get away from here. Right now there isn't a chance."

But there was a chance after all. One of the reasons for Rommel's decision to leave at this time was his own estimate of the Allies' intentions. Before him now on the desk was Army Group B's weekly report. This meticulously compiled evaluation was due to be sent by noon of the following day to Field Marshal von Rundstedt's headquarters, or, as it was generally known in military jargon, OB West (*Oberbefehlshaber West*). From there after further embroidery it would become part of the over-all theater report and then it would be forwarded to Hitler's head-quarters, OKW (*Oberkommando der Wehrmacht**).

Rommel's estimate read in part that the Allies had reached a "high degree of readiness" and that there was an "increased volume of messages going to the French resistance." But, it went on, "according to past experience this is not indicative that an invasion is imminent . . ."

This time Rommel had guessed wrong.

3

IN THE OFFICE of the chief of staff, down the corridor from the Field Marshal's study, Captain Hellmuth Lang, Rommel's thirty-six-year-old aide, picked up the morning report. It was always his first chore for the commander in chief. Rommel liked to get the report early so that he could discuss it with his staff at breakfast. But there was nothing much in it this morning; the invasion front remained quiet except for the con-tinuing nightly bombing of the Pas-de-Calais. There seemed no doubt about it: Besides all the other indications, this mar-athon bombing pointed to the Pas-de-Calais as the place the Allies had chosen for their attack. If they were going to invade at all it would be there. Nearly everybody seemed to think so.

Lang looked at his watch; it was a few minutes of 6 A.M. They

*Armed Forces High Command.

would leave at seven sharp and they should make good time. There was no escort, just two cars, Rommel's and one belonging to Colonel Hans George von Tempelhof, Army Group B's operations officer, who was going along with them. As usual, the various military commanders in the areas through which they would pass had not been informed of the Field Marshal's plans. Rommel liked it that way; he hated to be delayed by the fuss and protocol of heel-clicking commanders and motorcycle escorts awaiting him at the entrance to each city. So with a bit of luck they should reach Ulm about three.

There was the usual problem: what to take along for the Field Marshal's lunch. Rommel did not smoke, rarely drank, and cared so little for food that he sometimes forgot to eat. Often when going over the arrangements for a long journey with Lang, Rommel would run a pencil through the proposed luncheon and write in big black letters "Simple field kitchen meal." Sometimes he would confuse Lang even more by saying, "Of course, if you want to throw in a chop or two that won't bother me." The attentive Lang never quite knew what to order from the kitchen. This morning, besides a vacuum jug of consommé, he had ordered an assortment of sandwiches. His guess was that Rommel, as usual, would forget about lunch anyway.

Lang left the office and walked down the oak-paneled corridor. From the rooms on either side of him came the hum of conversation and the clacking of typewriters; Army Group B headquarters was an extremely busy place now. Lang had often wondered how the Duke and the Duchess, who occupied the floors above, could possibly sleep through all the noise.

At the end of the corridor Lang stopped before a massive door. He knocked gently, turned the handle and walked in. Rommel did not look up. He was so engrossed in the papers before him that he seemed quite unaware that his aide had entered the room, but Lang knew better than to interrupt. He stood waiting.

Rommel glanced up from his desk. "Good morning, Lang," he said.

"Good morning, Field Marshal. The report." Lang handed it over. Then he left the room and waited outside the door to escort Rommel down to breakfast. The Field Marshal seemed extremely busy this morning. Lang, who knew how impulsive and changeable Rommel could be, wondered if they were really leaving after all.

Rommel had no intention of canceling the trip. Although no definite appointment had yet been made, he hoped to see Hitler. All field marshals had access to the Führer, and Rommel had telephoned his old friend, Major General Rudolf Schmundt, Hitler's adjutant, requesting an appointment. Schmundt thought the meeting could be arranged sometime between the sixth and the ninth. It was typical of Rommel that nobody outside of his own staff knew that he intended to see Hitler. In the official diaries at Rundstedt's headquarters, it was simply noted that Rommel was spending a few days' leave at home.

Rommel was quite confident that he could leave his headquarters at this time. Now that May had passed—and it had been a month of perfect weather for the Allied attack—he had reached the conclusion that the invasion would not come for several more weeks. He was so confident of this that he had even set a deadline for the completion of all anti-invasion obstacle programs. On his desk was an order to the Seventh and Fifteenth armies. "Every possible effort," it read, "must be made to complete obstacles so as to make a low-tide landing possible only at extreme cost to the enemy . . . work must be pushed forward . . . completion is to be reported to my headquarters by June 20."

He now reasoned—as did Hitler and the German High Command—that the invasion would take place either simultaneously with the Red Army's summer offensive, or shortly after. The Russian attack, they knew, could not begin until the late thaw in Poland, and therefore they did not think the offensive could be mounted until the latter part of June.

In the west the weather had been bad for several days, and it promised to be even worse. The 5 A.M. report, prepared by Colonel Professor Walter Stöbe, the Luftwaffe's chief meteorologist in Paris, predicted increasing cloudiness, high winds and rain. Even now a twenty- to thirty-mile-an-hour wind was blowing in the Channel. To Rommel, it seemed hardly likely that the Allies would dare launch their attack during the next few days.

Even at La Roche-Guyon, during the night, the weather had changed. Almost opposite Rommel's desk two tall French windows opened out onto a terraced rose garden. It was not much of a rose garden this morning—rose petals, broken branches and twigs were strewn all over. Shortly before dawn a brief summer storm had come out of the English Channel, swept along part of the French coast and then passed on.

Rommel opened the door of his office and stepped out. "Good morning, Lang," he said, as though he had not seen his aide until that moment. "Are we ready to go?" Together they went down to breakfast.

Outside in the village of La Roche-Guyon the bell in the Church of St. Samson sounded the Angelus. Each note fought for its existence against the wind. It was 6 A.M.

4

BETWEEN Rommel and Lang an easy, informal relationship existed. They had been constantly together for months. Lang had joined Rommel in February and hardly a day had passed since without a long inspection trip somewhere. Usually they were on the road by 4:30 A.M., driving at top speed to some distant part of Rommel's command. One day it would be Holland, another day Belgium, the next day Normandy or Brittany. The determined Field Marshal had taken advantage of every moment. "I have only one real enemy now," he had told Lang, "and that is time." To conquer time Rommel spared neither himself nor his men; it had been that way from the moment he had been sent to France in November 1943.

That fall Von Rundstedt, responsible for the defense of all Western Europe, had asked Hitler for reinforcements. Instead, he had got the hardheaded, daring and ambitious Rommel. To the humiliation of the aristocratic sixty-eight-year-old Commander in Chief West, Rommel arrived with a *Gummi-befehl*, an "elastic directive," ordering him to inspect the coastal fortifications—Hitler's much-publicized "Atlantic Wall"—and then to report directly back to the Führer's headquarters, OKW. The embarrassed and disappointed Von Rundstedt was so upset by the arrival of the younger Rommel—he referred to him as the "*Marschall Bubi*" (roughly, the "Marshal Laddie")

—that he asked Field Marshal Wilhelm Keitel, Chief of OKW, if Rommel was being considered as his successor. He was told "not to draw any false conclusions," that with all "Rommel's capabilities he is not up to that job."

Shortly after his arrival, Rommel had made a whirlwind inspection of the Atlantic Wall—and what he saw appalled him. In only a few places were the massive concrete and steel fortifications along the coast completed: at the principal ports and river mouths and overlooking the straits, roughly from above Le Havre to Holland. Elsewhere the defenses were in various stages of completion. In some places work had not even begun. True, the Atlantic Wall was a formidable barrier even in its present state. Where it was finished, it fairly bristled with heavy guns. But there were not enough of them to suit Rommel. There was not enough of anything to stop the sort of onslaught that Rommel—always remembering his crushing defeat at the hands of Montgomery in North Africa the year before—knew must surely come. To his critical eye the Atlantic Wall was a farce. Using one of the most descriptive words in any language, he had denounced it as a "figment of Hitler's *Wolkenkuckucksheim* [cloud cuckoo land]."

Just two years before, the wall had hardly existed at all.

Up to 1942 victory had seemed so certain to the Führer and his strutting Nazis that there was no need for coastal fortifications. The swastika flew everywhere. Austria and Czechoslovakia had been picked off before the war even started. Poland had been carved up between Germany and Russia as long ago as 1939. The war was not even a year old when the countries of Western Europe began falling like so many rotten apples. Denmark fell in a day. Norway, infiltrated from within, took a little longer: six weeks. Then that May and June, in just twenty-seven days and without overture of any sort, Hitler's blitzkrieging troops had plunged into Holland, Belgium, Luxembourg, France, and, as an incredulous world watched, had driven the British into the sea at Dunkirk. After the collapse of France all that remained was England—standing alone. What need had Hitler for a "wall"?

But Hitler didn't invade England. His generals wanted him to, but Hitler waited, thinking the British would sue for peace. As time passed the situation rapidly changed. With U.S. aid,

Britain began staging a slow but sure recovery. Hitler, by now deeply involved in Russia—he attacked the Soviet Union in June 1941—saw that the coast of France was no longer an offensive springboard. It was now a soft spot in his defenses. By the fall of 1941 he began talking to his generals about making Europe an "impregnable fortress." And in December, after the U.S. had entered the war, the Führer ranted to the world that "a belt of strongpoints and gigantic fortifications runs from Kirkenes [on the Norwegian-Finnish frontier] . . . to the Pyrenees [on the Franco-Spanish border] . . . and it is my unshakable decision to make this front impregnable against every enemy."

It was a wild, impossible boast. Discounting the indentations, this coastline running from the Arctic Ocean in the north to the Bay of Biscay in the south stretched almost three thousand miles.

Even directly across from Britain at the narrowest part of the Channel, the fortifications didn't exist. But Hitler had become obsessed with the fortress concept. Colonel General Franz Halder, then Chief of the German General Staff, well remembers the first time Hitler outlined his fantastic scheme. Halder, who would never forgive Hitler for refusing to invade England, was cool to the whole idea. He ventured the opinion that fortifications "if they were needed" should be constructed "behind the coastline out of range of naval guns," otherwise troops might be pinned down. Hitler dashed across the room to a table on which there was a large map and for a full five minutes threw an unforgettable tantrum. Pounding the map with his clenched fist he screamed, "Bombs and shells will fall here . . . here . . . here . . . and here . . . in front of the wall, behind it and on it . . . but the troops will be safe in the wall! Then they'll come out and fight!"

Halder said nothing, but he knew, as did the other generals in the High Command, that despite all the Reich's intoxicating victories the Führer already feared a second front—an invasion.

Still, little work was done on the fortifications. In 1942, as the tide of war began to swing against Hitler, British commandos began raiding the "impregnable" fortress of Europe. Then came the bloodiest commando raid of the war, when more than five thousand heroic Canadians landed at Dieppe. It was a bloody curtain-raiser to the invasion. Allied planners learned just how strongly the Germans had fortified the ports. The Canadians had 3,369 casualties, of which 900 were dead. The raid was disastrous, but it shocked Hitler. The Atlantic Wall, he thundered at his generals, must be completed at top speed. Construction was to be rushed "fanatically."

It was. Thousands of slave laborers worked night and day to build the fortifications. Millions of tons of concrete were poured; so much was used that all over Hitler's Europe it became impossible to get concrete for anything else. Staggering quantities of steel were ordered, but this commodity was in such short supply that the engineers were forced to do without it. As a result few of the bunkers or blockhouses had swiveling cupolas, which required steel for the turrets, and the arc of fire from the guns was thereby restricted. So great was the demand for materials and equipment that parts of the old French Maginot Line and Germany's frontier fortifications (the Siegfried Line) were cannibalized for the Atlantic Wall. By the end of 1943, although the wall was far from finished, over half a million men were working on it and the fortifications had become a menacing reality.

Hitler knew that invasion was inevitable, and now he was faced with another great problem: finding the divisions to man his growing defenses. In Russia division after division was being chewed up as the Wehrmacht tried to hold a 2,000-mile front against relentless Soviet attacks. In Italy, knocked out of the war after the invasion of Sicily, thousands of troops were still pinned down. So, by 1944, Hitler was forced to bolster his garrisons in the west with a strange conglomeration of replacements—old men and young boys, the remnants of divisions shattered on the Russian front, impressed "volunteers" from occupied countries (there were units of Poles, Hungarians, Czechs, Roumanians and Yugoslavs, to mention just a few) and even two Russian divisions composed of men who preferred fighting for the Nazis to remaining in prison camps. Questionable as these troops might prove to be in combat, they filled out the gaps. He still had a hard core of battle-hardened troops and panzers. By D Day Hitler's strength in the west would total a formidable sixty divisions.

Not all these divisions would be up to full strength, but

Hitler was still relying on his Atlantic Wall; that would make the difference. Yet men like Rommel who had been fighting —and losing—on other fronts were shocked when they saw the fortifications. Rommel had not been in France since 1941. And he, like many other German generals, believing in Hitler's propaganda, had thought that the defenses were almost completed.

His scathing denunciation of the "wall" came as no surprise to Von Rundstedt at OB West. He heartily concurred; indeed, it was probably the only time that he completely agreed with Rommel on anything. The wise old Von Rundstedt had never believed in fixed defenses. He had masterminded the successful outflanking of the Maginot Line in 1940 that had led to the collapse of France. To him Hitler's Atlantic Wall was nothing more than an "enormous bluff . . . more for the German people than for the enemy . . . and the enemy, through his agents, knows more about it than we do." It would "temporarily obstruct" the Allied attack, but it would not stop it. Nothing, Von Rundstedt was convinced, could prevent the initial landings from being successful. His plan to defeat the invasion was to hold the great mass of his troops back from the coast and to attack *after* the Allied troops had landed. That would be the moment to strike, he believed—when the enemy was still weak, without adequate supply lines and struggling to organize in isolated bridgeheads.

With this theory Rommel disagreed completely. He was positive that there was only one way to smash the attack: meet it head on. There would be no time to bring up reinforcements from the rear; he was certain that they would be destroyed by incessant air attacks or the massive weight of naval or artillery bombardment. Everything, in his view, from troops to panzer divisions, had to be held ready at the coast or just behind it. His aide well remembered a day when Rommel had summed up his strategy. They had stood on a deserted beach, and Rommel, a short, stocky figure in a heavy greatcoat with an old muffler around his throat, had stalked up and down waving his "informal" marshal's baton, a two-foot-long silver-topped black stick with a red, black and white tassel. He had pointed to the sands with his baton and said, "The war will be won or lost on the beaches. We'll have only one chance to stop the enemy and that's while he's in the water . . . struggling to get ashore. Reserves will never get up to the point of attack and it's foolish even to consider them. The *Hauptkampflinie* [main line of resistance] will be here . . . everything we have must be on the coast. Believe me, Lang, the first twenty-four hours of the invasion will be decisive . . . for the Allies, as well as Germany, it will be the longest day."

Hitler had approved Rommel's plan in general, and from then on Von Rundstedt had become merely a figurehead. Rommel executed Von Rundstedt's orders only if they agreed with his own ideas. To get his way he would frequently use a single but powerful argument. "The Führer," Rommel would remark, "gave quite explicit orders to me." He never said this directly to the dignified Von Rundstedt, but rather to OB West's chief of staff, Major General Blumentritt.

With Hitler's backing and Von Rundstedt's reluctant acceptance ("That Bohemian corporal, Hitler," snapped the Commander in Chief West, "usually decides against himself") the determined Rommel had set out completely to overhaul the existing anti-invasion plans.

In a few short months Rommel's ruthless drive had changed the whole picture. On every beach where he considered a landing possible he had ordered his soldiers, working with local conscripted labor battalions, to erect barriers of crude anti-invasion obstacles. These obstacles—jagged triangles of steel, saw-toothed gatelike structures of iron, metal-tipped wooden stakes and concrete cones—were planted just below high- and low-tide water marks. Strapped to them were deadly mines. Where there were not enough mines, shells had been used, their noses pointing ominously out to sea. A touch would cause them to explode instantly.

Rommel's strange inventions (he had designed most of them himself) were both simple and deadly. Their object was to impale and destroy troop-filled landing craft or to obstruct them long enough for shore batteries to zero in. Either way, he reasoned, the enemy soldiers would be decimated long before they reached the beaches. More than half a million of these lethal underwater obstacles now stretched along the coastline.

Still Rommel, the perfectionist, was not satisfied. In the sands, in bluffs, in gullies and pathways leading off the beaches, he ordered mines laid—all varieties, from the large pancake type, capable of blowing off a tank's tracks, to the small S mine which when stepped on bounded into the air and exploded level with a man's midriff. Over five million of these mines now infested the coast. Before the attack came, Rommel hoped to have another six million planted. Eventually he hoped to girdle the invasion coast with sixty million mines.*

Overlooking the coastline, back of this jungle of mines and obstacles, Rommel's troops waited in pillboxes, concrete bunkers and communication trenches, all surrounded by layers of barbed wire. From these positions every piece of artillery that the Field Marshal had been able to lay hands on looked down on sands and sea, already sighted in to give overlapping fields of fire. Some guns were actually in positions on the seashore itself. These were hidden in concrete emplacements beneath innocent-looking seaside homes, their barrels aimed not toward the sea but directly down the beaches, so as to fire at point-blank range along the waves of assaulting troops.

Rommel took advantage of every new technique or development. Where he was short of guns, he positioned batteries of rocket launchers or multiple mortar throwers. At one place he even had miniature robot tanks called "Goliaths." These devices, capable of carrying more than half a ton of explosives, could be guided by remote control from the fortifications down onto the beaches and detonated among troops or landing craft.

About all that was missing from Rommel's medieval arsenal of weapons were crucibles of molten lead to pour down on the attackers—and in a way he had the modern equivalent:

---

*Rommel was fascinated by mines as a defensive weapon. On one inspection trip with the Field Marshal, Major General Alfred Gause (Rommel's chief of staff before Major General Dr. Hans Speidel) pointed to several acres of wild spring flowers and said, "Isn't that a wonderful sight?" Rommel nodded and said, "You might make a note, Gause—that area will take about one thousand mines." And on yet another occasion when they were en route to Paris, Gause suggested that they visit the famous porcelain china works at Sèvres. Gause was surprised when Rommel agreed. But Rommel was not interested in the works of art he was shown. He walked quickly through the display rooms and, turning to Gause, said, "Find out if they can make waterproof casings for my sea mines."

automatic flame throwers. At some places along the front, webs of piping ran out from concealed kerosene tanks to the grassy approaches leading off the beaches. At the press of a button, advancing troops would be instantly swallowed by flame.

Nor had Rommel forgotten the threat of parachutists or glider-borne infantry. Behind the fortifications low-lying areas had been flooded, and into every open field within seven or eight miles of the coast heavy stakes had been driven and booby-trapped. Trip wires were strung between these posts. When touched, they would immediately set off mines or shells.

Rommel had organized a bloody welcome for the Allied troops. Never in the history of modern warfare had a more powerful or deadly array of defenses been prepared for an invading force. Yet Rommel was not content. He wanted more pillboxes, more beach obstacles, more mines, more guns and troops. Most of all he wanted the massive panzer divisions which were lying in reserve far from the coast. He had won memorable battles with panzers in the North African deserts. Now, at this crucial moment, neither he nor Rundstedt could move these armored formations without Hitler's consent. The Führer insisted on holding them under his personal authority. Rommel needed at least five panzer divisions at the coast, ready to counterattack within the first few hours of the Allied assault. There was only one way to get them—he would see Hitler. Rommel had often told Lang, "The last man who sees Hitler wins the game." On this leaden morning in La Roche-Guyon, as he prepared to leave for Germany and the long drive home, Rommel was more determined than ever to win the game.

5

AT FIFTEENTH Army headquarters near the Belgian border, 125 miles away, one man was glad to see the morning of June 4 arrive. Lieutenant Colonel Hellmuth Meyer sat in his office, haggard and bleary-eyed. He had not really had a good night's sleep since June 1. But the night that had just passed had been the worst yet; he would never forget it.

Meyer had a frustrating, nerve-racking job. Besides being the Fifteenth Army's intelligence officer, he also headed up the only counterintelligence team on the invasion front. The heart of his setup was a thirty-man radio interception crew who worked in shifts around the clock in a concrete bunker crammed full of the most delicate radio equipment. Their job was to listen, nothing more. But each man was an expert who spoke three languages fluently, and there was hardly a word, hardly a single stutter of Morse code whispering through the ether from Allied sources that they did not hear.

Meyer's men were so experienced and their equipment was so sensitive that they were even able to pick up calls from radio transmitters in military-police jeeps in England more than a hundred miles away. This had been a great help to Meyer. American and British MPs, chatting with one another by radio as they directed troop convoys, had helped him no end in compiling a list of the various divisions stationed in England. But for some time now Meyer's operators had been unable to pick up any more of these calls. This was also significant to Meyer; it meant that a strict radio silence had been imposed. It was just one more clue to add to the many he already had that the invasion was close at hand.

With all the other intelligence reports available to him, items like this helped Meyer develop a picture of Allied planning. And he was good at his job. Several times a day he sifted through sheaves of monitored reports, always searching for the suspicious, the unusual—and even the unbelievable.

During the night his men had picked up the unbelievable. The message, a high-speed press cable, had been monitored just after dark. It read: "URGENT PRESS ASSOCIATED NYK FLASH EISENHOWER'S HQ ANNOUNCES ALLIED LANDINGS IN FRANCE."

Meyer was dumfounded. His first impulse was to alert the headquarters staff. But he had paused and calmed down, because Meyer knew the message had to be wrong.

There were two reasons why. First, there was the complete absence of any activity along the invasion front—he would have known immediately if there had been an attack. Second, in January Admiral Wilhelm Canaris, then chief of German intelligence, had given Meyer the details of a fantastic two-part signal which he said the Allies would use to alert the underground prior to the invasion.

Canaris had warned that the Allies would broadcast hundreds

of messages to the underground in the months preceding the attack. Only a few of these would actually relate to D Day; the remainder would be fake, deliberately designed to mislead and confuse. Canaris had been explicit: Meyer was to monitor all these messages in order not to miss the all-important one.

At first Meyer had been skeptical. It had seemed madness to him to depend entirely on only one message. Besides, he knew from past experience that Berlin's sources of information were inaccurate ninety per cent of the time. He had a whole file of false reports to prove his point; the Allies seemed to have fed every German agent from Stockholm to Ankara with the "exact" place and date of the invasion—and no two of the reports agreed.

But this time Meyer knew Berlin was right. On the night of June 1, Meyer's men, after months of monitoring, had intercepted the first part of the Allied message—exactly as described by Canaris. It was not unlike the hundreds of other coded sentences that Meyer's men had picked up during the previous months. Daily, after the regular BBC news broadcasts, coded instructions in French, Dutch, Danish and Norwegian were read out to the underground. Most of the messages were meaningless to Meyer, and it was exasperating not to be able to decode such cryptic fragments as "The Trojan War will not be held," "Molasses tomorrow will spurt forth cognac," "John has a long mustache," or "Sabine has just had mumps and jaundice." But the message that followed the 9 P.M. BBC news on the night of June 1 was one that Meyer understood only too well.

"Kindly listen now to a few personal messages," said the voice in French. Instantly Sergeant Walter Reichling switched on a wire recorder. There was a pause, and then: "*Les sanglots longs des violons de l'automne*" [The long sobs of the violins of autumn]."

Reichling suddenly clapped his hands over his earphones. Then he tore them off and rushed out of the bunker for Meyer's quarters. The sergeant burst into Meyer's office and excitedly said, "Sir, the first part of the message—it's here."

Together they returned to the radio bunker, where Meyer listened to the recording. There it was—the message that Canaris had warned them to expect. It was the first line of

"Chanson d'Automne [Song of Autumn]" by the nineteenth-century French poet Paul Verlaine. According to Canaris' information, this line from Verlaine was to be transmitted on the "first or fifteenth of a month . . . and will represent the first half of a message announcing the Anglo-American invasion."

The last half of the message would be the second line of the Verlaine poem, "*Blessent mon coeur d'une langueur monotone* [Wounding my heart with a monotonous languor]." When this was broadcast it would mean, according to Canaris, that "the invasion will begin within forty-eight hours . . . the count starting at 0000 hours of the day following the transmission."

Immediately on hearing the recording of the first line from Verlaine, Meyer informed the Fifteenth Army's chief of staff, Major General Rudolf Hofmann. "The first message has come," he told Hofmann. "Now something is going to happen."

"Are you absolutely sure?" Hofmann asked.

"We recorded it," Meyer replied.

Hofmann immediately gave the alarm to alert the whole of the Fifteenth Army.

Meyer meanwhile sent the message by teletype to OKW. Next he telephoned Rundstedt's headquarters (OB West) and Rommel's headquarters (Army Group B).

At OKW the message was delivered to Colonel General Alfred Jodl, Chief of Operations. The message remained on Jodl's desk. He did not order an alert. He assumed Rundstedt had done so; but Rundstedt thought Rommel's headquarters had issued the order.*

Along the invasion coast only one army was placed on readiness: the Fifteenth. The Seventh Army, holding the coast of Normandy, heard nothing about the message and was not alerted.

On the nights of the second and third of June the first part of the message was again broadcast. This worried Meyer; according to his information it should have been broadcast only once. He could only assume that the Allies were repeating the alert in order to make sure it was received by the underground.

---

*Rommel must have known about the message; but from his own estimate of Allied intentions it is obvious that he must have discounted it.

Within the hour after the message was repeated on the night
of June 3, the AP flash regarding the Allied landings in France
had been picked up. If the Canaris warning was right, the AP
report must be wrong. After his first moment of panic, Meyer
had bet on Canaris. Now he was weary, but elated. The coming of the dawn and the continued peacefulness along the front
had more than proved him right.

Now there was nothing to do but wait for the last half of
the vital alert, which might come at any moment. Its awesome
significance overwhelmed Meyer. The defeat of the Allied invasion, the lives of hundreds of thousands of his countrymen, the
very existence of his country would depend on the speed with
which he and his men monitored the broadcast and alerted the
front. Meyer and his men would be ready as never before. He
could only hope that his superiors also realized the importance
of the message.

As Meyer settled down to wait, 125 miles away the commander of Army Group B was preparing to leave for Germany.

6

FIELD MARSHAL ROMMEL carefully spread a little honey on a
slice of buttered bread. At the breakfast table sat his brilliant
chief of staff, Major General Dr. Hans Speidel, and several
members of his staff. There was no formality. The table talk
was easy and uninhibited; it was almost like a family gathering
with the father sitting at the head of the table. In a way it was
a kind of close-knit family. Each of the officers had been hand-
picked by Rommel and they were devoted to him. All of them
this morning had briefed Rommel on various questions which
they hoped he would raise with Hitler. Rommel had said little.
He had simply listened. Now he was impatient to leave. He
looked at his watch. "Gentlemen," he said abruptly, "I must
go."

Outside the main entrance Rommel's chauffeur, Daniel,
stood by the Field Marshal's car with the door open. Rommel
invited Colonel von Tempelhof, besides Lang the only other
staff officer going with them, to ride with him in the Horch.
Tempelhof's car could follow behind. Rommel shook hands

with each member of his official family, spoke briefly to his chief of staff and then took his usual seat next to the chauffeur. Lang and Colonel von Tempelhof sat in the back. "We can go now, Daniel," said Rommel.

Slowly the car circled the courtyard and drove out through the main gate, passing the sixteen square-cut linden trees along the driveway. In the village it turned left onto the main Paris road.

It was 7 A.M. Leaving La Roche-Guyon on this particular dismal Sunday morning, June 4, suited Rommel fine. The timing of the trip could not have been better. Beside him on the seat was a cardboard box containing a pair of handmade gray suède shoes, size five and a half, for his wife. There was a particular and very human reason why he wanted to be with her on Tuesday, June 6. It was her birthday.*

In England it was 8 A.M. (There was one hour's difference between British Double Summer Time and German Central Time.) In a house trailer in a wood near Portsmouth, General Dwight D. Eisenhower, the Allied Supreme Commander, was sound asleep after having been up nearly all night. For several hours now coded messages had been going out by telephone, by messenger and by radio from his headquarters nearby. Eisenhower, at about the time Rommel got up, had made a fateful decision: Because of unfavorable weather conditions he had postponed the Allied invasion by twenty-four hours. If conditions were right, D Day would be Tuesday, June 6.

---

*Since World War II, many of Rommel's senior officers have stood shoulder to shoulder in an effort to alibi the circumstances surrounding Rommel's absence from the front on June 4 and 5 and for the best part of D Day itself. In books, articles and interviews they have stated that Rommel left for Germany on June 5. This is not true. They also claim that Hitler ordered him to Germany. This is not true. The only person at Hitler's headquarters who knew of Rommel's intended visit was the Führer's adjutant, Major General Rudolf Schmundt. General Walter Warlimont, then Deputy Chief of Operations at OKW, has told me that neither Jodl, Keitel nor himself was even aware that Rommel was in Germany. Even on D Day Warlimont thought that Rommel was at his headquarters conducting the battle. As to the date of Rommel's departure from Normandy, it was June 4; the incontrovertible proof lies in the meticulously recorded Army Group B War Diary, which gives the exact time.

7

LIEUTENANT COMMANDER GEORGE D. HOFFMAN, thirty-three-year-old skipper of the destroyer U.S.S. *Corry*, looked through his binoculars at the long column of ships plowing steadily across the English Channel behind him. It seemed incredible to him that they had got this far without an attack of some sort. They were on course and exactly on time. The crawling convoy, following a circuitous route and moving less than four miles an hour, had sailed more than eighty miles since leaving Plymouth the night before. But at any moment now Hoffman expected to meet trouble—U-boat or aircraft attack or both. At the very least he expected to encounter mine fields, for as every minute passed they were sailing farther into enemy waters. France lay ahead, now only forty miles away.

The young commander—he had "fleeted up" on the *Corry* from a lieutenant to skipper in less than three years—was immensely proud to be leading this magnificent convoy. But as he looked at it through his glasses he knew that it was a sitting duck for the enemy.

Ahead were the mine sweepers, six small ships spread out in a diagonal formation, like one side of an inverted V, each one trailing in the water, off to its right, a long saw-toothed wire sweep to cut through the moorings and detonate floating mines. Behind the mine sweepers came the lean, sleek shapes of the "shepherds," the escorting destroyers. And behind them, stretching back as far as the eye could see, came the convoy, a great procession of lumbering, unwieldy landing ships carrying thousands of troops, tanks, guns, vehicles and ammunition. Each of the heavily laden ships flew an antiaircraft barrage balloon at the end of a stout cable. And because these protective balloons, all flying at the same altitude, swung out in the face of the brisk wind, the entire convoy appeared to be listing drunkenly to one side.

To Hoffman it was quite a sight. Estimating the distance separating one ship from the next and knowing the total number of vessels, he figured that the tail end of this fantastic parade must still be back in England, in Plymouth Harbor.

And this was only one convoy. Hoffman knew that dozens of others had been due to sail when he did, or would leave

England during the day. That night all of them would converge on the Bay of the Seine. By morning an immense fleet of five thousand ships would stand off the invasion beaches of Normandy.

Hoffman could hardly wait to see it. The convoy that he led had left England early because it had the farthest to go. It was part of a massive American force, the 4th Division, destined for a place that Hoffman, like millions of other Americans, had never heard of before—a stretch of wind-blown sand on the eastern side of the Cherbourg peninsula that had been given the code name "Utah." Twelve miles to the southeast, in front of the seaside villages of Vierville and Colleville, lay the other American beach, "Omaha," a crescent-shaped strip of silvery strand where the men of the 1st and 29th divisions would land.

The *Corry*'s captain had expected to see other convoys near him this morning, but he seemed to have the Channel all to himself. He wasn't disturbed. Somewhere in the vicinity, he knew, other convoys attached to either "Force U" or "Force O" were sailing for Normandy. Hoffman did not know that because of the uncertain weather conditions a worried Eisenhower had permitted fewer than a score of slow-moving convoys to set sail during the night.

Suddenly the bridge telephone buzzed. One of the deck officers reached for it but Hoffman, who was closer, picked up the phone. "Bridge," he said. "This is the captain." He listened for a moment. "Are you quite sure?" he asked. "Has the message been repeated?" Hoffman listened a moment longer, then he replaced the receiver on its cradle. It was unbelievable: the whole convoy had been ordered back to England—no reason given. What could have happened? Had the invasion been postponed?

Hoffman looked through his glasses at the mine sweepers ahead; they hadn't changed course. Neither had the destroyers behind them. Had they received the message? Before doing anything else he decided to see the turnabout message for himself—he had to be sure. Quickly he climbed down to the radio shack one deck below.

Radioman Third Class Bennie Glisson had made no mistake. Showing his skipper the radio logbook, he said, "I checked it twice just to be certain." Hoffman hurried back to the bridge.

His job and that of the other destroyers now was to wheel this monstrous convoy around, and quickly. Because he was in the lead his immediate concern was the flotilla of mine sweepers several miles ahead. He could not contact them by radio because a strict radio silence had been imposed. "All engines ahead full speed," Hoffman ordered. "Close up on the mine sweepers. Signalman on the light."

As the *Corry* raced forward Hoffman looked back and saw the destroyers behind him wheel and swing around the flanks of the convoy. Now, with signal lights blinking, they began the huge job of turning the convoy around. A worried Hoffman realized that they were dangerously close to France—just thirty-eight miles. Had they been spotted yet? It would be a miracle if they got away with the turnabout undetected.

Down in the radio shack Bennie Glisson continued to pick up the coded postponement message every fifteen minutes. To him it was the worst news he had received in a long time, for it seemed to confirm a nagging suspicion: that the Germans knew all about the invasion. Had D Day been called off because the Germans had found out? Like thousands of other men Bennie did not see how the invasion preparations—the convoys, the ships, men and supplies that filled every port, inlet and harbor from Land's End to Portsmouth—could possibly have gone unnoticed by Luftwaffe reconnaissance planes. And if the message simply meant that the invasion had been postponed for some other reason, then it followed that the Germans had still more time to spot the Allied armada.

The twenty-three-year-old radio operator turned the dial of another set and tuned in Radio Paris, the German propaganda station. He wanted to hear sexy-voiced "Axis Sally." Her taunting broadcasts were amusing because they were so inaccurate, but you never could tell. There was another reason: The "Berlin Bitch," as she was often irreverently called, seemed to have an inexhaustible supply of the latest hit tunes.

Bennie didn't get a chance to listen because just then a long string of coded weather reports began coming in. But as he finished typing up these messages "Axis Sally" put on her first record of the day. Bennie instantly recognized the opening bars of the popular wartime tune "I Double Dare You." But new lyrics had been written for the song. As he listened, they confirmed his worst fears. That morning a little before eight Bennie and many thousands of Allied troops who had steeled themselves for the invasion of Normandy on June 5, and who now had another agonizing twenty-four hours to wait, heard "I Double Dare You" with these pertinent, if chilling, lines:

> *"I double dare you to come over here.*
> *I double dare you to venture too near.*
> *Take off your high hat and quit that bragging.*
> *Cut out that claptrap and keep your hair on.*
> *Can't you take a dare on?*
>
> *I double dare you to venture a raid.*
> *I double dare you to try and invade.*
> *And if your loud propaganda means half of what it says,*
> *I double dare you to come over here.*
> *I double dare you."*

8

IN THE HUGE Operations Center at Allied naval headquarters in Southwick House outside Portsmouth, they waited for the ships to come back.

The long, high room with its white-and-gold wallpaper was the scene of intense activity. One entire wall was covered by a gigantic chart of the English Channel. Every few minutes two Wrens, working from a traveling stepladder, moved colored markers over the face of the chart as they plotted the new positions of each returning convoy. Clustered in groups of two and three, staff officers from the various Allied services watched in silence as each new report came in. Outwardly they appeared calm, but there was no disguising the strain that everybody felt. Not only must the convoys wheel about, almost under the very noses of the enemy, and return to England along specific, mine-swept tracks; they were now faced with the threat of another enemy—a storm at sea. For the slow-moving landing craft, heavily loaded with troops and supplies, a storm could be disastrous. Already the wind in the Channel was blowing up to thirty miles an hour, with waves up to five feet, and the weather was due to get worse.

As the minutes passed, the face of the chart reflected the orderly pattern of the recall. There were streams of markers backtracking up the Irish Sea, clustered in the vicinity of the Isle of Wight and huddled together in various ports and anchorages along the southwest coast of England. It would take some of the convoys nearly all day to put back to port.

The location of each convoy and that of nearly every other ship of the Allied fleet could be seen at a glance on the board. But two vessels were not shown—a pair of midget submarines. They seemed to have disappeared completely off the chart.

In an office nearby, a pretty twenty-four-year-old Wren lieutenant wondered how soon her husband would make it back to his home port. Naomi Coles Honour was a bit anxious but not unduly worried yet, even though her friends in "Ops" seemed to know nothing about the whereabouts of her husband, Lieutenant George Honour, and his 57-foot-long midget submarine, the X23.

One mile off the coast of France a periscope broke the surface of the water. Thirty feet below, crouching in the cramped control room of the X23, Lieutenant George Honour pushed his cap back. "Well, gentlemen," he recalls saying, "let's take a look-see."

Cushioning one eye against the rubber-cupped eyepiece, he slowly pivoted the periscope around, and as the distorting shimmer of water disappeared from the lens the blurred image before him straightened out and became the sleepy resort town of Ouistreham near the mouth of the Orne. They were so close in and his view was so magnified that Honour could see smoke rising from chimneys and, in the far distance, a plane that had just taken off from Carpiquet Airport near Caen. He could also see the enemy. Fascinated, he watched German troops calmly working among the anti-invasion obstacles on the sandy beaches that stretched away on either side.

It was a great moment for the twenty-six-year-old Royal Navy Reserve lieutenant. Standing back from the periscope, he said to Lieutenant Lionel G. Lyne, the navigational expert in charge of the operation, "Take a look, Thin—we're almost bang on the target."

In a way the invasion had already begun. The first craft and the first men of the Allied forces were in position off the beaches of Normandy. Directly ahead of the X23 lay the British-Canadian assault sector. Lieutenant Honour and his crew were not unaware of the significance of this particular date. On another June 4, four years earlier, at a place less than two hundred miles away, the last of 338,000 British troops had been evacuated from a blazing port called Dunkirk. On the X23 it was a tense, proud moment for the five specially chosen Englishmen. They were the British vanguard; the men of the X23 were leading the way back to France for the thousands of their countrymen who would soon follow.

These five men crouching in the tiny all-purpose cabin of the X23 wore rubber frogmen's suits, and they carried ingeniously falsified papers that would have passed the scrutiny of the most suspicious German sentry. Each had a false French identity card complete with photograph, plus work permits and ration cards bearing official-looking German rubber-stamped impressions, and other letters and documents. In case anything went wrong and the X23 was sunk or had to be abandoned, her crew members were to swim ashore and, armed with new identities, try to escape capture and make contact with the French underground.

The X23's mission was a particularly hazardous one. Twenty minutes before H Hour, the midget sub and her sister ship, the X20—some twenty miles farther down the coast, opposite the little village of Le Hamel—would boldly come to the surface to act as navigational markers, clearly defining the extreme limits of the British-Canadian assault zone: three beaches that had been given the code names Sword, Juno and Gold.

The plan they were to follow was involved and elaborate. An automatic radio beacon capable of sending out a continuous signal was to be switched on the moment they surfaced. At the same time sonar apparatus would automatically broadcast sound waves through the water which could be picked up by underwater listening devices. The fleet carrying British and Canadian troops would home in on either one or both of the signals.

Each midget also carried an 18-foot telescopic mast to which was attached a small but powerful searchlight that could send out a flashing beam capable of being seen more than five miles away. If the light showed green, it would mean that the subs were on target; if not, the light would be red.

As additional navigation aids, the plan called for each midget to launch a moored rubber dinghy with a man in it and allow it to drift a certain distance toward shore. The dinghies had been outfitted with searchlights which would be operated by their crewmen. By taking bearings on the lights of the midgets and their drifting dinghies, approaching ships would be able to pinpoint the exact positions of the three assault beaches.

Nothing had been forgotten, not even the danger that the little sub might be run over by some lumbering landing craft. As protection the X23 would be clearly marked by a large yellow flag. The point had not escaped Honour that the flag would also make them a fine target for the Germans. Notwithstanding, he planned to fly a second flag, a large white Navy "battle duster." Honour and his crew were prepared to risk enemy shellfire, but they were taking no chances on being rammed and sunk.

All this paraphernalia and more had been packed into the already cramped innards of the X23. Two extra crewmen, both navigation experts, had also been added to the sub's normal complement of three men. There was scarcely room now to stand up or sit down in the X23's single all-purpose cabin, which was only five feet eight inches high, five feet wide and barely eight feet long. Already it was hot and stuffy, and the atmosphere would get much worse before they dared surface, which would not be until after dark.

Even in daylight in these shallow coastal waters, Honour knew that there was always the possibility of being spotted by low-flying reconnaissance planes or patrol boats—and the longer they stayed at periscope depth the greater was the risk.

At the periscope Lieutenant Lyne took a series of bearings. He quickly identified several landmarks: the Ouistreham lighthouse, the town church and the spires of two others in the villages of Langrune and St.-Aubin-sur-Mer a few miles away. Honour had been right. They were almost "bang on the target," barely three quarters of a mile from their plotted position.

Honour was relieved to be this close. It had been a long, harrowing trip. They had covered the ninety miles from

Portsmouth in a little under two days, and much of that time they had traveled through mine fields. Now they would get into position and then drop to the bottom. "Operation Gambit" was off to a good start. Secretly he wished that some other code word had been chosen. Although he was not superstitious, on looking up the meaning of the word the young skipper had been shocked to discover that "gambit" meant "throwing away the opening pawns."

Honour took one last look through the periscope at the Germans working on the beaches. All hell would break loose on those beaches by this time tomorrow, he thought. "Down periscope," he ordered. Submerged, and out of radio communication with their base, Honour and the crew of the X23 did not know that the invasion had been postponed.

9

BY 11 A.M. the gale in the Channel was blowing hard. In the restricted coastal areas of Britain, sealed off from the remainder of the country, the invasion forces sweated it out. Their world now was the assembly areas, the airfields and the ships. It was almost as though they were physically severed from the mainland—caught up strangely between the familiar world of England and the unknown world of Normandy. Separating them from the world they knew was a tight curtain of security.

On the other side of that curtain life went on as usual. People went about their accustomed routines unaware that hundreds of thousands of men waited out an order that would mark the beginning of the end of World War II.

In the town of Leatherhead, Surrey, a slight, fifty-four-year-old physics teacher was walking his dog. Leonard Sidney Dawe was a quiet, unassuming sort of man and outside of a small circle of friends he was unknown. Yet the retiring Dawe enjoyed a public following far exceeding that of a film star. Every day upwards of a million people struggled over the crossword puzzle that he and his friend Melville Jones, another schoolteacher, prepared for each morning's London *Daily Telegraph*.

For more than twenty years Dawe had been the *Telegraph*'s senior crossword compiler and in that time his tough, intricate puzzles had both exasperated and satisfied countless millions. Some addicts claimed that the *Times*'s puzzle was tougher, but Dawe's fans were quick to point out that the *Telegraph*'s crossword had never repeated the same clue twice. That was a matter of considerable pride to the reserved Dawe.

Dawe would have been astonished to know that ever since May 2 he had been the subject of a most discreet inquiry by a certain department in Scotland Yard charged with counterespionage, M.I.5. For over a month his puzzles had thrown one scare after another into many sections of the Allied High Command.

On this particular Sunday morning M.I.5 had decided to talk to Dawe. When he returned home he found two men waiting for him. Dawe, like everybody else, had heard of M.I.5, but what could they possibly want with him?

"Mr. Dawe," said one of the men as the questioning began, "during the last month a number of highly confidential code words concerning a certain Allied operation have appeared in the *Telegraph* crossword puzzles. Can you tell us what prompted you to use them—or where you got them?"

Before the surprised Dawe could answer, the M.I.5 man pulled a list out of his pocket and said, "We are particularly interested in finding out how you came to choose this word." He pointed to the list. The prize competition crossword in the *Telegraph* for May 27 included the clue (11 across), "But some big-wig like this has stolen some of it at times." This mystifying clue through some strange alchemy made sense to Dawe's devoted followers. The answer, published just two days before on June 2, was the code name for the entire Allied invasion plan—"Overlord."

Dawe did not know what Allied operation they were talking about, so he was not unduly startled or even indignant at these questions. He could not explain, he told them, just how or why he had chosen that particular word. It was quite a common word in history books, he pointed out. "But how," he protested, "can I tell what is being used as a code word and what isn't?"

The two M.I.5 men were extremely courteous: they agreed that it was difficult. But wasn't it strange that all these code words should appear in the same month?

One by one they went over the list with the now slightly harassed bespectacled schoolmaster. In the puzzle for May 2, the clue "One of the U.S." (17 across) had produced the solution "Utah." The answer to three down, "Red Indian on the Missouri," on May 22, turned out to be "Omaha."

In the May 30 crossword (11 across), "This bush is a center of nursery revolutions" required the word "Mulberry"—the code name for the two artificial harbors that were to be placed in position off the beaches. And the solution to 15 down on June 1, "Britannia and he hold to the same thing," had been "Neptune"—the code word for the naval operations in the invasion.

Dawe had no explanation for the use of these words. For all he knew, he said, the crosswords mentioned on the list could have been completed six months before. Was there any explanation? Dawe could suggest only one: fantastic coincidence.

There had been other hair-raising scares. Three months before in Chicago's central post office a bulky, improperly wrapped envelope had burst open on the sorting table, revealing a number of suspicious-looking documents. At least a dozen sorters saw the contents: something about an operation called Overlord.

Intelligence officers were soon swarming all over the scene. The sorters were questioned and told to forget anything they might have seen. Next the completely innocent addressee was interrogated: a girl. She could not explain why these papers were en route to her, but she did recognize the handwriting on the envelope. Through her the papers were traced back to their point of origin, an equally innocent sergeant at American headquarters in London. He had wrongly addressed the envelope. By mistake he had sent it to his sister in Chicago.

Minor as this incident was it might have assumed even greater proportions had Supreme Headquarters known that the German intelligence service, the *Abwehr*, had already discovered the meaning of the code word "Overlord." One of their agents, an Albanian named Diello but better known to the *Abwehr* as "Cicero," had sent Berlin the information in January. At first Cicero had identified the plan as "Overlock," but later he had corrected it. And Berlin believed Cicero—he worked as a valet in the British Embassy in Turkey.

But Cicero was unable to discover the big Overlord secret: the time and place of D Day itself. So scrupulously guarded was this information that up to the end of April only a few hundred Allied officers knew it. But that month, despite constant warnings by counterintelligence that agents were active throughout the British Isles, two senior officers, an American general and a British colonel, carelessly violated security. At a cocktail party in Claridge's Hotel, London, the General mentioned to some brother officers that the invasion would take place before June 15. Elsewhere in England, the colonel, a battalion commander, was even more indiscreet. He told some civilian friends that his men were training to capture a specific target and he hinted that its location was in Normandy. Both officers were immediately demoted and removed from their commands.*

And now, on this tense Sunday, June 4, Supreme Headquarters was stunned by the news that there had been yet another leak, far worse than any that had occurred before. During the night an AP teletype operator had been practicing on an idle machine in an effort to improve her speed. By error the perforated tape carrying her practice "flash" somehow preceded the usual nightly Russian communiqué. It was corrected after only thirty seconds, but the word was out. The "bulletin" that reached the U.S. read: "URGENT PRESS ASSOCIATED NYK FLASH EISENHOWER'S HQ ANNOUNCED ALLIED LANDINGS IN FRANCE."

Grave as the consequences of the message might prove to be, it was much too late to do anything about it now. The gigantic machinery of the invasion had moved into high gear. Now, as the hours slipped by and the weather steadily worsened, the greatest airborne and amphibious force ever assembled waited for General Eisenhower's decision. Would Ike confirm June 6 as D Day? Or would he be compelled because of Channel weather—the worst in twenty years—to postpone the invasion once again?

---

*Although the American General had been a West Point classmate of General Eisenhower's there was nothing that the Supreme Commander could do but send him home. After D Day the General's case received wide publicity and later, as a colonel, he retired. There is no record that Eisenhower's HQ even heard about the Britisher's indiscretion. It was quietly handled by his own superiors. The Britisher went on to become a Member of Parliament.

IO

IN A rain-lashed wood two miles from the naval headquarters at Southwick House, the American who had to make that great decision wrestled with the problem and tried to relax in his sparsely furnished three-and-a-half-ton trailer. Although he could have moved into more comfortable quarters at the big, sprawling Southwick House, Eisenhower had decided against it. He wanted to be as close as possible to the ports where his troops were loading. Several days before he had ordered a small compact battle headquarters set up—a few tents for his immediate staff and several trailers, among them his own which he had long ago named "my circus wagon."

Eisenhower's trailer, a long, low caravan somewhat resembling a moving van, had three small compartments serving as bedroom, living room and study. Besides these, neatly fitted into the trailer's length was a tiny galley, a miniature switchboard, a chemical toilet and, at one end, a glass-enclosed observation deck. But the Supreme Commander was rarely around long enough to make full use of the trailer. He hardly ever used the living room or the study; when staff conferences were called he generally held them in a tent next to the trailer. Only his bedroom had a "lived-in" look. It was definitely his: there was a large pile of Western paperbacks on the table near his bunk, and here too were the only pictures—photographs of his wife, Mamie, and his twenty-one-year-old son, John, in West Point cadet's uniform.

From this trailer Eisenhower commanded almost three million Allied troops. More than half of his immense command were American: roughly 1,700,000 soldiers, sailors, airmen and coastguardmen. British and Canadian forces together totaled around one million and in addition there were Fighting French, Polish, Czech, Belgian, Norwegian and Dutch contingents. Never before had an American commanded so many men from so many nations or shouldered such an awesome burden of responsibility.

Yet despite the magnitude of his assignment and his vast powers there was little about this tall, sunburned Midwesterner with the infectious grin to indicate that he was the Supreme Commander. Unlike many other famous Allied commanders, who were instantly recognizable by some visible trade-mark such as eccentric headgear or garish uniforms layered shoulder-high with decorations, everything about Eisenhower was re-strained. Apart from the four stars of his rank, a single ribbon of decorations above his breast pocket and the flaming-sword shoulder patch of SHAEF (Supreme Headquarters Allied Ex-peditionary Force) Eisenhower shunned all distinguishing marks. Even in the trailer there was little evidence of his au-thority: no flags, maps, framed directives, or signed photo-graphs of the great or near-great who often visited him. But in his bedroom, close to his bunk, were three all-important telephones, each a different color; the red was for "scrambled" calls to Washington, the green was a direct line to Winston Churchill's residence at No. 10 Downing Street, London, and the black connected him to his brilliant chief of staff, Major General Walter Bedell Smith, the immediate headquarters, and other senior members of the Allied High Command.

It was on the black phone, to add to all his other worries, that Eisenhower heard of the erroneous "flash" concerning the "landings." He said nothing when he was told the news. His naval aide, Captain Harry C. Butcher, recalls that the Supreme Commander merely grunted an acknowledgment. What was there to say or do now?

Four months before, in the directive appointing him Su-preme Commander, the Combined Chiefs of Staff in Washing-ton had spelled out his assignment in one precise paragraph. It read: "You will enter the continent of Europe and, in conjunction with the other United Nations, undertake opera-tions aimed at the heart of Germany and the destruction of her armed forces . . ."

There in one sentence was the aim and purpose of the as-sault. But to the entire Allied world this was to be more than a military operation. Eisenhower called it "a great crusade"—a crusade to end once and for all a monstrous tyranny that had plunged the world into its bloodiest war, shattered a continent and placed upwards of 300 million people in bondage. (Actu-ally, nobody at this time could even imagine the full extent of the Nazi barbarism that had washed across Europe—the mil-lions who had disappeared into the gas chambers and furnaces of Heinrich Himmler's aseptic crematoria, the millions who

had been herded out of their countries to work as slave laborers, a tremendous percentage of whom would never return,
the millions more who had been tortured to death, executed
as hostages or exterminated by the simple expedient of starvation.) The great crusade's unalterable purpose was not only
to win the war, but to destroy Nazism and bring to an end an
era of savagery which had never been surpassed in the world's
history.

But first the invasion had to succeed. If it failed, the final
defeat of Germany might take years.

To prepare for the all-out invasion on which so much depended, intensive military planning had been going on for
more than a year. Long before anyone knew that Eisenhower
would be named Supreme Commander a small group of
Anglo-American officers under Britain's Lieutenant General
Sir Frederick Morgan had been laying the groundwork for
the assault. Their problems were incredibly involved—there
were few guideposts, few military precedents, but a plethora
of question marks. Where should the attack be launched and
when? How many divisions should be used? If X divisions were
needed would they be available, trained and ready to go by Y
date? How many transports would be required to carry them?
What about naval bombardment, support ships and escorts?
Where were all the landing craft going to come from—could
some be diverted from the Pacific and Mediterranean theaters
of war? How many airfields would be needed to accommodate
the thousands of planes necessary for the air attack? How long
would it take to stockpile all the supplies, the equipment, guns,
ammunition, transport, food, and how much was needed not
only for the attack but to follow it up?

These were just a few of the staggering questions that Allied
planners had to answer. There were thousands of others. Ultimately their studies, enlarged and modified into the final Overlord plan after Eisenhower took over, called for more men,
more ships, more planes, more equipment and matériel than
had ever been assembled before for a single military operation.

The build-up was enormous. Even before the plan reached
its final form an unprecedented flow of men and supplies began
pouring into England. Soon there were so many Americans in
the small towns and villages that the British who lived in them

were often hopelessly outnumbered. Their movie theaters, hotels, restaurants, dance halls and favorite pubs were suddenly swamped by a flood of troops from every state in the Union.

Airfields blossomed everywhere. For the great air offensive 163 bases were constructed in addition to the scores already in existence, until at last there were so many that a standard gag among 8th and 9th Air Force crewmen was that they could taxi the length and breadth of the island without scratching a wing. Ports were jammed. A great supporting naval fleet of almost nine hundred ships, from battleships to PT boats, began to assemble. Convoys arrived in such great numbers that by spring they had delivered almost two million tons of goods and supplies—so much that 170 miles of new railroad lines had to be laid down to move it.

By May southern England looked like a huge arsenal. Hidden in the forests were mountainous piles of ammunition. Stretching across the moors, bumper to bumper, were tanks, half-tracks, armored cars, trucks, jeeps and ambulances—more than fifty thousand of them. In the fields were long lines of howitzers and antiaircraft guns, great quantities of prefabricated materials from Nissen huts to airstrips, and huge stocks of earth-moving equipment from bulldozers to excavators. At central depots there were immense quantities of food, clothing and medical supplies, from pills for combating seasickness to 124,000 hospital beds. But the most staggering sight of all were the valleys filled with long lines of railroad rolling stock: almost one thousand brand-new locomotives, and nearly twenty thousand tanker cars and freight cars which would be used to replace the shattered French equipment after the beachhead had been established.

There were also strange new devices of war. There were tanks that could swim, others that carried great rolls of lath to be used in antitank ditches or as steppingstones over walls, and yet others equipped with great chain flails that beat the ground in front of them to explode mines. There were flat, block-long ships, each carrying a forest of pipes for the launching of warfare's newest weapon, rockets. Perhaps strangest of all were two man-made harbors that were to be towed across to the Normandy beaches. They were engineering miracles and one of the big Overlord secrets; they assured the constant flow

of men and supplies into the beachhead during the first critical weeks until a port could be captured. The harbors, called
"Mulberries," consisted first of an outer breakwater made up
of great steel floats. Next came 145 huge concrete caissons in
various sizes which were to be sunk butt to butt to make an inner breakwater. The largest of these caissons had crew quarters
and antiaircraft guns and, when it was being towed, looked like
a five-story apartment building lying on its side. Within these
man-made harbors freighters as large as Liberty ships could
unload into barges ferrying back and forth to the beaches.
Smaller ships, like coasters or landing craft, could dump their
cargoes at massive steel pierheads where waiting trucks would
run them to shore over floating pontoon-supported piers. Beyond the Mulberries a line of sixty concrete blockships was to
be sunk as an additional breakwater. In position off the invasion beaches of Normandy, each harbor would be the size of
the port of Dover.

All through May men and supplies began to move down to
the ports and the loading areas. Congestion was a major problem, but somehow the quartermasters, military police and British railroad authorities kept everything moving and on time.

Trains loaded with troops and supplies backed and filled on
every line as they waited to converge on the coast. Convoys
jammed every road. Every little village and hamlet was covered
with a fine dust, and throughout the quiet spring nights the
whole of southern England resounded with the low whining
sound of the trucks, the whirring and clacking of tanks and
the unmistakable voices of Americans, all of whom seemed to
be asking the same question: "How far away is this goddam
place?"

Almost overnight, cities of Nissen huts and tents sprang up
in the coastal regions as troops began to pour into the embarkation areas. Men slept in bunks stacked three and four deep.
Showers and latrines were usually several fields away and the
men had to queue up to use them. Chow lines were sometimes
a quarter of a mile long. There were so many troops that it
took some 54,000 men, 4,500 of them newly trained cooks,
just to service American installations. The last week in May
troops and supplies began loading onto the transports and the
landing ships. The time had finally come.

The statistics staggered the imagination; the force seemed overwhelming. Now this great weapon—the youth of the free world, the resources of the free world—waited on the decision of one man: Eisenhower.

Throughout most of June 4 Eisenhower remained alone in his trailer. He and his commanders had done everything to insure that the invasion would have every possible chance of success at the lowest cost in lives. But now, after all the months of political and military planning, Operation Overlord lay at the mercy of the elements. Eisenhower was helpless; all he could do was to wait and hope that the weather would improve. But no matter what happened he would be forced to make a momentous decision by the end of the day—to go or to postpone the assault once again. Either way the success or failure of Operation Overlord might depend on that decision. And nobody could make that decision for him. The responsibility would be his and his alone.

Eisenhower was faced with a dreadful dilemma. On May 17 he had decided that D Day would have to be one of three days in June—the fifth, sixth or seventh. Meteorological studies had shown that two of the vital weather requirements for the invasion could be expected for Normandy on those days: a late-rising moon and, shortly after dawn, a low tide.

The paratroopers and glider-borne infantry who would launch the assault, some eighteen thousand men of the U.S. 101st and 82nd divisions and the British 6th Division, needed the moonlight. But their surprise attack depended on darkness up to the time they arrived over the dropping zones. Thus their critical demand was for a late-rising moon.

The seaborne landings had to take place when the tide was low enough to expose Rommel's beach obstacles. On this tide the timing of the whole invasion would depend. And to complicate the meteorological calculations further, follow-up troops landing much later in the day would also need a low tide—and it had to come before darkness set in.

These two critical factors of moonlight and tide shackled Eisenhower. Tide alone reduced the number of days in any one month for the attack to six, and three of those were moonless.

But that was not all. There were many other considerations he had to take into account. First, all the services wanted long hours of daylight and good visibility—to identify the beaches; for the naval and air forces to spot their targets; and to reduce the hazard of collision when five thousand ships began maneuvering almost side by side in the Bay of the Seine. Second, a calm sea was required. Apart from the havoc a rough sea might cause to the fleet, seasickness could leave the troops helpless long before they even set foot on the beaches. Third, low winds, blowing inshore, were needed to clear the beaches of smoke so that targets would not be obscured. And finally the Allies required three more quiet days after D Day to facilitate the quick build-up of men and supplies.

Nobody at Supreme Headquarters expected perfect conditions on D Day, least of all Eisenhower. He had schooled himself, in countless dry runs with his meteorological staff, to recognize and weigh all the factors which would give him the bare minimum conditions acceptable for the attack. But according to his meteorologist the chances were about ten to one against Normandy having weather on any one day in June which would meet even the minimal requirements. On this stormy Sunday, as Eisenhower, alone in his trailer, considered every possibility, those odds appeared to have become astronomical.

Of the three possible days for the invasion he had chosen the fifth so that if there was a postponement he could launch the assault on the sixth. But if he ordered the landings for the sixth and then had to cancel them again, the problem of refueling the returning convoys might prevent him from attacking on the seventh. There would then be two alternatives. He could postpone D Day until the next period when the tides were right, June 19. But if he did that the airborne armies would be forced to attack in darkness—June 19 was moonless. The other alternative was to wait until July, and that long a postponement, as he was later to recall, "was too bitter to contemplate."

So terrifying was the thought of postponement that many of Eisenhower's most cautious commanders were even prepared to risk attack instead on the eighth or ninth. They did not see how more than 200,000 men, most of them already briefed, could be kept isolated and bottled up for weeks on ships, in embarkation areas and on airfields without the secret of the invasion leaking out. Even if security remained intact during the period, surely Luftwaffe reconnaissance aircraft would spot the massed fleet (if they hadn't done so already) or German agents would somehow learn of the plan. For everybody the prospect of a postponement was grim. But it was Eisenhower who would have to make the decision.

In the fading light of the afternoon the Supreme Commander occasionally came to the door of his trailer and gazed up through the wind-swept treetops at the blanket of clouds that covered the sky. At other times he would pace up and down outside the trailer, chain-smoking, kicking at the cinders on the little pathway—a tall figure, shoulders slightly hunched, hands rammed deep into his pockets.

On these solitary strolls Eisenhower scarcely seemed to notice anybody, but during the afternoon he spotted one of the four pool correspondents accredited to his advance headquarters—Merrill "Red" Mueller of NBC. "Let's take a walk, Red," said Ike abruptly, and without waiting for Mueller he strode off, hands in his pockets, at his usual brisk pace. The correspondent hurriedly caught up with him as he disappeared into the woods.

It was a strange, silent walk. Eisenhower uttered hardly a word. "Ike seemed completely preoccupied with his own thoughts, completely immersed in all his problems," Mueller remembers. "It was almost as though he had forgotten I was with him." There were many questions that Mueller wanted to put to the Supreme Commander, but he didn't ask them; he felt that he couldn't intrude.

When they returned to the encampment and Eisenhower had said goodbye, the correspondent watched him climb the little aluminum stairs leading to the trailer door. At that moment he appeared to Mueller to be "bowed down with worry . . . as though each of the four stars on either shoulder weighed a ton."

Shortly before nine-thirty that night, Eisenhower's senior commanders and their chiefs of staff gathered in the library of Southwick House. It was a large, comfortable room with a table covered by a green baize cloth, several easy chairs and two sofas. Dark oak bookcases lined three of the walls, but there were few books on the shelves and the room had a bare look. Heavy double blackout curtains hung at the windows and on this night they muffled the drumming of the rain and the flat buckling sound of the wind.

Standing about the room in little groups, the staff officers talked quietly. Near the fireplace Eisenhower's chief of staff, Major General Walter Bedell Smith, conversed with the pipe-smoking Deputy Supreme Commander, Air Chief Marshal Tedder. Seated to one side was the fiery Allied naval commander, Admiral Ramsay, and close by the Allied air commander, Air Chief Marshal Leigh-Mallory. Only one officer was dressed informally, General Smith recalls. The peppery Montgomery, who would be in charge of the D-Day assault, wore his usual corduroy slacks and roll-necked sweater. These were the men who would translate the order for the attack when Eisenhower gave the word to go. Now they and their staff officers—altogether there were twelve senior officers in the room—waited for the arrival of the Supreme Commander and the decisive conference that would begin at nine-thirty. At that time they would hear the latest forecasts of the meteorologists.

At exactly nine-thirty the door opened and Eisenhower, neat in his dark-green battle dress, strode in. There was just the faintest flicker of the old Eisenhower grin as he greeted his old friends, but the mask of worry quickly returned to his face as he opened the conference. There was no need for a preamble; everybody knew the seriousness of the decision that had to be made. So almost immediately the three senior Overlord meteorologists, led by their chief, Group Captain J. N. Stagg of the Royal Air Force, came into the room.

There was a hushed silence as Stagg opened the briefing. Quickly he sketched the weather picture of the previous twenty-four hours and then he quietly said, "Gentlemen . . . there have been some rapid and unexpected developments in the situation . . ." All eyes were on Stagg now, as he presented the anxious-faced Eisenhower and his commanders with a slender ray of hope.

A new weather front had been spotted which, he said, would move up the Channel within the next few hours and cause a gradual clearing over the assault areas. These improving conditions would last throughout the next day and continue up to the morning of June 6. After that the weather would begin to deteriorate again. During this promised period of fair weather,

the winds would drop appreciably and the skies would clear
—enough at least for bombers to operate on the night of the
fifth and throughout the morning of the sixth. By noon the
cloud layer would thicken and the skies would become overcast again. In short, what Eisenhower was being told was that
a barely tolerable period of fair conditions, far below the minimal requirements, would prevail *for just a little more than
twenty-four hours.*

The moment Stagg had finished, he and the other two meteorologists were subjected to a barrage of questions. Were all of
them confident about the accuracy of their predictions? Could
their forecasts be wrong—had they checked their reports with
every available source? Was there any chance of the weather
continuing to improve in the few days immediately after the
sixth?

Some of the questions were impossible for the weathermen
to answer. Their report had been checked and double-checked
and they were as optimistic as they could be about the forecast, but there was always the chance that the vagaries of the
weather might prove them wrong. They answered as best they
could, then they withdrew.

For the next fifteen minutes Eisenhower and his commanders deliberated. The urgency of making a decision was stressed
by Admiral Ramsay. The American task force for Omaha and
Utah beaches under the command of Rear Admiral A. G. Kirk
would have to get the order within a half hour if Overlord was
to take place on Tuesday. Ramsay's concern was prompted by
the refueling problem; if those forces sailed later and were then
recalled it would be impossible to get them ready again for a
possible attack on Wednesday, the seventh.

Eisenhower now polled his commanders one by one. General Smith thought that the attack should go in on the sixth—it
was a gamble, but one that should be taken. Tedder and Leigh-
Mallory were both fearful that even the predicted cloud cover
would prove too much for the air forces to operate effectively.
It might mean that the assault would take place without adequate air support. They thought it was going to be "chancy."
Montgomery stuck to the decision that he had made the night
before when the June 5 D Day had been postponed. "I would
say Go," he said.

It was now up to Ike. The moment had come when only he could make the decision. There was a long silence as Eisenhower weighed all the possibilities. General Smith, watching, was struck by the "isolation and loneliness" of the Supreme Commander as he sat, hands clasped before him, looking down at the table. The minutes ticked by; some say two minutes passed, others as many as five. Then Eisenhower, his face strained, looked up and announced his decision. Slowly he said, "I am quite positive we must give the order . . . I don't like it, but there it is. . . . I don't see how we can do anything else."

Eisenhower stood up. He looked tired, but some of the tension had left his face. Six hours later at a brief meeting to review the weather he would hold to his decision and reconfirm it—Tuesday, June 6, would be D Day.

Eisenhower and his commanders left the room, hurrying now to set the great assault in motion. Behind them in the silent library a haze of blue smoke hung over the conference table, the fire reflected itself in the polished floor, and on the mantelpiece the hands of a clock pointed to 9:45.

II

IT WAS about 10 P.M. when Private Arthur B. "Dutch" Schultz of the 82nd Airborne Division decided to get out of the crap game; he might never have this much money again. The game had been going on ever since the announcement that the airborne assault was off for at least twenty-four hours. It had begun behind a tent, next it had moved under the wing of a plane, and now the session was going full blast in the hangar, which had been converted into a huge dormitory. Even here it had done some traveling, moving up and down the corridors created by the rows of double-tiered bunks. And Dutch was one of the big winners.

How much he had won he didn't know. But he guessed that the bundle of crumpled greenbacks, English banknotes and fresh blue-green French invasion currency he held in his fist came to more than $2,500. That was more money than he had seen at any one time in all his twenty-one years.

Physically and spiritually he had done everything to prepare himself for the jump. Services for all denominations had been held on the airfield in the morning and Dutch, a Catholic, had gone to confession and Communion. Now he knew exactly what he was going to do with his winnings. He mentally figured out the distribution. He would leave $1,000 with the adjutant's office; he could use that on pass when he got back to England. Another $1,000 he planned to send to his mother in San Francisco to keep for him, but he wanted her to have $500 of it as a gift—she sure could use it. He had a special purpose for the remainder: that would go on a helluva blowout when his outfit, the 505th, reached Paris.

The young paratrooper felt good; he had taken care of everything—but had he? Why did the incident of the morning keep coming back, filling him with so much uneasiness?

At mail call that morning he had received a letter from his mother. As he tore open the envelope a rosary slid out and fell at his feet. Quickly, so that the wisecracking crowd around him wouldn't notice, he had snatched up the beads and stuffed them into a barracks bag that he was leaving behind.

Now the thought of the rosary beads suddenly gave rise to a question that hadn't struck him before: What was he doing gambling at a time like this? He looked at the folded and crumpled bills sticking out between his fingers—more money than he could have earned in a year. At that moment Private Dutch Schultz *knew* that if he pocketed all this money, he would surely be killed. Dutch decided to take no chances. "Move over," he said, "and let me get at the play." He glanced at his watch and wondered how long it would take to lose $2,500.

Schultz wasn't the only one who acted strangely this night. Nobody, from enlisted men to generals, seemed eager to challenge the fates. Over near Newbury at the headquarters of the 101st Airborne Division, the commander, Major General Maxwell D. Taylor, was holding a long, informal session with his senior officers. There were perhaps half a dozen men in the room and one of them, Brigadier General Don Pratt, the assistant division commander, sat on a bed. While they were talking another officer arrived. Taking off his cap, he tossed it onto the bed. General Pratt leaped up, swept the cap onto the floor and said, "My God, that's damn bad luck!" Everybody laughed, but Pratt didn't sit on the bed again. He had chosen to lead the 101st's glider forces into Normandy.

As the night closed in, the invasion forces all over England continued to wait. Keyed up by months of training, they were ready to go, and the postponement had made them jittery. It was now about eighteen hours since the stand-down, and each hour had taken its toll of the patience and readiness of the troops. They did not know that D Day now was barely twenty-six hours away; it was still much too early for the news to filter down. And so, on this stormy Sunday night, men waited, in loneliness, anxiety and secret fear, for something, anything, to happen.

They did precisely what the world expects men to do under such circumstances: They thought of their families, their wives, their children, their sweethearts. And everybody talked about the fighting that lay ahead. What would the beaches really be like? Would the landings be as tough as everybody seemed to think? Nobody could visualize D Day, but each man prepared for it in his own way.

On the dark, wave-tossed Irish Sea, aboard the destroyer U.S.S. *Herndon*, Lieutenant (j.g.) Bartow Farr, Jr., tried to concentrate on a bridge game. It was difficult; there were too many sober reminders all around him that this was not just another social evening. Taped to the walls of the wardroom were large aerial reconnaissance photographs of German gun positions overlooking the Normandy beaches. These guns were the *Herndon*'s D-Day targets. It occurred to Farr that the *Herndon* would also be theirs.

Farr was reasonably certain he would survive D Day. There had been a lot of kidding about who would come through and who wouldn't. Back in Belfast Harbor the crew of the *Corry*, their sister ship, had been giving odds of ten to one against the *Herndon*'s return. The *Herndon*'s crew retaliated by spreading the rumor that when the invasion fleet set out the *Corry* would remain in port, because of low morale aboard ship.

Lieutenant Farr had every confidence that the *Herndon* would return safe, and he with her. Still, he was glad he had written a long letter to his unborn son. It never occurred to

Farr that his wife, Anne, back in New York, might give birth to a girl instead. (She didn't. That November the Farrs had a boy.)

In a staging area near Newhaven, Corporal Reginald Dale of the British 3rd Division sat up in his bunk and worried about his wife, Hilda. They had been married in 1940, and ever since both had longed for a child. On his last leave, just a few days before, Hilda had announced that she was pregnant. Dale was furious; all along he had sensed that the invasion was close and that he'd be in on it. "This is a hell of a time, I must say," he had snapped. In his mind he saw again the quick hurt that had come into her eyes, and he berated himself once again for the hasty words.

But it was too late now. He could not even telephone her. He lay back down on his bunk and, like thousands of others in British staging areas, tried to will himself to sleep.

A few men, nerveless and cool, slept soundly. At a British 50th Division embarkation area one such man was Company Sergeant Major Stanley Hollis. Long ago he had learned to sleep whenever he could. The coming attack didn't worry Hollis too much; he had a good idea what to expect. He had been evacuated from Dunkirk, had fought with the Eighth Army in North Africa and had landed on the beaches of Sicily. Among the millions of troops in Britain that night Hollis was a rarity. He was looking forward to the invasion; he wanted to get back to France to kill some more Germans.

It was a personal matter with Hollis. He had been a dispatch rider at the time of Dunkirk, and in the town of Lille during the retreat he had seen a sight which he had never forgotten. Cut off from his unit, Hollis had taken a wrong turn in a part of the town that the Germans had apparently just passed through. He found himself in a cul-de-sac filled with the still warm bodies of over a hundred French men, women and children. They had been machine-gunned. Embedded in the wall behind the bodies and littering the ground were hundreds of spent bullets. From that moment Stan Hollis had become a superb hunter of the enemy. His score was now over ninety. At D Day's end, he would notch his Sten gun with his one hundred and second victory.

There were others who were also anxious to set foot in

France. The waiting seemed interminable to Commander Philippe Kieffer and his 171 tough French commandos. With the exception of the few friends they had made in England, there had been no one for them to say goodbye to—their families were still in France.

In their encampment near the mouth of the Hamble River, they spent the time checking weapons and studying the molded-foam-rubber terrain model of Sword Beach and their targets in the town of Ouistreham. One of the commandos, Count Guy de Montlaur, who was extremely proud to be a sergeant, was delighted to hear this night that there had been a slight change of plan: His squad would be leading the attack on the resort's gambling casino, now believed to be a strongly defended German command post. "It will be a pleasure," he told Commander Kieffer. "I have lost several fortunes in that place."

One hundred fifty miles away, in the U.S. 4th Infantry Division's staging area, near Plymouth, Sergeant Harry Brown came off duty and found a letter waiting for him. Many times he had seen the same sort of thing in war movies, but he never thought it would happen to him: the letter contained an advertisement for Adler Elevator Shoes. The ad particularly galled the sergeant. Everyone was so short in his section that they were called "Brown's midgets." The sergeant was the tallest —five feet five and a half inches.

While he was wondering who had given his name to the Adler Company, one of his squad showed up. Corporal John Gwiadosky had decided to repay a loan. Sergeant Brown couldn't get over it as Gwiadosky solemnly handed him the money. "Don't get any wrong ideas," explained Gwiadosky. "I just don't want you chasing me all over hell trying to collect."

Across the bay, on the transport *New Amsterdam* anchored near Weymouth, Second Lieutenant George Kerchner of the 2nd Ranger Battalion was occupied with a routine chore. He was censoring his platoon's mail. It was particularly heavy tonight; everybody seemed to have written long letters home. The 2nd and 5th Rangers had been given one of the toughest D-Day assignments. They were to scale the almost sheer 100-foot cliffs at a place called Pointe du Hoc and silence a battery of six long-range guns—guns so powerful that they could zero in on Omaha Beach or the transport area of Utah Beach. The Rangers would have just thirty minutes to do the job.

Casualties were expected to be heavy—some thought as high as sixty per cent—unless the air and naval bombardment could knock out the guns before the Rangers got there. Either way, nobody expected the attack to be a breeze. Nobody, that is, except Staff Sergeant Larry Johnson, one of Kerchner's section leaders.

The lieutenant was dumfounded when he read Johnson's letter. Although none of the mail would be sent out until after D Day—whenever that would be—this letter couldn't even be delivered through ordinary channels. Kerchner sent for Johnson and, when the sergeant arrived, gave him back the letter. "Larry," said Kerchner drily, "you better post this yourself— after you get to France." Johnson had written a girl asking for a date early in June. She lived in Paris.

It struck the lieutenant as the sergeant left the cabin that as long as there were optimists like Johnson nothing was impossible.

Almost every man in the invasion forces wrote a letter to someone during the long hours of waiting. They had been penned up for a long time, and the letters seemed to give them emotional release. Many of them recorded their thoughts in a way that men seldom do.

Captain John F. Dulligan of the 1st Infantry Division, slated to land on Omaha Beach, wrote his wife: "I love these men. They sleep all over the ship, on the decks, in, on top, and underneath the vehicles. They smoke, play cards, wrestle around and indulge in general horseplay. They gather around in groups and talk mostly about girls, home and experiences (with and without girls) . . . They are good soldiers, the best in the world . . . Before the invasion of North Africa, I was nervous and a little scared. During the Sicilian invasion I was so busy that the fear passed while I was working. . . . This time we will hit a beach in France and from there on only God knows the answer. I want you to know that I love you with all my heart. . . . I pray that God will see fit to spare me to you and Ann and Pat."

The men on heavy naval vessels or large transports, on airfields or in embarkation areas, were the lucky ones. They were restricted and overcrowded, but they were dry, warm and well. It was a different story for the troops on the flat-bottomed landing ships heaving at anchor outside nearly every harbor. Some men had been on these vessels for more than a week. The ships were overcrowded and foul, the men unbelievably miserable. For them the battle began long before they ever left England. It was a battle against continuous nausea and seasickness. Most of the men still remember that the ships smelled of just three things: diesel oil, backed-up toilets and vomit.

Conditions varied from ship to ship. On LCT 777 Signalman Third Class George Hackett, Jr., was amazed to see waves so high that they smashed over one end of the wallowing craft and rolled out the other. LCT 6, a British landing craft, was so overloaded that Lieutenant Colonel Clarence Hupfer of the U.S. 4th Division thought it would sink. Water lapped at the gunwales and at times washed over into the craft. The galley was flooded and the troops were forced to eat cold food—those who could eat at all.

LST 97, Sergeant Keith Bryan of the 5th Engineer Special Brigade remembers, was so overcrowded that men were stepping over one another, and it rolled so much that those lucky enough to have bunks had difficulty staying in them. And to Sergeant Morris Magee of the Canadian 3rd Division the heaving of his craft "was worse than being in a rowboat in the center of Lake Champlain." He was so sick he could no longer throw up.

But the troops who suffered most during the waiting period were the men in the recalled convoys. All day they had ridden out the storm in the Channel. Now, waterlogged and weary, they glumly lined the rails as the last of the straggling convoys dropped their anchors. By 11 P.M. all the ships were back.

Outside Plymouth Harbor, Lieutenant Commander Hoffman of the *Corry* stood on his bridge looking at the long lines of dark shadows, blacked-out landing ships of every size and description. It was cold. The wind was still high and he could hear the shallow-draft vessels slopping and slapping the water as they rolled in the trough of every wave.

Hoffman was weary. They had returned to port only a short while before to learn for the first time the reason for the postponement. Now they had been warned to stand to once again.

Below decks the news spread quickly. Bennie Glisson, the radio operator, heard it as he prepared to go on watch. He made his way to the mess hall and when he got there he found more than a dozen men having dinner—tonight it was turkey with all the trimmings. Everybody seemed depressed. "You guys," he said, "act like you're eating your last meal." Bennie was nearly right. At least half of those present would go down with the *Corry* a little after H Hour on D Day.

Nearby, on LCI 408, morale was also very low. The Coast Guard crew were convinced that the false start had been just another dry run. Private William Joseph Phillips of the 29th Infantry Division tried to cheer them up. "This outfit," he solemnly predicted, "will never see combat. We've been in England so long that our job won't start until the war is over. They're going to have us wipe the bluebird shit off the White Cliffs of Dover."

At midnight Coast Guard cutters and naval destroyers began the huge job of reassembling the convoys again. This time there would be no turning back.

Off the coast of France the midget submarine X23 slowly came to the surface. It was 1 A.M., June 5. Lieutenant George Honour quickly undid the hatch. Climbing up into the little conning tower, Honour and another crewman erected the antennae. Below, Lieutenant James Hodges flicked the dial on the radio to 1850 kilocycles and cupped his earphones with his hands. He hadn't long to wait. Very faintly he picked up their call sign: "PADFOOT . . . PADFOOT . . . PADFOOT." As he heard the one-word message that followed, he looked up in disbelief. Pressing his hands more firmly over the earphones, he listened again. But there was no mistake. He told the others. Nobody said anything. Glumly they looked at one another; ahead lay another full day under water.

12

IN THE early-morning light the beaches of Normandy were shrouded in mist. The intermittent rain of the previous day had become a steady drizzle, soaking everything. Beyond the beaches lay the ancient, irregularly shaped fields over which countless battles had been fought and countless more battles would be fought.

For four years the people of Normandy had lived with the Germans. This bondage had meant different things for different Normans. In the three major cities—Le Havre and Cherbourg, the ports which bracketed the area on east and west, and between them (both geographically and in size) Caen, lying ten miles inland—the occupation was a harsh and constant fact of life. Here were the headquarters of the Gestapo and the S.S. Here were the reminders of war—the nightly roundups of hostages, the never ending reprisals against the underground, the welcome but fearful Allied bombing attacks.

Beyond the cities, particularly between Caen and Cherbourg, lay the hedgerow country: the little fields bordered by great mounds of earth, each topped with thick bushes and saplings, that had been used as natural fortifications by invaders and defenders alike since the days of the Romans. Dotting the countryside were the timbered farm buildings with their thatched or red-tiled roofs, and here and there stood the towns and villages like miniature citadels, nearly all with square-cut Norman churches surrounded by centuries-old gray stone houses. To most of the world their names were unknown—Vierville, Colleville, La Madeleine, Ste.-Mère-Église, Chef-du-Pont, Ste.-Marie-du-Mont, Arromanches, Luc. Here, in the sparsely populated countryside, the occupation had a different meaning than in the big cities. Caught up in a kind of pastoral backwash of the war, the Norman peasant had done what he could to adjust to the situation. Thousands of men and women had been shipped out of the towns and villages as slave laborers, and those who remained were forced to work part of their time in labor battalions for the coastal garrisons. But the fiercely independent peasants did no more than was absolutely necessary. They lived from day to day, hating the Germans with Norman tenaciousness, and stoically watching and waiting for the day of liberation.

In his mother's house on a hill overlooking the sleepy village of Vierville, a thirty-one-year-old lawyer, Michel Hardelay, stood at the living-room windows, his binoculars focused on a German soldier riding a large farm horse down the road to the sea front. On either side of his saddle hung several tin cans. It was a preposterous sight: the massive rump of the horse, the bounding cans, and the soldier's bucketlike helmet topping it all.

As Hardelay watched, the German rode through the village, past the church with its tall, slender spire and on down to the concrete wall that sealed the main road off from the beach. Then he dismounted and took down all but one can. Suddenly three or four soldiers appeared mysteriously from around the cliffs and bluffs. They took the cans and disappeared again. Carrying the remaining can, the German climbed the wall and crossed to a large russet-colored summer villa surrounded by trees which stood astride the promenade at the end of the beach. There he got down on his knees and passed the can to a pair of waiting hands that appeared at ground level from under the building.

Every morning it was the same. The German was never late; he always brought the morning coffee down to the Vierville exit at this time. The day had begun for the gun crews in the cliffside pillboxes and camouflaged bunkers at this end of the beach—a peaceful-looking, gently curving strip of sand that would be known to the world by the next day as Omaha Beach.

Michel Hardelay knew it was exactly 6:15 A.M.

He had watched the ritual many times before. It always struck Hardelay as a little comic, partly because of the soldier's appearance, partly because he found it amusing that the much vaunted technical know-how of the Germans fell apart when it came to a simple job like supplying men in the field with morning coffee. But Hardelay's was a bitter amusement. Like all Normans he had hated the Germans for a long time and he hated them particularly now.

For some months Hardelay had watched German troops and conscripted labor battalions digging, burrowing and tunneling all along the bluffs which backed up the beach and in the cliffs at either end where the sands stopped. He had seen them trellis the sands with obstacles and plant thousands of lethal, ugly mines. And they had not stopped there. With methodical thoroughness, they had demolished the line of pretty pink, white and red summer cottages and villas below the bluffs along the sea front. Now only seven out of ninety buildings remained. They had been destroyed not only to give the gunners clear arcs of fire, but because the Germans wanted the wood to panel their bunkers. Of the seven houses still standing, the largest—an all-year-round house built of stone—belonged to Hardelay. A few days before he had been officially told by the local commandant that his house would be destroyed. The Germans had decided they needed the bricks and the stone.

Hardelay wondered if maybe somebody, somewhere wouldn't countermand the decision. In some matters, the Germans were often unpredictable. He'd know for certain within twenty-four hours; he had been told the house would come down tomorrow—Tuesday, June 6.

At six-thirty, Hardelay switched on his radio to catch the BBC news. It was forbidden, but like hundreds of thousands of Frenchmen he flouted the order. It was just one more way to resist. Still he kept the sound down to a whisper. As usual, at the end of the news "Colonel Britain"—Douglas Ritchie, who was always identified as the voice of Supreme Headquarters Allied Expeditionary Force—read an important message.

"Today, Monday, June fifth," he said, "the Supreme Commander directs me to say this: There now exists in these broadcasts a direct channel of communications between the Supreme Commander and yourselves in the occupied countries. . . . In due course instructions of great importance will be given, but it will not be possible always to give them at a previously announced time; therefore, you must get into the habit, either personally or by arrangement with your friends, of listening at all hours. This is not as difficult as it sounds . . ." Hardelay guessed that the "instructions" would have something to do with the invasion. Everyone knew it was coming. He thought the Allies would attack at the narrowest part of the English Channel—around Dunkirk or Calais, where there were ports. But certainly not here.

The Dubois and Davot families living in Vierville didn't hear the broadcast; they slept late this morning. They had held a big celebration the previous night that had gone on until the early hours. Similar family gatherings had taken place all over Normandy, for Sunday, June 4, had been set aside by the ecclesiastical authorities as First Communion Day. It was always a great occasion, an annual reason for families and relatives to get together.

Togged out in their best clothes, the Dubois and Davot children had made their first Communion in the little Vierville church before their proud parents and relatives. Some of these relatives, each armed with a special pass from the German authorities which had taken months to get, had come all the way from Paris. The trip had been exasperating and dangerous—exasperating because the overcrowded trains no longer ran on time, dangerous because all locomotives were targets for Allied fighter-bombers.

But it had been worth it; a trip to Normandy always was. The region was still rich in all those things that Parisians rarely saw now—fresh butter, cheese, eggs, meat and, of course, Calvados, the heady cider-and-apple-pulp cognac of the Normans. Besides, in these difficult times Normandy was a good place to be. It was quiet and peaceful, too far away from England to be invaded.

The reunion of the two families had been a great success. And it wasn't over yet. This evening everyone would sit down to another great meal with the best wines and cognacs that their hosts had been able to save. That would wind up the celebrations; the relatives would catch the train for Paris at dawn on Tuesday.

Their three-day Normandy vacation was due to last much longer; they would remain trapped in Vierville for the next four months.

Farther down the beach, near the Colleville exit, forty-year-old Fernand Broeckx was doing what he did every morning at six-thirty: he sat in his dripping barn, spectacles askew, head tucked down by the udders of a cow, directing a thin stream of milk into a pail. His farm, lying alongside a narrow dirt road, topped a slight rise barely a half mile from the sea. He hadn't been down that road or onto the beach in a long time—not since the Germans had closed it off.

He had been farming in Normandy for five years. In World War I, Broeckx, a Belgian, had seen his home destroyed. He had never forgotten it. In 1939 when World War II began he promptly gave up his job in an office and moved his wife and daughter to Normandy, where they would be safe.

Ten miles away in the cathedral town of Bayeux his pretty nineteen-year-old daughter Anne Marie prepared to set out for the school where she taught kindergarten. She was looking forward to the end of the day, for then summer vacations began. She would spend her holidays on the farm. She would cycle home tomorrow.

Tomorrow also, a tall, lean American from Rhode Island whom she had never met would land on the beach almost in line with her father's farm. She would marry him.

All along the Normandy coast people went about their usual daily chores. The farmers worked in the fields, tended their apple orchards, herded their white-and-liver-colored cows. In the little villages and town's the shops opened. For everyone it was just another routine day of occupation.

In the little hamlet of La Madeleine, back of the dunes and the wide expanse of sand that would soon be known as Utah Beach, Paul Gazengel opened up his tiny store and café as usual, although there was almost no business.

There had been a time when Gazengel had made a fair living —not much, but sufficient for the needs of himself, his wife Marthe and their twelve-year-old daughter Jeannine. But now the entire coastal area was sealed off. The families living just behind the seashore—roughly from the mouth of the Vire (which emptied into the sea nearby) and all along this side of the Cherbourg peninsula—had been moved out. Only those who owned farms had been permitted to remain. The café keeper's livelihood now depended on seven families that remained in La Madeleine and a few German troops in the vicinity whom he was forced to serve.

Gazengel would have liked to move away. As he sat in his café waiting for the first customer, he did not know that within twenty-four hours he would be making a trip. He and all the other men in the village would be rounded up and sent to England for questioning.

One of Gazengel's friends, the baker Pierre Caldron, had more serious problems on his mind this morning. In Dr. Jeanne's clinic at Carentan ten miles from the coast, he sat by the bedside of his five-year-old son Pierre, who had just had his tonsils removed. At midday Dr. Jeanne re-examined his son. "You've nothing to worry about," he told the anxious father. "He's all right. You'll be able to take him home tomorrow." But Caldron had been thinking. "No," he said. "I think his mother will be happier if I take little Pierre home today." Half an hour later, with the little boy in his arms, Caldron set out for his home in the village of Ste.-Marie-du-Mont, back of Utah Beach—where the paratroopers would link up with the men of the 4th Division on D Day.

The day was quiet and uneventful for the Germans too. Nothing was happening and nothing was expected to happen; the weather was much too bad. It was so bad, in fact, that in Paris, at the Luftwaffe's headquarters in the Luxembourg Palace, Colonel Professor Walter Stöbe, the chief meteorologist, told staff officers at the routine daily conference that they could relax. He doubted that Allied planes would even be operational this day. Antiaircraft crews were promptly ordered to stand down.

Next, Stöbe telephoned 20 Boulevard Victor Hugo in St.-Germain-en-Laye, a suburb of Paris just twelve miles away. His call went to an immense, three-floored blockhouse, one hundred yards long, sixty feet deep and embedded in the side of a slope beneath a girl's high school—OB West, Von Rundstedt's headquarters. Stöbe spoke to his liaison officer, weatherman Major Hermann Mueller, who dutifully recorded the forecast and then sent it along to the chief of staff, Major General Blumentritt. Weather reports were taken very seriously at OB West and Blumentritt was particularly anxious to see this one. He was putting the finishing touches to the itinerary of an inspection trip the Commander in Chief West planned to make. The report confirmed his belief that the trip could take place as scheduled. Von Rundstedt, accompanied by his son, a young lieutenant, planned to inspect the coastal defenses in Normandy on Tuesday.

Not many in St.-Germain-en-Laye were aware of the blockhouse's existence and even fewer knew that the most powerful field marshal in the German west lived in a small unpretentious villa back of the high school at 28 Rue Alexandre Dumas. It was surrounded by a high wall, the iron gates permanently closed. Entrance to the villa was by way of a specially constructed corridor that had been cut through the walls of the school, or by way of an unobtrusive door in the wall bordering the Rue Alexandre Dumas.

Von Rundstedt slept late as usual (the aged Field Marshal

rarely got up now before ten-thirty) and it was almost noon before he sat down at his desk in the villa's first-floor study. It was there that he conferred with his chief of staff and approved OB West's "Estimate of Allied Intentions" so that it could be forwarded to Hitler's headquarters, OKW, later in the day. The estimate was another typical wrong guess. It read:

> The systematic and distinct increase of air attacks indicates that the enemy has reached a high degree of readiness. The probable invasion front still remains the sector from the Scheldt [in Holland] to Normandy . . . and it is not impossible that the north front of Brittany might be included . . . [but] it is still not clear where the enemy will invade within this total area. Concentrated air attacks on the coast defenses between Dunkirk and Dieppe may mean that the main Allied invasion effort will be made there . . . [but] imminence of invasion is not recognizable . . .

With this vague estimate out of the way—an estimate that placed the possible invasion area someplace along almost eight hundred miles of coast—Von Rundstedt and his son set out for the Field Marshal's favorite restaurant, the Coq Hardi at Bougival nearby. It was a little after one; D Day was twelve hours away.

All along the chain of German command the continuing bad weather acted like a tranquilizer. The various headquarters were quite confident that there would be no attack in the immediate future. Their reasoning was based on carefully assessed weather evaluations that had been made of the Allied landings in North Africa, Italy and Sicily. In each case conditions had varied, but meteorologists like Stöbe and his chief in Berlin, Dr. Karl Sonntag, had noted that the Allies had never attempted a landing unless the prospects of favorable weather were almost certain, particularly for covering air operations. To the methodical German mind there was no deviation from this rule; the weather had to be just right or the Allies wouldn't attack. And the weather wasn't just right.

At Army Group B headquarters in La Roche-Guyon the work went on as though Rommel were still there, but the chief of staff, Major General Speidel, thought it was quiet enough to plan a little dinner party. He had invited several guests: Dr. Horst, his brother-in-law; Ernst Junger, the philosopher and author; and an old friend, Major Wilhelm von Schramm, one of the official "war reporters." The intellectual Speidel was looking forward to the dinner. He hoped they'd discuss his favorite subject, French literature. There was something else to be discussed: a twenty-page manuscript that Junger had drafted and secretly passed on to Rommel and Speidel. Both of them fervently believed in the document; it outlined a plan for bringing about peace—after Hitler had either been tried by a German court or been assassinated. "We can really have a night discussing things," Speidel had told Schramm.

In St.-Lô, at the headquarters of the 84th Corps, Major Friedrich Hayn, the intelligence officer, was making arrangements for another kind of party. He had ordered several bottles of excellent Chablis, for at midnight the staff planned to surprise the corps commander, General Erich Marcks. His birthday was June 6.

They were holding the surprise birthday party at midnight because Marcks had to leave for the city of Rennes in Brittany at daybreak. He and all the other senior commanders in Normandy were to take part in a big map exercise that was to begin early on Tuesday morning. Marcks was slightly amused at the role he was supposed to play: he would represent the "Allies." The war games had been arranged by General Eugen Meindl, and perhaps because he was a paratrooper the big feature of the exercise was to be an "invasion" beginning with a paratroop "assault" followed by "landings" from the sea. Everyone thought the *Kriegsspiel* would be interesting—the theoretical invasion was supposed to take place in Normandy.

The *Kriegsspiel* worried the Seventh Army's chief of staff, Major General Max Pemsel. All afternoon at the headquarters in Le Mans he'd been thinking about it. It was bad enough that his senior commanders in Normandy and the Cherbourg peninsula would be away from their commands all at the same time. But it might be extremely dangerous if they were away overnight. Rennes was a long way off for most of them and Pemsel was afraid that some might be planning to leave the front before dawn. It was the dawn that always worried Pemsel; if an invasion ever came in Normandy, he believed, the attack would be launched at first light. He decided to warn all those due to participate in the games. The order he sent out by teletype read: "Commanding generals and others scheduled to attend the *Kriegsspiel* are reminded not to leave for Rennes before dawn on June 6." But it was too late. Some had already gone.

And so it was that, one by one, senior officers from Rommel down had left the front on the very eve of the battle. All of them had reasons, but it was almost as though a capricious fate had manipulated their departure. Rommel was in Germany. So was Army Group B's operations officer, Von Tempelhof. Admiral Theodor Krancke, the naval commander in the west, after informing Rundstedt that patrol boats were unable to leave harbor because of rough seas, set out for Bordeaux. Lieutenant General Heinz Hellmich, commanding the 243rd Division, which was holding one side of the Cherbourg peninsula, departed for Rennes. So did Lieutenant General Karl von Schlieben of the 709th Division. Major General Wilhelm Falley of the tough 91st Air Landing Division, which had just moved into Normandy, prepared to go. Colonel Wilhelm Meyer-Detring, Rundstedt's intelligence officer, was on leave and the chief of staff of one division couldn't be reached at all—he was off hunting with his French mistress.*

At this point, with the officers in charge of beachhead defenses dispersed all over Europe, the German High Command decided to transfer the Luftwaffe's last remaining fighter squadrons in France far out of range of the Normandy beaches. The fliers were aghast.

---

*After D Day the coincidences of these multiple departures from the invasion front struck Hitler so forcibly that there was actually talk of an investigation to see whether British secret service could possibly have had anything to do with it.

The fact is that Hitler himself was no better prepared for the great day than his generals. The Führer was at his Berchtesgaden retreat in Bavaria. His naval aide, Admiral Karl Jesko von Puttkamer, remembers that Hitler got up late, held his usual military conference at noon and then had lunch at 4 P.M. Besides his mistress, Eva Braun, there were a number of Nazi dignitaries and their wives. The vegetarian Hitler apologized to the ladies for the meatless meal with his usual mealtime comment, "The elephant is the strongest animal; he also cannot stand meat." After lunch the group adjourned to the garden, where the Führer sipped lime blossom tea. He napped between six and seven, held another military conference at 11 P.M., then, a little before midnight, the ladies were called back. To the best of Puttkamer's recollection, the group then had to listen to four hours of Wagner, Lehar and Strauss.

The principal reason for the withdrawal was that the squadrons were needed for the defense of the Reich, which for months had been coming under increasingly heavy round-the-clock Allied bombing attack. Under the circumstances it just did not seem reasonable to the High Command to leave these vital planes on exposed airfields in France where they were being destroyed by Allied fighters and bombers. Hitler had promised his generals that a thousand Luftwaffe planes would hit the beaches on the day of invasion. Now that was patently impossible. On June 4 there were only 183 day fighter planes in the whole of France,* of which about 160 were considered serviceable. Of the 160 one wing of 124, the 26th Fighter Wing, was being moved back from the coast this very afternoon.

At the headquarters of the 26th at Lille in the zone of the Fifteenth Army, Colonel Josef "Pips" Priller, one of the Luftwaffe's top aces (he had shot down ninety-six planes), stood on the airfield and fumed. Overhead was one of his three squadrons, heading for Metz in northeast France. His second squadron was about to take off. It had been ordered to Rheims, roughly halfway between Paris and the German border. The third squadron had already left for the south of France.

There was nothing the wing commander could do but protest. Priller was a flamboyant, temperamental pilot renowned in the Luftwaffe for his short temper. He had a reputation for telling off generals, and now he telephoned his group commander. "This is crazy!" Priller shouted. "If we're expecting an invasion the squadrons should be moved up, not back! And what happens if the attack comes during the transfer? My supplies can't reach the new bases until tomorrow or maybe the day after. You're all crazy!"

"Listen, Priller," said the group commander. "The invasion is out of the question. The weather is much too bad."

Priller slammed down the receiver. He walked back out onto the airfield. There were only two planes left, his and the one belonging to Sergeant Heinz Wodarczyk, his wing man.

---

*In researching this book I found no less than five different figures for the number of fighter planes in France. The figure of 183 given here I believe to be accurate. My source is a recent Luftwaffe history written by Colonel Josef Priller (see next paragraph), whose work is now considered one of the most authoritative yet written on the Luftwaffe's activities.

"What can we do?" he said to Wodarczyk. "If the invasion comes they'll probably expect us to hold it off all by ourselves. So we might as well start getting drunk now."

Of all the millions who watched and waited throughout France only a few men and women actually knew that the invasion was imminent. There were less than a dozen of them. They went about their affairs calmly and casually as usual. Being calm and casual was part of their business; they were the leaders of the French underground.

Most of them were in Paris. From there they commanded a vast and complicated organization. It was in fact an army with a full chain of command and countless departments and bureaus handling everything from the rescue of downed Allied pilots to sabotage, from espionage to assassination. There were regional chiefs, area commanders, section leaders and thousands of men and women in the rank and file. On paper the organization had so many overlapping nets of activity that it appeared to be unnecessarily complex. This apparent confusion was deliberate. In it lay the underground's strength. Overlapping commands gave greater protection; multiple nets of activity guaranteed the success of each operation; and so secret was the entire structure that leaders rarely knew one another except by code names and never did one group know what another was doing. It had to be this way if the underground was to survive at all. Even with all those precautions German retaliatory measures had become so crushing that by May of 1944 the life expectancy of an active underground fighter was considered to be less than six months.

This great secret resistance army of men and women had been fighting a silent war for more than four years—a war that was often unspectacular, but always hazardous. Thousands had been executed, thousands more had died in concentration camps. But now, although the rank and file didn't know it yet, the day for which they had been fighting was close at hand.

In the previous days the underground's high command had picked up hundreds of coded messages from the BBC. A few of these had been alerts warning that the invasion might come at any moment. One of these messages had been the first line of the Verlaine poem, "Chanson d'Automne"—the same alert that Lieutenant Colonel Meyer's men at the German Fifteenth Army headquarters had intercepted on June 1. (Canaris had been right.)

Now, even more excited than Meyer, the underground leaders waited for the second line of this poem and for other messages which would confirm the previously received information. None of these alerts was expected to be broadcast until the very last moment in the hours preceding the actual day of invasion. Even then the underground leaders knew that they would not learn from these messages the exact area where the landings were due to take place. For the underground at large the real tip-off would come when the Allies ordered the prearranged sabotage plans to go into effect. Two messages would trigger off the attacks. One, "It is hot in Suez," would put into effect the "Green Plan"—the sabotaging of railroad tracks and equipment. The other, "The dice are on the table," would call for the "Red Plan"—the cutting of telephone lines and cables. All regional, area and sector leaders had been warned to listen for these two messages.

On this Monday evening, the eve of D Day, the first message was broadcast by the BBC at 6:30 P.M. "It is hot in Suez. . . . It is hot in Suez," said the voice of the announcer solemnly.

Guillaume Mercader, the intelligence chief for the Normandy coastal sector between Vierville and Port-en-Bessin (roughly the Omaha Beach area) was crouching by a hidden radio set in the cellar of his bicycle shop in Bayeux when he heard it. He was almost stunned by the impact of the words. It was a moment he would never forget. He didn't know where the invasion would take place or when, but it was coming at long last, after all these years.

There was a pause. Then came the second message that Mercader had been waiting for. "The dice are on the table," said the announcer. "The dice are on the table." This was immediately followed by a long string of messages, each one repeated: "Napoleon's hat is in the ring. . . . John loves Mary. . . . The Arrow will not pass. . . ." Mercader switched off the radio. He had heard the only two messages that concerned him. The others were specific alerts for groups elsewhere in France.

Hurrying upstairs, he said to his wife, Madeleine, "I have to go out. I'll be back late tonight." Then he wheeled out a low racing bike from his bicycle shop and pedaled off to tell his section leaders. Mercader was the former Normandy cycling champion and he had represented the province several times in the famed Tour de France race. He knew the Germans wouldn't stop him. They had given him a special permit so that he could practice.

Everywhere now resistance groups were quietly told the news by their immediate leaders. Each unit had its own plan and knew exactly what had to be done. Albert Augé, the stationmaster at Caen, and his men were to destroy water pumps in the yards, smash the steam injectors on locomotives. André Farine, a café owner from Lieu Fontaine, near Isigny, had the job of strangling Normandy's communications: his forty-man team would cut the massive telephone cable feeding out of Cherbourg. Yves Gresselin, a Cherbourg grocer, had one of the toughest jobs of all: his men were to dynamite a network of railway lines between Cherbourg, St.-Lô and Paris. And these were just a few of the teams. It was a large order for the underground. Time was short and the attacks couldn't begin before dark. But everywhere along the invasion coast from Brittany to the Belgian border men prepared, all hoping that the attack would come in their areas.

For some men the messages posed quite different problems. In the seaside resort town of Grandcamp near the mouth of the Vire and almost centered between Omaha and Utah beaches, sector chief Jean Marion had vital information to pass on to London. He wondered how he'd get it there—and if he still had time. Early in the afternoon his men had reported the arrival of a new antiaircraft battery group barely a mile away. Just to be sure, Marion had casually cycled over to see the guns. Even if he was stopped he knew he'd get through; among the many fake identification cards he had for such occasions was one stating that he was a construction worker on the Atlantic Wall.

Marion was shaken by the size of the unit and the area it covered. It was a motorized flak assault group with heavy, light and mixed antiaircraft guns. There were five batteries, twenty-five guns in all, and they were being moved into positions covering the area from the mouth of the Vire all the way to the outskirts of Grandcamp. Their crews, Marion noted, were toiling feverishly to emplace the guns, almost as though they were working against time. The frantic activity worried Marion. It could mean that the invasion would be here and that somehow the Germans had learned of it.

Although Marion did not know it, the guns covered the precise route the planes and gliders of the 82nd and 101st paratroopers would take within a few hours. Yet, if anybody in the German High Command had any knowledge of the impending attack they hadn't told Colonel Werner von Kistowski, commander of Flak Assault Regiment 1. He was still wondering why his 2,500-man flak unit had been rushed up here. But Kistowski was used to sudden moves. His outfit had once been sent into the Caucasus all by itself. Nothing surprised him any more.

Jean Marion, calmly cycling by the soldiers at work on the guns, began to wrestle with a big problem: how to get this vital information to the secret headquarters of Léonard Gille, Normandy's deputy military intelligence chief, in Caen, fifty miles away. Marion couldn't leave his sector now—there was too much to do. So he decided to take a chance on sending the message by a chain of couriers to Mercader in Bayeux. He knew it might take hours, but if there was still time Marion was sure that Mercader would somehow get it to Caen.

There was one more thing Marion wanted London to know about. It wasn't as important as the antiaircraft gun positions—simply a confirmation of the many messages he had sent in the previous days about the massive gun emplacements on the top of the nine-story-high cliffs at Pointe du Hoc. Marion wanted to pass on once again the news that the guns had not yet been installed. They were still en route, two miles away from the positions. (Despite Marion's frantic efforts to warn London, on D Day U.S. Rangers would lose 135 men out of 225 in their heroic attack to silence guns that had never been there.)

For some members of the underground, unaware of the imminence of the invasion, Tuesday, June 6, had a special significance of its own. For Léonard Gille it meant a meeting in Paris with his superiors. Even now, Gille was calmly sitting in a train bound for Paris, although he expected Green Plan sabotage teams to derail it at any moment. Gille was quite sure the invasion was not scheduled for Tuesday, at least not in his area.

Surely his superiors would have canceled the meeting if the attack was due in Normandy.

But the date did bother him. That afternoon in Caen, one of Gille's section chiefs, the leader of an affiliated Communist group, had told him quite emphatically that the invasion was due at dawn on the sixth. The man's information had proved invariably right in the past. This raised an old question again in Gille's mind. Did the man get his information direct from Moscow? Gille decided not; it seemed inconceivable to him that the Russians would deliberately jeopardize Allied plans by breaking security.

For Janine Boitard, Gille's fiancée, back in Caen, Tuesday couldn't come soon enough. In three years of underground work, she had hidden more than sixty Allied pilots in her little ground-floor apartment at 15 Rue Laplace. It was dangerous, unrewarding, nerve-racking work; a slip could mean the firing squad. After Tuesday Janine could breathe a little easier—until the next time she hid a flier who was down—for on Tuesday she was due to pass along the escape route two R.A.F. pilots who had been shot down over northern France. They had spent the last fifteen days in her apartment. She hoped her luck would continue to hold.

For others, luck had already run out. For Amélie Lechevalier, June 6 could mean nothing, or everything. She and her husband, Louis, had been arrested by the Gestapo on June 2. They had helped more than a hundred Allied fliers to escape; they had been turned in by one of their own farm boys. Now, in her cell in the Caen prison, Amélie Lechevalier sat on the bunk and wondered how soon she and her husband would be executed.

13

OFF THE French coast a little before 9 P.M. a dozen small ships appeared. They moved quietly along the horizon, so close that their crews could clearly see the houses of Normandy. The ships went unnoticed. They finished their job and then moved back. They were British mine sweepers—the vanguard of the mightiest fleet ever assembled.

For now back in the Channel, plowing through the choppy gray waters, a phalanx of ships bore down on Hitler's Europe —the might and fury of the free world unleashed at last. They came, rank after relentless rank, ten lanes wide, twenty miles across, five thousand ships of every description. There were fast new attack transports, slow rust-scarred freighters, small ocean liners, Channel steamers, hospital ships, weather-beaten tankers, coasters and swarms of fussing tugs. There were endless columns of shallow-draft landing ships—great wallowing vessels, some of them almost 350 feet long. Many of these and the other heavier transports carried smaller land-ing craft for the actual beach assault—more than 1,500 of them. Ahead of the convoys were processions of mine sweep-ers, Coast Guard cutters, buoy-layers and motor launches. Barrage balloons flew above the ships. Squadrons of fighter planes weaved below the clouds. And surrounding this fan-tastic cavalcade of ships packed with men, guns, tanks, motor vehicles and supplies, and excluding small naval vessels, was a formidable array of 702 warships.*

There was the heavy cruiser U.S.S. *Augusta*, Rear Admi-ral Kirk's flagship, leading the American task force—twenty-one convoys bound for Omaha and Utah beaches. Just four months before Pearl Harbor the queenly *Augusta* had carried President Roosevelt to a quiet Newfoundland bay for the first of his many historic meetings with Winston Churchill. Nearby, steaming majestically with all their battle flags flying, were the battleships: H.M.S. *Nelson*, *Ramillies* and *Warspite*, and U.S.S. *Texas*, *Arkansas* and the proud *Nevada* which the Japanese had sunk and written off at Pearl Harbor.

Leading the thirty-eight British and Canadian convoys bound for Sword, Juno and Gold beaches was the cruiser H.M.S. *Scylla*, the flagship of Rear Admiral Sir Philip Vian,

---

*There is considerable controversy as to the exact number of ships in the inva-sion fleet, but the most accurate military works on D Day—Gordon Harrison's *Cross-Channel Attack* (the official U.S. Army military history) and Admiral Samuel Eliot Morison's naval history *Invasion of France & Germany*—both agree on a figure of about five thousand. This includes the landing craft which were carried on board. *Operation Neptune* by the Royal Navy's Commander Kenneth Edwards gives a lower figure of around 4,500.

the man who tracked down the German battleship *Bismarck*. And close by was one of Britain's most famous light cruisers —H.M.S. *Ajax*, one of a trio which had hounded the pride of Hitler's fleet, the *Graf Spee*, to her doom in Montevideo harbor after the battle of the River Plate in December 1939. There were other famous cruisers—the U.S.S. *Tuscaloosa* and *Quincy*, H.M.S. *Enterprise* and *Black Prince*, France's *Georges Leygues*—twenty-two in all.

Along the edges of the convoys sailed a variety of ships: graceful sloops, chunky corvettes, slim gunboats like the Dutch *Soemba*, antisubmarine patrol craft, fast PT boats, and everywhere sleek destroyers. Besides the scores of American and British destroyers, there were Canada's *Qu'Appelle*, *Saskatchewan* and *Ristigouche*, Norway's *Svenner*, and even a contribution from the Polish forces, the *Poiron*.

Slowly, ponderously this great armada moved across the Channel. It followed a minute-by-minute traffic pattern of a kind never attempted before. Ships poured out of British ports and, moving down the coasts in two-convoy lanes, converged on the assembly area south of the Isle of Wight. There they sorted themselves out and each took a carefully predetermined position with the force heading for the particular beach to which it had been assigned. Out of the assembly area, which was promptly nicknamed "Piccadilly Circus," the convoys headed for France along five buoy-marked lanes. And as they approached Normandy these five paths split up into ten channels, two for each beach—one for fast traffic, the other for slow. Up front, just behind the spearhead of mine sweepers, battleships and cruisers, were the command ships, five attack transports bristling with radar and radio antennae. These floating command posts would be the nerve centers of the invasion.

Everywhere there were ships. To the men aboard, this historic armada is still remembered as "the most impressive, unforgettable" sight they had ever seen.

For the troops it was good to be on the way at last, despite the discomforts and the dangers ahead. Men were still tense, but some of the strain had lifted. Now everybody simply wanted to get the job over and done with. On the landing ships and transports men wrote last-minute letters, played cards, joined in long bull sessions. "Chaplains," Major Thomas

Spencer Dallas of the 29th Division recalls, "did a land-office business."

One minister on a jam-packed landing craft, Captain Lewis Fulmer Koon, chaplain for the 4th Division's 12th Infantry Regiment, found himself serving as pastor for all denominations. A Jewish officer, Captain Irving Gray, asked Chaplain Koon if he would lead his company in prayer "to the God in whom we all believe, whether Protestant, Roman Catholic or Jew, that our mission may be accomplished and that, if possible, we may be brought safely home again." Koon gladly obliged. And in the gathering dusk, Gunner's Mate Third Class William Sweeney of a Coast Guard cutter remembers, the attack transport *Samuel Chase* blinked out a signal, "Mass is going on."

For most of the men the first few hours of the journey were spent quietly. Many grew introspective and talked of things men usually keep to themselves. Hundreds later recalled that they found themselves admitting their fears and talking of other personal matters with unusual candor. They drew closer to one another on this strange night and confided in men they had never even met before. "We talked a lot about home and what we had experienced in the past and what we would experience at the landing and what it would all be like," P.F.C. Earlston Hern of the 146th Engineer Battalion recalls. On the slippery wet deck of his landing craft, Hern and a medic whose name he never learned had such a conversation. "The medic was having trouble at home. His wife, a model, wanted a divorce. He was a pretty worried guy. He said she'd have to wait until he got home. I remember, too, that the whole time we were talking there was a young kid nearby singing softly to himself. This kid made the remark that he could sing better than he ever had in the past and it really seemed to please him."

Aboard H.M.S. *Empire Anvil*, Corporal Michael Kurtz of the U.S. 1st Division, a veteran of the invasions of North Africa, Sicily and Italy, was approached by a new replacement, Private Joseph Steinber of Wisconsin.

"Corporal," said Steinber, "do you honestly think we've got a chance?"

"Hell, yes, boy," said Kurtz. "Don't ever worry about getting killed. In this outfit we worry about battles when we get to them."

Sergeant Bill "L-Rod" Petty of the 2nd Ranger Battalion was doing his worrying now. With his friend, P.F.C. Bill McHugh, Petty sat on the deck of the old Channel steamer *Isle of Man* watching the darkness close in. Petty took cold comfort from the long lines of ships all about them; his mind was on the cliffs at Pointe du Hoc. Turning to McHugh, he said, "We haven't got a hope in hell of coming out of this alive."

"You're just a goddam pessimist," said McHugh.

"Maybe," replied Petty, "but only one of us will make it, Mac."

McHugh was unimpressed. "When you gotta go, you gotta go," he said.

Some men tried to read. Corporal Alan Bodet of the 1st Division began *Kings Row* by Henry Bellamann, but he found it difficult to concentrate because he was worrying about his jeep. Would the waterproofing hold out when he drove it into three or four feet of water? Gunner Arthur Henry Boon of the Canadian 3rd Division, on board a landing craft loaded with tanks, tried to get through a pocket book intriguingly titled *A Maid and a Million Men*. Chaplain Lawrence E. Deery of the 1st Division on the transport H.M.S. *Empire Anvil* was amazed to see a British naval officer reading Horace's odes in Latin. But Deery himself, who would land on Omaha Beach in the first wave with the 16th Infantry Regiment, spent the evening reading Symonds' *Life of Michelangelo*. In another convoy, on a landing craft which was rolling so much that nearly everybody was seasick, Captain James Douglas Gillan, another Canadian, brought out the one volume which made sense this night. To quiet his own nerves and those of a brother officer, he opened to the Twenty-third Psalm and read aloud, "The Lord is my Shepherd; I shall not want. . . ."

It wasn't all solemn. There was lightheartedness too. Aboard the transport H.M.S. *Ben Machree*, some Rangers strung three-quarter-inch ropes from the masts to the decks and began climbing all over the ship, much to the astonishment of the British crew. On another ship, members of the Canadian 3rd Division held an amateur night with assorted recitations, jigs and reels and choral offerings. Sergeant James Percival "Paddy" de Lacy of the King's Regiment became so emotional listening to the "Rose of Tralee" played on the bagpipes that

he forgot where he was and stood up and offered a toast to
Ireland's Eamon de Valera for "keepin' us out of the war."

Many men who had spent hours worrying about their
chances of survival now couldn't wait to reach the beaches.
The boat trip was proving more terrible than their worst fear
of the Germans. Seasickness had struck through the fifty-nine
convoys like a plague, especially in the rolling landing craft.
Each man had been supplied with antiseasickness pills, plus an
article of equipment which was listed in the loading sheets with
typical Army thoroughness as "Bag, vomit, one."

This was military efficiency at its best, but it still wasn't
enough. "The puke bags were full, tin hats were full, the
fire buckets were emptied of sand and filled," Technical Sergeant William James Wiedefeld of the 29th Division recalls.
"The steel decks you couldn't stand on, and everywhere you
heard men say, 'If they are going to kill us, get us out of these
damn tubs.'" On some landing ships men were so ill that they
threatened—possibly more for effect than in earnest—to throw
themselves overboard. Private Gordon Laing of the Canadian 3rd Division found himself hanging on to a friend who
"begged me to let go his belt." A Royal Marine commando,
Sergeant Russell John Wither, remembers that on his landing
ship "the spew bags were soon used up and in the end only one
was left." It was passed from hand to hand.

Because of the seasickness thousands of the men lost the
best meals they would see for many months to come. Special arrangements had been made to give all ships the finest
food possible. The special menus, which the troops dubbed
the "last meal," varied from ship to ship, and appetites varied from man to man. On board the attack transport *Charles
Carroll*, Captain Carroll B. Smith of the 29th Division had
a steak with eggs on top, sunny side up, and then topped
it off with ice cream and loganberries. Two hours later he
was fighting for a position at the rail. Second Lieutenant Joseph Rosenblatt, Jr., of the 112th Engineer Battalion ate seven
helpings of chicken à la king and felt fine. So did Sergeant
Keith Bryan of the 5th Engineer Special Brigade. He put away
sandwiches and coffee and was still hungry. One of his buddies "lifted" a gallon of fruit cocktail from the galley and four
of them finished that.

Aboard the H.M.S. *Prince Charles*, Sergeant Avery J. Thornhill of the 5th Rangers avoided all discomforts. He took an overdose of seasick pills and slept through it all.

Despite the common miseries and fears of the men who were there some memories are etched with surprising clarity. Second Lieutenant Donald Anderson of the 29th Division remembers how the sun broke through about an hour before dark, silhouetting the entire fleet. In honor of Sergeant Tom Ryan of the 2nd Rangers, the men of F Company gathered around him and sang "Happy Birthday." He was twenty-two. And for homesick nineteen-year-old Private Robert Marion Allen of the 1st Division it was "a night ready-made for a boat ride on the Mississippi."

All over, throughout the ships of the fleet, the men who would make history at dawn settled down to get what rest they could. As Commander Philippe Kieffer of the lone French commando unit rolled himself into his blankets aboard his landing ship, there came to his mind the prayer of Sir Jacob Astley at the battle of Edgehill in England in 1642. "O Lord," prayed Kieffer, "Thou knowest how busy I must be this day. If I forget Thee, do not Thou forget me . . ." He drew up the blankets and was almost immediately asleep.

It was a little after 10:15 P.M. when Lieutenant Colonel Meyer, counterintelligence chief of the German Fifteenth Army, rushed out of his office. In his hand was probably the most important message the Germans had intercepted throughout the whole of World War II. Meyer now knew that the invasion would take place within forty-eight hours. With this information the Allies could be thrown back into the sea. The message picked up from a BBC broadcast to the French underground was the second line of the Verlaine poem: "*Blessent mon coeur d'une langueur monotone* [Wounding my heart with a monotonous languor]."

Meyer burst into the dining room where General Hans von Salmuth, the Fifteenth Army's commanding officer, was playing bridge with his chief of staff and two others. "General!" Meyer said breathlessly. "The message, the second part—it's here!"

Von Salmuth thought a moment, then gave the order to put the Fifteenth Army on full alert. As Meyer hurried out of the room, Von Salmuth was again looking at his bridge hand. "I'm too old a bunny," Von Salmuth recalls saying, "to get too excited about this."

Back in his office, Meyer and his staff immediately notified OB West, Von Rundstedt's headquarters, by telephone. They in turn alerted OKW, Hitler's headquarters. Simultaneously all other commands were informed by teletype.

Once again, for reasons that have never been explained satisfactorily, the Seventh Army was not notified.* It would take the Allied fleet a little more than four hours now to reach the transport areas off the five Normandy beaches; within three hours eighteen thousand paratroopers would drop over the darkening fields and hedgerows—into the zone of the one German army never alerted to D Day.

Private Arthur B. "Dutch" Schultz of the 82nd Airborne Division was ready. Like everybody else on the airfield, he was in his jump suit, a parachute hanging over his right arm. His face was blackened with charcoal; his head, in the crazy style affected by paratroopers everywhere this night, was shaven Iroquois fashion, with a narrow tuft of hair running back the center of his scalp. All around him was his gear; he was ready

---

*All times in this book are given in British Double Summer Time, which was one hour later than German Central Time. So to Meyer the time his men intercepted the message was 9:15 P.M. Just for the record the Fifteenth Army War Diary carries the exact teletype message that was sent out to the various commands. It reads: "Teletype No. 2117/26 urgent to 67th, 81st, 82nd, 89th Corps; Military Governor Belgium and Northern France; Army Group B; 16th Flak Division; Admiral Channel Coast; Luftwaffe Belgium and Northern France. Message of BBC, 2115, June 5 has been processed. According to our available records it means 'Expect invasion within 48 hours, starting 0000, June 6.'"

It will be noted that neither the Seventh Army nor its 84th Corps is included in the above list. It was not Meyer's job to notify these. The responsibility lay with Rommel's headquarters, as these units came under Army Group B. However, the biggest mystery of all is why OB West, Rundstedt's headquarters, failed to alert the whole invasion front from Holland to the Spanish border. The mystery is further compounded by the fact that at war's end the Germans claimed that at least fifteen messages pertaining to D Day were intercepted and correctly interpreted. The Verlaine messages are the only ones I found entered in the German war diaries.

in every respect. Of the $2,500 he had won a few hours before he now had just $20 left.

Now the men waited for the trucks to carry them to the planes. Private Gerald Columbi, one of Dutch's friends, broke away from a small crap game that was still going and came running up. "Lend me twenty bucks quick!" he said.

"What for?" asked Schultz. "You might get killed."

"I'll let you have this," said Columbi, undoing his wrist watch.

"Okay," said Dutch, handing over his last $20.

Columbi ran back to the game. Dutch looked at the watch; it was a gold Bulova graduation model with Columbi's name and an inscription from his parents on the back. Just then someone yelled, "Okay, here we go."

Dutch picked up his gear and with the other paratroopers left the hangar. As he climbed aboard a truck he passed Columbi. "Here," he said, as he gave him back the watch, "I don't need two of them." Now all Dutch had left were the rosary beads his mother had sent him. He had decided to take them after all. The trucks moved across the airfield toward the waiting planes.

All over England the Allied airborne armies boarded their planes and gliders. The planes carrying the pathfinders, the men who would light the dropping zones for the airborne troops, had already left. At the 101st Airborne Division's headquarters at Newbury, the Supreme Commander, General Dwight D. Eisenhower, with a small group of officers and four correspondents, watched the first planes get into position for take-off. He had spent more than an hour talking to the men. He was more worried about the airborne operation than about any other phase of the assault. Some of his commanders were convinced that the airborne assault might produce more than eighty per cent casualties.

Eisenhower had said goodbye to the 101st's commanding officer, Major General Maxwell D. Taylor, who was leading his men into battle. Taylor had walked away carrying himself very straight and stiff. He didn't want the Supreme Commander to know that he had torn a ligament in his right knee that afternoon playing squash. Eisenhower might have refused him permission to go.

Now Eisenhower stood watching as the planes trundled

down the runways and lifted slowly into the air. One by one they followed each other into the darkness. Above the field they circled as they assembled into formation. Eisenhower, his hands deep in his pockets, gazed up into the night sky. As the huge formation of planes roared one last time over the field and headed toward France, NBC's Red Mueller looked at the Supreme Commander. Eisenhower's eyes were filled with tears.

Minutes later, in the Channel, the men of the invasion fleet heard the roar of the planes. It grew louder by the second, and then wave after wave passed overhead. The formations took a long time to pass. Then the thunder of their engines began to fade. On the bridge of the U.S.S. *Herndon*, Lieutenant Bartow Farr, the watch officers and NEA's war correspondent, Tom Wolf, gazed up into the darkness. Nobody could say a word. And then as the last formation flew over, an amber light blinked down through the clouds on the fleet below. Slowly it flashed out in Morse code three dots and a dash: V for Victory.

PART TWO

THE NIGHT

I

OONLIGHT flooded the bedroom. Madame Angèle Levrault, sixty-year-old schoolmistress in Ste.-Mère-Église,
slowly opened her eyes. On the wall opposite her bed bunches
of red and white lights were flickering silently. Madame Levrault
sat bolt upright and stared. The winking lights seemed to be
slowly dripping down the wall.

As full consciousness came to her, the old lady realized she
was looking at reflections in the large mirror on her dressing
table. At that moment, too, she heard off in the distance the
low throbbing of planes, the muffled booming of explosions
and the sharp staccato of quick-firing flak batteries. Quickly she
went to the window.

Far up the coast, hanging eerily in the sky, were brilliant
clusters of flares. A red glow tinged the clouds. In the distance there were bright-pink explosions and streams of orange,
green, yellow and white tracer bullets. To Madame Levrault it
looked as if Cherbourg, twenty-seven miles away, was being
bombed again. She was glad she lived in quiet little Ste.-Mère-
Église this night.

The schoolmistress put on her shoes and a dressing gown
and headed through the kitchen and out the back door, bound
for the outhouse. In the garden everything was peaceful. The
flares and the moonlight made it seem bright as day. The
neighboring fields with their hedgerows were still and quiet,
filled with long shadows.

She had taken only a few steps when she heard the sound of
airplanes growing louder, heading for the town. Suddenly every flak battery in the district began firing. Madame Levrault,
frightened, rushed wildly for the protection of a tree. The
planes came in fast and low, accompanied by a thunderous barrage of antiaircraft fire, and she was momentarily deafened by
the din. Almost immediately the roar of the engines faded, the
firing ceased and, as though nothing had happened, there was
silence again.

It was then that she heard a strange fluttering sound from
somewhere above her. She looked up. Floating down, heading

straight for the garden, was a parachute with something bulky swinging beneath it. For a second the light of the moon was cut off, and at that moment Private Robert M. Murphy* of the 82nd Airborne's 505th Regiment, a pathfinder, fell with a thud twenty yards away and tumbled head over heels into the garden. Madame Levrault stood petrified.

Quickly the eighteen-year-old trooper whipped out a knife, cut himself loose from his chute, grabbed a large bag and stood up. Then he saw Madame Levrault. They stood looking at each other for a long moment. To the old Frenchwoman, the paratrooper looked weirdly frightening. He was tall and thin, his face was streaked with war paint, accentuating his cheekbones and nose. He seemed weighted down with weapons and equipment. Then, as the old lady watched in terror, unable to move, the strange apparition put a finger to his lips in a gesture of silence and swiftly disappeared. At that moment, Madame Levrault was galvanized to action. Grabbing up the skirts of her nightwear, she dashed madly for the house. What she had seen was one of the first Americans to land in Normandy. The time was 12:15 A.M., Tuesday, June 6. D Day had begun.

All over the area the pathfinders had jumped, some from only three hundred feet. The task of this advance guard of the invasion, a small, courageous group of volunteers, was to mark "drop zones" in a 50-mile-square area of the Cherbourg peninsula back of Utah Beach for the 82nd and 101st paratroopers and gliders. They had been trained in a special school set up by Brigadier General James M. "Jumpin' Jim" Gavin. "When you land in Normandy," he had told them, "you will have only one friend: God." At all costs they were to avoid trouble. Their vital mission depended on speed and stealth.

---

*As a war correspondent I interviewed Madame Levrault in June 1944. She had no idea of the man's name or unit, but she showed me three hundred rounds of ammunition, still in their pouches, which the paratrooper had dropped. In 1958 when I began writing and interviewing D-Day participants for this book I was able to locate only a dozen of the original American pathfinders. One of them, Mr. Murphy, now a prominent Boston lawyer, told me that "after hitting the ground . . . I took my trench knife from my boot and cut myself out of the harness. Without knowing it I also cut away pouches carrying three hundred rounds of ammunition." His story tallied in all respects with Madame Levrault's, told to me fourteen years before.

Hitler's "Atlantic Wall" was formidable. Never before had an attacking force encountered such defenses—yet the Wall was only *partially* completed. These photos (enlargements from a 16 mm. German propaganda film) give some idea of the heavily gunned steel and concrete fortifications which girdled the invasion coast. Communication trenches, machine-gun nests, mortar pits and mine fields supplemented the heavy gun blockhouses, and the sands were strewn with a maze of mined anti-invasion obstacles. (*Wide World*)

Rommel inspects defenses along French coast in February 1944. On his right (almost out of picture) is Maj. Gen. Alfred Gause, his Chief of Staff up to March 1944. Facing camera, directly behind unidentified officer who is pointing, is Rommel's aide, Capt. Hellmuth Lang.

One of Rommel's simple but deadly anti-invasion beach obstacles—a stake topped by Teller mine. Rommel designed most of these devices and proudly called them "my inventions."

"Usually Rommel would explain his ideas by whipping out a pad and making a sketch," recalls his aide. Shortly after his first inspection trip of the invasion coast in the fall of 1943, Rommel sketched the diagram above. It outlined his beach-obstacle plan more clearly than if his engineers had written a pamphlet. It was distributed by the thousands, and Rommel drove his troops so hard to get his program finished that some generals complained. Gen. Marcks of the 84th Corps once told Rommel that his troops were getting "neither training nor rest." Replied Rommel: "My dear Marcks, which would they rather be— tired or dead?" Rommel's drive paid off. Below, the way the beaches looked by April 1944. (*Author's Collection*)

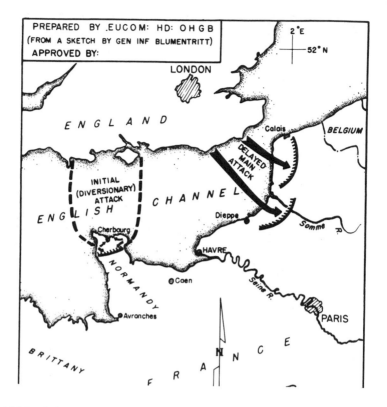

Field Marshal von Rundstedt [BELOW, LEFT] expected a two-pronged Allied invasion. The first, a diversionary attack against the Cherbourg peninsula and, later, the main assault against the Pas-de-Calais area, where Gen. Hans von Salmuth's massive 15th Army lay waiting. Even after D Day Hitler believed that the Pas-de-Calais attack would still come, and held the 15th Army in its positions until late July. Map prepared from sketches by Rundstedt's Chief of Staff, Maj. Gen. Gunther Blumentritt [BELOW, RIGHT].

Field Marshal Gerd von Rundstedt, German Supreme Commander in the West.

Maj. Gen. Gunther Blumentritt, Rundstedt's Chief of Staff.

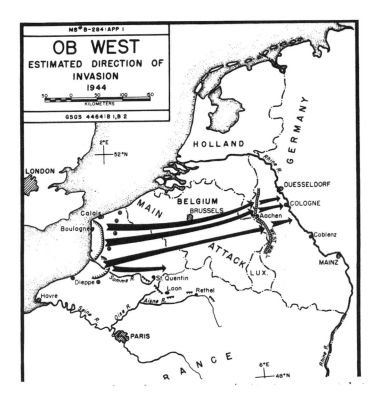

Blumentritt map, above, shows one reason why invasion was expected at Pas-de-Calais: it was the nearest point to the German border. Germans reasoned that Allies would pick the shortest route for their drive toward the Reich. Even after the Normandy invasion began, Rommel's Chief of Staff, Maj. Gen. Hans Speidel [BELOW, LEFT], thought it was a diversionary attack. The 7th Army's Chief of Staff, Maj. Gen. Max Pemsel [BELOW, RIGHT], was first German general to warn that Normandy assault was the real invasion.

Maj. Gen. Dr. Hans Speidel,
Rommel's Chief of Staff.

Maj. Gen. Max Pemsel,
7th Army's Chief of Staff.

General Dwight D. Eisenhower, the Supreme Commander, and Allied chiefs. [ABOVE LEFT TO RIGHT]: Lt. Gen. Omar N. Bradley, U.S. 1st Army Commander; Admiral Bertram Ramsey, Allied Naval Commander; Air Chief Marshal Tedder, Deputy Supreme Commander; Eisenhower; Field Marshal Bernard Montgomery, D Day's Assault Commander; Air Chief Marshal Leigh-Mallory, Allied Air Commander; Maj. Gen. Walter Bedell Smith, Eisenhower's Chief of Staff.

In last weeks of May, ports were jammed as men and equipment loaded for D Day attack. Picture below shows troops and vehicles going aboard three LSTs at Brixham. Notice concrete "hards," which were specially laid down to facilitate loading of shallow-draft landing craft.

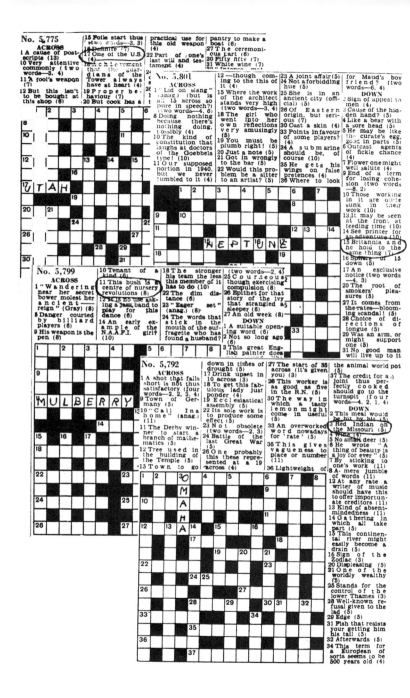

No. 5,775

ACROSS

1 A cause of post-scripta (13)
10 Very attentive commonly (two words—3, 4)
11 A fool's weapon (7)
12 But this isn't to be bought at this shop (6)
15 Foils start thus (two words—3, 3)
16 Definite (7)
17 One of the U.S. (4)
22 Part of one's last will and testament (4)
27 The ceremonious part (6)
30 Fifty fifty (7)
31 White wine (7)

...that the sundial of the Tower always have at heart (4)
19 Proper behaviour (7)
20 But cook has a...

U T A H

No. 5,801

ACROSS

1 "Lid on slang" (anag.) (but is all 15 across so pure in speech?) (two words—4, 6)
8 Doing nothing because there's nothing doing, possibly (4)
10 The kind of constitution that laughs at doctors of the Goebbels type! (10)
11 Our supposed portion in 1940, but we never tumbled to it (4)
12 —though coming to the this of it (4)
15 Where the work of the architect stands very high (two words—3, 4)
18 The girl who went into her own reflections very amusingly (5)
19 You must be plumb right! (5)
20 Just a note (5)
21 Got in wrongly to the bar (5)
22 Would this problem be a sitter to an artist? (5)
23 A joint affair (5)
24 Not a forbidding hue (5)
25 She is in an ancient city (official) (5)
26 Of Eastern origin, but serious (7)
30 Cast a skin (4)
33 Points in favour of some players? (4)
34 A submarine should be, of course (10)
35 He gets his wings on false pretences (4)
36 Where to look for Maud's boy friend? (two words—6, 4)

DOWN

2 Sign of appeal to men (4)
3 Cause of the hidden hand? (5)
4 Like a bear with a sore head (5)
5 He may be like the curate's egg, good in parts (5)
6 Outcast agents of fickle chance (4)
7 Flower one might well salute (4)
9 End of a term for losing cohesion (two words—8, 2)
10 Those working in it are quite sunk in their work (10)
13 It may be seen at the front at feeding time (10)
14 See printer for an adventure (10)
15 Britannia and he hold the same thing (7)
16 Sphere of 15 down (5)
17 An exclusive notice (two words—4, 3)
20 The root of smokers' pleasures (5)
27 It comes from the rates—blooming scandal! (5)
28 Choice of directions of tongue (5)
29 Was an arm, or might support one (5)
31 No good man will live up to it...

N E P T U N E

No. 5,799

ACROSS

1 "Wandering near her secret bower molest her ancient reign" (Gray) (8)
8 Danger courted by billiard players (8)
9 His weapon is the pen (8)
10 Tenant of a kind (6)
11 This bush is the centre of nursery revolutions (8)
12 It is no use asking a jazz band to play for this dance (6)
14 An early example of the N.A.A.F.I. (10)
18 The stronger his team the less has to do (10)
22 The dim distance (6)
23 "Eager" set (anag.) (8)
24 The words that stick in the mouth of the suffragette who has found a husband? (6)
25 Courteous though exercising compulsion (8)
26 Epithet for that story of the ivy that strangled a sleeper (8)
27 An old week (8)

DOWN

1 A suitable opening word (6)
3 This great English painter does...
33 [grid]
31 No good man will live up to it...

M U L B E R R Y

No. 5,792

ACROSS

1 A shot that falls short is not thus satisfactory (four words—2, 3, 3, 4)
9 Town of Germany (5)
10 "Call Ina home" (anag.) (11)
11 The Derby winner to start a branch of mathematics (5)
12 Tree used in the building of the Temple (5)
15 Town to go down in times of drought (5)
17 Drink upset in 10 across (3)
18 To get this fabulous lady just ponder (4)
19 Ecclesiastical assembly (5)
22 Its sole work is to produce some effect (5)
23 Not obsolete (two words—2, 3)
24 Battle of the last Great War (5)
26 One probably this these represented at a 19 across (4)
27 The start of 35 across (it's given you) (3)
28 This worker is as good as five in the R.N. (5)
30 The way in which a tasty lemon might come in useful (5)
33 An overworked word nowadays for 'rate' (5)
35 This gives vagueness to place or number (11)
36 Lightweight of the animal world pot (5)
37 The credit for a joint thus perfectly cooked should go to the turnspit (four words—4, 2, 1, 4)

DOWN

2 This meal would be hit by the (5)
3 Red Indian of the Missouri (5)
5 No amiss deer (5)
6 He wrote "A thing of beauty is a joy for ever" (5)
7 By sticking to one's work (11)
8 A mere jumble of words (11)
12 At any rate a writer of music should have this to offer importunate creditors (11)
13 Kind of absent-mindedness (11)
14 Gathering in which all take part (5)
15 This continental river might easily become a drain (5)
16 Sign of the Zodiac (3)
20 Displeasing (5)
21 One of the worldly wealthy (5)
25 Stands for the control of the lower Thames (5)
28 Well-known refusal given to the lad (5)
29 Edge (5)
31 Fish that resists your getting him his tall (5)
32 Afterwards (5)
34 This term for a European of sorts seems to be 500 years old (4)

M U L B E R R Y

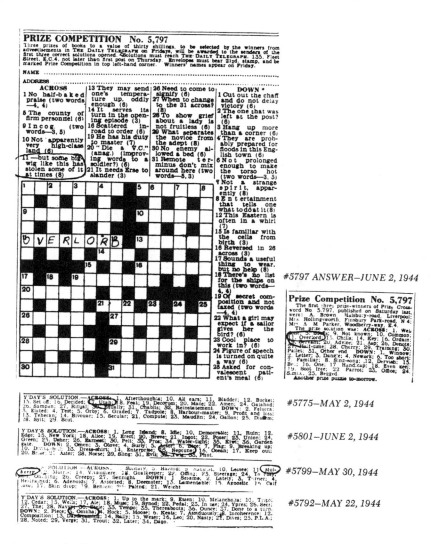

#5797 ANSWER–JUNE 2, 1944

#5775–MAY 2, 1944

#5801–JUNE 1, 1944

#5799–MAY 30, 1944

#5792–MAY 22, 1944

Here are the five *Daily Telegraph* crossword puzzles containing key D-Day code words, which scared Allied HQ. Although prepared months before, by some strange quirk of fate they all appeared in tense days prior to invasion. Note that "Overlord" and "Neptune," the principal code words, showed up on same day, June 2, four days before attack. (Reproductions courtesy Michael Berry, Editor, London *Daily Telegraph*)

This photo showing Eisenhower talking to 101st Division paratroops just before they boarded their planes on the evening of June 5 is probably the best known of all the pre-invasion pictures, but I have always wondered about the identities of the men. The 101st Airborne Association traced them for me. Among those surrounding the Supreme Commander are: Pfc. William Boyle, Cpl. Hans Sannes, Pfc. Ralph Pombano, Pfc. S. W. Jackson, Sgt. Delbert Williams, Cpl. William E. Hayes, Pfc. Carl Wickers, 1st Lt. William Strebel, Pfc. Henry Fuller, Pfc. Michael Babich and Pfc. William Noll.

Lt. Col. Hellmuth Meyer, 15th Army Intelligence chief, who picked up the Verlaine messages going to the French underground [SEE OPPOSITE PAGE], correctly interpreted them, and warned that the Allied invasion would take place in 48 hours. (*Author's Collection*)

Tag Uhrzeit Ort und Art der Unterkunft	Darstellung der Ereignisse (Dabei wichtig: Beurteilung der Lage [Feind- und eigene], Eingangs- und Abgangs- zeiten von Meldungen und Befehlen)
5 6.44	Am 1., 2. und 3.6.44 ist durch die Nast innerhalb der "Messages personelles" der französischen Sendungen des britischen Rundfunks folgende Meldung abgehört worden : "Les sanglots longs des violons de l'automne ".
	Nach vorhandenen Unterlagen soll dieser Spruch am 1. oder 15. eines Monats durchgegeben werden, nur die erste Hälfte eines ganzen Spruches darstellen und ankündigen, dass binnen 48 Stunden nach Durchgabe der zweiten Hälfte des Spruches, gerechnet von 00.00 Uhr des auf die Durchsage folgenden Tages ab, die anglo-amerikanische Invasion beginnt.
21.15 Uhr	Zweite Hälfte des Spruches "Blessent mon coeur d'une longeur monotone" wird durch Naet abgehört.
21.20 Uhr	Spruch an Ic-AO durchgegeben. Danach mit Invasionsbeginn ab 6.6. 00.00 Uhr innerhalb 48 Stunden zu rechnen.
	Überprüfung der Meldung durch Rückfrage beim Militärbe-fehlshaber Belgien/Nordfrankreich in Brüssel (Major von Wangenheim).
22.00 Uhr	Meldung an O.B. und Chef des Generalstabes.
22.15 Uhr	Weitergabe gemäss Fernschreiben (Anlage 1) an General-kommandos. Mündliche Weitergabe an 16.Flak-Division.

Photo of actual 15th Army War Diary page showing entries of two-part Verlaine message which indicated to Col. Meyer that invasion was imminent (see text). Note vital second line of the verse "Blessent mon coeur d'une longeur [sic] monotone" was picked up from BBC broadcast to French Underground at 9:15 (10:15 British time) and its meaning—that the invasion would begin within 48 hours starting 00:00, 6 June—was recorded five minutes later. Although other D Day messages were decoded, this is the only one recorded in German War Diaries. Ample evidence supports Col. Meyer's claim that Germans considered the Verlaine verse the all-important message. On June 8 Hitler's HQ demanded explanation from Rundstedt as to why full alert had not been ordered, and specifically referred to Verlaine passages. (*Author's Collection*)

Destination Normandy. [ABOVE] A "stick" of 101st Division paratroopers make final check before boarding DC 3. [BELOW] The convoys, protected by barrage balloons and fighter escorts, set sail for the beaches. (*Wide World*)

DC 3s of the 316th Troop Carrier Group towing Waco gliders over France.

First U.S. generals to land in Normandy. [LEFT TO RIGHT] Maj. Gen. Matthew B. Ridgway, 82nd Airborne's commanding officer; Brig. Gen. James M. Gavin, 82nd's Assistant Division Commander; Maj. Gen. Maxwell D. Taylor, 101st Airborne Commander. First senior British officer was 6th Airborne's Commander, Maj. Gen. Richard Gale.

Alexandre Renaud, Mayor of Ste.-Mère-Eglise, who witnessed slaughter in town square, and Father Louis Roulland, who ordered church bell rung.

This rare photo, the only one known to exist, shows a group of 82nd Airborne Pathfinders just before they took off for Normandy. These were among the first Americans to land in France. How many of the men pictured below survived the war and how many are still living? I was able to find only two 82nd Pathfinders. One of them, Pvt. Robert M. Murphy, who landed in Madame Levrault's back garden, is standing, third from right, wearing woolen cap. (*Courtesy Robert M. Murphy*)

Wrecked 30-man Horsa glider in field near Ste.-Mère-Eglise. Eight paratroopers died in crash.

Flooded areas at both ends of Normandy battlefield claimed greatest number of British and American paratroopers. In darkness, weighed down by equipment and often unable to extricate themselves from chutes, many men became casualties and drowned, often like the trooper below, in less than three feet of water. (*Courtesy Lt. Gen. James M. Gavin*)

Father Edward Waters conducts dockside service for 1st Division assault troops. The next stop would be Omaha Beach.

But the pathfinders ran into difficulties from the very beginning. They plunged into chaos. The Dakotas had swept in
over the targets so fast that the Germans at first thought they
were fighter planes. Surprised by the suddenness of the attack,
flak units opened up blindly, filling the sky with weaving patterns of glowing tracer bullets and deadly bursts of shrapnel. As
Sergeant Charles Asay of the 101st floated down, he watched
with a curious detachment as "long graceful arcs of multicolored bullets waved up from the ground," reminding him of the
Fourth of July. He thought "they were very pretty."

Just before Private Delbert Jones jumped, the plane he was
in got a direct hit. The shell slammed through without doing
much damage, but it missed Jones by only an inch. And as
Private Adrian Doss, burdened with upwards of one hundred
pounds of equipment, fell through the air, he was horrified
to find tracer bullets weaving all about him. They converged
above his head and he felt the tugging of his chute as the bullets ripped through the silk. Then a stream of bullets passed
through the equipment hanging in front of him. Miraculously
he wasn't hit, but a hole was ripped in his musette bag "large
enough for everything to fall out."

So intense was the flak fire that many planes were forced
off course. Only thirty-eight of the 120 pathfinders landed directly on their targets. The remainder came down miles away.
They dropped into fields, gardens, streams and swamps. They
crashed into trees and hedgerows and onto rooftops. Most of
these men were veteran paratroopers, but even so they were
utterly confused when they tried to get their initial bearings.
The fields were smaller, the hedgerows higher and the roads
narrower than those they had studied for so many months on
terrain maps. In those first awful moments of disorientation,
some men did foolhardy and even dangerous things. P.F.C.
Frederick Wilhelm was so dazed when he landed that he forgot he was behind enemy lines and switched on one of the
large marker lights he was carrying. He wanted to see if it still
worked. It did. Suddenly the field was flooded with light, scar-
ing Wilhelm more than if the Germans had actually opened fire
on him. And Captain Frank Lillyman, leader of the 101st teams,
almost gave his position away. Dropping into a pasture, he was
suddenly confronted by a huge bulk that bore down on him

out of the darkness. He almost shot it before it identified itself with a low moo.

Besides frightening themselves and startling the Normans, the pathfinders surprised and confused the few Germans who saw them. Two troopers actually landed outside the headquarters of Captain Ernst Düring of the German 352nd Division, more than five miles from the nearest drop zone. Düring, who commanded a heavy machine gun company stationed at Brevands, had been awakened by the low-flying formations and the flak barrage. Leaping out of bed, he dressed so quickly that he put his boots on the wrong feet (something he didn't notice until the end of D Day). In the street Düring saw the shadowy figures of the two men some distance away. He challenged them but got no answer. Immediately he sprayed the area with his *Schmeisser* submachine gun. There was no answering fire from the two well-trained pathfinders. They simply vanished. Rushing back to his headquarters, Düring called his battalion commander. Breathlessly he said into the phone, "*Fallschirmjäger* [Paratroopers]! *Fallschirmjäger!*"

Other pathfinders weren't as lucky. As Private Robert Murphy of the 82nd, lugging his bag (which contained a portable radar set), headed out of Madame Levrault's garden and started toward his drop zone north of Ste.-Mère-Église, he heard a short burst of firing off to his right. He was to learn later that his buddy, Private Leonard Devorchak, had been shot at that moment. Devorchak, who had sworn to "win a medal a day just to prove to myself that I can make it," may have been the first American to be killed on D Day.

All over the area pathfinders like Murphy tried to get their bearings. Silently moving from hedgerow to hedgerow, these fierce-looking paratroopers, bulky in their jump smocks and overloaded with guns, mines, lights, radar sets and fluorescent panels, set out for rendezvous points. They had barely one hour to mark the drop zones for the full-scale American airborne assault that would begin at 1:15 A.M.

Fifty miles away, at the eastern end of the Normandy battlefield, six planeloads of British pathfinders and six R.A.F. bombers towing gliders swept in over the coast. Ahead of them the sky stormed with vicious flak fire, and ghostly chandeliers of flares hung everywhere. In the little village of Ranville, a few miles from Caen, eleven-year-old Alain Doix had seen the flares, too. The firing had awakened him and now he stared transfixed, as had Madame Levrault, utterly fascinated by the kaleidoscopic reflections which he could see in the great brass knobs on the posts at the end of the bed. Shaking his grandmother, Madame Mathilde Doix, who was sleeping with him, Alain said excitedly, "Wake up! Wake up, Grandmama, I think something is happening."

Just then Alain's father, René Doix, rushed into the room. "Get dressed quickly," he urged them. "I think it's a heavy raid." From the window, father and son could see the planes coming in over the fields, but as he watched René realized that these planes made no sound. Suddenly it dawned on him what they were. "My God," he exclaimed, "these aren't planes! They're gliders!"

Like huge bats, the six gliders, each carrying approximately thirty men, swooped silently down. Immediately on crossing the coast, at a point some five miles from Ranville, they had been cast off by their tow planes from five to six thousand feet up. Now they headed for two parallel waterways shimmering in the moonlight, the Caen Canal and the Orne River. Two heavily guarded bridges, one leading to the other, crossed the twin channels just above and between Ranville and the village of Bénouville. These bridges were the objectives for this small band of British 6th Airborne glider infantry—volunteers from such proud units as the Oxfordshire and Buckinghamshire Light Infantry and the Royal Engineers. Their hazardous mission was to seize the bridges and overwhelm the garrison. If their task could be achieved a major artery between Caen and the sea would be severed, preventing the east-west movement of German reinforcements, particularly panzer units, from driving into the flank of the British and Canadian invasion area. Because the bridges were needed to expand the invasion bridgehead, they had to be captured intact before the guards could set off demolitions. A swift surprise assault was called for. The British had come up with a bold and dangerous solution. The men who now linked arms and held their breath as their gliders rustled softly down through the moonlit night were about to crash-land on the very approaches to the bridges.

Private Bill Gray, a Bren gunner, in one of three gliders heading for the Caen Canal bridge, closed his eyes and braced himself for the crash. It was eerily silent. There was no firing from the ground. The only sound came from the big machine, sighing gently through the air. Near the door, ready to push it open the moment they touched down, was Major John Howard, in charge of the assault. Gray remembers his platoon leader, Lieutenant H. D. "Danny" Brotheridge, saying, "Here we go, chaps." Then there was a splintering, rending crash. The undercarriage ripped off, splinters showered back from the smashed cockpit canopy, and, swaying from side to side like a truck out of control, the glider screeched across the ground, throwing up a hail of sparks. With a sickening half swing, the wrecked machine smashed to a halt, as Gray recalls, "with the nose buried in barbed wire and almost on the bridge."

Someone yelled, "Come on, lads!" and men came scrambling out, some piling through the door, others tumbling down from the stove-in nose. Almost at the same time and only yards away, the other two gliders skidded to a crashing halt and out of them poured the remainder of the assault force. Now everybody stormed the bridge. There was bedlam. The Germans were shocked and disorganized. Grenades came hurtling into their dugouts and communications trenches. Some Germans who were actually asleep in gun pits woke to the blinding crash of explosions and found themselves gazing into the business ends of Sten guns. Others, still dazed, grabbed rifles and machine guns and began firing haphazardly at the shadowy figures who seemed to have materialized from nowhere.

While teams mopped up resistance on the near side of the bridge, Gray and some forty men led by Lieutenant Brotheridge charged across to seize the all-important far bank. Halfway over, Gray saw a German sentry with a Very pistol in his right hand, ready to fire a warning flare. It was the last act of a courageous man. Gray fired from the hip with his Bren gun and, he thinks, so did everyone else. The sentry fell dead even as the flare burst over the bridge and arched into the night sky.

His warning, presumably intended for the Germans on the Orne bridge a few hundred yards ahead, was fired much too late. The garrison there had already been overrun, even though in that attack only two of the assaulting gliders found the target (the third came down seven miles away on the wrong bridge —a crossing over the Dives River). Both target bridges fell almost simultaneously. Stunned by the swiftness of the assault, the Germans were overwhelmed. Ironically, the Wehrmacht garrisons couldn't have destroyed the crossings even if they had had the time. Swarming over the bridges, the British sappers found that although demolition preparations had been completed, explosive charges had never been placed in position. They were found in a nearby hut.

Now there was that strange silence that seems always to follow a battle, when men partly dazed by the speed of events try to figure out how they lived through it and everybody wonders who else survived. The nineteen-year-old Gray, elated by his part in the assault, eagerly sought out his platoon leader, "Danny" Brotheridge, whom he had last seen leading the attack across the bridge. But there had been casualties, and one of them was the twenty-eight-year-old lieutenant. Gray found Brotheridge's body lying in front of a small café near the canal bridge. "He had been shot in the throat," Gray recalls, "and apparently hit by a phosphorous smoke grenade. His airborne smock was still burning."

Close by, in a captured pillbox, Lance Corporal Edward Tappenden sent out the success signal. Over and over he called into his walkie-talkie-like radio the code message, "Ham and jam . . . Ham and jam . . ." D Day's first battle was over. It had lasted barely fifteen minutes. Now Major Howard and his 150-odd men, deep in enemy territory and cut off for the moment from reinforcements, prepared to hold the vital bridges.

At least they knew where they were. The same couldn't be said for the majority of the sixty British paratroop pathfinders who jumped from six light bombers at 12:20 A.M.—the same time that Howard's gliders touched down.

These men took on one of the toughest of all D-Day jobs. The vanguard of the British 6th Airborne assault, they had volunteered to jump into the unknown and to mark three drop zones west of the Orne River with flashing lights, radar beacons and other guidance apparatus. These areas, all lying in a rectangle of roughly twenty square miles, were close to three small villages—Varaville, less than three miles from the coast; Ranville, near the bridges which Howard's men now held;

and Touffréville, barely five miles from the eastern outskirts of Caen. At twelve-fifty British paratroopers would begin dropping on these zones. The pathfinders had just thirty minutes to set them up.

Even in England in daylight, it would have been tricky to find and mark drop zones in thirty minutes. But at night, in enemy territory and in a country where few of them had ever been, their task was awesome. Like their comrades fifty miles away, the British pathfinders dropped headlong into trouble. They, too, were scattered widely and their drop was even more chaotic.

Their difficulties began with the weather. An unaccountable wind had sprung up (which the American pathfinders did not experience) and some areas were obscured by light patches of fog. The planes carrying the British pathfinder teams ran into curtains of flak fire. Their pilots instinctively took evasive action, with the result that targets were overshot or couldn't be found at all. Some pilots made two and three runs over the designated areas before all the pathfinders were dropped. One plane, flying very low, swept doggedly back and forth through intense antiaircraft fire for fourteen hair-raising minutes before unloading its pathfinders. The result of all this was that many pathfinders or their equipment plummeted down in the wrong places.

The troopers bound for Varaville landed accurately enough, but they soon discovered that most of their equipment had been smashed in the fall or had been dropped elsewhere. None of the Ranville pathfinders landed even close to their area in the initial drop; they were scattered miles away. But most unfortunate of all were the Touffréville teams. Two 10-man groups were to mark that area with lights, each one flashing up into the night sky the code letter K. One of these teams dropped on the Ranville zone. They assembled easily enough, found what they thought was their right area and a few minutes later flashed out the wrong signal.

The second Touffréville team did not reach the right area either. Of the ten men in this "stick," only four reached the ground safely. One of them, Private James Morrissey, watched with horror as the other six, suddenly caught by a heavy wind, sailed far off to the east. Helplessly Morrissey watched the men being swept away toward the flooded Dives valley, gleaming in the moonlight off in the distance—the area the Germans had inundated as part of their defenses. Morrissey never saw any of the men again.

Morrissey and the remaining three men landed quite close to Touffréville. They assembled and Lance Corporal Patrick O'Sullivan set out to reconnoiter the drop zone. Within minutes he was hit by fire which came from the very edge of the area they were supposed to mark. So Morrissey and the other two men positioned the Touffréville lights in the cornfield where they had landed.

Actually in these first confusing minutes few of the pathfinders encountered the enemy. Here and there men startled sentries and drew fire, and inevitably some became casualties. But it was the ominous silence of their surroundings which created the greatest terror. Men had expected to meet heavy German opposition the moment they landed. Instead, for the majority all was quiet—so quiet that men passed through nightmarish experiences of their own making. In several instances pathfinders stalked one another in fields and hedgerows, each man thinking the other was a German.

Groping through the Normandy night, near darkened farmhouses and on the outskirts of sleeping villages, the pathfinders and 210 men of the battalions' advance parties tried to get their bearings. As always, their immediate task was to find out exactly where they were. Those dropped accurately recognized the landmarks they had been shown on terrain maps back in England. Others, completely lost, tried to locate themselves with maps and compasses. Captain Anthony Windrum of an advance signal unit solved the problem in a more direct way. Like a motorist who has taken the wrong road on a dark night, Windrum shinnied up a signpost, calmly struck a match and discovered that Ranville, his rendezvous point, was only a few miles off.

But some pathfinders were irretrievably lost. Two of them plunged out of the night sky and dropped squarely on the lawn before the headquarters of Major General Josef Reichert, commanding officer of the German 711th Division. Reichert was playing cards when the planes roared over, and he and the other officers rushed out onto the veranda—just in time to see the two Britishers land on the lawn.

It would have been hard to tell who was the more aston-ished, Reichert or the two pathfinders. The General's intelli-gence officer captured and disarmed the two men and brought them up to the veranda. The astounded Reichert could only blurt out, "Where have you come from?" to which one of the pathfinders, with all the aplomb of a man who had just crashed a cocktail party, replied, "Awfully sorry, old man, but we simply landed here by accident."

Even as they were led away to be interrogated, 570 American and British paratroopers, the first of the Allied forces of liber-ation, were setting the stage for the battle of D Day. On the landing zones lights were already beginning to flash up into the night sky.

2

"WHAT'S HAPPENING?" yelled Major Werner Pluskat into the phone. Dazed and only half awake, he was still in his under-wear. The racket of planes and gunfire had awakened him, and every instinct told him that this was more than a raid. Two years of bitter experience on the Russian front had taught the major to rely heavily on his instincts.

Lieutenant Colonel Ocker, his regimental commander, seemed annoyed at Pluskat's phone call. "My dear Pluskat," he said icily, "we don't know yet what's going on. We'll let you know when we find out." There was a sharp click as Ocker hung up.

The reply didn't satisfy Pluskat. For the past twenty minutes planes had been droning through the flare-studded sky, bomb-ing the coast to the east and the west. Pluskat's coastal area in the middle was uncomfortably quiet. From his headquarters at Etreham, four miles from the coast, he commanded four bat-teries of the German 352nd Division—twenty guns in all. They covered one half of Omaha Beach.

Nervously, Pluskat decided to go over his regimental com-mander's head; he phoned division headquarters and spoke with the 352nd's intelligence officer, Major Block. "Probably just another bombing raid, Pluskat," Block told him. "It's not clear yet."

Feeling a little foolish, Pluskat hung up. He wondered if he had been too impetuous. After all, there had been no alarm. In fact, Pluskat recalls, after weeks of on-again, off-again alerts this was one of the few nights when his men had been ordered to stand down.

Pluskat was wide-awake now, too uneasy for sleep. He sat on the edge of his cot for some time. At his feet, Harras, his German shepherd, lay quietly. In the château all was still, but off in the distance Pluskat could still hear the droning of planes.

Suddenly the field telephone rang. Pluskat grabbed it. "Paratroopers are reported on the peninsula," said the calm voice of Colonel Ocker. "Alert your men and get down to the coast right away. This could be the invasion."

Minutes later Pluskat, Captain Ludz Wilkening, the commander of his second battery, and Lieutenant Fritz Theen, his gunnery officer, started out for their advance headquarters, an observation bunker built into the cliffs near the village of Ste.-Honorine. Harras went with them. It was crowded in the jeep-like Volkswagen and Pluskat recalls that in the few minutes it took them to reach the coast nobody talked. He had one big worry: his batteries had only enough ammunition for twenty-four hours. A few days before, General Marcks of the 84th Corps had inspected the guns and Pluskat had raised the question. "If an invasion ever does come in your area," Marcks had assured him, "you'll get more ammunition than you can fire."

Passing through the outer perimeter of the coastal defense zone, the Volkswagen reached Ste.-Honorine. There, with Harras on a leash, and followed by his men, Pluskat slowly climbed a narrow track back of the cliffs leading to the hidden headquarters. The path was clearly marked by several strands of barbed wire. It was the only entrance to the post and there were mine fields on either side. Almost at the top of the cliff the major dropped into a slit trench, went down a flight of concrete steps, followed a twisting tunnel and finally entered a large, single-roomed bunker manned by three men.

Quickly Pluskat positioned himself before the high-powered artillery glasses which stood on a pedestal opposite one of the bunker's two narrow apertures. The observation post couldn't have been better sited: it was more than one hundred feet above Omaha Beach and almost directly in the center of what was soon to be the Normandy beachhead. On a clear day from this vantage point, a spotter could see the whole Bay of the Seine, from the tip of the Cherbourg peninsula off to the left to Le Havre and beyond on the right.

Even now, in the moonlight, Pluskat had a remarkable view. Slowly moving the glasses from left to right, he scanned the bay. There was some mist. Black clouds occasionally blanketed out the dazzling moonlight and threw dark shadows on the sea, but there was nothing unusual to be seen. There were no lights, no sound. Several times he traversed the bay with the glasses, but it was quite empty of ships.

Finally Pluskat stood back. "There's nothing out there," he said to Lieutenant Theen as he called regimental headquarters. But Pluskat was still uneasy. "I'm going to stay here," he told Ocker. "Maybe it's just a false alarm, but something still could happen."

By now vague and contradictory reports were filtering into Seventh Army command posts all over Normandy, and everywhere officers were trying to assess them. They had little to go on—shadowy figures seen here, shots fired there, a parachute hanging from a tree somewhere else. Clues to something—but what? Only 570 Allied airborne troops had landed. This was just enough to create the worst kind of confusion.

Reports were fragmentary, inconclusive and so scattered that even experienced soldiers were skeptical and plagued by doubts. How many men had landed—two or two hundred? Were they bomber crews that had bailed out? Was this a series of French underground attacks? Nobody was sure, not even those like General Reichert of the 711th Division who had seen paratroopers face to face. Reichert thought that it was an airborne raid on his headquarters and that was the report he passed on to his corps commander. Much later the news reached Fifteenth Army headquarters, where it was duly recorded in the war diary with the cryptic note, "No details given."

There had been so many false alarms in the past that everyone was painfully cautious. Company commanders thought twice before passing reports on to battalion. They sent out patrols to check and recheck. Battalion commanders were even more careful before informing regimental officers. As to

what actually transpired at the various headquarters in these
first minutes of D Day, there are as many accounts as there
were participants. But one fact seems clear: On the basis of
such spotty reports nobody at this time was willing to raise the
alarm—an alarm that later might be proved wrong. And so the
minutes ticked by.

On the Cherbourg peninsula two generals had already departed for the map exercise in Rennes. Now a third, Major
General Wilhelm Falley of the 91st Air Landing Division,
chose this time to set out. Despite the order issued from Seventh Army headquarters forbidding commanding officers to
leave before dawn, Falley did not see how he could make the
Kriegsspiel unless he departed earlier. His decision was to cost
him his life.

At Seventh Army headquarters in Le Mans, the commanding officer, Colonel General Friedrich Dollmann, was asleep.
Presumably because of the weather, he had actually canceled a
practice alert scheduled for this very night. Tired out, he had
gone to bed early. His chief of staff, the very able and conscien-
tious Major General Max Pemsel, was preparing for bed.

In St.-Lô, at the headquarters of the 84th Corps, the next
level of command below army headquarters, all was set for
General Erich Marcks's surprise birthday party. Major Friedrich Hayn, the corps intelligence officer, had the wine ready.
The plan was for Hayn, Lieutenant Colonel Friedrich von
Criegern, the chief of staff, and several other senior officers to
walk into the General's room as the clock in St.-Lô Cathedral
struck midnight (1 A.M. British Double Summer Time). Everybody wondered how the stern-faced, one-legged Marcks (he
had lost a leg in Russia) would react. He was considered one
of the finest generals in Normandy, but he was also an austere
man not given to demonstrations of any kind. Still, the plans
were set and although everybody felt a little childish about the
whole idea the staff officers were determined to go through
with the party. They were almost ready to enter the General's
room when suddenly they heard a nearby flak battery open
up. Rushing outside, they were just in time to see an Allied
bomber spiraling down in flames and to hear the jubilant gun
crew yelling, "We got it! We got it!" General Marcks remained
in his room.

As the cathedral bells began chiming, the little group, with Major Hayn in the lead carrying the Chablis and several glasses, marched into the General's room, perhaps a shade self-consciously, to do honor to their commander. There was a slight pause as Marcks looked up and gazed at them mildly through his glasses. "His artificial leg creaked," recalls Hayn, "as he rose to greet us." With a friendly wave of the hand he immediately put everybody at ease. The wine was opened and, standing in a little group around the fifty-three-year-old general, his staff officers came to attention. Stiffly raising their glasses, they drank his health, blissfully unaware that forty miles away 4,255 British paratroopers were dropping on French soil.

3

ACROSS the moonlit fields of Normandy rolled the hoarse, haunting notes of an English hunting horn. The sound hung in the air, lonely, incongruous. Again and again the horn sounded. Scores of shadowy helmeted figures, in green-brown-and-yellow camouflaged jump smocks festooned with equipment, struggled across fields, along ditches, by the sides of hedgerows, all heading in the direction of the call. Other horns took up the chorus. Suddenly a bugle began trumpeting. For hundreds of men of the British 6th Airborne Division this was the overture to battle.

The strange cacophony came from the Ranville area. The calls were the assembly signals for two battalions of the 5th Parachute Brigade and they had to move fast. One was to rush to the assistance of Major Howard's tiny glider-borne force holding the bridges. The other was to seize and hold Ranville, at the eastern approaches to this vital crossing. Never before had paratroop commanders assembled men in this manner, but speed this night was essential. The 6th Airborne was racing against time. The first waves of American and British troops would land on Normandy's five invasion beaches between 6:30 and 7:30 A.M. The "Red Devils" had five and a half hours to secure the initial foothold and anchor the left flank of the entire invasion area.

The division had a variety of complex tasks, each one demanding almost minute-by-minute synchronization. The plan called for paratroopers to dominate the heights northeast of Caen, hold the bridges over the Orne and the Caen Canal, demolish five more on the Dives River and thus block enemy forces, particularly panzers, from driving into the side of the invasion bridgehead.

But the lightly armed paratroopers didn't have enough fire power to stop a concentrated armored attack. So the success of the holding action depended on the speedy and safe arrival of antitank guns and special armor-piercing ammunition. Because of the weight and size of the guns there was only one way of getting them safely into Normandy: by glider train. At 3:20 A.M. a fleet of sixty-nine gliders was due to sweep down out of the Normandy skies carrying men, vehicles, heavy equipment and the precious guns.

Their arrival posed a mammoth problem all by itself. The gliders were immense—each one larger than a DC-3. Four of them, the Hamilcars, were so big that they could even carry light tanks. To get the sixty-nine gliders in, the paratroopers had first to secure the chosen landing zones from enemy attack. Next they had to create a huge landing field out of the obstacle-studded meadows. This meant clearing a forest of mined tree trunks and railroad ties, in the dead of night, and in just under two and a half hours. The same field would be used for a second glider train due to land in the evening.

There was one more job to be done. It was perhaps the most important of all the 6th Airborne's missions: the destruction of a massive coastal battery near Merville. Allied intelligence believed that this battery's four powerful guns could harass the assembling invasion fleet and massacre the troops landing on Sword Beach. The 6th had been ordered to destroy the guns by 5 A.M.

To accomplish these tasks 4,255 paratroopers of the 3rd and 5th parachute brigades had jumped into Normandy. They dropped over a huge area, victims of navigational errors, bucketing planes forced off course by flak fire, badly marked drop zones and gusty winds. Some were fortunate, but thousands fell anywhere from five to thirty-five miles from the drop zones.

Of the two brigades the 5th fared best. Most of its soldiers were dropped close to their objectives near Ranville. Even so, it would take company commanders the better part of two hours to assemble even half their men. Scores of troopers, however, were already en route, guided in by the wavering notes of the horns.

Private Raymond Batten of the 13th Battalion heard the horns, but although he was almost at the edge of his drop zone he was momentarily unable to do anything about it. Batten had crashed through the thick, leafy roof of a small woods. He was hanging from a tree, slowly swaying back and forth in his harness, just fifteen feet from the ground. It was very still in the woods, but Batten could hear prolonged bursts of machine gun fire, the droning of planes and the firing of flak batteries off in the distance. As he pulled out his knife, ready to cut himself down, Batten heard the abrupt stutter of a *Schmeisser* machine pistol nearby. A minute later, there was a rustling of underbrush and somebody moved slowly toward him. Batten had lost his Sten gun in the drop and he didn't have a pistol. Helplessly he hung there, not knowing whether it was a German or another paratrooper moving toward him. "Whoever it was came and looked up at me," Batten recalls. "All I could do was to keep perfectly still and he, probably thinking I was dead, as I hoped he would, went away."

Batten got down from the tree as fast as he could and headed toward the rallying horns. But his ordeal was far from over. At the edge of the woods he found the corpse of a young paratrooper whose parachute had failed to open. Next, as he moved along a road a man rushed past him shouting crazily, "They got my mate! They got my mate!" And finally, catching up with a group of paratroopers heading toward the assembly point, Batten found himself beside a man who seemed to be in a state of complete shock. He strode along, looking neither to his left or right, totally oblivious of the fact that the rifle which he gripped tightly in his right hand was bent almost double.

In many places this night men like Batten were shocked almost immediately into the harsh realities of war. As he was struggling to get out of his harness, Lance Corporal Harold Tait of the 8th Battalion saw one of the Dakota transports hit by flak. The plane careened over his head like a searing comet and exploded with a tremendous noise about a mile away. Tait wondered if the stick of troopers it carried had already jumped.

Private Percival Liggins of the Canadian 1st Battalion saw

another flaming plane. It was "at full power, with pieces falling off it, blazing from end to end," and seemed to be heading for him. He was so fascinated by the sight that he was unable to move. It swept overhead and crashed in a field behind him. He and others tried to get to the plane in an effort to rescue anybody still in it, but "the ammo started to go and we couldn't get near it."

To twenty-year-old Private Colin Powell of the 12th Battalion, miles from his drop zone, the first sound of war was a moaning in the night. He knelt down beside a badly wounded trooper, an Irishman, who softly pleaded with Powell to "finish me off, lad, please." Powell could not do it. He made the trooper as comfortable as he could and hurried off, promising to send back help.

In these first few minutes their own resourcefulness became the measure of survival for many men. One paratrooper, Lieutenant Richard Hilborn of the Canadian 1st Battalion remembers, crashed through the top of a greenhouse, "shattering glass all over the place and making a hell of a lot of noise, but he was out and running before the glass had stopped falling." Another fell with pinpoint accuracy into a well. Hauling himself up hand over hand on his shroud lines, he set out for his assembly point as though nothing had happened.

Everywhere men extricated themselves from extraordinary predicaments. Most of their situations would have been bad enough in daylight; at night, in hostile territory, they were compounded by fear and imagination. Such was the case with Private Godfrey Maddison. He sat at the edge of a field imprisoned by a barbed-wire fence, unable to move. Both legs were twisted in the wire and the weight of his equipment—125 pounds, including four 10-pound mortar shells—had driven him so far forward into the wire that he was almost completely enmeshed. Maddison had been heading toward the rallying horns of the 5th when he missed his footing and crashed into the fence. "I started to panic a bit," he remembers, "and it was very dark and I felt sure someone would take a potshot at me." For a few moments he did nothing but wait and listen. Then, satisfied that he had escaped notice, Maddison began a slow and painful struggle to free himself. It seemed hours before he finally worked one arm free enough to get a pair of wire cutters from the back of his belt. In a few minutes he was out and heading in the direction of the horns again.

At about that same time Major Donald Wilkins of the Canadian 1st Battalion was crawling past what appeared to him to be a small factory building. Suddenly he saw a group of figures on the lawn. He instantly threw himself to the ground. The shadowy figures did not move. Wilkins stared hard at them and, after a minute, got up cursing and went over to confirm his suspicions. They were stone garden statues.

A sergeant of the same unit had a somewhat similar experience, except that the figures he saw were only too real. Private Henry Churchill, in a nearby ditch, saw the sergeant, who had landed in knee-deep water, shrug out of his harness and look about in desperation as two men approached. "The sergeant waited," Churchill remembers, "trying to decide whether they were British or Germans." The men came closer and their voices were unmistakably German. The sergeant's Sten gun barked and "he brought them down with a single fast burst."

The most sinister enemy in these opening minutes of D Day was not man but nature. Rommel's antiparatroop precautions had paid off well: the waters and swamps of the flooded Dives valley were deathtraps. Many of the men of the 3rd Brigade came down in this area like so much confetti shaken haphazardly out of a bag. For these paratroopers, mishap followed tragic mishap. Some pilots, caught in heavy cloud, mistook the mouth of the Dives for that of the Orne and let men out over a maze of marshes and swamps. One entire battalion of seven hundred whose drop was to be concentrated in an area roughly a mile square was scattered, instead, over fifty miles of countryside, most of it swampland. And this battalion, the highly trained 9th, had been given the toughest, most urgent job of the night—the assault on the Merville battery. It would take some of these men days to rejoin their unit; many would never return at all.

The number of troopers who died in the wastes of the Dives will never be known. Survivors say that the marshes were intersected by a maze of ditches about seven feet deep, four feet wide and bottomed with sticky slime. A man alone, weighed down with guns, ammunition and heavy equipment, could not negotiate these ditches. Wet kitbags nearly doubled in weight and men had to discard them in order to survive. Many men who somehow struggled through the marshes drowned in the river with dry land only a few yards away.

Private Henry Humberstone of the 224th Parachute Field Ambulance narrowly missed such a death. Humberstone landed waist-deep in the marshes, with no idea of where he was. He had expected to come down in the orchard area west of Varaville; instead he had landed on the east side of the drop zone. Between him and Varaville were not only the marshes but the Dives River itself. A low mist covered the area like a dirty white blanket, and all around Humberstone could hear the croaking of frogs. Then, ahead, came the unmistakable sound of rushing water. Humberstone stumbled on through the flooded fields and came upon the Dives. While he looked for some way to cross the river, he spotted two men on the opposite bank. They were members of the Canadian 1st Battalion. "How do I get across?" yelled Humberstone. "It's quite safe," one of them called back. The Canadian waded into the river, apparently to show him. "I was watching him one minute and the next minute he was gone," Humberstone remembers. "He didn't yell or scream or anything. He just drowned before either me or his buddy on the other bank could do anything."

Captain John Gwinnett, the chaplain of the 9th Battalion, was completely lost. He, too, had landed in the marshes. He was all alone and the silence around him was unnerving. Gwinnett had to get out of the swamps. He was certain the Merville assault would be a bloody one and he wanted to be with his men. "Fear," he had told them at the airfield just before take-off, "knocked at the door. Faith opened it, and there was nothing there." Gwinnett did not know it now, but it would be a full seventeen hours before he found his way out of the swamps.

At this moment the 9th's commander, Lieutenant Colonel Terence Otway, was in a towering rage. He had been dropped miles from the rendezvous point, and he knew that his battalion must have been thoroughly scattered. As Otway marched quickly through the night, small groups of his men appeared everywhere, confirming his worst suspicions. He wondered just how bad the drop had been. Had his special glider train been scattered, too?

Otway badly needed the glider-borne guns and other equipment if his plan of assault was to succeed, for Merville was no ordinary battery. Around it ranged a formidable series of defenses in depth. To get to the heart of the battery—four heavy guns in massive concrete emplacements—the 9th would have to pass through mine fields and over antitank ditches, penetrate a 15-foot-thick hedge of barbed wire, cross more mine fields and then fight through a maze of machine-gun-filled trenches. The Germans considered this deadly fortification with its garrison of two hundred men almost impregnable.

Otway didn't think it was, and his plan to destroy it was elaborate and incredibly detailed. He wanted to leave nothing to chance. One hundred Lancaster bombers were to saturate the battery first with 4,000-pound bombs. The glider trains were to bring in jeeps, antitank guns, flame throwers, "Bangalore" torpedoes (lengths of explosive-filled pipe to destroy the wire), mine detectors, mortars, and even lightweight aluminum scaling ladders. After collecting this special equipment from the gliders, Otway's men were to set out for the battery in eleven teams to begin the assault.

This called for dovetailed timing. Reconnaissance teams would lead off and scout the area. "Taping" parties would remove the mines and mark the approaches through the cleared areas. "Breaching" teams with the Bangalore torpedoes would destroy the barbed wire. Snipers, mortar men and machine gunners were to take up positions to cover the main charge.

Otway's plan had one final surprise: At the same time that his assault troops rushed the battery from the ground, three gliders filled with more troopers were to crash-land *on the top of the battery*, in a combined massive rush on the defenses from ground and air.

Parts of the plan seemed suicidal, but the risks were worth taking, for the Merville guns could kill thousands of British troops as they touched down on Sword Beach. Even if everything went according to schedule in the next few hours, by the time Otway and his men assembled, moved out and reached the battery they would have barely an hour to destroy the guns. He had been told plainly that if the 9th could not complete the task on time, naval gunfire would try to do it. That meant that Otway and his men had to be away from the battery, no matter what the outcome, by 5:30 A.M. At that time, if the signal of success had not come from Otway, the bombardment would begin.

That was the strategy. But, as Otway hurried anxiously toward the assembly point, the first part of the plan had already misfired. The air attack which had taken place at twelve-thirty had been a complete failure; not one bomb had hit the battery. And the errors were multiplying: the gliders with the vital supplies had failed to arrive.

In the center of the Normandy beachhead, in the German observation bunker overlooking Omaha Beach, Major Werner Pluskat still watched. He saw the white tops of the waves, nothing more. His uneasiness had not lessened; if anything, Pluskat felt more certain than ever that something was happening. Soon after he reached the bunker, formation after formation of planes had thundered over the coast far off to the right; Pluskat thought there must have been hundreds. From the first moment he heard them, he had expected a sudden call from regiment confirming his suspicions that the invasion was in fact beginning. But the phone had remained silent. There had been nothing from Ocker since the first call. Now Pluskat heard something else—the slowly swelling roar of a great number of planes off to his left. This time the sound was coming from behind him. The planes seemed to be approaching the Cherbourg peninsula from the west. Pluskat was more bewildered than ever. Instinctively he looked out through his glasses once again. The bay was completely empty. There was nothing to be seen.

4

IN STE.-MÈRE-ÉGLISE the sound of bombing was very close. Alexandre Renaud, the mayor and town pharmacist, could feel the very ground shaking. It seemed to him that planes were attacking the batteries at St.-Marcouf and St.-Martin-de-Varreville, and both places were only a few miles away. He was quite worried about the town and its people. About all the inhabitants could do was take shelter in garden trenches or cellars, for they could not leave their homes because of the

curfew. Renaud herded his wife, Simone, and their three children to the passageway leading off the living room. Its heavy
timbers afforded good protection. It was about 1:10 A.M. when
the family collected in the makeshift air raid shelter. Renaud
remembers the time (it was 12:10 A.M. to him), because just
then there was a persistent, urgent knocking at the street door.

Renaud left his family in their living quarters and walked
through his darkened pharmacist's shop, which fronted on the
Place de l'Église. Even before he reached the door, he could
see what the trouble was. Through the windows of his shop
the square, with its edging of chestnut trees and its great Norman church, appeared brilliantly lit up. M. Hairon's villa across
the square was on fire and blazing fiercely.

Renaud got the door open. The town's fire chief, resplendent in his polished, shoulder-length brass helmet, stood before him. "I think it was hit by a stray incendiary from one of
the planes," the man said without any preamble, motioning
toward the burning house. "The fire is spreading fast. Can you
get the commandant to lift the curfew? We need as much help
as we can get for the bucket brigade."

The mayor ran to the nearby German headquarters. He
quickly explained the situation to the sergeant on duty, who,
on his own authority, gave permission. At the same time the
German called out the guard, to watch the volunteers when
they assembled. Then Renaud went to the parish house and
told Father Louis Roulland. The curé sent his sexton to the
church to toll the bell, while he, Renaud and the others banged
on doors, calling for the inhabitants to help. Above them
the bell began to clang, booming out over the town. People
started to appear, some in their nightwear, others half dressed,
and soon more than one hundred men and women in two
long lines were passing buckets of water from hand to hand.
Surrounding them were about thirty German guards armed
with rifles and *Schmeissers*.

In the midst of this confusion, Renaud remembers, Father
Roulland took him aside. "I must talk to you—something very
important," the priest said. He led Renaud to the kitchen of
the parish house. There Madame Angèle Levrault, the aged
schoolmistress, awaited them. She was in a state of shock. "A
man has landed in my pea patch," she announced in a wavering

voice. Renaud had almost more trouble than he could handle, but he tried to calm her. "Don't worry," he said. "Please go home and stay indoors." Then he raced back to the fire.

The noise and confusion had intensified in his absence. The flames were higher now. Showers of sparks had spread to the outbuildings and they were already starting to burn. To Renaud the scene had a nightmarish quality. He stood almost rooted to the spot, seeing the flushed, excited faces of the fire fighters, the overdressed, ponderous German guards with their rifles and machine guns. And above the square the bell still tolled, adding its persistent clanging to the din. It was then they all heard the droning of the planes.

The sound came from the west—a steadily mounting roar, and with it the approaching racket of antiaircraft fire as battery after battery across the peninsula picked up the formations. In the square of Ste.-Mère-Église everybody looked up, transfixed, the burning house forgotten. Then the guns of the town began firing and the roaring was on top of them. The aircraft swept in, almost wing tip to wing tip, through a crisscrossing barrage of fire that hammered up from the ground. The planes' lights were on. They came in so low that people in the square instinctively ducked and Renaud remembers that the airplanes cast "great shadows on the ground and red lights seemed to be glowing inside them."

In wave after wave the formations flew over, the first planes of the biggest airborne operation ever attempted—882 planes carrying thirteen thousand men. These men of the U.S. 101st and veteran 82nd airborne divisions were heading for six drop zones all within a few miles of Ste.-Mère-Église. The troopers tumbled out of their planes, stick after stick. And as those destined for the zone outside the town drifted down, scores of them heard an incongruous sound over the clatter of battle: a church bell tolling in the night. For many it was the last sound they ever heard. Caught by a heavy wind, a number of soldiers floated down toward the inferno of the Place de l'Église—and the guns of the German guards that a twist of fate had placed there. Lieutenant Charles Santarsiero of the 101st's 506th Regiment was standing in the door of his plane as it passed over Ste.-Mère-Église. "We were about four hundred feet up," he remembers, "and I could see fires burning and Krauts running about. There seemed to be total confusion on the ground. All hell had broken loose. Flak and small-arms fire was coming up and those poor guys were caught right in the middle of it."

Almost as soon as he left his plane, Private John Steele of the 82nd's 505th Regiment saw that instead of landing in a lighted drop zone he was heading for the center of a town that seemed to be on fire. Then he saw German soldiers and French civilians running frantically about. Most of them, it seemed to Steele, were looking up at him. The next moment he was hit by something that felt "like the bite of a sharp knife." A bullet had smashed into his foot. Then Steele saw something that alarmed him even more. Swinging in his harness, unable to veer away from the town, he dangled helplessly as his chute carried him straight toward the church steeple at the edge of the square.

Above Steele, P.F.C. Ernest Blanchard heard the church bell ringing and saw the maelstrom of fire coming up all around him. The next minute he watched horrified as a man floating down almost beside him "exploded and completely disintegrated before my eyes," presumably a victim of the explosives he was carrying.

Blanchard began desperately to swing on his risers, trying to veer away from the mob in the square below. But it was too late. He landed with a crash in one of the trees. Around him men were being machine-gunned to death. There were shouts, yells, screams and moans—sounds that Blanchard will never forget. Frantically, as the machine-gunning came closer, Blanchard sawed at his harness. Then he dropped out of the tree and ran in panic, unaware that he had also sawed off the top of his thumb.

It must have seemed to the Germans that Ste.-Mère-Église was being smothered by paratroop assault, and certainly the townspeople in the square thought that they were at the center of a major battle. Actually very few Americans—perhaps thirty—dropped into the town, and no more than twenty came down in and about the square. But they were enough to cause the German garrison of slightly less than one hundred men to panic. Reinforcements rushed to the square, which seemed to be the focal point of the attack, and there some Germans, coming suddenly upon the bloody, burning scene, seemed to Renaud to lose all control.

About fifteen yards from where the mayor stood in the square a paratrooper plunged into a tree and almost immediately, as he tried frantically to get out of his harness, he was spotted. As Renaud watched, "about half a dozen Germans emptied the magazines of their submachine guns into him and the boy hung there with his eyes open, as though looking down at his own bullet holes."

Caught up in the slaughter all around them, the people in the square were now oblivious to the mighty airborne armada that was still droning ceaselessly overhead. Thousands of men were jumping for the 82nd's drop zones northwest of the town, and the 101st's zones east and slightly west, between Ste.-Mère-Église and the Utah invasion area. But every now and then, because the drop was so widely scattered, stray paratroopers from almost every regiment drifted into the holocaust of the little town. One or two of these men, loaded down with ammunition, grenades and plastic explosives, actually fell into the burning house. There were brief screams and then a fusillade of shots and explosions as the ammunition went up.

In all this horror and confusion one man tenaciously and precariously clung to life. Private Steele, his parachute draped over the steeple of the church, hung just under the eaves. He heard the shouts and the screams. He saw Germans and Americans firing at each other in the square and the streets. And, almost paralyzed by terror, he saw winking red flashes of machine guns as streams of stray bullets shot past and over him. Steele had tried to cut himself down, but his knife had somehow slipped out of his hand and dropped to the square below. Steele then decided that his only hope lay in playing dead. On the roof, only a few yards away from him, German machine gunners fired at everything in sight, but not at Steele. He hung so realistically "dead" in his harness that Lieutenant Willard Young of the 82nd, who passed by during the height of the fighting, still remembers "the dead man hanging from the steeple." In all, Steele dangled there for more than two hours before being cut down and taken captive by the Germans. Shocked and in pain from his shattered foot, he has absolutely no recollection of the tolling of the bell, only a few feet from his head.

The encounter at Ste.-Mère-Église was the prelude to the

main American airborne assault. But in the scheme of things this initial and bloody skirmish* was quite accidental. Although the town was one of the principal objectives of the 82nd Airborne, the real battle for Ste.-Mère-Église was still to come. Much had to be accomplished before then, for the 101st and 82nd divisions, like the British, were racing the clock.

To the Americans went the job of holding the right flank of the invasion area just as their British counterparts were holding on the left. But much more was riding on the American paratroopers: on them hung the fate of the whole Utah Beach operation.

The main obstacle to the success of the Utah landing was a body of water known as the Douve River. As part of their anti-invasion measures Rommel's engineers had taken brilliant advantage of the Douve and its principal tributary, the Merderet. These water barriers veining the lower part of the thumblike Cherbourg land mass flow south and southeast through low-lying land, link up with the Carentan Canal at the base of the peninsula and, flowing almost parallel with the Vire River, empty into the English Channel. By manipulating the century-old La Barquette locks just a few miles above the town of Carentan, the Germans had inundated so much ground that the peninsula, marshy to begin with, was almost isolated from the remainder of Normandy. Thus, by holding the few roads, bridges and causeways through these wastes the Germans could bottle up an invading force and eventually wipe it out. In the event of landings on the eastern coast German forces attacking from the north and west could close the trap and drive the invaders back into the sea.

---

*I have not been able to determine how many were killed and wounded in the square, because sporadic fighting continued all over the town until the actual attack which resulted in its capture. But the best estimates put casualties at about twelve killed, wounded and missing. Most of these men were from F Company, 2nd Battalion, 505th Regiment, and there is a pathetic little note in their official records which reads: "2nd Lt. Cadish and the following enlisted men dropped in the town and were killed almost instantly: Shearer, Blankenship, Bryant, Van Holsbeck and Tlapa." Private John Steele saw two men fall into the burning house, and one of those he believes was Private White of his own mortar squad, who dropped behind him.

Lieutenant Colonel William E. Ekman, commanding the 505th, also says that "one of the chaplains of the regiment . . . who dropped in Ste.-Mère-Église was captured and executed within minutes."

That, at least, was the general strategy. But the Germans had no intention of allowing an invasion to get even that far; as a further defense measure they had flooded more than twelve square miles of low-lying land behind the beaches on the eastern coast. Utah Beach lay almost in the center of these man-made lakes. There was only one way that the men of the 4th Infantry Division (plus their tanks, guns, vehicles and supplies) could force their way inland: along five causeways running through the floods. And German guns controlled these.

Holding the peninsula and these natural defense barriers were three German divisions: the 709th in the north and along the east coast, the 243rd defending the west coast, and the recently arrived 91st in the middle and spread about the base. Also, lying south of Carentan and within striking distance was one of the finest and toughest German units in Normandy—Baron von der Heydte's 6th Parachute Regiment. Exclusive of naval units manning coastal batteries, Luftwaffe antiaircraft contingents and a variety of personnel in the Cherbourg vicinity, the Germans could throw about forty thousand men almost immediately at an Allied attack of any sort. In this heavily defended area Major General Maxwell D. Taylor's 101st Airborne Division and Major General Matthew B. Ridgway's 82nd had been given the enormous task of carving out and holding an "airhead"—an island of defense running from the Utah Beach area to a point far to the west across the base of the peninsula. They were to open up the way for the 4th Division and hold until relieved. In and about the peninsula the American paratroopers were outnumbered more than three to one.

On the map the airhead looked like the imprint of a short, broad left foot with the small toes lying along the coast, the big toe at the La Barquette locks above Carentan, and the heel back and beyond the Merderet and Douve marshes. It was roughly twelve miles long, seven miles wide at the toes and four miles in width across the heel. It was a huge area to be held by thirteen thousand men, but it had to be taken in less than five hours.

Taylor's men were to seize a six-gun battery at St.-Martin-de-Varreville, almost directly behind Utah, and race for four of the five causeways between there and the coastal hamlet of Pouppeville. At the same time crossings and bridges along the Douve and the Carentan Canal, particularly the La Barquette locks, had to be seized or destroyed. While the Screaming Eagles of the 101st secured these objectives, Ridgway's men were to hold the heel and the left side of the foot. They were to defend crossings over the Douve and the Merderet, capture Ste.-Mère-Église and hold positions north of the town to prevent counterattacks from driving into the side of the bridgehead.

The men of the airborne divisions had one other vital mission. The enemy had to be cleared off glider landing areas, for big glider trains were coming in to reinforce the Americans, just as they were the British, before dawn and again in the evening. The first flight, more than one hundred gliders, was scheduled to arrive at 4 A.M.

From the beginning the Americans worked against staggering odds. Like the British, the U.S. divisions were critically scattered. Only one regiment, the 505th of the 82nd, fell accurately. Sixty per cent of all equipment was lost, including most of the radios, mortars and ammunition. Worse still, many of the men were lost too. They came down miles from any recognizable landmarks, confused and alone. The route of the planes was from west to east and it took just twelve minutes to cross the peninsula. Jumping too late meant landing in the English Channel; too early meant coming down somewhere between the west coast and the flooded areas. Some sticks were dropped so badly they actually landed closer to the western side of the peninsula than to their zones on the east. Hundreds of men, heavily weighted with equipment, fell into the treacherous swamps of the Merderet and the Douve. Many drowned, some in less than two feet of water. Others, jumping too late, fell into the darkness over what they thought was Normandy and were lost in the Channel.

One entire stick of 101st paratroopers—some fifteen or eighteen soldiers—met such a death. In the next plane Corporal Louis Merlano fell on a sandy beach in front of a sign reading "*Achtung Minen!*" He had been the second man in his stick to jump. Off in the darkness Merlano could hear the quiet slapping sound of waves. He was lying in sand dunes surrounded by Rommel's anti-invasion obstacles, just a few yards above Utah Beach. As he lay there, trying to get his breath, he heard screams far off in the distance. Merlano was not to find out until later that the screams were coming from the Channel, where the last eleven men from his plane were at that moment drowning.

Merlano got off the beach fast, ignoring the possibility that it was mined. He climbed over a barbed-wire fence and ran for a hedgerow. Someone else was already there; Merlano didn't stop. He ran across a road and started to climb a stone wall. Just then he heard an agonized cry behind him. He whirled around. A flame thrower was hosing the hedgerow he had just passed, and outlined in the flame was the figure of a fellow paratrooper. Stunned, Merlano crouched down by the wall. From the other side came the shouts of German voices and the firing of machine guns. Merlano was caught in a heavily fortified area, with Germans on all sides of him. He prepared to fight for his life. There was one thing he had to do first. Merlano, who was attached to a signal unit, pulled from his pocket a two-by-two-inch communications log containing codes and passwords for three days. Carefully he tore up the log and, page by page, ate it all.

On the other side of the airhead men were floundering in the dark swamps. The Merderet and the Douve were dotted with parachutes of all colors and the little lights on equipment bundles gleamed eerily from out of the marshes and the water. Men plummeted down from the sky, barely missing one another as they splashed beneath the surface of the water. Some never appeared again. Others came up gasping, fighting for air and sawing desperately at chutes and equipment that could drag them under again.

Like Chaplain John Gwinnett of the British 6th Airborne fifty miles away, the 101st chaplain, Captain Francis Sampson, landed in the wastes. The water was over his head. The priest was pinned by his equipment and his parachute, caught by a strong wind, remained open above him. Frantically he cut away the equipment hanging from him—including his Mass kit. Then, with his parachute acting like a great sail, he was blown along for about a hundred yards until he finally came to rest in shallow water. Exhausted, he lay there for about twenty minutes. At last, disregarding the machine gun and mortar fire that was beginning to come in, Father Sampson set out for the area where he had first gone under and doggedly began diving for his Mass kit. He got it on the fifth try.

It wasn't until much later that Father Sampson, thinking back about the experience, realized that the Act of Contrition he had so hurriedly said as he struggled in the water was actually the grace before meals.

In countless small fields and pastures between the Channel and the flooded areas, Americans came together in the night, drawn not by hunting horns but by the sound of a toy cricket. Their lives depended on a few cents' worth of tin fashioned in the shape of a child's snapper. One snap of the cricket had to be answered by a double snap and—for the 82nd alone—a password. Two snaps required one in reply. On these signals men came out of hiding, from trees and ditches, around the sides of buildings, to greet one another. Major General Maxwell D. Taylor and a bareheaded, unidentified rifleman met at the corner of a hedgerow and warmly hugged each other. Some paratroopers found their units right away. Others saw strange faces in the night and then the familiar, comforting sight of the tiny American flag stitched above the shoulder patch.

As confused as things were these men adapted quickly. The battle-tested troopers of the 82nd, with airborne assaults in Sicily and Salerno under their belts, knew what to expect. The 101st, on its first combat jump, was fiercely determined not to be outdone by its more illustrious partner. All these men wasted as little time as possible, for they had no time to waste. The lucky ones who knew where they were assembled promptly and set out for their objectives. The lost ones joined with small groups made up of men from different companies, battalions and regiments. 82nd troopers found themselves being led by 101st officers and vice versa. Men from both divisions fought side by side, often for objectives they had never heard of.

Hundreds of men found themselves in small fields, surrounded on all sides by tall hedgerows. The fields were silent little worlds, isolated and scary. In them every shadow, every rustle, every breaking twig was the enemy. Private Dutch Schultz, in one such shadowy world, was unable to find his way out. He decided to try his cricket. On the very first click he got a response he hadn't bargained for: machine gun fire. He threw himself to the ground, aimed his MI rifle in the direction of the machine gun position, and pressed the trigger. Nothing happened. He had forgotten to load it. The machine gun opened up again and Dutch ran for cover in the nearest hedgerow.

He made another careful reconnaissance of the field. Then he heard a twig crackle. Dutch felt a moment's panic, but he calmed down as his company commander, Lieutenant Jack Tallerday, came through the hedgerow. "Is that you, Dutch?" Tallerday called softly. Schultz hurried over to him. Together they left the field and joined a group that Tallerday had already assembled. There were men from the 101st Division and from all three of the 82nd's regiments. For the first time since the jump Dutch felt easy. He was no longer alone.

Tallerday moved down along the side of a hedgerow with his little group fanning out behind him. A short while later they heard and then saw a group of men coming toward them. Tallerday snapped his cricket and thought he heard an answering click. "As our two groups approached each other," Tallerday says, "it was quite evident by the configuration of their steel helmets that they were Germans." And then there occurred one of those curious and rare happenings in war. Each group silently walked past the other in a kind of frozen shock, without firing a shot. As the distance between them grew, the darkness obliterated the figures as though they had never existed.

All over Normandy this night paratroopers and German soldiers met unexpectedly. In these encounters men's lives depended on their keeping their wits and often on the fraction of a second it took to pull a trigger. Three miles from Ste.-Mère-Église, Lieutenant John Walas of the 82nd almost tripped over a German sentry who was in front of a machine gun nest. For a terrible moment, each man stared at the other. Then the German reacted. He fired a shot at Walas at point-blank range. The bullet struck the bolt mechanism of the lieutenant's rifle, which was directly in front of his stomach, nicked his hand and ricocheted off. Both men turned and fled.

One man, Major Lawrence Legere of the 101st, talked his way out of trouble. In a field between Ste.-Mère-Église and Utah Beach, Legere had collected a little group of men and was leading them toward the rendezvous point. Suddenly Legere was challenged in German. He knew no German but he was fluent in French. As the other men were some distance behind him and had not been seen, Legere, in the darkness of the field, posed as a young farmer and explained rapidly in French that he had been visiting his girl and was on his way home. He apologized for being out after curfew. As he talked, he was busily removing a strip of adhesive tape from a grenade, placed there to prevent the accidental release of the pin. Still talking, he yanked the pin, threw the grenade and hit the ground as it went off. He found he had killed three Germans. "When I backtracked to pick up my brave little band," Legere recalls, "I found they had scattered to the four winds."

There were many ludicrous moments. In a dark orchard one mile from Ste.-Mère-Église, Captain Lyle Putnam, one of the 82nd's battalion surgeons, found himself utterly alone. He gathered up all his medical equipment and began searching for a way out. Near one of the hedgerows he saw a figure approaching cautiously. Putnam froze in his tracks, leaned forward and loudly whispered the 82nd's password, "Flash." There was a moment of electric silence as Putnam waited for the countersign, "Thunder." Instead, to his amazement, Putnam recalls, the other man yelled, "Jesus Christ!" and turned and "fled like a maniac." The doctor was so angry he forgot to be frightened. Half a mile away his friend Captain George Wood, the 82nd's chaplain, was also alone and busily snapping his cricket. No one answered him. Then he jumped with fright as a voice behind him said: "For God's sake, Padre, stop that damn noise." Chastened, Chaplain Wood followed the paratrooper out of the field.

By afternoon these two men would be in Madame Angèle Levrault's schoolhouse in Ste.-Mère-Église fighting their own war—a war where uniforms made no difference. They would be tending the wounded and dying of both sides.

By 2 A.M., although more than an hour would pass before all the paratroopers were on the ground, many small groups of determined men were closing in on their objectives. One group was actually attacking its target, an enemy stronghold of dugouts and machine gun and antitank gun positions in the village of Foucarville just above Utah Beach. The position was of extreme importance, for it controlled all movement on the main road running behind the Utah Beach area—a road which enemy tanks would have to use to reach the beachhead. Storming Foucarville called for a full company, but only eleven men under Captain Cleveland Fitzgerald had as yet arrived. So determined were Fitzgerald and his little group that they assaulted the position without waiting for more men. In this, the first recorded 101st unit battle of the D-Day airborne assault, Fitzgerald and his men got as far as the enemy command post.

There was a short, bloody battle. Fitzgerald was shot in the lung by a sentry, but as he fell he killed the German. At last the outnumbered Americans had to pull back to the outskirts to await dawn and reinforcements. Unknown to them nine paratroopers had reached Foucarville some forty minutes earlier. They had dropped into the strongpoint itself. Now, under the eyes of their captors, they were sitting in a dugout, oblivious of the battle, listening to a German practicing on his harmonica.

These were crazy moments for everyone—particularly the generals. They were men without staffs, without communications, and without men to command. Major General Maxwell Taylor found himself with several officers but only two or three enlisted men. "Never," he told them, "have so few been commanded by so many."

Major General Matthew B. Ridgway was alone in a field, pistol in hand, counting himself lucky. As he was later to recall, "at least if no friends were visible neither were any foes." His assistant, Brigadier General James M. "Jumpin' Jim" Gavin, who at this time was in complete charge of the 82nd's parachute assault, was miles away in the swamps of the Merderet.

Gavin and a number of paratroopers were trying to salvage equipment bundles from the marshes. In them were the radios, bazookas, mortars and ammunition Gavin so desperately needed. He knew that by dawn the heel of the airhead which his men were to hold would be under heavy attack. As he stood knee-deep in cold water, alongside the troopers, other worries were crowding in on Gavin. He was not sure where he was, and he wondered what to do about the number of injured men who had found their way to his little group and were now lying along the edge of the swamp.

Nearly an hour earlier, seeing red and green lights on the far edge of the water, Gavin had sent his aide, Lieutenant Hugo Olson, to find out what they meant. He hoped they were the assembly lights of two of the 82nd's battalions. Olson had not returned and Gavin was getting anxious. One of his officers, Lieutenant John Devine, was out in the middle of the river, stark naked, diving for bundles. "Whenever he came up, he stood out like a white statue," Gavin recalls, "and I couldn't help thinking that he'd be a dead turkey if he was spotted by the Germans."

Suddenly a lone figure came struggling out of the swamps.

He was covered with mud and slime and was wringing wet. It was Olson coming to report that there was a railroad directly across from Gavin and his men, on a high embankment which snaked through the marshes. It was the first good news of the night. Gavin knew there was only one railroad in the district—the Cherbourg-Carentan track, which passed down the Merderet valley. The general began to feel better. For the first time he knew where he was.

In an apple orchard outside Ste.-Mère-Église, the man who was to hold the northern approaches to the town—the flank of the Utah invasion bridgehead—was in pain and trying not to show it. Lieutenant Colonel Benjamin Vandervoort of the 82nd had broken his ankle on the jump, but he had made up his mind to stay in the fighting no matter what happened.

Bad luck had dogged Vandervoort. He had always taken his job seriously, sometimes too seriously. Unlike many another Army officer, Vandervoort had never had a popular nickname, nor had he permitted himself the kind of close, easy relationship with his men that other officers enjoyed. Normandy was to change all that—and more. It was to make him, as General Matthew B. Ridgway later recalled, "one of the bravest, toughest battle commanders I ever knew." Vandervoort was to fight on his broken ankle for forty days, side by side with the men whose approval he wanted most.

Vandervoort's battalion surgeon, Captain Putnam, still fuming from his encounter with the strange paratrooper in the hedgerow, came across the colonel and some of his troopers in the orchard. Putnam still vividly remembers his first sight of Vandervoort: "He was seated with a rain cape over him, reading a map by flashlight. He recognized me and, calling me close, quietly asked that I take a look at his ankle with as little demonstration as possible. His ankle was obviously broken. He insisted on replacing his jump boot, and we laced it tightly." Then, as Putnam watched, Vandervoort picked up his rifle and, using it as a crutch, took a step forward. He looked at the men around him. "Well," he said, "let's go." He moved out across the field.

Like the British paratroopers to the east, the Americans—in humor, in sorrow, in terror and in pain—began the work they had come to Normandy to do.

*

This, then, was the beginning. The first invaders of D Day, almost eighteen thousand Americans, British and Canadians, were on the flanks of the Normandy battlefield. In between lay the five invasion beaches and beyond the horizon, steadily approaching, the mighty 5,000-ship invasion fleet. The first of the vessels, the U.S.S. *Bayfield*, carrying the commander of the Navy's Force U, Rear Admiral D. P. Moon, was now within twelve miles of Utah Beach and preparing to drop anchor.

Slowly the great invasion plan was beginning to unfold—and still the Germans remained blind. There were many reasons. The weather, their lack of reconnaissance (only a few planes had been sent over the embarkation areas in the preceding weeks, and all had been shot down), their stubborn belief that the invasion *must* come at the Pas-de-Calais, the confusion and overlapping of their own commands, and their failure to take the decoded underground messages seriously all played a part. Even their radar stations failed them this night. Those that had not been bombed had been confused by Allied planes flying along the coast dropping bundles of "window"—strips of tin-foil which snowed the screens. Only one station had made a report. It saw only "normal Channel traffic."

More than two hours had elapsed since the first paratroopers had landed. Only now were the German commanders in Normandy beginning to realize that something important might be happening. The first scattered reports were beginning to come in and slowly, like a patient coming out of an anesthetic, the Germans were awakening.

5

GENERAL ERICH MARCKS stood at a long table studying the war maps spread out before him. He was surrounded by his staff. They had been with him ever since his birthday party, briefing the 84th Corps commander for the war games in Rennes. Every now and then the General called for another map. It seemed to his intelligence officer, Major Friedrich Hayn, that Marcks was preparing for the *Kriegsspiel* as though it was a real battle, instead of merely a theoretical invasion of Normandy.

In the midst of their discussion, the phone rang. The conversation ceased as Marcks picked up the receiver. Hayn recalls that "as he listened, the General's body seemed to stiffen." Marcks motioned to his chief of staff to pick up the extension phone. The man who was calling was Major General Wilhelm Richter, commander of the 716th Division, holding the coast above Caen. "Parachutists have landed east of the Orne," Richter told Marcks. "The area seems to be around Bréville and Ranville . . . along the northern fringe of the Bavent Forest . . ."

This was the first official report of the Allied attack to reach a major German headquarters. "It struck us," Hayn says, "like lightning." The time was 2:11 A.M. (British Double Summer Time).

Marcks immediately telephoned Major General Max Pemsel, chief of staff of the Seventh Army. At 2:15 A.M. Pemsel placed the Seventh on *Alarmstruffe II*, the highest state of readiness. It was four hours since the second Verlaine message had been intercepted. Now at last the Seventh Army, in whose area the invasion had already begun, had been alerted.

Pemsel was taking no chances. He wakened the Seventh's commanding officer, Colonel General Friedrich Dollmann. "General," said Pemsel, "I believe this is the invasion. Will you please come over immediately?"

As he put down the phone, Pemsel suddenly remembered something. Among a sheaf of intelligence bulletins that had come in during the afternoon, one had been from an agent in Casablanca. He had specifically stated that the invasion would take place in Normandy on June 6.

As Pemsel waited for Dollmann to arrive, the 84th Corps reported again: ". . . Parachute drops near Montebourg and St.-Marcouf [on the Cherbourg peninsula] . . . Troops partly already engaged in battle."* Pemsel promptly called Rommel's chief of staff, Major General Dr. Hans Speidel at Army Group B. It was 2:35 A.M.

---

*There has been considerable controversy over the timing of the German reaction to the invasion and over the messages that were passed from one headquarters to another. When I began my research, Colonel General Franz Halder, the former Chief of the German General Staff (now attached to the U.S. Army's historical section in Germany) told me to "believe nothing on our side unless it tallies with the official war diaries of each headquarters." I have followed his advice. All times (corrected to British Double Summer Time), reports and telephone calls as they pertain to German activities come from these sources.

At about the same time, General Hans von Salmuth, from his Fifteenth Army headquarters near the Belgian border, was trying to get some firsthand information. Although the bulk of his army was far removed from the airborne attacks, one division, Major General Josef Reichert's 711th, held positions east of the Orne River on the boundary line between the Seventh and Fifteenth armies. Several messages had come in from the 711th. One reported that paratroopers actually were landing near the headquarters at Cabourg; a second announced that fighting was going on all around the command post.

Von Salmuth decided to find out for himself. He rang Reichert. "What the devil is going on down there?" Von Salmuth demanded.

"My General," came Reichert's harassed voice on the other end of the wire, "if you'll permit me, I'll let you hear for yourself." There was a pause, and then Von Salmuth could clearly hear the clatter of machine gun fire.

"Thank you," said Von Salmuth, and he hung up. Immediately he too called Army Group B, reporting that at the 711th's headquarters "the din of battle can be heard."

Pemsel's and Von Salmuth's calls, arriving almost simultaneously, gave Rommel's headquarters the first news of the Allied attack. Was it the long-expected invasion? Nobody at Army Group B at this time was prepared to say. In fact, Rommel's naval aide, Vice-Admiral Friedrich Ruge, distinctly remembers that as more reports came in of airborne troops "some said they were only dolls disguised as paratroopers."

Whoever made the observation was partly right. To add to the German confusion, the Allies had dropped hundreds of lifelike rubber dummies, dressed as paratroopers, south of the Normandy invasion area. Attached to each were strings of firecrackers which exploded on landing, giving the impression of a small-arms fight. For more than three hours a few of these dummies were to deceive General Marcks into believing that paratroopers had landed at Lessay some twenty-five miles southwest of his headquarters.

These were strange, confusing minutes for Von Rundstedt's staff at OB West in Paris and for Rommel's officers at La Roche-Guyon. Reports came piling in from everywhere—reports that were often inaccurate, sometimes incomprehensible, and always contradictory.

Luftwaffe headquarters in Paris announced that "fifty to sixty two-engined planes are coming in" over the Cherbourg peninsula and that paratroopers had landed "near Caen." Admiral Theodor Krancke's headquarters—*Marinegruppenkommando West*—confirmed the British paratroop landings, nervously pointed out that the enemy had fallen close to one of their coastal batteries, and then added that "part of the parachute drop consists of straw dummies." Neither report mentioned the Americans on the Cherbourg peninsula—yet at this time one of the naval batteries at St.-Marcouf, just above Utah Beach, had informed Cherbourg headquarters that a dozen Americans had been captured. Within minutes of their first message, the Luftwaffe phoned in another bulletin. Parachutists, they said, were down near Bayeux. Actually none had landed there at all.

At both headquarters men tried desperately to evaluate the rash of red spots sprouting over their maps. Officers at Army Group B rang their opposite numbers at OB West, hashed the situation over and came up with conclusions many of which, in the light of what was actually happening, seem incredible. When OB West's acting intelligence officer, Major Doertenbach, called Army Group B for a report, for example, he was told that "the Chief of Staff views the situation with equanimity" and that "there is a possibility that parachutists who have been reported are merely bailed-out bomber crews."

The Seventh Army didn't think so. By 3 A.M. Pemsel was convinced that the *Schwerpunkt*—the main thrust—was driving into Normandy. His maps showed paratroopers at each end of the Seventh's area—on the Cherbourg peninsula and east of the Orne. Now, too, there were alarming reports from naval stations at Cherbourg. Using sound direction apparatus and some radar equipment, the stations were picking up ships maneuvering in the Bay of the Seine.

There was no doubt now in Pemsel's mind—the invasion was on. He called Speidel. "The air landings," Pemsel said, "constitute the first phase of a larger enemy action." Then he added, "Engine noises are audible from out at sea." But Pemsel could not convince Rommel's chief of staff. Speidel's answer, as recorded in the Seventh Army telephone log, was that "the affair is still locally confined." The estimate that he gave Pemsel at this time was summarized in the war diary and reads: "Chief of Staff Army Group B believes that for the time being this is not to be considered as a large operation."

Even as Pemsel and Speidel talked, the last paratroopers of the 18,000-man airborne assault were floating down over the Cherbourg peninsula. Sixty-nine gliders, carrying men, guns and heavy equipment, were just crossing the coast of France, headed for the British landing areas near Ranville. And twelve miles off Normandy's five invasion beaches, the *Ancon*, headquarters ship of Task Force O, under the command of Rear Admiral John L. Hall, dropped anchor. Lining up behind her were the transports carrying the men who would land in the first wave on Omaha Beach.

But at La Roche-Guyon there was still nothing to indicate the immensity of the Allied attack, and in Paris OB West endorsed Speidel's first estimate of the situation. Rundstedt's able operations chief, Lieutenant General Bodo Zimmermann, informed of Speidel's conversation with Pemsel, sent back a message agreeing with Speidel: "Operations OB West holds that this is not a large-scale airborne operation, all the more because Admiral Channel Coast (Krancke's headquarters) has reported that the enemy has dropped straw dummies."

These officers can hardly be blamed for being so utterly confused. They were miles away from the actual fighting, entirely dependent on the reports coming in. These were so spotty and so misleading that even the most experienced officers found it impossible to gauge the magnitude of the airborne assault—or, for that matter, to see an over-all pattern emerging from the Allied attacks. If this was the invasion, was it aimed at Normandy? Only the Seventh Army seemed to think so. Perhaps the paratroop attacks were simply a diversion intended to draw attention from the real invasion—against General Hans von Salmuth's massive Fifteenth Army in the Pas-de-Calais, where nearly everybody thought the Allies would strike. The Fifteenth's chief of staff, Major General Rudolf Hofmann was so sure the main attack would come in the Fifteenth's area that he called Pemsel and bet him a dinner that he was right. "This is one bet you're going to lose," said Pemsel. Yet at this time neither Army Group B nor OB West had sufficient evidence to draw any conclusions. They alerted the invasion coast and ordered measures taken against the paratroop attacks. Then everybody waited for more information. There was little else they could do.

By now, messages were flooding into command posts all over Normandy. One of the first problems for some of the divisions was to find their own commanders—the generals who had already left for the *Kriegsspiel* in Rennes. Although most of them were located quickly, two—Lieutenant General Karl von Schlieben and Major General Wilhelm Falley, both commanding divisions in the Cherbourg peninsula—couldn't be found. Von Schlieben was asleep in his hotel in Rennes and Falley was still en route there by car.

Admiral Krancke, the naval commander in the west, was on an inspection trip to Bordeaux. His chief of staff awakened him in his hotel room. "Paratroop landings are taking place near Caen," Krancke was informed. "OB West insists that this is only a diversionary attack and not the real invasion, but we're picking up ships. We think it's the real thing." Krancke immediately alerted the few naval forces he had and then quickly set out for his headquarters in Paris.

One of the men who got his orders at Le Havre was already a legend in the German Navy. Lieutenant Commander Heinrich Hoffmann had made his name as an E-boat commander. Almost from the beginning of the war, his speedy, powerful flotillas of torpedo craft had ranged up and down the English Channel, attacking shipping wherever they found it. Hoffmann also had been in action during the Dieppe raid and had boldly escorted the German battleships *Scharnhorst*, *Gneisenau* and *Prinz Eugen* in their dramatic dash from Brest to Norway in 1942.

When the message from headquarters came in, Hoffmann was in the cabin of T-28, the lead E-boat of his 5th Flotilla, preparing to go out on a mine-laying operation. Immediately he called together the commanders of the other boats. They were all young men and although Hoffmann told them that "this must be the invasion," it did not surprise them. They had expected it. Only three of his six boats were ready, but Hoffmann could not wait for the others to be loaded with torpedoes. A few minutes later the three small boats left Le Havre. On the bridge of T-28, his white sailor's cap pushed back on his head as usual, the thirty-four-year-old Hoffmann peered out into the darkness. Behind him, the two little boats bounced along in Indian file, following the lead boat's every maneuver. They raced through the night at more than twenty-three knots—blindly heading straight toward the mightiest fleet ever assembled.

At least they were in action. Probably the most baffled men in Normandy this night were the 16,242 seasoned troops of the tough 21st Panzer Division, once a part of Rommel's famed *Afrika Korps*. Clogging every small village, hamlet and wood in the area just twenty-five miles southeast of Caen, these men were sitting almost on the edge of the battlefield, the only panzer division within immediate striking distance of the British airborne assault and the only veteran troops in that area.

Ever since the alert, officers and men had been standing alongside their tanks and vehicles, engines running, waiting for the order to move out. Colonel Hermann von Oppeln-Bronikowski, in command of the division's regiment of tanks, couldn't understand the delay. He had been awakened shortly after 2 A.M. by the 21st's commander, Lieutenant General Edgar Feuchtinger. "Oppeln," Feuchtinger had said breathlessly, "imagine! *They* have landed." He had briefed Bronikowski on the situation and told him that as soon as the division got its orders it would "clean out the area between Caen and the coast immediately." But no further word had come. With growing anger and impatience, Bronikowski continued to wait.

Miles away, the most puzzling reports of all were being received by the Luftwaffe's Lieutenant Colonel Priller. He and his wing man, Sergeant Wodarczyk, had stumbled into their beds about 1 A.M. at the 26th Fighter Wing's now deserted airfield near Lille. They had succeeded in drowning their anger at the Luftwaffe High Command with several bottles of excellent cognac. Now, in his drunken sleep, Priller heard the phone ring as though from a long way off. He came to slowly, his left hand groping over the bedside table for the phone.

Second Fighter Corps headquarters was on the wire. "Priller," said the operations officer, "it seems that some sort of an invasion is taking place. I suggest you put your wing on the alert."

Sleepy as he was, Pips Priller's temper promptly boiled over again. The 124 planes of his command had been moved away from the Lille area the previous afternoon and now the very thing he had feared was happening. Priller's language, as he remembers the conversation, is unprintable, but after telling his caller what was wrong with corps headquarters and the entire Luftwaffe High Command, the fighter ace roared, "Who in hell am I supposed to alert? *I'm* alert. Wodarczyk is alert! But you fatheads *know* I have only two damned planes!" With that he slammed down the receiver.

A few minutes later the phone rang again. "Now what?" yelled Priller. It was the same officer. "My dear Priller," he said, "I'm awfully sorry. It was all a mistake. We somehow got a wrong report. Everything is fine—there's no invasion." Priller was so furious he couldn't answer. Worse than that, he couldn't get back to sleep.

Despite the confusion, hesitancy and indecision in the higher levels of command, the German soldiers in actual contact with the enemy were reacting swiftly. Thousands of troops were already on the move and, unlike the generals at Army Group B and OB West, these soldiers had no doubts that the invasion was upon them. Many of them had been fighting it off in isolated, face-to-face skirmishes ever since the first British and Americans had dropped out of the sky. Thousands of other alerted troops waited behind their formidable coastal defenses, ready to repel an invasion no matter where it might come. They were apprehensive, but they were also determined.

At Seventh Army headquarters, the one top commander who was not confused called his staff together. In the brightly lighted map room, General Pemsel stood before his officers. His voice was as calm and quiet as usual. Only his words betrayed the deep concern he felt. "Gentlemen," he told them, "I am convinced the invasion will be upon us by dawn. Our future will depend on how we fight this day. I request of you all the effort and pain that you can give."

In Germany, five hundred miles away, the man who might have agreed with Pemsel—the one officer who had won many a battle by his uncanny ability to see clearly through the most confusing situations—was asleep. At Army Group B the situation was not considered serious enough yet to call Field Marshal Erwin Rommel.

6

ALREADY the first reinforcements had reached the airborne troops. In the British 6th Airborne's area sixty-nine gliders had landed, forty-nine of them on the correct landing strip near Ranville. Other small glider units had landed earlier—notably Major Howard's force on the bridges and a formation carrying heavy equipment for the division—but this was the main glider train. The sappers had done a good job. They had not had time to completely clear the long glider field of all its obstructions, but enough of these had been dynamited for the force to come in. After the arrival of the gliders the landing zone presented a fantastic sight. In the moonlight it looked like a Daliesque graveyard. Wrecked machines, with crumpled wings, squashed cabins and crazily canted tails, lay everywhere. It did not seem possible that anyone could have survived the splintering crashes, yet casualties had been low. More men had been injured from antiaircraft fire than in the landings.

The train had brought in the 6th Airborne's commander, Major General Richard Gale, and his headquarters staff with more troops, heavy equipment and the all-important antitank guns. Men had poured out of the gliders expecting to find the field under harassing enemy fire; instead they found a strange, pastoral silence. Sergeant John Hutley, piloting a Horsa, had expected a hot reception and had warned his copilot, "Get out as quick as you can the moment we hit, and make a dash for cover." But the only sign of battle was off in the distance where Hutley could see the multicolored flash of tracers and hear the sound of machine gun fire coming from nearby Ranville. Around him the landing field was bustling with activity as men salvaged equipment from the wrecks and hitched up the antitank guns to the backs of jeeps. There was even an air of cheerfulness now that the glider ride was over. Hutley and the men he had carried sat down in the wrecked cabin of their glider and had a cup of tea before setting out for Ranville.

On the other side of the Normandy battlefield, on the Cherbourg peninsula, the first American glider trains were just coming in. Sitting in the copilot's seat of the 101st lead glider was the assistant division commander, Brigadier General Don

Pratt, the officer who had been so alarmed back in England when a hat was tossed on the bed where he was sitting. Pratt was, reportedly, "as tickled as a schoolboy" to be making his first glider flight. Strung out behind was a procession of fifty-two gliders in formations of four, each towed by a Dakota. The train carried jeeps, antitank guns, an entire airborne medical unit, even a small bulldozer. High on the nose of Pratt's glider a big No. 1 was painted. A huge "Screaming Eagle," insignia of the 101st, and a U.S. flag adorned the canvas on either side of the pilots' compartment. In the same formation, Surgical Technician Emile Natalle looked down on shell bursts and burning vehicles below and saw "a wall of fire coming up to greet us." Still hitched to their planes, the gliders lurched from side to side scudding through "flak thick enough to land on."

Unlike the paratroopers' planes, the gliders came in from the Channel and approached the peninsula from the east. They were only seconds past the coast when they saw the lights of the landing zone at Hiesville, four miles from Ste.-Mère-Église. One by one the 300-yard-long nylon tow ropes parted and the gliders came soughing down. Natalle's glider overshot the zone and crashed into a field studded with "Rommel's asparagus" —lines of heavy posts embedded in the ground as antiglider obstacles. Sitting in a jeep inside the glider, Natalle gazed out through one of the small windows and watched with horrified fascination as the wings sheared off and the posts whizzed past. Then there was a ripping sound and the glider broke in two—directly behind the jeep in which Natalle was sitting. "It made it very easy to get out," he recalls.

A short distance away lay the wreckage of glider No. 1. Skidding down a sloping pasture, its brakes unable to halt its 100-m.p.h. rush, it had smashed headlong into a hedgerow. Natalle found the pilot, who had been hurled from the cockpit, lying in the hedgerow with both legs broken. General Pratt had been killed instantly, crushed by the crumpled framework of the cockpit. He was the first general officer on either side to be killed on D Day.

Pratt was one of the few casualties in the 101st landings. Almost all the division's gliders came down on or close to the field at Hiesville. Although most of them were totally wrecked, their equipment arrived largely intact. It was a remarkable achievement. Few of the pilots had made more than three or four practice landings and these had all been in daylight.*

Although the 101st was lucky, the 82nd was not. The inexperience of the pilots produced near-disaster in the 82nd's 50-glider train. Fewer than half their formations found the right landing zone northwest of Ste.-Mère-Église; the remainder plowed into hedgerows and buildings, dove into rivers or came down in the marshes of the Merderet. Equipment and vehicles so urgently needed were strewn everywhere and casualties were high. Eighteen pilots alone were killed within the first few minutes. One glider loaded with troops sailed directly over the head of Captain Robert Piper, the 505th Regiment's adjutant and, to his horror, "careened off the chimney of a house, dropped into the back yard, cartwheeled across the ground and smashed into a thick stone wall. There was not even a moan from the wreckage."

For the hard-pressed 82nd, the wide dispersion of the glider train was calamitous. It would take hours to salvage and collect the few guns and supplies that had arrived safely. In the meantime, troopers would have to fight on with the weapons they had carried with them. But this, after all, was standard operating procedure for paratroopers: they fought with what they had until relieved.

Now the 82nd men holding the rear of the airhead—the bridges over the Douve and the Merderet—were in position and already encountering the Germans' first probings. These paratroopers had no vehicles, no antitank guns, few bazookas, machine guns or mortars. Worse, they had no communications. They did not know what was happening around them, what positions were being held, what objectives had been taken. It was the same with the men of the 101st, except that the fortunes of war had given them most of their equipment.

---

*There was also a shortage of glider pilots. "At one time," General Gavin recalls, "we didn't think we'd have enough. In the invasion each copilot's seat was occupied by an airborne trooper. Incredible as it may seem, these troopers had been given no training in either flying or landing gliders. Some found themselves with a wounded pilot and a fully loaded glider on their hands as they came hurtling in through flak-filled space on June 6. Fortunately the type glider we were using was not too hard to fly or land. But having to do it for the first time in combat was a chastening experience; it really gave a man religion."

The soldiers of both divisions were still scattered and isolated, but little groups were fighting toward the principal objectives —and strongholds were beginning to fall.

In Ste.-Mère-Église, as the stunned townspeople watched from behind their shuttered windows, paratroopers of the 82nd's 505th Regiment slipped cautiously through the empty streets. The church bell was silent now. On the steeple Private John Steele's empty parachute hung limp, and every now and then the glowing embers of M. Hairon's villa erupted, briefly outlining the trees in the square. Occasionally a sniper's bullet whined angrily into the night, but that was the only sound; everywhere there was an uneasy silence.

Lieutenant Colonel Edward Krause, leading the attack, had expected to fight hard for Ste.-Mère-Église, but apart from a few snipers it appeared that the German garrison had pulled out. Krause's men swiftly took advantage of the situation: They occupied buildings, set up road blocks and machine gun posts, cut telephone cables and wires. Other squads continued the slow sweep through the town, moving like shadows from hedge to hedge and doorway to doorway, all converging on the town's center, the Place de l'Église.

Passing around the back of the church, P.F.C. William Tucker reached the square and set up his machine gun behind a tree. Then as he looked out on the moonlit square he saw a parachute and, lying next to him, a dead German. On the far side were the crumpled, sprawled shapes of other bodies. As Tucker sat there in the semidarkness trying to figure out what had happened, he began to feel that he was not alone—that somebody was standing behind him. Grabbing the cumbersome machine gun, he whirled around. His eyes came level with a pair of boots slowly swaying back and forth. Tucker hastily stepped back. A dead paratrooper was hanging in the tree looking down at him.

Now other paratroopers came into the square and suddenly they too saw the bodies hanging in the trees. Lieutenant Gus Sanders remembers that "men just stood there staring, filled with a terrible anger." Lieutenant Colonel Krause reached the square. As he stood looking at the dead troopers, he said just three words: "Oh, my God."

Then Krause pulled an American flag from his pocket. It was old and worn—the same flag that the 505th had raised over Naples. Krause had promised his men that "before dawn of D Day this flag will fly over Ste.-Mère-Église." He walked to the town hall and, on the flagpole by the side of the door, ran up the colors. There was no ceremony. In the square of the dead paratroopers the fighting was over. The Stars and Stripes flew over the first town to be liberated by the Americans in France.

At the German Seventh Army headquarters in Le Mans a message was received from General Marcks's 84th Corps. It read: "Communications with Ste.-Mère-Église cut off . . ." The time was 4:30 A.M.

The Îles-St.-Marcouf are two barren piles of rock just three miles off Utah Beach. In the vast and intricate invasion plan the islands had gone unnoticed until three weeks before D Day. Then Supreme Headquarters had decided that they could be the sites of heavy gun batteries. To ignore the islands, then, was a risk that no one was prepared to take. Hurriedly 132 men of the U.S. 4th and 24th cavalry squadrons were trained for a pre-H-Hour assault. These men had landed on the isles at about 4:30 A.M. They found no guns, no troops—only sudden death. For as Lieutenant Colonel Edward C. Dunn's men moved off the beaches they were trapped in a hideous labyrinth of mine fields. S mines—which bound into the air when stepped on and gut the attacker with bulletlike ball bearings—had been sown like grass seed. Within minutes the night was ripped by the flash of explosions, the screams of mangled men. Three lieutenants were injured almost immediately, two enlisted men were killed, and Lieutenant Alfred Rubin, who was also a casualty, would never forget "the sight of one man lying on the ground spitting up ball bearings." By the end of the day their losses would be nineteen killed and wounded. Surrounded by the dead and the dying, Lieutenant Colonel Dunn sent out the success signal, "Mission accomplished." These were the first Allied troops to invade Hitler's Europe from the sea. But in the scheme of things, their action was merely a D-Day footnote, a bitter and useless victory.

In the British zone, almost on the coast and just three miles east of Sword Beach, Lieutenant Colonel Terence Otway and his men lay under heavy machine gun fire at the edge of the barbed wire and the mine fields protecting the massive Mer-ville battery. Otway's situation was desperate. In all the months of training he had never expected every phase of his elaborate land-and-air assault of the coastal battery to work out exactly as planned. But neither had he been prepared for its total dis-integration. Yet, somehow, it had happened.

The bombing attack had failed. The special glider train had been lost and with it artillery, flame throwers, mortars, mine detectors and scaling ladders. Of his 700-man battalion, Ot-way had found only 150 soldiers and, to take the battery with its garrison of 200, these soldiers had only their rifles, Sten guns, grenades, a few Bangalore torpedoes and one heavy ma-chine gun. Despite these handicaps, Otway's men had grappled with each problem, improvising brilliantly.

With wire cutters they had already cut gaps through the outer barricade of wire and placed their few Bangalore tor-pedoes in position ready to blow the rest. One group of men had cleared a path through the mine fields. It had been a hair-raising job. They had crawled on hands and knees across the moonlit approaches to the battery, feeling for trip wires and prodding the ground ahead of them with bayonets. Now Ot-way's 150 men crouched in ditches and bomb craters and along the sides of hedges, waiting for the order to attack. The 6th Airborne's commander, General Gale, had instructed Otway, "Your attitude of mind must be that you cannot contemplate failure in the direct assault . . ." As he looked around at his men, Otway knew that his casualties would be high. But the guns of the battery had to be silenced—they could slaugh-ter the troops crossing Sword Beach. The situation was, he thought, desperately unfair, but there was no alternative. He had to attack. He knew this even as he knew that the last part of his carefully detailed plan was also doomed to failure. The three gliders due to crash-land on the battery as the ground attack went in would not come down unless they received a special signal—a star shell fired from a mortar. Otway had nei-ther the shell nor the mortar. He did have flares for a Very pistol, but they were to be used only to signal the success of the assault. His last chance for help was gone.

The gliders were on time. The tow planes signaled with their landing lights and then cast off the machines. There were only two gliders, each carrying about twenty men. The third, parting from its tow rope over the Channel, had glided safely back to England. Now the paratroopers heard the soft rustle of the machines as they came over the battery. Helplessly Otway watched as the gliders, silhouetted against the moon, gradually lost height and wheeled back and forth, their pilots searching desperately for the signal he could not send. As the gliders circled lower the Germans opened up. The machine guns which had pinned down the troopers now turned on the gliders. Streams of 20-millimeter tracers ripped into the unprotected canvas sides. Still the gliders circled, following the plan, doggedly looking for the signal. And Otway, agonized, almost in tears, could do nothing.

Then the gliders gave it up. One veered off, to land four miles away. The other passed so low over the waiting, anxious men that Privates Alan Mower and Pat Hawkins thought it was going to smash into the battery. At the last moment it lifted and crashed instead into a wood some distance away. Instinctively a few men pushed themselves up from hiding to go help the survivors. But they were stopped immediately. "Don't move! Don't leave your positions!" whispered their harassed officers. There was now nothing more to wait for. Otway ordered the attack. Private Mower heard him yell, "Everybody in! We're going to take this bloody battery!"

And in they went.

With a blinding roar the Bangalore torpedoes blasted great gaps in the wire. Lieutenant Mike Dowling yelled, "Move up! Move up!" Once again a hunting horn sounded in the night. Yelling and firing, Otway's paratroopers plunged into the smoke of the explosions and through the wire. Ahead of them, across the no man's land of mine fields, manned trenches and gun pits, loomed the battery. Suddenly red flares burst over the heads of the advancing paratroopers and immediately machine gun, *Schmeisser* and rifle fire poured out to meet them. Through the deadly barrage, the paratroopers crouched and crawled, ran, dropped to the ground, got up and ran some more. They dived into shell craters, pulled themselves out and went forward again. Mines exploded. Private Mower heard a scream and then someone yelled, "Stop! Stop! There's mines everywhere!" Over on his right, Mower saw a badly wounded corporal sitting on the ground waving men away, and shouting, "Don't come near me! Don't come near me!"

Above the firing, the bursting of mines and the yells of the men, Lieutenant Alan Jefferson, out ahead, continued to blow his hunting horn. Suddenly Private Sid Capon heard a mine explode and saw Jefferson go down. He ran toward the lieutenant, but Jefferson shouted at him, "Get in! Get in!" Then, lying on the ground, Jefferson raised the horn to his lips and began blowing it again. Now there were yells and screams and the flash of grenades as paratroopers piled into the trenches and fought hand to hand with the enemy. Private Capon, reaching one of the trenches, suddenly found himself facing two Germans. One of them hastily raised a Red Cross box high above his head in a token of surrender and said, "*Russki, Russki.*" They were Russian "volunteers." For a moment, Capon didn't know what to do. Then he saw other Germans surrendering and paratroopers leading them down the trench. He handed over his two captives and continued on toward the battery.

There Otway, Lieutenant Dowling and about forty men were already fighting fiercely. Troopers who had cleaned out trenches and gun pits were running around the sides of the earth-banked concrete fortifications, emptying their Sten guns and tossing grenades into the apertures. The battle was gory and wild. Privates Mower, Hawkins and a Bren gunner, racing through a torrent of mortar and machine gun fire, reached one side of the battery, found a door open and plunged inside. A dead German gunner was lying in the passageway; there seemed to be nobody else around. Mower left the other two men by the door and went along the passage. He came to a large room and saw a heavy field piece on a platform. Next to it great stacks of shells were piled. Mower rushed back to his friends and excitedly outlined his plan to "blow the whole business up by detonating grenades among the shells." But they didn't get the chance. As the three men stood talking there was the blast of an explosion. The Bren gunner died instantly. Hawkins was hit in the stomach. Mower thought his back had been "ripped open by a thousand red-hot needles." He couldn't control his legs. They twitched involuntarily—the way he had seen dead bodies twitch. He was sure he was going to die and he didn't

want to end this way and he began to call out for help. He
called for his mother.

Elsewhere in the battery Germans were surrendering. Private Capon caught up with Dowling's men just in time to see
"Germans pushing each other out of a doorway and almost
begging to surrender." Dowling's party split the barrels of two
guns by firing two shells simultaneously through each barrel,
and temporarily knocked out the other two. Then Dowling
found Otway. He stood before the colonel, his right hand
holding the left side of his chest. He said, "Battery taken as
ordered, sir. Guns destroyed." The battle was over; it had taken
just fifteen minutes. Otway fired a yellow flare—the success
signal—from the Very pistol. It was seen by an R.A.F. spotting
plane and radioed to H.M.S. *Arethusa* offshore exactly a quarter of an hour before the cruiser was to start bombarding the
battery. At the same time Otway's signal officer sent a confirming message out by pigeon. He had carried the bird all through
the battle. On its leg in a plastic capsule was a strip of paper
with the code word "Hammer." Moments later Otway found
the lifeless body of Lieutenant Dowling. He had been dying at
the time he made his report.

Otway led his battered battalion out of the bloody Merville
battery. He had not been told to hold the battery once the
guns were knocked out. His men had other D-Day missions.
They took only twenty-two prisoners. Of the two hundred Germans, no fewer than 178 were dead or dying, and Otway had
lost almost half of his own men—seventy killed or wounded.
Ironically, the four guns were only half the reported size. And
within forty-eight hours the Germans would be back in the
battery and two of the guns would be firing on the beaches.
But for the critical few hours ahead the Merville battery would
be silent and deserted.

Most of the badly injured had to be left behind, for Otway's
men had neither sufficient medical supplies nor transport to
carry them. Mower was carried out on a board. Hawkins was
too terribly wounded to be moved. Both men would survive
—even Mower, with fifty-seven pieces of shrapnel in his body.
The last thing Mower remembers as they moved away from
the battery was Hawkins yelling, "Mates, for God's sake, don't

leave me!" Then the voice grew fainter and fainter and Mower mercifully drifted into unconsciousness.

It was nearly dawn—the dawn that eighteen thousand para-troopers had been fighting toward. In less than five hours they had more than fulfilled the expectations of General Eisen-hower and his commanders. The airborne armies had confused the enemy and disrupted his communications, and now, hold-ing the flanks at either end of the Normandy invasion area, they had to a great extent blocked the movement of enemy reinforcements.

In the British zone Major Howard's glider-borne troops were firmly astride the vital Caen and Orne bridges. By dawn the five crossings over the Dives would be demolished. Lieutenant Colonel Otway and his emaciated battalion had knocked out the Merville battery, and paratroopers were now in position on the heights overlooking Caen. Thus the principal British assignments had been completed, and as long as the various arteries could be held German counterattacks would be slowed down or stopped altogether.

At the other end of Normandy's five invasion beaches the Americans, despite more difficult terrain and a greater variety of missions, had done equally well. Lieutenant Colonel Krause's men held the key communications center of Ste.-Mère-Église. North of the town Lieutenant Colonel Vandervoort's battalion had cut the main Cherbourg highway running down the pen-insula and stood ready to repel attacks driving in from there. Brigadier General Gavin and his troops were dug in around the strategic Merderet and Douve crossings and were holding the rear of the Utah invasion beachhead. General Maxwell Taylor's 101st was still widely scattered; by dawn the division's assem-bled strength would be only 1,100 out of a total of 6,600 men. Despite this handicap troopers had reached the St.-Martin-de-Varreville gun battery, only to discover that the guns had been removed. Others were in sight of the vital La Barquette locks, the key to the flooding across the neck of the peninsula. And although none of the causeways leading off Utah had been reached, groups of soldiers were driving for them and already held the western edge of the inundated areas back of the beach itself.

The men of the Allied airborne armies had invaded the Continent from the air and secured the initial foothold for the invasion from the sea. Now they awaited the arrival of the seaborne forces with whom they would drive into Hitler's Europe. The American task forces were already lying twelve miles off Utah and Omaha beaches. For U.S. troops H Hour—6:30 A.M.—was exactly one hour and forty-five minutes away.

7

AT 4:45 A.M., Lieutenant George Honour's midget submarine X23 broke the surface of a heaving sea one mile off the Normandy coast. Twenty miles away its sister sub the X20 also surfaced. These two 57-foot craft were now in position, each marking one end of the British-Canadian invasion area—the three beaches, Sword, Juno and Gold. Now each crew had to erect a mast with a flashing light, set up all the other visual and radio signaling apparatus and wait for the first British ships to home in on their signals.

On the X23 Honour pushed up the hatch and climbed stiffly out onto the narrow catwalk. Waves rolled over the little deck and he had to hang on to avoid being washed overboard. Behind him came his weary crew. They clung to the guide rails, water washing about their legs, and hungrily gulped in the cool night air. They had been off Sword Beach since before dawn on June 4 and they had been submerged for more than twenty-one hours out of each day. In all, since leaving Portsmouth on June 2 they had been under water some sixty-four hours.

Even now their ordeal was far from over. On the British beaches H Hour varied from 7 to 7:30 A.M. So for two more hours, until the first wave of assault craft came in, the midget subs would have to hold their positions. Until then the X23 and X20 would be exposed on the surface—small, fixed targets for the German beach batteries. And soon it would be daylight.

8

EVERYWHERE men waited for this dawn, but none so anxiously as the Germans. For by now a new and ominous note had begun to creep into the welter of messages pouring into

Rommel's and Rundstedt's headquarters. All along the invasion coast Admiral Krancke's naval stations were picking up the sound of ships—not just one or two as before, but ships by the score. For more than an hour the reports had been mounting. At last a little before 5 A.M. the persistent Major General Pemsel of the Seventh Army telephoned Rommel's chief of staff, Major General Speidel, and told him bluntly, "Ships are concentrating between the mouths of the Vire and the Orne. They lead to the conclusion that an enemy landing and large-scale attack against Normandy is imminent."

Field Marshal Gerd von Rundstedt at his headquarters, OB West, outside Paris had already reached a similar conclusion. To him the impending Normandy assault still looked like a "diversionary attack" and not the real invasion. Even so Rundstedt had moved fast. He had already ordered two massive panzer divisions—the 12th S.S. and the *Panzer Lehr*, both lying in reserve near Paris—to assemble and rush to the coast. Technically both these divisions came under Hitler's headquarters, OKW, and they were not to be committed without the Führer's specific approval. But Rundstedt had taken the chance; he could not believe that Hitler would object or countermand the order. Now, convinced that all the evidence pointed to Normandy as the area for the Allied "diversionary attack," Rundstedt sent an official request to OKW for the reserves. "OB West," explained his teletype message, "is fully aware that if this is actually a large-scale enemy operation it can only be met successfully if immediate action is taken. This involves the commitment on this day of the available strategic reserves . . . these are the 12th S.S. and *Panzer Lehr* divisions. If they assemble quickly and get an early start they can enter the battle on the coast during the day. Under the circumstances OB West therefore requests OKW to release the reserves . . ." It was a perfunctory message, simply for the record.

At Hitler's headquarters in Berchtesgaden in the balmy unrealistic climate of southern Bavaria, the message was delivered to the office of Colonel General Alfred Jodl, Chief of Operations. Jodl was asleep and his staff believed that the situation had not developed sufficiently enough yet for his sleep to be disturbed. The message could wait until later.

Not more than three miles away at Hitler's mountain retreat, the Führer and his mistress Eva Braun were also asleep.

Hitler had retired as usual at 4 A.M. and his personal physician, Dr. Morell, had given him a sleeping draught (he was unable to sleep now without it). At about 5 A.M. Hitler's naval aide, Admiral Karl Jesko von Puttkamer, was awakened by a call from Jodl's headquarters. Puttkamer's caller—he cannot recall now who it was—said that there had been "some sort of landings in France." Nothing precise was known yet—in fact, Puttkamer was told, "the first messages are extremely vague." Did Puttkamer think that the Führer should be informed? Both men hashed it over and then decided not to wake Hitler. Puttkamer remembers that "there wasn't much to tell him anyway and we both feared that if I woke him at this time he might start one of his endless nervous scenes which often led to the wildest decisions." Puttkamer decided that the morning would be time enough to give Hitler the news. He switched off the light and went back to sleep.

In France the generals at OB West and Army Group B sat down to wait. They had alerted their forces and called up the panzer reserves; now the next move was up to the Allies. Nobody could estimate the magnitude of the impending assault. Nobody knew—or could even guess—the size of the Allied fleet. And although everything pointed toward Normandy, nobody was really sure where the main attack would come. The German generals had done all they could. The rest depended on the ordinary Wehrmacht soldiers holding the coast. They had suddenly become important. From the coastal fortifications the soldiers of the Reich looked out toward the sea, wondering if this was a practice alert or the real thing at last.

Major Werner Pluskat in his bunker overlooking Omaha Beach had heard nothing from his superiors since 1 A.M. He was cold, tired and exasperated. He felt isolated. He couldn't understand why there had been no reports from either regimental or division headquarters. To be sure, the very fact that his phone had remained silent all night was a good sign; it must mean that nothing serious was happening. But what about the paratroopers, the massed formations of planes? Pluskat could not rid himself of his gnawing uneasiness. Once more he swung the artillery glasses over to the left, picked up the dark mass of the Cherbourg peninsula and began another slow sweep of the horizon. The same low banks of mist came into view, the same patches of shimmering moonlight, the same restless, white-flecked sea. Nothing was changed. Everything seemed peaceful.

Behind him in the bunker his dog, Harras, was stretched out asleep. Nearby, Captain Ludz Wilkening and Lieutenant Fritz Theen were talking quietly. Pluskat joined them. "Still nothing out there," he told them. "I'm about to give it up." But he walked back to the aperture and stood looking out as the first streaks of light began to lighten the sky. He decided to make another routine sweep.

Wearily, he swung the glasses over to the left again. Slowly he tracked across the horizon. He reached the dead center of the bay. The glasses stopped moving. Pluskat tensed, stared hard.

Through the scattering, thinning mist the horizon was magically filling with ships—ships of every size and description, ships that casually maneuvered back and forth as though they had been there for hours. There appeared to be thousands of them. It was a ghostly armada that somehow had appeared from nowhere. Pluskat stared in frozen disbelief, speechless, moved as he had never been before in his life. At that moment the world of the good soldier Pluskat began falling apart. He says that in those first few moments he knew, calmly and surely, that "this was the end for Germany."

He turned to Wilkening and Theen and, with a strange detachment, said simply, "It's the invasion. See for yourselves." Then he picked up the phone and called Major Block at the 352nd Division's headquarters.

"Block," said Pluskat, "it's the invasion. There must be ten thousand ships out here." Even as he said it, he knew his words must sound incredible.

"Get hold of yourself, Pluskat!" snapped Block. "The Americans and the British together don't have that many ships. Nobody has that many ships!"

Block's disbelief brought Pluskat out of his daze. "If you don't believe me," he suddenly yelled, "come up here and see for yourself. It's fantastic! It's unbelievable!"

There was a slight pause and then Block said, "What way are these ships heading?"

Pluskat, phone in hand, looked out the aperture of the bunker and replied, "Right for me."

PART THREE
THE DAY

I

NEVER had there been a dawn like this. In the murky, gray light, in majestic, fearful grandeur, the great Allied fleet lay off Normandy's five invasion beaches. The sea teemed with ships. Battle ensigns snapped in the wind all the way across the horizon from the edge of the Utah area on the Cherbourg peninsula to Sword Beach near the mouth of the Orne. Outlined against the sky were the big battlewagons, the menacing cruisers, the whippetlike destroyers. Behind them were the squat command ships, sprouting their forests of antennae. And behind them came the convoys of troop-filled transports and landing ships, lying low and sluggish in the water. Circling the lead transports, waiting for the signal to head for the beaches, were swarms of bobbing landing craft, jam-packed with the men who would land in the first waves.

The great spreading mass of ships seethed with noise and activity. Engines throbbed and whined as patrol boats dashed back and forth through the milling assault craft. Windlasses whirred as booms swung out amphibious vehicles. Chains rattled in the davits as assault boats were lowered away. Landing craft loaded with pallid-faced men shuddered and banged against the high steel sides of transports. Loud-hailers blared out, "Keep in line! Keep in line!" as coastguardmen shepherded the bobbing assault boats into formations. On the transports men jammed the rails, waiting their turn to climb down slippery ladders or scramble-nets into the heaving, spray-washed beaching craft. And through it all, over the ships' public-address systems came a steady flow of messages and exhortations: "Fight to get your troops ashore, fight to save your ships, and if you've got any strength left, fight to save yourselves." . . . "Get in there, Fourth Division, and give 'em hell!" . . . "Don't forget, the Big Red One is leading the way." . . . "U.S. Rangers, man your stations." . . . "Remember Dunkirk! Remember Coventry! God bless you all." . . . "*Nous mourrons sur le sable de notre France chérie, mais nous ne retournerons pas* [We shall die on the sands of our dear France but we shall not turn back]." . . . "This is it, men, pick it up and put it on, you've only got a one-way ticket and this is the end of the line.

Twenty-nine, let's go!" And then the two messages that most men still remember: "Away all boats," and "Our Father, which art in Heaven, hallowed be Thy Name . . ."

Along the crowded rails many men left their positions to say goodbye to buddies going in on other boats. Soldiers and seamen, who had become firm friends after the long hours spent aboard ships, wished one another good luck. And hundreds of men took time to exchange home addresses "just in case." Technical Sergeant Roy Stevens of the 29th Division fought his way across a crowded deck in search of his twin brother. "I finally found him," he says. "He smiled and extended his hand. I said, 'No, we will shake hands at the crossroads in France like we planned.' We said goodbye, and I never saw him again." On H.M.S. *Prince Leopold*, Lieutenant Joseph Lacy, the chaplain of the 5th and 2nd Ranger battalions, walked among the waiting men and P.F.C. Max Coleman heard him say, "I'll do your praying for you from here on in. What you're going to do today will be a prayer in itself."

All over the ships, officers wound up their pep talks with the kind of colorful or memorable phrases that they felt best suited the occasion—sometimes with unexpected results. Lieutenant Colonel John O'Neill, whose special combat engineers were to land on Omaha and Utah beaches in the first wave and destroy the mined obstacles, thought he had the ideal conclusion to his debarking talk when he thundered, "Come hell or high water, get those damned obstacles out!" From somewhere nearby, a voice remarked, "I believe that s.o.b. is scared, too." Captain Sherman Burroughs of the 29th Division told Captain Charles Cawthon that he planned to recite "The Shooting of Dan McGrew" on the way in to the beach. Lieutenant Colonel Elzie Moore, heading up an engineer brigade bound for Utah, was without a speech. He had wanted to recite a most appropriate excerpt from the story of another invasion of France, a battle scene from Shakespeare's *Henry V*, but all he could remember was the opening line, "Once more unto the breach, dear friends . . ." He decided to give up the idea. Major C. K. "Banger" King of the British 3rd Division, going in on the first wave to Sword Beach, planned to read from the same play. He had gone to the trouble of writing down the lines he wanted. They closed with the passage, "He that outlives this day, and comes safe home/Will stand a tip-toe when this day is named . . ."

The tempo was increasing. Off the American beaches more and more troop-filled boats were joining the churning assault craft endlessly circling the mother ships. Sodden, seasick and miserable, the men in these boats would lead the way into Normandy, across Omaha and Utah beaches. In the transport areas, debarking was now in full swing. It was a complex and hazardous operation. Soldiers carried so much equipment that they were barely able to move. Each had a rubber-tube life preserver and, besides weapons, musette bags, entrenching tools, gas masks, first-aid kits, canteens, knives and rations, everybody had extra quantities of grenades, explosives and ammunition —often as much as 250 rounds. In addition, many men were burdened with the special equipment that their particular jobs demanded. Some men estimate that they weighed at least three hundred pounds as they waddled across decks and prepared to get into the boats. All this paraphernalia was necessary, but it seemed to Major Gerden Johnson of the 4th Infantry Division that his men were "slowed down to the pace of a turtle." Lieutenant Bill Williams of the 29th thought his men were so overburdened that "they wouldn't be able to do much fighting," and Private Rudolph Mozgo, looking down the side of his transport at the assault craft that smashed against the hull and rose sickeningly up and down on the swells, figured that if he and his equipment could just get into a boat "half the battle would be won."

Many men, trying to balance themselves and their equipment as they climbed down the weblike scramble-nets, became casualties long before they were even fired on. Corporal Harold Janzen of a mortar unit, loaded down with two reels of cable and several field phones, tried to time the rise and fall of the assault craft beneath him. He jumped at what he thought was the right moment, misjudged, fell twelve feet to the bottom of the boat and knocked himself out with his carbine. There were more serious injuries. Sergeant Romeo Pompei heard someone scream below him, looked down and saw a man hanging in agony on the net as the assault boat ground his foot against the side of the transport. Pompei himself fell headlong from the net into the boat and smashed his front teeth.

Troops that boarded craft on the decks and were lowered down from davits were no better off. Major Thomas Dallas, one of the 29th's battalion commanders, and his headquarters staff were suspended about halfway between the rail and the water when the davits lowering their boat jammed. They hung there for about twenty minutes—just four feet beneath the sewage outlet from the "heads." "The heads were in constant use," he recalls, "and during these twenty minutes we received the entire discharge."

The waves were so high that many assault craft bounced like monstrous Yo-yos up and down on the davit chains. One boat-load of Rangers got halfway down the side of H.M.S. *Prince Charles* when a huge swell surged up and almost pitched them back on the deck. The swell receded and the boat dropped sickeningly down again on its cables, bouncing its seasick occupants about like so many dolls.

As they went into the small boats veteran soldiers told the new men with them what to expect. On H.M.S. *Empire Anvil*, Corporal Michael Kurtz of the 1st Division gathered his squad about him. "I want all of you Joes to keep your heads down below the gunwale," he warned them. "As soon as we're spotted we'll catch enemy fire. If you make it, O.K. If you don't, it's a helluva good place to die. Now let's go." As Kurtz and his men loaded into their boat in the davits they heard yells below them. Another boat had upended, spilling its men into the sea. Kurtz's boat was lowered away without trouble. Then they all saw the men swimming near the side of the transport. As Kurtz's boat moved off, one of the soldiers floating in the water yelled, "So long, suckers!" Kurtz looked at the men in his boat. On each face he saw the same waxy, expressionless look.

It was 5:30 A.M. Already the first-wave troops were well on the way to the beaches. For this great seaborne assault which the free world had toiled so hard to mount, only about three thousand men were leading the attack. They were the combat teams of the 1st, 29th and 4th divisions and attached units—Army and Navy underwater demolition teams, tank battalion groups, and Rangers. Each combat team was given a specific landing zone. For example, the 16th Regiment of Major General Clarence R. Huebner's 1st Division would assault one half of Omaha Beach, the 116th of Major General Charles

H. Gerhardt's 29th Division the other.* Those zones had been subdivided into sectors, each with a code name. Men of the 1st Division would land on Easy Red, Fox Green and Fox Red, the 29th on Charlie, Dog Green, Dog White, Dog Red and Easy Green.

The landing schedules for both Omaha and Utah beaches were planned on an almost minute-by-minute timetable. In the 29th Division's half of Omaha Beach at H Hour minus five minutes—6:25 A.M.—thirty-two amphibious tanks were to swim onto Dog White and Dog Green and take up firing positions at the water's edge to cover the first phase of the assault. At H Hour itself—6:30 A.M.—eight LCTs would bring in more tanks, landing them directly from the sea on Easy Green and Dog Red. One minute later—6:31 A.M.—the assault troops would swarm across the beach on all sectors. Two minutes after that—6:33 A.M.—the underwater demolition engineers were due; they had the tough job of clearing sixteen 50-yard paths through the mines and obstacles. They had just twenty-seven minutes to finish this ticklish job. At six-minute intervals from 7 A.M. on, five assault waves, the main body of troops, would begin landing.

This was the basic landing plan for both beaches. The build-up was so carefully timed that heavy equipment like artillery was expected to be landed on Omaha Beach within an hour and a half and even cranes, half-tracks and tank recovery vehicles were scheduled to come in by 10:30 A.M. It was an involved, elaborate timetable which looked as if it could not possibly hold up—and in all probability the planners had taken this into consideration, too.

The first-wave assault troops could not yet see the misty shores of Normandy. They were still more than nine miles away. Some warships were already dueling with German naval coastal batteries, but the action as yet was remote and impersonal for the soldiers in the boats—nobody was firing directly at them. Seasickness was still their biggest enemy. Few were immune. The assault boats, each loaded with about thirty men

---

*Although the 1st and 29th Divisions' combat teams shared the assault, the actual landings were technically under the command of the 1st Division in this opening phase.

and all their weighty equipment, rode so low in the water that waves rolled over the side and out again. With each wave the boats pitched and tossed, and Colonel Eugene Caffey of the 1st Engineers Special Brigade remembers that some of the men in his boat "just lay there with the water sloshing back and forth over them, not caring whether they lived or died." But for those among them not yet incapacitated by seasickness, the sight of the great invasion fleet looming up all about them was awesome and wonderful. In Corporal Gerald Burt's boatload of demolition engineers, one man wistfully remarked that he wished he'd brought his camera.

Thirty miles away Lieutenant Commander Heinrich Hoffmann, in the lead E-boat of his 5th Flotilla, saw a strange, unreal fog blanketing the sea ahead. As Hoffmann watched, a single plane flew out of the whiteness. That confirmed his suspicion—it must be a smoke screen. Hoffmann, followed by the other two E-boats, plunged into the haze to investigate—and got the shock of his life. On the other side he found himself face to face with a staggering array of warships—almost the entire British fleet. Everywhere he looked there were battleships, cruisers and destroyers towering over him. "I felt as though I were sitting in a rowboat," Hoffmann says. Almost instantly shells began to fall around his dodging, twisting boats. Without a moment's hesitation, the cocky Hoffmann, unbelievably outnumbered, ordered the attack. Seconds later, in the only German naval offensive of D Day, eighteen torpedoes knifed through the water toward the Allied fleet.

On the bridge of the Norwegian destroyer *Svenner*, the Royal Navy's Lieutenant Desmond Lloyd saw them coming. So did officers on the bridges of *Warspite*, *Ramillies* and *Largs*. *Largs* promptly slammed her engines to full speed astern. Two torpedoes sliced between *Warspite* and *Ramillies*. *Svenner* couldn't get out of the way. Her captain yelled, "Hard aport! Full ahead starboard! Full astern port!" in a vain effort to swing the destroyer so that the torpedoes would pass parallel to the ship. Lieutenant Lloyd, watching through his binoculars, saw that the torpedoes were going to hit directly beneath the bridge. All he could think of was, "How high will I fly?" With agonizing slowness *Svenner* turned to port and for a moment Lloyd thought they might escape. But the maneuver failed. A torpedo slammed into the boiler room. *Svenner* seemed to lift from the water, shuddered and broke in two. Nearby, Leading Stoker Robert Dowie, on the mine sweeper H.M.S. *Dunbar*, was amazed to see the destroyer slide beneath the water with "her bow and stern sticking up to form a perfect V." There were thirty casualties. Lieutenant Lloyd, unhurt, swam about for nearly twenty minutes, keeping a sailor with a broken leg afloat, until they were both picked up by the destroyer *Swift*.

To Hoffmann, safely back again on the other side of the smoke screen, the important thing now was to raise the alarm. He flashed the news to Le Havre, serenely unaware that his radio had been knocked out of commission in the brief battle that had just taken place.

On the flagship *Augusta* lying off the American beaches, Lieutenant General Omar N. Bradley plugged his ears with cotton and then trained his binoculars on the landing craft speeding toward the beaches. His troops, the men of the U.S. First Army, were moving steadily in. Bradley was deeply concerned. Up to a few hours before he had believed that an inferior and overextended German "static" division, the 716th, was holding the coastal area, roughly from Omaha Beach all the way east to the British zone. But just before he left England, Allied intelligence had passed on the information that an additional German division had moved into the invasion area. The news had arrived too late for Bradley to inform his already briefed and "sealed" troops. Now the men of the 1st and 29th divisions were heading for Omaha Beach, unaware that the tough, battle-tested 352nd Division manned the defenses.*

The naval bombardment which Bradley prayed would make their job easier was about to begin. A few miles away Contre-Amiral Jaujard, on the French light cruiser *Montcalm*, spoke to his officers and men. "*C'est une chose terrible et monstrueuse que d'être obligé de tirer sur notre propre patrie*," he said, his voice heavy with emotion, "*mais je vous demande de le faire*

---

*Allied intelligence was under the impression that the 352nd had only recently taken up these positions and then only for "a defense exercise." Actually units had been in the coastal zone and overlooking Omaha Beach for more than two months—and some even longer. Pluskat and his guns, for example, had been there since March. But up to June 4 Allied intelligence had still placed the 352nd around St.-Lô, more than twenty miles away.

aujourd'hui [It is a terrible and monstrous thing to have to fire on our homeland, but I want you to do it this day]." And four miles off Omaha Beach on the destroyer U.S.S. *Carmick*, Commander Robert O. Beer pressed a button on the ship's intercom and said, "Now hear this! This is probably going to be the biggest party you boys will ever go to—so let's all get out on the floor and dance!"

The time was 5:50 A.M. The British warships had been firing off their beaches for more than twenty minutes. Now the bombardment in the American zone began. The entire invasion area erupted with a roaring storm of fire. The maelstrom of sound thundered back and forth along the Normandy coast as the big ships slammed steadily away at their preselected targets. The gray sky brightened with the hot flash of their guns and along the beaches great clouds of black smoke began to bunch up into the air.

Off Sword, Juno and Gold the battleships *Warspite* and *Ramillies* lobbed tons of steel from their 15-inch guns toward powerful German gun batteries at Le Havre and around the mouth of the Orne. Maneuvering cruisers and destroyers poured streams of shells into pillboxes, concrete bunkers and redoubts. With incredible accuracy, the sharpshooting H.M.S. *Ajax* of River Plate fame knocked out a battery of four 6-inch guns from six miles offshore. Off Omaha, the big battleships *Texas* and *Arkansas*, mounting between them a total of ten 14-inch, twelve 12-inch and twelve 5-inch guns, pumped six hundred shells onto the coastal battery position atop Pointe du Hoc in an all-out attempt to ease the way for the Ranger battalions even now heading for the 100-foot-high sheer cliffs. Off Utah the battleship *Nevada* and the cruisers *Tuscaloosa*, *Quincy* and *Black Prince* seemed to lean back as they hurled salvo after salvo at the shore batteries. While the big ships blasted away from five to six miles offshore, the small destroyers pressed in to a mile or two off the beaches and, line astern, sent a saturating fire into targets all over the network of coastal fortifications.

The fearsome salvos of the naval bombardment made deep impressions on the men who saw and heard them. Sub-Lieutenant Richard Ryland of the Royal Navy felt immense pride in "the majestic appearance of the battleships," and wondered "whether this would be the last occasion such a sight would be seen." On the U.S.S. *Nevada*, Yeoman Third Class Charles Langley was almost frightened by the massive fire power of the fleet. He did not see "how any army could possibly withstand the bombardment" and believed that "the fleet would be able to pull out in two or three hours." And in the speeding assault boats, as this roaring canopy of steel flashed over their heads, the sodden, miserable, seasick men, bailing with their helmets, looked up and cheered.

Now a new sound throbbed over the fleet. Slowly at first, like the mumbling of some giant bee, and then building to a great crescendo of noise, the bombers and fighters appeared. They flew straight in over the massive fleet, flying wing tip to wing tip, formation after formation—nine thousand planes. Spitfires, Thunderbolts and Mustangs whistled in over the heads of the men. With apparent disregard for the rain of shells from the fleet, they strafed the invasion beaches and headlands, zoomed up, swept around and came in again. Above them, crisscrossing at every altitude, were the 9th Air Force's B-26 medium bombers, and above these, out of sight in the heavy cloud layer, droned the heavies—the R.A.F. and 8th Air Force Lancasters, Fortresses and Liberators. It seemed as though the sky could not possibly hold them all. Men looked up and stared, eyes damp, faces contorted with a sudden emotion almost too great to bear. It was going to be all right now, they thought. There was the air cover—the enemy would be pinned down, the guns knocked out, the beaches would be cratered with foxholes. But, unable to see through the cloud layers, and unwilling to risk bombing their own troops, 329 bombers assigned to the Omaha area were already unloading thirteen thousand bombs up to three miles inland from their targets, the deadly guns* of Omaha Beach.

The last explosion was very near. Major Werner Pluskat thought the bunker was shaking itself apart. Another shell hit the cliff face at the very base of the hidden position. The shock of it

---

*There were 8 concrete bunkers with guns of 75 millimeters or larger caliber; 35 pillboxes with artillery pieces of various sizes and/or automatic weapons; 4 batteries of artillery; 18 antitank guns; 6 mortar pits; 35 rocket-launching sites, each with four 380-millimeter rocket tubes; and no less than 85 machine gun nests.

spun Pluskat around and hurled him backward. He fell heavily to the ground. Dust, dirt and concrete splinters showered about him. He couldn't see through the clouds of white dust, but he could hear his men shouting. Again and again shells smashed into the cliff. Pluskat was so dazed by the concussion that he could hardly speak.

The phone was ringing. It was the 352nd Division headquarters. "What's the situation?" a voice asked.

"We're being shelled," Pluskat managed to say, "heavily shelled."

Somewhere far behind his position he now heard bombs exploding. Another salvo of shells landed on the cliff top, sending an avalanche of earth and stones in through the bunker's apertures. The phone rang again. This time Pluskat couldn't find it. He let it ring. He noticed that he was covered from head to foot with a fine white dust and his uniform was ripped.

For a moment the shelling lifted and through the thick haze of dust Pluskat saw Theen and Wilkening on the concrete floor. He yelled to Wilkening, "Better get to your position while you have a chance." Wilkening looked glumly at Pluskat —his observation post was in the next bunker, some distance away. Pluskat took advantage of the lull to phone his batteries. To his amazement not one of his twenty guns—all brand-new Krupps of various calibers—had been hit. He could not see how the batteries, only half a mile or so from the coast, had escaped; there were not even any casualties among the crews. Pluskat began to wonder if observation posts along the coast were being mistaken for gun positions. The damage around his own post seemed to indicate it.

The phone rang just as the shelling began again. The same voice he had heard earlier demanded to know "the exact location of the shelling."

"For God's sake," Pluskat yelled, "they're falling all over. What do you want me to do—go out and measure the holes with a ruler?" He banged down the phone and looked around him. Nobody in the bunker seemed to be hurt. Wilkening had already left for his own bunker; Theen was at one of the apertures. Then Pluskat noticed that Harras was gone. But he had little time to bother about the big dog now. He picked up the phone again, walked over to the second aperture and looked out. There seemed to be even more assault boats in the water than when he had last looked, and they were closer now. Soon they would be in range.

He called Colonel Ocker at regimental headquarters. "All my guns are intact," he reported.

"Good," said Ocker, "now you'd better get back to your headquarters immediately."

Pluskat rang his gunnery officers. "I'm going back," he told them. "Remember, no gun must fire until the enemy reaches the water's edge."

The landing craft carrying U.S. 1st Division troops to their sector on Omaha Beach had not far to go now. Behind the bluffs overlooking Easy Red, Fox Green and Fox Red, the gun crews in Pluskat's four batteries waited for the boats to get just a little nearer.

"This is London calling.

"I bring you an urgent instruction from the Supreme Commander. The lives of many of you depend upon the speed and thoroughness with which you obey it. It is particularly addressed to all who live within thirty-five kilometers of any part of the coast."

Michel Hardelay stood at the window of his mother's house in Vierville at the western end of Omaha Beach and watched the invasion fleet maneuver. The guns were still firing, and Hardelay could feel the concussion through the soles of his shoes. The whole family—Hardelay's mother, his brother, his niece and the maid—had gathered in the living room. There seemed no doubt about it now, they all agreed: the invasion was going to take place right at Vierville. Hardelay was philosophical about his own seaside villa; now it would most certainly come down. In the background the BBC message, which had been repeated over and over for more than an hour, continued.

"Leave your towns at once, informing, as you go, any neighbors who may not be aware of the warning. . . . Stay off frequented roads. . . . Go on foot and take nothing with you which you cannot easily carry. . . . Get as quickly as possible into the open country. . . . Do not gather in large groups which may be mistaken for troop concentrations. . . ."

Hardelay wondered if the German on horseback would make his usual trip down to the gun crews with the morning coffee. He looked at his watch; if the soldier was coming, it was nearly time. Then Hardelay saw him on the same big-rumped horse, with the same bouncing coffee cans that he always carried. The man rode calmly down the road, turned the bend— and saw the fleet. For a second or two he sat motionless. Then he jumped off the horse, stumbled and fell, picked himself up and ran for cover. The horse continued slowly on down the road to the village. The time was 6:15 A.M.

2

BY NOW the long, bobbing lines of assault craft were less than a mile from Omaha and Utah beaches. For the three thousand Americans in the first wave H Hour was just fifteen minutes away.

The noise was deafening as the boats, long white wakes streaming out behind them, churned steadily for the shore. In the slopping, bouncing craft the men had to shout to be heard over the roar of the diesels. Overhead, like a great steel umbrella, the shells of the fleet still thundered. And rolling out from the coast came the booming explosions of the Allied air forces' carpet bombing. Strangely, the guns of the Atlantic Wall were silent. Troops saw the coastline stretching ahead and wondered about the absence of enemy fire. Maybe, many thought, it would be an easy landing after all.

The great square-faced ramps of the assault craft butted into every wave, and chilling, frothing green water sloshed over everyone. There were no heroes in these boats—just cold, miserable, anxious men, so jam-packed together, so weighed down by equipment that often there was no place to be seasick except over one another. *Newsweek*'s Kenneth Crawford, in the first Utah wave, saw a young 4th Division soldier, covered in his own vomit, slowly shaking his head in abject misery and disgust. "That guy Higgins," he said, "ain't got nothin' to be proud of about inventin' this goddamned boat."

Some men had no time to think about their miseries—they were bailing for their lives. Almost from the moment the assault craft left the mother ships, many boats had begun to fill with water. At first men had paid little attention to the sea slopping about their legs; it was just another misery to be endured.

Lieutenant George Kerchner of the Rangers watched the water slowly rise in his craft and wondered if it was serious. He had been told that the LCA was unsinkable. But then over the radio Kerchner's soldiers heard a call for help: "This is LCA 860! . . . LCA 860! . . . We're sinking! . . . We're sinking!" There was a final exclamation: "My God, we're sunk!" Immediately Kerchner and his men began bailing.

Directly behind Kerchner's boat, Sergeant Regis McCloskey, also of the Rangers, had his own troubles. McCloskey and his men had been bailing for more than an hour. Their boat carried ammunition for the Pointe du Hoc attack and all of the Rangers' packs. The boat was so waterlogged McCloskey was sure it would sink. His only hope lay in lightening the wallowing craft. McCloskey ordered his men to toss all unnecessary equipment overboard. Rations, extra clothing and packs went over the side. McCloskey heaved them all into the swells. In one pack was $1,200 which Private Chuck Vella had won in a crap game; in another was First Sergeant Charles Frederick's false teeth.

Landing craft began to sink in both the Omaha and Utah areas—ten off Omaha, seven off Utah. Some men were picked up by rescue boats coming up behind, others would float around for hours before being rescued. And some soldiers, their yells and screams unheard, were dragged down by their equipment and ammunition. They drowned within sight of the beaches, without having fired a shot.

In an instant the war had become personal. Troops heading for Utah Beach saw a control boat leading one of the waves suddenly rear up out of the water and explode. Seconds later heads bobbed up and survivors tried to save themselves by clinging to the wreckage. Another explosion followed almost immediately. The crew of a landing barge trying to launch four of the thirty-two amphibious tanks bound for Utah had dropped the ramp right onto a submerged sea mine. The front of the craft shot up and Sergeant Orris Johnson on a nearby LCT watched in frozen horror as a tank "soared more than a hundred feet into the air, tumbled slowly end over end, plunged back into the water and disappeared." Among the many dead, Johnson learned later, was his buddy, Tanker Don Neill.

Scores of Utah-bound men saw the dead bodies and heard

the yells and screams of the drowning. One man, Lieutenant (j.g.) Francis X. Riley of the Coast Guard, remembers the scene vividly. The twenty-four-year-old officer, commanding an LCI, could only listen "to the anguished cries for help from wounded and shocked soldiers and sailors as they pleaded with us to pull them out of the water." But Riley's orders were to "disembark the troops on time regardless of casualties." Trying to close his mind to the screams, Riley ordered his craft on past the drowning men. There was nothing else he could do. The assault waves sped by, and as one boat carrying Lieutenant Colonel James Batte and the 4th Division's 8th Infantry Regiment troops threaded its way through the dead bodies, Batte heard one of his gray-faced men say, "Them lucky bastards—they ain't seasick no more."

The sight of the bodies in the water, the strain of the long trip in from the transport ships and now the ominous nearness of the flat sands and the dunes of Utah Beach jerked men out of their lethargy. Corporal Lee Cason, who had just turned twenty, suddenly found himself "cursing to high heaven against Hitler and Mussolini for getting us into this mess." His companions were startled at his vehemence—Cason had never before been known to swear. In many boats now soldiers nervously checked and rechecked their weapons. Men became so possessive of their ammunition that Colonel Eugene Caffey could not get a single man in his boat to give him a clip of bullets for his rifle. Caffey, who was not supposed to land until 9 A.M., had smuggled himself aboard an 8th Infantry craft in an effort to catch up with his veteran 1st Engineer Brigade. He had no equipment and although all the men in the boat were overloaded with ammunition, they were "hanging onto it for dear life." Caffey was finally able to load the rifle by taking up a collection of one bullet from each of eight men.

In the waters off Omaha Beach there had been a disaster. Nearly half of the amphibious tank force scheduled to support the assault troops had foundered. The plan was for sixty-four of these tanks to be launched two to three miles offshore. From there they were to swim in to the beach. Thirty-two of them had been allotted to the 1st Division's area—Easy Red, Fox Green and Fox Red. The landing barges carrying them reached their positions, the ramps were dropped and twenty-nine tanks were launched into the heaving swells. The weird-looking amphibious vehicles, their great balloonlike canvas skirts supporting them in the water, began breasting the waves, driving toward the shore. Then tragedy overtook the men of the 741st Tank Battalion. Under the pounding of the waves the canvas water wings ripped, supports broke, engines were flooded —and, one after another, twenty-seven tanks foundered and sank. Men came clawing up out of the hatches, inflating their life belts, plunging into the sea. Some succeeded in launching survival rafts. Others went down in the steel coffins.

Two tanks, battered and almost awash, were still heading for the shore. The crews of three others had the good fortune to be on a landing barge whose ramp jammed. They were put ashore later. The remaining thirty-two tanks—for the 29th Division's half of the beach—were safe. Officers in charge of the craft carrying them, overwhelmed by the disaster they had seen, wisely decided to take their force directly onto the beach. But the loss of the 1st Division tanks would cost hundreds of casualties within the next few minutes.

From two miles out the assault troops began to see the living and the dead in the water. The dead floated gently, moving with the tide toward the beach, as though determined to join their fellow Americans. The living bobbed up and down in the swells, savagely pleading for the help the assault boats could not tender. Sergeant Regis McCloskey, his ammunition boat again safely under way, saw the screaming men in the water, "yelling for help, begging us to stop—and we couldn't. Not for anything or anyone." Gritting his teeth, McCloskey looked away as his boat sped past, and then, seconds later, he vomited over the side. Captain Robert Cunningham and his men saw survivors struggling, too. Instinctively their Navy crew swung the boat toward the men in the water. A fast launch cut them off. Over its loud-speaker came the grim words, "You are not a rescue ship! Get on shore!" In another boat nearby, Sergeant Noel Dube of an engineer battalion said the Act of Contrition.

Now the deadly martial music of the bombardment seemed to grow and swell as the thin wavy lines of assault craft closed in on Omaha Beach. Landing ships lying about one thousand yards offshore joined in the shelling; and then thousands of flashing rockets whooshed over the heads of the men. To the troops it seemed inconceivable that anything could survive the massive weight of fire power that flayed the German defenses. The beach was wreathed in haze, and plumes of smoke from grass fires drifted lazily down from the bluffs. Still the German guns remained silent. The boats bored in. In the thrashing surf and running back up the beach men could now see the lethal jungles of steel-and-concrete obstacles. They were strewn everywhere, draped with barbed wire and capped with mines. They were as cruel and ugly as the men had expected. Back of the defenses the beach itself was deserted; nothing and no one moved upon it. Closer and closer the boats pressed in . . . 500 yards . . . 450 yards. Still no enemy fire. Through waves that were four to five feet high the assault craft surged forward, and now the great bombardment began to lift, shifting to targets farther inland. The first boats were barely 400 yards from the shore when the German guns—the guns that few believed could have survived the raging Allied air and sea bombardment —opened up.

Through the din and clamor one sound was nearer, deadlier than all the rest—the sound of machine gun bullets clanging across the steel, snoutlike noses of the boats. Artillery roared. Mortar shells rained down. All along the four miles of Omaha Beach German guns flayed the assault craft.

It was H Hour.

They came ashore on Omaha Beach, the slogging, unglamorous men that no one envied. No battle ensigns flew for them, no horns or bugles sounded. But they had history on their side. They came from regiments that had bivouacked at places like Valley Forge, Stoney Creek, Antietam, Gettysburg, that had fought in the Argonne. They had crossed the beaches of North Africa, Sicily and Salerno. Now they had one more beach to cross. They would call this one "Bloody Omaha."

The most intense fire came from the cliffs and high bluffs at either end of the crescent-shaped beach—in the 29th Division's Dog Green area to the west and the 1st Division's Fox Green sector to the east. Here the Germans had concentrated their heaviest defenses to hold two of the principal exits leading off the beach at Vierville and toward Colleville. Everywhere along the beach men encountered heavy fire as their boats came in, but the troops landing at Dog Green and Fox Green hadn't a chance. German gunners on the cliffs looked almost directly down on the waterlogged assault craft that heaved and pitched toward these sectors of the beach. Awkward and slow, the assault boats were nearly stationary in the water. They were sitting ducks. Coxswains at the tillers, trying desperately to maneuver their unwieldy craft through the forest of mined obstacles, now had to run the gantlet of fire from the cliffs.

Some boats, unable to find a way through the maze of obstacles and the withering cliff fire, were driven off and wandered aimlessly along the beach seeking a less heavily defended spot to land. Others, doggedly trying to come in at their assigned sectors, were shelled so badly that men plunged over the sides into deep water, where they were immediately picked off by machine gun fire. Some landing craft were blown apart as they came in. Second Lieutenant Edward Gearing's assault boat, filled with thirty men of the 29th Division, disintegrated in one blinding moment three hundred yards from the Vierville exit at Dog Green. Gearing and his men were blown out of the boat and strewn over the water. Shocked and half drowned, the nineteen-year-old lieutenant came to the surface yards away from where his boat had gone down. Other survivors began to bob up, too. Their weapons, helmets and equipment were gone. The coxswain had disappeared and nearby one of Gearing's men, struggling beneath the weight of a heavy radio set strapped to his back, screamed out, "For God's sake, I'm drowning!" Nobody could get to the radioman before he went under. For Gearing and the remnants of his section the ordeal was just beginning. It would be three hours before they got on the beach. Then Gearing would learn that he was the only surviving officer of his company. The others were dead or seriously wounded.

All along Omaha Beach the dropping of the ramps seemed to be the signal for renewed, more concentrated machine gun fire, and again the most murderous fire was in the Dog Green and Fox Green sectors. Boats of the 29th Division, coming into Dog Green, grounded on the sand bars. The ramps came down and men stepped out into water three to six feet deep. They had but one object in mind—to get through the water, cross two hundred yards of the obstacle-strewn sand, climb the gradually rising shingle and then take cover in the doubtful shelter of a sea wall. But, weighed down by their equipment, unable to run in the deep water and without cover of any kind, men were caught in crisscrossing machine gun and small-arms fire.

Seasick men, already exhausted by the long hours spent on the transports and in the assault boats, found themselves fighting for their lives in water which was often over their heads. Private David Silva saw the men in front of him being mowed down as they stepped off the ramp. When his turn came, he jumped into chest-high water and, bogged down by his equipment, watched spellbound as bullets flicked the surface all around him. Within seconds machine gun fire had riddled his pack, his clothing and his canteen. Silva felt like a "pigeon at a trap shoot." He thought he spotted the German machine gunner who was firing at him, but he could not fire back. His rifle was clogged with sand. Silva waded on, determined to make the sands ahead. He finally pulled himself up on the beach and dashed for the shelter of the sea wall, completely unaware that he had been wounded twice—once in the back, and once in the right leg.

Men fell all along the water's edge. Some were killed instantly, others called pitifully for the medics as the incoming tide slowly engulfed them. Among the dead was Captain Sherman Burroughs. His friend, Captain Charles Cawthon, saw the body washing back and forth in the surf. Cawthon wondered if Burroughs had recited "The Shooting of Dan McGrew" to his men on the run-in as he had planned. And when Captain Carroll Smith passed by, he could not help but think that Burroughs "would no longer suffer from his constant migraine headaches." Burroughs had been shot through the head.

Within the first few minutes of the carnage at Dog Green one entire company was put out of action. Less than a third of the men survived the bloody walk from the boats to the edge of the beach. Their officers were killed, severely wounded or missing, and the men, weaponless and shocked, huddled at the base of the cliffs all day. Another company in the same sector suffered even higher casualties. Company C of the 2nd Ranger Battalion had been ordered to knock out enemy strongpoints at Pointe de la Percée, slightly west of Vierville. The Rangers

landed in two assault craft with the first wave on Dog Green.
They were decimated. The lead craft was sunk almost immediately by artillery fire, and twelve men were killed outright. The
moment the ramp of the second craft dropped down machine
gun fire sprayed the debarking Rangers, killing and wounding
fifteen. The remainder set out for the cliffs. Men fell one after
another. P.F.C. Nelson Noyes, staggering under the weight of
a bazooka, made a hundred yards before he was forced to hit
the ground. A few moments later he got up and ran forward
again. When he reached the shingle he was machine-gunned in
the leg. As he lay there Noyes saw the two Germans who had
fired looking down on him from the cliff. Propping himself on
his elbows he opened up with his Tommy gun and brought
both of them down. By the time Captain Ralph E. Goranson,
the company commander, reached the base of the cliff, he had
only thirty-five Rangers left out of his seventy-man team. By
nightfall these thirty-five would be cut down to twelve.

Misfortune piled upon misfortune for the men of Omaha
Beach. Soldiers now discovered that they had been landed in
the wrong sectors. Some came in almost two miles away from
their original landing areas. Boat sections from the 29th Division found themselves intermingled with men of the 1st Division. For example, units scheduled to land on Easy Green and
fight toward an exit at Les Moulins discovered themselves at the
eastern end of the beach in the hell of Fox Green. Nearly all the
landing craft came in slightly east of their touch-down points.
A control boat drifting off station, a strong current running
eastward along the beach, the haze and smoke from grass fires
which obscured landmarks—all these contributed to the mis-
landings. Companies that had been trained to capture certain
objectives never got near them. Small groups found themselves
pinned down by German fire and isolated in unrecognizable
terrain, often without officers or communications.

The special Army-Navy demolition engineers who had the
job of blowing paths through the beach obstacles were not
only widely scattered, they were brought in crucial minutes
behind schedule. These frustrated men set to work wherever
they found themselves. But they fought a losing battle. In the
few minutes they had before the following waves of troops

bore down on the beaches, the engineers cleared only five
and a half paths instead of the sixteen planned. Working with
desperate haste, the demolition parties were impeded at every
turn—infantrymen waded in among them, soldiers took shelter behind the obstacles they were about to blow, and landing
craft, buffeted by the swells, came in almost on top of them.
Sergeant Barton A. Davis of the 299th Engineer Combat Battalion saw an assault boat bearing down on him. It was filled
with 1st Division men and was coming straight in through the
obstacles. There was a tremendous explosion and the boat disintegrated. It seemed to Davis that everyone in it was thrown
into the air all at once. Bodies and parts of bodies landed all
around the flaming wreckage. "I saw black dots of men trying
to swim through the gasoline that had spread on the water and
as we wondered what to do a headless torso flew a good fifty
feet through the air and landed with a sickening thud near us."
Davis did not see how anyone could have lived through the explosion, but two men did. They were pulled out of the water,
badly burned but alive.

But the disaster that Davis had seen was no greater than
that which had overtaken the heroic men of his own unit, the
Army-Navy Special Engineer Task Force. The landing boats
carrying their explosives had been shelled, and the hulks of
these craft lay blazing at the edge of the beach. Engineers with
small rubber boats loaded with plastic charges and detonators
were blown apart in the water when enemy fire touched off the
explosives. The Germans, seeing the engineers working among
the obstacles, seemed to single them out for special attention.
As the teams tied on their charges, snipers took careful aim at
the mines on the obstacles. At other times they seemed to wait
until the engineers had prepared whole lines of steel trestles
and tetrahedra obstacles for blowing. Then the Germans themselves would detonate the obstacles with mortar fire—before
the engineers could get out of the area. By the end of the day
casualties would be almost fifty per cent. Sergeant Davis himself would be one. Nightfall would find him aboard a hospital
ship with a wounded leg, heading back for England.

It was 7 A.M. The second wave of troops arrived on the
shambles that was Omaha Beach. Men splashed ashore under
the saturating fire of the enemy. Landing craft joined the ever

growing graveyard of wrecked, blazing hulks. Each wave of boats gave up its own bloody contribution to the incoming tide, and all along the crescent-shaped strip of beach dead Americans gently nudged each other in the water.

Piling up along the shore was the flotsam and jetsam of the invasion. Heavy equipment and supplies, boxes of ammunition, smashed radios, field telephones, gas masks, entrenching tools, canteens, steel helmets and life preservers were strewn everywhere. Great reels of wire, ropes, ration boxes, mine detectors and scores of weapons, from broken rifles to stove-in bazookas, littered the sand. The twisted wrecks of landing craft canted up crazily out of the water. Burning tanks threw great spirals of black smoke into the air. Bulldozers lay on their sides among the obstacles. Off Easy Red, floating in and out among all the cast-off materials of war, men saw a guitar.

Small islands of wounded men dotted the sand. Passing troops noticed that those who could sat bolt upright as though now immune to any further hurt. They were quiet men, seemingly oblivious to the sights and sounds around them. Staff Sergeant Alfred Eigenberg, a medic attached to the 6th Engineers Special Brigade, remembers "a terrible politeness among the more seriously injured." In his first few minutes on the beach, Eigenberg found so many wounded that he did not know "where to start or with whom." On Dog Red he came across a young soldier sitting in the sand with his leg "laid open from the knee to the pelvis as neatly as though a surgeon had done it with a scalpel." The wound was so deep that Eigenberg could clearly see the femoral artery pulsing. The soldier was in deep shock. Calmly he informed Eigenberg, "I've taken my sulfa pills and I've shaken all my sulfa powder into the wound. I'll be all right, won't I?" The nineteen-year-old Eigenberg didn't quite know what to say. He gave the soldier a shot of morphine and told him, "Sure, you'll be all right." Then, folding the neatly sliced halves of the man's leg together, Eigenberg did the only thing he could think of—he carefully closed the wound with safety pins.

Into the chaos, confusion and death on the beach poured the men of the third wave—and stopped. Minutes later the fourth wave came in—and they stopped. Men lay shoulder to shoulder on the sands, stones and shale. They crouched down behind obstacles; they sheltered among the bodies of the dead. Pinned down by the enemy fire which they had expected to be neutralized, confused by their landings in the wrong sectors, bewildered by the absence of the sheltering craters they had expected from the air force bombing, and shocked by the devastation and death all around them, the men froze on the beaches. They seemed in the grip of a strange paralysis. Overwhelmed by it all, some men believed the day was lost. Technical Sergeant William McClintock of the 741st Tank Battalion came upon a man sitting at the edge of the water, seemingly unaware of the machine gun fire which rippled all over the area. He sat there "throwing stones into the water and softly crying as if his heart would break."

The shock would not last long. Even now a few men here and there, realizing that to stay on the beach meant certain death, were on their feet and moving.

Ten miles away on Utah Beach the men of the 4th Division were swarming ashore and driving inland fast. The third wave of assault boats was coming in and still there was virtually no opposition. A few shells fell on the beach, some scattered machine gun and rifle fire rattled along it, but there was none of the fierce infighting that the tense, keyed-up men of the 4th had expected. To many of the men the landing was almost routine. P.F.C. Donald N. Jones in the second wave felt as though it was "just another practice invasion." Other men thought the assault was an anticlimax; the long months of training at Slapton Sands in England had been tougher. P.F.C. Ray Mann felt a little "let down" because "the landing just wasn't a big deal after all." Even the obstacles were not as bad as everyone had feared. Only a few concrete cones and triangles and hedgehogs of steel cluttered the beach. Few of these were mined and all of them were lying exposed, easy for the engineers to get at. Demolition teams were already at work. They had blown one 50-yard gap through the defenses and had breached the sea wall, and within the hour they would have the entire beach cleared.

Strung out along the mile of beach, their canvas skirts hanging limply down, were the amphibious tanks—one of the big reasons why the assault had been so successful. Lumbering out of the water with the first waves, they had given a roaring support to the troops as they dashed across the beach. The tanks and the preassault bombardment seemed to have shattered and demoralized the German troops holding positions back of this beach. Still, the assault had not been without its share of misery and death. Almost as soon as he got ashore, P.F.C. Rudolph Mozgo saw his first dead man. A tank had received a direct hit and Mozgo found "one of the crew lying half in and half out of the hatch." Second Lieutenant Herbert Taylor of the 1st Engineer Special Brigade was numbed by the sight of a man "decapitated by an artillery burst just twenty feet away." And P.F.C. Edward Wolfe passed a dead American "who was sitting on the beach, his back resting against a post, as though asleep." So natural and peaceful did he seem that Wolfe "had an urge to reach over and shake him awake."

Stomping up and down the sands, occasionally massaging his arthritic shoulder, was Brigadier General Theodore Roosevelt. The fifty-seven-year-old officer—the only general to land with first-wave troops—had insisted on this assignment. His first request had been turned down, but Roosevelt had promptly countered with another. In a handwritten note to the 4th's commanding officer, Major General Raymond O. Barton, Roosevelt pleaded his case on the grounds that "it will steady the boys to know I am with them." Barton reluctantly agreed, but the decision preyed on his mind. "When I said goodbye to Ted in England," he recalls, "I never expected to see him alive again." The determined Roosevelt was very much alive. Sergeant Harry Brown of the 8th Infantry saw him "with a cane in one hand, a map in the other, walking around as if he was looking over some real estate." Every now and then a mortar burst on the beach, sending showers of sand into the air. It seemed to annoy Roosevelt; impatiently he would brush himself off.

As the third-wave boats beached and men began to wade ashore, there was the sudden whine of German 88 fire and shells burst among the incoming troops. A dozen men went down. Seconds later, a lone figure emerged from the smoke of the artillery burst. His face was black, his helmet and equipment were gone. He came walking up the beach in complete shock, eyes staring. Yelling for a medic, Roosevelt ran over to the man. He put his arm around the soldier. "Son," he said gently, "I think we'll get you back on a boat."

As yet only Roosevelt and a few of his officers knew that the Utah landings had been made in the wrong place. It had been a fortunate error; heavy batteries that could have decimated the troops were still intact, sited in along the planned assault area. There had been a number of reasons for the mislanding. Confused by smoke from the naval bombardment which had obscured landmarks, caught by a strong current moving down the coast, a solitary control boat had guided the first wave into a landing more than a mile south of the original beach. Instead of invading the beach opposite Exits 3 and 4—two of the vital five causeways toward which the 101st Airborne was driving—the entire beachhead had slipped almost two thousand yards and was now astride Exit 2. Ironically, at this moment Lieutenant Colonel Robert G. Cole and a miscellaneous band of seventy-five 101st and 82nd troopers had just reached the western end of Exit 3. They were the first paratroopers to get to a causeway. Cole and his men concealed themselves in the swamps and settled down to wait; he expected the men of the 4th Division along at any moment.

On the beach, near the approach to Exit 2, Roosevelt was about to make an important decision. Every few minutes from now on wave after wave of men and vehicles were due to land —thirty thousand men and 3,500 vehicles. Roosevelt had to decide whether to bring succeeding waves into this new, relatively quiet area with only one causeway, or to divert all other assault troops and take their equipment to the original Utah Beach with its two causeways. If the single exit could not be opened and held, a nightmarish jumble of men and vehicles would be trapped on the beach. The General huddled with his battalion commanders. The decision was made. Instead of fighting for the planned objectives which lay back of the original beach, the 4th would drive inland on the single causeway and take out German positions when and where they found them. Everything now depended on moving as fast as possible before the enemy recovered from the initial shock of the landings. Resistance was light and the men of the 4th were moving off the beach fast. Roosevelt turned to Colonel Eugene Caffey of the 1st Engineer Special Brigade. "I'm going ahead with the troops," he told Caffey. "You get word to the Navy to bring them in. We're going to start the war from here."

Off Utah the U.S.S. *Corry*'s guns were red-hot. They were firing so fast that sailors stood on the turrets playing hoses on the barrels. Almost from the moment Lieutenant Commander George Hoffman had maneuvered his destroyer into firing position and dropped anchor, the *Corry*'s guns had been slamming shells inland at the rate of eight 5-inchers a minute. One German battery would never bother anyone again; the *Corry* had ripped it open with 110 well-placed rounds. The Germans had been firing back—and hard. The *Corry* was the one destroyer the enemy spotters could see. Smoke-laying planes had been assigned to protect the "inshore close support" bombarding group, but the *Corry*'s plane had been shot down. One battery in particular, on the bluffs overlooking the coast above Utah—the gun flashes located it near the village of St.-Marcouf—seemed to be concentrating all its fury on the exposed destroyer. Hoffman decided to move back before it was too late. "We swung around," recalls Radioman Third Class Bennie Glisson, "and showed them our fantail like an old maid to a Marine."

But the *Corry* was in shallow water, close to a number of knife-edged reefs. Her skipper could not make the dash for safety until he was clear. For a few minutes he was forced to play a tense cat-and-mouse game with the German gunners. Trying to anticipate their salvos, Hoffman put the *Corry* through a series of jolting maneuvers. He shot forward, went astern, swung to port, then to starboard, stopped dead, went forward again. All the while his guns engaged the battery. Nearby, the destroyer U.S.S. *Fitch* saw his predicament and began firing on the St.-Marcouf guns too. But there was no letup from the sharpshooting Germans. Almost bracketed by their shells, Hoffman inched the *Corry* out. Finally, satisfied that he was away from the reefs, he ordered, "Hard right rudder! Full speed ahead!" and the *Corry* leaped forward. Hoffman looked behind him. Salvos were smacking into their wake, throwing up great plumes of spray. He breathed easier; he had made it.

It was at that instant that his luck ran out. Tearing through the water at more than twenty-eight knots the *Corry* ran headlong onto a submerged mine.

There was a great rending explosion that seemed to throw the destroyer sideways out of the water. The shock was so great that Hoffman was stunned. It seemed to him "that the ship had been lifted by an earthquake." In his radio shack Bennie Glisson, who had been looking out a porthole, suddenly felt that he had been "dropped into a concrete mixer." Jerked off his feet, he was hurled upward against the ceiling, and then he crashed down and smashed his knee.

The mine had cut the *Corry* almost in half. Running across the main deck was a rip more than one foot in width. The bow and the stern pointed crazily upward; about all that held the destroyer together was the deck superstructure. The fireroom and engine room were flooded. There were few survivors in the number two boiler room—the men there were almost instantly scalded to death when the boiler blew up. The rudder was jammed. There was no power, yet somehow in the steam and fire of her death agonies the *Corry* continued to charge crazily through the water. Hoffman became suddenly aware that some of his guns were still firing—his gunners, without power, continued to load and fire manually.

The twisted pile of steel that had once been the *Corry* thrashed through the sea for more than a thousand yards before finally coming to a halt. Then the German batteries zeroed in. "Abandon ship!" Hoffman ordered. Within the next few minutes at least nine shells plowed into the wreck. One blew up the 40-millimeter ammunition. Another set off the smoke generator on the fantail, almost asphyxiating the crew as they struggled into boats and rafts.

The sea was two feet above the main deck when Hoffman, taking one last look around, dived overboard and swam toward a raft. Behind him the *Corry* settled on the bottom, her masts and part of her superstructure remaining above the waves—the U.S. Navy's only major D-Day loss. Of Hoffman's 294-man crew thirteen were dead or missing and thirty-three injured, more casualties than had been suffered in the Utah Beach landings up to this time.

Hoffman thought he was the last to leave the *Corry*. But he wasn't. Nobody knows now who the last man was, but as the boats and rafts pulled away, men on the other ships saw a sailor climb the *Corry*'s stern. He removed the ensign, which had been shot down, and then, swimming and climbing over the wreckage, he reached the main mast. From the U.S.S. *Butler* Coxswain Dick Scrimshaw watched in amazement and admiration as the sailor, shells still falling about him, calmly tied on the flag and ran it up the mast. Then he swam away. Above the wreck of the *Corry* Scrimshaw saw the flag hang limp for a moment. Then it stretched out and fluttered in the breeze.

Rockets trailing ropes shot up toward the 100-foot-high cliff at Pointe du Hoc. Between Utah and Omaha beaches the third American seaborne attack was going in. Small-arms fire poured down on Lt. Col. James E. Rudder's three Ranger companies as they began the assault to silence the massive coastal batteries which intelligence said menaced the American beaches on either side. The nine LCAs carrying the 225 men of the 2nd Ranger Battalion clustered along the little strip of beach beneath the cliff overhang. It afforded some protection from the machine gun fire and from the grenades that the Germans were now rolling down on them—but not much. Offshore the British destroyer *Talybont* and the U.S. destroyer *Satterlee* lobbed in shell after shell onto the cliff top.

Rudder's Rangers were supposed to touch down at the base of the cliff at H Hour. But the lead boat had strayed and led the little flotilla straight toward Pointe de la Percée, three miles east. Rudder had spotted the mistake, but by the time he got the assault craft back on course, precious time had been lost. The delay would cost him his 500-man support force—the rest of the 2nd Rangers and Lieutenant Colonel Max Schneider's 5th Ranger Battalion. The plan had been for Rudder to fire flares as soon as his men had scaled the cliff, as a signal for the other Rangers waiting in their boats some miles offshore to follow in. If no signal was received by 7 A.M., Colonel Schneider was to assume that the Pointe du Hoc assault had failed and head for Omaha Beach four miles away. There, following in behind the 29th Division, his Rangers would swing west and drive for the Pointe to take the guns from the rear. It was now 7:10 A.M. No signal had been given, so Schneider's force was already heading for Omaha. Rudder and his 225 Rangers were on their own.

It was a wild, frenzied scene. Again and again the rockets roared, shooting the ropes and rope ladders with grapnels attached. Shells and 40-millimeter machine guns raked the cliff top, shaking down great chunks of earth on the Rangers. Men spurted across the narrow, cratered beach trailing scaling ladders, ropes and hand rockets. Here and there at the cliff top Germans bobbed up, throwing down "potato masher" hand grenades or firing *Schmeissers*. Somehow the Rangers dodged from cover to cover, unloaded their boats and fired up the cliff—all at the same time. And off the Pointe, two DUKWs—amphibious vehicles—with tall, extended ladders, borrowed for the occasion from the London Fire Brigade, tried to maneuver closer in. From the tops of the ladders Rangers blasted the headlands with Browning automatic rifles and Tommy guns.

The assault was furious. Some men didn't wait for the ropes to catch. Weapons slung over their shoulders, they cut handholds with their knives and started up the nine-story-high cliff like flies. Some of the grapnels now began to catch and men swarmed up the ropes. Then there were wild yells as the Germans cut the ropes and Rangers hurtled back down the cliff. P.F.C. Harry Robert's rope was cut twice. On his third try he finally got to a cratered niche just under the edge of the cliff. Sergeant Bill "L-Rod" Petty tried going up hand over hand on a plain rope but, although he was an expert free climber, the rope was so wet and muddy he couldn't make it. Then Petty tried a ladder, got thirty feet up and slid back when it was cut. He started back up again. Sergeant Herman Stein climbing another ladder, was almost pushed off the cliff face when he accidentally inflated his Mae West. He "struggled for an eternity" with the life preserver but there were men ahead and behind him on the ladder. Somehow Stein kept on going.

Now men were scrambling up a score of ropes that twisted and snaked down from the top of the cliff. Suddenly Sergeant Petty, on his way up for the third time, was peppered by chunks of earth flying out all around him. The Germans were leaning out over the edge of the cliff, machine-gunning the Rangers as they climbed. The Germans fought desperately, despite the fire that was still raining on them from the Rangers on the fire ladders and from the destroyers offshore. Petty saw the climber next to him stiffen and swing out from the cliff. Stein saw him, too. So did twenty-year-old P.F.C. Carl Bombardier. As they watched, horrified, the man slid down the rope and fell, bouncing from ledges and rock outcroppings, and it seemed to Petty "a lifetime before his body hit the beach." Petty froze on the rope. He could not make his hand move up to the next rung. He remembers saying to himself, "This is just too hard to climb." But the German machine guns got him going again. As they began to spray the cliff dangerously near him, Petty "unfroze real fast." Desperately he hauled himself up the last few yards.

Everywhere men were throwing themselves over the top and into shell holes. To Sergeant Regis McCloskey, who had successfully brought his half-sinking ammunition boat in to the beach, the high plateau of Pointe du Hoc presented a weird, incredible sight. The ground was so pitted by the shells and bombs of the pre-H-Hour naval and air bombardment that it looked like "the craters of the moon." There was an eerie silence now as men pulled themselves up and into the protective craters. The fire had stopped for the moment, there was not a German to be seen, and everywhere men looked the yawning craters stretched back toward the mainland—a violent, terrible no man's land.

Colonel Rudder had already established his first command post, a niche at the edge of the cliff. From it his signal officer, Lieutenant James Eikner, sent out the message "Praise the Lord." It meant "All men up cliff." But it was not quite true. At the base of the cliff the Rangers' medical officer, a pediatrician in private practice, was tending the dead and the dying on the beach—perhaps twenty-five men. Minute by minute the valiant Ranger force was being chipped away. By the end of the day there would only be ninety of the original 225 still able to bear arms. Worse, it had been a heroic and futile effort—to silence guns which were not there. The information which Jean Marion, the French underground sector chief, had tried to send to London was true. The battered bunkers atop Pointe du Hoc were empty—the guns had never been mounted.*

---

*Some two hours later a Ranger patrol found a deserted five-gun battery in a camouflaged position more than a mile inland. Stacks of shells surrounded each gun and they were ready to fire, but the Rangers could find no evidence that they had ever been manned. Presumably these were the guns for the Pointe du Hoc emplacements.

In his bomb crater at the top of the cliff, Sergeant Petty and his four-man BAR team sat exhausted after the climb. A little haze drifted over the churned, pitted earth and the smell of cordite was heavy in the air. Petty stared almost dreamily around him. Then on the edge of the crater he saw two sparrows eating worms. "Look," said Petty to the others, "they're having breakfast."

Now on this great and awful morning the last phase of the assault from the sea began. Along the eastern half of the Normandy invasion coast, Lieutenant General M. C. Dempsey's British Second Army was coming ashore, with grimness and gaiety, with pomp and ceremony, with all the studied nonchalance the British traditionally assume in moments of great emotion. They had waited four long years for this day. They were assaulting not just beaches but bitter memories—memories of Munich and Dunkirk, of one hateful and humiliating retreat after another, of countless devastating bombing raids, of dark days when they had stood alone. With them were the Canadians, with a score of their own to settle for the bloody losses at Dieppe. And with them, too, were the French, fierce and eager on this homecoming morning.

There was a curious jubilance in the air. As the troops headed toward the beaches the loud-speaker in a rescue launch off Sword roared out "Roll Out the Barrel." From a rocket-firing barge off Gold came the strains of "We Don't Know Where We're Going." Canadians going to Juno heard the rasping notes of a bugle blaring across the water. Some men were even singing. Marine Denis Lovell remembers that "the boys were standing up, singing all the usual Army and Navy songs." And Lord Lovat's 1st Special Service Brigade commandos, spruce and resplendent in their green berets (the commandos refused to wear tin helmets), were serenaded into battle by the eerie wailing of the bagpipes. As their landing boats drew abreast of Admiral Vian's flagship H.M.S. *Scylla*, the commandos gave the "thumbs-up" salute. Looking down on them, eighteen-year-old Able Seaman Ronald Northwood thought they were "the finest set of chaps I ever came across."

Even the obstacles and the enemy fire now lacing out at the boats were viewed with a certain detachment by many men.

On one LCT, Telegraphist John Webber watched a Royal Marine captain study the maze of mined obstacles clotting the coastline, then remark casually to the skipper, "I say, old man, you really must get my chaps on shore, there's a good fellow." Aboard another landing craft a 50th Division major stared thoughtfully at the round Teller mines clearly visible on top of the obstacles and said to the coxswain, "For Christ's sake, don't knock those bloody coconuts down or we'll all get a free trip to hell." One boatload of 48th Royal Marine commandos were met by heavy machine gun fire off Juno and men dived for cover behind the deck superstructure. Not the adjutant, Captain Daniel Flunder. He tucked his swagger stick under his arm and calmly paraded up and down the foredeck. "I thought," he explained later, "it was the thing to do." (While he was doing it, a bullet plowed through his map case.) And in a landing craft charging for Sword Major C. K. "Banger" King, just as he had promised, was reading *Henry V*. Amid the roar of the diesels, the hissing of the spray and the sound of gunfire, King spoke into the loud-hailer, "And gentlemen in England now a-bed/ Shall think themselves accurs'd they were not here . . ."

Some men could hardly wait for the fighting to begin. Two Irish sergeants, James Percival "Paddy" de Lacy, who had toasted De Valera hours before for "keepin' us out of the war," and his side-kick, Paddy McQuaid, stood at the ramps of an LST and, fortified by good Royal Navy rum, solemnly contemplated the troops. "De Lacy," said McQuaid, staring hard at the Englishmen all around them, "don't you think now that some of these boys seem a wee bit timid?" As the beaches neared, De Lacy called out to his men, "All right, now! Here we go! At the run!" The LST ground to a halt. As the men ran out, McQuaid yelled at the shell-smoked shore line, "Come out, ye bastards, and fight us now!" Then he disappeared under water. An instant later he came up spluttering. "Oh, the evil of it!" he bellowed. "Tryin' to drown me before I even get up on the beach!"

Off Sword, Private Hubert Victor Baxter of the British 3rd Division revved up his Bren gun carrier and, peering over the top of the armored plating, plunged into the water. Sitting exposed on the raised seat above him was his bitter enemy, Sergeant "Dinger" Bell, with whom Baxter had been fighting for months. Bell yelled, "Baxter, wind up that seat so you can see where you're going!" Baxter shouted back, "Not bloody likely! I can see!" Then, as they swept up the beach, the sergeant, caught up in the excitement of the moment, resorted to the very thing that had begun the feud in the first place. He slammed down his fist again and again on Baxter's helmet and roared, "Bash on! Bash on!"

As the commandos touched down on Sword, Lord Lovat's piper, William Millin, plunged off his landing craft into water up to his armpits. He could see smoke piling up from the beach ahead and hear the crump of exploding mortar shells. As Millin floundered toward the shore, Lovat shouted at him, "Give us 'Highland Laddie,' man!" Waist-deep in the water, Millin put the mouthpiece to his lips and splashed on through the surf, the pipes keening crazily. At the water's edge, oblivious to the gunfire, he halted and, parading up and down along the beach, piped the commandos ashore. The men streamed past him, and mingling with the whine of bullets and the screams of shells came the wild skirl of the pipes as Millin now played "The Road to the Isles." "That's the stuff, Jock," yelled a commando. Said another, "Get down, you mad bugger."

All along Sword, Juno and Gold—for almost twenty miles, from Ouistreham near the mouth of the Orne to the village of Le Hamel on the west—the British swarmed ashore. The beaches were choked with landing craft disgorging troops, and nearly everywhere along the assault area the high seas and underwater obstacles were causing more trouble than the enemy.

The first men in had been the frogmen—120 underwater demolition experts whose job it was to cut 30-yard gaps through the obstacles. They had only twenty minutes to work before the first waves bore down upon them. The obstacles were formidable—at places more densely sown than in any other part of the Normandy invasion area. Sergeant Peter Henry Jones of the Royal Marines swam into a maze of steel pylons, gates and hedgehogs and concrete cones. In the 30-yard gap Jones had to blow, he found twelve major obstacles, some of them fourteen feet long. When another frogman, Lieutenant John B. Taylor of the Royal Navy, saw the fantastic array of underwater defenses surrounding him, he yelled out to his unit leader that "this bloody job is impossible." But he did not give it up. Working under fire, Taylor, like the other frog-men, methodically set to work. They blew the obstacles singly, because they were too large to blow in groups. Even as they worked, amphibious tanks came swimming in among them, followed almost immediately by first-wave troops. Frogmen rushing out of the water saw landing craft, turned sideways by the heavy seas, crash into the obstacles. Mines exploded, steel spikes and hedgehogs ripped along the hulls, and up and down the beaches landing craft began to flounder. The waters offshore became a junkyard as boats piled up almost on top of one another. Telegraphist Webber remembers thinking that "the beaching is a tragedy." As his craft came in Webber saw "LCTs stranded and ablaze, twisted masses of metal on the shore, burning tanks and bulldozers." And as one LCT passed them, heading for the open sea, Webber was horrified to see "its well deck engulfed in a terrifying fire."

On Gold Beach, where frogman Jones was now working with the Royal Engineers trying to clear the obstacles, he saw an LCI approach with troops standing on the deck ready to disembark. Caught by a sudden swell, the craft swerved side-ways, lifted and crashed down on a series of mined steel trian-gles. Jones saw it explode with a shattering blast. It reminded him of a "slow-motion cartoon—the men, standing to atten-tion, shot up into the air as though lifted by a water spout . . . at the top of the spout bodies and parts of bodies spread like drops of water."

Boat after boat got hung up on the obstacles. Of the sixteen landing craft carrying the 47th Royal Marine commandos in to Gold Beach, four boats were lost, eleven were damaged and beached and only one made it back to the parent ship. Ser-geant Donald Gardner of the 47th and his men were dumped into the water about fifty yards from shore. They lost all of their equipment and had to swim in under machine gun fire. As they struggled in the water, Gardner heard someone say, "Perhaps we're intruding, this seems to be a private beach." Going into Juno the 48th Royal Marine commandos not only ran afoul of the obstacles, they also came under intense mor-tar fire. Lieutenant Michael Aldworth and about forty of his men crouched down in the forward hold of their LCI as shells exploded all about them. Aldworth shoved his head up to see what was happening and saw men from the aft hold running along the deck. Aldworth's men yelled out, "How soon do we get out of here?" Aldworth called back, "Wait a minute, chaps. It's not our turn." There was a moment's pause and then someone inquired, "Well, just how long do you think it will be, old man? The ruddy hold is filling full of water."

The men from the sinking LCI were quickly picked up by a variety of craft. There were so many boats around, Aldworth recalls, that "it was rather like hailing a taxi in Bond Street." Some men were delivered safely onto the beaches; others were taken out to a Canadian destroyer, but fifty commandos discovered themselves on an LCT which had unloaded its tanks and was under instructions to proceed directly back to England. Nothing the infuriated men could say or do would persuade the skipper to change his course. One officer, Major de Stackpoole, had been wounded in the thighs on the run-in, but on hearing the LCT's destination he roared, "Nonsense! You're all bloody well mad!" With that he dived overboard and swam for shore.

For most men the obstacles proved to be the toughest part of the assault. Once they were through these defenses, troops found the enemy opposition along the three beaches spotty—fierce in some sectors, light and even nonexistent in others. On the western half of Gold men of the 1st Hampshire Regiment were almost decimated as they waded through water that was at places three to six feet deep. Struggling through the heaving sea line abreast, they were caught by heavy mortar bursts and crisscrossing machine gun fire that poured out from the village of Le Hamel, a stronghold occupied by the tough German 352nd Division. Men went down one after another. Private Charles Wilson heard a surprised voice say, "I've bought it, mates!" Turning, Wilson saw the man, a strange look of disbelief on his face, slide beneath the water without another word. Wilson plowed on. He had been machine-gunned in the water before—except that at Dunkirk he had been going the other way. Private George Stunell saw men going down all around him too. He came across a Bren gun carrier standing in about three feet of water, its motor running and the driver "frozen at the wheel, too terrified to drive the machine onto the shore." Stunell pushed him to one side and with machine gun bullets whipping all around drove up onto the beach. Stunell was elated to have made it. Then he suddenly pitched headlong to the ground; a bullet had slammed into a can of cigarettes in his tunic pocket with terrific impact. Minutes later he discovered that he was bleeding from wounds in his back and ribs. The same bullet had passed cleanly through his body.

It would take the Hampshires almost eight hours to knock out the Le Hamel defenses, and at the end of D Day their casualties would total almost two hundred. Strangely, apart from the obstacles, troops landing on either side encountered little trouble. There were casualties, but they were fewer than had been anticipated. On the left of the Hampshires, men of the 1st Dorset Regiment were off the beach in forty minutes. Next to them the Green Howards landed with such dash and determination that they moved inland and captured their first objective in less than an hour. Company Sergeant Major Stanley Hollis, killer of ninety Germans up to now, waded ashore and promptly captured a pillbox singlehanded. The nerveless Hollis, using grenades and his Sten gun, killed two and captured twenty in the start of a day that would see him kill another ten.

On the beach to the right of Le Hamel it was so quiet that some men were disappointed. Medic Geoffrey Leach saw troops and vehicles pouring ashore and found that there was nothing "for the medics to do but help unload ammunition." To Marine Denis Lovell, the landing was like "just another exercise back home." His unit, the 47th Royal Marine commandos, moved quickly off the beach, avoided all enemy contact, turned west and set out on a seven-mile forced march to link up with the Americans near Port-en-Bessin. They expected to see the first Yanks from Omaha Beach around noon.

But this was not to be—unlike the Americans on Omaha, who were still pinned down by the rugged German 352nd Division, the British and the Canadians were more than a match for the tired and inferior 716th Division with its impressed Russian and Polish "volunteers." In addition, the British had made the fullest possible use of amphibious tanks and a Rube Goldberg-like collection of armored vehicles. Some, like the "flail" tanks, lashed the ground ahead of them with chains that detonated mines. Other armored vehicles carried small bridges or great reels of steel matting which, when unrolled, made a temporary roadway over soft ground. One group even carried giant bundles of logs for use as steppingstones over walls or to fill in antitank ditches. These inventions, and the extra-long period of bombardment that the British beaches had received, gave the assaulting troops additional protection.

Still some strong pockets of resistance were encountered. On one half of Juno Beach men of the Canadian 3rd Division fought through lines of pillboxes and trenches, through fortified houses, and from street to street in the town of Courseulles before finally breaking through and pushing inland. But all resistance there would be mopped up within two hours. In many places it was being done with quickness and dispatch. Able Seaman Edward Ashworth, off an LCT which had brought troops and tanks in to the Courseulles beach, saw Canadian soldiers march six German prisoners behind a dune some distance away. Ashworth thought that this was his chance to get a German helmet for a souvenir. He ran up the beach and in the dunes discovered the six Germans "all lying crumpled up." Ashworth bent over one of the bodies, still determined to get a helmet. But he found "the man's throat was cut—every one of them had had his throat cut," and Ashworth "turned away, sick as a parrot. I didn't get my tin hat."

Sergeant Paddy de Lacy, also in the Courseulles area, had captured twelve Germans who had come almost eagerly out of a trench, their arms raised high above their heads. De Lacy stood staring at them for a moment; he had lost a brother in North Africa. Then he said to the soldier with him, "Look at the super blokes—just look at them. Here, take them out of my sight." He walked away to make himself a cup of tea to soothe his anger. While he was heating a canteen of water over a Sterno can a young officer "with the down still on his chin" walked over and said sternly, "Now look here, Sergeant, this is no time to be making tea." De Lacy looked up and, as patiently as his twenty-one years of Army service would allow, replied, "Sir, we are not playing at soldiers now—this is real war. Why don't you come back in five minutes and have a nice cup of tea?" The officer did.

Even as the fighting was going on in the Courseulles area, men, guns, tanks, vehicles and supplies were pouring ashore. The movement inland was smoothly and efficiently handled.

The beachmaster, Captain Colin Maud, allowed no loiterers on Juno. Most men, like Sub-Lieutenant John Beynon, were a little taken aback at the sight of the tall, bearded officer with the imposing bearing and the booming voice who met each new contingent with the same greeting, "I'm chairman of the reception committee and of this party, so get a move on." Few men cared to argue with the custodian of Juno Beach; Beynon remembers he had a cudgel in one hand and the other held tight to the leash of a fierce-looking Alsatian dog. The effect was all he could have hoped for. INS correspondent Joseph Willicombe recalls a futile argument he had with the beachmaster. Willicombe, who had landed in the first wave of Canadians, had been assured that he would be allowed to send a twenty-five-word message via the beachmaster's two-way radio to the command ship for transmission to the U.S. Apparently no one had bothered to so inform Maud. Staring stonily at Willicombe, he growled, "My dear chap, there's a bit of a war going on here." Willicombe had to admit that the beachmaster had a point.* A few yards away, in the coarse beach grass, lay the mangled bodies of fifteen Canadians who had trod on mines as they dashed ashore.

All along Juno the Canadians suffered. Of the three British beaches theirs was the bloodiest. Rough seas had delayed the landings. Razor-edged reefs on the eastern half of the beach and barricades of obstacles created havoc among the assault craft. Worse, the naval and air bombardment had failed to knock out the coastal defenses or had missed them altogether, and in some sectors troops came ashore without the protection of tanks. Opposite the towns of Bernières and St.-Aubin-sur-Mer men of the Canadian 8th Brigade and the 48th Marine

---

*Correspondents on Juno had no communications until Ronald Clark of United Press came ashore with two baskets of carrier pigeons. The correspondents quickly wrote brief stories, placed them in the plastic capsules attached to the pigeons' legs and released the birds. Unfortunately the pigeons were so overloaded that most of them fell back to earth. Some, however, circled overhead for a few moments—and then headed toward the German lines. Charles Lynch of Reuter's stood on the beach, waved his fist at the pigeons and roared, "Traitors! Damned traitors!" Four pigeons, Willicombe says, "proved loyal." They actually got to the Ministry of Information in London within a few hours.

commandos came in under heavy fire. One company lost nearly half its men in the dash up the beach. Artillery fire from St.-Aubin-sur-Mer was so concentrated that it led to one particular horror on the beach. A tank, buttoned up for protection and thrashing wildly up the beach to get out of the line of fire, ran over the dead and the dying. Captain Daniel Flunder of the commandos, looking back from the sand dunes, saw what was happening and oblivious of the bursting shells ran back down the beach shouting at the top of his voice, "They're my men!" The enraged Flunder beat on the tank's hatch with his swagger stick, but the tank kept on going. Pulling the pin on a grenade, Flunder blew one of the tank's tracks off. It wasn't until the startled tankers opened the hatch that they realized what had happened.

Although the fighting was bitter while it lasted, the Canadians and the commandos got off the Bernières–St.-Aubin beaches in less than thirty minutes and plunged inland. Follow-up waves experienced little difficulty and within an hour it was so quiet on the beaches that Leading Aircraftman John Murphy of a barrage balloon unit found that "the worst enemy was the sand lice that drove us crazy as the tide came in." Back of the beaches street fighting would occupy troops for nearly two hours, but this section of Juno, like the western half, was now secure.

The 48th commandos fought their way through St.-Aubin-sur-Mer and, turning east, headed along the coast. They had a particularly tough assignment. Juno lay seven miles away from Sword Beach. To close this gap and link up the two beaches, the 48th was to make a forced march toward Sword. Another commando unit, the 41st, was to land at Lion-sur-Mer on the edge of Sword Beach, swing right and head west. Both forces were expected to join up within a few hours at a point roughly halfway between the two beachheads. That was the plan, but almost simultaneously the commandos ran into trouble. At Langrune, about a mile east of Juno, men of the 48th found themselves in a fortified area of the town that defied penetration. Every house was a strongpoint. Mines, barbed wire and concrete walls—some of them six feet high and five feet thick —sealed off the streets. From these positions heavy fire greeted the invaders. Without tanks or artillery the 48th was stopped cold.

On Sword, six miles away, the 41st after a rough landing turned west and headed through Lion-sur-Mer. They were told by the French that the German garrison had pulled out. The information seemed correct—until the commandos reached the edge of the town. There artillery fire knocked out three supporting tanks. Sniper and machine gun fire came from innocent-looking villas that had been converted into block-houses, and a rain of mortar shells fell among the commandos. Like the 48th, the 41st came to a standstill.

Now, although no one in the Allied High Command knew about it yet, a vital gap six miles wide existed in the beachhead—a gap through which Rommel's tanks, if they moved fast enough, could reach the coast and, by attacking left and right along the shore, could roll up the British landings.

Lion-sur-Mer was one of the few real trouble spots on Sword. Of the three British beaches, Sword was expected to be the most heavily defended. Troops had been briefed that casualties would be very high. Private John Gale of the 1st South Lancashire Regiment was "cold-bloodedly told that all of us in the first wave would probably be wiped out." The picture was painted in even blacker terms to the commandos. It was drilled into them that "no matter what happens we must get on the beaches, for there will be no evacuation . . . no going back." The 4th commandos expected to be "written off on the beaches," as Corporal James Colley and Private Stanley Stewart remember, for they were told their casualties would run as "high as eighty-four per cent." And the men who were to land ahead of the infantry in amphibious tanks were warned that "even those of you who reach the beach can expect sixty per cent casualties." Private Christopher Smith, driver of an amphibious tank, thought his chances of survival were slim. Rumor had increased the casualty figure to ninety per cent and Smith was inclined to believe it, for as his unit left England men saw canvas screens being set up on Gosport Beach and "it was said that these were being erected to sort out the returned dead."

For a while it looked as though the worst of the predictions might come true. In some sectors first-wave troops were heavily machine-gunned and mortared. In the Ouistreham half of Sword, men of the 2nd East York Regiment lay dead and dying from the water's edge all the way up the beach. Although nobody would ever know how many men were lost in this bloody dash from the boats, it seems likely that the East Yorks suffered most of their two hundred D-Day casualties in these first few minutes. The shock of seeing these crumpled khaki forms seemed to confirm the most dreadful fears of follow-up troops. Some saw "bodies stacked like cordwood" and counted "more than 150 dead." Private John Mason of the 4th commandos, who landed half an hour later, was shocked to find himself "running through piles of dead infantry who had been knocked down like nine pins." And Corporal Fred Mears of Lord Lovat's commandos was "aghast to see the East Yorks lying in bunches. . . . It would probably never have happened had they spread out." As he charged up the beach determined to make "Jesse Owens look like a turtle," he remembers cynically thinking that "they would know better the next time."

Although bloody, the beach fight was brief.* Except for initial losses, the assault on Sword went forward speedily, meeting little sustained opposition. The landings were so successful that many men coming in minutes after the first wave were surprised to find only sniper fire. They saw the beaches shrouded in smoke, medics working among the wounded, flail tanks detonating mines, burning tanks and vehicles littering the shore line, and sand shooting up from occasional shell bursts, but nowhere was there the slaughter they had expected. To these tense troops, primed to expect a holocaust, the beaches were an anticlimax.

In many places along Sword there was even a bank holiday atmosphere. Here and there along the seafront little groups of elated French waved to the troops and yelled, "*Vive*

---

*There will always be differences of opinion about the nature of the fighting on Sword. Men of the East Yorks disagree with their own history, which says that it was "just like a training show, only easier." The troops of the 4th commandos claim that when they landed at H-plus-30 they found the East Yorks still at the water's edge. According to Brigadier E. E. E. Cass, in command of the 8th Brigade that assaulted Sword, the East Yorks were off the beach by the time the 4th commandos landed. It is estimated that the 4th lost thirty men as they came ashore. On the western half of the beach, says Cass, "opposition had been overcome by eight-thirty except for isolated snipers." Men of the 1st South Lancashire Regiment landing there had light casualties and moved inland fast. The 1st Suffolks coming in behind them had just four casualties.

les Anglais!" Royal Marine Signalman Leslie Ford noticed a Frenchman "practically on the beach itself who appeared to be giving a running commentary on the battle to a group of townspeople." Ford thought they were crazy, for the beaches and the foreshore were still infested with mines and under occasional fire. But it was happening everywhere. Men were hugged and kissed and embraced by the French, who seemed quite unaware of the dangers around them. Corporal Harry Norfield and Gunner Ronald Allen were astonished to see "a person all dressed up in splendid regalia and wearing a bright brass helmet making his way down to the beaches." He turned out to be the mayor of Colleville-sur-Orne, a small village about a mile inland, who had decided to come down and officially greet the invasion forces.

Some of the Germans seemed no less eager than the French to greet the troops. Sapper Henry Jennings had no sooner disembarked than he was "confronted with a collection of Germans—most of them Russian and Polish 'volunteers'—anxious to surrender." But Captain Gerald Norton of a Royal Artillery unit got the biggest surprise of all: he was met "by four Germans with their suitcases packed, who appeared to be awaiting the first available transportation out of France."

Out of the confusion on Gold, Juno and Sword, the British and the Canadians swarmed inland. The advance was business-like and efficient and there was a kind of grandeur about it all. As troops fought into towns and villages examples of heroism and courage were all around them. Some remember a Royal Marine commando major, both arms gone, who urged his men along by shouting at them to "get inland, chaps, before Fritz gets wise to this party." Others remember the cocky cheerfulness and bright faith of the wounded as they waited for the medics to catch up with them. Some waved as the troops passed, others yelled, "See you in Berlin, mates!" Gunner Ronald Allen would never forget one soldier who had been badly wounded in the stomach. He was propped up against a wall calmly reading a book.

Now speed was essential. From Gold troops headed for the cathedral town of Bayeux, roughly seven miles inland. From Juno the Canadians drove for the Bayeux-Caen highway and Carpiquet Airport, about ten miles away. And out of Sword the

British headed for the city of Caen. They were so sure of capturing this objective that even correspondents, as the London *Daily Mail*'s Noel Monks was later to recall, were told that a briefing would be held "at point X in Caen at 4 P.M." Lord Lovat's commandos marching out of the Sword area wasted no time. They were going to the relief of General Gale's embattled 6th Airborne troops holding the Orne and Caen bridges four miles away and "Shimy" Lovat had promised Gale that he would be there "sharp at noon." Behind a tank at the head of the column Lord Lovat's piper Bill Millin played "Blue Bonnets over the Border."

For ten Britishers, the crews of the midget submarines X20 and X23, D Day was over. Off Sword Beach Lieutenant George Honour's X23 threaded through waves of landing craft streaming steadily in toward the shore. In the heavy seas, with her flat superstructure almost awash, all that could be seen of the X23 were her identifying flags whipping in the wind. Coxswain Charles Wilson on an LCT "almost fell overboard with surprise" when he saw what appeared to be "two large flags apparently unsupported" moving steadily toward him through the water. As the X23 passed, Wilson couldn't help wondering "what the devil a midget sub had to do with the invasion." Plowing by, the X23 headed out into the transport area in search of her tow ship, a trawler with the appropriate name of *En Avant.* Operation Gambit was over. Lieutenant Honour and his four-man crew were going home.

The men for whom they had marked the beaches marched into France. Everyone was optimistic. The Atlantic Wall had been breached. Now the big question was, how fast would the Germans recover from the shock?

3

BERCHTESGADEN lay quiet and peaceful in the early morning. The day was already warm and sultry, and the clouds hung low on the surrounding mountains. At Hitler's fortress-like mountain retreat on the Obersalzberg, all was still. The Führer was asleep. A few miles away at his headquarters, the *Reichskanzlei*, it was just another routine morning. Colonel General

Alfred Jodl, OKW's Chief of Operations, had been up since six. He had eaten his customary light breakfast (one cup of coffee, a soft-boiled egg and a thin slice of toast) and now, in his small soundproofed office, he was leisurely reading the night's reports.

The news from Italy continued to be bad. Rome had fallen twenty-four hours before and Field Marshal Albert Kesselring's troops were being hard pressed as they pulled back. Jodl thought that there might be an Allied breakthrough even before Kesselring disengaged his troops and withdrew to new positions in the north. So concerned was Jodl about the threatened collapse in Italy that he had ordered his deputy, General Walter Warlimont, to proceed to Kesselring's headquarters on a fact-finding trip. Warlimont was to leave by the end of the day.

There was nothing new from Russia. Although Jodl's sphere of authority did not officially include the eastern theater, he had long ago maneuvered himself into a position whereby he "advised" the Führer on the conduct of the Russian war. The Soviet summer offensive would begin any day now, and all along the 2,000-mile front two hundred German divisions —more than 1,500,000 men—were poised, waiting for it. But this morning the Russian front was quiet. Jodl's aide had also passed on several reports from Rundstedt's headquarters about an Allied attack in Normandy. Jodl did not think that the situation there was serious, at least not yet. At the moment his big concern was Italy.

In the barracks at Strub a few miles away, Jodl's deputy, General Warlimont, had been carefully following the Normandy attack since 4 A.M. He had received OB West's teletype message requesting the release of the panzer reserves—the *Panzer Lehr* and 12th S.S. divisions—and he had discussed this by phone with Von Rundstedt's chief of staff, Major General Günther Blumentritt. Now Warlimont rang Jodl.

"Blumentritt has called about the panzer reserves," Warlimont reported. "OB West wants to move them into the invasion areas immediately."

As Warlimont recalls, there was a long silence as Jodl pondered the question. "Are you so sure that this *is* the invasion?"

asked Jodl. Before Warlimont could answer, Jodl went on, "According to the reports I have received it could be a diversionary
attack . . . part of a deception plan. OB West has sufficient
reserves right now. . . . OB West should endeavor to clean
up the attack with the forces at their disposal. . . . I do not
think that this is the time to release the OKW reserves. . . .
We must wait for further clarification of the situation."

Warlimont knew that there was little use in arguing the
point, although he thought the Normandy landings were more
serious than Jodl seemed to believe. He said to Jodl, "Sir, in
view of the Normandy situation, shall I proceed to Italy as
planned?" Jodl answered, "Yes, yes, I don't see why not." Then
he hung up.

Warlimont put down his phone. Turning to Major General von Buttlar-Brandenfels, the Army Operations Chief, he
told him of Jodl's decision. "I sympathize with Blumentritt,"
Warlimont said. "This decision is absolutely contrary to my
understanding of what the plan was to be in the event of an
invasion."

Warlimont was "shocked" by Jodl's literal interpretation of
the Hitler edict concerning the control of the panzers. True,
they were OKW reserves and therefore they came under Hitler's direct authority. But, like Von Rundstedt, Warlimont
had always understood that "in the event of an Allied attack,
whether diversionary or not, the panzers would be immediately released—automatically released, in fact." To Warlimont,
such a move seemed only logical; the man on the spot, fighting
off the invasion, should have all the available forces to use as
he saw fit, especially when that man happened to be the last
of Germany's "Black Knights," the venerable strategist Von
Rundstedt. Jodl could have released the force, but he was taking no chances. As Warlimont was later to recall, "Jodl's decision was the one he thought Hitler would have made." Jodl's
attitude, Warlimont felt, was just another example of "the
chaos of leadership in the Leader State." But nobody argued
with Jodl. Warlimont put through a call to Blumentritt at OB
West. Now the decision to release the panzers would depend
on the capricious whim of the man whom Jodl considered to
be a military genius—Hitler.

The officer who had anticipated just such a situation and who had hoped to discuss it with Hitler was less than a two hours' drive from Berchtesgaden. Field Marshal Erwin Rommel, at his home in Herrlingen, Ulm, seems somehow to have been completely forgotten in all the confusion. There is no record in the meticulously kept Army Group B War Diary that Rommel had even heard as yet about the Normandy landings.

At OB West outside Paris, Jodl's decision produced shock and incredulity. Lieutenant General Bodo Zimmermann, chief of operations, remembers that Von Rundstedt "was fuming with rage, red in the face, and his anger made his speech unintelligible." Zimmermann couldn't believe it either. During the night, in a phone call to OKW, Zimmermann had informed Jodl's duty officer, Lieutenant Colonel Friedel, that OB West had alerted the two panzer divisions. "No objections whatsoever were made against the movement," Zimmermann bitterly recalls. Now he called OKW again and spoke to the Army Operations Chief, Major General von Buttlar-Brandenfels. He got a frigid reception—Von Buttlar had picked up his cue from Jodl. In an angry outburst Von Buttlar ranted, "These divisions are under the direct control of OKW! You had no right to alert them without our prior approval. You are to halt the panzers immediately—nothing is to be done before the Führer makes his decision!" When Zimmermann tried to argue back, Von Buttlar shut him up by saying sharply, "Do as you are told!"

The next move should have been up to Von Rundstedt. As a field marshal, he could have called Hitler directly, and it is even likely that the panzers might have been immediately released. But Von Rundstedt did not telephone the Führer now or at any time during D Day. Not even the overwhelming importance of the invasion could compel the aristocratic Von Rundstedt to plead with the man he habitually referred to as "that Bohemian corporal."*

But his officers continued to bombard OKW with telephone calls in vain and futile efforts to get the decision reversed. They

---

*According to Von Buttlar-Brandenfels, Hitler was well aware of Von Rundstedt's contempt. "As long as the Field Marshal grumbles," Hitler had once said, "everything is all right."

called Warlimont, Von Buttlar-Brandenfels, and even Hitler's adjutant, Major General Rudolf Schmundt. It was a strange, long-distance struggle that would go on for hours. Zimmermann summed it up this way: "When we warned that if we didn't get the panzers the Normandy landings would succeed and that unforeseeable consequences would follow, we were simply told that *we* were in no position to judge—that the main landing was going to come at an entirely different place anyway."* And Hitler, protected by his inner circle of military sycophants, in the balmy, make-believe world of Berchtesgaden, slept through it all.

At Rommel's headquarters in La Roche-Guyon, the chief of staff, Major General Speidel, knew nothing of Jodl's decision as yet. He was under the impression that the two reserve panzer divisions had been alerted and were already en route. Also Speidel knew the 21st Panzer was moving into an assembly area south of Caen, and although it would be some time before their tanks could move up, some of their reconnaissance forces and infantry were already engaging the enemy. So there was a definite air of optimism at the headquarters. Colonel Leodegard Freyberg recalls that "the general impression was that the Allies would be thrown back into the sea by the end of the day." Vice-Admiral Friedrich Ruge, Rommel's naval aide, shared in the general elation. But Ruge noticed one peculiar thing: The household staff of the Duke and Duchess de La Rochefoucauld was quietly going through the castle taking the priceless Gobelin tapestries down from the walls.

There seemed greater reason for optimism at the headquarters of the Seventh Army, the army that was actually fighting the Allied attack. To staff officers there it looked as though the 352nd Division had thrown the invaders back into the sea in the area between Vierville and Colleville—Omaha Beach.

---

*Hitler had become so convinced that the "real" invasion would take place in the Pas-de-Calais area that he held Von Salmuth's 15th Army in its positions until July 24. By then it was too late. Ironically Hitler seems to have been the only one who originally believed that the invasion would take place in Normandy. General Blumentritt says that "I well remember a call from Jodl some time in April in which he said 'The Führer has definite information to the effect that a landing in Normandy is not unlikely.'"

What had happened was that an officer in a bunker overlooking the beach had finally been able to get through to his headquarters with an encouraging report on the progress of the battle. The report was considered so important that it was taken down word for word. "At the water's edge," said the observer, "the enemy is in search of cover behind the coastal-zone obstacles. A great many motor vehicles—among them ten tanks—stand burning on the beach. The obstacle demolition squads have given up their activities. Debarkation from the landing boats has ceased . . . the boats keep farther out to sea. The fire of our battle positions and artillery is well placed and has inflicted considerable casualties on the enemy. A great many wounded and dead lie on the beach . . ."*

This was the first good news that the Seventh Army had received. Spirits were so high as a result that when the Fifteenth Army's commanding officer, General von Salmuth, suggested that he send his 346th Infantry Division to help the Seventh out, he was haughtily turned down. "We don't need them," he was told.

Even though everyone was confident, the Seventh Army's chief of staff, General Pemsel, was still trying to piece together an accurate picture of the situation. It was difficult, for he had practically no communications. Wires and cables had been cut or otherwise destroyed by the French underground, by the paratroopers or by the naval and air bombardment. Pemsel told Rommel's headquarters, "I'm fighting the sort of battle that William the Conqueror must have fought—by ear and sight alone." Actually Pemsel did not know how bad his communications really were. He thought that only paratroopers had landed on the Cherbourg peninsula. At this time he had

---

*This report was given, sometime between eight and nine, directly to the 352nd's operations chief, Lieutenant Colonel Ziegelmann, by a certain Colonel Goth who commanded the fortifications on Pointe et Raz de la Percée overlooking the Vierville end of Omaha Beach. It caused such elation that Ziegelmann, according to his own account written after the war, considered that he was dealing with "inferior enemy forces." Later reports were even more optimistic and by 11 A.M. General Kraiss, the 352nd's commanding officer, was so convinced that he had rubbed out the Omaha beachhead that he diverted reserves to strengthen the division's right wing in the British sector.

no idea that seaborne landings had taken place on the east coast of the peninsula, at Utah Beach.

Difficult as it was for Pemsel to define the exact geographic limits of the attack, he was certain of one thing—the Normandy assault *was* the invasion. He continued to point this out to his superiors at Rommel's and Von Rundstedt's headquarters, but he remained very much in the minority. As both Army Group B and OB West stated in their morning reports, "at the present time, it is still too early to say whether this is a large-scale diversionary attack or the main effort." The generals continued to look for the *Schwerpunkt*. Along the Normandy coast any private could have told them where it was.

Half a mile from Sword Beach Lance Corporal Josef Häger, dazed and trembling, somehow found the trigger of his machine gun and began firing again. The earth seemed to be blowing up all about him. The noise was deafening. His head roared and the eighteen-year-old machine gunner was sick with fear. He had fought well, helping to cover the retreat of his company ever since the 716th Division's line broke back of Sword. How many Tommies he had hit Häger did not know. Fascinated, he had watched them come off the beach and had chopped them down one after another. Often in the past he had wondered what it would be like to kill the enemy. Many times he had talked about it with his friends Huf, Saxler and "Ferdi" Klug. Now Häger had found out: it was terribly easy. Huf hadn't lived long enough to discover how easy it was—he had been killed as they ran back. Häger had left him lying in a hedgerow, his mouth open, a hole where his forehead had been. Häger didn't know where Saxler was, but Ferdi was still beside him, half blind, blood running down his face from a shrapnel burst. And now Häger knew that it was only a question of time before they were all killed. He and nineteen men —all that remained of the company—were in a trench before a small bunker. They were being hit from all sides by machine gun, mortar and rifle fire. They were surrounded. It was either surrender or be killed. Everyone knew this—everyone except the captain firing the machine gun behind them in the bunker. He wouldn't let them in. "We must hold! We must hold!" he kept yelling.

This was the most terrible time of Häger's life. He no longer knew what he was firing at. Every time the shelling lifted he automatically pulled the trigger and felt the machine gun pound. It gave him courage. Then the shelling would begin again and everyone would yell at the captain, "Let us in! Let us in!"

Perhaps it was the tanks that made the captain change his mind. They all heard the whirring and clanking. There were two of them. One stopped a field away. The other ambled slowly on, crushing its way across a hedge, passing three cows that munched unconcernedly in a nearby meadow. Then the men in the trench saw its gun slowly lower, ready to fire at point-blank range. At that moment the tank suddenly, unbelievably blew up. A bazooka man in the trench, down to his last bulbous-nosed rocket projectile, had scored a direct hit. Spellbound, not quite sure how it had all happened, Häger and his friend Ferdi saw the hatch of the blazing tank open and through the billowing black smoke a man desperately trying to climb out. Screaming, his clothes on fire, he got halfway though the opening and then collapsed, his body hanging down the side of the tank. Häger said to Ferdi, "I hope God gives us a better death."

The second tank, prudently remaining out of bazooka range, began firing and at last the captain ordered everyone into the bunker. Häger and the other survivors stumbled inside—into a fresh nightmare. The bunker, barely the size of a living room, was filled with dead and dying soldiers. More than thirty other men in the bunker were so jammed together that they were unable to sit down or even turn about. It was hot and dark and hideously noisy. The wounded were moaning. Men were talking in several different languages—many of them were Poles or Russians. And all the time, the captain, oblivious to the yells of the wounded to "Surrender! Surrender!" fired his machine gun through the single aperture.

For an instant there was a lull and Häger and the suffocating men in the bunker heard someone outside shout, "All right, Herman—you better come out!" The captain angrily began firing his machine gun. A few minutes later they heard the same voice again. *"You better give up, Fritz!"*

Men were coughing now from the acrid gaseous discharge of the captain's machine gun, which was fouling the already stifling atmosphere. Each time the captain stopped to reload the voice demanded that they surrender. Finally somebody outside called to them in German and Häger would always remember that one of the wounded, apparently using the only two words of English he knew, began chanting back, "Hello, boys! Hello, boys! Hello, boys!"

The firing outside stopped and it seemed to Häger that everyone realized almost at the same moment what was about to happen. There was a small peephole in a cupola over their heads. Häger and several others lifted a man up so that he could see what was happening. Suddenly he yelled, "Flame thrower! They're bringing up a flame thrower!"

Häger knew that the flames could not reach them because the metal air shaft which entered the bunker from the back was built in staggered sections. But the heat could kill them. Suddenly they heard the "woof" of the flame thrower. Now the only way that air could get into the bunker was through the narrow aperture, where the captain continued to blaze away with his machine gun, and through the peephole in the roof.

Gradually the temperature began to rise. Some men panicked. Clawing and pushing and yelling, "We've got to get out!" they tried to drop to the floor and burrow through the legs of the others toward the door. But, pinioned by the press of men around them, they were unable even to reach the floor. Everyone was now begging the captain to surrender. The captain, still firing, didn't even turn from the aperture. The air was getting indescribably foul.

"We'll all breathe in and out on my command," yelled a lieutenant. "*In! . . . Out! . . . In! . . . Out! . . .*" Häger watched the metal fairing of the air shaft go from pink to red and then to a glowing white. "*In! . . . Out! . . . In! . . . Out!*" yelled the officer. "Hello, boys! Hello, boys!" cried the wounded man. And at a radio set in one corner Häger could hear the operator saying over and over, "Come in, Spinach! Come in, Spinach!"

"Sir!" yelled the lieutenant. "The wounded are suffocating —we must surrender!"

"It's out of the question!" roared the captain. "We're going to fight our way out! Count the men and their weapons!"

"No! No!" men yelled from every corner of the bunker.

Ferdi said to Häger, "You're the only one besides the captain with a machine gun. That madman will send you out first, believe me."

By now, many of the men were defiantly pulling the bolts of their rifles and throwing them on the floor. "I won't go," Häger told Ferdi. He pulled the locking pin on his machine gun and threw it away.

Men began to collapse from the heat. Knees buckling, heads lolling, they remained in a partly upright position; they could not fall to the floor. The young lieutenant continued to plead with the captain, but to no avail. No one could get to the door, because the aperture was next to it and the captain was there with his machine gun.

Suddenly the captain stopped firing and turning to the radio operator he said, "Have you made contact?" The operator said, "Nothing, sir." It was then that the captain looked about him as though seeing the jam-packed bunker for the first time. He seemed dazed and bewildered. Then he threw down his machine gun and said resignedly, "Open the door."

Häger saw somebody stick a rifle with a piece of torn white cloth on it through the aperture. From outside a voice said, "All right, Fritz, out you come—one at a time!"

Gasping for air, dazzled by the light, the men reeled out of the dark bunker. If they did not drop their weapons and helmets fast enough, British troops standing on either side of the trench fired into the ground behind them. As they reached the end of the trench their captors cut their belts, laces and tunics and sliced the buttons off the flies of their pants. Then they were made to lie face downward in a field.

Häger and Ferdi ran down the trench, their hands in the air. As Ferdi's belt was cut, a British officer said to him, "In two weeks we'll be seeing your pals in Berlin, Fritz." Ferdi, his face bloody and puffed up from the shrapnel splinters, tried to joke. He said, "By that time we'll be in England." He meant that they would be in a prisoner-of-war camp, but the Britisher misunderstood. "Take these men to the beaches!" he roared. Holding up their pants, they were marched away, passing the still burning tank and the same cows munching quietly in the meadow.

Fifteen minutes later, Häger and the others were working among the obstacles in the surf, removing mines. Ferdi said to Häger, "I bet you never thought when you were putting these things in that one day you'd be taking them up again."*

Private Aloysius Damski had no heart for the fight at all. Damski, a Pole who had been impressed into the 716th Division, had long ago decided that if the invasion ever came he would run up the ramp of the nearest landing craft and surrender. But Damski didn't get the chance. The British landed under such a fierce protective bombardment of naval and tank fire that Damski's battery commander, in a position near the western edge of Gold Beach, promptly ordered a withdrawal. Damski realized that to run forward would mean certain death —either at the hands of the Germans behind or at those of the advancing British ahead. But in the confusion of the withdrawal he struck out for the village of Tracy, where he was billeted in the home of an old French lady. If he stayed there, Damski reasoned, he could surrender when the village was captured.

As he was making his way across the fields he ran into a hard-bitten Wehrmacht sergeant on horseback. Marching ahead of the sergeant was another private, a Russian. The sergeant looked down at Damski and with a broad smile asked, "Now, just where do you think you're going all by yourself?" They looked at each other for a moment and Damski knew that the sergeant had guessed he was running away. Then, still smiling, the sergeant said, "I think you'd better come with us." Damski wasn't surprised. As they marched off he bitterly thought that his luck had never been good and that it certainly wasn't improving.

Ten miles away, roughly in the vicinity of Caen, Private Wilhelm Voigt of a mobile radio monitoring unit was also wondering how he could surrender. Voigt had lived seventeen years in Chicago, but he had never taken out naturalization papers. In

---

*I was not able to locate the fanatical captain who tried to hold the bunker, but Häger believes that his name was Gundlach and that the junior officer was a Lieutenant Lutke. Later in the day Häger found his missing friend Saxler —he too was working among the obstacles. That night they were taken to England and six days later Häger and 150 other Germans landed in New York en route to a Canadian prisoner-of-war camp.

1939 his wife, visiting her home in Germany, had been forced to stay because of an ailing mother. In 1940, against the advice of friends, Voigt had set out to bring her home. Unable to reach wartime Germany by regular routes, he had made a tortuous journey across the Pacific to Japan, then to Vladivostok and via the Trans-Siberian railway to Moscow. From there he had traveled to Poland and into Germany. The journey took nearly four months—and once across the border Voigt could not get out. He and his wife were trapped. Now, for the first time in four years, he could hear American voices in his earphones. For hours he had been planning what he would say when he saw the first U.S. troops. He was going to run up to them yelling, "Hi, you guys, I'm from Chicago!" But his unit was being held too far back. He had made almost a complete circle of the world just to get back to Chicago—and now all he could do was sit in his truck and listen to the voices, only a few short miles away,* that to him spelled home.

Behind Omaha Beach Major Werner Pluskat lay gasping in a ditch. He was almost unrecognizable. He had lost his helmet. His clothes were ripped and torn. His face was scratched and bloody. For more than an hour and a half, ever since he had left his bunker at Ste.-Honorine to return to his headquarters, Pluskat had been crawling through a burning, erupting no man's land. Scores of fighter planes, flying back and forth just behind the bluffs, were strafing everything that moved, and all the while naval gunfire was plowing up the area. His Volkswagen was somewhere behind him, a burning, twisted wreck. Smoke billowed up from burning hedgerows and grass fires. Here and there he had come across trenches filled with dead troops, blasted either by artillery or by the merciless strafing. At first he had tried to run, but he had been pounced on by the planes. Again and again he had been strafed. Now Pluskat crawled. He figured he had made just one mile and he was still three miles from his headquarters at Etreham. Painfully he moved on. Ahead he saw a farmhouse. He decided that when he came abreast of it he would sprint the twenty

*Voigt never did make it back. He still lives in Germany, where he works for Pan American Airways.

yards or so from the ditch and ask the occupants for a drink of water. As he drew near, he was amazed to see two French-women sitting calmly in the open door, as though immune from the shelling and strafing. They looked across at him and one, laughing spitefully, called out, "*C'est terrible, n'est-ce pas?*" Pluskat crawled past, the laughter still ringing in his ears. At that moment he hated the French, the Normans and the whole rotten stinking war.

Corporal Anton Wuensch of the 6th Parachute Regiment saw the parachute hanging high in the branches of a tree. It was blue and there was a large canvas container swinging below it. In the distance there was a lot of rifle and machine gun fire, but so far Wuensch and his mortar unit had seen nothing of the enemy. They had been marching for almost three hours and now they were in a small wood above Carentan, roughly ten miles southwest of Utah Beach.

Lance Corporal Richter looked at the parachute and said, "It belongs to the Amis [Americans]. Probably contains ammo." Private Fritz "Friedolin" Wendt thought there might be food in it. "God, I'm so hungry," he said. Wuensch told them all to stay in the ditch while he crawled forward. It might be a trick; they might be ambushed when they tried to get the container down, or it could be a booby trap.

Wuensch carefully reconnoitered ahead. Then, satisfied that everything was quiet, he tied two grenades around the tree trunk and pulled the pins. The tree crashed down and with it the parachute container. Wuensch waited, but apparently the explosions had gone unnoticed. He waved his unit in. "Let's see what the Amis have sent us," he yelled.

Friedolin ran forward with his knife and cut through the canvas. He was ecstatic. "Oh, my God," he yelled, "it's food! Food!"

For the next half hour the seven tough paratroopers had the time of their lives. They found cans of pineapple and orange juice, cartons of chocolate and cigarettes, and an assortment of foods the like of which they had not seen in years. Friedolin gorged himself. He even poured powdered Nescafé down his throat and tried to wash it down with condensed milk. "I don't know what it is," he said, "but it tastes wonderful."

Finally, over Friedolin's protest, Wuensch decided that they had better "move on and find the war." Stuffed, their pockets bulging with all the cigarettes they could carry, Wuensch and his men moved out of the wood and headed in single file toward the distant firing. Minutes later the war found them. One of Wuensch's men fell, shot through the temple.

"Sniper!" yelled Wuensch. Everyone dived for cover as shots began to whistle about them.

"Look," yelled one of the men, pointing toward a clump of trees off to the right, "I'm sure I saw him up there."

Wuensch took out his binoculars and, focusing his glasses on the treetops, began a careful search. He thought he saw a slight movement of the branches in one tree, but he wasn't sure. For a long time he held the glasses steady and then he saw the foliage move again. Picking up his rifle, he said, "Now we'll see who's the man and who's the fake." He fired.

At first Wuensch thought he had missed, for as he watched he saw the sniper climbing down the tree. Again Wuensch aimed, this time for a spot on the tree trunk which was clear of branches and foliage. "My boy," he said aloud, "I'm going to get you now." He saw the sniper's legs appear and then his torso. Wuensch fired, again and again. Very slowly the sniper fell backward out of the tree. Wuensch's men cheered and then everybody ran over to the body. They stood looking down at the first American paratrooper they had seen. "He was dark-haired, he was very handsome and very young. There was a trickle of blood at the side of his mouth," Wuensch recalls.

Lance Corporal Richter went through the dead man's pockets and found a wallet with two photographs and a letter. Wuensch remembers that one of them "showed the soldier sitting next to a girl and we all concluded that maybe it was his wife." The other was a snapshot "of the young man and the girl sitting on a veranda with a family, presumably his family." Richter began putting the photographs and the letter into his pocket.

Wuensch said, "What do you want to do that for?"

Richter said, "I thought I'd send this stuff to the address on the envelope after the war."

Wuensch thought he was crazy. "We may be captured by the Amis," he said, "and if they find this stuff on you . . ." He drew his finger across his throat. "Leave it for the medics," said Wuensch, "and let's get out of here."

As his men moved on, Wuensch remained for a moment and stared at the dead American, lying limp and still "like a dog who had been run over." He hurried after his men.

A few miles away a German staff car, its black, white and red pennant flying, raced along the secondary road leading toward the village of Picauville. Major General Wilhelm Falley of the 91st Air Landing Division, together with his aide and a driver, had been in his Horch for almost seven hours, ever since he set out for Rennes and the war games a little before 1 A.M. Sometime between 3 and 4 A.M., the continuous droning of planes and the distant explosions of bombs had caused the concerned Falley to turn back.

They were only a few miles from the headquarters north of Picauville when machine gun bullets ripped across the front of the car. The windshield shattered and Falley's aide, sitting beside the driver, slumped down in his seat. Swaying from side to side, tires screaming, the Horch swerved and smashed into a low wall. The doors flew open with the impact and the driver and Falley were hurled out. Falley's gun slithered out in front of him. He crawled across the road toward it. The driver, shaken and dazed, saw several American soldiers rushing up to the car. Falley was shouting, "Don't kill! Don't kill!" but he continued to crawl toward the gun. There was a shot and Falley collapsed in the road, one hand still stretched out toward the gun.

Lieutenant Malcolm Brannen of the 82nd Airborne looked down at the dead man. Then he stooped and picked up the officer's cap. Stenciled on the sweatband was the name "Falley." The German wore a greenish-gray uniform with red stripes down the seam of the trousers. There were narrow gold epaulets at the shoulders of his tunic and red tabs decorated with gold-braided oak leaves at the collar. An Iron Cross hung from a black ribbon around the man's neck. Brannen wasn't sure, but it looked to him as though he'd killed a general.

On the airfield near Lille, Wing Commander Josef "Pips" Priller and Sergeant Heinz Wodarczyk ran for their two solitary FW-190 fighter planes.

Minutes before H Hour and Omaha Beach looms ahead. Spray-drenched
assault troops crouch down in Coast Guard LCA racing for shore.

[BELOW] Waves of assault boats thrash past cruiser, U.S.S. *Augusta*. On bridge [TOP, LEFT] bespectacled Lt. Gen. Omar N. Bradley, U.S. 1st Army Commander, watches landing craft heading in for Omaha Beach. Next to him is Rear Admiral Alan Kirk, Overlord Western Task Force Commander. Landing craft [MIDDLE, LEFT] receives direct hit and bursts into flame off Omaha. Survivors of another damaged craft struggle ashore from life raft [BOTTOM, LEFT].

[TOP, LEFT] H Hour on Omaha Beach. Assault troops struggling through obstacles and heavy surf while under fire. This photo, taken by the late Bob Capa of *Life*, is probably the best remembered picture of D Day. (*Wide World*)

[MIDDLE, LEFT] H Hour plus 15 minutes. Pinned down by enemy fire, troops take cover behind obstacles. (*Courtesy Col. John T. O'Neill*)

[BOTTOM, LEFT] H Hour plus 25 minutes. Engineers of Assault Team 10 move in. Note troops behind obstacles and taking cover back of engineers' tankdozer. (*Courtesy Col. John T. O'Neill*)

[BELOW] Omaha Beach wounded sheltering behind sea wall, waiting to be evacuated.

Headquarters 1st Infantry Division
APO # 1, U. S. Army
G-3 Journal
Appendix V

From 0001B

Date; 6 June 1944

Time:

To.: 2400B

CP Location: USS ANCON, ENGLISH CHA
off Coast of France

Time	No.	From	Synopsis	Rec'd Via	Disposition
0230	1		Arrived in Transport Area at 0230.		
0251	2		Dropped Anchor at 0251.		
0630	3	CG	Land CT 115 at H/4 unless otherwise directed.		Comdr CTF 124
0708	4		1st wave landed 0635 2d wave landed 0636	Rad	J
0830	5		16 Inf and 116 Inf touched down 060635.	Rad	J
0630	6	Talley	It 1 DUKW No one waterborne	Rad	V Corps & J
0636	7	Talley	It 3 Dog Dogs Launched Saw empty LCT returning.	Rad	V Corps & J
0655	8	PC 552	NK First wave foundered.	Rad	Navy & J
0702	9	Javelin	LCA unit is landing half on DOG GREEN half on CHARLIE.	Rad	Navy & J
0700	10	Talley	Brilliant white flare seen near POINTE DE HOE.	Rad	V Corps & J
0641	11	PC 552	Entire first wave foundered.	Rad	Chase & J
0807	17	Thomas Jefferson	Returning boats report floating mines near beach endangering landings. Many boats have swamped because of them. Many persons in water.	R d	COMTRANSDIV 3 &
0730	23	DC/S V Corps	LC IL 94 and 493 landed 0740. Firing heavy on beach.	Rad	V Corps & J
0838	24	Control Vessel Dog Red	The obstacles are mined. No chance of destroying mines by demolition yet.	Rad	J
0816	25	LCT 535	There are DUKWS in distress between here and the beach.	Rad	Ancon & J
0710	27	CTG 124.4 (Rngr Co)	Two L TS knocked out by enemy btry back of center of Beach Dog Green.	Rad	Ancon & J
0809	28	Control Craft	All of DD Tks for Fox Green beach sank between disembarkation point and line of departure.	Rad	CG, G-3, J
0824	29	CTG 124.9	Btrys at MAISY still in commission. Being kept under fire.	Rad	CG, G-3, J
0830	30	50th Div	Request progress of your trs. Progress of 50th Div going according to plan.	Rad	CG, G-3, J
0833	31	LCT 538	Failed to unload due to indirect fire of 88's. Hit. 5 Army casualties.	Rad	PC 617, G-3

3	32	V Corps	Wave Claude & Eric touched down at 0720. Obstacles not breached. Four tks held up by enemy fire, heavy this area. Wave E & C forced to withdraw. Casualties appeared heavy.	Rad	CG V Corps, CG, G-3, J.
9	34	1st Bn 116Ct	Held up by enemy MG fire. Request fire support.	Rad	Co CT 116, CG, G-3, J
69	35	Rngr Co	Brit Off reports on Dog Green Beach. Heavy MG fire. Obstacles not cleared.	Rad	CG, G-3, J.
0	36	Rngr Co	Tide rising rapidly. Obstacles still on beach. Need demolition squad.	Rad	CG, G-3, J.
909	44	CG	Enemy btry back of center of beach Dog Green. Find and Silence.	Rad	CTG, 124. 9
930	46	Prince Leopold	Rngrs landed safely. Heavy opposition. Beach not cleared of obstruction. Very dangerous for LCA's.	Rad	Prince Charles, CG, G-3, J.
	48	Control Vessel	Do not know whether firing on beach is friendly or enemy. Keeping LCI'S from landing.	Rad	USS Chase, CG, G-3, J.
945	49	Div Bat 5	Btrys at MAISY completely destroyed.	Rad	CG, G-3, J.
946	50	CG	Firing on Beach Easy Red is keeping LCI's from landing.	Rad	CTG 124.8, J.
950	52	ACG	Beach too many vehs. Send combat trs.	Rad	CG, G-3, J.
	63	CTG 124.8	Control vessel reports many wounded at DOG RED beach needing immediate evacuation. Many LCTS standing by bouy but cannot unload because of heavy shell fire on beach.	Rad	TF 124 + V Corps & J.
40	75	CG 1st Div	Reinforce 2d Bn 16th Inf at once.	Rad	Co. CT 18, &
	76	Beachmaster Easy Red	Send in H Plus 195 wave at once.	Rad	Ancon & J
5	93	Comdesron 18	Inf advancing send reinforcements. Also Dog Green needs inf.	Rad	CG & CTG 124.9 G-3 & J
37	99	Thomas Jefferson	Fire support on Easy Green beach reported excellent. Germans reported leaving positions and surrendering to American soldiers.	Rad	Comtransdiv 3, CG, G-3, J.
	154	CG	16th Inf at COLLEVILLE SUR MER 687882. Other units progressing slowly- Beaches not yet clear of fire 061315.	Rad	50 Div & J.
	155	Navy	Beaches DOG GREEN WHITE RED are entirely clear of opposition and ready for landing trs. No opposition on beach. EASY GREEN AND RED trs ashore apparently waiting infantry reinforcements. All fire support ships are waiting on Army for target assignments. Request you get this info to Army ashore.	Rad	CG & J.

These excerpts from U.S. 1st Division's operations journal give almost minute-by-minute account of the seven-hour crisis on Omaha Beach up to time troops began to move inland shortly after 1 P.M. Note that in first twenty-five minutes after H Hour, Patrol Craft 552, in messages number 8 and 11, reported entire first wave had foundered. (*Author's Collection*)

[ABOVE] Men of U.S. 4th Division wade ashore on Utah Beach. First-wave casualties were light, but heavy artillery fire flayed beach later in morning. [BELOW] 4th Division medics tend wounded on sands.

"Now listen, there's just the two of us. We can't afford to break up. For God's sake, do exactly as I do. Fly behind me and follow every move. We're going in alone—and I don't think we're coming back." These were the instructions Wing Commander Josef Priller [LEFT] gave his wingman, Sergeant Heinz Wodarczyk, just before they took off in the only Luftwaffe air attack made during the initial Allied landings. (*Author's Collection*)

German 88 shell explodes among assault troops on Utah Beach. In foreground, right, men crouch for safety by sea wall.

Rangers march German POWs down cliff face after Colonel Rudder's force had been relieved on D + 2. The American flag is protection against these troops being shelled by their own men.

4th Division's commanding officer, Maj. Gen. Raymond O. Barton (*center*), holds conference at first command post, 300 yards in from Utah Beach. On his right, wearing woolen cap, Brig. Gen. Theodore Roosevelt, Assistant Division Commander, who landed with first wave. Left: Lt. Col. Clarence G. Hupfer, Commander, 746th Tank Battalion. (*Courtesy Maj. Gen. Barton*)

The heroic Brig. Gen. Norman Cota, 29th Division Asst. Commander, who, completely oblivious of the rain of enemy fire, calmly walked up and down Omaha Beach and sparked the move of 29th Div. troops inland.

Major Werner Pluskat, Omaha Beach battery commander who spotted the huge invasion fleet from his forward observation post, a coastal bunker almost in the dead center of the Normandy beachhead. (*Author's Collection*)

British troops land under fire. Beach is unidentified, but it is probably Gold. Note, at left, wounded men lying in water and others falling, while at right trooper strides calmly along beach. This is one of the most human of all D Day photos, for it shows what every invasion veteran remembers—sudden death in one place, false security in another. (*Wide World*)

[TOP, RIGHT] Canadian troops jam LCI as it heads for Juno. Note collapsible bicycles at left. [BOTTOM, RIGHT] Led by amphibious tanks, their balloonlike canvas "water wings" now deflated, British troops assault unidentified beach—possibly the western half of Sword.

Picture above is historic and a rarity—it has never appeared before. It shows Col. Ernest R. Dupuy, Eisenhower's press officer, rising to broadcast the news the free world had been waiting for—that Allied troops had landed in Europe. The time was 9:33 A.M. (*Courtesy Col. Ernest Dupuy*)

Greatest American success on D Day was Utah Beach assault. Fourth Division troops moved inland faster than anyone had anticipated. Above, troops slosh through inundated area heading for link-up with paratroopers. By roadside is sight that was to become all too common as Normandy battle progressed—bodies of Germans and Americans alike.

At dusk on D Day, troops on Utah watch glider trains fly over to reinforce still-beleaguered airborne troops.

The beginning of the end for Hitler's Third Reich. German prisoners trudge down Omaha Beach.

The Luftwaffe's 2nd Fighter Corps headquarters had telephoned. "Priller," the operations officer had said, "the invasion has started. You'd better get up there."

Priller had exploded: "Now you've dropped it! You damned fools! What the hell do you expect me to do with just two planes? Where are my squadrons? Can you call them back?"

The operations officer had remained perfectly cool. "Priller," he had said soothingly, "we don't know yet exactly where your squadrons have landed, but we're going to divert them back to the field at Poix. Move all your ground personnel there immediately. Meanwhile you better get up to the invasion area. Good luck, Priller."

As quietly as his anger would allow Priller had said, "Would you mind telling me where the invasion is?"

The officer, unruffled, had said, "Normandy, Pips—somewhere above Caen."

It had taken Priller the best part of an hour to make the necessary arrangements for the movement of his ground personnel. Now he and Wodarczyk were ready—ready to make the Luftwaffe's only daylight attack against the invasion.*

Just before they got into their planes, Priller went over to his wing man. "Now listen," he said, "there's just the two of us. We can't afford to break up. For God's sake, do exactly as I do. Fly behind me and follow every move." They had been together a long time and Priller felt he must make the situation quite clear. "We're going in alone," he said, "and I don't think we're coming back."

It was 9 A.M. when they took off (8 A.M. to Priller). They flew due west, hugging the ground. Just over Abbeville, high above them, they began to see Allied fighters. Priller noticed that they were not flying in tight formation as they should have been. He remembers thinking that "if I only had some planes, they'd be sitting ducks." As they approached Le Havre, Priller climbed for cover in the clouds. They flew for a few more

*In some accounts it has been written that eight JU-88 bombers attacked the beaches during the initial landings. Bombers were over the beachhead on the night of June 6–7, but there is no record that I could find of a D-Day morning raid other than Priller's fighter attack.

minutes and then broke through. Below them was a fantastic fleet—hundreds of ships of every size and type, stretching endlessly, it seemed, all the way back across the Channel. There was a steady procession of landing craft carrying men toward shore, and Priller could see the white puffs of explosions on and behind the beaches. The sands were black with troops, and tanks and equipment of all sorts littered the shore line. Priller swept back into the clouds to consider what to do. There were so many planes, so many battleships offshore, so many men on the beaches, that he figured he'd have time for just one pass over the beaches before being shot down.

There was no need for radio silence now. Almost lightheartedly, Priller spoke into his microphone. "What a show! What a show!" he said. "There's everything out here—everywhere you look. Believe me, this is the invasion!" Then he said, "Wodarczyk, we're going in! Good luck!"

They hurtled down toward the British beaches at over 400 m.p.h., coming in at less than 150 feet. Priller had no time to aim. He simply pressed the button on his control stick and felt his guns pounding. Skimming along just over the tops of men's heads, he saw upturned, startled faces.

On Sword, Commander Philippe Kieffer of the French commandos saw Priller and Wodarczyk coming. He dived for cover. Six German prisoners took advantage of the confusion and tried to bolt. Kieffer's men promptly mowed them down. On Juno Private Robert Rogge of the Canadian 8th Infantry Brigade heard the scream of the planes and saw them "coming in so low that I could clearly see the pilots' faces." He threw himself flat like everyone else, but he was amazed to see one man "calmly standing up, blazing away with a Sten gun." On the eastern edge of Omaha, Lieutenant (j.g.) William J. Eisemann of the U.S. Navy gasped as the two FW-190s, guns chattering, zoomed down "at less than fifty feet and dodged through the barrage balloons." And on H.M.S. *Dunbar*, Leading Stoker Robert Dowie watched every antiaircraft gun in the fleet open up on Priller and Wodarczyk. The two fighters flew through it all unscathed, then turned inland and streaked up into the clouds. "Jerry or not," said Dowie, unbelievingly, "the best of luck to you. You've got guts."

4

ALL ALONG the Normandy coastline the invasion stormed. For the French, caught up in the battle, these were hours of chaos, elation and terror. Around Ste.-Mère-Église, which was now being heavily shelled, 82nd paratroopers saw farmers calmly working in the fields as though nothing were happening. Every now and then one of them would fall, either wounded or killed. In the town itself paratroopers watched the local barber remove the sign "*Friseur*" from the front of his shop and put up a new one that said "Barber."

A few miles away, in the little coastal hamlet of La Madeleine, Paul Gazengel was bitter and in pain. Not only had the roof of his store and café been blown off, but he had been wounded during the shelling, and now 4th Division troops were taking him and seven other men down to Utah Beach.

"Where are you taking my husband?" demanded his wife of the young lieutenant in charge.

The officer answered in perfect French. "For questioning, madame," he said. "We can't talk to him here, so we're taking him and all the other men to England."

Madame Gazengel couldn't believe her ears. "To England!" she exclaimed. "Why? What has he done?"

The young officer was embarrassed. Patiently he explained that he was simply carrying out instructions.

"What happens if my husband gets killed in the bombing?" asked Madame Gazengel tearfully.

"There's a ninety per cent chance that won't happen, madame," he said.

Gazengel kissed his wife goodbye and was marched off. He had no idea what it was all about—and he never would find out. Two weeks later he would be back in Normandy, with the lame excuse from his American captors that "it was all a mistake."

Jean Marion, French underground sector chief in the seaside town of Grandcamp, was frustrated. He could see the fleet off Utah Beach to his left and Omaha Beach to his right and he knew troops were landing. But it looked to him as though Grandcamp had been forgotten. All morning he had waited in vain for soldiers to come in. But he was heartened when his wife pointed out a destroyer that was slowly maneuvering opposite the town. "The gun!" exclaimed Marion. "The gun I told them about!" A few days earlier he had informed London that a small artillery piece had been mounted on the sea wall, sited so that it would fire only to the left, in the direction of what was now Utah Beach. Now Marion was sure that his message had been received, for he saw the destroyer carefully move into position on the gun's blind side and commence firing. With tears in his eyes Marion jumped up and down each time the destroyer fired. "They got the message!" he cried. "They got the message!" The destroyer—which may have been the *Herndon*—blasted the artillery piece with round after round. Suddenly there was a violent explosion as the gun's ammunition blew up. "*Merveilleux!*" yelled the excited Marion. "*Magnifique!*"

In the cathedral town of Bayeux, roughly fifteen miles away, Guillaume Mercader, the underground intelligence chief for the Omaha Beach area, stood at the window of his living room with his wife Madeleine. Mercader was having a hard time fighting back his tears. After four terrible years, the main body of German troops billeted in the town seemed to be pulling out. He could hear the cannonading in the distance and he knew that heavy fighting must be taking place. Now he had a strong urge to organize his resistance fighters and drive the remainder of the Nazis out. But the radio had warned them to be calm, that there must be no uprising. It was difficult, but Mercader had learned to wait. "We'll be free soon," he told his wife.

Everyone in Bayeux seemed to feel the same way. Although the Germans had posted notices ordering the townspeople to stay indoors, people had gathered quite openly in the cathedral courtyard to hear a running commentary on the invasion from one of the priests. From his vantage point he could clearly see the beaches; hands cupped around his mouth he was yelling down from the belfry of the steeple.

Among those who heard of the invasion from the priest was Anne Marie Broeckx, the nineteen-year-old kindergarten teacher who would find her future husband among the American invaders. At seven she had calmly set out on her bicycle for her father's farm at Colleville, back of Omaha Beach. Pedaling furiously, she had cycled past German machine gun positions and troops marching toward the coast. Some Germans had waved to her and one had warned her to be careful, but nobody stopped her. She had seen planes strafing and Germans diving for cover, but Anne Marie, her tresses flying in the wind and her blue skirt ballooning around her, kept on. She felt perfectly safe; it never dawned on her that her life was in danger.

Now she was less than a mile from Colleville. The roads were deserted. Clouds of smoke drifted inland. Here and there fires were burning. Then she saw the wreckage of several farmhouses. For the first time Anne Marie felt frightened. Frantically she raced on. By the time she reached the crossroads at Colleville she was thoroughly alarmed. The thunder of gunfire rolled all about her and the entire area seemed strangely desolated and uninhabited. Her father's farm lay between Colleville and the beach. Anne Marie decided to continue on foot. Hitching her bicycle over her shoulder, she hiked across the fields. Then, topping a little rise, she saw the farmhouse—still standing. She ran the remainder of the way.

At first Anne Marie thought the farm was deserted, for she could see no movement. Calling to her parents, she dashed into the little farmyard. The windows of the house had been blown out. Part of the roof had disappeared and there was a gaping hole in the door. Suddenly the wrecked door opened and there stood her father and mother. She threw her arms around both of them.

"My daughter," said her father, "this is a great day for France." Anne Marie burst into tears.

Half a mile away, fighting for his life amid the horrors of Omaha Beach, was nineteen-year-old P.F.C. Leo Heroux, the man who would marry Anne Marie.*

While the Allied attack raged in Normandy, one of the region's top underground officials was fuming on a train just

*Anne Marie is one war bride who does not live in the U.S. She and Leo Heroux now live where they first met on June 8—at the Broeckx farm near Colleville back of Omaha Beach. They have three children and Heroux runs an auto-driving school.

.

outside Paris. Léonard Gille, Normandy's deputy military intelligence chief, had been riding the Paris-bound train for more than twelve hours. The journey seemed interminable. They had crawled through the night, stopping at every station. Now, ironically, the intelligence chief had heard the news from one of the porters. Gille had no idea where in Normandy the assault had taken place, but he could hardly wait to get back to Caen. He was bitter that after all the years of work, his superiors had chosen this of all days to order him to the capital. Worse, there was no way now for him to get off the train. The next stop was Paris.

But back in Caen his fiancée, Janine Boitard, had been busy ever since she had heard the news. At seven she had roused the two R.A.F. pilots she was hiding. "We must hurry," she told them. "I'm taking you to a farm in the village of Gavrus, twelve kilometers from here."

Their destination came as a shock to the two Britishers. Freedom was only ten short miles away, yet they were going to head inland. Gavrus lay southwest of Caen. One of the Britishers, Wing Commander K. T. Lofts, thought they should take a chance and go north to meet the troops.

"Be patient," said Janine. "The area between here and the coast is swarming with Germans. It will be safer to wait."

Shortly after seven they set out on bicycles, the two Britishers dressed in rough farm clothes. The journey was uneventful. Although they were stopped several times by German patrols, their fake identity papers stood the test and they were passed on. At Gavrus, Janine's responsibility ended—two more fliers were a step closer to home. Janine would have liked to have gone farther with them, but she had to return to Caen—to wait for the next downed pilots who would pass along the escape route, and the moment of liberation that she knew was close. Waving goodbye, she jumped on her bicycle and cycled off.

In the prison at Caen, Madame Amélie Lechevalier, expecting to be executed for her part in saving Allied pilots, heard a whisper as the tin plate with her breakfast was slid under the cell door. "Hope, hope," said the voice. "The British have landed." Madame Lechevalier began to pray. She wondered if her husband, Louis, in a cell nearby, had heard the news. All night there had been explosions, but she had thought that it was the usual Allied bombing. Now there was a chance; maybe they would be saved before it was too late.

Suddenly Madame Lechevalier heard a commotion in the corridor. She got down on her knees by the slit beneath the door and listened. She could hear shouting and the word "*Raus! Raus!* [Out! Out!]" repeated over and over. Then there was the tramping of feet, the slamming of cell doors and then silence again. A few minutes later, somewhere outside the prison she heard prolonged machine gun fire.

The Gestapo guards had panicked. Within minutes of the news of the landings, two machine guns had been set up in the prison courtyard. In groups of ten the male prisoners were led out, placed against the wall and executed. They had been picked up on a variety of charges, some true, some false. There were Guy de Saint Pol and René Loslier, farmers; Pierre Audige, a dentist; Maurice Primault, a shop assistant; Colonel Antoine de Touchet, a retired officer; Anatole Lelièvre, the town hall secretary; Georges Thomine, a fisherman; Pierre Menochet, a policeman; Maurice Dutacq, Achille Boutrois, Joseph Picquenot and his son, French railway workers; Albert Anne; Désiré Lemière; Roger Veillat; Robert Boulard—ninety-two in all, of whom only forty were members of the French underground. On this day, the day that began the great liberation, these men, without explanation, without a hearing, without a trial, were slaughtered. Among them was Madame Lechevalier's husband, Louis.

The firing went on for an hour. In her cell Madame Lechevalier wondered what was happening.

5

IN ENGLAND it was 9:30 A.M. All night General Eisenhower had paced the floor of his trailer, waiting for the reports to come in. He had tried to relax in his usual manner by reading Westerns, but with little success. Then the first messages began to arrive. They were fragmentary, but the news was good. His air and naval commanders were more than satisfied with the progress of the attack and troops were ashore on all five beaches. Overlord was going well. Although the foothold was slight, there would be no need now for him to release the communiqué he had quietly scribbled just twenty-four hours before. In case the attempt to land troops was defeated, he had written: "Our landings in the Cherbourg-Havre area have failed to gain a satisfactory foothold and I have withdrawn the troops. My decision to attack at this time and place was based upon the best information available. The troops, the air and Navy did all that bravery and devotion to duty could do. If there is any blame or fault attached to the attempt, it is mine alone."

Certain that his troops were ashore on the invasion beaches, Eisenhower had authorized the release of a far different communiqué. At 9:33 A.M. his press aide, Colonel Ernest Dupuy, broadcast the news to the world. "Under the command of General Eisenhower," he said, "Allied naval forces, supported by strong air forces, began landing Allied armies this morning on the northern coast of France."

This was the moment the free world had been waiting for —and now that it had come people responded with a curious mixture of relief, exhilaration and anxiety. "At last," said the London *Times* in a D-Day editorial, "the tension has broken."

Most Britons heard the news at work. In some war plants the bulletin was read out over loud-speakers and men and women stood back from their lathes and sang "God Save the King." Village churches threw open their doors. Total strangers talked to one another on commuter trains. On city streets civilians walked up to American soldiers and shook hands. Small crowds gathered on corners to gaze upward at the heaviest air traffic Britons had ever seen.

Wren Lieutenant Naomi Coles Honour, wife of the skipper of the midget sub X23, heard the news and immediately knew where her husband was. Sometime later she got a call from one of the operations officers at naval headquarters: "George is all right, but you'll never guess what he's been up to." Naomi could hear all that later; the important thing now was that he was safe.

The mother of eighteen-year-old Able Seaman Ronald Northwood of the flagship *Scylla* got so excited she ran across the street to tell her neighbor Mrs. Spurdgeon that "my Ron must be there." Mrs. Spurdgeon wasn't to be outdone. She had "a relative on the *Warspite*" and she was certain he was there too. (With minor variations the same conversation was taking place all over England.)

Grace Gale, wife of Private John Gale, who had landed in the first wave on Sword Beach, was bathing the youngest of their three children when she heard the bulletin. She tried to hold back her tears, but couldn't—she was certain that her husband was in France. "Dear God," she whispered, "bring him back." Then she told her daughter Evelyn to turn off the radio. "We're not going to let your dad down by worrying," she said.

In the cathedral-like atmosphere of the Westminster Bank at Bridgeport in Dorset, Audrey Duckworth was hard at work and didn't hear about the assault until much later in the day. It was just as well. Her American husband, Captain Edmund Duckworth of the 1st Division, had been killed as he stepped onto Omaha Beach. They had been married just five days.

En route to Eisenhower's headquarters at Portsmouth, Lieutenant General Sir Frederick Morgan heard the BBC warn listeners to stand by for a special announcement. Morgan told his driver to stop the car for a moment. He turned up the volume on his radio—and then the author of the original invasion plan heard the news of the attack.

For most of the United States the report came in the middle of the night; on the East Coast it was 3:33 A.M., on the West Coast 12:33 A.M. Most people were asleep, but among the first to hear of D Day were the thousands working on the swing shifts, the men and women who had toiled to produce most of the guns, tanks, ships and planes that were being used in the assault. Everywhere in the great pulsing war plants work stopped for a moment of solemn meditation. In a Brooklyn shipyard, under the harsh glare of arc lamps, hundreds of men and women knelt down on the decks of partially finished Liberty ships and began to say the Lord's Prayer.

Across the nation, in sleeping towns and villages, lights flashed on. Quiet streets suddenly filled with sound as radios were turned up. People woke their neighbors to tell them the news, and so many phoned friends and relatives that telephone switchboards were jammed. In Coffeyville, Kansas, men and women in their night attire knelt on porches and prayed. On a train between Washington and New York a clergyman was asked to hold an impromptu service. In Marietta, Georgia, people thronged into churches at 4 A.M. The Liberty Bell was rung in Philadelphia, and throughout historic Virginia, the home of the 29th Division, church bells tolled in the night just as they had during the Revolution. In little Bedford, Virginia (population 3,800), the news had a special significance. Nearly everyone had a son, brother, sweetheart or husband in the 29th. In Bedford they did not know it yet, but all of their men had landed on Omaha Beach. Out of forty-six Bedford men in the 116th Regiment, only twenty-three would come home again.

Wave Ensign Lois Hoffman, wife of the skipper of the *Corry*, was on duty at the Norfolk, Virginia, naval base when she heard about D Day. From time to time she had kept track of her husband's destroyer through friends in the operations room. The news had no personal significance for her. She still believed her husband was escorting a munitions convoy in the North Atlantic.

In San Francisco, Mrs. Lucille M. Schultz, a nurse at the Veterans Hospital at Fort Miley, was on night duty when the first announcement was made. She wanted to stay by the radio in the hope that the 82nd Airborne would be mentioned; she suspected the division was in the assault. But she was also afraid the radio might excite her cardiac patient, a World War I veteran. He wanted to listen to the reports. "I wish I was there," he said. "You've had your war," said Nurse Schultz as she turned off the radio. Sitting in the darkness, weeping silently, she said the Rosary over and over for her twenty-one-year-old paratrooper son, Arthur, better known to the 505th Regiment as Private Dutch Schultz.

At her home on Long Island, Mrs. Theodore Roosevelt had slept fitfully. About 3 A.M. she awoke and could not get back to sleep. Automatically she turned on the radio—just in time to catch the official D-Day announcement. She knew that it was characteristic of her husband to be somewhere in the thick of the fighting. She did not know that she was probably the only woman in the nation to have a husband on Utah Beach and a son—twenty-five-year-old Captain Quentin Roosevelt of the 1st Division—on Omaha Beach. Sitting up in bed, she closed her eyes and said an old and familiar family prayer: "O Lord support us this day . . . until the shadows lengthen and the evening falls."

In Stalag 17B near Krems, Austria, the news was received with a rejoicing that could hardly be contained. U.S. Air Force enlisted men had picked up the electrifying announcement on tiny handmade crystal sets, some of them built to fit in tooth-brush holders, others camouflaged to look like lead pencils. Staff Sergeant James Lang, who had been shot down over Ger-many more than a year before, was almost afraid to believe the report. The camp's "news monitoring committee" tried to warn the four thousand POWs against overoptimism. "Don't get your hopes up," they cautioned. "Give us time to verify or deny." But in barracks after barracks men were already at work drawing secret maps of the Normandy coast on which they intended to plot the victorious advance of the Allied armies.

At this time the prisoners of war knew more about the in-vasion than the German people. So far the man in the street had heard nothing officially. It was ironic, because Radio Ber-lin, beating the Eisenhower communiqué by three hours, had been the first to announce the Allied landings. From six-thirty on, the Germans had showered a somewhat doubting world with a steady stream of newscasts. These short-wave broadcasts could not be heard by the German public. Still, thousands had learned of the landings from other sources. Although listening to foreign broadcasts was forbidden and punishable by a stiff prison term, some Germans had tuned in Swiss, Swedish or Spanish stations. The news had spread swiftly. Many of those who did hear it were skeptical. But there were some, particu-larly women with husbands in Normandy, who got the report and were deeply concerned. One of these was Frau Werner Pluskat.

She had planned to go to a movie in the afternoon with Frau Sauer, another officer's wife. But when she heard that the Allies were rumored to have landed in Normandy, she became almost hysterical. Immediately she called Frau Sauer, who had also heard something about the attack, and canceled the movie date. "I must know what has happened to Werner," she said. "I may never see him again."

Frau Sauer was very abrupt and very Prussian. "You shouldn't act like this!" snapped Frau Sauer. "You should believe in the Führer and act like a good officer's wife."

Frau Pluskat shot back, "I'll never talk to you again!" Then she slammed down the phone.

In Berchtesgaden it almost seemed as though the men around Hitler had waited for the official Allied communiqué before daring to break the news to him. It was about 10 A.M. (9 A.M. German time) when Hitler's naval aide, Admiral Karl Jesko von Puttkamer, called Jodl's office for the latest report. He was told that there were "definite indications that an important landing has taken place." Gathering all the information he could, Puttkamer and his staff quickly prepared a map. Then Major General Rudolf Schmundt, the Führer's adjutant, awakened Hitler. He was in a dressing gown when he came out of his bedroom. He listened calmly to the report of his aides and then sent for OKW's Chief, Field Marshal Wilhelm Keitel, and Jodl. By the time they arrived Hitler was dressed and waiting —and excited.

The conference that followed was, as Puttkamer recalls, "extremely agitated." Information was scanty, but on the basis of what was known Hitler was convinced that this was not the main invasion, and he kept repeating that over and over again. The conference lasted only a few minutes and ended abruptly, as Jodl was later to remember, when Hitler suddenly thundered at him and Keitel, "Well, is it or isn't it the invasion?" and then turned on his heel and left the room.

The subject of the release of the OKW panzer divisions, which Von Rundstedt so urgently needed, did not even come up.

At ten-fifteen the phone rang in Field Marshal Erwin Rommel's home at Herrlingen. The caller was his chief of staff, Major General Hans Speidel. The purpose: the first complete briefing on the invasion.* Rommel listened, shocked and shaken.

It was not a "Dieppe-type raid." With all the canny instinct that had served him so well for most of his life, Rommel knew

---

* General Speidel has told me that he called Rommel "around 6 A.M. on a private wire." He says the same thing in his own book *Invasion 1944*. But General Speidel had his times confused. For example, his book states that the Field Marshal left La Roche-Guyon on June 5—not on June 4, as Captain Hellmuth Lang and Colonel Hans George von Tempelhof have stated and as the Army Group B War Diary records. On D Day the diary lists only one call to Rommel: the 10:15 A.M. call. The entry reads: "Speidel informs Field Marshal Rommel by phone on the situation. Commander in Chief Army Group B is going to return to his headquarters today."

that it was the day he had been waiting for—the one he had said would be "the longest day." He waited patiently until Speidel had finished the report and then he said quietly, with no tinge of emotion in his voice, "How stupid of me. How stupid of me."

He turned from the phone and Frau Rommel saw that "the call had changed him . . . there was a terrible tension." During the next forty-five minutes, Rommel twice called his aide, Captain Hellmuth Lang, at his home near Strasbourg. Each time he gave Lang a different hour for their return to La Roche-Guyon. That in itself worried Lang; it was unlike the Field Marshal to be so undecisive. "He sounded terribly depressed on the phone," Lang recalls, "and that was not like him, either." The departure time was finally set. "We will leave at one o'clock sharp from Freudenstadt," Rommel told his aide. As Lang hung up the phone he reasoned that Rommel was delaying their departure in order to see Hitler. He did not know that at Berchtesgaden no one but Hitler's adjutant, Major General Schmundt, was even aware that Rommel was in Germany.

6

ON UTAH BEACH the roar of trucks, tanks, half-tracks and jeeps almost drowned out the sporadic whine of German 88s. It was the noise of victory; the 4th Division was moving inland faster than anyone had anticipated.

On Exit 2, the only open causeway running in from the beach, two men stood directing the flood of traffic. Both were generals. On one side of the road stood Major General Raymond O. Barton, commander of the 4th Division, on the other the boyishly exuberant Brigadier General Teddy Roosevelt. As Major Gerden Johnson of the 12th Infantry Regiment came up he saw Roosevelt "stomping up and down the dusty road, leaning on his cane and smoking his pipe almost as unperturbed as though he were in the middle of Times Square." Roosevelt spotted Johnson and yelled, "Hi, Johnny! Keep right on this road, you're doing fine! It's a great day for hunting, isn't it?" It was a triumphant moment for Roosevelt. His decision to bring the 4th in two thousand yards from the planned touch-down point could have been disastrous. Now he watched the long lines of vehicles and men moving inland and felt an immense personal satisfaction.*

But Barton and Roosevelt, despite their air of unconcern, shared a secret fear: Unless the traffic could be kept constantly moving, the 4th could be stopped dead in its tracks by a determined German counterattack. Again and again the two generals unsnarled traffic jams. Stalled trucks were ruthlessly pushed off the road. Here and there blazing vehicles, victims of enemy shells, threatened to halt the advance. Tanks bulldozed them into the inundated area where troops were sloshing inland. About 11 A.M. Barton got the good news: Exit 3, just one mile away, was open. To ease the pressure Barton immediately sent his tanks rumbling off in the direction of the newly opened exit. The 4th was rolling, rushing toward the link-up with the hard-pressed paratroopers.

When it came, the link-up was unspectacular—lone men meeting one another in unexpected places, often with humorous and emotional results. Corporal Louis Merlano of the 101st may well have been the first airborne soldier to encounter troops of the 4th Division. With two other paratroopers, Merlano, who had landed among the beach obstacles just above the original Utah Beach, had fought his way almost two miles down the coast. He was tired, dirty and battered when he met the 4th Division soldiers. He stared at them for a moment and then asked irritably, "Where the hell have you guys been?"

Sergeant Thomas Bruff of the 101st watched a 4th Division scout come off the causeway near Pouppeville, "carrying his rifle like a squirrel gun." The scout looked at the weary Bruff. "Where's the war?" he inquired. Bruff, who had landed eight miles from his drop zone and had fought all night with a small group under the command of General Maxwell Taylor, growled at the soldier, "Anywhere from here on back. Keep going, buddy, you'll find it."

Near Audouville-la-Hubert, Captain Thomas Mulvey of the 101st was hurrying toward the coast along a dirt road when

---

*For his performance on Utah Roosevelt was awarded the Congressional Medal of Honor. On July 12 General Eisenhower confirmed his appointment as the 90th Division's commanding general. Roosevelt never learned of the appointment. He died that same evening of a heart attack.

"a soldier with a rifle popped into view from the edge of the bushes, about seventy-five yards ahead." Both men dived for cover. Cautiously they emerged, rifles ready, and in wary silence stared at each other. The other man demanded that Mulvey drop his rifle and advance with arms raised. Mulvey suggested that the stranger do the same. "This," says Mulvey, "went on for several go-rounds, with neither of us giving an inch." Finally Mulvey, who could now see that the other man was a U.S. soldier, stood up. The two met in the middle of the road, shook hands and slapped each other on the back.

In Ste.-Marie-du-Mont, Pierre Caldron, the baker, saw paratroopers high in the steeple of the church waving a big orange identification panel. Within a few moments a long line of men, marching in single file, came down the road. As the 4th Division passed through, Caldron lifted his little son high on his shoulders. The boy was not fully recovered from his tonsillectomy of the day before, but this was a sight Caldron did not want his son to miss. Suddenly the baker found himself crying. A stocky U.S. soldier grinned at Caldron and shouted, "*Vive la France!*" Caldron smiled back, nodding his head. He could not trust himself to speak.

Out of the Utah Beach area the 4th Division poured inland. Their D-Day losses were light: 197 casualties, sixty of whom were lost at sea. Terrible fighting lay ahead for the 4th in the next weeks, but this was their day. By evening 22,000 men and 1,800 vehicles would be ashore. With the paratroopers, the 4th Division had secured the first major American beachhead in France.

Savagely, inch by inch, men fought their way off Bloody Omaha. From the sea the beach presented an incredible picture of waste and destruction. The situation was so critical that at noon General Omar Bradley aboard the *Augusta* began to contemplate the possible evacuation of his troops and the diversion of follow-up forces to Utah and the British beaches. But even as Bradley wrestled with the problem, the men in the chaos of Omaha were moving.

Along Dog Green and Dog White, a crusty fifty-one-year-old general named Norman Cota strode up and down in the hail of fire, waving a .45 and yelling at men to get off the beach.

Along the shingle, behind the sea wall and in the coarse beach grass at the base of the bluffs, men crouched shoulder to shoulder, peering at the General, unwilling to believe that a man could stand upright and live.

A group of Rangers lay huddled near the Vierville exit. "Lead the way, Rangers!" Cota shouted. Men began to rise to their feet. Farther down the beach was an abandoned bulldozer loaded with TNT. It was just what was needed to blow the antitank wall at the Vierville exit. "Who drives this thing?" he thundered. No one answered. Men seemed still paralyzed by the merciless gunfire that flayed the beach. Cota began to lose his temper. "Hasn't anyone got guts enough to drive the damn thing?" he roared.

A red-haired soldier got slowly up from the sand and with great deliberation walked over to Cota. "I'll do it," he said.

Cota slapped him on the back. "That's the stuff," the General said. "Now let's get off the beach." He walked away without looking back. Behind him, men began to stir.

This was the pattern. Brigadier General Cota, the 29th Division's assistant commander, had been setting an example almost from the moment he arrived on the beach. He had taken the right half of the 29th's sector; Colonel Charles D. Canham, commanding the 116th, had taken the left. Canham, a bloody handkerchief tied around a wrist wound, moved through the dead, the dying and the shocked, waving groups of men forward. "They're murdering us here!" he said. "Let's move inland and get murdered!" P.F.C. Charles Ferguson looked up in amazement as the Colonel went by. "Who the hell is that son of a bitch?" he asked and then he and the other men with him got up and headed toward the bluffs.

In the 1st Division's half of Omaha Beach, the veterans of Sicily and Salerno came out of the shock faster. Sergeant Raymond Strojny rallied his men and led them up the bluffs through a mine field. On top he knocked out a pillbox with a bazooka. Strojny had become "just a little mad." A hundred yards away Sergeant Philip Streczyk had had his fill of being pinned down, too. Some soldiers remember that Streczyk almost booted men off the beach and up the mined headlands, where he breached the enemy barbed wire. A short while later, Captain Edward Wozenski met Streczyk on a trail running down the bluffs. Horrified, Wozenski saw Streczyk step on a Teller mine. Streczyk said coolly, "It didn't go off when I stepped on it going up, either, Captain."

Ranging up and down the 1st Division sector, oblivious to the artillery and machine gun fire that raked the sands, was the 16th's commanding officer, Colonel George A. Taylor. "Two kinds of people are staying on this beach," he yelled, "the dead and those who are going to die. Now let's get the hell out of here."

Everywhere intrepid leaders, privates and generals alike, were showing the way, getting the men off the beach. Once started, the troops did not stop again. Technical Sergeant William Wiedefeld, Jr., stepped over the dead bodies of a score of his friends and, with face set, went up the hill through the mine fields. Second Lieutenant Donald Anderson, nursing a wound —he had been shot in the back of the neck and the bullet had come out through his mouth—found that he had "the courage to get up, and at that point I changed from a rookie in combat to a veteran." Sergeant Bill Courtney of the 2nd Rangers climbed to the top of a ridge and yelled down to his squad, "Come on up! The s.o.b.s are cleaned out!" Immediately there was a burst of machine gun fire to his left. Courtney wheeled, hurled a couple of grenades and then yelled again, "Come on! Come on! The s.o.b.s are cleaned out *now*!"

Even as the troops began to advance, the first few landing craft began driving right up on the beaches, ramming their way through the obstacles. Coxswains on other boats saw it could be done and followed. Some destroyers, backing up the advance, came so close to the shore that they ran the risk of foundering and, at point-blank range, fired at enemy strongpoints all along the bluffs. Under the covering barrage, engineers began to complete the demolition job they had begun almost seven hours earlier. Everywhere along Omaha Beach the deadlock was breaking up.

As the men found it possible to move forward, their fear and frustration gave way to an overpowering anger. Near the top of the Vierville bluff, Ranger P.F.C. Carl Weast and his company commander, Captain George Whittington, spotted a machine gun nest manned by three Germans. As Weast and the captain circled it cautiously, one of the Germans suddenly turned, saw the two Americans and yelled, "*Bitte! Bitte! Bitte!*" Whittington fired, killing all three. Turning to Weast he said, "I wonder what *bitte* means."

Out of the horror that had been Omaha Beach troops pressed inland. At one-thirty General Bradley would receive the message: "Troops formerly pinned down on beaches Easy Red, Easy Green, Fox Red advancing up heights behind beaches." By the end of the day men of the 1st and 29th divisions would be one mile inland. The cost on Omaha: an estimated 2,500 dead, wounded and missing.

7

It was 1 p.m. when Major Werner Pluskat got back to his headquarters at Etreham. The apparition that came through the door bore little resemblance to the commander his officers knew. Pluskat was shivering like a man with the palsy, and all he could say was, "Brandy. Brandy." When it came his hands shook so uncontrollably that he was almost unable to lift the glass.

One of his officers said, "Sir, the Americans have landed." Pluskat glared and waved him away. His staff crowded around him, one problem uppermost in their minds. The batteries, they informed Pluskat, would soon be low on ammunition. The matter had been reported to regiment, he was told, and Lieutenant Colonel Ocker had said that supplies were on the way. But nothing had arrived as yet. Pluskat rang Ocker.

"My dear Plus," came Ocker's airy voice over the wire, "are you still alive?"

Pluskat ignored the question. "What's happening about the ammunition?" he asked bluntly.

"It's on the way," said Ocker.

The colonel's calmness maddened Pluskat. "When?" he shouted. "When will it arrive? You people don't seem to realize what it's like up here."

Ten minutes later Pluskat was summoned to the phone. "I've got bad news," Ocker told him. "I've just learned that the ammunition convoy has been wiped out. It will be nightfall before anything gets up to you."

Pluskat wasn't surprised; he knew from bitter personal experience that nothing could move along the roads. He also knew that at the rate his guns were firing, the batteries would be out of ammunition by nightfall. The question was, which would reach his guns first—the ammunition or the Americans? Pluskat gave orders for his troops to prepare for close combat and then he wandered aimlessly through the château. He felt suddenly useless and alone. He wished he knew where his dog Harras was.

8

BY NOW the British soldiers who had fought D Day's first battle had been holding on to their prize, the bridges over the Orne and the Caen Canal, for more than thirteen hours. Although Major Howard's glider-borne troops had been re-inforced at dawn by other 6th Airborne paratroopers, their numbers had been steadily dwindling under fierce mortar and small-arms fire. Howard's men had stopped several small, probing counterattacks. Now the tired, anxious troopers in the captured German positions on either side of the bridge eagerly awaited the link-up from the sea.

In his foxhole near the approaches to the Caen Canal bridge, Private Bill Gray looked at his watch again. Lord Lovat's commandos were almost an hour and a half overdue. He wondered what had happened back up on the beaches. Gray didn't think the fighting could be much worse there than it was at the bridges. He was almost afraid to lift his head; it seemed to him the snipers were becoming more accurate by the minute.

It was during a lull in the firing that Gray's friend, Private John Wilkes, lying beside him, suddenly said, "You know, I think I hear bagpipes." Gray looked at him scornfully. "You're daft," he said. A few seconds later, Wilkes turned to his friend again. "I do hear bagpipes," he insisted. Now Gray could hear them too.

Down the road came Lord Lovat's commandos, cocky in their green berets. Bill Millin marched at the head of the col-umn, his pipes blaring out "Blue Bonnets over the Border." On both sides the firing suddenly ceased, as soldiers gazed at the spectacle. But the shock didn't last long. As the com-mandos headed across the bridges the Germans began firing again. Bill Millin remembers that he was "just trusting to luck that I did not get hit, as I could not hear very much for the drone of the pipes." Halfway across, Millin turned around to look at Lord Lovat. "He was striding along as if he was out for a walk round his estate," Millin recalls, "and he gave me the signal to carry on."

Disregarding the heavy German fire, the paratroopers rushed out to greet the commandos. Lovat apologized "for being a few minutes late." To the weary 6th Airborne troopers, it was a stirring moment. Although it would be hours before the main body of British troops reached the farthermost points of the defense line held by the paratroopers, the first reinforcements had arrived. As the red and green berets intermingled, there was a sudden, perceptible lightening of the spirits. Nineteen-year-old Bill Gray felt "years younger."

9

NOW, on this fateful day for Hitler's Third Reich, as Rommel raced frantically for Normandy, as his commanders on the invasion front tried desperately to halt the storming Allied assault, everything depended on the panzers: the 21st Panzer Division just behind the British beaches, and the 12th S.S. and the *Panzer Lehr* still held back by Hitler.

Field Marshal Rommel watched the white ribbon of road stretching out ahead and urged his driver on. "*Tempo! Tempo! Tempo!*" he said. The car roared as Daniel put his foot down. They had left Freudenstadt just two hours before and Rommel had uttered hardly a word. His aide, Captain Lang, sitting in back, had never seen the Field Marshal so depressed. Lang wanted to talk about the landings, but Rommel showed no inclination for conversation. Suddenly Rommel turned around and looked at Lang. "I was right all along," he said, "all along." Then he stared at the road again.

The 21st Panzer Division couldn't get through Caen. Colonel Hermann von Oppeln-Bronikowski, commanding the division's regiment of tanks, drove up and down the column in a Volkswagen. The city was a shambles. It had been bombed some time earlier and the bombers had done a good job. Streets were piled up with debris, and it seemed to Bronikowski that "everyone in the city was on the move trying to get out." The roads were choked with men and women on bicycles. There was no hope for the panzers. Bronikowski decided to pull back and go around the city. It would take hours, he knew, but there was no other way. And where was the regiment of troops that was supposed to support his attack when he did get through?

Nineteen-year-old Private Walter Hermes of the 21st Panzer Division's 192nd Regiment had never been so happy. It was glorious. He was leading the attack against the British! Hermes sat astride his motorcycle, weaving ahead of the advance company. They were heading toward the coast and soon they would pick up the tanks and then the 21st would drive the British into the sea. Everybody said so. Nearby on other motorcycles were his friends, Tetzlaw, Mattusch and Schard. All of them had expected to be attacked by the British before now, but nothing had happened. It seemed strange that they hadn't caught up with the tanks yet. But Hermes guessed that they must be somewhere ahead, probably attacking already on the coast. Hermes drove happily on, leading the advance company of the regiment up into the eight-mile gap that the British commandos still hadn't closed between Juno and Gold. This was a gap the panzers could have exploited to split the British beaches wide open and menace the entire Allied assault—a gap that Colonel von Oppeln-Bronikowski knew nothing whatever about.

In Paris at OB West, Major General Blumentritt, Rundstedt's chief of staff, called Speidel at Rommel's headquarters. The one-sentence conversation was duly recorded in Army Group B's War Diary. "OKW," said Blumentritt, "has released the 12th S.S. and *Panzer Lehr* divisions." The time was 3:40 P.M. Both generals knew that it was too late. Hitler and his senior officers had held up the two panzer divisions for more than ten hours. There was no hope of either division reaching the invasion area on this vital day. The 12th S.S. would not get to the beachhead until the morning of June 7. The *Panzer Lehr*, almost decimated by continuous air attacks, would not arrive until the ninth. The only chance of catching the Allied assault off balance now lay with the 21st Panzer Division.

Close on 6 P.M., Rommel's Horch pulled up in Rheims. In the city commander's headquarters Lang placed a call to La Roche-Guyon. Rommel spent fifteen minutes on the phone, getting a briefing from his chief of staff. When Rommel came out of the office, Lang saw that the news must have been bad. There was silence in the car as they drove off. Sometime later Rommel drove his gloved fist into the palm of his other hand and said, bitterly, "My friendly enemy, Montgomery." Still later, he said, "My God! If the Twenty-first Panzer can make it, we might just be able to drive them back in three days."

North of Caen, Bronikowski gave the order to attack. He sent thirty-five tanks, under the command of Captain Wilhelm von Gottberg, ahead to take the heights at Périers four miles from the coast. Bronikowski himself would try for the ridge at Biéville two miles away with another twenty-five tanks.

General Edgar Feuchtinger, commander of the 21st Panzer, and General Marcks, the 84th Corps commander, had come to see the attack go in. Marcks came over to Bronikowski. He said, "Oppeln, the future of Germany may very well rest on your shoulders. If you don't push the British back into the sea, we've lost the war."

Bronikowski saluted and replied, "General, I intend to do my best."

As they moved up, the tanks fanning out across the fields, Bronikowski was halted by Major General Wilhelm Richter, commander of the 716th Division. Bronikowski saw that Richter "was almost demented with grief." Tears came to his eyes as he told Bronikowski, "My troops are lost. My whole division is finished."

Bronikowski asked, "What can I do, sir? We'll help as best we can." He got out his map and showed it to Richter. "Where are their positions, sir? Will you point them out?"

Richter just shook his head. "I don't know," he said, "I don't know."

Rommel turned half around on the front seat of the Horch and said to Lang, "I hope there isn't a second landing right now from the Mediterranean." He paused for a moment. "Do you know, Lang," he said thoughtfully, "if I was commander of the Allied forces right now, I could finish off the war in fourteen days." He turned back and stared ahead. Lang watched him, miserable, unable to help. The Horch roared on through the evening.

*

Bronikowski's tanks rumbled up the rise at Biéville. So far they had encountered no enemy resistance. Then as the first of his Mark IV tanks neared the top, there was the sudden roar of guns opening up somewhere in the distance. He couldn't tell whether he had run headlong onto British tanks or whether the firing was from antitank guns. But it was accurate and fierce. It seemed to be coming from half a dozen places all at once. Suddenly his lead tank blew up without having fired a shot. Two more tanks moved up, their guns firing. But they seemed to make no impression on the British gunners. Bronikowski began to see why: he was being outgunned. The British guns seemed to have a tremendous range. One after the other Bronikowski's tanks were knocked out. In less than fifteen minutes he lost six tanks. He had never seen such shooting. There was nothing Bronikowski could do. He halted the attack and gave the order to pull back.

Private Walter Hermes couldn't understand where the tanks were. The advance company of the 192nd Regiment had reached the coast at Luc-sur-Mer, but there was no sign of the panzers. There was no sign of the British, either, and Hermes was a little disappointed. But the sight of the invasion fleet almost made up for it. On the coast, off to Hermes' left and right, he saw hundreds of ships and craft moving back and forth, and a mile or so offshore were warships of every description. "Beautiful," he said to his friend Schard. "Just like a parade." Hermes and his friends stretched out on the grass and took out their cigarettes. Nothing seemed to be happening and no one had given them any orders.

The British were already in position on the Périers heights. They stopped Captain Wilhelm von Gottberg's thirty-five tanks even before the panzers got into firing range. In a matter of minutes Gottberg lost ten tanks. The delay in orders, the time wasted trying to get around Caen had given the British the opportunity to consolidate fully their positions on the strategic heights. Gottberg roundly cursed everyone he could think of. He pulled back to the edge of a wood near the village of Lebisey. There he ordered his men to dig in their tanks, hulls down, with only the turrets showing. He was sure the British would drive on Caen within a few hours.

But to Gottberg's surprise time passed without an attack. Then, a little after 9 P.M., Gottberg saw a fantastic sight. There was the slowly mounting roar of planes and, off in the distance against the still-bright evening sun, he saw swarms of gliders coming in over the coast. There were scores of them, flying steadily in formation behind their tow planes. Then as he watched, the gliders were cast off and, wheeling and banking, they came soughing down, to land out of sight somewhere between him and the coast. Gottberg swore angrily.

At Biéville Bronikowski had dug in his tanks, too. As he stood by the side of the road, he watched "German officers with twenty to thirty men apiece, marching back from the front —retreating toward Caen." Bronikowski couldn't understand why the British didn't attack. It seemed to him that "Caen and the whole area could be taken within a few hours."* At the end of the procession Bronikowski saw a sergeant, his arms around two hefty German Wacs. They were "as drunk as pigs, their faces were dirty and they swayed from side to side." Reeling by, oblivious to everything, they sang "Deutschland über Alles" at the top of their voices. Bronikowski watched them until they were out of sight. "The war is lost," he said aloud.

Rommel's Horch purred quietly through La Roche-Guyon, moving slowly by the little houses that shouldered each other on either side of the road. The big black car turned off the highway, passed the sixteen square-cut linden trees and entered the gates of the castle of the Dukes de La Rochefoucauld. As they came to a halt before the door, Lang jumped out and ran ahead to inform Major General Speidel of the Field Marshal's return. In the main corridor he heard the strains of a Wagnerian opera coming from the chief of staff's office. The music welled up as the door suddenly opened and Speidel came out.

Lang was angry and shocked. Forgetting for a moment that

*Although the British made D Day's greatest advances, they failed to capture their principal objective—Caen. Bronikowski was to stay in position with his tanks for more than six weeks—until the city finally fell.

he was talking to a general, he snapped, "How can you possibly play opera at a time like this?"

Speidel smiled and said, "My dear Lang, you don't think that my playing a little music is going to stop the invasion, now do you?"

Down the corridor strode Rommel in his long blue-gray field coat, his silver-topped marshal's baton in his right hand. He walked into Speidel's office and, hands clasped behind his back, stood looking at the map. Speidel closed the door, and Lang, knowing that this conference would last some time, made his way to the dining room. Wearily he sat down at one of the long tables and ordered a cup of coffee from the orderly. Nearby another officer was reading a paper. He looked up. "How was the trip?" he asked pleasantly. Lang just stared at him.

On the Cherbourg peninsula near Ste.-Mère-Église, Private Dutch Schultz of the 82nd Airborne leaned against the side of a foxhole and listened to a distant church bell sounding eleven. He could hardly keep his eyes open. He figured he had been awake now almost seventy-two hours—ever since the postponement on the night of June 4 when he had joined in the crap game. It struck him as funny that he had gone to so much trouble to lose all his winnings—nothing at all had happened to him. In fact, Dutch felt a little sheepish. He had not fired a single shot all day.

Back of Omaha Beach, beneath the bluffs, Medic Staff Sergeant Alfred Eigenberg flopped wearily into a crater. He had lost count of the number of casualties he had treated. He was bone-tired, but there was one thing he wanted to do before he fell asleep. Eigenberg fished a crumpled sheet of V-mail paper out of his pocket and, with the aid of a flashlight, settled down to write home. He scribbled, "Somewhere in France," and then began, "Dear Mom and Dad, I know that by now you've heard of the invasion. Well, I'm all right." Then the nineteen-year-old medic stopped. He couldn't think of anything more to say.

Down on the beach Brigadier General Norman Cota watched the "cat's eyes" blackout lights of trucks and heard the shouts of the MPs and beachmasters as they moved men and vehicles inland. Here and there landing craft still burned, throwing a ruddy glare into the night sky. The surf pounded the shore, and somewhere off in the distance Cota heard the lonely stutter of a machine gun. Suddenly Cota felt very tired. A truck rumbled toward him and Cota flagged it down. He stepped up onto the running board and hooked one arm around the door. For just a moment he looked back at the beach, then he said to the driver, "Run me up the hill, son."

At Rommel's headquarters Lang, like everyone else, had heard the bad news: the 21st Panzer attack had failed. Lang was very depressed. He said to the Field Marshal, "Sir, do you think we can drive them back?"

Rommel shrugged, spread his hands and said, "Lang, I hope we can. I've nearly always succeeded up to now." Then he patted Lang on the shoulder. "You look tired," he said. "Why don't you go to bed? It's been a long day." He turned away and Lang watched him walk down the corridor to his office. The door closed softly behind him.

Outside, nothing stirred in the two great cobbled courtyards. La Roche-Guyon was silent. Soon this most occupied of all French villages would be free—as would the whole of Hitler's Europe. From this day on the Third Reich had less than one year to live. Beyond the castle gates the main road stretched broad and empty and the windows of the red-roofed houses were shuttered. In the Church of St. Samson the bell tolled midnight.

A NOTE ON CASUALTIES

Over the years a variety of vague and contradictory figures have been given on the losses sustained by Allied troops during the twenty-four-hour period of the assault. None of them can be said to be accurate. At best they must remain estimates, for by the very nature of the assault it was impossible for anyone to arrive at an exact figure. In general most military historians agree that the total Allied casualties reached 10,000; some even put the figure at 12,000.

American casualties are put at 6,603. This figure is based on the U.S. First Army's after-action report, which gives the following breakdown: 1,465 killed, 3,184 wounded, 1,928 missing and 26 captured. Included in this compilation are 82nd and 101st Airborne losses, which alone are estimated at 2,499 killed, wounded and missing.

The Canadians had 946 casualties, of which 335 were killed. No British figures have ever been issued, but it is estimated that they had at least 2,500 to 3,000 casualties, of which the 6th Airborne suffered losses of 650 killed, wounded and missing.

What were the German D-Day losses? No one can say. In my interviews with senior German officers I was given estimates ranging from 4,000 to 9,000. But by the end of June, Rommel was to report that his casualties for the month were "28 generals, 354 commanders and approximately 250,000 men."

D-DAY VETERANS

What They Do Today

In the following lists of contributors, all ranks shown are those as of D Day. Occupations may have changed for some men during the months since the lists were compiled.

AMERICAN

Accardo, Nick J., Lt. [4th Div.] *Orthopedic surgeon, New Orleans, La.*

Adams, Ernest C., Lt. Col. [1st Eng. Sp. Brig.] *Col., U.S. Army*

Adams, Jonathan E., Jr., Capt. [82nd Airborne] *Lt. Col., U.S. Army*

Albanese, Salvatore A., S/Sgt. [1st Div.] *Payroll clerk, Verplanck, N.Y.*

Albrecht, Denver, 2nd Lt. [82nd Airborne] *W/Off., U.S. Army*

Allen, Miles L., Pfc. [101st Airborne] *SFC, U.S. Army*

Allen, Robert M., Pfc. [1st Div.] *High-school teacher, athletic coach, Oelwein, Iowa*

Allen, Walter K., T/S [467th AAA (AW) Bn.] *Farmer, Monmouth, Iowa*

Allison, Jack L., Pvt. [237th Eng.] *Accountant, Chester, W. Va.*

Alpaugh, Stanley H., 2nd Lt. [4th Div.] *Maj., U.S. Army*

Anderson, C. W., Pfc. [4th Div.] *Sgt., Military Police supervisor, U.S. Army*

Anderson, Donald C., Lt. [29th Div.] *Flight test engineer*, General Dynamics, *Edwards, Cal.*

Anderson, Donald D., Sgt. [4th Div.] *Dealer, timber products, Effie, Minn.*

Anderson, Martin H., Stm 1/c [11th & 12th Amphibious Force, USN] *A/2c, U.S.A.F.*

Apel, Joel H., 1st Lt. [457th Bomb Group] *Squadron Cdr., U.S.A.F.*

Apostolas, George N., T/4 [397th AAA Bn.] *Service officer*, Illinois Veterans Commission

Appleby, Sam, Jr., Cpl. [82nd Airborne] *Attorney, Ozark, Mo.*

Araiza, Joe L., Sgt. [446th Bomb Group] *M/Sgt., U.S.A.F.*

Arman, Robert C., Lt. [2nd Rangers] *Capt., Disability retirement, Lafayette, Ind.*

Armellino, John R., Capt. [1st Div.] *Mayor, West New York, N.J.*

Armstrong, Louis M., T/Sgt. [29th Div.] *Post-office clerk, Staunton, Va.*

Arnold, Edgar L., Capt. [2nd Rangers] *Lt. Col., U.S. Army*

Asay, Charles V., Sgt. [101st Airborne] *Linotype operator*, Placer Herald, *Auburn, Cal.*

Ashby, Carroll A., S/Sgt. [29th Div.] Lt.; *Advisor, Army reserve unit, Arlington, Va.*

Azbill, Boyce, Q.M. 2/c [U.S.C.G. LCI (L) 94] *Branch manager*, U.S. Pipe & Supply Co., *Tucson, Ariz.*

Baechle, Joseph W., Sgt. [5th Eng. Spec. Brig.] *Accountant, Cleveland, Ohio*

Bagley, Frank H., Lt. [U.S.S. *Herndon*] *Branch manager*, De Laval Steam Turbine Co., *Milwaukee, Wis.*

Baier, Harold L., Ens. [7th Naval Beach Bn.] *Doctor (Biological research), Frederick, Md.*

Bailey, Edward A., Lt. Col. [65th Armored Field Artillery Bn.] *Col., U.S. Army*

Bailey, Rand S., Lt. Col. [1st Eng. Sp. Brig.] *Ret'd; Part time, Consultant,* Rural Electrification Administration, *Washington, D.C.*

Baker, Richard J., Lt. [344th Bomb Group] *Maj., U.S.A.F.*

Balcer, Charles I., Lt. [HQ VII Corps] *Maj., U.S. Army*

Ball, Sam H., Jr., Capt. [146th Eng.] *Television account executive*, KCMC-TV, *Texarkana, Tex.*

Barber, Alex W., Pfc. [5th Rangers] *Chiropractor, Johnstown, Pa.*

Barber, George R., Capt. (chaplain), [1st Div.] *Minister & investment adviser, Montebello, Cal.*

Barrett, Carlton W., Pvt. [1st Div.] *SFC, U.S. Army*

Barton, Raymond O., Maj. Gen. [C.O. 4th Div.] Southern Finance Corp., *Augusta, Ga.*

Bass, Hubert S., Capt. [82nd Airborne] *Maj. (retired), Houston, Tex.*

Bassett, Leroy A., Pvt. [29th Div.] *Claims examiner*, Veterans Administration, *Fargo, N. Dak.*

Batte, James H., Lt. Col. [87th Chem. Mortar Bn.] *Col., U.S. Army*

Bearden, Robert L., Sgt. [82nd Airborne] Bearden's Personal Service, *Fort Hood, Tex.*

Beaver, Neal W., 2nd Lt. [82nd Airborne] *Cost accountant, Toledo, Ohio*

Beck, Carl A., Pvt. [82nd Airborne] *Engineering parts inspector*, IBM, *Poughkeepsie, N.Y.*

Beeks, Edward A., Pfc. [457th AAA AW Bn.] *Foreman mechanic, Scobey, Montana*

Beer, Robert O., Comdr. [U.S.S. *Carmick*] *Capt., U.S. Navy*

Belisle, Maurice A., Capt. [1st Div.] *Lt. Col., U.S. Army*

Belmont, Gail H., S/Sgt. [2nd Rangers] *Capt., U.S. Army*

Bengel, Wayne P., Pvt. [101st Airborne] *Senior clerk*, Cunard Steamship Co., Ltd., *Pittsburgh, Pa.*

Billings, Henry J., Cpl. [101st Airborne] *Chief W/Off., U.S. Army*

Billiter, Norman W., Sgt. [101st Airborne] *Chief parachute inspector, Fort Benning, Ga.*

Bingham, Sidney V., Maj. [29th Div.] *Col., U.S. Army*

Blackstock, James P., S/Sgt. [4th Div.] *Optician, Philadelphia, Pa.*

Blakeley, Harold W., Brig. Gen., C.O. [4th Div., Artillery] *Maj. Gen., U.S. Army (retired)*

Blanchard, Ernest R., Pfc. [82nd Airborne] *Machinist*, E. Ingraham Clock Co., *Bristol, Conn.*

Bodet, Alan C., Cpl. [1st Div.] *Assistant cashier*, Guaranty Bank & Trust Co., *Jackson, Miss.*

Boice, William S., Capt. (chaplain) [4th Div.] *Minister*, First Christian Church, *Phoenix, Ariz.*

Boling, Rufus C., Jr., Pvt. [4th Div.] *Apartment-house superintendent, Brooklyn, N.Y.*

Bombardier, Carl E., Pfc. [2nd Rangers] *Tractor operator, shipper*, Procter & Gamble Mfg. Co., *North Abington, Mass.*

Bour, Lawrence J., Capt. [1st Div.] *Lt. Col., U.S. Army*

Boyd, Dale E., Lt. [1st Div.] *Editor*, Pocahontas Democrat, *Pocahontas, Iowa*

Bradley, Omar N., Lieut. Gen. [C.O. U.S. 1st Army] *General of the Army; Chairman*, Bulova Watch Co., *New York, N.Y.*

Brandt, Jerome N., Capt. [5th Eng. Sp. Brig.] *Lt. Col., U.S. Army*

Brannen, Malcolm D., Lt. [82nd Airborne] *Maj.*; Stetson University ROTC, *DeLand, Fla.*

Brewer, S. D., Seaman 1/c [U.S.S. *Arkansas*] *Post-office clerk, Hackleburg, Ala.*

Briel, Raymond C., Sgt. [1st Div.] *M/Sgt., U.S.A.F.*

Brinson, William L., Capt. [315th Troop Carrier Group] *Lt. Col., U.S.A.F.*

Broughman, Warner A., Capt. [101st Airborne] *Vocational-education director*, U.S. Public Health Hospital, *Lexington, Ky.*

Brown, Harry, Sgt. [4th Div.] *Optometrist, Clawson, Mich.*

Bruen, James J., Sgt. [29th Div.] *Police officer, Cleveland, Ohio*

Bruff, Thomas B., Sgt. [101st Airborne] *Capt., U.S. Army*

Bruno, Joseph J., Seaman 1/c [U.S.S. *Texas*] *Freight traffic clerk, U.S. Army, Pittsburgh, Pa.*

Bryan, Keith, Sgt. [5th Eng. Sp. Brig.] *Veteran's service officer, Columbus, Neb.*

Buckheit, John P., Seaman 1/c [U.S.S. *Herndon*] *Guard*, Olmsted A.F. Base, *Harrisburg, Pa.*

Buckley, Walter, Jr., Lt. Comdr. [U.S.S. *Nevada*] *Capt., U.S. Navy*

Buffalo Boy, Herbert J., S/Sgt. [82nd Airborne] *Ranch hand, farmer, Fort Yates, N. Dak.*

Burke, John L., Cpl. [5th Rangers] *Sales supervisor*, A. H. Robins Inc., *Delmar, N.Y.*

Burlingame, William G., Lt. [355th Fighter Group] *Maj., U.S.A.F.*

Burt, Gerald H., Cpl. [299th Engrs.] *Pipe fitter, Niagara Falls, N.Y.*

Busby, Louis A., Jr., Watertender 1/c [U.S.S. *Carmick*] *Chief boilerman*, U.S.S. *Saratoga*

Butler, John C., Jr., Capt. [5th Eng. Sp. Brig.] *Realty officer*, Bureau of Indian Affairs, *Arlington, Va.*

Byers, John C., T/Sgt. [441st Troop Carrier Group] *Mechanical engineer, San Pedro, Cal.*

Caffey, Eugene M., Col. [1st Eng. Sp. Brig.] *Maj. Gen.* (*retired*); *attorney*, Darden & Caffey, *Las Cruces, N.M.*

Callahan, William R., Capt. [29th Div.] *Maj., U.S. Army*

Canham, Charles D. W., Col. [29th Div.] *Maj. Gen., U.S. Army*

Canoe, Buffalo Boy, T/Sgt. [82nd Airborne] *Judo instructor, Venice, Calif.*

Capobianco, Gaetano, Pfc. [4th Div.] *Butcher, Easton, Pa.*

Carden, Fred J., Pfc. [82nd Airborne] *Airborne technician, U.S. Army*

Carey, James R., Jr., Sgt. [8th AF] *Carey's West Side Service, Ossian, Iowa*

Carlo, Joseph W., Hosp. Corpsman [LST 288] *Lt.* (*chaplain*), *U.S. Navy*

Carlstead, Harold C., Ensign [U.S.S. *Herndon*] *Accountant; teacher*, Northwestern University School of Business, *Chicago, Ill.*

Carpenter, Joseph B., F/O [410th Bomb Group] *M/Sgt., U.S.A.F.*

Carroll, John B., Lt. [1st Div.] *Public relations*, Glass Container & Mfrs. Assn., *New York, N.Y.*

Cascio, Charles J., Seaman 2/c [LST 312] *Mail carrier, Endicott, N.Y.*

Cason, Lee B., Cpl. [4th Div.] *M/Sgt., U.S. Army*

Cassel, Thomas E., Specialist 2/c [Task Force 122-3] *Capt., fire department, New York, N.Y.*

Cator, Richard D., Pfc. [101st Airborne] *Lt., U.S. Army*

Cawthon, Charles R., Capt. [29th Div.] *Lt. Col., U.S. Army*

Chance, Donald L., S/Sgt. [5th Rangers] *Safety engineer*, Yale & Towne Mfg. Co., *Philadelphia, Pa.*

Chase, Charles H., Lt. Col. [101st Airborne] *Brig. Gen., U.S. Army*

Chase, Lucius P., Col. [6th Eng. Sp. Brig.] *General counsel & director*, Kohler Co., *Kohler, Wis.*

Chesnut, Webb W., Lt. [1st Div.] Production Credit Association, *Campbellsville, Ky.*

Chontos, Ernest J., Pvt. [1st Div.] *Realtor, Ashtabula, Ohio*

Ciarpelli, Frank, Pvt. [1st Div.] *Sanitation inspector*, Health Department, *Rochester, N.Y.*

Cirinese, Salvatore, Pfc. [4th Div.] *Shoe repairman, Miami, Fla.*

Clark, William R., Capt. [5th Eng. Sp. Brig.] *Postmaster, Loysville, Pa.*

Clayton, William J., S/Sgt. [4th Div.] *Clerk*, Railway Express Agency, *Philadelphia, Pa.*

Clements, Edgar, S/Sgt. [4th Div.] *Painter, Dunbar, Pa.*

Cleveland, William H., Col. [HQ 325th Recon. Wing] *Col., U.S.A.F.*

Clifford, Richard W., Capt. [4th Div.] *Dental surgeon, Hudson Falls, N.Y.*

Cochran, Sam L., T/Sgt. [4th Div.] *Capt., U.S. Army*

Coffey, Vernon C., Pvt. [37th Engrs.] *Owner, meat packing, frozen-food-processing firm, Houghton, Iowa*

Coffman, Ralph S., S/Sgt. [29th Div.] *Truck driver*, Southern States Augusta Petroleum Cooperative, *Staunton, Va.*

Coffman, Warren G., Pfc. [1st Div.] *Capt., U.S. Army*

Coleman, Max D., Pfc. [5th Rangers] *Baptist minister, Clarkston, Mo.*

Collins, J. Lawton, Maj. Gen. [C.O., 7th Corps] *Gen. (retired); Chairman*, Charles Pfizer Co., *Washington, D.C.*

Collins, Thomas E., 2nd Lt. [93rd Bomb Group] *Statistician*, Northrop Aircraft Inc., *Gardena, Calif.*

Conley, Richard H., 2nd Lt. [1st Div.] *Capt., U.S. Army*

Conover, Charles M., Lt. [1st Div.] *Lt. Col., U.S. Army*

Cook, William, Ensign [LCT 588] *Comdr., U.S. Navy*

Cook, William S., Signalman 3/c [2nd Beach Bn.] *Manager, grain elevator, Flasher, N. Dak.*

Cooper, John P., Jr., Col. [29th Div.] *Brig. Gen. (retired); executive*, Baltimore Telephone Co. *Baltimore, Md.*

Copas, Marshall, Sgt. [101st Airborne] *M/Sgt., U.S. Army*

Corky, John T., Lt. Col. [1st Div.] *Col., U.S. Army*

Cota, Norman D., Brig. Gen. [29th Div.] *Maj. Gen. (retired), Civil Defense director, Montgomery Co., Pa.*

Couch, Riley C., Jr., Capt. [90th Div.] *Farmer and rancher, Haskell, Texas*

Cox, John F., Cpl. [434th Troop Carrier Group] *Lt., fire department, Binghamton, N.Y.*

Coyle, James J., 2nd Lt. [82nd Airborne] *Accountant,* American Tobacco Co., *New York, N.Y.*

Crawford, Ralph O., Chief W/Off. [1st Eng. Sp. Brig.] *Postmaster, Dilley, Texas*

Crispen, Frederick J., 2nd Lt. [436th Troop Carrier Group] *M/Sgt., U.S.A.F.*

Cross, Herbert A., 2nd Lt. [4th Div.] *Principal, elementary school, Oneida, Tenn.*

Crowder, Ralph H., Cpl. [4th Div.] *Owner,* Mick's Glass Shop, *Radford, Va.*

Crowley, Thomas T., Maj. [1st Div.] *General manager,* Division of Crucible Steel Corp., *Pittsburgh, Pa.*

Cryer, William J., Jr., 2nd Lt. [96th Bomb Group] *Partner and General Manager, boat-building and repair yard, Oakland, Calif.*

Cunningham, Robt. E., Capt. [1st Div.] *Photoengraving; author, Stillwater, Okla.*

Dahlen, Johan B., Capt. (chaplain) [1st Div.] *Pastor, Lutheran church, Churchs Ferry, N. Dak.*

Dallas, Thomas S., Maj. [29th Div.] *Lt. Col., U.S. Army*

Danahy, Paul A., Maj. [101st Airborne] *Manufacturer's Representative, Minneapolis, Minn.*

Dance, Eugene A., Lt. [101st Airborne] *Maj., U.S. Army*

Daniel, Derrill M., Lt. Col. [1st Div.] *Maj. Gen., U.S. Army*

Dasher, Benedict J., Capt. [6th Eng. Sp. Brig.] *President,* Universe Life Insurance Co., *Reno, Nev.*

Daughtrey, John E., Lt. (j.g.) [6th Beach Bn.,] *Doctor (general surgery), Lakeland, Fla.*

Davis, Barton A., Sgt. [299th Engrs.] *Assistant treasurer,* Hardinge Brothers, Inc., *Elmira, N.Y.*

Davis, Kenneth S., Comdr. U.S.C.G. [U.S.S. *Bayfield*] *Capt., U.S. Coast Guard*

Dawson, Francis W., Lt. [5th Rangers] *Maj., U.S. Army*

De Benedetto, Russell J., Pfc. [90th Div.] *Realtor, Port Allen, La.*

de Chiara, Albert, Jr., Ens. [U.S.S. *Herndon*] *Manufacturer's representative, Passaic, N.J.*

Deery, Lawrence E., Capt. (chaplain) [1st Div.] *Priest,* St. Joseph's, *Newport, R.I.*

Degnan, Irwin J., 2nd Lt. [HQ V Corps] *Insurance agent, Guttenberg, Iowa*

DeMayo, Anthony J., Pfc. [82nd Airborne] *Foreman, electrical construction, New York, N.Y.*

Depace, V. N., Pvt. [29th Div.] *Internal Revenue agent, Pittsburgh, Pa.*

Derda, Fred, Signalman 1/c U.S.C.G. [LCI (L) 90] *Chiropractor, St. Louis, Mo.*

Derickson, Richard B., Lt. Comdr. [U.S.S. *Texas*] *Capt., U.S. Navy*

Desjardins, J. L., CM 3/c [3rd Naval Const. Bn.] *Police Department Custodian, Leominster, Mass.*

Di Benedetto, Angelo, Pfc. [4th Div.] *Letter carrier, Brooklyn, N.Y.*

Dickson, Archie L., Lt. [434th Troop Carrier Group] *Insurance agent, Gulfport, Miss.*

Dokich, Nicholas, Jr., Torpedoman [PT boat] *Torpedoman 3/c, U.S. Navy*

Dolan, John J., Lt. [82nd Airborne] *Attorney, Boston, Mass.*

Donahue, Thomas F., Pfc. [82nd Airborne] *Clerk,* A. and P. Tea Co., *Brooklyn, N.Y.*

Doss, Adrian R., Sr., Pfc. [101st Airborne] *Spec. 1/c, U.S. Army*

Doyle, George T., Pfc. [90th Div.] *Printer, Parma Heights, Ohio*

Dube, Noel A., Sgt. [121st Engrs.] *Administrative Assistant, Air Force Commissary, Pease A.F. Base, N.H.*

Dulligan, John F., Capt. [1st Div.] *Veteran's Administration, Boston, Mass.*

Dunn, Edward C., Lt. Col. [4th Cav. Recon.] *Col., U.S. Army*

Duquette, Donald M., Sgt. [254th Engrs.] *M/Sgt., U.S. Army*

Dwyer, Harry A., Chief Signalman [5th Div. Amphibious Force] *Storekeeper, Veterans Hospital, Sepulveda, Calif.*

Eades, Jerry W., Sgt. [62nd Armored Bn.] *Lead-man, aircraft factory, Arlington, Texas*

East, Charles W., Capt. [29th Div.] *Underwriter, Staunton, Va.*

Eastus, Dalton L., Pvt. [4th Div.] *Meterman,* Indiana and Michigan Electric Co., *Marion, Ind.*

Eaton, Ralph P., Col. [82nd Airborne] *Brig. Gen. (retired), U.S. Army*

Echols, Eugene S., Maj. [5th Eng. Sp. Brig.] *City Engineer, Memphis, Tenn.*

Edelman, Hyman, Pvt. [4th Div.] *Liquor-store owner, Brooklyn, N.Y.*

Edlin, Robert T., Lt. [2nd Rangers] *Insurance agent supervisor,* Universal Life Insurance Co., *Bloomington, Ind.*

Edmond, Emil V. B., Capt. [1st Div.] *Lt. Col., U.S. Army*

Eichelbaum, Arthur, Lt. [29th Div.] *Vice-president, sales, Sands Point, L.I., N.Y.*

Eigenberg, Alfred, S/Sgt. [6th Eng. Sp. Brig.] *Lt., U.S. Army*

Eisemann, William J., Lt. (j.g.) [Rocket Support Div.] *Staff Assistant,* New England Mutual Life Insurance Co., *Bethpage, L.I., N.Y.*

Ekman, William E., Lt. Col. [82nd Airborne] *Col., U.S. Army*

Elinski, John, Pfc. [4th Div.] *Night shipper,* Keebler Biscuit Co., *Philadelphia, Pa.*

Ellery, John B., S/Sgt. [1st Div.] *Professor,* Wayne State University, *Royal Oak, Mich.*

Elliott, Robert C., Pvt. [4th Div.] *Disabled, Passaic, N.J.*

Erd, Claude G., Ch. W/Off. [1st Div.] *M/Sgt.,* University of Kentucky, *ROTC, Lexington, Ky.*

Erwin, Leo F., Pvt. [101st Airborne] *SFC Mess Steward, U.S. Army*

Ewell, Julian J., Lt. Col. [101st Airborne] *Col., U.S. Army*

Fainter, Francis, F., Col. [6th Armored Grp.] *Rep., N.Y. Stock Exchange,* Westheimer & Co., *Charleston, W. Va.*

Fanning, Arthur E., Lt. U.S.C.G. [LCI (L) 319] *Insurance, Philadelphia, Pa.*

Fanto, James A., Radioman 1/c [6th Beach Bn.] *Chief Radioman, U.S. Navy*

Farr, H. Bartow, Lt. (j.g.) [U.S.S. *Herndon*] *Attorney*, IBM, *New York, N.Y.*

Faulk, Willie T., S/Sgt. [409th Bomb Group] *M/Sgt., U.S.A.F.*

Ferguson, Charles A., Pfc. [6th Eng. Sp. Brig.] *Price specialist*, Western Electric Co., Inc., *New York, N.Y.*

Ferguson, Vernon V., Lt. [452nd Bomb Group] *Occupation unknown*

Ferro, Samuel Joseph, Pfc. [299th Engrs.] *Machinist, Binghamton, N.Y.*

Finnigan, William E., Pvt. [4th Div.] *Personnel assistant*, U.S. Military Academy, *West Point, N.Y.*

Fish, Lincoln D., Capt. [1st Div.] *President, paper company, Worcester, Mass.*

Fitzsimmons, Robert C., Lt. [2nd Rangers] *Police lieutenant, Niagara Falls, N.Y.*

Flanagan, Larry, Pvt. [4th Div.] *Salesman, Philadelphia, Pa.*

Flora, John L., Jr., Capt. [29th Div.] *Real-estate appraiser*, FHA, *Roanoke, Va.*

Flowers, Melvin L., 2nd Lt. [441st Troop Carrier Grp.] *Capt., U.S.A.F.*

Flynn, Bernard J., 2nd Lt. [1st Div.] *Supervisor, package design*, General Mills Inc., *Minneapolis, Minn.*

Forgy, Samuel W., Lt. Col. [1st Eng. Sp. Brig.] *President*, The Carabela Trading Co., Inc., *Manhasset, L.I., N.Y.*

Fowler, Rollin B., F/Off. [435th Troop Carrier Group] *M/Sgt., U.S.A.F.*

Fox, Jack, S/Sgt. [4th Div.] *Capt., U.S. Army*

Francis, Jack L., Cpl. [82nd Airborne] *Roofer, Sacramento, Calif.*

Franco, Robert, Capt. [82nd Airborne] *Surgeon, Richland, Wash.*

French, Gerald M., Lt. [450th Bomb Group] *Capt., U.S.A.F.*

Frey, Leo, Ch. Machinist Mate [LST 16] *W/Off., U.S.C.G.*

Friedman, William, Capt. [1st Div.] *Lt. Col., U.S. Army*

Frisby, Ralph E., 2nd Lt. [29th Div.] *Grocery-store owner, Okmulgee, Okla.*

Frische, William C., Jr., S/Sgt. [4th Div.] *Draftsman*, Gibson Art Co., *Cincinnati, Ohio*

Frohman, Howard J., S/Sgt. [401st Bomb Grp.] *Capt., U.S.A.F.*

Funderburke, Arthur, S/Sgt. [20th Engrs.] *Salesman*, Coca-Cola Bottling Co., *Macon, Ga.*

Gagliardi, Edmund J., SC/3c [LCT 637] *Police officer, Ambridge, Pa.*

Gardner, Edwin E., Pfc. [29th Div.] *Letter carrier, Plainville, Kansas*

Gaskins, Charles Ray, Cpl. [4th Div.] *Owner and operator*, Esso Service Center, *Kannapolis, N.C.*

Gavin, James M., Brig. Gen. [82nd Airborne, Ass't Div. Comdr.] *Lt. Gen. (retired); vice-president*, Arthur D. Little Inc., *Wellesley Hills, Mass.*

Gearing, Edward M., 2nd Lt. [29th Div.] *Assistant division comptroller*, NEMS, Division of Vitro Corp. of America, *Chevy Chase, Md.*

Gee, Ernest L., T/Sgt. [82nd Airborne] *Owner*, Mission Yellow Cab Co., *San Jose, Calif.*

Gerhardt, Charles H., Maj. Gen. [C.O., 29th Div.] *Maj. Gen. (retired), Florida*

Gerow, Leonard T., Maj. Gen. [C.O., 5th Corps] *Gen. (retired); Bank director, Petersburg, Va.*

Gervasi, Frank M., S/Sgt. [1st Div.] *Plant guard, Monroeville, Pa.*

Gibbons, Joseph H., Lt. Comdr. [C.O. Naval Combat Demolition units] *Sales Manager*, N.Y. Telephone Co., *New York, N.Y.*

Gibbons, Ulrich G., Lt. Col. [4th Div.] *Col., U.S. Army*

Gift, Melvin R., Pvt. [87th Chem. Mortar Bn.] *Dispatch clerk, Chambersburg, Pa.*

Gilhooly, John, Pfc. [2nd Rangers] *Store manager*, A. & P. Tea Co., *Roosevelt, L.I., N.Y.*

Gill, Dean Dethroe, Sgt. [4th Cav. Recon.] *Cook, Veterans Hosp., Lincoln, Neb.*

Gillette, John Lewis, Signalman 3/c [2nd Beach Bn.] *Teacher*, Wheatland-Chili Central School, *Scottsville, N.Y.*

Glisson, Bennie W., Radioman 3/c [U.S.S. *Corry*] *Teletype operator*

Goldman, Murray, S/Sgt. [82nd Airborne] *Sales supervisor*, Reddi-Wip Corp., *Monticello, N.Y.*

Goldstein, Joseph I., Pvt. [4th Div.] *Insurance, Sioux City, Iowa*

Goode, Robert Lee, Sgt. [29th Div.] *Mechanic, Bedford, Va.*

Goodmundson, Carl T., Signalman 2/c [U.S.S. *Quincy*] *Telegrapher*, Great Northern Railroad, *Minneapolis, Minn.*

Goranson, Ralph E., Capt. [2nd Rangers] *Director of Overseas Operations*, The E. F. MacDonald Co., *Dayton, Ohio*

Gordon, Fred, SPC [90th Div.] *SP-3, U.S. Army*

Gowdy, George, Lt. [65th Armored Bn.] *Fisherman, St. Petersburg, Fla.*

Greco, Joseph J., Pfc. [299th Engrs.] *Manager*, United Whelan Corp., *Syracuse, N.Y.*

Greenstein, Carl R., 2nd Lt. [93rd Bomb Group] *Capt., U.S.A.F.*

Greenstein, Murray, Lt. [95th Bomb Group] *Installment sales, owner, Bradley Beach, N.J.*

Griffiths, William H., Ens. [U.S.S. *Herndon*] *Comdr., U.S. Navy*

Grissinger, John P., 2nd Lt. [29th Div.] *General Agency for* Mutual Trust Life Insurance Co. of Chicago, *Harrisburg, Pa.*

Grogan, Harold M., T/5 [4th Div.] *U.S. Post Office, Vicksburg, Miss.*

Gudehus, Judson, Lt. [389th Bomb Group] *Salesman*, Toledo Optical Laboratory, *Toledo, Ohio*

Hackett, George R., Jr., Signalman 3/c [LCT Flot. 17] *Q/M 2/c, U.S. Navy*

Hahn, William I., Seaman 1/c [Husky Support Boat Crew] *Coal-mine operator, Wilkes-Barre, Pa.*

Hale, Bartley E., 2nd Lt. [82nd Airborne] *Student*, University of Georgia

Haley, James W., Capt. [4th Div.] *Col., U.S. Army*

Hall, Charles G., 1st Sgt. [4th Div.] *Chief W/Off., U.S.A.F.*

Hall, John Leslie, Jr., Rear Admiral [Assault Force O, Comdr.] *Rear Adm. (retired), U.S. Navy*

Hamlin, Paul A., Jr., Pvt. [299th Eng.] *Reclamation analyst*, IBM, *Vestal, N.Y.*

Hamner, Theodore S., Jr., S/Sgt. [82nd Airborne] *Floor foreman*, B. F. Goodrich Co., *Tuscaloosa, Ala.*

Hanson, Howard K., Pvt. [90th Div.] *Postmaster and farmer, Argusville, N. Dak.*

Harken, Delbert C., MoMM 3/c [LST 134] *Acting postmaster, Ackley, Iowa*

Harker, George S., Lt. [5th Eng. Sp. Brig.] *Research psychologist, Fort Knox, Ky.*

Harrington, James C., Lt. [355th Fighter Group] *Maj., U.S.A.F.*

Harrison, Thomas C., Capt. [4th Div.] *Sales manager*, Henry I. Christal Co., *Chappaqua, N.Y.*

Harrisson, Charles B., Pfc. [1st Eng. Sp. Brig.] *Insurance, Lansdowne, Pa.*

Harwood, Jonathan H., Jr., Capt. [2nd Rangers] *Deceased*

Hass, William R., Jr., Fl/Off. [441st Troop Carrier Group] *Capt., U.S.A.F.*

Hatch, James J., Capt. [101st Airborne] *Col., U.S. Army*

Havener, John K., Lt. [344th Bomb Group] *Materials controller*, International Harvester Co., *Sterling, Ill.*

Haynie, Ernest W., Sgt. [29th Div.] *Store clerk, marine engine supplies, Warsaw, Va.*

Heefner, Mervin C., Pfc. [29th Div.] *Occupation unknown*

Heikkila, Frank E., Lt. Col. [6th Eng. Sp. Brig.] *Customer relations*, Westinghouse Electric Corp., *Pittsburgh, Pa.*

Henley, Clifford M., Capt. [4th Div.] *Road contracting, Summerville, S.C.*

Hennon, Robert M., Capt. (chaplain) [82nd Airborne] *Minister, Supervisor*, Evangelical Children's Home, *Brentwood, Miss.*

Herlihy, Raymond M., Sgt. [5th Rangers] *Tax Representative*, Prentice-Hall publishers, *Bronx, N.Y.*

Hermann, LeRoy W., Pfc. [1st Div.] *Parcel-post carrier, Akron, Ohio*

Hern, Earlston E., Pfc. [146th Engrs.] *Agent telegrapher*, Atchison, Topeka & Santa Fe Railway Co., *Medford, Okla.*

Herron, Beryl A., Pfc. [4th Div.] *Farmer, Coon Rapids, Iowa*

Hicks, Herbert C., Jr., Lt. Col. [1st Div.] *Col., U.S. Army*

Hicks, Joseph A., Capt. [531st Eng. Shore Regt.] *Board chairman*, Commonwealth Fertilizer Co., *Russellville, Ky.*

Hill, Joel G., T/4 [102nd Cavalry Recon.] *Sawmill and logging operation, Lookout, Pa.*

Hodgson, John C., Sgt. [5th Rangers] *Post-office worker, Silver Spring, Md.*

Hoffmann, Arthur F., Capt. [1st Div.] *Landscaping, Simsbury, Conn.*

Hoffman, George D., Lt. Comdr. [U.S.S. *Corry*] *Capt., U.S. Navy*

Hogue, Clyde E., Cpl. [743rd Tank Bn.] *Letter carrier, Diagonal, Iowa*

Holland, Harrison H., Lt. [29th Div.] *Coach, U.S. Army pistol team*

Holman, John N., Jr., Seaman 1/c [U.S.S. *Hobson*] *Boy Scout field executive, Macon, Miss.*

Hooper, Joseph O., Pfc. [1st Div.] *Fire-fighter, Chemical Corps, U.S. Army*

Hoppler, Wendell L., Q/master 3/c [LST 515] *Agency instructor*, N.Y. Life Insurance Co., *Forest Park, Ill.*

House, Francis J. E., Pfc. [90th Div.] *Potter*, Homer Laughlin China Co., *E. Liverpool, Ohio*

Huebner, Clarence R., Maj. Gen. [C.O., 1st Div.] *Lieut. Gen. (retired); Director*, Civil Defense, *New York, N.Y.*

Huggins, Spencer J., Pfc. [90th Div.] *M/Sgt., U.S. Army*

Hughes, Melvin T., Pfc. [1st Div.] *Salesman*, Adams & Morrow Inc., *Patoka, Ind.*

Hunter, Robert F., Maj. [5th Eng. Sp. Brig.] *Civil engineer, Tulsa, Okla.*

Hupfer, Clarence G., Lt. Col. [746th Tank Bn.] *Col. (retired), U.S. Army*

Imlay, M. H., Capt. [U.S.C.G. Commdr. LCI (L) Flot. 10] *Rear Adm. (retired), U.S.C.G.*

Infinger, Mark H., S/Sgt. [5th Eng. Sp. Brig.] *SFC, U.S. Army*

Irwin, John T., Pfc. [1st Div.] *Sgt. (retired), mail clerk, U.S. Army*

Isaacs, Jack R., Lt. [82nd Airborne] *Pharmacist, Coffeyville, Kan.*

Jakeway, Donald I., Pfc. [82nd Airborne] *Bookkeeper,* Rice Oil Co., *Johnstown, Ohio*

James, Francis W., Pfc. [87th Chem. Mortar Bn.] *Police officer, Winnetka, Ill.*

James, George D., Jr., Lt. [67th Tactical Recon. Group] *Insurance, Umadilla, N.Y.*

Jancik, Stanley W., S/c [LST 538] *Salesman,* Singer Sewing Machine Co., *Lincoln, Neb.*

Janzen, Harold G., Cpl. [87th Chem. Mortar Bn.] *Electrotyper, Elmhurst, Ill.*

Jarvis, Robert C., Cpl. [743rd Tank Bn.] *Pumpman,* Socony Mobil Oil Co., *Brooklyn, N.Y.*

Jewet, Milton A., Maj. [299th Engrs.] *Col., Manager power plant,* New York City Transit Authority, *New York, N.Y.*

Johnson, Fancher B., Pvt. [HQ V Corps] *Timekeeper,* California Packing Corp., *Kingsburg, Calif.*

Johnson, Gerden F., Maj. [4th Div.] *Accountant, Schenectady, N.Y.*

Johnson, Orris H., Sgt. [70th Tank Bn.] *Café owner, Leeds, N. Dak.*

Jones, Allen E., Pfc. [4th Div.] *SFC, U.S. Army*

Jones, Delbert F., Pfc. [101st Airborne] *Mushroom grower, Avondale, Pa.*

Jones, Desmond D., Pfc. [101st Airborne] *Metallurgical inspector,* Sun Oil Co., *Greenridge, Pa.*

Jones, Donald N., Pfc. [4th Div.] *Cemetery superintendent, Cadiz, Ohio*

Jones, Henry W., Lt. [743rd Tank Bn.] *Rancher, Cedar City, Utah*

Jones, Raymond E., Lt. [401st Bomb Sqdn.] *Operator,* Petroleum Chemicals Inc., *Lake Charles, La.*

Jones, Stanson R., Sgt. [1st Div.] *Lt., U.S. Army*

Jordan, Harold L., Pfc. [457th AAA AW Bn.] *Tool and die apprentice, Indianapolis, Ind.*

Jordan, Hubert H., M/Sgt. [82nd Airborne] *M/Sgt., U.S. Army*

Jordan, James H., Pvt. [1st Div.] *Maintenance, Pittsburgh, Pa.*

Joseph, William S., Lt. [1st Div.] *Painting contractor, San Jose, Calif.*

Joyner, Jonathan S., Sgt. [101st Airborne] *Post-office worker, Lawton, Okla.*

Judy, Bruce P., Ships Cook 1/c U.S.C.G. [LCI (L) 319] Bruce Judy Catering Service, *Kirkland, Wash.*

Kalisch, Bertram, Lt. Col. [Signal Corps, 1st Army] *Col., U.S. Army*

Kanarek, Paul, Sgt. [29th Div.] *Procedure analyst,* U.S. Steel Corp., *South Gate, Calif.*

Karper, A. Samuel, T/5 [4th Div.] *Judge's clerk, New York, N.Y.*

Kaufman, Joseph, Cpl. [743rd Tank Bn.] *Accounting, Monsey, N.Y.*

Keashen, Francis X., Pvt. [29th Div.] *Medical Division*, Veterans Administration, *Philadelphia, Pa.*

Keck, William S., Tech/Sgt. [5th Eng. Sp. Brig.] *Sgt/Maj., U.S. Army*

Keller, John W., Pvt. [82nd Airborne] *Tool and diemaker, Sea Cliff, N.Y.*

Kelly, John J., Capt. [1st Div.] *Attorney*, DeGraff, Foy, Conway & Hall-Harris, *Albany, N.Y.*

Kelly, Timothy G., Ch. Elec. Mate [81st Naval Const. Bn.] *Telephone company employee, Amityville, L.I., N.Y.*

Kennedy, Harold T., Fl/Off. [437th Troop Carrier Grp.] *M/Sgt., U.S.A.F.*

Kerchner, George F., 2nd Lt. [2nd Rangers] *Supervisor, luncheonette chain, Baltimore, Md.*

Kesler, Robert E., S/Sgt. [29th Div.] *Clerk*, Norfolk & Western Railroad, *Roanoke, Va.*

Kidd, Charles W., 2nd Lt. [87th Chem. Mortar Bn.] *Executive vice-president*, First Bank of Sitka, *Sitka, Alaska*

Kiefer, Norbert L., Sgt. [1st Div.] *Sales representative*, Benrus Watch Co., *E. Providence, R.I.*

Kindig, George, Pfc. [4th Div.] *Disabled, Brook, Indiana*

King, Wm. M., Capt. [741st Tank Bn.] *Director of Student Activities*, Clarkson College of Technology, *Potsdam, N.Y.*

Kinnard, Harry W. O., Lt. Col. [101st Airborne] *Col., U.S. Army*

Kinney, Prentis McLeod, Capt. [37th Engrs.] *Doctor, Bennettsville, S.C.*

Kirk, Alan Goodrich, Rear Admiral [Comdr., Western Naval Task Force] *Admiral (retired), U.S. Navy*

Kline, Nathan, S/Sgt. [323rd Bomb Grp.] *Partner*, Kline-Auto Supply Co., *Allentown, Pa.*

Kloth, Glenn C., S/Sgt. [112th Engrs.] *Carpenter, Cleveland, Ohio*

Knauss, Niles H., Pfc. [1st Div.] *Test operator-generators, Allentown, Pa.*

Koester, Wilbert J., Pfc. [1st Div.] *Farmer, Watseka, Ill.*

Kolody, Walter J., Capt. [447th Bomb Group] *Maj., U.S.A.F.*

Koluder, Joseph G., S/Sgt. [387th Bomb Grp.] *Quality control inspector*

Koon, Lewis Fulmer, Capt. (Chaplain) [4th Div.] *Supervisory staff*, Shenandoah County Public Schools, *Woodstock, Va.*

Kraft, Paul C., Pvt. [1st Div.] *Post-office clerk and farmer, Canton, Miss.*

Kratzel, Siegfried F., S/Sgt. [4th Div.] *Post-office worker, Palmertown, Pa.*

Krause, Edward, Lt. Col. [82nd Airborne] *Col., U.S. Army (retired)*

Krausnick, Clarence E., Sgt. [299th Engrs.] *Carpenter, Syracuse, N.Y.*

Krzyzanowski, Henry S., S/Sgt. [1st Div.] *Sgt. 1/c, U.S. Army*

Kucipak, Harry S., Pfc. [29th Div.] *Electrician, Tupper Lake, N.Y.*

Kuhre, Leland B., Col. [Hqtrs., Eng. Sp. Brig.] *Writer and teacher, San Antonio, Tex.*

Kurtz, Michael, Cpl. [1st Div.] *Coal miner, New Salem, Pa.*

Lacy, Joseph R., Lt. (chaplain) [2nd & 5th Rangers] *Priest*, St. Michael's Church, *Hartford, Conn.*

Lagrassa, Edward, Pfc. [4th Div.] *Power press operator and liquor salesman, Brooklyn, N.Y.*

Lamar, Kenneth W., Fireman 1/c, U.S.C.G. [LST 27] *Chief Engineman, U.S. Coast Guard*

Lanaro, Americo, T/5 [87th Mortar Bn.] *Painter, Stratford, Conn.*

Lang, James H., S/Sgt. [12th Bomb Grp.] *T/Sgt., U.S.A.F.*

Langley, Charles H., Yeoman 3/c [U.S.S. *Nevada*] *Rural mail carrier, Loganville, Ga.*

Lapres, Theodore E., Jr., Lt. [2nd Rangers] *Attorney, Margate, N.J.*

Lassen, Donald D., Pvt. [82nd Airborne] *Production Foreman*, Victor Chemical Works, *Harvey, Ill.*

Law, Robert W., Jr., Lt. [82nd Airborne] *Insurance, Bishopville, S.C.*

Lawton, John III, Cpl. [5th Corps Artillery] *Insurance, Fillmore, Calif.*

Lay, Kenneth E., Maj. [4th Div.] *Col., U.S. Army*

Leary, James E., Jr., Lt. [29th Div.] *Attorney, manager, Personal Health Division*, John Hancock Mutual Insurance Co., *Boston, Mass.*

LeBlanc, Joseph L., S/Sgt., [29th Div.] *Social worker, Lynn, Mass.*

Leever, Lawrence C., Comdr. [6th Eng. Sp. Brig.] *Rear Admiral, U.S.N.R.; Chief Deputy Division Civil Defense, Phoenix, Ariz.*

LeFebvre, Henry E., Lt. [82nd Airborne] *Maj., U.S. Army*

Legere, Lawrence J., Jr., Maj. [101st Airborne] *Lt. Col., U.S. Army*

Leister, Kermit R., Pfc. [29th Div.] *Trainman*, Pennsylvania Railroad, *Philadelphia, Pa.*

Lepicier, Leonard R., Lt. [29th Div.] *Maj., U.S. Army*

Lillyman, Frank L., Capt. [101st Airborne] *Lt. Col., U.S. Army*

Lindquist, Roy E., Col. [82nd Airborne] *Maj. Gen., U.S. Army*

Linn, Herschel E., Lt. Col. [237th Engrs.] *Lt. Col., U.S. Army*

Littlefield, Gordon A., Comdr. [U.S.S. *Bayfield*] *Rear Adm. (retired), U.S.C.G.*

Litzler, Frank Henry, Pfc. [4th Div.] *Rancher, Sweeny, Tex.*

Lord, Kenneth P., Maj. [1st Div.] *Assistant to president*, Security Mutual Life Insurance Co., *Binghamton, N.Y.*

Luckett, James S., Lt. Col. [4th Div.] *Col., U.S. Army*

Lund, Melvin C., Pfc. [29th Div.] *Shipping room*, Smith, Follett & Crowl, *Fargo, N. Dak.*

Luther, Edward S., Capt. [5th Rangers] *Vice-president and sales manager*, Hews Body Co., *Portland, Me.*

MacFadyen, Alexander G., Lt. [U.S.S. *Herndon*] Consolidated Brass Inc., *Charlotte, N.C.*

Mack, William M., Fl/Off. [437th Troop Carrier Command] *Capt., U.S.A.F.*

Magro, Domenick L., Sgt. [4th Div.] *Casting conditioner*, Bethlehem Steel Co., *Buffalo, N.Y.*

Maloney, Arthur A., Lt. Col. [82nd Airborne] *Col., U.S. Army*

Mann, Lawrence S., Capt. [6th Eng. Sp. Brig.] *Assistant Professor of Surgery*, Chicago Medical School, *Chicago, Ill.*

Mann, Ray A., Pfc. [4th Div.] *Feed-mill operator, Laureldale, Pa.*

Marble, Harrison A., Sgt. [299th Engrs.] *Contractor, Syracuse, N.Y.*

Marsden, William M., Lt. [4th Div.] *Civil Defense coordinator, Richmond, Va.*

Marshall, Leonard S., Capt. [834th Eng. Aviation Bn.] *Lt. Col., U.S.A.F.*

Masny, Otto, Capt. [2nd Rangers] *Salesman*, Oil-Rite Corp., *Manitowoc, Wis.*

Mason, Charles W., M/Sgt. [82nd Airborne] *Editor*, Airborne Quarterly, *Fayetteville, N.C.*

Matthews, John P., S/Sgt. [1st Div.] *Supervisor, fire-alarm and traffic-signal systems, Hempstead, L.I., N.Y.*

Mazza, Albert, Sgt. [4th Div.] *Police officer, Carbondale, Pa.*

McCabe, Jerome J., Maj. [48th Fighter Group] *Col., U.S.A.F.*

McCain, James W., 2nd Lt. [5th Eng. Sp. Brig.] *Sgt. Maj., U.S. Army*

McCall, Hobby H., Capt. [90th Div.] *Attorney*, McCall, Parkhurst & Crowe, *Dallas, Tex.*

McCardle, Kermit R., Radioman 3/c [U.S.S. *Augusta*] *Terminal Foreman*, Shell Oil Co., *Louisville, Ky.*

McClean, Thomas J., 2nd Lt. [82nd Airborne] *Police officer, New York, N.Y.*

McClintock, William D., T/Sgt. [741st Tank Bn.] *Disabled, N. Hollywood, Cal.*

McCloskey, Regis F., Sgt. [2nd Rangers] *SFC, U.S. Army*

McCormick, Paul O., Pfc. [1st Div.] *Auto Mechanic, Baltimore, Md.*

McDonald, Gordon D., M/Sgt. [29th Div.] *Shipping foreman*, American Viscose Corp., *Roanoke, Va.*

McElyea, Atwood M., 2nd Lt. [1st Div.] *Part-time salesman; Summer Camp Director, Candler, N.C.*

McIlvoy, Daniel B., Jr., Maj. [82nd Airborne] *Pediatrician, Bowling Green, Ky.*

McIntosh, Joseph R., Capt. [29th Div.] *Business and law, Baltimore, Md.*

McKearney, James B., S/Sgt. [101st Airborne] *Air-conditioning and refrigeration, Pennsauken, N.J.*

McKnight, John L., Maj. [5th Eng. Sp. Brig.] *Civil engineer, Vicksburg, Miss.*

McManaway, Fred., Maj. [29th Div.] *Col., U.S. Army*

Meason, Richard P., Lt. [101st Airborne] *Attorney, Phoenix, Ariz.*

Meddaugh, William J., Lt. [82nd Airborne] *Project manager*, IBM, *Hyde Park, N.Y.*

Medeiros, Paul L., Pfc. [2nd Rangers] *Biology teacher*, Father Judge High School, *Philadelphia, Pa.*

Merendino, Thomas N., Capt. [1st Div.] *Motor vehicle inspector, Margate City, N.J.*

Mergler, Edward F., W/Off. [5th Eng. Sp. Brig.] *Attorney*, Matson and Mergler, *Bolivar, N.Y.*

Merical, Dillon H., Cpl. [149th Engrs.] *Bank assistant, vice-president*, Dallas County State Bank, *Van Meter, Iowa*

Merlano, Louis P., Cpl. [101st Airborne] *District sales manager*, Facit, Inc., *New York, N.Y.*

Merrick, Robert L., S 1/c [U.S. Coast Guard] *Fire department captain, New Bedford, Mass.*

Merrick, Theodore, Sgt. [6th Eng. Sp. Brig.] *Insurance Consultant, Park Forrest, Ill.*

Mikula, John, Torpedoman 3/c [U.S.S. *Murphy*] *Reporter, Ford City, Pa.*

Miller, George R., Lt. [5th Rangers] *Part owner, acid plant; farming, Pecos, Tex.*

Miller, Howard G., Pfc. [101st Airborne] *SFC, U.S. Army*

Mills, William L., Jr., Lt. [4th Div.] *Attorney*, Hartsell & Hartsell, *Concord, N.C.*

Milne, Walter J., S/Sgt. [386th Bomb Group] *T/Sgt., U.S.A.F.*

Mockrud, Paul R., Cpl. [4th Div.] *Veterans service officer, Westby, Wis.*

Moglia, John J., S/Sgt. [1st Div.] *Capt., U.S. Army*

Montgomery, Lester I., Pfc. [1st Div.] *Gas-station operator, Pittsburg, Kan.*

Moody, Lloyd B., Ens. [5th Div. Amphibious Force] *Hardware store operator, Lake View, Iowa*

Moore, Elzie K., Lt. Col. [First Eng. Sp. Brig.] *Counselor; teacher*, Culver Military Academy, *Culver, Ind.*

Mordenga, Christopher J., Pvt. [299th Engrs.] *Maintenance*, Treesweet Products, *Fort Pierce, Fla.*

Morecock, Bernard J., Jr., Sgt. [29th Div.] *Administrative supply technician, Virginia National Guard, Glen Allen, Va.*

Moreno, John A., Comdr. [U.S.S. *Bayfield*] *Capt., U.S. Navy*

Morrow, George M., Pfc. [1st Div.] *Brick-company employee; Farmer, Rose, Kan.*

Moser, Hyatt W., Cpl. [1st Eng. Sp. Brig.] *Chief W/Off., U.S. Army*

Moulton, Bernard W., Lt. (j.g.) [U.S.S. *Herndon*] *Comdr., U.S. Navy*

Mozgo, Rudolph S., Pfc. [4th Div.] *Capt., U.S. Army*

Mueller, David C., Capt. [435th Troop Carrier Group] *Capt., U.S.A.F.*

Muller, Charles, Jr., Cpl. [231st Engrs.] *Grocery clerk*, A. & P. Tea Co., *Newark, N.J.*

Mulvey, Thomas P., Capt. [101st Airborne] *Lt. Col., U.S. Army*

Murphy, Robert M., Pvt. [82nd Airborne] *Attorney, Boston, Mass.*

Nagel, Gordon L., Pfc. [82nd Airborne] *Senior mechanic*, American Airlines, *Tulsa, Okla.*

Natalle, E. Keith, Cpl. [101st Airborne] *School administrator, San Francisco, Cal.*

Nederlander, Samuel H., Cpl. [518th Port Bn.] *Scrap Inspector*, Bethlehem Steel Co., *Portage, Pa.*

Negro, Frank E., Sgt. [1st Div.] *Post-office clerk, Brooklyn, N.Y.*

Neild, Arthur W., Mach. Mate 1/c [U.S.S. *Augusta*] *Lt., U.S. Navy*

Nelson, Emil, Jr., S/Sgt. [5th Rangers] *Auto dealer, assistant service manager, Cedar Lake, Ind.*

Nelson, Glen C., Pfc. [4th Div.] *Rural mail carrier, Milboro, S. Dak.*

Nelson, Raider, Pfc. [82nd Airborne] Accro Plastics, *Chicago, Ill.*

Nero, Anthony R., Pvt. [2nd Division] *Disabled; part-time realtor, Cleveland, Ohio*

Newcomb, Jesse L., Jr., Cpl. [29th Div.] *Merchant and farmer, Keysville, Va.*

Nickrent, Roy W., S/Sgt. [101st Airborne] *Town marshal and waterworks superintendent, Saybrook, Ill.*

Norgaard, Arnold, Pfc. [29th Div.] *Farming, Arlington, S. Dak.*

Obert, Edward Jules, Jr., Pfc. [747th Tank Bn.] *Supervisor*, Sikorsky Aircraft, *Milford, Conn.*

O'Connell, Thomas C., Capt. [1st Div.] *Maj., U.S. Army*

Olds, Robin, Lt. [8th AF] *Col., U.S.A.F.*

O'Loughlin, Dennis G., Pfc. [82nd Airborne] *Construction, Missoula, Montana*

Olwell, John J., Pvt. [1st Div.] Veterans Administration, *Lyons, N.J.*

O'Mahoney, Michael, Sgt. [6th Eng. Sp. Brig.] *Fabricating plant operator, Mercer, Pa.*

O'Neill, John T., Lt. Col. [C.O. Sp. Eng. Task Force (Prov. Eng. Comb. Grp.)] *Col., U.S. Army*

Orlandi, Mark, S/Sgt. [1st Div.] *Truck driver, Smithport, Pa.*

Owen, Joseph K., Capt. [4th Div.] *Assistant Director of Hospitals, Va., Richmond, Va.*

Owen, Thomas O., 2nd Lt. [2nd Air Div.] *Athletics director and coach, Nashville, Tenn.*

Owens, William D., Sgt. [82nd Airborne] *Office manager, Temple City, Cal.*

Paez, Robert O., Bugler 1/c [U.S.S. *Nevada*] *Film editor*, Atomic Energy Commission, *Eniwetok Atoll, Marshall Islands*

Paige, Edmund M., Cpl. [1st Div.] *Exporter, New Rochelle, N.Y.*

Palmer, Wayne E., S/Sgt. [1st Div.] *Assistant Manager, invoicing and estimating department, Oshkosh, Wis.*

Parker, Donald E., S/Sgt. [1st Div.] *Farmer, Stillwell, Ill.*

Patch, Lloyd E., Capt. [101st Airborne] *Lt. Col., U.S. Army*

Patrick, Glenn, T/5 [4th Div.] *Bulldozer operator, Stockport, Ohio*

Pattillo, Lewis C., Lt. Col. [V Corps] *Civil engineer, Hartselle, Ala.*

Payne, Windrew C., Lt. [90th Div.] *County supervisor*, Farmer's Home Administration, U.S. Dept. of Agriculture, *San Augustine, Tex.*

Pearson, Ben F., Maj. [82nd Airborne] *Paint company vice-president, Savannah, Ga.*

Pence, James L., Capt. [1st Div.] *Supervisor, pharmaceutical laboratories, Elkhart, Ind.*

Perry, Edwin R., Capt. [299th Engrs.] *Lt. Col., U.S. Army*

Perry, John J., Sgt. [5th Rangers] *SFC, U.S. Army*

Peterson, Theodore L., Lt. [82nd Airborne] *occupation unknown, Birmingham, Mich.*

Petty, William L., Sgt. [2nd Rangers] *Boys' camp director, Carmel, N.Y.*

Phillips, Archie C., S/Sgt. [101st Airborne] *Flower grower, Jensen Beach, Fla.*

Phillips, William J., Pvt. [29th Div.] *Electric power company dispatcher, Hyattsville, Md.*

Picchiarini, Ilvo, Motor Mach. Mate 1/c [LST 374] *Steel company employee, Belle Vernon, Pa.*

Pike, Malvin R., T/Sgt. [4th Div.] *Company burner and welder*, Esso Oil, *Baker, La.*

Piper, Robert M., Capt. [82nd Airborne] *Lt. Col., U.S. Army*

Plude, Warren M., S/Sgt. [1st Div.] *Sgt., U.S. Army*

Polanin, Joseph J., Cpl. [834th Eng. Aviation Bn.] *Baked-goods distributor, Dickson City, Pa.*

Polezoes, Stanley, 2nd Lt. [1st Air Div.] *Maj., U.S.A.F.*

Polyniak, John, Sgt. [29th Div.] *Accountant, Baltimore, Md.*

Pompei, Romeo T., Sgt. [87th Chemical Mortar Bn.] *Builder, Philadelphia, Pa.*

Potts, Amos P., Jr., Lt. [2nd Rangers] *Materials engineer, Loveland, Ohio*

Powell, Joseph C., Ch. W/Off. [4th Div.] *Ch. W/Off., U.S. Army*

Pratt, Robert H., Lt. Col. [HQ V Corps] *President, manufacturing corporation, Milwaukee, Wis.*

Presley, Walter G., Pfc. [101st Airborne] *Appliance repair business, Odessa, Tex.*

Preston, Albert G., Jr., Capt. [1st Div.] *Tax consultant, Greenwich, Conn.*

Price, Howard P., Lt. [1st Div.] *Sgt., National Guard*

Priesman, Maynard J., T/Sgt. [2nd Rangers] *Fishery proprietor, Oak Harbor, Ohio*

Provost, William B., Jr., Lt. (j.g.) [LST 492] *Comdr., university ROTC, Oxford, Ohio*

Pruitt, Lanceford B., Lt. Comdr. [LCT Flot. 19] *Comdr., U.S.N. (ret.), San Francisco, Calif.*

Pulcinella, Vincent J., T/Sgt. [1st Div.] *M/Sgt., U.S. Army*

Purnell, William C., Lt. Col. [29th Div.] *Gen. (retired); Railway vice-president and general counsel, Baltimore, Md.*

Purvis, Clay S., M/Sgt. [29th Div.] *Manager concessions,* Alumni Association, University of Virginia, *Charlottesville, Va.*

Putnam, Lyle B., Capt. [82nd Airborne] *Surgeon and general practitioner, Wichita, Kan.*

Quinn, Kenneth R., S/Sgt. [1st Div.] *Manager,* Inter-Plan Bank, New Jersey Blue Cross, *Hillsdale, N.J.*

Raff, Edson D., Col. [82nd Airborne] *Col., U.S. Army*

Raftery, Patrick H., Jr., 2nd Lt. [440th Troop Carrier Group] *Self-employed, elevator construction, Metairie, La.*

Rankin, Wayne W., Pfc. [29th Div.] *Teacher, Homes City, Pa.*

Rankins, William F., Jr., Pvt. [518th Port Bn.] *Telephone-company employee, Houston, Tex.*

Ranney, Burton E., S/Sgt. [5th Rangers] *Electrician, Decatur, Ill.*

Raudstein, Knut H., Capt. [101st Airborne] *Lt. Col., U.S. Army*

Rayburn, Warren D., Lt. [316th Troop Carrier Group] *Maj., U.S.A.F.*

Read, Wesley J., Cpl. [746th Tank Bn.] *Railroad carman, Du Bois, Pa.*

Reams, Quinton F., Pfc. [1st Div.] *Railroad engineer, Punxsutawney, Pa.*

Reed, Charles D., Capt. (chaplain) [29th Div.] *Methodist minister, Troy, Ohio*

Reeder, Russel P., Jr., Col. [4th Div.] *Col. (retired); Assistant Mgr. Athletics, West Point, N.Y.*

Rennison, Francis A., Lt. [U.S. Navy] *Realtor, New York, N.Y.*

Reville, John J., Lt. [5th Rangers] *Police Officer, New York, N.Y.*

Ricci, Joseph J., Sgt. [82nd Airborne] *Pharmacist, Bethalto, Ill.*

Richmond, Alvis, Pvt. [82nd Airborne] *Clerk, Portsmouth, Va.*

Ridgway, Matthew B., Maj. Gen. [C.O. 82nd Airborne] *Gen. (retired); Chairman of the Board,* The Mellon Institute, *Pittsburgh, Pa.*

Riekse, Robert J., Lt. [1st Div.] *Company division manager, Owosso, Mich.*

Riley, Francis X., Lt. (j.g.), U.S.C.G. [LCI (L) 319] *Comdr., U.S. Coast Guard*

Ritter, Leonard C., Cpl. [3807 QM Truck Co.] *Public relations, Chicago, Ill.*

Robb, Robert W., Lt. Col. [HQ VII Corps] *Vice-president, advertising, New York, N.Y.*

Roberts, George G., T/Sgt. [306th Bomb Group] *Educational advisor, U.S.A.F., Belleville, Ill.*

Roberts, Milnor, Capt. [HQ Co., V Corps] *President, advertising company, Pittsburgh, Pa.*

Robertson, Francis C., Capt. [365th Fighter Group] *Lt. Col., U.S.A.F.*

Robinson, Robert M., Pfc. [82nd Airborne] *Capt., U.S. Army*

Robison, Charles, Jr., Lt. (j.g.) [U.S.S. *Glennon*] *Comdr., U.S. Navy*

Rocca, Francis A., Pfc. [101st Airborne] *Machine operator, Pittsfield, Mass.*

Rodwell, James S., Col. [4th Div.] *Brig. Gen. (retired), Denver, Colo.*

Rogers, T. DeF., Lt. Col. [1106th Engrs.] *Col., U.S. Army*

Roginski, E. J., S/Sgt. [29th Div.] *Sales manager*, Spaulding Bakeries, Inc., *Shamokin, Pa.*

Roncalio Teno, 2nd Lt. [1st Div.] *Attorney, Cheyenne, Wyo.*

Rosemond, St. Julien P., Capt. [101st Airborne] *Assistant county attorney, Miami, Fla.*

Rosenblatt, Joseph K., Jr., 2nd Lt. [112th Engrs.] *M/Sgt., U.S. Army*

Ross, Robert P., Lt. [37th Engrs.] *Box manufacturer, Waukesha, Wis.*

Ross, Wesley R., 2nd Lt. [146th Engrs.] *Sales engineer*, Western XRay Co., *Tacoma, Wash.*

Rosson, Walter E., Lt. [389th Bomb Group] *Optometrist, San Antonio, Tex.*

Rountree, Robert E., Lt., U.S.C.G. [U.S.S. *Bayfield*] *Comdr., U.S. Coast Guard*

Roworth, Wallace H., Radioman 3/c [U.S.S. *Joseph T. Dickman*] *Engineer, Garden City, L.I., N.Y.*

Rubin, Alfred, Lt. [24th Cav. Recon. Sqdn.] *Catering and restaurateur, Napierville, Ill.*

Rudder, James E., Lt. Col. [2nd Rangers] *College vice-president, College Station, Tex.*

Ruggles, John F., Lt. Col. [4th Div.] *Brig. Gen., U.S. Army*

Runge, William M., Capt. [5th Rangers] *Funeral director, Davenport, Iowa*

Russell, Clyde R., Capt. [82nd Airborne] *Lt. Col., U.S. Army*

Russell, John E., Jr., Sgt. [1st Div.] *Personnel department, steel company, New Kensington, Pa.*

Russell, Joseph D., Pvt. [299th Engrs.] *Telephone-company employee, Moores Hill, Ind.*

Russell, Kenneth, Pfc. [82nd Airborne] *Bank official, New York, N.Y.*

Ryals, Robert W., T/4 [101st Airborne] *SPF, U.S. Army*

Ryan, Thomas F., S/Sgt. [2nd Rangers] *Police Officer, Chicago, Ill.*

Sammon, Charles E., Lt. [82nd Airborne] *Occupation unknown*

Sampson, Francis L., Capt. (chaplain) [101st Airborne] *Lt. Col., chaplain, U.S. Army*

Sanders, Gus L., 2nd Lt. [82nd Airborne] *Credit-bureau operator, Springdale, Ark.*

Sands, William H., Brig. Gen. [29th Div.] *Attorney, Norfolk, Va.*

Santarsiero, Charles J., Lt. [101st Airborne] *Occupation unknown*

Saxion, Homer J., Pfc. [4th Div.] *Extrusion press*, Titan Metal Mfg. Co., *Bellefonte, Pa.*

Scala, Nick A., T/Sgt. [4th Div.] *Order interpreter, engineering service department*, Westinghouse Electric Corp., *Beaver, Pa.*

Scharfenstein, Charles F., Jr., Lt., U.S.C.G. [LCI (L) 87] *Comdr., U.S. Coast Guard*

Schechter, James H., Cpl. [38th Recon. Sqdn.] *Quarry driller, St. Cloud, Minn.*

Schmid, Earl W., 2nd Lt. [101st Airborne] *Insurance, Fayetteville, N.C.*

Schneider, Max, Lt. Col. [5th Rangers] *Col., U.S. Army (deceased)*

Schoenberg, Julius, T/Sgt. [453rd Bomb Group] *Letter carrier, New York, N.Y.*

Schopp, Dan D., Cpl. [5th Rangers] *M/Sgt., U.S.A.F.*

Schroeder, Leonard T., Jr., Capt. [4th Div.] *Lt. Col., U.S. Army*

Schultz, Arthur B., Pfc. [82nd Airborne] *Security officer, U.S. Army*

Schweiter, Leo H., Capt. [101st Airborne] *Lt. Col., U.S. Army*

Scott, Arthur R., Lt. (j.g.) [U.S.S. *Herndon*] *Salesman, Arcadia, Calif.*

Scott, Harold A., S/Sgt. [4042 QM Truck Co.] *Post-office employee, Yeadon, Pa.*

Scott, Leslie J., S/Sgt. [1st Div.] *Sgt. Maj., U.S. Army*

Scrimshaw, Richard E., B.M. 3/c [15th Destroyer Sqdn.] *Aircraft mechanic, Washington, D.C.*

Seelye, Irvin W., Pfc. [82nd Airborne] *Teacher, Crete, Ill.*

Settineri, John, Capt. [1st Div.] *Doctor, Jamesville, N.Y.*

Shanley, Thomas J., Lt. Col. [82nd Airborne] *Col., U.S. Army*

Sherman, Herbert A., Jr., Pfc. [1st Div.] *Salesman, South Norwalk, Conn.*

Shindle, Elmer G., T/4 [29th Div.] *Plastics factory worker, Lancaster, Pa.*

Shoemaker, William J., Pvt. [37th Engrs.] *Mechanic, Santa Ana, Calif.*

Shollenberger, Joseph H., Jr., 2nd Lt. [90th Div.] *Maj., U.S. Army*

Shoop, Clarence A., Lt. Col. [C.O. 7th Recon. Group] *Maj. Gen. (retired); Vice-president*, Hughes Aircraft Company, *Culver City, Calif.*

Shoop, Dale L., Pvt. [1st Engrs.] *Government-ammunition inspector, Chambersburg, Pa.*

Shorter, Paul R., Sgt. [1st Div.] *SFC, U.S. Army*

Shumway, Hyrum S., 2nd Lt. [1st Div.] *Director, Department of Deaf and Blind, State Department of Education, Cheyenne, Wyo.*

Silva, David E., Pvt. [29th Div.] *Priest, Akron, Ohio*

Simeone, Francis L., Pvt. [29th Div.] *Underwriter, Rocky Hill, Conn.*

Simmons, Stanley R., Gunner's Mate 3/c [Amphibious Unit] *Stone-quarry worker, Swanton, Ohio*

Sink, James D., Capt. [29th Div.] *Superintendent, traffic engineering and communications, Roanoke, Va.*

Sink, Robert F., Col. [101st Airborne] *Maj. Gen., U.S. Army*

Skaggs, Robert N., Lt. Col. [741st Tank Bn.] *Col. (retired); marine sales, Ft. Lauderdale, Fla.*

Slappey, Eugene N., Col. [29th Div.] *Col. (retired), Leesburg, Va.*

Sledge, Edward S., II, Lt. [741st Tank Bn.] *Bank vice-president, Mobile, Ala.*

Smith, Carroll B., Capt. [29th Div.] *Lt. Col., U.S. Army*

Smith, Charles H., Lt. [U.S.S. *Carmick*] *Advertising, Evanston, Ill.*

Smith, Frank R., Pfc. [4th Div.] *Veterans service officer, Waupaca, Wis.*

Smith, Franklin M., Cpl. [4th Div.] *Wholesale electrical distributor, Philadelphia, Pa.*

Smith, Gordon K., Maj. [82nd Airborne] *Lt. Col., U.S. Army*

Smith, Harold H., Maj. [4th Div.] *Attorney, White Oak, Va.*

Smith, Joseph R., Cpl. [81st Chem. Mortar Bn.] *Science teacher, Eagle Pass, Tex.*

Smith, Owen, Pvt. [5th Eng. Sp. Brig.] *Post-office clerk, Los Angeles, Calif.*

Smith, Ralph R., Pvt. [101st Airborne] *Post-office clerk, St. Petersburg, Fla.*

Smith, Raymond, Pvt. [101st Airborne] *Glass-company owner, Whitesburg, Ky.*

Smith, Wilbert L., Pfc. [29th Div.] *Farmer, Woodburn, Iowa*

Snyder, Jack A., Lt. [5th Rangers] *Lt. Col., U.S. Army*

Sorriero, Armand J., Pfc. [4th Div.] *Commercial artist, Philadelphia, Pa.*

Spalding, John M., 2nd Lt. [1st Div.] *Department manager*, Interstate Stores Co., *Owensboro, Ky.*

Spencer, Lyndon, Capt., U.S.C.G. [U.S.S. *Bayfield*] *Vice Admiral (retired)*, *President*, Lake Carrier's Assn., *Cleveland, Ohio*

Spiers, James C., Pvt. [82nd Airborne] *Rancher, Picayune, Miss.*

Spitzer, Arthur D., Cpl. [29th Div.] *Employee*, E. I. du Pont Co., *Staunton, Va.*

Sproul, Archibald A., Maj. [29th Div.] *Executive vice-president*, W. J. Perry Corp.

Steele, John M., Pvt. [82nd Airborne] *Cost engineer, Hartsville, S.C.*

Stein, Herman E., T/5 [2nd Rangers] *Sheet-metal worker, Ardsley, N.Y.*

Steinhoff, Ralph, Cpl. [467th AAA Bn.] *Butcher, Chicago, Ill.*

Stephenson, William, Lt. [U.S.S. *Herndon*] *Attorney, Sante Fe, N.M.*

Stevens, Roy O., T/Sgt. [29th Div.] *Employee*, Rubatex Division of Bedford, *Bedford, Va.*

Stivison, William J., S/Sgt. [2nd Rangers] *Postmaster, Homer City, Pa.*

Strayer, Robert L., Lt. Col. [101st Airborne] *Insurance, Springfield, Pa.*

Street, Thomas F., MoM 1/c U.S.C.G. [LST 16] *Post-office worker, River Edge, N.J.*

Strojny, Raymond F., S/Sgt. [1st Div.] *Spi, U.S. Army*

Stults, Dallas M., Pfc. [1st Div.] *Coal miner, Monterey, Tenn.*

Stumbaugh, Leo A., 2nd Lt. [1st Div.] *Capt., U.S. Army*

Sturdivant, Hubert N., Lt. Col. [492nd Bomb Group] *Col., U.S.A.F.*

Sullivan, Fred P., Lt. [4th Div.] *Salesman*, Mississippi Chemical Corporation, *Winona, Miss.*

Sullivan, Richard P., Maj. [5th Rangers] *Engineering, Dorchester, Mass.*

Swatosh, Robert B., Maj. [4th Div.] *Lt. Col., U.S. Army*

Sweeney, William F., Gunner's Mate 3/c [U.S.C.G. Reserve Flotilla] *Telephone-company employee, East Providence, R.I.*

Swenson, J. Elmore, Maj. [29th Div.] *Lt. Col., U.S. Army*

Tabb, Robert P., Jr., Capt. [237th Eng. Combat Bn.] *Col., U.S. Army*

Tait, John H., Jr., Pharmacist's Mate 1/c, U.S.C.G. [LCI (L) 349] *Zanjero, Salt River Valley Users Association, Tempe, Ariz.*

Tallerday, Jack, Lt. [82nd Airborne] *Lt. Col., U.S. Army*

Talley, Benjamin B., Col. [HQ V Corps] *Brig. Gen. (retired); vice-president, construction company, New York, N.Y.*

Taylor, Beryl F., Hosp. App. 1/c [LST 338] *Diving instructor, U.S. Navy*

Taylor, Charles A., Ens. [LCT Amphibious Unit] *Assistant director, athletics,* Stanford University, *Palo Alto, Calif.*

Taylor, Edward G., Ens. [LST 331] *Lt. Comdr., U.S. Coast Guard*

Taylor, H. Afton, 2nd Lt. [1st Eng. Sp. Brig.] Hallmark Cards, Inc., *Independence, Mo.*

Taylor, Ira D., T/Sgt. [4th Div.] *Capt., U.S. Army*

Taylor, Maxwell D., Maj. Gen. [C.O. 101st Airborne] *General, Chief of Staff (retired); Chairman,* Mexican Light & Power Co.

Taylor, William R., Ens. [U.S. Navy, Liaison Off. communications] *Retailer, building materials, South Hill, Va.*

Telinda, Benjamin E., S/Sgt. [1st Div.] *Locomotive fireman,* Chicago Great Western Railroad, *St. Paul, Minn.*

Thomason, Joel F., Lt. Col. [4th Div.] *Col., U.S. Army*

Thompson, Egbert W., Jr., Lt. [4th Div.] *County Supervisor,* Farmers Home Administration, U.S.D.A., *Bedford, Va.*

Thompson, Melvin, Pvt. [5th Eng. Sp. Brig.] *Mechanic, Yardville, N.J.*

Thompson, Paul W., Col. [6th Eng. Sp. Brig.] *Brig. Gen. (retired); Manager International Editions,* The Reader's Digest, *Pleasantville, N.Y.*

Thornhill, Avery J., Sgt. [5th Rangers] *Chief W/Off., U.S. Army*

Trathen, Robert D., Capt. [87th Chem. Mortar Bn.] *Lt. Col. (retired); Asst. Chief Plans & Training, U.S. Army Chem. Corps, Fort McClellan, Ala.*

Tregoning, Wm. H., Lt. (j.g.), U.S.C.G. [Flot. 4] *Manager, service department,* Fairbanks Morse & Co., *East Point, Ga.*

Tribolet, Hervey A., Col. [4th Div.] *Col. (retired), U.S. Army*

Trusty, Lewis, S/Sgt. [8th Air Force] *M/Sgt., U.S.A.F.*

Tucker, William H., Pfc. [82nd Airborne] *Attorney, Athol, Mass.*

Tuminello, Vincent J., Cpl. [1st Div.] *Bricklayer, Massapequa, L.I., N.Y.*

Vandervoort, Benjamin H., Lt. Col. [82nd Airborne] *Col. (retired), U.S. Army, Washington, D.C.*

Vantrease, Glen W., Sgt. [82nd Airborne] *Accountant, Gary, Ind.*

Vaughn, James H., Motor Mach. Mate 1/c [LST 49] *Construction superintendent, McIntyre, Ga.*

Ventrelli, William E., Sgt. [4th Div.] *Foreman,* Department of Sanitation, New York City, *Mount Vernon, N.Y.*

Vickery, Grady M., T/Sgt. [4th Div.] *M/Sgt., U.S. Army*

Viscardi, Peter, Pvt. [4th Div.] *Taxi driver, New York, N.Y.*

Visco, Serafino R., Pvt. [456th AAA AW Bn.] *Post-office worker, Dania, Fla.*

Volponi, Raymond R., Sgt. [29th Div.] *Disabled;* Veterans Administration Hospital, *Altoona, Pa.*

Von Heimburg, Herman E., Capt. [11th Amphibious Force] *Rear Adm., Naval Reserve Training Command*

Wade, James Melvin, 2nd Lt. [82nd Airborne] *Maj., U.S. Army*

Wadham, Lester B., Capt. [1st Eng. Sp. Brig.] Wadham Mutual Investments, *Frankfurt, Germany*

Wadsworth, Loring L., Pfc. [2nd Rangers] Sparrell Funeral Service, *Norwell, Mass.*

Wagner, Clarence D., Radioman 1/c [LST 357] *CPO, U.S. Navy*

Walker, Francis M., Sgt. [6th Eng. Spec. Brig.] *Sgt. 1/c, U.S. Army*

Wall, Charles A., Lt. Col. [Eng. Spec. Brig. Grp.] *President*, Associated Music Publishers, *New York, N.Y.*

Wall, Herman V., Capt. [165 Signal Photo Co.] *Director of photography*, Los Angeles State College Foundation

Wallace, Dale E., Seaman 2/c [SC 1332] *Salesman*, Capitol Tobacco Co., *Jackson, Miss.*

Ward, Charles R., Cpl. [29th Div.] *Investigator*, Ohio Department of Liquor Control, *Ashtabula, Ohio*

Washington, Wm. R., Maj. [1st Div.] *Lt. Col., U.S. Army*

Weast, Carl F., Pfc. [5th Rangers] *Machine operator*, Babcock & Wilcox Co., *Alliance, Ohio*

Weatherley, Marion D., Cpl. [237th Engrs.] *Disabled veteran, Laurel, Del.*

Weintraub, Louis, Cpl. [Photog. Army Pict. Svce., 1st Div.] *Public relations*, Louis Weintraub Associates, Inc., *New York, N.Y.*

Welborn, John C., Lt. Col. [4th Div.] *Col.; president*, U.S. Army Armor Board

Weller, Malcolm R., Maj. [29th Div.] *Chief W/Off., U.S. Army*

Wellner, Herman C., Cpl. [37th Engrs.] *Mason, Boscobel, Wis.*

Welsch, Woodrow J., Cpl. [29th Div.] *Construction engineer, Pittsburgh, Pa.*

Wertz, Raymond J., Cpl. [5th Eng. Spec. Brig.] *Self-employed, construction business, Bassett, Wis.*

Whelan, Thomas J., Cpl. [101st Airborne] *Department-store buyer, Smithtown, L.I., N.Y.*

White, John F., 2nd Lt. [29th Div.] *Prosthetic specialist*, Veterans Administration, *Roanoke, Va.*

White, Maurice C., Sgt. [101st Airborne] *Chief W/Off., U.S. Army*

Wiedefeld, William J., Jr., T/Sgt. [29th Div.] *Postal clerk, Annapolis, Md.*

Walsh, Richard J., Sgt. [452nd Bomb Group] *Sgt., U.S.A.F.*

Wilhelm, Frederick A., Pfc. [101st Airborne] *Painter, Pittsburgh, Pa.*

Wilhoit, William L., Ens. [LCT 540] *Special agent*, Insurance Co. of North America, *Jackson, Miss.*

Willett, John D., Jr., Pfc. [29th Div.] *Employee*, General Electric, *Roanoke, Ind.*

Williams, William B., Lt. [29th Div.] *Secretary-treasurer*, Acme Wire Co., *Hamden, Conn.*

Williamson, Jack L., S/Sgt. [101st Airborne] *Post-office clerk, Tyler, Tex.*

Wolf, Edwin J., Lt. Col. [6th Eng. Spec. Brig.] *Attorney*, Wolf & Wolf, *Baltimore, Md.*

Wolf, Karl E., Lt. [1st Div.] *Assistant professor of law*, U.S. Military Academy, *West Point, N.Y.*

Wolfe, Edward, Pfc. [4th Div.] *Assistant manager*, Singer Sewing Machine Co., *Westbury, L.I., N.Y.*

Wood, George B., Capt. (chaplain) [82nd Airborne] Trinity Episcopal Church, *Fort Wayne, Ind.*

Woodward, Robert W., Capt. [1st Div.] *Manufacturer, textiles and textile machines, Rockland, Mass.*

Wordeman, Harold E., Pvt. [5th Eng. Spec. Brig.] *Unemployed—partly disabled, V.A. Hospital, Brooklyn, N.Y.*

Worozbyt, John B., Pfc. [1st Div.] *M/Sgt., U.S. Army*

Wozenski, Edward F., Capt. [1st Div.] *Foreman*, Wallace Barnes Co., *Bristol, Conn.*

Wylie, James M., Capt. [93rd Bomb Group] *Maj., U.S.A.F.*

Wyman, Willard G., Brig. Gen. [Asst. C.O. 1st Div.] *Gen.*; Aeroneutronic Systems, Inc., *Santa Ana, Calif.*

Yates, Douglas R., Pfc. [6th Eng. Spec. Brig.] *Farmer, Yoder, Wyo.*

Yeatts, Lynn M., Maj. [746th Tank Bn.] *Operations manager*, Commercial Oil Transport Co., *Fort Worth, Tex.*

Young, Wallace W., Pfc. [2nd Rangers] *Electrician, Beaver Falls, Pa.*

Young, Willard, Lt. [82nd Airborne] *Lt. Col., U.S. Army*

Zaleski, Roman, Pvt. [4th Div.] *Molder, aluminum foundry, Paterson, N.J.*

Zmudzinski, John J., Pfc. [5th Eng. Spec. Brig.] *Letter carrier, South Bend, Ind.*

Zush, Walter J., T/4 [1st Div.] *Occupation unknown*

BRITISH

Aldworth, Michael, Lt. [48th (Royal Marine) Commando] *Advertising*

Allen, Ronald H. D., Gunner [3rd Div.] *Cashier*

Ashover, Claude G., Coxswain [Royal Navy] *Electrician*

Ashworth, Edward P., Ab/Seaman [Royal Navy] *Furnace man, alloy foundry*

Avis, Cecil, Pvt. [Pioneer Corps] *Landscape gardener*

Bagley, Anthony F., Midshipman [Royal Navy] *Banking, office worker*

Baker, Alfred G., Ab/Seaman [Royal Navy] *Chemical worker*

Bald, Peter W., Pvt. [Pioneer Corps.] *Foreman mechanic, garage*

Batten, Raymond W., Pvt. [6th Airborne] *Male nurse*

Baxter, Hubert V., Pvt. [3rd Div.] *Printer*

Beck, Sidney, J. T., Lt. [50th Div.] *Civil servant*

Beynon, John P., Sub Lt. [R.N.V.R.] *Import manager*

Bicknell, Sidney R., Telegraphist [Royal Navy] *Copy editor*

Bidmead, William H., Pvt. [No. 4 Commando] *Bricklayer*

Blackman, Arthur John, Leading/Stoker [Royal Navy] *Dock engineer*

Bowley, Eric, F. J., Pvt. [50th Div.] *Inspector, aircraft components*

Brayshaw, Walter, Pvt. [50th Div.] *Factory worker*

Brierley, Denys S. C., Fl/Lt. [Royal Air Force] *Textile manufacturer*

Brookes, John S., Pvt. [50th Div.] *Factory worker*

Cadogan, Roy, Trooper [27th Armoured Brig.] *Surveyor*

Capon, Sidney F., Pvt. [6th Airborne] *Master builder*

Cass, E. E. E., Brigadier [3rd Div.] *Brigadier, British Army (retired)*

Cheesman, Arthur B., SubLt. R.N.V.R. [LCS 254] *Quarry manager*

Cheshire, Jack, Sgt. [No. 6 Beach Grp.] *Printer*

Cloudsley-Thompson, John L., Capt. [7th Armoured Div.] *Lecturer, zoology,* University of London

Cole, Thomas A. W., Gunner [50th Div.] *Inspector, machine tools*

Colley, James S. F., Cpl. [4th Commando] *Occupation unknown*

Collins, Charles L., Cpl. [6th Airborne] *Detective sergeant*

Collinson, Joseph A., Lance/Cpl. [3rd Div.] *Engineering draughtsman*

Cooksey, Frank, Cpl. [No. 9 Beach Grp.] *Aircraft fitter*

Cooper, John B., Ab/Seaman [LCT 597] *Occupation unknown*

Corkill, William A., Signalman ["O" LCT Sqdn.] *Senior clerk, accounting office*

Cowley, Ernest J., Stoker/1c [LCT 7045] *Maintenance engineer*

Cox, Leonard H., Cpl. [6th Airborne] *Engraver*

Cox, Norman V., Lt. R.N.V.R. [4th Flotilla] *Civil servant*

Cullum, Percy E., Petty Officer [Mobile Radio Unit] *Inland Revenue officer*

Cutlack, Edward B., Lt. Comdr. R.N.V.R. [9th Minesweeping Flotilla] *Chief instructor,* East Midland Gas Board

Dale, Reginald G., Cpl. [3rd Div.] *Self-employed*

Deaken, B., Pvt. [6th Airborne] *Shoe repairing*

deLacy, James Percival, Sgt. [8th (Irish) Bn. (att. 3rd Can. Div.)] *Travel agent*

Devereux, Roy P., Trooper [6th Airborne] *Travel agency, branch manager*

Dowie, Robert A., Leading/Stoker [H.M.S. *Dunbar*] *Turbine operator*

Dunn, Arthur H., Maj. [50th Div.] *Retired*

Edgson, Charles L., Capt. [Royal Engrs.] *Schoolteacher*

Ellis, F., Pvt. [50th Div.] *Occupation unknown*

Emery, William H., Pvt. [50th Div.] *Van driver*

Emmett, Frederick W., Lance/Bombardier [50th Div.] *Chemical worker*

Finch, Harold, Pvt. [50th Div.] *Policeman*

Flood, Bernard A., Sapper [3rd Div.] *Post-office supervisor*

Flunder, Daniel J., Capt. [48th (Royal Marine) Commando] *Branch manager,* Dunlop Ltd.

Ford, Leslie W., Royal Marine Signalman 2/c [1st S.S. Brig.] *Occupation unknown*

Fortnam, Stanley, Driver/Mech. [6th Airborne] *Compositor*

Fowler, William R., Lt. [H.M.S. *Halsted*] *Advertising salesman*

Fox, Geoffrey R., Leading/Seaman [48th Landing Craft Flotilla] *Policeman*

Fox, Hubert C., Lt. Comdr. [Naval Assault Grp.] *Dairy Farmer*

Gale, John T. J., Pvt. [3rd Div.] *Post-office worker*

Gardner, Donald H., Sgt. [47th (Royal Marine) Commando] *Civil servant*

Gardner, Thomas H., Maj. [3rd Div.] *Managing director,* Leather Manufacturers

Gibbs, Leslie R., Sgt. [50th Div.] *Charge-hand, steel-works production*

Girling, Donald B., Maj. [50th Div.] *Occupation unknown*

Glew, George W., Gunner [3rd Div.] *Clerk*

Gough, J. G., Maj. [3rd Div.] *Dairy farmer*

Gray, William J., Pvt. [6th Airborne] *Occupation unknown*

Grundy, Ernest, Capt. [50th Div.] *Doctor*

Gunning, Hugh, Capt. [3rd Div.] *Syndication manager*, Daily News Ltd.

Gwinnett, John, Capt. (chaplain) [6th Airborne] *Pastor*, Tower of London

Hammond, William, Cpl. [79th Armoured Div.] *Sqdn. Sgt. Maj., British Army*

Hanneson, Hannes, Capt. [R.A.M.C., LST 21] *Specialist physician*

Hardie, I., Lt. Col. [50th Div.] *British Army, active service*

Hargreaves, Edward R., Maj. [3rd Div.] *Deputy County Medical Officer*

Harris, Harry, Ab/Seaman [H.M.S. *Adventure*] *Coal miner*

Harrison, Roger H., Lt. R.N.V.R. [4th LCT Flot.] *Inspection staff, bank*

Harvey, Adolphus J., Acting Col. [Royal Marine Armoured Support Group] *Market gardener*

Hayden, A. C., Pvt. [3rd Div.] *Laborer*

Hollis, Stanley E. V., Co./Sgt./Maj. [50th Div.] *Sand blaster*

Honour, George B., Lt. R.N.V.R. [Midget Submarine X23] *Area Sales Manager*, Schweppes Ltd.

Horton, Harry, Trooper [No. 3 Commando] *Cpl., H.M. Forces*

Humberstone, Henry F., Pvt. [6th Airborne] *Clothing factory worker*

Hutley, John C., S/Sgt. [Glider Pilot Regt.] *Canteen manager*

Hynes, William, Sgt. [50th Div.] *British Army, active service*

Ingram, Ronald A., Gunner [3rd Div.] *Painter and decorator*

James, Leonard K., Cpl. [3rd Div.] *Advertising*

Jankel, Herbert, Capt. [20th Beach Recovery Section] *Garage proprietor*

Jennings, Henry, Sapper [Royal Engrs.] *Contracting*

John, Frederick R., Trooper [No. 6 Commando] *Senior assistant, accounting office*

Johnson, Frank C., Lance/Bombardier [50th Div.] *Wood machinist*

Jones, Edward, Maj. [3rd Div.] *Classics master*

Jones, Peter H., Sgt. [Royal Marines, Frogman] *Building contractor*

Kendall, Hubert O., Cpl. [6th Airborne] *Shipping and forwarding agent*

Kimber, Donald E., Marine [609 Flotilla LCM] *Machine operator*

King, Gordon W., Lt. [6th Airborne] *Representative, paint firm*

Leach, Geoffrey, J., Pvt. [50th Div.] *Laboratory assistant*

Lee, Arthur W., Ab/Seaman [LCT 564] *Local government officer*

Lee, Norton, SubLt. R.N.V.R. [550 LCA Flotilla] *Painter, interior decorating*

Lloyd, Desmond C., Lt. R.N. [Norwegian destroyer *Svenner*] *Company director*

Lovell, Denis, Marine [4th Commando] *Engineering*

Maddison, Godfrey, Pvt. [6th Airborne] *Miner*

March, Desmond C., Lt. [3rd Div.] *Company director*

Markham, Lewis S., T/O Signalman [R.N. LST 301] *Shipping clerk*

Mason, John T., Pvt. [No. 4 Commando] *Schoolteacher*

Masters, Peter F., Lance/Cpl. [No. 10 Commando] *Art director*, WTOP Television, *Washington, D.C.*

Mathers, George H., Cpl. [Royal Engrs.] *Clerk*

May, John McCallon, Sgt. [6th Airborne] *British Army, active service*

McGowan, Alfred, L/Cpl. [6th Airborne] *Packer, flour mill*

Mears, Frederick G., Cpl. [No. 3 Commando] *Accounting machines factory worker*

Millin, W., Piper [1st S.S. Brig.] *Male nurse*

Minnis, James C., Sub/Lt. R.N.V.R. [LCT 665] *Teacher*

Mitchell, John D., Cpl. [54 Beach Balloon Unit, RAF] *Company director*

Montgomery, Sir Bernard Law, Gen.; *Field Marshal (retired)*

Moore, William J. D., L/Cpl. [3rd Div.] *Male nurse*

Morgan, Vincent H., Pvt. [50th Div.] *Post-office worker*

Morris, Ernest, Cpl. [50th Div.] *Occupation unknown*

Morrissey, James F., Pvt. [6th Airborne] *Docker*

Mower, Alan C., Pvt. [6th Airborne] *Security officer, research labs*

Murphy, John, Leading Aircraftman [RAF, Balloon Command] *Post-office worker*

Neilsen, Henry R., Capt. [6th Airborne] *Knitwear manufacturer*

Newton, Reginald V., Pvt. [6th Airborne] *Company director*

Nissen, Derek A., Lt. [3rd Div.] *Works manager*

Norfield, Harry T., Cpl. [3rd Div.] *British Admiralty messenger*

Northwood, Ronald J., Ab/Seaman [H.M.S. *Scylla*] *Hairdresser*

Norton, Gerald Ivor D., Capt. [3rd Div.] *Company secretary*

Oliver, Arthur E., L/Cpl. [No. 4 Commando] *Coal miner*

Otway, Terence, Lt. Col. [6th Airborne] *Executive*, Kemsley Newspapers

Pargeter, George S., Cpl. [Royal Marines] *Production control clerk*

Paris, Sydney F., Leading Seaman [H.M.S. *Melbreak*] *Police constable*

Parker, William, Sapper [50th Div.] *Bus driver*

Peachey, Sidney, Chief P.O. [H.M.S. *Warspite*] *Engineer*

Peskett, Stanley V., Lt. Col. [1st R.M. Armoured Support Regt.] *Royal Marines, active service*

Phillips, Sir Farndale, Lt. Col. [47th (Royal Marine) Commando CO] *Maj. Gen.; President*, British Trades Federation

Porter, Walter S., Pfc. [53 Pioneer Corps] *Painter, decorator*

Powell, Colin E., Pvt. [6th Airborne] *Sales department, steel company*

Purver, Raymond, Sapper [50th Div.] *Stores foreman*

Purvis, Joseph, Pvt. [5th Div.] *Laborer*

Raphaelli, Cyril, Cpl. [3rd Div.] *British Army, active service*

Ringland, John, Trooper [8th Armoured Brigade] *Post and telegraph officer*

Robertson, D. J., Lt. [27th Armoured Brig.] *Solicitor's managing clerk*

Rolles, John R., Cpl. [3rd Div.] *Lighterman*

Ruthen, Walter S., Pvt. [3rd Div.] *Postman*

Rutter, William I., Pvt. [6th Airborne] *Poultry farmer*

Ryland, Richard A., Sub/Lt. R.N.V.R. [7th Landing Barge Flotilla] *Cultivating oysters and writing*

Sawyer, David J., Trooper [79th Armoured Div.] *Power station foreman*

Scarfe, Norman, Lt. [3rd Div.] *Lecturer, history*, University of Leicester

Scoot, J. E., Marine [48th (Royal Marine) Commando] *Department manager, factory*

Sharr, Leonard G., S/Sgt. [6th Airborne] *Partner, textile agency*

Sheard, Edgar T., Trooper [6th Airborne] *Sergeant, British Army*

Sim, John A., Capt. [6th Airborne] *Active service*

Slade, John H., Sapper [50th Div.] *Railway clerk*

Slapp, John A., Cpl. [3rd Div.] *Chief clerk*

Smith, Christopher N., Trooper [27th Armoured Brig.] *Area representative, gas board*

Smith, Robert A., Signalman [3rd Div.] *Guard, railways*

Spence, Basil, Capt. [3rd Div.] *Architect*, Coventry Cathedral

Stannard, Ernest W., Dvr/Operator [50th Div.] *Maintenance fitter*

Stevenson, Douglas A., Coder [LCI 100] *Fishmonger*

Stewart, Stanley, Pvt. [4th Commando] *Occupation unknown*

Stokes, Albert J., Pvt. [3rd Div.] *Exterminator*

Stott, Frederick, Pvt. [3rd Div.] *Clergyman*

Strevens, George A., Cpl. [3rd Div.] *Inshore fisherman*

Stunell, George C., Pvt. [50th Div.] *Occupation unknown*

Sullivan, Bernard J., Lt. R.N.V.R. [553 Assault Flotilla] *Bank clerk*

Swan, Robert M., L/Cpl. [50th Div.] *Bank clerk*

Tait, Harold G., L/Cpl. [6th Airborne] *Grocery manager*

Tappenden, Edward, L/Cpl. [6th Airborne] *Clerk*

Taylor, John B., Lt. [Frogman, Team No. 4] *Tobacconist*

Thomas, William J., Cpl. [50th Div.] *Diesel operator*

Thomson, Roger W. D., Comdr. R.N. [H.M.S. *Sidmouth*] *Manufacturing plant*

Todd, Richard, Lt. [6th Airborne] *Movie actor*

Tomlinson, Percy, W/OP [Mobile Signals Unit R.A.F.] *Plasterer*

Vickers, Francis W., Pvt. [50th Div.] *Occupation unknown*

Warburton, Geoffrey A., Signalman [8th Armoured Brig.] *Accounts clerk*

Ward, Patrick A., Lt. R.N.V.R. [115th Minesweeping Flotilla] *Occupation unknown*

Ward, Percy, CO Sgt/Maj. [50th Div.] *Telephone engineer*

Webber, Dennis J., Lt. [9th Beach Grp.] *Bank clerk*

Webber, John, Telegraphist/O [200 LCT Flotilla] *Opthalmic optician*

Webber, John J., Capt. [6th Airborne] *Accountant*

West, Leonard C., W/O [3rd Div.] *Clerical office, Admiralty*

Weston, Ronald, L/Cpl. [50th Div.] *Chief clerk, Army*

White, Niels W., 2/Lt. [50th Div.] *Fur broker*

Wiggins, John R., Lt. R.N.V.R. [LST 423] *Headmaster*

Wightman, Leslie, Pvt. [3rd Div.] *Chief cinema projectionist*

Wilson, Charles S., Pvt. [50th Div.] *Subway railway clerk*

Wilson, Gordon C., 2nd Lt. [47th (Royal Marine) Commando] *Advertising agency*

Windrum, Anthony W., Maj. [6th Airborne] *Foreign Service officer (retired)*

Winter, John E., Stoker/1c [R.N. (Combined Ops)] *Bookmaker*

Wither, Russell J., Sgt. [41st (Royal Marine) Commando] *Wages clerk*

Yelland, Charles H., Sgt. [50th Div.] *Foundry worker*

CANADIAN

Anderson, James, Maj. [3rd Can. Div.] *Department minister, social services, New Brunswick*

Arbuckle, Robert, Gunner [19th Can. Field Regt.] *Sectionman*, Canadian National Railways

Axford, Douglas S., Sgt. [3rd Can. Div.] *W/Off., Canadian Army*

Backosti, John, Leading Stoker [H.M.C.S. *Prince Henry*] *A. E. Tech., RCAF*

Bayliss, Gilbert, Fl/Off. [RAF] *Fl/Off., RCAF*

Blackader, K. G., Brigadier [3rd Can. Div.] *Accountant*

Blake, John J., Steward [H.M.C.S. *Prince Henry*] *Ground-Technician, RCAF*

Boon, Arthur, Gunner [3rd Can. Div.] *Employee*, Canadian National Railways

Brebner, Dr. Colin N., Capt. [1st Can. Parachute Bn., 6th Airborne] *Surgeon*

Chalcraft, William R., Fl/Lt. [419 Sqdn.] *Fl/Off., RCAF*

Champoux, Robert A., Cpl. [3rd Can. Div.] *Canadian Army*

Cherrington, Horace D., Sgt. [570th Sqdn.] *Engineer*

Churchill, Henry L., Pvt. [1st Can. Para. Bn., 6th Airborne] *Occupation unknown*

Cockroft, Gordon, Leading Coder [H.M.C.S. *Lindsay*] *Cpl., Canadian Army, Ordnance Corps*

Couture, George J., Rifleman [3rd Can. Div.] *Recruiting sergeant, Canadian Army*

Cox, Kenneth W., Pvt. [14th Can./Field Ambulance] *Sgt., RCAF*

Cresine, Ellis R., Gunner [3rd Can. Div.] *RCAF, Air Force police*

Davies, Francis J., Lance/Bombardier [3rd Can. Div.] *S/Sgt., Canadian Army*

Dewey, Clarence J., Cpl. [1st TAC Air Force Police] *Fire Fighter, RCAF*

Dunn, Clifford E., Pvt. [3rd Can. Div.] *Dairy business*

Dutton, Eldon R., Signalman [3rd Can. Div.] *Sgt., Canadian Army*

Eldridge, Victor, W./Off. [415 RCAF Sqdn.] *RCAF*

Elmes, William J., Lance/Cpl. [2nd Can. Army] *Canadian Army*

Evans, Cyril, Tpr. [3rd Can. Div.] *Electrician*

Farrell, J. A., Pvt. [3rd Can. Div.] *Broadcaster and writer*

Fitzpatrick, Carl L., Ab/Seaman [H.M.C.S. *Blairmore*] *Lt., Canadian Army*

Forbes, Robert B., Maj. [3rd Can. Div.] *Purchasing manager*

Forth, John W., Maj. [Asst. Sr. Chaplain, 3rd Can. Div.] *Col., director of chaplains, Canadian Army*

Fowler, Donald M., Pvt. [3rd Can. Div.] *Pricing supervisor*

Fuller, Clayton, Maj. [1st Can. Parachute Bn., 6th Airborne] Canadian Brass Company, *Galt, Ont.*

Fraser, George C., Cpl. [3rd Can. Div.] *Clerk*

Gammon, Clinton C. L., Capt. [3rd Can. Div.] *Papermaker*

Gardiner, George J., Sgt. [3rd Can. Div.] *Cpl., Canadian Army*

Gillan, James D. M., Capt. [3rd Can. Div.] *Canadian Army*

Goeres, Raymond J., F/Lt. [RAF 101 Sqdn.] *F/Lt., RCAF*

Graham, Robert J., Sapper [3rd Can. Div.] *Office Supervisor*

Griffin, Peter, Capt. [1st Can. Parachute Bn., 6th Airborne] *Occupation unknown*

Gunnarson, Gunnar H., Rifleman [3rd Can. Div.] *Farming*

Haines, Charles W. R., Pvt. [3rd Can. Div.] *Air Force police, RCAF*

Hall, John T., Fl/Off. [51 Bomber Sqdn.] *Sqdn. Leader, RCAF*

Hamilton, John H., Lance/Cpl. [3rd Can. Div.] *Buyer, wholesale grocery firm*

Hickey, R. M., Capt. (Chaplain) [3rd Can. Div.] *Pastor*

Hilborn, Richard, Lt. [1st Can. Parachute Bn., 6th Airborne] Preston Furniture Co., *Preston, Ont.*

Hillock, Frank W., Wing Comdr. [143 Wing RCAF] *Wing Comdr., RCAF*

Hurtick, Walter J., Fl/Off. [524 Sqdn.] *Sgt., RCAF*

Jeans, Ernest A., Cpl. [1st Can. Parachute Bn., 6th Airborne] *Teacher*

Johnston, Alexand, Sapper [3rd Can. Div.] *Royal Canadian Ordnance Corps*

Johnston, John R., Signalman [3rd Can. Div.] *Telegraph technician, RCAF*

Johnstone, T., Sgt. [2nd Arm. Brig.] *Instructor, Canadian Army*

Labelle, Placide, Capt. [3rd Can. Div.] *Publicity services*

Laing, Gordon K., Pvt. [3rd Can. Div.] *Industrial painter*

Langell, Louis, Pvt. [3rd Can. Div.] *Canadian Army*

LeBlanc, Joseph E. H., Capt. [3rd Can. Div.] *Maj., Canadian Army*

Leroux, Roland A., Sgt. [3rd Can. Div.] *Customs officer*

Liggins, Percival, Pvt. [1st Can. Parachute Bn., 6th Airborne] *Parachute rescue jumper*

Lind, Jack B., Capt. [3rd Can. Div.] *Canadian Army*

Little, Edward T., Lance/Cpl. [1st Can. Parachute Bn., 6th Airborne] *Canadian Army*

Lockhart, Lloyd J., Leading Seaman [H.M.C.S. *Saskatchewan*] *Fire fighter, RCAF*

Lynch, C. Lawrence, Lt. [3rd Can. Div.] *Bank employee*

MacKenzie, Donald L., Pvt. [3rd Can. Div.] *RCAF*

MacLean, Richard O., Sgt. [1st Can. Parachute Bn., 6th Airborne] *Oil and gas distributor*

MacRae, John, Lt. [3rd Can. Div.] *Member of Parliament*

Magee, Morris H., Sgt. [3rd Can. Div.] *Cardiographer*

Mandin, Joseph A., Rifleman [3rd Can. Div.] *Airman, RCAF*

Manning, Robert F., C/Petty Off. [Minesweeping Flotilla] *Maintenance superintendent, hydroelectric plant*

Mathieu, Paul, Lt. Col. [3rd Can. Div.] *Assistant Department Minister, Department of National Defence*

McCumber, John M., Cpl. [2nd Armoured Brig.] *Canadian Army*

McDonald, James W., Cpl. [3rd Can. Div.] *Immigration officer on U.S.–Canadian border*

McDougall, Colin C., Capt. [3rd Can. Div.] *Department director, public relations, Canadian Army*

McFeat, William P., Gunner [3rd Can. Div.] *Special placements officer*, Canadian Employment Service

McGechie, William, Fl/Off. [298th Sqdn.] *Assessor, Canadian Department of Mines and Minerals*

McKee, Robert, Fl/Off. [296th Sqdn.] *Sqdn. leader, RCAF*

McLean, Charles W., Maj. [3rd Can. Div.] *General Sales manager, textiles*

McMurray, Robert M., Lance/Cpl. [3rd Can. Div.] *Insurance underwriter*
McNamee, Gordon A., Fl/Off. [405th Sqdn.] *Fl/Lt., RCAF*
McPhatter, Roderick H., Leading Coder [H.M.C.S. *Caraquet*] *Fl/Lt., RCAF*
McTavish, Frank A., Maj. [3rd Can. Div.] *Maj., Canadian Army*
Millar, Ian A. L., Maj. [3rd Can. Div.] *Lt. Col., Canadian Army*
Mitchell, James F., Sqdn. Leader [83rd Sqdn.] *RCAF*
Moffatt, John L., Fl/Off. [575th Sqdn.] *Schoolteacher*
Mosher, Albert B., Pvt. [3rd Can. Div.] *Ground defence instructor, RCAF*
Murch, Hewitt J., Signalman [3rd Can. Div.] *Farmer*
Newin, Harry J., F/Sgt. [625 Sqdn.] *RCAF*
Olmsted, Earl A., Capt. [3rd Can. Div.] *Lt. Col., Canadian Army*
O'Regan, Robert B., Gunner [3rd Can. Div.] *Public relations, Canadian Army*
Osborne, Daniel N., Capt. [3rd Can. Div.] *Maj., Canadian Army*
Paterson, William, Pvt. [6th Airborne] *High-school teacher*
Pearson, Clifford A., Lance/Cpl. [3rd Can. Div.] *Sgt., Canadian Army*
Piers, Desmond W., Lt. Comdr. [H.M.C.S. *Algonquin*] *Commodore, Royal Canadian Navy*
Raich, Jack, Cpl. [3rd Can. Div.] *Sgt., Canadian Army*
Rehill, Cecil, Lt. [3rd Can. Div.] *Canadian Army*
Rogge, Robert E., Pvt. [3rd Can. Div.] *T/Sgt., USAF*
Ruffee, George E. M., Lt. [3rd Can. Div.] *Canadian Army*
Saunders, Frederick T., Lance/Cpl. [3rd Can. Div.] *Foreman supervisor, power station*
Schaupmeyer, John E., Sapper [3rd Can. Div.] *Farming*
Scott, Charles J., Lt. [LCT 926] *Editor*
Shawcross, Ronald G., Capt. [3rd Can. Div.] *Manager, envelope company*
Smith, Stanley A. E., Leading Aircadet [2nd T.A.F.] *Cpl., RCAF*
Somerville, Joseph, Pvt. [3rd Can. Div.] *Employee, paper company*
Stanley, Robert W., Pvt. [1st Can. Parachute Bn., 6th Airborne] *Metal worker*
Stewart, Angus A., Pvt. [3rd Can. Div.] *Farming*
Stothart, Jack G., Capt. [3rd Can. Div.] *Agricultural research*
Thompson, Robert J., Gunner [3rd Can. Div.] *Fire fighter, RCAF*
Thomson, Thomas A., P/Off. [425 Sqdn.] *Fl/Sgt., RCAF*
Todd, Percy A. S., Brig. [3rd Can. Div. (Artillery Comdr.)] *Railway, general manager*
Velux, Gene, Sapper [3rd Can. Div.] *Cpl., Canadian Army*
Vidler, Douglas R., Pvt. [3rd Can. Div.] *Film tester*
Warburton, James A., Lt. [3rd Can. Div.] *Engineer*
Washburn, Arthur S., Lance/Sgt. [3rd Can. Div.] *Civil servant*
Webber, John L., Sgt. [86th Sqdn.] *Flt/Engineer*
White, William B., Pvt. [1st Can. Parachute Bn., 6th Airborne] *Sgt., Canadian Army*
Widenoja, Edwin T., Fl/Off. [433rd Sqdn.] *Pulp and paper tester*
Wilkins, Donald, Maj. [1st Can. Parachute Bn., 6th Airborne] *Investment broker*
Zack, Theodore, Trooper [3rd Can. Div.] *Farmer*

FRENCH

Kieffer, Philippe, Commander [CO French Commandos, Att. No. 4 Commando] *NATO Paris*

French Underground
Auge, Albert—*Caen, French Railways*
Gille, Léonard—*Caen, Normandy Deputy Military Intelligence Chief*
Gille, Louise "Janine" Boitard—*Caen, Allied Pilot Escape Network*
Lechevalier, Amélie—*Caen, Allied Pilot Escape Network*
Marion, Jean—*Grandcamp, Omaha Sector Chief*
Mercader, Guillaume—*Bayeux, Coastal Section Chief*
Picard, Roger—*Southern France, Intelligence*
Rémy, George Jean—*Paris, Radio Communication*

GERMAN

Blumentritt, Gunther, Maj. Gen. [OB West—Rundstedt's Chief of Staff] *Lt. Gen. (retired)*
Bürkner, Leopold, Vice Admiral [Chief of Protocol, Hitler's HQ-OKW] *Airline personnel director*
Damski, Aloysius, Pvt. [716th Div.] *Occupation unknown*
Düring, Ernst, Capt. [352nd Div.] *Businessman*
Feuchtinger, Edgar, Lt. Gen. [CO 21st Panzer Div.] *Technical Adviser, German industrial combine*
Freyberg, Leodegard, Col. [Personnel Chief, Army Group B] *Official*, Federation of German Soldiers
Gause, Alfred, Maj. Gen. [Rommel's Chief of Staff (to Mar. 1944)] *U.S. Army Historical Division, Germany*
Häger, Josef, Lance Cpl. [716th Div.] *Machinist*
Halder, Franz, Col. Gen. [Chief of German General Staff (to Sept. 1942)] *U.S. Army Historical Division, Germany*
Hayn, Friedrich, Maj. [Intelligence Officer, 84th Corps] *Author*
Hermes, Walter, Pvt. [192nd Regt., 21st Panzer Div.] *Postman*
Hildebrand, Otto, Lt. [21st Panzer Div.] *Occupation unknown*
Hoffmann, Heinrich, Lt. Comdr. [5th E-boat Flotilla] *German Navy, Bonn Defense Ministry*
Hoffner, Hans, Brig. Gen. [Rail Transportation Chief for France, OB West] *German Army*
Hofmann, Rudolf, Maj. Gen. [Chief of Staff, 15th Army] *Retired; consultant to U.S. Army Historical Division, Germany*
Hummerich, Wilhelm, Capt. [709th Div.] *Deputy Commander, German Support Unit, NATO—Allied Forces Central Europe*
Krancke, Theodor, Admiral [Naval Comdr.-in-Chief, West] *Now pensioned and retired. (Until recently employed as laborer)*
Lang, Hellmuth, Capt. [Rommel's Aide] *Storekeeper*
Meyer, Hellmuth, Lt. Col. [Intelligence Officer, 15th Army] *German Army*

Meyer-Detring, Wilhelm, Brig. Gen. [Intelligence Chief, OB West] *Chief, Intelligence, NATO—Allied Forces Central Europe*

Ohmsen, Walter, Capt. [Comdr., Marcouf Battery] *Harbor control officer*

Pemsel, Max, Maj. Gen. [Chief of Staff, 7th Army] *Lt. Gen., German Army*

Pluskat, Werner, Maj. [352nd Div.] *Engineer*

Priller, Josef, Col. [Wing Comdr., 26th Fighter Wing] *Brewery manager*

Reichert, Josef, Maj. Gen. [CO 711th Div.] *Lt. Gen. (retired)*

Richter, Wilhelm, Maj. Gen. [CO 716th Inf. Div.] *Lt. Gen. (retired)*

Ruge, Friedrich, Vice-Admiral [Rommel's Naval Aide] *Inspector of German Naval Forces*

Saul, Carl, Lt. Dr. [709th Inf. Div.] *High-school teacher*

Schenck Zu Schweinsberg, Maj., Baron Hans [21st Panzer Div.] *Private income*

Speidel, Hans, Maj. Gen., Dr. [Rommel's Chief of Staff] *Lt. Gen.; NATO—Commander, Allied Land Forces, Central Europe*

Staubwasser, Anton, Lt. Col. [Intelligence Chief, Army Group B] *German Army*

Stenzel, Willy, Lance/Cpl. [6th Parachute Regiment] *Salesman*

Stöbe, Walter, Prof., Dr. [Chief Meteorologist, Luftwaffe (West)] *Teacher*

Voigt, Wilhelm, Pvt. [Radio Monitoring Group] *Public relations*, Pan American Airways, *Frankfurt, Germany*

von Gottberg, Wilhelm, Capt. [22nd Regt., 21st Panzer] *Manager, automobile agency*

von Kistowski, Werner, Col. [1st Regt., 3rd Flak Corps] *Lightning-rod salesman*

von Oppeln-Bronikowski, Hermann, Col. [22nd Regt., 21st Panzer Div.] *Gen. (retired); estate steward*

von Puttkamer, Karl Jesko, Adm. [Hitler's Naval Aide] *Personnel director, export firm*

von Salmuth, Hans, Gen. [CO 15th Army] *Gen. (retired)*

von Schramm, Wilhelm, Maj. [Official War Reporter] *Author*

Warlimont, Walter, Gen. [Ass't Chief of Operations, OKW] *Gen. (retired)*

Wuensch, Anton, Cpl. [6th Parachute Regt.] *Occupation unknown*

Zimmermann, Bodo, Lt. Gen. [Chief of Operations, OB West] *Lt. Gen. (retired); magazine and book publisher*

ACKNOWLEDGMENTS

THE PRINCIPAL sources of information for this book came from Allied and German D-Day survivors, French underground workers and civilians—more than 1,000 in all. Freely and unselfishly they gave of their time, and no inconvenience seemed too great. They filled out questionnaires, and after these forms had been collated and cross-checked with those of other veterans they cheerfully provided additional information. They answered my many letters and queries. They supplied me with a wealth of documentation and memorabilia—water-stained maps, tattered diaries, after-action reports, logs, message pads, company rosters, casualty lists, personal letters and photographs —and they made themselves available for interview. I am deeply indebted to these contributors. On preceding pages the reader will find a complete list of all military personnel and French underground workers who helped. To my knowledge this partial list of D-Day participants is the only one of its kind in existence.

Of the total number of survivors located—a task that took the best part of three years—some 700 were interviewed in the U.S., Canada, Great Britain, France and Germany. Some 383 accounts were blended into the text. For a variety of editorial reasons—principally that of repetition—it was impossible to include everyone's account. However, the framework of the book was constructed on the information supplied by all the participants, plus Allied and German after-action reports, war diaries, histories or other official records (such as the magnificent combat interviews conducted during and after the war by Brigadier General S. L. A. Marshall, U.S.A.R., the European Theater Military Historian).

At the onset I wish to thank De Witt Wallace, editor and publisher of *The Reader's Digest*, for underwriting nearly all of the costs and thus making this book possible.

Next I must pay tribute to the U.S. Secretary of Defense; General Maxwell D. Taylor, until recently the U.S. Army's Chief of Staff; Major General H. P. Storke, the Army's Chief of Information; Colonel G. Chesnutt, Lieutenant Colonel John S. Cheseboro and Lieutenant Colonel C. J. Owen of the Army's Magazine and Book branch; Commander Herbert Gimpel of the U.S. Navy's Magazine and Book branch; Major J. Sunderman and Captain W. M. Mack of the U.S. Air Force's Information Division; Mrs. Martha Holler of the Defense Department's Accreditation and Travel Division; and the many public-relations officers in Europe and elsewhere who assisted me at every turn. All of these people aided not only in helping me locate veterans but by opening doors everywhere, granting me permission to examine hitherto classified documents, supplying me with detailed maps, transporting me to and from Europe, and in setting up interviews.

I must also acknowledge the gracious assistance and co-operation of Dr. Kent Roberts Greenfield, until recently Chief of Military History, and the members of his staff—Major William F. Heinz, Mr. Israel Wice, Mr. Charles

Finke and Mr. Charles von Luttichau—for giving me permission to draw on official histories and records and for their constant guidance and advice. I would like to mention here the work of Charles von Luttichau, who spent all of his spare time over a period of nearly eight months translating bale loads of German documents and the all important German war diaries.

Among the contributors to the book I would like to thank in particular the following: Sergeant William Petty for meticulously reconstructing the Rangers' action at Pointe du Hoc; Corporal Michael Kurtz of the 1st Division, Second Lieutenant Edward Gearing and Brigadier General Norman Cota of the 29th for their vivid descriptions of Omaha Beach; Colonel Gerden Johnson of the 4th Division for his careful breakdown of the equipment carried by first-wave assault troops; Colonel Eugene Caffey and Sergeant Harry Brown for their portrayals of Brigadier General Theodore Roosevelt on Utah Beach; Major General Raymond O. Barton, the 4th Division's Commanding Officer on D Day, for his guidance and for loaning me his maps and official papers; Brigadier E. E. E. Cass, whose 8th British Brigade led the assault on Sword Beach, for his detailed memorandums and papers and his kind efforts in trying to research the British casualty figures; Mrs. Theodore Roosevelt for her many kindnesses, thoughtful suggestions and criticisms; William Walton, formerly of *Time* and *Life*, the only war correspondent to jump with the 82nd, for digging through his trunks and finding his old notebooks and then over a two-day session re-creating the atmosphere of the assault; Captain Daniel J. Flunder and Lieutenant Michael Aldworth of the 48th Royal Marine Commandos for painting the scene on Juno; and Piper Bill Millin of Lord Lovat's Commandos for his diligent search to find the list of tunes that he played throughout the day.

I would also like to express my appreciation to General Maxwell D. Taylor, who took time out from his grueling schedule to take me step by step through the 101st Airborne's assault and who later read pertinent parts of the manuscript for accuracy. Others who checked for errors and who read two or three versions of the manuscript were Lieutenant General Sir Frederick Morgan, the architect of the original Overlord plan, and Lieutenant General James M. Gavin, who commanded the 82nd's parachute drop into Normandy.

I am also indebted to General Omar N. Bradley, who commanded the U.S. First Army; Lieutenant General Walter B. Smith, who was Chief of Staff to General Dwight D. Eisenhower; Lieutenant General J. T. Crocker, who commanded the 1st British Corps; and General Sir Richard Gale, who commanded the British 6th Airborne. These men kindly answered my queries, or granted me interviews or made available to me their wartime maps and papers.

On the German side I wish to acknowledge the generous co-operation of the Bonn Government and the many service associations who located veterans and set up appointments.

For assistance from the many German contributors I am particularly grateful to Colonel General Franz Halder, former Chief of the German General Staff; Captain Hellmuth Lang, Rommel's aide; Major General Günther Blumentritt, Field Marshal von Rundstedt's Chief of Staff; Lieutenant General Dr. Hans

Speidel, Rommel's Chief of Staff; Frau Lucie Maria Rommel and her son, Manfred; Lieutenant General Max Pemsel, the 7th Army's Chief of Staff; General Hans von Salmuth, the 15th Army's commanding officer; General von Oppeln-Bronikowski of the 21st Panzer; Colonel Josef Priller of the Luftwaffe's 26th Fighter Wing; Lieutenant Colonel Hellmuth Meyer of the 15th Army; and Major Werner Pluskat of the 352nd Division. All these and scores of others were kind enough to grant me interviews, spending hours reconstructing various phases of the battle.

In addition to the information collected from D-Day participants, many works by eminent historians and authors were consulted during the research. I would like to express my gratitude to Gordon A. Harrison, author of the official D-Day history, *Cross-Channel Attack*, and Dr. Forest Pogue, author of the U.S. Army's *The Supreme Command*, both of whom gave me guidance and helped me solve many a controversial point. Their books proved invaluable in giving me an over-all picture both politically and militarily of the events leading up to the invasion and in detailing the attack itself. Other books that I found most helpful were *The Invasion of France and Germany* by Samuel E. Morison; *Omaha Beachhead* by Charles H. Taylor; *Utah to Cherbourg* by R. G. Ruppenthal; *Rendezvous with Destiny* by Leonard Rapport and Arthur Norwood, Jr.; *Men Against Fire* by Brigadier General S. L. A. Marshall, U.S.A.R.; and *The Canadian Army: 1939–1945* by Colonel C. P. Stacey. A bibliography of books referred to is appended.

In locating veterans, gathering research and in the final interviewing I was ably assisted by *Reader's Digest* researchers, bureau representatives and editors in the U.S., Canada, Great Britain, France and Germany. In New York Miss Frances Ward and Miss Sally Roberts, under the guidance of Department Editor Gertrude Arundel, waded through piles of documents, questionnaires and correspondence and somehow kept abreast of it all. In London Miss Joan Isaacs did a similar job, including many interviews. With the help of the Canadian War Office, the *Digest's* Shane McKay and Miss Nancy Vail Bashant found and interviewed dozens of Canadian veterans. The European end of the operation was the most difficult, and I must thank Max C. Schreiber, editor of the *Digest's* German edition, for his advice; and especially Associate Editor George Révay, John D. Panitza and Yvonne Fourcade of the *Digest's* European editorial office in Paris for their magnificent work in organizing and researching the project and for their tireless interviewing. My earnest thanks also to the *Digest's* Assistant Managing Editor, Hobart Lewis, for believing in the project in the first place and for holding my hand through the long months of work.

There are many, many others to whom I owe debts of gratitude. To mention just a few: Jerry Korn for his thoughtful criticisms and editorial assistance; Don Lassen for his many letters regarding the 82nd Airborne; Don Brice of the Dictaphone Corp., and David Kerr for help in interviewing; Colonel John Verdon of the *Army Times*, Kenneth Crouch of the *Bedford Democrat*, Dave Parsons of Pan-American Airways, Ted Rowe of IBM, and Pat Sullivan of General Dynamics—all of whom through their organizations helped me trace survivors; Suzanne Gleaves, Theodore H. White, Peter Schwed, and Phyllis

Jackson for their careful readings of each version of the work; Lillian Lang for her secretarial work; Anne Wright, who filed, cross-indexed, handled correspondence and did all the typing; and above all my dear wife, Kathryn, who collated, organized the research, helped in final revision of the manuscript, and contributed more than anyone else—for she had to live through the writing.

C. R.

BIBLIOGRAPHY

Babington-Smith, Constance, *Air Spy*. New York: Harper & Bros., 1957.

Baldwin, Hanson W., *Great Mistakes of the War*. New York: Harper & Bros., 1950.

Baumgartner, Lt. John W.; DePoto, 1st Sgt. Al; Fraccio, Sgt. William; Fuller, Cpl. Sammy, *The 16th Infantry, 1798–1946*. Privately printed.

Bird, Will R., *No Retreating Footsteps*. Nova Scotia: Kentville Publishing Co.

Blond, Georges, *Le Débarquement, 6 Juin 1944*. Paris: Arthème Fayard, 1951.

Bradley, General Omar N., *A Soldier's Story*. New York: Henry Holt, 1951.

Bredin, Lt. Col. A. E. C., *Three Assault Landings*. London: Gale & Polden, 1946.

British First and Sixth Airborne Divisions, the Official Account of, *By Air to Battle*. London: His Majesty's Stationery Office, 1945.

Brown, John Mason, *Many a Watchful Night*. New York: Whittlesey House, 1944.

Butcher, Captain Harry C., *My Three Years with Eisenhower*. New York: Simon and Schuster, 1946.

Canadian Department of National Defence, *Canada's Battle in Normandy*. Ottawa: King's Printer, 1946.

Chaplin, W. W., *The Fifty-Two Days*. Indianapolis and New York: Bobbs-Merrill, 1944.

Churchill, Winston S., *The Second World War* (Vols. I–VI). Boston: Houghton Mifflin, 1948–1953.

Clay, Major Ewart W., *The Path of the 50th*. London: Gale & Polden, 1950.

Colvin, Ian, *Master Spy*. New York: McGraw-Hill, 1951.

Cooper, John P., Jr., *The History of the 110th Field Artillery*. Baltimore: War Records Division, Maryland Historical Society, 1953.

Crankshaw, Edward, *Gestapo*. New York: Viking Press, 1956.

Danckwerts, P. V., *King Red and Co*. Royal Armoured Corps *Journal*, Vol. 1, July 1946.

Dawson, W. Forrest, *Saga of the All American* (82nd Airborne Div.). Privately printed.

Dempsey, Lt. Gen. M. C., *Operations of the 2nd Army in Europe*. London: War Office, 1957.

Edwards, Commander Kenneth, R.N., *Operation Neptune*. London: The Albatross Ltd., 1947.

Eisenhower, Dwight D., *Crusade in Europe*. New York: Doubleday, 1948.

First Infantry Division, with introduction by Hanson Baldwin: H. R. Knickerbocker, Jack Thompson, Jack Belden, Don Whitehead, A. J. Liebling, Mark Watson, Cy Peterman, Iris Carpenter, Col. R. Ernest Dupuy, Drew Middleton and former officers: *Danger Forward*. Atlanta: Albert Love Enterprises, 1947.

First U.S. Army Report of Operations, 20 Oct. '43 to Aug. '44. *Field Artillery Journal*.

Fleming, Peter, *Operation Sea Lion*. New York: Simon and Schuster, 1947.

457 AAA AW Battalion, *From Texas to Teismach*. Nancy, France: Imprimerie A. Humblot, 1945.

Fuller, Major General J. F. C., *The Second World War*. New York: Duell, Sloan and Pearce, 1949.

Gale, Lt. Gen. Sir Richard, *With the 6th Airborne Division in Normandy*. London: Sampson, Lowe, Marston & Co. Ltd., 1948.

Gavin, Lt. Gen. James M., *Airborne Warfare*. Washington, D.C.: Infantry Journal Press, 1947.

Glider Pilot Regimental Association, *The Eagle* (Vol. 2). London, 1954.

Goerlitz, Walter, *The German General Staff* (Introduction by Walter Millis). New York: Frederick A. Praeger, 1953.

Guderian, General Heinz, *Panzer Leader*. New York: E. P. Dutton, 1952.

Gunning, Hugh, *Borderers in Battle*. Berwick-on-Tweed, England: Martin and Co., 1948.

Hansen, Harold A.; Herndon, John G.; Langsdorf, William B., *Fighting for Freedom*. Philadelphia: John C. Winston, 1947.

Harrison, Gordon A., *Cross-Channel Attack*. Washington, D.C.: Office of the Chief of Military History, Department of the Army, 1951.

Hart, B. H. Liddell, *The German Generals Talk*. New York: William Morrow, 1948.

Hart, B. H. Liddell (editor), *The Rommel Papers*. New York: Harcourt, Brace, 1953.

Hayn, Friedrich, *Die Invasion*. Heidelberg: Kurt Vowinckel Verlag, 1954.

Herval, René, *Bataille de Normandie*. Paris: Editions de Notre-Dame.

Hickey, Rev. R. M., *The Scarlet Dawn*. Campbellton, N.B.: Tribune Publishers, Ltd., 1949.

Hollister, Paul, and Strunsky, Robert (editors), *D-Day Through Victory in Europe*. New York: Columbia Broadcasting System, 1945.

Holman, Gordon, *Stand By to Beach!* London: Hodder & Stoughton, 1944.

Jackson, Lt. Col. G. S., *Operations of Eighth Corps*. London: St. Clements Press, 1948.

Johnson, Franklyn A., *One More Hill*. New York: Funk & Wagnalls, 1949.

Karig, Commander Walter, USNR, *Battle Report*. New York: Farrar & Rinehart, 1946.

Lemonnier-Gruhier, François, *La Brèche de Sainte-Marie-du-Mont*. Paris: Editions Spes.

Life (editors of), *Life's Picture History of World War II*.

Lockhart, Robert Bruce, *Comes the Reckoning*. London: Putnam, 1947.

Lockhart, Robert Bruce, *The Marines Were There*. London: Putnam, 1950.

Lowman, Major F. H., *Dropping into Normandy*. Oxfordshire and Bucks Light Infantry Journal, January 1951.

Madden, Capt. J. R., *Ex Coelis*. Canadian Army *Journal*, Vol. XI, No. 1.

Marshall, S. L. A., *Men Against Fire*. New York: William Morrow, 1947.

McDougall, Murdoch C., *Swiftly They Struck*. London: Odhams Press, 1954.

Millar, Ian A. L., *The Story of the Royal Canadian Corps*. Privately printed.

Monks, Noel, *Eye-Witness*. London: Frederick Muller, 1955.

Montgomery, Field Marshal Sir Bernard, *The Memoirs of Field Marshal Montgomery*. Cleveland and New York: The World Publishing Company, 1958.

Moorehead, Alan, *Eclipse*. New York: Coward-McCann, 1945.

Morgan, Lt. Gen. Sir Frederick, *Overture to Overlord*. London: Hodder & Stoughton, 1950.

Morison, Samuel Eliot, *The Invasion of France and Germany*. Boston: Little, Brown, 1957.

Munro, Ross, *Gauntlet to Overlord*. Toronto: The Macmillan Company of Canada, 1945.

Nightingale, Lt. Col. P. R., *A History of the East Yorkshire Regiment*. Privately printed.

Norman, Albert, *Operation Overlord*. Harrisburg, Penna.: The Military Service Publishing Co., 1952.

North, John, *North-West Europe 1944–5*. London: His Majesty's Stationery Office, 1953.

Otway, Col. Terence, *The Second World War, 1939–1945—Airborne Forces*. London: War Office, 1946.

Parachute Field Ambulance (members of 224), *Red Devils*. Privately printed.

Pawle, Gerald, *The Secret War*. New York: William Sloan, 1957.

Pogue, Forrest C., *The Supreme Command*. Washington, D.C.: Office of the Chief of Military History, Department of the Army, 1954.

Pyle, Ernie, *Brave Men*. New York: Henry Holt, 1944.

Rapport, Leonard, and Northwood, Arthur Jr., *Rendezvous with Destiny*. Washington, D.C.: Washington Infantry Journal Press, 1948.

Ridgway, Matthew B., *Soldier: The Memoirs of Matthew B. Ridgway*. New York: Harper & Bros., 1956.

Roberts, Derek Mills, *Clash by Night*. London: Kimber, 1956.

Royal Armoured Corps *Journal*, Vol. IV, *Anti-Invasion*. London: Gale & Polden, 1950.

Ruppenthal, R. G., *Utah to Cherbourg*. Washington, D.C.: Office of the Chief of Military History, Department of the Army, 1946.

Salmond, J. B., *The History of the 51st Highland Division, 1939–1945*. Edinburgh and London: William Blackwood & Sons, Ltd., 1953.

Saunders, Hilary St. George, *The Green Beret*. London: Michael Joseph, 1949.

Saunders, Hilary St. George, *The Red Beret*. London: Michael Joseph, 1950.

Semain, Bryan, *Commando Men*. London: Stevens & Sons, 1948.

Shulman, Milton, *Defeat in the West*. London: Secker and Warburg, 1947.

Smith, Gen. Walter Bedell (with Stewart Beach), *Eisenhower's Six Great Decisions*. New York: Longmans, Green, 1956.

Special Troops of the 4th Infantry Division, *4th Infantry Division*. Baton Rouge, La.: Army & Navy Publishing Co., 1946.

Speidel, Lt. Gen. Dr. Hans, *Invasion 1944*. Chicago: Henry Regnery, 1950.

Stacey, Col. C. P., *The Canadian Army: 1939–1945*. Ottawa: King's Printer, 1948.

Stanford, Alfred, *Force Mulberry*. New York: William Morrow, 1951.

Story of the 79th Armoured Division, The. Hamburg. Privately printed.

Synge, Capt. W. A. T., *The Story of the Green Howards*. London. Privately printed.

Taylor, Charles H., *Omaha Beachhead*. Washington, D.C.: Office of the Chief of Military History, Department of the Army, 1946.

Von Schweppenburg, General Baron Leo Geyr, "Invasion without Laurels" in *An Cosantoir*, Vol. IX, No. 12, and Vol. X, No. 1. Dublin, 1949–50.

Waldron, Tom, and Gleeson, James, *The Frogmen*. London: Evans Bros., 1950.

Weller, George, *The Story of the Paratroops*. New York: Random House, 1958.

Wertenbaker, Charles Christian, *Invasion!* New York: D. Appleton-Century, 1944.

Wilmot, Chester, *The Struggle for Europe*. New York: Harper & Bros., 1952.

Young, Brig. Gen. Desmond, *Rommel the Desert Fox*. New York: Harper & Bros., 1950.

GERMAN MANUSCRIPTS AND CAPTURED DOCUMENTS

Blumentritt, Lt. Gen. Gunther, *OB West and the Normandy Campaign, 6 June– 24 July 1944*, MS. B-284; *A Study in Command*, Vols. I, II, III, MS. B-344.

Dihm, Lt. Gen. Friedrich, *Rommel and the Atlantic Wall* (Dec. '43–Jul. '44), MSS. B-259, B-352, B-353.

Feuchtinger, Lt. Gen. Edgar, *21st Panzer Division in Combat Against American Troops in France and Germany*, MS. A-871.

Guderian, Gen. Heinz, *Panzer Tactics in Normandy*.

Hausser, Gen. Paul, *Seventh Army in Normandy*.

Jodl, General Alfred, *Invasion and Normandy Campaign*, MS. A-913.

Keitel, Field Marshal Wilhelm, and Jodl, General Alfred, *Answers to Questions on Normandy. The Invasion*, MS. A-915.

Pemsel, Lt. Gen. Max, *Seventh Army* (June '42–5 June '44), MS. B-234; *Seventh Army* (6 June–29 July '44), MS. B-763.

Remer, Major General Otto, *The 20 July '44 Plot Against Hitler; The Battle of the 716 Division in Normandy*. (6 June–23 June '44), MS. B-621.

Roge, Commander, *Part Played by the French Forces of the Interior During the Occupation of France, Before and After D-Day*, MS. B-035.

Rommel, Field Marshal Erwin: Captured documents—private papers, photographs and 40 letters to Mrs. Lucia Maria Rommel and son, Manfred (translated by Charles von Luttichau).

Ruge, Admiral Friedrich, *Rommel and the Atlantic Wall* (Dec. '43–July '44), MSS. A-982, B-282.

Scheidt, Wilhelm, *Hitler's Conduct of the War*, MS. ML-864.

Schramm, Major Percy E., *The West* (1 Apr. '44–16 Dec. '44), MS. B-034; *Notes on the Execution of War Diaries*, MS. A-860.

Speidel, Lt. Gen. Dr. Hans, *The Battle in Normandy: Rommel, His Generalship, His Ideas and His End*, MS. C-017; *A Study in Command*, Vols. I, II, III, MS. B-718.

Staubwasser, Lt. Col. Anton, *The Tactical Situation of the Enemy During the Normandy Battle*, MS. B-782; *Army Group B—Intelligence Estimate*, MS. B-675.

Von Buttlar, Maj. Gen. Horst, *A Study in Command*, Vols. I, II, III, MS. B-672.

Von Criegern, Friedrich, *84th Corps* (17 Jan.–June '44), MS. B-784.

Von der Heydte, Lt. Col. Baron Friedrich, *A German Parachute Regiment in Normandy*, MS. B-839.

Von Gersdorff, Maj. Gen., *A Critique of the Defense Against the Invasion*, MS. A-895. *German Defense in the Invasion*, MS. B-122.

Von Rundstedt, Field Marshal Gerd, *A Study in Command*, Vols. I, II, III, MS. B-633.

Von Salmuth, General Hans, *15th Army Operations in Normandy*, MS. B-746.

Von Schlieben, Lt. Col. Karl Wilhelm, *The German 709th Infantry Division During the Fighting in Normandy*, MS. B-845.

Von Schweppenburg, Gen. Baron Leo Geyr, *Panzer Group West* (Mid-'43–5 Jul. '44), MS. B-258.

War Diaries: Army Group B (Rommel's headquarters); OB West (Rundstedt's headquarters); Seventh Army (and Telephone Log); Fifteenth Army. All translated by Charles von Luttichau.

Warlimont, General Walter, *From the Invasion to the Siegfried Line*.

Ziegelman, Lt. Col., *History of the 352 Infantry Division*, MS. B-432.

Zimmermann, Lt. Gen. Bodo, *A Study in Command*, Vols. I, II, III, MS. B-308.

A BRIDGE TOO FAR

For Them All

MAPS BY RAFAEL PALACIOS

The photographs in this book are from the collection of the author, who gratefully acknowledges the assistance of the Imperial War Museum in London, the U.S. Department of Defense, the Dutch Historical Military Archives, the Dutch Municipal Archives, and the many individuals who provided photographs of events and themselves.

CONTENTS

On the narrow corridor that would carry the armored drive, there were five major bridges to take. They had to be seized intact by airborne assault. It was the fifth, the crucial bridge over the Lower Rhine at a place called Arnhem, sixty-four miles behind the German lines, that worried Lieutenant General Frederick Browning, Deputy Commander, First Allied Airborne Army. Pointing to the Arnhem bridge on the map he asked, "How long will it take the armor to reach us?" Field Marshal Montgomery replied briskly, "Two days." Still looking at the map, Browning said, "We can hold it for four." Then he added, "But, sir, I think we might be going a bridge too far."

> The final conference at Montgomery's Headquarters on Operation Market-Garden, September 10, 1944, as recalled in Major General Roy E. Urquhart's memoirs, *Arnhem*.

FOREWORD

OPERATION MARKET-GARDEN
September 17–24, 1944

SHORTLY AFTER 10 A.M. on Sunday, September 17, 1944, from airfields all over southern England the greatest armada of troop-carrying aircraft ever assembled for a single operation took to the air. In this, the 263rd week of World War II, the Supreme Allied Commander, General Dwight David Eisenhower, unleashed Market-Garden, one of the most daring and imaginative operations of the war. Surprisingly, Market-Garden, a combined airborne and ground offensive, was authored by one of the most cautious of all the Allied commanders, Field Marshal Bernard Law Montgomery.

Market, the airborne phase of the operation, was monumental: it involved almost five thousand fighters, bombers, transports and more than 2500 gliders. That Sunday afternoon, at exactly 1:30 P.M., in an unprecedented daylight assault, an entire Allied airborne army, complete with vehicles and equipment, began dropping behind the German lines. The target for this bold and historic invasion from the sky: Nazi-occupied Holland.

On the ground, poised along the Dutch-Belgian border, were the Garden forces, massed tank columns of the British Second Army. At 2:35 P.M., preceded by artillery and led by swarms of rocket-firing fighters, the tanks began a dash up the backbone of Holland along a strategic route the paratroopers were already fighting to capture and hold open.

Montgomery's ambitious plan was designed to sprint the troops and tanks through Holland, springboard across the Rhine and into Germany itself. Operation Market-Garden, Montgomery reasoned, was the lightning stroke needed to topple the Third Reich and effect the end of the war in 1944.

PART ONE
THE RETREAT

I

IN THE THOUSAND-YEAR-OLD Dutch village of Driel, people listened intently. Even before dawn, restless sleepers woke and lights came on behind shuttered windows. Initially there was only a sense of something unaccountable taking place somewhere beyond the immediate, physical surroundings. Gradually vague impressions took form. In the far distance came a muted, continuous mutter.

Barely audible, but persistent, the sound reached the village in waves. Unable to identify the subtle noise, many listened instinctively for some change in the flow of the nearby Lower Rhine. In Holland, half of which lies below sea level, water is the constant enemy, dikes the major weapon in a never-ending battle that has gone on since before the eleventh century. Driel, sitting in a great bend of the Lower Rhine, southwest of Arnhem, capital of Gelderland, has an ever-present reminder of the struggle. A few hundred yards to the north, protecting the village and the region from the restless 400-yard-wide river, a massive dike, topped by a road, rises at places more than twenty feet high. But this morning the river gave no cause for alarm. The Neder Rijn swept peacefully toward the North Sea at its customary speed of two miles per hour. The sounds reverberating off the stone face of the protective dike came from another, far more ruthless, enemy.

As the sky lightened and the sun began to burn off the mist, the commotion grew louder. From roads due east of Driel the villagers could clearly hear the sound of traffic—traffic that seemed to grow heavier by the minute. Now their uneasiness turned to alarm, for there was no doubt about the identity of the movement: in this fifth year of World War II and after fifty-one months of Nazi occupation, everyone recognized the rumble of German convoys.

Even more alarming was the size of the procession. Some people later recalled that only once before had they heard such a flow of traffic—in May, 1940, when the Germans had invaded the Netherlands. At that time, swarming across the Reich frontier ten to fifteen miles from Driel, Hitler's mechanized armies had reached the main highways and spread swiftly throughout the country. Now, over those same roads convoys seemed once more to be moving endlessly.

Strange sounds came from the nearest main road—a two-lane highway connecting Arnhem, on the northern bank of the Lower Rhine, with the eighth-century city of Nijmegen, on the broad river Waal, eleven miles to the south. Against the low background throb of engines, people could plainly identify individual noises which seemed curiously out of place in a military convoy—the scrape of wagon wheels, the whir of countless bicycles and the slow, unpaced shuffling of feet.

What kind of convoy could this be? And, more important, where was it heading? At this moment in the war Holland's future could well depend on the answer to that question. Most people believed the convoys carried heavy reinforcements—either pouring into the country to bolster the German garrison or rushing south to halt the Allied advance. Allied troops had liberated northern France with spectacular speed. Now they were fighting in Belgium and were said to be close to the capital, Brussels, less than one hundred miles away. Rumors persisted that powerful Allied armored units were driving for the Dutch border. But no one in Driel could tell for sure exactly the direction the convoys were taking. Distance and the diffusion of sound made that impossible. And because of the nightly curfew the villagers were unable to leave their houses to investigate.

Plagued by uncertainty, they could only wait. They could not know that shortly before dawn the three young soldiers who constituted little Driel's entire German garrison had left the village on stolen bicycles and pedaled off into the mist. There was no longer any military authority in the village to enforce the curfew regulations.

Unaware, people kept to their homes. But the more curious among them were too impatient to wait and decided to risk using the telephone. In her home at 12 Honingveldsestraat, next to her family's jam-and-preserves factory, young Cora Baltussen called friends in Arnhem. She could scarcely believe their eyewitness report. The convoys were *not* heading south to the western front. On this misty morning, September 4, 1944, the Germans and their supporters appeared to be fleeing from Holland, traveling in anything that would move.

The fighting that everyone had expected, Cora thought, would now pass them by. She was wrong. For the insignificant village of Driel, untouched until now, the war had only begun.

2

FIFTY MILES SOUTH, in towns and villages close to the Belgian border, the Dutch were jubilant. They watched incredulously as the shattered remnants of Hitler's armies in northern France and Belgium streamed past their windows. The collapse seemed infectious; besides military units, thousands of German civilians and Dutch Nazis were pulling out. And for these fleeing forces all roads seemed to lead to the German border.

Because the withdrawal began so slowly—a trickle of staff cars and vehicles crossing the Belgian frontier—few Dutch could tell exactly when it had started. Some believed the retreat began on September 2; others, the third. But by the fourth, the movement of the Germans and their followers had assumed the characteristics of a rout, a frenzied exodus that reached its peak on September 5, a day later to be known in Dutch history as *Dolle Dinsdag*, "Mad Tuesday."

Panic and disorganization seemed to characterize the German flight. Every kind of conveyance was in use. Thronging the roads from the Belgian border north to Arnhem and beyond were trucks, buses, staff cars, half-track vehicles, armored cars, horse-drawn farm carts and civilian automobiles running on charcoal or wood. Everywhere throughout the disorderly convoys were swarms of tired, dusty soldiers on hastily commandeered bicycles.

There were even more bizarre forms of transportation. In the town of Valkenswaard, a few miles north of the Belgian frontier, people saw heavily laden German troopers laboriously pushing along on children's scooters. Sixty miles away, in Arnhem, crowds standing on the Amsterdamseweg watched as a massive black-and-silver hearse pulled by two plodding farm horses passed slowly by. Crowded in the casket space in back were a score of disheveled, exhausted Germans.

Trudging in these wretched convoys were German soldiers from many units. There were Panzer troops, minus tanks, in their black battle suits; Luftwaffe men, presumably all that remained of German air force units that had been shattered in either France or Belgium; Wehrmacht soldiers from a score of divisions; and Waffen SS troops, their skull-and-crossbones insignia a macabre identification. Looking at these apparently leaderless, dazed troops moving aimlessly along, young Wilhelmina Coppens in St. Oedenrode thought that "most of them had no idea where they were or even where they were going." Some soldiers, to the bitter amusement of Dutch bystanders, were so disoriented that they asked for directions to the German frontier.

In the industrial town of Eindhoven, home of the giant Philips electrical works, the population had heard the low sound of artillery fire from Belgium for days. Now, watching the dregs of the beaten German army thronging the roads, people expected Allied troops to arrive within hours. So did the Germans. It appeared to Frans Kortie, twenty-four-year-old employee in the town's finance department, that these troops had no intention of making a stand. From the nearby airfield came the roar of explosions as engineers blew up runways, ammunition dumps, gasoline storage tanks and hangars; and through a pall of smoke drifting across the town, Kortie saw squads of troops rapidly working to dismantle heavy anti-aircraft guns on the roofs of the Philips buildings.

All through the area, from Eindhoven north to the city of Nijmegen, German engineers were hard at work. In the Zuid Willemsvaart Canal running below the town of Veghel, Cornelis de Visser, an elementary-school teacher, saw a heavily loaded barge blown skyward, shooting out airplane engine parts like a deadly rain of shrapnel. Not far away, in the village of Uden, Johannes de Groot, forty-five-year-old car-body builder, was watching the retreat with his family when Germans set fire to a former Dutch barracks barely 300 yards from his home. Minutes later heavy bombs stored in the building exploded, killing four of de Groot's children, aged five to eighteen.

In places such as Eindhoven, where school buildings were set ablaze, fire brigades were prevented from operating and whole blocks were burned down. Still, the sappers, in contrast to the fleeing columns on the roads, gave evidence of following some definite plan.

The most frantic and confused among the escapees were the civilians, German, Dutch, Belgian and French Nazis. They got no sympathy from the Dutch. To farmer Johannes Hulsen at St. Oedenrode, they looked "scared stiff"; and they had reason to be, he thought with satisfaction, for with the Allies "snapping at their heels these traitors knew it was *Bijltjesdag* ['Hatchet Day']."

The frantic flight of Dutch Nazis and German civilians had been triggered by the *Reichskommissar* in Holland, the notorious fifty-two-year-old Dr. Arthur Seyss-Inquart, and by the ambitious and brutal Dutch Nazi Party leader, Anton Mussert. Nervously watching the fate of the Germans in France and Belgium, Seyss-Inquart on September 1 ordered the evacuation of German civilians to the east of Holland, closer to the Reich border. The fifty-year-old Mussert followed suit, alerting members of his Dutch Nazi Party. Seyss-Inquart and Mussert were themselves among the first to leave: they moved from The Hague east to Apeldoorn, fifteen miles north of Arnhem.* Mussert rushed his family even closer to the Reich, moving them into the frontier region at Twente, in the province of Overijssel. At first most of the German and Dutch civilians moved at a leisurely pace. Then a sequence of events produced bedlam. On September 3 the British captured Brussels. The next day Antwerp fell. Now, British tanks and troops were only miles from the Dutch border.

On the heels of these stunning victories, the aged Queen of the Netherlands, Wilhelmina, told her people in a radio broadcast from London that liberation was at hand. She announced that her son-in-law, His Royal Highness Prince Bernhard, had been named Commander in Chief of the Netherlands Forces and would also assume leadership of all underground resistance groups. These factions, comprising three distinct organizations

---

*Seyss-Inquart was terrified. At Apeldoorn, he took to his underground headquarters—a massive concrete and brick bunker constructed at a cost of more than $250,000—complete with conference rooms, communications and personal suites. It still exists. Scratched on the concrete exterior near the entrance are the figures "6 1/4," the nickname for the hated commissioner. The Netherlanders couldn't resist it; in Dutch, Seyss-Inquart and "6 1/4" sound almost the same—*zes en een kwart.*

ranging politically from the left to the extreme right, would now be grouped together and officially known as *Binnenlandse Strijdkrachten* (Forces of the Interior). The thirty-three-year-old Prince Bernhard, husband of Princess Juliana, heir to the throne, followed the Queen's announcement with one of his own. He asked the underground to have armlets ready "displaying in distinct letters the word 'Orange,'" but not to use them "without my order." He warned them to "refrain in the enthusiasm of the moment from premature and independent actions, for these would compromise yourselves and the military operations underway."

Next, a special message was broadcast from General Dwight D. Eisenhower, Supreme Commander of the Allied Forces, confirming that freedom was imminent. "The hour of liberation the Netherlands have awaited so long is now very near," he promised. And within a few hours these broadcasts were followed by the most optimistic statement of all, from the prime minister of the Dutch government in exile, Pieter S. Gerbrandy. He told his listeners, "Now that the Allied armies, in their irresistible advance, have crossed the Netherlands frontier . . . I want all of you to bid our Allies a hearty welcome to our native soil. . . ."

The Dutch were hysterical with joy, and the Dutch Nazis fled for their lives. Anton Mussert had long boasted that his party had more than 50,000 Nazis. If so, it seemed to the Dutch that they all took to the roads at the same time. In scores of towns and villages all over Holland, Nazi-appointed mayors and officials suddenly bolted—but often not before demanding back pay. The mayor of Eindhoven and some of his officials insisted on their salaries. The town clerk, Gerardus Legius, thought their posture ridiculous, but he didn't even feel badly about paying them off. Watching them scurry out of town "on everything with wheels" he wondered: "How far can they get? Where can they go?" There was also a run on the banks. When Nicolaas van de Weerd, twenty-four-year-old bank clerk, got to work in the town of Wageningen on Monday, September 4, he saw a queue of Dutch Nazis waiting outside the bank. Once the doors were opened they hurriedly closed accounts and emptied safety deposit boxes.

Railway stations were overrun by terrified civilians. Trains leaving for Germany were crammed to capacity. Stepping off a train on its arrival in Arnhem, young Frans Wiessing was engulfed by a sea of people fighting to get aboard. So great was the rush that after the train left, Wiessing saw a mountain of luggage lying abandoned on the platform. In the village of Zetten, west of Nijmegen, student Paul van Wely watched as Dutch Nazis crowding the railroad station waited all day for a Germany-bound train, which never arrived. Women and children were crying and to Van Wely "the waiting room looked like a junk store full of tramps." In every town there were similar incidents. Dutch collaborators fled on anything that would move. Municipal architect Willem Tiemans, from his office window near the great Arnhem bridge, watched as Dutch Nazis "scrambled like mad" to get onto a barge heading up the Rhine for the Reich.

Hour after hour the traffic mounted, and even during darkness it went on. So desperate were the Germans to reach safety that on the nights of September 3 and 4, in total disregard of Allied air attacks, soldiers set up searchlights at some crossroads and many overloaded vehicles crawled by, headlights blazing. German officers seemed to have lost control. Dr. Anton Laterveer, a general practitioner in Arnhem, saw soldiers throwing away rifles—some even tried to sell their weapons to the Dutch. Joop Muselaars, a teen-ager, watched a lieutenant attempt to stop a virtually empty army vehicle, but the driver, ignoring the command, drove on through. Furious, the officer fired his pistol irrationally into the cobblestones.

Everywhere soldiers tried to desert. In the village of Eerde, Adrianus Marinus, an eighteen-year-old clerk, noticed a soldier jumping off a truck. He ran toward a farm and disappeared. Later Marinus learned that the soldier was a Russian prisoner of war who had been conscripted into the Wehrmacht. Two miles from Nijmegen, in the village of Lent on the northern bank of the Waal, Dr. Frans Huygen, while making his rounds, saw troops begging for civilian clothing, which the villagers refused. In Nijmegen deserters were not so abject. In many cases they demanded clothing at gunpoint. The Reverend Wilhelmus Peterse, forty-year-old Carmelite, saw soldiers hurriedly remove uniforms, change to suits and set off on foot for the German border. "The Germans were totally fed up with the war," recalls Garrit Memelink, Arnhem's Chief Forestry Inspector. "They were doing their damnedest to evade the military police."

With officers losing control, discipline broke down. Unruly gangs of soldiers stole horses, wagons, cars and bicycles. Some ordered farmers at gunpoint to haul them in their wagons toward Germany. All through the convoys the Dutch saw trucks, farm wagons, hand carts—even perambulators pushed by fleeing troops—piled high with loot filched from France, Belgium and Luxembourg. It ranged from statuary and furniture to lingerie. In Nijmegen soldiers tried to sell sewing machines, rolls of cloth, paintings, typewriters—and one soldier even offered a parrot in a large cage.

Among the retreating Germans there was no shortage of alcohol. Barely five miles from the German border in the town of Groesbeek, Father Herman Hoek watched horse-drawn carts loaded down with large quantities of wines and liquors. In Arnhem, the Reverend Reinhold Dijker spotted boisterous Wehrmacht troops on a truck drinking from a huge vat of wine which they had apparently brought all the way from France. Sixteen-year-old Agatha Schulte, daughter of the chief pharmacist of Arnhem's municipal hospital, was convinced that most of the soldiers she saw were drunk. They were throwing handfuls of French and Belgian coins to the youngsters and trying to sell bottles of wine, champagne and cognac to the adults. Her mother, Hendrina Schulte, vividly recalls seeing a German truck carrying another kind of booty. It was a large double bed —and in the bed was a woman.*

Besides the columns straggling up from the south, heavy German and civilian traffic was coming in from western Holland

---

* "Scenes were witnessed which nobody would ever have deemed possible in the German army," writes Walter Goerlitz, the German historian, in his *History of the German General Staff*. "Naval troops marched northward without weapons, selling their spare uniforms . . . They told people that the war was over and they were going home. Lorries loaded with officers, their mistresses and large quantities of champagne and brandy contrived to get back as far as the Rhineland, and it was necessary to set up special courts-martial to deal with such cases."

and the coast. It flooded through Arnhem and headed east for Germany. In the prosperous Arnhem suburb of Oosterbeek, Jan Voskuil, a thirty-eight-year-old chemical engineer, was hiding out at the home of his father-in-law. Learning that he was on a list of Dutch hostages to be arrested by the Germans, he had fled from his home in the town of Geldermalsen, twenty miles away, bringing his wife, Bertha, and their nine-year-old son. He had arrived in Oosterbeek just in time to see the evacuation. Jan's father-in-law told him not to "worry anymore about the Germans; you won't have to 'dive' now." Looking down the main street of Oosterbeek, Voskuil saw "utter confusion." There were dozens of German-filled trucks, nose-to-tail, "all dangerously overloaded." He saw soldiers "on bicycles, pedaling furiously, with suitcases and grips looped over their handlebars." Voskuil was sure that the war would be over in a matter of days.

In Arnhem itself, Jan Mijnhart, sexton of the Grote Kerk —the massive fifteenth-century Church of St. Eusebius with a famed 305-foot-high tower—saw the *Moffen* (a Dutch nickname for the Germans, equivalent to the English "Jerry") filing through the town "four abreast in the direction of Germany." Some looked old and sick. In the nearby village of Ede an aged German begged young Rudolph van der Aa to notify his family in Germany that they had met. "I have a bad heart," he added, "and probably won't live much longer." Lucianus Vroemen, a teen-ager in Arnhem, noticed the Germans were exhausted and had "no fighting spirit or pride left." He saw officers trying, with little or no success, to restore order among the disorganized soldiers. They did not even react to the Dutch, who were yelling, "Go home! The British and Americans will be here in a few hours."

Watching the Germans moving east from Arnhem, Dr. Pieter de Graaff, forty-four-year-old surgeon, was sure he was seeing "the end, the apparent collapse of the German army." And Suze van Zweden, high-school mathematics teacher, had a special reason to remember this day. Her husband, Johan, a respected and well-known sculptor, had been in Dachau concentration camp since 1942 for hiding Dutch Jews. Now he might soon be freed, for obviously the war was nearly over. Suze was determined to witness this historic moment—the departure of the Germans and the arrival of the Allied liberators. Her son Robert was too young to realize what was happening but she decided to take her daughter Sonja, aged nine, into town. As she dressed Sonja, Suze said, "This is something you have to see. I want you to try and remember it all your life."

Everywhere the Dutch rejoiced. Dutch flags made their appearance. Enterprising merchants sold orange buttons and large stocks of ribbon to the eager crowds. In the village of Renkum there was a run on the local drapery shop, where manager Johannes Snoek sold orange ribbon as fast as he could cut it. To his amazement, villagers fashioned bows then and there and proudly pinned them on. Johannes, who was a member of the underground, thought "this was going a bit too far." To protect the villagers from their own excesses, he stopped selling the ribbon. His sister Maria, caught up in the excitement, noted happily in her diary that there was "a mood in the streets almost as though it was *Koninginnedag*, the Queen's birthday." Cheering crowds stood on sidewalks yelling, "Long live the Queen!" People sang the "Wilhelmus" (the Dutch national anthem) and "Oranje Boven!" ("Orange Above All!"). Cloaks flying, Sisters Antonia Stranzky and Christine van Dijk from St. Elisabeth's Hospital in Arnhem cycled down to the main square, the Velperplein, where they joined crowds on the terraces of cafés who were sipping coffee and eating potato pancakes as the Germans and Dutch Nazis streamed by.

At St. Canisius Hospital in Nijmegen, Sister M. Dosithèe Symons saw nurses dance with joy in the convent corridors. People brought out long-hidden radios and, while watching the retreat flood by their windows, listened openly for the first time in long months to the special Dutch service, Radio Orange, from London's BBC. So excited by the broadcasts was fruit grower Joannes Hurkx, in St. Oedenrode, that he failed to spot a group of Germans back of his house stealing the family bicycles.

In scores of places schools closed and work came to a halt. Employees at the cigar factories in Valkenswaard promptly left their machines and crowded into the streets. Streetcars stopped running in The Hague, the seat of government. In the capital, Amsterdam, the atmosphere was tense and unreal. Offices closed, and trading ceased on the stock exchange. Military units suddenly disappeared from the main thoroughfares, and the central station was mobbed by Germans and Dutch Nazis. On the outskirts of Amsterdam, Rotterdam and The Hague, crowds carrying flags and flowers stood along main roads leading into the cities—hoping to be the first to see British tanks coming from the south.

Rumors grew with every hour. Many in Amsterdam believed that British troops had already freed The Hague, near the coast about thirty miles to the southwest. In The Hague people thought the great port of Rotterdam, fifteen miles away, had been liberated. Rail travelers got a different story every time their trains stopped. One of them, Henri Peijnenburg, a twenty-five-year-old resistance leader traveling from The Hague to his home in Nijmegen, a distance of less than eighty miles, heard at the beginning of his journey that the British had entered the ancient border city of Maastricht. In Utrecht he was told they had reached Roermond. Then, in Arnhem he was assured that the British had taken Venlo, a few miles from the German border. "When I finally got home," he recalls, "I expected to see the Allies in the streets, but all I saw were the retreating Germans." Peijnenburg felt confused and uneasy.

Others shared his concern—especially the underground high command meeting secretly in The Hague. To them, tensely watching the situation, Holland seemed on the threshold of freedom. Allied tanks could easily slice through the country all the way from the Belgian border to the Zuider Zee. The underground was certain that the "gateway"—through Holland, across the Rhine and into Germany—was wide open.

The resistance leaders knew the Germans had virtually no fighting forces capable of stopping a determined Allied drive. They were almost scornful of the one weak and undermanned division composed of old men guarding coastal defenses (they had been sitting in concrete bunkers since 1940 without firing a shot), and of a number of other low-grade troops, whose combat capabilities were extremely doubtful, among them Dutch SS, scratch garrison troops, convalescents and the medically unfit—these last grouped into units aptly known as "stomach" and "ear" battalions, because most of the men suffered from ulcers or were hard of hearing.

To the Dutch the Allied move seemed obvious, invasion

imminent. But its success depended on the speed of British forces driving from the south, and about this the underground high command was puzzled: they were unable to determine the precise extent of the Allied advance.

Checking on the validity of Prime Minister Gerbrandy's statement that Allied troops had already crossed the frontier was no simple matter. Holland was small—only about two thirds the size of Ireland—but it had a dense population of more than nine million, and as a result the Germans had difficulty controlling subversive activity. There were underground cells in every town and village. Still, transmitting information was hazardous. The principal, and most dangerous, method was the telephone. In an emergency, using complicated circuitry, secret lines and coded information, resistance leaders could call all over the country. Thus, on this occasion, underground officials knew within minutes that Gerbrandy's announcement was premature: British troops had not crossed the border.

Other Radio Orange broadcasts further compounded the confusion. Twice in a little more than twelve hours (at 11:45 P.M. on September 4 and again on the morning of September 5) the Dutch Service of the BBC announced that the fortress city of Breda, seven miles from the Dutch-Belgian border, had been liberated. The news spread rapidly. Illegal, secretly printed newspapers promptly prepared liberation editions featuring the "fall of Breda." But the Arnhem regional resistance chief, thirty-eight-year-old Pieter Kruyff, whose group was one of the nation's most highly skilled and disciplined, seriously doubted the Radio Orange bulletin. He had his communications expert Johannes Steinfort, a young telephone-company instrument maker, check the report. Quickly tying in to a secret circuit connecting him with the underground in Breda, Steinfort became one of the first to learn the bitter truth: the city was still in German hands. No one had seen Allied troops, either American or British.

Because of the spate of rumors, many resistance groups hurriedly met to discuss what should be done. Although Prince Bernhard and SHAEF (Supreme Headquarters Allied Expeditionary Forces) had cautioned against a general uprising, some underground members had run out of patience. The time had come, they believed, to directly confront the enemy and thus aid the advancing Allies. It was obvious that the Germans feared a general revolt. In the retreating columns, the underground noted, sentries were now sitting on the fenders of vehicles with rifles and submachine guns at the ready. Undeterred, many resistance men were eager to fight.

In the village of Ede, a few miles northwest of Oosterbeek, twenty-five-year-old Menno "Tony" de Nooy tried to persuade the leader of his group, Bill Wildeboer, to attack. It had long been planned, Tony argued, that the group should take over Ede in the event of an Allied invasion. The barracks at Ede, which had been used to train German marines, were now practically empty. De Nooy wanted to occupy the buildings. The older Wildeboer, a former sergeant major in the Dutch Army, disagreed. "I don't trust this situation," he told them. "The time is not yet ripe. We must wait."

Not all resistance movements were held in check. In Rotterdam, underground members occupied the offices of the water-supply company. Just over the Dutch-Belgian border in the village of Axel, the town hall with its ancient ramparts was seized and hundreds of German soldiers surrendered to the civilian fighters. In many towns Dutch Nazi officials were captured as they tried to bolt. West of Arnhem, in the village of Wolfheze, noted principally for its hospital for the mentally ill, the district police commissioner was seized in his car. He was locked up temporarily in the nearest available quarters, the asylum, for delivery to the British "when they arrived."

These were the exceptions. In general, underground units remained calm. Yet, everywhere they took advantage of the confusion to prepare for the arrival of Allied forces. In Arnhem, Charles Labouchère, forty-two, descendant of an old French family and active in an intelligence unit, was much too busy to bother about rumors. He sat, hour after hour, by the windows of an office in the neighborhood of the Arnhem bridge and, with a number of assistants, watched German units heading east and northeast along the Zevenaar and Zutphen roads toward Germany. It was Labouchère's job to estimate the number of troops and, where possible, to identify the units. The vital information he noted down was sent to Amsterdam by courier and from there via a secret network to London.

In suburban Oosterbeek, young Jan Eijkelhoff, threading his

way unobtrusively through the crowds, cycled all over the area, delivering forged food ration cards to Dutchmen hiding out from the Germans. And the leader of one group in Arnhem, fifty-seven-year-old Johannus Penseel, called "the Old One," reacted in the kind of wily manner that had made him a legend among his men. He decided the moment had come to move his arsenal of weapons. Openly, with German troops all about, he and a few hand-picked assistants calmly drove up in a baker's van to the Municipal Hospital, where the weapons were hidden. Quickly wrapping the arms in brown paper they transported the entire cache to Penseel's home, whose basement windows conveniently overlooked the main square. Penseel and his coleader, Toon van Daalen, thought it was a perfect position from which to open fire on the Germans when the time came. They were determined to live up to the name of their militant subdivision—*Landelyke Knokploegen* ("Strong-arm Boys").

Everywhere men and women of the vast underground army poised for battle; and in southern towns and villages, people who believed that parts of Holland were already free ran out of their homes to welcome the liberators. There was a kind of madness in the air, thought Carmelite Father Tiburtius Noordermeer as he observed the joyful crowds in the village of Oss, southeast of Nijmegen. He saw people slapping one another on the back in a congratulatory mood. Comparing the demoralized Germans on the roads with the jubilant Dutch spectators, he noted "wild fear on the one hand and crazy, unlimited, joy on the other." "Nobody," the stolid Dutch priest recalled, "acted normally."

Many grew more anxious as time passed. In the drugstore on the main street in Oosterbeek, Karel de Wit was worried. He told his wife and chief pharmacist, Johanna, that he couldn't understand why Allied planes had not attacked the German traffic. Frans Schulte, a retired Dutch major, thought the general enthusiasm was premature. Although his brother and sister-in-law were overjoyed at what appeared to be a German debacle, Schulte was not convinced. "Things may get worse," he warned. "The Germans are far from beaten. If the Allies try to cross the Rhine, believe me, we may see a major battle."

3

HITLER'S CRUCIAL MEASURES were already underway. On September 4 at the Führer's headquarters deep in the forest of Görlitz, Rastenburg, East Prussia, sixty-nine-year-old Field Marshal Gerd von Rundstedt prepared to leave for the western front. He had not expected a new command.

Called abruptly out of enforced retirement, Von Rundstedt had been ordered to Rastenburg four days before. On July 2, two months earlier, Hitler had fired him as Commander in Chief West (or, as it was known in German military terms, OB West—*Oberbefehlshaber* West) while Von Rundstedt, who had never lost a battle, was trying to cope with the aftermath of Germany's greatest crisis of the war, the Allied invasion of Normandy.

The Führer and Germany's most distinguished soldier had never agreed on how best to meet that threat. Before the invasion, appealing for reinforcements, Von Rundstedt had bluntly informed Hitler's headquarters (OKW—Oberkommando der Wehrmacht)* that the Western Allies, superior in men, equipment and planes, could "land anywhere they want to." Not so, Hitler declared. The Atlantic Wall, the partly completed coastal fortifications which, Hitler boasted, ran almost three thousand miles from Kirkenes (on the Norwegian-Finnish frontier) to the Pyrenees (on the Franco-Spanish border) would make "this front impregnable against any enemy." Von Rundstedt knew only too well that the fortifications were more propaganda than fact. He summed up the Atlantic Wall in one word: "Humbug."

The legendary Field Marshal Erwin Rommel, renowned for his victories in the North African deserts in the first years of the war and sent by Hitler to command Army Group B under Von Rundstedt, was equally appalled by the Führer's confidence. To Rommel, the coastal defenses were a "figment of Hitler's *Wolkenkuckkuksheim* [cloud cuckoo land]." The aristocratic, tradition-bound Von Rundstedt and the younger, ambitious Rommel found themselves, probably for the first time, in

*Armed Forces High Command

agreement. On another point, however, they clashed. With the crushing defeat of his Afrika Korps by Britain's Montgomery at El Alamein in 1942 always in his mind, and well aware of what the Allied invasion would be like, Rommel believed that the invaders must be stopped on the beaches. Von Rundstedt icily disagreed with his junior—whom he sarcastically referred to as the "Marschall Bubi" ("Marshal Laddie"); Allied troops should be wiped out *after* they landed, he contended. Hitler backed Rommel. On D Day, despite Rommel's brilliant improvisations, Allied troops breached the "impregnable" wall within hours.

In the terrible days that followed, overwhelmed by the Allies, who enjoyed almost total air supremacy over the Normandy battlefield, and shackled by Hitler's "no withdrawal" orders ("Every man shall fight and fall where he stands"), Von Rundstedt's straining lines cracked everywhere. Desperately he plugged the gaps, but hard as his men fought and counterattacked, the outcome was never seriously in doubt. Von Rundstedt could neither "drive the invaders into the sea" nor "annihilate them" (the words were Hitler's).

On the night of July 1, at the height of the Normandy battle, Hitler's chief of staff, Field Marshal Wilhelm Keitel, called Von Rundstedt and plaintively asked, "What shall we do?" Characteristically blunt, Von Rundstedt snapped, "End the war, you fools. What else can you do?" Hitler's comment on hearing the remark was mild. "The old man has lost his nerve and can't master the situation any longer. He'll have to go." Twenty-four hours later, in a polite handwritten note, Hitler informed Von Rundstedt that, "in consideration of your health and of the increased exertions to be expected in the near future," he was relieved of command.

Von Rundstedt, the senior and most dependable field marshal in the Wehrmacht, was incredulous. For the five years of war his military genius had served the Third Reich well. In 1939, when Hitler cold-bloodedly attacked Poland, thereby igniting the conflict that eventually engulfed the world, Von Rundstedt had clearly demonstrated the German formula for conquest—*Blitzkrieg* ("lightning war")—when his Panzer spearheads reached the outskirts of Warsaw in less than a week. One year later, when Hitler turned west and with devastating speed overwhelmed most of western Europe, Von Rundstedt was in charge of an entire Panzer army. And in 1941 he was in the forefront again when Hitler attacked Russia. Now, outraged at the jeopardy to his career and reputation, Von Rundstedt told his chief of staff, Major General Gunther Blumentritt, that he had been "dismissed in disgrace by an amateur strategist." That "Bohemian corporal," he fumed, had used "my age and ill health as an excuse to relieve me in order to have a scapegoat." Given a free hand, Von Rundstedt had planned a slow withdrawal to the German frontier, during which, as he outlined his plans to Blumentritt, he would have "exacted a terrible price for every foot of ground given up." But, as he had said to his staff many times, because of the constant "tutelage from above," about the only authority he had as OB West was "to change the guard in front of the gate."*

From the moment of his recall and his arrival at the end of August at the Rastenburg *Wolfsschanze* ("Wolf's Lair"), as it was named by Hitler, Von Rundstedt, at the Führer's invitation, attended the daily briefing conference. Hitler, according to the Deputy Chief of Operations General Walter Warlimont, greeted his senior field marshal warmly, treating him with "unwonted diffidence and respect." Warlimont also noted that throughout the long sessions Von Rundstedt simply sat "motionless and monosyllabic."[†] The precise, practical field marshal had nothing to say. He was appalled by the situation.

The briefings clearly showed that in the east the Red Army now held a front more than 1,400 miles long, from Finland in the north to the Vistula in Poland, and from there to the Carpathian Mountains in Rumania and Yugoslavia. In fact, Russian armor had reached the borders of East Prussia, barely a hundred miles from the Führer's headquarters.

In the west Von Rundstedt saw that his worst fears had

---

*"Von Rundstedt was hurt by the implication in Hitler's letter that he had 'requested' relief," the late General Blumentritt told me in an interview. "Some of us at Headquarters actually thought he had, but this was not so. Von Rundstedt denied that he had ever asked to be relieved—or that he had ever thought of doing so. He was extremely angry—so angry in fact that he swore he would never again take a command under Hitler. I knew he did not mean it for, to Von Rundstedt, military obedience was unconditional and absolute."

[†]Warlimont, *Inside Hitler's Headquarters, 1939–45*, p. 477.

been realized. Division after division was now destroyed, the entire German line thrown helplessly back. Rear-guard units, although surrounded and cut off, still clung to vital ports such as Dunkirk, Calais, Boulogne, Le Havre, Brest, Lorient and St. Nazaire, forcing the Allies to continue bringing supplies in from the distant invasion beaches. But now, with the sudden, stunning capture of Antwerp, one of Europe's greatest deep seaports, the Allies might well have solved their supply problem. Von Rundstedt noted, too, that the tactic of *Blitzkrieg*, perfected by himself and others, was being borrowed with devastating effect by Eisenhower's armies. And Field Marshal Walter Model, the fifty-four-year-old new Commander in Chief, West (he took over on August 17), was clearly unable to bring order out of the chaos. His front had been ripped apart, slashed in the north by tanks of the British Second Army and the U.S. First Army driving through Belgium toward Holland; and, south of the Ardennes, armored columns of the U.S. Third Army under General George S. Patton were heading for Metz and the Saar. To Von Rundstedt the situation was no longer merely ominous. It was cataclysmic.

He had time to dwell on the inevitability of the end. Almost four days elapsed before Hitler allowed Von Rundstedt a private audience. During his wait the Field Marshal stayed in the former country inn reserved for senior officers in the center of the vast headquarters—a barbed-wire-enclosed enclave of wooden huts and concrete bunkers built over a catacomb of underground installations. Von Rundstedt vented his impatience at the delay on Keitel, the chief of staff. "Why have I been sent for?" he demanded. "What sort of game is going on?" Keitel was unable to tell him. Hitler had given Keitel no particular reason, short of an innocuous mention of the Field Marshal's health. Hitler seemed to have convinced himself of his own manufactured version for Von Rundstedt's dismissal on "health grounds" back in July. To Keitel, Hitler had merely said, "I want to see if the old man's health has improved."

Twice Keitel reminded the Führer that the Field Marshal was waiting. Finally, on the afternoon of September 4, Von Rundstedt was summoned to Hitler's presence, and, uncharacteristically, the Führer came to the point immediately. "I would like to entrust you once more with the western front."

Stiffly erect, both hands on his gold baton, Von Rundstedt

merely nodded. Despite his knowledge and experience, his distaste for Hitler and the Nazis, Von Rundstedt, in whom the Prussian military tradition of devotion to service was ingrained, did not decline the appointment. As he was later to recall, "it would have been useless to protest anyway."*

Almost cursorily, Hitler outlined Von Rundstedt's task. Once more Hitler was improvising. Before D Day he had insisted that the Atlantic Wall was invulnerable. Now, to Von Rundstedt's dismay, the Führer stressed the impregnability of the Westwall—the long-neglected, unmanned but still formidable frontier fortifications better known to the Allies as the Siegfried Line. Von Rundstedt, Hitler ordered, was not only to stop the Allies as far west as possible, but to counterattack for, as the Führer saw it, the most dangerous Allied threats were no more than "armored spearheads." Clearly, however, Hitler was shaken by the capture of Antwerp. Its vital port was to be denied the Allies at all costs. Thus, since the other ports were still in German hands, Hitler said, he fully expected the Allied drive to come to a halt because of overextended supply lines. He was confident that the western front could be stabilized and, with the coming of winter, the initiative regained. Hitler assured Von Rundstedt that he was "not unduly worried about the situation in the west."

It was a variation of a monologue Von Rundstedt had heard many times in the past. The Westwall, to Hitler, had now become an *idée fixe*, and Von Rundstedt once again was being ordered "not to give an inch," and "to hold under all conditions."

By ordering Von Rundstedt to replace Field Marshal Model, Hitler was making his third change of command of OB West within two months—from Von Rundstedt to Field Marshal Gunther von Kluge, to Model, and now once again to Von Rundstedt. Model, in the job just eighteen days, would now command only Army Group B under Von Rundstedt, Hitler said. Von Rundstedt had long regarded Model with less than enthusiasm. Model, he felt, had not earned his promotion the

*According to Walter Goerlitz, editor of *The Memoirs of Field Marshal Keitel* (Chapter 10, p. 347), Von Rundstedt said to Hitler, "My Führer, whatever you may command, I will do my duty to my last breath." My version of Von Rundstedt's reaction is based on the recollections of his former chief of staff, Major General Blumentritt. "I said nothing," Von Rundstedt told him. "If I'd opened my mouth, Hitler would have talked 'at me' for three hours."

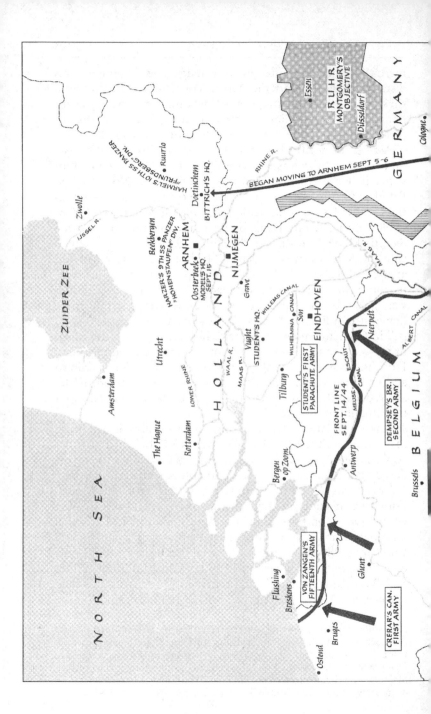

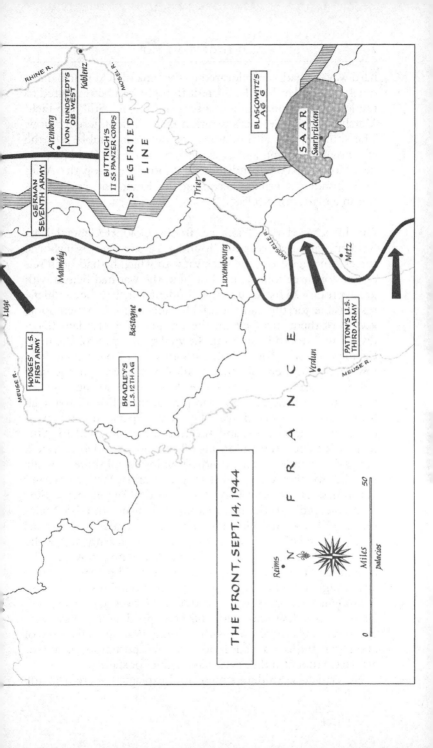

THE FRONT, SEPT. 14, 1944

hard way; he had been elevated to the rank of field marshal too quickly by Hitler. Von Rundstedt thought him better suited to the job of a "good regimental sergeant major." Still, the Field Marshal felt that Model's position made little difference now. The situation was all but hopeless, defeat inevitable. On the afternoon of September 4, as he set out for his headquarters near Koblenz, Von Rundstedt saw nothing to stop the Allies from invading Germany, crossing the Rhine and ending the war in a matter of weeks.

On this same day in Wannsee, Berlin, Colonel General Kurt Student, fifty-four-year-old founder of Germany's airborne forces, emerged from the backwater to which he had been relegated for three long years. For him, the war had begun with great promise. His paratroops, Student felt, had been chiefly responsible for the capture of Holland in 1940, when some 4,000 of them dropped on the bridges of Rotterdam, Dordrecht and Moerdijk, holding the vital spans open for the main German invasion force. Student's losses had been incredibly low—only 180 men. But the situation was different in the 1941 airborne assault of Crete. There, losses were so high—more than a third of the 22,000-man force—that Hitler forbade all future airborne operations. "The day of parachute troops is over," the Führer said, and the future had dimmed for Student. Ever since, the ambitious officer had been tied to a desk job as commander of an airborne-training establishment, while his elite troopers were used strictly as infantry. With shattering abruptness, at precisely 3 P.M. on this critical September 4, Student emerged into the mainstream once again. In a brief telephone call, Colonel General Alfred Jodl, Hitler's operations chief, ordered him to immediately organize an army, which the Führer had designated as the "First Parachute Army." As the astounded Student listened, it occurred to him that "it was a rather high-sounding title for a force that didn't exist."

Student's troopers were scattered all over Germany, and apart from a few seasoned, fully equipped units, they were green recruits armed only with training weapons. His force of about ten thousand had almost no transportation, armor or artillery. Student didn't even have a chief of staff.

Nevertheless, Student's men, Jodl explained, were urgently

needed in the west. They were to "close a gigantic hole" between Antwerp and the area of Liège-Maastricht by "holding
a line along the Albert Canal." With all possible speed, Student was ordered to rush his forces to Holland and Belgium.
Weapons and equipment would be issued at the "railheads of
destination." Besides his paratroopers, two divisions had been
earmarked for his new "army." One of them, the 719th, Student soon learned, was "made up of old men stationed along
the Dutch coast who had not as yet fired a single shot." His
second division, the 176th, was even worse. It consisted of
"semi-invalids and convalescents who, for convenience, had
been grouped together in separate battalions according to
their various ailments." They even had special "diet" kitchens
for those suffering from stomach trouble. Besides these units,
he would get a grab bag of other forces scattered in Holland
and Belgium—Luftwaffe troops, sailors and antiaircraft crews
—and twenty-five tanks. To Student, the expert in paratroop
warfare and supertrained airborne shock troops, his makeshift
army was a "grotesque improvisation on a grand scale." Still,
he was back in the war again.

All through the afternoon, by telephone and teletype, Student mustered and moved his men out. It would take at least
four days for his entire force to reach the front, he estimated.
But his toughest and best troops, rushed in special trains to
Holland in what Student called a "blitz move," would be in
position on the Albert Canal, as part of Model's Army Group
B, within twenty-four hours.

Jodl's call and the information he himself had since gathered
alarmed Student. It seemed apparent that his most seasoned
group—the 6th Parachute Regiment plus one other battalion,
together totaling about three thousand men—probably constituted the only combat-ready reserve in the whole of Germany.
He found the situation ominous.

Frantically, Field Marshal Walter Model, Commander in Chief,
West, tried to plug the yawning gap east of Antwerp and halt
the disorderly retreat from Belgium into Holland. As yet no
news of Von Rundstedt's appointment as his successor had
reached him. His forces were so entangled, so disorganized
that Model had all but lost control. He no longer had contact

with the second half of his command, Army Group G in the south. Had General Johannes Blaskowitz, its commander, successfully withdrawn from France? Model wasn't sure. To the harassed Field Marshal the predicament of Army Group G was secondary. The crisis was clearly in the north.

With dispatch and ferocity, Army Group B had been split in two by armored columns of the British and Americans. Of the two armies composing Army Group B, the Fifteenth was bottled up, its back to the North Sea, roughly between Calais and a point northwest of Antwerp. The Seventh Army had been almost destroyed, and thrown back toward Maastricht and Aachen. Between the two armies lay a 75-mile gap and the British had driven through it straight to Antwerp. Plunging along the same route were Model's own demoralized, retreating forces.

In a desperate effort to halt their flight, Model issued an emotional plea to his troops.

> . . . With the enemy's advance and the withdrawal of our front, several hundred thousand soldiers are falling back—army, air force and armored units—troops which must re-form as planned and hold in new strong points or lines.
>
> In this stream are the remnants of broken units which, for the moment, have no set objectives and are not even in a position to receive clear orders. Whenever orderly columns turn off the road to reorganize, streams of disorganized elements push on. With their wagons move whispers, rumors, haste, endless disorder and vicious self-interest. This atmosphere is being brought back to the rear areas, infecting units still intact and in this moment of extreme tension must be prevented by the strongest means.
>
> I appeal to your honor as soldiers. We have lost a battle, but I assure you of this: We will win this war! I cannot tell you more at the present, although I know that questions are burning on your lips. Whatever has happened, never lose your faith in the future of Germany. At the same time you must be aware of the gravity of the situation. This moment will and should separate men from weaklings. Now every soldier has the same responsibility. When his commander falls, he must be ready to step into his shoes and carry on . . .

There followed a long series of instructions in which Model "categorically" demanded that retreating troops should immediately "report to the nearest command point," instill in others "confidence, self-reliance, self-control and optimism," and repudiate "stupid gossip, rumors and irresponsible reports." The enemy, he said, was "not everywhere at once" and, indeed, "if all the tanks reported by rumormongers were counted, there would have to be a hundred thousand of them." He begged his men not to give up important positions or demolish equipment, weapons or installations "before it is necessary." The astonishing document wound up by stressing that everything depended on "gaining time, which the Führer needs to put new weapons and new troops into operation."

Virtually without communications, depending for the most part on radio, Model could only hope that his Order of the Day reached all his troops. In the confusion he was not even sure of the latest position of his disorganized and shattered units; nor did he know precisely how far Allied tanks and troops had advanced. And where was the *Schwerpunkt* (main thrust) of the Allied drive—with the British and Americans in the north heading for the Siegfried Line and thence across the Rhine and into the Ruhr? Was it with Patton's massive U.S. Third Army driving for the Saar, the Siegfried Line and over the Rhine into Frankfurt?

Model's dilemma was the outgrowth of a situation that had occurred nearly two months earlier at the time of Von Rundstedt's dismissal and Hitler's swift appointment of Von Kluge as the old Field Marshal's successor. On sick leave for months from his command in Russia, Von Kluge happened to be making a courtesy call on the Führer at the precise moment when Hitler decided to dismiss Von Rundstedt. With no preamble, and possibly because Von Kluge happened to be the only senior officer in sight, Hitler had named the astonished Von Kluge Commander in Chief, West.

Von Kluge, a veteran front commander, took over on July 4. He was to last forty-four days. Exactly as predicted by Von Rundstedt, the Allied breakout occurred. "The whole western front has been ripped open," Von Kluge informed Hitler. Overwhelmed by the Allied tide pouring across France, Von Kluge, like Von Rundstedt before him, found his hands tied by Hitler's insistent "no withdrawal" orders. The German armies in France were encircled and all but destroyed. It was during

this period that another convulsion racked the Third Reich—
an abortive assassination attempt on Hitler's life.

During one of the endless conferences at the Führer's headquarters, a time bomb in a briefcase, placed by Colonel Claus
Graf von Stauffenberg beneath a table close to Hitler, exploded, killing and wounding many in the room. The Führer
escaped with minor injuries. Although only a small elite group
of officers were involved in the plot, Hitler's revenge was bar-
baric. Anyone connected with the plotters, or with their families, was arrested; and many individuals, innocent or not, were
summarily executed.* Some five thousand people lost their
lives. Von Kluge had been indirectly implicated, and Hitler also
suspected him of trying to negotiate a surrender with the enemy. Von Kluge was replaced by Model and ordered to report
immediately to the Führer. Before leaving his headquarters the
despairing Von Kluge wrote a letter to Hitler. Then, en route
to Germany, he took poison.

> *When you receive these lines I shall be no more* [he wrote to the
> Führer]. . . . *I did everything within my power to be equal to
> the situation . . . Both Rommel and I, and probably all the other
> commanders here in the west with experience of battle against the
> Anglo-Americans, with their preponderance of material, foresaw
> the present developments. We were not listened to. Our appreci-
> ations were not dictated by pessimism, but from sober knowledge
> of the facts. I do not know whether Field Marshal Model, who has
> been proved in every sphere, will master the situation. From my
> heart I hope so. Should it not be so, however, and your new weapons
> . . . not succeed, then, my Führer, make up your mind to end the
> war. It is time to put an end to this frightfulness. . . . I have
> always admired your greatness . . . and your iron will . . .
> Show yourself now also great enough to put an end to this hopeless
> struggle. . . .*

Hitler had no intention of conceding victory to the Allies,
even though the Third Reich that he had boasted would last a

---

*Hitler took advantage of his most senior officer, Von Rundstedt, once again
by making him President of the Court of Honor that passed judgment on the
officers suspected. Von Rundstedt quietly acceded to the Führer's request. "If
I had not," he later explained, "I too might have been considered a traitor."
Von Rundstedt's explanation has never satisfied many of his brother generals,
who privately denounced him for bending to Hitler's request.

millennium was undermined and tottering. On every front he was attempting to stave off defeat. Yet each move the Führer made seemed more desperate than the last.

Model's appointment as OB West had not helped. Unlike Von Rundstedt or, briefly, Von Kluge, Model did not have the combat genius of Rommel as support. After Rommel was badly wounded by a strafing Allied plane on July 17, no one had been sent to replace him.* Model did not at first appear to feel the need. Confident that he could right the situation, he took on Rommel's old command as well, becoming not only OB West but also Commander of Army Group B. Despite Model's expertise, the situation was too grave for any one commander.

At this time Army Group B was battling for survival along a line roughly between the Belgian coast and the Franco-Luxembourg border. From there, south to Switzerland, the remainder of Model's command—Army Group G under General Blaskowitz—had already been written off. Following the second Allied invasion on August 15, by French and American forces in the Marseilles area, Blaskowitz's group had hurriedly departed southern France. Under continuous pressure they were now falling back in disarray to the German border.

Along Model's disintegrating northern front, where Allied armor had torn the 75-mile-wide gap in the line, the route from Belgium into Holland and from there across Germany's vulnerable northwest frontier lay open and undefended. Allied forces driving into Holland could outflank the Siegfried Line where the massive belt of fortifications extending along Germany's frontiers from Switzerland terminated at Kleve on the Dutch-German border. By turning this northern tip of Hitler's Westwall and crossing the Rhine, the Allies could swing into the Ruhr, the industrial heart of the Reich. That maneuver might well bring about the total collapse of Germany.

Twice in seventy-two hours Model appealed desperately to Hitler for reinforcements. The situation of his forces in the

---

*Rommel, who was also suspected by Hitler of being involved in the assassination attempt, died three months later. While convalescing at his home, Hitler gave him a choice: stand trial for treason or commit suicide. On October 14, Rommel swallowed cyanide, and Hitler announced that the Reich's most popular field marshal had "died of wounds sustained on the battlefield."

undefended gap was chaotic. Order had to be restored and the breach closed. Model's latest report, which he had sent to Hitler in the early hours of September 4, warned that the crisis was approaching and unless he received a minimum of "twenty-five fresh divisions and an armored reserve of five or six panzer divisions," the entire front might collapse, thereby opening the "gateway into northwest Germany."

Model's greatest concern was the British entry into Antwerp. He did not know whether the huge port, the second-largest in Europe, was captured intact or destroyed by the German garrison. The city of Antwerp itself, lying far inland, was not the crux. To use the port, the Allies needed to control its seaward approach, an inlet 54 miles long and 3 miles wide at its mouth, running into Holland from the North Sea past Walcheren Island and looping alongside the South Beveland peninsula. So long as German guns commanded the Schelde estuary, the port of Antwerp could be denied the Allies.

Unfortunately for Model, apart from antiaircraft batteries and heavy coastal guns on Walcheren Island, he had almost no forces along the northern bank. But on the other side of the Schelde and almost isolated in the Pas de Calais was General Gustav von Zangen's Fifteenth Army—a force of more than 80,000 men. Though pocketed—the sea lay behind them to the north and west, and Canadians and British were pressing in from the south and east—they nevertheless controlled most of the southern bank of the estuary.

By now, Model believed, British tanks, exploiting the situation, would surely be moving along the northern bank and sweeping it clear. Before long the entire South Beveland peninsula could be in their hands and sealed off from the Dutch mainland at its narrow base north of the Belgian border, barely 18 miles from Antwerp. Next, to open the port, the British would turn on the trapped Fifteenth Army and clear the southern bank. Von Zangen's forces had to be extricated.

Late in the afternoon of September 4 at Army Group B's headquarters southeast of Liège in the village of La Chaude Fontaine, Model issued a series of orders. By radio he commanded Von Zangen to hold the southern bank of the Schelde and reinforce the lesser ports of Dunkirk, Boulogne and Calais, which Hitler had earlier decreed were to be held with "fanatical determination as fortresses." With the remainder of his troops the hapless Von Zangen was to attack northeast into the avalanche of British armor. It was a desperate measure, yet Model saw no other course. If Von Zangen's attack was successful, it might isolate the British in Antwerp and cut off Montgomery's armored spearheads driving north. Even if the attack failed, Von Zangen's effort might buy time, slowing up the Allied drive long enough for reserves to arrive and hold a new front along the Albert Canal.

Exactly what reinforcements were on the way, Model did not know. As darkness fell he finally received Hitler's answer to his pleas for new divisions to stabilize the front. It was the terse news of his replacement as Commander in Chief, West, by Field Marshal von Rundstedt. Von Kluge had lasted forty-four days as OB West, Model barely eighteen. Normally temperamental and ambitious, Model reacted calmly on this occasion. He was more aware of his shortcomings as an administrator than his critics believed.* Now he could concentrate on the job he knew best: being a front-line commander, solely in charge of Army Group B. But, among the flurry of frantic orders Model issued on this last day as OB West, one would prove momentous. It concerned the relocation of his II SS Panzer Corps.

The commander of the Corps, fifty-year-old Obergruppen-führer (Lieutenant General) Wilhelm Bittrich, had been out of touch with Model for more than seventy-two hours. His forces, fighting almost continuously since Normandy, had been badly mauled. Bittrich's tank losses were staggering, his men short on ammunition and fuel. In addition, because of the breakdown of communications, the few orders he had received by radio were already out of date when Bittrich got them. Uncertain

---

*Twice Model informed Hitler of his inability to command both OB West and Army Group B. "We rarely saw him," OB West's Chief of Staff Blumentritt recalled. "Model hated paper work and spent most of his time in the field." Lieutenant General Bodo Zimmermann, OB West's operations chief, wrote after the war (OCMH MS 308, pp. 153–154) that though Model "was a thoroughly capable soldier," he often "demanded too much and that too quickly," hence "losing sight of what was practically possible." He had a tendency to "dissipate his forces," added Zimmermann, and "staff work suffered under his too-frequent absences and erratic, inconsistent demands."

of the enemy's movements and badly in need of direction, Bittrich set out on foot to find Model. He finally located the Field Marshal at Army Group B headquarters near Liège. "I had not seen him since the Russian front in 1941," Bittrich later recalled. "Monocle in his eye, wearing his usual short leather coat, Model was standing looking at a map and snapping out commands one after the other. There was little time for conversation. Pending official orders, which would follow, I was told to move my Corps headquarters north into Holland." With all possible speed Bittrich was directed to "supervise the refitting and rehabilitation of the 9th and 10th SS Panzer divisions." The battered units, Model told him, were to "slowly disengage from the battle and immediately head north."*

The almost unknown Bittrich could hardly foresee the critical role his 9th and 10th SS Panzer divisions would play within the next two weeks. The site Model chose for Bittrich was in a quiet zone, at this point some seventy-five miles behind the front. By a historic fluke, the area included the city of Arnhem.

4

THE HEADLONG RETREAT of the Germans out of Holland was slowing, although few of the jubilant Dutch realized it as yet. From the Belgian border north to Arnhem, roads were still choked, but there was a difference in the movement. From his post in the Provincial Building above the Arnhem bridge, Charles Labouchère saw no letup in the flood of vehicles, troops and Nazi sympathizers streaming across the bridge.

---

*Understandably perhaps, German records of this period are vague and often inexplicable. Commands were issued, never received, re-sent, countermanded or changed. Considerable confusion exists about Model's order. According to Army Group B's war diary, movement orders for the 9th and 10th SS Panzer divisions were sent on the night of September 3. If so, they were never received. Also, it is recorded that Bittrich received his instructions forty-eight hours later to supervise the regrouping and rehabilitation of not only the 9th but the 2nd and 116th Panzer units. Curiously, the 10th is not mentioned. I can find no evidence that either the 2nd or 116th ever reached the Arnhem area. (It appears they continued fighting at the front.) According to Bittrich's own papers and logs, he received Model's orders orally on September 4 and duly directed only the 9th and 10th to proceed north. Both units, according to their commanders, began slowly withdrawing on September 5–6.

But a few blocks north of Labouchère's location, Gerhardus Gysbers, a seller of antique books, saw a change take place. German troops entering Arnhem from the west were not moving on. The compound of the Willems Barracks next to Gysbers' home and the streets in the immediate vicinity were filling with horse-drawn vehicles and disheveled soldiers. Gysbers noted Luftwaffe battalions, antiaircraft personnel, Dutch SS and elderly men of the 719th Coastal Division. It was clear to Arnhem's resistance chief, Pieter Kruyff, that this was no temporary halt. These troops were not heading back into Germany. They were slowly regrouping; some horse-drawn units of the 719th were starting to move south. Kruyff's chief of intelligence for the Arnhem region, thirty-three-year-old Henri Knap, unobtrusively cycling through the area, spotted the subtle change, too. He was puzzled. He wondered if the optimistic broadcasts from London were false. If so, they were cruel deceptions. Everywhere he saw the Dutch rejoicing. Everyone knew that Montgomery's troops had taken Antwerp. Surely Holland would be liberated within hours. Knap could see the Germans were reorganizing. While they still had little strength, he knew that if the British did not come soon that strength would grow.

In Nijmegen, eleven miles to the south, German military police were closing off roads leading to the German frontier. Elias Broekkamp, a wine importer, saw some troops moving north toward Arnhem, but the majority were being funneled back and traffic was being broken up, processed and fanned out. As in Arnhem, the casual spectator seemed unaware of the difference. Broekkamp observed Dutch civilians laughing and jeering at what they believed to be the Germans' bewildering predicament.

In fact the predicament was growing much less. Nijmegen was turning into a troop staging area, once more in the firm control of German military.

Farther south, in Eindhoven, barely ten miles from the Belgian border, the retreat had all but stopped. In the straggling convoys moving north there were now more Nazi civilians than troops. Frans Kortie, who had seen the Germans dismantling antiaircraft guns on the roofs of the Philips factories, noted a new development. In a railway siding near the station he watched a train pulling flatcars into position. On the cars were heavy antiaircraft guns. Kortie experienced a feeling of dread.

Far more disheartening for observant Dutch was the discovery that reinforcements were coming in from Germany. In Tilburg, Eindhoven, Helmond and Weert, people saw contingents of fresh troops arrive by train. Unloaded quickly and formed up, they set out for the Dutch-Belgian border. They were not regular Wehrmacht soldiers. They were seasoned, well-equipped and disciplined, and their distinctive helmets and camouflaged smocks instantly identified them as veteran German paratroopers.

5

BY LATE AFTERNOON of September 5 Colonel General Kurt Student's first paratroop formations were digging in at points along the north side of Belgium's Albert Canal. Their haste was almost frantic. Student, on his arrival at noon, had discovered that Model's "new German line" was strictly the 80-foot-wide water barrier itself. Defense positions had not been prepared. There were no strong points, trenches or fortifications. And, to make matters worse for the defenders, Student noted, "almost everywhere the southern bank dominated the northern side." Even the bridges over the canal were still standing. Only now were engineers placing demolition charges. In all the confusion no one apparently had ordered the crossings destroyed.

Nevertheless, Student's timetable was well planned. The "blitz move" of his airborne forces was a spectacular success. "Considering that these paratroopers were rushed in from all over Germany, from Güstrow in Mecklenburg to Bitsch in Lothringen," he later recalled, "and arms and equipment, brought in from still other parts of Germany, were waiting for them at the railheads, the speed of the move was remarkable." Student could only admire "the astonishing precision of the general staff and the entire German organization." Lieutenant General Karl Sievers' 719th Coastal Division had made good time, too. Student was heartened to see their columns heading for positions north of Antwerp "clattering down the roads to the front, their transports and artillery pulled by heavy draft horses."* Hour by hour, his hastily formed First Parachute Army was arriving. Also, by extraordinary good fortune, help had come from a most unexpected source.

The headlong retreat from Belgium into Holland had been slowed and then virtually stopped by the doggedness and ingenuity of one man: Lieutenant General Kurt Chill. Because his 85th Infantry Division was almost totally destroyed, Chill had been ordered to save whatever remained and move back into Germany. But the strong-willed general, watching the near-panic on the roads and prompted by Model's Order of the Day, decided to disregard orders. Chill concluded that the only way to avert catastrophe was to organize a line along the Albert Canal. He welded what remained of his 85th Division with the remnants of two others and quickly dispersed these men to strategic points on the northern bank of the canal. Next, he turned his attention to the bridges and set up "reception centers" at their northern exits. In twenty-four hours Chill succeeded in netting thousands of servicemen from nearly every branch of the German armed forces. It was a "crazy-quilt mob,"† including Luftwaffe mechanics, military-government personnel, naval coastal units and soldiers from a dozen different divisions, but these stragglers, armed at best with rifles, were already on the canal when Student arrived.

Student called Chill's virtuoso performance in halting the near-rout "miraculous." With remarkable speed he had established a defense line of sorts, helping to buy a little time for all

---

*Despite the confusion, horse-lover Student took the time to note in his diary that "these huge animals were Clydesdale, Percheron, Danish and Frisian types." Contrary to general belief, Hitler's armies, unlike the Allies', were never totally motorized. Even at the pinnacle of German strength more than 50 percent of their transport was horse-drawn.

†Charles B. MacDonald, *The Siegfried Line Campaign*, p. 124. Published in the official U.S. Army History series, MacDonald's volume and Martin Blumenson's *Breakout and Pursuit* together give the most accurate military picture of the German debacle in the west and the events that followed. Another valuable work on the period, more vivid perhaps because it was written shortly after the war, is Milton Shulman's *Defeat in the West*.

of Student's forces to arrive. This would still take several days. Even with the boost from Chill, Student's patchwork First Parachute Army might total at best 18,000–20,000 men, plus some artillery, antiaircraft guns and twenty-five tanks—hardly the equivalent of an American division. And racing toward this scanty force—so thin that Student could not even man the 75-mile Antwerp-Maastricht gap, let alone close it—were the awesome armored forces of the British Second Army and part of the U.S. First Army. Student was outgunned and outnumbered; about all that stood between him and disaster was the Albert Canal itself.

At what point along it would the enemy attack? Student's line was vulnerable everywhere, but some areas were more critical than others. He was particularly concerned about the sector north of Antwerp, where the weak 719th Coastal Division was only now taking up position. Was there still time to take advantage of the 80-foot-wide water barrier and turn it into a major defense line that would delay the Allies long enough for additional reinforcements to reach the canal? This was Student's greatest hope.

He expected to be attacked at any moment, yet there were still no reports of Allied armor. Student was particularly surprised that there was almost no enemy contact north of Antwerp. He had by now expected that British tanks, after capturing the city, would strike north, cut off the Beveland peninsula, and smash into Holland. It seemed to Student that the British had slowed down. But why?

Four times in eighteen days the vast complex of the German Supreme Headquarters in the West had been forced to move. Bombed, shelled, almost overrun by Allied tanks, OB West had finally come to a halt behind the borders of the Reich. And shortly after 2 P.M. on September 5 the new commander in chief found his headquarters in the little town of Aremberg near Koblenz.

Tired and irritable after his long journey, Field Marshal Gerd von Rundstedt dispensed with the usual military courtesies and fanfare that often accompanied a German change of command. Immediately he plunged into a series of staff conferences that were to last long into the evening. Officers not personally acquainted with the field marshal were startled by the speed of his takeover. To older hands, it was as though he had never been away. For everyone, the very presence of Von Rundstedt brought feelings of relief and renewed confidence.

Von Rundstedt's task was formidable, his problems were massive. He must produce, as quickly as possible, a strategic blueprint for the 400-mile western front running from the North Sea all the way to the Swiss border—a plan which Field Marshal Model had candidly found beyond his capability. With the battered forces at Von Rundstedt's disposal—Army Group B in the north and G in the south—he was expected to hold everywhere and even to counterattack, as Hitler had directed. Simultaneously, to stave off invasion of the Reich, he was to make a reality of Hitler's "impregnable" Siegfried Line—the long-obsolete, unfinished concrete fortifications which had lain neglected, unmanned, and stripped of guns since 1940. There was more, but on this afternoon Von Rundstedt gave first priority to the immediate problems. They were far worse than even he had anticipated.

The picture was bleak. Before his dismissal by Hitler in July, Von Rundstedt had command of sixty-two divisions. Now his operations chief, Lieutenant General Bodo Zimmermann, produced an ominous balance sheet. In the two army groups, he told the Field Marshal, there were "forty-eight 'paper' divisions, fifteen panzer divisions and four brigades with almost no tanks." So weak in men, equipment and artillery were these forty-eight divisions, Zimmermann said, that in his view they constituted "a combat power equivalent to only twenty-seven divisions." This force was less than "half the strength of the Allies." Von Rundstedt learned that his staff believed Eisenhower had at least sixty divisions, completely motorized and at full strength. (This estimate was wrong. Eisenhower had, at this moment, forty-nine divisions on the Continent.)

As for German panzer forces, they were virtually nonexistent. Along the entire front, against the Allies' estimated strength of more than two thousand tanks, there were only one hundred panzers left. The Luftwaffe had been virtually destroyed; above the battlefield, the Allies had complete aerial supremacy. Von Rundstedt's own grim summation was that in troops, most of whom were exhausted and demoralized, he was outnumbered more than 2 to 1; in artillery by 2½ guns to 1; in tanks, 20 to 1; and in planes, 25 to 1.* Besides there were grave shortages in gasoline, transportation and ammunition. Von Rundstedt's new chief of staff, General Siegfried Westphal, was later to recall, "The situation was desperate. A major defeat anywhere along the front—which was so full of gaps that it did not deserve the name—would lead to catastrophe if the enemy were to fully exploit the opportunities."

Lieutenant General Blumentritt, fully agreeing with Westphal's view, was even more specific.† In his opinion, if the Allies mounted "a major thrust resulting in a breakthrough anywhere," collapse would follow. The only capable troops Von Rundstedt had were those facing General George S. Patton's U.S. Third Army driving toward Metz and heading for the industrial region of the Saar. These forces might delay Patton, but they were not strong enough to stop him. Rather than waste precious time, it seemed to Blumentritt that the Allies would strike where the Germans were weakest—by attempting a powerful thrust in the north to cross the Rhine and move into the Ruhr. That drive, he believed, might be given priority by the Americans and the British, because, as he later put it, "He who holds northern Germany, holds Germany."

Von Rundstedt had already reached the same conclusion. Seizing the Ruhr was undoubtedly the major Allied objective.

---

* German losses in men and matériel had been staggering. In the ninety-two days since the invasion of Normandy, 300,000 German troops had been killed or wounded or were missing; another 200,000 were surrounded, holding "last-ditch fortresses" such as ports or in the Channel Islands. Some 53 German divisions had been destroyed, and strewn across France and Belgium were vast quantities of matériel including at least 1,700 tanks, 3,500 guns, thousands of armored vehicles and horse-drawn or motorized transports and mountains of equipment and supplies ranging from small arms to vast ammunition dumps. The casualties included two field marshals and more than twenty generals.

† To Von Rundstedt's annoyance, General Blumentritt, who had long been his chief of staff and most trusted confidant, was replaced by General Westphal on September 5 and ordered back to Germany. Von Rundstedt protested the change, to no avail. Blumentritt did, however, attend the early conferences in Aremberg and did not leave the headquarters until September 8.

The British and Americans in the north were driving in that direction, toward the frontier at Aachen. There was little to stop them from penetrating the unmanned, outdated Siegfried Line, crossing Germany's last natural barrier, the vital Rhine, and striking into the Reich's industrial heart.

Von Rundstedt's analytical mind had seized on one more fact. Eisenhower's skilled and highly trained airborne forces, used so successfully in the Normandy invasion, had disappeared off German situation maps. They were not being used as infantry. Obviously these forces had been withdrawn, preparatory to another airborne operation. But where and when? It was logical that an airborne drop would coincide with a drive on the Ruhr. In Von Rundstedt's view such an attack might come at either of two key areas: behind the Westwall fortifications, or east of the Rhine to seize bridgeheads. In fact, Field Marshal Model, several days earlier, had expressed the same fear in a message to Hitler, stressing the possibility as an "acute threat." Equally, Von Rundstedt could not discount the possibility of the entire Allied front moving forward simultaneously toward the Ruhr *and* the Saar with airborne troops committed at the same time. The Field Marshal could see no solution to any of these impending threats. Allied opportunities were too many and too varied. His only option was to try to bring order out of chaos and to buy time by outguessing Allied intentions, if he could.

Von Rundstedt did not underestimate Eisenhower's intelligence of the German predicament. But, he pondered, was the Allied command really aware how desperate the situation was? The truth was that he was fighting, as he put it to Blumentritt, with "rundown old men" and the pillboxes of the Westwall would be "absolutely useless against an Allied onslaught." It was "madness," he said, "to defend these mouse holes for reasons of prestige." Nevertheless, the ghostly Siegfried Line must be given substance, its fortifications readied and manned. Tersely, Von Rundstedt told his staff: "We must somehow hold for at least six weeks."

Studying each aspect of the situation confronting him, diagraming possible Allied moves and weighing each alternative, he noted that the most vigorous attacks were still being made by Patton, heading for the Saar. In the north British and

American pressure was noticeably less. Von Rundstedt thought he detected an absence of movement, almost a pause, in that area. Turning his attention to Montgomery's front, as Blumentritt was later to remember, Von Rundstedt concentrated on the situation at Antwerp. He was intrigued by reports that, for more than thirty-six hours now, the British had mounted no drive north from the city, nor had they cut the South Beveland peninsula. Obviously, Antwerp's great harbor facilities would solve Allied supply problems. But they could not use the port if both sides of the 54-mile-long estuary leading to it remained in German hands. To the Field Marshal, it seemed clear that the letup he had noted was real; a definite Allied slowdown had occurred, particularly in Montgomery's area.

Throughout his career, Von Rundstedt had closely studied British military tactics; he had also, to his own misfortune, been able to observe American warfare at first hand. He had found the Americans more imaginative and daring in the use of armor, the British superb with infantry. In each case, however, commanders made the difference. Thus, Von Rundstedt considered Patton a far more dangerous opponent than Montgomery. According to Blumentritt, Von Rundstedt viewed Field Marshal Montgomery as "overly cautious, habit-ridden and systematic." Now the Field Marshal weighed the significance of Montgomery's tardiness. With the other Channel ports still in German hands, Von Rundstedt saw Antwerp as essential to Eisenhower's advance—so why had Montgomery not moved for thirty-six hours and apparently failed to secure the second-largest port in Europe? There could be only one reason: Montgomery was not ready to continue the attack. Von Rundstedt was certain that he would not depart from habit. The British would never attack until the meticulous, detail-minded Montgomery was fully prepared and supplied. The answer therefore, Von Rundstedt reasoned, was that the British had overextended themselves. This was not a pause, Von Rundstedt told his staff. Montgomery's pursuit, he was convinced, had ground to a halt.

Quickly, Von Rundstedt turned his attention to Model's orders of the previous twenty-four hours. Because now, if his theory was right, Von Rundstedt saw a chance not only to deny the port of Antwerp to the Allies but, equally important, to save General Von Zangen's trapped Fifteenth Army, a force of more than 80,000 men—men that Von Rundstedt desperately needed.

From Model's orders he saw that, while Von Zangen had been told to hold the southern bank of the Schelde and reinforce the Channel ports, he had also been ordered to attack with the remainder of his troops northeast into the flank of the British drive—an attack scheduled to take place on the morning of the sixth. Without hesitation, Von Rundstedt canceled that attack. Under the circumstances, he saw no merit to it. Besides, he had a bolder, more imaginative plan. The first part of Model's orders could stand, because now holding the Channel ports was more important than ever. But instead of attacking northeast, Von Zangen was ordered to evacuate his remaining troops by sea, across the waters of the Schelde to the island of Walcheren. Once on the northern bank of the estuary, Von Zangen's troops could march eastward along the one road running from Walcheren Island, across the South Beveland peninsula until they reached the Dutch mainland north of Antwerp. Because of Allied air power, ferrying operations across the 3-mile mouth of the Schelde, between the ports of Breskens and Flushing, would have to take place at night. Nevertheless, with luck, a good portion of the Fifteenth Army might be safely withdrawn within two weeks. Von Rundstedt knew that the plan was hazardous, but he saw no other course, for, if successful, he would have almost an entire German army, battered though it might be, at his disposal. More than that he would still—unbelievably—control the vital port of Antwerp. But the success of the operation would depend entirely on Von Rundstedt's hunch that Montgomery's drive had indeed come to a halt.

Von Rundstedt was sure of it. Further, he was banking on it that Montgomery's slowdown held a far deeper significance. Because of overextended communications and supply lines, he was convinced, the Allied breakneck pursuit had reached its limit. At the close of the conference, as Blumentritt was later to recall, "Von Rundstedt looked at us and suggested the incredible possibility that, for once, Hitler might be right."

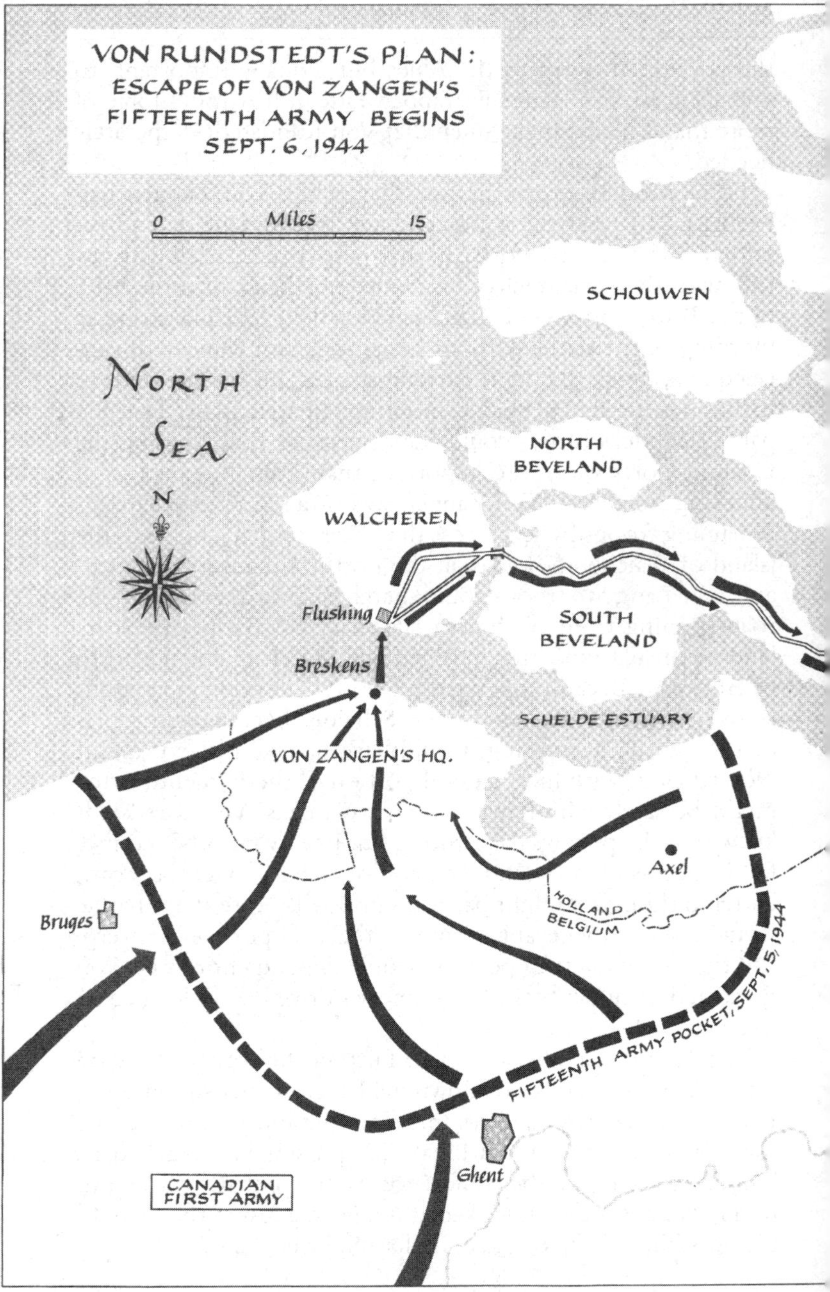

VON RUNDSTEDT'S PLAN:
ESCAPE OF VON ZANGEN'S
FIFTEENTH ARMY BEGINS
SEPT. 6, 1944

0   Miles   15

SCHOUWEN

NORTH SEA

N

NORTH BEVELAND

WALCHEREN

Flushing

SOUTH BEVELAND

Breskens

SCHELDE ESTUARY

VON ZANGEN'S HQ.

Bruges

HOLLAND
BELGIUM

Axel

FIFTEENTH ARMY POCKET, SEPT. 5, 1944

CANADIAN
FIRST ARMY

Ghent

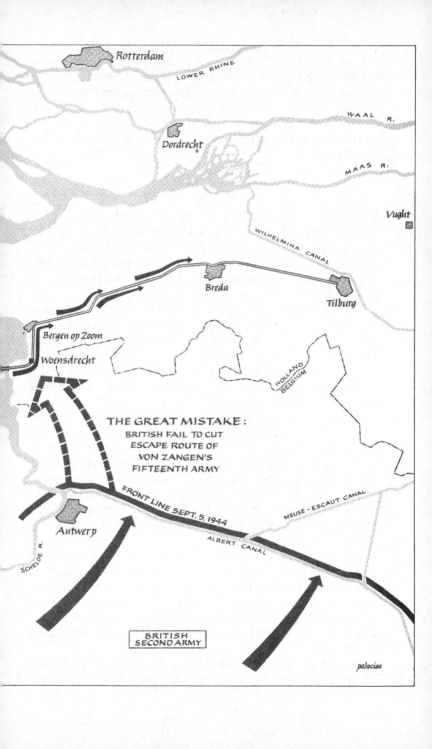

Rotterdam

LOWER RHINE

WAAL R.

Dordrecht

MAAS R.

Vught

WILHELMINA CANAL

Breda

Tilburg

Bergen op Zoom

Woensdrecht

HOLLAND
BELGIUM

THE GREAT MISTAKE:
BRITISH FAIL TO CUT
ESCAPE ROUTE OF
VON ZANGEN'S
FIFTEENTH ARMY

FRONT LINE SEPT. 5, 1944

MEUSE - ESCAUT CANAL

Antwerp

ALBERT CANAL

SCHELDE R.

BRITISH
SECOND ARMY

palacios

Hitler's and Von Rundstedt's estimates of the situation, although only partly correct, were far more accurate than either realized. The precious time Von Rundstedt needed to stabilize his front was being provided by the Allies themselves. The truth was that the Germans were losing faster than the Allies could win.

6

EVEN AS VON RUNDSTEDT gambled desperately to save the trapped Fifteenth Army, Major General George Philip Roberts, commander of the British 11th Armored Division, 150 miles away in Antwerp, was jubilantly informing his superiors of a startling development. His men had captured not only the city but the huge port as well.

Together with the Guards Armored Division, Roberts' tanks had made an extraordinary dash of more than 250 miles in just five days. The spearhead of Lieutenant General Miles C. Dempsey's great British Second Army had been ordered by Lieutenant General Brian Horrocks, XXX Corps commander, to "keep going like mad." Leaving the Guards to capture Brussels, Roberts' division bypassed the city and in the early hours of September 4, with the courageous help of the Belgian underground, entered Antwerp. Now, some thirty-six hours later, after clearing the deep-sea complex of a stunned and panic-stricken enemy, Roberts reported that his men had captured Antwerp's huge 1,000-acre harbor area intact. Warehouses, cranes, bridges, 3½ miles of wharves, quays, locks, drydocks, rolling stock—and, unbelievably, even the all-important electrically controlled sluice gates, in full working order—had been seized.

German plans to demolish the port had failed. Explosives had been placed on major bridges and other key installations, but, overwhelmed by the spectacular speed of the British and resistance groups (among them Belgian engineers who knew exactly where the demolitions were planted), the disorganized German garrison never had a chance to destroy the vast harbor facilities.

The thirty-seven-year-old Roberts had brilliantly executed his orders. Unfortunately, in one of the greatest miscalculations of the European war, no one had directed him to take advantage of the situation—that is, strike north, grab bridgeheads over the Albert Canal in the northern suburbs, and then make a dash for the base of the South Beveland peninsula only eighteen miles away. By holding its 2-mile-wide neck, Roberts could have bottled up German forces on the isthmus, preparatory to clearing the vital northern bank. It was a momentous oversight.* The port of Antwerp, one of the war's major prizes, was secured; but its approaches, still held by the Germans, were not. This great facility, which could have shortened and fed Allied supply lines all along the front, was useless. Yet nobody, in the heady atmosphere of the moment, saw this oversight as more than a temporary condition. Indeed, there seemed no need to hurry. With the Germans reeling, the mop-up could take place at any time. The 11th Armored, its assignment completed, held its positions awaiting new orders.

The magnificent drive of Dempsey's armored forces in the north, equaling that of Patton's south of the Ardennes, had run its course, though at this moment few realized it. Roberts' men were exhausted, short on gasoline and supplies. The same was true of the remainder of General Brian Horrocks' XXX Corps. Thus, on this same afternoon, the relentless pressure that had thrown the Germans back in the north, shattered and demoralized, suddenly relaxed. The blunder at Antwerp was compounded as the British came to a halt to "refit, refuel, and rest."

---

*The late B. H. Liddell Hart, the celebrated British historian, in his *History of the Second World War* wrote: "It was a multiple lapse—by four commanders from Montgomery downwards . . ." Charles B. MacDonald, the American historian in *The Mighty Endeavor*, agrees with Liddell Hart. He called the failure "one of the greatest tactical mistakes of the war." The best and most detailed account on the cost of Antwerp is undoubtedly R. W. Thompson, *The 85 Days*, and I agree with him that one of the main reasons for the missed opportunity was "weariness." Men of the 11th Armored, he wrote, "slept where they sat, stood or lay, drained of emotion, and in utter exhaustion." If we accept his theory it is doubtful that Roberts' 11th could have continued its drive with the same vigor. Nevertheless, Antwerp and its vital approaches, argues Thompson, might have been taken with ease "had there been a commander following the battle, hour by hour, day by day, and with the flexibility of command to see the prospect."

General Horrocks, the XXX Corps's capable and dynamic commander, was not even thinking about Antwerp.* Like Field Marshal Montgomery, commander of the British 21st Army Group, his attention was focused on another target: the crossing of the Rhine and a swift end to the war. Only a few hours earlier, elated at the verve and dash of his armies, Montgomery had cabled the Supreme Commander, General Dwight D. Eisenhower: "We have now reached a stage where a really powerful and full-blooded thrust towards Berlin is likely to get there and thus end the war."

In London, His Royal Highness, the Prince of the Netherlands conferred with Queen Wilhelmina and then telephoned his wife, the Princess Juliana, in Canada. He urged her to fly immediately to England, ready to return to the Netherlands the moment the country was freed. Their long exile was about to end. The liberation, when it came, would be swift. They must be ready. Yet Bernhard was uneasy.

Over the past seventy-two hours messages reaching him from the resistance had again and again underscored the German panic in Holland and repeated the news that the retreat, begun on September 2, was still in progress. Now, on the fifth, underground leaders reported that although the Germans were still disorganized, the exodus appeared to be slowing down. Bernhard had also heard from the Dutch Prime Minister in exile. Prime Minister Gerbrandy was somewhat embarrassed. Obviously his September 3 broadcast was premature; Allied troops had most certainly not crossed the Dutch border as yet. The Prince and the Prime Minister pondered the reason. Why had

---

*Horrocks, in his memoirs, gives a very frank explanation. "My excuse is that my eyes were fixed entirely on the Rhine and everything else seemed of subsidiary importance. It never entered my head that the Schelde would be mined and that we would not be able to use Antwerp until the channel had been swept and the Germans cleared from the coastlines on either side. . . . Napoleon would, no doubt, have realized these things but Horrocks didn't." He also readily admits there was little opposition ahead of him and "we still had 100 miles of petrol per vehicle and one further day's supply within reach." There would have been "considerable risk" but "I believe that if we had taken the chance and carried straight on with our advance, instead of halting in Brussels, the whole course of the war in Europe might have been changed."

the British not moved? Surely, from the underground messages they received, the situation in Holland was clear.

Bernhard had little military training and was dependent on his own advisers, yet he was puzzled.* If the Germans were still disorganized and, as his resistance leaders believed, a "thrust by a few tanks" could liberate the country "in a matter of hours" —why, then, didn't the British proceed? Perhaps Montgomery disbelieved the reports of the Dutch resistance because he considered them amateurish or unreliable. Bernhard could find no other explanation. Why else would the British hesitate, instead of instantly crossing the border? Although he was in constant touch with his ministers, the United States ambassador at large, Anthony Biddle, and Eisenhower's chief of staff, Bedell Smith, and as a result was well aware that, at this moment, the advance was so fluid that the situation was changing almost hour by hour, nevertheless Bernhard thought he would like firsthand information. He made a decision: he would request permission of SHAEF to fly to Belgium and see Field Marshal Montgomery himself as soon as possible. He had every faith in the Allied high command and, in particular, Montgomery. Still, if something was wrong, Bernhard had to know.

At his spartan, tented headquarters in the Royal Palace Gardens at Laeken, a few miles from the center of Brussels, Field Marshal Bernard Law Montgomery impatiently waited for an answer to his coded "Personal for Eisenhower Eyes Only" message. Its urgent demand for a powerful and full-blooded thrust to Berlin was sent in the late hours of September 4. Now, by

---

*The young Prince, although named Commander in Chief of the Netherlands Forces by the Queen, was quite frank in interviews with the author regarding his military background. "I had no tactical experience," he told me, "except for a course at the War College before the war. I followed this up with courses in England, but most of my military knowledge was learned in a practical way by reading and by discussions with my officers. However, I never considered myself experienced enough to make a tactical decision. I depended on my staff, who were very well qualified." Nevertheless Bernhard took his job very seriously. In his meticulously kept personal diary for 1944, which he kindly placed at my disposal, he recorded in minuscule handwriting each movement, almost minute by minute, from telephone calls and military conferences to official functions. During this period, based on his own notations, I would estimate that his average working day was about sixteen hours.

midday on September 5, the brusque, wiry fifty-eight-year-old hero of El Alamein waited for a reply and impatiently fretted about the future course of the war. Two months before the invasion of Normandy he had said, "If we do our stuff properly and no mistakes are made, then I believe that Germany will be out of the war this year." In Montgomery's unalterable opinion, a momentous strategic mistake had been made just before the Allies captured Paris and crossed the Seine. Eisenhower's "broad-front policy"—moving his armies steadily forward to the borders of the Reich, then up to the Rhine—may have been valid when planned before the invasion, but with the sudden disorderly collapse of the Germans, the Britisher believed, it was now obsolete. As Montgomery put it, that strategy had become "unstitched." And all his military training told him "we could not get away with it and . . . would be faced with a long winter campaign with all that that entailed for the British people."

On August 17 he had proposed to General Omar N. Bradley, the U.S. 12th Army Group commander, a single-thrust plan. Both his own and Bradley's army group should stay "together as a solid mass of forty divisions, which would be so strong that it need fear nothing. This force should advance northeastward." Montgomery's 21st Army Group would clear the Channel coast, and secure Antwerp and southern Holland. Bradley's U.S. 12th Army Group, its right flank on the Ardennes, would head for Aachen and Cologne. The basic objective of Montgomery's proposed drive was to "secure bridgeheads over the Rhine before the winter began and to seize the Ruhr quickly." In all probability, he theorized, it would also end the war. Montgomery's plan called for three of Eisenhower's four armies—the British Second, the U.S. First and the Canadian First. The fourth, Patton's U.S. Third Army, at this moment making headlines around the world for its spectacular advances, Montgomery dismissed. He calmly suggested it should be brought to a halt.

Some forty-eight hours later Montgomery learned that Bradley, who he had believed was responsive to his own idea, actually favored an American thrust, a Patton drive toward the Rhine and Frankfurt. Eisenhower rejected both plans; he was not prepared to change his strategic concept. The Supreme Commander wanted to remain flexible enough to thrust both to the Ruhr and the Saar as the occasion permitted. To Montgomery, this was no longer the "broad-front policy" but a double-thrust plan. Everybody now, he felt, was "going his own way"—especially Patton, who seemed to be allowed enormous latitude. Eisenhower's determination to persist in his original concept revealed quite clearly, in Montgomery's opinion, that the Supreme Commander was "in fact, completely out of touch with the land battle."

Montgomery's view was based on a recent development which angered him and, he felt, demeaned his own role. He was no longer the over-all coordinator of the land battle. On September 1 Eisenhower had personally taken over command. Because the Supreme Commander believed Montgomery "a master of the set battle piece," he had given the British general operational control of the D-Day assault and the initial period of fighting thereafter. Thus, General Omar N. Bradley's 12th Army Group was under Montgomery. Press stories appearing in the United States at the end of August revealing that Bradley's army group still operated under Montgomery created such a public furor that Eisenhower was promptly ordered by General George C. Marshall, U.S. Chief of Staff, to "immediately assume direct command" of all ground forces. American armies reverted back to their own command. The move caught Montgomery off base. As his chief of staff, General Francis de Guingand, later put it: "Montgomery . . . never, I believe, thought that the day would come so soon. Possibly he hoped that the initial command set up was there to stay for a long time. He was, I think, apt to give insufficient weight to the dictates of prestige and national feelings, or to the increasing contribution of America, in both men and arms . . . it was obvious, however, to most of us that it would have been an impossible situation for a British general and a British headquarters to retain command of these more numerous American formations indefinitely."* It may have been obvious to his staff but not to Montgomery. He felt publicly humiliated.†

It was hardly a secret that Monty and his superior, Sir Alan

---

*Major General Francis de Guingand, *Generals at War*, pp. 100–101.
†Montgomery and the British public, as outraged as he, were somewhat mollified when George VI, at Churchill's strong urging, made Montgomery a field marshal on September 1.

Brooke, Chief of the Imperial General Staff, were highly critical of Eisenhower. Both men considered him ambivalent and
indecisive. In a letter to Montgomery on July 28, Brooke
commented that Eisenhower had only "the very vaguest conception of war!" On another occasion he summarized the
Supreme Commander as "a most attractive personality," but
with "a very, very limited brain from a strategic point of view."
Montgomery, never a man to mince words, saw "right from
the beginning that Ike had simply no experience for the job,"
and while history, he felt, would record Eisenhower "as a very
good Supreme Commander, as a field commander he was very
bad, very bad."* Angrily, Montgomery began promoting the
idea of an over-all "Land Forces Commander," a post sand-
wiched between the army groups and Eisenhower. He knew
just the man for the job—himself. Eisenhower was well aware
of the underground campaign. He remained calm. The Supreme Commander was, in his way, as obstinate as Montgomery. His orders from General Marshall were clear and he had
no intention of entertaining the idea of any over-all ground
commander other than himself.

Montgomery had no opportunity to discuss his single-
thrust plan or his thoughts about a land-forces commander
directly with Eisenhower until August 23, when the Supreme
Commander came to lunch at 21st Army Group headquarters. Then the fractious Montgomery, with extraordinary tact-
lessness, insisted on a private conversation with the Supreme
Commander. He demanded that Eisenhower's chief of staff,
General Bedell Smith, be excluded from the conference. Smith
left the tent, and for an hour Eisenhower, grimly keeping his
temper, was lectured by his subordinate on the need for "a
firm and sound plan." Montgomery demanded that Eisenhower "decide where the main effort would be" so that "we
could be certain of decisive results quickly." Again and again
he pressed for the "single thrust," warning that if the Supreme
Commander continued the "broad-front strategy with the
whole line advancing and everyone fighting all the time, the
advance would inevitably peter out." If that happened, Montgomery warned, "the Germans would gain time to recover,

*Author's interview with Field Marshal Montgomery.

and the war would go on all through the winter and well into 1945. If we split the maintenance," Montgomery said, "and advance on a broad front we shall be so weak everywhere we'll have no chance of success." To his mind there was only one policy: "to halt the right and strike with the left, or halt the left and strike with the right." There could only be one thrust and everything should support it.

Eisenhower saw Montgomery's proposal as a gigantic gamble. It might produce speedy and decisive victory. It might instead result in disaster. He was not prepared to accept the risks involved. Nevertheless he found himself caught between Montgomery on one side and Bradley and Patton on the other —each advocating "the main thrust," each wanting to be entrusted with it.

Up to this point, Montgomery, notorious for his slow-moving, if successful, tactics, had yet to prove that he could exploit a situation with the speed of Patton; and at this moment Patton's army, far ahead of everyone else, had crossed the Seine and was racing toward Germany. Diplomatically, Eisenhower explained to Montgomery that, whatever the merits of a single thrust, he could hardly hold back Patton and stop the U.S. Third Army in its tracks. "The American people," said the Supreme Commander, "would never stand for it, and public opinion wins wars." Montgomery heatedly disagreed. "Victories win wars," he announced. "Give people victory and they won't care who won it."

Eisenhower was not impressed. Although he did not say so at the time, he thought Montgomery's view was "much too narrow," and that the Field Marshal did not "understand the over-all situation." Eisenhower explained to Montgomery that he wanted Patton to continue eastward so that a link-up might be effected with the American and French forces advancing from the south. In short, he made it quite clear that his "broad-front policy" would continue.

Montgomery turned for the moment to the subject of a land commander. "Someone must run the land battle for you." Eisenhower, Montgomery declared, should "sit on a very lofty perch in order to be able to take a detached view of the whole intricate problem, which involves land, sea, air, et cetera." He retreated from arrogance to humility. If the matter of "public opinion in America was involved," Montgomery declared, he would gladly "let Bradley control the battle and serve under him."

Eisenhower quickly dismissed the suggestion. Placing Bradley over Montgomery would be as unacceptable to the British people as the reverse would be to the Americans. As for his own role he could not, he explained, deviate from the plan to take personal control of the battle. But, in seeking a solution to some of the immediate problems, he was ready to make some concessions to Montgomery. He needed the Channel ports and Antwerp. They were vital to the entire Allied supply problem. Thus, for the moment, Eisenhower said, priority would be given to the 21st Army Group's northern thrust. Montgomery could use the Allied First Airborne Army in England—at the time SHAEF's only reserve. Additionally, he could have the support of the U.S. First Army moving on his right.

Montgomery had, in the words of General Bradley, "won the initial skirmish," but the Britisher was far from satisfied. It was his firm conviction that Eisenhower had missed the "great opportunity." Patton shared that view—for different reasons—when the news reached him. Not only had Eisenhower given supply priority to Montgomery at the expense of the U.S. Third Army, but he had also rejected Patton's proposed drive to the Saar. To Patton, it was "the most momentous error of the war."

In the two weeks since this clash of personalities and conflicting military philosophies had taken place, much had happened. Montgomery's 21st Army Group now rivaled Patton's in speed. By September 5, with his advance units already in Antwerp, Montgomery was more convinced than ever that his single-thrust concept was right. He was determined to reverse the Supreme Commander's decision. A crucial turning point in the conflict had been reached. The Germans, Montgomery was convinced, were teetering on the verge of collapse.

He was not alone in this view. On nearly every level of command, intelligence officers were forecasting the imminent end of the war. The most optimistic estimate came from the Combined Allied Intelligence Committee in London. The German situation had deteriorated to such an extent that the group believed the enemy incapable of recovery. There was every indication, their estimate said, that "organized resistance under the control of the German high command is unlikely to continue beyond December 1, 1944, and . . . may end even sooner." Supreme Headquarters shared this optimism. At the end of August, SHAEF's intelligence summary declared that "the August battles have done it and the enemy in the west has had it. Two and one half months of bitter fighting have brought the end of the war in Europe in sight, almost within reach." Now, one week later, they considered the German army "no longer a cohesive force but a number of fugitive battle groups, disorganized and even demoralized, short of equipment and arms." Even the conservative director of military operations at the British War Office, Major General John Kennedy, noted on September 6 that "If we go at the same pace as of late, we should be in Berlin by the 28th. . . ."

In this chorus of optimistic predictions there seemed only one dissenting voice. The U.S. Third Army's intelligence chief, Colonel Oscar W. Koch, believed the enemy still capable of waging a last-ditch struggle and warned that "barring internal upheaval in the homeland and the remote possibility of insurrection within the Wehrmacht . . . the German armies will continue to fight until destroyed or captured."* But his own intelligence officer's cautious appraisal meant little to the Third Army's ebullient commander, Lieutenant General George S. Patton. Like Montgomery in the north, Patton in the south was now only one hundred miles from the Rhine. He too believed the time had come, as Montgomery had put it, "to stick our neck out in a single deep thrust into enemy territory," and finish off the war. The only difference lay in their views of who was to stick out his neck. Both commanders, flushed with victory and bidding for glory, now vied for that opportunity. In his zeal, Montgomery had narrowed his rivalry down to Patton alone: a British field marshal in charge of an entire army group was trying to outrace an American lieutenant general in charge of a single army.

But all along the front the fever of success gripped battle commanders. After the spectacular sweep across France and Belgium and with evidence of German defeat all around, men now confidently believed that nothing could stop the victorious

---

*For a more detailed version of Allied intelligence estimates see Dr. Forrest C. Pogue, *The Supreme Command*, pp. 244–45.

surge from continuing through the Siegfried Line and beyond, into the heart of Germany. Yet, keeping the enemy off balance and disorganized demanded constant, unremitting Allied pressure. Supporting that pressure had now produced a crisis that few seemed aware of. The heady optimism bordered on self-deception for, at this moment, Eisenhower's great armies, after a hectic dash of more than two hundred miles from the Seine, were caught up in a gigantic maintenance and supply problem. After six weeks of almost nonstop advance against little opposition, few noted the sudden loss of momentum. But as the first tanks approached Germany's threshold and at places began probing the Westwall itself, the advance began to slow. The Allied pursuit was over, strangled by its own success.

The chief problem crippling the advance was the lack of ports. There was no shortage of supplies, but these were stockpiled in Normandy, still being brought in across the beaches or through the only workable port, Cherbourg—some 450 miles behind the forward elements. Supplying four great armies in full pursuit from that far back was a nightmarish task. A lack of transportation added to the creeping paralysis. Rail networks, bombed in preinvasion days or destroyed by the French underground, could not be repaired fast enough. Gasoline pipelines were only now being laid and extended. As a result, everything from rations to gasoline was being hauled by road, and there was a frustrating shortage of trucks.

To keep abreast of the pursuit which, day by day, pushed farther east, every kind of vehicle was being pressed into service. Artillery, antiaircraft guns and spare tanks had been unloaded from their conveyors and left behind so that the conveyors could be used to carry supplies. Divisions had been stripped of their transport companies. The British had left one entire corps west of the Seine so that its transport could service the rest of the speeding army. Montgomery's difficulties mounted with the discovery that 1,400 British three-ton trucks were useless because of faulty pistons.

Now, in herculean efforts to keep the pursuit going without pause, a ceaseless belt of trucks—the "Red Ball Express" —hammered east, delivered their supplies and then swung back to the west for more, some convoys often making a grueling round trip of between six and eight hundred miles. Even with all available transport moving around the clock and with commanders in the field applying the most stringent economies, the supply demands of the armies could not be met. Taxed beyond its capabilities, the makeshift supply structure had almost reached the breaking point.

Besides the acute transportation problem, men were tired, equipment worn out after the catapultlike advance from Normandy. Tanks, half-tracks and vehicles of every description had been driven so long without proper maintenance that they were breaking down. Overshadowing everything was a critical shortage of gasoline. Eisenhower's armies, needing one million gallons per day, were receiving only a fraction of that amount.

The effect was critical. In Belgium, as the enemy fled before it, an entire corps of the U.S. First Army was halted for four days, its tanks dry. Patton's U.S. Third Army, more than a hundred miles ahead of everyone else, and meeting little opposition, was forced to halt for five days on the Meuse, because armored columns were out of gas. Patton was furious when he discovered that of the 400,000 gallons of gasoline ordered, he had received only 32,000 due to priority cutbacks. He promptly ordered his leading corps commander: "Get off your fanny as fast as you can and move on until your engines run dry, then get out and walk, goddammit!" To his headquarters staff, Patton raged that he was "up against two enemies —the Germans and our own high command. I can take care of the Germans, but I'm not sure I can win against Montgomery and Eisenhower." He tried. Convinced that he could bludgeon his way into Germany in a matter of days, Patton furiously appealed to Bradley and Eisenhower. "My men can eat their belts," he stormed, "but my tanks have gotta have gas."

The crushing defeat of the Germans in Normandy and the systematic and speedy annihilation of their forces following the breakout had caused the logistic crisis. On the assumption that the enemy would hold and fight on the various historic river lines, invasion planners had anticipated a more conservative advance. A pause for regrouping and massing of supplies, it was assumed, would take place after the Normandy beachhead had been secured and Channel ports captured. The lodgment area was expected to lie west of the river Seine which, according to the projected timetable, would not be reached until September 4 (D plus 90 days). The sudden disintegration of the enemy's forces and their headlong flight eastward had made the

Allied timetable meaningless. Who could have foreseen that by September 4 Allied tanks would be two hundred miles east of the Seine and in Antwerp? Eisenhower's staff had estimated that it would take approximately eleven months to reach the German frontier at Aachen. Now, as tank columns approached the Reich, the Allies were almost seven months ahead of their advance schedule. That the supply and transportation system, designed for a much slower rate of progress, had stood up to the strain of the hectic pursuit at all was close to miraculous.

Yet, in spite of the critical logistic situation, no one was ready to admit that the armies must soon halt or that the pursuit was over. "Every commander from division upwards," Eisenhower later wrote, was "obsessed with the idea that with only a few more tons of supply, he could rush right on and win the war. . . . Each commander, therefore, begged and demanded priority over all others, and it was quite undeniable that in front of each were opportunities for quick exploitation that made the demands completely logical." Still, the optimism had infected even the Supreme Commander. It was obvious that he believed the impetus of the advance could be maintained long enough for the Allied armies to overrun the Siegfried Line before the Germans had a chance to defend it, for he saw signs of "collapse" on the "entire front." On September 4 he directed that Bradley's "12th Army Group will capture the Saar and the Frankfurt area." Montgomery's "21st Army Group will capture the Ruhr and Antwerp."

Even Patton seemed appeased by the announcement. Now he was sure that, given adequate supplies, his powerful U.S. Third Army could, by itself, reach the industrial Saar and then dash on all the way to the Rhine.* And in the unparalleled

---

*Patton's weekly press conferences were always newsworthy, but especially memorable for the General's off-the-record remarks, which, because of his colorful vocabulary, could never have been printed anyway. That first week of September, as a war correspondent for the London *Daily Telegraph*, I was present when, in typical fashion, he expounded on his plans for the Germans. In his high-pitched voice and pounding the map, Patton declared that, "Maybe there are five thousand, maybe ten thousand, Nazi bastards in their concrete foxholes before the Third Army. Now, if Ike stops holding Monty's hand and gives me the supplies, I'll go through the Siegfried Line like shit through a goose."

atmosphere of victory that prevailed, Montgomery, with his coded message of September 4, once again doggedly pressed his case. This time he went far beyond his proposal of August 17 and his conversation with Eisenhower on August 23. Convinced that the Germans were broken, the commander of the British 21st Army Group believed that he could not only reach the Ruhr but race all the way to Berlin itself.

In his nine-paragraph message to Eisenhower, Montgomery spelled out again the reasons that convinced him that the moment had come for a "really powerful and full-blooded thrust." There were two strategic opportunities open to the Allies, "one via the Ruhr and the other via Metz and the Saar." But, he argued, because "we have not enough resources, two such drives could not be maintained." There was a chance for only one—his. That thrust, the northern one "via the Ruhr," was, in Montgomery's opinion, "likely to give the best and quickest results." To guarantee its success, Monty's single thrust would need "all the maintenance resources . . . without qualification." He was now clearly impatient of any other considerations. He was going on record both as to the worth of his own plan and his skill and belief in himself as the one man to carry it off. Other operations would have to get along with whatever logistic support remained. There could be no compromise, he warned the Supreme Commander. He dismissed the possibility of two drives, because "it would split our maintenance resources so that neither thrust is full-blooded" and as a result "prolong the war." As Montgomery saw the problem it was "very simple and clear-cut." But time was of "such vital importance . . . that a decision is required at once."

Acrid and autocratic, the most popular British commander since Wellington was obsessed by his own beliefs. Considering the acute logistic situation, he reasoned that his single-thrust theory was now more valid than it had been two weeks before. In his intractable way—and indifferent as to how the tone of his message might be received—Montgomery was not merely suggesting a course of action for the Supreme Commander; the Field Marshal was dictating one. Eisenhower must halt all other armies in their tracks—in particular Patton's—so that all resources could be put behind his single drive. And his Signal

No. M-160 closed with a typical example of Montgomery's arrogance. "If you are coming this way perhaps you would look in and discuss it," he proposed. "If so, delighted to see you lunch tomorrow. Do not feel I can leave this battle just at present." That his closing words bordered on the insolent seemed not to occur to Montgomery in his anxiety that this last chance to finish off the Germans must not be lost. Limpetlike, he clung to his single-thrust plan. For now he was sure that even Eisenhower must realize that the time had come to strike the final blow.

In the bedroom of his villa at Granville on the western side of the Cherbourg peninsula, the Supreme Commander read Montgomery's Signal No. M-160 with angry disbelief. The fifty-five-year-old Eisenhower thought Montgomery's proposal "unrealistic" and "fantastic." Three times Montgomery had nagged him to exasperation about single-thrust schemes. Eisenhower thought he had settled the strategy conflict once and for all on August 23. Yet, now Montgomery was not only advocating his theory once again but was proposing to rush all the way to Berlin. Usually calm and congenial, Eisenhower now lost his temper. "There isn't a single soul who believes this can be done, except Montgomery," he exploded to members of his staff. At this moment, to Eisenhower's mind, the most urgent matter was the opening of the Channel ports, especially Antwerp. Why could Montgomery not understand that? The Supreme Commander was only too well aware of the glittering opportunities that existed. But, as he told the Deputy Supreme Commander, Marshal of the Royal Air Force Sir Arthur Tedder, and SHAEF's assistant chief of staff Lieutenant General Frederick Morgan, for Montgomery "to talk of marching to Berlin with an army which is still drawing the great bulk of its supplies over the beaches is fantastic."

The Field Marshal's message could hardly have come at a worse time. The Supreme Commander was propped up in bed, his right knee in a cast, as a consequence of an injury of which Montgomery, at the moment, was unaware. Eisenhower had more cause than this, however, to be edgy. Leaving the main body of SHAEF in London, he had come to the Continent to take personal control on September 1, four days earlier. His small advance command headquarters at Jullouville near Granville was totally inadequate. Because of the phenomenal movement of his armies, Eisenhower was stranded more than four hundred miles from the front—and there were, as yet, no telephone or teletype facilities. Except for radio and a rudimentary courier system, he was unable to communicate immediately with his commanders in the field. The physical injury which added to these tactical discomforts had occurred after one of his routine flying visits to his principal commanders. On September 2, returning from a conference at Chartres with senior American generals, Eisenhower's plane, because of high winds and bad visibility, had been unable to land at the headquarters' airfield. Instead, it had put down—safely—on the beach near his villa. But then, trying to help the pilot pull the plane away from the water's edge, Eisenhower had badly wrenched his right knee. Thus, at this vital juncture in the war, as the Supreme Commander tried to take control of the land battle and with events happening so fast that immediate decisions were necessary, Eisenhower was physically immobilized.

Although Montgomery—or, for that matter, Bradley and Patton—might feel that Eisenhower "was out of touch with the land battle," only distance made that argument valid. His excellent, integrated Anglo-American staff was much more cognizant of the day-to-day situation in the field than his generals realized. And while he expected combat commanders to display initiative and boldness, only the Supreme Commander and his staff could view the over-all situation and make decisions accordingly. But it was true that, in this transitional period, while Eisenhower was assuming personal control, there appeared to be a lack of clear-cut direction, due in part to the complexity of the Supreme Commander's role. Coalition command was far from easy. Yet, Eisenhower, maintaining a delicate balance, and following to the letter the plans of the Combined Chiefs of Staff, made the system work. In the interest of Allied amity, he might modify strategy, but Eisenhower had no intention of throwing caution to the winds and allowing Montgomery, as the Supreme

Commander later put it, to make a "single, knifelike drive toward Berlin."*

He had been more than tolerant with Montgomery, granting him concession after concession, often incurring the anger of his own American generals. Yet, it seemed that Monty "always wanted everything and he never did anything fast in his life."† Eisenhower said he understood Montgomery's peculiarities better than the Britisher realized. "Look, people have told me about his boyhood," Eisenhower recalled, "and when you have a contest between Eton and Harrow on one side and some of the lesser schools on the other, some of these juniors coming into the army felt sort of inferior. The man, all his life, has been trying to prove that he was somebody." Clearly, however, the Field Marshal's views reflected his British superiors' beliefs on how the Allies should proceed.

---

*In all fairness to Montgomery, it must be said that he, himself, never used this phrase. His idea was to throw forty divisions together and drive toward Berlin —certainly no knifelike thrust—but he has been credited with the remark and in my opinion it hurt his cause at SHAEF during the many strategic meetings that took place.

†To the author. In a taped interview, President Eisenhower almost relived for me his emotions at the time of this bitter argument with Montgomery. When I told him I had interviewed the Field Marshal, Eisenhower cut me short and said, "You don't have to tell me what he told you—he said I knew nothing about war—right? Look, I'm interested only in getting this thing down truthfully and logically, because any historian has to make deductions. . . . Personally, I don't believe I would put too much weight on what generals remember, including me. Because memory is a fallible thing . . . Goddammit, I don't know what you heard in Britain, but the British have never understood the American system of command. . . . When the whole damned thing [WW II] was done . . . I never heard from the British any goldarn paeans of praise. And you're not going to hear it now, particularly from people like Montgomery. . . . His associates—they've said things about him that I would never dream of repeating. . . . I don't care if he goes down as the greatest soldier in the world. He isn't, but if he goes down that way it's all right with me. . . . He got so damn personal to make sure that the Americans and me, in particular, had no credit, had nothing to do with the war, that I eventually just stopped communicating with him . . . I was just not interested in keeping up communications with a man that just can't tell the truth." The reader is urged to remember that never, during the war, did the Supreme Commander publicly discuss the Field Marshal, and his views expressed here are revealed for the first time.

Understandable as this might be, Montgomery's arrogance in presenting such views invariably set American commanders' teeth on edge. As Supreme Commander, armed by the Combined Chiefs of Staff with sweeping powers, Eisenhower had one prime concern: to hold the Allies together and win the war swiftly. Although some of SHAEF's staff, including many Britishers, considered Montgomery insufferable and said so, Eisenhower never commented on him except in private to his chief of staff, Bedell Smith. But, in fact, the Supreme Commander's exasperation with Montgomery went far deeper than anyone knew. Eisenhower felt that the Field Marshal was "a psychopath . . . such an egocentric" that everything he had ever done "was perfect . . . he never made a mistake in his life." Eisenhower was not going to let him make one now. "Robbing the American Peter who is fed from Cherbourg," he told Tedder, "will certainly not get the British Paul to Berlin."

Nevertheless, Eisenhower was deeply disturbed at the widening rift between him and Britain's favorite general. Within the next few days, the Supreme Commander decided, he would meet with Montgomery in an effort to clarify what he considered to be a misunderstanding. Once more he would attempt to spell out his strategy and hope for agreement, however grudgingly it might come. In the interim before the meeting, he made one thing clear. He firmly rejected Montgomery's single-thrust plan and his bid for Berlin. On the evening of September 5, in a coded message to the Field Marshal, he said, "While agreeing with your conception of a powerful and full-blooded thrust toward Berlin, I do not agree that it should be initiated at this moment to the exclusion of all other maneuvers." As the Supreme Commander saw it, "the bulk of the German army in the west has now been destroyed," and that success should be exploited "by promptly breaching the Siegfried Line, crossing the Rhine on a wide front and seizing the Saar and the Ruhr. This I intend to do with all possible speed." These moves, Eisenhower believed, would place a "strangle hold on Germany's main industrial areas and largely destroy her capacity to wage war. . . ." Opening the ports of Le Havre and Antwerp was essential, Eisenhower went on, before any "powerful thrust" into Germany could be launched.

But, at the moment, Eisenhower emphasized, "no relocation of our present resources would be adequate to sustain a thrust to Berlin. . . ."

Eisenhower's decision took thirty-six hours to reach Montgomery, and then only the last half of the message arrived. The concluding two paragraphs were received by Montgomery at 9 A.M. on the morning of September 7. The opening section did not arrive until September 9, another forty-eight hours later. As Montgomery saw it, Eisenhower's communication was one more confirmation that the Supreme Commander was "too far removed from the battle."

From the first fragment of the message that Montgomery received, it was abundantly clear that Eisenhower had rejected his plan, for it contained the sentence, "No relocation of our present resources would be adequate to sustain a thrust to Berlin." Montgomery immediately sent off a message disagreeing heatedly.

With the slackening of the pursuit, Montgomery's worst fears were being realized. German opposition was stiffening. In his message, focusing in particular on the shortage of supplies, Montgomery claimed that he was getting only half his requirements, and "I cannot go on for long like this." He refused to be diverted from his plan to drive to Berlin. The obvious necessity of immediately opening up the vital port of Antwerp was not even mentioned in his dispatch, yet he stressed that "as soon as I have a Pas de Calais port working, I would then require about 2,500 additional three-ton lorries, plus an assured airlift averaging about 1,000 tons a day to enable me to get to the Ruhr and finally Berlin." Because it was all "very difficult to explain," the Field Marshal "wondered if it was possible" for Eisenhower to come and see him. Unshaken in his conviction that the Supreme Commander's decision was a grave error and confident that his own plan would work, Montgomery refused to accept Eisenhower's rejection as final. Yet he had no intention of flying to Jullouville in an attempt to change Eisenhower's mind. Such diplomacy was not part of his makeup, although he was fully aware that the only hope of selling his proposal was via a face-to-face meeting with the Supreme Commander. Outraged and seething, Montgomery awaited a reply from Eisenhower.

The British Field Marshal was in near-seclusion, impatient and irritable, at the moment when Prince Bernhard arrived at the headquarters to pay his respects.

Bernhard had arrived in France on the evening of the sixth. With a small staff, three jeeps, his Sealyham terrier Martin and a bulging briefcase containing Dutch underground reports, he and his party flew to the Continent, guarded by two fighter planes, in three Dakotas with Bernhard at the controls of one. From the airfield at Amiens they drove to Douai, fifty miles north, and early on the seventh set out for Belgium and Brussels. At the Laeken headquarters the Prince was met by General Horrocks, introduced to Montgomery's staff and ushered into the presence of the Field Marshal. "He was in a bad humor and obviously not happy to see me," Bernhard recalled. "He had a lot on his mind, and the presence of royalty in his area was understandably a responsibility that he could easily do without."

The Field Marshal's renown as the greatest British soldier of the war had made him, in Bernhard's words, "the idol of millions of Britishers." And the thirty-three-year-old Prince was in awe of Montgomery. Unlike Eisenhower's relaxed, almost casual manner, Montgomery's demeanor made it difficult for Bernhard to converse easily with him. Sharp and blunt from the outset, Montgomery made it clear that Bernhard's presence in his area "worried" him. With justification untempered by tact or explanation, Montgomery told the Prince that it would be unwise for Bernhard to visit the headquarters of the Dutch unit—the Princess Irene Brigade—attached to the British Second Army, quartered in the area around Diest, barely ten miles from the front line. Bernhard, who, as Commander in Chief of the Netherlands Forces, had every intention of visiting Diest, for the moment did not respond. Instead, he began to discuss the Dutch resistance reports. Montgomery overrode him. Returning to the matter, he told the Prince, "You must not live in Diest. I cannot allow it." Irked, Bernhard felt compelled to point out that he was "serving directly under Eisenhower and did not come under the Field Marshal's command." Thus, from the start, as Bernhard remembers the meeting, "rightly or wrongly, we got off on the wrong foot." (Later, in fact, Eisenhower backed Montgomery regarding Diest, but he did say that Bernhard could stay in Brussels "close to 21st Army Group headquarters, where your presence may be needed.")

Bernhard went on to review the situation in Holland as reflected in the underground reports. Montgomery was told of the retreat and disorganization of the Germans, which had been going on since September 2, and of the makeup of the resistance groups. To the best of his knowledge, Bernhard said, the reports were accurate. Montgomery, according to the Prince, retorted, "I don't think your resistance people can be of much use to us. Therefore, I believe all this is quite unnecessary." Startled by the Field Marshal's bluntness, Bernhard "began to realize that Montgomery apparently did not believe *any* of the messages coming from my agents in Holland. In a way, I could hardly blame him. I gathered he was a bit fed up with misleading information that he had received from the French and Belgian resistance during his advance. But, in this instance, I knew the Dutch groups involved, the people who were running them and I knew the information was, indeed, correct." He persisted. Showing the Field Marshal the message file and quoting from report after report, Bernhard posed a question: "In view of this, why can't you attack right away?"

"We can't depend on these reports," Montgomery told him. "Just because the Dutch resistance claim the Germans have been retreating from September 2 doesn't necessarily mean they are still retreating." Bernhard had to admit the retreat "was slowing down," and there were "signs of reorganization." Still, in his opinion, there was valid reason for an immediate attack.

Montgomery remained adamant. "Anyway," he said, "much as I would like to attack and liberate Holland, I can't do it because of supplies. We are short of ammunition. We are short of petrol for the tanks and if we did attack, in all probability they would become stranded." Bernhard was astounded. The information he received in England from both SHAEF and his own advisers had convinced him that the liberation of Holland would be accomplished in a matter of days. "Naturally I automatically assumed that Montgomery, commander on the spot, knew the situation better than anyone else," Bernhard later said. "Yet we had absolutely every detail on the Germans—troop strength, the number of tanks and armored vehicles, the position of antiaircraft guns—and I knew, apart from immediate front-line opposition, that there was little strength behind it. I was sick at heart, because I knew that German strength would grow with each passing day. I was unable to persuade Montgomery. In fact, nothing I said seemed to matter."

Then Montgomery made an extraordinary disclosure. "I am just as eager to liberate the Netherlands as you are," he said, "but we intend to do it in another, even better way." He paused, thought a moment and then, almost reluctantly, said, "I am planning an airborne operation ahead of my troops." Bernhard was startled. Instantly a number of questions came to his mind. In what area were the drops planned? When would the operation take place? How was it being developed? Yet he refrained from asking. Montgomery's manner indicated he would say no more. The operation was obviously still in the planning stage and the Prince's impression was that only the Field Marshal and a few of his staff officers knew of the plan. Although he was given no more details, Bernhard was now hopeful that the liberation of Holland, despite Montgomery's earlier talk of lack of supplies, was imminent. He must be patient and wait. The Field Marshal's reputation was awesome. Bernhard believed in it and in the man himself. The Prince felt a renewal of hope, for "anything Montgomery did, he would do well."

Eisenhower, acceding to Montgomery's request, set Sunday, September 10, as the date for a meeting. He was not particularly looking forward to his meeting with Montgomery and the usual temperamental arguments he had come to expect from the Field Marshal. He was, however, interested in learning what progress had been made in one aspect of the Montgomery operation. Although the Supreme Commander must approve all airborne plans, he had given Montgomery tactical use of the First Allied Airborne Army and permission to work out a possible plan involving that force. He knew that Montgomery, at least since the fourth, had been quietly exploring the possibility of an airborne operation to seize a bridgehead across the Rhine.

Ever since the formation of the First Allied Airborne Army under its American commander, Lieutenant General Lewis Hyde Brereton, six weeks earlier, Eisenhower had been searching for both a target and a suitable opportunity to employ the force. To that end he had been pressing Brereton and the various army commanders to develop bold and imaginative airborne plans calling for large-scale mass attacks deep behind the enemy's lines. Various missions had been proposed and accepted, but all had been canceled. In nearly every case the speeding land armies had already arrived at the objectives planned for the paratroops.

Montgomery's original proposal had called for units of Brereton's airborne force to grab a crossing west of the town of Wesel, just over the Dutch-German border. However, heavy antiaircraft defenses in that area had forced the Field Marshal to make a change. The site he then chose was farther west in Holland: the Lower Rhine bridge at Arnhem—at this juncture more than seventy-five miles behind the German front lines.

By September 7, Operation Comet, as the plan was called, was in readiness; then bad weather, coupled with Montgomery's concern about the ever-increasing German opposition his troops were encountering, forced a postponement. What might have succeeded on the sixth or seventh seemed risky by the tenth. Eisenhower too was concerned; for one thing he felt that the launching of an airborne attack at this juncture would mean a delay in opening the port of Antwerp. Yet the Supreme Commander remained fascinated by the possibilities of an airborne attack.

The abortive operations, some of them canceled almost at the last minute, had created a major problem for Eisenhower. Each time a mission reached the jump-off stage, troop-carrier planes, hauling gasoline to the front, had to be grounded and made ready. This loss of precious air-supply tonnage brought cries of protest from Bradley and Patton. At this moment of relentless pursuit, the airlift of gasoline, they declared, was far more vital than airborne missions. Eisenhower, anxious to use the paratroopers and urged by Washington to do so—both General Marshall and General Henry H. Arnold, commander of the U.S. Army air forces, wanted to see what Brereton's

new Allied Airborne Army could accomplish—was not prepared to ground his highly trained airborne divisions. On the
contrary, he was insisting that they be used at the earliest opportunity.* In fact, it might be a way to catapult his troops
across the Rhine at the very moment when the pursuit was
slowing down. But on this morning of September 10, as he
flew to Brussels, all other considerations were secondary in his
mind to the opening of the vital port of Antwerp.

Not so Montgomery. Anxious and determined, he was wait-
ing at Brussels airport as Eisenhower's plane touched down.
With characteristic preciseness, he had honed and refined his
arguments preparatory to the meeting. He had talked with
General Miles C. Dempsey of the British Second Army, and
Lieutenant General Frederick Browning, commander of the
British I Airborne Corps, who was also deputy chief of the First
Allied Airborne Army. Browning was waiting in the wings for
the outcome of the conference. Dempsey, concerned at the
ever-stiffening enemy resistance before him and aware from
the intelligence reports that new units were moving in, asked
Montgomery to abandon the plan for an airborne attack on
the bridge at Arnhem. Instead, he suggested concentrating on
seizing the Rhine crossing at Wesel. Even in conjunction with
an airborne mission, Dempsey contended, the British Second
Army probably was not strong enough to drive due north to
Arnhem by itself. It would be better, he believed, to advance in
conjunction with the U.S. First Army northeast toward Wesel.

A drive into Holland was, in any case, now imperative. The
British War Office had informed Montgomery that V-2's—the
first German rockets—had landed in London on September 8.
Their launch sites were believed to be somewhere in western
Holland. Whether before or after receiving this information,
Montgomery altered his plans. Operation Comet, as originally
devised, called for only a division and a half—the British 1st
Airborne and the Polish 1st Parachute Brigade; that force was
too weak to be effective, he believed. As a result, he canceled
Comet. In its place, Montgomery came up with an even more
ambitious airborne proposal. As yet, only a few of the Field

* Pogue, *The Supreme Command*, p. 280.

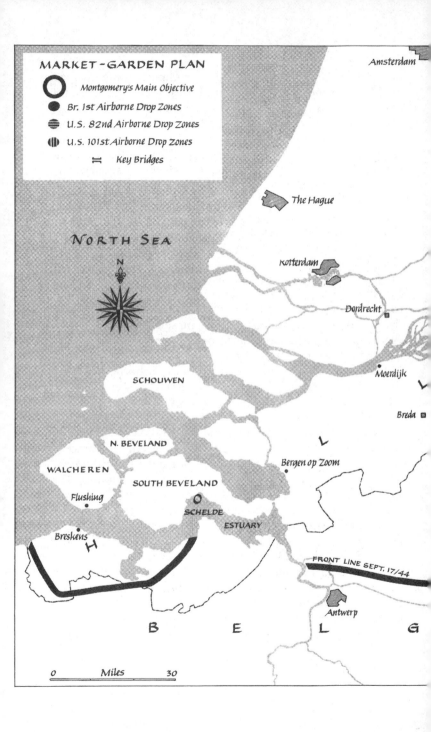

MARKET-GARDEN PLAN

○ Montgomery's Main Objective
● Br. 1st Airborne Drop Zones
◉ U.S. 82nd Airborne Drop Zones
◉ U.S. 101st Airborne Drop Zones
⚌ Key Bridges

NORTH SEA

N

Amsterdam

The Hague

Rotterdam

Dordrecht

Moerdijk

Breda

SCHOUWEN

N. BEVELAND

Bergen op Zoom

WALCHEREN
SOUTH BEVELAND

Flushing

O

SCHELDE

ESTUARY

Breskens

FRONT LINE SEPT. 17/44

B   E   L   G

Antwerp

0   Miles   30

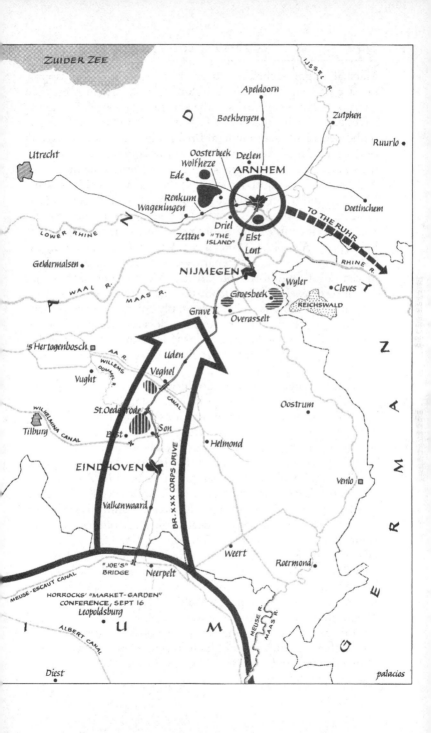

Marshal's upper-echelon officers knew about it and, apprehensive of General Bradley's influence with Eisenhower, they had taken great pains to see that no hint of the plan reached American liaison officers at the British headquarters. Like Eisenhower, Lieutenant General Browning and the headquarters of the First Allied Airborne Army in England were, at this moment, unaware of Montgomery's new airborne scheme.

Because of his injured knee, Eisenhower was unable to leave his plane, and the conference was held on board. Montgomery, as he had done on August 23, determined who should be present at the meeting. The Supreme Commander had brought his deputy, Air Chief Marshal Sir Arthur Tedder, and an assistant chief of staff, Lieutenant General Sir Humphrey Gale, in charge of administration. Curtly, Montgomery asked that Eisenhower exclude Gale from the conference while insisting that his own administrative and supply chief, Lieutenant General Miles Graham, remain. Another, less acquiescent superior might well have taken issue with Montgomery's attitude. Eisenhower patiently granted the Field Marshal's demand. General Gale left.

Almost immediately Montgomery denounced the Supreme Commander's broad-front policy. Constantly referring to a sheaf of Eisenhower's communications that had arrived during the previous week, he called attention to the Supreme Commander's inconsistencies in not clearly defining what was meant by "priority." He argued that his 21st Army Group was not getting the "priority" in supplies promised by Eisenhower; that Patton's drive to the Saar was being allowed to proceed at the expense of Montgomery's forces. Calmly Eisenhower answered that he had never meant to give Montgomery "absolute priority" to the exclusion of everyone else. Eisenhower's strategy, Montgomery reiterated, was wrong and would have "dire consequences." So long as these two "jerky and disjointed thrusts were continued," with supplies split between himself and Patton, "neither could succeed." It was essential, Montgomery said, that Eisenhower decide between him and Patton. So fierce and unrestrained was Montgomery's language that Eisenhower suddenly reached out, patted Montgomery's knee and told him, "Steady, Monty! You can't speak to me like that. I'm your boss." Montgomery's anger vanished. "I'm sorry, Ike," he said quietly.*

The uncharacteristic but seemingly genuine apology was not the end of the matter. Doggedly, though with less acrimony, Montgomery continued to argue for his "single thrust." Eisenhower listened intently and with sympathy to the arguments, but his own view remained unchanged. His broad-front advance would continue. He told Montgomery clearly why. As Eisenhower was later to recall,[†] he said, "What you're proposing is this—if I give you all of the supplies you want, you could go straight to Berlin—right straight to Berlin? Monty, you're nuts. You can't do it. What the hell! If you try a long column like that in a single thrust you'd have to throw off division after division to protect your flanks from attack. Now suppose you did get a bridge across the Rhine. You couldn't depend for long on that one bridge to supply your drive. Monty, you can't do it."

Montgomery, according to Eisenhower, replied, "I'll supply them all right. Just give me what I need and I'll reach Berlin and end the war."

Eisenhower's rejection was firm. Antwerp, he stressed, must be opened before any major drive into Germany could even be contemplated. Montgomery then played his trump card. The most recent development—the rocket attack on London from sites in the Netherlands—necessitated an immediate advance into Holland. He knew exactly how such a drive should begin. To strike into Germany, Montgomery proposed to use almost the entire First Allied Airborne Army in a stunning mass attack.

His plan was an expanded, grandiose version of Operation Comet. Montgomery now wanted to use three and a half divisions—the U.S. 82nd and 101st, the British 1st Airborne

---

*In his memoirs, Montgomery, in discussing the meeting, says that "we had a good talk." But he does state that, during these days of strategy arguments, "Possibly I went a bit far in urging on him my own plan, and did not give sufficient weight to the heavy political burden he bore. . . . Looking back on it all I often wonder if I paid sufficient heed to Eisenhower's notions before refuting them. I think I did. Anyhow . . . I never cease to marvel at his patience and forbearance. . . ."

[†]To the author.

and the Polish 1st Parachute Brigade. The airborne forces were to seize a succession of river crossings in Holland ahead of his troops, with the major objective being the Lower Rhine bridge at Arnhem. Anticipating that the Germans would expect him to take the shortest route and drive northeast for the Rhine and the Ruhr, Montgomery had deliberately chosen a northern "back door" route to the Reich. The surprise airborne attack would open a corridor for the tanks of his British Second Army, which would race across the captured bridges to Arnhem, over the Rhine and beyond. Once all this was accomplished, Montgomery could wheel east, outflank the Siegfried Line, and dash into the Ruhr.

Eisenhower was intrigued and impressed. It was a bold, brilliantly imaginative plan, exactly the kind of mass attack he had been seeking for his long-idle airborne divisions. But now the Supreme Commander was caught between the hammer and the anvil: if he agreed to the attack, the opening of Antwerp would temporarily have to be delayed and supplies diverted from Patton. Yet, Montgomery's proposal could revitalize the dying advance and perhaps propel the pursuit across the Rhine and into the Ruhr. Eisenhower, fascinated by the audaciousness of the plan, not only gave his approval,* but insisted that the operation take place at the earliest possible moment.

Yet the Supreme Commander stressed that the attack was a "limited one." And he emphasized to Montgomery that he considered the combined airborne-ground operation "merely an extension of the northern advance to the Rhine and the Ruhr." As Eisenhower remembered the conversation, he said to Montgomery, "I'll tell you what I'll do, Monty. I'll give you whatever you ask to get you over the Rhine because I want a bridgehead . . . but let's get over the Rhine first before we discuss anything else." Montgomery continued to argue, but Eisenhower would not budge. Frustrated, the Field Marshal had to accept what he called a "half measure," and on this note the conference ended.

---

*Eisenhower told Stephen E. Ambrose, according to his book, *The Supreme Commander*, p. 518 fn.: "I not only approved . . . I insisted upon it. What we needed was a bridgehead over the Rhine. If that could be accomplished, I was quite willing to wait on all other operations. . . ."

After Eisenhower's departure, Montgomery outlined the proposed operation on a map for Lieutenant General Browning. The elegant Browning, one of Britain's pioneer airborne advocates, saw that the paratroopers and glider-borne forces were being called upon to secure a series of crossings—five of them major bridges including the wide rivers of the Maas, the Waal and the Lower Rhine—over a stretch approximately sixty-four miles long between the Dutch border and Arnhem. Additionally, they were charged with holding open the corridor—in most places a single highway running north—over which British armor would drive. All of the bridges had to be seized intact if the armored dash was to succeed. The dangers were obvious, but this was precisely the kind of surprise assault for which the airborne forces had been trained. Still, Browning was uneasy. Pointing to the most northern bridge over the Lower Rhine at Arnhem, he asked, "How long will it take the armor to reach us?" Montgomery replied briskly, "Two days." Still intent on the map, Browning said, "We can hold it for four." Then he added, "But sir, I think we might be going a bridge too far."

The embryo concept (which thereafter would bear the code name "Operation Market-Garden"—"Market" covering the airborne drop and "Garden" for the armored drive) was to be developed with the utmost speed, Montgomery ordered. He insisted that the attack had to be launched in a few days. Otherwise, he told Browning, it would be too late. Montgomery asked: "How soon can you get ready?" Browning, at this moment, could only hazard a guess. "The earliest scheduling of the operation would be the fifteenth or sixteenth,"* he told the Field Marshal.

Carrying Montgomery's skeleton plan and weighed with the urgency of preparing for such a massive mission in only a few days, Browning flew back to England immediately. On landing at his Moor Park Golf Course base near Rickmansworth on the outskirts of London, he telephoned the First Allied Airborne headquarters, twenty miles away, and notified the commander, Lieutenant General Brereton, and his chief of staff, Brigadier

* Minutes of the first planning meeting, First Allied Airborne Army operational file 1014–1017.

General Floyd L. Parks. The time was 2:30 P.M., and Parks noted that Browning's message contained "the first mention of 'Market' at this headquarters."

The airborne commanders were not the only officers caught unaware. Montgomery's daring plan so impressed and surprised the Field Marshal's greatest critic, General Omar N. Bradley, that he later recalled, "Had the pious, teetotalling Montgomery wobbled into SHAEF with a hangover, I could not have been more astonished. . . . Although I never reconciled myself to the venture, I nevertheless freely concede that it was one of the most imaginative of the war."*

It was, but Montgomery remained unhappy. He now prodded the Supreme Commander even further, reverting to the cautious, perfectionist thinking that was characteristic of his military career. Unless the 21st Army Group received additional supplies and transport for the "selected thrust," Montgomery warned Eisenhower, Market-Garden could not be launched before September 23 at the earliest, and might even be delayed until September 26. Browning had estimated that Market could be ready by the fifteenth or sixteenth, but Montgomery was concerned about Garden, the land operation. Once again he was demanding what he had always wanted: absolute priority, which to his mind would guarantee success. Eisenhower noted in his desk diary for September 12: "Monty's suggestion is simple—'give him everything.'" Fearing that any delay might jeopardize Market-Garden, Eisenhower complied. He promptly sent his chief of staff, General Bedell Smith, to see Montgomery; Smith assured the Field Marshal of a thousand tons of supplies per day plus transport. Additionally, Montgomery was promised that Patton's drive to the Saar would be checked. Elated at the "electric" response—as the Field Marshal called it—Montgomery believed he had finally won the Supreme Commander over to his point of view.

Although opposition before Montgomery's troops had stiffened, he believed that the Germans in Holland, behind the hard crust of their front lines, had little strength. Allied

---

*General Omar N. Bradley, *A Soldier's Story*, p. 416. Bradley also added, "I had not been brought into the plan. In fact, Montgomery devised and sold it to Ike several days before I even learned of it from our own liaison officer at 21st Army Group."

intelligence confirmed his estimate. Eisenhower's headquarters reported "few infantry reserves" in the Netherlands, and even these were considered to be "troops of low category." The enemy, it was thought, was still "disorganized after his long and hasty retreat . . . and though there might be numerous small bodies of Germans in the area," they were hardly capable of any great organized resistance. Montgomery now believed he could quickly crack the German defenses. Then, once he was over the Rhine and headed for the Ruhr, he did not see how Eisenhower could halt his drive. The Supreme Commander would have little choice, he reasoned, but to let him continue toward Berlin—thus ending the war, as Montgomery put it, "reasonably quickly." Confidently, Montgomery set Sunday, September 17, as D Day for Operation Market-Garden. The brilliant scheme he had devised was to become the greatest airborne operation of the entire war.

Not everyone shared Montgomery's certainty about Market-Garden. At least one of his senior officers had reason to be worried. General Miles Dempsey, commander of the British Second Army, unlike the Field Marshal, did not dispute the authenticity of Dutch resistance reports. From these, Dempsey's intelligence staff had put together a picture indicating rapidly increasing German strength between Eindhoven and Arnhem, in the very area of the planned airborne drop. There was even a Dutch report that "battered panzer formations have been sent to Holland to refit," and these too were said to be in the Market-Garden area. Dempsey sent along this news to Browning's British I Airborne Corps, but the information lacked any back-up endorsement by Montgomery or his staff. The ominous note was not even included in intelligence summaries. In fact, in the mood of optimism prevailing at 21st Army Group headquarters, the report was completely discounted.

7

FIELD MARSHAL GERD VON RUNDSTEDT's high-risk gamble to rescue the remains of General Von Zangen's encircled Fifteenth Army in the Pas de Calais was paying off. Under cover of darkness, ever since September 6, a hastily assembled fleet consisting of two ancient Dutch freighters, several Rhine barges and some small boats and rafts had been plying back and forth across the three-mile mouth of the Schelde estuary ferrying men, artillery, vehicles and even horses.

Although powerful coastal guns on Walcheren Island protected against attack from the sea, the Germans were surprised that Allied naval forces made no effort to interfere. Major General Walter Poppe expected the convoy carrying his splintered 59th Infantry Division to be "blown out of the water." To him the one-hour trip between Breskens and Flushing "in completely darkened ships, exposed and defenseless, was a most unpleasant experience." The Allies, the Germans suspected, completely underestimated the size of the evacuation. Certainly they knew about it. Because both Von Rundstedt and Army Group B's commander, Field Marshal Walter Model, desperately in need of reinforcements, were demanding speed, some daylight trips had been made. Immediately, fighters pounced on the small convoys. Darkness, however unpleasant, was much safer.

The most hazardous part of the journey was on the Schelde's northern bank. There, under the constant threat of Allied air attack, Von Zangen's forces had to follow a single main road, running east from Walcheren Island, across the Beveland peninsula and into Holland. Part of the escape route, at the narrow neck joining the mainland, was only a few miles from Antwerp and British lines on the Albert Canal. Inexplicably the British even now made no serious effort to attack north, spring the trap, and cut the base of the isthmus. The escape route remained open. Although hammered by incessant Allied air attacks Von Zangen's Fifteenth Army would eventually reach Holland—at a most crucial moment for Montgomery's Market-Garden operation.

While the Fifteenth Army had been extricated more by calculated design than by luck, now the opposite occurred: fate, the unexpected and unpredictable, took a hand. Some eighty miles away the battered armored units of Lieutenant General Wilhelm Bittrich's elite, veteran II SS Panzer Corps reached bivouac areas in the vicinity of Arnhem. As directed by Field Marshal Model on September 4, Bittrich had slowly disengaged the 9th and 10th SS Panzer divisions for "refitting and rehabilitation." Model had chosen the Arnhem area. The two reduced, but still tough, divisions were fanned out to the north, east and south of the town. Bittrich assigned the 9th SS to a huge rectangular sector north and northeast of Arnhem, where most of the division's men and vehicles were on high ground and conveniently hidden in a densely wooded national park. The 10th was encamped in a semicircle to the northeast, east and southeast. Thus, camouflaged and hidden in nearby woods, villages and towns—Beekbergen, Apeldoorn, Zutphen, Ruurlo and Doetinchem—both divisions were within striking distance of Arnhem; some units were within a mile or two of the suburbs. As Bittrich was later to recall, "there was no particular significance in Model choosing the Arnhem vicinity—except that it was a peaceful sector where nothing was happening."

The possibility that this remote backwater might have any strategic value to the Allies was obviously discounted. On the morning of September 11, a small group of Model's staff officers was dispatched in search of a new site for Army Group B's headquarters—in Arnhem.

One of Model's aides, his general headquarters administration and transportation officer, thirty-five-year-old Lieutenant Gustav Sedelhauser, later remembered that "we visited the 9th and 10th SS division headquarters at Beekbergen and Ruurlo and General Bittrich's command post at Doetinchem. Then we inspected Arnhem itself. It had everything we wanted: a fine road net and excellent accommodations. But it was not until we drove west to the outlying district of Oosterbeek that we found what we were looking for." In the wealthy, residential village just two and a half miles from the center of Arnhem was a group of hotels, among them the gracious, white Hartenstein, with its broad expanse of crescent-shaped lawn, stretching back into parklike surroundings where deer roamed undisturbed, and the smaller, two-story, tree-shaded Tafelberg with its glassed-in veranda and paneled rooms. Impressed by the facilities and, as Sedelhauser recalled, "especially the accommodations," the group promptly recommended Oosterbeek to the chief of staff, Lieutenant General Hans Krebs, as "perfect for Army Group B's headquarters." Model approved the decision. Part of the staff, he decided, would live at the Hartenstein, while he would occupy the more secluded, less ostentatious Tafelberg. Lieutenant Sedelhauser was delighted.

Since his tenure the headquarters had never remained anywhere for more than a few days, and now Sedelhauser "was looking forward to some peace and a chance to get my laundry done." By September 15, Model directed, Army Group B's headquarters was to be fully operational in Oosterbeek—approximately three miles from the broad expanse of heaths and pastureland where the British 1st Airborne Division was due to land on September 17.

PART TWO
THE PLAN

I

IN THE EARLY EVENING of September 10, within hours of General Browning's meeting with Field Marshal Montgomery, Lieutenant General Lewis H. Brereton held the first basic planning conference on Operation Market. At his Sunninghill Park headquarters near the fashionable Ascot racecourse thirty-five miles from London, twenty-seven senior officers crowded into Brereton's large map-lined office. After General Browning briefed the group on Montgomery's plan, Brereton told them that, because there was so little time, "major decisions arrived at now must stand—and these have to be made immediately."

The task was monumental, and there were few guidelines. Never before had there been an attempt to send a mammoth airborne force, complete with vehicles, artillery and equipment, capable of fighting on its own, deep behind enemy front lines. In comparison with Market, previous airborne attacks had been small; yet months had gone into their planning. Now, to prepare for the greatest paratroop and glider-borne infantry operation ever conceived, Brereton and his planners had barely seven days.

Brereton's greatest concern was not the deadline, but the possibility that this operation, like its predecessors, might be canceled. His long-idle airborne troops were impatient for action, and a serious morale problem had developed as a consequence. For weeks his elite, highly trained divisions had stood down while ground forces on the Continent swept victoriously across France and Belgium. There was a widespread feeling that victory was so near that the war might end before the First Allied Airborne Army got into battle.

The General harbored no doubts about the ability of his staff to meet the tight, one-week Market schedule. There had been so many "dry runs" in developing previous airborne schemes that his headquarters and division staffs had reached a stage of high-speed efficiency. Additionally, much of the planning that had gone into Comet and other canceled operations could be readily adapted to Market. In preparing for the aborted Comet mission, for example, the British 1st Airborne Division and the Polish Brigade, charged with that operation, had made a thorough study of the Arnhem area. Still, most of the Market concept meant vastly expanded planning—and all of it was time-consuming.

General Brereton was outwardly confident and calm, but members of his staff noted that he smoked one cigarette after another. On his desk was a framed quotation which the General often pointed out to his staff. It read: "Where is the Prince who can afford so to cover his country with troops for its defense, as that 10,000 men descending from the clouds, might not, in many places, do an infinite deal of mischief before a force could be brought together to repel them?" It had been written in 1784 by Benjamin Franklin.

Brereton was fascinated by the vision of the eighteenth-century statesman and scientist. "Even after a hundred sixty years," he had told his staff, "the idea remains the same." But Franklin would have been bewildered by the complexities and size of Operation Market. To invade Holland from the sky, Brereton planned to land almost 35,000 men—nearly twice the number of paratroops and glider-borne infantry used in the invasion of Normandy.

To "grab the bridges with thunderclap surprise," as Brereton put it, and hold open the narrow, one-highway advance corridor for the British Garden ground forces—from their attack line near the Dutch-Belgian border to Arnhem sixty-four miles north—three and one half airborne divisions were to be used. Two would be American. Almost directly ahead of General Horrocks' XXX Corps tanks, Major General Maxwell D. Taylor's 101st Airborne Division was to capture canal and river crossings over a fifteen-mile stretch between Eindhoven and Veghel. North of them, Brigadier General James M. Gavin's veteran 82nd Division was charged with the area between Grave and the city of Nijmegen, approximately a ten-mile stretch. They were to seize crossings over the great Maas and Waal rivers, in particular the huge multispan bridge at Nijmegen, which, with its approaches, was almost a half-mile long. The single most important objective of Operation Market-Garden was Arnhem and its vital crossing over the 400-yard-wide Lower Rhine. The great concrete-and-steel, three-span highway bridge, together with its concrete ramps, was almost 2,000 feet long. Its capture was assigned to the British and Poles—Major General Robert "Roy" E. Urquhart's 1st Airborne Division and, under his command, Major General Stanislaw Sosabowski's Polish 1st Parachute Brigade. Arnhem, lying farthest away from the Garden forces, was the prize. Without the Rhine crossing, Montgomery's bold stroke to liberate Holland, outflank the Siegfried Line and springboard into Germany's industrial Ruhr would fail.

To carry the huge force to targets three hundred miles away, an intricate air plan had to be designed. Three distinct operations were required: transportation, protection and resupply. No fewer than twenty-four different airfields would be needed for takeoff. Brereton planned to use every operable glider in his command—an immense fleet of more than 2,500. Besides hauling heavy equipment such as jeeps and artillery, the gliders were to ferry more than a third of the 35,000-man force; the rest would drop by parachute. All the craft had to be checked out, loading space allotted, heavy equipment and cargo stowed, and troop complements prepared.

Gliders posed only a single problem in the air planning. Transports to carry paratroops and tow planes to pull the gliders must be diverted from their normal task of supplying the advancing armies and grounded in order to be readied for Market. The crews of bomber squadrons had to be alerted and briefed for missions in the Market-Garden area prior to, and during, the attack. Swarms of fighter squadrons from all over England—more than 1,500 planes—would be needed to escort the airborne force. Intricate aerial traffic patterns were of prime importance. Routes between England and Holland had to be laid out to avoid heavy enemy antiaircraft fire and the equally dangerous possibility of air collision. Air-sea rescue operations, resupply missions, even a dummy parachute drop in another area of Holland to deceive the enemy, were also planned. In all, it was estimated that almost 5,000 aircraft of all types would be involved in Market. To develop plans and ready this vast air armada would take a minimum of seventy-two hours.

The most pressing question of the conference, in Brereton's opinion, was whether the operation should be undertaken by day or by night. Previous major airborne operations had taken place in moonlight. But semidarkness had led to confusion in finding landing zones, lack of troop concentration and unnecessary casualties. The General decreed that the huge airborne assault would take place in broad daylight. It was an unprecedented decision. In the history of airborne operations, a daylight drop of such proportions had never before been made.

Brereton had other reasons than the desire to avoid confusion. The week scheduled for Operation Market was a no-moon period and night landings on a large scale were therefore impossible. Apart from that, Brereton chose a daylight attack because, for the first time in the war, it was feasible. Allied fighters held such overwhelming superiority over the battlefields that now interference from the Luftwaffe was practically nonexistent. But the Germans did have night fighters. In a night drop, against columns of slow-moving troop-carrying planes and gliders, they might prove devastatingly effective. German antiaircraft strength was another consideration: flak maps of the approaches to the Market drop areas were dotted with antiaircraft positions. The charts, based on photo-reconnaissance flights and the experience of bomber crews flying over Holland en route to Germany, looked formidable—particularly so because gliders were without protective armor, except in the cockpits, and C-47 troop-carriers and tow planes had no self-sealing gas tanks. Nevertheless, Brereton believed that enemy antiaircraft positions could be neutralized by concentrated bomber and fighter attacks preceding and during the assault. In any event, most antiaircraft was radar-directed, and therefore was as effective after dark as it was during the day. Either way, losses were to be expected. Still, unless bad weather and high winds intervened, the airborne force, by attacking in daylight, could be dropped with almost pinpoint accuracy on the landing zones, thus guaranteeing a quick concentration of troops in the corridor. "The advantages," Brereton told his commanders, "far outweigh the risks."

Brereton made his final announcement. To command the giant operation he appointed his deputy, the fastidious forty-seven-year-old Lieutenant General Frederick "Boy" Browning, head of the British I Airborne Corps. It was an excellent choice, though disappointing to Lieutenant General Matthew B. Ridgway, commander of the other corps in the airborne army—the XVIII Airborne Corps. Still, Browning had been slated to command the aborted Operation Comet, which, though smaller and utilizing only British and Polish airborne troops, was similar in concept to Market-Garden. Now, under the enlarged and innovative plan Montgomery had devised, American paratroops would serve under a British airborne commander for the first time.

To the assembled airborne commanders Browning delivered an optimistic summation. He ended his talk with the kind of picturesque confidence that had always made him a heroic figure to his men. As his chief of staff, Brigadier Gordon Walch, remembers, "General Browning was in high spirits, delighted that at last we were going. 'The object,' he told us, 'is to lay a carpet of airborne troops down over which our ground forces can pass.' He believed this single operation held the key to the duration of the war."

Browning's enthusiasm was catching. As the large meeting broke up, to be replaced by smaller staff conferences which would last throughout the night, few officers were aware that an underlying friction existed between Brereton and Browning. Originally, when the First Allied Airborne Army was formed, British hopes ran high that Browning, Britain's senior airborne authority and one of the pioneers in the use of paratroops, would be named commander. Because of the preponderance of American troops and equipment within the newly organized army, the coveted post went to an American, General Brereton.

In rank, Browning was six months Brereton's senior; and although the American was a distinguished tactical air force officer, he had never before commanded airborne forces. Additionally, there were wide personality differences between the two men. Brereton had been a World War I flyer and had served brilliantly in World War II, first in the Far and Middle East and later as commanding general of the U.S. Ninth Air Force in England. He was tenacious and single-minded, but his zeal to achieve was cloaked by a quiet, stolid demeanor. Now Brereton proceeded on the awesome assignment he had been handed with the determination and bulldozing tactics that characterized many of his fellow American career officers.

Browning, a Grenadier Guards officer, was also a perfectionist, equally determined to prove the worth of paratroops. But he had never commanded an airborne corps before. In contrast to Brereton, "Boy" Browning was a somewhat glamorous figure, elegant and impeccably groomed, with an air of easy assurance often misunderstood for arrogance, not only by Americans but by some of his own commanders. Though he was temperamental and sometimes overly impatient, his reputation as an airborne theorist was legendary among his admirers. Still, he lacked the battle experience of some other officers, such as General Richard Gale of the British 6th Airborne Division and the veteran American commanders, Generals Gavin and Taylor. And, Browning had yet to prove that he possessed the administrative genius of the most experienced of all airborne commanders, General Ridgway.

Only days before, an incident had occurred that pointed up the differences between Brereton and Browning. On September 3, Browning had protested to Brereton the dangers of trying to launch an airborne assault on just thirty-six hours' notice. Since D Day on June 6, seventeen airborne operations had been prepared and canceled. In the thirty-three days of Brereton's command, in his eagerness to get into action, plans had been processed at the rate of almost one a week. None reached the launching stage. Browning, watching the mass production of airborne schemes, was deeply concerned about the haste and the risks being run. When Operation Linnet I —a drop before the British army in Belgium—was canceled on September 2, Brereton quickly found new objectives ahead of the speeding armies and proposed Operation Linnet II, as a substitute attack to take place on the morning of September 4.

As Brereton later recalled the incident, "Browning was quite agitated about Operation Linnet II in which there was a serious shortage of information, photographs and, in particular, maps. As a result, 'Boy' claimed his troops could not be briefed properly." Airborne operations, Browning contended, "should not be attempted on such short notice." In principle Brereton had agreed, but he had told his deputy that "the disorganization of the enemy demands that chances be taken." The disagreement between the two men had ended with Browning stiffly stating that he intended to submit his protest in writing. A few hours later his letter had arrived. Because "of our sharp differences of opinion," Browning wrote, he could no longer "continue as Deputy Commander of the First Allied Airborne Army."

Brereton, unintimidated, had begun at once to consider the problem of Browning's replacement. He had alerted General Ridgway to "stand by to take over." The delicate problem was solved when Operation Linnet II was canceled; the following day Brereton had persuaded Browning to withdraw his letter of resignation.

Now, their differences set aside, both men faced the huge, complex task of preparing Market. Whatever reservations Browning entertained were now secondary to the job ahead.

There was one decision Brereton could not make at the initial meeting: exactly how the airborne troops comprising the carpet were to be carried to the targets. The airborne commanders could not make detailed plans until this greatest of all problems was solved. The fact was that the airborne army was only as mobile as the planes that would carry it. Apart from gliders, Brereton had no transports of his own. To achieve complete surprise, the ideal plan called for the three and one-half divisions in Market to be delivered to landing zones on the same day at the same hour. But the immense size of the operation ruled out this possibility. There was an acute shortage of both aircraft and gliders; the planes would have to make more than one trip. Other factors also forced a different approach. Each division had separate combat requirements. For example, it was essential that the transport for General Taylor's 101st Airborne carry more men than equipment when the attack began so that the division could carry out its assigned task of achieving a link-up with the Garden forces within the first few hours. Also, Taylor's men had to join quickly with the 82nd Airborne on the corridor north of them. There, General Gavin's troops not only had to secure the formidable bridges across the Maas and the Waal but also hold the Groesbeek ridge to the southeast, terrain which had to be denied the Germans because it dominated the countryside. Gavin's special assignment also imposed special requirements. Because the 82nd Airborne would have to fight longer than the 101st before the link-up occurred, Gavin needed not only troops but artillery.

Farther north, the problems of the British 1st Airborne under General Urquhart were different still. The British 1st was to hold the Arnhem bridge until relieved. With luck, German reaction would be sluggish enough so that ground forces could reach the lightly armed British troopers before any real enemy strength developed. But until Horrocks' tanks arrived, Urquhart's men would have to hang on. Urquhart could not dissipate his strength by sending units south to link up with Gavin. Lying at the farthest end of the airborne carpet, the British 1st Airborne would have to hold longer than anyone else. For this reason, Urquhart's force was the largest, his division bolstered by the addition of Polish paratroops, plus the 52nd Lowland Division, which was to be flown in as soon as air strips could be located and prepared in the Arnhem area.

On the morning of the eleventh, after a hectic night of assessing and analyzing aircraft availability for the attack, Major General Paul L. Williams, commander of the U.S. IX Troop Carrier Command, and in charge of all Market air operations, gave his estimate to Brereton. There was such a shortage of gliders and planes, he reported, that even with an all-out effort, at best only half the troop strength of Browning's total force could be flown in on D Day. Essential items such as artillery, jeeps and other heavy cargo scheduled for the gliders could be included only on a strict priority basis. Brereton urged his air commander to explore the possibility of two D-Day airlifts but the suggestion was found impractical. "Owing to the reduced hours of daylight and the distances involved, it would not be possible to consider more than one lift per day," General Williams said. It was too risky. There would be no time for maintenance or battle-damage repair, he pointed out, and almost certainly "casualties would result from pilot and crew fatigue."

Hamstrung by the shortage of aircraft and the time limit, Brereton made some general assessments. A full day would be required to take aerial-reconnaissance photographs of the Dutch bridges and terrain; two days must go into the preparation and distribution of maps of the areas; intelligence had to be gathered and analyzed; detailed battle plans must be prepared. The most crucial decision of all: Brereton was forced to tailor the Market plan to suit the existing airlift capability. He must transport his force in installments, flying the three and one half divisions to their targets over a period of three days. The risks were great: German reinforcements might reach the Market-Garden area faster than anyone anticipated; antiaircraft fire could intensify; and there was always the possibility of bad weather. Fog, high winds, a sudden storm—all likely at this time of the year—could cause disaster.

Worse, once on the ground, the paratroopers and glider-borne infantry, arriving without heavy artillery or tanks, would be highly vulnerable. General Horrocks' XXX Corps tank columns, using one narrow highway, could not make the 64-mile dash to Arnhem and beyond unless Brereton's men seized the bridges and held open the advance route. Conversely, the airborne army had to be relieved at top speed. Cut off far behind enemy lines and dependent on supplies by air, the airborne forces could expect German reinforcements to increase with each passing day. At best the beleaguered troopers might hold out in their "airheads" for only a few days. If the British armored drive was held up or failed to move fast enough, the airborne troops would inevitably be overrun and destroyed.

More could go wrong. If General Taylor's "Screaming Eagles" failed to secure the bridges directly ahead of the British Second Army's tank spearheads, it would make little difference whether or not the men under General Gavin's or General Urquhart's command secured their objectives in Nijmegen and Arnhem. Their forces would be isolated.

Certain classic airborne risks had to be accepted: divisions might be dropped or landed by gliders in the wrong areas; crossings might be destroyed by the enemy even as the attack began; bad weather could make air resupply impossible; and even if all the bridges were seized, the corridor might be cut at any point. These were but a few of the imponderables. The planners were gambling on speed, boldness, accuracy and surprise—all deriving from a precise synchronized land-and-airborne plan that, in its turn, gambled on German disorganization and inadequate strength. Each link in Market-Garden was interlocked with the next. If one gave way, disaster might result for all.

In Brereton's opinion, such risks had to be accepted. The opportunity might never arise again. Additionally, on the basis of the latest information of enemy strength, from Montgomery's 21st Army Group, Allied Airborne headquarters still felt that Brereton's forces would meet an "ill-organized enemy of varying standards." It was not expected that "any mobile force larger than a brigade group [about 3,000 men] with very few tanks and guns could be concentrated against the airborne troops before relief by the ground forces." It was expected "that the flight and landings would be hazardous, that the capture intact of the bridge objectives was more a matter of surprise and confusion than hard fighting." There was nothing here that the planners had not already taken under consideration. The last words of the intelligence summation seemed almost superfluous—"the advance of the ground forces would be very swift if the airborne operations were successful."

Major Brian Urquhart was deeply disturbed by the optimism permeating General Browning's British I Airborne Corps headquarters. The twenty-five-year-old intelligence chief felt that he was probably the only one on the staff with any doubts about Market-Garden. Urquhart (no relation to the British 1st Airborne Division commander, Major General Robert Urquhart) did not believe the optimistic estimates on enemy strength which arrived almost daily from Montgomery's 21st Army command. By the morning of Tuesday, September 12, with D Day only five days away, his doubts about Market-Garden amounted to near-panic.

His feeling had been triggered by a cautious message from General Dempsey's British Second Army headquarters. Quoting a Dutch report, Dempsey's intelligence staff warned of an increase in German strength in the Market-Garden area and spoke of the presence of "battered panzer formations believed to be in Holland to refit." Admittedly, the information was vague. Lacking any kind of confirmation, Dempsey's report was not included in the latest intelligence summaries of either Montgomery's or Eisenhower's headquarters. Urquhart could not understand why. He had been receiving similar disquieting news from Dutch liaison officers at Corps headquarters itself. And, like General Dempsey's staff, he believed them. Adding his own information to that received from Dempsey's command, Major Urquhart felt reasonably certain that elements of at least two panzer divisions were somewhere in the Arnhem area. The evidence was thin. The units were unidentified, with strength unknown, and he could not tell whether they were actually being refitted or merely passing through Arnhem.

Nevertheless, Urquhart, as he later recalled, "was really very shook up."

Ever since the inception of Operation Comet and its evolution into Market-Garden, Major Urquhart's fears had been growing. Repeatedly, he had voiced his objections to the operation to "anybody who would listen on the staff." He was "quite frankly horrified by Market-Garden, because its weakness seemed to be the assumption that the Germans would put up no effective resistance." Urquhart himself was convinced that the Germans were rapidly recovering and might well have more men and equipment in Holland than anyone realized. Yet the whole essence of the scheme, as he saw it, "depended on the unbelievable notion that once the bridges were captured, XXX Corps's tanks could drive up this abominably narrow corridor—which was little more than a causeway, allowing no maneuverability—and then walk into Germany like a bride into a church. I simply did not believe that the Germans were going to roll over and surrender."

At planning conferences, Major Urquhart became increasingly alarmed at what he saw as "the desperate desire on everybody's part to get the airborne into action." There were constant comparisons between the current situation and the collapse of the Germans in 1918. Urquhart remembers that General Browning, perhaps reflecting Montgomery's views and those of "several other British commanders, was thinking about another great breakthrough." It seemed to the worried intelligence officer that everyone around him thought the war would be over by winter and "the Arnhem attack might be the airborne's last chance of getting into action." Urquhart was appalled at the lighthearted metaphor—"it was described as a 'party'"—used in reference to Market-Garden. And, in particular, he was upset by General Browning's statement that the object of the airborne attack was to "lay a carpet of airborne troops down over which our ground forces can pass." He believed that "that single cliché had the psychological effect of lulling many commanders into a passive and absolutely unimaginative state of mind in which no reaction to German resistance, apart from dogged gallantry, was envisaged." He considered the atmosphere at headquarters so unrealistic that,

at one of the planning conferences, he asked "whether the 'carpet' was to consist of live airborne troops or dead ones."

"It was absolutely impossible," he said later, "to get them to
face the realities of the situation; their personal longing to get
into the campaign before it ended completely blinded them."
But young Urquhart was convinced that General Dempsey's
warning was accurate. He believed there was German armor
in the vicinity of Arnhem, but he needed to substantiate the
report by getting more evidence. A Spitfire fighter squadron
equipped with special cameras for taking oblique pictures was
stationed, Urquhart knew, at nearby Benson in Oxfordshire.
The squadron was currently searching out rocket sites along
the Dutch coast.

On the afternoon of September 12, Major Urquhart requested low-level R.A.F. reconnaissance sweeps of the Arnhem area. To avoid detection, enemy tanks would be hidden
in forests or beneath camouflaged netting and might well escape high-altitude photographic flights. Urquhart's request
was acknowledged; low-level missions would be flown over the
Arnhem area, and he would get the results as fast as possible.
Photographs of the tanks, if they were there, might prove to all
concerned that Major Urquhart's fears were justified.

There was too little time now for airborne division commanders to check out intelligence reports firsthand. They were dependent on Corps or First Allied Airborne headquarters for the
latest estimates. From experience, each commander knew that
even this information would be several days old by the time he
received it. Still, in the general view, there was little reason to
anticipate any powerful enemy resistance. The risks involved in
Market-Garden were, as a result, considered acceptable.

Once Generals Brereton and Browning had outlined the
plan, determined the objectives and decided on airlift capability, each commander developed his own combat plans. The
choice of drop zones and landing sites had priority. From previous operations, veteran airborne commanders knew that the
best chance of success depended on how close to their objectives assaulting troops could be dropped. Ideally, they should
be landed almost on their targets or within quick marching
distance, especially if they were expected to seize a bridge.

With the meager ground transport available, the pinpointing of these sites was vital.

Major General Maxwell D. Taylor was all too aware that his sites must be chosen for maximum effect. While Taylor would have the majority of his Screaming Eagle paratroops on D Day, his engineering units, artillery and most of the 101st transport would not arrive until D plus 1 and 2. Studying the southernmost part of the corridor where the 101st Airborne Division was to hold between Eindhoven and Veghel, Taylor quickly noted that over the fifteen-mile stretch of highway, his troops must capture two major canal crossings and no less than nine highway and railroad bridges. At Veghel, over the river Aa and the Willems Canal, there were four bridges, one a major canal crossing. Five miles south in St. Oedenrode, a bridge over the Lower Dommel had to be seized; four miles from there was the second major canal crossing, over the Wilhelmina Canal near the village of Son, and to the west a bridge near the hamlet of Best. Five miles farther south in Eindhoven, four bridges over the Upper Dommel had to be taken.

After studying the flat terrain between Eindhoven and Veghel, with its veining waterways, dikes, ditches and tree-lined roads, Taylor decided to pinpoint his major landing site almost in the center of his assault area, by the edge of a forest barely one and one half miles from Son and roughly equidistant between Eindhoven and Veghel. He would land two of his regiments, the 502nd and the 506th, on this zone. The 502nd was charged with objectives in St. Oedenrode and Best; the 506th with those in Son and Eindhoven. The third regiment, the 501st, was to land in two areas north and west of Veghel, within a few hundred yards of the vital four bridges. It was a formidable assignment for his men to accomplish on D Day without their back-up auxiliary units, but Taylor believed that "with luck, we can make it."

The task of the 82nd Airborne was more intricate. Its ten-mile sector was wider than that of the 101st. In this central segment of the corridor, the huge, nine-span, 1,500-foot-long bridge over the Maas river at Grave and at least one of four smaller railroad and highway crossings over the Maas-Waal Canal must be seized. The great bridge over the Waal river at Nijmegen, almost in the center of this city of 90,000, was also a prime objective. None of these could be called "secured" unless the Groesbeek Heights, dominating the area two miles southwest of Nijmegen, were held. Also, to the east was the great belt of forest along the German border—the Reichswald —where the Germans might assemble for attack. When General Gavin explained to his headquarters' officers what was expected of them, his chief of staff, Colonel Robert H. Wienecke, protested, "We'll need two divisions to do all that." Gavin was terse. "There it is, and we're going to do it with one."

Remembering the 82nd Airborne's attacks in Sicily and Italy, when his troops were scattered sometimes as far as thirty-five miles from their drop zone (the standard division joke was that "we always use blind pilots"), Gavin was determined to land his men this time almost on their targets. In order of priority, he decided that his objectives were: first, the Groesbeek Heights; second, the bridge at Grave; third, the crossings on the Maas-Waal Canal; and fourth, the Waal bridge at Nijmegen. "Because of probable quick enemy reaction," Gavin later recalled, "I decided to drop the largest part of my paratroops between the Groesbeek Heights and the Reichswald." He chose two landing zones in the Groesbeek vicinity less than a mile and a half from the ridge itself and three to four miles southwest of Nijmegen. There, his 508th and 505th regiments, plus the headquarters staff, would land. The third regiment, the 504th, was to drop on the western side of the Groesbeek Heights in the triangle between the Maas river and the Maas-Waal Canal, a mile from the eastern end of the Grave bridge and two miles west of the Maas-Waal Canal bridges. To insure the capture of the vital Grave bridge, which might be prepared for demolition, an additional phase of his plan was developed in which a company of the 504th was to be dropped a half mile from the western end of the bridge. Before the enemy could retaliate, the 504th would rush the bridge from both ends.

Obviously, the great Nijmegen bridge was the most important of all his objectives and crucial to the entire Market-Garden operation. Yet Gavin was well aware that, without holding the other objectives, the Waal river crossing by itself would be useless. General Browning agreed with him. If the first bridges were not taken or if the enemy held the Groesbeek Heights, the corridor for the Garden forces would never be opened.

Therefore, Browning specifically directed, Gavin was not to attempt an attack on the Nijmegen bridge until the primary objectives were secured.

Although he was concerned about the wide dispersal of his troops, Gavin was satisfied with the plan. One aspect bothered him, as it had bothered Taylor. His entire division would not be organically complete until supporting units arrived on D plus 1 and 2, and he wondered how his men—who knew nothing about Market-Garden as yet—would react. Still, in the experienced 82nd, morale was high as always; many of his men had made three combat jumps already. "Jumping Jim" Gavin, at thirty-seven the youngest brigadier general in the U.S. Army, had no doubts that his "fugitives from the law of averages," as they called themselves, would do their job.

The most difficult and dangerous assignment, by far, had been given to a modest, reticent career officer, Major General Robert "Roy" Urquhart, forty-two-year-old commander of the British 1st Airborne Division and the attached Polish Brigade.

Unlike General Browning and his American colleagues, Urquhart, a highly professional soldier who had fought with great distinction in North Africa, Sicily and Italy, had no airborne warfare experience. He would be commanding an airborne division in battle for the first time. Browning had chosen him because he was "hot from battle," but Urquhart had been surprised at his appointment. He had always considered airborne units "tightly knit organizations, closed family affairs and quite exclusive." Yet Urquhart had confidence in his ability to lead the elite unit. Once the force was on the ground the basic fighting rules remained the same, and he viewed his airborne division as "very highly trained infantry troops."

Despite his long combat experience, Urquhart was bothered about one thing: he had never parachuted or been in a glider. "I was even prone to airsickness," he was later to remark. On taking command in January, 1944, nine months before, Urquhart had suggested to General Browning that perhaps, as the new division commander, he ought to have some parachute training. Browning, who impressed Urquhart as a "lithe, immaculately turned-out man who gave the appearance of a restless hawk," answered that Urquhart's job was to get his division ready for an invasion of the Continent. Looking over the six-foot, 200-pound Scotsman, Browning added, "Leave the parachuting to younger chaps. Not only are you too large, but you're getting on."*

Throughout the long months of training, Urquhart "often felt like an outsider, a kind of military landlubber." He was aware of "being watched closely; not with hostility, though some airborne officers had reservations and a few did not bother to conceal them. I was on trial; my actions were being judged. It was an unenviable position, but one I accepted." Slowly, Urquhart's confident, assured handling of the division won over his officers. And among the troopers, Urquhart was far more popular than he knew. Private James W. Sims, of the 1st Airborne Division's 1st Parachute Brigade, remembers "the General's supreme confidence and his calmness." Sergeant John Rate, of Division headquarters, had the impression that "General Urquhart did whatever job had to be done. He didn't just ask someone else to do it. The General didn't stand on ceremony." Signalman Kenneth John Pearce called him "a big wonderful fellow. He called us 'son' or used our first names if he knew them." And from Sergeant Roy Ernest Hatch, of the Glider Pilot Regiment, Urquhart earned the supreme compliment. "He was," Hatch asserted, "a bloody general who didn't mind doin' the job of a sergeant."

To Urquhart's frustration, his division had not been chosen for the Normandy invasion, and "the summer passed interminably, planning one operation after another, only to see each canceled." Now, his "Red Devils" were "hungering for a fight." They had almost given up. "We were calling ourselves 'The Stillborn Division,'" recalls Major George S. Powell of the 4th Parachute Brigade. "We figured we were being kept in reserve for use in the victory parade." As Urquhart saw it, "there was a dangerous mixture of ennui and cynicism slowly creeping into our lives. We were trained to a fine edge and I knew that if we didn't get into battle soon, we would lose it. We were ready and willing to accept anything, with all the 'ifs.'"

---

*At their first interview Urquhart was still wearing his Brigadier's badges and tight-fitting Tartan trousers (trews) and spats of the Highland Division. As the meeting broke up, Browning, pointing to Urquhart's pants, said, "You might also get yourself properly dressed and get rid of those trews."

Urquhart's principal target—the prize of Operation Market-Garden—was Arnhem's concrete-and-steel highway bridge over the Lower Rhine. Additionally, Urquhart's men had two secondary objectives: a nearby floating pontoon bridge and a double-track railway crossing upriver, two and a half miles west of the town.

Urquhart's assignment presented a series of problems. Two were particularly worrisome. Reports of heavy antiaircraft defenses in the area indicated that some enemy units were massing in the vicinity of the Arnhem bridge itself. And Urquhart was uneasy about the three days it would take to airlift his entire force of British and Polish paratroops to their objectives. Both these problems had a direct bearing on Urquhart's choice of landing sites. Unlike the 82nd and 101st Airborne Divisions, he could not pick zones almost on or even close to the principal target. Ideally, he should land his forces near the Arnhem bridge on both sides of the river; but Urquhart's terrain was by no means ideal. The northern exit of the crossing ran directly into the densely populated, built-up center of Arnhem itself. Near the southern exit, low-level polder land was, according to reports, too marshy for men or gliders. "Many of my own commanders," Urquhart remembers, "were quite willing to land on the southern side, even though it was marshy. Indeed, some were ready to risk injury by parachuting on the northern side—on the town itself."

In the previous week, bomber crews returning from other missions had reported a 30 percent increase in antiaircraft fire near the Arnhem crossing and from Deelen airfield seven miles to the north. Consequently, R.A.F. commanders whose pilots were scheduled to tow Urquhart's glider-borne troops raised strong objections to landing zones close to the Arnhem bridge. If sites were located near the southern exit, tug aircraft wheeling north after releasing gliders would run into heavy flak over the airfield. Turning south was almost as bad; planes might risk collision with aircraft dropping the 82nd Airborne near Nijmegen, eleven miles away. Urquhart was confronted with a dilemma: he could insist that the R.A.F. place his troops in proximity to the bridge, or he could choose drop zones much farther away, outside Arnhem itself, with all the dangers that choice entailed—delay, loss of surprise, possible German opposition. The risks were multiplied because on D Day Urquhart would have only a part of his division. "My problem was to get enough men down on the first lift," Urquhart recalled, "not only to seize the main bridge in the town itself, but also to guard and defend the drop zones and landing areas for the succeeding lifts. To seize the main bridge on the first day my strength was reduced to just one parachute brigade."

Faced with these restrictions, Urquhart appealed to Browning for extra planes. It seemed to him, he told the Corps commander, "that the Americans are getting all they need." Browning disagreed. The allocation of aircraft, he assured Urquhart, was "entirely due to priorities and not to any high-level American pressure." The entire operation, he explained, had to be planned from south to north, "bottom to top"; objectives in the southern and central sections of the corridor must be "seized first to get the ground forces through. Otherwise, the 1st Airborne would be wiped out."

In his command caravan on the Moor Park golf course near the clubhouse that General Browning used as headquarters, Urquhart pored over his maps and pondered the situation. Some open sectors existed north of Arnhem in a national park, but these were too small and the terrain was unsuitable. At best, these spots might accommodate a small parachute force but no gliders. The only alternative was to land in some broad expanses of open heaths and pasture land bordered by pine woods, 250 feet above sea level, lying west and northwest of Arnhem. The heathlands were firm and flat, perfect for gliders and parachutists. They were ideal in every way—except one: the areas lay between six and eight miles from the Arnhem bridge. Faced with the R.A.F.'s continued opposition to a drop in the immediate vicinity of the bridge, Urquhart reluctantly decided on the distant sites. "There was nothing else to do," he recalled, "but to accept the risks and plan for them. I was left with no choice."*

By September 12, Urquhart had his plan ready. Outlined on the map were five landing and drop zones straddling the

---

*Colonel George S. Chatterton, commanding the Glider Pilot Regiment, recalls that he wanted a *coup de main*, "a force of five or six gliders to land near the bridge and take it. I saw no reason why we could not do it, but apparently nobody else saw the need for it, and I distinctly remember being called a bloody murderer and assassin for suggesting it."

Arnhem-Amsterdam railroad in the vicinity of Wolfheze, approximately four miles northwest of Arnhem. Three sites lay north of Wolfheze and two south, the southern zones together making up an irregular box-shaped tract more than a mile square. All were at least six miles away from the bridge at Arnhem; the farthest, northwest of Wolfheze, was eight.

On D Day two brigades would go in—Brigadier Philip "Pip" Hicks's 1st Airlanding Brigade, scheduled to hold the drop zones, and Brigadier Gerald Lathbury's 1st Parachute Brigade, which would make a dash for Arnhem and its highway, railroad and pontoon bridges. Leading the way would be a motorized reconnaissance squadron of jeeps and motorcycles. Urquhart was counting on Major C. F. H. "Freddie" Gough's highly specialized force of some 275 men in four troops—the only unit of its kind in the British army—to reach the highway bridge and hold it until the main body of the brigade arrived.

The next day, D plus 1, Brigadier John "Shan" Hackett's 4th Parachute Brigade was due to arrive, together with the remainder of the Airlanding Brigade; and on the third day, Major General Stanislaw Sosabowski's Polish 1st Parachute Brigade was to be landed. Urquhart had marked in a sixth drop zone for the Poles. Because it was anticipated that, by D plus 2, the bridge would be captured and the flak batteries knocked out, the Poles were to drop on the southern bank of the Lower Rhine near the village of Elden about one mile south of the Arnhem crossing.

Despite the risks he must accept, Urquhart felt confident. He believed he had "a reasonable operation and a good plan." Casualties, he thought, might be "somewhere in the neighborhood of 30 percent"; considering the intricate nature of the attack, he did not think the cost was too high. In the early evening of September 12, he briefed his commanders on the operation and, Urquhart remembers, "everybody seemed quite content with the plan."

One commander, however, had grave misgivings. Major General Stanislaw Sosabowski, the trim, fifty-two-year-old leader of the Polish 1st Parachute Brigade, was quite sure that "we were in for a bitter struggle." The former Polish War Academy professor had already stated his position to Generals Urquhart and Browning when he first heard about Operation Comet. At that time he had demanded that Urquhart give him his orders in writing so that "I would not be held responsible for the disaster." With Urquhart he had visited Browning and told him "this mission cannot possibly succeed." Browning asked why. As Sosabowski remembered, "I told him it would be suicide to attempt it with the forces we had and Browning answered, 'But, my dear Sosabowski, the Red Devils and the gallant Poles can do anything!'"

Now, one week later, as he listened to Urquhart, Sosabowski thought, "the British are not only grossly underestimating German strength in the Arnhem area, but they seem ignorant of the significance Arnhem has for the Fatherland." Sosabowski believed that to the Germans Arnhem represented "the gateway to Germany, and I did not expect the Germans to leave it open." He did not believe that "troops in the area were of very low caliber, with only a few battered tanks sitting around." He was appalled when Urquhart told the assembled brigade commanders that the 1st Airborne was to be dropped "at least six miles from the objective." To reach the bridge the main body of troops would have "a five-hour march; so how could surprise be achieved? Any fool of a German would immediately know our plans."

There was another part of the plan Sosabowski did not like. Heavy equipment and ammunition for his brigade was to go in by glider on an earlier lift. Thus, his stores would be on a northern landing zone when his troops landed on the southern bank. What would happen if the bridge was not taken by the time the Poles landed? As Urquhart spelled out the plan, Sosabowski learned to his astonishment that, if the bridge was still in German hands by that time, his Polish troops would be expected to take it.

Despite Sosabowski's anxieties, at the September 12 briefing he remained silent. "I remember Urquhart asking for questions and nobody raised any," he recalled. "Everyone sat nonchalantly, legs crossed, looking bored. I wanted to say something about this impossible plan, but I just couldn't. I was unpopular as it was, and anyway who would have listened?"

Later, when the entire airborne operation was reviewed for all commanders at General Browning's headquarters, others had grave misgivings about the British part of the plan but they too remained silent. Brigadier General James M. Gavin, commander of the American 82nd Airborne, was so astonished when he heard of Urquhart's choice of landing sites that he said to his operations chief, Lieutenant Colonel John Norton, "My God, he can't mean it." Norton was equally appalled. "He does," he said grimly, "but I wouldn't care to try it." In Gavin's view, it was far better to take "10 percent initial casualties by dropping either on or close to the bridge than to run the risk of landing on distant drop zones." He was "surprised that General Browning did not question Urquhart's plan." Still, Gavin said nothing "for I assumed that the British, with their extensive combat experience, knew exactly what they were doing."

2

SS STURMBANNFÜHRER (MAJOR) SEPP KRAFFT did not intend to move again if he could avoid it. In the past few weeks his understrength SS Panzer Grenadier Training and Reserve Battalion had been ordered back and forth across Holland. Now, after only five days, the unit was being ordered out of the village of Oosterbeek—and not by a superior of Krafft's, but by a Wehrmacht major.

Krafft protested vehemently. The main body of his three companies of men was billeted in the village, with the rest in Arnhem, and another 1,000 SS recruits were due to arrive momentarily for training. The Wehrmacht major was adamant. "I don't care about that," he told Krafft bluntly, "you've got to get out." Krafft fought back. The ambitious thirty-seven-year-old officer took orders only from his SS superiors. "I refuse," he said. The Wehrmacht officer was not intimidated. "Let me make things clear to you," he said. "You're moving out of Oosterbeek because Model's headquarters is moving in."

Krafft quickly calmed down. He had no wish to run afoul of Field Marshal Walter Model. Still, the order rankled. Krafft moved, but not very far. He decided to bivouac his troops in the woods and farms northwest of Oosterbeek, not far from the village of Wolfheze. The spot he happened to choose was alongside the Wolfheze road, almost between the zones marked on maps in England for the men of the British 1st Airborne Division to land, and blocking the route into Arnhem itself.

3

HENRI KNAP, Arnhem's underground intelligence chief, felt safe in his new role. To protect his wife and two daughters from complicity in his activities, he had left home four months earlier and moved a few blocks away. His headquarters were now in the offices of a general practitioner, Dr. Leo C. Breebaart. The white-coated Knap was now the doctor's "assistant," and certain "patients" were messengers and couriers belonging to his intelligence network: forty men and women and a few teen-agers.

Knap's was a time-consuming and frustrating job. He had to evaluate the information he received and then pass it along by phone. Arnhem's resistance chief, Pieter Kruyff, had given Knap three telephone numbers, each with twelve to fifteen digits, and told him to commit them to memory. Knap never knew where or to whom he was calling. His instructions were to dial each number in turn until contact was made.*

Gathering intelligence was even more complicated. Knap's requests were passed down through the network chain, and he never knew what agent procured the information. If a report seemed dubious, Knap investigated on his own. At the moment he was intrigued and puzzled by several reports that had reached him about enemy activity in Oosterbeek.

A German officer wearing staff insignia, Major Horst Smöckel, had visited a number of stores in Renkum, Oosterbeek and Arnhem and ordered a variety of supplies to be delivered to Oosterbeek's Tafelberg Hotel. What Knap found curious were the requisitions; among them were hard-to-find foods and other specialty items which the Dutch population rarely saw anymore, such as *Genever* gin.

Additionally, German signalmen had been busy laying a welter of telephone cables to a number of hotels in the suburbs,

---

*Knap has never learned who his contacts were except that his reports were passed on to a top-secret unit known as the "Albrecht Group." He knew the calls he made were long distance. At the time, Dutch telephone numbers consisted of four digits. A brilliant telephone technician named Nicolaas Tjalling de Bode devised a method for underground members under which, by using certain telephone numbers, they could bypass local switchboards and automatically call all over Holland.

including the Tafelberg. The conclusion, Knap felt, was obvious: a high-ranking headquarters was moving into Oosterbeek. But which one? Who was the general? And had he arrived?

It was even more important for Knap to keep abreast of the enemy strength in and around the Arnhem region. He knew there were other intelligence men sending back information in each town and that he was "only a small cog in a vast collection system." As a result, there was probably "much duplication of effort." Nevertheless, everything was important, for "what one cell might miss, we might pick up."

Two weeks before, as he later recalled, "there was almost no German strength in the Arnhem region." Since then, the military picture had changed dramatically. Now, Knap was alarmed at the German buildup. From his network sources, over the previous seven days, Knap had reported that "the remains of several divisions, including panzer units, were in the process of reorganizing in and around Arnhem or were moving into Germany." By now, more specific news had come. His sources reported the presence of tanks north and northeast of Arnhem. Knap believed that "parts of at least one or even two panzer divisions" were in the area, but their identity and exact location were, so far, not known.

Knap wanted details quickly. Urgently, he passed the word to his network. He demanded more exact information on the panzer activity and he wanted to know immediately the identity of the "new occupant" in the Tafelberg Hotel.

Twenty-five-year-old Wouter van de Kraats had never heard of Henri Knap. His contact in the underground was a man he knew only as "Jansen" who lived somewhere in Arnhem. Jansen had a new assignment for him—the Tafelberg Hotel. A high-ranking German officer had arrived, he was told, and Van de Kraats was to see if any of the staff cars outside "carried an identifying pennant or flag." If so, he was to report the colors and symbols on the standard.

Van de Kraats had noticed an influx of German activity around the hotel. German military police and sentries had moved into the area. His problem was how to get through the sentries along the road—the Pietersbergweg—running past the Tafelberg. He decided to bluff his way through.

As he made for the hotel, he was immediately stopped by a sentry. "But I must get through," Van de Kraats told the German. "I work at the petrol station up the street." The German let him pass. Three other sentries gave him only a cursory glance. Then, as Van de Kraats passed the Tafelberg, he quickly looked at the entrance and the driveway. None of the parked cars had any identifying markings, but near the front door of the hotel stood a checkerboard black, red and white metal pennant—the insignia of a German army group commander.

On the afternoon of Thursday, September 14, Henri Knap heard from his network. Several sources reported large formations of panzer troops, tanks and armored vehicles encamped in a semicircle to the north of Arnhem. There were units at Beekbergen, Epse and along the Ijssel River. There was even a startling report of "20 to 30 Tiger tanks." Exactly how many units were involved, he was unable to ascertain. He was able to clearly identify only one, and that by a fluke. One of his agents noted "strange markings—reverse *F*'s with a ball at the foot of them"—on some tanks. Checking through a special German manual, Knap was able to identify the unit. He immediately called his telephone contact and reported the presence of the 9th SS Panzer Division Hohenstaufen. From the agent's report, Knap located its position as lying approximately to the north between Arnhem and Apeldoorn and from there, eastward to Zutphen.

Shortly afterward he received word about the Tafelberg Hotel. He passed this report on, too. The significant black, red and white checkerboard pennant told its own story. There was only one German army group commander in this part of the western front. Although Knap reported the news as hearsay, it seemed to him the officer had to be Field Marshal Walter Model.

4

TWENTY-FIVE MILES EAST of Oosterbeek at his II SS Panzer Corps headquarters in a small castle on the outskirts of Doetinchem, General Wilhelm Bittrich held a meeting with his two remaining division commanders. Bittrich was in a bad mood, barely able to contain his temper. The outlook for his battered panzer corps was now far worse than it had been a week earlier. Impatiently Bittrich had awaited replacements in men, armor and equipment. None had arrived. On the contrary, his force had been whittled down even more. He had been ordered to send two combat groups to the front. One was with the German Seventh Army trying to hold the Americans near Aachen; the other was dispatched to bolster General Kurt Student's First Parachute Army after British tanks successfully breached the Albert Canal line, crossed the Meuse-Escaut Canal and grabbed a bridgehead at Neerpelt almost on the Dutch border. Now, at a time when the British were massing to renew their offensive—an attack that the intelligence chief at Army Group B called "imminent"—Bittrich had received through Field Marshal Model a "crazy directive from the fools in Berlin." One of his shattered divisions was to be cannibalized and pulled back into Germany.

A once-ardent Nazi, Bittrich denounced the order acridly. He "was sick and tired of Berlin's orders and the sycophants around Hitler who were indulging in all kinds of gimmickry." Courageous and able, Bittrich had spent most of his adult life in uniform. In World War I, he had served as a lieutenant in the German air force and had been twice wounded. Later, for a few years, he worked in a stockbroker's office. Then, rejoining the armed forces, Bittrich became a member of a secret German air-force team and for eight years taught flying to the Russians. When Hitler came to power, Bittrich joined the newly formed Luftwaffe but in the mid-thirties he switched to the Waffen SS, where promotion was faster.*

In Normandy, Bittrich's faith in Hitler's leadership began to waver. He sided with Field Marshal Rommel against Hitler's "insane fight-to-the-last-man" philosophy. Once he confided to Rommel that "we are being so badly led from above that I

---

*As a suspected war criminal, Bittrich spent eight years in prison after World War II; on June 22, 1953, he was found innocent and released. Waffen SS commanders are difficult to locate and interview, but Bittrich and his officers were extremely helpful to me in setting the record straight on many hitherto unknown events in the Arnhem battle. Bittrich wanted me to clarify one minor matter relating to his personal life. In various British accounts "I have been described as a musician who hoped to be a conductor," he told me. "But the authors have confused me with my brother, Dr. Gerhard Bittrich, an extremely talented pianist and conductor."

can no longer carry out senseless orders. I have never been a robot and don't intend to become one." After the July 20 plot, when he learned that his former commander Colonel General Erich Hoepner, as a conspirator, had been condemned to death by hanging, Bittrich raged to his staff that "this is the blackest day for the German army." Bittrich's outspoken criticism of Hitler's military leadership soon reached Berlin. As Bittrich later recalled, "my remarks were reported to the chief of the SS, Reichsführer Heinrich Himmler, and the name Bittrich was no longer mentioned around Hitler's headquarters." Only the near-collapse of the German front in the west, a situation demanding Bittrich's kind of expertise, and the attitude of sympathetic commanders had saved him from being recalled. Even so, Himmler was still "eager for me to return to Germany for a little talk." Bittrich had no illusions about Himmler's invitation. Nor had Model; he was determined to keep Bittrich in the west and flatly refused to entertain Himmler's repeated requests to send Bittrich home.

Now the outraged Bittrich outlined Berlin's latest plan to the commanders of his divisions—SS Brigadeführer (Brigadier General) Heinz Harmel of the 10th Frundsberg Division and SS Obersturmbannführer (Lieutenant Colonel) Walter Harzer of the 9th Hohenstaufen Division. Bittrich told Harzer—who had already learned something about the plan from Model's chief of staff, Lieutenant General Hans Krebs—that his 9th Hohenstaufen Division was to entrain immediately for Germany, where it would be located near Siegen, northeast of Koblenz. Harmel's 10th Division was to remain in Holland. It would be refitted and brought up to strength in its present location east and southeast of Arnhem, ready to be committed again.

The thirty-eight-year-old Harmel, whose bluff heartiness had earned him the affectionate nickname of "*der alte Frundsberg*" from his men, was not pleased with the decision. It seemed to him that "Bittrich was, as usual, showing preference for the Hohenstaufen Division, perhaps because it had been his own before he became corps commander and perhaps, too, because Harzer had been his chief of staff." Although he did not think "Bittrich was consciously unfair, it always seemed to work out that the Hohenstaufen got the cushy jobs."

His younger counterpart, thirty-two-year-old Walter Harzer, was elated at the news, even though he thought "the likelihood of getting Berlin leave seemed doubtful." Ideally, after refitting he expected to have a "brand-new Hohenstaufen Division." Privately, too, the tough Harzer, his face marked by a saber scar, had high hopes now of achieving his ambition: to be promoted to the rank befitting an SS division commander —brigadier general. Still, as Bittrich outlined the entire plan, one segment was not to Harzer's liking.

Although badly depleted, his division was still stronger than Harmel's. Instead of the usual 9,000 men, the Hohenstaufen had barely 6,000, the Frundsberg about 3,500. Harzer had close to twenty Mark V Panther tanks, but not all were serviceable. He did, however, have a considerable number of armored vehicles: self-propelled guns, armored cars and forty armored personnel carriers, all with heavy machine guns, some mounted with artillery pieces. Harmel's Frundsberg Division had almost no tanks and was desperately short of all kinds of armored vehicles. Both divisions still had formidable artillery, mortar and antiaircraft units. To build up the Frundsberg Division, which would remain behind, Bittrich said, Harzer was to transfer as much of his transportation and equipment as he could to Harmel. Harzer was skeptical. "In my heart," Harzer later recalled, "I knew damn well that if I gave over my few tanks or the armored personnel carriers to Harmel, they'd never be replaced." Harzer did not protest the decision, but he had no intention of giving up all his vehicles.

Harzer had long ago learned to husband his division's resources. He had more vehicles than even Bittrich realized— including American jeeps he had captured during the long retreat from France. He decided to ignore the order by "some paper maneuvering." By removing caterpillar tracks, wheels or guns from his vehicles, he could make them temporarily unserviceable until he reached Germany. In the meantime they would be listed on his armored strength returns as disabled.

Even with the extra men and vehicles from Harzer's cannibalized division, Bittrich continued, the Frundsberg would still be understrength. There was only one way to stress the urgency of the situation to Berlin: by presenting the facts directly to SS operational headquarters. Maybe then, replacements and reinforcements would be forthcoming. But Bittrich had no intention of visiting Berlin; Harmel was made the emissary, to his surprise. "I don't know why he chose me rather than Harzer," Harmel remembers. "But we urgently needed men and armor, and perhaps Bittrich thought a general might carry more weight. The whole matter was to be kept secret from Field Marshal Model. So, as we were not expecting any trouble in the Arnhem area, it was decided that I would leave for Berlin on the evening of September 16."

The exchange of equipment between Harzer and Harmel and the move of the cannibalized Hohenstaufen Division to Germany, Bittrich ordered, was to begin immediately. While the operation was in process, he added, Field Marshal Model wanted small mobile attack groups to be readied as *Alarmeinheiten* ("alarm units") which could be committed in case of emergency. As a result, Harzer privately decided that his "best units would be entrained last." Bittrich expected the entire equipment transfer and move completed by September 22. Because six trains a day left for Germany, Harzer thought the task could be completed much earlier. He believed his last and best units could leave for the Fatherland in just three more days— probably on the afternoon of September 17.

A demoralizing rumor was making the rounds. By September 14, several senior German officers in Holland were saying that an airborne drop would take place.

The talk originated from a conversation between Hitler's operations chief, Colonel General Alfred Jodl, and the Commander in Chief, West, Field Marshal von Rundstedt. Jodl was concerned that the Allies might invade Holland from the sea. If Eisenhower followed his usual tactics, Jodl said, airborne troops would be dropped as a prelude to the seaborne attack. Von Rundstedt, though skeptical of the suggestion (he, by contrast, was convinced that paratroopers would be dropped in conjunction with an attack on the Ruhr), passed the information on to Army Group B's commander, Field Marshal Model. Model's view was the same as Von Rundstedt's. Nevertheless, he could not ignore Jodl's warning. He ordered the German armed forces commander in Holland, the jittery Luftwaffe general, Friedrich Christiansen, to dispatch units of his meager grab bag of army, navy, Luftwaffe and Dutch Waffen SS personnel to the coast.

Since Jodl's call on September 11, the scare had traveled down the various echelons of command, particularly through Luftwaffe channels. Although the invasion had so far failed to materialize, the fear of an airborne drop was still mounting. Everyone was speculating on possible sites. From their maps, some Luftwaffe commanders saw the large open areas between the north coast and Arnhem as possible landing zones. Others, nervously awaiting the renewal of the British offensive into Holland from the bridgehead over the Meuse-Escaut Canal at Neerpelt, wondered if paratroopers might be used in conjunction with that attack and dropped into the area of Nijmegen.

On September 13, Luftwaffe Colonel General Otto Dessloch, commander of the 3rd Air Fleet, heard about Berlin's fears at Von Rundstedt's headquarters in Koblenz. Dessloch was so concerned that he telephoned Field Marshal Model the following day. Model, he recalls, thought Berlin's invasion scare was "nonsense." The Field Marshal was so unconcerned "that he invited me to dinner at his new headquarters in the Tafelberg Hotel in Oosterbeek." Dessloch refused. "I have no intention of being made a prisoner," he told Model. Just before he hung up, Dessloch added: "If I were you, I would get out of that area." Model, Dessloch remembers, merely laughed.

At Deelen airfield north of Arnhem word of a possible airborne attack reached Luftwaffe fighter commander Major General Walter Grabmann. He drove to Oosterbeek for a conference with Model's chief of staff, Lieutenant General Hans Krebs. When Grabmann expressed the Luftwaffe's fears, Krebs said, "For God's sake, don't talk about such things. Anyway, where would they land?" Grabmann went to a map and, pointing to areas west of Arnhem, said, "Anywhere here. The heath is perfect for paratroopers." Krebs, Grabmann later recalled, "laughed and warned me that if I continued to talk this way, I'd make myself look ridiculous."

Holland's notorious police chief, SS Lieutenant General Hanns Albin Rauter, heard the rumor too, possibly from his superior General Christiansen. Rauter was convinced that anything was possible, including an airborne attack. Rauter, chief architect

of Nazi terror in the Netherlands, expected the Dutch underground to attack and the population to rise at any moment. He
was determined to stamp out any kind of insurrection by the
simple expedient of executing three Dutch nationals for each
Nazi killed. Rauter had declared an "emergency" immediately
after the German retreat and the stampede of Dutch Nazis to
Germany two weeks before. His police had taken bitter revenge against anyone even remotely involved with the Dutch
resistance. Men and women were arrested, shot or sent off
into concentration camps. Ordinary citizens fared little better.
All travel between provinces was forbidden. More restrictive
rules were imposed. Anyone found on the streets during curfew risked being fired on without warning. All over southern
Holland, in anticipation of the British offensive, the Dutch
were pressed into service as laborers digging trenches for the
Wehrmacht. In Nijmegen, Rauter filled his workforce quota by
threatening to throw entire families into concentration camps.
Gatherings of any kind were forbidden. "Where more than five
persons are seen together," one of Rauter's posters warned,
"they will be fired on by the Wehrmacht, SS or police troops."

Now, with the British attack from the south imminent and
Berlin's warning of a possible air and sea attack in the north,
Rauter's world was beginning to come apart. He was terrified.* Learning that Model was in Holland, Rauter decided to
seek reassurance and set out for the Tafelberg Hotel. On the
evening of September 14, Rauter met with Model and his chief
of staff, General Krebs. He was "convinced," Rauter told them,
"that the Allies would now use airborne forces in southern
Holland." He felt that it was the right psychological moment.
Model and Krebs disagreed. Elite airborne formations, Model
said, were too "precious, their training too costly" for indis-
criminate use. The Field Marshal did indeed expect Montgomery to attack into Holland from Neerpelt, but the situation

---

*In the safety of his prison cell after the war, Rauter admitted to Dutch in-
terrogators that "at the time I was very nervous. . . . I had to paralyze the
resistance." Rauter was found guilty by a Dutch court on January 12, 1949,
of a wide range of offenses, including "persecution of the Jews, deportation
of inhabitants for slave labor, pillage, confiscation of property, illegal arrests,
detentions . . . and the killings of innocent civilians as reprisals for offenses
. . . against the occupying authorities." He was executed on March 25, 1949.

was not critical enough to justify the use of airborne troops. Also, since assault forces would be separated by three broad rivers to the south, he did not think that a British attack toward Arnhem was possible. Both Nijmegen and Arnhem were too far from the British forces. Besides, Model continued, Montgomery was "tactically a very cautious man. He would never use airborne forces in a reckless adventure."

By the time the prisoner reached Major Friedrich Kieswetter's headquarters in the village of Driebergen, west of Oosterbeek, on September 15, the deputy chief of Wehrmacht counterintelligence in Holland knew a great deal about him. There was an ample file on slow-witted, twenty-eight-year-old Christiaan Antonius Lindemans, better known, because of his huge size (6'3", 260 lbs.), as "King Kong." Lindemans had been captured by a patrol near the Dutch-Belgian border, in the no man's land between the British and German lines. At first, because of his British battle dress, Lindemans was taken for a soldier but, at the battalion command post near Valkenswaard, to the amazement of his interrogators, he demanded to see Lieutenant Colonel Hermann Giskes—German spy chief in Holland and Kieswetter's superior. After a series of phone calls, Lindemans' captors were even more astonished to receive orders to drive the prisoner immediately to Driebergen. Lindemans alone displayed no surprise. Some of his compatriots thought him to be a stanch member of the Dutch underground; but the Germans knew him in another capacity —as a spy. King Kong was a double agent.

Lindemans had turned traitor in 1943. At that time he offered to work for Giskes in return for the release of his current mistress and younger brother, Henk, arrested by the Gestapo as a member of the underground and said to be awaiting execution. Giskes had readily agreed; and ever since, Lindemans had served the Germans well. His perfidy had resulted in the penetration of many underground cells and the arrest and execution of numerous Dutch and Belgian patriots. Although he was crude and boastful, given to wild, drunken excesses and possessed of an insatiable appetite for women, Lindemans had so far miraculously escaped exposure. However, many resistance leaders considered him a dangerous risk, unlike certain

Allied officers in Brussels who were so impressed by King Kong that Lindemans now worked for a British intelligence unit under the command of a Canadian captain.

In Giskes' absence, Kieswetter dealt with Lindemans for the first time. He found the towering braggart, who introduced himself to everyone in the office as the "great King Kong," disgusting. Lindemans told the major of his latest mission. The Canadian intelligence officer had sent him to warn underground leaders in Eindhoven that downed Allied pilots were no longer to be sent through the "escape line" into Belgium. Because the British were due to break out from the Neerpelt bridgehead toward Eindhoven, the pilots were to be kept hidden. Lindemans, who had spent five days coming through the lines, was able to give Kieswetter some details on the British buildup. The attack, he said flatly, would take place on September 17.

The imminence of the British move was hardly news. Kieswetter, like everyone else, had been expecting it momentarily. Lindemans also informed Kieswetter of another development: coincidental with the British attack, he reported, a paratroop drop was planned beyond Eindhoven to help capture the town.* The revelation made no sense to Kieswetter. Why use

---

*After the war, some British newspapers charged that it was because Lindemans pinpointed Arnhem as the main airborne objective that the panzer divisions were waiting. Obviously this is not so. Bittrich's corps reached its positions before Eisenhower and Montgomery met on September 10 and decided on Market-Garden. Neither could Lindemans have known anything about the Arnhem attack or the massive dimensions of the operation. Again, Allied decisions on dates, placement of drop zones, etc. were made long after Lindemans left Brussels to cross the German lines. A second often-repeated story is that Lindemans was taken to Colonel General Kurt Student's headquarters at Vught for questioning, and it has been suggested that the airborne expert correctly evaluated the report and gave the alert. Student flatly denies this allegation. "It is a large fat lie," he told me. "I never met Lindemans. Indeed, I first heard of the whole affair in a prison camp after the war." Student adds, "The truth is, nobody in the German command knew anything about the attack until it happened." Shortly after Market-Garden, suspicion fell on Lindemans and he was arrested by the Dutch. King Kong, the great Lothario, lived up to his reputation to the very end. In July, 1946, forty-eight hours before his trial, Lindemans, in a prison hospital, was found unconscious with a prison nurse nearby. Both of them, in a bizarre "love pact," had taken overdoses of sleeping pills. Lindemans died, the girl survived.

paratroopers when the British army could easily reach Eindhoven by itself? Perhaps because Lindemans' information seemed unrealistic or more likely because of his antipathy toward King Kong, Kieswetter told Lindemans to continue on with his mission and then return to the British lines. Kieswetter took no immediate action. He thought so little of Lindemans' information that he did not pass it on directly to Wehrmacht headquarters. He sent it, instead, through the Sicherheitsdienst (SS security and intelligence service). He also dictated a brief memorandum of his conversation with Lindemans for Giskes, at the moment away on another assignment. Giskes, who had always considered King Kong reliable, would not receive it until the afternoon of September 17.

5

OPERATION MARKET-GARDEN was now less than forty-eight hours away. In his office Lieutenant General Walter Bedell Smith, Eisenhower's chief of staff, listened to SHAEF's intelligence chief, British Major General Kenneth W. Strong, disclose his latest news with growing alarm. Beyond doubt, Strong said, there was German armor in the Market-Garden area.

For days, Strong and his staff had been sifting and assessing every intelligence report in an effort to determine the whereabouts of the 9th and 10th SS Panzer divisions. Since the first week in September there had been no contact with the units. Both were badly cut up, but it was considered unlikely that they had been completely destroyed. One theory held that the units might have been ordered back into Germany. Now Dutch underground messages told a different story. The lost divisions had been spotted.

The 9th and, presumably, the 10th SS Panzer divisions were in Holland, Strong reported to Smith, "in all probability to be refitted with tanks." Exactly what remained of the units or their fighting capability no one could say, but there was no longer any doubt about their location, Strong reported. They were definitely in the vicinity of Arnhem.

Deeply concerned about Market-Garden and, in his own words, "alarmed over the possibility of failure," Smith immediately conferred with the Supreme Commander. The British 1st Airborne Division, due to land at Arnhem, "could not hold out against two armored divisions," Smith told Eisenhower. To be sure, there was a question—a big question —about the strength of the units, but to be on the safe side Smith thought that Market-Garden should be reinforced. He believed two airborne divisions would be required in the Arnhem area. (Presumably, Smith had in mind as the additional unit the veteran British 6th Airborne Division, commanded by Major General Richard Gale, which had been used successfully during the Normandy invasion, but was not included in Market-Garden.) Otherwise, Smith told Eisenhower, the plan must be revised. "My feeling," he later said, "was that if we could not drop the equivalent of another division in the area, then we should shift one of the American airborne divisions, which were to form the 'carpet' further north, to reinforce the British."

Eisenhower considered the problem and its risks. On the basis of this intelligence report and almost on the eve of the attack, he was being urged to override Monty's plan—one that Eisenhower himself had approved. It meant challenging Montgomery's generalship and upsetting an already delicate command situation. As Supreme Commander, he had another option open: Market-Garden could be canceled; but the only grounds for such a decision would be this single piece of intelligence. Eisenhower had obviously to assume that Montgomery was the best judge of enemy strength before him and that he would plan accordingly. As Eisenhower explained to Smith, "I cannot tell Monty how to dispose of his troops," nor could he "call off the operation, since I have already given Monty the green light." If changes were to be made, Montgomery would have to make them. Still, Eisenhower was prepared to let Smith "fly to 21st Army Group headquarters and argue it out with Montgomery."

Bedell Smith set out immediately for Brussels. He found Montgomery confident and enthusiastic. Smith explained his fears about the panzer units in the Arnhem area and strongly suggested that the plan might need revision. Montgomery "ridiculed the idea. Monty felt the greatest opposition would come more from terrain difficulties than from the Germans. All would go well, he kept repeating, if we at SHAEF would help him surmount his logistical difficulties. He was not worried about the German armor. He thought Market-Garden would go all right as set." The conference was fruitless. "At least I tried to stop him," Smith said, "but I got nowhere. Montgomery simply waved my objections airily aside."*

Even as Montgomery and Smith conferred, across the Channel startling evidence reached British I Airborne Corps headquarters. Earlier in the day, fighters of the R.A.F.'s specially equipped photo-reconnaissance squadron returning from The Hague had made a low-level sweep over the Arnhem area. Now, in his office, intelligence officer Major Brian Urquhart took up a magnifying glass and examined five oblique-angle pictures—an "end of the run" strip from one of the fighters. Hundreds of aerial photographs of the Market-Garden area had been taken and evaluated in the previous seventy-two hours, but only these five shots showed what Urquhart had long feared—the unmistakable presence of German armor. "It was the straw that broke the camel's back," Urquhart later recalled. "There, in the photos, I could clearly see tanks—if not on the very Arnhem landing and drop zones, then certainly close to them."

Major Urquhart rushed to General Browning's office with the photographic confirmation. Browning saw him immediately. Placing the pictures on the desk before Browning, Urquhart said, "Take a look at these." The General studied them one by one. Although Urquhart no longer remembers the exact wording, to the best of his recollection, Browning said, "I wouldn't trouble myself about these if I were you." Then, referring to the tanks in the photos, he continued, "They're probably not serviceable at any rate." Urquhart was stunned. Helplessly he pointed out that the armor, "whether serviceable or not, were still tanks and they had guns." Looking back,

*I have based this entire section on information supplied to me by General S. L. A. Marshall, Chief Historian for the European Theatre of Operations during World War II, who kindly allowed me to see his various monographs on Market-Garden and also his 1945 interview with General Bedell Smith on the meeting with Eisenhower and later Montgomery.

Urquhart feels that "perhaps because of information I knew nothing about, General Browning was not prepared to accept my evaluation of the photos. My feeling remained the same —that everyone was so *gung-ho* to go that nothing could stop them."

Urquhart was unaware that some members of Browning's staff considered the young intelligence officer almost too zealous. The show was about to begin, and most officers were anxious and eager to get on with it. Urquhart's pessimistic warnings irritated them. As one senior staff officer put it, "His views were colored by nervous exhaustion. He was inclined to be a bit hysterical, no doubt brought on by overwork."

Shortly after his meeting with Browning, Urquhart was visited by the corps medical officer. "I was told," Urquhart recalls, "that I was exhausted—who wasn't?—and that perhaps I should take a rest and go on leave. I was out. I had become such a pain around headquarters that on the very eve of the attack I was being removed from the scene. I was told to go home. There was nothing I could say. Although I disagreed with the plan and feared the worst, still, this was going to be the big show and, curiously, I did not want to be left behind."

6

By NOON ON SATURDAY, September 16, the German proclamation was plastered on bulletin boards all over Arnhem.

By order of the Security Police, the following is announced:

During the night an attack with explosives was made on the railroad viaduct at Schaapsdrift.

The population is called upon to cooperate in tracing the culprits of this attack.

If they have not been found before 12 o'clock noon on Sunday, September 17, 1944, a number of hostages will be shot.

I appeal to the cooperation of all of you in order that needless victims be spared.

The acting Burgomaster,

LIERA

In a cellar, leading members of the Arnhem underground met in an emergency meeting. The sabotage of the railroad viaduct had been badly botched. Henri Knap, the Arnhem intelligence chief, had not been happy about the mission from its inception. He felt that, "at best, we are all rank amateurs when it comes to sabotage." In his view, "it is far better to concentrate on feeding intelligence to the Allies and to leave demolition jobs to men who know what they are doing." The chief of the Arnhem underground, thirty-eight-year-old Pieter Kruyff, asked for the others' opinions. Nicolaas Tjalling de Bode voted that the members give themselves up. Knap remembers thinking "this was a very steep price to pay—the lives of the hostages, innocent people—for a small hole in a bridge." Gijsbert Jan Numan was conscience-stricken. He had been involved along with Harry Montfroy, Albert Deuss, Toon van Daalen and others in procuring the materials for the explosives and in planning the sabotage, and no one wanted innocent men to suffer. Yet what was to be done? Kruyff heard everyone out, then he made his decision. "The organization must stay intact even though innocent people may be shot," he decreed. Looking around at the assembled leaders, as Nicolaas de Bode remembers, Kruyff told them, "No one will give himself up to the Germans. That's my order." Henri Knap had a feeling of dread. He knew that if the Germans followed their usual procedure, ten or twelve leading citizens—doctors, lawyers and teachers among them—would be publicly executed in an Arnhem square at noon on Sunday.

7

ALL DOWN THE ALLIED LINE of command the evaluation of intelligence on the panzers in the Arnhem area was magnificently bungled. SHAEF's Intelligence Summary No. 26 issued on September 16, the eve of Market-Garden—containing the ominous warning that had caused General Bedell Smith's alarm—was disregarded. In part, it read, "9th SS Panzer Division, and presumably the 10th, has been reported withdrawing to the Arnhem area in Holland; there, they will probably collect new tanks from a depot reported in the area of Cleves."

The information, already discredited by Montgomery at his meeting with Smith, was now discounted by General Dempsey's British Second Army headquarters—the same headquarters that had originally noted the presence in Holland of "battered panzer formations" on September 10. In the most serious blunder of all, Dempsey's intelligence staff, on September 14, described the Germans in the Market-Garden area as "weak, demoralized and likely to collapse entirely if confronted with a large airborne attack." Now, in a complete reversal of their original position, they dismissed the presence of the panzers, *because Dempsey's staff officers were unable to spot enemy armor on any reconnaissance photos.*

At First Allied Airborne Army headquarters, General Brereton's chief intelligence officer, British Lieutenant Colonel Anthony Tasker, was not prepared to accept SHAEF's report either. Reviewing all the information available, he decided there was no direct evidence that the Arnhem area contained "much more than the considerable flak defenses already known to exist."

Everyone, it seemed, accepted the optimistic outlook of Montgomery's headquarters. As the British I Airborne Corps's chief of staff, Brigadier Gordon Walch, remembers, "21st Army Group headquarters was the principal source of our intelligence, and we took what they gave us to be true." General Urquhart, commander of the British 1st Airborne Division, put it another way. "Nothing," he said, "was allowed to mar the optimism prevailing across the Channel."

Yet, besides SHAEF's report on the "missing" panzers, there was other evidence of German buildup, again almost cursorily noted. At the front, ahead of General Horrocks' XXX Corps Garden forces, it was plain that an increasing number of German units were moving into the line. Now the strategic error at Antwerp ten days before was beginning to build and threaten the grand design of Operation Market-Garden. The German troops filling out General Student's front were none other than units of the splintered divisions that had escaped across the mouth of the Schelde—the battered men of Von Zangen's Fifteenth Army, the army the Allies had practically written off. Intelligence officers did note that, though the Germans had increased in number, the new units in the line were "believed to be in no fit state to resist any determined advance." Any British Tommy along the Belgium-Dutch frontier could have told them otherwise.*

The cobblestone streets of the dingy mining town of Leopoldsburg in northern Belgium, barely ten miles from the front, were choked with jeeps and scout cars. All roads seemed to lead to a cinema opposite the railway station—and never before had the nondescript theater held such an audience. Officers of Lieutenant General Horrocks' XXX Corps—the Garden forces that would drive north through Holland to link up with the paratroopers—crowded the street and milled around the entrance as their credentials were inspected by red-capped military police. It was a colorful, exuberant group and it reminded Brigadier Hubert Essame, commanding officer of the 214th Brigade, 43rd Wessex Infantry Division, of "an army assembly at a point-to-point race or a demonstration on Salisbury Plain in time of peace." He was fascinated by the colorful dress of the commanders. There was a striking variety of headgear. No one had a steel helmet, but berets of many colors bore the proud badges of famous regiments, among them the Irish, Grenadier, Coldstream, Scotch, Welsh and Royal Horse Guards, the Royal Army Service Corps and Royal Artillery. There was a regal casualness about everyone's attire. Essame noted that most commanders were dressed in "sniper's smocks, parachutists' jackets and jeep coats over brightly colored slacks, corduroys, riding

*British Major General Hubert Essame (retired) in his excellent book *The Battle for Germany* (p. 13), writes: "In misappreciation of the actual situation at the end of August and the first half of September, Allied intelligence staffs sank to a level only reached by Brigadier John Charteris, Haig's Chief Intelligence Officer at the time of the Passchendaele Battles in 1917." At that time the wartime Prime Minister David Lloyd George alleged that Charteris "selected only those figures and facts which suited his fancy and then issued hopeful reports accordingly." At various times during the 1917 Flanders campaign Charteris reported the enemy as "cracking," "mangled," "with few reserves," and even "on the run." In the dreadful battles that ensued around Passchendaele between July 31 and November 12, casualties, according to the official British history, totaled a staggering 244,897.

britches or even jodhpurs." Instead of ties many sported ascots or "scarves of various colors."*

The renowned Lieutenant Colonel J.O.E. ("Joe") Vandeleur, the solidly built, ruddy-faced, six-foot commander of the Irish Guards Armored Group, personified the kind of devil-may-care elegance of the Guards' officers. The forty-one-year-old Vandeleur was wearing his usual combat garb: black beret, a multicolored camouflaged parachutist's jacket, and corduroy trousers above high rubber boots. Additionally, Vandeleur wore, as always, a .45 Colt automatic strapped to his hip and, tucked into his jacket, what had become a symbol for his tankers, a flamboyant emerald-green scarf. The fastidious General "Boy" Browning, back in England, would have winced. Even Horrocks had once dryly admonished Vandeleur. "If the Germans ever get you, Joe," he said, "they'll think they've captured a peasant." But on this September 16 even Horrocks lacked the usual elegance of the impeccably dressed British staff officer. Instead of a shirt he wore a ribbed polo sweater and, over his battle dress, a sleeveless leather jerkin reminiscent of a British yeoman's dress.

As the popular Horrocks made his way down the aisle of the crowded theater he was greeted on all sides. The meeting he had called had sparked high excitement. Men were eager to get going again. From the Seine to Antwerp, Horrocks' tanks had often averaged fifty miles in a single day, but ever since the disastrous three-day halt on September 4 to "refit, refuel and rest," the going had been rough. With the British momentum gone, the enemy had quickly recovered. In the two vital weeks since, the British advance had been reduced to a crawl. It had taken four days for the Guards Armored Division —led by Joe Vandeleur's Irish Guards Group—to advance ten miles and capture the vital bridge over the Meuse-Escaut Canal near Neerpelt, from which the attack into Holland would begin the next day. Horrocks had no illusions about the German

---

*In his history of *The 43rd Wessex Division at War* (p. 115), Essame writes: "Sartorial disciplinarians of the future" might remember "that when the morale of the British Army was as high as at any time in its history, officers wore the clothing they found most suitable to the conditions under which they had to live and fight."

opposition, but he was confident that his forces could break through the enemy crust.

At precisely 11 A.M. Horrocks stepped onto the stage. All those assembled knew that the British offensive was about to be renewed, but so great was the security surrounding Montgomery's plan that only a few general officers present knew the details. With D Day for Operation Market-Garden barely twenty-four hours away, the Field Marshal's commanders now learned of the attack for the first time.

Attached to the cinema screen was a huge map of Holland. Colored tape snaked north along a single highway, crossing the great river obstacles and passing through the towns of Valkenswaard, Eindhoven, Veghel, Uden, Nijmegen and thence to Arnhem, a distance of some sixty-four miles. From there the tape continued for another thirty-odd miles to the Zuider Zee. Horrocks took a long pointer and began the briefing. "This is a tale you will tell your grandchildren," he told his audience. Then he paused and, much to the delight of the assembled officers, added: "And mightily bored they'll be."

In the audience, Lieutenant Colonel Curtis D. Renfro, liaison officer from the 101st Airborne Division and one of the few Americans present, was impressed by the Corps commander's enthusiasm and confidence. He talked for an hour, Curtis recorded, "with only an occasional reference to notes."

Step by step Horrocks explained the complexities of Market-Garden. The airborne army would go in first, he said. Its objectives: to capture the bridges in front of XXX Corps. Horrocks would give the word for the attack to begin. Depending on the weather, zero hour for the ground forces was expected to be 2 P.M. At that moment 350 guns would open fire and lay down a massive artillery barrage that would last thirty-five minutes. Then, at 2:35 P.M., led by waves of rocket-firing Typhoons, XXX Corps tanks would break out of their bridgehead and "blast down the main road." The Guards Armored Division would have the honor of leading the attack. They would be followed by the 43rd Wessex and 50th Northumberland divisions, and then by the 8th Armored Brigade and the Dutch Princess Irene Brigade.

There was to be "no pause, no stop," Horrocks emphasized. The Guards Armored was "to keep going like hell" all the way to Arnhem. The breakout from the bridgehead, Horrocks believed, would be "almost immediate." He expected the first Guards tanks to be in Eindhoven within two or three hours. If the enemy reacted fast enough to blow all the bridges before the airborne troops could secure them, then the 43rd Wessex Infantry Division engineers, coming up behind, would rush forward with men and bridging equipment. This massive engineering operation, should it be required, Horrocks explained, could involve 9,000 engineers and some 2,277 vehicles already in the Leopoldsburg area. The entire XXX Corps armored column was to be fed up the main road with the vehicles two abreast, thirty-five vehicles per mile. Traffic would be one way, and Horrocks expected "to pass 20,000 vehicles over the highway to Arnhem in sixty hours."

General Allan Adair, the forty-six-year-old commander of the famed Guards Armored Division, listening to Horrocks, thought Market-Garden was a bold plan, but he also believed "it might be tricky." He expected the worst moment to be the breakout from the Meuse-Escaut Canal bridgehead. Once through that, although he fully expected German resistance, he thought the going would "not be difficult." Besides, he had every faith in the unit that would lead off the attack—Lieutenant Colonel Joe Vandeleur's Irish Guards Group.

Joe Vandeleur, as he learned that his tanks would spearhead the breakout, remembers thinking to himself, "Oh, Christ! Not us again." Vandeleur was proud that his veteran unit had been chosen, yet he knew his troops were tired and his units understrength. Since the breakout from Normandy he had received very few replacements in either men or tanks; furthermore, "they weren't allowing a hell of a lot of time for planning." But then he thought, how much time do you really need to plan for a straight bash through the German lines? Next to him, his cousin, thirty-three-year-old Lieutenant Colonel Giles Vandeleur, who commanded the 2nd Battalion under Joe, was "struck with horror at the plan to blast through the German resistance on a one-tank front." To him, it was not proper armored warfare. But he recalls "swallowing whatever misgivings I had and succumbing to a strange, tense excitement, like being at the pole at the start of a horse race."

To three men in the theater, the announcement produced

deep personal feelings. The senior officers of the Dutch Princess Irene Brigade had led their men in battle all the way from
Normandy. First they had fought alongside the Canadians;
then, after the fall of Brussels, they were transferred to the British Second Army. Now they would be coming home. Much
as they looked forward to the liberation of Holland, the commander, Colonel Albert "Steve" de Ruyter van Steveninck; his
second in command, Lieutenant Colonel Charles Pahud de
Mortanges; and the chief of staff, Major Jonkheer Jan Beelaerts
van Blokland, had grave misgivings about the manner in which
it was to be accomplished. Steveninck considered the entire
plan risky. Mortanges' impression was that the British were
more offhand about what lay ahead than the facts justified. As
he put it, "It was made to seem quite elementary. First, we'll
take this bridge; then that one and hop this river. . . . The
terrain ahead with its rivers, marshes, dikes and lowlands, was
extremely difficult—as the British well knew from our many
presentations." The thirty-three-year-old chief of staff, Beelaerts van Blokland, could not help thinking of past military
history. "We seemed to be violating Napoleon's maxim about
never fighting unless you are at least 75 percent sure of success. Then, the other 25 percent can be left to chance. The
British were reversing the process; we were leaving 75 percent
to chance. We had only forty-eight hours to get to Arnhem,
and if the slightest thing went wrong—a bridge blown, stiffer
German resistance than anticipated—we'd be off schedule."
Blokland had a private worry, too. His parents lived in the village of Oosterbeek, just two and a half miles from the Arnhem
bridge.

One of the few officers below the rank of brigade major who
heard the briefing was twenty-one-year-old Lieutenant John
Gorman of the Irish Guards. He was stimulated by the whole
affair and thought Horrocks was "at his finest." The Corps
commander, Gorman later recalled, "called into play all his
wit and humor, interspersing the more dramatic or technical
points with humorous little asides. He really was quite a show-
man." Gorman was particularly pleased with Operation Garden because "the Guards were to lead out and obviously their
role would be tremendously dramatic."

When the meeting had ended and commanders headed

out to brief their troops, young Gorman felt his first "private doubts about the chances of success." Lingering in front of a map, he remembers thinking that Market-Garden was "a feasible operation—but only just feasible." There were simply "too many bridges." Nor was he enthusiastic about the terrain itself. He thought it was poor tank country and advancing on "a one-tank front, we would be very vulnerable." But the promise of support from rocket-firing Typhoons was reassuring. So was another promise of sorts. Gorman remembered the day, months before, when he had received the Military Cross for bravery from Montgomery himself.* At the investiture, Monty had said, "If I were a betting man I should say it would be an even bet that the war will be over by Christmas." And Horrocks, Gorman recalls, had "told us that this attack could end the war." The only alternative Gorman could find to "going north seemed to be a long dreary winter camped on or near the Escaut Canal." Monty's plan, he believed, "had just the right amount of dash and daring to work. If there was a chance to win the war by Christmas, then I was for pushing on."

Now, in the flat, gray Belgian countryside with its coal fields and slag heaps which reminded so many of Wales, the men who would lead the way for General Dempsey's British Second Army heard of the plan and the promise of Arnhem. Along side roads, in bivouac areas and in encampments, soldiers gathered around their officers to learn the part they would play in Operation Market-Garden. When Lieutenant Colonel Giles Vandeleur told his officers that the Irish would be leading out, twenty-nine-year-old Major Edward G. Tyler remembers that a "half moan" went up from the assembled officers. "We figured," he recalls, "that we deserved a bit of a break after taking the bridge over the Escaut Canal, which we named 'Joe's bridge' after Joe Vandeleur. But our commanding officer told us that it was a great honor for us to be chosen." Despite his desire for a reprieve, Tyler thought so too. "We were used

---

*Gorman won his Military Cross during the fighting at Caen, Normandy. Leading a trio of Sherman tanks, he was suddenly confronted by four German tanks, one a 60-ton Tiger. His men dispatched the German armor and Gorman rammed the huge Tiger tank, destroyed its gun and killed its crew as they tried to escape.

to one-tank fronts," he remembers, "and in this case we were trusting to speed and support. No one seemed worried."

But Lieutenant Barry Quinan, who had just turned twenty-one, was "filled with trepidation." He was going into action for the first time with the lead Guards Armored tank squadron under Captain Mick O'Cock. Quinan's infantry would travel on the backs of the tanks, Russian-style. To him, "the number of rivers ahead seemed ominous. We were not amphibious." Yet Quinan felt proud that his men would be "leading the entire British Second Army."

Lieutenant Rupert Mahaffey, also twenty-one, vividly remembers being told that "if the operation was a success the wives and children at home would be relieved from the threat of the Germans' V-2 rockets." Mahaffey's mother lived in London, which by that time was under intense bombardment. Although he was excited at the prospect of the attack, the single road leading all the way up to Arnhem was, he thought, "an awfully long way to go."

Captain Roland S. Langton, twenty-three, just returned from five days in a field hospital after receiving shrapnel wounds, learned that he was no longer adjutant of the 2nd Irish Guards Battalion. Instead, he was assigned as second in command of Captain Mick O'Cock's breakout squadron. He was jubilant about the assignment. The breakout seemed to Langton a straightforward thing. Garden could not be anything but a success. It was "obvious to all that the Germans were disorganized and shaken, lacking cohesion, and capable only of fighting in small pockets."

Not everyone was so confident. As Lieutenant A. G. C. "Tony" Jones, twenty-one, of the Royal Engineers, listened to the plan, he thought it was "clearly going to be very difficult." The bridges were the key to the entire operation and, as one officer remarked, "The drive of the XXX Corps will be like threading seven needles with one piece of cotton and we only have to miss one to be in trouble." To veteran Guardsman Tim Smith, twenty-four, the attack was "just another battle." On this day his greatest concern was the famed St. Leger race at Newmarket. He had a tip that a horse called Tehran, to be ridden by the famous jockey Gordon Richards, was "a sure thing." He placed every penny he had on Tehran with a lance corporal at battalion headquarters. If Market-Garden was the operation that would win the war, this was just the day to win the St. Leger. To his amazement, Tehran won. He was quite sure now that Market-Garden would succeed.

One man was "decidedly uncomfortable." Flight Lieutenant Donald Love, twenty-eight, an R.A.F. fighter-reconnaissance pilot, felt completely out of place among the officers of the Guards Armored. He was part of the air liaison team which would call in the rocket-firing Typhoon fighters from the ground when the breakout began. His lightly armored vehicle (code-named "Winecup"), with its canvas roof and its maze of communications equipment, would be up front close to Lieutenant Colonel Joe Vandeleur's command car. Love felt naked and defenseless: the only weapons the R.A.F. team possessed were revolvers. As he listened to Vandeleur talking about "a rolling barrage that would move forward at a speed of 200 yards per minute" and heard the burly Irishman describe Love's little scout car as an "armored signal tender for direct communication with pilots in the sky," Love's concern mounted. "I got the distinct impression that I would be the one responsible for calling in the 'cab rank' of Typhoons overhead." The thought was not reassuring. Love knew very little about the radio setup, and he had never before acted as a ground-to-air tactical officer. Then, to his acute relief, he learned that an expert, Squadron Leader Max Sutherland, would join him the following day to handle the communications for the initial breakout. Thereafter, Love would be in charge. Love began to wonder whether he should have volunteered in the first place. He had only taken the job "because I thought it might be a nice change of pace."

A change of a different sort bothered the commander of the Irish Guards. During the capture of the bridgehead over the Escaut Canal, Joe Vandeleur had lost "a close and distinguished friend." His broadcasting van, with its huge trumpet-like loudspeaker on the roof, had been destroyed by a German shell. All through training back in England and in the great advance from Normandy, Joe had used the van to broadcast to his troops and after each session, being a lover of classical music, he had always put on a record or two—selections that didn't always please the Guardsmen. The van had been blown to pieces and shards of the classical records—along with Vandeleur's favorite popular tune—had showered down over the countryside. Joe was saddened by his loss; not so, his Irish Guardsmen. They thought the drive to Arnhem would be arduous enough without having to listen to Joe's loudspeaker blaring out his current theme song, "Praise the Lord and Pass the Ammunition."

Meanwhile, in England the paratroopers and glider-borne infantry of the First Allied Airborne Army were even now in marshaling areas, ready for the moment of takeoff. Over the previous forty-eight hours, using maps, photographs and scale models, officers had briefed and rebriefed their men. The preparations were immense and meticulous. At twenty-four air bases (8 British, 16 American), vast fleets of troop-carrying aircraft, tow planes and gliders were checked out, fueled and loaded with equipment ranging from artillery to jeeps. Some ninety miles north of London, Brigadier General James M. Gavin's "All-American" 82nd Airborne Division was already shut off from the outside world at a cluster of airfields around Grantham in Lincolnshire. So were part of General Roy Urquhart's Red Devils, the British 1st Airborne Division, and Major General Stanislaw Sosabowski's Polish 1st Parachute Brigade. To the south around Newbury, roughly eighty miles west of London, Major General Maxwell D. Taylor's Screaming Eagles, the 101st Airborne Division, were also "sealed in." In the same area, and stretching as far down as Dorsetshire, was the remainder of Urquhart's division. The majority of his units would not move to the airfields until the morning of the seventeenth, but in hamlets, villages and bivouac areas close to the departure points, they too made ready. Everywhere now, the airborne forces of Market-Garden waited out the time until takeoff and the historic invasion of Holland from the sky.

Some men felt more concern at being sealed in than about the mission itself. At an airfield near the village of Ramsbury, the security precautions made Corporal Hansford Vest, of the 101st Division's 502nd Regiment, distinctly uneasy. Aircraft and gliders "were parked for miles all over the countryside and there were guards everywhere." He noted that the airfield was surrounded by a barbed-wire fence with "British guards on the outside and our own guards on the inside." Vest had the "feeling that our freedom was gone." Private James Allardyce of the 508th Regiment, in his crowded tent city, tried to ignore the barbed wire and guards. He checked and rechecked his equipment "until it was almost worn out." Allardyce could not shake off the feeling that "we were like condemned men waiting to be led off."

Other men worried principally about their chances of going on the mission. So many previous operations had been canceled that one new recruit, nineteen-year-old Private Melvin Isenekev, of the 506th Regiment (he had arrived from the States on June 6, the day the 101st had jumped into Normandy), still didn't believe they would go when they reached the marshaling area. Isenekev felt he had trained "long and hard for this and I didn't want to be held back." Yet he almost was. Trying to light a makeshift oil burner used for heating water, he threw a lighted match into an oil drum. When nothing happened, Isenekev "put my head over it to look in and it exploded." Temporarily blinded, he instantly thought, "Now I've done it. They won't let me go." However within a few minutes his eyes stopped burning and he could see again. But he believes he was the only member of the 101st jumping into Holland with no eyebrows.

First Sergeant Daniel Zapalski, twenty-four, of the 502nd, "sweated out the jump; hoping the chute was packed right; hoping the field was soft; and hoping I didn't land in a tree." He was eager to go. Although he had not fully recovered from a Normandy leg wound, Zapalski believed his injury "was not serious enough to keep me from doing my normal duty." His battalion commander, the popular Lieutenant Colonel Robert G. Cole, disagreed. He had turned down Zapalski's pleas. Undeterred, Zapalski had bypassed Cole and obtained a written release certifying his combat readiness from the regimental surgeon. Though Zapalski and Cole had fought together in Normandy, the sergeant now got a "typical Cole chewing out. He called me 'a fatheaded Polack, impractical, burdensome and unreasonable.'" But he let Zapalski go.

Captain Raymond S. Hall, the 502nd's regimental chaplain, had a somewhat similar problem. He was "most anxious to return to action and to be with my men." But he too had been wounded in Normandy. Now the doctors would not let him jump. He was finally told that he could go in by glider. The chaplain was horrified. A veteran paratrooper, he considered gliders distinctly unsafe.

Fear of death or of failure to perform well disturbed others. Captain LeGrand Johnson, twenty-two-year-old company commander, remembering "the horrors and narrow escapes" during the 101st's night airborne attack preceding the Normandy invasion, was fatalistically "resigned." He was convinced that he would not return from this mission. Still, the young officer "fully intended to raise as much hell as I could." Johnson was not sure he liked the idea of a daylight drop. It might produce more casualties. On the other hand, this time "we would be able to see the enemy." To hide his nervousness, Johnson made bets with his fellow troopers on who would get the first Dutch beer. One of Johnson's staff sergeants, Charles Dohun, was "almost numb" with worry. He did "not know how to compare this daylight jump with Normandy or what to expect." Within forty-eight hours, his numbness forgotten, Staff Sergeant Dohun would heroically save the life of the fatalistic Captain Johnson.

Technical Sergeant Marshall Copas, twenty-two, had perhaps more reason than most for anxiety. He was one of the "pathfinders" who would jump first to mark the drop zones for the 101st. In the Normandy drop, Copas recalled, "we had forty-five minutes before the main body of troopers began jumping—now we had only twelve minutes." Copas and his friend Sergeant John Rudolph Brandt, twenty-nine, had one concern in common: both would have felt better "had General Patton's Third Army been on the ground below us, rather than the British. We had never fought with the Tommies before."

In the Grantham area, Private John Garzia, a veteran of three combat jumps with the 82nd Airborne Division, was stunned. To him, Market-Garden "was sheer insanity." He thought "Ike had transferred to the German side."

Now that Operation Market-Garden was actually on, Lieutenant Colonel Louis Mendez, battalion commander of the 82nd's 508th Regiment, had no hesitation in speaking out on one particular subject. With the nighttime experiences of his regiment in Normandy still painfully clear in his mind, Colonel Mendez delivered a scathing warning to the pilots who would carry his battalion into action the next day. "Gentlemen," Mendez said coldly, "my officers know this map of Holland and the drop zones by heart and we're ready to go. When I brought my battalion to the briefing prior to Normandy, I had the finest combat-ready force of its size that will ever be known. By the time I gathered them together in Normandy, half were gone. I charge you: put us down in Holland or put us down in hell, but put us all down together in one place."

Private First Class John Allen, twenty-four, a three-jump veteran and still recovering from wounds sustained in Normandy, was philosophical about the operation: "They never got me in a night jump," he solemnly told his buddies, "so now they'll be able to see me and get off a good shot." Staff Sergeant Russell O'Neal, with three night combat jumps behind him, was convinced that his "Irish luck was about to run out." When he heard the 82nd was to jump in daylight, he composed a letter he never sent—"You can hang a gold star in your window tonight, Mother. The Germans have a good chance to hit us before we even land." To lighten the atmosphere—though in doing so he may have made it worse—Private Philip H. Nadler, of the 504th Regiment, spread a few rumors. The one he liked best was that a large German camp of SS men were bivouacked on one of the 82nd drop zones.

Nadler had not been overly impressed by the briefing of the platoon. One of the 504th's objectives was the bridge at Grave. Gathering the men around him, the briefing lieutenant threw back the cover on a sandtable model and said, "Men, this is your destination." He rested a pointer on the bridge which bore the single word "Grave." Nadler was the first to comment. "Yeah, we know that, Lieutenant," he said, "but what country are we droppin' on?"

Major Edward Wellems, of the 504th's 2nd Battalion, thought the name of the bridge was rather ominous, too, despite the fact that the officers who briefed his group suddenly began to change the pronunciation, referring to it as the "gravey bridge."

The briefings caused mixed reactions. Nineteen-year-old Corporal Jack Bommer thought that "six or eight weeks would see us home and then they'd send us on to the Pacific." Private Leo Hart, twenty-one, did not believe they were going at all.

He had heard—probably as a result of Private Nadler's rumor —that there were 4,000 SS troops in the general jump area.

Major Edwin Bedell, thirty-eight, remembers that one private's sole concern was the safety of a live hare that he had won in a local village raffle. The private was fearful that his pet, which was so tame that it followed him everywhere, would not survive the jump, and that if it did it might still wind up in a stew pot.

Near Spanhoe airfield in the Grantham area, Lieutenant "Pat" Glover of the British 1st Airborne Division's 4th Parachute Brigade worried about Myrtle, a reddish-brown chicken that had been Glover's special pet since early summer. With parachute wings fastened to an elastic band around her neck, Myrtle "the parachick" had made six training jumps. At first she rode in a small zippered canvas bag attached to Glover's left shoulder. Later, he released her at fifty feet above the ground. By now Myrtle was an expert, and Glover could free her at three hundred feet. With a frenzied flutter of wings and raucous squawking, Myrtle gracelessly floated down to earth. There, Glover recalls, "this rather gentle pet would wait patiently on the ground for me to land and collect her." Myrtle the parachick was going to Arnhem. It would be her first combat jump. But Glover did not intend to tempt fate. He planned to keep Myrtle in her bag until he hit the ground in Holland.

Lance Corporal Sydney Nunn, twenty-three, of the 1st Airlanding Brigade, based in the south near Keevil, was only too glad to get away from his "pet." He thought the camp was "a nightmare." Nunn couldn't wait to get to Arnhem or anyplace else, so long as it was far enough away from the persistent mole who kept burrowing into his mattress.

For the men of the British 1st Airborne Division, now standing by in bases stretching from the Midlands south to Dorsetshire, the prevailing mood was one of relief that, at last, they were going into action. Besides, briefing officers stressed the fact that Market-Garden could shorten the war. For the British, fighting since 1939, the news was heady. Sergeant Ron Kent, of the 21st Independent Parachute Company, heard that "the success of the operation might even give us Berlin" and that ground opposition in Arnhem "would consist mainly of Hitler Youth and old men on bicycles." Sergeant Walter Inglis, of the 1st Parachute Brigade, was equally confident. The attack, he thought, would be "a piece of cake." All the Red Devils had to do was "hang on to the Arnhem bridge for forty-eight hours until XXX Corps tanks arrived; then the war would be practically over." Inglis expected to be back home in England in a week. Lance Corporal Gordon Spicer, of the 1st Parachute Brigade, offhandedly considered the operation "a fairly simple affair with a few backstage Germans recoiling in horror at our approach"; while Lance Bombardier Percy Parkes, of the 1st Airlanding Brigade, felt, after his briefing, that "all we would encounter at Arnhem was a mixed bag of Jerry cooks and clerks." The presence of tanks, Parkes says, was "mentioned only in passing, and we were told our air cover would be so strong that it would darken the sky above us." Confidence was such that Medic Geoffrey Stanners expected only "a couple of hernia battalions" and Signalman Victor Read was "looking forward to seeing German WAAF's who," he thought, "would be the only Germans defending Arnhem."

Some men who could legitimately remain behind were eager to go. Sergeant Alfred Roullier, of the 1st Airlanding Brigade's Artillery, was one of these. The thirty-one-year-old trooper discovered that he was not slated for the Arnhem operation. Although Roullier had been trained as an artilleryman, he was currently the acting mess sergeant at his battalion headquarters. Because of his culinary expertise, it appeared that he might spend the remainder of the war in the job. Twice, Alf Roullier had appealed to Sergeant Major John Siely to be included in the attack, but each time he was turned down. For the third time Alf pressed his case. "I know this operation can shorten the war," he told Siely. "I've got a wife and two children, but if this attack will get me home quicker and guarantee them a better future, then I want to go." Siely pulled a few strings. Alf Roullier's name was added to the list of those who would go to Arnhem—where, within the next week, the assistant mess sergeant would become something of a legend.

In the prevailing high mood before the onset of Market-Garden, there were undercurrents of doubt among some officers and enlisted men. They were troubled for a variety of reasons, although most took care to hide their feelings. Corporal Daniel Morgans, of the 1st Parachute Brigade, considered

"Market a snorter of an operation." Still, "to drop six or seven miles from the objective and then to fight through a city to get there, was really asking for trouble." Regimental Sergeant Major J. C. Lord, with a lifetime in the army behind him, thought so, too. "The plan was a bit dicey," he felt. Nor did Lord give much credence to the talk of an understrength, worn-out enemy. He knew that "the German is no fool and a mighty warrior." Still, J. C. Lord, whose demeanor could intimidate even the veterans in his charge (almost in awe, some called him "Jesus Christ" behind his back), did not reveal his uneasiness, because "it would have been catastrophic to morale."

Captain Eric Mackay, whose engineers were, among other tasks, to race to the main road bridge in Arnhem and remove expected German charges, was suspicious of the entire operation. He thought the division "might just as well be dropped a hundred miles away from the objective as eight." The advantage of surprise and "a quick lightning stroke" would surely be lost. Mackay quietly ordered his men to double the amount of ammunition and grenades each would carry and personally briefed everyone in the troop on escape techniques.*

Major Anthony Deane-Drummond, twenty-seven, second in command of 1st Airborne Division Signals, was particularly concerned about his communications. Apart from the main command units, he was worried about the smaller "22" sets that would be used between Urquhart and the various brigades during the Arnhem attack. The "22's" could best transmit and receive within a diameter of three to five miles. With drop zones seven to eight miles from the objective, performance was expected to be erratic. Worse, the sets must also contact General Browning's Airborne Corps headquarters, planned for Nijmegen, from the drop zones approximately fifteen miles to the south. Adding to the problem was the terrain. Between the main road bridge at Arnhem and the landing areas was the town itself, plus heavily wooded sections and suburban developments. On the other hand, an independent fact-gathering liaison unit, called "Phantom"—organized to collect and pass

---

*One of the most accurate accounts of the First British Airborne's activities on the Arnhem bridge is to be found in "The Battle of Arnhem Bridge" by Eric Mackay, *Blackwood's* Magazine, October 1945.

on intelligence estimates and immediate reports to each commander in the field, in this case General Browning of Airborne
Corps—was not worried about the range of its own "22's."
Twenty-five-year-old Lieutenant Neville Hay, in charge of the
Phantom team's highly trained specialists, was even a "little
disdainful of the Royal Corps of Signals," whom his group was
inclined to treat "as poor cousins." By using a special kind of
antenna, Hay and his operators had been able to transmit at
distances of over one hundred miles on a "22."

Even with Hay's success and although various forms of
communications* would be used in the event of emergency,
Deane-Drummond was uneasy. He mentioned to his superior,
Lieutenant Colonel Tom Stephenson, that "the likelihood of
the sets working satisfactorily in the initial phases of the operation is very doubtful." Stephenson agreed. Still, it would
hardly matter. In the surprise assault, troops were expected to
close up on the Arnhem bridge very quickly. Therefore, it was
believed that units would not be out of touch with headquarters for more than one or two hours, by which time, Deane-
Drummond heard, "things would have sorted themselves out
and Urquhart's command post would be with the 1st Parachute Brigade on the bridge itself." Although not entirely reassured, Deane-Drummond recalled that, "like almost everyone
else, I was swept along with the prevailing attitude: 'Don't be
negative; and for God's sake, don't rock the boat; let's get on
with the attack.'"

Now the final word depended not on men but on the weather.
From Supreme Command headquarters down, senior officers
anxiously awaited meteorological reports. Given less than seven
days to meet Montgomery's deadline, Market-Garden was as
ready as it would ever be, but a minimum forecast of three full
days of fair weather was needed. In the early evening of September 16, the weather experts issued their findings: apart from
some early morning fog, the weather for the next three days

---

* Included in the communications setup were 82 pigeons provided from R.A.F.
sources. The lofts for these birds were situated in the London area—meaning
that the birds, if they survived the airborne landing and the Germans, would
have to fly approximately 240 miles to deliver a message.

would be fair, with little cloud and virtually no winds. At First
Allied Airborne Army headquarters Lieutenant General Brereton quickly made his decision. The coded teleprinter message
that went out to his commanders at 7:45 P.M. read, "CONFIRM
MARKET SUNDAY 17TH. ACKNOWLEDGE." In his diary, Brereton
recorded, "At last we are going into action." He thought he
would sleep well this night for, as he told his staff, "Now that
I've made the decision, I've quit worrying."

In crowded hangars, cities of tents and Nissen huts, the waiting men were given the news. On a large mirror over the fireplace in the sergeants' mess of the British 1st Airborne Division
Signals near Grantham, someone chalked up "14 hours to
go . . . no cancellation." Sergeant Horace "Hocker" Spivey
noted that, as each hour passed, the number was rechalked. To
Spivey, tired of being briefed for operations that never came
off, the ever-diminishing number on the mirror was the best
proof yet that this time "we were definitely going."
   On all their bases the men of the First Allied Airborne Army
made last-minute preparations. They had been fully briefed,
their weapons had been checked and their currency exchanged
for Dutch guilders, and there was little now for the isolated
troopers to do but wait. Some spent the time writing letters,
"celebrating" their departure the following morning, packing
personal belongings, sleeping or participating in marathon
card games ranging from blackjack and poker to bridge.
Twenty-year-old Sergeant Francis Moncur, of the 1st Parachute
Brigade's 2nd Battalion, played blackjack hour after hour. To
his surprise, he won steadily. Looking at the ever-growing pile
of guilders before him, Moncur felt like a millionaire. He expected to have a "whale of a time in Arnhem after the battle,"
which, in his opinion, would "last only forty-eight hours." That
would be long enough for the sergeant to settle a score with
the Germans. Seventy-two hours earlier, Moncur's brother, a
seventeen-year-old R.A.F. flight sergeant, had been killed in
an attempt to jump from his disabled bomber at 200 feet. His
parachute had failed to open completely.
   South of Grantham at a base in Cottesmore, Sergeant "Joe"
Sunley of the 4th Parachute Brigade was on security patrol,
making sure that "no paratroopers had slipped off base into

the village." Returning to the airdrome, Sunley saw Sergeant "Ginger" Green, a physical-training instructor and a "gentle giant of a man," tossing a deflated football up in the air. Green deftly caught the ball and threw it to Sunley. "What the hell are you doing with this?" Sunley asked. Ginger explained that he was taking the deflated ball to Arnhem, "so we can have a little game on the drop zone after we're finished."

At Manston, Kent, Staff Sergeant George Baylis of the Glider Pilot Regiment was also looking forward to some recreation. He had heard that the Dutch liked to dance; so George carefully packed his dancing pumps. Signalman Stanley G. Copley of the 1st Parachute Brigade Signals bought extra film for his camera. As little opposition was expected he thought it was "a perfect chance to get some pictures of the Dutch countryside and towns."

One man was taking presents that he had bought in London a few days earlier. When the Netherlands was overrun, thirty-two-year-old Lieutenant Commander Arnoldus Wolters of the Dutch navy had escaped in his minesweeper and sailed to England. Since that time, he had been attached to the Netherlands government in exile, holding a variety of desk jobs dealing with information and intelligence. A few days earlier, Wolters had been asked to go to Holland as part of the military government and civil affairs team attached to General Urquhart's headquarters. It was proposed that Wolters become military commissioner of the Netherlands territories to be liberated by the airborne forces. "It was a startling suggestion—going from a desk chair to a glider," he recalled. He was attached to a unit under Colonel Hilaro Barlow, second in command of the 1st Airlanding Brigade, who was designated to become the town commandant in Arnhem after its capture. Wolters would be his assistant. Now, excited about the prospect of returning to Holland, Wolters "was struck by the optimism, and I believed everything I was told. I really did not expect the operation to be very difficult. It seemed that the war was virtually over and the attack dead easy. I expected to land on Sunday and be home on Tuesday with my wife and child at Hilversum." For his wife, Maria, Wolters had bought a watch, and for his daughter, whom he had last seen as a baby four years before, he had a two-foot Teddy bear. He hoped nobody would mind if he took it in the glider.

Lieutenant Colonel John Frost, thirty-one, who was to lead the battalion assigned to capture the Arnhem bridge, packed his copper fox-hunting horn with the rest of his battle gear. It had been presented to him by the members of the Royal Exodus Hunt, of which he was Master in 1939–40. During training, Frost had used the horn to rally his men. He would do so on this operation. Frost had no qualms about a daylight jump. From the information given at briefings, "we were made to feel that the Germans were weak and demoralized and German troops in the area were of a decidedly low category and badly equipped." Frost did have misgivings about the drop zones. He had been told that the "polder on the southern side of the bridge was unsuitable for parachutists and gliders." Why then, he wondered, were the Poles to drop on the southern side of the bridge "if it was so unsuitable?"

Though he was anxious to get into action, Frost "hated to leave for Holland." Secretly, he hoped for a last-minute cancellation or postponement. He had enjoyed the area of Stoke Rochford in Lincolnshire and wished for "perhaps another day or two just doing all the pleasant things I had done in the past." But with these thoughts were others, "telling me that we had been here long enough and it was time to get away." Frost slept soundly on September 16. Although he wasn't naïve enough to think the battle of Arnhem would be "much of a lark," he did tell his batman, Wicks, to pack his gun, cartridges, golf clubs and dinner jacket in the staff car that would follow.

On the mirror above the fireplace in the sergeants' mess, now empty, there was one last notation, scrawled before men became too busy to bother. It read: "2 hours to go . . . no cancellation."

PART THREE

THE ATTACK

I

THE THUNDER OF THE HUGE FORMATIONS was earsplitting. Around British glider bases in Oxfordshire and Gloucestershire, horses and cattle panicked and bolted in the fields. In southern and eastern England thousands of people watched in amazement. In some villages and towns road traffic jammed and came to a halt. Passengers in speeding trains crowded one another to stare out of windows. Everywhere people gaped, dumfounded, at a spectacle no one had ever seen before. The mightiest airborne force in history was off the ground and heading for its targets.

By coincidence on this bright Sunday morning, September 17, 1944, special services were being held all over England to commemorate "the valiant few," the handful of R.A.F. pilots who had boldly challenged Hitler's Luftwaffe four years before and fought them to a standstill. As worshipers knelt in prayer, the steady, overpowering drone of propellers completely drowned out some services. In London's great Westminster Cathedral the soaring organ tones of the solemn Magnificat could not be heard. In twos and threes, people left their pews to join the crowds already gathered in the streets. There, Londoners stared upward, overwhelmed by the din as formation after formation of aircraft passed overhead at low altitude. In north London, a Salvation Army band overpowered by the noise gave up, but the bass drummer, his eyes on the sky, thumped out a symbolic beat: three dots and a dash—in Morse code, *V* for *victory*.

To the onlookers, the nature of the attack was clearly revealed by the great streams of planes towing gliders. But it would be six more hours before the British people learned that they had witnessed the opening phase of the most momentous airborne offensive ever conceived. A Red Cross worker, Angela Hawkings, may have best summed up the reactions of those who saw the vast armada pass. From the window of a train, she stared up, astonished, as wave after wave of planes flew over like "droves of starlings." She was convinced that "this attack, wherever bound, must surely bring about the end of the war."

The men of the First Allied Airborne Army were as unprepared as the civilians on the ground for the awesome spectacle
of their own departure. The paratroopers, glider-borne infantry and pilots who set out for Holland were staggered by the
size and majesty of the air fleets. Captain Arie D. Bestebreurtje,
a Dutch officer attached to the 82nd Airborne, thought the
sight was "unbelievable. Every plane the Allies possessed must
have been engaged in this single scheme." In fact, some 4,700
aircraft were involved—the greatest number ever used on a single airborne mission.

The operation had begun in the predawn hours and continued on throughout the morning. First, more than 1,400
Allied bombers had taken off from British airfields and had
pounded German antiaircraft positions and troop concentrations in the Market-Garden area. Then, at 9:45 A.M. and for
two and one quarter hours more, 2,023 troop-carrying planes,
gliders and their tugs swarmed into the air from twenty-four
U.S. and British bases.* C-47's carrying paratroopers flew in
long 45-plane formations. More C-47's and British bombers
—Halifaxes, Stirlings and Albemarles—pulled 478 gliders.
In seemingly endless sky trains, these huge equipment- and
troop-carrying gliders bounced behind their tow planes at the
end of 300-foot-long ropes. Swaying among the smaller Horsa
and Waco gliders were massive slabsided Hamilcars, each with
a cargo capacity of eight tons; they could hold a small tank
or two 3-ton trucks with artillery or ammunition. Above,
below and on the flanks, protecting these huge formations,
were almost 1,500 Allied fighters and fighter-bombers—British
Spitfires, rocket-firing Typhoons, Tempests and Mosquitoes;
U.S. Thunderbolts, Lightnings, Mustangs and low-level dive
bombers. There were so many planes in the air that Captain
Neil Sweeney of the 101st Airborne Division remembered that
"it looked like we could get out on the wings and walk all the
way to Holland."

---

*Many official accounts give 10:25 A.M. as the time when the first Market air-
craft left the ground. Perhaps they had in mind the departure of the pathfinders, who arrived first. From an examination of log books and air controllers'
time schedules, it is clear that the airlift began at 9:45 A.M.

The British glider forces were the first to take off. Farther north on the Market-Garden corridor than the Americans and with different requirements, General Urquhart needed the maximum in men, equipment and artillery—especially antitank guns—in the first lift, to capture and hold his objectives until the land forces could link up. Therefore, the bulk of his division was glider-borne; 320 gliders carried the men, transport and artillery of Brigadier Philip "Pips" Hicks's 1st Airlanding Brigade. They would reach landing zones west of Arnhem a little after 1 P.M. Thirty minutes later, Brigadier Gerald Lathbury's 1st Parachute Brigade, in 145 troop-carrying planes, would begin dropping. Because the unwieldy gliders and tugs were slower—120 miles per hour versus 140 for the paratroopcarrier planes—these immense "sky trains"—or serials, as the airborne called them—had to be launched first. From eight bases in Gloucestershire and Oxfordshire, gliders and tugs rolled down runways and rose in the air at a launch rate never before attempted: one combination per minute. Forming up was especially intricate and dangerous. Climbing slowly to altitude, the planes headed west over the Bristol Channel. Then, speeds synchronized, the tugs and gliders echeloned to the right in pairs, turned back, flew over the takeoff bases and headed for a marshaling point above the town of Hatfield, north of London.

Even as the first British glider serials were forming up above the Bristol Channel, twelve British Stirling bombers and six U.S. C-47's began taking off at 10:25 A.M. for Holland. In them were U.S. and British pathfinders—the men who would land first to mark landing and drop zones for the Market forces.

Simultaneously, the men of the U.S. 82nd Airborne and the paratroop elements of the British First Division took off from bases around Grantham, Lincolnshire, in 625 troop-carrier planes and 50 C-47's towing gliders. With astonishing precision, the planes of the IX Troop Carrier Command left the ground at five- to twenty-second intervals. In wave after wave they rendezvoused above the town of March, Cambridgeshire, and from there set out in three parallel streams to cross the coast at Aldeburgh.

At the same time, from southern airfields around Greenham

Common, the 101st Airborne took to the air, in 424 C-47's plus 70 gliders and tugs. Forming up, they too passed over the traffic control point at Hatfield and flew east to cross the coast at Bradwell Bay.

In immense triple columns, together at least ten miles across and approximately a hundred miles long, the vast armada swept over the English countryside. The 82nd Airborne and British 1st Division, enroute to Nijmegen and Arnhem, flew along the northern track. A special serial of 38 gliders carrying General Browning's Corps headquarters, bound for Nijmegen, traveled with them. On the southern route, passing over Bradwell Bay, the 101st Airborne headed for its drop zones slightly north of Eindhoven. By 11:55 A.M., the entire force—more than 20,000 troops, 511 vehicles, 330 artillery pieces and 590 tons of equipment—was off the ground. First Lieutenant James J. Coyle of the 82nd Airborne, looking down on the English countryside from an altitude of only 1,500 feet, saw nuns waving from the courtyard of a convent. He thought "the beautiful day and the nuns made a picture that had the quality of an oil painting." Waving back, he wondered "if they could possibly know who we were and where we were going."

For the majority of the airborne troops, the mood of the initial part of the journey, across England, was lighthearted. To Private Roy Edwards of the 1st Parachute Brigade, "everything was so serene it was like going on a bus outing to the seaside." Private A. G. Warrender remembers that "this was a perfect Sunday; a morning for a walk down a country lane and a pint at the local."

The commanding officer of the Glider Pilot Regiment, Colonel George S. Chatterton, piloting the glider carrying General Browning, described the Sunday as "an extremely fine day. It did not seem possible that we were taking off for one of the greatest battles in history." Chatterton was struck by Browning's entourage and equipment. With the General were his batman, headquarters' medical officer, cook, as well as his tent and personal jeep. Browning sat on an empty Worthington Beer crate between the pilot and copilot, and Chatterton noted that he was "immaculately dressed in a Barathea battle dress, with a highly polished Sam Browne belt, knife-edge-creased trousers, leather holster gleaming like glass, a swagger stick and spotless

gray kid gloves." The General, says Chatterton, "was in tremendous form, because he realized he had reached one of the
climaxes of his career. There was an air of immense gaiety."

In another glider serial, the quiet Scot with the most difficult
Market-Garden assignment, the 1st Airborne Division's General
Roy Urquhart, thought it was "difficult not to feel excited that
we were off at last." Yet the popular officer's mind, as always,
was on his men and the job that lay ahead. Like Browning, he
had an entourage. Now, looking down the length of the Horsa
glider—which was carrying his aide Roberts, batman Hancock,
the Reverend G. A. Pare, padre of the Glider Pilot Regiment,
a signaler, two military police, their motorcycles and the General's jeep—Urquhart felt a pang of conscience. He thought of
his paratroopers, laden down with packs, guns and equipment,
crowded into heavy transport planes. Urquhart carried only
a small shoulder pack, two hand grenades, a map case and a
notebook. He was bothered by his own comfort.

Almost up to the moment of takeoff Urquhart had been
called on to make difficult decisions. Some hours before leaving, his chief of staff, Colonel Charles Mackenzie, had received
a telephone call from a senior American air force officer. Was
the mental asylum at Wolfheze to be bombed? The American, Mackenzie had reported, "wanted a personal assurance
from Urquhart that there were Germans in it and not lunatics;
otherwise the Americans could not accept responsibility." The
asylum was dangerously close to the division's assembly point,
and Urquhart's staff believed it to be held by the Germans.
Mackenzie had accepted responsibility. "On your head be it,"
the American had replied. Urquhart had approved his chief of
staff's action. "I meant to be as prepared as possible and that's
all there was to it," he remembered.

As Mackenzie was about to leave for his own glider, Urquhart had taken him privately aside. "Look, Charles," he had
told Mackenzie, "if anything happens to me the succession
of command should be as follows: first, Lathbury, then Hicks
and Hackett in that order." Urquhart's choice was based on
experience. "Everyone knew that Lathbury was my deputy,"
he later recalled. "Hackett was senior in rank to Hicks, but
he was much younger and I was quite convinced that Hicks
had more experience in handling infantry. My decision was

no reflection on Hackett's ability to command." Perhaps, Urquhart reflected, he should have informed each of his brigadiers of his decision earlier, but he had "frankly considered the whole question quite academic." The chance of the division losing both Urquhart and Lathbury was remote.

Now, all decisions made, Urquhart idly watched "squadrons of fighters flashing past the glider trains." This was his first operational trip in a glider, and earlier he had taken a couple of airsickness pills. His throat was dry and he had difficulty swallowing. He was conscious, too, that "Hancock, my batman, was watching me, a look of concern on his face. Like everyone else, he expected me to be airsick." Urquhart did not oblige. "We were in a huge stream of aircraft and I concentrated on impressions. We were committed. We had made a good plan. I still wished we could have gotten closer to the bridge, but I did not brood on it."

In spite of the operational efficiency displayed in launching the giant armada, mishaps occurred almost immediately. Just before takeoff, the port wing of one glider was chewed off by the propeller of a Stirling bomber. No one was hurt. As the glider carrying Lieutenant Alan Harvey Cox of the Airlanding Brigade lumbered into the air, it ran into trouble. Low clouds obstructed the glider pilot's view and he was unable to line up with the tail of his tug. The glider went in one direction, the plane in another, the tow rope threatening to loop the glider's wing and overturn it. Unable to realign with his tug, the glider pilot grabbed for the red-topped release lever and cast off. Cox's glider landed without damage in a hay field at Sandford-on-Thames. A more bizarre incident occurred in a C-47 carrying the men of the 82nd Airborne, who sat facing each other on opposite sides of the plane. Five minutes after takeoff, Corporal Jack Bommer saw "the cargo hatch directly behind the men facing me spring open." The force of air almost sucked the men through the hatchway into space. As they desperately hung on, recalls Bommer, "the pilot did a beautiful tail flip and the hatch slammed shut."

Lance Corporal Sydney Nunn, who was so anxious to leave his base near Keevil and the activities of the mole in his mattress, now felt lucky to be alive. After more than an hour of uneventful flight, his glider ran into cloud. Emerging from

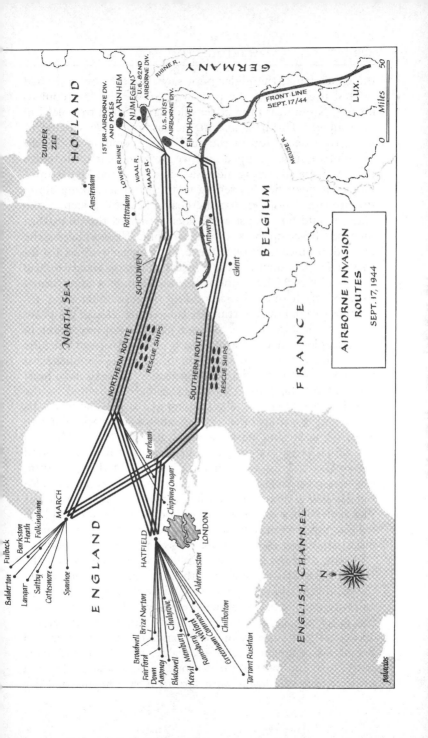

AIRBORNE INVASION ROUTES
SEPT. 17, 1944

the cloud bank, the glider pilot saw that the tow rope had twisted itself around the port wing. Over the intercom to his tug, Nunn heard the glider pilot say, "I'm in trouble! I'm in trouble!" The next instant, he cast off. "We seemed to come to a dead stop in the air," Nunn remembers. "Then the glider's nose dropped and we careened earthward with the tow rope streaming alongside like a broken kite string." Nunn sat "petrified," listening to the wind screaming along the fuselage, "hoping that the chains holding a jeep in the glider would take the strain." Then he heard the pilot warn them to "Brace up, blokes. Here we come." The glider hit the ground, bounced, hit once more, and came slowly to a stop. In the sudden silence, Nunn heard the pilot ask, "Are you blokes all right?" Everyone was, and the men were returned to Keevil to fly out in the second lift on September 18.

Others were not so fortunate. Tragedy struck one glider serial over Wiltshire. R.A.F. Sergeant Walter Simpson, sitting in the plexiglass turret of a Stirling bomber, was watching the Horsa glider trailing along behind. Suddenly, "The glider just seemed to part in the middle; it looked as if the back end just dropped off the front." Horrified, Simpson shouted to the captain, "My God, the glider's coming apart!" The tow rope broke and the front of the glider sank "like a rock falling to earth." The Stirling left formation, gradually lost height, and turned back to locate the wreckage. The front half was spotted in a field. The tail was nowhere to be seen. Marking the spot, the crew returned to Keevil and drove by jeep to the crash location. There, Simpson saw what appeared "like a match box that had been stepped on." The bodies of the men had remained inside. Simpson had no way of estimating how many dead there were—"it was just a mass of arms, legs and bodies."

By the time the last serials reached the English coast—the northern streams passing over the checkpoint at Aldeburgh, the southern columns flying over Bradwell Bay—thirty troop- and equipment-carrying gliders were down. Tug engine failure, broken tow ropes, and, in places, heavy clouds had caused the abortions. Although by military standards the operation had begun with eminent success—casualties were light, and many of the men and most of the downed cargo would be flown in on later lifts—the losses were sure to hurt. On this vital day when every man, vehicle and piece of equipment was important to General Urquhart, twenty-three of his glider loads were already lost. Not until the Arnhem force reached its drop and landing zones would commanders discover just how crucial these losses would be.

Now, as the long sky trains swarmed out over the English Channel and the land fell behind, a new kind of expectancy began to permeate the armada. The "Sunday outing" mood was fast disappearing. As American serials passed over the seaside resort of Margate, Private Melvin Isenekev of the 101st Airborne saw the white cliffs of Dover off to the right. From the distance, they looked like the wintry hillsides of the Adirondacks near his home in upper New York State. Corporal D. Thomas of the 1st British Airborne, staring out through an open plane door until his country's coastline disappeared, felt his eyes fill with tears.

From the marshaling points at March and Hatfield, the airborne columns had been aided by various navigational devices: radar beacons, special hooded lights and radio direction-finding signals. Now, beacons on ships in the North Sea began to guide the planes. Additionally, strings of launches—17 along the northern route; 10 below the southern flight path —stretched away across the water. To Flight Sergeant William Tompson, at the controls of a plane towing a four-ton Horsa glider, "there wasn't much navigating to do. The launches below us were set out like stepping stones across the Channel." But these fast naval vessels were much more than directional aids. They were part of a vast air-sea rescue operation, and they were already busy.

In the thirty-minute trip across the North Sea, men saw gliders bobbing on the gray waters as low-flying amphibious planes circled to mark their positions until rescue launches could reach the spot. Lieutenant Neville Hay, of the Phantom fact-gathering liaison unit, watched "with complete detachment two downed gliders and another ditching." He tapped his corporal on the shoulder. "Have a look down there, Hobkirk," Hay shouted. The corporal glanced down and, as Hay remembers, "I could almost see him turn green." Hay hurriedly reassured the man. "There's nothing to worry about. Look at the boats already picking them up."

Staff Sergeant Joseph Kitchener, piloting a glider, was equally impressed by the speed of the air-sea rescue launch that came alongside a floating glider he had spotted. "They picked up the men so fast I don't even think they got their feet wet," he recalls. Men in a glider piloted by Staff Sergeant Cyril Line were less fortunate—but lucky to be alive. In an aerial train of swaying black Horsas, Line observed one combination drop slowly out of position. Mesmerized, he watched the Horsa cut loose and descend almost leisurely toward the sea. A ring of white foam appeared as it hit the water. He wondered "who the poor devils were." At that moment, the starboard propellers on the Stirling pulling his glider slowed, and stopped. As the plane's speed was reduced Line found himself "in the embarrassing position of overtaking my own tug." He immediately released the tow line and his copilot called out, "Stand by for ditching!" From behind in the cabin, they could hear rifle butts crashing against the side of the glider's plywood fuselage as the frantic passengers tried to open up an escape route. Rapidly losing altitude, Line looked back and was horrified to see that the desperate troopers had "cut through the top of the glider and the sides were just beginning to go." Line screamed out, "Stop that! Strap yourselves in!" Then, with a heavy thud, the glider hit the water. When Line surfaced, he saw the wreckage floating some thirty feet away. There was no sign whatever of the cabin, but every one of his passengers was accounted for. Within minutes, all were picked up.

In all, eight gliders ditched safely during this first lift; once they were on the water, the air-sea rescue service, in a spectacular performance, saved nearly all crews and passengers. Once again, however, it was Urquhart's force that was whittled down. Of the eight gliders, five were Arnhem-bound.

Apart from some long-range inaccurate shelling of a downed glider, there was no serious enemy opposition during the Channel crossing. The 101st Airborne Division, following the southern route, which would bring it over Allied-held Belgium, was experiencing an almost perfect flight. But as the Dutch coastline appeared in the distance, the 82nd and the British troopers in the northern columns began to see the ominous telltale gray and black puffs of flak—German antiaircraft fire. As they flew on, at an altitude of only 1,500 feet, enemy guns firing from the outer Dutch isles of Walcheren, North Beveland and Schouwen were clearly visible. So were flak ships and barges around the mouth of the Schelde.

Escorting fighters began peeling out of formation, engaging the gun positions. In the planes men could hear spent shrapnel scraping against the metal sides of the C-47's. Veteran paratrooper Private Leo Hart of the 82nd heard a rookie aboard his plane ask, "Are these bucket seats bullet proof?" Hart just glowered at him; the light metal seats wouldn't have offered protection against a well-thrown stone. Private Harold Brockley, in another C-47, remembers one replacement wondering, "Hey, what are all those little black and gray puffs below?" Before anyone could answer, a piece of shrapnel came through the bottom of the ship and pinged harmlessly against a mess kit.

Veteran troopers hid their fears in different ways. When Staff Sergeant Paul Nunan saw the "familiar golf balls of red tracer bullets weaving up toward us" he pretended to doze off. Tracers barely missed Private Kenneth Truax's plane. "No one said anything," he recalls. "There was only a weak smile or two." Sergeant Bill Tucker, who had gone through antiaircraft fire in Normandy, was haunted by a "horrible fear of getting hit from underneath." He felt "less naked" sitting on three air-force flak jackets. And Private Rudolph Kos remembers that he felt "like sitting on my helmet, but I knew I would need it on my head."

One man was more concerned with the danger within than that without. Copilot Sergeant Bill Oakes, struggling to hold his Horsa glider steady in the air, looked back to see how his passengers were faring. To his horror, three troopers were "calmly sitting on the floor brewing up a mess tin of tea over a small cooker. Five others were standing around with their mugs, waiting to be served." Oakes was galvanized into action. He handed the controls over to the pilot and hurried aft, expecting the glider's plywood floor to catch fire at any minute. "Or, worse still, the mortar bombs in the trailer we were carrying could explode. The heat from that little field stove was terrific." He was livid with anger. "We're just having a little brew up," one of the troopers told him soothingly. Oakes hurried back to the cockpit and reported the matter to the pilot, Staff Sergeant Bert Watkins. The pilot smiled. "Tell 'em not to forget us when the tea's ready," he said. Oakes sank into his seat and buried his head in his hands.

Although the escort fighters silenced most of the coastal flak positions, some planes were damaged and one tug, its glider and a troop-carrier C-47 were shot down over Schouwen Island. The tug crash-landed, and its crew was killed. The glider, an 82nd Airborne Waco, broke up in mid-air and may have been seen by Major Dennis Munford, flying in a British column nearby. He watched, aghast, as the Waco disintegrated and "men and equipment spilt out of it like toys from a Christmas cracker." Others saw the troop-carrier go down. Equipment bundles attached beneath the C-47 were set on fire by tracer bullets. "Yellow and red streamers of flame appeared in the black smoke," recalls Captain Arthur Ferguson, who was flying in a nearby plane. Within minutes the C-47 was blazing. First Lieutenant Virgil Carmichael, standing in the door of his plane, watched as paratroopers jumped from the stricken aircraft. "As our men were using camouflaged chutes, I was able to count them as they left and saw that all had escaped safely."

The pilot, although the aircraft was engulfed in flames, somehow kept the plane steady until the paratroopers jumped. Then Carmichael saw one more figure leave. "The Air Corps used white parachutes, so I figured he had to be the crew chief." He was the last man out. Almost immediately the blazing plane nosedived and, at full throttle, plowed into a flooded area of Schouwen Island below. Carmichael remembers that, "on impact, a white chute billowed out in front of the plane, probably ejected by the force of the crash." To First Lieutenant James Megellas the sight of the downed C-47 had a "terrible effect." As jumpmaster in his plane, he had previously told his men that he would give the command "to stand up and hook up five minutes before reaching the drop zone." Now, he immediately gave the order. In many other planes, jumpmasters reacted as Megellas had and gave similar commands. To them, the battle was already joined—and, in fact, the drop and landing zones for the airborne men were now only thirty to forty minutes away.

2

INCREDIBLY, DESPITE THE NIGHT'S widespread bombing, and now the aerial attacks against Arnhem, Nijmegen and Eindhoven, the Germans failed to realize what was happening. Throughout the chain of command, attention was focused on a single threat: the renewal of the British Second Army's offensive from its bridgehead over the Meuse-Escaut Canal.

"Commanders and troops, myself and my staff in particular, were so overtaxed and under such severe strain in the face of our difficulties that we thought only in terms of ground operations," recalls Colonel General Kurt Student. Germany's illustrious airborne expert was at his headquarters in a cottage near Vught, approximately twenty-one miles northwest of Eindhoven, working on "red tape—a mountain of papers that followed me even into the battlefield." Student walked out onto a balcony, watched the bombers for a few moments, then, unconcerned, returned to his paper work.

Lieutenant Colonel Walter Harzer, commanding officer of the 9th SS Panzer Division Hohenstaufen, had by now transferred as much equipment as he intended to his rival, General Heinz Harmel of the 10th SS Panzer Division Frundsberg. Harmel, on Bittrich's orders and without Model's knowledge, was by now in Berlin. The last flatcars containing Harzer's "disabled" armored personnel carriers were ready to leave on a 2 P.M. train for Germany. Having been bombed repeatedly from Normandy onward, Harzer "paid little attention to planes." He saw nothing unusual about the huge bomber formations over Holland. He and his veteran tankers knew "it was routine to see bombers traveling east to Germany and returning several times a day. My men and I were numb from constant shelling and bombing." With Major Egon Skalka, the 9th Panzer's chief medical officer, Harzer set out from his headquarters at Beekbergen for the Hoenderloo barracks, about eight miles north of Arnhem. In a ceremony before the 600-man reconnaissance battalion of the division, he would decorate its commander, Captain Paul Gräbner, with the Knight's Cross. Afterward there would be champagne and a special luncheon.

At II SS Panzer Corps headquarters at Doetinchem, Lieutenant General Wilhelm Bittrich was equally unconcerned

about the air attacks. To him, "it was routine fare." Field
Marshal Walter Model, in his headquarters at the Tafelberg
Hotel in Oosterbeek, had been watching the bomber formations for some time. The view at headquarters was unanimous:
the squadrons of Flying Fortresses were returning from their
nightly bombing of Germany, and as usual, other streams of
Fortresses in the never-ending bombing of Germany were enroute east heading for other targets. As for the local bombing, it was not uncommon for bombers to jettison any unused
bombs over the Ruhr and often, as a result, into Holland itself. Model and his chief of staff, Lieutenant General Hans
Krebs, believed the bombardment and low-level strafing were
"softening-up operations"—a prelude to the opening of the
British ground offensive.

One officer was mildly concerned by the increased aerial activity over Holland. At the headquarters of OB West
in Aremberg near Koblenz, approximately 120 miles away,
Field Marshal Gerd von Rundstedt—although he still believed that airborne forces would be used only in an attack
against the Ruhr—wanted more information. In Annex 2227
of the morning report for September 17, his operations chief
recorded that Von Rundstedt had asked Model to investigate
the possibility that a combined sea and airborne invasion was
underway against northern Holland. The notation read, "The
general situation and notable increase of enemy reconnaissance
activities . . . has caused the Commander in Chief, West, to
again examine the possibilities of ship assault and air landing
operations. . . . Results of the survey are to be reported to
OKW [Hitler]."

The message reached Model's headquarters at about the
time the first planes of the armada crossed the coast.

Over Arnhem at 11:30 A.M. columns of black smoke rose in
the sky as fires burned throughout the city in the aftermath of
a three-hour near-saturation bombing. In Wolfheze, Oosterbeek, Nijmegen and Eindhoven, whole buildings were leveled,
streets were cratered and littered with debris and glass, and casualties were mounting minute by minute. Even now, low-level
fighters were strafing machine-gun and antiaircraft positions all
over the area. The mood of the Dutch, huddling in churches,

homes, cellars and shelters or, with foolhardy courage, cycling the streets or staring from rooftops, alternated between terror and exultation. No one knew what to believe or what would happen next. To the south, eighty-three miles from Nijmegen, Maastricht, the first Dutch city to be liberated, had been entered by the U.S. First Army on September 14. Many Dutch expected American infantry to arrive at any moment in their own towns and villages. Radio Orange, broadcasting from London, fed this impression in a flurry of bulletins: "The time is nearly here. What we have been waiting for is about to happen at last. . . . Owing to the rapid advance of the Allied armies . . . it is possible that the troops will not carry Dutch money yet. If our Allies offer French or Belgian notes . . . cooperate and accept this money in payment. . . . Farmers should finish off and deliver their harvest. . . ." Prince Bernhard, in a radio message, urged the Dutch "not to show joy by offering flowers or fruit when Allied troops liberate Netherlands territory . . . in the past the enemy has concealed explosives among offerings presented to the liberators." Uppermost in the minds of most Dutchmen was the certainty that these intensive bombings were the prelude to Allied invasion—the opening of the ground offensive. Like their German conquerors, the Dutch had no inkling of the impending airborne attack.

Jan and Bertha Voskuil, taking shelter in the home of Voskuil's father-in-law in Oosterbeek, thought the bombers in their area were aiming for Model's headquarters in the Tafelberg Hotel. The bright day, Voskuil remembers, "was perfect bombing weather." Yet he found it hard to "reconcile the war that was coming with the smell of ripe beetroots and sight of hundreds of sunflowers, their stems bent under the weight of their great heads. It did not seem possible that men were dying and buildings burning." Voskuil felt strangely calm. From his father-in-law's front veranda, he watched fighters flashing overhead and was sure they were strafing the hotel. Suddenly, a German soldier appeared in the garden without helmet or rifle and dressed only in a shirt and trousers. Politely he asked Voskuil, "May I take shelter here?" Voskuil stared at the man. "Why?" he asked. "You have your trenches." The German smiled. "I know," he answered, "but they are full." The soldier came up on the porch. "It is a very heavy bombing," he told

Voskuil, "but I don't think Oosterbeek is the target. They seem to be concentrating more to the east and west of the village."

From inside the house, Voskuil heard voices. A friend of the family had just arrived from the Wolfheze area. It had been heavily hit, she told them, and many people were dead. "I am afraid," she said, tremblingly, "it is our Last Supper." Voskuil looked at the German. "Perhaps they're bombing the Tafelberg because of Model," he said mildly. The German's face was impassive. "No," he told Voskuil, "I don't think so. No bombs fell there." Later, after the soldier had gone, Voskuil went out to survey the damage. Rumors abounded. He heard that Arnhem had been heavily hit and that Wolfheze was almost leveled. Surely, he thought, the Allies were now under march and would arrive at any hour. He was both elated and saddened. Caen, in Normandy, he remembered, had been reduced to rubble during the invasion. He was convinced that Oosterbeek, where he and his family had found shelter, would become a ruined village.

Around Wolfheze, German ammunition caches in the woods were exploding, and the famed mental institute had received direct hits. Four pavilions surrounding the administration building were leveled, forty-five patients were dead (the toll would increase to over eighty), and countless more were wounded. Sixty terrified inmates, mostly women, were wandering about in the adjoining woods. The electricity had failed, and Dr. Marius van der Beek, the deputy medical superintendent, could not summon help. Impatiently he awaited the arrival of doctors from Oosterbeek and Arnhem, who, he knew, would surely hear the news and come. He needed to set up two operating theaters with surgical teams as quickly as possible.

One of the "inmates," Hendrik Wijburg, was in reality a member of the underground hiding out in the asylum. "The Germans," he recalls, "were not actually inside the institute at the moment, although they did have positions nearby and artillery and ammunition stored in the woods." During the bombings when the dump was hit, Wijburg, on the veranda of one building, was knocked to the floor. "There was a huge explosion," he remembers, "and shells from the dump began whizzing into the hospital, killing and injuring many." Wijburg hastily scrambled to his feet and helped nurses, at the height of the strafing attacks, to lay out white sheets forming a huge cross on the grass. The entire area had been so badly hit that it looked to him as if "the place would soon be filled to the rafters with the dead and dying."

In Arnhem, fire brigades fought desperately to bring the spreading flames under control. Dirk Hiddink, in charge of a fifteen-man outdated fire-fighting unit (his men pushed two carts—one loaded with coiled hoses, the other with ladders), was ordered to the German-occupied Willems Barracks, which had received direct hits from low-flying Mosquitoes. Although the barracks were blazing, Hiddink's instructions from the Arnhem Fire Brigade Headquarters were unusual: let them burn down, he was told, but protect the surrounding houses. When his unit arrived, Hiddink saw that it would have been impossible to save the barracks in any case. The fires were too far advanced.

From his father's apartment at Willemsplein 28, Gerhardus Gysbers saw everything around him engulfed in flames. Not only the barracks, but the nearby high school and the Royal Restaurant, opposite, were burning. The heat was so intense that Gysbers remembers "the glass in our windows suddenly became wavy and then melted completely." The family evacuated the building immediately, scrambling over bricks and lumber into the square. Gysbers saw Germans stumbling from the blasted rubble of the barracks with blood pouring from their noses and ears. Streetcar driver Hendrik Karel reached the Willemsplein unintentionally. With the electric power cut by the bombing, Karel's pale-yellow streetcar coasted down a slight incline to reach a stop at the square. There he found a jumble of other streetcars which, like his own, had coasted into the square and were unable to leave. Through the smoke, crowds and debris, Karel saw waiters from the Royal Restaurant make their escape from the burning building. Abandoning the few diners who were heading for the doors, the waiters jumped right through the windows.

At the Municipal Gas Works just southeast of the great Arnhem bridge, technician Nicolaas Unck admired the skill of the bombardiers. Looking across the Rhine, he saw that twelve antiaircraft positions had been knocked out. Only one gun was left but its barrels were twisted and bent. Now that the city was without electricity, Unck was faced with his own problems. The technicians could no longer make gas. After the fuel remaining in the three huge gasometers was exhausted, there would be no more. Aside from coal and firewood, Arnhem was now without electricity, heating or cooking fuels.

Thousands of people remained cloistered in their churches. In the huge Dutch Reformed "Grote Kerk" Church alone, there were 1,200 people, Sexton Jan Mijnhart remembers. "Even though we had clearly heard the bombs exploding outside," he says, "the Reverend Johan Gerritsen had calmly continued his sermon. When the power was cut off, the organ stopped. Some one of the congregation came forward and began pumping the bellows manually." Then, against a background of sirens, explosions and thundering planes, the organ pealed out and the entire congregation stood up to sing the "Wilhelmus," the Dutch national anthem.

In the nearby Calvinist church, near the Arnhem railroad station, Gijsbert Numan of the resistance listened to a sermon delivered by Dominee Both. Numan felt that even the intense bombing would not deter the Germans from carrying out their threat to execute civilian hostages sometime during the day in reprisal for the resistance's attack on the viaduct. His conscience bothered him as he listened to Dominee Both's sermon on "the responsibility for your acts toward God and your fellow man," and he decided that once the service had ended, he would give himself up to the Germans. Leaving the church, Numan made his way through the littered streets to a telephone. There, he called Pieter Kruyff and told the regional commander his decision. Kruyff was blunt and to the point. "Rejected," he told Numan. "Carry on with your work." But Kruyff's was not to be the final decision. Market-Garden would save the hostages.

In Nijmegen, eleven miles to the south, bombers had hit German antiaircraft positions with such accuracy that only one was still firing. The great, towering PGEM power station, supplying electricity for the entire province of Gelderland, had received only superficial damage, but high-tension wires were severed, cutting off power throughout the area. A rayon factory near the PGEM station was badly damaged and ablaze. Houses in many parts of the city had received direct hits. Bombs had fallen on a girls' school and a large Catholic social center. Across the Waal in the village of Lent, a factory was destroyed and ammunition dumps exploded.

In the city's air-raid command post, the staff worked by candlelight. The air-raid workers were more and more puzzled by the stream of reports piling in. Working at his desk in semi-darkness, Albertus Uijen registered the incoming reports and found himself growing more confused by the moment. The widespread bombings gave no clear picture of what was happening, except that all German positions on Nijmegen's perimeter had been attacked. The principal approaches to the city —Waalbrug, St. Annastraat and Groesbeekseweg—were now blocked off. It almost seemed that an effort had been made to isolate the city.

As in Arnhem, most people in Nijmegen sought shelter from the fighters continually strafing the streets, but Elias Broekkamp, whose house was not far from the Waal bridge, had climbed to the roof for a better look. To Broekkamp's astonishment, so had the personnel of the German Town Major's office, five houses from Broekkamp's. The Germans, Broekkamp remembers, "looked very anxious. I looked, obviously, full of delight. I even remarked that the weather was lovely."

Nurse Johanna Breman watched Germans panic during the strafing. From a second-floor window of an apartment building south of the Waal bridge, Nurse Breman looked down at "wounded German soldiers helping each other along. Some were limping quite badly and I could see many with bandages. Their tunics were open and most had not even bothered to put their helmets on. On their heels came German infantrymen. As they headed toward the bridge, they fired into the windows whenever they saw Dutch peering out." When the Germans reached the bridge approaches, they began digging foxholes. "They dug everywhere," Miss Breman remembers, "next to the street leading up to the bridge, in grassy areas nearby and beneath trees. I was sure the invasion was coming and I remember thinking, 'What a beautiful view of the battle we shall have from here.' I had a feeling of expectancy." Nurse Breman's expectations did not include her marriage some months later to Master Sergeant Charles Mason of the 82nd, who would land in Glider 13 near the Groesbeek Heights, two miles southwest of her apartment.

Some towns and villages on the edges of the major Market-Garden objectives suffered damage as severe as the principal targets and had little, if any, rescue services. Close by the hamlet of Zeelst, approximately five miles west of Eindhoven, Gerardus de Wit had taken shelter in a beet field during the bombings. There had been no air raid alarm. He had seen planes high in the sky, and suddenly bombs rained down. De Wit, on a visit to his brother in the village of Veldhoven, four miles south, had turned around, pulled off the road and dived into a ditch adjoining the field. Now, he was frantic to get back to his wife and their eleven children.

Although planes were strafing, De Wit decided to risk the trip. Raising his head to look across the field, he saw that "even the leaves were scorched." Leaving his cycle behind, he climbed out of the ditch and ran across the open field. As he neared the village, he noted that bombs presumably intended for the Welschap airfield outside Eindhoven had fallen, instead, directly on little Zeelst. De Wit could see nothing but ruins. Several houses were burning, others had collapsed; and people stood about dazed and crying. One of De Wit's acquaintances, Mrs. Van Helmont, a widow, spotted him and begged him to come with her to cover a dead boy with a sheet. Tearfully, she explained that she could not do it herself. The child had been decapitated, but De Wit recognized the body as a neighbor's son. Quickly, he covered the corpse. "I didn't look at anything more," he remembers. "I just tried to get home as quickly as possible." As he neared his own house, a neighbor who lived opposite tried to detain him. "I'm bleeding to death," the man called out. "I've been hit by a bomb splinter."

At that moment, De Wit saw his wife, Adriana, standing in the street crying. She ran to him. "I thought you'd never get here," she told him. "Come quickly. Our Tiny has been hit." De Wit went past his injured neighbor. "I never thought of anything but my son. When I got to him I saw that the whole of his right side was open and his right leg was cut almost through. He was still fully conscious and asked for water. I saw that his right arm was missing. He asked me about his arm and, to comfort him, I said, 'You're lying on it.'" As De Wit knelt by the boy, a doctor arrived. "He told me not to hope anymore," De Wit remembers, "because our son was going to die." Cradling the boy, De Wit set out for the Duc George cigar factory, where a Red Cross post had been set up. Before he reached the factory, his fourteen-year-old son died in his arms.

In all the terror, confusion and hope, few of the Dutch saw the vanguard of the Allied Airborne Army. At approximately 12:40 P.M., twelve British Stirling bombers swept in over the Arnhem area. At 12:47, four U.S. C-47's appeared over the heaths north of Eindhoven, while two others flew across the open fields southwest of Nijmegen, close to the town of Overasselt. In the planes were British and American pathfinders.

Returning to his farm bordering Renkum heath, less than a mile from Wolfheze, Jan Pennings saw planes coming from the west, flying low. He thought they had returned to bomb the railway line. He watched them warily, ready to dive for cover if bombs dropped. As the planes came over Renkum heath, the astounded Pennings saw "bundles dropped, and then parachutists coming out. I knew that in Normandy the Allies had used parachutists and I was sure this was the beginning of *our* invasion."

Minutes later, cycling up to his farm, Jan shouted to his wife, "Come out! We're free!" Then, the first paratroopers he had ever seen walked into the farmyard. Dazed and awed, Pennings shook their hands. Within half an hour, they told him, "hundreds more of us will arrive."

Chauffeur Jan Peelen too saw the pathfinders land on Renkum heath. He recalls that "they came down almost silently. They were well-disciplined and immediately began to peg out the heath." Like other pathfinders north of the railway line, they were marking out the landing and dropping zones.

Fifteen miles south, near the town of Overasselt, nineteen-year-old Theodorus Roelofs, in hiding from the Germans, was suddenly liberated by 82nd Airborne pathfinders who landed in the vicinity of the family farm. The Americans, he remembers, were "scouts, and my big fear was that this small group of braves could easily be done away with." The pathfinders wasted little time. Discovering that the young Dutchman spoke English, they quickly enlisted Roelofs to help as guide and interpreter. Confirming positions on their maps and directing them to the designated landing sites, Roelofs watched with fascination as the troopers marked the area with "colored strips and smoke stoves." Within three minutes a yellow-paneled "O" and violet smoke clearly outlined the area.

The four C-47's carrying the 101st pathfinders to zones north of Eindhoven ran into heavy antiaircraft fire. One planeload was shot down in flames. There were only four survivors. The other three planes continued on, and the pathfinders dropped accurately on the 101st's two zones. By 12:54 P.M. dropping and landing zones throughout the entire Market-Garden area were located and marked. Incredibly, the Germans still had not raised an alarm.

At Hoenderloo barracks, Lieutenant Colonel Walter Harzer, commander of the Hohenstaufen Division, toasted newly decorated Captain Paul Gräbner. A few minutes before, Harzer had seen a few parachutes fall to the west of Arnhem. He was not surprised. He thought they were bailed-out bomber crews. In Oosterbeek, at the Tafelberg Hotel, Field Marshal Model was having a preluncheon aperitif—a glass of chilled Moselle—with his chief of staff, Lieutenant General Hans Krebs, the operations officer Colonel Hans von Tempelhof and the headquarters adjutant Colonel Leodegard Freyberg. As administrations officer Lieutenant Gustav Sedelhauser remembers, "Whenever he was at the headquarters, the Field Marshal was punctual to a fault. We always sat down to luncheon at precisely 1300 hours." That time was H Hour for the Market forces.

3

Now, IN TIGHT FORMATIONS, the great procession of C-47's carrying the 101st Airborne thundered across Allied-held Belgium. Some twenty-five miles beyond Brussels, the serials swung north heading for the Dutch border. Then, men in the planes looked down and, for the first time, saw their earth-bound counterpart, the Garden forces whose ground attack was to be synchronized with the air assault. It was a spectacular, unforgettable sight. The vast panoply of General Horrocks' XXX Corps spread out over every field, trail and road.

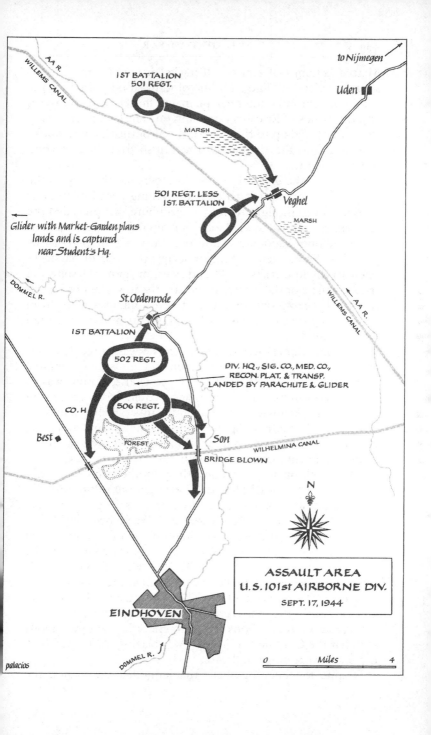

ST BATALION
501 REGT.

to Nijmegen

Uden

AA R.

WILLEMS CANAL

MARSH

501 REGT. LESS
1ST. BATTALION

Veghel

MARSH

Glider with Market-Garden plans
lands and is captured
near Student's Hq.

DOMMEL R.

St.Oedenrode

AA R.

WILLEMS CANAL

1ST BATTALION

502 REGT.

DIV. HQ., SIG. CO., MED. CO.,
RECON. PLAT. & TRANSP.
LANDED BY PARACHUTE & GLIDER

CO. H

506 REGT.

Best

FOREST

Son

WILHELMINA CANAL

BRIDGE BLOWN

N

ASSAULT AREA
U.S. 101st AIRBORNE DIV.
SEPT. 17, 1944

EINDHOVEN

palacios

DOMMEL R.

0   Miles   4

Massed columns of tanks, half-tracks, armored cars and personnel carriers and line after line of guns stood poised for the breakout. On tank antennas pennants fluttered in the wind, and thousands of Britishers standing on vehicles and crowding the fields waved up to the men of the airborne. Orange smoke billowing into the air marked the British front line. Beyond was the enemy.

Skimming the ground, fighter-bombers led the way to the drop zones, attempting to clear everything ahead of the formations. Even though the intense bombing that preceded the airborne assault had leveled many antiaircraft batteries, camouflaged nettings suddenly swung back to reveal hidden enemy positions. Some men remember seeing the tops of haystacks open to disclose nests of 88 and 20 mm. guns. Despite the thoroughness of the fighter-plane attacks, it was impossible to silence all enemy opposition. Just seven minutes away from their drop zones north of Eindhoven, the men of the 101st ran into intense flak.

Pfc. John Cipolla was dozing when he was suddenly awakened by "the sharp crack of antiaircraft guns, and shrapnel ripped through our plane." Like everyone else, Cipolla was so weighted down by equipment that he could hardly move. Besides his rifle, knapsack, raincoat and blanket, he had ammunition belts draping his shoulders, pockets full of hand grenades, rations and his main parachute plus reserve. In addition, in his plane, each man carried a land mine. As he recalls, "a C-47 on our left flank burst into flames, then another, and I thought 'My God, we are next! How will I ever get out of this plane!'"

His C-47 was shuddering and everyone seemed to be yelling at the same time, "Let's get out! We've been hit!" The jumpmaster gave the order to "Stand up and hook up." Then he calmly began an equipment check. Cipolla could hear the men as they called out, "One O.K. Two O.K. Three O.K." It seemed hours before Cipolla, the last man of the stick, was able to shout, "Twenty-one O.K." Then the green light went on and, in a rush, the men were out and falling, parachutes blossoming above them. Looking up to check his canopy, Cipolla saw that the C-47 he had just left was blazing. As he watched, the plane went down in flames.

Despite the bursting shells that engulfed the planes, the

formations did not waver. The pilots of the IX Troop Carrier Command held to their courses without deviating. Second Lieutenant Robert O'Connell remembers that his formation flew so tight, "I thought our pilot was going to stick his wing into the ear of the pilot flying on our left." O'Connell's plane was on fire. The red prejump warning light was on, and "so much smoke was fogging the aisle that I could not see back to the end of my stick." Men were coughing and yelling to get out. O'Connell "braced himself against the door to keep them in." The pilots flew on steadily, without taking evasive action, and O'Connell saw that the formation was gradually losing altitude and slowing down, preparatory to the jump. O'Connell hoped that "if the pilot thought the ship was going down, he would give us the green in time for the troops to get out." Calmly, the pilot held his flaming plane on course until he was right over the drop zone. Then the green light went on and O'Connell and his men jumped safely. O'Connell learned later that the plane crash-landed but the crew survived.

In total disregard for their own safety, troop-carrier pilots brought their planes through the flak and over the drop zones. "Don't worry about me," Second Lieutenant Herbert E. Shulman, the pilot of one burning C-47, radioed his flight commander. "I'm going to drop these troops right on the DZ." He did. Paratroopers left the plane safely. Moments later, it crashed in flames. Staff Sergeant Charles A. Mitchell watched in horror as the plane to his left streamed flame from its port engine. As the pilot held it steady on course, Mitchell saw the entire stick of paratroopers jump right through the fire.

Tragedies did not end there. Pfc. Paul Johnson was forward next to the pilot's cabin when his plane was hit dead center and both fuel tanks caught fire. Of the sixteen paratroopers, pilot and copilot, only Johnson and two other troopers got out. They had to climb over the dead in the plane to make their jumps. Each survivor was badly burned and Johnson's hair was completely seared away. The three came down in a German tank-bivouac area. For half an hour they fought off the enemy from a ditch. Then, all three injured, they were overwhelmed and taken prisoner.

Just as the green light went on in another plane, the lead paratrooper, standing in the door, was killed. He fell back on

Corporal John Altomare. His body was quickly moved aside and the rest of the group jumped. And, as another stick of troopers floated to the ground, a C-47 out of control hit two of them, its propellers chopping them to pieces.

Typically, the Americans found humor even in the terrifying approach to the drop zones. Just after Captain Cecil Lee stood to hook up, his plane was hit. Shrapnel ripped a hole through the seat he had just vacated. Nearby, a trooper shouted disgustedly, "*Now* they give us a latrine!" In another plane, Second Lieutenant Anthony Borrelli was sure he was paralyzed. The red light went on and everyone hooked up—except Borrelli, who couldn't move. An officer for only two weeks and on his first combat mission, Borrelli, who was Number 1 in the stick, was conscious of all eyes on him. To his embarrassment, he discovered he had hooked his belt to the seat. Private Robert Boyce made the trip despite the good intentions of the division dentist, who had marked him "L.O.B." (Left Out of Battle) because of his dental problems. With the intervention of his company commander, Boyce, a Normandy veteran, was permitted to go. Besides a bad tooth, he had other worries. Several new paratroop innovations—leg packs for machine guns, quick-release harness on some chutes and combat instead of jump boots—made him and many other men nervous. In particular, the troopers were concerned that their shroud lines might catch on the buckles of their new combat boots. As his plane flew low in its approach, Boyce saw Dutch civilians below holding up two fingers in the *V*-for-victory salute. That was all Boyce needed. "Hey, look," he called to the others, "they're giving us two to one we don't make it."

The odds against their ever reaching their drop zones seemed at least that high to many. Colonel Robert F. Sink, commander of the 506th Regiment, saw "a tremendous volume of flak coming up to greet us." As he was looking out the door, the plane shuddered violently and Sink saw a part of the wing tear and dangle. He turned to the men in his stick and said, "Well, there goes the wing." To Sink's relief, "nobody seemed to think much about it. They figured by this time we were practically in."

In plane Number 2, Sink's executive officer, Lieutenant Colonel Charles Chase, saw that their left wing was afire. Captain

Thomas Mulvey remembers that Chase stared at it for a minute and then remarked mildly, "I guess they're catching up on us. We'd better go." As the green light went on in both planes, the men jumped safely. The plane in which Chase was traveling burned on the ground. Sink's plane, with its damaged wing, is thought to have made the journey back to England safely.

Similar intense flak engulfed the serials of the 502nd Regiment, and planes of two groups almost collided. One serial, slightly off course, strayed into the path of a second group, causing the latter to climb for altitude and its troopers to make a higher jump than had been planned. In the lead plane of one of the serials was the division commander, General Maxwell D. Taylor, and the 502nd's 1st Battalion commander, Lieutenant Colonel Patrick Cassidy. Standing in the doorway, Cassidy saw one of the planes in the group burst into flames. He counted only seven parachutes. Then fire broke out in another C-47 just off to the left. All the paratroopers jumped from it. Mesmerized by the blazing plane, Cassidy failed to notice that the green light was on. General Taylor, standing behind him, said quietly, "Cassidy, the light's on." Automatically Cassidy answered, "Yes, sir. I know it," and jumped. Taylor was right behind him.

To General Taylor, the 101st jump was "unusually successful; almost like an exercise." In the initial planning, Taylor's staff had anticipated casualties as high as 30 percent. Of the 6,695 paratroopers who enplaned in England, 6,669 actually jumped. Despite the intense flak, the bravery of the C-47 and fighter pilots gave the 101st an almost perfect jump. Although some units were dropped from one to three miles north of the drop zones, they landed so close together that assembly was quick. Only two planes failed to reach the drop zone, and the IX Troop Carrier Command took the brunt of all casualties by their heroic determination to get the troopers to their targets. Of the 424 C-47's carrying the 101st, every fourth plane was damaged, and sixteen went down, killing their crews.

Glider losses were heavy, too. Later, as these serials began to come in, only 53 of the original 70 would arrive without mishap on the landing zone near Son. Still, despite abortions, enemy flak and crash-landings, the gliders would eventually deliver nearly 80 percent of the men and 75 percent of the jeeps

and trailers they carried.* Now, Taylor's Screaming Eagles began to move on their objectives—the bridges and crossings
over the vital fifteen-mile stretch of corridor ahead of the British ground forces.

4

COLONEL GENERAL KURT STUDENT and his chief of staff, Colonel Reinhard, stood on the balcony of the General's cottage
near Vught and "simply stared, stunned, like fools." Student
remembers clearly that "everywhere we looked, we saw chains
of planes—fighters, troop carriers and cargo planes—flying
over us. We climbed onto the roof of the house to get a better
idea of just where these units were going." Streams of planes
seemed to be heading in the direction of Grave and Nijmegen
and, only a few miles to the south near Eindhoven and Son, he
could clearly see troop carriers—one after the other—coming
in and dropping paratroopers and equipment. Some aircraft
flew so low that Student and Reinhard instinctively ducked.
"On the grounds of the headquarters, our clerks, quartermasters, drivers and signalmen were out in the open, firing with
all sorts of weapons. As usual, there was no sign of our own
fighter planes." Student was completely baffled. "I could not
tell what was happening or where these airborne units were
going. In these moments, I never once thought of the danger of our own position." But Student, the paratroop expert,
was filled with admiration and envy. "This mighty spectacle
deeply impressed me. I thought with reflection and longing

---

*Because Market-Garden was considered an all-British operation, few Ameri-
can correspondents were accredited to cover the attack. None was at Arnhem.
One of the Americans attached to the 101st was a United Press reporter named
Walter Cronkite, who landed by glider. Cronkite recalls that "I thought the
wheels of the glider were for landing. Imagine my surprise when we skidded
along the ground and the wheels came up through the floor. I got another
shock. Our helmets, which we all swore were hooked, came flying off on impact and seemed more dangerous than the incoming shells. After landing I
grabbed the first helmet I saw, my trusty musette bag with the Olivetti typewriter inside and began crawling toward the canal which was the rendezvous
point. When I looked back, I found a half dozen guys crawling after me. It
seems that I had grabbed the wrong helmet. The one I wore had two neat
stripes down the back indicating that I was a lieutenant."

of our own airborne operations and I said to Reinhard, 'Oh, if ever I'd had such means at my disposal. Just once, to have this many planes!'" Reinhard's feelings were very much in the present. "Herr General," he told Student, "we've got to *do* something!" They left the roof and went back to Student's office.

Only the previous evening, Student, in his daily report, had warned, "Heavy columns of traffic south of the Maas-Schelde Canal indicate an impending attack." The problem was: had it already begun? If so, then these airborne units were after the bridges around Eindhoven, Grave and Nijmegen. All the spans were prepared for demolition and protected by special engineer parties and security detachments. A bridge commander had been assigned to each crossing with strict orders to destroy the bridge in case of attack. "The obvious move for the Allies," it occurred to Student, "was to use airborne troops in this situation to seize the bridges before we could destroy them." At this time, Student did not even think of the importance of the Lower Rhine bridge at Arnhem. "Get me Model," he told Reinhard.

Reinhard picked up the phone to discover that the telephone lines were out. The headquarters was already cut off.

In Oosterbeek, some thirty-seven miles away, at the Tafelberg Hotel, Lieutenant Gustav Sedelhauser, Model's administration officer, was angry. "Are you hung over from last night?" he shouted into a field phone. Unteroffizier Youppinger, one of the 250-man company which, under Sedelhauser, was assigned to protect Model, repeated what he had said. At Wolfheze, "gliders are landing in our laps," he insisted. Sedelhauser slammed down the phone and rushed into the operations office, where he reported the message to a startled lieutenant colonel. Together, they hurried to the dining room, where Model and his chief of staff General Krebs were at lunch. "I've just had news that gliders are landing at Wolfheze," the colonel said. The operations officer, Colonel Tempelhof, stared; the monocle fell out of Krebs's eye. "Well, now we're for it," Tempelhof said.

Model jumped to his feet and issued a flurry of orders to evacuate the headquarters. As he headed out of the dining room to collect his own belongings, he shouted back over his shoulder, "They're after me and this headquarters!" Moments later, carrying only a small case, Model rushed through the Tafelberg's entrance. On the sidewalk he dropped the case, which flew open, spilling his linens and toilet articles.

Krebs followed Model outside in such haste that, Sedelhauser saw, "he had even forgotten his cap, pistol and belt." Tempelhof had not even had time to remove the war maps in the operations office. Colonel Freyberg, the headquarters adjutant, was equally rushed. As he passed Sedelhauser, he shouted, "Don't forget my cigars." At his car, Model told his driver, Frombeck, "Quick! Doetinchem! Bittrich's headquarters!"

Sedelhauser waited until the car drove off and then returned to the hotel. In the operations office, he saw the war maps —showing positions all the way from Holland to Switzerland —still on a table. He rolled them up and took them with him. Then he ordered the Hartenstein Hotel and the Tafelberg immediately evacuated; all transport, he said, "every car, truck and motorbike, is to leave here immediately." The last report he received before leaving for Doetinchem was that the British were less than two miles away. In all the confusion he completely forgot Freyberg's cigars.

5

SURROUNDED BY GROUND HAZE and the smoke and fire of burning buildings, the mighty British glider fleet was landing. Already the areas marked by orange and crimson nylon strips were beginning to look like vast aircraft parking lots. Blue smoke eddied up from the two landing zones—"Reyers Camp Farm" to the north and "Renkum Heath" to the southwest— near Wolfheze. From these zones, in chain after chain, tugs and gliders stretched back almost twenty miles to their approach point near the town of s'Hertogenbosch, southwest of Nijmegen. Swarms of fighters protected these ponderous columns. Traffic was so dense that pilots were reminded of the rush-hour congestion around London's busy Piccadilly Circus.

The serials—each group separated from the next by a four-minute interval—flew slowly over the flat, water-veined Dutch countryside. The landmarks pilots had been briefed to recognize now began to pass beneath them: the great wide rivers

Maas and Waal and up ahead, the Lower Rhine. Then, as each formation began its descent, men saw Arnhem off to the right and their vital objectives: the rail and highway bridges. Incredibly, despite the R.A.F. prediction of intense antiaircraft fire, the immense glider cavalcade encountered virtually no resistance. The preassault bombings had been far more effective around Arnhem than in the Eindhoven area. Not a single tug or glider was shot down in making the approach.

With clocklike precision, the skilled pilots of the R.A.F. and the Glider Pilot Regiment came over the zones. As gliders cast off, their tugs made climbing turns to free air space for the combinations coming up behind. These intricate maneuvers and the heavy traffic were causing problems of their own. Sergeant Pilot Bryan Tomblin remembers chaotic congestion over the landing zones. "There were gliders, tugs, ropes and all sorts of things in the sky," he recalls. "You had to be on the lookout all the time."

Staff Sergeant Victor Miller, piloting a Horsa, recalls coming in over the Lower Rhine and finding it "unbelievably calm." Beyond, he suddenly spotted his landing zone, with its "triangular-shaped woods and little farm nestling in the far corner." Seconds later, Miller heard the voice of his Stirling tug's navigator. "O.K. Number 2. When you're ready." Miller acknowledged. "Good luck, Number 2," the navigator told him. Miller immediately cast off. His tug disappeared, the tow rope flapping in its wake. It would be dropped, Miller knew, "on the enemy as a parting gift before the Stirling turned onto its homeward course."

The glider's air speed fell off and the field loomed nearer. Miller called for half-flaps and his copilot, Sergeant Tom Hollingsworth, instantly pushed a lever. For a moment the glider bucked, "as the great flaps descending from underneath each wing braked against our speed." The landing zone, Miller estimated, was now less than a mile away. "I reminded Tom to look out for gliders on his side. One slid across and above us less than fifty yards away," and, to Miller's amazement, "swung in on the same course. Another glider seemed to be drifting into us from starboard. I don't think the pilot even saw us, he was so intent on getting down in the field." To avoid collision, Miller deliberately dived under the incoming glider. "A great

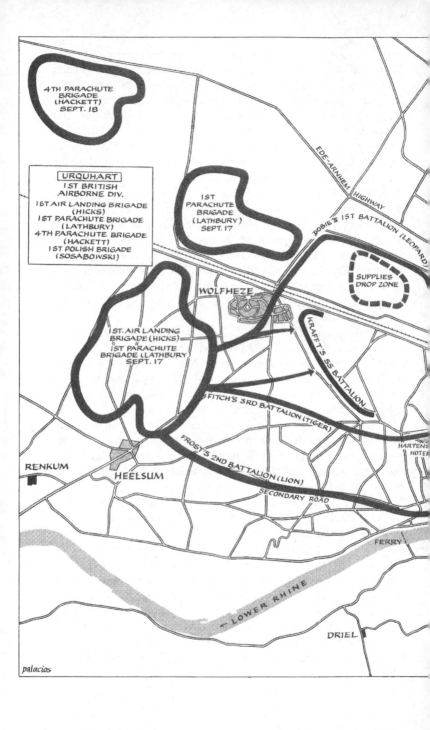

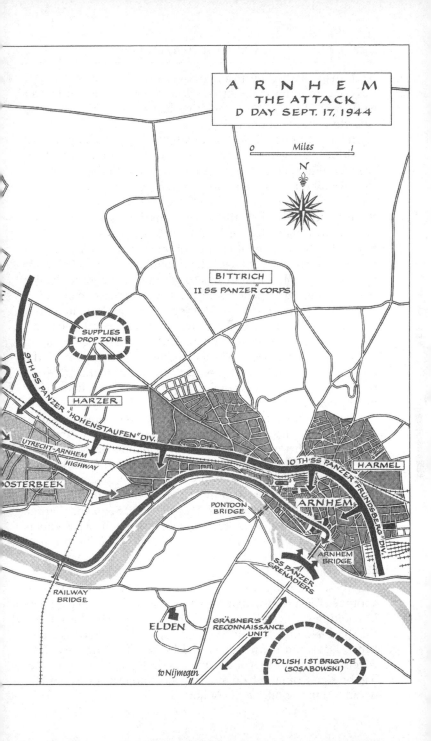

ARNHEM
THE ATTACK
D DAY SEPT. 17, 1944

0   Miles   1

N

BITTRICH
II SS PANZER CORPS

SUPPLIES DROP ZONE

9TH SS PANZER "HOHENSTAUFEN" DIV.

HARZER

UTRECHT-ARNHEM HIGHWAY

OOSTERBEEK

10 TH SS PANZER "FRUNDSBERG" DIV.

HARMEL

ARNHEM

PONTOON BRIDGE

SS PANZER GRENADIERS

ARNHEM BRIDGE

RAILWAY BRIDGE

ELDEN

GRÄBNER'S RECONNAISSANCE UNIT

POLISH 1ST BRIGADE (SOSABOWSKI)

to Nijmegen

black shape flashed over our cockpit, too close for my liking. I was concentrating so hard to set down in one piece that I never wondered if the enemy was firing at us—not that we could have done much about it."

Miller continued his descent with "tree tops leaping toward our floor boards and past the wings. As the ground rushed up, another glider came alongside. I pulled back on the wheel, leveled, we hit once, bounced about three feet, and came down to stay. Tom had slammed on the brakes and we careened across the plowed field. Then the wheels sank into soft soil and we ground to a halt fifty yards short of a heavy-looking line of trees." In the silence, after the continuous deafening roar of the slip stream, Miller heard the distant crackle of small-arms fire, "but my one thought was to get out of the glider before another crashed or landed on us. I was the last man out. I didn't even pause, but jumped straight through the ramp door and hit the ground of Holland, four feet below, rather hard."

The glider in which Signalman Graham Marples was riding circled and came back over its landing zone because of the congestion. "But, by then, we had run out of wind," Marples remembers. "I saw trees coming through the glider floor. They just ripped the floor to pieces, and the next thing I knew, we nosed over and came down. I could hear everything breaking, like dry twigs snapping. We landed squarely on our nose but no one was hurt except for a few scratches and bruises." Later, the pilot told Marples he had pulled up to avoid collision with another glider.

Many gliders, having surmounted all the problems of the long trip, touched down to disaster. Staff Sergeant George Davis stood near his empty Horsa and watched other gliders come in. One of the first to land, Davis had brought in thirty-two men of the 1st Airlanding Brigade. He saw two gliders "almost side by side bump across the landing zone and into the trees. The wings of both were sheared off." Seconds later, another Horsa rumbled in. Its speed was such that Davis knew it would never be able to stop in time. The glider plowed into the trees. No one got out. With his copilot, Staff Sergeant Williams, Davis ran to the glider and looked into the plexiglass-covered cockpit. Everyone inside was dead. A 75 mm. howitzer had broken from its chain mooring, crushing the gun crew and decapitating the pilot and copilot.

Lieutenant Michael Dauncey had just landed his glider—carrying a jeep, trailer and six gunners from an artillery battery—when he saw a huge eight-ton Hamilcar touch down. "The field was soft," he recalls, "and I saw the nose of the Hamilcar digging up earth in front of it." Weight and ground speed drove it deeper until the huge tail rose up in the air and the Hamilcar flipped over on its back. Dauncey knew "it was useless to try to dig them out. A Horsa's flat on top but a Hamilcar's got a hump where the pilots sit, and we knew the pilots were finished."

Making his approach in another Hamilcar, Staff Sergeant Gordon Jenks saw the same crash and immediately deduced that the ground ahead was too soft. Instantly, he decided against landing in the field. "I reckoned if we went into a dive right then," he remembers, "we would have enough speed for me to hold her off the deck until we had cleared the fence and got safely into the next field." Jenks pushed the control column forward, dived, then leveled out a few feet above the ground. Easing the huge aircraft gently over the fence, Jenks "put her down in the far field as lightly as a feather."

All over the landing zones now the tails of gliders were being unbolted and swung back, and artillery pieces, equipment, stores, jeeps and trailers were being unloaded. The men in Lance Corporal Henry Brook's glider, like many others, found that the unloading maneuver was fine in theory but more difficult in practice. "There were eight pins with a protective wire holding the glider tail on," Brook explained. "Back in England in practice exercises, you could always get the tail off and jeep and trailer out in two minutes flat. In action, it was different. We cut the wire and got the pins out but the tail wouldn't budge." Brook and the other troopers finally chopped it off. Lance Bombardier J. W. Crook was similarly frustrated, but a nearby jeep came to the aid of his men and, with its hawser, yanked off the tail.

All over the two zones men were beginning to salvage cargo from wrecked gliders. The crash of two giant Hamilcars was a serious loss. They contained a pair of 17-pounder artillery pieces plus three-ton trucks and ammunition trailers. But all of the fifteen 75 mm. pack howitzers of the 1st Airlanding Light Regiment artillery arrived safely.

Most men who came in by glider recall a strange, almost

eerie silence immediately after landing. Then, from the assembly point, men heard the skirl of bagpipes playing "Blue
Bonnets." At about the same time, soldiers on the edge of Renkum Heath saw Dutch civilians wandering aimlessly through
the woods or hiding in fright. Lieutenant Neville Hay of the
Phantom unit remembers that "it was a sobering sight. Some
were in white hospital gowns and seemed to be herded along
by attendants. Men and women capered about, waving, laughing and jabbering. They were obviously quite mad." Glider
Pilot Victor Miller was startled by voices in the woods. Then,
"groups of weird white-clothed men and women filed past." It
was only later that the troopers learned the strangely behaved
civilians were inmates from the bombed Wolfheze Psychiatric
Institute.

General Urquhart had landed at Renkum Heath. He too was
struck by the stillness. "It was," he recalls, "incredibly quiet.
Unreal." While his chief of staff, Colonel Charles Mackenzie,
set up the division's tactical headquarters at the edge of the
woods, Urquhart headed for the parachute dropping zones,
four hundred yards away. It was nearly time for Brigadier Lathbury's 1st Parachute Brigade to arrive. From the distance came
the drone of approaching aircraft. The bustle and activity all
over the glider zones paused as men looked up to see the long
lines of C-47's. Small-arms and antiaircraft fire during the paratroop drop was as limited and spasmodic as during the glider
landings. At exactly 1:53 P.M., and for the next fifteen minutes,
the sky was filled with brilliant-colored parachutes as the 1st
Brigade began jumping. Some 650 parapacks with bright-
yellow, red and brown chutes—carrying guns, ammunition
and equipment—fell rapidly through the streams of troopers.
Other supply chutes, pushed out of the planes before the men
jumped, floated down with a variety of cargo, including miniature foldable motorcycles. Many already overburdened paratroopers also jumped with large kitbags. In theory, these were
to be lowered by a cord just before the men touched ground.
Scores of the packs broke away from troopers and smashed on
the zones. Several contained precious radio sets.

British Private Harry Wright jumped from an American
C-47. As he fell through the air, he lost both his helmet and kit-
bag. He hit the ground very hard. Regimental Quartermaster

Sergeant Robertson came running up. Wright's forehead was streaming blood. "Were you hit by flak?" Robertson asked. Wright slowly shook his head. "No, sarge," he said. "It was that bloody Yank. We were going too fast when we jumped." Robertson applied a dressing and then, to Wright's surprise, offered the injured man a pork pie from his haversack. "I nearly died right then of the shock," Wright recalls. "First, Robertson was a Scot, and then, as a quartermaster, he never offered anyone anything."

Odd things seemed to be happening all over the drop zones. The first person Sergeant Norman Swift saw when he landed was Sergeant Major Les Ellis, who was passing by holding a dead partridge. The amazed Swift asked where the bird had come from. "I landed on it," Ellis explained. "Who knows? It'll be a bit of all right later on, in case we're hungry."

Sapper Ronald Emery had just slipped out of his chute when an elderly Dutch lady scuttled across the field, grabbed it up and raced away, leaving the startled Emery staring after her. In another part of the field, Corporal Geoffrey Stanners, loaded down with equipment, landed on the top of a glider wing. Like a trampoline, the wing sprang up, flipping Stanners back into the air. He landed with both feet on the ground.

Dazed after a hard fall, Lieutenant Robin Vlasto lay still for a few moments, trying to orient himself. He was conscious of "an incredible number of bodies and containers coming down all around me and planes continued to pour out paratroopers." Vlasto decided to get off the drop zone quickly. As he struggled to get out of his harness, he heard a weird sound. Looking around, he saw Lieutenant Colonel John Frost, the 2nd Battalion's commander, walking past, blowing his copper hunting horn.

Frost was also observed by Private James W. Sims. Sims had already gone through quite a day even before he landed. Having always flown with the R.A.F.—whose attitude, Sims recalls, was: "Don't worry, lads, whatever it's like, we'll get you through"—Sims received quite a shock on seeing his American pilot. "He was a lieutenant colonel with one of those soft hats. His flying jacket was hanging open and he was smoking a big cigar. Our lieutenant saluted him quite smartly and asked if the men should move up to the front of the plane on takeoff." The

American grinned. "Why, hell, no, lieutenant," Sims remembers him saying. "I'll get this goddam crate off the ground if I have to drag its ass halfway down the runway." Sims's officer was too startled to speak. Now, although he was fond of his colonel, Sims, watching Frost go by, had reached the limit of his patience. Surrounded by his equipment, he sat on the ground and muttered, "There goes old Johnny Frost, a .45 in one hand and that bloody horn in the other."

All over the drop and landing zones, where 5,191 men of the division had arrived safely, units were assembling, forming up and moving out. General Urquhart "couldn't have been more pleased. Everything appeared to be going splendidly." The same thought occurred to Sergeant Major John C. Lord. The veteran paratrooper recalls that "this was one of the best exercises I'd ever been on. Everyone was calm and businesslike." But the reservations he'd had before takeoff still bothered Lord. As he looked about, seeing the men assembling rapidly, with no enemy to contend with, he remembers thinking, "It's all too good to be true." Others had the same thought. As one group prepared to move off, Lieutenant Peter Stainforth heard Lieutenant Dennis Simpson say quietly, "Everything is going too well for my liking."

The man with the most urgent task on landing was forty-three-year-old Major Freddie Gough of the 1st Airborne Division reconnaissance unit. Leading a four-troop squadron in heavily armed jeeps, Gough was to make a dash for the bridge before Colonel John Frost's marching battalion reached it. Gough and his men parachuted in, and then sought their ground transport, which was being flown in by glider. Quickly Gough located his second in command, Captain David Allsop, on the landing zone and received some bad news. The entire transport for one of the four units—approximately twenty-two vehicles—had failed to arrive, Allsop reported. Thirty-six of the 320 gliders scheduled for Arnhem had been lost, and with them were lost the jeeps of Gough's A troop. Nevertheless, both Gough and Allsop believed that there were enough vehicles to race for the Arnhem bridge. Gough gave the order to move out. With his force whittled down, everything now depended on the reaction of the Germans.

6

IN ALL THE PANIC and confusion, the first German senior officer to raise the alert was General Wilhelm Bittrich, commander of the II SS Panzer Corps. At 1:30 P.M., Bittrich received his first report from the Luftwaffe communications net that airborne troops were landing in the Arnhem vicinity. A second report, arriving minutes later, gave the assault area as Arnhem and Nijmegen. Bittrich could not raise anybody at Field Marshal Model's headquarters at the Tafelberg in Oosterbeek. Nor was he able to contact either the town commander of Arnhem or General Student at his headquarters in Vught. Although the situation was obscure, Bittrich immediately thought of General Von Zangen's Fifteenth Army, most of which had escaped across the mouth of the Schelde and into Holland. "My first thought was that this airborne attack was designed to contain Von Zangen's army and prevent it from joining with the remainder of our forces. Then, probably, the objective would be a drive by the British Army across the Rhine and into Germany." If his reasoning was correct, Bittrich believed that the key to such an operation would be the Arnhem-Nijmegen bridges. Immediately he alerted the 9th Hohenstaufen and the 10th Frundsberg SS Panzer divisions.

Lieutenant Colonel Walter Harzer, commander of the Hohenstaufen, attending the luncheon following the decoration of Captain Paul Gräbner, was "in the middle of my soup" when Bittrich's call reached him. Tersely, Bittrich explained the situation and ordered Harzer to "reconnoiter in the direction of Arnhem and Nijmegen." The Hohenstaufen was to move out immediately, hold the Arnhem area and destroy airborne troops west of Arnhem near Oosterbeek. Bittrich warned Harzer that "quick action is imperative. The taking and securing of the Arnhem bridge is of decisive importance." At the same time, Bittrich ordered the Frundsberg Division—whose commander, General Harmel, was in Berlin—to move toward Nijmegen, "to take, hold and defend the city's bridges."

Harzer was now faced with the problem of unloading the last Hohenstaufen units, due to leave by train for Germany in less than an hour—including the "disabled" tanks, half-tracks and armored personnel carriers he had been determined to keep from Harmel. Harzer looked at Gräbner. "Now what are we going to do?" he asked. "The vehicles are dismantled and on the train." Of these, forty vehicles belonged to Gräbner's reconnaissance battalion. "How soon can you have the tracks and guns put back?" Harzer demanded. Gräbner immediately called his engineers. "We'll be ready to move within three to five hours," he told Harzer. "Get it done in three," Harzer snapped as he headed for his headquarters.

Although he had guessed right for the wrong reasons, General Bittrich had set in motion the panzer divisions that Montgomery's intelligence officers had totally dismissed.

The officer who had been ordered out of Oosterbeek to make way for Field Marshal Model's headquarters found himself and his men based almost on the British landing zones. SS Major Sepp Krafft, commander of the Panzer Grenadier Training and Reserve Battalion, was "sick to my stomach" with fright. His latest headquarters, in the Wolfheze Hotel, was less than one mile from Renkum Heath. Bivouacked nearby were two of his companies; a third was in reserve in Arnhem. From the hotel, Krafft could see the heath "jammed with gliders and troops, some only a few hundred yards away." He had always believed that it took hours for airborne troops to organize, but as he watched "the English were assembling everywhere and moving off ready to fight." He could not understand why such a force would land in this area. "The only military objective I could think of with any importance was the Arnhem bridge."

The terrified commander knew of no German infantry close by, other than his own understrength battalion. Until help could arrive, Krafft decided that "it was up to me to stop them from getting to the bridge—if that's where they were going." His companies were positioned in a rough triangle, its base— the Wolfheze road—almost bordering Renkum Heath. North of Krafft's headquarters was the main Ede–Arnhem road and the Amsterdam–Utrecht–Arnhem railway line; to the south, the Utrecht road ran via Renkum and Oosterbeek into Arnhem. Because he lacked the strength to maintain a line from one road to the other, Krafft decided to hold positions roughly from the railroad on the north to the Utrecht–Arnhem road to the south. Hurriedly, he ordered his reserve company out of Arnhem to join the rest of the battalion at Wolfheze. Machine-gun platoons were dispatched to hold each end of his line while the remainder of his troops fanned out in the woods.

Although lacking men, Krafft had a new experimental weapon at his disposal: a multibarreled, rocket-propelled launcher capable of throwing oversized mortar shells.* Several of these units had been left with him for training purposes. Now he planned to use them to confuse the British and give an impression of greater strength; at the same time, he ordered twenty-five-man attack groups to make sharp forays which might throw the paratroops off balance.

As Krafft was issuing his directions, a staff car roared up to his headquarters and Major General Kussin, Arnhem's town commander, hurried inside. Kussin had driven out of Arnhem at breakneck speed to see at first-hand what was happening. On the way he had met Field Marshal Model heading east toward Doetinchem. Stopping briefly on the road, Model had instructed Kussin to raise the alert and to inform Berlin of the developments. Now, looking across the heath, Kussin was flabbergasted at the sight of the vast British drop. Almost desperately he told Krafft that somehow he would get reinforcements to the area by 6 P.M. As Kussin started out to make the drive back to Arnhem, Krafft warned him not to take the Utrecht–Arnhem road. Already he had received a report that British troopers were moving along it. "Take the side roads," Krafft told Kussin. "The main road may already be blocked." Kussin was grim-faced. "I'll get through all right," he answered. Krafft watched as the staff car raced off toward the highway.

He was convinced that Kussin's replacements would never reach him, and that it was only a matter of time before his small force would be overpowered. Even as he positioned his troops along the Wolfheze road, Krafft sent his driver, Private

*This weapon should not be confused with the smaller German mortar thrower, *Nebelwerfer*. Krafft maintains that there were only four of these experimental launchers in existence. I have not been able to check this fact, but I can find no record of a similar weapon on the western front. There is no doubt that it was used with devastating effect against the British. Countless witnesses describe the scream and impact of the oversized mortars, but, inexplicably, there is no discussion of the weapon in any of the British after-action reports.

Wilhelm Rauh, to collect his personal possessions. "Pack them in the car and head for Germany," Krafft told Rauh. "I don't expect to get out of this alive."

At Bad Saarnow near Berlin, the commander of the 10th Frundsberg Division, General Heinz Harmel, conferred with the chief of Waffen SS Operations, Major General Hans Juttner, and outlined the plight of Bittrich's understrength II Panzer Corps. If the corps was to continue as an effective combat unit, Harmel insisted, "Bittrich's urgent request for men, armor, vehicles and guns must be honored." Juttner promised to do what he could, but he warned that "at this moment the strength of every combat unit is depleted." Everyone wanted priorities, and Juttner could not promise any immediate help. As the two men talked, Juttner's aide entered the office with a radio message. Juttner read it and wordlessly passed it to Harmel. The message read: "Airborne attack Arnhem. Return immediately. Bittrich." Harmel rushed out of the office and got into his car. Arnhem was an eleven-and-a-half-hour drive from Bad Saarnow. To his driver, Corporal Sepp Hinterholzer, Harmel said: "Back to Arnhem—and drive like the devil!"

7

MAJOR ANTHONY DEANE-DRUMMOND, second in command of the British 1st Airborne Division Signals, could not understand what was wrong. At one moment his radio sets were getting perfect reception from Brigadier Lathbury's brigade as it headed for its objectives, including the Arnhem bridge. But now, as Lathbury's battalions moved closer to Arnhem, radio signals were fading by the minute. From Deane-Drummond's signalmen came a constant stream of reports that disturbed and puzzled him. They were unable to contact some jeep-borne sets at all, and the signals they received from others were so weak as to be barely audible. Yet the various battalions of Lathbury's brigade and Major Freddie Gough's reconnaissance units could scarcely be more than two to three miles away.

Of particular concern to Deane-Drummond was Lathbury's messages. They were vital to General Urquhart in his direction of the battle. Deane-Drummond decided to send out a jeep with a radio and operator to pick up Lathbury's signals and relay them back to Division. He instructed the team to set up at a point midway between Division and Lathbury's mobile communications. A short time later, Deane-Drummond heard signals from the relay team. The range of their set seemed drastically reduced—at minimum, the "22's" should have operated efficiently at least up to five miles—and the signal was faint. Either the set was not functioning properly, he reasoned, or the operator was poorly located to send. Even as he listened, the signal faded completely. Deane-Drummond was unable to raise anybody. Nor could a special team of American communications operators with two radio jeeps. Hastily assembled and rushed to British Airborne Division headquarters only a few hours before takeoff on the seventeenth, the Americans were to operate ground-to-air "very high frequency" sets to call in fighters for close support. In the first few hours of the battle, these radio jeeps might have made all the difference. Instead, they were found to be useless. Neither jeep's set had been adjusted to the frequencies necessary to call in planes. At this moment, with the battle barely begun, British radio communications had totally broken down.*

8

As if on signal, German guns opened up as the planes carrying the 82nd Airborne Division made their approach to the drop zones. Looking down, Brigadier General James M. Gavin saw ground fire spurting from a line of trenches paralleling the Maas-Waal Canal. In wooded areas, enemy batteries that had remained silent and hidden until now also began to fire. Watching, Gavin wondered if his battle plan for the 82nd, which had been based on a calculated risk, might founder.

---

*In Christopher Hibbert's *The Battle of Arnhem*, p. 96, dealing specifically with the British at Arnhem and equally critical of British communications, he claims that "American air-support parties were insufficiently trained . . . the disastrous consequence was that not until the last day of the operation . . . was any effective close air support given to the airborne troops." There appears to be no information on who erred in the allocation of the frequencies, nor are the names of the Americans known. The two teams, who found themselves in the middle of the battle with the means of perhaps changing the entire course of history on that vital day, have never been found. Yet these two combat units are the only American ones known to have been in the Arnhem battle.

Charged with holding the middle sector of the Market-Garden corridor, the division had widespread objectives, running ten miles south-to-north and twelve miles west-to-east. Besides the drop of one paratroop company near the western end of the Grave bridge, which was to be seized by a surprise *coup de main* assault, Gavin had chosen three drop areas and one large landing zone. The latter would accommodate his fifty Waco gliders and the thirty-eight Horsas and Wacos of General Frederick Browning's British I Airborne Corps headquarters. But Gavin had ordered only one drop zone, north of Overasselt, to be marked by pathfinders. The other three, lying close to the Groesbeek ridge and the German border, were deliberately left unmarked. Gavin's paratroopers and gliders would land without identifying beacons or smoke in order to confuse the enemy as to their touchdown areas. Some thirteen minutes after the 82nd was down, Browning's Corps headquarters would land.

Because Gavin's primary concern was that enemy tanks might suddenly emerge from the Reichswald along the German border east of his largest glider and drop zone, he had given two unusual orders. To protect both his division and Browning's headquarters, he had instructed paratroopers to jump close to any antiaircraft batteries they were able to spot from the air and render them useless as quickly as possible. And, for the first time in airborne history, he was parachuting in a complete battalion of field artillery, dropping it onto the large zone directly facing the forest and approximately one and one-half miles from the German border itself. Now, looking at the intense antiaircraft fire and thinking of the possibility of enemy tanks in the Reichswald, Gavin knew that while he had planned for nearly all eventualities, the men of the 82nd faced a tough task.

Gavin's Normandy veterans had never forgotten the slaughter of their own in Ste. Mère Église. Dropped by accident on that village, men had been machine-gunned by the Germans as they came down; many were killed as they hung helpless in their parachutes, from telephone lines and trees around the village square. Not until Ste. Mère Église was finally secured by Lieutenant Colonel Ben Vandervoort were the dead troopers cut down and buried. Now, as the 82nd prepared to jump over Holland, some men called out to troopers still hooked up behind them: "Remember Ste. Mère Église." Although it was a risky procedure, many troopers jumped with their guns blazing.

Captain Briand Beaudin, coming down over his drop zone near the Groesbeek Ridge, saw that he was descending directly over a German antiaircraft emplacement with guns aiming at him. Beaudin began firing with his Colt .45. "Suddenly I realized," Beaudin remembers, "how futile it was, aiming my little peashooter while oscillating in the air above large-caliber guns." Landing close to the flak site, Beaudin took the entire crew prisoner. He thinks the Germans "were so startled they couldn't fire a single shot."

First Lieutenant James J. Coyle thought he was heading for a landing on a German tent hospital. Suddenly, enemy troops poured out of the tent and began running for 20 mm. antiaircraft guns around the perimeter. He, too, worked his .45 from its holster but his parachute began to oscillate and Coyle drifted away from the tent. One of the Germans started to run in Coyle's direction. "I couldn't get off a shot at the Kraut," Coyle recalls. "One second I'd be pointing the pistol at the ground; the next, I'd be aiming at the sky. I did have enough sense left to put the Colt back into the holster so I wouldn't drop it or shoot myself when I hit." On the ground, even before he tried to get out of his harness, Coyle drew his pistol once more. "The Kraut was now only a few feet away, but he was acting as though he didn't know I existed. Suddenly I realized that he wasn't running toward me; he was just running away." As the German hurried past Coyle he threw away his gun and helmet, and Coyle could see "he was only a kid, about eighteen years old. I just couldn't shoot an unarmed man. The last I saw of the boy he was running for the German border."

When tracer bullets began ripping through his canopy, Private Edwin C. Raub became so enraged that he deliberately side-slipped his chute so as to land next to the antiaircraft gun. Without removing his harness, and dragging his parachute behind him, Raub rushed the Germans with his Tommy gun. He killed one, captured the others and then, with plastic explosives, destroyed the flak-gun barrels.

Although enemy opposition to the 505th and 508th regiments in the Groesbeek area was officially considered negligible, a considerable amount of antiaircraft and small-arms fire came from the woods surrounding the zones. Without waiting to assemble, 82nd troopers, individually and in small groups, swarmed over these pockets of resistance, quickly subduing them and taking prisoners. Simultaneously, fighter planes skimmed over the tree tops, machine-gunning the enemy emplacements. The Germans scored heavily against these low-level attacks. Within a matter of minutes, three fighters were hit and crashed near the woods. Staff Sergeant Michael Vuletich saw one of them. It cartwheeled across the drop zone and when it finally stopped, only the plane's fuselage was intact. Moments later, the pilot emerged unscathed and stopped by the wreckage to light a cigarette. Vuletich remembers that the downed flier remained with the company as an infantryman.

From the ground, Staff Sergeant James Jones saw a P-47 aflame at about 1,500 feet. He expected the pilot to bail out but the plane came down, skidded across the drop zone and broke apart. The tail snapped off, the motor rolled away, and the cockpit came to rest on the field. Jones was sure the pilot was dead but, as he watched, the canopy slid back and "a little tow-headed guy with no hat on and a .45 under his arm ran toward us." Jones remembers asking, "Man, why in the devil didn't you jump?" The pilot grinned. "Hell, I was afraid to," he told Jones.

Just after landing and assembling his gear, Staff Sergeant Russell O'Neal watched a P-51 fighter dive and strafe a hidden German position near his field. After the plane had made two passes over the machine-gun nest, it was hit; but the pilot was able to circle and make a safe belly landing. According to O'Neal, "this guy jumped out and ran up to me, shouting, 'Give me a gun, quick! I know right where that Kraut s.o.b. is and I'm gonna get him.'" As O'Neal stared after him, the pilot grabbed a gun and raced off toward the woods.

Within eighteen minutes, 4,511 men of the 82nd's 505th and 508th regiments, along with engineers and seventy tons of equipment, were down on or near their drop zones straddling the town of Groesbeek on the eastern side of the wooded heights. As the men assembled, cleared the zones and struck out for objectives, special pathfinder teams marked the areas for the artillery drop, the 82nd's glider force, and the British Corps headquarters. So far, General Gavin's calculated risk was succeeding. Yet, although radio contact between the regiments was established almost immediately, it was still too early for Gavin, who had jumped with the 505th, to learn what was occurring eight miles west, where the 504th Regiment had dropped north of Overasselt. Nor did he know whether the special assault against the Grave bridge was proceeding according to plan.

Like the rest of the division's planes, the 137 C-47's carrying Colonel Reuben H. Tucker's 504th Regiment ran into spasmodic antiaircraft fire as they neared the Overasselt drop zone. As in the other areas, pilots held their courses, and at 1:15 P.M., some 2,016 men began to jump. Eleven planes swung slightly west and headed for a small drop site near the vital nine-span, 1,500-foot-long bridge over the Maas river near Grave. These C-47's carried Company E of Major Edward Wellems' 2nd Battalion to the most crucial of the 82nd's immediate objectives. Their job was to rush the bridges from the western approach; the remainder of Wellems' battalion would strike out from Overasselt and head for the eastern side. If the Grave bridge was not taken quickly and intact, the tight Market-Garden schedule could not be maintained. Loss of the bridge might mean failure for the entire operation.

As E Company's planes headed for the western assault site, platoon leader Lieutenant John S. Thompson could clearly see the Maas river, the town of Grave, the mass jump of the 504th to his right near Overasselt and then, coming up, the ditch-lined fields where the company was to drop. As Thompson watched, other men from the company were already out of their planes and falling toward the Grave bridge zone; but in the lieutenant's C-47 the green light had not yet flashed on. When it did, Thompson saw that they were directly over some buildings. He waited for a few seconds, saw fields beyond and jumped with his platoon. By a fortuitous error, he and his men came down only some five or six hundred yards from the southwestern edge of the bridge.

Thompson could hear erratic firing from the direction of Grave itself, but around the bridge everything seemed quiet. He did not know whether he should wait until the remainder of the company came up or attack with the sixteen men in his platoon. "Since this was our primary mission, I decided to attack," Thompson says. Sending Corporal Hugh H. Perry back to the company commander, Thompson gave him a laconic message to deliver: "We are proceeding toward the bridge."

Firing from the town and nearby buildings was now more intense, and Thompson led the platoon to cover in nearby drainage ditches. Working their way toward the bridge, men waded in water up to their necks. They began to receive fire from a flak tower close to the bridge and Thompson noticed enemy soldiers with bags in their arms running to and from a building near the crossing. He thought it must be a maintenance or power plant. Fearful that the Germans were carrying demolition charges to the bridge in preparation for destroying it, Thompson quickly deployed his men, encircled the building and opened fire. "We raked the area with machine guns, overran the power plant, found four dead Germans and one wounded," Thompson recalls. "Apparently they had been carrying their personal equipment and blankets." Suddenly, two trucks came racing down the highway from Grave, heading toward the bridge. One of Thompson's men killed a driver whose truck careened off the road as its load of German soldiers scrambled to get out. The second vehicle stopped immediately and the soldiers in it jumped to the ground. Thompson's men opened up, but the Germans showed no desire to fight. Without returning fire, they ran away.

Fire was still coming from the flak tower, but by now it was passing over the heads of the platoon. "The gunners were unable to depress the 20 mm. flak gun sufficiently to get us," Thompson remembers. The platoon's bazooka man, Private Robert McGraw, crawled forward and, at a range of about seventy-five yards, fired three rounds, two of them into the top of the tower, and the gun ceased firing.

Although a twin 20 mm. gun in a tower across the river near the far end of the bridge was firing, Thompson and his men nonetheless destroyed electrical equipment and cables that they suspected were hooked up to demolitions. The platoon then set up a roadblock and placed land mines across the highway at the southwestern approach to the bridge. In the flak tower they had knocked out, they found the gunner dead but his 20 mm. weapon undamaged. Thompson's men promptly began firing it at the flak tower across the river. The platoon, he knew, would soon be reinforced by the rest of E Company coming up behind and, shortly after, by Major Wellems' battalion even now rushing from Overasselt to grab the northeastern end of the bridge. But, as far as Lieutenant Thompson was concerned, the prime objective was already taken.*

By now, the remaining battalions of Tucker's 504th Regiment were moving eastward, like spokes on a wheel, for the three road crossings and the railroad bridge over the Maas-Waal Canal. Rushing toward the bridge also were units of the 505th and 508th regiments, bent on seizing the crossings from the opposite ends. Not all these objectives were essential to the Market-Garden advance. In the surprise of the assault and the ensuing confusion, Gavin hoped to seize them all; but one, in addition to the all-important Grave bridge, would suffice.

To keep the enemy off balance, defend his positions, protect General Browning's Corps headquarters and aid his paratroopers as they moved on their objectives, Gavin was depending heavily on his howitzers; and now the guns of the 376th Parachute Field Artillery were coming in. Small artillery units had been dropped in previous operations, but they had been badly scattered and slow to assemble and fire. The unit of 544 men now approaching was hand-picked, every soldier a veteran paratrooper. Among the forty-eight planes carrying the battalion was the artillery—twelve 75 mm. howitzers, each broken down into seven pieces. The howitzers would be dropped first, followed by some 700 rounds of ammunition. Lining up, the C-47's came in and, in quick succession, the guns rolled

---

*The 82nd's after-action report and that of the 504th commander, Colonel Tucker, state the bridge was "taken" at 2:30 P.M. But Major Wellems' account states that because the bridge was still under harassing fire, the first men to actually cross from the northeastern end went over at 3:35 P.M. Still, the E Company platoon under Lieutenant Thompson held the bridge and prevented its demolition from 1:45 P.M. until it was described as "secure" at 5 P.M.

out. Ammunition and men followed, all making a near-perfect landing.

One accident caused scarcely a pause. Lieutenant Colonel Wilbur Griffith, commanding the 376th, broke his ankle on the jump but his men quickly liberated a Dutch wheelbarrow in which to carry him. "I shall never forget the Colonel being trundled from place to place," Major Augustin Hart recalls, "and barking out orders for everybody to get assembled at top speed." When the job was complete, Griffith was wheeled over to General Gavin. There he reported: "Guns in position, sir, and ready to fire on call." In just over an hour, in the most successful drop of its kind ever made, the entire battalion was assembled and ten of its howitzers were already firing.

Fourteen minutes after the 82nd's field artillery landed, Waco gliders carrying an airborne antitank battalion, engineers, elements of Division headquarters, guns, ammunition, trailers and jeeps began to come in. Of the original fifty gliders leaving England, all but four reached Holland. Not all, however, touched down on their landing zone. Some gliders ended up a mile or two away. One, copiloted by Captain Anthony Jedrziewski, cut loose late from its tug and Jedrziewski saw with horror that "we were heading straight for Germany on a one-glider invasion." The pilot made a 180-degree turn and began to look for a place to land. As they came in, Jedrziewski remembers, "we lost one wing on a haystack, the other on a fence and ended up with the glider nose in the ground. Seeing earth up to my knees, I wasn't sure if my feet were still a part of me. Then, we heard the unwelcome sound of an 88 and, in nothing flat, we had the jeep out and were racing back toward our own area."

They were luckier than Captain John Connelly, whose pilot was killed during the approach. Connelly, who had never flown a glider before, took the controls and landed the Waco just inside the German border, six to seven miles away, near the town of Wyler. Only Connelly and one other man escaped capture. They were to hide out until darkness and finally reached their units by midmorning of September 18.

Yet, in all, the 82nd Airborne had successfully brought in 7,467 paratroopers and glider-borne men. The last elements to touch down in the area were 35 Horsas and Wacos carrying

General Frederick Browning's Corps headquarters. Three gliders had been lost en route to the drop zone, two before reaching the Continent; the third, south of Vught, had crash-landed in the vicinity of General Student's headquarters. Browning's headquarters landed almost on the German frontier. "There was little flak, if any, and almost no enemy opposition," Browning's chief of staff, Brigadier Gordon Walch, remembers. "We set down about a hundred yards west of the Reichswald Forest and my glider was roughly fifty yards away from Browning's."

Colonel George S. Chatterton, commanding the Glider Pilot Regiment, was at the controls of Browning's Horsa. After clipping off a front wheel on an electric cable, Chatterton slid into a cabbage patch. "We got out," Chatterton recalls, "and Browning, looking around, said, 'By God, we're here, George!'" Nearby, Brigadier Walch saw Browning run across the landing zone toward the Reichswald. When he returned a few minutes later, he explained to Walch, "I wanted to be the first British officer to pee in Germany."

While Browning's jeep was being unloaded, a few German shells exploded nearby. Colonel Chatterton promptly threw himself into the closest ditch. "I shall never forget Browning standing above me, looking like some sort of explorer, and asking, 'George, whatever in the world are you doing down there?'" Chatterton was frank. "I'm bloody well hiding, sir," he said. "Well, you can bloody well stop hiding," Browning told him. "It's time we were going." From a pocket in his tunic, Browning took out a parcel wrapped in tissue paper. Handing it to Chatterton, he said, "Put it on my jeep." Chatterton unfolded the tissue and saw that it contained a pennant bearing a light-blue Pegasus against a maroon background, the insignia of the British Airborne.* With the pennant fluttering from the jeep's fender, the commander of the Market forces drove away.

---

*Some accounts have stated that Browning's pennant was made by his wife, the novelist Daphne du Maurier. "I am sorry," she writes, "to disappoint the mythmakers . . . but anyone who has seen my attempts to thread a needle would know this was beyond me. It is a delightful thought, however, and would have greatly amused my husband." Actually, the pennant was made by Hobson & Sons Ltd., London, under the supervision of Miss Claire Miller, who also, at Browning's direction, hand-sewed tiny compasses into 500 shirt collars and belts just prior to Market-Garden.

*

At Renkum Heath west of Arnhem, Lieutenant Neville Hay, the highly trained specialist in charge of the fact-gathering liaison unit "Phantom," was totally baffled. His team of experts had assembled their radio set with its special antenna and expected immediate contact with General Browning's Corps headquarters. Hay's first priority on landing was to get through to Corps and give his position. Earlier, he had learned that Division communications had broken down. While he might have anticipated that problems would arise among the less experienced Royal Signal Corps operators, he was not prepared to believe that the difficulties he was having stemmed from his own men. "We were set up on the landing zone and, although it was screened by pine woods, we had got through in considerably worse country than this," he remembers. "We kept trying and getting absolutely nothing." Until he could discover where the trouble lay, there was no way of informing General Browning of the progress of General Urquhart's division or of relaying Browning's orders to the British 1st Airborne. Ironically, the Dutch telephone system was in full operation, including a special network owned and operated by the PGEM power station authorities at Nijmegen and connected with the entire province. Had he known, all Hay had to do, with the aid of the Dutch resistance, was to pick up a telephone.

Fifteen miles away there was already anxiety at General Browning's headquarters, now set up on the edge of the Groesbeek ridge. Both of the 82nd Airborne's large communication sets had been damaged on landing. Browning's had come through safely, and one of these was allocated to the 82nd, insuring immediate communication with General Gavin. The Corps communications section had also made radio contact with General Dempsey's British 2nd Army and Airborne Corps rear headquarters in England and Browning had radio contact with the 101st. But the signal section was unable to raise Urquhart's division. Brigadier Walch believes that Corps signals was to blame. "Before the operation was planned, we asked for a proper headquarters signals section," he says. "We were frightfully cognizant that our sets were inadequate and our headquarters signals staff weak and inexperienced." While Browning could direct and influence the movements of the

82nd, the 101st and Horrocks' XXX Corps, at this vital junction the all-important battle at Arnhem was beyond his control. As Walch says, "We had absolutely no idea what was happening in Arnhem."

A kind of creeping paralysis was already beginning to affect Montgomery's plan. But at this early stage no one knew it. Throughout the entire Market-Garden area, some 20,000 Allied soldiers were in Holland, heading out to secure the bridges and hold open the corridor for the massive Garden units whose lead tanks were expected to link up with 101st paratroopers by nightfall.

9

FROM THE FLAT ROOF of a large factory near the Meuse-Escaut Canal, General Brian Horrocks, commander of the British XXX Corps, watched the last of the huge airborne glider formations pass over his waiting tanks. He had been on the roof since 11 A.M., and as he put it, "I had plenty of time to think." The sight of the vast armada was "comforting, but I was under no illusion that this was going to be an easy battle," Horrocks remembers. Meticulously, he had covered every possible contingency, even to ordering his men to take as much food, gas and ammunition as they could carry, "since we were likely to be out in the blue on our own." There was one worry the General could not eliminate, but he had not discussed it with anyone—he did not like a Sunday attack. "No assault or attack in which I had taken part during the war which started on a Sunday had ever been completely successful." Bringing up his binoculars, he studied the white ribbon of road stretching away north toward Valkenswaard and Eindhoven. Satisfied that the airborne assault had now begun, Horrocks gave the order for the Garden forces to attack. At precisely 2:15 P.M., with a thunderous roar, some 350 guns opened fire.

The bombardment was devastating. Ton after ton of explosives flayed the enemy positions up ahead. The hurricane of fire, ranging five miles in depth and concentrated over a one-mile front, caused the earth to shake beneath the tanks of the Irish Guards as they lumbered up to the start line. Behind the lead squadrons, hundreds of tanks and armored vehicles began to move slowly out of their parking positions, ready to fall into line as the first tanks moved off. And up above, a "cab rank" of rocket-firing Typhoon fighters circled endlessly, waiting on call for the commander of the Irish Guards Group, Lieutenant Colonel Joe Vandeleur, to direct them to targets up ahead. At 2:35 P.M., standing in the turret of the lead tank of No. 3 Squadron, Lieutenant Keith Heathcote shouted into his microphone, "Driver, advance!"

Slowly the tanks rumbled out of the bridgehead and moved up the road at eight miles an hour. Now, the curtain of artillery fire lifted to creep ahead of the armor at exactly the same speed. Tankers could see shells bursting barely one hundred yards in front of them. As the squadrons moved forward, engulfed in the dust of the barrage, men could not tell at times whether the tanks were safely back of their own fire.

Behind the lead squadrons came the scout cars of Lieutenant Colonel Joe Vandeleur and his cousin Giles. Standing in his car, Vandeleur could see, both in front of and behind him, infantry riding on the tanks, each tank marked with yellow streamers to identify it to the Typhoons above. "The din was unimaginable," Vandeleur remembers, "but everything was going according to plan." By now, the lead tanks had burst out of the bridgehead and were across the Dutch frontier. Captain "Mick" O'Cock, commanding No. 3 Squadron, radioed back, "Advance going well. Leading squadron has got through." Then, in seconds, the picture changed. As Vandeleur recalls, "The Germans really began to paste us."

Ensconced in well-hidden, fortified positions on both sides of the road, German gunners had not only survived the tremendous barrage but had waited until it passed over them. Holding their fire, the Germans let the first few tanks go through. Then, within two minutes three tanks of the lead squadron and six of the next were knocked out of action. Burning and disabled, they littered a half mile of road. "We had just crossed the border when we were ambushed," Lieutenant Cyril Russell recalls. "Suddenly the tanks in front either slewed across the road or burned where they stood. The awful realization dawned on me that the next one to go was the one I was sitting on. We jumped into the ditches by the roadside." As Russell went forward to see how the remainder of his platoon was faring, a machine gun opened up; he was hit in the arm and fell back into the ditch. For Russell, the war was over.

Lance Corporal James Doggart's tank was hit. "I don't remember seeing or hearing the explosion," he says. "I was suddenly flat on my back in a ditch with the tank leaning over me. I had a Bren gun across my chest and next to me was a young lad with his arm nearly severed. Nearby, another of our men was dead. The tank was on fire and I don't recall seeing any of the crew get out."

Lieutenant Barry Quinan, in the last tank of the lead squadron, remembers that his Sherman swung left into a ditch, and Quinan thought the driver was trying to bypass the burning tanks ahead. But the tank had been hit by a shell which killed both the driver and codriver. The Sherman began to burn and Quinan's gunner, "trying to scramble out of the hatch, half lifted me out of the turret before I realized we were 'brewing up.'" As the two men climbed out of the tank, Quinan saw others coming up behind. One after the other, the tanks were hit. "I actually saw the commander of one tank trying to shield his face from a sheet of flame that engulfed the entire machine."

The breakout had been stopped before it had really begun and nine disabled tanks now blocked the road. Squadrons coming up could not advance. Even if they could bypass the burning hulks, hidden German gunners would pick them off. To get the advance rolling again, Vandeleur called in the rocket-firing Typhoons and, aided by purple smoke shells fired from the tanks to indicate suspected German positions, the fighters screamed down. "It was the first time I had ever seen Typhoons in action," Vandeleur recalls, "and I was amazed at the guts of those pilots. They came in, one at a time, head to tail, flying right through our own barrage. One disintegrated right above me. It was incredible—guns firing, the roar of planes, the shouts and curses of the men. In the middle of it all, Division asked how the battle was going. My second in command just held up the microphone and said, 'Listen.'"

As the planes swooped down on their targets, Vandeleur sent forward an armored bulldozer to push the burning tanks off the road. The bedlam of the battle now raged over several

miles of highway, stretching back as far as Vandeleur's own car
and the R.A.F. communications tender, which called the Typhoons down on demand. Flight Lieutenant Donald Love, the
fighter reconnaissance pilot attached to the communications
unit, was now convinced that he should never have volunteered for the job. While Squadron Leader Max Sutherland directed the Typhoons, Love got out to see what was happening.
Black smoke billowed up from the road ahead and an antitank
gun carrier, almost in front of the communications tender, was
afire. As Love watched, a Bren gun carrier came back along the
road carrying wounded. One man's shoulder was blown off,
and his clothes were burned and charred. "I was sure we were
surrounded," says Love. "I was horrified and I kept wondering
why hadn't I stayed with the Air Force, where I belonged."

The waiting tankers farther back in the halted columns felt,
as Captain Roland Langton describes it, "a strange sense of
powerlessness. We could go neither forward nor backward."
Langton watched infantry moving up to clean out the woods
on either side of the road with two Bren gun carriers out in
front. Langton thought the soldiers might be an advance party
of the 43rd Infantry Division. "Suddenly I saw both carriers
catapulted into the air," Langton remembers. "They had run
over enemy land mines." When the smoke cleared, Langton
saw "bodies in the trees. I don't know how many, it was impossible to tell. There were pieces of men hanging from every
limb."

With the Typhoons firing only yards away from them, the
British infantry men grimly began to dig out the Germans
from their hidden trenches. Lance Corporal Doggart had escaped from the ditch where he landed when his tank was hit.
He raced across the road and jumped into an empty enemy slit
trench. "At the same moment, two Germans—one a young
fellow without a jacket, the other a tough-looking bastard of
about thirty—jumped in after me from the opposite direction,"
Doggart says. Without hesitating, Doggart kicked the older
German in the face. The younger man, immediately cowed,
surrendered. Covering both with his rifle, Doggart sent them
marching back along the road "with streams of other Germans, all running with their hands behind their heads. Those
that were too slow got a fast kick in the backside."

From the woods, in ditches, around haystacks and along the roadway, now being slowly cleared of the disabled tanks, came the stutter of Sten guns as the infantry mopped up. The Guardsmen showed no quarter, particularly toward snipers. Men remember that prisoners were made to double-time down the road, and when they slowed they were promptly prodded with bayonets. One prisoner in the now-growing lines tried to break away, but there was more than a company of infantry in the vicinity and several men recall that—in the words of one— "he was dead the second the thought entered his mind."

Joe Vandeleur watched the prisoners being marched past his scout car. As one German came along, Vandeleur caught a sudden movement. "The bastard had taken a grenade he'd concealed and lobbed it into one of our gun carriers. It went off with a tremendous explosion and I saw one of my sergeants lying in the road with his leg blown off. The German was cut down on all sides by machine guns."

At his command post, General Horrocks received word that the road was gradually being cleared and that the infantry, although suffering heavy casualties, had routed the Germans on the flanks. As he later put it, "The Micks were getting tired of being shot at, and as so often happens with these great fighters, they suddenly lost their tempers."

Perhaps no one was more enraged than Captain Eamon Fitzgerald, the 2nd Battalion's intelligence officer, who interrogated the captured crew of an antitank gun. According to Lieutenant Colonel Giles Vandeleur, "Fitzgerald had an interesting way of extracting information. A huge giant of a man, he spoke German well, but with an atrocious accent. His normal custom was to produce his pistol, poke it into the German's belly and, standing as close as possible, shout questions in the man's face." The results, Vandeleur always thought, "were positively splendid. Within a few minutes after interrogating this crew, our tanks were picking off the German camouflaged antitank positions with creditable accuracy and the road was being sufficiently cleared to allow us to continue the advance."

Many Irish Guardsmen believe Sergeant Bertie Cowan turned the tide of the battle. Commanding a 17-pounder Sherman, Cowan had spotted a German antitank position and demolished it with a single shot. During the fight, Major Edward

G. Tyler, in command of the squadron, was astonished to see that a German was standing on Cowan's tank directing operations. He saw the tank cross the road and open fire; then, busy himself, Tyler forgot the incident. Later, Tyler learned that Cowan had knocked out three German guns. "When I could take a moment, I went to congratulate him," Tyler says. "Cowan told me the Jerry on his tank had been a crew chief in the first position he'd overrun who had surrendered." He had been interrogated by Captain Fitzgerald and then returned to Cowan where he had proven "most cooperative."

The Irish Guards were on the way again, but constant fighting continued. The German crust was far tougher than anyone had anticipated. Among the prisoners were men of renowned parachute battalions and—to the complete surprise of the British—veteran infantrymen from the 9th and 10th SS Panzer divisions: elements of the combat groups General Wilhelm Bittrich had sent to bolster Student's First Parachute Army. To compound the surprise, some prisoners were discovered to belong to General von Zangen's Fifteenth Army. As the Irish Guards' war diary notes, "Our intelligence spent the day in a state of indignant surprise: one German regiment after another appeared which had no right to be there."

General Horrocks had expected that his lead tanks would drive the thirteen miles to Eindhoven "within two to three hours." Precious time had been lost, and the Irish Guards would cover only seven miles, reaching Valkenswaard by nightfall. Market-Garden was already ominously behind schedule.

In order to be as mobile as possible, General Maxwell D. Taylor's gliders had brought in mostly jeeps—no artillery. The fact that the British were late in reaching Eindhoven was a blow. Taylor had hoped for the support of the tankers' guns along the fifteen-mile stretch of corridor the Screaming Eagles must control. Taylor's Dutch liaison officers discovered the true situation—that the 101st would have to operate independently for longer than planned—almost immediately; with the aid of the resistance, they simply used the telephone to learn what was happening with the British.

With lightning speed Taylor's paratroopers took Veghel, the northernmost objective along the corridor, and its four crossings—the rail and highway bridges over the river Aa and the Willems Canal. Heavy fighting would ensue; nevertheless, these four objectives were seized within two hours. Farther south, midway between Veghel and Son, the town of St. Oedenrode and its highway crossing over the Dommel river were captured with relative ease. According to official Dutch telephone log books, Johanna Lathouwers, a loyal operator with the state telephone exchange, heard "an unmistakable American voice came on the Oed 1 (St. Oedenrode) line, at 1425 hours, asking for Valkenswaard, a connection that lasted forty minutes."*

The Americans quickly learned that the spearhead of the Garden forces had not as yet even reached Valkenswaard. It now seemed unlikely that Horrocks' tanks, already delayed, would reach Eindhoven at the southern end of the corridor before nightfall; and that would be too late to help the Americans seize and control their widespread targets. The men of the 101st had achieved spectacular success. Now, they ran into problems.

The most pressing of Taylor's objectives was the highway bridge over the Wilhelmina Canal at Son, approximately five miles north of Eindhoven. As a contingency plan in case this main traffic artery was blown, Taylor had decided to seize a bridge over the canal at Best, four miles to the west. Because the bridge was considered secondary, only a single company of the 502nd Regiment was detailed to Best, and it was thought that only a few Germans would be in the area. Taylor's intelligence was unaware that Colonel General Student's headquarters lay only ten miles northwest of the 101st drop zones and that recent arrivals of Von Zangen's Fifteenth Army were quartered at nearby Tilburg. Among these forces was Major General Walter Poppe's battered 59th Infantry Division plus a considerable amount of artillery.

Almost immediately upon approaching the bridge, H Company radioed that it had run into enemy roadblocks and was meeting strong resistance. The message signaled the beginning of a bloody battle that would last throughout the night and most of the following two days. What had begun as a single-company operation eventually involved more than an entire

---

*By Allied clocks it was actually 1525 hours; there was a one-hour difference between German and British times.

regiment. But already the heroic men of H Company, though taking heavy casualties, were blunting the first, unexpectedly strong, German blows.

While H Company was setting out for the bridge at Best, Colonel Robert F. Sink's 506th Regiment was going for the main highway bridge at Son. There was almost no opposition until troops reached the northern outskirts of the village. Then they were fired on by a German 88 artillery piece. In less than ten minutes, the advance party destroyed the gun emplacement with a bazooka and killed its crew. Fighting through the streets, the Americans were a bare fifty yards from the canal itself when the bridge was blown up, debris falling all around the paratroopers. For Colonel Sink, who was to take Eindhoven and its crossings by 8 P.M., the loss of the bridge was a bitter blow. Reacting quickly and still under fire, three men—Major James LaPrade, Second Lieutenant Millford F. Weller and Sergeant John Dunning—dived into the canal and swam to the far side. Other members of the battalion followed their lead or went across in rowboats. On the southern bank, they subdued the German opposition and set up a bridgehead.

The central column of the bridge was still intact, and 101st engineers immediately began the construction of a temporary crossing. Help came from an unexpected source. Dutch civilians reported that a considerable amount of black-market lumber was being stored by a contractor in a nearby garage. Within one and a half hours the engineers, utilizing the bridge's center trestle and the liberated lumber, spanned the canal. As Colonel Sink recalled, "the bridge was unsatisfactory from every point of view, except that it did enable me to put the rest of the regiment across, single file." Until bridging equipment could be brought up, the Market-Garden corridor at Son was reduced to a single wooden footpath.

10

FIELD MARSHAL MODEL was still shaken when he reached General Bittrich's headquarters at Doetinchem. Normally, it would have taken him no longer than half an hour to cover the distance, but today, because he had made numerous stops along the way to alert area commanders to the airborne assault, the trip had lasted well over an hour. Although the Field Marshal seemed calm, Bittrich remembers "his first words to me were, 'They almost got me! They were after the headquarters. Imagine! They almost got me!'"

Bittrich immediately brought Model up to date on the latest information received by II SS Panzer Corps. No clear picture of the Allied intent was emerging as yet, but Bittrich told Model his own theory: that the assault was aimed at containing the Fifteenth Army while the British Second Army drove for the Ruhr. That would require the Allies to capture the Nijmegen and Arnhem bridges. Model disagreed completely. The Arnhem bridge was not the objective, he said. These airborne troops would swerve and march northeast for the Ruhr. The situation, Model believed, was still too obscure for any final conclusions. He was puzzled as to why airborne forces had landed in the Nijmegen area. Nevertheless, he approved the measures Bittrich had already taken.

Bittrich still pressed the subject of the bridges. "Herr Field Marshal, I strongly urge that the bridges at Nijmegen and Arnhem be immediately destroyed," he said. Model looked at him in amazement. "They will not be destroyed," he told Bittrich firmly. "No matter what the English plan, these bridges can be defended. No. Absolutely not. The bridges are not to be blown." Then, dismissing the subject, Model said, "I'm looking for a new headquarters, Bittrich." Before Bittrich could answer, Model said again musingly, "You know, they almost got me."

At his headquarters at Vught, Colonel General Kurt Student faced a dilemma: his First Parachute Army had been split in two by the airborne assault. Without telephone communications and now solely dependent on radio, he was unable to direct his divided army. For the moment units were fighting on their own without any cohesive direction. Then, by a momentous and fantastic stroke of luck, an undamaged briefcase found in a downed Waco glider near his headquarters was rushed to him.

"It was incredible," Student says. "In the case was the complete enemy attack order for the operation." Student and his staff officers pored over the captured plans. "They showed us everything—the dropping zones, the corridor, the objectives,

even the names of the divisions involved. Everything! Immediately we could see the strategic implications. They had to grab
the bridges before we could destroy them. All I could think
of was, 'This is retribution. Retribution! History is repeating
itself.' During our airborne operation in Holland in 1940, one
of my officers, against strict orders, had taken into battle papers
that detailed our entire attack, and these had fallen into enemy
hands. Now the wheel had turned full circle. I knew exactly
what I had to do."*

Model, as yet, did not. Student had never felt so frustrated.
Because of his communications breakdown, it would be nearly
ten hours before he could place the secret of Market-Garden
in Model's possession. The secret was that the Arnhem bridge
was of crucial importance. The captured plans clearly showed
that it was Montgomery's route into the Ruhr.

This was the kind of battle that Model liked best: one that
demanded improvisation, daring and, above all, speed. From
Bittrich's headquarters, Model telephoned OB West, Von
Rundstedt. With characteristic abruptness, he described the situation and asked for immediate reinforcements. "The only way
this airborne assault can be defeated is to strike hard within the
first twenty-four hours," he told Von Rundstedt. Model asked
for antiaircraft units, self-propelled guns, tanks and infantry;
and he wanted them on the move to Arnhem by nightfall. Von
Rundstedt told him that such reinforcements as were available
would be on the way. Turning to Bittrich, Model said trium-
phantly, "Now, we'll get reinforcements!" Model had decided

*In the legend of Arnhem the story of the captured documents, like that of
the spy Lindemans, is always included. Some accounts claim that the Market-
Garden plan was found on the body of a dead American captain. I interviewed
Student and examined all his documents. At no point does he confirm that
the briefcase was carried by a captain. Nor is there any such mention in official
British and American records. Perhaps, since Student says that the plans came
from "a Waco freight glider," it was generally assumed that only American personnel were aboard. However, part of General Browning's Corps headquarters flew to Holland in Wacos; and one of these did crash-land near Student's
headquarters. In any case, whether the personnel were British or American, I
think it highly unlikely that the entire Market-Garden operational plan could
have been in the possession of a captain. First, great care was taken in the distribution of the plan; and second, each copy was both numbered and restricted
solely to officers of staff rank.

to operate from Doetinchem; but, although he was apparently recovered from the shock of his hasty departure from Oosterbeek, this time he was taking no chances of being caught unawares. He refused accommodations at the castle; he would direct the battle from the gardener's cottage on the grounds.

Bittrich's early foresight was already having its effect. Sections of Harzer's Hohenstaufen Division were heading swiftly toward the battle zone. Harmel's Frundsberg Division—Harmel himself was expected back from Germany during the night—were on the move, too. Bittrich had ordered Harzer to set up his headquarters in a high school in the northern Arnhem suburbs overlooking the city, and that transfer was underway. But Harzer was chafing with impatience. The armored vehicles that had been scheduled to leave for Germany in the early afternoon were still being refitted with tracks and guns. Harzer had already moved the units closest to the British landing and drop zones into blocking positions at points west of Arnhem. For the moment, he had only a few armored cars, several self-propelled guns, a few tanks and some infantry. Still, Harzer hoped that by employing hit-and-run tactics he could halt and confuse British troops until the bulk of his division was again battle-ready.

Curiously, Harzer did not even know that Major Sepp Krafft's SS Panzer Grenadier Training and Reserve Battalion was in the area and, at the moment, the only unit in the path of the British airborne forces. Harzer concentrated his own strength on the two major highways running into Arnhem: the Ede-Arnhem road and the Utrecht-Arnhem road. Certain that the paratroopers must use these main arteries, he placed his units in a semicircular screen across the two highways. By oversight, or perhaps because he lacked sufficient forces at the moment, Harzer failed to position any groups along a quiet secondary road running parallel to the northern bank of the Rhine. It was the single unprotected route the British could take to the Arnhem bridge.

II

In their camouflage battle smocks and distinctive crash helmets, laden with weapons and ammunition, the men of Brigadier Lathbury's 1st Parachute Brigade were on the way to Arnhem. Interspersed among the columns of marching troopers were jeeps pulling artillery pieces and four-wheeled carts loaded with guns and stores. As General Roy Urquhart watched them pass, he remembered a compliment paid him some months before by General Horrocks. "Your men are killers," Horrocks had said admiringly. At the time, Urquhart had considered the remark an overstatement. On this Sunday, he was not so sure. As the 1st Brigade had moved off, Urquhart had felt a surge of pride.

The plan called for the three battalions of Lathbury's brigade to converge on Arnhem, each from a different direction. Lieutenant Colonel John Frost's 2nd Battalion was given the prime objective: marching along a secondary road running close to the north bank of the Rhine, Frost's men were to capture the main highway bridge. En route, they were to take the railway and pontoon bridges west of the great highway crossing. The 3rd Battalion, under Lieutenant Colonel J. A. C. Fitch, would move along the Utrecht-Arnhem road and approach the bridge from the north, reinforcing Frost. Once these two battalions had been successfully launched, Lieutenant Colonel D. Dobie's 1st Battalion was to advance along the main Ede-Arnhem highway—the most northerly route—and occupy the high ground north of the city. Lathbury had given each route a code name. Dobie's, farthest north, was designated "Leopard"; Fitch's, in the middle, was "Tiger"; and Frost's, the most crucial route, was "Lion." Speeding ahead of the entire brigade, the jeeps of Major Freddie Gough's reconnaissance squadron were expected to reach the bridge, seize it in a *coup de main*, and hold until Frost arrived.

So far, Urquhart thought, the initial phase was going well. He was not unduly alarmed by the breakdown of communications within the division at this time. He had experienced temporary signals disruption often in the North African desert campaigns. Since he could not raise Brigadier Hicks's 1st Airlanding Brigade, whose job it was to hold the landing and drop zones for the air lifts on the following two days, Urquhart drove to Hicks's headquarters. The Airlanding Brigade, he learned, was in position, and Hicks was for the moment away directing the disposition of his battalions. However, at Hicks's headquarters, Urquhart received news that one vital part of the plan to take the Arnhem bridge had gone wrong. He was told—erroneously—that most of Major Freddie Gough's reconnaissance vehicles had been lost in glider crashes; no one at Hicks's headquarters knew where Gough had gone. Without waiting for Hicks to return, Urquhart drove back to his own headquarters. He had to find Gough quickly and devise some alternative plan, but his greatest concern now was to warn Lathbury and, in particular, Frost, that the 2nd Battalion was on its own. Frost would have to take the main Arnhem bridge without the aid of Gough's planned surprise attack.

At Division, further bad news awaited Urquhart. "Not only was there no word of Gough," Urquhart recalls, "but apart from some short-range radio signals, headquarters communications had completely failed. The 1st Parachute Brigade and, indeed, the outside world, could not be contacted." Colonel Charles Mackenzie, Urquhart's chief of staff, watched the General pace up and down, "restive and anxious for news." Urquhart ordered his signals officer, Major Anthony Deane-Drummond, to investigate the "communications foul-up, see what had happened to the radio equipment and then set it right." Messengers were also sent out in search of Gough. As time passed without any new information, the worried Urquhart decided to wait no longer. Normally, he would have directed the battle from Division headquarters; but now, as each moment passed without communications, he was beginning to feel that this battle was anything but normal. Turning to Mackenzie, he said, "I think I'll go and have a look myself, Charles." Mackenzie did not try to stop him. "At the time," Mackenzie recalls, "since we were getting practically no information, it didn't seem a particularly bad thing to do." Taking only his driver and a signalman in his jeep, Urquhart set out after Lathbury. The time was 4:30 P.M.

Moving along the northern, Leopard route—the Ede-Arnhem road—Major Freddie Gough of the 1st Airlanding reconnaissance unit was making good time. Although the vehicles of A troop had failed to arrive, Gough had started off from the landing zone with the rest of the squadrons at 3:30 P.M. He was confident that he had sufficient jeeps for the *coup de main* attempt on the bridge. "In fact," he remembered, "I left several jeeps behind on the landing zone in reserve. We had more than enough to get to Arnhem." Gough had even detached twelve men from his unit to make their way south to join the 2nd Battalion, moving on the Lion route to the bridge. He was unaware that the loss of A troop's jeeps had raised a flurry of rumors and misinformation.*

From the beginning, Gough had had reservations about his recco unit's role in the Arnhem plan. Instead of a *coup de main*, Gough had urged that a screen of reconnaissance jeeps be sent ahead of each of the three battalions. "In that way," he says, "we would have quickly discovered the best and easiest way to reach the bridge." Failing that, he had asked that a troop of light tanks be brought in by glider to escort the *coup de main* force. Both requests had been turned down. Yet Gough had remained optimistic. "I wasn't the least bit concerned. There were supposed to be only a few old, gray Germans in Arnhem and some ancient tanks and guns. I expected it to be a pushover."

Now, as they moved swiftly along Leopard, the lead jeeps of the unit were suddenly ambushed by German armored cars and 20 mm. guns. Gough's second in command, Captain David Allsop, happened to note the time. It was exactly 4 P.M. Gough pulled out to drive to the head of the column and investigate. "Just as I was on the point of going forward, I got a message saying that Urquhart wanted to see me immediately. I didn't know what the hell to do," Gough says. "I was under Lathbury, and I thought I should at least tell him I was going, but I had no idea where he was. The unit was now in a heavy fire fight and pinned down in defensive positions near the railroad tracks on the outskirts of Wolfheze. I reckoned they would be all right for a time, so I turned around and headed back to Division headquarters on the landing zone. That was at 4:30."

---

*Some accounts of the Arnhem battle claim that Gough's unit could not operate because so many of his vehicles failed to arrive by glider. "The failure, if it can be called that," Gough says, "was not due to a lack of jeeps, but to the fact that no one had warned us that the 9th and 10th SS Panzer divisions were in the area."

At the precise moment that General Urquhart set out to find Lathbury, Gough was speeding back to Division to report to Urquhart.

All along the three strategic lines of march, the men of the 1st Parachute Brigade were encountering jubilant, hysterical throngs of Dutch. Many civilians from farms and outlying hamlets had followed the paratroopers from the time they left the landing zones, and as the crowds grew, the welcome seemed almost to overwhelm the march itself. Captain Eric Mackay, traveling the southernmost, Lion route with Colonel Frost's 2nd Battalion, was disturbed by the holiday atmosphere. "We were hampered by Dutch civilians," he says. "Waving, cheering and clapping their hands, they offered us apples, pears, something to drink. But they interfered with our progress and filled me with dread that they would give our positions away." Lieutenant Robin Vlasto remembers that "the first part of our march was in the nature of a victory parade, and the civilians were quite delirious with joy. It all seemed so unbelievable that we almost expected to see Horrocks' XXX Corps tanks coming out of Arnhem to meet us. People lined the road and great trays of beer, milk and fruit were offered. We had the greatest difficulty forcing the men to keep alive to the possibility of a German attack."

Young Anje van Maanen, whose father was a doctor in Oosterbeek, recalls receiving an exuberant call from the Tromp family in Heelsum, just south of the British landing zone on Renkum Heath. "We are free. Free!" the Tromps told her. "The Tommies dropped behind our house and they are on their way to Oosterbeek. They are so nice! We are smoking Players and eating chocolate." Anje put the phone down, "crazy with joy. We all jumped and danced around. This is it! An invasion! Lovely!" Seventeen-year-old Anje could hardly wait for her father to come home. Dr. van Maanen was delivering a baby at a patient's home, and Anje thought it "very annoying, particularly now, because the husband of the woman was a Dutch Nazi." Mrs. Ida Clous, the wife of an Oosterbeek dentist and a friend of the Van Maanens, also heard that the airborne troops were on their way. She worked feverishly, hunting through boxes and sewing scraps to find every bit of orange cloth she possessed. When the British got to Oosterbeek, she intended to rush outside with her three small children and greet the deliverers with small handmade orange flags.

Jan Voskuil, hiding out in the home of his wife's parents in Oosterbeek, was torn between his own desire to head up the Utrecht road to greet the paratroopers and the need to prevent his father-in-law from coming with him. The elder man was adamant. "I'm seventy-eight years old and I've never been in a war before and I want to see it." Voskuil's father-in-law was finally persuaded to stay in the garden and Voskuil, joining streams of other civilians heading out to meet the British, was turned back by a policeman on the outskirts of Oosterbeek. "It's too dangerous," the officer told the crowds. "Go back." Voskuil walked slowly home. There he ran into the same German soldier who had asked for shelter when the bombing had begun during the morning. Now the soldier was in full uniform, with camouflage jacket, helmet and rifle. He offered Voskuil some chocolates and cigarettes. "I am going away now," he said. "The Tommies will come." Voskuil smiled. "Now, you will go back to Germany," he said. The soldier studied Voskuil for several seconds. Then he shook his head slowly. "No, sir," he told Voskuil. "We will fight." The Dutchman watched the German walk away. "It begins now," Voskuil thought, "but what can I do?" Impatiently he paced the yard. There was nothing to do but wait.

Unhampered by police restraints or warnings to stay indoors, Dutch farmers and their families lined each route of march in throngs. Sergeant Major Harry Callaghan, on the middle, Tiger route, remembers a farm woman breaking through the crowds and running toward him with a pitcher of milk. He thanked her and the woman smiled and said, "Good, Tommy. Good." But, like Eric Mackay on the lower road, Callaghan, a Dunkirk veteran, was bothered by the number of civilians surrounding the troops. "They ran along beside us wearing armbands, aprons, and little pieces of ribbon, all orange," he remembers. "Children, with little snippets of orange cloth pinned to their skirts or blouses, skipped along, shrieking with delight. Most of the men were reaching in their packs to hand them chocolate. It was such a different atmosphere that the men were behaving as if they were on an exercise. I began to be concerned about snipers."

As Callaghan had feared, the victory parade came to a sudden halt. "It all happened so quickly," he says. "One moment we were marching steadily toward Arnhem; the next, we were scattered in the ditches. Snipers had opened fire, and three dead airborne soldiers lay across the road." The veteran sergeant major wasted no time. He had spotted a burst of flame from trees about fifty yards ahead. As the Dutch scattered, Callaghan took a party of twelve men forward. He stopped short of one tree and looked up. Something flashed. Raising his Sten gun, he fired directly into the tree. A Schmeisser automatic pistol clattered to the ground and, as Callaghan sighted up along the trunk of the tree, he saw a German dangling limply from a rope.

Now, too, on the middle route, other men from Lieutenant Colonel Fitch's 3rd Battalion were suddenly engaged in an unexpected encounter. Private Frederick Bennett had just passed around some apples to other troopers when a German staff car came speeding down the road. Bennett opened up with his Sten gun. The car screeched to a stop and tried to back up. But it was too late. Everyone near Bennett began firing and the car came to an abrupt halt, riddled with bullets. As the troopers cautiously approached, they saw that the driver was hanging halfway out of the car. The body of a senior German officer had been thrown partly out another door. To Bennett "he looked like some high-ranking Jerry officer," as indeed he was. Major General Kussin, the Arnhem town commander, had disregarded the warning of SS Major Sepp Krafft to avoid the main Utrecht-Arnhem road.*

---

*Kussin, on Model's orders issued as the Field Marshal fled east that morning, had informed Hitler's headquarters of the landings and of Model's narrow escape. The Allied assault had caused Hitler hysterical concern. "If such a mess happens here," he conjectured, "here I sit with my own Supreme Command —Goering, Himmler, Ribbentrop. Well, then, this is a most worthwhile catch. That's obvious. I would not hesitate to risk two parachute divisions here if with one blow I could get my hands on the whole German command."

Many men recall that the first serious German opposition began after the first hour of march—around 4:30 P.M. Then two of the three battalions—Dobie's, on the northern route, and Fitch's, in the center—were unexpectedly engaged in fierce enemy hit-and-run attacks. Major Gough's reconnaissance unit, now commanded by Captain Allsop, was desperately trying to find a way to outflank the German forces and clear a path for Dobie's 1st Battalion. But, according to Allsop, "each movement we made was blunted by an enemy force in front of us." Trooper William Chandler of the reconnaissance unit remembers that as his C Troop explored the terrain, "German bullets came so close and so thick that they almost stung as they went by."

As the battalion approached Wolfheze, it was almost completely stopped. "We halted," Private Walter Boldock recalls. "Then we started off again. Then we halted and dug in. Next, we moved on again, changing direction. Our progress was dictated by the success of the lead companies. Mortar bombs and bullets harassed us all the way." Beside a hedge, Boldock saw a sergeant he knew, lying seriously wounded. Farther ahead, he came upon the smoldering body of a lieutenant. He had been hit by a phosphorus bomb. To another soldier, Private Roy Edwards, "it just seemed we kept making a detour of the countryside and getting into running battles all afternoon."

The paratroopers were stunned by the ferociousness of the unanticipated enemy attacks. Private Andrew Milbourne, on the northern route, heard firing in the distance off to the south and was momentarily glad that the 1st Battalion had been given the assignment to hold the high ground north of Arnhem. Then, nearing Wolfheze, Milbourne realized that the column had swung south off the main road. He saw the railway station and, close to it, a tank. His first reaction was one of elation. "My God!" he thought, "Monty was right. The Second Army's here already!" Then, as the turret swung slowly around, Milbourne saw that a black cross was painted on the tank. Suddenly, he seemed to see Germans everywhere. He dived into a ditch and, raising his head cautiously, began looking for a good spot to position his Vickers machine gun.

Sergeant Reginald Isherwood saw the same tank. A jeep towing a light artillery piece drove up and started to turn around in order to engage it. "One of their sergeants yelled, 'We'd better fire before they do. Otherwise we've had it,'" Isherwood recalls. "The gun was swung around like lightning, but as our man yelled 'Fire!' I heard the German commander do the same. The Jerries must have got their shell off one tenth of a second sooner than us." The tank scored a direct hit. The jeep exploded and the gun crew were killed.

In the mounting confusion and the intense fire from all sides, it was now clear to Colonel Dobie that the opposition in front of him was heavier than anyone had expected. Nor did he believe it was still possible to occupy the high ground north of Arnhem. He was unable to raise Brigadier Lathbury by radio, and his casualties were mounting by the minute. Dobie decided to side-slip the battalion still farther south and attempt to join up with Frost going for the main Arnhem bridge.

The breakdown of communications and subsequent lack of direction was making it impossible for battalion commanders to know with any clarity what was happening now. In the unfamiliar countryside, with maps that often proved highly inaccurate, companies and platoons were frequently out of touch with one another. At a crossroads near the stretch of highway where men of Colonel Fitch's 3rd Battalion had killed General Kussin, the British caught the full brunt of SS Major Krafft's rocket-propelled mortars and machine guns. The marching columns broke as men scattered into the woods. The screeching mortars, exploding in air bursts above their heads, hurled deadly fragments in every direction.

Signalman Stanley Heyes remembers the intense enemy harassment vividly. He sprinted for some woods and dropped a spare radio transmitter; bending to recover it he was struck in the ankle. Heyes managed to crawl into the woods. As he sank down in the underbrush, he realized that the man alongside him was German. "He was young and as frightened as I was," Heyes says, "but he used my field dressing on my ankle. A short time later we both were wounded again by the mortar fire and we just lay there waiting for someone to pick us up." Heyes and the young German would remain together until well after dark, when British stretcher-bearers found and evacuated them.

Like the 1st Battalion, the 3rd too was pinned down. After

two hours on the road, both battalions had covered a bare two and a half miles. Now, Colonel Fitch reached the same conclusion as Dobie on the upper road; he too would have to find an alternate route to the Arnhem bridge. Time was precious, and the bridge was still a good four miles away.

In the woods around Wolfheze SS Major Sepp Krafft was convinced he was surrounded. He estimated that the British outnumbered his understrength battalion by twenty to one. But, although he considered his defense "insane," he could hardly believe the success of his blocking action. The rocket-propelled mortars had created havoc among the British, and his men now reported that paratroopers moving along the Utrecht-Arnhem road were halted in some places, and at others appeared to be abandoning the main road entirely. Krafft still believed that his was the only German unit in the area, and he had no illusions about stopping the British for long. He was running out of mortar ammunition and suffering heavy casualties, and one of his lieutenants had deserted. Still, Krafft was ebullient about "the courageous impetuosity of my young lads." The ambitious Krafft, who would later write a fulsome self-serving report to Himmler on his Grenadier Training and Reserve Battalion's actions, had no idea that his "young lads" were now being bolstered by the tanks, artillery and armored cars of Lieutenant Colonel Walter Harzer's Hohenstaufen Division only a mile or two east of Krafft's own headquarters.

Major Freddie Gough was totally baffled. Urquhart's message summoning him back to Division had carried no hint of what the General had in mind. When he left the Leopard route of the 1st Battalion, Gough brought back with him four escort jeeps and troops of his reconnaissance unit. Now, at Division headquarters, Urquhart's chief of staff, Colonel Charles Mackenzie, could not enlighten him either. The General, Mackenzie said, had gone off in search of Brigadier Lathbury, whose headquarters was following Colonel Frost's battalion along the southern, Lion route. Taking his escort, Gough set out once more. Surely, someplace along the route, he would find either one officer or the other.

THE PRIZE [FOLLOWING SPREAD]

The most northern of all crossings to be seized by Anglo-American and Polish airborne forces was the Arnhem bridge over the Lower Rhine. Assigned to Major General Urquhart's British 1st Airborne Division and Major General Sosabowski's Polish 1st Parachute Brigade, it was the key to Montgomery's plan to end the war in 1944. Photo shows bridge with long boulevards stretching back to the concert hall complex, Musis Sacrum (left foreground).

The Bridges: Urquhart's men were also to capture the Arnhem railroad crossing and the pontoon bridge. The Germans blew up the former, and the middle section of the latter was found missing. Mystery surrounds RAF photo of pontoon bridge [LEFT] taken eleven days before attack: were Germans replacing or removing the center? No one could tell, but attack was ordered just the same.

Major General Gavin's 82nd Airborne swiftly captured the 1,500-foot-long Grave bridge over the Maas River [OPPOSITE TOP] and, among others, the Heumen Canal bridge [OPPOSITE CENTER]. But due to confusion in orders and quick German reaction, they failed to capture on the first day Nijmegen bridge, over the Waal [BELOW], eleven miles from Arnhem. Crossing fell in combined Anglo-American attack on the 20th when the 82nd made a daring river assault which has been called a "second Omaha Beach landing."

outh of 82nd's positions, Major General Taylor's 101st Airborne captured
l bridges but one: the crossing at Son [BOTTOM] was blown up, throwing
Iarket-Garden's schedule off by 36 hours.

Eisenhower and Montgomery were bitterly opposed on war strategy. Montgomery thought Supreme Commander indecisi with "no experience for the job"; Eisenhower considered Britain's popular Field Marsha "an egocentric who never mad a mistake in his life."

New chief of First Allied Airborne Army, Lieutenant General Brereton, had never commanded paratroops before. He was in disagreement with British deputy, Lieutenant General Browning. Hours before attack planning began, Brereton received a letter of resignation from Browning.

Browning, Britain's foremost airborne authority, withdrew his resignation whe named to command Market-Garden. He had never had operational control o an airborne corps before.

Left to right) Major General Adair, commander of Guards Armored Division; Field Marshal Montgomery; Lieutenant General Horrocks, whose XXX Corps tanks and infantry would make drive; and Major General Roberts, whose Eleventh Armored captured Antwerp but was halted to "refuel, refit and rest," thus allowing bulk of German Fifteenth Army to reach Holland and participate in Market-Garden offensive.

[BELOW LEFT] Major General Taylor, commander of the U.S. 101st Airborne, meets with Lieutenant General Ritchie, of 12th British Corps; and [RIGHT] General Dempsey, chief of Second British Army, confers with Brigadier General Gavin, U.S. 82nd Airborne Commander.

Dutch intelligence man Henri Knap [TOP LEFT] with Arnhem underground chief Pieter Kruyff [TOP RIGHT] warned London of Panzer divisions in Arnhem area on September 14th. • [ABOVE] Major Brian Urquhart, Browning's intelligence chief, also spotted German tanks on RAF reconnaissance photos. Warnings went unheeded. • [LOWER LEFT] Major General "Roy" Urquhart, commander of British 1st Airborne, though veteran combat leader, was commanding paratroop division for first time. He was not only unaware of German armor but was forced to land his units from six to eight miles from crucial Arnhem bridge. Hardly had the attack begun than communications failed, and General Urquhart, cut off from headquarters behind German lines, was forced to hide out for 39 vital hours.

With Urquhart "missing," Brigadier Hicks [TOP LEFT] was forced to lead the division. • When 4th Parachute Brigade landed, September 18th, Brigadier Hackett [TOP RIGHT], because of seniority, challenged Hicks over division command. • Urquhart's Chief of Staff, Colonel Mackenzie [CENTER LEFT], calmed down arguing brigadiers. • Meanwhile, unaware of true situation in Arnhem, General Sosabowski [CENTER RIGHT] and his Polish 1st Parachute Brigade were delayed more than two days because of bad weather. • Brigadier Lathbury [RIGHT], commander of 1st Parachute Brigade, should have assumed division leadership, but was wounded and, like General Urquhart, considered "missing."

Holding northern approaches to Arnhem bridge and outnumbered by at least 10 to 1, Colonel John Frost [LEFT], with his men, in one of history's greatest feats of arms, held off elements of two German Panzer divisions.

Another bridge hero, Captain Eric Mackay [CENTER, AS HE IS TODAY], though almost out of ammunition, actually called on Germans to surrender. Wounded and captured, Mackay [BELOW AT TILLER] refused to give up; he escaped and floated downstream to Nijmegen with companions.

rish Guards tank group led the armored breakout from Dutch-Belgian border. Shown here are its commander, Colonel J. O. E. Vandeleur [ABOVE LEFT], and his cousin Giles, a battalion commander [ABOVE RIGHT]. [BELOW] The two men as they appeared in 1944. The Germans succeeded in halting Vandeleur's tanks barely six miles short of Frost's men on Arnhem bridge.

RAF Flight Lieutenant Love [TOP], ground-to-air communications officer during tank drive, wondered why he had volunteered for job. • Lord Wrottesley [LEFT CENTER], who made first contact with Urquhart's isolated troops. • Lieutenant Hay [RIGHT CENTER], whose "Phantom" radio unit finally contacted ground forces for Urquhart. • Colonel Chatterton [RIGHT], Glider Pilot Regiment commander, who pressed for a daring glider *coup-de-main* on Arnhem bridge. Had his plan been adopted, the bridge might have been taken within hours. Instead, Chatterton was called "an assassin and a bloody murderer" for suggesting the idea.

In his division's last stand at Oosterbeek, Major Cain [ABOVE LEFT], though wounded again and again, continued to fight back against enemy tanks. • Miss Clair Miller [ABOVE RIGHT], of London's Hobson & Sons Ltd., made Browning's Pegasus flag, contrary to the Arnhem myth that it was the work of his wife, novelist Daphne du Maurier. Miss Miller also sewed 500 tiny compasses into troopers' uniforms, which later aided many in making an escape. • Major Lonsdale [BELOW LEFT], whose "Lonsdale Force" held out to the very end.

In the Anglo-American attack on Nijmegen bridge, 82nd Airborne's Major Cook [ABOVE RIGHT] led the unprecedented crossing of Waal River to seize bridge's northern end. Simultaneously Lieutenant Colonel Vandervoort [ABOVE LEFT], together with British forces, attacked southern approaches.

Military Cross winner Lieutenant Gorman [ABOVE LEFT] had his "doubts" about the entire operation. He felt that no one was moving fast enough to rescue Frost's men on Arnhem bridge. • Lieutenant Wierzbowski [ABOVE RIGHT] was sent with a company to capture the bridge at Best, which was believed to be "lightly held." The area actually contained more than 1,000 German troops of the forgotten Fifteenth Army and in the end involved an entire regiment of the 101st Airborne.

Lieutenant Glover [ABOVE LEFT], who took his pet chicken, Myrtle, on the Arnhem jump. "Myrtle, the parachick" was killed and in the midst of the fighting was given a formal burial. • Major Deane-Drummond [ABOVE RIGHT], second in command, 1st Airborne Division Signals, had doubts that his communications would work, but like everyone else was "swept along with the prevailing attitude," which was "For God's sake, don't rock the boat." • Colonel Tucker [RIGHT], 504th regimental commander, whose units crossed Waal River, was appalled at slowness of British tanks. He had expected a special task force to make the eleven-mile dash to Arnhem and relieve bridge defenders. Instead, Tucker said, the British "stopped for tea."

Fired by Hitler after the Normandy débacle, Von Rundstedt [LEFT], the Reich's most competent Field Marshal, was recalled in September. The situation on the western front was so catastrophic that Von Rundstedt believed the Allies could invade the Reich and end the war within two weeks. His strategy in saving Fifteenth Army was a major factor in defeating Montgomery's Market-Garden plan. Field Marshal Model [BELOW], whom Von Rundstedt called a "good regimental sergeant major," had been unable to halt Allied drive across western Europe, but by chance had moved the II SS Panzer Corps into the Arnhem area days before the airborne attack. Captured Market-Garden plans were in his hands within 48 hours, but, incredibly, Model refused to believe them.

I SS Panzer Corps commander, Lieutenant General Bittrich [SHOWN ABOVE S HE IS TODAY AND IN 1944], knew nothing of captured Market-Garden lans, but correctly deduced that main objective was Arnhem bridge.

'he Reich's airborne expert, Colonel General Student [IN 1944 AND TODAY], as stunned by the size of airborne drop and "only wished I had had such orces at my disposal."

The British landed virtually amidst two Panzer divisions in the Arnhem area, to the surprise of their commanders: Lieutenant Colonel Harzer [ABOVE AS HE IS TODAY AND IN 1944] of 9th SS "Hohenstaufen" Division; Major General Harmel [BELOW] of 10th SS "Frundsberg" Division.

Double agent "King Kong" Lindemanns [RIGHT] crossed front lines to inform Germans of British ground attack on September 17th. Contrary to British newspaper reports after the war, Lindemanns knew nothing about scope of airborne attack.

Luftwaffe General Dessloch [ABOVE LEFT] was so worried about possibility of airborne attack that he refused to visit Model. The battalion of Major Krafft [ABOVE RIGHT] was by chance in position on the edge of British drop zones.

The first man at Model's headquarters in Tafelberg Hotel to learn of airborne drop barely two miles away was Lieutenant Sedelhauser [RIGHT]. "They are dropping in our laps," he was told.

Prince Bernhard [ABOVE] shown as he arrived in liberated Eindhoven and [OPPOSITE] as he is today. Neither Bernhard nor his general staff were consulted about terrain difficulty in the Market-Garden plan until it was too late, and detailed information which the Prince had from Dutch underground sources regarding German armor in Arnhem was discounted.

Expecting liberation, the Dutch in Oosterbeek found themselves caught up in brutal battle. "Montgomery will be here soon," optimistic Britishers told 17-year-old Anje van Maanen [ABOVE LEFT]. • Jan Voskuil [ABOVE RIGHT] could not rid himself of a "feeling of hopelessness." • Hendrika van der Vlist [BELOW] wrote in her diary that Oosterbeek had become "one of the bloodiest battlefields."

Kate ter Horst [ABOVE] with son Michiel during war and [BELOW] with husband, Jan, as they are today, courageously made her home available to British wounded. At one time during battle more than 300 casualties crowded the house.

A former Dutch captain, Jan could not understand why the British failed to use Driel ferry [NEXT PAGE] to cross the Rhine. In Market-Garden planning the ferry was completely overlooked.

12

GENERAL URQUHART'S JEEP sped down the Utrecht-Arnhem highway and turned south off the main artery onto a side road that led him to Frost's Lion route. Within a few minutes he caught up with the rear elements of the 2nd Battalion. They were moving single file, along both sides of the road. Urquhart could hear firing in the distance, but it seemed to him "there was a lack of urgency. Everyone appeared to be moving slowly." Driving swiftly along the cobbled road, Urquhart reached Frost's headquarters company only to discover that Frost was up with the leading units, which had run into German opposition. "I tried to impart a sense of urgency that I hoped would be conveyed to Frost," Urquhart writes, "and told them about the ill-fortune of the Recco Squadron." Learning that Lathbury had gone up to the middle road to see how the 3rd Battalion was doing, Urquhart retraced his route. Once again, he and Gough would miss each other by minutes.

Reaching the rear elements of the 3rd Battalion on the Tiger route, the General was told that Lathbury had gone forward. He followed. At a crossroads on the Utrecht-Arnhem road, Urquhart found the Brigadier. The area was under devastating mortar fire. "Some of these bombs were falling with unsettling accuracy on the crossroads and in the woodland where many of the Third Battalion were under cover," Urquhart was later to write. "This was the first real evidence to come my way of the speed and determination of the German reaction."*

Taking cover in a slit trench, Urquhart and Lathbury discussed the situation. Both officers were worried about the slow progress of the brigade, and now the critical lack of communications was paralyzing their own efforts to command. Lathbury was completely out of touch with the 1st Battalion and had only intermittent communication with Frost. It was apparent that both were able to direct operations only in the area where they physically happened to be. For the moment,

---

*Major General R. E. Urquhart, C.B., D.S.O. (with Wilfred Greatorex), *Arnhem*, p. 40.

Lathbury's concern was to get the 3rd Battalion off the cross-roads, out of the surrounding woods and on the move again. Urquhart decided to try to contact Division headquarters on his jeep's radio. As he neared the vehicle, he saw it had been struck by a mortar and his signalman was badly wounded. Although the radio set seemed undamaged, Urquhart could not raise Division. "I cursed the appalling communications," Urquhart later wrote. "Lathbury dissuaded me from attempting to go back to my own headquarters. The enemy was now thick between us and the landing zones . . . I decided he was right . . . and I stayed. But it was at this point that I realized I was losing control of the situation."

The men of the 1st and 3rd battalions were engaging in constant, bitter skirmishes. Hardened and desperate Waffen SS troopers, inferior in numbers but bolstered by half-tracks, artillery and tanks, were reducing the British advance on the two upper roads to a crawl. In the confusion, men were separated from their officers and from one another as companies scattered into the woods or fought along side roads and in the back gardens of houses. The Red Devils had recovered from the initial surprise of the German armored strength and, though taking heavy casualties, individually and in small groups they were striking back tenaciously. Still, there was little chance that the 1st and 3rd battalions could reach their Arnhem objectives as planned. Now everything depended upon Colonel John Frost's 2nd Battalion, moving steadily along the lower Rhine road, the secondary route that the Germans had largely dismissed.

Although Frost's battalion had been held up briefly several times by enemy fire, he had refused to allow his men to scatter or deploy. His spearheading A Company, commanded by Major Digby Tatham-Warter, pressed forward, leaving stragglers to join the companies coming up behind. From prisoners taken by the advance parties, Frost learned that an SS company was believed to be covering the western approaches of Arnhem. Using some captured transport as well as their own jeeps to scout ahead and to the sides, the battalion moved steadily on. A little after 6 P.M., the first of Frost's objectives, the railway bridge over the Lower Rhine slightly southeast of Oosterbeek, came into view. According to plan, Major Victor Dover's C

Company peeled off and headed for the river. The bridge looked empty and undefended as they approached. Lieutenant Peter Barry, twenty-one, was ordered to take his platoon across. "It was quiet when we started out," Barry recalls. "As we ran across the fields I noticed that there were dead cattle everywhere." Barry's platoon was within 300 yards of the bridge when he saw "a German run onto the bridge from the other side. He reached the middle, knelt down, and started doing something. Immediately, I told one section to open fire and a second section to rush the bridge. By this time, the German had disappeared."

Barry recalls that they "got onto the bridge and began racing across at full speed. Suddenly, there was a tremendous explosion and the bridge went up in our faces." Captain Eric Mackay of the Royal Engineers felt the ground shake under the impact. "A yellow-orange flame punched up and then black smoke rose over the bridge. I think the second span from the south bank was blown," Mackay says. On the bridge, under cover of smoke bombs, Lieutenant Barry ordered his men off the wreckage and back to the northern bank. As the platoon began to move, Germans hidden across the river opened fire. Barry was hit in the leg and arm and two other men were wounded. Watching the troopers return through the smoke and fire, Mackay, who had been uneasy about the operation from the beginning, remembers thinking, "Well, there goes number one." Colonel Frost was more philosophical. "I knew one of the three bridges was gone, but it was the least important. I didn't realize then what a disadvantage it would be." It was now 6:30 P.M. and there were two more bridges to go.

13

IT HAD TAKEN THE Hohenstaufen Division engineers five hours to reassemble all the tanks, half-tracks and armored personnel carriers that Harzer had planned to send back to Germany. Newly decorated Captain Paul Gräbner, his forty-vehicle reconnaissance battalion ready, now set out from Hoenderloo Barracks, north of Arnhem, and drove quickly south. Harzer had instructed him to make a sweep of the area between Arnhem and Nijmegen to assess the strength of the Allied airborne troops in that area. Gräbner raced swiftly through Arnhem and, by radio, informed Hohenstaufen headquarters that the city seemed almost deserted. There was no sign of enemy troops. A little before 7 P.M., Gräbner's unit crossed over the great Arnhem highway bridge. A mile past the southern end, Gräbner stopped his car to report, "No enemy. No paratroopers." Mile after mile, his light armored cars slowly patrolling both sides of the highway, Gräbner's radio messages conveyed the same information. At Nijmegen itself the news was unchanged. On orders of Hohenstaufen headquarters, Gräbner was then instructed to further patrol the outskirts of Nijmegen and then return to headquarters.

Gräbner's unit and the forward elements of Frost's 2nd Battalion had missed each other by approximately an hour. Even as Gräbner had driven out of Arnhem, Frost's men were in the city itself and were stealthily approaching their remaining objectives. Inexplicably, despite General Bittrich's explicit instructions, Harzer had completely failed to safeguard the Arnhem bridge.

14

IT WAS GROWING DARK as Colonel Frost quickened the battalion's pace toward the next objective, the pontoon crossing less than a mile west of the Arnhem bridge. Major Digby Tatham-Warter's A Company, still in the lead, was again momentarily held up on the high ground at the western outskirts of Arnhem. Enemy armored cars and machine guns had forced the company off the road and into the back gardens of nearby houses. Coming up behind, Frost found ten Germans guarded by a lone A Company man and, as he was later to write, surmised that "Digby's back-garden maneuver had been completely successful and that the company had rushed on again." Frost returned to the battalion. In the dusk, bursts of fire sporadically swept the road but as the men moved along, they passed damaged vehicles and a number of dead and wounded Germans—clear evidence, Frost thought, of "Digby's quite satisfactory progress."

Moving rapidly through the streets of Arnhem, the battalion reached the pontoon bridge and halted, faced with their second setback. The center section of the bridge had been removed and it was useless. As Captain Mackay stood looking at the dismantled crossing, he decided that "it was typical of the whole cocked-up operation. My one thought was, 'Now we've *got* to get that other bloody bridge.'" He stared off in the distance. Barely a mile away, the great concrete-and-steel span was silhouetted against the last light.

On the 3rd Battalion's Tiger route, moving haltingly toward Arnhem, General Urquhart knew with certainty that he was stranded. In the growing darkness, with enemy forays constantly harassing the march, there was no possibility of his returning to Division headquarters. His mood was bleak. "I wished with every step that I knew what was going on elsewhere." Just before nightfall, Urquhart learned that the 3rd's leading companies had reached the outskirts of Oosterbeek "near someplace called the Hartenstein Hotel. . . . We were making little progress," Urquhart was later to write, "and Lathbury, after a discussion with Fitch, the battalion commander, called a halt."

In a large house set well back from the road, Urquhart and Lathbury prepared to spend the night. The owner of the house, a tall, middle-aged Dutchman, brushed aside the General's apologies for inconveniencing him and his wife, and gave the two officers a downstairs front room overlooking the main road. Urquhart was restless and unable to relax. "I kept checking to see if any contact had been made with either Gough or Frost, but there was nothing from my headquarters or from anyone else."

The great bridge loomed ahead. The concrete ramps alone were immense complexes unto themselves with roads running beneath them and along the river bank from west to east. On either side the rooftops of houses and factory buildings came up to the level of the ramps. In the twilight, the massive approaches and the high-arched girders spanning the Rhine looked awesome and intimidating. Here finally was the main objective—the pivot of Montgomery's audacious plan—and to reach it Frost's men had fought on the march for nearly seven hours.

Now, as lead elements of the 2nd Battalion neared the bridge, Lieutenant Robin Vlasto, in command of one of A Company's platoons, was amazed by "its incredible great height." Vlasto noted "pillboxes at each end, and even in the general air of desertion, they looked threatening." In darkness A Company quietly took up positions beneath the huge supports at the northern end. From above them came the slow rumble of traffic.

Captain Eric Mackay of the Royal Engineers, approaching the bridge through a mosaic of streets, reached a small square leading to the ramp. He remembers that "the quietness as we went through the streets was oppressive, and all around us there seemed to be soft movement. Men were beginning to feel the strain, and I wanted to get that bridge as quickly as we could." Suddenly the darkness was ripped by German fire from a side street. One of the engineers' explosives trolleys went up in flames, and the men were clearly illuminated. Instantly, Mackay ordered his men with their equipment across the square. They dashed over, defying the German fire. Within a few minutes, without losing a man, they were at the bridge. Studying the terrain below the northern ramp, Mackay saw four houses on the east side. "One of them was a school and it was on the corner of a crossroads," he remembers. "I thought that whoever held these houses held the bridge." Mackay promptly ordered his engineers into the school.

Shortly after 8 P.M., Colonel Frost and the battalion headquarters arrived. Frost had sent Major Douglas Crawley's B Company to the high ground above the nearby railway embankment with antitank guns to protect the battalion's left flank, freeing A Company to dash for the bridge.* C Company, under Major Dover, was instructed to follow the forward elements into the city and seize the German commandant's headquarters. Now, at the bridge, Frost was unable to raise either company by radio. Quickly he dispatched messengers to determine their whereabouts.

Deciding not to wait, Frost ordered A Company platoons onto the bridge. As the men began to move across, the Germans came to life. Troopers were raked with fire from the

---

*Frost recalls that "a map I had taken from a German prisoner . . . showed the routes of an enemy armored-car patrol unit and I realized that the German strength was to my left."

pillbox at the northern end and by a lone armored car on the southern end of the bridge itself. A platoon, aided by Eric Mackay's sappers carrying flamethrowers, began to move through the top floors of houses whose roofs and attics were at eye level with the ramp. Simultaneously, Lieutenant Vlasto's platoon worked its way through basements and cellars, going from house to house until it reached Mackay's locations. In position, they attacked the pillbox. As the flamethrowers went into action, Frost recalls that "all hell seemed to be let loose. The sky lit up, and there was the noise of machine-gun fire, a succession of explosions, the crackling of burning ammunition and the thump of a cannon. A wooden building nearby was wreathed in flames, and there were screams of agony and fear."* Now, too, Frost could hear the crash of Vlasto's Piat† bombs smashing into the pillbox. Suddenly, the brief savage battle was over. The guns in the pillbox fell silent and through the fires, Frost saw German soldiers staggering toward his men. A Company had successfully cleared the north end of the bridge and it was theirs. But now, hampering fires and exploding ammunition made it suicidal to risk a second rush to grab the southern side. Only half an hour earlier, Frost could have succeeded.‡ But now, on the south bank, a group of SS Panzer Grenadiers had taken up positions.

Frost attempted to contact Major Crawley once more. He wanted to locate boats or barges in which Crawley's company could cross the river and attack the Germans on the southern side. Again, radio communications were out. Worse, messengers could not even find the company; and, they reported, there were no boats to be seen. As for C Company, the patrol sent out to contact them were pinned down and heavily engaged near the German commandant's headquarters.

---

*Several accounts state that the flamethrowers' aim was diverted and instead of hitting the pillbox, the fiery liquid hit several huts containing explosives.

†A short-range, spring-loaded British antitank gun weighing 33 pounds and capable of firing a projectile that could penetrate four inches of tempered armor plate.

‡According to Dutch Police Sergeant Johannes van Kuijk the bridge was deserted and without guards when he came on duty at 7:30 that evening. Earlier, according to Van Kuijk, when the airborne landings began, the bridge garrison of twenty-five World War I veterans deserted their post.

Grimly Frost's men looked across the Arnhem bridge. How strong were the Germans holding the southern end? Even now, A Company believed there was a chance of seizing the southern end by a surprise attack across the river, if only the men and boats could be found.

But that opportunity had passed. In one of the great ironies of the Arnhem battle, the Lower Rhine could have been crossed within the first hour of landing. Exactly seven miles west, at the village of Heveadorp—through which Frost's battalion had marched en route to their objectives—a large cable ferry, capable of carrying automobiles and passengers, had operated back and forth all day on its normal passage across the Lower Rhine between Heveadorp on the north bank and Driel on the south. Frost knew nothing about the ferry. Nor was it ever listed as one of Urquhart's objectives. In the meticulous planning of Market-Garden an important key to the taking of the Arnhem bridge—the ferry at Driel—had been totally overlooked.*

Major Freddie Gough had finally overtaken Lathbury's brigade headquarters, following Frost's battalion on the Lion route. Quickly he sought out Major Tony Hibbert, the second in command. "Where's the General and the Brigadier?" Gough asked. Hibbert didn't know. "They're together someplace," he told Gough, "but they've both gone off." Gough was now totally confused. "I didn't know what to do," he recalls. "I tried to contact Division without success, so I just decided to keep

---

*In the official orders issued to Urquhart, no reference to the Driel ferry as an objective seems to exist. R.A.F. reconnaissance photographs, used at briefings, show it clearly and one must assume that at some stage of the planning it was discussed. However, General Urquhart, when I interviewed him on the subject, told me "I can't recall that the ferry ever came up." When Urquhart finally learned of the ferry's existence, it was too late to be of any use. Says Urquhart, "By that time I did not have enough men to put across the river." In oral orders, however, the engineers were warned that "the seizure of all ferries, barges and tugs becomes of paramount importance to assist the subsequent advance of XXX Corps." Obviously, however, in the last-minute stages of the planning these orders apparently carried lower priority, for they were never formally issued. "No one told us about the ferry at Driel," Colonel Frost told the author, "and it could have made all the difference."

on going after Frost." Leaving Hibbert, Gough set out once more.

It was dark when Gough and his troopers drove into Arnhem and found Frost and his men holding positions near the northern end of the bridge. Immediately Gough asked where Urquhart was. Like Hibbert, Frost had no idea. He assumed Urquhart was back with Division. Once more Gough tried his radio. Now adding to his anxiety was the absence of any news of his own reconnaissance forces near Wolfheze. But again he could make no contact with anyone. Ordering his tired men to a building close by the bridge, Gough climbed to the roof just in time to see the whole southern end of the bridge "go up in flames" as Frost's men made their first attempt to seize the far end. "I heard this tremendous explosion and the whole end of the bridge seemed to be on fire. I remember somebody saying 'We've come all this way just to have the damn bridge burn down.'" Gough himself was momentarily alarmed. Then, through the smoke he saw that only the pillbox and some ammunition shacks were destroyed. Concerned and weary, Gough turned in for a few hours' rest. He had traveled route after route all day in search of Urquhart. Now, at the bridge, at least one problem was solved. He was where he had set out to be and there he would stay.

There was little more that Lieutenant Colonel Frost could do this night, except to guard the northern end of the bridge from enemy attacks on the southern side. He still had no contact with his missing companies and now, in a house on a corner overlooking the bridge, Frost set up battalion headquarters. Lance Corporal Harold Back of the 2nd Battalion's cipher section remembers that from the front window of the house, the headquarters personnel could look out on the ramp. "The side window of the room gave us a direct view of the bridge itself," says Back. "Our signalers stuck their antennas through the roof and moved their sets constantly, but they couldn't make contact with anybody."

Shortly after, Brigade headquarters arrived and set up in the attic of a house near Frost's. After conferring with his officers, Frost thought it was now obvious that the 1st and 3rd battalions had either been held up on the Tiger and Leopard routes

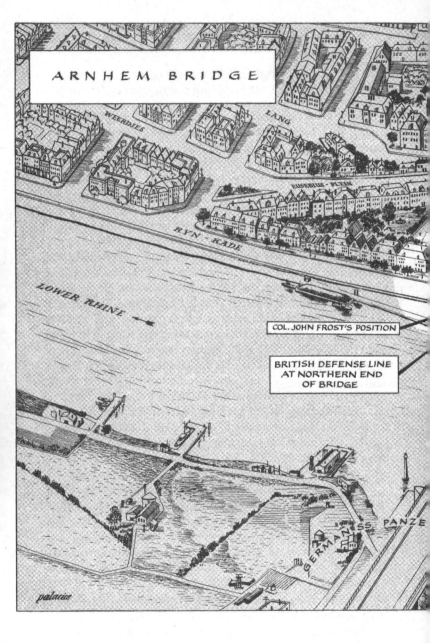

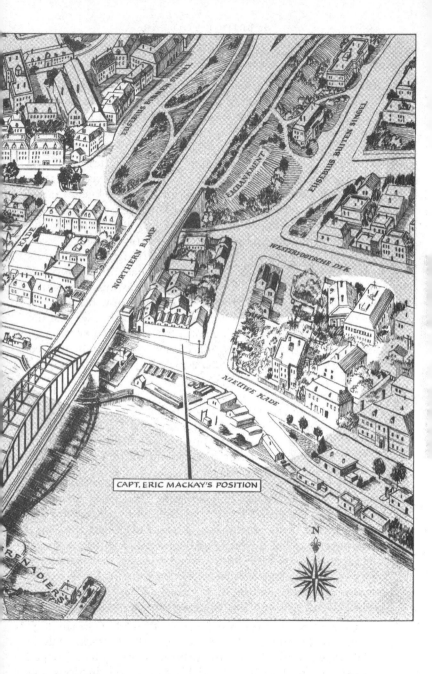

or were fighting north of the bridge somewhere in Arnhem. Without communications, it was impossible to tell what had happened. But if the two battalions did not reach Arnhem during the hours of darkness, the Germans would have the precious time necessary to close the area between Frost's men and the rest of the division. Additionally, Frost was worried that the great bridge might still be blown. In the opinion of the engineers, the heat from fires had already destroyed any fuses laid from the bridge to the town and all visible cables had already been cut by sappers. Still, no one knew exactly where other cables might be hidden. And, as Frost recalls, "the fires prevented even one man from being able to get on to the bridge to remove any charges that might still be there."

But the northern end of the Arnhem bridge was in Frost's hands and he and his courageous men had no intention of giving it up. Although he worried about his missing companies and the rest of the division, he did not show his concern. Visiting various sections now billeted in several houses near the ramp, he found his men "in great heart, as they had every reason to be." As Private James Sims recalls, "We felt quite pleased with ourselves, with the Colonel making jokes and inquiring about our comfort."

At battalion headquarters, Frost himself now settled down for the first time during the day. Sipping from a large mug of tea, he thought that, all in all, the situation was not too bad. "We had come eight miles through close, difficult country, to capture our objective within seven hours of landing in Holland . . . a very fine feat of arms indeed." Although restless, Frost, like his men, was optimistic. He now had a force numbering about five hundred men of various units, and he had every faith that his own missing companies would reach him at the bridge. In any case, he would only have to hold, at most, for another forty-eight hours—until the tanks of General Horrocks' XXX Corps arrived.

15

FROM BERLIN TO THE WESTERN FRONT, the German high command was stunned by the sudden Allied attack. Only in Arnhem, where the British 1st Airborne Division had dropped almost on top of General Bittrich's two panzer divisions, was the reaction both fierce and quick. Elsewhere, baffled and confused commanders tried to determine whether the startling events of September 17 were indeed the opening phase of an invasion of the Reich. A ground attack by the British out of Belgium had been anticipated. All available reserves, including General Von Zangen's Fifteenth Army, so worn down that men had little else but the rifles they carried, had been thrown into defense positions to hold against that threat. Trenches had been dug and strategic positions built in an all-out effort to force the British to fight for every foot of ground.

No one had foreseen that airborne forces would be used simultaneously with the British land advance. Were these airborne attacks the prelude to an invasion of Holland by sea, as Berlin feared? In the hours of darkness, while staff officers tried to analyze the situation, reports of additional airborne attacks further confused the picture. American paratroopers, their strength unknown and their units still unidentified, were in the Eindhoven-Nijmegen area; and the British 1st Airborne Division had clearly landed around Arnhem. But now new messages told of paratroopers in the vicinity of Utrecht, and a totally bewildering report claimed that airborne forces had landed in Warsaw, Poland.*

At Field Marshal Gerd von Rundstedt's headquarters in Koblenz, the general reaction was one of astonishment.† The crusty, aristocratic Von Rundstedt was not so much surprised at the nature of the attack as by the man who, he reasoned, must be directing it—Montgomery. Initially, Von Rundstedt doubted that these sudden and apparently combined land-and-air operations were the opening of Eisenhower's offensive to invade the Reich. The Field Marshal had long been certain that Patton and the American Third Army driving toward the Saar posed the real danger. To combat that threat, Von Rundstedt had committed his best troops to repulse Patton's racing tanks.

---

*The R.A.F. did drop dummy paratroops over a wide area around Utrecht, diverting some German troops for days. No troops were dropped on Warsaw and the report may have been garbled in transmission or, more simply, may have been the result of unfounded rumor.

†"When we first informed Von Rundstedt's headquarters of the airborne attack," Colonel Hans von Tempelhof, Model's operations chief, told me, "OB West seemed hardly perturbed. In fact the reaction was almost callously normal. It quickly changed."

Now Germany's most renowned soldier was caught temporarily off balance. Never had he expected Eisenhower's main offensive to be led by Montgomery, whom he had always considered "overly cautious, habit-ridden and systematic."

He was astounded by the boldness of Montgomery's move. The messages pouring in from Model's headquarters carried a note of hysteria attesting all the more to the surprise and gravity of the attack: "We must reckon with more airborne landings being made at night . . . the enemy obviously believes his attack to be of major importance and the British have achieved considerable initial success against Student and pushed forward to Valkenswaard . . . the position here is particularly critical . . . the lack of fast, strong reserves is increasing our difficulties . . . the general situation of Army Group B, stretched as it is to the limits, is critical . . . we require, as fast as possible, panzers, artillery, heavy mobile antitank weapons, antiaircraft units, and it is absolutely essential that we have fighters in the sky day and night . . ."

Model ended with these words: ". . . the main concentration of the Allies is on the northern wing of our front." It was one of the few times Von Rundstedt had ever respected the opinion of the officer he had caustically referred to as having the makings of a good sergeant major. In that fragment of his message, Model had stripped away Von Rundstedt's last doubts about who was responsible for the startling developments. The "northern wing" of Army Group B *was* Montgomery.

During the night hours it was impossible to estimate the strength of the Allied airborne forces in Holland, but Von Rundstedt was convinced that further landings could be expected. It would now be necessary not only to plug gaps all along the German front but to find reserves for Model's Army Group B at the same time. Once again, Von Rundstedt was forced to gamble. Messages went out from his headquarters transferring units from their positions facing the Americans at Aachen. The moves were risky but essential. These units would have to travel north immediately, and their commitment in the line might take forty-eight hours at minimum. Von Rundstedt issued further orders to defense areas along Germany's northwest frontier, calling for all available armor and antiaircraft units to proceed to the quiet backwater of Holland where, the Field

Marshal was now convinced, imminent danger to the Third
Reich lay. Even as he worked steadily on through the night to
shore up his defenses, Germany's Iron Knight pondered the
strangeness of the situation. He was still amazed that the officer in charge of this great Allied offensive was Montgomery.

It was late evening when the staff car carrying General Wilhelm
Bittrich from his headquarters at Doetinchem arrived in the
darkened streets of Arnhem. Bittrich was determined to see for
himself what was happening. As he reconnoitered through the
city, fires were still burning and debris littered the streets—the
effect of the morning's bombing. Dead soldiers and smoldering vehicles in many areas attested, as Bittrich was later to say,
to "the turbulent fighting that had taken place." Yet, he had
no clear picture of what was happening. Returning to his own
headquarters, Bittrich learned from reports received from two
women telephone operators in the Arnhem Post headquarters
—whom he was later to decorate with the Iron Cross—that the
great highway bridge had been taken by British paratroopers.
Bittrich was infuriated. His specific order to Harzer to hold
the bridge had not been carried out. Now it was crucial that
the Nijmegen bridge over the Waal river be secured before the
Americans in the south could seize it. Bittrich's only chance
of success was to crush the Allied assault along the corridor
and squeeze the British to a standstill in the Arnhem area. The
paratroopers now on the north end of the Arnhem bridge and
the scattered battalions struggling to reach them must be totally destroyed.

The top-secret Market-Garden plan that had fallen into Colonel General Kurt Student's possession finally reached Field
Marshal Model at his new headquarters. He had abandoned
the gardener's cottage on the Doetinchem castle grounds and
moved about five miles southeast near the small village of Terborg. It had taken Student the best part of ten hours to locate the Field Marshal and transmit the document by radio.
Arriving in three parts and now decoded, Market-Garden lay
revealed.

Model and his staff studied it intently. Before them was
Montgomery's entire plan: the names of the airborne divisions

employed, the successive air and resupply lifts ranging over a three-day period, the exact location of the landing and drop zones, the crucial bridge objectives—even the flight routes of the aircraft involved. Model, as Harzer was later to learn from the Field Marshal himself, called the plan "fantastic." It was so fantastic that in these critical hours Model refused to believe it.

The plans were too pat, too detailed for credibility. Model suggested to his staff that the very preciseness of the document argued against its authenticity. He stressed again his own firm conviction that the landings west of Arnhem were the spearhead of a large-scale airborne attack toward the Ruhr, via Bocholt and Münster, some forty miles east. Additional airborne landings should be expected, he warned, and once assembled would undoubtedly swerve north and then east. Model's reasoning was not without validity. As he told his staff, "If we are to believe these plans and are to assume that the Arnhem bridge is the true objective, why were not troops dropped directly on the bridge? Here, they arrive on vast open areas suitable for assembly, and moreover, eight miles to the west."

Model did not inform General Bittrich of the document. "I never realized until after the war," says Bittrich, "that the Market-Garden plans had fallen into our hands. I have no idea why Model did not tell me. In any case, the plans would simply have confirmed my own opinion that the important thing to do was prevent the link-up between the airborne troops and the British Second Army—and for that, they certainly needed the bridges."* One officer under Bittrich's command did learn of the document. Lieutenant Colonel Harzer seemed to be the only officer outside the Field Marshal's staff with whom Model talked about the plan. Harzer recalls that "Model was always prepared for the worst, so he did not discount it entirely. As he told me, he had no intention of being caught by the short hairs." Only time would tell the Germans whether the document was, in fact, genuine. Although the temperamental, erratic Field Marshal was not fully prepared to accept

---

*OB West was not informed of the captured Market-Garden plans either; nor is there any mention in Model's reports to Von Rundstedt of the documents. For some reason Model thought so little of the plans that he did not pass them on to higher headquarters.

the evidence before him, most of his staff were impressed. With the Market-Garden plan in their hands, Model's headquarters alerted all antiaircraft units already on the move of the drops that the plan said would take place a few hours later.

One assumption, at least, was laid to rest. Lieutenant Gustav Sedelhauser, the general-headquarters administrative officer, recalls that on the basis of the captured documents, Model was now of the opinion that he and his Oosterbeek headquarters had not been the objective of the airborne assault after all.

16

AT THE PRECISE TIME that Lieutenant Colonel John Frost secured the northern end of the Arnhem bridge, a cautious approach to another prime objective eleven miles away was only just beginning. The five-span highway bridge over the Waal river at Nijmegen in the 82nd Airborne's central sector of the corridor was the last crossing over which the tanks of General Horrocks' XXX Corps would pass on their drive to Arnhem.

With spectacular success, Brigadier General James M. Gavin's 504th paratroopers had grabbed the crucial Grave bridge eight miles southwest of Nijmegen; and, at about 7:30 P.M., units of the 504th and 505th regiments secured a crossing over the Maas-Waal Canal at the village of Heumen, less than five miles due east of Grave. Gavin's hope of capturing all three canal crossings and a railroad bridge was in vain. The bridges were blown or severely damaged by the Germans before the 82nd could grab them. Yet, within six hours of landing, Gavin's troopers had forged a route over which the British ground forces would travel. Additionally, patrols of the 505th Regiment probing the area between the 82nd's drop zones near the Groesbeek Heights and the Reichswald encountered only light resistance; and, by nightfall, other troopers of the 508th Regiment had secured a 3½-mile stretch of woods along the Holland-German border north of the Groesbeek drop zone and running to the southeastern outskirts of Nijmegen. Now, with three of the 82nd's four key objectives in hand, everything depended upon the capture of the 1,960-foot-long road bridge at Nijmegen.

Although General Browning had directed Gavin not to

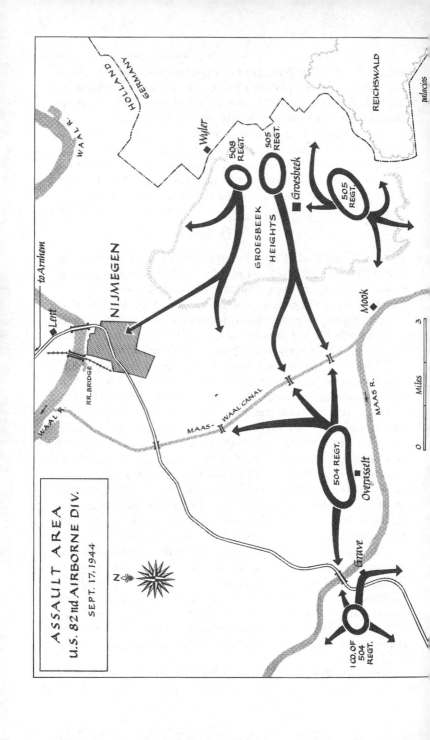

ASSAULT AREA
U.S. 82nd AIRBORNE DIV.
SEPT. 17, 1944

N

to Arnhem

WAAL R.

NIJMEGEN

RR. BRIDGE

Lent

Waal R.

MAAS-WAAL CANAL

504 REGT.

Overasselt

Grave

1 CO. OF
504 REGT.

Miles
0   3

HOLLAND
GERMANY

Wyler

508 REGT.

505 REGT.

Groesbeek

GROESBEEK HEIGHTS

505 REGT.

REICHSWALD

palacids

Mook

MAAS R.

go for the Nijmegen crossing until the high ground around Groesbeek was secured, Gavin was confident that all the 82nd's objectives could be taken on this first day. Evaluating the situation some twenty-four hours before the jump, Gavin had called in the 508th's commander, Colonel Roy E. Lindquist, and directed him to send one battalion racing for the bridge. In the surprise and confusion of the airborne landings, Gavin reasoned, the gamble was well worth taking. "I cautioned Lindquist about the dangers of getting caught in streets," Gavin remembers, "and pointed out that the way to get the bridge was to approach from east of the city without going through built-up areas." Whether by misunderstanding or a desire to clean up his initial assignments, Lindquist's own recollection was that he was not to commit his troopers in an assault on the bridge until the regiment's other objectives had been achieved. To the 1st Battalion, commanded by Lieutenant Colonel Shields Warren, Jr., Lindquist assigned the task of holding protective positions along the Groesbeek-Nijmegen highway about a mile and a quarter southeast of the city. Warren was to defend the area and link up with the regiment's remaining two battalions to the west and east. Only when these missions were accomplished, Warren recalled, was he to prepare to go into Nijmegen. Thus, instead of driving for the bridge from the flat farming areas to the east, Warren's battalion found itself squarely in the center of those very built-up areas Gavin had sought to avoid.

It was nightfall before Warren achieved his other objectives. Now with precious time lost, lead companies began to move slowly through the quiet, almost deserted streets of Nijmegen. The main objective was to reach the traffic circle leading to the southern approaches of the bridge. There was a diversionary target as well. The Dutch underground reported that the detonating mechanism for destroying the great crossing was situated in the main post-office building. This vital information reached Warren's units only after they had begun moving toward the bridge. A platoon was hurriedly sent to the post office, where, after subduing the German guards, engineers cut wires and blew up what they believed to be the detonating controls. Whether this apparatus was, in fact, actually hooked up to explosives on the bridge, no one would ever know for certain, but now, at least, electrical circuits and switchboards were destroyed. When the platoon attempted to withdraw to rejoin the main force they found that the enemy had closed in behind them. They were cut off and for the next three days would be forced to hold out in the post office until help arrived.

Meanwhile, as the remainder of Warren's force approached a park that led toward the bridge, they came suddenly under intense machine-gun and armored-car fire. Captain Arie D. Bestebreurtje, the Dutch officer assigned to the 82nd, remembers that "guns suddenly opened up on us, and I could see the flashes of fire from the muzzles. They seemed to be all around us." Before he could raise his carbine to fire, Bestebreurtje was hit in the left hand and elbow and the right index finger.* To Corporal James R. Blue, the eerie battle raging in the blacked-out streets was like a nightmare. "Right away we were engaged in hand-to-hand combat," Blue remembers. He was moving through the streets with Private First Class Ray Johnson, both armed with M-1 rifles with fixed bayonets, when they came face to face with SS troops. As Johnson tried to get one of the Germans with his bayonet, Blue went after an officer with a trench knife. "Our orders were not to fire. If we came to close combat we were to use knives and bayonets. But," Blue recalls, "that trench knife seemed mighty short, so I used my Tommy gun. That closed that chapter, but almost immediately a self-propelled gun began to fire in our direction and we moved up to the park and tied in with other platoons." Private James Allardyce remembers hearing a call for medics up front, but "bullets were whistling down the street and there was so much confusion in the darkness that men did not know where others were. We set up a perimeter defense around a modern brick schoolhouse. Out front we heard German voices and the moaning and cries of the wounded. We couldn't make it to the bridge. Finally it came through to us that the Jerries had stopped us."

---

*Several days later, Bestebreurtje was told by doctors that the finger must be amputated. "I told them absolutely not," Bestebreurtje says. "It was my finger and I was not going to have it amputated. Besides, it would have ruined my piano playing." He still has the finger.

As indeed they had. Captain Paul Gräbner's Reconnaissance Battalion, which had missed Frost at the Arnhem bridge, had arrived in Nijmegen well in advance of the late-starting Americans.

By midnight on this first day of the mightiest airborne assault in history, British and American paratroops were on, or fighting toward, their major objectives. Through long hours of march and savage encounters with an unexpectedly strong and tenacious enemy, they had gained most of the objectives that the planners had expected them to take swiftly and with ease. From the gallant men of Colonel John Frost's 2nd Battalion clinging to the north end of the Arnhem bridge, all along the corridor south to where Colonel Robert Sink's 101st troopers struggled to repair the bridge at Son, the mood was one of fierce determination; they must hold open the highway along which the British Second Army tanks and infantry would drive. On this midnight, troopers did not doubt that relief was on the way or that reinforcements and supplies, scheduled to arrive on the eighteenth, would further bolster their position. Despite heavy casualties, confusion, and communications setbacks, the men of the airborne army were completely optimistic. All in all, it had not been a bad Sunday outing.

17

THERE WAS A RED GLOW in the sky over Arnhem as the speeding car bringing Major General Heinz Harmel back from Berlin neared the city. Apprehensive and tired after the long trip, Harmel arrived at the Frundsberg Division headquarters in Ruurlo, only to find that his command post was now situated in Velp, approximately three miles northeast of Arnhem. There, he found his chief of staff, Lieutenant Colonel Paetsch, looking exhausted. "Thank God you're back!" Paetsch said. Quickly he briefed Harmel on the day's events and on the orders received from General Bittrich. "I was dumfounded," Harmel recalls. "Everything seemed confused and uncertain. I was very tired, yet the gravity of the situation was such that I called Bittrich and told him I was coming to see him."

Bittrich had not slept either. As Harmel was shown in, Bittrich began immediately to outline the situation. Angry and frustrated, he bent over his maps. "British paratroopers have landed here, west of Arnhem," he told Harmel. "We have no idea of their actual strength or intentions." Pointing to Nijmegen and Eindhoven, the corps commander said, "American airborne forces have secured lodgments in these two areas. Simultaneously, Montgomery's forces have attacked north from the Meuse-Escaut Canal. My belief is that the object is to split our forces. In my opinion, the objectives are the bridges. Once these are secured, Montgomery can drive directly up to the center of Holland and from there, into the Ruhr." Bittrich waved his hands. "Model disagrees. He still believes further airborne forces will be dropped north of the Rhine, east and west of Arnhem and march toward the Ruhr."

Harzer's Hohenstaufen Division, Bittrich went on to explain, had been ordered to mop up the British west and north of Arnhem. The armed forces commander in the Netherlands, General Christiansen, had been directed to send in his forces—a mixture of defense and training battalions—under command of Lieutenant General Hans von Tettau. Their mission was to aid the Hohenstaufen Division on the flanks in an effort to overrun the British landing and drop zones.

The Frundsberg Division, Bittrich continued, was charged with all activities to the east of Arnhem and south to Nijmegen. Stabbing the map with his finger, Bittrich told Harmel, "The Nijmegen bridge must be held at all costs. Additionally the Arnhem bridge and the area all the way south to Nijmegen is your responsibility." Bittrich paused and paced the room. "Your problems," he told Harmel, "have been made more difficult. Harzer failed to leave armored units at the north end of the Arnhem bridge. The British are now there."

As he listened, Harmel realized with growing alarm that with the Arnhem bridge in British hands, there was no way to get his armor quickly across the Rhine and down to Nijmegen. Nor was there another bridge crossing over the river east of the Arnhem bridge. His entire division would have to be taken over the Rhine at a ferry landing in the village of Pannerden, some eight miles southeast of Arnhem. Bittrich, anticipating the problem, had already ordered the ferry operations to begin. It would be a slow, tedious, roundabout way of reaching Nijmegen, and to ferry the division's trucks, armor and men would take all of Harmel's resources.

As he left Bittrich's headquarters, Harmel asked his commander, "Why not destroy the Nijmegen bridge before it's too late?" Bittrich's tone was ironic. "Model has flatly refused to consider the idea. We may need it to counterattack." Harmel stared in amazement. "With what?" he asked.

In the dark, Harmel set out once again, heading for Pannerden. His units were already on the move toward the ferry crossing and the roads were choked with troops and vehicles. In Pannerden itself, Harmel saw the reason for the chaotic conditions he had witnessed on the road. Vehicles congested the streets in one gigantic traffic jam. At the river's edge, makeshift ferries composed of rubber rafts were slowly floating trucks across the river. From his chief of staff, Harmel learned that one battalion had reached the far shore and was already en route to Nijmegen. Some trucks and smaller vehicles were also across. But as yet, heavier armored equipment had not even been loaded. In Paetsch's opinion, Harmel's Frundsberg units might not be in action in the Arnhem-Nijmegen area until September 24 if the slow, cumbersome ferrying could not be speeded up.

Harmel knew there was only one solution to the problem. He would have to retake the Arnhem bridge and open the highway route to Nijmegen. As this first day of Market-Garden, September 17, ended all the German frustrations now focused on a single obstinate man—Colonel John Frost at the Arnhem bridge.

PART FOUR

THE SIEGE

I

ARLY MORNING MIST rising from the Rhine swirled around the Arnhem bridge and the silent darkened houses surrounding it. A short distance from the northern ramp, the Eusebius Buiten Singel—a long, landscaped boulevard bordering the historic inner city—stretched back toward the outlying areas north and east and ended at the Musis Sacrum, Arnhem's popular concert hall. On this Monday, September 18, in the thin, indistinct light, the ancient capital of Gelderland appeared deserted. Nothing moved in the streets, gardens, squares or parks.

From their positions around the northern end of the bridge, Colonel Frost's men could begin to see for the first time the whole sprawl of the city with its houses and municipal buildings: the Court of Justice, Provincial Government House, State Archives buildings, the town hall, general post office and the railroad station less than a mile to the northwest. Nearer, the Church of St. Eusebius, with its 305-foot-high steeple, dominated the city. Few of Frost's men, looking warily out from shattered windows and freshly dug foxholes in a perimeter composed of eighteen houses, realized that the great church now had a sinister significance. German snipers had moved into the tower during the night. Carefully concealed, they, like the British, waited tensely for full light.

The battle for the bridge had raged all night. A midnight lull had been short-lived. When the fighting broke out again, it almost seemed that each man was engaged in individual contest. Twice during the night Frost's men had tried to rush the southern end of the bridge, only to be beaten back. Lieutenant John Grayburn, leading both charges, had been badly wounded in the face, but stayed on the bridge and oversaw the evacuation of all his men to safety.* Later, truckloads of

---

*Grayburn was killed in the battle for Arnhem. On September 20 he stood in full view of an enemy tank and directed the withdrawal of his men to a main defense perimeter. For supreme courage, leadership and devotion to duty during the entire engagement, he was posthumously awarded Britain's highest military honor, the Victoria Cross.

German infantry tried to ram their way across the bridge, only to be met by the concentrated fire of the British troopers. With flamethrowers, Frost's men had set the vehicles on fire. Panzer Grenadiers were burned alive in the inferno and fell screaming to the Rhine one hundred feet below. The acrid smell of burning rubber and thick black smoke eddying up from the debris hampered rescue parties from both sides searching for their wounded among the bodies littering the bridge. Lance Corporal Harold Back, in one such party, was helping to carry wounded into the basement of one of the houses held by Frost's men. In the darkness of the cellar, he saw what he thought were a few candles burning. Injured troopers were laid out all over the floor and suddenly Back realized that what he saw were tiny fragments glowing on the bodies of some of the wounded. Hit by splinters from phosphorous shells, the men were glowing in the dark.

Inexplicably, in these first moments of daylight, the battle halted again. It was almost as though both sides were drawing a deep breath. Across the road from Frost's battalion headquarters, on a side street under the ramp itself, Captain Eric Mackay made a quiet reconnaissance of the houses that his little force of engineers and small groups of men from other units now controlled. During a vicious nighttime battle, Mackay had managed to hang on to two of the four houses in the area and set up a command post in one of them, a brick schoolhouse. The Germans, counterattacking, had crept through the landscaped grounds to toss hand grenades into the houses. Infiltrating the buildings, the Germans fought a deadly, almost silent hand-to-hand battle with the British. Ranging through the cellars and from room to room, Mackay's men drove back swarms of the enemy with bayonets and knives. Then, taking a small group of men, Mackay went out into the bushes after the retreating Germans. Again, with bayonets and grenades, the British routed the enemy. Mackay was hit in the legs by shrapnel and a bullet punctured his helmet, grazing his scalp.

Now, checking his troopers, Mackay discovered casualties similar to his own. Adding to his problems, the supply situation was not good. There were six Bren guns, ammunition, grenades and some explosives. But Mackay had no antitank weapons, little food and no medical supplies except morphia and field dressings. Additionally, the Germans had cut off the water. Now, all that was available was what the men still had in their canteens.

Terrible as the nighttime fighting had been, Mackay maintained a fierce determination. "We were doing well and our casualties were comparatively light," he recalls. "Besides, now with the coming of daylight, we could see what we were doing and we were ready." Still, Mackay, like Frost, had few illusions. In this most deadly kind of fighting—street by street, house by house and room by room—he knew it was only a question of time before the British garrison at the bridge was overwhelmed. The Germans obviously hoped to crush Frost's small force, by sheer weight of numbers, within a matter of hours. Against such powerful and concentrated attacks, all that could save the courageous defenders at the bridge was the arrival of XXX Corps or the remaining battalions of the 1st Parachute Brigade still fighting their way into the city.

It had been a night of unceasing horror for the SS soldiers who fought near the bridge. Colonel Harzer, apparently satisfied that he had halted Urquhart's battalions, had underestimated both the number and the caliber of the men who had reached the northern end. Harzer did not even bother to order his few self-propelled guns to be brought up as support. Instead, squad after squad of SS were thrown against the British positions in the buildings around the ramp. These tough units met a foe most of them remember as the fiercest soldiers they had ever encountered.

SS Squad Leader Alfred Ringsdorf, twenty-one, an experienced soldier who had fought in Russia, was on a freight train heading toward Arnhem where, he was told, his group was to be refitted. There was utter confusion at the Arnhem station when Ringsdorf and his men arrived. Troops from a hodgepodge of units were milling about, being lined up and marched off. Ringsdorf's unit was told to report immediately to a command post in the city. There, a major attached them to a company of the 21st Panzer Grenadier Regiment. The squad had arrived without arms, but by late Sunday afternoon they were outfitted with machine guns, carbines, hand grenades and

a few *Panzerfäuste.** Questioning the limited amount of ammunition, they were told that supplies were en route. "At this
time," says Ringsdorf, "I had no idea where we were going to
fight, where the battle was, and I had never been in Arnhem
before."

In the center of the city, there was evidence that heavy street
fighting had already taken place. For the first time, Ringsdorf
learned that British paratroopers had landed and were holding
the northern end of the Arnhem bridge. No one seemed to
know how large the force was. His squad was assembled in a
church and given their orders. They were to infiltrate behind
the buildings on either side of the bridge ramp and rout out
the British. Ringsdorf knew how deadly this kind of fighting
was. His experiences at the Russian front had taught him that.
Yet, the men in his command were seasoned young veterans.
They thought the battle would be brief.

All through the area leading to the bridge, the squad saw
houses heavily damaged by bombing, and the men had to work
their way through the rubble. As they neared the perimeter
positions the British had set up around the north end of the
bridge, they came under intense machine-gun fire. Pinned
down, the squad was unable to get within six hundred yards
of the bridge approach. A lieutenant called for a volunteer to
cross the square and toss a demolition charge into the house
where the heaviest machine-gun fire seemed to be centered.
Ringsdorf volunteered. Under covering fire, he dashed across
the square. "I stopped behind a tree near a cellar window
where the shooting was coming from and tossed the charge
inside. Then I ran back to my men." Lying in rubble waiting
for the explosion to go off, Ringsdorf looked back just as a
tall house on a corner, where a number of German engineers
were sheltering, was suddenly hit by shells. The entire front of
the house crumbled, burying everybody. It struck Ringsdorf
that had his own men been there, the entire squad would have
been wiped out. At that moment, the demolition charge he
had thrown into the cellar exploded on the street not far from
where he lay. The British had tossed it back out the window.

---

*A German version of the American recoilless antitank bazooka capable of
firing a 20-pound projectile with extreme accuracy.

At nightfall various squads began to infiltrate the buildings to dig the British out. Ringsdorf's objective was a big red building which, he was told, was a school. Heading toward it, his squad quickly encountered alert British marksmen who forced the Germans to take refuge in a nearby house. Smashing the windows, the SS men opened fire. The British immediately took cover in the house next door and a vicious fire fight began. "The British shooting was deadly," Ringsdorf recalls. "We could hardly show ourselves. They aimed for the head, and men began to fall beside me, each one with a small, neat hole through the forehead."

With losses mounting, the Germans fired a panzerfaust directly at the British-occupied house. As the shell crashed into the building, Ringsdorf's squad charged. "The fighting was cruel," he remembers. "We pushed them back room by room, yard by yard, suffering terrible losses." In the middle of the melee, the young squad leader was ordered to report to his battalion commander; the British, he was told, must be driven out at all costs. Back with his men, Ringsdorf ordered the squad to dash forward, lobbing showers of grenades to keep the English under constant attack. "Only in this way," says Ringsdorf, "were we able to gain ground and continue our advance. But I certainly had not expected when I came from Germany to find myself suddenly engaged in bitter fighting in a restricted area. This was a harder battle than any I had fought in Russia. It was constant, close-range, hand-to-hand fighting. The English were everywhere. The streets, for the most part, were narrow, sometimes not more than fifteen feet wide, and we fired at each other from only yards away. We fought to gain inches, cleaning out one room after the other. It was absolute hell!"

Advancing cautiously toward one house, Ringsdorf caught a glimpse of an English helmet with camouflage netting momentarily outlined in an open cellar doorway. As he raised his arm to throw a grenade, he heard a low voice and the sound of moaning. Ringsdorf did not lob the grenade. Silently he moved down the cellar steps, then yelled, "Hands up." The command was unnecessary. In Ringsdorf's words, "Before me was a frightening sight. The cellar was a charnel house full of wounded English soldiers." Ringsdorf spoke soothingly, knowing that the British would not understand his words, but might comprehend his meaning. "It's O.K.," he told the wounded men. "It's all right." He called for medics and, collecting his prisoners, ordered the British moved back of his own lines for attention.

As the troopers were brought out of the cellar, Ringsdorf began to search one of the walking wounded. To his astonishment, the man uttered a low moan and crumpled at Ringsdorf's feet, dead. "It was a bullet meant for me," Ringsdorf says. "The English were protecting their own. They couldn't know we were trying to save their wounded. But for one moment, I was paralyzed. Then I broke out in a cold sweat and ran."

As the British troopers hung on grimly around the school, Ringsdorf knew that even his elite unit was not strong enough to force a surrender. As dawn broke on Monday, he and the depleted squad retreated back up the Eusebius Buiten Singel. Encountering an artillery commander, Ringsdorf told him that "the only way to get the British out is to blast the buildings down, brick by brick. Believe me, these are real men. They won't give up that bridge until we carry them out feet first."

Master Sergeant Emil Petersen had good reason to reach the same conclusion. He was attached to the Reichsarbeitsdienst (Reich Work Service) and, as Germany's manpower shortage became increasingly acute, Petersen and his thirty-five-man platoon had been transferred to a heavy antiaircraft unit, then to an infantry outfit. They had retreated all the way from France.

On Sunday afternoon, waiting at the Arnhem station for transportation back to Germany where they were to be reorganized, Petersen's platoon had been mobilized and told by a lieutenant that they were to be committed against British airborne troops who had landed in the city. "The unit we joined consisted of 250 men," Petersen recalls. "No one had any weapons. Only I and four others had machine pistols."

Petersen's men were tired. They had been without food for twenty-four hours, and the sergeant remembers thinking that had the train been on time, the platoon would have been fed, would have missed the battle and would have reached home in Germany.

At an SS barracks, the group was issued weapons. "The situation was laughable," Petersen says. "First, none of us liked fighting with the Waffen SS. They had a reputation for being merciless. The arms they gave us were ancient carbines. To break open mine, I had to bang it against a table. The morale of my men was not exactly high when they saw these old weapons."

It took some time to make the guns serviceable and, as yet, the unit had not received any orders. Nobody seemed to know what was happening or where the men were to be committed.

Finally, at dusk, the group was marched off to the town commander's headquarters. Arriving, they found the building deserted. Again, they waited. "All we could think about was food," says Petersen. Eventually, an SS lieutenant arrived and announced that the men were to push through the center of the city to the Rhine bridge.

The unit marched in platoons down Markt Street toward the Rhine. In the dark they could see nothing; but, Petersen recalls, "we were conscious of movement all around us. Occasionally we heard shooting in the distance and the sound of vehicles. Once or twice I thought I saw the dull silhouette of a helmet."

Less than three hundred yards from the bridge, Petersen was aware that they were passing through lines of soldiers and he guessed the group he was with must be replacing these men. Then one of the soldiers said something that, to Petersen, was unintelligible. Instantly Petersen realized that the man had spoken English. "We were marching alongside a British unit heading, like us, for the bridge." The mistaken identity was suddenly apparent to everyone. An English voice yelled out, "They're Jerries!" Petersen remembers shouting, "Fire!"

Within seconds the street reverberated with machine-gun and rifle fire as the two forces fought face to face. A stream of bullets missed Petersen by inches, ripping through his knapsack. The force of the fire slammed him to the ground. Quickly, he took cover behind a dead comrade.

"Everywhere you looked, men were firing from scattered positions, often mistakenly at their own side," Petersen remembers. Slowly he began to crawl forward. He came to an iron fence enclosing a small park and climbed the fence. There, he found most of the other survivors of the German platoons sheltering among trees and shrubs. The British had drawn back to a group of houses on both sides of the park, and now in the little square the Germans were caught in a crossfire. "I could hear the screams of the wounded," Petersen says. "The British fired flares pinpointing our positions and cut our group to pieces. Fifteen men in my platoon were killed in less than five minutes."

Just at dawn the British stopped firing. The Germans also halted. In the early light, Petersen saw that of the 250 men who had set out for the bridge, more than half were either dead or wounded. "We never did get near the approaches to the bridge. We just lay there and suffered, without support from the vaunted SS or a single self-propelled gun. That," Petersen says, "was our introduction to the Arnhem battle. For us, it was nothing less than a massacre."

Hour by hour, men of the two missing battalions of the 1st British Airborne Division somehow reached the bridge. They had managed, by twos and threes, to fight through Colonel Harzer's defense ring to the north and west. Many were wounded, hungry and cold. They would add to the medical and supply problems of Colonel Frost's group. But in these hours, the stragglers were proud and in high spirits, despite their exhaustion and wounds. They had arrived where briefing officers back in England and their own commanders had told them to come. They streamed in from every unit that had started out so confidently for the Arnhem bridge the previous afternoon, and by dawn on the eighteenth Frost estimated that he now had between 600 and 700 men on the northern approach. But each hour that brought more troopers to the bridge brought, too, the increasing sounds of mechanized equipment as General Harmel's armored units entered the city and took up positions.

Even the German armor found Arnhem a hazardous and frightening place. Along various routes throughout the city, ordinary Dutch civilians had blocked the roads. Braving German and British bullets, men and women living in the fighting areas had begun to collect the dead—British, German, and their own countrymen. Sergeant Reginald Isherwood, of the 1st Battalion, finally found his way to the center of Arnhem at daybreak, after a hazardous night on the roads. There he saw "a sight that will live with me until the end of my days." The Dutch, emerging from basements, cellars, gardens and wrecked buildings, were collecting bodies. "They carried the wounded to makeshift dressing stations and shelters in the basements," Isherwood recalls, "but the bodies of the dead were stacked like sandbags in long rows, the heads and feet placed alternately." The proud, grieving citizens of Arnhem were laying the bodies of friend and foe alike across the streets in five-to-six-foot-high human roadblocks to prevent German tanks from reaching Frost at the bridge.

For the civilians in the inner city, dawn brought no release from the terror and confusion. Fires were out of control and spreading rapidly. Huddled in cellars and basements, few people had slept. The night had been punctuated by the crash of shells, the dull crump of mortars, the whine of snipers' bullets and the staccato burst of machine guns. Strangely, outside the older part of town, the citizens of Arnhem were untouched by what was happening, and they were totally confused. They telephoned friends in the inner city seeking information, only to learn from the frightened householders that a pitched battle was taking place on the northern end of the bridge, which the British were holding against repeated German attacks. It was obvious to the callers that German troops and vehicles were moving into the city from all directions. Yet the faith of the Dutch did not falter. They believed that liberation by the British and Americans was imminent. In these outer parts of the city, people prepared for work as usual. Bakeries opened, milkmen made their rounds, telephone operators, railroad employees, utility workers—all were on their jobs. Civil servants were planning to go to work, firemen still attempted to keep up with the ever-growing number of burning buildings and, a few miles north of Arnhem, Dr. Reinier van Hooff, director of Burgers Zoological Gardens, tended his nervous, skittish animals.* Perhaps the only Dutch who knew the extent of the battle were doctors and nurses who answered calls constantly

---

*In the zoo were 12,000 carrier pigeons which the Germans had collected from bird keepers throughout Arnhem. Fearing that the Dutch might use the pigeons to carry reports, the birds had been confiscated and housed in the zoo. German soldiers appeared daily to count the birds and even dead pigeons were ordered kept until the Germans could check their registration numbers.

throughout the night. Ambulances raced through the city, collecting casualties and rushing them to St. Elisabeth's Hospital on the northwestern outskirts and to smaller nursing homes within the city. No one in Arnhem realized as yet that the city was already a no man's land and that the situation would grow steadily worse. Arnhem, one of the most scenic spots in the Netherlands, would soon become a miniature Stalingrad.

The Dutch in the inner city were, however, aware almost from the beginning that liberation would not come easily. In the middle of the night at the government police station on Eusebiusplein, less than a quarter of a mile from the bridge, twenty-seven-year-old Sergeant Joannes van Kuijk heard a quiet tapping at the station door. Opening up, he saw British soldiers standing outside. Immediately Van Kuijk asked them in. "They wanted the answers to all sorts of questions bearing on the locations of buildings and landmarks," he remembers. "Then a number of them left and began digging themselves in across the road in the direction of the bridge—all of it done as silently as possible." In front of a doctor's house nearby, Van Kuijk watched as the British set up a mortar site and then positioned a 6-pounder antitank gun in a corner of the doctor's garden. By dawn, Van Kuijk saw that the British had formed a tight perimeter around the northern extremity of the bridge. To him, these soldiers acted less like liberators than like grim-faced defenders.

On the other side of Eusebius Buiten Singel, the winding, grass-stripped boulevard close by the bridge, Coenraad Hulleman, a labor mediator staying with his fiancée, Truid van der Sande, and her parents in their villa, had been up all night listening to the firing and explosions around the schoolhouse a street away, where Captain Mackay's men were fighting off the Germans. Because of the intensity of the battle, the Van der Sandes and Hulleman had taken refuge in a small, windowless cellar beneath the central portion of the house.

Now, at dawn, Hulleman and his future father-in-law stole cautiously upstairs to a second-floor room overlooking the boulevard. There, they stared down in amazement. A dead German lay in the middle of a patch of marigolds in the landscaped street, and all through the grass plots they saw Germans in one-man slit trenches. Glancing along the boulevard to his right, Hulleman saw several German armored vehicles parked beside a high brick wall, drawn up and waiting. Even as the two men watched, a new battle broke out. Machine guns on the tanks suddenly fired into the towers of the nearby Walburg Church, and Hulleman saw a fine red dust spew out. He could only assume that paratroopers were in lookout positions in the church. Almost immediately the tank fire was answered, and the Germans in slit trenches began to machine-gun the houses on the opposite side of the street. One of them was a costume shop and in its windows were knights in armor. As Hulleman looked on, the bullets shattered the show window and toppled the knights. Moved to tears, Hulleman turned away. He hoped the sight was not prophetic.

A few blocks north, in a house near the concert hall, Willem Onck was awakened shortly after dawn by the sound of troop movements in the street. Someone hammered on his door and a German voice ordered Onck and his family to stay inside and to draw the blinds. Onck did not immediately obey. Running to the front window, he saw Germans with machine guns at every corner of the street. In front of the Musis Sacrum was an 88 mm. battery, and to Onck's utter amazement, German soldiers were sitting next to it on the auditorium's chairs which they had carried into the street. Watching them chatting casually with one another, Onck thought they looked as if they were only waiting for the concert to begin.

The most frustrated and angry civilians in the area were the members of the Dutch underground. Several of them had contacted the British almost immediately at the bridge, but their help had been politely refused. Earlier, Arnhem's underground chief, Pieter Kruyff, had sent Toon van Daalen and Gijsbert Numan to Oosterbeek to establish contact with the British. They too had found that their assistance was not needed. Numan remembers warning the troopers of snipers in the area and advising them to avoid main roads. "One of them told me their orders were to proceed to the bridge only, and they would follow their indicated routes," Numan says. "I got the impression that they were in dread of provocateurs and simply did not trust us."

Now, at dawn, Johannus Penseel held a meeting in his cellar with his resistance workers. Penseel planned to take over a local radio station and broadcast a proclamation that the city was free. A telephone call from Numan changed his mind. "It goes badly," Numan reported. "The situation is critical, and I think everything is already lost." Penseel was stunned. "What do you mean?" he asked. Numan was now near St. Elisabeth's Hospital. The British were finding it impossible to get through the German lines and march to the bridge, he said. Penseel immediately telephoned Pieter Kruyff, who advised the group to hold back any planned activities—"a temporary nonintervention," as Henri Knap, who attended the meeting, recalls. But the long-term hopes of the resistance workers were crushed. "We were prepared to do anything," Penseel recalls, "even sacrifice our lives if necessary. Instead, we sat useless and unwanted. It was now increasingly clear that the British neither trusted us nor intended to use us."

Ironically, in these early hours of Monday, September 18, when neither SHAEF, Montgomery nor any Market-Garden commander had a clear picture of the situation, members of the Dutch underground passed a report through secret telephone lines to the 82nd Airborne's Dutch liaison officer, Captain Arie Bestebreurtje, that the British were being overwhelmed by panzer divisions at Arnhem. In the 82nd's message logs, the notation appears: "Dutch report Germans winning over British at Arnhem." In the absence of any direct communications from the Arnhem battle area, this message was actually the first indication that the Allied High Command received of the crisis that was overtaking the 1st British Airborne Division.

2

AT THE FERRY LANDING STAGE in the little village of Driel, seven miles southwest of the Arnhem bridge, Pieter, the ferryman, prepared for his first trip of the day across the Lower Rhine. The early-morning commuters, who worked in the towns and villages on the northern side of the river, huddled together in small groups, chilled by the morning mist. Pieter took no part in the talk of his passengers about the fighting going on west of Arnhem and in the city itself. His concern was with the operation of the ferry and the daily schedules he must maintain, as he had done for years.

A few cars, and farm carts filled with produce for stores and
markets to the north, were loaded first. Then men and women
pushing bicycles came aboard. At exactly 7 A.M. Pieter swung
out into the river, the ferry running smoothly along its cable.
The trip took only a few minutes. Edging up to the ramp below the village of Heveadorp on the northern bank, passengers
and vehicles disembarked. Above them, the Westerbouwing,
a hundred-foot-high hill, dominated the countryside. On the
northern bank, most commuters set off on roads leading east
to Oosterbeek, whose tenth-century church tower rose above
groves of oaks and lupine-covered moors. Beyond was Arnhem.

Other passengers waited to cross back to Driel. There, once
again, Pieter took on northbound travelers. One of them was
young Cora Baltussen. Only two weeks earlier, on September
5, which would always be remembered by the Dutch as Mad
Tuesday, she had watched the Germans' frantic retreat. In
Driel, the conquerors had not returned. For the first time in
months, Cora had felt free. Now, once again, she was apprehensive. The joy of the news of the paratroop landings the day
before had been diminished by rumors of the intense fighting
in Arnhem. Still, Cora could not believe the Germans would
ever defeat the powerful Allied forces that had come to liberate
her country.

At the Heveadorp landing on the north side of the river,
Cora pushed her bicycle off the ferry and pedaled to Oosterbeek and the local baker's shop. She had given her meager
hoard of sugar rations to the pastry shop for a special occasion.
On this Monday, September 18, the Baltussen preserves factory was observing its seventy-fifth year in business and Cora's
mother was celebrating her sixty-second birthday. For the first
time in months all of the family would be together. Cora had
come to Oosterbeek early to pick up the birthday cake, which
would mark both the company's anniversary and Mrs. Baltussen's birthday.

Friends had tried to dissuade Cora from making the trip.
Cora refused to listen. "What can possibly happen?" she had
asked one friend. "The British are in Oosterbeek and Arnhem.
The war is almost over."

Her trip was uneventful. In these early hours Oosterbeek
seemed peaceful. There were British troops in the streets, the

shops were open, and a holiday mood prevailed. For the moment, although gunfire could be heard only a few miles away, Oosterbeek was tranquil, not yet touched by the battle. Although her order was ready, the baker was amazed that she had come. "The war is all but over," she told him. With her parcels, she cycled back to Heveadorp and waited until Pieter brought the ferry in again. On the southern bank she returned to the somnolent peace of little Driel, where, as usual, absolutely nothing was happening.

3

ON THE BRITISH LANDING and drop zones, the officer with perhaps the least glamorous job of all was going about it with his usual capability. All through the night the men of Brigadier Philip "Pip" Hicks's 1st Airlanding Brigade had staved off a series of vicious enemy attacks, as the motley groups under Von Tettau's command harassed the brigade. Hicks's men were dug in around the perimeters to hold the zones for the expected 10 A.M. drop of Brigadier Shan Hackett's 4th Parachute Brigade, and the resupply missions that would follow. The zones under Hicks's protection were also the supply dumps for the British airborne.

Neither Hicks nor his men had managed more than an hour or two of sleep. The Germans, attacking from the woods, had set the forest on fire in some areas in the hope of burning out the British defenders. The Red Devils promptly responded. Slipping behind the enemy, they charged with fixed bayonets and forced the Germans into their own fire. Signalman Graham Marples remembers the bitter nighttime battles vividly. He and a few others came upon a platoon of dead British troopers who had been overrun and completely wiped out. "No one said anything," Marples remembers. "We just fixed bayonets and went right on into the woods. We came out, but the Jerries didn't." Private Robert Edwards, who had seen action in North Africa, Sicily and Italy, recalls that "I had managed to come through all those actions more or less unscathed, but in one day in Holland I had been in more fire fights than all else put together."

The unending skirmishes had taken their toll. Several times during the night Hicks had called upon Lieutenant Colonel W. F. K. "Sheriff" Thompson for artillery support to force back the persistent enemy attacks. His real fear was that German armor, which he now knew was holding up the battalions going for the bridge, would break through his meager defenses and drive him off the landing and drop zones. "I went through some of the worst few hours I have ever spent in my life," Hicks recalls. "Two things were clear: although we did not know it at the time we had landed virtually on top of two panzer divisions—which weren't supposed to be there—and the Germans had reacted with extraordinary speed." Under attack from Von Tettau's groups from the west and Harzer's armor from the east, Hicks's lightly armed paratroopers had no option but to hold until relieved, or until reinforcements and supplies were safely down.

Colonel Charles Mackenzie, General Urquhart's chief of staff, had spent the night on the Renkum Heath landing zone, about three miles away from Hicks's command post. The intense fighting had caused Division to move out of the woods and back onto the field. There the headquarters staff took shelter in gliders for the rest of the night. Mackenzie was concerned about the absence of any word from Urquhart. "For more than nine hours, we had heard nothing whatsoever from the General," he recalls. "I assumed that he was with Lathbury's 1st Brigade, but communications were out and we had heard nothing from either officer. I knew that a decision would soon have to be made about the command of the division. There always existed the possibility that Urquhart had been captured or killed."

Early Monday, still without news, Mackenzie decided to confer with two senior staff officers, Lieutenant Colonel R. G. Loder-Symonds and Lieutenant Colonel P. H. Preston. Mackenzie informed them of Urquhart's conversation with him prior to takeoff in England: the succession of command, in case anything happened to Urquhart, should be Lathbury, Hicks, then Hackett. Now, with Lathbury missing as well, Mackenzie felt that Brigadier Hicks should be contacted. The other officers agreed. Immediately they drove to Hicks's headquarters. There, in a house close by the Heelsum-Arnhem road, Mackenzie told Hicks what he knew. "We had a scanty report that Frost had taken the bridge, but that the First and Third battalions were caught up in street fighting and had not as yet been able to reinforce him," Mackenzie remembers.

The best course of action now, Mackenzie believed, was for Hicks to release one of his Airlanding battalions and send it to the bridge. It could be reinforced later by elements of Hackett's 4th Paratroop Brigade when it arrived later in the morning. At the same time, Hicks was asked to take command of the division immediately.

Hicks seemed stunned. His forces were already understrength and he did not have a full battalion to send to the bridge. Yet it appeared the British battle plan was faltering. If Frost failed to get help immediately, the bridge might be lost; and if the landing areas were overrun, Hackett's 4th Brigade could be destroyed before it was even assembled.

Additionally, there seemed to be a tacit acknowledgment that Hicks was being asked to assume command of a division already in the process of disintegration through a total breakdown of communications and the absence of the commanding officer. Reluctantly, Hicks released half of one battalion—all he could spare—for defense of the bridge.* Obviously, that decision was most urgent. The bridge had to be held. Then, as Mackenzie remembers, "We finally convinced Hicks that he must take command of the division."

Few men had ever been asked to accept battleground responsibility for an entire division under such a complexity of circumstances. Hicks quickly discovered how critically the communications breakdown was affecting all operations. The few messages from Frost at the bridge were being received via Lieutenant Colonel Sheriff Thompson, commanding the Airlanding Light Regiment artillery. From an observation post in the steeple of the Oosterbeek Laag church, two and one-half

---

*He ordered half of the South Staffords to start off for Arnhem. The other half of this battalion would not arrive until the second lift, when, supplementing the advance of Hackett's 11th Battalion, these units would also move out.

miles from the bridge, Thompson had established a radio link with Major D. S. Munford's artillery command post at Brigade headquarters in a waterworks building near the bridge. The Thompson-Munford link afforded the only dependable radio communications at Hicks's disposal.

Equally critical, Division had no communications with General Browning's Corps headquarters near Nijmegen, or with the special "Phantom Net" sets at Montgomery's headquarters. Of the few vital messages that did reach England, most were sent over a BBC set, which had been specially flown in for British war correspondents. Its signal was weak and distorted. A high-powered German station and the British set were operating on the same frequency. Ironically, Division could pick up signals from rear Corps headquarters back in England, but were unable to transmit messages back. What sparse communications did get through via the BBC set were picked up at Browning's rear Corps headquarters at Moor Park and then relayed to the Continent. The transmission took hours and when the messages arrived they were outdated and often virtually meaningless.

Frustrated and worried, Hicks had three immediate concerns: the weather over England; the inability to confirm the planned arrival time of the second lift; and his lack of a means of informing anyone of the true situation in the Arnhem area. Additionally he could not warn Hackett of the perilous hold the British had on the landing areas where the 4th Brigade would expect to drop in cleared and protected zones.

Less crucial, but nonetheless troublesome, was the forthcoming encounter with Brigadier Shan Hackett. The volatile Hackett, Mackenzie told Hicks, would be informed of Urquhart's decision regarding the chain of command the moment he landed. "I knew Hackett's temperament," Mackenzie recalls, "and I was not looking forward to the meeting. But telling him was my job and I was following General Urquhart's orders. I could no longer take the chance that something had not happened to both the General and Lathbury."

At least Hicks was relieved of that delicate confrontation. The new division commander had enough on his mind. "The situation was more than just confusing," he remembers. "It was a bloody mess."

4

IN THE WESTERN SUBURBS of Arnhem, the once tidy parks and clean-swept streets were scarred and pitted by the battle as the British 1st and 3rd battalions struggled to reach the bridge. Glass, debris and the broken boughs of copper beech trees littered the cobblestone streets. Rhododendron bushes and thick borders of bronze, orange and yellow marigolds lay torn and crushed, and vegetable gardens in back of the neat Dutch houses were in ruins. The snouts of British antitank guns protruded from the shattered windows of shops and stores, while German half-tracks, deliberately backed into houses and concealed by their rubble, menaced the streets. Black smoke spewed up from burning British and German vehicles and constant showers of debris rained down as shells slammed into strong points. The crumpled bodies of the wounded and dead lay everywhere. Many soldiers remember seeing Dutch men and women, wearing white helmets and overalls emblazoned with red crosses, dashing heedlessly through the fire from both sides, to drag the injured and dying to shelter.

This strange, deadly battle now devastating the outskirts of the city barely two miles from the Arnhem bridge seemed to have no plan or strategy. Like all street fighting, it had become one massive, fierce, man-to-man encounter in a checkerboard of streets.

The Red Devils were cold, unshaven, dirty and hungry. The fighting had been too constant to allow men more than an occasional "brew-up" of tea. Ammunition was running short and casualties were mounting; some companies had lost as much as 50 percent of their strength. Sleep had been impossible, except in brief snatches. Many men, weary and on the move for hours, had lost all sense of time. Few knew exactly where they were or how far away the bridge still was, but they were grimly determined to get there. Years later, men like Private Henry Bennett of Colonel Fitch's 3rd Battalion, on the middle, Tiger route, would remember that throughout the constant skirmishes, sniping and mortar fire, one command was constant: "Move! Move! Move!"

Yet to General Urquhart, now absent from Division headquarters for nearly sixteen hours and without radio contact, the progress of the attack was agonizingly slow. Since 3 A.M., when he had been roused at the villa where he had spent a restless few hours, Urquhart, along with Brigadier Lathbury, had been on the road continuously with the 3rd Battalion. "Sharp encounters, brief bursts of fire, kept bringing the entire column to a stop," Urquhart says. The psychological effectiveness of German snipers disturbed the General. He had anticipated that some of his men who had not been in action before would be "a bit bullet-shy initially," but would rally quickly. Instead, along some streets, sniper fire alone was slowing up the progress of the entire battalion. Yet, rather than interfere with Fitch's command, Urquhart remained silent. "As a divisional commander mixed up in a battalion encounter . . . I was in the worst possible position to intervene, but all the time I was conscious of each precious second that was being wasted." German snipers were dealt with effectively, but Urquhart was appalled at the time it took to dig them out.

So was Regimental Sergeant Major John C. Lord. Like the General, Lord was chafing at the delay. "German resistance was fierce and continuous, but at least a large part of our delay was caused by the Dutch as well. They were out in the streets early, waving, smiling, offering us ersatz coffee. Some of them had even draped Union Jacks over their hedges. There they were, right in the midst of the fighting, and they didn't even seem to realize it was going on. They, with all their good intentions, were holding us up as much as the Germans."

Suddenly the intensive sniper fire was replaced by something far more serious: the piercing crack of the enemy's 88 mm. artillery and self-propelled guns. At this point the forward units of Fitch's battalion were close by the massive St. Elisabeth's Hospital, less than two miles northwest of the Arnhem bridge. The hospital lay almost at the confluence of the two main highways leading into Arnhem, along which the 1st and 3rd battalions were attempting to march to the bridge. Here, elements of the Hohenstaufen Division's armor had been positioned throughout the night. Both Colonel Dobie's 1st Battalion on the Ede-Arnhem road and Fitch's 3rd Battalion on the Utrecht road must pass on either side of the junction to get to the bridge. Dobie's battalion was the first to feel the force of Colonel Harzer's fanatical SS units.

From a horseshoe-shaped perimeter covering the northern and western approaches of the city, the Germans had forced Dobie's men off the upper road and into cover in the surrounding built-up areas. SS men, hidden on the rooftops, and snipers in attics had allowed forward units to pass unhindered before opening up with a murderous fire on troops coming up behind. In the confusion of the surprise attack, companies and platoons were dispersed in all directions.

Now, employing the same tactics, the Germans were concentrating on Fitch's 3rd Battalion. And, in a situation that could have disastrous consequences, four critical officers—the commanders of the 1st and 3rd battalions, the officer in charge of the 1st Parachute Brigade and the commander of the 1st British Airborne Division—all found themselves bottled up in the same small, heavily populated area. Ironically, as in the case of Model and his commanders at Oosterbeek, General Urquhart and Brigadier Lathbury were surrounded by an enemy oblivious to their presence.

Trapped by fire from ahead and behind, the British columns scattered. Some men headed for buildings along the Rhine, more took to the nearby woods and others—among them, Urquhart and Lathbury—ran for safety into narrow streets of identical brick houses.

Urquhart and his group had just reached a three-story house in a block of buildings near the main Utrecht-Arnhem road when the Germans shelled the building. The British were uninjured, but German armor, Urquhart was later to note, "moved through the streets with almost casual immunity." As one tank rumbled down the street, its commander standing in the open hatch looking for targets, Major Peter Waddy leaned out of an upper-floor window of a house next to Urquhart's and expertly dropped a plastic explosive into the open turret, blowing the tank to pieces.* Other men, following Waddy's example, demolished two more tanks. But, although the British fought fiercely, the lightly armed troopers were no match for the German armor.

---

*A short time later, reconnoitering the British positions, Waddy was killed by a mortar blast.

Urquhart's own predicament was increasing by the minute. He was desperately anxious to get back to Division headquarters and gain control of the battle. Caught up in the fighting, he believed his only means of escape was to take to the streets and, in the confusion, try to get through the German positions. His officers, fearful for his safety, disagreed, but Urquhart was adamant. The intense fighting was, as he saw it, still only "company-size action" and, as the buildings the British occupied were not yet surrounded, he felt the group should get out quickly before German strength increased and the ring tightened.

During the hasty conference amid the noise of the battle, Urquhart and his officers were dumfounded to see a British Bren gun carrier clatter down the street, as though unaware of the German fire, and pull up outside the building. A Canadian lieutenant, Leo Heaps, who in Urquhart's words "seemed to have a charmed existence," leaped out of the driver's seat and raced for the building. Behind Heaps was Charles "Frenchie" Labouchère, of the Dutch resistance, who was acting as Heaps's guide. The carrier was loaded with supplies and ammunition which Heaps hoped to deliver to Colonel Frost on the bridge. With German armor everywhere, the small vehicle and its two occupants had miraculously survived enemy fire and en route had, by chance, discovered Urquhart's whereabouts. Now, for the first time in hours, Urquhart learned from Heaps what was happening. "The news was far from encouraging," Urquhart later recalled. "Communications were still out. Frost was on the northern end of the bridge under heavy attack, but holding, and I was reported missing or captured." After listening to Heaps, Urquhart told Lathbury that it was now imperative "before we're completely bottled up to take a chance and break out."

Turning to Heaps, Urquhart told the Canadian that if he reached Division headquarters after completing his mission at the bridge, he was to urge Mackenzie to "organize as much help as he could for Frost's battalion." At all costs, including his own safety, Urquhart was determined that Frost must get the supplies and men needed to hold until Horrocks' tanks reached Arnhem.

As Heaps and Labouchère left, Urquhart and Lathbury set about making their escape. The street outside was now being swept constantly by enemy fire and buildings were crumpling under the pounding of shells. Urquhart noted "a growing pile of dead around the houses we occupied," and concluded that any exit via the street would be impossible. The commanders, along with others, decided to leave from the rear of the building, where, under covering fire and smoke bombs, they might be able to get away. Then, taking advantage of plantings in the back gardens of the row houses, Urquhart and Lathbury hoped eventually to reach a quiet area and make their way back to headquarters.

The route was nightmarish. While paratroopers laid down a heavy smoke screen, Urquhart's group dashed out the back door, sprinted through a vegetable garden and climbed a fence separating the house from its neighbor. As they paused for a moment near the next enclosure, Lathbury's Sten gun went off accidentally, barely missing the General's right foot. As Urquhart was later to write, "I chided Lathbury about soldiers who could not keep their Stens under control. It was bad enough for a division commander to be jinking about . . . and it would have been too ironic for words to be laid low by a bullet fired by one of my own brigadiers."

Climbing fence after fence, and once a ten-foot-high brick wall, the men moved down the entire block of houses until, finally, they reached an intersecting cobbled street. Then, confused and weary, they made a drastic miscalculation. Instead of veering left, which might have given them a margin of safety, they turned right toward St. Elisabeth's Hospital, directly into the German fire.

Running ahead of Urquhart and Lathbury were two other officers, Captain William Taylor of the Brigade's headquarters staff and Captain James Cleminson of the 3rd Battalion. One of them called out suddenly but neither Urquhart nor Lathbury understood his words. Before Taylor and Cleminson could head them off, the two senior officers came upon a maze of intersecting streets where, it seemed to Urquhart, "a German machine gun was firing down each one." As the four men attempted to run past one of these narrow crossings, Lathbury was hit.

Quickly the others dragged him off the street and into a house. There, Urquhart saw that a bullet had entered the Brigadier's lower back and he appeared to be temporarily paralyzed. "All of us knew," Urquhart recalls, "that he could travel no farther." Lathbury urged the General to leave immediately without him. "You'll only get cut off if you stay, sir," he told Urquhart. As they talked, Urquhart saw a German soldier appear at the window. He raised his automatic and fired at point-blank range. The bloodied mass of the German's face disappeared. Now, with the Germans so near, there was no longer any question that Urquhart must leave quickly. Before going, he talked with the middle-aged couple who owned the house and spoke some English. They promised to get Lathbury to St. Elisabeth's Hospital as soon as there was a lull in the fighting. In order to save the owners from German reprisal, Urquhart and his party hid Lathbury in a cellar beneath a stairway until he could be removed to the hospital. Then, Urquhart remembers, "we left by the back door and into yet another maze of tiny, fenced gardens." The three men did not get far, but Urquhart's life may well have been saved by the prompt action of fifty-five-year-old Antoon Derksen, owner of a terrace house at Zwarteweg 14.

In the maelstrom of firing, Antoon, his wife Anna, their son Jan, and daughter Hermina were sheltering in the kitchen at the rear of the house. Glancing through a window, Derksen was amazed to see three British officers vault over the fence into his back garden and head for the kitchen door. Quickly, he let them in.

Unable to communicate—he didn't speak English and no one in Urquhart's party knew Dutch—Antoon, gesturing, tried to warn the Britishers that the area was surrounded. "There were Germans in the street," he later recalled, "and at the back, in the direction the officers had been going. At the end of the row of gardens there were Germans in position at the corner."

Derksen hastily ushered his visitors up a narrow staircase to a landing and from there into a bedroom. In the ceiling was a pull-down door with steps leading to the attic. Cautiously looking out the bedroom window the three men saw the reason for Derksen's wild pantomime. Only a few feet below them, in positions all along the street, were German troops.

"We were so close to them," Urquhart remembers, "we could hear them talking."

Urquhart was unable to guess whether the Germans had spotted his group as they entered the rear of the house, or whether they might burst in at any moment. In spite of Derksen's warning that the area was surrounded, he pondered the twin risks of continuing through the chain of back gardens or making a dash down the front street, using hand grenades to clear the way. He was ready to take any chance to return to his command. His officers, fearful for him, were not. At the moment, the odds were simply too great. It was far better, they argued, to wait until British troops overran the sector than for the commanding general to risk capture or possible death.

The advice, Urquhart knew, was sound, and he did not want to compel his officers to take risks that might prove suicidal. Yet, "my long absence from Division headquarters was all I could think about, and anything seemed better to me than to stay out of the battle in this way."

The familiar creaking clack of caterpillar treads forced Urquhart to stay put. From the window the three officers saw a German self-propelled gun come slowly down the street. Directly outside the Derksen house, it came to a halt. The top of the armored vehicle was almost level with the bedroom window, and the crew, dismounting, now sat talking and smoking directly below. Obviously, they were not moving on and at any moment the Britishers expected them to enter the house.

Quickly Captain Taylor pulled down the attic steps and the three officers hurriedly climbed up. Crouched down and looking about him, the six-foot Urquhart saw that the attic was little more than a crawl space. He felt "idiotic, ridiculous, as ineffectual in the battle as a spectator."

The house was now silent. Antoon Derksen, as a loyal Dutchman, had sheltered the British. Now, fearing possible reprisal if Urquhart was found, he prudently evacuated his family to a neighboring house. In the nearly airless attic, and without food or water, Urquhart and his officers could only wait anxiously, hoping either for the Germans to pull back or for British troops to arrive. On this Monday, September 18, with Market-Garden only a day old, the Germans had almost brought the Arnhem battle to a halt and, compounding all the errors and miscalculations of the operation, Urquhart, the one man who might have brought cohesion to the British attack, was isolated in an attic, trapped within the German lines.

It had been a long, tedious mission for Captain Paul Gräbner and his 9th SS Panzer Reconnaissance Battalion. Allied paratroopers had not landed in the eleven-mile stretch between Arnhem and Nijmegen. Of that, Gräbner was quite certain. But enemy units were in Nijmegen. Immediately after a few of Gräbner's vehicles had crossed the great Waal river bridge, there had been a short, brisk small-arms encounter. In the darkness, the enemy had seemed to show no great inclination to continue the fight against his armored vehicles, and Gräbner had reported to headquarters that the Allies seemed to have little strength in the city as yet.

Now, his scouting mission completed, Gräbner ordered a few self-propelled guns from his forty-vehicle unit to guard the southern approaches to the Nijmegen bridge. With the rest of the patrol, he headed back north to Arnhem. He had seen neither paratroopers nor any enemy activity when crossing the Arnhem bridge the night before. However, from radio messages, he had learned that some British troops were on one side of the bridge. Harzer's headquarters had merely called them "advance units." Gräbner halted once more, this time at the town of Elst, approximately midway between Arnhem and Nijmegen. There again, to be within striking distance of either highway bridge, he left off part of his column. With the remaining twenty-two vehicles, he sped back toward the Arnhem bridge to clear it of whatever small enemy units were there. Against paratroopers armed with only rifles or machine guns, Gräbner expected little difficulty. His powerful armored units would simply smash through the lightly held British defenses and knock them out.

At precisely 9:30 A.M., Corporal Don Lumb, from his rooftop position near the bridge, yelled out excitedly, "Tanks! It's XXX Corps!" At Battalion headquarters nearby, Colonel John Frost heard his own spotter call out. Like Corporal Lumb, Frost felt a moment's heady exhilaration. "I remember thinking that we would have the honor of welcoming XXX Corps into Arnhem all by ourselves," he recalls. Other men were equally cheered. On the opposite side of the northern approach, the men under the ramp near Captain Eric Mackay's command post could already hear the sound of heavy vehicles reverberating on the bridge above. Sergeant Charles Storey pounded up the stairs to Corporal Lumb's lookout. Peering toward the smoke still rising from the southern approach, Storey saw the column Lumb had spotted. His reaction was immediate. Racing back downstairs, the pre-Dunkirk veteran shouted, "They're Germans! Armored cars on the bridge!"

At top speed, the vanguard of Captain Paul Gräbner's assault force came on across the bridge. With extraordinary skill, German drivers, swerving left and right, not only avoided the smoldering wreckage cluttering the bridge, but drove straight through a mine field—a string of platelike Teller mines that the British had laid during the night. Only one of Gräbner's five lead vehicles touched off a mine—and only superficially damaged, kept on coming. On his side of the ramp, Captain Mackay stared with amazement as the first of the squat camouflaged cars, machine guns firing constantly, barreled off the ramp, smashed through the British perimeter defenses, and kept on going straight toward the center of Arnhem. Almost immediately, Mackay saw another go past. "We had no antitank guns on our side," Mackay says, "and I just watched helplessly as three more armored cars sped right past us and took off up the avenue."

Gräbner's daring plan to smash across the bridge by force and speed was underway. Out of the sight of the British, on the southern approach to the bridge, he had lined up his column. Now, half-tracks, more armored cars, personnel carriers and even a few truckloads of infantry, firing from behind heavy sacks of grain, began to advance. Crouching behind the half-tracks were other German soldiers, firing steadily.

The sudden surprise breakthrough of Gräbner's lead vehicles had stunned the British. They recovered quickly. Antitank guns from Frost's side of the bridge began to get the range. From the entire northern area a lethal fire enveloped the German column. From parapets, rooftops, windows and slit trenches, troopers opened fire with every weapon available, from machine guns to hand grenades. Sapper Ronald Emery, on Mackay's side of the ramp, shot the driver and codriver of the first half-track to cross. As the second came into view, Emery shot its drivers, too. The half-track came to a dead halt just off the ramp, whereupon the remainder of its crew of six, abandoning the vehicle, were shot one by one.

Relentlessly, Gräbner's column pressed on. Two more half-tracks nosed across the bridge. Suddenly, chaos overtook the German assault. The driver of the third half-track was wounded. Panicked, he threw his vehicle into reverse, colliding with the half-track behind. The two vehicles, now inextricably tangled, slewed across the road, one bursting into flames. Doggedly the Germans coming up behind tried to force a passage. Accelerating their vehicles, frantic to gain the northern side, they rammed into one another and into the growing piles of debris tossed up by shells and mortar bursts. Out of control, some half-tracks hit the edge of the ramp with such force that they toppled over the edge and down into the streets below. Supporting German infantrymen following the half-tracks were mercilessly cut down. Unable to advance beyond the center of the bridge, the survivors raced back to the southern side. A storm of fire ricocheted against the girders of the bridge. Now, too, shells from Lieutenant Colonel Sheriff Thompson's artillery, situated in Oosterbeek, and called in by Major Dennis Munford from the attic of Brigade headquarters near Frost's own building, screamed into Gräbner's stricken vehicles. Through all the din came the yelling of the now-exuberant British paratroopers as they shouted the war cry, "Whoa Mohammed," which the Red Devils had first used in the dry hills of North Africa in 1942.*

The fierceness of the raging battle stunned the Dutch in the area. Lambert Schaap, who lived with his family on the Rijnkade —the street running east and west of the bridge—hurried his wife and nine children off to a shelter. Schaap himself remained

---

*In that campaign, paratroopers noted that the Arabs, shouting messages to one another, seemed to begin each communication with these two words. In Arnhem, the war cry was to take on special meaning. It enabled paratroopers on both sides of the northern ramp to determine who was friend or foe in the various buildings and positions, since the Germans seemed unable to pronounce the words. According to Hilary St. George Saunders in *By Air to Battle*, the war cry "seemed to rouse the men to their highest endeavours."

in his house until a hail of bullets came through the windows, pitting walls and smashing furniture. Under this intense barrage Schaap fled. To Police Sergeant Joannes van Kuijk, the battle seemed endless. "The firing was furious," he recalls, "and one building after another seemed to be hit or burning. Telephone calls from colleagues and friends were constant, asking for information about what was happening. We were having a hard time of it in our building, and neighboring premises were catching fire. The houses on Eusebius Buiten Singel were also alight."

On that wide boulevard near the northern approach, Coenraad Hulleman, in his fiancée's house only a few doors away from Captain Mackay's command post, now stayed with the rest of the Van der Sande family in their basement shelter. "There was a funny sound overriding all the other noise and someone said it was raining," Hulleman remembers. "I went up to the first floor, looked out, and saw that it was fire. Soldiers were running in every direction, and the entire block seemed to be in flames. The battle moved right up the boulevard, and suddenly it was our turn. Bullets smacked into the house, smashing windows, and upstairs we heard musical notes as the piano was hit. Then, amazingly, a sound like someone typing in Mr. Van der Sande's office. The bullets were simply chewing up the typewriter." Hulleman's fiancée, Truid, who had followed him up, saw that shots were hitting the tower of the massive Church of St. Eusibius. As she watched in amazement the gold hands of the huge clock on the church spun crazily as though, Truid remembers, "time was racing by."

To the bridge fighters, time had lost all meaning. The shock, speed and ferocity of the battle caused many men to think that the fight had gone on for many hours. Actually, Gräbner's attack had lasted less than two. Of the armored vehicles that Colonel Harzer had jealously guarded from General Harmel, twelve lay wrecked or burning on the northern side. The remainder disengaged from the carnage and moved back to Elst, minus their commander. In the bitter no-quarter fighting, Captain Paul Gräbner had been killed.

Now the British, in pride and triumph, began to assess the damage. Medics and stretcher-bearers, braving the unrelenting sniper fire, moved through the smoke and litter, carrying the wounded of both sides to shelter. The Red Devils on the bridge had repulsed and survived the horror of an armored attack and, almost as though they were being congratulated on their success, 2nd Battalion signalmen suddenly picked up a strong clear message from XXX Corps. The grimy, weary troopers imagined that their ordeal was all but over. Now, beyond any doubt, Horrocks' tanks must be a scant few hours away.

From airfields behind the German border, swarms of fighters took to the air. To amass and fuel the planes, the nearly depleted Luftwaffe had mounted an all-out effort. Now, after a frantic, sleepless night, during which fighters had been rushed in from all over Germany, some 190 planes gathered over Holland between 9 and 10 A.M. Their mission was to destroy the second lift of Market. Unlike the skeptical Field Marshal Model, the Luftwaffe generals believed the captured Market-Garden plans to be authentic. They saw a glittering opportunity to achieve a major success. From the plans, German air commanders knew the routes, landing zones and drop times of the Monday lift. Squadrons of German fighters patrolling the Dutch coast across the known Allied flight paths and drop zones waited to pounce on the airborne columns, due to begin their drops at 10 A.M. Zero hour passed with no sign of the Allied air fleet. The short-range fighters were ordered to land, refuel and take off again. But the sky remained empty. None of the anticipated targets materialized. Baffled and dismayed, the Luftwaffe high command could only wonder what had happened.

What had happened was simple. Unlike Holland, where the weather was clear, Britain was covered by fog. On the bases, British and American airborne troops, ready to go, waited impatiently by their planes and gliders. On this crucial morning, when every hour mattered, General Lewis H. Brereton, the First Allied Airborne Army commander, was, like the men of the second lift, at the mercy of the weather. After consultation with the meteorologists, Brereton was forced to reschedule zero hour. The men in and around Arnhem and the Americans down the corridor—all holding against the increasing German buildup—must now wait four long hours more. The second lift could not reach the drop zones before 2 P.M.

5

AT VALKENSWAARD, fifty-seven miles south of Arnhem, ground fog had held up the planned 6:30 A.M. jump-off time for the tanks of XXX Corps. Scout cars, however, had set out on schedule. Patrolling ahead and to the east and west since daybreak, they were feeling out the German strength. To the east, heather-covered sand and small streams made the area barely negotiable even for reconnaissance vehicles. West of the village, wooden bridges over streams and rivers were considered too light to support tanks. As scout cars in the center moved along the narrow, one-tank-wide main road out of Valkenswaard, they suddenly encountered a German tank and two self-propelled guns, which drove off toward Eindhoven as the patrol approached. From all reports it seemed clear that the quickest route into Eindhoven was still the highway, despite the sighting of German armor and the expectation of running into more as the British approached the city. Now, three hours later, General Horrocks' tanks were only just beginning to roll again. As Colonel Frost's men engaged Captain Gräbner's units at the Arnhem bridge, the spearheading Irish Guards were finally on the move, heading up the main road toward Eindhoven.

Stiff German resistance had thwarted Horrocks' plan to smash out from the Meuse-Escaut Canal on Sunday and link up with General Taylor's 101st Airborne Division in Eindhoven in less than three hours. By nightfall on the seventeenth, Lieutenant Colonel Joe Vandeleur's tankers had come only seven miles to Valkenswaard, six miles short of the day's objective. There had seemed little reason to push on during the night. Brigadier Norman Gwatkin, chief of staff of the Guards Armored Division, had told Vandeleur that the Son bridge beyond Eindhoven was destroyed. Bridging equipment would have to be brought up before Vandeleur's tanks could cross. As Vandeleur remembers, Gwatkin said, "Push on to Eindhoven tomorrow, old boy, but take your time. We've lost a bridge."

Unaware of the setback, men were impatient at the delay. Lieutenant John Gorman, who had attended General Horrocks' briefing in Leopoldsburg prior to the break-out, had thought at the time that there were too many bridges to cross.

Now Gorman, recipient of the Military Cross a few weeks earlier, was edgy and irritable. His original fears seemed justified. Anxious to be off, Gorman could not understand why the Guards Armored had spent the night in Valkenswaard. Habit, he noted, "seemed to dictate that one slept at night and worked by day," but now, Gorman felt, such behavior should not apply. "We must get on," he remembers saying. "We can't wait." Lieutenant Rupert Mahaffey was equally disturbed at the Guards' slow advance. "I began having the first faint traces of conscience," he says. "Our advance seemed slower than intended, and I knew that if we did not pick up the pace soon we weren't going to get to Arnhem on time."

Although the scouting patrols of the Household Cavalry had warned of waiting German armor and infantry, the tanks of the Irish Guards met little opposition until they reached the village of Aalst, halfway to Eindhoven. Then, from the pinewood forests flanking the highway, a hail of infantry fire engulfed the column, and a lone self-propelled gun engaged the leading tanks. It was quickly put out of action and Vandeleur's force rumbled on through the village. Two miles north, at a small bridge over the river Dommel, the Irish were held up again, this time by heavy artillery fire. Four 88 mm. guns covered the bridge. Infantry with heavy machine guns were hidden in nearby houses and behind concrete walls. Immediately the lead vehicles halted and British troops, jumping from the tanks, fought back.

To move on as quickly as possible, Vandeleur decided to call in the rocket-firing Typhoons that had aided the column so expertly during the previous day's advance. Flight Lieutenant Donald Love, now in complete charge of ground-to-air communication, put through the request. To his astonishment, he was turned down. In Belgium, the squadrons were weathered in by fog. Vandeleur, Love recalls, "was livid." Squinting into the bright weather over Holland, he asked Love sarcastically "if the R.A.F. is frightened by sunshine."

By now the entire column, stretching back almost to the Belgian border, was stalled by the well-sited enemy guns. Lead tanks tried to edge forward, and one gun, firing directly down the road, stopped them at point-blank range. As his tanks opened up against the Germans, Vandeleur called for heavy artillery and quickly ordered patrols to move out west along the river in search of a bridge or ford where his vehicles might cross, outflank the German battery and attack from the rear.

A barrage of steel whistled over the lead tanks as British batteries began to engage the enemy. Well positioned and fiercely determined, the Germans continued to fire. For two hours the battle went on. Fuming at the delay, Vandeleur was helpless. All he could do was wait.

But, barely four miles to the north, one of the reconnaissance units had met with unexpected success. After a circuitous cross-country trip through water-veined terrain and marshes, and across fragile wooden bridges, one troop of scout cars, skirting the German positions, came suddenly upon American paratroopers north of Eindhoven. Shortly before noon, Lieutenant John Palmer, commanding the Household Cavalry scout unit, was warmly greeted by Brigadier General Gerald Higgins, deputy commander of the 101st Screaming Eagles. By radio, Palmer jubilantly informed his headquarters that the "Stable Boys have contacted our Feathered Friends." The first of three vital link-ups along the corridor had been made, eighteen hours behind Market-Garden's schedule.

With contact finally established, discussion immediately turned to the Son bridge. Waiting British engineering units needed complete details in order to bring forward the materials and equipment needed to repair the damaged crossing. Sappers, moving up alongside Vandeleur's lead columns, prepared to rush to the bridge the moment the advance picked up again. Information could have been passed by radio, but the Americans had already discovered a simpler method. The surprised British were radioed to ask their engineers to telephone "Son 244." The call went immediately through the German-controlled automatic telephone exchange, and within minutes the Americans at the Son bridge had given British engineers the vital information they needed to bring up the proper bridging equipment.

In the village of Aalst, Vandeleur's tankers were startled by a sudden abrupt end to the German fire which had kept them immobilized so long on the main road. One of their own squadrons had opened the way. Working slowly down the western bank of the Dommel river, a British reconnaissance force came upon a crossing a mile north of Aalst and behind the German positions. The squadron charged the German guns from the rear, overran their positions and ended the battle.

Unaware of the move, the stalled tankers at Aalst thought the sudden silence was a lull in the fighting. Major Edward Tyler, in charge of the lead Number 2 Squadron, was debating whether he should take advantage of the cessation and order his tanks to smash on, when he spotted a man cycling down the main road toward the column. Stopping on the far bank, the man jumped off the bicycle and, waving frantically, ran across the bridge. The astounded Tyler heard him say: "Your General! Your General! The Boche have gone!"

Breathlessly, the Dutchman introduced himself. Cornelis Los, forty-one, was an engineer employed in Eindhoven but living in Aalst. "The road," Los told Tyler, "is open and you have put out of action the only German tank at the village entrance." Then, Tyler recalls, "he produced a detailed sketch of all the German positions between Aalst and Eindhoven."

Immediately, Tyler gave the order to advance. The tanks moved over the bridge and up the road, passing the now ruined and deserted German artillery positions. Within the hour, Tyler saw the sprawl of Eindhoven up ahead and what appeared to be thousands of Dutch thronging the road, cheering and waving flags. "The only obstruction holding us up now are the Dutch crowds," Major E. Fisher-Rowe radioed back down the column. In the heady carnival atmosphere, the cumbersome tanks of XXX Corps would take more than four hours to move through the city. Not until shortly after 7 P.M. did advance units reach the Son bridge, where Colonel Robert F. Sink's weary engineers were working, as they had been ever since it was destroyed, to repair the vital span.

From the outset, the synchronized Market-Garden schedule had allowed little margin for error. Now, like the thwarted advance of the British battalions into Arnhem, the damage to the bridge at Son was a major setback that threatened the entire operation. Twenty-eight miles of the corridor—from the Belgian border north to Veghel—were now controlled by the

Anglo-Americans. With extraordinary speed, the 101st Division had covered its fifteen-mile stretch of highway, capturing the principal towns of Eindhoven, St. Oedenrode and Veghel, and all but two of eleven crossings. Yet Horrocks' 20,000-vehicle relief column could advance no farther until the Son crossing was repaired. British engineers and equipment, moving up with the lead tanks, must work against time to repair the bridge and move XXX Corps over the Wilhelmina Canal, for there was no longer an alternative route that Horrocks' tanks could take.

In the planning stages General Maxwell Taylor, knowing that the Son bridge was vital to a straight dash up the corridor, had included a secondary target as well. To counteract just such a setback as had occurred at Son, Taylor had ordered a one-hundred-foot-long concrete road bridge over the canal at the village of Best to be taken as well. Four miles west of the main road, the bridge could still be used in an emergency. Since intelligence sources believed that the area held few German troops, a lone company had been assigned to grab the bridge and a nearby railway crossing.

Best was to become a tragic misnomer for the American troopers sent to secure it. Lieutenant Edward L. Wierzbowski's reinforced company had been greatly reduced during ferocious night fighting on the seventeenth. Infiltrating along dikes and canal banks, and through marshes, the dogged troopers under Wierzbowski's command pressed on against overwhelming German forces; once they were within fifteen feet of the bridge before being stopped by a barrage of fire. At various times during the night, word filtered back that the bridge had been taken. Other reports claimed that Wierzbowski's company had been wiped out. Reinforcements, like the original company, became quickly engulfed in the desperate, unequal struggle. At 101st headquarters, it was soon clear that German forces were heavily concentrated at Best. Far from being lightly held, the village contained upwards of one thousand troops—units of the forgotten German Fifteenth Army. And like a sponge, Best was drawing more and more American forces. As fighting raged throughout the area, Wierzbowski and the few survivors of his company were almost in the dead center of the battle. So surrounded that their own reinforcements did not know they were there, they continued to fight for the bridge.

Around noon, as advance parties of British and Americans linked up in Eindhoven, the bridge at Best was blown by the Germans. So close were Wierzbowski and his men that falling debris added to the wounds they had already sustained. Elsewhere in the area, casualties were also heavy. One of the most colorful and acerbic of the 101st commanders, Lieutenant Colonel Robert Cole, who held the Congressional Medal of Honor, was killed. The medal also would be awarded posthumously to another soldier. Private Joe E. Mann, so badly wounded at the bridge that both arms were bandaged and tied to his sides, saw a German grenade land among the men he was with. Unable to free his arms, Mann fell on the grenade, saving the others around him. As Wierzbowski reached him, Mann spoke just once. "My back is gone," he told the lieutenant. Then he was dead.

With the Best bridge gone, the success of Market-Garden now hinged more critically than ever on the speed with which engineers could repair the Son crossing. In the interlocking phases of the plan—each link dependent on the next—the road beyond Son was empty of the tanks that should have moved along it hours before. Montgomery's daring attack was moving into ever-deepening trouble.

The farther up the corridor, the more compounded the problems became. Isolated in the center from General Taylor's Screaming Eagles to the south and the Red Devils in Arnhem, General Gavin's 82nd Airborne were holding firmly to the 1,500-foot-long bridge at Grave and the smaller one near Heumen. To the southwest, after a brisk fight, platoons of the 504th and 508th, attacking simultaneously from opposite sides of the Maas-Waal Canal, seized another bridge over the Grave-Nijmegen highway at the village of Honinghutie, opening an alternate route into Nijmegen for Horrocks' tanks. But just as the damaged Son bridge was holding up the British advance into the middle sector of the corridor, so the inability of the 82nd to seize the Nijmegen crossing quickly had created its own problems. There, SS troops were now dug in at the southern approaches. Well protected and concealed, they repeatedly repulsed attacks by a company of the 508th. As each hour passed, German strength was building, and Gavin could not spare more men in an all-out effort to get the bridge; for throughout the 82nd's vast lodgment—an area ranging ten miles north to south and twelve miles east to west—a series of wild, apparently uncoordinated enemy attacks threatened disaster.

Patrols along the Grave-Nijmegen highway were being constantly attacked by infiltrating enemy troops. Corporal Earl Oldfather, on the lookout for snipers, saw three men in a field the 504th was occupying. "One was bailing water out of his hole, the other two were digging," Oldfather recalls. "I waved and saw one of them pick up his rifle. They were Jerries who had gotten right into our field and were firing at us from our own foxholes."

Farther east, the two vital landing zones between the Groesbeek Heights and the German frontier quickly became battlefields as waves of low-caliber German infantry were thrown against the troopers. Among them were naval and Luftwaffe personnel, communications troops, soldiers on furlough, hospital orderlies, and even recently discharged convalescents. Corporal Frank Ruppe remembers that the first Germans he saw wore a bewildering variety of uniforms and rank insignia. The attack began so suddenly, he recalls, that "we were ambushed practically next to our own outposts." Units appeared as though from nowhere. In the first few minutes Lieutenant Harold Gensemer captured an overconfident German colonel who boasted that "my men will soon kick you right off this hill." They almost did.

Swarming across the German border from the town of Wyler and out of the Reichswald in overwhelming numbers, the Germans burst through the 82nd's perimeter defenses and quickly overran the zones, capturing supply and ammunition dumps. For a time the fighting was chaotic. The 82nd defenders held their positions as long as they could, then slowly pulled back. All over the area troops were alerted to rush to the scene. Men on the edge of Nijmegen force-marched all the way to the drop zones to give additional support.

A kind of panic seemed to set in among the Dutch also. Private Pat O'Hagan observed that as his platoon withdrew from the Nijmegen outskirts, the Dutch flags he had seen in profusion on the march into the city were being hurriedly taken down. Private Arthur "Dutch" Schultz,* a Normandy veteran and a Browning automatic gunner for his platoon, noticed that "everyone was nervous, and all I could hear was the chant 'BAR front and center.'" Everywhere he looked he saw Germans. "They were all around us and determined to rush us off our zones." It was clear to everyone that until German armor and seasoned reinforcements arrived, the enemy units, estimated at being close to two battalions, had been sent on a suicide mission: to wipe out the 82nd at any cost and hold the drop zones—the division's lifeline for reinforcements and supplies. If the Germans succeeded they might annihilate the second lift even as it landed.

At this time, General Gavin believed that the scheduled lift had already left England. There was no way of stopping or diverting them in time. Thus, Gavin had barely two hours to clear the areas and he needed every available trooper. Besides those already engaged, the only readily available reserves were two companies of engineers. Immediately Gavin threw them into the battle.

Bolstered by mortar and artillery fire, the troopers, outnumbered sometimes five to one, fought all through the morning to clear the zones.[†] Then with fixed bayonets many men went after the Germans down the slopes. It was only at the height of the battle that Gavin learned that the second lift would not arrive until 2 P.M. The woods remained infested with a hodgepodge of German infantry and it was obvious that these enemy forays heralded more concentrated and determined attacks. By juggling his troops from one area to another, Gavin was confident of holding, but he was only too well aware that for the moment the 82nd's situation was precarious. And now with information that the Son bridge was out and being repaired, he could not expect a British link-up before D plus 2. Impatiently and with growing concern, Gavin waited for the second lift, which would bring him desperately needed artillery, ammunition and men.

---

*See Cornelius Ryan, *The Longest Day*, pp. 50, 223.

[†]In the wild, chaotic fighting that ensued over a period of four hours on the zones, one of the most beloved officers in the 82nd, the heavyweight champion of the division, Captain Anthony Stefanich, was killed. "We've come a long way together," he told his men. "Tell the boys to do a good job." Then he died.

6

FROM THE SMOKING RUINS OF ARNHEM to the damaged crossing at Son, in foxholes, forests, alongside dikes, in the rubble of demolished buildings, on tanks and near the approaches of vital bridges, the men of Market-Garden and the Germans they fought heard the low rumble come out of the west. In column after column, darkening the sky, the planes and gliders of the second lift were approaching. The steady, mounting drone of motors caused a buoyant renewal of vigor and hope in the Anglo-Americans and the Dutch people. For most Germans, the sound was like a forerunner of doom. Combatants and civilians alike stared skyward, waiting. The time was a little before 2 P.M. Monday, September 18th.

The armada was gigantic, dwarfing even the spectacle of the day before. On the seventeenth, flights had followed two distinct northern and southern paths. Now, bad weather and the hope of effecting greater protection from the Luftwaffe had caused the entire second lift to be routed along the northern path to Holland. Condensed into one immense column covering mile after mile of sky, almost four thousand aircraft were layered at altitudes from 1,000 to 2,500 feet.

Flying wing tip to wing tip, 1,336 American C-47's and 340 British Stirling bombers made up the bulk of the sky train. Some of the planes carried troops. Others towed a staggering number of gliders—1,205 Horsas, Wacos and mammoth Hamilcars. Positioned at the rear of the 100-mile-long convoy, 252 four-engined Liberator bombers were ferrying cargo. Protecting the formations above and on the flanks, 867 fighters —ranging from squadrons of British Spitfires and rocket-firing Typhoons to American Thunderbolts and Lightnings—flew escort. In all, at time of takeoff, the second lift carried 6,674 airborne troops, 681 vehicles plus loaded trailers, 60 artillery pieces with ammunition and nearly 600 tons of supplies, including two bulldozers.*

---

*In the compilation of plane figures there are some discrepancies. American sources give a total of 3,807 aircraft; British figures list 4,000. The count used above comes from General Browning's after-action Corps report, indicating that the difference in figures seems to lie in the number of fighter planes. According to U.S. sources, 674 England-based fighters flew escort for the second

Wreathed by flak bursts, the huge armada made landfall over the Dutch coast at Schouwen Island, then headed inland due east to a traffic-control point south of the town of s'Hertogen-bosch. There, with fighters leading the way, the column split into three sections. With timed precision, executing difficult and dangerous maneuvers, the American contingents swung south and east for the zones of the 101st and 82nd as British formations headed due north for Arnhem.

As on the previous day, there were problems, although they were somewhat diminished. Confusion, abortions and fatal mishaps struck the glider fleets in particular. Long before the second lift reached the drop zones, 54 gliders were downed by structural or human error. Some 26 machines aborted over England and the Channel; two were seen to disintegrate during flight, and 26 more prematurely released on the 80-mile flight over enemy territory, landing far from their zones in Belgium and Holland and behind the German frontier. In one bizarre incident a distraught trooper rushed to the cockpit and yanked the release lever separating the glider from its tow plane. But troop casualties over-all were low. The greatest loss, as on the previous day, was in precious cargo. Once again Urquhart's men seemed plagued by fate—more than half of the lost cargo gliders were bound for Arnhem.

Fate had ruled the Luftwaffe too. At 10 A.M., with no sign of the expected Allied fleet, German air commanders pulled back more than half the 190-plane force to their bases, while the remainder patrolled the skies over northern and southern Holland. Half of these squadrons were caught in the wrong sector or were being refueled as the second lift came in. As a result, fewer than a hundred Messerschmitts and FW-190's rushed to battle in the Arnhem and Eindhoven areas. Not a single enemy plane was able to penetrate the massive Allied fighter screen protecting the troop carrier columns. After the mission Allied pilots claimed 29 Messerschmitts destroyed against a loss of only five American fighters.

---

lift, but not included in that number were 193 Belgium-based planes, which brings the over-all total of fighters to 867. By far the best account of the air action in Market-Garden, particularly as it pertains to the troop carriers, is the official U.S.A.F. Historical Division's Study No. 97, by Dr. John C. Warren, entitled *Airborne Operations in World War II, European Theater.*

Intense ground fire began to envelop the air fleet as it neared the landing zones. Approaching the 101st's drop areas north of Son, slow-moving glider trains encountered low ground haze and rain, cloaking them to some extent from German gunners. But sustained and deadly flak fire from the Best region ripped into the oncoming columns. One glider, probably carrying ammunition, caught a full antiaircraft burst, exploded, and completely disappeared. Releasing their gliders, four tow planes were hit, one after the other. Two immediately caught fire; one crashed, the other made a safe landing. Three gliders riddled with bullets crash-landed on the zones with their occupants miraculously untouched. In all, of the 450 gliders destined for General Taylor's 101st, 428 reached the zones with 2,656 troopers, their vehicles and trailers.

Fifteen miles to the north, General Gavin's second lift was threatened by the battles still raging on the drop zones as the gliders began to come in. Losses to the 82nd were higher than in the 101st area. Planes and gliders ran into a hail of antiaircraft fire. Although less accurate than on the day before, German gunners managed to shoot down six tow planes as they turned steeply away after releasing their gliders. The wing of one was blasted off, three others crashed in flames, another came down in Germany. The desperate fire fight for possession of the zones forced many gliders to land elsewhere. Some came down three to five miles from their targets; others ended up in Germany; still more decided to put down fast on their assigned landing zones. Pitted by shells and mortar, crisscrossed by machine-gun fire, each zone was a no man's land. Coming in quickly to hard landings, many gliders smashed undercarriages or nosed over completely. Yet the pilots' drastic maneuvers worked. Troops and cargo alike sustained surprisingly few casualties. Not a man was reported hurt in landing accidents, and only forty-five men were killed or wounded by enemy fire in flight or on the zones. Of 454 gliders, 385 arrived in the 82nd's area, bringing 1,782 artillerymen, 177 jeeps and 60 guns. Initially, more than a hundred paratroopers were thought to have been lost, but later more than half the number made their way to the 82nd's lines after distant landings. The grimly determined glider pilots sustained the heaviest casualties; fifty-four were killed or listed as missing.

Although the Germans failed to seriously impede the arrival of the second lift, they scored heavily against the bomber resupply missions arriving after the troop-carrier and glider trains. By the time the first of the 252 huge four-engined B-24 Liberators approached the 101st and 82nd zones, antiaircraft gunners had found the range. Swooping down ahead of the supply planes, fighters attempted to neutralize the flak guns. But, just as German batteries had done when Horrocks' tanks began their break-out on the seventeenth, so now the enemy forces held their fire until the fighters passed over. Then, suddenly they opened up. Within minutes, some 21 escort planes were shot down.

Following the fighters, bomber formations came in at altitudes varying from 800 to 50 feet. Fire and haze over the zones hid the identifying smoke and ground markers, so that even experienced dropmasters aboard the planes could not locate the proper fields. From the bays of the B-24s, each carrying approximately two tons of cargo, supplies began to fall haphazardly, scattering over a wide area. Racing back and forth throughout their drop zones, 82nd troopers managed to recover 80 percent of their supplies, almost in the faces of the Germans. The 101st was not so fortunate. Many of their equipment bundles landed almost directly among the Germans in the Best area. Less than 50 percent of their resupply was recovered. For General Taylor's men in the lower part of the corridor, the loss was serious, since more than a hundred tons of cargo intended for them consisted of gasoline, ammunition and food. So devastating was the German assault that about 130 bombers were damaged by ground fire, seven were shot down, and four others crash-landed. The day that had begun with so much hope for the beleaguered Americans along the corridor was rapidly becoming a grim fight for survival.

Lieutenant Pat Glover of Brigadier Shan Hackett's 4th Parachute Brigade was out of the plane and falling toward the drop zone south of the Ede-Arnhem road. He felt the jerk as his chute opened, and instinctively reached across and patted the zippered canvas bag attached to the harness over his left shoulder. Inside the bag, Myrtle the parachick squawked and Glover was reassured. Just as he had planned it back in England, Myrtle was making her first combat jump.

As Glover looked down it seemed to him that the entire heath below was on fire. He could see shells and mortars bursting all over the landing zone. Smoke and flames billowed up, and some paratroopers, unable to correct their descent, were landing in the inferno. Off in the distance where gliders were bringing in the remainder of Brigadier Pip Hicks's Airlanding Brigade, Glover could see wreckage and men running in all directions. Something had gone terribly wrong. According to the briefings, Glover knew that Arnhem was supposed to be lightly held and the drop zones, by now, should certainly be cleared and quiet. There had been no indication before the second lift left from England that anything was wrong. Yet it seemed to Glover that a full-scale battle was going on right beneath him. He wondered if by some mistake they were jumping in the wrong place.

As he neared the ground the stutter of machine guns and the dull thud of mortar bursts seemed to engulf him. He hit ground, careful to roll onto his right shoulder to protect Myrtle, and quickly shucked off his harness. Nearby, Glover's batman, Private Joe Scott, had just set down. Glover handed him Myrtle's bag. "Take good care of her," he told Scott. Through the haze covering the field, Glover spotted yellow smoke which marked the rendezvous point. "Let's go," he yelled to Scott. Weaving and crouching, the two men started out. Everywhere Glover looked there was utter confusion. His heart sank. It was obvious that the situation was going badly.

As Major J. L. Waddy came down, he too heard the ominous sound of machine-gun fire that seemed to be flaying the area on all sides. "I couldn't understand it," he recalls. "We had been given the impression that the Germans were in flight, that there was disorder in their ranks." Swinging down in his parachute, Waddy found that the drop zone was almost obscured by smoke from raging fires. At the southern end of the field where he landed, Waddy set out for the battalion's rendezvous area. "Mortars were bursting everywhere, and I saw countless casualties as I went along." When he neared the assembly point, Waddy was confronted by an irate captain from Battalion headquarters who had jumped into Holland the previous day. "You're bloody late," Waddy recalls the man shouting. "Do you realize we've been waiting here for four hours?" Agitatedly, the officer immediately began to brief Waddy. "I was shocked as I listened," Waddy remembers. "It was the first news we had that things weren't going as well as had been planned. We immediately got organized, and as I looked around, it seemed to me that the whole sky up ahead was a mass of flames."

On both landing zones west of the Wolfheze railway station —at Ginkel Heath and Reyers-Camp—paratroopers and glider-borne infantrymen were dropping into what appeared to be a raging battle. From the captured Market-Garden documents the Germans had known the location of the landing areas. And through enemy radar installations in the still-occupied Channel ports such as Dunkirk, they, unlike the British on the ground, could calculate with accuracy the time the second lift was due to arrive. SS units and antiaircraft, hurriedly disengaged in Arnhem, were rushed to the zones. Twenty Luftwaffe fighters, vectored in, continuously strafed the sectors. Ground fighting was equally intense. To clear parts of the heath of the encroaching enemy, the British, as they had during the night and early morning, charged with fixed bayonets.

Mortar bursts, hitting gliders that had landed the day before, turned them into flaming masses that in turn ignited the heath. Infiltrating enemy units used some gliders as cover for their attacks and the British set the machines on fire themselves, rather than let them fall into enemy hands. Nearly fifty gliders blazed in a vast inferno on one section of the field. Yet Brigadier Pip Hicks's Airlanding Brigade—minus the half battalion that had been sent into Arnhem—was managing with dogged courage to hold the zones. The paratroop and glider landings, bringing in 2,119 men, were far more successful than the men in the air or on the ground could believe. Even with the battle underway, 90 percent of the lift was landing—and in the right places.

Flight Sergeant Ronald Bedford, a rear gunner in a four-engined Stirling, found Monday's mission far different from the one he had flown on Sunday. Then, the nineteen-year-old Bedford had been frankly bored with the routineness of the flight. Now, as they neared the landing zone, firing was continuous and intense. Spotting an antiaircraft battery mounted on a truck at the edge of the field, Bedford tried desperately to turn his guns on it. He could see his tracers curving down, and then the battery stopped firing. Bedford was exuberant. "I got him!" he shouted. "Listen, I got him!" As the Stirling held steady on its course, Bedford noticed that gliders all around seemed to be breaking away from their tugs prematurely. He could only assume that the heavy fire had caused many glider pilots to release and try to get down as fast as possible. Then he saw the tow rope attached to their own Horsa falling away. Watching the glider swoop down, Bedford was sure it would collide with others before it could land. "The entire scene was chaotic," he recalls. "The gliders seemed to be going into very steep dives, leveling off, and coasting down, often, it looked, right into each other. I wondered how any of them would make it."

Sergeant Roy Hatch, copiloting a Horsa carrying a jeep, two trailers filled with mortar ammunition, and three men, wondered how they were going to get down when he saw the anti-aircraft fire ahead of them on the run-in. As Staff Sergeant Alec Young, the pilot, put the glider into a steep dive and leveled off, Hatch noticed to his amazement that everyone seemed to be heading toward the same touch-down point—including a cow which was frantically running just in front of them. Somehow Young put the glider down safely. Immediately the men jumped out and began unbolting the tail section. Nearby, Hatch noticed three gliders lying on their backs. Suddenly, with a tearing, rasping sound, another Horsa crash-landed on top of them. The glider came straight in, sliced off the nose of Hatch's glider, including the canopy and the cockpit where Hatch and Young had been sitting only moments before, then slid forward, coming to a halt directly in front of them.

Other gliders missed the zones altogether, some crash-landing as far as three miles away. Two came down on the southern bank of the Rhine, one near the village of Driel. Leaving casualties in the care of Dutch civilians, the men rejoined their units by crossing the Rhine on the forgotten but still active Driel ferry.*

---

*The story is probably apocryphal but the Dutch like to tell it. According to Mrs. Ter Horst of Oosterbeek, when the British troopers and their equipment, including an antitank gun, boarded the Driel ferry, Pieter was faced with a dilemma: whether or not to charge them for the trip. By the time they reached the northern bank, Pieter had decided to give them the ride free.

Several C-47's were hit and set afire as they made their approach to the zones. About ten minutes from landing, Sergeant Francis Fitzpatrick noticed that flak was coming up thick. A young trooper, Private Ginger MacFadden, jerked and cried out, his hands reaching for his right leg. "I'm hit," MacFadden mumbled. Fitzpatrick examined him quickly and gave him a shot of morphia. Then the sergeant noticed that the plane seemed to be laboring. As he bent to look out the window, the door to the pilot's compartment opened and the dispatcher came out, his face tense. "Stand by for a quick red and green," he said. Fitzpatrick looked down the line of paratroopers, now hooked up and ready to go. He could see smoke pouring from the port engine. Leading the way, Fitzpatrick jumped. As his chute opened, the plane went into a racing dive. Before Fitzpatrick hit the ground he saw the C-47 plow into a field off to his right and nose over. He was sure the crew and Ginger MacFadden had not escaped.

In another C-47 the American crew chief jokingly told Captain Frank D. King, "You'll soon be down there and I'll be heading home for bacon and eggs." The American sat down opposite King. Minutes later the green light went on. King glanced over at the crew chief. He seemed to have fallen asleep, slumped back with his chin on his chest, his hands in his lap. King had a feeling something was not quite right. He shook the American by the shoulder and the man fell sideways. He was dead. Behind him, King saw a large hole in the fuselage which looked as though it had been made by a .50-caliber machine-gun bullet. Standing in the doorway ready to jump, King saw that flames were streaming from the port wing. "We're on fire," he shouted to Sergeant Major George Gatland, "Check with the pilot." Gatland went forward. As he opened the cockpit door a sheet of flame shot out, sweeping the entire length of the plane. Gatland slammed the door shut and King ordered the men to jump. He believed they were now pilotless.

As the troopers went out the door, Gatland estimated the plane was between two and three hundred feet off the ground. He landed with a jar and began a head count. Four men were missing. One man had been killed by gun fire in the doorway before he had a chance to leave the plane. Another had jumped but his chute had caught fire; and a third, Gatland and King learned, had landed a short distance away. Then the fourth man arrived still in his parachute. He had come down with the plane. The crew, he told them, had somehow crash-landed the plane and they had miraculously walked away from it. Now, fifteen miles from Oosterbeek and far from the British lines, King's group set out to make their way back. As they moved out, the C-47, blazing a quarter of a mile away, blew up.

In some areas paratroopers jumped safely only to find themselves falling through waves of incendiary fire. Tugging desperately at parachute lines to avoid the tracers, many men landed on the edges of the zones in dense forests. Some, as they struggled to shed their chutes, were shot by snipers. Others landed far away from their zones. In one area, part of a battalion came down behind the Germans, then marched for the rendezvous point bringing eighty prisoners with them.

Under fire on the zones, troopers, discarding their chutes, ran swiftly for cover. Small clusters of badly wounded men lay everywhere. Private Reginald Bryant was caught by the blast of a mortar shell and so severely concussed that he was temporarily paralyzed. Aware of what was happening around him, he could not move a muscle. He stared helplessly as the men from his plane, believing Bryant dead, picked up his rifle and ammunition and hurriedly struck out for the assembly point.

Many men, surprised by the unexpected and unremitting machine-gun and sniper fire that swept the zones, sprinted for cover in the woods. In minutes the areas were deserted except for the dead and wounded. Sergeant Ginger Green, the physical-training instructor who had optimistically brought along a football to have a game on the zone after the expected easy action, jumped and hit the ground so hard that he broke two ribs. How long he lay there, Green does not know. When he regained consciousness, he was alone except for casualties. Painfully he sat up and almost immediately a sniper fired at him. Green got to his feet and began to dart and weave his way toward the woods. Bullets pinged all around him. Again and again, the pain in his ribs forced Green to the ground. He was certain that he would be hit. In the billowing smoke rolling across the heath, his strange duel with the sniper went on for what seemed like hours. "I could only make five or six yards at a time," he remembers, "and I figured I was up against either a sadistic bastard or a damned bad shot." Finally, hugging his injured ribs, Green made one last dash for the woods. Reaching them, he threw himself into the undergrowth and rolled against a tree just as a last bullet smacked harmlessly into the branches above his head. He had gained vital yardage under the most desperate circumstances of his life. Spent and aching, Green slowly removed the deflated football from inside his camouflage smock and painfully threw it away.

Many men would remember the first terrible moments after they jumped. Running for their lives from bullets and burning brush on Ginkel Heath at least a dozen troopers recall a young twenty-year-old lieutenant who lay in the gorse badly wounded. He had been shot in the legs and chest by incendiary bullets as he swung helplessly in his parachute. Lieutenant Pat Glover saw the young officer as he moved off the zone. "He was in horrible pain," Glover remembers, "and he just couldn't be moved. I gave him a shot of morphia and promised to send back a medic as soon as I could." Private Reginald Bryant, after recovering from his paralysis on the drop zone, came across the officer as he was heading for the assembly area. "When I got to him, smoke was coming from wounds in his chest. His agony was awful. A few of us had come upon him at the same time and he begged us to kill him." Someone, Bryant does not remember who, slowly reached down and gave the lieutenant his own pistol, cocked. As the men hurried off, the fire on the heath was slowly moving toward the area where the stricken officer lay. Later, rescue parties came across the body. It was concluded that the lieutenant had committed suicide.*

With characteristic precision Brigadier Shan Hackett, commander of the 4th Parachute Brigade, landed within three hundred yards of the spot he had chosen for his headquarters. In spite of enemy fire, the Brigadier's first concern was to find his walking stick, which he had dropped on the way down. As he was searching for it, he came across a group of Germans. "I was more scared than they were," he recalled, "but they seemed eager to surrender." Hackett, who spoke German

---

*Although numerous witnesses confirm the story, I have withheld the officer's name. There is still doubt that he shot himself. He was both popular and brave. He may, indeed, have used his pistol, or he may have been killed by a sniper.

fluently, brusquely told them to wait; then, recovering his stick, the trim, neatly mustached Brigadier calmly marched his prisoners off.

Impatient, prickly and temperamental at best of times, Hackett did not like what he saw. He, too, had expected the zones to be secure and organized. Now, surrounded by his officers, he prepared to move out his brigade. At this moment, Colonel Charles Mackenzie, General Urquhart's chief of staff, drove up to perform his painful duty. Taking Hackett aside, Mackenzie —in his own words—"told him what had been decided and concluded with the touchy matter of command." Brigadier Pip Hicks had been placed in charge of the division in Urquhart's and Lathbury's absence. Mackenzie went on to explain that Urquhart had made the decision back in England that Hicks was to take over in the event both he and Lathbury should be missing or killed.

Hackett was none too happy, Mackenzie recalls. "Now look here, Charles, I'm senior to Hicks," he told Mackenzie. "I should therefore command this division." Mackenzie was firm. "I quite understand, sir, but the General did give me the order of succession and we must stick to it. Further, Brigadier Hicks has been here twenty-four hours and is now much more familiar with the situation." Hackett, Mackenzie said, might only make matters worse if he "upset the works and tried to do something about it."

But it was obvious to Mackenzie that the matter would not end there. A delicate rift had always existed between Urquhart and Hackett. Although the volatile Brigadier was eminently fit for command, in Urquhart's opinion he lacked the older Hicks's infantry experience. Additionally, Hackett was a cavalryman, and Urquhart was known to hold a lesser opinion of cavalry brigadiers than of the infantrymen with whom he had long been associated. He had once jestingly referred to Hackett in public as "that broken-down cavalryman"—a remark that Hackett had not found amusing.

Mackenzie told Hackett that his 11th Battalion was to be detached from the brigade. It would move out immediately for Arnhem and the bridge. To Hackett, this was the final insult. His pride in the brigade stemmed, in part, from its qualities as a highly trained integrated unit that fought as an independent team. He was appalled that it was being separated and broken into parts. "I do not like being told to give up a battalion without being consulted," he told Mackenzie hotly. Then, on reflection, he added, "Of course, if any battalion should go, it is the 11th. It has been dropped in the southeastern corner of the zone and is closest to Arnhem and the bridge." But he requested another battalion in exchange and Mackenzie replied that he thought Hicks would give him one. And there the matter ended for the moment. The brilliant, explosive and dynamic Hackett bowed to inevitability. For the time, Hicks could run the battle, but Hackett was determined to run his own brigade.

For the British it was a grim and bloody afternoon. With a problem-ridden second lift, the fate of General Urquhart and Brigadier Lathbury still unknown, with Colonel Frost's small force precariously clinging to the north end of the Arnhem bridge, and with a swelling clash of personalities developing between two brigadiers, one more unforeseen disaster had taken place.

Depleted in numbers, worn out by constant fighting, the troopers of Hicks's Airlanding Brigade watched in despair as thirty-five Stirling bomber-cargo planes dropped supplies everywhere but on the zones. Of the eighty-seven tons of ammunition, food and supplies destined for the men of Arnhem, only twelve tons reached the troops. The remainder, widely scattered to the southwest, fell among the Germans.

In Antoon Derksen's house less than five miles away, General Urquhart was still surrounded by Germans. The self-propelled gun and crew on the street below were so close that Urquhart and the two officers with him had not dared risk talk or movement. Apart from some chocolate and hard candy, the men were without food. The water had been cut off and there were no sanitary arrangements. Urquhart felt a sense of desperation. Unable to rest or sleep, he brooded about the progress of the battle and the arrival of the second lift, unaware of its delayed start. He wondered how far Horrocks' tanks had advanced and if Frost still held at the bridge. "Had I known the situation at that moment," he later recalled, "I would have disregarded the concern of my officers and made a break for it, Germans or no Germans." Silent and withdrawn, Urquhart found himself staring fixedly at Captain James Cleminson's mustache. "The enormity in hirsute handlebars had earlier been lost on me," he wrote, "but now there was little else to look at." The mustache irritated him. It looked "damned silly."

With all his preoccupation, Urquhart had never thought of the decision he had made regarding chain of command within the division, a last-minute instruction that was fast building toward a complex confrontation between Hicks and Hackett. By now, at 4 P.M. on Monday, September 18, Urquhart had been absent from his headquarters for almost one full day.

General Wilhelm Bittrich, commander of the II SS Panzer Corps, was shocked by the enormous size of the second lift. Badgered by Field Marshal Model to quickly capture the Arnhem bridge and pressed by Colonel Harzer and General Harmel for reinforcements, Bittrich found his problems growing increasingly acute. As he grimly watched the skies west of Arnhem blossom with hundreds of multicolored parachutes, then fill with an apparently unceasing stream of gliders, he despaired. From the Luftwaffe communications net, he learned that two other massive drops had taken place. Trying to guess the Allied strength, Bittrich greatly overestimated the number of Anglo-Americans now in Holland. He believed that maybe another division had landed, enough to tilt the balance in favor of the attackers.

To Bittrich, the buildup of Allied strength versus the arrival of German reinforcements had become a deadly race. So far only a trickle of men and matériel had reached him. By comparison, the Allies seemed to have inexhaustible resources. He feared that they might mount yet another airborne drop the following day. In the narrow confines of Holland, with its difficult terrain, bridges, and proximity to the undefended frontiers of Germany, a force that size could mean catastrophe.

There was little coordination between Bittrich's forces and Colonel General Student's First Parachute Army to the south. Although Student's men were being constantly reinforced by the remnants of Von Zangen's Fifteenth Army, that shattered force was desperately short of transport, guns and ammunition. Days, perhaps weeks, would be needed to re-equip them. Meanwhile, the entire responsibility for halting Montgomery's attack lay with Bittrich, and his most pressing problems remained the crossing at Nijmegen and the unbelievable defense by the British at the northern approach of the Arnhem bridge.

So long as the Allied troopers held out there, Bittrich was prevented from moving his own forces down the highway to Nijmegen. Harmel's Frundsberg Division, trying to get across the Rhine, was dependent entirely on the ferry at Pannerden —a slow, tedious method of crossing. Ironically, while the British at Arnhem were experiencing their first tentative doubts of their ability to hang on, Bittrich was gravely concerned about the outcome of the battle. He saw the Reich as dangerously close to invasion. The next twenty-four hours might tell the story.

Bittrich's superiors had problems of wider scope. All along Army Group B's vast front, Field Marshal Model was juggling forces, trying to stem the relentless attacks of the American First and Third Armies. Although the reinstatement of the illustrious Von Rundstedt to his old command had brought a renewal of order and cohesion, he was scraping the bottom of the nation's manpower barrel for reinforcements. Locating gasoline to move units from one area to another was also becoming an increasingly critical problem, and there was little help from Hitler's headquarters. Berlin seemed more preoccupied with the Russian menace from the east than with the Allied drive from the west.

Despite his other worries, Model seemed confident of overcoming the threat in Holland. He remained convinced that the country's marshes, dikes and water barriers could work for him in providing time to halt and defeat Montgomery's attack. Bittrich had no such optimism. He urged Model to take several important steps before the situation worsened. In Bittrich's view, the destruction of the Nijmegen and Arnhem bridges was necessary immediately, but that proposal irritated Model every time Bittrich suggested it. "Pragmatic, always demanding the impossible, Model visited me every day," Bittrich was to recall. "On the spot, he would issue a stream of orders referring to immediate situations, but he never stayed long enough at any conference to hear out or approve long-range plans." Model, Bittrich feared, did not grasp the appalling eventualities that could ensue for Germany if an Allied breakthrough occurred. Instead, he seemed obsessed with details; he was particularly concerned about the German failure to recapture the Arnhem bridge. Stung by the implied criticism, Bittrich told the Field Marshal, "In all my years as a soldier, I have never seen men fight so hard." Model was unimpressed. "I want that bridge," he said coldly.

On the afternoon of the eighteenth Bittrich tried again to explain his view of the over-all situation to an impatient Model. The Nijmegen bridge was the key to the entire operation, he argued. Destroy it and the head of the Allied attack would be severed from its body. "Herr Field Marshal, we should demolish the Waal crossing before it is too late," Bittrich said. Model was adamant. "No!" he said. "The answer is no!" Not only did Model insist that the bridge could be defended; he demanded that Student's army and the Frundsberg Division halt the Anglo-Americans before they ever reached it. Bittrich said bluntly that he was far from sure the Allies could be contained. As yet there was almost no German armor in the area and, he told Model, there was grave danger that Montgomery's overwhelming tank strength would achieve a breakthrough. Then Bittrich expressed his fears that further airborne drops could be expected. "If the Allies succeed in their drive from the south and if they drop one more airborne division in the Arnhem area, we're finished," he said. "The route to the Ruhr and Germany will be open." Model would not be swayed. "My orders stand," he said. "The Nijmegen bridge is not to be destroyed, and I want the Arnhem bridge captured within twenty-four hours."

Others knew the difficulty of carrying out Model's commands. Lieutenant Colonel Harzer, commander of the Hohenstaufen Division, had run out of men. All his forces were fully engaged. No additional reinforcements had arrived, and the size of the second lift posed grave doubts as to the ability of his soldiers to halt and contain the enemy. Like Bittrich, Harzer was convinced that "the Allies had dropped no more than an airborne spearhead. I was sure that more would follow and then they would drive for the Reich." With limited armor, Harzer did not know whether he could stop the enemy. He had, however, succeeded in making one place secure—the grounds of his own headquarters. There, with cynical disregard for the rights of prisoners, he had ordered several hundred

British troopers to be held under guard in wire enclosures. "I was quite sure," he was to recall, "that the R.A.F. would not bomb their own troops."

Harzer, a self-professed Anglophile ("I had a real weakness for the English"), had once studied as an exchange student in Great Britain. He enjoyed sauntering among the prisoners trying to engage in conversation to practice his English and, hopefully, to elicit information. He was struck by the British morale. "They were contemptuous and self-assured, as only veteran soldiers can be," he recalled. The caliber of his prisoners convinced Harzer that the battle was far from won. To keep Urquhart's forces off balance and to prevent any kind of cohesive attack, he ordered his Hohenstaufen Division on the evening of the eighteenth "to attack unceasingly at whatever cost throughout the night."

The commander of the Frundsberg Division, General Harmel, was "too busy to worry about what might happen next. I had my hands full fighting the Lower Rhine." Charged with the capture of the Arnhem bridge and the defense of the Waal crossing and the area in between, Harmel's problems were far more acute than Harzer's. The move of his division by ferry across the river was proceeding at a snail's pace. Troops, equipment and tanks were loaded on makeshift rubber or log rafts. Roads leading down to the water's edge had become quagmires. Tanks and vehicles had slid off rafts, and some had even been swept away. Worse, because of constant strafing by Allied planes, nearly all ferrying and convoying operations had to take place during darkness. In twenty-four hours Harmel's engineers had succeeded in moving only two battalions with their vehicles and equipment into the Arnhem-Nijmegen area. To speed up operations, truck shuttles carrying troops ran back and forth between the south bank landing stage and Nijmegen. But the movement was far too slow. To be sure, Harmel's men were now in the center of Nijmegen and on the southern side of the highway bridge, but he doubted that they could stop a determined attack by the Anglo-Americans. Although he had been ordered not to destroy it, Harmel was prepared for the eventuality. His engineers had already laid charges and set up detonating apparatus in a roadside bunker near the village of Lent on the northern bank. He hoped Bittrich would approve the blowing of the highway and railroad bridges if they could not be held. But if he did not, Harmel's decision was already made. If British tanks broke through and started across, he would defy his superiors and destroy the bridges.

7

THE PROSPEROUS VILLAGE OF OOSTERBEEK seemed infused with a strange mixture of gaiety and uneasiness. Like an island in the middle of the battle, the village was assaulted by the noise of fighting on three sides. From the drop zones to the west came the nearly constant thunder of guns. To the northwest the chattering of machine guns and the steady cough of mortars could be clearly heard in the flower-lined streets, and to the east, two and a half miles away in Arnhem, black smoke hung over the horizon, a somber backdrop to the unceasing timpani of heavy artillery.

The bombing and strafing preceding the troop and glider landings on the previous day had produced casualties among the villagers and some damage to shops and houses, as had infiltrating snipers and ill-directed mortar bursts, but the war had not so far made serious inroads into Oosterbeek. The neat resort hotels, landscaped villas and tree-lined streets were still largely untouched. Yet it was becoming obvious with every hour that the fighting was coming closer. Here and there, concussion from distant explosions splintered panes of glass with startling suddenness. Charred particles of paper, cloth and wood, carried like confetti by the wind, rained down into the streets, and the air was acrid with the smell of cordite.

On Sunday Oosterbeek had been filled with troops as the British arrived almost on the heels of a frantic German departure. No one had slept during the night. A nervous excitement, heightened by the low whine of jeeps, the clatter of Bren gun carriers and the tramp of marching men, made rest impossible. Throughout most of the eighteenth the movement had continued. The villagers, joyous and yet apprehensive, had decked the streets and houses with Dutch flags and plied their liberators with food, fruit and drink as the British Tommies hurried through. To almost everyone the war seemed all but over. Now, subtly, the atmosphere was changing. Some British units were apparently firmly established in the village, and

Lieutenant Colonel Sheriff Thompson's artillery spotters occupied the tower of the tenth-century Dutch Reformed church
near the Rhine in lower Oosterbeek, but troop movement had
noticeably slowed. By late afternoon most thoroughfares were
disquietingly empty, and the Dutch noted that antitank and
Bren gun positions were now sited at strategic points on the
main road. Seeing them, villagers had a sense of foreboding.

As he walked through Oosterbeek trying to discover exactly
what was happening, Jan Voskuil recalls seeing a British officer
ordering civilians to take in their flags. "This is war," he heard
the officer tell one villager, "and you are in the middle of it."
Throughout his walk, Voskuil noted that the mood of the people was changing. From Jaap Koning, a local baker, Voskuil
learned that many Dutch were pessimistic. There were rumors,
Koning said, that "things are not going well." Apprehension
was replacing the heady sense of liberation. "The British,"
Koning said, "are being pushed back everywhere." Voskuil was
profoundly concerned. Koning was always well informed, and
although his was the first bad news Voskuil had heard, it confirmed his own fears. As each hour passed, Voskuil thought that
the canopy of shells screaming over the town toward Arnhem
was growing heavier. Remembering anew the terrible destruction of the Normandy villages, Voskuil could not rid himself of
an overwhelming feeling of hopelessness.

A second tradesman, baker Dirk van Beek, was as depressed
as Koning and Voskuil. The news he had heard on his delivery rounds had dampened his first excited reaction to the Allied drop. "What if the war comes here—what will we do?" he
asked his wife, Riek. But he already knew the answer: he would
remain in Oosterbeek and keep on baking. "People have to
eat," he told Riek. "Anyway, where would we go if we left the
shop?" Absorbing himself in work, Van Beek tried to reassure
himself that everything would work out for the best. He had
received his monthly allotment of wheat and yeast a few days
earlier. Now, determined to stay and to keep his shop open, he
remembered that an old baker had once told him of a method
of making bread that required less than half the usual amount
of yeast. He decided to stretch his supplies to the limit. He
would continue to bake until everything was gone.

At the Tafelberg, Schoonoord and Vreewijk Hotels it was
obvious that the battle had taken a serious turn: the airy,

comfortable resorts were being turned into casualty stations. At the Schoonoord British medics and Dutch civilians began a full-scale house cleaning to make ready to receive the wounded. Jan Eijkelhoff, of the underground, saw that the Germans, in their hasty departure, had left the hotel "looking like a pig pen. Food was all over the place. Tables had been overturned, plates broken, clothing and equipment were scattered around. Papers and rubbish littered every room." From surrounding houses extra mattresses were brought in and placed on the ground floor. Rows of beds were set up in the main reception rooms and stretchers were placed along the glassed-in veranda. Every room, including the cellars, would be needed by nightfall, the Dutch were told. Eijkelhoff learned that St. Elisabeth's Hospital in Arnhem was already filled to capacity. Yet the British medics with whom he worked remained optimistic. "Don't worry," one of them told him, "Monty will be here soon."

At the Tafelberg Hotel, where Dr. Gerrit van Maanen was setting up a hospital, seventeen-year-old Anje van Maanen, who had come to help her father, noted the startling change in other volunteers. "We are afraid," she wrote in her diary, "but we don't know why. We have a queer feeling that weeks have passed between yesterday and today." As at the Schoonoord, there were rumors at the Tafelberg that Montgomery's forces were on the way. On the lookout for their quick arrival, Anje wrote, "We stare constantly out of the upstairs windows. The shooting is stronger. There are lights and fires, but the great army is not here yet."

A few blocks away, the ornate twelve-room Hartenstein Hotel, sited amid its parklike surroundings, wore a gaunt, deserted look. In Daliesque disarray, tables and chairs were scattered across the fine green lawn and among them, the result of a sharp fire fight the day before, lay the crumpled bodies of several Germans.

As he cycled up to the building, twenty-seven-year-old William Giebing was sickened by the appearance of the once elegant hotel. A few months after he took possession of the building, leasing it from the town of Oosterbeek in 1942, the Germans had moved into the village and requisitioned the hotel. From that time on, Giebing and his wife, Truus, were relegated to the position of servants. The Germans allowed them to clean the Hartenstein and to oversee the cuisine, but the management of the hotel was in German hands. Finally, on September 6, Giebing was summarily ordered to leave, but his wife and two maids were allowed to return each day to keep the place clean.

On the seventeenth, "crazy with joy at the landings," Giebing jumped on a bicycle and set out for the Hartenstein from Westerbouwing, where his father-in-law, Johan van Kalkschoten, operated the hilltop restaurant overlooking the Heveadorp-Driel ferry. He was just in time to see the last of the Germans departing. Running into the building, he felt for the first time that "the hotel was finally mine." But the air of desertion was unnerving. In the dining room two long tables covered with white damask tablecloths were set for twenty. There were soup bowls, silver, napkins and wine glasses and, in the center of each table, a large tureen of vermicelli soup. Touching it, Giebing found it still warm. In silver servers on the sideboard was the main course: fried sole.

Giebing wandered from room to room looking at the rich, gold-covered damask walls, the ornate plaster angels and garlands, the bridal suite where gold stars speckled the sky-blue ceiling. The Germans, he was relieved to find, had not looted the hotel. Not a spoon was missing and the refrigerators were still full of food. Making the rounds, Giebing heard voices coming from the veranda. Rushing out he found several British soldiers drinking his sherry. Eight empty bottles lay on the floor. Unaccountably, after all the days of occupation, Giebing lost his temper. The Germans had, at least, left his beloved hotel clean. "So this is the first thing you do," he yelled at the troopers. "Break open my cellar and steal my sherry." The British were embarrassed and apologetic, and Giebing was mollified, but once again he was told he could not remain. However, the British assured him that his property would be respected.

Now, a day later, hoping that the British had passed through and left his hotel, Giebing returned. His heart sank as he approached the building. Jeeps were parked in the rear of the building and, behind the wire netting of the tennis courts, he saw German prisoners. Slit trenches and gun positions had been dug in around the perimeter of the grounds and staff officers seemed to be everywhere. Disheartened, Giebing returned to Westerbouwing. In the afternoon his wife visited the Hartenstein and explained who she was. "I was treated very politely," she recalls, "but we were not permitted to move back. The British, like the Germans, had requisitioned the hotel." There was one consolation, she thought: the war would soon be over and then the Giebings could truly operate what they considered the best hotel in Oosterbeek. The courteous English officers with whom she talked did not inform her that the Hartenstein, as of 5 P.M. on September 18, was now the headquarters of the 1st British Airborne Division.

In the strange mixture of anxiety and joy that permeated Oosterbeek, one incident terrified many of the inhabitants more than the thought of the encroaching battle. During the day prisoners had been released from the Arnhem jail. Many were resistance fighters, but others were dangerous convicts. In their striped prison garb, they flooded out of Arnhem, and more than fifty ended up in Oosterbeek. "They added a final touch of madness," recalls Jan ter Horst, a former Dutch army artillery captain, a lawyer and a leading member of the Oosterbeek resistance. "We rounded the convicts up and put them temporarily in the concert hall. But the question was, what to do with them? They seemed harmless enough at the moment, but many of these felons had been imprisoned for years. We feared the worst—especially for our women folk—when they finally realized that they were free."

Talking with the convicts Ter Horst found that they wanted only to get out of the immediate combat zone. The sole route across the Rhine was by the Heveadorp-Driel ferry. Pieter, the ferryman, flatly refused to cooperate. He did not want fifty convicts running loose on the southern bank. Further, the ferry was now moored on the north side and Pieter wanted it to remain there. After several hours of testy negotiations, Ter Horst was finally able to get Pieter to take the prisoners across. "We were glad to see them go," he remembers. "The women were more scared of the convicts than they had been of the Germans." Prudently Ter Horst insisted that the ferry be returned to the northern bank, where it could be used by the British.

As a former army officer, Ter Horst was puzzled as to why the Heveadorp-Driel ferry had not been immediately seized by the British. When the troopers entered Oosterbeek he had questioned them about the ferry. To his amazement, he discovered they knew nothing about it. A former artilleryman, he was astounded that the British had not occupied nearby Westerbouwing, the only high ground overlooking the Rhine. Whoever held these heights with artillery controlled the ferry. Further, the choice of the Hartenstein as British headquarters disturbed him. Surely, he thought, the restaurant and its buildings on the heights at Westerbouwing were a far preferable site. "Hold the ferry and Westerbouwing," he urged several British staff officers. They were polite, but uninterested. One officer told Ter Horst, "We don't intend to stay here. With the bridge in our hands and the arrival of Horrocks' tanks, we don't need the ferry." Ter Horst hoped the man was right. If the Germans reached Westerbouwing, less than two miles away, their guns not only could command the ferry but could totally demolish British headquarters at the Hartenstein. The British now knew about the ferry and they had been briefed about Westerbouwing. There was little else Ter Horst could do. The former Dutch officer had, in fact, pointed out one of the most crucial oversights in the entire operation—the failure of the British to realize the strategic importance of the ferry and the Westerbouwing heights. Had General Urquhart stayed at his headquarters and in control of the battle the situation might have been rectified in time.*

Brigadier Hicks, commanding the division in Urquhart's absence, was facing almost hourly the bewildering problem of orienting himself to the complex, constantly shifting moves of the hard-pressed airborne unit. With the breakdown of radio communications between headquarters and the battalions, there was little precise information about what was happening, nor could Hicks gauge the strength and potential of the

---

*The same point is made in several monographs written by the eminent Dutch military historian, Lieutenant Colonel Theodor A. Boeree. "Had Urquhart been there," he writes, "he might well have abandoned the defense of the bridge, recalled Frost's battalion, if possible, concentrated his six original battalions and the three of the 4th Parachute Brigade that had just landed, and established a firm bridgehead somewhere else on the northern side of Lower Rhine . . . with the high ground at Westerbouwing . . . as the center of the bridgehead. There they could have awaited the arrival of the British Second Army."

enemy forces opposing him. What scant news reached him was brought by spent, dirt-streaked messengers, who risked their lives to bring him information, which was often hopelessly out of date by the time they arrived at headquarters, or by the various members of the Dutch underground, whose reports were often disregarded or viewed as suspect. Hicks found himself depending strongly on one slender channel of communication —the tenuous Thompson-to-Munford artillery radio link existing between Oosterbeek and Frost's forces at the bridge.

Mauled and battered, the 2nd Battalion and the valiant stragglers who had reached it were still holding, but Frost's situation had been desperate for hours and was deteriorating rapidly. "We were getting constant messages from the bridge asking for relief and ammunition," Hicks recalled. "Enemy pressure and the steadily increasing strength of German armor was building everywhere, and there was absolutely no contact with Urquhart, Lathbury, Dobie or Fitch. We could not raise Browning at Corps headquarters to explain the gravity of the situation, and we were desperate for help." From prisoner interrogations Hicks now knew that the troopers were up against battle-hardened SS men of the 9th Hohenstaufen and 10th Frundsberg divisions. No one had been able to tell him how strong these units were or to estimate the number of tanks that were being thrown against him. Worse, Hicks did not know whether the original preattack plan could withstand the present German pressure. If the enemy was heavily reinforced the entire mission might founder.

Help, he knew, was coming. On the nineteenth, Major General Stanislaw Sosabowski's Polish Brigade would arrive in the third lift. Horrocks' tanks should also be arriving and were, indeed, already late. How close were they to Arnhem and could they arrive in time to relieve and balance the situation? "In spite of everything," Hicks recalls, "I believed Frost would hold the northern end of the bridge until Monty's tanks got to it. The bridge was still our objective, after all, and my decisions and actions were centered solely on seizing and holding that objective." Balancing all the factors, Hicks felt he must stick to the original plan, and so did Brigadier Hackett at this time.

The original task of Hackett's 4th Parachute Brigade was to occupy the high ground north of Arnhem to prevent German reinforcements from reaching the bridge. But at the time that plan was conceived it was thought that enemy strength would prove negligible and, at worst, manageable. In fact, enemy reaction had been so fast, concentrated and effective that Hicks could not assess the true situation. Bittrich's corps held the north of Arnhem; his troops had bottled up Frost at the bridge and successfully prevented Dobie and Fitch's battalions from relieving them. The advance of these two units was now virtually sheared off. In the built-up areas around St. Elisabeth's Hospital barely a mile or so from the bridge, the battalions were stopped in their tracks. The South Staffordshires, already en route to help, and the 11th Battalion from Hackett's brigade were faring no better. "We now came to the wide-open, exposed riverside stretch of road in front of St. Elisabeth's Hospital, and then everything suddenly let loose," remembers Private Robert C. Edwards of the South Staffordshires. "We must have looked like targets in a shooting gallery. All Jerry had to do was line up his guns and mortars on this one gap —about a quarter of a mile wide—and fire. He couldn't miss." Edwards saw Captain Edward Weiss, second in command of his company, running tirelessly up and down the column "totally ignoring all the metal flying about him, his voice growing ever hoarser as he yelled out 'On, on, on, D Company, on.'"

Weiss seemed to be everywhere. Men were falling all around. If troopers halted or hesitated, Weiss was "immediately beside them urging them on. You just couldn't crawl and watch him stand upright. You had to follow his lead through that hell of fire." Edwards threw some smoke bombs to try to hide their advance and "then put my head down and ran like a hare." He stumbled over "heaps of dead, slithered in pools of blood, until I reached the partial shelter afforded by houses and buildings on the far side of the road." There he discovered that Captain Weiss had been hit as he ran across. "Major Phillips had been badly wounded. No one seemed to have much idea of what was going on or what we should do next." As for D Company, when a count was made, "only 20 percent remained, and quite obviously we couldn't continue against such overwhelming German strength. Hopefully we waited for the dawn."

It was as if a solid wall had been built between the division and Frost's pitiful few at the bridge.

In exchange for his 11th Battalion, Hackett had been given the 7th Battalion of the King's Own Scottish Borderers (KOSB's).

They had guarded the drop zones since landing on the seventeenth. Now they moved out with Hackett's 10th and 156th battalions via Wolfheze northwest of Oosterbeek. In that area the KOSB's would guard Johannahoeve Farm, a landing zone where transport and artillery of the Polish Brigade were due to arrive by glider in the third lift.

After the initial fighting on the zones, Hackett's brigade moved off without incident, and by nightfall the KOSB's had taken up positions around Johannahoeve Farm. There, suddenly, the battalions ran into heavy German opposition from strongly held machine-gun positions. A pitched battle began. In the growing darkness, commands went out to hold positions and then attempt to rout the enemy at dawn. It was vitally important to secure the area. Sosabowski's paratroopers were scheduled to land on the nineteenth on the southern side of the Arnhem bridge, in the polder land that Urquhart and the R.A.F. had deemed unsuitable—because of antiaircraft considerations—for the large-scale initial landings. By the time the Poles were to arrive, it had been expected that the bridge would be in British hands. If it was not, the Poles had been assigned to take it. At Browning's rear Corps headquarters in England, where no one was aware of the compounding setbacks developing at Arnhem, the Polish drop was still scheduled to take place as planned. If Frost could hold out and the Polish drop was successful, there was still a chance even now that Market-Garden could succeed.

Everywhere men were still struggling toward the bridge. On the lower road that Frost had taken on what now seemed to many a long-ago day, Private Andrew Milbourne and a small group of stragglers from other battalions passed stealthily near the ruins of the railway bridge that Frost's men had tried to capture on their march to the prime objective. In fields to his left, Milbourne saw white mounds gleaming in the darkness. "They were dozens of dead bodies, and the Dutch were moving quietly around the area, covering our comrades with white sheets," he recalls. Up ahead, fires reddened the sky and an occasional flash of guns outlined the great bridge. All afternoon the little band had been held up by superior German forces. Now, once more, they were pinned down. As they took refuge in a boathouse on the edge of the river, Milbourne began to despair of ever reaching the bridge. A lone signalman in the group began to work his radio set and, as the men gathered around, he suddenly picked up the BBC from London. Milbourne listened as the clear, precise voice of the announcer recounted the day's happenings on the western front. "British troops in Holland," he reported, "are meeting only slight opposition." In the gloomy boathouse someone laughed derisively. "Bloody liar," Milbourne said.

Now, as the courageous men of the 1st British Airborne Division fought for their very existence, two of His Majesty's brigadiers chose to have a heated argument over which of them should command the division. The dispute was triggered by a smolderingly angry Brigadier Shan Hackett who, by evening of the eighteenth, saw the situation as not only disquieting but "grossly untidy." The enemy seemed to have the upper hand everywhere. British battalions were scattered and fighting uncohesively, without knowledge of one another's whereabouts. Lacking communications, pinned down in built-up areas, many units came upon one another quite by chance. It appeared to Hackett that there was no over-all command or coordination of effort. Late in the evening, still smarting over the startling announcement by Mackenzie concerning the command of the division, the temperamental Hackett drove to the Hartenstein Hotel in Oosterbeek to have it out with Hicks. "He arrived about midnight," Hicks recalls. "I was in the operations room, and from the very beginning it was perfectly clear that, as he was senior in grade to me, he was less than happy that I had been given command. He was young, with firm ideas and rather argumentative."

Initially, Hackett's displeasure focused on the fact that Hicks had detached the 11th Battalion from him. He demanded to know what orders it had been given and who was in command of the sector. "He thought," recalls Hicks, "that the situation was too fluid, and obviously disagreed with the decisions I had made." Patiently the older Hicks explained that because of strong German resistance, the present battle situation had been totally unforeseen. Each battalion, therefore, was now fighting individually to reach the bridge and, although instructed to follow specific routes, battalions had been warned that due to the unusual conditions some overlapping might occur. Two or more units might well find themselves forced into the same vicinity. Hackett brusquely commented that "the command setup was clearly unsatisfactory."

Hicks agreed, but the object, he told Hackett, "was to help Frost at the bridge in whatever way we can and as fast as possible." While agreeing that Frost had to be reinforced quickly, Hackett sarcastically suggested that this might be done in a "more coordinated manner with more drive and cohesion." There was much to be said for Hackett's argument: a coordinated drive might indeed succeed in breaking through the German ring and reaching Frost; but, lacking communications and kept off balance by constant German attacks, Hicks had had little time to organize such an all-out attack.

The two men then turned to the role that Hackett's brigade would play the next day. In Hicks's view, Hackett should not attempt to occupy the high ground north of Arnhem. "I felt he could aid Frost better by driving into Arnhem and helping to hold the northern end of the bridge." Hackett objected strongly. He wanted a definite objective, and he appeared to know what it should be. He would take the high ground east of Johannahoeve first, he announced, and then "see what I can do to assist the operations in Arnhem." In the quiet, understated but bitter verbal fencing, Hackett insisted that he be given a time schedule so that he could relate "my actions to everyone else." He wanted "a sensible plan." Otherwise, Hackett said, he would be compelled "to raise the question of command of the division."

Lieutenant Colonel P. H. Preston, the headquarters administrative officer, was present at what Hicks has since tactfully called "our discussion." Preston remembers that Hicks, "his face tightly drawn," turned to him and said, "Brigadier Hackett thinks he ought to be in command of the division." Hackett protested the choice of words. Preston, sensing that the conversation was becoming overly tense, immediately left the room and sent the duty officer, Gordon Grieve, in search of the chief of staff, Colonel Mackenzie.

In a room upstairs Mackenzie was resting, unable to sleep. "I had been there about half an hour when Gordon Grieve

came in. He told me that I should come downstairs immediately, that the two Brigadiers, Hicks and Hackett, 'were having
a flaming row.' I was already dressed. On the way down I tried
to think quickly. I knew what the row was about and that it
might be necessary for me to take decisive action. I had no
intention of going into the operations room and exchanging
pleasantries. I felt at this point that General Urquhart's orders were being questioned and I intended to back Hicks in
everything."

As Mackenzie entered the room the conversation between
the two brigadiers abruptly ceased. "Both men had begun to
compose themselves," recalls Mackenzie, "and it was immediately clear that the worst was over." Hicks, glancing up at
Mackenzie, was almost casual. "Oh, hello, Charles," Mackenzie remembers him saying, "Brigadier Hackett and I have had
a bit of a row, but it is all right now." Hicks was certain that
"things had settled back to normal. I was rather firm with
Hackett and when he left I knew he would follow my orders."
However much he may have appeared to accept Hicks's new
role, Hackett's view was largely unchanged. "I intended to take
orders from Pip if they made sense," he remembers. "What
I was told to do was far from that. Therefore, I was inclined
to assert my position as senior brigadier of the two and issue
the sort of orders for my brigade's operation which did make
sense."*

Under any other circumstances, the confrontation between
the brigadiers would have been merely an historical footnote.
Two courageous, dedicated men, under intense strain and with
identical aims, lost their tempers for a moment. In the balance
sheet of Market-Garden when the plan was in such jeopardy
and every soldier was needed if a coordinated effort to seize
the Arnhem bridge was to succeed, cooperation among commanders and cohesion in the ranks were vital. Particularly so,
since the fate of the First Allied Airborne Army had taken yet

---

*I believe the row was far more heated than related above, but understandably
Hicks and Hackett, good friends, are reluctant to discuss the matter in greater
detail. There are at least four different versions of what transpired, and none of
them may be entirely accurate. My reconstruction is based on interviews with
Hackett, Hicks and Mackenzie, and on accounts in Urquhart's *Arnhem*, pp.
77–90, and Hibbert's *The Battle of Arnhem*, pp. 101–3.

another turn: throughout the Market-Garden area, Field Marshal Von Rundstedt's promised reinforcements were arriving from all over the western front in a steady, unceasing flow.

Nicolaas de Bode, the highly skilled technician who had made the first secret telephone connection for the underground between north and south Holland, had remained in his room all day. On instructions from the regional resistance chief Pieter Kruyff, De Bode sat by a small side window which looked out on the Velper Weg, the wide street leading from the eastern side of Arnhem to Zutphen in the north. Although he had not strayed from his post, calls had reached him from outlying areas to the west and had deeply disturbed him. In the Wolfheze and Oosterbeek areas, underground members reported trouble. The excited talk of liberation had stopped. For some hours now, all he had heard was that the situation was worsening. De Bode was asked to keep a constant watch for any sign of heavy German movement from the north and east. So far he had seen nothing. His messages, phoned to underground headquarters hourly, contained the same terse information. "The road is empty," he had reported again and again.

In the late evening, some twenty minutes before his next call, he heard "the sound of armored cars running on rubber tires and the clanking of armor." Wearily he walked to the window, and gazed up the Velper Weg. The road seemed empty as before. Then in the distance, visible in the fiery glow that hung over the city, he saw two massive tanks coming into view. Moving side by side along the wide street, they were heading straight down the road leading into the old part of the city. As De Bode watched wide-eyed, besides the tanks he saw trucks "carrying clean-looking soldiers, sitting straight up on the seats with their rifles in front of them. Then, more tanks and more soldiers in rows on trucks." Promptly he called Kruyff and said, "It looks like an entire German army complete with tanks and other weapons is heading straight into Arnhem."

The man who had warned London on September 14 about the presence of Bittrich's II SS Panzer Corps, Henri Knap, Arnhem's underground intelligence chief, was now receiving a steady stream of reports of German reinforcements from his network. Knap abandoned caution. He telephoned British headquarters at the Hartenstein directly and spoke to a duty officer. Without preamble Knap told him that "a column of tanks, among them some Tigers, is moving into Arnhem and some are heading toward Oosterbeek." The officer politely asked Knap to hold on. A few minutes later he came back on the line. Thanking Knap, he explained that "the Captain is doubtful about the report. After all, he's heard a lot of fairy tales." But the skepticism at British headquarters quickly disappeared when Pieter Kruyff confirmed through Lieutenant Commander Arnoldus Wolters, of the Royal Dutch Navy, acting as an intelligence liaison officer for the division, that at least "fifty tanks are heading into Arnhem from the northeast."

The stench of battle permeated the inner city. On the bridge, wreckage jutted high above the concrete shoulders and littered streets along the Rhine. Heavy smoke smeared buildings and yards with a greasy film. All along the waterfront hundreds of fires burned unattended, and men remember that the ground shook constantly from the concussion of heavy explosives as the Germans, in the final hours of this second day of battle, battered British strongholds along the northern ramp in the bitter contest for possession of Montgomery's prime objective.

Around midnight Lieutenant Colonel John Frost left his headquarters on the western side of the ramp and made his way around the perimeter, checking his men. Although the battle had continued almost without letup since Gräbner's armored attack during the morning, morale was still high. Frost was proud of his tired, dirty troopers. All day long they had doggedly repelled attack after attack. Not a single German or vehicle had reached the north end of the bridge.

During the afternoon the Germans had changed their tactics. With phosphorous ammunition, they attempted to burn the British out of their strong points. A long-barreled 150 mm. gun hurled 100-pound shells directly against Frost's headquarters building, forcing the men to the cellar. Then British mortars got the range and scored a direct hit, killing the gun crew. As the troopers cheered and hooted derisively, other Germans rushed out under fire and towed the gun away. Houses around the perimeter were burning fiercely, but the British held out in them until the very last minute before moving to other positions. Damage was awesome. Burning trucks and vehicles, wrecked half-tracks and smoking piles of debris cluttered every street. Sergeant Robert H. Jones remembers the sight as "a Sargasso sea of blazing collapsed buildings, half-tracks, trucks and jeeps." The battle had become an endurance contest, one that Frost knew his men could not win without help.

Cellars and basements were filled with wounded. One of the battalion chaplains, the Reverend Father Bernard Egan, and the battalion medical officer, Captain James Logan—who had been friends since the North African campaign—tended the casualties from a rapidly dwindling stock of medical supplies. There was almost no morphia left and even field dressings were almost gone. The men had set out for the bridge with only enough light rations for forty-eight hours. Now, these were almost exhausted, and the Germans had cut off the water. Forced to scrounge for food, the troopers were existing on apples and a few pears stored in the cellars and basements of the houses they occupied. Private G. W. Jukes remembers his sergeant telling the men, "You don't need water if you eat lots of apples." Jukes had a vision of "being eventually relieved, standing back-to-back defiantly in bloodstained bandages, surrounded by dead Germans, spent cartridge cases and apple cores."

Hour after hour Frost waited vainly for Dobie's or Fitch's relieving battalions to break through the German ring and reach the bridge. Although sounds of battle came from the direction of western Arnhem, there was no sign of large-scale troop movements. All through the day Frost had expected some further word from Horrocks' XXX Corps. Nothing had been heard from them since the single strong radio signal picked up during the morning. Stragglers from the 3rd Battalion who had managed to get through to Frost brought news that Horrocks' tanks were still far down the corridor. Some had even heard from Dutch underground sources that the column had not reached Nijmegen as yet. Worried and uncertain, Frost decided to keep this information to himself. He had already begun to believe that the men of his proud 2nd Battalion, which he had commanded since its inception, would be alone far longer than he believed it possible to hold.

In the last hours of Monday, Frost's hopes hinged on the third lift and the expected arrival of Major General Stanislaw Sosabowski's 1st Polish Parachute Brigade. "They were to drop south of the bridge," Frost later wrote, "and I dreaded the reception they would have . . . but it was important that

they find a handful of friends to meet them." To prepare for
the Poles' arrival, Frost organized a "mobile storming party."
Using two of Major Freddie Gough's armored reconnaissance
jeeps and a Bren-gun carrier, Frost hoped to rush across the
bridge and, in the surprise and confusion of the assault, open
a passage and bring the Poles through. Major Gough, who
was to lead the group, was "thoroughly miserable and quite
unenthusiastic about the idea." He had celebrated his forty-
third birthday on September 16. If Frost's plan was carried out,
Gough felt quite certain he would not see his forty-fourth.*

The Poles were not expected to land before 10 A.M., on the
nineteenth. Now, making his rounds of men in slit trenches,
machine-gun emplacements, basements and cellars, Frost
warned them to save precious ammunition. They were to
fire only at close quarters, to make every shot count. Signalman James Haysom was sighting his rifle on a German when
the Colonel's order was passed along. "Stand still, you sod,"
Haysom shouted. "These bullets cost money."

While Frost knew that reducing the rate of fire would help
the enemy improve his positions, he also believed that the Germans would be misled into thinking the British had lost heart
as well as numbers. This attitude, Frost was certain, would cost
the Germans dearly.

On the opposite side of the ramp, the little band of men with
Captain Eric Mackay was already proving Frost's theory.

In the scarred and pitted schoolhouse under the ramp,
Mackay had compressed his small force into two rooms and
posted a handful of men in the hall outside to ward off any
enemy attempt at infiltration. Mackay had barely positioned
his men when the Germans launched a murderous machine-
gun and mortar attack. Lance Corporal Arthur Hendy remembers the firing was so intense that bullets "whizzed through
the shattered windows, chopped up the floorboards and we
dodged as many flying splinters as we did actual bullets."

As men ducked for cover, Mackay discovered that the

---

*After the war Gough learned that General Horrocks had been thinking about
a similar idea. Remembering how a fast reconnaissance unit had gone ahead
of the British column and linked up with the 101st, he thought that a similar
fast patrol might well take its chances and reach the Arnhem bridge. "Colonel
Vincent Dunkerly was alerted to lead the group," Gough says, "and, like me,
he admitted that he spent the entire day peeing in his knickers at the thought."

Germans had brought up a flamethrower, and within minutes a demolished half-track near the school was set afire. Then, Mackay recalls, "the Germans set fire to the house to our north and it burned merrily, sending down showers of sparks on our wooden roof which promptly caught fire." In the pandemonium, men sprinted for the roof, where for over three hours, using fire extinguishers from the school and their own camouflage smocks, they worked frantically to extinguish the flames. To Lance Corporal Hendy the stench was "like burning cheese and burning flesh. The whole area was lit up. The heat in the attic was intense and all the time the Germans were sniping away at us. Finally the fire was put out."

As the exhausted troopers collected once again in the two rooms, Mackay ordered his soldiers to bind their feet with their smocks and shirts. "The stone floors were thick with glass, plaster and metal fragments and the stairs were slippery with blood. Everything scrunched under our feet and made a terrific racket." As Mackay was about to go to the cellar to check on his wounded, he remembers "a blinding flash and a terrific explosion. The next thing I knew, someone was slapping my face." During the fire the Germans had brought up antitank Panzerfäuste in an effort to demolish the little force once and for all. With dazed disbelief Mackay saw that the entire southwest corner of the school and part of the still-smoldering roof had been blown away. Worse, the classrooms now resembled a charnel house with dead and wounded everywhere. "Only a few minutes later," Mackay recalls, "someone came over and said he thought we were surrounded. I looked out one of the windows. Down below was a mass of Germans. Funnily enough, they weren't doing anything, just standing around on the grass. They were on all sides of us except the west. They must have thought the Panzerfäuste had finished us off, because we had stopped firing."

Making his way carefully around the bodies on the floor, Mackay ordered his men to take up grenades. "When I yell 'Fire!' open up with everything you have," he said. Back at the southeast window, Mackay gave the order. "The boys dropped grenades on the heads below and we instantly followed up with all we had left: six Brens and fourteen Sten guns, firing at maximum rate." In the din, paratroopers stood silhouetted in the windows, firing their machine guns from the hip and yelling their war cry, "Whoa Mohammed." Within minutes the counterattack was over. As Mackay recalls, "when I looked out again, all I could see below was a carpet of gray. We must have wiped out between thirty and fifty Germans."

Now his men went about collecting the dead and wounded. One man was dying with fifteen bullets in the chest. Five other men were critically injured and almost all the troopers had sustained burns trying to save the blazing roof. Mackay had also been hit again by shrapnel and he discovered that his foot was pinned to his boot. Neither Mackay nor Sapper Pinky White, the acting medical orderly, could remove the metal and Mackay laced his boot tighter to keep the swelling down. Out of fifty men, Mackay now had only twenty-one in good shape; four were dead, and twenty-five wounded. Although he had no food and only a little water, he had collected a plentiful supply of morphia and was able to ease the pains of the injured. "Almost everybody was suffering from shock and fatigue," he remembers, "but we had gotten ourselves another temporary breathing space. I just didn't think things looked too bright, but we'd heard the BBC and they told us that everything was going according to plan. I got on the wireless to the Colonel, gave in our strength return and said we were all happy and holding our own."

As Lance Corporal Hendy tried to catch a few minutes' sleep he heard a church bell off in the distance. At first he thought that it was ringing to announce the approach of Horrocks' tanks, but the sound was not measured and consistent. Hendy realized that bullets or shell fragments must be hitting the bell. He thought of the men around Colonel Frost's headquarters on the other side of the ramp and wondered if they were holding safe. He heard the bell again and felt himself shivering. He could not rid himself of an eerie, doomed feeling.

The help that Frost so urgently needed was agonizingly close —barely more than a mile away. Four battalions spread between St. Elisabeth's Hospital and the Rhine were desperately trying to reach him. Lieutenant Colonel J. A. C. Fitch's 3rd Battalion had been attempting to force its way along the Lion route—the Rhine river road that Frost had used in reaching the bridge two days before. In darkness, without communications, Fitch was unaware that three other battalions were also on the move—Lieutenant Colonel David Dobie's 1st, Lieutenant Colonel G. H. Lea's 11th, and Lieutenant Colonel W. D. H. McCardie's 2nd South Staffordshires; Dobie's men were separated from him by only a few hundred yards.

At 4 A.M. on Tuesday, September 19, the 11th Battalion and the 2nd South Staffs began to move through the heavily built-up area between St. Elisabeth's Hospital and the Arnhem Town Museum. South of them, on the Lion route, where Fitch had already encountered devastating opposition, the 1st Battalion was now attempting to push its way through. Initially the three battalions, coordinating their movements, gained ground. Then, with dawn, their cover disappeared. German opposition, uneven throughout the night, was suddenly fiercely concentrated. The advance ground to a halt as the battalions found themselves in a tight net, trapped on three sides by an enemy who seemed almost to have waited for them to arrive at a preplanned position. And the Germans were prepared for a massacre.

Forward elements were hit and stopped in their tracks by German tanks and half-tracks blocking the streets ahead. From the windows of houses on the high escarpment of the railway marshaling yards to the north, waiting machine-gun crews opened up. And from the brickworks across the Rhine multi-barreled flak guns, firing horizontally, ripped into Dobie's battalion and flayed Fitch's men as they tried to move along the lower Rhine road. Fitch's battalion, already badly mauled in the fighting since landing two days before, was now so cut to pieces by the unremitting flak fire that it could no longer exist as an effective unit. Men broke in confusion. They could go neither forward nor back. With virtually no protection on the open road, they were methodically mowed down. "It was painfully obvious," says Captain Ernest Seccombe, "that the Jerries had much more ammunition than we did. We tried to move in spurts, from cover to cover. I had just begun one dash when I was caught in a murderous crossfire. I fell like a sack of potatoes. I couldn't even crawl." Seccombe, who had been hit in both legs, watched helplessly as two Germans approached him. The British captain, who spoke fluent German, asked them to look at his legs. They bent down and examined his wounds. Then one of the Germans straightened up. "I'm sorry, Herr Hauptmann," he told Seccombe. "I'm afraid for you the war is over." The Germans called their own medics and Seccombe was taken to St. Elisabeth's Hospital.*

By chance one of Fitch's officers discovered the presence of Dobie's forces on the lower road, and the men of the 1st Battalion, despite their own heavy casualties, hurried forward, toward the pitiable remnants of Fitch's group. Dobie was now hell bent on reaching the bridge, but the odds were enormous. As he moved up into the intense fire and leapfrogged over Fitch's men, Dobie himself was wounded and captured (he later succeeded in making his escape); by the end of the day it was estimated that only forty men of his battalion remained. Private Walter Boldock was one of them. "We kept trying to make it, but it was a disaster. We were constantly mortared, and German tanks whirled right up to us. I tried to get one with my Bren gun and then we seemed to be going backwards. I passed a broken water main. A dead civilian in blue overalls lay in the gutter, the water lapping gently around his body. As we left the outskirts of Arnhem, I knew somehow we wouldn't be going back."

Fitch's men, attempting to follow Dobie's battalion, were shredded once again. The march had lost all meaning; after-action reports indicate the total confusion within the battalion at this point. "Progress was satisfactory until we reached the area of the dismantled pontoon bridge," reads the 3rd Battalion's report. "Then casualties from the 1st Battalion began passing through us. Heavy machine guns, 20 mm. and intense mortar fire began . . . casualties were being suffered at an ever-increasing rate, and the wounded were being rushed back in small groups every minute."

With his force in danger of total destruction, Fitch ordered his men back to the Rhine Pavilion, a large restaurant-building complex on the bank of the river, where the remnants of the

---

*Throughout most of the Arnhem battle, the hospital was used by both British and German doctors and medics to care for their wounded. Seccombe, as a German prisoner, was moved to the small Dutch town of Enschede, about five miles from the German border. During his stay there, both legs were amputated. He was liberated in April, 1945.

battalion could regroup and take up positions. "Every officer and man must make his way back as best he can," Fitch told his troopers. "The whole area seems covered by fire, and the only hope of getting out safely is individually." Private Robert Edwards remembers a sergeant "whose boots were squelching blood from his wounds, telling us to get out and make our way back to the first organized unit we came to." Colonel Fitch did not reach the Rhine Pavilion. On the deadly road back, he was killed by mortar fire.

By an odd set of circumstances, two men who should never have been there actually made their way into Arnhem. Major Anthony Deane-Drummond, the second in command of Division signals, had become so alarmed over the breakdown of communications that, with his batman-driver, Lance Corporal Arthur Turner, he had gone forward to discover the trouble. Deane-Drummond and Turner had been on the road since early Monday. First they had located Dobie's battalion, where they had learned that Frost was on the bridge and Dobie was preparing an attack to get through to him. Setting off on the river road, Deane-Drummond caught up with elements of the 3rd Battalion struggling toward Arnhem and traveled with them. Heavy fire engulfed the group and in the fighting that ensued Deane-Drummond found himself leading the remnants of a company whose officer had been killed.

Under constant small-arms fire and so surrounded that Deane-Drummond remembers the Germans were tossing stick grenades at the men, he led the group along the road to some houses near a small inlet. Ahead, he could see the bridge. "The last couple of hundred yards to the houses I had decided on, the men were literally dropping like flies," he recalls. "We were down to about twenty men, and I realized the rest of the battalion was now far to the rear and not likely to reach us." Dividing the men into three parties, Deane-Drummond decided to wait until darkness, move down to the river, swim across it, then try to recross and join Division to the west. In a small corner house with the Germans all around, he settled down to wait. A banging began on the front door. Deane-Drummond and the three men with him raced to the back of the house and locked themselves in a small lavatory. From the noise from outside the little room, it was clear that the Germans were busy converting the house into a strong point. Deane-Drummond was trapped. He and the others would remain in the tiny room for the better part of three more days.*

Meanwhile, the 11th Battalion and the South Staffordshires, after several hours of relentless street fighting, had also come to a standstill. Counterattacking German tanks hammered the battalions, forcing them to pull slowly back.

Private Maurice Faulkner remembers that elements of the battalions reached the museum with heavy casualties, only to encounter the tanks. "I saw one man jump out of a window on top of a tank and try to put a grenade in," Faulkner recalls. "He was killed by a sniper, but I think he was probably trapped anyway, and he may have figured that was the only way out." Private William O'Brien says that the situation was "suddenly chaotic. Nobody knew what to do. The Germans had brought up those *Nebelwerfer* mortar throwers and we were scared out of our minds at the screaming sound. It began to seem to me that the generals had gotten us into something they had no business doing. I kept wondering where the hell was the goddam Second Army."

Private Andrew Milbourne, near the church at Oosterbeek, heard the call go out for machine-gunners. Milbourne stepped forward and was told to take his gun and a crew to the juncture of the road near St. Elisabeth's Hospital to help cover and protect the two battalions as they disengaged. Putting his Vickers machine gun in a jeep, Milbourne set off with three others. Milbourne positioned his gun in the garden of a house at the crossroads. Almost immediately he seemed to be engulfed in his own private battle. Mortar bursts and shells appeared to be

---

*Deane-Drummond was captured on Friday, September 22, shortly after he left the house near the Arnhem bridge. In an old villa near Velp, used as a P.O.W. compound, he discovered a wall cupboard in which to hide. In these cramped confines, he remained for thirteen days, rationing himself to a few sips of water and a small amount of bread. On October 5 he escaped, contacted the Dutch underground and on the night of October 22, was taken to the 1st Airborne Casualty Clearing Station at Nijmegen. One of the three men with him in Arnhem, Deane-Drummond's batman, Lance Corporal Arthur Turner, was also captured and taken to the Velp house. Eventually he was shipped to a P.O.W. camp in Germany and was liberated in April, 1945. Deane-Drummond's own story is told most effectively in his own book, *Return Ticket.*

aimed directly at him. As troopers began to fall back around him, Milbourne sent a constant arc of bullets out in front of them. He remembers hearing a rushing sound, like wind, and then a flash. Seconds later he knew that something was wrong with his eyes and hands. He remembers someone saying, "Lord, he's copped it."

Private Thomas Pritchard heard the voice and ran to where men were now standing over Milbourne. "He was lying over the twisted Vickers with both hands hanging by a thread of skin and an eye out of its socket. We started yelling for a medic." Not far away Milbourne's best friend, Corporal Terry "Taffy" Brace of the 16th Field Ambulance, heard someone shout. Leaving a shrapnel case he had treated, Brace sprinted forward. "Quick," a man called out to him, "the Vickers has caught it." As he ran, Brace remembers, he could hear an almost steady sound of machine-gun fire, and shells and mortars seemed to be dropping everywhere. Approaching a cluster of men, he pushed his way through and, to his horror, saw Milbourne lying on the ground. Working frantically, Brace wrapped Milbourne's arms and put a dressing just below the injured man's cheekbone to cushion his left eye. Brace remembers talking constantly as he worked. "It's just a scratch, Andy," he kept saying. "It's just a scratch." Picking up his friend, Brace carried Milbourne to a nearby dressing station where a Dutch doctor immediately set to work. Then he went back to battle.*

Brace passed what seemed to be hundreds of men lying in the fields and along the road. "I stopped at every one," he recalls. "The only thing I could do for most of them was take off their smocks and cover their faces." Brace treated one injured sergeant as best he could and then as he prepared to set out again, the man reached out to him. "I'm not going to make it," he told Brace. "Please hold my hand." Brace sat down and cupped the sergeant's hand in both of his. He thought of Milbourne, his best friend, and of the many men who had come streaming back through the lines this day. A few minutes later,

---

*Milbourne was later captured in the cellar of the Ter Horst house in Oosterbeek. He lost his left eye and both hands were amputated by a German surgeon in Apeldoorn. He spent the rest of the war in a prisoner-of-war camp in Germany.

Brace felt a slight pull. Looking down, he saw that the sergeant was dead.

By now the British were in confusion, without antitank guns, out of Piat ammunition and suffering heavy casualties. The attack had become a shambles. The two battalions could not drive beyond the built-up areas around St. Elisabeth's Hospital. But in that maze of streets one action was both positive and successful. The attack had overrun a terrace house at Zwarteweg 14, the building from which General Roy Urquhart had been unable to escape.

"We heard the wheeze of the self-propelled gun outside and the rattle of its track," Urquhart later wrote. "It was moving off." Antoon Derksen then appeared and "announced excitedly that the British were at the end of the road. We ran down the street and I thanked God we had made contact again."

Urquhart, learning from an officer of the South Staffordshires that his headquarters was now in a hotel called the Hartenstein in Oosterbeek, commandeered a jeep and, driving at full speed through a constant hail of sniper fire, at last reached Division.

The time was 7:25 A.M. He had been absent and lacking control of the battle in its most crucial period, for almost thirty-nine hours.

At the Hartenstein, one of the first men to see Urquhart was Chaplain G. A. Pare. "The news had not been so good," he recalls. "The General had been reported a prisoner and there was no sign of the Second Army." As Pare came down the steps of the hotel "who should be ascending but the General. Several of us saw him, but nobody said a word. We just stared —completely taken aback." Dirty and with "two days' beard on my face I must have been something to see," Urquhart says. At that moment Colonel Charles Mackenzie, the chief of staff, came rushing out. Staring at Urquhart, Mackenzie told him, "We had assumed, sir, that you had gone for good."

Quickly Mackenzie briefed the anxious Urquhart on the events that had occurred during his absence and gave him the situation—as Division knew it—at the moment. The picture was appalling. Bitterly, Urquhart saw that his proud division was being scattered and cut to ribbons. He thought of all the setbacks that had dogged his Market forces: the distance from the drop zones to the bridge; the near-total breakdown of communications; the weather delay of Hackett's 4th Brigade plus the loss of precious resupply cargo; and the slow progress of Horrocks' tanks. Urquhart was stunned to learn that XXX Corps was not reported to have reached even Nijmegen as yet. The command dispute between Hackett and Hicks was upsetting, particularly as it stemmed from Urquhart's and Lathbury's own unforeseeable absence in the crucial hours when precise direction was required in the battle. Above all, Urquhart rued the incredible overoptimism of the initial planning stages that had failed to give due importance to the presence of Bittrich's Panzer Corps.

All these factors, one compounding another, had brought the division close to catastrophe. Only superb discipline and unbelievable courage were holding the battered Red Devils together. Urquhart was determined to somehow instill new hope, to coordinate the efforts of his men down even to company level. In doing so, he knew that he must demand more of his weary and wounded men than any airborne commander ever had demanded. He had no choices. With the steady inflow of German reinforcements, the dedicated, soft-spoken Scotsman saw that unless he acted immediately "my division would be utterly destroyed." Even now, it might be too late to save his beloved command from annihilation.

A look at the map told its own desperate story. Quite simply, there was no front line. Now that all his troopers but the Polish Brigade had arrived, the main dropping zones to the west had been abandoned and, apart from resupply areas, the lines around them held by Hicks's men had been shortened and pulled in. Hackett was going for the high ground northeast of Wolfheze and Johannahoeve Farm, he saw. The 11th Battalion and the South Staffordshires were fighting near St. Elisabeth's Hospital. There was no news of the progress of the 1st and 3rd battalions on the lower Rhine road. Yet Frost, Urquhart learned with pride, still held at the bridge. Everywhere on the situation map red arrows indicated newly reported concentrations of enemy tanks and troops; some actually appeared to be positioned *behind* the British units. Urquhart did not know if there was time enough remaining to reorganize and coordinate the advance of his dwindling forces and send them toward the bridge in one last desperate drive. Ignorant for now of the cruel damage done to the 1st and 3rd battalions, Urquhart believed there might still be a chance.

"The thing that hit me was this," he remembers. "Who was running the battle in the town? Who was coordinating it? Lathbury was wounded and no longer there. No one had been nominated to make a plan." As he began to work on the problem Brigadier Hicks arrived. He was extremely happy to see Urquhart and to return the division to his care. "I told him," Urquhart says, "that we would have to get somebody into town immediately. A senior officer, to coordinate Lea and McCardie's attack. I realized that they had been only a few hundred yards away from me, and it would have been better if I had remained in town to direct. Now, I sent Colonel Hilaro Barlow, Hicks's deputy. He was the man for the job. I told him to get into town and tie up the loose ends. I explained exactly where Lea and McCardie were and sent him off with a jeep and wireless set and ordered him to produce a properly coordinated attack."

Barlow never reached the battalions. Somewhere en route he was killed. "He simply vanished," Urquhart recalls, and the body was never found.

The arrival of the Poles in the third lift was of almost equal urgency. They would now land directly on a prepared enemy on the southern approaches of the bridge, as Frost knew only too well; and by now, Urquhart reasoned, the Germans were obviously reinforced by armor. The drop could be a slaughter. In an effort to stop them and even though communications were uncertain—no one knew whether messages were getting through—Urquhart sent a warning message and requested a new drop zone. At rear Corps headquarters the signal was never received. But it was irrelevant. In yet another setback, fog covered many of the airfields in England where the planes and gliders of the vital third lift were readying to go.

The corridor through which Horrocks' tanks had to drive was open once again. At Son, forty-six miles south of Arnhem, engineers watched the first British armor thud across the temporary Bailey bridge they had erected. The Guards Armored Division was once more on its way, the drive now led by the

Grenadiers. Now, at 6:45 A.M. on September 19, the Garden forces were behind schedule by thirty-six hours.

No one in this sector of the corridor could guess as yet what that time loss would mean in the final reckoning—and worse was to come. The great Waal bridge at Nijmegen, thirty-five miles north, was still in German hands. If it was not taken intact and soon, airborne commanders feared the Germans would blow it up.

That fear gave urgency to the armored drive. To General Gavin, General Browning, the Corps commander, and to Horrocks, the Nijmegen bridge was now the most critical piece in the plan. As yet the commanders did not know the true plight of the 1st British Airborne Division. German propaganda broadcasts had boasted that General Urquhart was dead* and his division smashed, but there had been no news at all from Division itself. In the tank columns men believed that Market-Garden was going well. So did General Taylor's Screaming Eagles. "To the individual 101st trooper, the sound of the tanks, the sight of their guns was both an assurance and a promise," General S. L. A. Marshall was later to write—"an assurance that there was a plan and a promise that the plan might work."

As the tanks rumbled by, the watching troopers of General Taylor's 101st took just pride in their own achievements. Against unexpectedly strong resistance they had taken and held the fifteen-mile stretch of road from Eindhoven up to Veghel. Along the route men waved and cheered as armored cars of the Household Cavalry, the tanks of the Grenadiers and the mighty mass of XXX Corps swept by. In minutes the column moved from Son to Veghel. Then, with the kind of dash that Montgomery had envisioned for the entire drive, the armored spearhead, flanked by cheering, flag-waving Dutch crowds, sped on, reaching its first destination at Grave at 8:30 A.M. There, the tanks linked up with Gavin's 82nd. "I knew we had reached them," recalls Corporal William Chennell, who was in one of the lead armored cars, "because the Americans, taking no chances, halted us with warning fire."

---

*According to Bittrich the Germans learned from P.O.W.'s that Urquhart was either dead or missing and also, he claims, "we were monitoring radio messages and listening to phone calls."

Moving quickly on, the first tanks reached the Nijmegen suburbs at midday. Now two thirds of the vital Market-Garden corridor had been traversed. The single road, jammed with vehicles, could have been severed at any time had it not been for the vigilant, tenacious paratroopers who had fought and died to keep it open. If Montgomery's bold strategy was to succeed, the corridor was the lifeline which alone could sustain it. Men felt the heady excitement of success. According to official pronouncements, including those from Eisenhower's headquarters, everything was going according to plan. There was not even a hint of the dire predicament that was slowly engulfing the men at Arnhem.

Yet, General Frederick Browning was uneasy. During the afternoon of the eighteenth he met with General Gavin. The Corps commander had received no news from Arnhem. Other than scant Dutch underground information, Browning's communications men had not received a single situation report. Despite official announcements that the operation was proceeding satisfactorily, messages relayed to Browning from his own rear headquarters and from General Dempsey's Second Army had roused in him a gnawing concern. Browning could not rid himself of the feeling that Urquhart might be in grievous trouble.

Two reports in particular fed his anxiety. German strength and reaction in Arnhem had unquestionably proved heavier and faster than the planners had ever anticipated. And R.A.F. photo-reconnaissance information indicated that only the northern end of the Arnhem bridge was held by the British. But even now, Browning was unaware that two panzer divisions were in Urquhart's sector. Disturbed by the lack of communications and nagged by his suspicions, Browning warned Gavin that the "Nijmegen bridge must be taken today. At the latest, tomorrow." From the moment he had first learned of Market-Garden, the bridge at Arnhem had worried Browning. Montgomery had confidently expected Horrocks to reach it within forty-eight hours. At the time, Browning's view was that Urquhart's paratroopers could hold for four days. Now, on D plus two—one day short of Browning's estimate of the division's ability to function alone—although unaware of the grave condition of the 1st British Airborne

Division, Browning told Gavin, "we must get to Arnhem as quickly as possible.*

Immediately after the link-up in the 82nd's sector, Browning called a conference. The Guards' lead armored cars were sent back to pick up the XXX Corps commander, General Horrocks, and the commander of the Guards Armored Division, General Allan Adair. With Browning, the two officers drove to a site northeast of Nijmegen, overlooking the river. From there Corporal William Chennell, whose vehicle had picked up one of the two officers, stood with the little group observing the bridge. "To my amazement," Chennell remembers, "we could see German troops and vehicles moving back and forth across it, apparently completely unconcerned. Not a shot was fired, yet we were hardly more than a few hundred yards away."

Back at Browning's headquarters, Horrocks and Adair learned for the first time of the fierce German opposition in the 82nd's area. "I was surprised to discover upon arrival that we did not have the Nijmegen bridge," Adair says. "I assumed it would be in airborne hands by the time we reached it and we'd simply sweep on through." Gavin's troopers, the generals now learned, had been so hard-pressed to hold the airhead that companies had been recalled from Nijmegen to protect the landing zones from massed enemy assaults. Elements of the 508th Battalion had been unable to make any headway against the strong SS units holding the bridge approaches. The only way to take the bridge quickly, Browning believed, was by a combined tank and infantry assault. "We're going to have to winkle these Germans out with more than airborne troops," Browning told Adair.

*Many British accounts of Arnhem, including Chester Wilmot's excellent *Struggle for Europe*, imply that Browning knew more about Urquhart's situation at this time than he actually did. A careful check of the scattered and inconclusive information passed on to Corps headquarters shows that the first direct message from the Arnhem sector reached Browning at 8:25 A.M. on the nineteenth. Two others arrived during the course of the day and dealt with the bridge, troop locations and a request for air support. Although many messages giving the true picture had been sent, they had not been received, and these three gave no indication that Urquhart's division was being methodically destroyed. In some quarters, Montgomery and Browning have been unjustly criticized for not taking more immediate and positive steps. At this time they knew virtually nothing of Urquhart's critical problems.

The Nijmegen bridge was the last crucial link in the Market-Garden plan. With the time limit that Browning had placed on the British paratroopers' ability to hold out about to expire, the pace of the operation must be accelerated. Eleven miles of corridor remained to be forced open. The Nijmegen bridge, Browning stressed, had to be captured in record time.

Major General Heinz Harmel, the Frundsberg Division commander, was irritable and more than a little frustrated. Despite constant pressure from General Bittrich, he had still been unable to bludgeon Frost and his men from the Arnhem bridge. "I was beginning to feel damn foolish," Harmel recalls.

By now he knew that the paratroopers were nearing the end of their supplies and ammunition. Also their casualties, if his own were an example, were extremely high. "I had determined to bring tanks and artillery fire to bear and level every single building they held," Harmel says, "but in view of the fight they were putting up, I felt I should first ask for their surrender." Harmel ordered his staff to arrange for a temporary truce. They were to pick a British prisoner of war to go to Frost with Harmel's ultimatum. The soldier selected was a newly captured engineer, twenty-five-year-old Sergeant Stanley Halliwell, one of Captain Mackay's sappers.

Halliwell was told to enter the British perimeter under a flag of truce. There he was to tell Frost that a German officer would arrive to confer with him about surrender terms. If Frost agreed, Halliwell would once more return to the bridge to stand unarmed with Frost until the German officer joined them. "As a P.O.W. I was supposed to return to the Jerries as soon as I delivered the message and got the Colonel's answer and I didn't like that part of the business at all," Halliwell says. The Germans brought Halliwell close to the British perimeter, where, carrying the truce flag, he crossed into the British-held sector and arrived at Frost's headquarters. Nervously, Halliwell explained the situation to Frost. The Germans, he said, believed it pointless for the fight to continue. The British were surrounded with no hope of relief. They had no choice but to die or surrender. Questioning Halliwell, Frost learned that "the enemy seemed to be most disheartened at their own losses." His own spirits lifted momentarily at the news, and he remembers thinking that "if only more ammunition would arrive, we would soon have our SS opponents in the bag." As to the German request for negotiations, Frost's answer to Halliwell was explicit. "Tell them to go to hell," he said.

Halliwell was in full agreement. As a P.O.W. he was expected to return, but he did not relish the idea of repeating the Colonel's exact words and, he pointed out to Frost, it might prove difficult to return through the lines. "It is up to you to make that decision," Frost said. Halliwell had already done so. "If it's all the same with you, Colonel," he told Frost, "I'll stay. Jerry will get the message sooner or later."

On the far side of the ramp Captain Eric Mackay had just received a similar invitation, but he chose to misinterpret it. "I looked out and saw a Jerry standing with a not-very-white hanky tied to a rifle. He shouted 'Surrender!' I promptly assumed that they wanted to surrender, but perhaps they meant us." In the now nearly demolished schoolhouse in which his small force was holding out, Mackay, still thinking the German was making a surrender offer, thought the whole idea impractical. "We only had two rooms," he says. "We would have been a bit cramped with prisoners."

Waving his arms at the German, Mackay shouted, "Get the hell out of here. We're taking no prisoners." The medical orderly, Pinky White, joined Mackay at the window. "*Raus!*" he shouted. "Beat it!" Amid a series of hoots and catcalls, other troopers took up the cry. "Bugger off! Go back and fight it out, you bastard." The German seemed to get the point. As Mackay recalls, he turned around and walked quickly back to his own building, "still waving his dirty hanky."

Harmel's attempt to seek a surrender from the spirited, beleaguered men on the bridge had failed. The battle began again in all its fury.

8

At fog-covered bases near Grantham, England, the 1st Polish Parachute Brigade was waiting to take off. Zero hour for the drop had been scheduled for 10 a.m., but weather had forced a five-hour postponement. The brigade was now due to come in at 3 p.m. Major General Stanislaw Sosabowski, the Poles' fiercely independent, mercurial commander, had kept his men by their planes during the wait. It seemed to the fifty-two-year-old Sosabowski that England was fogged in every morning. If the weather cleared more quickly than expected, orders might change and Sosabowski intended to be ready to go on short notice. He felt that every hour mattered now. Urquhart, Sosabowski believed, was in trouble.

Apart from instinct, there was no specific reason for Sosabowski's feeling. But the Market-Garden concept had not appealed to him from the outset. He was certain that the drop zones were too far from the bridge to effect surprise. Further, no one in England appeared to know what was happening in Arnhem, and Sosabowski had been alarmed to discover at headquarters that communications with the 1st British Airborne Division had broken down. All that was known was that the north end of the Arnhem bridge was in British hands. Since there had been no change in the plan, Sosabowski's men, dropping to the south near the village of Elden, would take the other end.

But the General was worried about the lack of information. He could not be sure that Urquhart's men were still on the bridge. Liaison officers from Browning's rear headquarters, on whom Sosabowski was dependent for news, seemed to know little about what was actually happening. He had thought of going to First Allied Airborne Army Headquarters at Ascot to talk directly with General Lewis Brereton, the commanding officer. Protocol dictated otherwise. His troops were under General Browning's command, and Sosabowski was reluctant to bypass military channels. Any alterations in the plan should come only from Browning, and none had been received. Yet, Sosabowski felt that something had gone wrong. If the British were holding only the north end of the bridge, the enemy had to be in strength to the south and the Poles might well have the fight of their lives. Sosabowski's transport and artillery, due to leave in forty-six gliders from the southern Down Ampney and Torrant Rushton bases, were still scheduled for a midday takeoff. Since that part of the plan remained unchanged, Sosabowski tried to convince himself that all would go well.

Lieutenant Albert Smaczny was equally uneasy. He was to lead his company across the Arnhem bridge and occupy some buildings in the eastern part of the city. If the bridge had not been captured, he wondered how he would put his men across the Rhine. Smaczny had been assured that the crossing would be in British hands, but ever since his escape from the Germans in 1939 (his sixteen-year-old brother had been shot by the Gestapo in reprisal) Smaczny had schooled himself "to expect the unexpected."

Hour after hour the Poles waited, while the fog in the Midlands persisted. Corporal Wladijslaw Korob "was beginning to get nervous. I wanted to go," he remembers. "Standing around the airdrome wasn't my idea of the best way to kill Germans." Looking at the assemblage of planes on the field, Lieutenant Stefan Kaczmarek felt "a joy that almost hurt." He, too, was getting tired of standing around idle. The operation, he told his men, "is the second-best alternative to liberating Warsaw. If we succeed, we'll walk into Germany right through the kitchen."

But the Poles were to be disappointed. At noon Sosabowski received fresh orders. Although planes were operating from the southern fields, in the Midlands the bases remained weathered in. The jump was canceled for the day. "It's no good, General," the chief liaison officer, Lieutenant Colonel George Stevens, told the protesting Sosabowski. "We can't get you out." The assault was postponed until the following morning, Wednesday, September 20. "We'll try it then at 10 A.M.," he was told. There was no time to transfer troop loads to bases in the south. To Sosabowski's chagrin, he learned that his glider supply lift had already left and was on the way to Holland. The General fumed with impatience. Each hour that passed meant greater enemy resistance, and the following day might bring an infinitely harder fight—unless his nagging fears were completely unjustified.

They were not. Sosabowski's glider supply lift with men, artillery and transport was heading for near annihilation. The third air lift would be a disaster.

Low-scudding clouds blanketed the southern route all the way across the Channel. The third lift, heading for the 101st, 82nd and British drop zones, encountered trouble right from the beginning. Clear weather had been predicted by afternoon. Instead, conditions were deteriorating even as the formations took to the air. Squadrons of fighters, caught in cloud and unable to see ground targets, were forced to turn back. In zero visibility, unable to see their tow planes, many gliders cut loose to make emergency landings in England or in the Channel and whole serials were forced to abort and return to base.

Of the 655 troop carriers and 431 gliders that did take off, little more than half reached the drop and landing zones, although most of the plane-glider combinations carrying troops were able to land safely back in England or elsewhere. But over the Continent intense enemy ground fire and Luftwaffe attacks, combined with the poor weather, caused the loss of some 112 gliders and 40 transports. Only 1,341 out of 2,310 troops and only 40 out of 68 artillery pieces bound for the 101st Airborne Division got through. So hard-pressed were General Taylor's men that the 40 guns went into action almost as soon as they landed.

General Gavin's 82nd Airborne fared even worse. At this time, when every trooper was needed for the attack on the critical Nijmegen bridges, Gavin's 325th Glider Infantry Regiment did not arrive at all. Like the Polish paratroops, the 325th's planes and gliders, also based in the Grantham area, were unable to leave the ground. Worse, out of 265 tons of stores and ammunition destined for the 82nd, only about 40 tons were recovered.

In the British sector, where Urquhart was expecting not only the Poles but a full-cargo resupply mission, tragedy struck. The supply dropping zones had been overrun by the enemy, and although intensive efforts were made to divert the 163-plane mission to a new area south of the Hartenstein Hotel, the effort failed. Desperately short of everything, particularly ammunition, Urquhart's men saw the formations approach through a blizzard of antiaircraft fire. Then enemy fighters appeared, firing on the formations and strafing the new supply dropping zones.

At about 4 P.M., the Reverend G. A. Pare, chaplain of the Glider Pilot Regiment, heard the cry, "Third lift coming!" Suddenly, the chaplain remembers, "there was the most awful crescendo of sound and the very air vibrated to a tremendous barrage of guns. All we could do was gaze in stupefaction at our friends going to inevitable death."

Pare watched "in agony, for these bombers, used to flying at

15,000 feet at night, were coming in at 1,500 feet in daylight. We saw more than one machine blazing, yet carrying on its course until every container was dropped. It now became obvious to us that we had terrible opposition. A signal had been sent asking that supplies be dropped near our headquarters, but hardly anything did."

Without fighter escort and doggedly holding course, the unwavering formations released supplies on the old dropping zones. Men on the ground tried desperately to attract attention by firing flares, igniting smoke bombs, waving parachutes and even setting parts of the heath on fire—and as they did they were strafed by diving enemy Messerschmitts.

Many soldiers recall one British Dakota, its starboard wing on fire, coming in over the drop zone now held by the Germans. Sergeant Victor Miller, one of the glider pilots who had landed in the first lift on Sunday, was "sick at heart to see flames envelop almost the whole of the lower half of the fuselage." Watching for the crew to bail out, Miller found himself muttering, "Jump! Jump!" As the plane flew low, Miller saw the dispatcher standing in the door, pushing out containers. Mesmerized, he watched the flaming Dakota turn and make another run in, and through the smoke he saw more containers tumbling out. Sergeant Douglas Atwell, another glider pilot, remembers that men climbed out of their trenches staring silently at the sky. "We were dead tired, and we had little to eat or drink, but I couldn't think of anything but that plane at the moment. It was as if it was the only one in the sky. Men were just riveted where they stood—and all the time that dispatcher kept on pushing out bundles." The pilot held his burning plane steady, making a second slow pass. Major George Powell "was awestruck that he would do this. I couldn't take my eyes off the craft. Suddenly it wasn't a plane any more, just a big orange ball of fire." As the burning plane plunged to the ground, its pilot, thirty-one-year-old Flight Lieutenant David Lord, still at the controls, Miller saw beyond the trees "only an oily column of smoke to mark the resting place of a brave crew who died that we might have the chance to live."

But Sergeant Miller was wrong. One member of the crew of the ill-fated Dakota did survive. Flying Officer Henry Arthur King, the navigator on that flight, remembers that just a few minutes before 4 P.M. as the plane was approaching the drop zone, flak set the starboard engine afire. Over the intercom Lord said, "Everyone O.K.? How far to the drop zone, Harry?" King called back, "Three minutes' flying time." The plane was listing heavily to the right and King saw that they were losing altitude rapidly. Flames had begun to spread along the wing toward the main fuel tank. "They need the stuff down there," he heard Lord say. "We'll go in and bail out afterwards. Everyone get your chutes on."

King spotted the drop zone and informed Lord. "O.K., Harry, I can see it," the pilot said. "Go back and give them a hand with the baskets." King made his way back to the open door. Flak had hit the rollers used to move the heavy supply bundles, and the dispatcher, Corporal Philip Nixon, and three soldiers from the Royal Army Service Corps were already man-handling eight heavy panniers of ammunition to the door. The men had taken off their parachutes in order to tug the baskets forward. Together the five men had pushed out six baskets when the red light, indicating that the plane was now off the drop zone, came on. King went on the intercom. "Dave," he called to Lord, "we've got two left." Lord put the plane in a tight left turn. "We'll come round again," he answered. "Hang on."

King saw they were then at about 500 feet and Lord "was handling that ship like a fighter plane. I was trying to help the R.A.S.C. boys get their chutes back on. The green light flashed and we pushed out our bundles. The next thing I remember is Lord shouting, 'Bail out! Bail out! For God's sake, bail out!' There was a tremendous explosion and I found myself hurtling through the air. I don't remember pulling the ripcord but I must have done it instinctively. I landed flat and hard on my back. I remember looking at my watch and seeing it was only nine minutes since we took the flak. My uniform was badly scorched and I couldn't find my shoes."

Nearly an hour later, King stumbled across a company of the 10th Battalion. Someone gave him tea and a bar of chocolate. "That's all we've got," the trooper told him. King stared at him. "What do you mean, that's all you've got? We just dropped supplies to you." The soldier shook his head. "You dropped our tins of sardines all right, but the Jerries got them.

We got nothing." King was speechless. He thought of Flight Lieutenant Lord, and the crew and men who had shed their chutes in a desperate effort to get precious ammunition bundles out to the anxious troops below. Of all these men, only King was alive. And now he had just learned that the sacrifice of his crew had been for nothing.*

Planes crash-landed throughout the area, mainly around Wageningen and Renkum. Some ended up on the southern side of the Rhine. Sergeant Walter Simpson remembers hearing his pilot shout over the intercom, "My God, we've been hit!" Looking out, Simpson saw that the port engine was on fire. He heard the engines being throttled back and then the plane went into a dive. The frightened Simpson remembers that the plane "dragged its tail across the north bank of the river, lifted slightly, then catapulted across the water and came down on the southern side."

On impact Simpson was hurtled forward and thrown to one side of the fuselage. The wireless operator, Sergeant Runsdale, crashed into him and lay huddled across Simpson's body. The interior of the plane was a shambles, fuel was burning, and Simpson could hear the crackling of flames. As he tried to ease his legs from under the wireless operator, Runsdale screamed and fainted. His back was broken. Simpson staggered up and carried the sergeant out through the escape hatch. Four crew members, dazed and in shock, were already there. Simpson went back for the others still inside. He found the bombardier unconscious. "His shoe had been blown off, part of his heel was missing and both arms were broken," he recalls. Simpson picked up this man, too, and carried him out. Although the plane was now burning fiercely, Simpson went back a third time for the engineer, whose leg was broken. He, too, was brought to safety.

In the village of Driel, young Cora Baltussen, her sister Reat and their brother Albert saw Simpson's plane come down. The

---

*Flight Lieutenant David Lord, holder of the Distinguished Flying Cross, was posthumously awarded the Victoria Cross. The bodies of the three R.A.F. officers and the four Army dispatchers—Pilot Officer R. E. H. Medhurst, Flying Officer A. Ballantyne, Corporal Nixon, Drivers James Ricketts, Leonard Sidney Harper and Arthur Rowbotham—were all identified and are buried in the British Military Cemetery at Arnhem.

three immediately set out for the site of the crash. "It was horrible," Cora recalls. "There were eight men and some of them were terribly injured. We dragged them away from the burning plane just as it exploded. I knew that the Germans would be looking for the crew. I told the pilot, Flight Officer Jeffrey Liggens, who was unharmed, that we'd have to hide him out while we took the injured men to the small surgery in the village. We hid him and two others in a nearby brickworks and told them we'd return at dark." That evening Cora assisted the lone physician in the village, a woman, Dr. Sanderbobrorg, as she amputated the bombardier's foot. The war had finally reached both Cora and little Driel.

In all, out of 100 bombers and 63 Dakotas, 97 were damaged and 13 were shot down—and, in spite of the heroism of pilots and crews, Urquhart's stricken division had not been bolstered. Of 390 tons of stores and ammunition dropped, nearly all fell into German hands. Only an estimated 21 tons was retrieved.

Worse problems were to engulf the Polish transport and artillery lift. Before leaving England in the Polish lift, Sergeant Pilot Kenneth Travis-Davison, copilot of a Horsa glider, was struck by the almost complete absence of information relating to conditions at their destination. Routes were laid out on maps, and the drop zones for the Poles' artillery and transport were marked; but, says Travis-Davison, "we were told that the situation was unknown." The only landing instruction was that "gliders should land on the area marked by purple smoke." In Travis-Davison's opinion, "the briefing was ludicrous."

Yet, despite the inadequacy of information, R.A.F. planes correctly located the drop zone near Johannahoeve Farm and 31 out of 46 gliders reached the zone. As they came in, the air erupted with fire. A squadron of Messerschmitts hit many of the machines, riddling the thin canvas-and-plywood hulls, puncturing the gas tanks of jeeps and setting some afire. Antiaircraft bursts caught others. Those that made it to the ground landed in the midst of a battlefield. Troopers of Hackett's 4th Brigade, struggling to disengage from an enemy that threatened to overrun them, were unable to reach the high ground and the drop zone beyond in time to protect the area. As the British and Germans fought fiercely, the Poles landed directly in the middle of the cataclysmic battle. In the terror and confusion the Poles were fired on from both sides. Gliders, many already on fire, crash-landed on the field or plowed into nearby trees. Polish artillerymen, caught in the crossfire and unable to tell friend from foe, fired back at both the Germans and British. Then, hastily unloading the usable jeeps and artillery, the dazed men ran a gauntlet of fire as they left the landing zone. Surprisingly, ground casualties were light, but many of the men, bewildered and shocked, were taken prisoner. Most of the jeeps and supplies were destroyed and of eight desperately needed six-pounder antitank guns, only three came through undamaged. General Stanislaw Sosabowski's fears were more than justified. And the ordeal of the 1st Polish Parachute Brigade was only just beginning.

Some forty miles south along the highway, General Maxwell Taylor's 101st troopers were now fighting hard to keep the corridor open. But the German Fifteenth Army's fierce defense at Best was draining Taylor's forces. More and more men were being caught up in the bitter engagement that one division intelligence officer wryly termed "a minor error in estimate." Pressure was building all along Taylor's 15-mile sector, which the Screaming Eagles had newly named "Hell's Highway." It was now obvious that the enemy's intent was to cut off Horrocks' tank spearhead, using Best as the base.

The jammed columns of vehicles massing the highway were easy targets for artillery fire. Bulldozers and tanks roamed constantly up and down the road, pushing wreckage out of the convoys to keep the columns rolling. Since Sunday, Best, the minor secondary objective, had grown to such proportions that it threatened to overpower all other action along Taylor's stretch of road. Now, the 101st commander was determined to crush the enemy at Best completely.

Early Tuesday afternoon, with the support of British tanks, Taylor threw almost the entire 502nd Regiment against Von Zangen's men at Best. The mammoth attack caught the enemy by surprise. Bolstered by the recently arrived 327th Glider Infantry Regiment and by British armor on the highway, the 2nd and 3rd battalions relentlessly swept the forested areas east of Best. Caught in a giant ring and forced back toward the Wilhelmina Canal, the Germans suddenly broke. With the commitment of fresh forces, the battle that had continued without letup for close to forty-six hours was suddenly over in two. Taylor's men had achieved the first major victory of Market-Garden. More than three hundred of the enemy were killed and over a thousand captured, along with fifteen 88 mm. artillery pieces. "By late afternoon," reads the official history, "as hundreds of Germans gave up, the word went out to send all Military Police available." Lieutenant Edward Wierzbowski, the platoon leader who had come closest to seizing the Best bridge before it was blown, brought in his own prisoners after having first been captured himself. Out of grenades and ammunition, with his casualties all about him—only three men of his valiant platoon had not been wounded—Wierzbowski had finally surrendered. Now, dead tired and begrimed, Wierzbowski and his men, including some of the wounded, disarmed the doctors and orderlies in the German field hospital to which the men had been taken and marched back to Division, bringing their prisoners with them.

Successful as the engagement had been, General Taylor's difficulties were far from over. Even as the battle at Best ended, German armor struck out for the newly installed bridge at Son in yet another attempt to sever the corridor. Taylor himself, leading his headquarters troops—his only available reinforcements—rushed to the scene. With bazooka fire and a single antitank gun, a German Panther tank was knocked out almost as it reached the bridge. Similarly, several other tanks were quickly dispatched. The German attack collapsed, and traffic continued to move. But the vigilance of the Screaming Eagles could not be relaxed. "Our situation," Taylor later noted, "reminded me of the early American West, where small garrisons had to contend with sudden Indian attacks at any point along great stretches of vital railroad."

The Germans' hard, fast, hit-and-run tactics were taking their toll. Almost 300 men of the 101st had been killed or wounded or were missing in ground actions. Men in slit trenches holding positions on either side of the highway or in the fields around Best were in constant danger of being overrun from the flanks, and each night brought its own particular fear. In darkness, with the Germans infiltrating the 101st's perimeter, no one knew whether the man in the next foxhole would be alive by the following morning. In the confusion and surprise of these sharp enemy actions men suddenly disappeared, and when the fire fights were over their friends searched for them among the dead and wounded on the battle ground and at aid stations and field hospitals.

As the Best battle ended and the long lines of prisoners were being herded back to Division, thirty-one-year-old Staff Sergeant Charles Dohun set out to find his officer, Captain LeGrand Johnson. Back in England prior to the jump, Dohun had been almost "numb with worry." The twenty-two-year-old Johnson had felt much the same. He was "resigned to never coming back." The morning of the nineteenth Johnson had thrown his company into an attack near Best. "It was that or be slaughtered," he recalls. In the fierce battle, which Johnson remembers as "the worst I have ever seen or heard," he was shot in the left shoulder. With his company reduced from 180 to 38 and surrounded in a field of burning haystacks, Johnson held off the Germans until relieving companies, driving back the enemy, could reach and evacuate the survivors. As Johnson was being helped back to an aid station he was shot once again, this time through the head. At the battalion aid station his body was placed among other fatally wounded men in what the medics called the "dead pile." There, after a long search, Sergeant Dohun found him. Kneeling down, Dohun was convinced there was a flicker of life.

Picking up the inert officer, Dohun laid Johnson and four other casualties from his company in a jeep and set out for the field hospital at Son. Cut off by Germans, Dohun drove the jeep into the woods and hid. When the German patrol moved on, he set out again. Arriving at the hospital, he found long lines of casualties waiting for treatment. Dohun, certain that Johnson might die at any minute, passed down the lines of wounded until he came to a surgeon who was checking the casualties to determine who was in need of immediate aid. "Major," Dohun told the doctor, "my captain needs attention right away." The major shook his head. "I'm sorry, sergeant," he told Dohun. "We'll get to him. He'll have to wait his turn." Dohun tried again. "Major, he'll die if you don't look at him quick." The doctor was firm. "We've got a lot of injured men here," he said. "Your captain will be attended to as soon as we can get to him." Dohun pulled out his .45 and cocked the trigger. "It's not soon enough," he said calmly. "Major, I'll kill you right where you stand if you don't look at him right now." Astonished, the surgeon stared at Dohun. "Bring him in," he said.

In the operating theater Dohun stood by, his .45 in hand as the doctor and a medical team worked on Johnson. As the sergeant watched, Johnson was given a blood transfusion, his wounds cleaned and a bullet was removed from his skull and another from his left shoulder. When the operation was completed and Johnson was bandaged, Dohun moved. Stepping up to the doctor, he handed over his .45. "O.K.," he said, "thanks. Now you can turn me in."

Dohun was sent back to the 2nd Battalion of the 502nd. There, he was brought before the commanding officer. Dohun snapped to attention. He was asked if he was aware of exactly what he had done and that his action constituted a court-martial offense. Dohun replied, "Yes, sir, I do." Pacing up and down, the commander suddenly stopped. "Sergeant," he said, "I'm placing you under arrest"—he paused and looked at his watch—"for exactly one minute." The two men waited in silence. Then the officer looked at Dohun. "Dismissed," he said. "Now get back to your unit." Dohun saluted smartly. "Yes, sir," he said, and left.*

Now, in General Gavin's sector of the corridor, as Horrocks' tanks rolled forward toward Nijmegen, the quick capture of the city's crossings assumed critical importance. On the seventeenth the Germans had had only a few soldiers guarding the approaches to the Waal river bridge. By afternoon of the

*I am indebted to Mrs. Johnson for this story. She first learned of it from the adjutant of the 502nd, Captain Hugh Roberts. Although Captain Roberts did not mention the commanding officer's name, I must assume that it was Lieutenant Colonel Steve Chappuis of the 2nd Battalion. Captain Johnson remembers only that he "woke up in England six weeks later—blind, deaf, dumb, forty pounds lighter and with a big plate in my head." Except for partial blindness, he recovered. Sergeant Dohun, in his correspondence and interview for this book, made little mention of the role he played in saving Captain Johnson's life. But he acknowledges that it happened. "I don't know to this day," he wrote, "if I would have shot that medic or not."

nineteenth Gavin estimated that he was opposed by more than
five hundred SS Grenadiers, well-positioned and supported by
artillery and armor. The main body of the Guards Armored
Division was still en route to the city. Only the spearhead of the
British column—elements of the 1st Battalion of the Grenadier
Guards under the command of Lieutenant Colonel Edward
H. Goulburn—was available for an attack and Gavin's 82nd
troopers in their ten-mile stretch of corridor were widely dispersed by their efforts to fight off a constantly encroaching
enemy. Since Gavin's Glider Infantry Regiment, based in the
fogbound Midlands of England, had been unable to take off,
he could afford to release only one battalion for a combined attack with the British spearhead tanks. Gavin chose the 2nd Battalion of the 505th under the command of Lieutenant Colonel
Ben Vandervoort. There was a chance that the attack, based
on speed and surprise, might succeed. If anyone could help effect it, Gavin believed it was the reserved, soft-spoken Vandervoort.* Still, the operation carried heavy risks. Gavin thought
the British appeared to underestimate the German strength,
as indeed they did. The Grenadier Guards' after-action report
noted that "It was thought that a display in the shape of tanks
would probably cause the enemy to withdraw."

At 3:30 P.M. the combined attack began. The force quickly
penetrated the center of the city without encountering serious opposition. There, approximately forty British tanks and
armored vehicles split into two columns, with American troops
riding on the tanks and following behind them. On top of lead
tanks and in reconnaissance cars were twelve specially chosen
Dutch underground scouts guiding the way—among them a
twenty-two-year-old university student named Jan van Hoof,
whose later actions would become a subject of sharp dispute. "I
was reluctant to use him," recalls the 82nd's Dutch liaison officer, Captain Arie D. Bestebreurtje. "He seemed highly excited,
but another underground member vouched for his record. He
went in with a British scout car and that was the last I ever
saw of him." As the force divided, one column headed for the

---

*In Normandy, Vandervoort had fought for forty days with a broken ankle.
See *The Longest Day*, pp. 118, 136.

railroad bridge and the second, with Goulburn and Vandervoort, approached the main highway crossing over the Waal.

At both objectives the Germans were waiting in strength.
Staff Sergeant Paul Nunan remembers that as his platoon approached an underpass near the railroad bridge, "we began
receiving sniper fire. With a thousand places for snipers to hide,
it was hard to tell where fire was coming from." Men dived for
cover and slowly began to pull back. British armor fared no
better. As tanks began to roll toward the bridge, 88's, firing
down the street at almost point-blank range, knocked them
out. A wide street, the Kraijenhoff Laan, led to a triangular
park west of the crossing. There, in buildings facing the park
on three sides, the paratroopers regrouped for another attack.
But again the Germans held them off. Snipers on roofs and
machine guns firing from a railroad overpass kept the men
pinned down.

Some troopers remember Lieutenant Russ Parker, a cigar
clenched in his teeth, moving into the open and spraying the
rooftops to keep snipers' heads down. A call went out for tanks,
and Nunan remembers that "at that instant the entire park
seemed filled with tracer slugs coming from a fast-firing automatic weapon sited to our left across the street." Nunan turned
to Herbert Buffalo Boy, a Sioux Indian and a veteran 82nd
trooper. "I think they're sending a German tank," he said. Buffalo Boy grinned. "Well, if they've got infantry with them, it
could get to be a very tough day," he told Nunan. The German
tank did not materialize, but a 20 mm. antiaircraft gun opened
up. With grenades, machine guns and bazookas, the troopers
fought on until word was passed for forward platoons to pull
back and consolidate for the night. As men moved out, the
Germans set buildings along the river's edge on fire, making
it impossible for Vandervoort's men to infiltrate, overrun artillery positions and clear out pockets of resistance. The railroad
bridge attack had ground to a halt.

Under cover of heavy American artillery fire, the second column had made for Huner Park, the ornamental gardens leading to the approaches of the highway bridge. Here, in a traffic
circle, all roads leading to the bridge converged and an ancient
ruin with a sixteen-sided chapel—the Valkhof—once the palace
of Charlemagne and later rebuilt by Barbarossa, commanded

the area. In this citadel the enemy was concentrated. It almost seemed to Colonel Goulburn that "the Boche had some sort of an idea of what we were trying to do." As indeed they had.

Captain Karl Heinz Euling's battalion of SS Panzer Grenadiers was one of the first units to cross the Rhine at Pannerden. Acting on General Harmel's orders to protect the bridge at all costs, Euling had ringed the Huner Park area with self-propelled guns and had positioned men in the chapel of the old ruin. As British tanks rattled around the corners of the streets leading to the park, they came under Euling's guns. Meeting a punishing artillery barrage, the tanks pulled back. Colonel Vandervoort immediately took to the street, and getting a mortar crew into action with covering fire, he moved one company forward. As the company's lead platoon, under First Lieutenant James J. Coyle, sprinted for a row of attached houses facing the park, they came under small-arms and mortar fire. Lieutenant William J. Meddaugh, second in command, saw that this was "observed fire. The guns and snipers were being directed by radio. British tanks covered our front as Lieutenant Coyle moved into a block of buildings overlooking the entire enemy position. Other platoons were stopped, unable to move, and the situation looked rotten."

Covered by British smoke bombs Meddaugh succeeded in bringing the rest of the company forward, and the commander, Lieutenant J. J. Smith, consolidated his men in houses around Coyle. As Meddaugh recalls, "Coyle's platoon now had a perfect view of the enemy, but as we started to move tanks up, some high-velocity guns opened up that had not done any firing as yet. Two tanks were knocked out, and the others retired." As Coyle's men replied with machine guns, they immediately drew antitank gun fire from across the streets. When darkness closed in, Euling's SS men attempted to infiltrate the American positions. One group got to within a few feet of Coyle's platoon before they were spotted and a fierce fire fight broke out. Coyle's men suffered casualties, and three of the Germans were killed before the attack was driven back. Later, Euling sent medics to pick up his wounded, and Coyle's paratroopers waited until the injured Germans were evacuated before resuming the fight. In the middle of the action, Private First Class John Keller heard a low pounding noise. Going to a window, he was amazed to see a Dutchman on a stepladder calmly replacing the shingles on the house next door as though nothing was happening.

In late evening, with small-arms fire continuing, any further attempt to advance was postponed until daylight. The Anglo-American assault had been abruptly stopped barely 400 yards from the Waal river bridge—the last water obstacle on the road to Arnhem.

To the Allied commanders it was now clear that the Germans were in complete control of the bridges. Browning, worried that the crossings might be destroyed at any moment, called another conference late on the nineteenth. A way must be found to cross the 400-yard-wide Waal river. General Gavin had devised a plan which he had mentioned to Browning at the time of the link-up. Then the Corps commander had turned down the scheme. At this second conference Gavin proposed it again. "There's only one way to take this bridge," he told the assembled officers. "We've got to get it simultaneously— from both ends." Gavin urged that "any boats in Horrocks' engineering columns should be rushed forward immediately, because we're going to need them." The British looked at him in bewilderment. What the 82nd commander had in mind was an assault crossing of the river—by paratroops.

Gavin went on to explain. In nearly three days of fighting, his casualties were high—upwards of 200 dead and nearly 700 injured. Several hundred more men were cut off or scattered and were listed as missing. His losses, Gavin reasoned, would grow progressively worse if blunt head-on attacks continued. What was needed was a means of capturing the bridge quickly and cheaply. Gavin's plan was to throw a force in boats across the river a mile downstream while the attack continued for possession of the southern approaches. Under a barrage of tank fire the troopers were to storm the enemy defenses on the northern side before the Germans fully realized what was happening.

Yet total surprise was out of the question. The river was too wide to enable boatloads of men to escape detection, and the bank on the far side was so exposed that troopers, once across the river, would have to negotiate 200 yards of flat ground. Beyond was an embankment from which German gunners could fire down upon the invading paratroopers. That defense position would have to be overrun too. Although heavy casualties could be expected initially, in Gavin's opinion they would still be less than if the assault were continued against the southern approaches alone. "The attempt has to be made," he told Browning, "if Market-Garden is to succeed."

Colonel George S. Chatterton, commander of the British Glider Pilot Regiment, remembers that, besides Browning and Horrocks, commanders of the Irish, Scots, and Grenadier Guards were present at the conference. So was cigar-chewing Colonel Reuben Tucker, commander of the 82nd's 504th Regiment, whose men Gavin had picked to make the river assault if his plan won approval. Although intent on Gavin's words, Chatterton could not help noting the differences in the men assembled. "One brigadier wore suede shoes and sat on a shooting stick," he recalls. "Three Guards' commanders had on rather worn corduroy trousers, chukka boots and old school scarves." Chatterton thought "they seemed relaxed, as though they were discussing an exercise, and I couldn't help contrast them to the Americans present, especially Colonel Tucker, who was wearing a helmet that almost covered his face. His pistol was in a holster under his left arm, and he had a knife strapped to his thigh." To Chatterton's great amusement, "Tucker occasionally removed his cigar long enough to spit and every time he did faint looks of surprise flickered over the faces of the Guards' officers."

But the daring of Gavin's plan provided the real surprise. "I knew it sounded outlandish," Gavin recalls, "but speed was essential. There was no time even for a reconnaissance. As I continued to talk, Tucker was the only man in the room who seemed unfazed. He had made the landing at Anzio and knew what to expect. To him the crossing was like the kind of exercise the 504th had practiced at Fort Bragg." Still, for paratroopers, it was unorthodox and Browning's chief of staff, Brigadier Gordon Walch, recalls that the Corps commander was "by now filled with admiration at the daring of the idea." This time Browning gave his approval.

The immediate problem was to find boats. Checking with his engineers, Horrocks learned they carried some twenty-eight small canvas and plywood craft. These would be rushed to Nijmegen during the night. If the planning could be completed in

time, Gavin's miniature Normandy-like amphibious assault of
the Waal would take place at 1 P.M. the next day, on the twentieth. Never before had paratroopers attempted such a combat
operation. But Gavin's plan seemed to offer the best hope of
grabbing the Nijmegen bridge intact; and then, as everyone
still believed, another quick dash up the corridor would unite
them with the men at Arnhem.

In the grassy expanse of the Eusebius Buiten Singel, General
Heinz Harmel personally directed the opening of the bombardment against Frost's men at the bridge. His attempt to
persuade Frost to surrender had failed. Now, to the assembled
tank and artillery commanders his instructions were specific:
they were to level every building held by the paratroopers.
"Since the British won't come out of their holes, we'll blast
them out," Harmel said. He told gunners to "aim right under
the gables and shoot meter by meter, floor by floor, until each
house collapses." Harmel was determined that the siege would
end, and since everything else had failed this was the only
course. "By the time we're finished," Harmel added, "there'll
be nothing left but a pile of bricks." Lying flat on the ground
between two artillery pieces, Harmel trained his binoculars on
the British strongholds and directed the fire. As the opening
salvos zeroed in he stood up, satisfied, and handed over to his
officers. "I would have liked to stay," he recalls. "It was a new
experience in fighting for me. But with the Anglo-Americans
attacking the bridges at Nijmegen I had to rush down there."
As Harmel left, his gunners, with methodical, scythelike precision, began the job of reducing Frost's remaining positions
to rubble.
   Of the eighteen buildings that the 2nd Battalion had initially
occupied, Frost's men now held only about ten. While tanks
hit positions from the east and west, artillery slammed shells
into those facing north. The barrage was merciless. "It was the
best, most effective fire I have ever seen," remembers SS Grenadier Private Horst Weber. "Starting from the rooftops, buildings collapsed like doll houses. I did not see how anyone could
live through this inferno. I felt truly sorry for the British."
   Weber watched three Tiger tanks rumble slowly down the
Groote Markt, and while machine guns sprayed every window
in a block of buildings opposite the northern approaches to

the bridge, the tanks "pumped shell after shell into each house, one after the other." He remembers a corner building where "the roof fell in, the two top stories began to crumble and then, like the skin peeling off a skeleton, the whole front wall fell into the street revealing each floor on which the British were scrambling like mad." Dust and debris, Weber remembers, "soon made it impossible to see anything more. The din was awful but even so, above it all we could hear the wounded screaming."

In relays, tanks smashed houses along the Rhine waterfront and under the bridge itself. Often, as the British darted out, tanks rammed the ruins like bulldozers, completely leveling the sites. At Captain Mackay's headquarters under the ramp in the nearly destroyed schoolhouse, Lieutenant Peter Stainforth estimated that "high-explosive shells came through the southern face of the building at the rate of one every ten seconds." It became "rather hot," he recalls, "and everyone had some sort of wound or other." Yet the troopers obstinately hung on, evacuating each room in its turn "as ceilings collapsed, cracks appeared in the walls, and rooms became untenable." In the rubble, making every shot count, the Red Devils, Stainforth recalls proudly, "survived like moles. Jerry just couldn't dig us out." But elsewhere men were finding their positions almost unendurable. "The Germans had decided to shell us out of existence," Private James W. Sims explains. "It seemed impossible for the shelling and mortaring to get any heavier, but it did. Burst after burst, shell after shell rained down, the separate explosions merging into one continuous rolling detonation." With each salvo Sims repeated a desperate litany, "Hold on! Hold on! It can't last much longer." As he crouched alone in his slit trench the thought struck Sims that he was "lying in a freshly dug grave just waiting to be buried alive." He remembers thinking that "unless XXX Corps hurries, we have had it."

Colonel Frost realized that disaster had finally overtaken the 2nd Battalion. The relieving battalions had not broken through, and Frost was sure they were no longer able to come to his aid. The Polish drop had failed to materialize. Ammunition was all but gone. Casualties were now so high that every available cellar was full, and the men had been fighting without letup for over fifty hours. Frost knew they could not endure this punishment much longer. All about his defensive perimeter, houses were in flames, buildings had collapsed, and positions were being overrun. He did not know how much longer he could hold out. His beloved 2nd Battalion was being buried in the ruins of the buildings around him. Yet Frost was not ready to oblige his enemy. Beyond hope, he was determined to deny the Germans the Arnhem bridge to the last.

He was not alone in his emotions. Their ordeal seemed to affect his men much as it did Frost. Troopers shared their ammunition and took what little they could find from their wounded, preparing for the doom that was engulfing them. There was little evidence of fear. In their exhaustion, hunger and pain, the men seemed to develop a sense of humor about themselves and their situation which grew even as their sacrifice became increasingly apparent.

Father Egan remembers meeting Frost coming out of a toilet. "The Colonel's face—tired, grimy, and wearing a stubble of beard—lit up with a smile," Egan recalls. "'Father,' he told me, 'the window is shattered, there's a hole in the wall, and the roof's gone. But it has a chain and it works.'"

Later, Egan was trying to make his way across one street to visit wounded in the cellars. The area was being heavily mortared and the chaplain was taking cover wherever he could. "Outside, strolling unconcernedly up the street was Major Digby Tatham-Warter, whose company had taken the bridge initially," he recalls. "The major saw me cowering down and walked over. In his hand was an umbrella." As Egan recalls, Tatham-Warter "opened the umbrella and held it over my head. With mortar shells raining down everywhere, he said, 'Come along, Padre.'" When Egan showed reluctance, Tatham-Warter reassured him. "Don't worry," he said, "I've got an umbrella." Lieutenant Patrick Barnett encountered the redoubtable major soon afterward. Barnett was sprinting across the street to a new defense area Frost had ordered him to hold. Tatham-Warter, returning from escorting Father Egan, was out visiting his men in the shrinking perimeter defenses and holding the umbrella over his head. Barnett was so surprised that he stopped in his tracks. "That thing won't do you much good," he told the major. Tatham-Warter looked at him in mock surprise. "Oh, my goodness, Pat," he said. "What if it rains?"

During the afternoon, as the bombardment continued, Major Freddie Gough saw Tatham-Warter leading his company,

umbrella in hand. Tanks were thundering down the streets firing at everything. "I almost fainted when I saw those huge
Mark IV's firing at us at almost point-blank range," recalls
Gough. Then the tension was suddenly relieved. "There, out
in the street leading his men in a bayonet charge against some
Germans who had managed to infiltrate, was Tatham-Warter,"
Gough recalls. "He had found an old bowler someplace and he
was rushing along, twirling that battered umbrella, looking for
all the world like Charlie Chaplin."

There were other moments of humor equally memorable.
As the afternoon wore on, battalion headquarters was heavily bombarded and caught fire. Father Egan went down to
the cellar to see the wounded. "Well, Padre," said Sergeant
Jack Spratt, who was regarded as the battalion comic, "they're
throwing everything at us but the kitchen stove." He had
barely said the words when the building suffered another direct hit. "The ceiling fell in, showering us with dirt and plaster.
When we picked ourselves up, there right in front of us was a
kitchen stove." Spratt looked at it and shook his head. "I knew
the bastards were close," he said, "but I didn't believe they
could hear us talking."

Toward evening it began to rain, and the German attack
seemed to intensify. Captain Mackay, on the opposite side of
the bridge, contacted Frost. "I told the Colonel I could not
hold out another night if the attack continued on the same
scale," Mackay wrote. "He said he could not help me, but I was
to hold on at all costs."

Mackay could see the Germans were slowly compressing
Frost's force. He saw British troopers scurrying from burning
houses along the riverbank toward a couple almost opposite
him, which were still standing. "They were beginning to hem
us in," he noted, "and it was obvious that if we didn't get help
soon, they'd winkle us out. I went up to the attic and tuned into
the 6 o'clock BBC news. To my utter amazement the newscaster
said that British armor had reached the airborne troops."*

Almost immediately Mackay heard a cry from the floor below, "Tiger tanks are heading for the bridge." (It was exactly 7

---

*Mackay thought the report referred to Arnhem; in fact, it related to the
link-up of Horrocks' tanks with the 82nd Airborne in Nijmegen.

P.M. German time; 6 P.M. British time.) Two of the huge 60-ton tanks were heading in from the north. On his side of the bridge Frost saw them, too. "They looked incredibly sinister in the half light," he noted. "Like some prehistoric monsters, as their great guns swung from side to side breathing flame. Their shells burst through the walls. The dust and slowly settling debris following their explosions filled the passages and rooms."

One complete side of Mackay's building was hit. "Some of the shells must have been armor-piercing," Lieutenant Peter Stainforth says, "because they went through the school from end to end, knocking a four-foot hole in every room." Ceilings came down, walls cracked and "the whole structure rocked." Staring at the two tanks on the ramp, Mackay thought the end had come. "A couple more rounds like that and we'll be finished," he said. Still, with the stubborn and fearless resistance that the fighters at the bridge had shown since their arrival, Mackay thought that he might "be able to take a party out and blow them up. But just then the two tanks reversed and pulled back. We were still alive."

At Frost's headquarters, Father Egan had been hit. Caught on a stairway when shells began coming in, he fell two flights to the first floor. When he recovered consciousness, the priest was alone except for one man. Crawling to him, Egan saw that the trooper was near death. At that moment another barrage hit the building and Egan again lost consciousness. He awoke to find that the room and his clothes were on fire. Desperately he rolled along the floor, beating the flames out with his hands. The injured man he had seen earlier was dead. Now Egan could not use his legs. Slowly, in excruciating pain, he hauled himself toward a window. Someone called his name, and the intelligence officer, Lieutenant Bucky Buchanan, helped him through the window and dropped him into the arms of Sergeant Jack Spratt. In the cellar, where Dr. James Logan was at work, the priest was put on the floor with other wounded. His right leg was broken and his back and hands were peppered with shrapnel splinters. "I was pretty well out of it," Egan recalls. "I couldn't do much now but lie there on my stomach." Nearby, slightly wounded, was the incredible Tatham-Warter, still trying to keep men's spirits up, and still hanging on to his umbrella.

Occasionally there was a pause in the terrible pounding, and Captain Mackay believed the Germans were stocking up with more ammunition. As darkness set in during one of these intervals, Mackay issued benzedrine tablets to his tired force, two pills per man. The effect on the exhausted, weary men was unexpected and acute. Some troopers became irritable and argumentative. Others suffered double vision and for a time could not aim straight. Among the shocked and wounded, men became euphoric and some began to hallucinate. Corporal Arthur Hendy remembers being grabbed by one trooper, who pulled him to a window. "Look," he commanded Hendy in a whisper. "It's the Second Army. On the far bank. Look. Do you see them?" Sadly, Hendy shook his head. The man became enraged. "They're right over there," he shouted, "plain as anything."

Mackay wondered if his small force would see out the night. Fatigue and wounds were taking their toll. "I was thinking clearly," Mackay remembers, "but we had had nothing to eat and no sleep. We were limited to one cup of water daily, and everyone was wounded." With his ammunition nearly gone, Mackay set his men to making homemade bombs from the small stock of explosives still remaining. He intended to be ready when the German tanks returned. Taking a head count, Mackay now reported to Frost that he had only thirteen men left capable of fighting.

From his position on the far side of the bridge, as the night of Tuesday, September 19, closed in, Frost saw that the entire city appeared to be burning. The spires of two great churches were flaming fiercely and as Frost watched, "the cross which hung between two lovely towers was silhouetted against the clouds rising far into the sky." He noted that "the crackle of burning wood and the strange echoes of falling buildings seemed unearthly." Upstairs, Signalman Stanley Copley, sitting at his radio set, had abandoned sending in Morse code. Now he was broadcasting in the clear. Continually he kept repeating, "This is the 1st Para Brigade calling Second Army. . . . Come in Second Army. . . . Come in Second Army."

At his headquarters in Oosterbeek's Hartenstein Hotel, General Urquhart tried desperately to save what remained of his division. Frost was cut off. Every attempt to reach him at the bridge had been mercilessly beaten back. German reinforcements were pouring in. From the west, north and east, Bittrich's forces were steadily chopping the gallant 1st British Airborne to pieces. Cold, wet, worn out, but still uncomplaining, the Red Devils were trying to hold out— fighting off tanks with rifles and Sten guns. The situation was heartbreaking for Urquhart. Only quick action could save his heroic men. By Wednesday morning, September 20, Urquhart had developed a plan to salvage the remnants of his command and perhaps turn the tide in his favor.

September 19—"a dark and fateful day," in Urquhart's words —had been the turning point. The cohesion and drive that he had hoped to instill had come too late. Everything had failed: the Polish forces had not arrived; the cargo drops had been disastrous; and battalions had been devastated in their attempts to reach Frost. The division was being pushed closer and closer to destruction. The tally of Urquhart's remaining men told a frightful story. All through the night of the nineteenth, battalion units still in contact with division headquarters reported their strength. Inconclusive and inaccurate as the figures were, they presented a grim accounting: Urquhart's division was on the verge of disappearing.

Of Lathbury's 1st Parachute Brigade, only Frost's force was fighting as a coordinated unit, but Urquhart had no idea how many men were left in the 2nd Battalion. Fitch's 3rd Battalion listed some 50 men, and its commander was dead. Dobie's 1st totaled 116, and Dobie had been wounded and captured. The 11th Battalion's strength was down to 150, the 2nd South Staffordshires to 100. The commanders of both units, Lea and McCardie, were wounded. In Hackett's 10th Battalion there were now 250 men, and his 156th reported 270. Although Urquhart's total division strength was more—the figures did not include other units such as a battalion of the Border Regiment, the 7th KOSB's engineers, reconnaissance and service troops, glider pilots and others—his attack battalions had almost ceased to exist. The men of these proud units were now dispersed in small groups, dazed, shocked and often leaderless.

The fighting had been so bloody and so terrible that even battle-hardened veterans had broken. Urquhart and his chief of staff had sensed an atmosphere of panic seeping through headquarters as small groups of stragglers ran across the lawn yelling, "The Germans are coming." Often, they were young soldiers, "whose self-control had momentarily deserted them," Urquhart later wrote. "Mackenzie and I had to intervene physically." But others fought on against formidable odds. Captain L. E. Queripel, wounded in the face and arms, led an attack on a German twin machine-gun nest and killed the crews. As other Germans, throwing grenades, began to close in on Queripel and his party, Queripel hurled the "potato mashers" back. Ordering his men to leave him, the officer covered their retreat, throwing grenades until he was killed.*

Now, what remained of Urquhart's shattered and bloodied division was being squeezed and driven back upon itself. All roads seemed to end in the Oosterbeek area, with the main body of troops centered around the Hartenstein in a few square miles running between Heveadorp and Wolfheze on the west, and from Oosterbeek to Johannahoeve Farm on the east. Within that rough corridor, ending on the Rhine at Heveadorp, Urquhart planned to make a stand. By pulling in his troops, he hoped to husband his strength and hang on until Horrocks' armor reached him.

All through the night of the nineteenth orders went out for troops to pull back into the Oosterbeek perimeter, and in the early hours of the twentieth, Hackett was told to abandon his planned attack toward the Arnhem bridge with his 10th and 156th battalions and disengage them too. "It was a terrible decision to make," Urquhart said later. "It meant abandoning the 2nd Battalion at the bridge, but I knew I had no more chance of reaching them than I had of getting to Berlin." In his view, the only hope "was to consolidate, form a defensive box and try to hold on to a small bridgehead north of the river so that XXX Corps could cross to us."

The discovery of the ferry operating between Heveadorp and Driel had been an important factor in Urquhart's decision. It was vital to his plan for survival; for on it, theoretically, help could arrive from the southern bank. Additionally, at the ferry's landing stages on either bank, there were ramps that would help the engineers to throw a Bailey bridge across the Rhine. Admittedly the odds were great. But if the Nijmegen bridge could be taken swiftly and if Horrocks moved fast and

---

*Queripel was posthumously awarded the Victoria Cross.

if Urquhart's men could hold out long enough in their perimeter for engineers to span the river—a great many *if*'s—there was still a chance that Montgomery might get his bridgehead across the Rhine and drive for the Ruhr, even though Frost might be overrun at Arnhem.

All through the nineteenth, messages had been sent from Urquhart's headquarters requesting a new drop zone for the Poles. Communications, though still erratic, were slightly improved. Lieutenant Neville Hay of the Phantom net was passing some messages to British Second Army headquarters, who in turn relayed them to Browning. At 3 A.M. on the twentieth, Urquhart received a message from Corps asking for the General's suggestions regarding the Poles' drop zone. As Urquhart saw it, only one possible area remained. In view of his new plan he requested the 1,500-man brigade be landed near the southern terminal of the ferry in the vicinity of the little village of Driel.

Abandoning Frost and his men was the most bitter part of the plan. At 8 A.M. on Wednesday, Urquhart had an opportunity to explain the position to Frost and Gough at the bridge. Using the Munford-Thompson radio link, Gough called division headquarters and got through to Urquhart. It was the first contact Gough had had with the General since the seventeenth, when he had been ordered back to Division only to discover that Urquhart was somewhere along the line of march. "My goodness," Urquhart said, "I thought you were dead." Gough sketched in the situation at the bridge. "Morale is still high," he recalls saying, "but we're short of everything. Despite that, we'll continue to hold out." Then, as Urquhart remembers, "Gough asked if they could expect reinforcements."

Answering was not easy. "I told him," Urquhart recalls, "that I was not certain if it was a case of me coming for them or they coming for us. I'm afraid you can only hope for relief from the south." Frost then came on the line. "It was very cheering to hear the General," Frost wrote, "but he could not tell me anything really encouraging. . . . they were obviously having great difficulties themselves." Urquhart requested that his "personal congratulations on a fine effort be passed on to everyone concerned and I wished them the best of luck." There was nothing more to be said.

Twenty minutes later, Urquhart received a message from Lieutenant Neville Hay's Phantom net. It read:

200820 (From 2nd Army). Attack at Nijmegen held up by strongpoint south of town. 5 Guards Brigade halfway in town. Bridge intact but held by enemy. Intention attack at 1300 hours today.

Urquhart immediately told his staff to inform all units. It was the first good news he had had this day.

Tragically, Urquhart had an outstanding force at his disposal whose contributions, had they been accepted, might well have altered the grim situation of the British 1st Airborne Division. The Dutch resistance ranked among the most dedicated and disciplined underground units in all of occupied Europe. In the 101st and 82nd sectors Dutchmen were fighting alongside the American paratroopers. One of the first orders Generals Taylor and Gavin had given on landing was that arms and explosives be issued to the underground groups. But in Arnhem the British virtually ignored the presence of these spirited, brave civilians. Armed and poised to give immediate help to Frost at the bridge, the Arnhem groups were largely unheeded, and their assistance was politely rejected. By a strange series of events only one man had held the power to coordinate and weld the resistance into the British assault, and he was dead. Lieutenant Colonel Hilaro Barlow, the officer Urquhart had sent to coordinate the faltering attacks of the battalions in the western suburbs, was killed before he could put his own mission into full effect.

In the original plan, Barlow was to have assumed the role of Arnhem's town major and military-government chief once the battle ended. His assistant and the Dutch representative for the Gelderland province had also been named. He was Lieutenant Commander Arnoldus Wolters of the Dutch Navy. Prior to Market-Garden, an Anglo-Dutch intelligence committee had given Barlow top-secret lists of Dutch underground personnel who were known to be completely trustworthy. "From these lists," recalls Wolters, "Barlow and I were to screen the groups and use them in their various capabilities: intelligence, sabotage, combat and the like. Barlow was the only other man who knew what our mission really was. When he disappeared, the plan collapsed." At division headquarters, Wolters was thought to be either a civil-affairs or an intelligence officer. When he produced the secret lists and made recommendations, he was looked on with suspicion. "Barlow trusted me completely," Wolters says. "I regret to say that others at headquarters did not."

With Barlow's death, Wolters' hands were tied. "The British wondered why a Dutch Navy type should be with them at all," he remembers. Gradually he won limited acceptance and although some members of the resistance were put to work, they were too few and their help was too late. "We hadn't time any longer to check everybody out to the satisfaction of headquarters," Wolters says, "and the attitude there was simply: 'Who can we trust?'" The opportunity to effectively organize and collate the underground forces in the Arnhem area had been lost.*

In England, a little before 7 A.M. on the twentieth, Major General Stanislaw Sosabowski learned that his drop zone had been changed. The Polish Brigade would now land in an area a few miles west of the original site, near the village of Driel. Sosabowski was stunned by the news his liaison officer, Lieutenant

---

*The British had long been wary of the Dutch underground. In 1942, Major Herman Giskes, Nazi spy chief in Holland, succeeded in infiltrating Dutch intelligence networks. Agents sent from England were captured and forced to work for him. For twenty months, in perhaps the most spectacular counter-intelligence operation of World War II, nearly every agent parachuted into Holland was intercepted by the Germans. As a security check, monitors in England were instructed to listen for deliberate errors in Morse code radio transmissions. Yet messages from these "double agents" were accepted without question by British intelligence. It was not until two agents escaped that Giskes' Operation North Pole came to an end. Having hoodwinked the Allies for so long, Giskes could not resist boasting of his coup. In a plain-text message to the British on November 23, 1943, he wired: "To Messrs. Hunt, Bingham & Co., Successors Ltd., London. We understand you have been endeavoring for some time to do business in Holland without our assistance. We regret this . . . since we have acted for so long as your sole representative in this country. Nevertheless . . . should you be thinking of paying us a visit on the Continent on an extensive scale we shall give your emissaries the same attention as we have hitherto. . . ." As a result, although intelligence networks were purged and completely revamped—and although Dutch resistance groups were separate from these covert activities—nevertheless, many British senior officers were warned before Operation Market-Garden against placing too much trust in the underground.

Colonel George Stevens, had brought. The brigade was already on the airfield and scheduled to leave for Holland in three hours. Within that time Sosabowski had to completely redesign his attack for an area that had not even been studied. Days had gone into the planning for the drop near Elden on the southern approaches of the Arnhem bridge. Now, he was to recall, "I was given the bare bones of a scheme, with only a few hours to develop a plan."

There was still very little news of Arnhem, but, as Stevens briefed him on the new plan to ferry his troops across the Rhine from Driel to Heveadorp, it was obvious to Sosabowski that Urquhart's situation had taken a turn for the worse. He foresaw countless problems, but he noted that "nobody else seemed unduly alarmed. All Stevens had learned was that the picture was pretty confusing." Quickly informing his staff of the new developments, Sosabowski postponed the 10 A.M. takeoff until 1:00 P.M. He would need that time to reorient his troopers and to devise new attack plans, and the three-hour delay might enable Stevens to get more up-to-date information on Arnhem. Sosabowski doubted that his force could have been flown out at 10 A.M. in any case. Fog again covered the Midlands, and the forecast was not reassuring. "That and the paucity of information we received made me most anxious," Sosabowski recalled. "I did not think that Urquhart's operation was going well. I began to believe that we might be dropping into Holland to reinforce defeat."

9

AT THE ARNHEM BRIDGE the massive defiance by the valiant few was nearly over. At dawn the Germans had renewed their terrifying bombardment. In the morning light the stark pitted wrecks that had once been houses and office buildings were again subjected to punishing fire. On each side of the bridge and along the churned, mangled ruins of the Eusebius Buiten Singel, the few strongholds that still remained were being systematically blown apart. The semicircular defense line that had protected the northern approaches had almost ceased to exist. Yet, ringed by flames and sheltering behind rubble, small groups of obstinate men continued to fight on, denying the Germans the bridge.

Only the rawest kind of courage had sustained Frost's men up to now, but it had been fierce enough and constant enough to hold off the Germans for three nights and two days. The 2nd Battalion and the men from other units who had come by twos and threes to join it (a force that by Frost's highest estimate never totaled more than six or seven hundred men) had been welded together in their ordeal. Pride and common purpose had fused them. Alone they had reached the objective of an entire airborne division—and held out longer than the division was meant to do. In the desperate, anxious hours, awaiting help that never came, their common frame of mind was perhaps best summed up in the thoughts of Lance Corporal Gordon Spicer, who wrote, "Who's failing in their job? Not us!"

But now the time of their endurance had nearly run its course. Holed up in ruins and slit trenches, struggling to protect themselves and cellars full of wounded, shocked and concussed by nearly unceasing enemy fire, and wearing their filthy bloodstained bandages and impudent manners like badges of honor, the Red Devils knew, finally, that they could no longer hold.

The discovery produced a curious calmness, totally devoid of panic. It was as if men decided privately that they would fight until they dropped—if only to provoke the Germans more. Despite their knowledge that the fight was all but over, men invented still new ways to keep it going. Troopers of mortar platoons fired their last few bombs without tripods or base plates by standing the barrel up and holding it with ropes. Others, discovering there were no more detonators for the spring-loaded, Piat missile-throwers, tried instead to detonate the bombs with fuses made from boxes of matches. All about them friends lay dead or dying, and still they found the will to resist and, in doing so, often amused one another. Men remember an Irish trooper knocked unconscious by a shell burst opening his eyes at last to say, "I'm dead." Then, thinking it over, he remarked, "I can't be. I'm talking."

To Colonel John Frost, whose hunting horn had called them to him on the sunny Sunday that was to be the opening of their victory march, they would always remain unbeaten. Yet now, on this dark and tragic Wednesday, he knew there was "practically no possibility for relief."

The number of men still capable of fighting was, at best, between 150 and 200, concentrated mainly about the damaged headquarters buildings on the western side of the ramp. Over 300 British and German wounded filled the cellars. "They were crowded almost on top of each other," Frost noted, "making it difficult for doctors and orderlies to get around and attend them." Soon he would have to make a decision about these casualties. If the headquarters building was hit again, as it was almost certain to be, Frost told Major Freddie Gough, he "did not see how I can fight it out to the last minute, then go, and have our wounded be roasted." Measures would have to be taken to get out casualties before the building was demolished or overrun. Frost did not know how much time was left. He still believed he could control the approaches for a time, perhaps even another twenty-four hours, but his perimeter defenses were now so weak that he knew "a determined rush by the enemy could carry them into our midst."

On Captain Mackay's side of the ramp, the pulverized schoolhouse looked, he thought, "like a sieve." As Mackay later recalled, "We were alone. All the houses on the eastern side had been burned down, except for one to the south, which was held by the Germans." And in the schoolhouse, horror had piled on horror. "The men were exhausted and filthy," Mackay wrote, "and I was sick to my stomach every time I looked at them. Haggard, with bloodshot and red-rimmed eyes, almost everyone had some sort of dirty field dressing and blood was everywhere." As wounded were carried down the stairway to the cellar, Mackay noted that "on each landing blood had formed in pools and ran in small rivulets down the stairs." His remaining thirteen men were huddled "in twos and threes, manning positions that required twice that number. The only things that were clean were the men's weapons." In the shell of the schoolhouse Mackay and his men fought off three enemy attacks in two hours, leaving around four times their number in enemy dead.

As morning wore on, the fighting continued. Then, around noon, the man who had so stubbornly defied the Germans was wounded. As Frost met with Major Douglas Crawley to discuss a fighting patrol to clear the area, he remembers "a tremendous explosion" that lifted him off his feet and threw him face

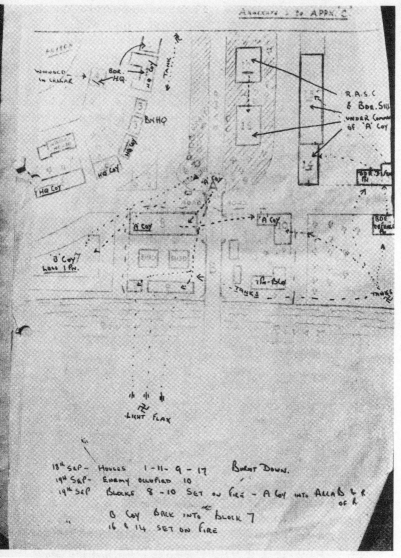

Colonel Frost's position around northern approaches of Arnhem bridge, from after action report.

downward several yards away. A mortar bomb had exploded almost between the two men. Miraculously both were alive, but shrapnel had torn into Frost's left ankle and right shinbone and Crawley was hit in both legs and his right arm. Frost, barely conscious, felt ashamed that he could not "resist the groans that seemed to force themselves out of me, more particularly as Doug never made a sound." Wicks, Frost's batman, helped drag the two officers to cover and stretcher-bearers carried them to the cellar with the other wounded.

In the crowded basement Father Egan tried to orient himself. In the dim recesses of the chilly room, Lieutenant Bucky Buchanan, the intelligence officer who had earlier helped to rescue Egan, appeared to have propped himself up wearily against the wall. But Buchanan was dead. A bomb blast had killed him outright without leaving a mark. Then, dazed and still in shock, Egan saw Frost being carried in. "I remember his face," Egan says. "He looked dead-tired and dejected." Other wounded in the cellar saw their battalion commander, too. To Lieutenant John Blunt, a friend of the dead Buchanan, the sight of the Colonel on a stretcher was a crushing blow. "We subalterns had always considered him irrepressible," Blunt wrote. "It hurt to see him carried in like that. He had never given in to anything."

Across the room Private James Sims, who also had a shrapnel wound, remembers somebody anxiously calling out to Frost, "Sir, can we still hold out?"

In England, Major General Sosabowski watched his brigade board the long lines of troop-carrier Dakotas. Ever since Sunday he had felt the tension build as his Poles waited to go. They had made the trip from their billets to the airfield on Tuesday only to have the operation canceled. This Wednesday morning, learning of the change in his drop zone, Sosabowski himself had postponed the flight by three hours in order to work out new plans. Now, a little before 1 P.M., as the heavily laden paratroopers moved toward the planes, the atmosphere of impatience was gone. The men were on the way at last, and Sosabowski noted "an almost lighthearted attitude among them."

His frame of mind was far different. In the few short hours since the switch in plans he had tried to learn everything he could about Urquhart's situation and the new drop zone. He had briefed his three-battalion brigade down to platoon level but the information he could give them was sparse. Sosabowski felt that they were ill-prepared, almost "jumping into the unknown."

Now, as propellers ticked over, his battalions began to climb aboard the 114 Dakotas that would take them to Holland. Satisfied with the loading, Sosabowski hoisted himself into the lead plane. With engines revving, the Dakota moved out, rolled slowly down the runway, turned and made ready for takeoff. Then it paused. To Sosabowski's dismay, the engines were throttled back. Minutes passed, and his anxiety grew. He wondered what was delaying takeoff.

Suddenly the door opened and an R.A.F. officer climbed in. Making his way up the aisle to the General, he informed Sosabowski that control had just received word to halt the takeoff. The situation was a repeat of Tuesday: the southern fields were open and bomber resupply planes were taking off, but in the Grantham area a heavy overcast was settling in. Sosabowski was incredulous. He could hear the curses of his officers and men as the news was relayed. The flight was canceled for twenty-four hours more—until 1 P.M. Thursday, September 21.

General Gavin's Glider Infantry Regiment too was grounded once again. On this day of the vital Waal river assault at Nijmegen, Gavin's sorely needed 3,400 men, with their guns and equipment, could not get out. The Driel-Heveadorp ferry was still in operation. On this crucial Wednesday, D plus 3, when the Polish Brigade might have been ferried across the Rhine to strengthen Urquhart's flagging troopers, the weather had struck again at Market-Garden.

Field Marshal Walter Model was finally ready to open his counteroffensive against the British and Americans in Holland. On this critical Wednesday, September 20, the entire corridor erupted in one German attack after another.

Model, his reinforcements steadily arriving, was certain that his forces were now strong enough to wipe out Montgomery's attack. He planned to pinch off the Allied corridor at Son, Veghel and Nijmegen. The Arnhem bridge, he knew, was almost in his hands. And Von Zangen's Fifteenth Army—the army that had been forgotten at Antwerp by Montgomery

—was now slowly renewing its strength. Staffs were being newly organized, ammunition and supplies were arriving daily. Within forty-eight hours, in Army Group B's war diary, Annex 2342, Model would report Von Zangen's status to Von Rundstedt in these terms: "The total number of personnel and equipment ferried across the Schelde by the Fifteenth Army totals 82,000 men; 530 guns; 4,600 vehicles; over 4,000 horses and a large amount of valuable material. . . ."*

Model was now so confident of Von Zangen's ability to take over that within seventy-two hours he planned to completely reorganize his own command structure. Von Zangen would command all Army Group B forces west of the Allied corridor; General Student's First Parachute Army, now being systematically reinforced, would be assigned the eastern side. The moment had come for Model to begin his offensive with sharp probing attacks.

At the Son bridge on the morning of the twentieth, panzer forces, striking into the 101st's area, almost succeeded in taking the bridge. Only quick action by General Taylor's men and British tanks held off the attack. Simultaneously, as Horrocks' columns sped toward Nijmegen, the entire stretch of Taylor's sector came under pressure.

At 11 A.M. in General Gavin's area, German troops, preceded by a heavy bombardment, advanced out of the Reichswald and attacked the 82nd's eastern flank. Within a few hours a full-scale drive was in progress in the Mook area, threatening the Heumen bridge. Rushing to the scene from Nijmegen, where his men were preparing to assault the Waal, Gavin saw that "the only bridge we owned that would take armor" was in serious jeopardy. "It was essential to the survival of the British and Americans crowded into Nijmegen," he recalls. His problem was acute; every available 82nd unit was already committed. Hurriedly Gavin asked for help from the Coldstream Guards.

---

*Although these are the exact figures quoted from Army Group B's diary, they seem excessive particularly in the number of guns, vehicles and horses. The evacuation of the Fifteenth Army across the Schelde and around Antwerp was directed by General Eugene Felix Schwalbe. In 1946 he gave the following estimate: 65,000 men, 225 guns, 750 trucks and wagons and 1,000 horses (see Milton Shulman, *Defeat in the West*, p. 180). I cannot explain the discrepancy, but Schwalbe's figures seem much more realistic.

Then, with Gavin personally leading the counterattack, a bitter, unrelenting battle began that was to last all day. Shifting his forces back and forth like chess men, Gavin held out and eventually forced the Germans to withdraw. He had always feared attack from the Reichswald. Now Gavin and the Corps commander, General Browning, knew that a new and more terrible phase of the fighting had begun. Among the prisoners taken were men from General Mendl's tough II Parachute Corps. Model's intention was now obvious: key bridges were to be grabbed, the corridor was to be squeezed and Horrocks' columns crushed.

For his part, Model was convinced that the Allies would never cross at Nijmegen and drive the last eleven miles to Arnhem. Within the week, he confidently told General Bittrich, he expected the battle to be over. Bittrich was less assured. He would feel happier, he told Model, if the Nijmegen bridges were destroyed. Model looked at him and angrily shouted, "No!"

Major General Heinz Harmel was annoyed by the attitude of his superior, General Wilhelm Bittrich. The II SS Panzer Corps commander had adopted too far-sighted a view of the battle, Harmel felt. Bittrich "seemed to have closed his mind completely to the ferrying problems at Pannerden." Those problems had hampered Harmel from the beginning, yet it appeared to him that Bittrich never remained long enough at the site "to see for himself the almost impossible task of getting twenty tanks across the river—and three of them were Royal Tigers." It had taken Harmel's engineers nearly three days to build a ferry capable of carrying an estimated 40-ton load across the Rhine. Although Harmel believed the operation could now be accelerated, only three platoons of tanks (twelve Panthers) had so far reached the vicinity of Nijmegen. The remainder, including his Tiger tanks, were fighting at the Arnhem bridge under the veteran eastern front commander, Major Hans Peter Knaust.

The thirty-eight-year-old Knaust had lost a leg in battle near Moscow in 1941. As Harmel recalls, "he stomped about with a wooden one and, although he was always in pain, he never once complained." Yet, Knaust too was the target for much of Harmel's displeasure.

To reinforce the Frundsberg Division, the "Knaust *Kampf-gruppe*" had been rushed to Holland with thirty-five tanks, five armored personnel carriers and one self-propelled gun. But Knaust's veterans were of low caliber. Almost all of them had been badly wounded at one time or another; in Harmel's view they were "close to being invalids." Under normal conditions the men would not have been in active service. Additionally, Knaust's replacements were young, and many had had only eight weeks' training. The Arnhem bridge battle had gone on so long that Harmel was now fearful of the situation at Nijmegen. In case the British broke through, he would need Knaust's tanks to hold the bridge and defense positions between Nijmegen and Arnhem. More armored reinforcements were on the way, including fifteen to twenty Tiger tanks and another twenty Panthers. But Harmel had no idea when they would arrive or whether the Arnhem bridge would be open to speed their drive south. Even after its capture, Harmel envisioned a full day to clear the wreckage and get vehicles moving.

To oversee all operations, Harmel had set up an advance command post near the village of Doornenburg, two miles west of Pannerden and six miles northeast of Nijmegen. From there he drove west to roughly the mid-point of the Nijmegen-Arnhem highway to study the terrain, automatically fixing in his mind defense positions that might be used if a breakthrough occurred. His reconnaissance produced one clear impression: it seemed impossible for either British or German tanks to leave the highway. Only light vehicles could travel the thinly sur-faced, brick-paved, secondary roads. His own tanks, moving to Nijmegen after crossing at Pannerden, had bogged down on just such roads, their weight crumbling the pavement. The main Nijmegen-Arnhem highway was, in places, a dike road, nine to twelve feet above soft polder on either side. Tanks mov-ing along these high stretches would be completely exposed, silhouetted against the sky. Well-sited artillery could easily pick them off. At the moment, Harmel had almost no artillery cov-ering the highway; thus it was imperative that Knaust's tanks and guns get across the Rhine and in position before a British breakthrough could occur at Nijmegen.

Returning to his headquarters at Doornenburg, Harmel heard the latest reports from his chief of staff, Colonel Paetsch.

There was good news from Arnhem: more prisoners were being taken, and the fighting at the bridge was beginning to break up. Knaust now believed he might have the crossing by late afternoon. Fighting continued in Nijmegen, but Captain Karl Heinz Euling, although taking heavy casualties, was containing all efforts to seize the railway and road bridges there. The Americans and British had been stopped at both approaches. In the center of the city British forces had been held up too, but that situation was more precarious.

Euling's report reflected an optimism that Harmel did not share. Eventually, by sheer weight of numbers, British armor would surely overrun the German line. Lighting a cigar, Harmel told Paetsch that he "expected the full weight of the Anglo-American attack to be thrown at the highway bridge within forty-eight hours." If Knaust's tanks and artillerymen secured the Arnhem bridge quickly, they might halt the British armored drive. Should the panzers be slow in forcing the little band of British from the Arnhem bridge and clearing it of wreckage, Harmel knew that, against all orders, he must blow the Nijmegen highway bridge.

For all his careful consideration, he did not envision a most preposterous scheme: that the American paratroopers might try to ford the river in a major amphibious assault.

10

WAITING PARATROOPERS CROWDED THE AREA not far from the crossing site, one mile downstream from the Nijmegen railway bridge. Throughout Tuesday night and well into Wednesday morning, as the Anglo-American forces under Lieutenant Colonel Goulburn and Lieutenant Colonel Vandervoort continued the battle for the railroad and highway bridges to the east, American and British soldiers labored to widen the area leading to the river bank so that the tanks and heavy artillery of the Guards Armored Division could take up firing positions to support the assault. Typhoons were scheduled to fly low over the northern bank thirty minutes before H Hour, spraying the entire area with rocket and machine-gun fire. On the ground, tanks and artillery would pound the site for another fifteen minutes. Then, under a smoke screen laid down by tanks, the first wave of men led by twenty-seven-year-old Major Julian Cook were to set out in one of the most daring river crossings ever made.

The plan was as thorough as commanders working throughout the night could make it. But the boats in which Cook's troopers would cross the 400-yard-wide river had not arrived. H Hour, originally set for 1 P.M., was postponed until 3 P.M.

In small groups the Americans waited as Cook paced up and down. "Where are the damned boats?" he wondered. Ever since he had been told by General Gavin and the 504th regimental commander, Colonel Tucker, that his 3rd Battalion would make the Waal assault crossing, Cook had been "shocked and dumfounded." It seemed to the young West Pointer that "we were being asked to make an Omaha beach landing all by ourselves." Many of his men had never even been in a small boat.

Cook was not the only one anxiously awaiting the arrival of the boats. Before noon General Frederick Browning had received the first clear indication of the seriousness of Urquhart's situation. Received via British Second Army communications, the Phantom message read in part:

> (201105) . . . senior formation still in vicinity north end of main bridge but not in touch and unable resupply . . . Arnhem entirely in enemy hands. Request all possible steps expedite relief. Fighting intense and opposition extremely strong. Position not too good.

Browning was deeply disturbed. Every hour now mattered and the quick seizure of the Nijmegen bridges was vital to the survival of Urquhart's men. The relief of the Arnhem defenders was, at this moment, almost solely up to Cook and the 3rd Battalion—a fact of which Cook was unaware.

In any event, the boats were not at hand, and no one even knew what they were like. All through the night General Horrocks and his staff had been trying to speed their arrival. Far back in the engineering convoys three trucks carrying the craft had been inching their way up the jam-packed road. Back in Eindhoven they had been held up by a fierce Luftwaffe bombing attack. The whole center of the city was devastated. Scores of supply trucks had been destroyed and an entire ammunition convoy had been ignited, adding to the carnage. Now, at the Waal crossing less than one hour before H hour, there was still no sign of the trucks and the vital boats.

The assault site lay to the east of the massive PGEM electrical power plant, and originally it was believed that the crossing could be made from the plant itself. There, at the river's edge, a small inlet afforded protection for the loading, unobserved by the Germans. Colonel Tucker had rejected the site; it was too close to the enemy-held railway bridge. As the troopers emerged from the dock area, the Germans could sweep each assault wave with machine-gun fire. Here, too, at the mouth of the inlet, the 8- to 10-mile-an-hour current swirled stronger. Shifting farther west, Tucker planned to have the men rush the boats at double time down to the river's edge, launch them and paddle across. That, too, worried Cook. From the little he had learned, each craft weighed about 200 pounds; when they were loaded with the men's equipment and ammunition, that figure would probably double.

Once launched, each boat would carry thirteen paratroopers and a crew of three engineers to row the men across. The operation would be continuous. In wave after wave the assault craft were to cross back and forth until the whole of Cook's battalion and part of another, under Captain John Harrison, were across. Major Edward G. Tyler of the Irish Guards, whose tanks were to give fire support, was appalled by the whole concept. "It put the fear of God in me," Tyler recalls. He asked the cigar-chewing Colonel Tucker if his men had ever practiced this kind of operation before. "No," Tucker replied laconically. "They're getting on-the-job training."

From the ninth floor of the power plant, Cook and Lieutenant Colonel Giles Vandeleur, commanding the Irish Guards' 2nd Battalion, observed the north shore through binoculars. Directly across from where they stood, flat ground ran inland from the river's edge for 200 to 800 yards. Cook's men would have to cross this unprotected stretch after they landed. Beyond the level shore, a sloping dike embankment rose some 15 to 20 feet high, and topping it was a 20-foot-wide road running west to east. A squat building, called Fort Hof Van Holland, stood about 800 yards beyond the road. Cook and Vandeleur could clearly see enemy troops in position along the top of the embankment, and they were almost sure that observation and artillery posts were positioned inside the fort. "Somebody," Cook remembers thinking, "has come up with a real nightmare." Yet, effective H-Hour air and artillery support could soften the German resistance and enable the troopers to command the northern bank quickly. Cook was counting heavily on that support.

Vandeleur thought the crossing might prove "ghastly, with heavy casualties." But he intended his tanks to support the Americans to the utmost. He planned to use about thirty Sherman tanks—two squadrons under command of Major Edward G. Tyler and Major Desmond FitzGerald. At 2:30 P.M., the tanks were to move toward the river and mount the embankment, "track-to-track," their 75 mm. guns lined up to pound the far shore. This British bombardment would be reinforced by the 82nd's mortar and artillery fire. In all, 100 guns would batter the northern bank.

Cook's men, who had not seen the actual assault area as yet, had taken the briefing in their stride. But the width of the river shocked everyone. "At first when we were briefed, we thought they were joking," recalls Second Lieutenant John Holabird. "It all sounded too fantastic." Sergeant Theodore Finkbeiner, scheduled for the first wave, was sure that "our chances were pretty good because of the smoke screen." But Captain T. Moffatt Burriss, commander of I Company, believed the plan was nothing short of a suicide mission.

So did the 504th's Protestant chaplain, Captain Delbert Kuehl. Normally Kuehl would not have gone in with assault troops. Now he requested permission to be with Cook's men. "It was the hardest decision I ever made," he recalls, "because I was going on my own volition. The plan seemed absolutely impossible, and I felt if ever the men needed me, it would be on this operation."

Captain Henry Baldwin Keep, who was known as the battalion's millionaire because he was a member of the Philadelphia Biddle family, considered that "the odds were very much against us. In eighteen months of almost steady combat we had done everything from parachute jumps to establishing bridgeheads to acting as mountain troops and as regular infantry. But a river crossing was something else! It sounded impossible."

Cook, according to Lieutenant Virgil Carmichael, tried to lighten the atmosphere by announcing that he would imitate George Washington by "standing erect in the boat and, with clenched right fist pushed forward, shout, 'Onward, men! Onward!'" Captain Carl W. Kappel, commander of H Company, who had heard that the Arnhem attack was in trouble, was deeply concerned. He wanted "to get in the damn boat and get the hell across." He had a good friend in the British 1st Airborne, and he felt if anyone was on the Arnhem bridge it was "Frosty"—Colonel John Frost.

By 2 P.M. there was still no sign of the assault craft, and now it was too late to recall the approaching squadrons of Typhoons. Back of the jump-off site, hidden behind the river embankment, Cook's men and Vandeleur's tanks waited. At precisely 2:30 P.M. the Typhoon strike began. Flashing overhead, the planes peeled off and screamed down, one after another, shooting rockets and machine-gun fire at the enemy positions. Ten minutes later, as Vandeleur's tanks began taking up positions on the embankment, the three trucks carrying the assault craft arrived. With only twenty minutes to go, Cook's men saw, for the first time, the flimsy collapsible green boats.

Each boat was nineteen feet long with a flat, reinforced plywood bottom. The canvas sides, held in place by wooden pegs, measured thirty inches from floor to gunwales. Eight paddles, four feet long, were supposed to accompany each boat, but in many there were only two. Men would have to use their rifle butts to paddle.

Quickly engineers began assembling the boats. As each was put together, the paratroopers assigned to the craft loaded their equipment on board and got ready to dash for the bank. Against the deafening din of the barrage now lashing the far shore, the twenty-six boats were finally assembled. "Somebody yelled, 'Go!'" First Lieutenant Patrick Mulloy recalls, "and everybody grabbed the gunwales and started to lug the boats down to the river." From the rear, shells screamed over the men's heads; tank guns barked from the embankment ahead of them, and white smoke, "looking fairly thick" to Mulloy, drifted over the width of the river. The assault was on.

As the first wave of some 260 men—two companies, H and I, plus headquarters staff and engineers—got to the water the launching immediately began to assume the proportions of a disaster. Boats put into too-shallow water bogged down in the mud and would not budge. Struggling and thrashing in the shallows, men carried them to deeper parts, pushed them out and then climbed in. As some troopers tried to hoist themselves aboard, their boats overturned. Other boats, overloaded, were caught by the current and began circling out of control. Some sank under their heavy loads. Paddles were lost; men fell overboard. Captain Carl Kappel saw the scene as one "of mass confusion." His boat began to founder. "Private Legacie was in the water and starting to go down," Kappel remembers. Diving in after him, Kappel was surprised at the swiftness of the current. He was able to grab Legacie and pull him to safety "but by the time I got him to the bank I was an old man and worn out." Jumping into another boat Kappel started out again. First Lieutenant Tom MacLeod's craft was almost awash, and he thought they were sinking. "Paddles were flaying like mad," he remembers, and all he could hear above the din was Cook's voice, from a nearby boat, yelling, "Keep going! Keep going!"

The Major, a devout Catholic, was also praying out loud. Lieutenant Virgil Carmichael noticed that he had developed a kind of cadence with each line. "Hail Mary—full of Grace—Hail Mary—full of Grace," Cook chanted with every stroke of the paddle.* Then, in the midst of the confusion, the Germans opened up.

The fire was so intense and concentrated that it reminded Lieutenant Mulloy of "the worst we ever took at Anzio. They were blazing away with heavy machine guns and mortars, most of it coming from the embankment and the railroad bridge. I felt like a sitting duck." Chaplain Kuehl was sick with horror. The head of the man sitting next to him was blown off. Over and over Kuehl kept repeating "Lord, Thy will be done."

From his command post in the PGEM building, Lieutenant Colonel Vandeleur, along with General Browning and General Horrocks, watched in grim silence. "It was a horrible, horrible

---

* "'The Lord is with Thee' was too long," Cook says, "so I kept repeating, 'Hail Mary' (one stroke), 'Full of Grace' (second stroke)." Captain Keep tried to remember his crewing days at Princeton but he found himself nervously counting "7-6-7-7-7-8-9."

sight," Vandeleur remembers. "Boats were literally blown out of the water. Huge geysers shot up as shells hit and small-arms fire from the northern bank made the river look like a seething cauldron." Instinctively men began to crouch in the boats. Lieutenant Holabird, staring at the fragile canvas sides, felt "totally exposed and defenseless." Even his helmet "seemed about as small as a beanie."

Shrapnel ripped through the little fleet. The boat carrying half of First Lieutenant James Megellas' platoon sank without a trace. There were no survivors. First Lieutenant Allen McLain saw two craft blown apart and troopers thrown into the water. Around Captain T. Moffatt Burriss' boat fire was coming down "like a hailstorm," and finally the engineer steering the boat said, "Take the rudder. I'm hit." His wrist was shattered. As Burriss leaned over to help, the engineer was hit again, this time in the head. Shell fragments caught Burriss in the side. As the engineer fell overboard, his foot caught the gunwale, causing his body to act like a rudder and swinging the boat around. Burriss had to heave the dead man into the water. By then two more troopers sitting in front had also been killed.

Under a brisk wind the smoke screen had been blown to tatters. Now German gunners raked each boat individually. Sergeant Clark Fuller saw that some men, in their haste to get across quickly, and desperately trying to avoid the fire, "rowed against each other, causing their boats to swing around in circles." The Germans picked them off easily. Fuller was "so scared that he felt paralyzed." Halfway across, Private Leonard G. Tremble was suddenly slammed into the bottom of the boat. His craft had taken a direct hit. Wounded in the face, shoulder, right arm and left leg, Tremble was sure he was bleeding to death. Taking water, the boat swung crazily in circles, then drifted slowly back to the southern shore, everyone in it dead but Tremble.

In the command post Vandeleur saw that "huge gaps had begun to appear in the smoke screen." His tankers had fired smoke shells for more than ten minutes, but now the Guardsmen were running low on every kind of ammunition. "The Germans had switched ammunition and were beginning to use big stuff, and I remember almost trying to will the Americans to go faster. It was obvious that these young paratroopers were inexperienced in handling assault boats, which are not the easiest things to maneuver. They were zigzagging all over the water."

Then the first wave reached the northern bank. Men struggled out of the boats, guns firing, and started across the exposed flat land. Sergeant Clark Fuller, who a few minutes before had been paralyzed with fear, was so happy to be alive that he felt "exhilarated. My fear had been replaced by a surge of recklessness. I felt I could lick the whole German army." Vandeleur, watching the landing, "saw one or two boats hit the beach, followed immediately by three or four others. Nobody paused. Men got out and began running toward the embankment. My God, what a courageous sight it was! They just moved steadily across that open ground. I never saw a single man lie down until he was hit. I didn't think more than half the fleet made it across." Then, to Vandeleur's amazement, "the boats turned around and started back for the second wave." Turning to Horrocks, General Browning said, "I have never seen a more gallant action."

As Julian Cook's assault craft neared the beach he jumped out and pulled the boat, eager to get ashore. Suddenly to his right he saw a bubbling commotion in the gray water. "It looked like a large air bubble, steadily approaching the bank," he remembers. "I thought I was seeing things when the top of a helmet broke the surface and continued on moving. Then a face appeared under the helmet. It was the little machine-gunner, Private Joseph Jedlicka. He had bandoliers of 30-caliber machine-gun bullets draped around his shoulders and a box in either hand." Jedlicka had fallen overboard in eight feet of water and, holding his breath, had calmly walked across the river bottom until he emerged.

Medics were already working on the beach and as First Lieutenant Tom MacLeod prepared to return across the Waal for another boatload of troopers, he saw that rifles had been stuck in the ground next to the fallen.

Shortly after 4 P.M., General Heinz Harmel received an alarming message at his headquarters in Doornenburg. It was reported that "a white smoke screen has been thrown across the river opposite Fort Hof Van Holland." Harmel, with some of his staff, rushed by car to the village of Lent, on the northern bank of the Waal, a mile from the Nijmegen highway bridge. The smoke could mean only one thing: the Anglo-Americans were trying to cross the Waal by boat. Still, Harmel could not believe his own analysis. The width of the river, the forces manning the northern bank, Euling's optimistic report of the morning, and his own estimate of the British and American forces in Nijmegen—all argued against the operation. But Harmel decided to see for himself. He remembers that "I had no intention of being arrested and shot by Berlin for letting the bridges fall into enemy hands—no matter how Model felt about it."

Major Julian Cook knew his losses were appalling, but he had no time to assess them now. His companies had landed everywhere along the exposed stretch of beach. Units were inextricably mixed up and, for the time, without organization. The Germans were flaying the beach with machine-gun fire, yet his stubborn troopers refused to be pinned down. Individually and in twos and threes they headed for the embankment. "It was either stay and get riddled or move," Cook remembers. Struggling forward, the men, armed with machine guns, grenades and fixed bayonets, charged the embankment and viciously dug the Germans out. Sergeant Theodore Finkbeiner believes he was one of the first to reach the high dike roadway. "I stuck my head over the top, and stared right into the muzzle of a machine gun," he recalls. He ducked, but "the muzzle blast blew my helmet off." Finkbeiner tossed a grenade into the German emplacement, heard the explosion and the sound of men screaming. Then he quickly hoisted himself up onto the embankment road and headed for the next machine-gun nest.

Captain Moffatt Burriss had no time to think about the shrapnel wound in his side. When he landed he was "so happy to be alive that I vomited." He ran straight for the dike, yelling to his men to get "one machine gun firing on the left flank, another on the right." They did. Burriss saw several houses back of the dike. Kicking the door of one open, he surprised "several Germans who had been sleeping, apparently unaware of what was happening." Reaching quickly for a hand grenade, Burriss pulled the pin, threw it into the room and slammed the door.

In the smoke, noise and confusion, some men in the first wave did not remember how they got off the beach. Corporal Jack Bommer, a communications man laden down with equipment, simply ran forward. He "had only one thing in mind: to survive if possible." He knew he had to get to the embankment and wait for further instructions. On reaching the crest he saw "dead bodies everywhere, and Germans—some no more than fifteen years old, others in their sixties—who a few minutes before had been slaughtering us in the boats were now begging for mercy, trying to surrender." Men were too shocked by their ordeal and too angry at the death of friends to take many prisoners. Bommer recalls that some Germans "were shot out of hand at point-blank range."

Sickened and exhausted by the crossing, their dead and wounded lying on the beach, the men of the first wave subdued the German defenders on the dike road in less than thirty minutes. Not all the enemy positions had been overrun, but now troopers hunched down in former German machine-gun nests to protect the arrival of succeeding waves. Two more craft were lost in the second crossing. And, still under heavy shellfire, exhausted engineers in the eleven remaining craft made five more trips to bring all the Americans across the bloodstained Waal. Speed was all that mattered now. Cook's men had to grab the northern ends of the crossings before the Germans fully realized what was happening—and before they blew the bridges.

By now the embankment defense line had been overrun, and the Germans were pulling back to secondary positions. Cook's troopers gave them no quarter. Captain Henry Keep comments that "what remained of the battalion seemed driven to fever pitch and, rendered crazy by rage, men temporarily forgot the meaning of fear. I have never witnessed this human metamorphosis so acutely displayed as on this day. It was an awe-inspiring sight but not a pretty one."

Individually and in small groups, men who had sat helpless in the boats as friends died all around them took on four and five times their number with grenades, submachine guns and bayonets. With brutal efficiency they dug the Germans out and, without stopping to rest or regroup, continued their rampaging assault. They fought through fields, orchards and houses back of the embankment under the fire of machine guns and antiaircraft batteries hammering at them from Fort Hof Van Holland directly ahead. As some groups headed due

east along the sunken dike road for the bridges, others stormed
the fort, almost oblivious to the German guns. Some troopers, laden with grenades, swam the moat surrounding the fortress and began climbing the walls. Sergeant Leroy Richmond,
swimming underwater, took the enemy soldier guarding the
causeway by surprise, then waved his men across. According
to First Lieutenant Virgil F. Carmichael, troopers "somehow
climbed to the top of the fort, then others below tossed up
hand grenades which were promptly dropped into the turret
portholes, one after the other." The German defenders quickly
surrendered.

Meanwhile, units from two companies—Captain Burriss' I
Company and Captain Kappel's H Company—were sprinting
for the bridges. At the railroad bridge, H Company found the
German defense so fierce that it looked as though the American attack might stall.* Then the continuing pressure from the
British and American forces at the southern end and in Nijmegen itself caused the enemy suddenly to crack. To Kappel's
amazement the Germans began to retreat across the bridge
"in wholesale numbers"—right into the American guns. From
his tank near the PGEM factory, Lieutenant John Gorman
"could see what looked like hundreds of Germans, confused
and panic-stricken, running across the bridge right toward the
Americans." On the northern bank First Lieutenant Richard
La Riviere and Lieutenant E. J. Sims also saw them coming. In
disbelief, they watched as the Germans abandoned their guns
and hurried toward the northern exit. "They were coming
across in a mass," recalls La Riviere, "and we let them come—
two thirds of the way." Then the Americans opened fire.

A hail of bullets ripped into the defenders. Germans fell
everywhere—some into the girders under the bridge; others to the water below. More than 260 lay dead, many were
wounded, and scores more were taken prisoner before the firing ceased. Within two hours of the Waal river assault, the first
of the bridges had fallen. Major Edward G. Tyler of the Irish

---

*According to Charles B. MacDonald, in *The Siegfried Line Campaign*, p.
181, the Germans on the bridge had a formidable array of armament which
included 34 machine guns, two 20 mm. antiaircraft guns and one 88 mm.
dual-purpose gun.

Guards saw "someone waving. I had been concentrating so long on that railroad bridge that, for me, it was the only one in existence. I got on the wireless and radioed Battalion, 'They're on the bridge! They've got the bridge!'" The time was 5 P.M. Captain Tony Heywood of the Grenadier Guards received Major Tyler's message and found it "utterly confusing." Which bridge did the message refer to? The Grenadiers under Lieutenant Colonel Goulburn were still fighting alongside Colonel Vandervoort's troopers near the Valkhof, where Euling's SS forces continued to deny them the highway bridge. If the message meant that the highway bridge had been taken, Heywood remembers, "I couldn't figure how they had gotten across."

The railroad bridge was intact and physically in Anglo-American hands, but Germans—either prepared to fight to the last or too frightened to leave their positions—were still on it. The Americans had made a quick search for demolition charges at the northern end. Although they had found nothing, there was still a chance that the bridge was wired and ready to be destroyed. Captain Kappel now radioed Major Cook, urging him to get British tanks across as quickly as possible. With these as support, he and Captain Burriss of I Company believed, they could grab the big prize, the Nijmegen highway bridge, slightly less than a mile east. Then, recalls Kappel, Colonel Tucker arrived. The request, Tucker said, "had been relayed, but the Germans might blow both bridges at any moment." Without hesitation Cook's troopers pushed on for the highway bridge.

General Harmel could not make out what was happening. Binoculars to his eyes, he stood on the roof of a bunker near the village of Lent. From this position on the northern bank of the Waal barely a mile from the main Nijmegen highway bridge, he could see smoke and haze off to his right and hear the crash of battle. But no one seemed to know exactly what was taking place, except that an attempt had been made to cross the river near the railroad bridge. He could see the highway bridge quite clearly; there was nothing on it. Then, as Harmel recalls, "the wounded started to arrive, and I began to get conflicting reports." Americans, he learned, had crossed the river, "but everything was exaggerated. I could not tell if they had come across in ten boats or a hundred." His mind "working furiously trying to decide what to do next," Harmel checked with his engineers. "I was informed that both bridges were ready to go," he remembers. "The local commander was instructed to destroy the railroad bridge. The detonator for the highway bridge was hidden in a garden near the bunker at Lent, and a man was stationed there awaiting orders to press the plunger." Then Harmel received his first clear report: only a few boats had crossed the river, and the battle was still in progress. Looking through his binoculars again, he saw that the highway bridge was still clear and free of movement. Although his "instinct was to get this troublesome bridge weighing on my shoulders destroyed, I had no intention of doing anything until I was absolutely sure that it was lost." If he was forced to blow the highway bridge, Harmel decided, he would make sure that "it was crowded with British tanks and let them go up in the blast, too."

In Huner Park and in the Valkhof close by the southern approaches to the highway bridge, Captain Karl Euling's SS Panzer Grenadiers were fighting for their lives. The Anglo-American attack by Lieutenant Colonel Edward Goulburn's Grenadier Guards and Lieutenant Colonel Ben Vandervoort's 2nd Battalion of the 82nd's 505th Regiment was methodical and relentless. Vandervoort's mortars and artillery pounded the German defense line as his men sprinted from house to house. Closing the gap between themselves and Euling's steadily shrinking defenses, Goulburn's tanks moved up the converging streets, driving the Germans before them, their 17-pounders and machine guns blasting.

The Germans fought back hard. "It was the heaviest volume of fire I ever encountered," recalls Sergeant Spencer Wurst, then a nineteen-year-old veteran who had been with the 82nd since North Africa. "I had the feeling I could reach up and grab bullets with each hand." From his vantage point on the ledge of a house some twenty-five yards from the Valkhof, Wurst could look down into the German positions. "There were foxholes all over the park," he remembers, "and all the action seemed to be centered from these and from a medieval tower. I watched our men break out from right and left and charge right up to the traffic circle. We were so anxious to get that bridge that I saw some men crawl over to the foxholes and literally drag the Germans out." Wurst's own rifle barrel was so hot that cosmoline began to ooze from the wood stock.

As the murderous fire fight continued Wurst was astounded to see Colonel Vandervoort "stroll across the street, smoking a cigarette. He stopped in front of the house I was in, looked up and said, 'Sergeant, I think you better go see if you can get that tank moving.'" Vandervoort pointed to the entrance to the park where a British tank was sitting, its turret closed. Clambering off the roof, Wurst ran to the tank and rapped on its side with his helmet. The turret opened. "Colonel wants you to move it," Wurst said. "Come on. I'll show you where to fire." Advancing beside the tank in full view of the Germans, Wurst pointed out targets. As the intense fire coming from Vandervoort's men and Goulburn's tanks increased, the enemy defense ring began to collapse. The formidable line of antitank guns that had stopped each previous attack was obliterated. Finally only four self-propelled guns dug into the center of the traffic circle remained firing. Then, a little after 4 P.M., in an all-out tank and infantry assault, these too were overrun. As Vandervoort's troopers charged with bayonets and grenades, Goulburn lined his tanks up four abreast and sent them charging into the park. In panic the Germans broke. As they retreated, some tried to take cover in the girders of the bridge; others, farther away, raced through the American and British fire toward the medieval fort. As the Germans passed, scores of troopers lobbed grenades into their midst. The assault was over. "They had given us a real tough time," Wurst says. "We watched them charging right past us, up over the road leading onto the bridge and some went off to the east. We felt pretty good."

General Allan Adair, commander of the Guards Armored Division, directing operations in a nearby building, remembers "gritting my teeth, dreading the sound of an explosion that would tell me the Germans had blown the bridge." He heard nothing. The approaches to the great Waal bridge lay open, the span itself apparently intact.

Sergeant Peter Robinson's troop of four tanks had been waiting for just this moment. Now they moved out for the bridge.* The twenty-nine-year-old Dunkirk veteran had been alerted a few hours earlier by his squadron leader, Major John Trotter, "to stand ready to go for the bridge." Germans were still on the crossing, and Trotter now warned Robinson, "We don't know what to expect when you cross, but the bridge has to be taken. Don't stop for anything." Shaking hands with the sergeant, Trotter added jokingly, "Don't worry. I know where your wife lives and if anything happens, I'll let her know." Robinson was not amused. "You're bloody cheerful, aren't you, sir?" he asked Trotter. Climbing onto his tank, Robinson led off for the bridge.

The troop of four tanks came into Huner Park by the right of the roundabout. To Robinson it appeared that "the whole town was burning. Buildings to my left and right were on fire." Wreathed in smoke, the great crossing looked "damned big." As Robinson's tank rumbled forward he reported constantly by radio to division headquarters. "Everyone else had been ordered off the air," he recalls. Clanking onto the approaches, Robinson remembers, "We came under heavy fire. There was an explosion. One of the idler wheels carrying the track on one side of the tank had been hit." The tank was still running, although "the wireless was dead and I had lost touch with headquarters." Shouting to his driver to reverse, Robinson backed his tank to the side of the road. Quickly the sergeant jumped out, ran to the tank behind him and told its commander, Sergeant Billingham, to get out. Billingham began to argue. Robinson shouted that he was giving "a direct order. Get out of that tank damned quick and follow along in mine." The third tank in line, commanded by Sergeant Charles W. Pacey, had pulled out and was leading the way onto the bridge. Jumping

---

*It has been said that an American flag was raised on the north end of the railroad bridge and, in the smoke and confusion, British tankers thought it was flying on the far end of the highway bridge—signaling the American seizure of that end. The story may be true, but in scores of interviews I have not found a single participant who confirmed it. I have walked over the entire area and it seems inconceivable that anyone looking across the highway bridge could mistake a flag flying a mile to the west as the terminus of this crossing.

aboard Billingham's tank, Robinson ordered the others to follow. As the four tanks advanced, Robinson recalls, they came
under fire from a "big 88 parked on the other side of the river,
near some burning houses and from what appeared to be a self-
propelled gun in the far distance."

Colonel Vandervoort, watching the tanks, saw the 88 begin to fire. "It was pretty spectacular," he recalls. "The 88 was
sandbagged into the side of the highway about one hundred
yards from the north end of the bridge. One tank and the 88
exchanged about four rounds apiece with the tank spitting 30-
caliber tracers all the while. In the gathering dusk it was quite
a show." Then Robinson's gunner, Guardsman Leslie Johnson,
got the 88 with another shot. Germans with grenades, rifles
and machine guns clung to the girders of the bridge, Robinson
remembers. The tank machine guns began "to knock them
off like ninepins." And Johnson, answering the heavy enemy
artillery fire, "pumped shells through his gun as fast as the
loader could run them through." In a hail of fire Robinson's
troop rattled forward, now approaching the halfway mark on
the highway bridge.

In the twilight, billowing smoke clogged the distant Waal
highway bridge. At his forward position near Lent, General
Heinz Harmel stared through his binoculars. Guns were banging all around him, and troops were moving back through the
village to take up new positions. Harmel's worst fear had now
been realized. The Americans, against all expectations, had
succeeded in making a bold, successful crossing of the Waal.
In Nijmegen itself the optimism of Captain Karl Euling had
proved unfounded. The last message received from him had
been terse: Euling said he was encircled with only sixty men
left. Now Harmel knew beyond doubt that the bridges were
lost. He did not know whether the railroad bridge had been
destroyed, but if he was to demolish the highway bridge, it
must be done immediately.

"Everything seemed to pass through my mind all at once,"
he recalled. "What must be done first? What is the most urgent, most important action to take? It all came down to the
bridges." He had not contacted Bittrich "beforehand to warn
him that I might have to demolish the highway crossing. I

presumed that it was Bittrich who had ordered the bridges readied for demolition." So, Harmel reasoned, in spite of Model's order, "if Bittrich had been in my shoes, he would have blown the main bridge. In my opinion, Model's order was now automatically canceled anyway." At any moment he expected tanks to appear on the highway bridge.

Standing next to the engineer by the detonator box, Harmel scanned the crossing. At first he could detect no movement. Then suddenly he saw "a single tank reach the center, then a second behind and to its right." To the engineer he said, "Get ready." Two more tanks appeared in view, and Harmel waited for the line to reach the exact middle before giving the order. He shouted, "Let it blow!" The engineer jammed the plunger down. Nothing happened. The British tanks continued to advance. Harmel yelled, "Again!" Once more the engineer slammed down the detonator handle, but again the huge explosions that Harmel had expected failed to occur. "I was waiting to see the bridge collapse and the tanks plunge into the river," he recalled. "Instead, they moved forward relentlessly, getting bigger and bigger, closer and closer." He yelled to his anxious staff, "My God, they'll be here in two minutes!"

Rapping out orders to his officers, Harmel told them "to block the roads between Elst and Lent with every available antitank gun and artillery piece because if we don't, they'll roll straight through to Arnhem." Then, to his dismay he learned that the railroad bridge was also still standing. Hurrying to a radio unit in one of the nearby command posts, he contacted his advance headquarters and spoke with his operations officer. "Stolley," Harmel said, "tell Bittrich. They're over the Waal."*

Sergeant Peter Robinson's four tanks pressed on across the bridge. A second 88 had stopped firing, and Robinson "reckoned we had put it out of operation, too." Looming ahead was a roadblock of heavy concrete cubes with a gap of approximately ten feet in the middle. Robinson saw Sergeant Pacey's tank make it through and stop on the far side. Then Robinson got past and, as Pacey covered the three tanks, took the lead

---

*This is the first account of the German attempt to destroy the Nijmegen highway bridge. General Harmel had never before given an interview to anyone on

once more. Robinson remembers that "visibility was terrible. I was shouting like hell, trying to direct the gunner, the driver, and inform headquarters all at the same time. The noise was unbelievable, with all sorts of fire clanging off the girders." Three to four hundred yards ahead on the right, alongside the roadbed, Robinson saw another 88. He shouted to the gunner: "Traverse right 400 yards and fire." Guardsman Johnson blew the gun to pieces. As infantry around it began to run, Johnson opened up with his machine gun. "It was a massacre," he recalled. "I didn't even have to bother looking through the periscope. There were so many of them that I just pulled the trigger." He could feel the tank "bumping over the bodies lying in the road."

From the turret Robinson saw that his three tanks were still coming on unharmed. He radioed to them to "close up and get a move on!" The troop was now nearing the northern end of the bridge. Within seconds a self-propelled gun began to fire. "There were two big bangs in front of us," Robinson recalls. "My tin hat was blown off, but I wasn't hit." Johnson fired off three or four shells. The gun and a nearby house "burst into flame and the whole area was lit up like day." Before he realized it, Robinson's tanks were across the bridge.

He ordered the gunners to cease fire, and as the dust cleared, he caught sight of some figures in the ditch. At first he thought they were German. Then "from the shape of their helmets I knew they were Yanks. Suddenly there were Americans swarming all over the tank, hugging and kissing me, even kissing the

------

the subject. The failure of the demolition charge remains a mystery to this day. Many Dutch believe that the main crossing was saved by a young underground worker, Jan van Hoof, who had been sent into Nijmegen on the nineteenth by the 82nd's Dutch liaison officer, Captain Arie Bestebreurtje, as a guide to the paratroopers. Van Hoof is thought to have succeeded in penetrating the German lines and to have reached the bridge, where he cut cables leading to the explosives. He may well have done so. In 1949 a Dutch commission investigating the story was satisfied that Van Hoof had cut some lines, but could not confirm that these alone actually saved the bridge. The charges and transmission lines were on the Lent side of the Waal and Van Hoof's detractors maintain that it would have been impossible for him to have reached them without being detected. The controversy still rages. Although the evidence is against him, personally I would like to believe that the young Dutchman, who was shot by the Germans for his role in the underground during the battle, was indeed responsible.

tank." Captain T. Moffatt Burriss, his clothes still damp and blood-soaked from the shrapnel wound he had received during the Waal crossing, grinned up at Johnson. "You guys are the most beautiful sight I've seen in years," he said. The huge, multispanned Nijmegen crossing, together with its approaches almost a half mile long, had fallen intact. Of the Market-Garden bridges, the last but one was now in Allied hands. The time was 7:15 P.M., September 20. Arnhem lay only eleven miles away.

Lieutenant Tony Jones of the Royal Engineers—a man whom General Horrocks was later to describe as "the bravest of the brave"—had followed Robinson's troop across the bridge. Searching carefully for demolitions, Jones worked so intently that he was unaware that Germans, still on the girders, were shooting at him. In fact, he recalls, "I don't ever remember seeing any." Near the roadblock in the center of the bridge he found "six or eight wires coming over the railing and lying on the footpath." Jones promptly cut the wires. Nearby he found a dozen Teller mines neatly stacked in a slit trench. He reasoned that "they were presumably to be used to close the ten-foot gap in the roadblock, but the Germans hadn't had the time to do it." Jones removed the detonators and threw them into the river. At the bridge's northern end he found the main explosive charges in one of the piers. He was "staggered by the preparations for the German demolition job." The tin demolition boxes, painted green to match the color of the bridge, "were manufactured precisely to fit the girders they were attached to. Each had a matching serial number, and altogether they were packed with about five hundred pounds of TNT." The explosives were designed to be fired electrically and the detonators were still in place and attached to the wires Jones had just cut on the bridge. He could not understand why the Germans had not destroyed the bridge unless the sudden smashing Anglo-American drive had given them no time. With the detonators now removed and all wires cut, the bridge was safe for vehicles and tanks.

But the British armored task force that the Americans had expected would move out immediately for Arnhem did not appear.

The link-up with the British 1st Airborne at the farthest end of the corridor weighed heavily on the minds of the Americans.

Paratroopers themselves, they felt a strong kinship with the men still fighting up ahead. Cook's battalion had suffered brutally in crossing the Waal. He had lost more than half of his two companies—134 men had been killed, wounded or were missing—but the mission to capture the Nijmegen bridges from both ends and open the road north had been accomplished. Now, Cook's officers quickly pushed their units out into a perimeter defense about the northern end of the highway bridge and waited, expecting to see tanks race past them to relieve the British paratroopers up ahead. But there was no further movement over the bridge. Cook could not understand what was happening. He had expected the tanks to "go like hell" toward Arnhem before light failed.

Captain Carl Kappel, commander of H Company, whose friend Colonel John Frost was "somewhere up there," was on edge. His men had also found and cut wires on the northern end. He was certain that the bridge was safe. As he and Lieutenant La Riviere continued to watch the empty bridge, Kappel said impatiently, "Perhaps we should take a patrol and lead them over by the hand."

Second Lieutenant Ernest Murphy of Cook's battalion ran up to Sergeant Peter Robinson, whose troops had crossed the bridge, and reported to him that "we've cleared the area ahead for about a quarter of a mile. Now it's up to you guys to carry on the attack to Arnhem." Robinson wanted to go, but he had been told to "hold the road and the end of the bridge at all costs." He had no orders to move out.

Colonel Tucker, the 504th regimental commander, was fuming at the British delay. Tucker had supposed that a special task force would make a dash up the road the moment the bridge was taken and cleared of demolitions. The time to do it, he believed, "was right then, before the Germans could recover their balance." As he later wrote, "We had killed ourselves crossing the Waal to grab the north end of the bridge. We just stood there, seething, as the British settled in for the night, failing to take advantage of the situation. We couldn't understand it. It simply wasn't the way we did things in the American army—especially if it had been our guys hanging by their fingernails eleven miles away. We'd have been going, rolling without stop. That's what Georgie Patton would have done, whether it was daylight or dark."

Lieutenant A. D. Demetras overheard Tucker arguing with a major from the Guards Armored Division. "I think a most incredible decision was being made right there on the spot," he recalls. From inside a small bungalow being used as a command post, Demetras heard Tucker say angrily, "Your boys are hurting up there at Arnhem. You'd better go. It's only eleven miles." The major "told the Colonel that British armor could not proceed until infantry came up," Demetras recalls. "They were fighting the war by the book," Colonel Tucker said. "They had 'harbored' for the night. As usual, they stopped for tea."

Although his men were at less than half strength and almost out of ammunition, Tucker thought of sending the 82nd troopers north toward Arnhem on their own. Yet, he knew that General Gavin would never have approved his action. The 82nd, strung out along its section of the corridor, could not afford the manpower. But Gavin's sympathies were with his men: the British should have driven ahead. As he was later to put it, "there was no better soldier than the Corps commander, General Browning. Still, he was a theorist. Had Ridgway been in command at that moment, we would have been ordered up the road in spite of all our difficulties, to save the men at Arnhem."*

Despite their apparent casualness, the British officers—Browning, Horrocks, Dempsey and Adair—were well aware of the urgency of moving on. Yet, the problems were immense. Horrocks' corps was short of gasoline and ammunition. He saw indications that his columns might be pinched off south of Nijmegen at any moment. Fighting was still going on in the center of the city, and Major General G. I. Thomas' 43rd Wessex Division, far back in the column, had not even reached the bridge at Grave, eight miles to the south. Cautious and methodical, Thomas had not been able to keep pace with the British columns. The Germans had cut the road at several

---

*Says General Gavin, "I cannot tell you the anger and bitterness of my men. I found Tucker at dawn so irate that he was almost unable to speak. There is no soldier in the world that I admire more than the British, but British infantry leaders somehow did not understand the camaraderie of airborne troops. To our men there was only one objective: to save their brother paratroopers in Arnhem. It was tragic. I knew Tucker wanted to go, but I could never have allowed it. I had my hands full. Besides, Tucker and my other line officers did not appreciate some of the problems that the British had at that moment."

points and Thomas' men had battled fiercely to resecure it and drive back attacks. Although worried by the viciousness of the German attacks that were now pressing on both sides of the narrow corridor running to Nijmegen, General Browning believed that Thomas could have moved faster. Horrocks was not so sure. Concerned by the massive traffic jams along the road, he told General Gavin, "Jim, never try to supply a corps up just one road."

Terrain—the difficulty Montgomery had foreseen and Model had counted on—greatly influenced the tactical considerations involved in moving on from the Nijmegen bridge. It was clear to General Adair, commanding the Guards Armored Division, that the tanks had reached the worst part of the Market-Garden corridor. The dead-straight high-dike road ahead between Nijmegen and Arnhem looked like an "island." "When I saw that island my heart sank," Adair later recalled. "You can't imagine anything more unsuitable for tanks: steep banks with ditches on each side that could be easily covered by German guns." In spite of his misgivings Adair knew they would "have to have a shot at it," but he had virtually no infantry and "to get along that road was obviously first a job for infantry." Horrocks had reached the same conclusion. The tanks would have to wait until infantry could move up and pass through the Guards Armored columns. It would be almost eighteen hours before a tank attack toward Arnhem could begin.

Yet the Corps commander, like the Americans, had held out hope for a quick move up the corridor. Immediately upon the capture of the Nijmegen crossing, believing that the northern end of the Arnhem bridge was still in British hands, General Browning had informed Urquhart that tanks were across. At two minutes to midnight, still optimistic about an early start, Browning sent the following message:

> 202358 . . . intention Guards Armored Division . . . at first light to go all-out for bridges at Arnhem . . .

Some forty-five minutes later, learning of the delay in bringing up infantry, Browning sent Urquhart a third message:

> 210045 . . . tomorrow attack 1st Airborne Division will be first priority but do not expect another advance possibly before 1200 hours.

In Arnhem the "first priority" was far too late. The men of Colonel John Frost's 2nd Battalion had already been enveloped by their tragic fate. Three hours before Sergeant Robinson's troop had rattled across the great Nijmegen span, the first three tanks under Major Hans Peter Knaust's command had at last bludgeoned their way onto the Arnhem bridge.

II

IN THE AFTERNOON, as the first wave of Major Cook's paratroopers began to cross the Waal, Captain Eric Mackay gave the order to evacuate the Arnhem schoolhouse his men had held for more than sixty hours—since evening on September 17. From seventy yards away a Tiger tank fired shell after shell into the southern face of the building. "The house was burning now," Mackay remembers, "and I heard my little stock of explosives, which we had left upstairs, blow up." Of the thirteen men still able to move about, each was down to just one clip of ammunition. Hobbling about the cellar, Mackay decided that his troopers would break out, fighting to the end.

He had no intention of leaving his wounded behind. With Lieutenant Dennis Simpson leading the way, Mackay and two men acted as rear guard as the paratroopers brought their casualties up from the cellar. While Simpson covered them, the injured were moved into a side garden. "Then just as Simpson moved toward the next house a mortar bombardment began and I heard him shout, 'Six more wounded.' I knew," Mackay recalls, "that we would be massacred—or the wounded would, at any rate—if we tried to escape with them. I yelled to Simpson to surrender."

Collecting the remaining five men, each armed with a Bren gun, Mackay headed east—the one direction, he believed, the Germans would not expect him to take. His plan was to "lay low for the night and try to make our way back west to join the main force." Mackay led his men across the road, through ruined houses on the opposite side and onto the next street. There, they came face to face with two tanks accompanied by fifty or sixty soldiers. Quickly moving line abreast, the six paratroopers riddled the mass of startled Germans. "We had time for only a single magazine apiece," Mackay recalls. "It was all over in two or three seconds. The Germans just dropped like half-filled sacks of grain." As Mackay shouted to his group to head for a nearby house, another man was killed and a second wounded. Reaching temporary shelter, Mackay told the three remaining men, "This fight is over." He suggested the troopers move out individually. "With luck," he said, "we might all meet together again by the bridge tonight."

One by one the men left. Ducking into a garden, Mackay crawled under a rose bush. There he took off his badges of rank and threw them away. "I figured I would sleep a bit," he recalls. "I had just shut my eyes and reached that drowsy stage when I heard German voices. I tried to breathe more softly and, with my charred and bloody clothes, I thought I might look convincingly dead." Suddenly he received "a terrific kick in the ribs." He took it limply, "like a newly dead corpse." Then he "felt a bayonet go into my buttocks and lodge with a jar against my pelvis." Strangely, Mackay recalls, "it didn't hurt, just shocked me a bit when it hit the pelvis. It was when the bayonet came out that I felt the pain." It triggered Mackay's anger. Pulling himself to his feet, he drew his Colt. "What the bloody hell do you mean stabbing a bayonet into a British officer?" he yelled. Unprepared for Mackay's outburst, the Germans drew back and Mackay realized that he could have "shot some of them if I had had any bullets. They couldn't shoot back," he remembers, "because they were ringed all around me. They would have hit one of their own. Their situation was so funny I laughed." As the Germans stared at him, Mackay contemptuously threw his Colt over a garden wall "so they couldn't get it as a souvenir."

Forcing Mackay to lean against a wall, the Germans began to search him. His watch and an empty silver flask that had been his father's were taken from him, but an escape map in his breast pocket was overlooked. An officer returned the flask. When Mackay asked about his watch he was told, "You won't need it where you're going, and we're rather short on watches." Hands above his head, he was marched off to a building where other British prisoners of war were being held. Going from group to group Mackay reminded the men that it was their duty to escape. Suddenly Mackay, the only officer present, was taken into another room for interrogation. "I decided to go on the offensive," he recalls. "There was a German lieutenant who spoke perfect English, and I told him, firmly but politely, that it was all over for the Germans and I was quite prepared to take their surrender." The lieutenant stared at him in amazement but, Mackay remembers, "that was the end of the interrogation."

Shortly before dusk the prisoners were herded out to trucks, which took them east toward Germany. "They got a guard on the back, which made it harder to try to get away," Mackay says, "but I told the lads to scrunch up and crowd him so he couldn't use his gun." As the truck in which he was riding slowed down at a bend in the road, Mackay jumped off and tried to make his escape. "Unfortunately I had chosen the worst possible place," he recalls. "I dropped within three feet of a sentry. I jumped him and was trying to break his neck. Others arrived just then and they beat me senseless." When he came to, Mackay found himself crowded with other prisoners into a room in a small Dutch inn. He managed to drag himself up to a sitting position against a wall and then, for the first time in ninety hours, the young officer fell sound asleep.*

In the dusk around Colonel Frost's headquarters' building and alongside the ramp, nearly a hundred men in small groups were still fighting fiercely to hang on. The headquarters roof was burning and nearly every man was down to his last few rounds of ammunition. Yet the troopers seemed spirited as ever. Major Freddie Gough believed that "even now, if we could just hold out a few hours longer, we would be relieved."

At around 7 P.M. the 2nd Battalion's wounded commander awoke, annoyed to find that he had slept at all. Frost heard "the gibbering of some shell-shock cases" in the darkness of the cellar. The Germans were still pounding the building and Frost became aware that the heat in the cellar, now filled with over two hundred casualties, was intense. Attempting to move, he felt a shock of pain run through his legs. He asked that

---

*The following day Mackay and three others escaped from the German town of Emmerich. One of the men with him was Lieutenant Dennis Simpson, who had led the breakout of the little group from the schoolhouse. The four men made their way across country and reached the Rhine. In a stolen boat they paddled all the way down to the Allied lines at Nijmegen.

Gough be sent to him. "You'll have to take over," Frost told
the major, "but don't make any crucial decisions without first
referring them to me." By now Frost was becoming aware that
what he had most feared had begun to happen: the building
was burning down and the wounded were in danger "of being roasted alive." All over the dark room men were coughing
from the acrid smoke. Dr. James Logan, the battalion's chief
medical officer, knelt down beside Frost. The time had come,
Logan said, to get the casualties out. "We've got to arrange a
truce with the Germans, sir," Logan insisted. "We can't wait
any longer." Turning to Gough, Frost ordered him to make
the arrangements, "but to get the fighting soldiers to other
buildings and carry on. I felt that even though the bridge was
lost we could still control the approach for a time, perhaps
enough time for our tanks to come."

Gough and Logan left to make arrangements for the truce.
Logan proposed to unbolt the heavy front doors of the building and go out under a Red Cross flag. Gough was skeptical of
the idea. He did not trust the SS; they might well open fire in
spite of the flag. Going back to Frost, Logan received permission to proceed. As the doctor headed toward the doors, Frost
removed his badges of rank. He hoped to "fade into the ranks
and possibly get away later." Wicks, his batman, went in search
of a stretcher.

Nearby, Private James Sims, one of the wounded, glumly
heard the evacuation plans being made. Logically he knew
there was no alternative. "Our position was obviously hopeless," he recalls. "Ammunition was all but exhausted, nearly all
the officers and NCO's were dead or wounded, and the building was well alight; the smoke was nearly choking everyone."
He heard Frost tell the able-bodied and the walking wounded
"to get out and make a run for it." Sims knew it was "the only
sensible course, but the news that we were to be left behind
was not well received."

Upstairs Doctor Logan unlocked the front door. Accompanied by two orderlies and carrying a Red Cross flag, Logan
walked out to meet the Germans. The noise of battle halted. "I
saw some Germans run around to the back where we had our
jeeps and carriers parked," Gough remembers. "They needed
them to move the wounded, and I mentally waved goodbye to
our remaining transport forever."

In the cellar men heard German voices in the passageways and Sims noticed "the heavy thud of German jackboots on the stairway." The cellar was suddenly quiet. Looking up Sims saw a German officer appear in the doorway. To his horror, "a badly wounded paratrooper brought up his Sten gun, but he was quickly overpowered. The officer," Sims remembers, "took stock of the situation and rapped out some orders. German soldiers filed in and began carrying the wounded upstairs." They were almost too late. As Sims was being moved, "a huge piece of burning timber nearly fell on top of us." He was acutely aware that the Germans were "nervous, decidedly trigger-happy, and a lot of them were armed with British rifles and Sten guns."

With the help of a shell-shocked paratrooper, Frost was carried up and laid on the embankment beside the bridge he had so desperately tried to hold. All about him he saw buildings burning fiercely. He watched as Germans and British together "worked at top speed to get us out, while the whole scene was brilliantly lit by the flames." Only minutes after the last casualty was carried up, there was a sudden roar and the building collapsed into a heap of fiery rubble. Turning to Major Douglas Crawley, lying on a stretcher beside him, Frost said tiredly, "Well, Doug, we didn't get away with it this time, did we?" Crawley shook his head. "No, sir," he said, "but we gave them a damn good run for their money."

As the British wounded watched in wary surprise, the Germans moved among them with extraordinary camaraderie, handing out cigarettes, chocolate and brandy. Bitterly, the paratroopers noticed that most of the supplies were their own, obviously collected from resupply drops that had fallen into German hands. As the hungry, thirsty men began to eat, German soldiers knelt beside them, congratulating them on the battle. Private Sims stared at a line of Mark IV tanks stretching back along the road. Seeing his expression a German nodded. "Yes, Tommy," he told Sims, "those were for you in the morning if you had not surrendered."

But Frost's stubborn able-bodied men had not given up. As the last wounded man was brought out of the cellar the battle began again, as intensely as an hour before. "It was a nightmare," Gough recalls. "Everywhere you turned there were Germans—in front, in back and on the sides. They had managed to infiltrate a large force into the area during the truce. They now held practically every house. We were literally overrun."

Gough ordered troopers to disperse and hide out for the night. At dawn he hoped to concentrate the force in a group of half-gutted buildings by the river bank. Even now he expected relief by morning, and "I thought that somehow we could hold till then." As the men moved off into the darkness, Gough crouched down beside his radio. Bringing the microphone close to his mouth, he said, "This is the First Para Brigade. We cannot hold out much longer. Our position is desperate. Please hurry. Please hurry."

The Germans knew the fight was over. All that now remained was a mopping-up operation. Ironically, although there were tanks on the bridge, they could not cross. As General Harmel had predicted, the massed wreckage would take hours to remove. Not until early Thursday, September 21, would a single pathway be finally cleared and movement across the bridge begin.

At first light on Thursday Gough and the scattered men remaining in the perimeter emerged from their hiding places. Relief had not come. Systematically the Germans overran positions, forcing men now out of ammunition to surrender. By ones and twos, survivors, undetected, scattered to attempt to make their escape. Slowly, defiantly, the last British resistance came to an end.

Major Gough had headed for the waterworks, hoping to hide and rest for a time and then attempt to make his way west toward the main body of troops under Urquhart's command. Just outside the waterworks building he heard German voices. Sprinting for a pile of wood, Gough tried to burrow under it. The heel of his boot protruded and a German grasped it and pulled Gough out. "I was so damn tired I just looked up at them and laughed," Gough says. Hands over his head, he was led away.

In a roomful of other prisoners a German major sent for Gough. He gave the British officer a Hitler salute. "I understand you are in command," the German said. Gough looked at him warily. "Yes," he said. "I wish to congratulate you and your men," the German told him. "You are gallant soldiers. I fought at Stalingrad and it is obvious that you British have

had a great deal of experience in street fighting." Gough stared
at the enemy officer. "No," he said. "This was our first effort.
We'll be much better next time."

At some moment during these last hours one final message
was radioed from someone near the bridge. It was not picked
up by either Urquhart's headquarters or by the British Second Army, but at the 9th SS Hohenstaufen headquarters Lieutenant Colonel Harzer's listening monitors heard it clearly.
Years later Harzer could not recall the complete message, but
he was struck by the last two sentences: "Out of ammunition.
God Save the King."

A few miles to the north near Apeldoorn, Private James
Sims lay on the grass outside a German military hospital, surrounded by other wounded paratroopers awaiting processing
and treatment. The men were quiet, drawn into themselves.
"The thought that we had fought for nothing was a natural
one," Sims wrote, "but I couldn't help but think about the
main army, so strong, and yet unable to make those last few
miles to us. The hardest thing to bear was the feeling that we
had just been written off."

12

AT EXACTLY 10:40 A.M. ON THURSDAY, September 21, Captain Roland Langton of the Irish Guards was told that his
Number 1 Squadron was to dash out of the newly acquired
Nijmegen bridgehead and make for Arnhem. H Hour, he was
informed by Lieutenant Colonel Joe Vandeleur, would be 11
A.M. Langton was incredulous. He thought Vandeleur must
be joking. He was being given just twenty minutes to brief his
squadron and prepare them for a major attack. Langton, himself, was quickly briefed on a captured map. "The only other
one we had was a road map devoid of details," he says. Information about enemy gun positions was contained in a single reconnaissance photo showing an antiaircraft site between
the villages of Lent and Elst, and "the supposition was that it
might no longer be there."

In Langton's view, everything about the plan was wrong—in
particular, the fact that "they were actually going to launch
this thing in twenty minutes." His squadron was to strike out
with a second unit coming up behind. Two tanks would carry

infantry; and more troops, Langton was told, would follow. Yet he could expect little artillery support, and the Typhoon "cab rank" air cover, used so successfully in the initial breakout, would not be immediately available: in Belgium the Typhoons were grounded by weather. Nevertheless, Langton was instructed "to go like hell and get on up to Arnhem."

Although he did not betray his feelings to Langton, Joe Vandeleur was pessimistic about the outcome of the attack. Earlier, he and others, including his cousin Lieutenant Colonel Giles Vandeleur, had crossed the Nijmegen bridge to study the elevated "island" highway running due north to Arnhem. To these officers the road seemed ominous. Joe Vandeleur's second in command, Major Desmond FitzGerald, was the first to speak. "Sir," he said, "we're not going to get a yard up this bloody road." Giles Vandeleur agreed. "It's a ridiculous place to try to operate tanks." Up to this point in the corridor advance, although vehicles had moved on a one-tank front, it had always been possible when necessary to maneuver off the main road. "Here," Giles Vandeleur recalls, "there was no possibility of getting off the road. A dike embankment with a highway running along its top is excellent for defense but it's hardly the place for tanks." Turning to the others, Giles said, "I can just imagine the Germans sitting there, rubbing their hands with glee, as they see us coming." Joe Vandeleur stared silently at the scene. Then he said, "Nevertheless, we've got to try. We've got to chance that bloody road." As Giles remembers, "Our advance was based on a time program. We were to proceed at a speed of fifteen miles in two hours." Brigadier Gwatkin, the Guards Armored chief of staff, had told them tersely, "Simply get through."

At exactly 11 A.M., Captain Langton picked up the microphone in his scout car and radioed: "Go! Go! Go! Don't stop for anything!" His tanks rumbled past the Lent post office and up the main road. Fatalistically, Langton thought, It is now or never. After fifteen or twenty minutes, he began to breathe easier. There was no enemy action, and Langton felt "a little ashamed for being so upset earlier. I began to wonder what I was going to do when I reached the Arnhem bridge. I hadn't really thought about it before."

Behind the lead tanks came the Vandeleurs in their scout

car and, back of them, Flight Lieutenant Donald Love in his
R.A.F. ground-to-air communications tender. With him once
more was Squadron Leader Max Sutherland, quiet and anxious.
As he climbed aboard the white armored scout car, Sutherland
—who had directed the Typhoon strike at the breakout from
the Meuse-Escaut Canal—told Love that "the airborne boys
in Arnhem are in deep trouble and desperate for help." Love
scanned the skies looking for the Typhoons. He was sure they
would need them. Remembering the horrors of the breakout,
Love "wasn't at all anxious to find himself in a similar position
to the one I had been in the previous Sunday, when the Germans had stopped us cold."

The tanks of the Irish Guards moved steadily forward, passing the village of Oosterhout off to the left and the hamlets of
Ressen and Bemmel on the right. From his scout car Captain
Langton could hear Lieutenant Tony Samuelson, troop commander of the lead tanks, announce the locations. Samuelson
called out that the first tank was approaching the outskirts of
Elst. The Irish were approximately halfway to Arnhem. As he
listened Langton realized that "we were out on our own."
But tension was relaxing throughout the column. Flight Lieutenant Love heard a droning in the sky and saw the first Typhoons appear. The weather had cleared in Belgium, and now
the squadrons came into view, one at a time. As they began
to circle overhead, Love and Sutherland settled back relieved.

In his scout car, Captain Langton was examining his map.
The entire column had passed the secondary Bemmel turning,
off to the right. At that moment, Langton heard a violent explosion. Looking up, he saw "a Sherman sprocket wheel lift
lazily into the air over some trees up ahead." He knew immediately that one of the lead tanks had been hit. Lieutenant Samuelson, much farther up the road, quickly confirmed the fact.

In the distance guns began to bark and black smoke boiled
up into the sky. Far down the line Lieutenant Rupert Mahaffey
knew that something had gone wrong. Abruptly the column
halted. There was confusion as to what had happened, and
voices on the radio became distorted and jumbled as the battle
was joined. "There seemed to be a great deal of shouting," Giles
Vandeleur remembers, "and I told Joe I had better go forward
and see what the hell was happening." The commander of the

Irish Guards agreed. "Let me know as quickly as you can," he told Giles.

Captain Langton was already on his way forward. Inching by the standing armor, Langton came to a bend in the road. Ahead he saw that all four lead tanks, including Samuelson's, had been knocked out and some were ablaze. The shells were coming from a self-propelled gun in the woods to the left, near Elst. Langton ordered his driver to pull into a yard of a house near the bend. A few minutes later Giles Vandeleur joined him. Immediately machine-gun fire forced the men to take cover. Vandeleur was unable to get back to his armored car and report to his cousin Joe. Each time he called out to his driver, Corporal Goldman, to back up the vehicle—a Humber with a top hatch and a door at the side—"Goldman would lift the lid and the Germans would pour a burst of fire over his head, causing him to slam it shut again." Finally, exasperated, Giles crawled back along a ditch to Joe's command car.

Joe Vandeleur was already rapping out orders. Over the radio he called for artillery support; then, seeing the Typhoons overhead, he ordered Love to call them in. In the R.A.F. car Sutherland picked up the microphone. "This is Winecup . . . Winecup . . ." he said. "Come in please." The Typhoons continued to circle overhead. Desperate, Sutherland called again. "This is Winecup . . . Winecup . . . Come in." There was no response. Sutherland and Love stared at each other. "The set was dead," Love says. "We were getting no signal whatsoever. The Typhoons were milling around above us and, on the ground, shelling was going on. It was the most hopeless, frustrating thing I have ever lived through, watching them up there and not being able to do a damn thing about it." Love knew the pilots of the slowly wheeling Typhoons "had instructions not to attack anything on speculation." By now Giles Vandeleur had reached his cousin. "Joe," he said, "if we send any more tanks up along this road it's going to be a bloody murder." Together the two men set out for Captain Langton's position.

Now the infantry of the Irish Guards were off their tanks and moving up into orchards on both sides of the road. Langton had taken over one of the tanks. Unable to find cover or move off the road, he was maneuvering backward and forward, trying to fire at the self-propelled gun in the woods. Each time he fired a round, "the gun responded with five of its own."

The infantry captain, whose troops were also after the same target but were now huddling in a ditch, was livid with rage. "What the bloody hell do you think you're doing?" he yelled at Langton. The young officer stayed calm. "I'm trying to knock out a gun so we can get to Arnhem," he said.

As the Vandeleurs appeared, Langton, unsuccessful in his attempts to knock out the gun, climbed out to meet them. "It was a mess up there," Joe Vandeleur remembers. "We tried everything. There was no way to move the tanks off the road and down the steep sides of that damn dike. The only artillery support I could get was from one field battery, and it was too slow registering on its targets." His lone infantry company was pinned down and he was unable to call in the Typhoons. "Surely we can get support somewhere," Langton said. Vandeleur slowly shook his head, "I'm afraid not." Langton persisted. "We could get there," he pleaded. "We can go if we get support." Vandeleur shook his head again. "I'm sorry," he said. "You stay where you are until you get further orders."

To Vandeleur it was clear that the attack could not be resumed until the infantry of Major General G. I. Thomas' 43rd Wessex Division could reach the Irish Guards. Until then, Vandeleur's tanks were stranded alone on the high exposed road. A single self-propelled gun trained on the elevated highway had effectively stopped the entire relief column almost exactly six miles from Arnhem.

Farther back in the line of tanks, opposite a greenhouse near Elst, whose windows had miraculously remained almost wholly intact, Lieutenant John Gorman stared angrily up the road. Ever since the column had been halted at Valkenswaard far down the corridor, Gorman had felt driven to move faster. "We had come all the way from Normandy, taken Brussels, fought halfway through Holland and crossed the Nijmegen bridge," he said. "Arnhem and those paratroopers were just up ahead and, almost within sight of that last bloody bridge, we were stopped. I never felt such morbid despair."

PART FIVE

DER HEXENKESSEL
[The Witches' Cauldron]

"MONTY'S TANKS ARE ON THE WAY!" All along the shrunken Oosterbeek perimeter—from slit trenches, houses now turned into strong points, crossroads positions, and in woods and fields—grimy, ashen-faced men cheered and passed the news along. To them, it seemed the long, isolated ordeal was coming to its end. General Urquhart's Rhine bridgehead had become a fingertip-shaped spot on the map. Now in an area barely two miles long, one and a half miles wide at its center, and one mile along its base on the Rhine, the Red Devils were surrounded and were being attacked and slowly annihilated from three sides. Water, medical supplies, food and ammunition were lacking or dwindling away. As a division the British 1st Airborne had virtually ceased to exist. Now men were once again heartened by the hope of relief. Now, too, a storm of fire roared overhead as British medium and heavy guns eleven miles south across the Rhine lashed the Germans only a few hundred yards from Urquhart's front lines.

By signal, General Browning had promised Urquhart that the batteries of XXX Corps's 64th Medium Regiment would be in range by Thursday and regiment artillery officers had asked for targets in order of priority. Without regard for their own safety, Urquhart's steely veterans had quickly complied. In good radio contact for the first time, via the 64th's communications net, the Red Devils savagely called down artillery fire almost on top of their own positions. The accuracy of the fire was heartening, its effect on the Germans unnerving. Again and again British guns broke up heavy tank attacks that threatened to swamp the bearded, tattered paratroopers.

Even with this welcome relief, Urquhart knew that a massed coordinated German attack could wipe out his minuscule force. Yet now the men believed there was a modicum of hope —a chance to snatch victory at the eleventh hour. On this Thursday, the outlook was slightly brighter. Urquhart had limited communications and a link by way of the 64th's artillery support. The Nijmegen bridge was safe and open; the tanks of the Guards Armored were on the way; and, if the weather held, 1,500 fresh paratroopers of General Sosabowski's Polish

1st Brigade would land by late afternoon. If the Poles could be ferried quickly across the Rhine between Driel and Heveadorp, the bleak picture could well change.

Yet, if Urquhart was to hold, supplies were as urgent as the arrival of Sosabowski's men. On the previous day, out of a total of 300 tons, R.A.F. bombers had delivered only 41 to the Hartenstein zone. Until antitank guns and artillery arrived in number, close-in air support was critically important. Lacking ground-to-air communications—the special American ultra-high-frequency equipment, rushed to the British only hours before takeoff on D Day, the seventeenth, had been set to the wrong wavelength and was useless—division officers were forced to acknowledge that the R.A.F. seemed unprepared to abandon caution and make the kind of daring forays the airborne men knew to be essential and were prepared to risk. Urquhart had sent a continual stream of messages to Browning, urging fighters and fighter-bombers to attack "targets of opportunity" without regard to the Red Devils' own positions. It was the airborne way of operating; it was not the R.A.F.'s. Even at this critical stage, pilots insisted that enemy targets be pinpointed with near-cartographic accuracy—an utter impossibility for the beleaguered paratroopers pinned down in their diminishing airhead. Not a single low-level air attack had been made, yet every road, field and woods around the perimeter and spreading east to Arnhem held enemy vehicles or positions.

Lacking the air strikes they so desperately urged, hemmed into the perimeter, suffering almost constant mortar bombardment and, in places, fighting hand-to-hand, the Red Devils placed their hopes on the Guards' columns, which they believed were rolling toward them. Urquhart was less optimistic. Outnumbered at least four to one, pounded by artillery and tanks, and with steadily mounting casualties, Urquhart knew that only a mammoth, all-out effort could save his fragmented division. Keenly aware that the Germans could steam-roller his pathetically small force, the dogged, courageous Scot kept his own lonely counsel even as he told his staff, "We must hold the bridgehead at all costs."

The perimeter defenses were now divided into two commands. Brigadier Pip Hicks held the western side; Brigadier

Shan Hackett was to the east. Hicks's western arm was manned by soldiers from the Glider Pilot Regiment, Royal Engineers, remnants of the Border Regiment, some Poles and a polyglot collection of other troopers from various units. To the east were the survivors of Hackett's 10th and 156th battalions, more glider pilots and the 1st Airlanding Light Regiment, R.A. Curving up from these prime defenses the northern shoulders (close to the Wolfheze railroad line) were held by men of Major Boy Wilson's 21st Independent Parachute Company—the pathfinders who had led the way—and by Lieutenant Colonel R. Payton-Reid's 7th King's Own Scottish Borderers. Along the southern base, stretching roughly from east of the medieval church in lower Oosterbeek to the heights at Westerbouwing on the west, Hackett commanded additional elements of the Border Regiment and a miscellaneous group composed of the remains of the South Staffordshires, the 1st, 3rd and 11th battalions and a variety of service troops under the twice-wounded Major Dickie Lonsdale—the "Lonsdale Force." In the heart of that area was Lieutenant Colonel Sheriff Thompson's main force, the hard-pressed artillerymen whose batteries sought continually to serve the tight defense line and whose precious supply of ammunition was dwindling fast.*

On neat after-action report maps, each unit has its carefully inked-in place; but survivors would recall years later that there was really no perimeter, no front line, no distinction between

---

*The consolidation of the southeastern end of the perimeter owed much to the quick thinking of Colonel Sheriff Thompson who, in the confusion of battle when men retreating from Arnhem on September 19 found themselves leaderless, quickly organized them in defense of the last piece of high ground before his gun positions. These forces, together with others who had earlier become separated from their units—some 150 glider pilots and his own artillery men, about 800 in all—were known as the "Thompson Force." Subsequently augmented, they were placed under the command of Major Lonsdale. They withdrew late on September 20 and were deployed by Thompson about his gun positions. Owing to command changes and the general situation, some confusion has continued to exist regarding these events, but immediately before Thompson was wounded on September 21 all infantry in the gun area came under the command of what was later to be known as the "Lonsdale Force." The glider pilots remained under the command of the 1st Airlanding Brigade.

units, no fighting as integrated groups. There were only shocked, bandaged, bloodstained men, running to fill gaps wherever and whenever they occurred. As Brigadier Hicks visited his exhausted men, tenaciously defending their sectors of the bridgehead, he knew "it was the beginning of the end, and I think we were all aware of it, although we tried to keep a reasonable face."

Unaware that Frost's gallant stand at the bridge had ended —although Lieutenant Colonel Sheriff Thompson suspected it had when his artillery radio link with Major Dennis Munford abruptly closed down—Urquhart could only place his hope in the Guards tanks' reaching the remnants of the 2nd Battalion in time.* That single bridge spanning the Rhine—the Reich's last natural defense line—had been the principal objective all along, Montgomery's springboard to a quick ending of the war. Without it, the 1st Airborne's predicament and, in particular, the suffering of Frost's brave men, would be for nothing. As Urquhart had told Frost and Gough, there was nothing more that he could do for them. Their help must come from the speed and armored strength of XXX Corps.

For Urquhart now the immediate priority was to get Sosabowski's Poles across the river and into the perimeter as quickly as they landed. The cable ferry was particularly suited to the operation. Urquhart's engineers had signaled Corps headquarters that it was "a class-24 type and capable of carrying three tanks." Although Urquhart was worried about the heights of Westerbouwing and the possibility of German artillery controlling the ferry crossing from there, as yet no enemy troops had reached the area. With so few men to hold the perimeter, only a single platoon of the 1st Borderers had been detached to defend the position. In fact, the heights were unguarded by either side. Major Charles Osborne's D Company of the Border

---

*Munford destroyed his wireless set shortly after dawn on Thursday as the Germans began rounding up the few men still attempting to hang on. "Enemy tanks and infantry were right up to the bridge," Munford recalls. "I helped carry some more wounded to a collecting point and then I bashed in the set. There was nothing more that Colonel Thompson could do for us and everybody who could wanted to get back to the division at Oosterbeek." Munford was captured on the outskirts of Arnhem as he tried to reach the British lines.

Regiment had been given the assignment soon after landing on Sunday but, Osborne says, "we never did hold Westerbouwing. I was sent on a reconnaissance patrol to lay out battalion positions. However, by the time I'd done this and returned to headquarters, plans had changed." By Thursday, Osborne's men "were moved rather piecemeal into a position near the Hartenstein Hotel." No one was on the vital heights.

On Wednesday engineers had sent reconnaissance patrols down to the Rhine to report back on the ferry, the depth, condition of the banks and speed of the current. Sapper Tom Hicks thought the survey was to "aid the Second Army when it tried bridging the river." Along with three other sappers and a Dutch guide, Hicks had crossed the Rhine on the ferry. Pieter, he saw, "operated it with a cable that the old man wound in by hand and it seemed that the current helped work it across." Tying a grenade to a length of parachute rigging and knotting the cord every foot along its length, Hicks took soundings and measured the current. On Wednesday night, after the Poles' drop zone had been changed to Driel, another patrol was sent to the ferry site. "It was a volunteer job," recalls Private Robert Edwards of the South Staffordshires. "We were to go down to the river at Heveadorp, find the ferry and stay there to protect it."

In darkness a sergeant, a corporal, six privates and four glider pilots set out. "Mortar bombs and shells were falling heavily as we plunged into the thickly wooded country between us and Heveadorp," says Edwards. Several times the group was fired on, and a glider pilot was wounded. Reaching the riverbank at the site marked on their maps, the patrol found no sign of the ferry. It had completely disappeared. Although the possibility remained that the craft was moored on the southern bank, the patrol had been told they would find it on their own side. Immediately the men spread out, searching along a quarter-mile strip on either side of the ferry's northern landing stage. The hunt was fruitless. Pieter's ferry could not be found. As Edwards remembers, the sergeant in charge of the patrol reached the conclusion that the boat had either been sunk or simply never existed. At first light the men gave up the search and began their dangerous journey back.

Only minutes later heavy machine-gun fire wounded three more of the patrol and the group was pulled back to the river. There the sergeant decided the men would have a better chance of getting back by splitting up. Edwards left with the corporal and two of the glider pilots. After "minor encounters and brushes with the Germans," his group reached the church in lower Oosterbeek just as a mortar burst landed. Edwards was thrown to the ground, both legs filled with "tiny pieces of shrapnel and my boots full of blood." In the house next to the church an orderly dressed his wounds and told the injured private to take a rest. "He didn't say where, though," Edwards recalls, "and every inch of space in the house was packed with badly wounded. The stench of wounds and death was something awful." He decided to leave and head for company headquarters, located in a laundry, "in order to find somebody to make my report to. I told an officer about the ferry and then I got into a weapons' pit with a glider pilot. I don't know if the others made it back or what happened to the men who got to the church with me."

Sometime later General Urquhart, still ignorant of Frost's fate, signaled Browning:

> Enemy attacking main bridge in strength. Situation critical for slender force. Enemy attacking east from Heelsum and west from Arnhem. Situation serious but am forming close perimeter around Hartenstein with remainder of division. Relief essential both areas earliest possible. Still maintain control ferry point at Heveadorp.

Even as the message was being sent via the 64th Medium Regiment's communications net, Division headquarters learned that the ferry had not been found. Urquhart's officers believed the Germans had sunk it. But Pieter's ferry was still afloat. Presumably artillery fire had cut its moorings. Far too late to be of use, it was eventually found by Dutch civilians near the demolished railroad bridge about a mile away, washed up but still intact. "If we had been able to search a few hundred yards closer to Oosterbeek, we would have found it," Edwards says.

As Urquhart returned to his headquarters on Thursday morning after an inspection of the Hartenstein defenses, he heard the crushing news. With the Poles' drop only hours away, his only quick way of reinforcing the perimeter with Sosabowski's men was gone.*

Looking down from a window in the lead Dakota, as the long columns of planes carrying the Polish 1st Parachute Brigade headed for the drop zone at Driel, Major General Stanislaw Sosabowski "learned the real truth, and what I had suspected all along." From Eindhoven, where the formations turned north, he saw "hundreds of vehicles below in chaotic traffic jams all along the corridor." Smoke churned up from the road. At various points along the highway enemy shells were landing, trucks and vehicles were ablaze, and "everywhere wreckage was piled up on the sides." Yet, somehow, the convoys were still moving. Then, beyond Nijmegen, movement stopped. Through low clouds off to his right, Sosabowski could see the "island" road and the clogged, halted tanks on it. Enemy fire was falling on the head of the column. Moments later, as the planes banked toward Driel, the Arnhem bridge loomed into view. Tanks were crossing over it, driving north to south, and Sosabowski realized they were German. Shocked and stunned, he knew now that the British had lost the bridge.

On Wednesday night, agitated by the lack of information regarding Urquhart's situation, and "as I had visions of being court-martialed by my own government," Sosabowski had thrown caution to the winds. He demanded to see General Brereton, the First Allied Airborne Army commander. To Colonel George Stevens, the liaison officer with the Polish Brigade, Sosabowski had emotionally insisted that unless he was "given

---

*The true account of the ferry appears here for the first time. Even official histories state that it was sunk. Other versions imply that, to prevent its use, the Germans either destroyed the ferry with artillery fire or moved it to another location under their control. There is no reference in any German war diary, log, or after-action report to sustain these conjectures. Interviewing German officers—such as Bittrich, Harzer, Harmel and Krafft—I found that none of them could recall ordering any such action. Assuming that the Germans wanted to seize the ferry, I believe they would have encountered the same difficulties in locating it that Edwards reported. In any case, no German officer remembers ordering the cable cut in order to prevent the British from using it.

Urquhart's exact situation around Arnhem, the Polish Parachute Brigade will not take off." Startled, Stevens had rushed off to First Allied Airborne headquarters with Sosabowski's ultimatum. At 7 A.M. on Thursday morning, he returned with news from Brereton. There was confusion, Stevens admitted, but the attack was going as planned; the drop zone at Driel had not been changed and "the Heveadorp ferry was in British hands." Sosabowski was mollified. Now, looking down on the panorama of battle, he realized he "knew more than Brereton." Enraged as he saw what was obviously German armor about Oosterbeek and ahead a hail of antiaircraft fire coming up to greet his men, Sosabowski believed his brigade was "being sacrificed in a complete British disaster." Moments later he was out the door, falling through weaving curtains of antiaircraft fire. The time, the precise fifty-year-old general noted, was exactly 5:08 P.M.

As Sosabowski had feared, the Poles jumped into a holocaust. As before, the Germans were waiting. They had tracked and timed the formations from Dunkirk on and now, with far more reinforcements than before, the area bristled with antiaircraft guns. As the transports approached, twenty-five Messerschmitts suddenly appeared and, diving out of the clouds, raked the approaching planes.

As he fell through the air Sosabowski saw one Dakota, both engines flaming, fall toward the ground. Corporal Alexander Kochalski saw another go down. Only a dozen paratroopers escaped before it crashed and burned. First Lieutenant Stefan Kaczmarek prayed as he hung below his chute. He saw so many tracer bullets that "every gun on the ground seemed to be aimed at me." Corporal Wladijslaw Korob, his parachute full of holes, landed alongside a fellow Pole who had been decapitated.

In the Oosterbeek perimeter the Polish drop, barely two and one-half miles away, caused a momentary halt in the battle. Every German gun seemed to be concentrating on the swaying, defenseless men. "It was as if all the enemy guns lifted together and let fly simultaneously," Gunner Robert Christie noted. The reprieve from the constant shelling was too precious to waste: men quickly took the opportunity to move jeeps and equipment, dig new gun pits, bring up spare ammunition, rearrange camouflage nets and toss empty shell cases out of crowded slit trenches.

Six miles away on the elevated "island" road, Captain Roland Langton, whose lead tank squadron had been halted en route to Arnhem some six hours previously, watched the drop in agony. It was the most horrible sight he had ever seen. German planes dived at the defenseless Polish transports, "blasting them out of the air." Parachutists tried to get out of burning aircraft, "some of which had nosed over and were diving to the ground." Bodies of men "tumbled through the air, inert forms drifting slowly down, dead before they hit the ground." Langton was close to tears. "Where the hell is the air support?" he wondered. "We were told in the afternoon we couldn't have any for our attack toward Arnhem, because all available air effort had to go for the Poles. Where was it now? The weather? Nonsense. The Germans flew; why couldn't we?" Langton had never felt so frustrated. With all his heart, he knew that with air support his tanks "could have got through to those poor bastards at Arnhem." In anxiety and desperation he suddenly found himself violently sick.

Though they were shocked by the savagery of the combined air and antiaircraft assault, most of the Polish Brigade miraculously made the drop zone. Even as they landed, flak and high-explosive mortar shells—fired from tanks and antiaircraft guns along the Nijmegen-Arnhem elevated highway and by batteries north of Driel—burst among them, and Sosabowski saw that even machine guns seemed to be ranged in on the entire area. Hammered in the air and caught in a deadly crossfire on the ground, the men now had to fight their way off the drop zones. Sosabowski landed near a canal. As he ran for cover he came across the body of one trooper. "He lay on the grass, stretched out as if on a cross," Sosabowski later wrote. "A bullet or piece of shrapnel had neatly sliced off the top of his head. I wondered how many more of my men would I see like this before the battle was over and whether their sacrifice would be worthwhile."*

* Stanislaw Sosabowski, *Freely I Served*, p. 124.

Aghast at the fierce German reception, the entire population of Driel was engulfed by the paratroop drop. Polish troopers came down all about the hamlet, landing in orchards, irrigation canals, on the top of the dikes, on the polder and in the village itself. Some men fell into the Rhine and, unable to shed their parachutes, were swept away and drowned. Disregarding the shell and machine-gun fire all about them, the Dutch ran to help the ill-fated Poles. Among them, as a member of a Red Cross team, was Cora Baltussen.

The landing, centered on drop zones less than two miles south of Driel, had come as a complete surprise to the villagers. No pathfinders had been used, and the Dutch underground was ignorant of the plan. Riding a bicycle with wooden tires, Cora Baltussen headed south on a narrow dike road toward a place known as Honingsveld, where many of the paratroopers appeared to have landed. Shocked and terrified, she did not see how anyone could have lived through the German fire. She expected enormous numbers of casualties. To her surprise, Cora saw men, under attack, forming up and running in groups toward the safety of dike embankments. She could hardly believe so many were still alive but "at last," she thought, "the Tommies have arrived in Driel."

She had not spoken English in years, but Cora was the only inhabitant of Driel familiar with the language. While her services as a trained Red Cross nurse would be required, Cora also hoped to act as an interpreter. Hurrying forward, she saw men waving wildly at her, obviously "warning me to get off the road because of the fire." But in her "excitement and foolishness," Cora was unaware of the fusillade of enemy steel storming all about her. Shouting "Hello Tommies" to the first group she encountered, she was nonplused by their reply. These men spoke another language—not English. For a moment she listened. A number of Poles, impressed into the German Army, had been stationed in Driel some years before. Almost immediately she recognized the language as Polish. This puzzled her still more.

After years of living under enemy occupation, Cora was wary. Hiding in the Baltussen factory at this moment were several British troopers and the crew of a downed plane. The

Poles seemed equally suspicious, as they eyed her carefully. They spoke no Dutch, but some men ventured guarded questions in broken English or German. Where, they asked, had she come from? How many people were in Driel? Were there any Germans in the village? Where was Baarskamp farm? The mention of Baarskamp brought a torrent of words in both German and English from Cora. The farm lay slightly east of the village and, although Cora was not a member of the tiny underground force in Driel, she had heard her brother, Josephus, an active member, refer to the owner of the farm as a Dutch Nazi. She knew there were some German troops around Baarskamp, along the Rhine dike road, and manning antiaircraft gun sites in the brickworks along the riverbank. "Don't go there," she pleaded. "German troops are all about the place." The Poles seemed unconvinced. "They were not sure whether to trust me or not," Cora recalls. "I did not know what to do. Yet I was desperately afraid these men would set out for Baarskamp and into some sort of a trap." Among the group around her was General Sosabowski. "As he wore no distinctive markings and looked like all the others," Cora remembers, "it was not until the next day that I learned that the short, wiry little man was the general." Sosabowski, she remembers, was calmly eating an apple. He was intensely interested in her information about Baarskamp farm; by sheer accident it had been chosen as the main rendezvous point for his brigade. Although Cora thought that no one in the group believed her, Sosabowski's officers now immediately sent off runners to inform other groups about Baarskamp. The compact little man with the apple now asked, "Where is the ferry site?"

One of the officers produced a map, and Cora pointed out the location. "But," she informed them, "it is not running." The people of Driel had not seen the tender since Wednesday. They had learned from Pieter that the cable had been cut, and they presumed that the ferry had been destroyed.

Sosabowski listened with dismay. On landing, he had sent out a reconnaissance patrol to locate the site. Now his fear had been confirmed. "I still waited for the patrol's report," he recalled, "but this young woman's information seemed accurate.

I thanked her warmly."* A formidable task now lay before him. To send help quickly to Urquhart's beleaguered men in the perimeter, Sosabowski would have to put his force across the 400-yard-wide Rhine by boat or raft—and in darkness. He did not know whether Urquhart's engineers had found boats, or where he might find enough himself. His radiomen, Sosabowski learned, were unable to raise British 1st Airborne headquarters. He was ignorant of any new plans that might have been formulated.

Now, as Cora and her team set out to help the wounded, Sosabowski watched his men move up under the cover of smoke bombs, overrunning what little opposition there was in the area. So far, the only major resistance his brigade had encountered came from artillery shells and mortars. As yet no armor had appeared. The soft polder seemed inadequate for tanks. Perplexed and grim, Sosabowski set up brigade headquarters in a farmhouse and waited for news from Urquhart. His mood was not improved when he learned that of his 1,500-man brigade, 500 troops had failed to arrive. Bad weather had forced the planes carrying almost one entire battalion to abort and return to their bases in England. In casualties, his remaining force had already paid a cruel price: although he did not have the exact figures, by nightfall only about 750 men had been assembled, among them scores of wounded.

At 9 P.M. news arrived, rather dramatically, from Urquhart. Unable to raise Sosabowski by radio, the Polish liaison officer at Urquhart's headquarters, Captain Zwolanski, swam across the Rhine. "I was working on a map," Sosabowski remembered, "and suddenly this incredible figure, dripping with water and covered with mud, clad in undershorts and camouflaged netting, came in."

Zwolanski told the General that Urquhart "wanted us to cross that night and he would have rafts ready to ferry us over." Sosabowski immediately ordered some of his men up to the

---

*Some accounts claim that Cora was a member of the underground and was sent to inform Sosabowski that the ferry was in German hands. "Nothing could be further from the truth," says Cora. "I was never a member of the resistance, though my brothers were involved. The British did not trust the underground and certainly we in Driel knew nothing about the drop until the Poles were right on us."

river line to wait. They remained there most of the night, but the rafts did not come. "At 3 A.M.," says Sosabowski, "I knew the scheme, for some reason, had failed. I pulled my men back into a defensive perimeter." By dawn he expected "German infantry attacks and heavy artillery fire." Any chance of getting across the Rhine "under cover of darkness this night was gone."

At the Hartenstein Hotel across the river, Urquhart had earlier sent an urgent message to Browning. It read:

> (212144) No knowledge of elements of division in Arnhem for 24 hours. Balance of division in very tight perimeter. Heavy mortaring and machine-gun fire followed by local attacks. Main nuisance self-propelled guns. Our casualties heavy. Resources stretched to utmost. Relief within 24 hours vital.

At his small post in Brussels, near Montgomery's 21st Army Group headquarters, Prince Bernhard, Commander in Chief of the Netherlands Forces, followed each harrowing new development with anguish. Holland, which might have been liberated with ease in the first days of September, was being turned into a vast battlefield. Bernhard blamed no one. American and British fighting men were giving their lives to rid the Netherlands of a cruel oppressor. Still, Bernhard had rapidly become disenchanted with Montgomery and his staff. By Friday, September 22, when Bernhard learned that the Guards Armored tanks had been stopped at Elst and the Poles dropped near Driel rather than on the southern side of the Arnhem bridge, the thirty-three-year-old Prince lost his temper. "Why?" he angrily demanded of his chief of staff, Major General "Pete" Doorman. "Why wouldn't the British listen to us? Why?"

Senior Dutch military advisers had been excluded from the planning for Market-Garden; their counsel might have been invaluable. "For example," Bernhard recalls, "if we had known in time about the choice of drop zones and the distance between them and the Arnhem bridge, my people would certainly have said something." Because of "Montgomery's vast experience," Bernhard and his staff "had questioned nothing and accepted everything." But, from the moment Dutch generals learned of the route that Horrocks' XXX Corps columns proposed to take, they had anxiously tried to dissuade anyone who would listen, warning of the dangers of using exposed dike roads. "In our military staff colleges," Bernhard says, "we had run countless studies on the problem. We knew tanks simply could not operate along these roads without infantry." Again and again Dutch officers had told Montgomery's staff that the Market-Garden schedule could not be maintained unless infantry accompanied the tanks. General Doorman described how he had "personally held trials with armor in that precise area before the war."

The British, Bernhard says, "were simply not impressed by our negative attitude." Although everyone was "exceptionally polite, the British preferred to do their own planning, and our views were turned down. The prevailing attitude was, 'Don't worry, old boy, we'll get this thing cracking.'" Even now, Bernhard noted, "everything was being blamed on the weather. The general impression among my staff was that the British considered us a bunch of idiots for daring to question their military tactics." With the exception of a few senior officers, Bernhard knew that he was "not particularly loved at Montgomery's headquarters, because I was saying things that now unfortunately were turning out to be true—and the average Englishman doesn't like being told by a bloody foreigner that he's wrong."*

From his Brussels headquarters Bernhard had kept the sixty-four-year-old Queen Wilhelmina and the Dutch government in exile in London fully informed of events. "They could not have influenced British military decisions either," Bernhard says. "It would have done no good for the Queen or our government to take the matter up with Churchill. He would never have interfered with a military operation in the field. Monty's

---

*Lieutenant Rupert Mahaffey of the Irish Guards remembers that an officer of the Dutch Princess Irene Brigade came to the Guards' mess for dinner shortly after the tanks were stopped at Elst. Looking around the table, the Dutch officer said, "You would have failed the examination." He explained that one of the problems in the Dutch Staff College examination dealt solely with the correct way to attack Arnhem from Nijmegen. There were two choices: a) attack up the main road; or b) drive up it for 1–2 miles, turn left, effect a crossing of the Rhine and come around in a flanking movement. "Those who chose to go straight up the road failed the examination," the officer said. "Those who turned left and then moved up to the river, passed."

reputation was too big. There wasn't anything we could really do."

Queen Wilhelmina followed the battle anxiously. Like her son-in-law, she had expected a quick liberation of the Netherlands. Now, if Market-Garden failed, the royal family feared "the terrible reprisals the Germans would exact from our people. The Queen expected no sympathy from the Germans, whom she hated with a passion."

In the early progress of the operation, Bernhard had informed Wilhelmina that "soon we will be overrunning some of the royal castles and estates." The Queen replied, "Burn them all." Startled, Bernhard stammered, "I beg your pardon?" Wilhelmina said, "I will never again set foot in a place where the Germans have been sitting in my chairs, in my rooms. Never!" Bernhard attempted to mollify her. "Mother, you are exaggerating things a bit. After all, they are quite useful buildings. We can steam them out, use DDT." The Queen was adamant. "Burn the palaces down," she commanded. "I will never set foot in one of them." The Prince refused. "The Queen was angry because I occupied the palace with my staff (without destroying it) and not asking her first. She didn't talk to me for weeks, except on official matters."

Now Bernhard and his staff could only "wait and hope. We were bitter and frustrated at the turn of events. It had never entered our minds that costly mistakes could be made at the top." The fate of Holland itself made Bernhard even more apprehensive. "If the British were driven back at Arnhem, I knew the repercussions against the Dutch people in the winter ahead would be frightful."

2

OOSTERBEEK, THE QUIET ISLAND in the midst of the war, was now the very center of the fighting. In less than seventy-two hours—from Wednesday on—the village had been pounded to a shambles. Artillery and mortar fire had reduced it to one vast junk heap. The serene order of the town was gone. In its place was a ravaged raw landscape, pitted with shell craters, scarred by slit trenches, littered with splinters of wood and steel, and thick with red brick dust and ashes. From fire-blackened trees, fragments of cloth and curtains blew eerily in the wind. Spent brass cartridge cases glinted in the ankle-high dust along the streets. Roads were barricaded with burned-out jeeps and vehicles, trees, doors, sandbags, furniture—even bathtubs and pianos. Behind half-demolished houses and sheds, by the sides of streets and in ruined gardens lay the bodies of soldiers and civilians, side by side. Resort hotels, now turned into hospitals, stood among lawns littered with furniture, paintings and smashed lamps; and the gaily striped canopies, which had shaded the wide verandas, hung down in soiled, ragged strips. Nearly every house had been hit; some had burned down; and there were few windows left in the town. In this sea of devastation, which the Germans were now calling *Der Hexenkessel* (the witches' cauldron), the Dutch—some eight to ten thousand men, women and children—struggled to survive. Crowded into cellars, without gas, water or electricity and, like the troops in many sectors, almost without food, the civilians nursed their wounded, the British defenders and, when the occasion arose, their German conquerors.

In the Schoonoord Hotel, now one of the main casualty stations sitting squarely on the front line, Hendrika van der Vlist, the daughter of the owner, noted in her diary:

> We are no longer afraid; we are past all that. There are wounded lying all around us—some of them are dying. Why shouldn't we do the same if this is asked of us? In this short time we have become detached from everything we have always clung to before. Our belongings are gone. Our hotel has been damaged on all sides. We don't even give it a thought. We have no time for that. If this strife is to claim us as well as the British, we shall give ourselves.

Along lanes, in fields and on rooftops, behind barricaded windows in the ruins of houses, near the church in lower Oosterbeek, in the deer park about the wrecked Hartenstein, tense, hollow-eyed paratroopers manned positions. The noise of the bombardment was now almost continuous. Soldiers and civilians alike were deafened by it. In Oosterbeek the British and Dutch were shocked into a kind of numbness. Time had little meaning, and events had become blurred. Yet soldiers and civilians helped to comfort each other, hoping for rescue, but almost too exhausted to worry about survival. Lieutenant Colonel R. Payton-Reid, commander of the 7th KOSB's, noted: "Lack of sleep is the most difficult of all hardships to combat. Men reached the stage when the only important thing in life seemed to be sleep." As Captain Benjamin Clegg of the 10th Parachute Battalion put it, "I remember more than anything the tiredness—almost to the point that being killed would be worth it." And Sergeant Lawrence Goldthorpe, a glider pilot, was so worn out that "I sometimes wished I could get wounded in order to lie down and get some rest." But there was no rest for anyone.

All about the perimeter—from the white Dreyeroord Hotel (known to the troops as the "White House") in the northern extremity of the fingertip-shaped salient, down to the tenth-century church in lower Oosterbeek—men fought a fiercely confused kind of battle in which the equipment and forces of defender and attacker were crazily intermingled. British troopers often found themselves using captured German ammunition and weapons. German tanks were being destroyed by their own mines. The Germans were driving British jeeps and were bolstered by the captured supplies intended for the airborne. "It was the cheapest battle we ever fought," Colonel Harzer, the Hohenstaufen commander, recalls. "We had free food, cigarettes and ammunition." Both sides captured and recaptured each other's positions so often that few men knew with certainty from hour to hour who occupied the site next to them. For the Dutch sheltering in cellars along the perimeter, the constant switching was terrifying.

Jan Voskuil, the chemical engineer, moved his entire family —his parents-in-law, his wife, Bertha, and their nine-year-old son, Henri—to the home of Dr. Onderwater, because the doctor's reinforced sand-bagged cellar seemed safer. At the height of one period of incessant shooting, a British antitank team fought from the floor above them. Minutes later the cellar door burst open and an SS officer, accompanied by several of his men, demanded to know if the group was hiding any British. Young Henri was playing with a shell case from a British fighter's wing gun. The German officer held up the casing. "This is from a British gun," he shouted. "Everyone upstairs!" Voskuil was quite sure that the cellar's occupants would all be shot. Quickly he intervened. "Look," he told the officer, "this is a shell from an English plane. My son found it and has simply been playing with it." Abruptly the German motioned to his men and the group moved to the upper floor, leaving the Dutch unharmed. Some time later, the cellar door burst open again. To everyone's relief, British paratroopers entered, looking, Voskuil thought, "unearthly, with their camouflage jackets and helmets still sprouting twigs. Like St. Nicholas they handed around chocolates and cigarettes which they had just captured from a German supply truck."

Private Alfred Jones, of Major Boy Wilson's pathfinders, was also caught up in the confusion of battle. Holding positions in a house at the crossroads near the Schoonoord Hotel, Jones and other members of a platoon saw a German staff car approach. The bewildered troopers stared as the car pulled up at the house next to them. "We watched openmouthed," Jones remembers, "as the driver opened the door for the officer and gave the Hitler salute and the officer made for the house." Then, Jones recalls, "we all woke up, the platoon opened fire, and we got them both."

Some brushes with the enemy were less impersonal. Leading a fighting patrol through dense undergrowth on the northern shoulder of the perimeter near the Dennenkamp crossroads, Lieutenant Michael Long of the Glider Pilot Regiment came face to face with a young German. He was carrying a Schmeisser submachine gun; Long had a revolver. Yelling to his men to scatter, the lieutenant opened fire, but the German was faster "by a split second." Long was hit in the thigh and fell to the ground; the German was "only nicked in the right ear." To Long's horror the German tossed a grenade "which landed about eighteen inches from me." Frantically Long kicked the "potato masher" away. It exploded harmlessly. "He searched me," Long remembers, "took two grenades from my pockets and threw them into the woods after my men. Then he calmly sat on my chest and opened fire with the Schmeisser." As the German sprayed the undergrowth, the hot shell cases dropped down into the open neck of Long's battle dress. Irate, Long nudged the German and, pointing at the shell cases, yelled, "*Sehr warm*." Still firing, the German said, "Oh, *ja!*" and shifted his position so that the spent ammunition fell on the ground. After a few moments the German ceased firing and again searched Long. He was about to throw away the lieutenant's first-aid kit, when Long pointed to his thigh. The German pointed to his ear which Long's bullet had grazed. In the undergrowth, with firing going on all around them, the two men bandaged each other's wounds. Then Long was led away into captivity.

Slowly but surely the perimeter was being squeezed as men were killed, wounded or taken prisoner. Staff Sergeant George Baylis, the glider pilot who had brought his dancing pumps to Holland because he believed the Dutch loved to dance, was "winkled out" of a camouflaged slit trench in a garden by German soldiers. Lined up against a wall, Baylis was searched and interrogated. Ignoring his questioner, Baylis calmly took out a hand mirror and examining his grimy, unshaven face, asked the German, "You don't happen to know if there's a dance in town tonight, do you?" He was marched off.

Other paratroopers actually did hear dance music. From German loudspeakers came one of World War II's popular songs, Glenn Miller's "In the Mood." In trenches and fortified positions, haggard troopers listened silently. As the record ended, a voice speaking English told them, "Men of the First Airborne Division, you are surrounded. Surrender or die!" Sergeant Leonard Overton of the Glider Pilot Regiment "fully expected now not to leave Holland alive anyway." Overton and everyone nearby answered with machine-gun fire. Sergeant Lawrence Goldthorpe heard the loudspeaker, too. A few hours earlier he had risked his life to retrieve a resupply pannier—only to discover that it contained, not food or ammunition, but red berets. Now, when he heard the call to "Give yourselves up, while you still have time," he yelled: "Bugger off, you silly bastards!" As he lifted his rifle he heard other men in woods and trenches take up the cry. There was a blaze of machine-gun and rifle fire as enraged troopers trained their guns in the direction of the loudspeaker. Abruptly the voice stopped.

To the Germans, surrender seemed the only sensible course left to the British—as Major Richard Stewart of the 1st Airlanding Brigade discovered. Stewart, captured and found to speak German fluently, was taken to a large headquarters. He remembers the commanding officer vividly. General Bittrich "was a tall, slender man, probably in his early or middle forties, wearing a long black leather coat and cap," Stewart recalls. Bittrich did not interrogate him. "He simply told me that he wanted me to go to my division commander and persuade him to surrender to save the division from annihilation." Stewart politely refused. The General went into "a long dissertation. He told me it was in my power to save the 'flowering manhood of the nation.'" Again, Stewart said, "I cannot do it." Bittrich urged him once more. Stewart asked, "Sir, if our places were reversed, what would your answer be?" The German commander slowly shook his head. "My answer would be No." Stewart said, "That's mine too."

Although Bittrich "had never seen men fight as hard as the British at Oosterbeek and Arnhem," he continued to underestimate the determination of Urquhart's troopers, and he wrongly interpreted the Polish drop at Driel. While he considered the arrival of the Poles "a morale booster" for the embattled 1st British Airborne, Bittrich believed Sosabowski's principal task was to attack the German rear and prevent Harmel's Frundsberg Division, now using the Arnhem bridge, from reaching the Nijmegen area. He considered the Polish threat so serious that he "intervened in the operations against Oosterbeek" and ordered Major Hans Peter Knaust to rush his armored battalion south. The powerful Knaust *Kampfgruppe*, now reinforced with twenty-five 60-ton Tiger tanks and twenty Panthers, was to defend Elst and prevent the Poles from reaching the southern end of the Arnhem bridge and Horrocks' tanks from linking up with them. Harmel's Frundsberg Division, after it reformed, was ordered "to throw the Anglo-Americans in the Nijmegen area back across the Waal." To Bittrich, the British drive from Nijmegen was of utmost importance. Urquhart's division, Bittrich believed, was contained and finished. He had never considered that the Poles' objective was to reinforce Urquhart's bridgehead. Nevertheless, Bittrich's strategy —developed for the wrong reasons—would seal the fate of the 1st Airborne Division.

Early in the morning of Friday, September 22, as the last of Knaust's tanks arrived at Elst, General Urquhart heard from Horrocks, the XXX Corps commander. In two Phantom messages sent during the night Urquhart had informed British

Second Army headquarters that the ferry was no longer held. Horrocks apparently had not been informed. The Corps commander's message read: "43rd Division ordered to take all risks to effect relief today and are directed on ferry. If situation warrants you should withdraw to or cross ferry." Urquhart replied, "We shall be glad to see you."

In the wine cellar of the wrecked Hartenstein Hotel—"the only place remaining that was relatively safe," Urquhart recalls —the General conferred with his chief of staff, Colonel Charles Mackenzie. "The last thing we wanted to be was alarmist," Urquhart remembers, "but I felt I had to do something to effect relief—and effect it immediately."

Outside, the "morning hate," as the troopers called the usual dawn mortaring, had begun. The shattered Hartenstein shook and reverberated from the concussion of near hits, and the harried Urquhart wondered how long they could hold. Of the 10,005 airborne troops—8,905 from the division and 1,100 glider pilots and copilots—that had landed on the Arnhem drop zones, Urquhart now estimated that he had fewer than 3,000 men. In slightly less than five days he had lost more than two thirds of his division. Although he now had communication with Horrocks and Browning, Urquhart did not believe they understood what was happening. "I was convinced," Urquhart says, "that Horrocks was not fully aware of our predicament, and I had to do something to acquaint them with the urgency and desperateness of the situation." He decided to send Colonel Mackenzie and Lieutenant Colonel Eddie Myers, the chief engineer, "who would handle the special arrangements for ferrying across men and supplies," to Nijmegen to see Browning and Horrocks. "I was told," Mackenzie says, "that it was absolutely vital to impress Horrocks and Browning with the fact that the division as such had ceased to exist—that we were merely a collection of individuals hanging on." The limit of endurance had been reached, Urquhart believed, and Mackenzie was to impress on them "that if we don't get men and supplies over by tonight, it may be too late."

Urquhart stood by as Mackenzie and Myers prepared to leave. He knew that the trip would be dangerous, perhaps impossible, yet it seemed reasonable to assume—if Horrocks' messages were to be believed and the 43rd Wessex attack was launched on schedule—that some kind of route would be open to Nijmegen by the time Mackenzie and Myers crossed the river. As the men left Urquhart had "one final word for Charles. I told him to try and make them realize what a fix we were in. Charles said he would do his best, and I knew he would." Taking a rubber boat, Myers and Mackenzie set out by jeep for lower Oosterbeek and the Rhine.

Ten miles away, in the Nijmegen area north of the Waal, twenty-six-year-old Captain Lord Richard Wrottesley, commanding a troop of the 2nd Household Cavalry, sat in an armored car ready to give the command to move out. During the night his reconnaissance unit had been ordered to lead the squadron ahead of the attacking 43rd Wessex Division and make contact with the airborne forces. Since the day before, when the Irish Guards had been stopped, Wrottesley had been "fully aware of the German strength north of Nijmegen." No news had been received from either the Poles at Driel or the 1st Airborne, "so somebody had to find out what was happening." The squadron's role, young Wrottesley remembers, was to "find a way past the enemy defenses by bashing through." By avoiding the main Nijmegen-Arnhem highway and traveling the gridiron of secondary roads to the west, Wrottesley believed, there was a good chance of sprinting through the enemy defenses under cover of an early morning mist "which could contribute to our luck." At first light Wrottesley gave the order to move out. Quickly his two armored cars and two scout cars disappeared into the fog. Following behind him came a second troop under Lieutenant Arthur Young. Traveling fast, the force swung west of the village of Oosterhout, following the Waal riverbank for about six miles. Then, looping back, they headed due north for Driel. "At one point we saw several Germans," Wrottesley remembers, "but they seemed to be more startled than we were." Two and a half hours later, at 8 A.M., Friday, September 22, the first link between the Market-Garden ground forces and the 1st British Airborne was made. The forty-eight hours that Montgomery had envisioned before the link-up had been stretched out to four days and eighteen hours. Wrottesley and Lieutenant Young, surpassing the attempt of the Guards Armored tanks on Thursday, had reached Driel and the Rhine without firing a shot.

Lieutenant H. S. Hopkinson's third troop, coming up behind them, ran into trouble. The morning mist suddenly lifted and as the unit was sighted, enemy armor opened up. "Driver Read in the first car was immediately killed," Hopkinson says. "I went forward to help, but the scout car was blazing and enemy tanks continued to fire on us. We were forced to retire." For the moment, the Germans once more had closed off a relief route to Urquhart's 1st Airborne Division.

The strange, crippling paralysis that had steadily invaded the Market-Garden plan from its very beginning was intensifying. At dawn on Friday, September 22, General Thomas' long-awaited 43rd Wessex Division was to break out from Nijmegen to aid the Guards Armored column still stalled at Elst. The plan called for one brigade—the 129th—to advance along each side of the elevated highway, through Elst and on to Arnhem; simultaneously, a second brigade, the 214th, was to attack farther west through the town of Oosterhout and strike for Driel and the ferry site. Incredibly, it had taken the Wessexes almost three days to travel from the Escaut Canal—a distance of a little more than sixty miles. In part this was due to the constant enemy attacks against the corridor; but some would later charge that it was also due to the excessive cautiousness of the methodical Thomas. His division might have covered the distance more quickly on foot.*

Now, mishap overtook the 43rd Wessex again. To the bitter disappointment of General Essame, commander of the 214th Brigade, one of his lead battalions, the 7th Somersets, had lost its way and had failed to cross the Waal during the night of the twenty-first. "Where the hell have you been?" Essame heatedly demanded of its commander when the force finally arrived. The Somersets had been held up by crowds and roadblocks in Nijmegen; several companies were separated in the confusion and directed over the wrong bridge. Essame's plan to take advantage of the dawn mist and drive toward Driel was lost. The two-pronged attack did not jump off until 8:30 A.M. In full light the enemy, alerted by the Household Cavalry's reconnaissance unit, was prepared. By 9:30 a resourceful German commander at Oosterhout, skillfully using tanks and

* Chester Wilmot, *The Struggle for Europe*, p. 516.

artillery, had successfully pinned down the 214th Brigade; and the 129th, heading toward Elst and trying to support Colonel Vandeleur's Irish Guards, came under fire from Major Knaust's massed tanks, which General Bittrich had ordered south to crush the Anglo-American drive. On this critical Friday, when, in Urquhart's opinion, the fate of the British 1st Airborne was dependent on immediate relief, it would be late afternoon before the 43rd Wessex would capture Oosterhout —too late to move troops in mass to help the surrounded men in Oosterbeek.

Like Essame, others were angered by the sluggish progress of the attack. Lieutenant Colonel George Taylor, commanding the 5th Duke of Cornwall's Light Infantry,* could not understand "what was holding everything up." He knew the Garden forces were already three days behind schedule in reaching the 1st Airborne. He was uncomfortably aware that higher command headquarters was worried, too. On Thursday he had met General Horrocks, the Corps commander, who had asked him, "George, what would you do?" Without hesitation, Taylor had suggested rushing a special task force to the Rhine on Thursday night carrying 2½-ton amphibious vehicles (DUKWs) filled with supplies. "My idea was a shot in the dark," Taylor recalls. "Horrocks looked slightly startled and, as people do sometimes when they consider a suggestion impractical, he quickly changed the conversation."

Taylor now waited impatiently for orders to move his battalion across the Waal river. It was not until midday Friday that a major, a staff officer from XXX Corps, arrived to tell him that his battalion would be given two DUKWs loaded with supplies and ammunition to take up to Driel. Additionally, Taylor would have a squadron of tanks of the Dragoon Guards. "The situation at Arnhem is desperate," the major said. "The DUKWs must be moved across the river tonight." Looking at the heavily laden DUKWs that arrived in the assembly area at

---

*The names of the famous British regiments involved always caused confusion for Americans—especially when they were abbreviated. At First Allied Airborne headquarters a message concerning the Duke of Cornwall's Light Infantry arrived, reading, "5DCLI are to make contact with 1 Airborne Division . . ." The puzzled duty officer finally decoded the message. He reported "Five Duck Craft Landing Infantry" were on their way to Urquhart.

3:00 P.M. on Friday afternoon, Taylor wondered if they carried enough supplies. "Surely," he remarked to his intelligence officer, Lieutenant David Wilcox, "we've got to get more than this across to them."

Even as the infantry was moving out of the Nijmegen bridge-head, Colonel Mackenzie and Lieutenant Colonel Myers had reached Sosabowski and the Poles at Driel. Their crossing of the Rhine had been surprisingly uneventful. "Only a few shots were fired at us," Mackenzie says, "and they went over our heads." On the southern side a full-scale battle was in progress and the Poles were hard pressed, holding off enemy infantry attacks from the direction of Elst and Arnhem. For some time Mackenzie and Myers had waited on the Rhine's southern bank for the Poles. "They had been told by radio to watch out for us," Mackenzie says. "But there was quite a battle going on, and Sosabowski had his hands full." Finally, riding bicycles, they were escorted to Sosabowski's headquarters.

Mackenzie was heartened to discover the Household Cavalry units. But his hopes of reaching General Browning at Nijmegen quickly were dashed. To Lord Wrottesley and Lieutenant Arthur Young, the failure of Hopkinson's third troop of reconnaissance vehicles to reach Driel meant that the Germans had closed in behind them; nor had the attack of the 43rd Wessex yet broken through. Mackenzie and Myers would have to wait until a route was opened.

Wrottesley recalls that "Mackenzie immediately asked to use my radio to contact Corps headquarters." He began to relay a long message via Wrottesley's squadron commander for Horrocks and Browning. Urquhart's chief of staff made no effort to encode his signal. Standing beside him, Wrottesley heard Mackenzie "in the clear" say, "'We are short of food, ammunition and medical supplies. We cannot hold out for more than twenty-four hours. All we can do is wait and pray.'" For the first time Wrottesley realized "that Urquhart's division must be in a very bad way."

Mackenzie and Myers then conferred with Sosabowski about the urgency of getting the Poles across. "Even a few men now can make a difference," Mackenzie told him. Sosabowski agreed, but asked where the boats and rafts were to come from. Hopefully DUKWs, which had been requested, would arrive by night. Meanwhile, Myers thought, several two-man rubber dinghies, which the airborne had, could be used. Linked by hawser they could be pulled back and forth across the river. Sosabowski was "delighted with the idea." It would be painfully slow, he said, but "if unopposed, perhaps two hundred men might be shipped across during the night." By radio, Myers quickly contacted the Hartenstein to make arrangements for the dinghies. The pathetic and desperate operation, it was decided, would begin at nightfall.

In the bridgehead across the river, Urquhart's men continued to fight with extraordinary courage and resolution. Yet, at places about the perimeter, even the most resolute were voicing worry about relief. Here and there a looming sense of isolation was growing, infecting the Dutch as well.

Douw van der Krap, a former Dutch naval officer, had earlier been placed in command of a twenty-five-man Dutch underground unit which was to fight alongside the British. The group had been organized at the instigation of Lieutenant Commander Arnoldus Wolters, the Dutch liaison officer at Urquhart's headquarters. Jan Eijkelhoff, who had helped make ready the Schoonoord Hotel for casualties on Monday, was charged with finding German weapons for the group. The British could give each man only five rounds of ammunition—if weapons could be found. Driving as far as Wolfheze, Eijkelhoff found only three or four rifles. At first the newly appointed commander of the unit, Van der Krap, was elated at the idea, but his hopes dimmed. His men would be instantly executed if captured while fighting with the paratroopers. "Without relief and supplies for themselves, it was obvious the British couldn't last," Van der Krap recalls. "They couldn't arm us and they couldn't feed us and I decided to disband the group." Van der Krap, however, remained with the paratroopers. "I wanted to fight," he says, "but I didn't think we had a chance."

Young Anje van Maanen, who had been so excited by the paratroopers' arrival and the daily expectation of seeing "Monty's tanks," was now terrified by the continuous shelling and constantly changing battle lines. "The noise and the hell go on," she wrote in her diary. "I can't bear it any longer. I'm so scared and I can't think of anything but shells and death."

Anje's father, Dr. Gerritt van Maanen, working alongside British doctors at the Tafelberg Hotel, brought news to his family whenever he could, but to Anje the battle had assumed unrealistic proportions. "I don't understand," she wrote. "One side of a street is British, the other German, and people kill each other from both sides. There are house, floor and room fights." On Friday, Anje wrote, "the British say Monty will be here at any moment. I don't believe that. Monty can go to hell! He will never come."

In the Schoonoord Hotel, where British and German wounded crowded the wide veranda and lay in the reception rooms, passageways and bedrooms, Hendrika van der Vlist could hardly believe it was Friday. The hospital was constantly changing hands. On Wednesday the hotel had been taken by the Germans, on Thursday by the British; and by Friday morning it had been recaptured by the Germans. Control of the Schoonoord was less important than the need to prevent it being fired on. A large Red Cross flag flew on the roof, and numerous smaller ones were spotted around the grounds, but the dust and flying debris often obscured the pennants. Orderlies, nurses and doctors worked on, seemingly oblivious to anything but the constant flow of wounded men.

Hendrika had slept in her clothes for only a few hours each night, getting up to assist doctors and orderlies as fresh casualties were carried in. Fluent in English and German, she had originally noted a pessimism among the Germans in contrast to the patient cheerfulness of the British. Now many of the severely wounded Red Devils seemed stoically prepared to accept their fate. As she brought one trooper the minuscule portion of soup and a biscuit that constituted the only meal the hospital could provide, he pointed to a newly arrived casualty. "Give it to him," he told Hendrika. Pulling down the man's blanket, she saw he wore a German uniform. "German, eh?" the trooper asked. Hendrika nodded. "Give him the food anyway," the Britisher said, "I ate yesterday." Hendrika stared at him. "Why is there a war on, really?" she asked. Tiredly, he shook his head. In her diary she put down her private fears: "Has our village become one of the bloodiest battlefields? What is holding up the main army? It cannot go on like this any longer."

In Dr. Onderwater's cellar, where the Voskuil family was sheltering along with some twenty others, both Dutch and British, Mrs. Voskuil noticed for the first time that the floor was slippery with blood. During the night two wounded officers, Major Peter Warr and Lieutenant Colonel Ken Smyth, had been brought in by British troopers. Both men were seriously wounded, Warr in the thigh and Smyth in the stomach. Shortly after the injured men were laid on the floor, the Germans burst in. One of them threw a grenade. Lance Corporal George Wyllie of Colonel Smyth's 10th Battalion remembers "a flash of light and then a deafening explosion." Mrs. Voskuil, sitting behind Major Warr, felt "red hot pain" in her legs. In the now-dark cellar she heard someone shouting, "Kill them! Kill them!" She felt a man's body fall heavily across her. It was Private Albert Willingham, who had apparently jumped in front of Mrs. Voskuil to protect her. Corporal Wyllie saw a gaping wound open in Willingham's back. He remembers the woman sitting on a chair with a child beside her, the dead paratrooper across her lap. The child seemed covered with blood. "My God!" Wyllie thought as he lost consciousness, "we've killed a child." Suddenly the fierce battle was over. Someone shone a torch. "Do you still live?" Mrs. Voskuil called out to her husband. Then she reached for her son, Henri. The child did not respond to her cries. She was sure he was dead. "Suddenly I didn't care what happened," she says. "It just didn't matter any more."

She saw that soldiers and civilians alike were terribly wounded and screaming. In front of her, Major Warr's tunic was "bloody and gaping open." Everyone was shouting or sobbing. "Silence," Mrs. Voskuil yelled in English. "Silence!" The heavy burden across her body was pulled away and then she saw Wyllie nearby. "The English boy got up, shaking visibly. He had his rifle butt on the floor and the bayonet, almost level with my eyes, jerked back and forth as he tried to steady himself. Low animal-like sounds—almost like a dog or a wolf —were coming from him."

Corporal Wyllie's head began to clear. Someone had now lit a candle in the cellar, and a German officer gave him a sip of brandy. Wyllie noticed the bottle bore a Red Cross insignia, and underneath the words, "His Majesty's Forces." As he was led out Wyllie looked back at the lady "whose child was dead." He wanted to say something to her but "couldn't find the words."*

The German officer asked Mrs. Voskuil to tell the British "they have fought gallantly and behaved like gentlemen, but now they must surrender. Tell them it is over." As the paratroopers were taken out, a German medical orderly examined Henri. "He is in a coma," he told Mrs. Voskuil. "He is grazed along the stomach and his eyes are discolored and swollen, but he will be all right." Mutely she nodded her head.

On the floor Major Warr, his shoulder bones protruding through the skin from the explosion, shouted, cursed and then fell unconscious again. Leaning over, Mrs. Voskuil moistened her handkerchief and wiped the blood from his lips. A short distance away Colonel Smyth mumbled something. A German guard turned, questioningly, toward Mrs. Voskuil. "He wants a doctor," she said softly. The soldier left the cellar and returned a few minutes later with a German doctor. Examining Smyth, the physician said, "Tell the officer I am sorry to have to hurt him but I must look at his wound. Tell him to grit his teeth." As he began pulling away the clothing, Smyth fainted.

At daylight the civilians were ordered to leave. Two SS men carried Mrs. Voskuil and Henri out into the street, and a Dutch Red Cross worker directed them to the cellar of a dentist, Dr. Phillip Clous. Voskuil's parents-in-law did not go. They preferred to take their chances at home. In the Clous house, the dentist warmly welcomed the family. "Don't worry," he told Voskuil. "It's going to be all right. The British will win." Voskuil, standing beside his wounded wife and child, his mind still filled with the night's horrors, stared at the man. "No," he said quietly, "they will not."

Though they were unwilling to recognize that their endurance had nearly run its course, many paratroopers knew that they could not hold on alone much longer. Staff Sergeant Dudley Pearson was tired "of being pushed around by the Germans." On the northern edge of the perimeter, he and his men

---

*Wyllie never again saw the Voskuils, nor did he know their names. For years he worried about the woman in the cellar and the child he believed dead. Today young Henri Voskuil is a doctor.

had been chased by tanks, pinned down in woods and forced to fight off the Germans with bayonets. Finally, on Thursday night, as the perimeter tightened, Pearson's group was ordered to pull back. He was told to cover the withdrawal with a smoke grenade. Nearby he heard a lone Bren gun firing. Scrambling through underbrush he discovered a corporal hidden in a deep hollow in the woods. "Get out," Pearson told him. "I'm the last one here." The corporal shook his head. "Not me, sergeant," he said. "I'm staying. I won't let those bastards by." As Pearson made his way back he could hear the Bren-gunner firing. He thought the situation was hopeless. He began to wonder if it wouldn't be better to surrender.

In a slit trench near the tennis courts at the Hartenstein —where the earth was now crisscrossed with foxholes that the German prisoners had been allowed to dig for their own protection—Glider Pilot Victor Miller stared at the body of another pilot, who lay sprawled a few yards away. Firing had been so intense that men had not been able to remove the dead. Miller saw that since the last mortaring the body was half buried by leaves and shattered branches. He kept staring at the corpse, wondering if anyone would come to pick it up. He was frightened that the features of his dead friend would change, and he was certain there was a "strong smell of death." He felt sick. He remembers thinking wildly that "if something isn't done soon, we'll all be corpses. The shells will eliminate us one by one, until this will be only a park of the dead."

Other men felt they were being exhorted to keep up courage without access to the facts. Private William O'Brien, near the church in lower Oosterbeek, remembers that "every night an officer came around and told us to hang on, the Second Army would arrive the next day. There was a helluva lot of apathy. Everyone was asking what the hell they were there for and where the hell was the goddam army. We'd had it." Sergeant Edward Mitchell, a glider pilot, in a position opposite the church, remembers one man locked himself in a nearby shed. "He would let no one near. Every now and again he'd shout, 'Come on, you bastards,' and empty a magazine all around the shed." For hours, the lone trooper alternately shouted and fired, then lapsed into periods of silence. As Mitchell and others debated how to get him out, there was another sharp burst of fire and then silence. Reaching the shed, they found the paratrooper dead.

Here and there shell-shocked, concussed, battle-fatigued men roamed the Hartenstein area, finally oblivious to the battle. Medic Taffy Brace, who on Tuesday had tended the mangled body of his friend, Andy Milbourne, was encountering these tragic, pathetic men as he treated the wounded. By now Brace had run out of morphia, and he was using paper bandages. He could not bring himself to reveal that he had no medication. "What would you be wanting morphia for?" he asked one critically wounded trooper. "Morphia's for people who are really hurt. You're doing fine."

As Brace bandaged the man, he was aware of a strange hooting sound behind him. Turning he saw a totally naked paratrooper, pumping his arms up and down and "sounding like a locomotive." As Brace caught his eye, the soldier began to curse. "Blast this fireman," the trooper said, "he was never any good." In one house near the perimeter Brace, arriving with a casualty, heard a man softly singing "The White Cliffs of Dover." Thinking the trooper was soothing the other injured, Brace smiled at him and nodded encouragement. The soldier lunged at Brace and tried to choke him. "I'll kill you," he yelled. "What do you know about Dover?" Brace loosened the fingers at his throat. "It's all right," he said gently, "I've been there." The man stepped back. "Oh," he said, "that's all right then." Minutes later he began to sing again. Others remember a shell-shocked trooper who walked among them at night. Bending over the huddled forms of men trying to sleep he would shake them roughly awake, stare into their eyes and ask them all the same question: "Have you got faith?"

Despite those pitiable, shocked and desperate men whose faith was gone, hundreds of others were bolstered by the actions of eccentric, undaunted soldiers who seemed utterly fearless and who refused to give in to wounds or hardships. Major Dickie Lonsdale, commander of the "Lonsdale Force," holding positions about the church in lower Oosterbeek, seemed to be everywhere. "His was a figure that would inspire terror," recalls Sergeant Dudley Pearson. "He had one arm in a bloodstained

sling, an equally bloody wrapping around his head and a giant bandage on one leg." Hobbling about exhorting his men,
Lonsdale led attack after attack.

Sergeant Major Harry Callaghan, who had added extra
touches to his uniform—he had found a tall black hat in a
hearse and wore it everywhere, explaining to the men that
he had been named "the Airborne representative to Hitler's
funeral"—remembers the awesome-looking Lonsdale deliver a
ringing, defiant speech to men in the church. Officers and non-
coms had rounded up troopers and sent them to the ancient
ruined building. "The roof was gone," Callaghan remembers,
"and each new explosion sent plaster cascading down." As soldiers leaned listlessly against walls and broken pews—smoking,
lounging, half-asleep—Lonsdale climbed into the pulpit. Men
stared upward at the fierce-looking, bloodstained figure.
"We've fought the Germans in North Africa, Sicily and Italy,"
Callaghan remembers Lonsdale saying. "They weren't good
enough for us then! They're bloody well not good enough for
us now!" Captain Michael Corrie of the Glider Pilot Regiment
had been struck as he entered the church "by the weariness I
saw. But Lonsdale's speech was stirring. I felt stunned by his
words, and proud. The men went in looking beaten, but as
they came out, they had new spirit. You could read it on their
faces."

Some men seemed to have overcome even the paralyzing
fear that the brute force of enemy armored attacks instilled.
With few antitank guns, troopers were helpless against tanks
and self-propelled guns that roamed the perimeter, pulverizing
position after position. Yet, somehow the foot soldiers were
fighting back. Even 60-ton Tigers were destroyed—often by
men who had never before fired an antitank gun. Lance Corporal Sydney Nunn, who had eagerly looked forward to Arnhem as an escape from the "nightmare" of his camp in England
and the mole which had invaded his mattress, now faced a far
more dreadful nightmare with outward calm. He and another
paratrooper, Private Nobby Clarke, had become friendly with a
glider pilot in an adjoining slit trench. During a lull in the mortaring, the pilot called over to Nunn, "I don't know whether
you know it, old lad, but there's a whopping great tank out
in front to our right. One of the Tiger family." Clarke looked

at Nunn. "What are we supposed to do?" he asked. "Go drill holes in it?"

Cautiously Nunn looked over the edge of the trench. The tank was "enormous." Nearby in the bushes an antitank gun was concealed, but its crew had been killed, and no one in Nunn's group knew how to load or fire the weapon. Nunn and the glider pilot decided to crawl to it. As the men climbed out they were spotted and the tank's gun began firing. "We dug grooves in the soil with our noses, we were that low," Nunn recalls. "Our little woods began to look like a logging camp as trees came down all around us." The two men reached the gun just as the Tiger "began to give us personal attention with its machine gun." The pilot sighted down the barrel of the gun and shouted happily. "Our gun was pointed directly at the tank. If we'd known how to do it, we couldn't have aimed it better." Looking at Nunn, the glider pilot said, "I hope this thing works." He pulled the trigger. In the heavy explosion that followed, both men were thrown on their backs. "When our ears stopped ringing, I heard other men around us begin to laugh and cheer," Nunn says. As he stared disbelievingly, he saw the Tiger engulfed in flames, its ammunition exploding. Turning to Nunn, the glider pilot solemnly shook hands. "Our game, I think," he said.

Many men remember Major Robert Cain of the 2nd South Staffordshires as the real expert against tanks and self-propelled guns. It seemed to Cain that he and his men had been pursued and threatened by Tigers ever since they had arrived. Now, with his small force positioned at the church in lower Oosterbeek, in houses and gardens across the road, and in a laundry owned by a family named Van Dolderen, Cain was determined to knock out every piece of armor he saw. Searching for the best site from which to operate, Cain picked the Van Dolderen house. The laundry owner was unwilling to leave. Surveying the back garden, Cain said, "Well, be that as it may, I'm going to dig in out there. I'm using your place for my ammo dump."

Cain was using the bazookalike antitank weapon known as a Piat to hunt down armor. On Friday, as the street battles grew in intensity, Cain's eardrums burst from his constant firing. Stuffing pieces of field dressing into his ears he continued lobbing bombs.

Suddenly someone called out to Cain that two tanks were coming up the road. At the corner of a building, Cain loaded the Piat and aimed it. Staff Sergeant Richard Long, a glider pilot, looked on aghast. "He was the bravest man I've ever seen," Long says. "He was only about a hundred yards away when he started to fire." The tank fired back before Cain could reload, and the shell hit the building in back of him. In the thick swirl of dust and debris, Cain fired again and then again. He saw the crew of the first tank bail out, spraying the street with machine-gun bullets. Immediately around Cain, paratroopers opened up with Bren guns and, Cain remembers, "the Germans were just cut off their feet." Reloading again, he fired, and Sergeant Long saw "a tremendous flash. The bomb had gone off inside the Piat. Major Cain threw his hands in the air and fell backward. When we got to him, his face was black. His first words were, 'I think I'm blind.'" Staff Sergeant Walton Ashworth, one of the Bren-gunners who had shot up the German tank crew, stared stonily as Cain was taken away. "All I could think was 'that poor bloody bastard.'"

Within half an hour Cain's sight had returned, but his face was imbedded with bits of metal. He refused morphia and, deciding that he "wasn't wounded enough to stay where he was," went back to the battle—as Captain W. A. Taylor described it, "to add to his bag of enemy tanks." By Friday afternoon, the thirty-five-year-old Cain had a bagful. Since landing on the eighteenth he had put out of action or driven off a total of six tanks, plus a number of self-propelled guns.

Ferocious men throughout the airhead were making heroic stands, unmindful of their own safety. By dusk on Friday Corporal Leonard Formoy, one of the survivors of Colonel Fitch's 3rd Battalion, who had made the desperate march to reach Frost's men at the Arnhem bridge, occupied a position on the western outskirts not far from Division headquarters at the Hartenstein. "We were being hit from practically all sides," Formoy remembers. Suddenly a Tiger tank, coming from the direction of Arnhem, rumbled toward the cluster of men around Formoy. In the twilight Formoy saw the turret swivel. Sergeant "Cab" Calloway picked up a Piat and rushed forward. "You're going where I'm going!" Formoy heard him yell. Approximately fifty yards away from the tank, Calloway fired. The bomb exploded against the tracks and the tank stopped, but Calloway was killed at almost the same moment by its guns. "It was an act of desperation," Formoy remembers. "He was just ripped in half, but he saved our lives."

Private James Jones remembers an unknown major who asked Jones and three others to go with him outside the perimeter on a search for guns and ammunition. The small party came suddenly upon some Germans in a machine-gun nest. Leaping up, the major fired, yelling, "There's some more of those bastards who won't live!" As the Germans opened up, the group scattered and Jones was trapped behind a disabled jeep. "I said a prayer, waited for another burst from the gun, and got back to the lines," Jones recalls. He never saw the major again.

Senior officers, often unaware of the impression they made, set examples their men would never forget. Brigadier Pip Hicks refused to wear a helmet throughout the battle. Trooper William Chandler, one of Major Freddie Gough's Reconnaissance Squadron men whose group had been cut off on the northern, Leopard route on Sunday and had been moved back to a crossroads at Oosterbeek, remembers Hicks's red beret standing out among groups of helmeted men. "Hey, Brigadier," someone called out, "put your bloody helmet on." Hicks just smiled and waved. "I wasn't trying to be debonair," Hicks explains. "I just couldn't stand the damn thing bouncing around on my head." His activities might have had something to do with that. Some men recall Hicks's frequent daily trips to Urquhart's headquarters. He started each journey at a jog and ended up sprinting a step ahead of German shellfire. "I felt fully my age when I finished those mad dashes," Hicks confesses.

Brigadier Shan Hackett, who had brought his battered 10th and 156th battalions back to the Oosterbeek area after their brave but futile attempt to break through the German defenses to the north and east and get to Arnhem, visited his men constantly, offering them quiet words of praise. Major George Powell was commanding two platoons of the 156th in perimeter positions to the north. "We were short on food, ammunition and water," Powell remembers, "and we had few medical supplies." On Friday Hackett suddenly appeared at Powell's command post, where, says Powell, "we were literally poking right into the enemy's lines." Hackett explained that he had not had time to visit Powell until now, "but you've been holding so well, George, I wasn't worried about you." Powell was pleased. "The only real mistake I've made so far, sir," he said, "is putting the headquarters in a chicken run. We're all alive with fleas." To Staff Sergeant Dudley Pearson, chief clerk of the 4th Brigade, Hackett earned respect because "he shared with us as though he had no rank. If we ate, he did, and if we went hungry, so did he. He didn't seem to have a mess kit. On Friday he sat down with us and ate a little piece of food with his fingers." Pearson went to find a knife and fork. On the way back he was wounded in the heel; but, he says, "I thought the Brigadier rather deserved something better than the way he was living among us."

And Signalman Kenneth Pearce, attached to Command Artillery Signals at Division headquarters, will always remember the man who came to his aid. Pearce was in charge of the heavy storage batteries, called "Dags"—each weighing approximately twenty-five pounds and encased in a wooden box with cast-iron handles—that powered the signal sets. In the late evening Pearce was struggling to move a fresh Dag from the deep trench in which they were stored. Above him, he heard someone say, "Here, let me help you." Pearce directed the man to grab one handle and pull up the set. Together the two dragged the cumbersome box to the command-post trench. "There's one more," Pearce said. "Let's go get it." The men made the second trip and, back at the command post, Pearce jumped into the trench as the other man hoisted the boxes down to him. As they walked away Pearce suddenly noticed that the man wore red staff officer's tabs. Stopping dead, he stammered, "Thank you very much, sir." General Urquhart nodded. "That's all right, son," he said.

Step by terrible step the crisis was mounting; nothing went right on this day, which General Horrocks was to call "Black Friday." Weather conditions in both England and Holland again grounded Allied planes, preventing resupply missions. In answer to Urquhart's plea for fighter strikes, the R.A.F. replied: ". . . After most careful examination regret owing to storm unable to accept . . ." And, at this moment, when

Horrocks needed every man, tank and ton of supplies to retain Montgomery's bridgehead over the Rhine and break through to the Red Devils, Field Marshal Model's counteroffensive finally succeeded in cutting the corridor. Thirty minutes after receiving Mackenzie's message that Urquhart might be overrun in twenty-four hours, General Horrocks received another message: in the 101st Airborne's sector, powerful German armored forces had cut the corridor north of Veghel.

Model could hardly have chosen a more vital spot or timed his attack better. British infantry forces of the XII and VIII Corps, advancing on either side of the highway, had only now reached Son, barely five miles into the 101st's area. Fighting against stiff resistance, they had made agonizingly slow progress. The 101st's commander, General Taylor, had expected the British to reach his sector of "Hell's Highway" long before. After more than five days of continuous fighting without support, Taylor's hard-pressed troopers were thinly spread and vulnerable. Along some stretches the highway was unguarded except by the British armor and infantry moving along it on the way north. Elsewhere, the "front" was literally the sides of the road. Field Marshal Model had chosen to counterattack at Veghel for a particular reason: throughout the entire length of the Market-Garden corridor the Veghel area contained the greatest cluster of bridges—no fewer than four, of which one was a major canal crossing. With one stroke Model hoped to strangle the Allied lifeline. He almost did. He might have succeeded, but for the Dutch underground.

During the night and early morning, in villages and hamlets east of Veghel, the Dutch spotted the German buildup; they promptly phoned liaison officers with the 101st. The warning came not a moment too soon. Massed German armor almost overwhelmed Taylor's men. Twice in four hours, in a wild melee that ranged over a five-mile stretch of the corridor, German tanks tried to push through to the bridges. Desperately, Taylor's men, aided by British artillery and armor on the road, threw back the attacks. But four miles to the north, at Uden, the Germans succeeded in cutting the corridor. Now, with the battle still raging and the forces in the rear cut off and isolated, Horrocks was forced to make a fateful decision: he would have to send armored units—urgently needed in his efforts to reach Urquhart—back south down the corridor to help General Taylor, whose need was now even more urgent. The 32nd Guards Brigade was sent rushing south to support the 101st in reopening the highway. The gallant 101st would hang on to the bridges, but even with the help of the Guards, not a man, tank or supply vehicle would move north along the corridor for the next twenty-four hours. Model's counteroffensive, though unsuccessful for the moment, had still paid enormous dividends. In the end, the battle for the corridor would decide the fate of Arnhem.

By 4 P.M. on Friday, September 22, in the Nijmegen-Arnhem area—six and one-half hours after they had first been pinned down by German tanks and artillery—British infantrymen finally bludgeoned their way through Oosterhout. The village was in flames, and SS prisoners were being rounded up. The relief route west of the "island" highway, the low-lying secondary roads used by the enterprising Household Cavalry in their race to Driel at dawn, was now believed to be free or, at worst, only lightly held by the enemy. The 5th Duke of Cornwall's Light Infantry, supported by a squadron of Dragoon Guards' tanks and carrying the precious two amphibious vehicles loaded with supplies, was ready to slam through whatever opposition remained and dash for the Rhine. Lieutenant Colonel George Taylor, commanding the force, was so eager to get to Urquhart that he "felt a mad desire to sweep my infantry onto the tanks with my hands and get moving."

In a small wood north of Oosterhout, his loaded vehicles waited to move out. Suddenly, off in the distance, Taylor spotted two Tiger tanks. Quietly he warned Lieutenant David Wilcox, his intelligence officer, "Don't say anything. I don't want anyone to know about those tanks. We can't stop now." Taylor waved the relief column up the road. "If we had waited five minutes more," he says, "I knew the route would have been closed again."

At full speed—his infantry mounted on tanks, carriers and trucks—Taylor's column rolled through Dutch hamlets and villages. Everywhere they were met by surprised, cheering villagers, but there was no slowdown. Taylor's only concern was to get to the Rhine. "I felt a sense of great urgency," he says.

"Any time lost would give the enemy an opportunity to move up a blocking force." The convoy met no opposition, and for Taylor, "it was an exhilarating feeling as the light faded rapidly and the head of the column reached Driel." They had covered the ten-mile journey in just thirty minutes. At 5:30 P.M. the first tanks of the Dragoon Guards reached the Rhine and, skirting northeast along its banks, moved into the outskirts of the village. Taylor heard an explosion and guessed immediately what it was: on the cautious Sosabowski's defense perimeter, one of the tanks had run over a Polish mine.

It was dark when Taylor reached Sosabowski's headquarters. The information he had about Urquhart's division was vague. "I had no idea where they were in Arnhem or if they still held one end of the bridge." But Taylor planned to send his infantry and tanks immediately toward the southern end. He knew the DUKWs must get "across as soon as possible and if the bridge was still held it would be obviously quicker to drive them across than to float them over." At Sosabowski's headquarters, Taylor was astonished to find Colonel Charles Mackenzie and Lieutenant Colonel Myers. Quickly they dissuaded him from heading out for the Arnhem bridge. Nothing had been heard from Frost, Mackenzie explained, since Wednesday night and it was presumed at headquarters that "it was all over at the bridge."

Reluctantly Taylor gave up his plan and ordered out a reconnaissance group to scout along the riverbank for a site from which the DUKWs might be launched. Sosabowski's engineers were not optimistic; the awkward amphibious vehicles would prove cumbersome to manhandle across ditches and banks down to the river, especially in the dark. A short while later Taylor's reconnaissance group confirmed the Poles' opinion. The river could be approached, they thought, only by one narrow ditch-lined road. In spite of the serious obstacles, Taylor's men believed they could get the DUKWs down to the Rhine. Colonel Mackenzie, still unable to continue on to Nijmegen, would oversee the launching. The DUKWs would cross the river at 2 A.M. on Saturday, the twenty-third. First priority, however, was to get men into the bridgehead: Sosabowski's Poles had to be ferried over in the little string of rubber boats.

At 9 P.M. on Friday night that operation began. Silently crouching along the riverbank, the Polish soldiers waited. On both sides of the river engineers, under the direction of Lieutenant Colonel Myers, stood ready to pull the hawser attaching the rubber dinghies back and forth. In just four boats—two 2-man and two 1-man dinghies—only six men could cross the 400-yard-wide Rhine at a time. Supplementing the craft were several wooden rafts that the Polish engineers had constructed to carry small supplies and stores. On Sosabowski's order the first six men got into the boats and moved out. Within a few minutes the men were across. Behind them came a string of rafts. As fast as men landed on the northern bank the boats and rafts were hauled back. "It was a slow, laborious process," Sosabowski noted, "but so far the Germans seemed to suspect nothing."

Then, from a point to the west of the landing site across the river a light shot up into the sky, and almost immediately the whole area was brilliantly lit by a magnesium parachute flare. Instantly Spandau machine guns began raking the river, "stirring up small waves and making the water boil with hot steel," Sosabowski recalls. Simultaneously, mortar shells began to fall among the waiting Poles. Within minutes two rubber boats were riddled, their occupants heaved into the river. On the southern bank, men scattered, firing at the parachute flare. In the wild melee, Sosabowski halted the operation. Men moved back and took up new positions, trying to avoid the bursting mortar shells. The moment the flare dimmed and burned out, they ran to the boats and rafts, climbed in, and the crossings began again. Another flare burst in the sky. In this cruel game of hide-and-seek the Poles, suffering terrible casualties, continued to cross the river all night in the remaining boats. At the schoolhouse in Driel which had been temporarily turned into a casualty station, Cora Baltussen tended the injured as they were brought in. "We can't get across," a Pole told her. "It's a slaughter up there—and we can't even fire back."

At 2 A.M., Taylor's amphibious DUKWs began moving down to the river. Because of heavy rain during the day, the low, narrow, ditch-lined road was inches thick in mud. And, as the DUKWs, surrounded by sixty men, slowly approached the river, a heavy ground mist formed. Men could not see either the road or the river. Again and again, struggling soldiers labored to straighten the vehicles as they slid off the road. Supplies were unloaded to lighten the DUKWs, but even this was not enough. Finally, despite strenuous efforts to hold them back, the cumbersome vehicles slid into the ditch only yards from the Rhine. "It's no good," the despairing Mackenzie told Taylor. "It's just hopeless." At 3 A.M., the entire operation came to a halt. Only fifty men and almost no supplies had been ferried across the river into Urquhart's bridgehead.

3

BY THE TIME COLONEL CHARLES MACKENZIE finally reached General Browning's headquarters in Nijmegen on Saturday morning, September 23, he was "dead tired, frozen stiff, and his teeth were chattering," Brigadier Gordon Walch, the chief of staff, remembers. In spite of his determination to see Browning immediately, Mackenzie was promptly "put in a bath to thaw out."

British forces using the relief route west of, and parallel to, the "island" highway were now moving steadily up to Driel, but the roads were far from clear of the enemy. Still, Lord Wrottesley had decided to try to get Mackenzie and Lieutenant Colonel Myers back to Nijmegen. The brief trip, in a small convoy of reconnaissance vehicles, was hair-raising. As the party approached a crossroads, they found a partly destroyed German half-track lying slewed across it. Wrottesley got out to guide his vehicles, and at that point, a Tiger tank appeared farther down the road. To avoid an encounter, the armored car carrying Mackenzie began backing away, when suddenly the road collapsed beneath it and the car turned over. Mackenzie and the crew were forced to hide out from German infantry in a field as Wrottesley, yelling to the driver of his scout car "to go like hell," headed up the road toward Nijmegen to find British troops. Organizing a relief force, Wrottesley sped back down the road to find Mackenzie. When the little force arrived the German tank was gone and Mackenzie and the crew of the armored car came up to meet them from the field where they had taken cover. In the confusion Myers, following in a second armored car, became separated from the troop.

General Browning greeted Mackenzie anxiously. According to his staff, "the week had been a series of agonizing and tragic setbacks." More than anything else the lack of full communications with Urquhart had contributed to Browning's concern. Even now, although messages were passing between the British 1st Airborne Division and Corps, Browning's picture of Urquhart's situation was apparently very vague. In the original Market-Garden plan the 52nd Lowland Division was to have been flown into the Arnhem area once Urquhart's men had found a suitable landing site—ideally by Thursday, September 21. When Urquhart's desperate situation became known, the 52nd's commanding officer, Major General Edmund Hakewill Smith, promptly offered to risk taking in part of his unit by glider, to land as close as possible to the beleaguered 1st Airborne. On Friday morning Browning had rejected the proposal, radioing: "Thanks for your message but offer not repeat not required as situation better than you think . . . 2nd Army definitely . . . intend fly you in to Deelen airfield as soon as situation allows." Later General Brereton, First Allied Airborne Army commander, noting the message in his diary, commented, "General Browning was over-optimistic and apparently then did not fully appreciate the plight of the Red Devils." At the time, Brereton seemed no better informed than Browning. In a report to Eisenhower, which was sent on to General Marshall in Washington on Friday night, Brereton said of the Nijmegen-Arnhem area: "the situation in this sector is showing great improvement."

Within hours the optimism of Brereton and Browning had faded. Friday's futile efforts to reach Urquhart seemed to have been the turning point for the Corps commander. According to his staff, "he was disgusted with General Thomas and the 43rd Wessex Division." He felt they had not moved fast enough. Thomas, he told them, had been "too anxious to tidy things up as he went along." Additionally, Browning's authority extended only so far: the moment British ground troops entered the Nijmegen area, administrative control passed over to General Horrocks, the XXX Corps commander; decisions would be made by Horrocks and by his chief, the British Second Army's General Miles C. Dempsey. There was little that Browning could do.

Convinced that Holland was on the verge of liberation and completely oblivious to the dangers, the Dutch climbed on their roofs to watch the vast armada of troop-carrier planes and gliders.

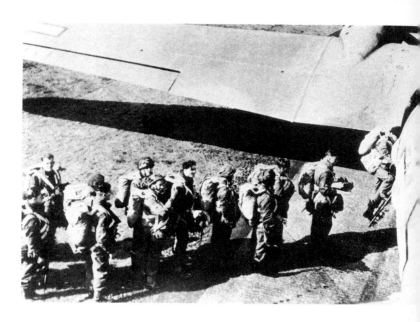

British troopers enplane for Holland [ABOVE], and an American Waco glider [BELOW] is loaded. • [OPPOSITE] Planes tow gliders of 101st Airborne over Eindhoven, and [NEXT PAGE] men of 82nd Airborne land over Groesbeek in mass jump.

Gliders and paratroopers of British 1st Airborne [ABOVE] land near Arnhem, and a supply drop [BELOW] in the British Paratroop sector.

A tow plane behind the Waco glider [ABOVE] crash-lands and explodes on Arnhem drop zone. Tail of the huge Horsa glider [BELOW] was quickly removed to unload the cargo.

In spite of warnings, Arnhem's German commander, General Kussin, took the wrong road and was killed by British troopers.

Artillery chief Lieutenant Colonel "Sheriff" Thompson (*at left*) unloads gear from Horsa glider.

A Guards Armored tank passes a knocked-out German armored vehicle. Terrain difficulties and narrow, one-tank-width roads hindered the advance of the armored drive.

In the corridor a supply truck explodes after receiving direct hit.

A German patrol moves up during first hours of battle.

Flight Lieutenant David Lord [BELOW, AT RIGHT], in an unprecedented act of courage witnessed by British paratroopers, circled his flaming Dakota again and again over the drop zone in a successful attempt to parachute precious supplies. The only survivor was Flying Officer Henry King [ABOVE LEFT]. • Typical of courageous glider pilots was Sergeant Victor Miller [ABOVE RIGHT], who successfully landed his huge, unwieldy craft. His one concern was that another glider might "crash-land on top of me."

Lieutenant Tony Jones [ABOVE LEFT], called by General Horrocks the "bravest of the brave," rushed across Nijmegen bridge in wake of tanks and cut the German detonating explosive wires. • A badly wounded paratrooper [RIGHT] is rushed to casualty station. • 82nd Airborne troopers [BELOW] move through outskirts of Nijmegen.

[ABOVE] British "Red Devils" move forward through the debris at Arnhem. [BELOW] Antoon Derksen's house at 14 Zwarteweg, where General Urquhart hid out when caught behind German lines.

101st Airborne troopers are greeted by Dutch [ABOVE] as they pass through Eindhoven. • Terrain difficulties are clearly shown [BELOW] on one-tank front, where Guards Armored column has been halted on "island" dike-top road.

On Arnhem bridge Colonel Frost's and Captain Mackay's men successfully repulsed a German armored attack, knocking out twelve lead vehicles. The German commander, Gräbner, was killed in the attack.

(*Below, left to right*) Field Marshal Mode[l], General Bittrich; the one-legged Major Knaust (*also shown above left as he is toda[y]*) and Major General Heinz Harmel conf[er] during battle. Knaust's Tiger tanks stop[ped] the last drive of British to relieve the Arnhem bridge defenders. • Major Ego[n] Skalka [ABOVE, RIGHT], Hohenstaufen Division medical officer, who cooperate[d] in exchanging the wounded during the [...] The SS man, obviously worried about h[is] future, requested a letter of commendat[ion] from a British medical officer.

Dutch women who had collaborated with Germans [ABOVE] were quickly rounded up by the Resistance and had their heads shaved [BELOW].

[LEFT] The Hartenstein Hotel in Oosterbeek, General Urquhart's headquarters during the battle. [CENTER] The Schoonoord Hotel and [BOTTOM] the Tafelberg Hotel, shown before and during the battle.

Perhaps the finest journalistic coverage of the war came out of Arnhem. Sergeants Lewis and Walker, Army cameramen [ABOVE], share a meal with Dutch girl. • London *Daily Express* war correspondent Alan Wood [BELOW] electrified Britain with his brilliant dispatches from the field.

The build-up of the 35,000-man Allied Airborne Army was slowed by inclement weather. Parachutes of 101st Airborne troopers [ABOVE] dot countryside on second day of attack. • At Arnhem bridge, Major Digby Tatham-Warter [SHOWN BELOW AS HE IS TODAY AND IN 1944] bolstered the men's morale by his eccentric charges against the enemy under an open umbrella.

In Oosterbeek perimeter, cut off and without supplies, Medic "Taffy" Brace [RIGHT] used makeshift paper bandages to save the life of machine gunner Corporal Andrew Milbourne [SHOWN ABOVE THEN AND NOW], who lost an eye and both hands. • Another British hero was Sergeant Alfred Roullier [SHOWN BELOW THEN AND NOW], who cooked and served hot stew in the midst of battle to the hungry troops.

A major British miscalculation was the failure to use the Dutch underground. The most frustrated of all were Dutch liaison officer Lieutenant Commander Arnoldus Wolters [ABOVE LEFT] and Douw van der Krap [ABOVE RIGHT], whose efforts to form a fighting unit proved fruitless.

In Oosterbeek, baker Dirk van Beek [LEFT] saw that "things were going bad," but vowed to continue "baking to the last." • Rare book seller Gerhardus Gysbers [RIGHT], whose shop was next to the German barracks, was one of the first to realize that the British Arnhem attack was doomed to failure.

In the pre-attack bombing, Resistance worker Albertus Uijen [BELOW LEFT] saw that Nijmegen was being isolated by bombers. • Telephone technician Nicolaas de Bode [BELOW RIGHT], using secret lines, was able to pass on vital information to the underground and Allies. • Johannus Penseel [ABOVE LEFT] took advantage of German confusion to move an arsenal of weapons "beneath Germans' noses." • Gysbert Numan [ABOVE RIGHT] wanted to surrender himself and others rather than allow twelve innocent men to be executed for the abortive sabotage of a viaduct on September 15th. Arnhem Resistance chief Kruyff refused the request.

The Germans systematically destroyed British strongholds. • British troopers hold positions around the Hartenstein Hotel. In background is the tennis court where German prisoners were held.

A knocked-out German tank lies amidst the ruins • [OPPOSITE] Church in lower Oosterbeek was almost totally destroyed.

"They are throwing us away," Colonel Tilly [ABOVE RIGHT] confided to his second-in-command, Major Grafton [ABOVE LEFT], after he learned that his Dorset unit was to cross the Lower Rhine and make a last stand while the remnants of Urquhart's division were evacuated. Of 10,000 Britishers in the Arnhem attack, only 2,323 crossed the river to safety. Some of the survivors are shown below.

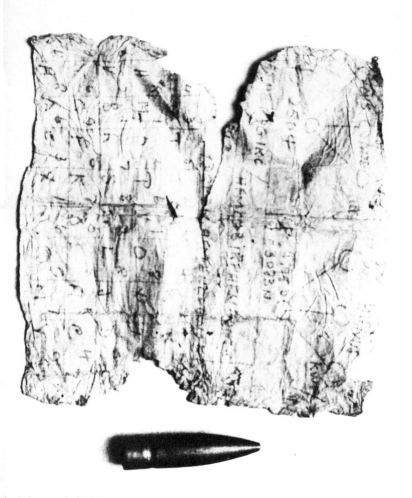

A cipher code hidden in a .303 cartridge was supposed to be fired before evacuation. In the excitement of escape, Signaler James Cockrill forgot his instructions and later found the code and bullet in his battle dress pocket.

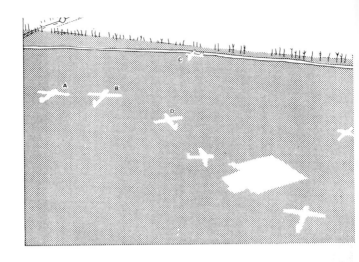

In the late sixties, during a photo-mapping of Holland by KLM Airlines, experts were mystified by what appeared to be aircraft on the heaths near Arnhem [OPPOSITE]. On careful examination cartographers discovered that the ghostly images were outlines of gliders. During and after the battle in 1944, wrecked gliders were burned, indelibly branding the heath. Confirmation of the silhouettes was made by Robert Voskuil, son of Jan and Bertha, who compared the wartime aerial photographs with KLM pictures and presented his findings in the *Journal of the Royal Geographic Society.*

The chief personalities of the airborne attack as they are today
General James M. Gavin of 82nd Airborne [ABOVE LEFT]; General Maxwell
D. Taylor of 101st Airborne [ABOVE RIGHT] [BELOW, LEFT TO RIGHT, IN 1966]
General Stanislaw Sosabowski; General John Hackett; General Roy Urquhart;
Colonel C. F. Gough; General John Frost; and Brigadier Graeme Warrack. •
Refusing to return to Communist-dominated Poland at war's end, Sosabowski
worked for a time in Britain as a common laborer. He died as this book was
being written.

Sitting with the somewhat revived Mackenzie, Browning now learned for the first time the details of Urquhart's appalling predicament. Mackenzie, sparing nothing, recounted everything that had happened. Brigadier Walch remembers Mackenzie telling Browning that "the division is in a very tight perimeter and low in everything—food, ammunition and medical supplies." While the situation was acute, Mackenzie said, "if there is a chance of the Second Army getting to us, we can hold—but not for long." Walch recollects Mackenzie's grim summation. "There isn't much left," he said. Browning listened in silence. Then he assured Mackenzie that he had not given up hope. Plans were now afoot to get men and supplies into the bridgehead during Saturday night. But, Brigadier Walch says, "I do remember Browning telling Charles that there did not seem to be much chance of getting a good party across."

As Mackenzie set out for Driel once more, he was struck by the ambivalence of the thinking at Corps headquarters—and by the dilemma that created for him. Obviously the fate of the British 1st Airborne still hung in the balance. No one had as yet made any definite decisions. But what should he tell Urquhart? "After seeing the situation on both sides of the river," he says, "I was convinced a crossing from the south would not be successful and I could tell him that. Or, I could report, as I was told, that everyone was doing his best, that there would be a crossing and we should hold on. Which was better? Tell him that in my opinion there wasn't a chance in hell of anyone getting over? Or that help was on the way?" Mackenzie decided on the latter, for he felt it would help Urquhart "to keep people going if I put it that way."

Like Browning, the Allied high command was only now learning the true facts of the 1st Airborne's plight. In off-the-record briefings at Eisenhower's, at Brereton's and at Montgomery's headquarters, war correspondents were told that the "situation is serious, but every measure is being taken to relieve Urquhart." That minor note of concern represented a radical change in attitude. Since its inception, Market-Garden had been painted in public reports as an overwhelming success. On Thursday, September 21, under a headline announcing that a "tank paradise lies ahead," one British newspaper's lead story stated: "Hitler's northern flank is crumbling. Field Marshal

Montgomery, with the brilliant aid of the First Airborne Army, has paved the way into the Ruhr—and to the end of the war." Even the staid London *Times* on Friday had such headlines as "On the Road to Arnhem; Tanks Across the Rhine"; only the subhead hinted of possible trouble ahead: "Coming Fight for Arnhem; Airborne Forces' Hard Time." Correspondents could hardly be blamed. Lack of communications, overenthusiasm on the part of Allied commanders and strict censorship prevented accurate reporting. Then, overnight, the picture changed. On Saturday, the twenty-third, the *Times*'s headline read: "2nd Army Meets Tough Opposition; Airborne Forces' Grim Fight," and the London *Daily Express* was calling Arnhem a "Patch of Hell."*

Yet hopes remained high. On this Saturday, the seventh day of Market-Garden, the weather over England cleared and Allied planes took to the air again.† The last of the great fleet of gliders, grounded in the Grantham area since Tuesday, set out finally for Gavin's 82nd with 3,385 troops—his long-awaited 325th Glider Infantry Regiment—and Taylor's hard-pressed 101st Division was brought up to full strength by nearly 3,000 more men. But Sosabowski, under heavy attack at Driel, could not be reinforced with the remainder of his brigade. Browning was forced to direct the rest of the Poles to drop zones in the 82nd's area. Because of weather Brereton's three-day air plan

---

*Some of the war's finest reporting came out of Arnhem. The ten-man press team attached to the 1st Airborne Division included Major Roy Oliver, a public information officer; censors Flight Lieutenant Billy Williams and Captain Peter Brett; army photographers Sergeants Lewis and Walker; and correspondents Alan Wood, London *Daily Express*; Stanley Maxted and Guy Byam, BBC; Jack Smyth, Reuter's, and Marek Swiecicki, a Polish correspondent attached to Sosabowski's brigade. Although limited by sparse communications to bulletins of only a few hundred words per day, these men, in the finest tradition of war reporting, portrayed the agonies of Urquhart's men. I have been unable to locate a single correspondent of the original team. Presumably, all are dead.

†Inexplicably, some official and semiofficial British accounts contend that bad weather prevented aerial activity on Saturday, September 23. Meteorological, Corps and Allied Air Force after-action reports all record Saturday's weather as fair, with more missions flown than on any day since Tuesday, the nineteenth. In the semiofficial *Struggle for Europe*, Chester Wilmot erred in stating that on Saturday "aerial resupply had been thwarted by bad weather." The phrase altered his chronology of the battle thereafter. Other accounts, using Wilmot as a guide, have compounded the inaccuracies.

to deliver some 35,000 men in the greatest airborne operation ever conceived had taken more than double the planned time.

Once again, although resupply missions were successful elsewhere, Urquhart's men, in their rapidly diminishing pocket about Oosterbeek, watched cargo fall into enemy hands. Unable to locate the Hartenstein drop zone, and flying through savage antiaircraft fire, the supply planes were in constant trouble; 6 of the 123 planes were shot down and 63 damaged. In a message to Browning, Urquhart reported:

> 231605 . . . Resupply by air; very small quantity picked up. Snipers now severely curtailing movement and therefore collection. Also roads so blocked by falling trees, branches and houses that movement in jeeps virtually impossible. Jeeps in any case practically out of action.

Close-in fighter support was inadequate, too. In the Arnhem area the weather had been bad throughout the morning, clearing only by midday. As a result only a few flights of R.A.F. Spitfires and Typhoons attacked targets about the perimeter. Urquhart was baffled. "In view of our complete aerial superiority," he later recollected, "I was bitterly disappointed by the lack of fighter support." But to his men, who had not seen a fighter since D Day, the previous Sunday, the attacks were heartening. By now, too, most of them had learned that British troops had finally reached the southern bank of the Rhine at Driel. Relief, they believed, was close at hand.

In spite of all the setbacks, now that General Thomas' troops were moving up the side roads to Driel, General Horrocks believed that Urquhart's worsening situation could be alleviated. Brilliant, imaginative and determined, Horrocks was opposed to throwing away all that had been gained. Yet he must find some way to move troops and supplies into the bridgehead. "I am certain," he later put it, "that these were about the blackest moments in my life." He was so distressed at "the picture of the airborne troops fighting their desperate battle on the other side of the river" that he could not sleep; and the severing of the corridor north of Veghel, cut since Friday afternoon, threatened the life of the entire operation.

Now every hour was vital. Like Horrocks, General Thomas was determined to get men across the river. His 43rd Wessex was going all-out in a two-phase operation: attacking to seize Elst and driving toward Driel. Although by now no one had any illusions that the Arnhem bridge could be captured—from aerial reconnaissance photos it was clear the enemy held it in strength—Thomas' right flank, terminating at Elst, had to be protected if any operations were to be conducted across the Rhine from Driel. And Horrocks had hopes that, in addition to the Poles, some British infantry might cross into the bridge-head on Saturday night.

His optimism was premature. On the low-lying secondary roads west of the main Nijmegen-Arnhem highway a giant bottleneck developed as Thomas' two brigades, each totaling about 3,000 men—one brigade attacking northeast toward Elst, the other driving north for Driel—attempted to move through the same crossroads. Enemy shelling added to the crowding and confusion. Thus, it was dark by the time the bulk of Thomas' 130th Brigade began to reach Driel—too late to join the Poles in an organized attempt to cross the river.

Shortly after midnight, Sosabowski's men, heavily supported by artillery, began crossing, this time in sixteen boats left from the 82nd's assault across the Waal. They came under intense fire and suffered heavy losses. Only 250 Poles made it to the northern bank, and of these only 200 reached the Hartenstein perimeter.

On this grim day Horrocks and Thomas received just one piece of good news: at 4 P.M. the corridor north of Veghel was reopened and traffic began flowing again. In the engineering columns were more assault craft, and the stubborn Horrocks was hopeful that they could be rushed forward in time to pour infantry across the river on Sunday night.

But could the division hang on another twenty-four hours? Urquhart's plight was rapidly growing worse. In his situation report to Browning on Saturday night, Urquhart had said:

> 232015: Many attacks during day by small parties infantry, SP guns, tanks including flame thrower tanks. Each attack accompanied by very heavy mortaring and shelling within Div perimeter. After many alarms and excursions the latter remains substantially unchanged, although very thinly held. Physical contact not yet made with those on south bank of river.

> Resupply a flop, small quantities of ammo only gathered in. Still no food and all ranks extremely dirty owing to shortage of water. Morale still adequate, but continued heavy mortaring and shelling is having obvious effects. We shall hold but at the same time hope for a brighter 24 hours ahead.

The afternoon's giant Allied glider lift had caught Field Marshal Walter Model by surprise. At this late date in the battle he had not anticipated any further Allied airborne landings. These new reinforcements, coming just as his counteroffensive was gaining momentum, could change the tide of battle—and even more might be on the way. For the first time since the beginning of the Allied attack he began to have doubts about the outcome.

Driving to Doetinchem he conferred with General Bittrich, demanding, as the II SS Panzer Corps commander remembers, "a quick finish to the British at Oosterbeek." Model needed every man and tank. Too great a force was being tied down in a battle that "should have been brought to an end days before." Model was "very excited," Bittrich says, "and kept repeating, 'When will things finally be over here?'"

Bittrich insisted that "we are fighting as we have never fought before." At Elst, Major Hans Peter Knaust was staving off British tank and infantry columns trying to proceed up the main highway to Arnhem. But Knaust could not hold at Elst and also attack west against the Poles and British at Driel. The moment his heavy Tigers moved onto the polder they bogged down. The assault toward Driel was a task for infantry and lighter vehicles, Bittrich explained. "Model was never interested in excuses," Bittrich says, "but he understood me. Still, he gave me only twenty-four hours to finish the British off."

Bittrich drove to Elst to see Knaust. The major was worried. All day the forces against him had appeared to be growing stronger. While he knew British tanks could not leave the main highway, the possibility of attacks from the west concerned him. "A British breakthrough must be halted at all costs," Bittrich warned. "Can you hold for another twenty-four hours, while we clean up Oosterbeek?" Knaust assured Bittrich that he could. Leaving Knaust, the Panzer Corps commander immediately ordered Colonel Harzer of the Hohenstaufen Division to "intensify all attacks against the airborne tomorrow. I want the whole affair ended."

Harzer's problems were also difficult. Although Oosterbeek was completely encircled, its narrow streets were proving almost impossible for maneuvering tanks—especially for the 60-ton Tigers, "which tore up the road foundations, making them look like plowed fields, and ripped off the pavement when they turned." Additionally, Harzer told Bittrich, "everytime we compress the airborne pocket and shrink it even tighter, the British seem to fight harder." Bittrich advised that "strong attacks should be thrown from east and west at the base of the perimeter to cut the British off from the Rhine."

The Frundsberg Division commander, General Harmel, charged with holding and driving back the Allied forces in the Nijmegen-Arnhem area, heard from Bittrich, too. The assembling of his whole division delayed by the wreckage on the Arnhem bridge, Harmel had not been able to form a blocking front on both sides of the elevated "island" highway. The British attack at Oosterbeek had split his forces. Only part of his division had been in position on the western side when the British attacked. Now, what remained of his men and equipment was east of the highway. Elst would be held, Harmel assured Bittrich. The British could not advance up the main road. But he was powerless to halt the drive to Driel. "I cannot prevent them going up or coming back," he told Bittrich. The II SS Panzer Corps leader was firm. The next twenty-four hours would be critical, he warned Harmel. "The British will try everything to reinforce their bridgehead and also drive for Arnhem." Harzer's attacks against the Oosterbeek perimeter would succeed—provided that Harmel held. As Bittrich put it, "We'll get the nail. You must amputate the finger."

The guns of the 43rd were thundering, and in the southwest corner of the Oosterbeek perimeter a big gasometer blazed, throwing an eerie, flickering, yellowish light over the Rhine. As he climbed out of a boat on the northern bank, Colonel Charles Mackenzie could see why he had been warned by radio to wait for a guide. The shoreline was unrecognizable; boat wreckage, fallen trees, and shell craters had buried the road running back into the bridgehead. If he had tried to set out by himself he would certainly have become lost. Now, following an engineer, he was guided to the Hartenstein.

Mackenzie had not changed his mind about the report he would make to Urquhart. Once again, while waiting to be rowed over to the division perimeter, he had thought about his options. In spite of all the preparations that he had seen in Driel and on the southern bank, he remained skeptical that help would ever reach the division in time. He felt guilty about the report he had decided to make. Yet, there was still the chance that his own view was far too pessimistic.

In the cellar of the shattered Hartenstein, Urquhart was waiting. Mackenzie gave the Airborne commander the official view: "Help is on the way. We should hang on." Urquhart, Mackenzie remembers, "listened impassively, neither disheartened nor gladdened by the news." The unspoken question for both men remained the same: How much *longer* must they hold? At this time, in the first hours of Sunday, September 24, after eight days of battle, Urquhart's estimated strength was down to fewer than 2,500 men. And for all of them there was only one question: When will Monty's forces arrive? They had thought about it in the loneliness of trenches, gunpits and outposts, in the wrecks of houses and shops, and in the hospitals and dressing stations, where anxious uncomplaining men lay wounded on pallets, mattresses and bare floors.

With infantry on the south bank of the river, the paratroopers did not doubt that the Second Army would eventually cross. They wondered only if any of them would be alive to see the relief for which they had waited so long. In these last tragic hours annihilation was their constant fear, and to allay this dread, men tried to raise one another's morale by any means they could. Jokes made the rounds. Wounded men, still holding at their posts, disregarded their injuries, and examples of extraordinary daring were becoming commonplace. Above all, Urquhart's men were proud. They shared a spirit in those days that was stronger, they said later, than they would ever know again.

From his kit Lance Bombardier James Jones of an artillery troop took out the single nonmilitary item he had brought along—the flute he had used as a boy. "I just wanted to play it again," he remembers. "It was raining mortar bombs for three or four days straight and I was frightened to death. I got out the flute and began to play." Nearby, Lieutenant James Woods, the gun-position officer, had an idea. With Jones leading, Lieutenant Woods and two other gunners climbed out of their trenches and began to march around the gun positions. As they proceeded single file, Lieutenant Woods began to sing. Behind him the two troopers removed their helmets and drummed on them with sticks. Battered men heard the strains of "British Grenadiers" and "Scotland the Brave" filtering softly through the area. Faintly at first, other men began to sing and then, with Woods "going at the top of his voice," the artillery positions erupted in song.

In the Schoonoord Hotel on the Utrecht-Arnhem road, approximately midway along the eastern side of the perimeter, Dutch volunteers and British medics cared for hundreds of wounded under the watchful eyes of German guards. Hendrika van der Vlist wrote in her diary:

> Sunday, September 24. This is the day of the Lord. War rages outside. The building is shaking. That is why the doctors cannot operate or fix casts. We cannot wash the wounded because nobody can venture out to find water under these conditions. The army chaplain scribbles in his notebook. I ask him what time the service will be held.

Padre G. A. Pare finished his notes. With Hendrika he made the rounds of all the rooms in the hotel. The shelling seemed "particularly noisy," he recalls, "and I could hardly hear my own voice above the battle outside." Yet, "looking into the faces of men stretched out all over the floor," Chaplain Pare "felt inspired to fight the noise outside with God's peace inside." Quoting from St. Matthew, Pare said, "'Take no thought for the morrow. What ye shall eat or what ye shall drink, or where withal ye shall be clothed.'" Then he, like the men in the artillery positions, began to sing. As he began "Abide With Me," men just listened. Then they began to hum and sing softly themselves. Against the thunderous barrage outside the Schoonoord, hundreds of wounded and dying men took up the words, "'When other helpers fail and comforts flee, God of the helpless, O abide with me.'"

Across the street from the church in lower Oosterbeek, Kate ter Horst left her five children and the eleven other civilians sheltering in the ten-by-six-foot cellar of her house and made her way past the wounded on the upper floor. The fourteen-room, 200-year-old house, a former vicarage, was totally unrecognizable. The windows were gone and "every foot of space in the main hall, dining room, study, garden room, bedrooms, corridors, kitchen, boiler room and attic was crowded with wounded," Mrs. ter Horst recalls. They lay, too, in the garage and even under the stairs. In all, more than three hundred injured men crowded the house and grounds, and others were being brought in by the minute. Outdoors on this Sunday morning Kate ter Horst saw that a haze hung over the battlefield. "The sky is yellow," she wrote, "and there are dark clouds hanging down like wet rags. The earth has been torn open." On the grounds she saw "the dead, our dead, wet through from rain, and stiff. Lying on their faces, just as they were yesterday and the day before—the man with the tousled beard and the one with the black face and many, many others." Eventually, fifty-seven men would be buried in the garden, "one of them a mere boy," Mrs. ter Horst wrote, "who died inside the house for lack of space." The lone doctor among the medical teams in the house, Captain Randall Martin, had told Mrs. ter Horst that the boy "had simply banged his head against a radiator until he was gone."

Picking her way gingerly about the rooms, Kate ter Horst thought of her husband, Jan, who had left on Tuesday night by bicycle to scout the area and bring back information about German positions to an artillery officer. The perimeter had been formed while he was gone and, in the heavy fighting, Jan was unable to get back home. They would not see each other for two more weeks. Working with Dr. Martin and the orderlies ever since Wednesday, Mrs. ter Horst had hardly slept. Going from room to room, she prayed with the wounded and read to them from the 91st Psalm, "Thou shalt not be afraid for the terror by night, nor for the arrow that flieth by day."

Now, all this morning, snipers, infiltrating into the perimeter during the night, were firing "shamelessly into a house from which never a shot was fired," she wrote. "Bullets whizzed through rooms and corridors crowded with helpless people."

Carrying a stretcher past a window, two orderlies were shot. Then, what everyone feared most might happen occurred: Dr. Martin was wounded. "It's only my ankle," he told Mrs. ter Horst. "In the afternoon I'll go hopping around again."

Outside the sniping gave way to shelling. The thunder and crash of mortar bursts "defies description," Kate ter Horst recorded. To Private Michael Growe, "the lady seemed terribly calm and unflustered." Growe, already wounded in the thigh from shrapnel, was now hit again in the left foot by a shell burst. Hastily medics moved Growe and other newly injured men away from a line of French windows.

Corporal Daniel Morgans, hit in the head and right knee as he was holding a position near the Oosterbeek church, was carried to the Ter Horst house just as a German tank came up the road. As an orderly was explaining to Morgans that "they were practically out of dressings and had no anesthetics or food, and only a little water," the tank sent a shell crashing against the house. In an upstairs room, Private Walter Boldock, with bullet wounds in the side and back, stared in horror as the tank "ground and wheeled. I could hear the gibberish chatter of machine guns and then a shell tore through the wall above my back. Plaster and debris began falling everywhere and many of the wounded were killed." Downstairs Bombardier E. C. Bolden, a medical orderly, was in a white-hot rage. Grabbing a Red Cross flag, he rushed out of the house and straight for the tank. Corporal Morgans heard him clearly. "What the hell are you doing?" Bolden screamed at the German tank commander. "This house is clearly marked with a Red Cross flag. Get the hell away from here!" As the anxious wounded listened, they heard the sound of the tank backing off. Bolden returned to the house, "almost as angry," Morgans remembers, "as when he left. We asked him what happened." Bolden replied tersely: "The German apologized but he also got the hell out."

Although the house was not shelled again, there was no letup in the fire about them. Kate ter Horst wrote: "All around these men are dying. Must they breathe their last in such a hurricane? Oh, God! Give us a moment's silence. Give us quiet, if only for a short moment, so that they at least can die. Grant them a moment's holy silence while they pass on to Eternity."

All about the perimeter, tanks crashed through defenses as weary, groggy troopers reached the limits of exhaustion. There were horrors everywhere—particularly from flamethrowers. In one incident of SS brutality, a jeep carrying wounded under a Red Cross flag was stopped by four Germans. One of the medics tried to explain that he was carrying wounded to a casualty station. The Germans turned a flamethrower on him, then walked away. But throughout the battle, both at the Arnhem bridge and in the perimeter, there were singular examples of chivalry.

On Brigadier Hackett's eastern perimeter defenses a German officer drove up to the British positions under a white flag and asked to see the commander. Hackett met him and learned that the Germans "were about to attack, first laying down mortar and artillery fire on my forward positions." As the Germans knew that one of the casualty stations was in the line of attack, Hackett was requested to move his forward positions back 600 yards. "We do not want to put down a barrage that will hit the wounded," the German explained. Hackett knew he could not comply. "If the line had been moved back the distance demanded by the Germans," General Urquhart later wrote, "it would have put Divisional headquarters 200 yards behind the German lines." Despite his inability to move, Hackett noted that when the attack finally came the barrage was carefully laid down to the south of the casualty station.

At the Tafelberg, another doctor, Major Guy Rigby-Jones, who had been operating on a billiard table in the game room of the hotel, lost all his equipment when an 88 shell came through the roof of the building. He had not been able to operate since Thursday, although one of the field ambulance teams had set up a theater in the Petersburg Hotel. "We had 1,200 to 1,300 casualties and neither the nursing facilities nor the staff to properly treat them," he remembers. "All we had was morphia to kill the pain. Our main problem was food and water. We had already drained the central heating system to get water, but now, having ceased operating, I became more or less a quartermaster, trying to feed the wounded." One of them, Major John Waddy of the 156th Battalion, shot in the groin by a sniper on Tuesday, had been wounded again. A mortar shell landing on the window sill of a large bay window exploded and a shell fragment embedded itself in Waddy's left foot. Then the room took a direct hit. Waddy's right shoulder, face and chin were lacerated by falling bricks and wood splinters. Dr. Graeme Warrack, the division's chief medical officer, whose headquarters were at the Tafelberg, rushed outside. Waddy hauled himself up to see Warrack standing in the street shouting at the Germans: "You bloody bastards! Can't anybody recognize a Red Cross?"

The Van Maanen family—Anje, her brother Paul and her aunt—were working around the clock in the Tafelberg, under direction of Dr. van Maanen. Paul, who was a medical student, remembers that "Sunday was terrible. We seemed to be hit all the time. I remembered that we mustn't show fear in front of the patients, but I was ready to jump out of the room and scream. I didn't, because the wounded stayed so calm." As injured men were carried from one damaged room to another, Paul remembers that "we began to sing. We sang for the British, for the Germans, for ourselves. Then everyone seemed to be doing it and with all the emotion people would stop because they were crying, but they would start up again."

For young Anje van Maanen, the romantic dream of liberation by the bright stalwart young men who had dropped from the skies was ending in despair. Many Dutch civilians brought to the Tafelberg had died of their wounds; two, Anje noted in her diary, were "lovely girls and good skaters, as old as I am, just seventeen. Now I will never see them again." To Anje the hotel now seemed to be constantly hit by shells. In the cellar she began to cry. "I am afraid to die," she wrote. "The explosions are enormous and every shell kills. How can God allow this hell?"

By 9:30 A.M. on Sunday morning Dr. Warrack decided to do something about the hell. The nine casualty stations and hospitals in the area were so jammed with wounded from both sides that he began to feel that "the battle could no longer continue in this fashion." Medical teams "were working under impossible conditions, some without surgical instruments." And under the intensified German attacks, casualties were steadily mounting—among them now the courageous Brigadier Shan Hackett, who suffered severe leg and stomach wounds from a mortar-shell burst shortly before 8 A.M.

Warrack had determined on a plan which needed General Urquhart's consent, and he set out for the Hartenstein. "I told the General," Warrack says, "that despite Red Cross flags, all the hospitals were being shelled. One had taken six hits and was set afire, forcing us to quickly evacuate a hundred fifty injured." The wounded, he said, were being "badly knocked about, and the time had come to make some sort of arrangement with the Germans." As it was quite impossible to evacuate wounded across the Rhine, Warrack believed that many lives would be saved "if casualties were handed over to the Germans for treatment in their hospitals in Arnhem."

Urquhart, Warrack recalls, "seemed resigned." He agreed to the plan. But under no circumstances, he warned Warrack, "must the enemy be allowed to think that this was the beginning of a crack in the formation's position." Warrack was to make clear to the Germans that the step was being taken solely on humane grounds. Negotiations could take place, Urquhart said, "on condition that the Germans understand you are a doctor representing your patients, not an official emissary from the division." Warrack was permitted to ask for a truce period during the afternoon so that the battlefield could be cleared of wounded before "both sides got on with the fight."

Warrack hurried off to find Lieutenant Commander Arnoldus Wolters, the Dutch liaison officer, and Dr. Gerritt van Maanen, both of whom he asked to help in the negotiations. Because Wolters, who would act as interpreter, was in the Dutch military and "might run a great risk going to a German headquarters," Warrack gave him the pseudonym "Johnson." The three men quickly headed for the Schoonoord Hotel to contact the German division medical officer.

By coincidence, that officer, twenty-nine-year-old Major Egon Skalka, claims he had reached the same conclusion as Warrack. As Skalka recalls that Sunday morning, he felt "something had to be done not only for our wounded but the British in *der Hexenkessel*." In the Schoonoord Hotel "casualties lay everywhere—even on the floor." According to Skalka, he had come to see "the British chief medical officer to suggest a battlefield clearing" before Warrack arrived. Whoever first had the idea, they did meet. Warrack's impression of the young German doctor was that "he was effeminate in appearance, but sympathetic and apparently quite anxious to ingratiate himself with the British—just in case." Confronting the slender, dapper officer, handsome in his finely cut uniform, Warrack, with "Johnson" interpreting, made his proposal. As they talked, Skalka studied Warrack, "a tall, lanky, dark-haired fellow, phlegmatic like all Englishmen. He seemed terribly tired but otherwise not in bad shape." Skalka was prepared to agree to the evacuation plan, but, he told Warrack, "first we will have to go to my headquarters to make sure there are no objections from my General." Skalka refused to take Dr. van Maanen with them. In a captured British jeep, Skalka, Warrack and "Johnson" set out for Arnhem with Skalka driving. Skalka recalls that he "drove very fast, zigzagging back and forth. I did not want Warrack to orient himself and he would have had a tough time of it the way I drove. We went very fast, part of the time under fire, and twisted and turned into the city."

To Wolters, the short drive into Arnhem was "sad and miserable." Wreckage lay everywhere. Houses were still smoking or in ruins. Some of the roads they followed, chewed up by tank tracks and cratered by shellfire, "looked like plowed fields." Wrecked guns, overturned jeeps, charred armored vehicles and "the crumpled bodies of the dead" lay like a trail all the way into Arnhem. Skalka had not blindfolded the two men, nor did Wolters feel he made any attempt to conceal the route he took. It struck him that the elegant SS medical officer seemed "eager for us to see the German strength." Through the still-smoking, debris-strewn streets of Arnhem, Skalka drove northeast and pulled up outside Lieutenant Colonel Harzer's headquarters, the high school on Hezelbergherweg.

Although the arrival of Warrack and Wolters created surprise among the staff officers, Harzer, alerted by phone, was waiting for them. Skalka, leaving the two officers in an outer room, reported to his commander. Harzer was angry. "I was amazed," he says, "that Skalka had not blindfolded them. Now they knew the exact location of my headquarters." Skalka had laughed. "The way I drove I would be very surprised if they could find their way anywhere," he assured Harzer.

The two Germans sat down with the British emissaries. "The medical officer proposed that his British wounded be evacuated from the perimeter since they no longer had the room or supplies to care for them," Harzer says. "It meant calling a truce for a couple of hours. I told him I was sorry our countries were fighting. Why should we fight, after all? I agreed to his proposal."

Wolters—"a Canadian soldier named Johnson," as Warrack introduced him—remembers the conference in a completely different context. "At first the German SS colonel refused to even consider a truce," he says. "There were several other staff officers in the room, including the acting chief of staff, Captain Schwarz, who finally turned to Harzer and said that the whole matter would have to be taken up with the General." The Germans left the room. "As we waited," Wolters says, "we were offered sandwiches and brandy. Warrack warned me not to drink on an empty stomach. Whatever kind of filling was in the sandwiches was covered with sliced onions."

As the Germans reentered the room, "everyone snapped to attention and there was much 'Heil Hitlering.'" General Bittrich, hatless, in his long black leather coat, came in. "He stayed only a moment," Wolters remembers. Studying the two men, Bittrich said, "*Ich bedauere sehr diesen Krieg zwischen unseren Vaterländern*" (I regret this war between our two nations). The General listened quietly to Warrack's evacuation plan and gave his consent. "I agreed," Bittrich says, "because a man cannot—provided, of course, that he has such feelings to start with—lose all humanity, even during the most bitter fight." Then Bittrich handed Warrack a bottle of brandy. "This is for your General," he told Warrack, and he withdrew.

By 10:30 A.M. Sunday, agreement on the partial truce was reached, although Wolters recollects "that the Germans seemed worried. Both the Tafelberg and the Schoonoord hotels were sitting on the front lines and the Germans could not guarantee to stop mortaring and shelling." Harzer was mainly concerned about the long-range shelling of the British south of the Rhine and whether it could be controlled during the casualty evacuation. Skalka says that after assurances had been given on this point, he received a radio message from British Second Army headquarters. "It was simply addressed to the medical officer, 9th SS Panzer Division, thanking me and asking if a cease-fire could extend long enough for the British to bring up medical supplies, drugs and bandages from across the Rhine." Skalka radioed back, "We do not need your help but request only that your air force refrain from bombing our Red Cross trucks continually." He was answered immediately: "Unfortunately, such attacks occur on both sides." Skalka thought the message "ridiculous." Angrily he replied, "Sorry, but I have not seen our air force in two years." Back came the British message: "Just stick to the agreement." Skalka was now enraged, so much so, he claims, that he radioed back, "Lick my ————."*

The arrangement, as finally worked out, called for a two-hour truce beginning at 3 P.M. The wounded would leave the perimeter by a designated route near the Tafelberg Hotel. Every effort was to be made "to slacken fire or stop completely." Troops on both sides holding front-line positions were warned to hold their fire. As Skalka began to order "every available ambulance and jeep to assemble behind the front lines," Warrack and Wolters, about to head back to their own lines, were allowed to fill their pockets with morphia and medical supplies. Wolters "was glad to get out of there, especially from the moment Schwarz said to me, 'You don't speak German like a Britisher.'"

En route back to the perimeter, a Red Cross flag flying from their jeep and escorted by another German medical officer, Warrack and Wolters were permitted to stop at St. Elisabeth's Hospital to inspect conditions and visit the British wounded —among them Brigadier Lathbury, who, with badges of rank removed, was now "Lance Corporal" Lathbury. They were greeted by the chief British medical officer, Captain Lipmann Kessel; the head of the surgical team, Major Cedric Longland; and the senior Dutch surgeon, Dr. van Hengel—all of whom, Warrack remembers, "were desperately anxious for news." Heavy fighting had taken place about the hospital. At one point there had even been a pitched battle in the building with Germans firing over the heads of patients in the wards, Kessel reported. But since Thursday the area had been quiet and

*Skalka's account that some exchange of messages took place is probably true. Yet the wording of the messages is certainly questionable, especially his answer regarding the Luftwaffe, which was in the air during the week, harassing the British drops. Further, it is a belittlement of forces of his own country. Such a contemptuous assessment of one's own side to an enemy was certainly uncommon among the SS.

Warrack discovered that, in contrast to the harrowing ordeal of the wounded in the perimeter, in St. Elisabeth's "British casualties were in beds with blankets and sheets, and well cared for by Dutch nuns and doctors." Warning Kessel to be prepared for a heavy flow of casualties, the two men returned to Oosterbeek, just in time, Warrack recalls, "to step into a packet of mortaring near the Tafelberg."

At 3 P.M. the partial truce began. The firing suddenly diminished and then stopped altogether. Lance Bombardier Percy Parkes, for whom the "overwhelming noise had become normal, found the silence so unreal that for a second I thought I was dead." With British and German medical officers and orderlies supervising the moves, ambulances and jeeps from both sides began loading casualties. Sergeant Dudley R. Pearson, the 4th Parachute Brigade's chief clerk, was put beside his Brigadier's stretcher on a jeep. "So you got it too, Pearson," said Hackett. Pearson was wearing only his boots and trousers. His right shoulder was heavily bandaged "where shrapnel had torn a huge hole." Hackett was gray-faced and obviously in great pain from his stomach wound. As they moved off toward Arnhem, Hackett said, "Pearson, I hope you won't think I'm pulling rank, but I think I'm a bit worse off than you are. At the hospital do you mind if they get to me first?"*

---

*Both Lathbury and Hackett became "lance corporals" in the hospital. Sergeant Dave Morris, who gave blood to Hackett before his operation, was cautioned that the Brigadier's identity was not to be revealed. Lathbury, in the hospital since the nineteenth, got his first news of the division when the Oosterbeek wounded arrived—including the information that Urquhart had been able to rejoin the division and that Frost's men had held the Arnhem bridge for almost four days. Both brigadiers later escaped from the hospital with the help of the Dutch and hid out. Lathbury eventually joined the irrepressible Major Digby Tatham-Warter, who, dressed in civilian clothes and working with the Dutch underground, "went about quite openly and on one occasion helped to push a German staff car out of a ditch." With a group of approximately 120 troopers, medics and pilots who had been hidden by the Dutch, and led by a Dutch guide, Lathbury reached American troops south of the Rhine on the evening of October 22. The incredible Tatham-Warter helped about 150 British soldiers to escape. Incidentally, it took the author seven years to discover his whereabouts—then by accident. My British publisher met him in Kenya where he has been living since the end of the war. Tatham-Warter says that he "carried the umbrella in battle more for identification purposes than for anything else, because I was always forgetting the password."

Lieutenant Pat Glover, who had jumped with Myrtle the "parachick," was moved to St. Elisabeth's in agony. A bullet had severed two veins in his right hand and on the way to the Schoonoord dressing station he was hit again by shrapnel in the right calf. There was so little morphia that he was told he could not be given a shot unless he deemed it absolutely necessary. Glover did not ask for any. Now, sleeping fitfully, he found himself thinking of Myrtle. He could not remember what day she had been killed. During the fighting he and his batman, Private Joe Scott, had traded Myrtle's satchel back and forth. Then, in a slit trench under fire, Glover suddenly realized that Myrtle's bag was not there. "Where's Myrtle?" he had yelled to Scott. "She's up there, sir." Scott pointed to the top of Glover's trench. Inside her bag, Myrtle lay on her back, feet in the air. During the night Glover and Scott buried the chicken in a shallow little grave near a hedge. As Scott brushed earth over the spot, he looked at Glover and said, "Well, Myrtle was game to the last, sir." Glover remembered he had not taken off Myrtle's parachute wings. Now, in a haze of pain, he was glad that he had buried her with honor and properly—with her badge of rank—as befitted those who died in action.

At the Schoonoord, Hendrika van der Vlist watched as German orderlies began to move casualties out. Suddenly firing began. One of the Germans yelled, "If it does not stop we will open fire and not a casualty, a doctor or a nurse will come out alive." Hendrika paid no attention. "It is always the youngest soldiers who yell the loudest," she noted, "and we're used to the German threats by now." The firing ceased and the loading continued.

Several times again firing broke out as the long lines of walking wounded and convoys of jeeps, ambulances and trucks moved out toward Arnhem. "Inevitably," General Urquhart recalled, "there were misunderstandings. It is not easy to still a battle temporarily." Doctors at the Tafelberg had "some uneasy moments as they cleared combative Germans off the premises." And nearly everyone remembers that the recently arrived Poles could not understand the necessity for the partial cease-fire. "They had many old scores to settle," says Urquhart, "and saw no legitimate reason for holding their fire." Ultimately, they were "prevailed upon to curb their eagerness until the evacuation was completed."

Major Skalka, along with Dr. Warrack, kept the convoys moving throughout the afternoon. Some 200 walking wounded were led out and more than 250 men were carried in the medical convoys. "I have never seen anything like the conditions at Oosterbeek," Skalka says. "It was nothing but death and wreckage."

At St. Elisabeth's, Lieutenant Peter Stainforth, recovering from a chest wound received in Arnhem, heard the first walking wounded coming in. "I felt a shiver of excitement run up my spine," he says. "I have never been so proud. They came in and the rest of us were horror-stricken. Every man had a week's growth of beard. Their battle dress was torn and stained; and filthy, blood-soaked bandages poked out from all of them. The most compelling thing was their eyes—red-rimmed, deep-sunk, peering out from drawn, mud-caked faces made haggard by lack of sleep, and yet they walked in undefeated. They looked fierce enough to take over the place right then and there."

As the last convoy left Oosterbeek, Warrack thanked the SS medical officer for his help. "Skalka looked me in the eye and said, 'Can I have that in writing?'" Warrack ignored the remark. At 5 P.M. the battle began again as though it had never stopped.

At Lance Bombardier Percy Parkes's gun position near the Dolderen laundry, "all hell broke loose again. The Jerries threw everything at us." After the relative quiet during the evacuation of the wounded, Parkes felt a sense of relief. "Everything had returned to normal, and I could orient to that. I was back in business again." Germans, taking advantage of the temporary truce, had infiltrated many areas. Men heard screaming and firing from all directions as Germans and British chased one another through streets and gardens. From his trench Parkes saw a tank coming across a cabbage patch toward battery headquarters. Two artillerymen sprinted for a 6-pounder on the road. As the troopers began to fire, Parkes looked up in amazement as cabbages began to sail over his trench. "The force of the gun was sucking up the cabbages, pulling them right out of the ground and hurling them through the air. Then there was a tremendous bang and we saw a shell hit the tank."

Major Robert Cain heard someone yell, "Tigers!" and he raced for the small antitank gun set up alongside a building in his block. A gunner ran up the street to help him. Together the two men rolled the gun into position. "Fire!" Cain shouted. He saw that the shell had hit the tank, disabling it. "Let's have another go to be sure," he yelled. The gunner looked at Cain and shook his head. "Can't, sir," he said. "She's finished. The recoil mechanism's gone."

Inside the Ter Horst house the noise was so loud that everyone was numbed and deafened. Suddenly Kate ter Horst felt "a tremendous shock. There was a thunder of bricks. Timbers cracked and there were stifled cries from all sides." The force of the explosion had jammed the cellar door. In the choking dust that swirled through the little room, she heard "men working with spades and tools . . . sawing and the breaking of timbers . . . footsteps crunching through bricks and mortar . . . and heavy things dragged back and forth." The cellar door was broken open and fresh air poured in. Upstairs Kate saw that part of the corridor and the garden room were open to the outdoors and a section of one wall had been blown in. Men lay everywhere, tossed about by the explosion. Dr. Martin had been hit again and was unable to get about at all. A soldier who had been brought in several days earlier suffering from shell shock roamed through the carnage in the house. Staring at Kate ter Horst, he said, "I think I've seen you someplace before." Gently she led him to the cellar and found room for him on the stone floor. Almost immediately he fell asleep. Wakening later, he moved over to Mrs. ter Horst. "We can be taken at any moment now," he said quietly. He went to sleep again. Leaning tiredly against a wall, her five children beside her, Kate waited, as "the ghastly hours stretched slowly."

In a trench not far from Major Cain's position, Sergeant Alf Roullier saw another tank appear in the street. He and a gunner dashed to the only antitank gun that seemed to be left in the artillery troop he was with. The two men reached the gun just as the tank turned toward them. They fired and saw a flash as the tank was hit. At that moment a machine gun opened up. The gunner with Roullier gasped and sagged against him.

As Roullier turned to ease the man down, a bullet tore into his left hand. It began to shake uncontrollably and Roullier assumed the bullet had hit a nerve. Easing the gunner over his back, Roullier made it to his trench. "I'll go get help," he told the bloodstained trooper. At the Ter Horst house Roullier stopped, unwilling to go in. He heard men screaming and babbling, begging for water, crying out the names of relatives. "Oh, God!" Roullier said. "What have I come here for?" Bombardier E. C. Bolden appeared at that moment. "Blimey, mate," Bolden said, looking at Roullier's shaking hand, "you been out typewriting?" Roullier explained that he had come for help for the wounded gunner. "All right," Bolden said, bandaging Roullier's hand, "I'll get there." Returning to his position, Roullier passed the Ter Horst garden and stopped, staring in horror. He had never seen so many dead in one place before. Some had smocks over their faces but others were uncovered and "their eyes stared off in all directions." There were piles of dead, so many that a man could not step between them.

At the trench Roullier waited until Bolden arrived with two stretcher-bearers. "Don't worry," Bolden told Roullier. He raised his thumb. "Everything will be O.K." Roullier didn't think so. Back in England, the thirty-one-year-old trooper had pleaded to go on the mission. His age was against it, and although Roullier was an artilleryman, he had become acting mess sergeant. But he had won out, and finally had been allowed to go. Now, staring at the tired, thirsty, hungry troopers around him, he remembers that "something clicked in my mind. I just forgot the battle. I was obsessed with getting us something to eat." He does not know how long he crawled through torn-up gardens and half-demolished houses in the area, ransacking shelves and searching cellars for bits and pieces of food. Someplace he found an undamaged galvanized tub. Into it he threw everything he found—a few withered carrots, some onions, a bag of potatoes, salt and some bouillon cubes. Near the house he found a chicken coop. Only one bird was still alive. Roullier took it along.

On the stone floor of a ruined house he built a circle of bricks to hold the tub. Tearing strips of wallpaper off walls and using pieces of wood, he built a fire. He does not remember the battle still raging in the streets as he made one more trip outside to find water—but he staggered back with the tub partly filled. He killed and plucked the chicken, and dropped it into the tub. Just at dusk when he decided the stew was finished he pulled a pair of curtains off a window frame to wrap the hot handles of the pot and, with the help of another trooper, set out for the trenches. For the first time in hours he was aware of mortars coming in. The two men moved at intervals, stopping at each near burst, then going on again. At the artillery position, Roullier yelled out, "Come and get it!" Amazed, bleary troopers appeared in cautious groups with battered ration cans and mess kits. Dazedly mumbling their thanks, they dipped into the hot tub and disappeared into the growing darkness. In ten minutes the stew was gone. Peering into the bottom of the tub, Alf Roullier could just make out a few small chunks of potatoes. He picked them out and, for the first time that day, ate some food. He had never felt happier.

On the grounds of the Hartenstein Hotel in a five-man trench, Sergeant Leonard Overton, the glider pilot, stared out into the growing dusk. The four men who shared his trench had disappeared. Suddenly Overton saw dark shapes approaching. "It's only us," someone said quietly. As the four soldiers dropped into the trench, Overton saw that they carried a gas cape bundled together. Carefully the men opened the cape and, holding a can at one edge, emptied almost a pint of rain water into the container. One man produced a cube of tea and began to stir the liquid. Overton looked on, dazed. "We had had nothing to eat or drink that day and only two hard biscuits which we had shared on Saturday," he says. Then, to Overton's surprise, the troopers offered the tin can to him. He took a sip and passed it on. "Many happy returns," each man told him softly. Overton had forgotten that Sunday, September 24, was his twenty-third birthday.

In the Schoonoord the critical cases and the walking wounded were gone, but shell-shocked men still lingered in the big hotel. As Chaplain Pare walked through a half-deserted room, he heard a thin shaking voice somewhere in the echoing building singing "Just a song at twilight." Climbing to an upstairs room, Pare knelt beside a badly shocked young trooper. "Padre," the boy said, "will you tuck me in? I get so frightened with all the noise." Pare had no blanket but he pretended to cover the trooper. "That feels fine, Padre. I feel very well now.

Will you do me one more favor?" Pare nodded. "Say the Lord's Prayer with me." Pare did. He soothed back the young man's hair. "Now close your eyes," Pare told him. "Sleep well. God bless you." The trooper smiled. "Good night, Padre. God bless you." Two hours later a medic came for Pare. "You know that lad you said the prayers with?" Pare asked, "What's wrong?" The medic shook his head. "He died just now. He said to tell you he couldn't stand the noise outside."

As evening set in, Colonel R. Payton-Reid in the KOSB's area of the perimeter was not unhappy to see "the twenty-fourth grow to its melancholy close. The high hopes of early support by the ground forces was a subject now, by mutual consent, taboo."

Late Sunday night Lieutenant Neville Hay, the Phantom Net operator, was called into General Urquhart's room in the cellar of the Hartenstein. "He handed me a long message," Hay says, "and told me when I had finished encoding it to return it to him. I remember him saying that perhaps by that time he wouldn't have to send it." Hay was stunned as he read the message. "What it really meant was that they had to come and get us or we would be wiped out." Hay encoded the signal and returned it to Urquhart. "I hoped he wouldn't have to send it, either," Hay says. As sent out, the message read:

> Urquhart to Browning. Must warn you unless physical contact is made with us early 25 Sept. consider it unlikely we can hold out long enough. All ranks now exhausted. Lack of rations, water, ammunition and weapons with high officer casualty rate. Even slight enemy offensive action may cause complete disintegration. If this happens all will be ordered to break toward bridgehead if anything rather than surrender. Any movement at present in face of enemy impossible. Have attempted our best and will do so as long as possible.*

Over two consecutive nights, attempts to move men and supplies into Urquhart's lodgment had failed. Yet the stubborn XXX Corps commander, General Horrocks, refused to

---

*Several versions of this message have appeared in other accounts of the battle. The one above is the original. Lieutenant Neville Hay retained his timed Phantom message logs and made them available to me. I am extremely grateful for his cooperation.

51. From Phantom   Source G Ops 1330 hrs. Enemy continues to
      1 Airborne Div   attack in small parties with SP guns in suppor
                    Small numbers of Pz Kw IV area 694788. Mortar
                    fire continues. Poles who crossed last night
                    now fighting area 698782.

                    TOO 241330   THI   241945

52. From Phantom   Source G Ops 0845 hrs. Only 300 Polish over
      1 Airborne Div   last night. Water and food and ammunition sho
                    Shelling and mortaring continues and intense.

                    TOO 241630   THI   241805

53. From Phantom   Perimeter very weak and casualties mounting.
      1 Airborne Div   Essential relieving troops make contact
                    immediately on crossing. Enemy attacks
                    made with SP guns or tanks and following
                    infantry were NOT formidable. Heavy shelling
                    and mortaring continues.

                    TOO   242205   THI   242330

54. From Phantom   URQUHART TO BROWNING. MUST WARN YOU UNLESS
      1 Airborne Div   PHYSICAL CONTACT IS MADE WITH US **EARLY** 25
                    SEP CONSIDER IT UNLIKELY WE CAN HOLD OUT LONG
                    ENOUGH, ALL RANKS NOW EXHAUSTED. LACK OF
                    RATIONS, WATER, AMMUNITION AND WEAPONS WITH
                    HIGH OFFICER CASUALTY RATE. EVEN SLIGHT
                    ENEMY OFFENSIVE ACTION MAY CAUSE COMPLETE
                    DISINTEGRATION. IF THIS HAPPENS, ALL WILL
                    BE ORDERED TO BREAK TOWARD BRIDGEHEAD IF
                    ANYTHING RATHER THAN SURRENDER. ANY MOVEMENT
                    AT PRESENT IN FACE OF ENEMY IMPOSSIBLE.
                    HAVE ATTEMPTED OUR BEST AND WILL DO SO AS
                    LONG AS POSSIBLE.

                    TOO 250830   THI   251040

55. From Phantom   Source G2 Ops 1330 hrs. Perimeter still
      1 Airborne Div   holding though situation so fluid impossible
                    state exact locations.

                    TOO 251345   THI 252035

*Extract from Lieutenant Hay's "Phantom" log, showing memorable Urquhart
message to Browning.*

abandon the effort. If the bridgehead was to be saved and the relief of Urquhart's men effected, it must take place this Sunday night. Once again the weather was unfavorable; no help could be expected from England-based planes flying supply or support missions. But troops were now in strength in the Driel-Nijmegen area, and Horrocks—achieving the near-impossible by driving his entire corps up the narrow, one-tank-wide corridor to his spear-point on the Rhine—was obsessed by the 400 yards of river that separated him from the airborne forces. Success was tantalizingly close. He ordered General Thomas' 43rd Wessex to make one last push: with the remaining Poles, troops of Lieutenant Colonel Gerald Tilly's 4th Dorsets would assault the river and try to cross into the bridgehead beginning at 10 P.M.

Tilly's move would be a first step in a wider plan. "If things went well," Horrocks later wrote, "I hoped to side-slip the 43rd Division across the Rhine farther to the west and carry out a left hook against the German force attacking the airborne perimeter." The alternative was withdrawal. On this eighth day of Market-Garden, Horrocks obstinately refused to face that choice. Others, however, were now seriously planning how it might be done.

According to his chief of staff, Brigadier Gordon Walch, the First Airborne Corps commander, General Browning, now spoke "quite openly about withdrawing." While the 43rd Wessex was moving up to Driel the decision had been in the balance, but "as soon as they became stuck, Browning became convinced we would have to get Urquhart's men out." The British Second Army commander, General Miles C. Dempsey, had reached the same conclusion. He had not met with Horrocks since the beginning of the attack. Now, as time ran out, Dempsey ordered Horrocks to a meeting down the corridor at St. Oedenrode. In line of command, Dempsey, on authority from Montgomery, would have the last word. The agonizing decision would be forced on them by one man—Field Marshal Model.

As Horrocks drove south to St. Oedenrode, Lieutenant Colonel Tilly of the 4th Dorsets prepared for the night's river crossing. His battalion was rushing up to the assembly area in Driel, and assault craft, now that the corridor was open again,

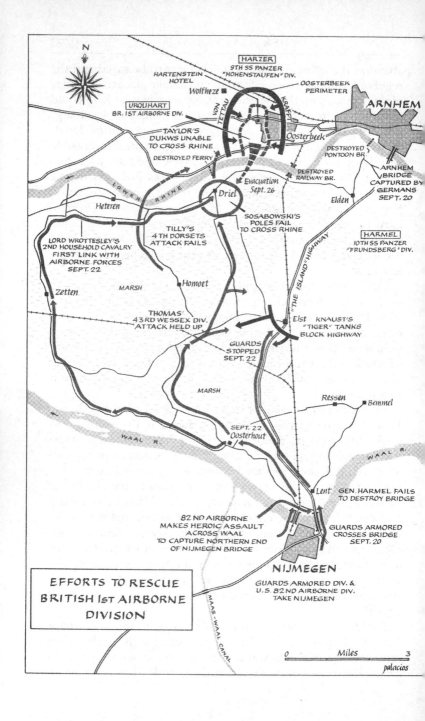

N

HARZER
9TH SS PANZER
"HOHENSTAUFEN" DIV.

HARTENSTEIN
HOTEL

OOSTERBEEK
PERIMETER

Wolfheze

ARNHEM

URQUHART
BR. 1ST AIRBORNE DIV.

TAYLOR'S
DUKWS UNABLE
TO CROSS RHINE

Oosterbeek

DESTROYED
PONTOON BR.

DESTROYED FERRY

ARNHEM
BRIDGE
CAPTURED BY
GERMANS
SEPT. 20

DESTROYED
RAILWAY BR.

Evacuation
Sept. 26

LOWER RHINE

Driel

Elden

Heteren

SOSABOWSKI'S
POLES FAIL
TO CROSS RHINE

TILLY'S
4TH DORSETS
ATTACK FAILS

LORD WROTTESLEY'S
2ND HOUSEHOLD CAVALRY
FIRST LINK WITH
AIRBORNE FORCES
SEPT. 22

HARMEL
10TH SS PANZER
"FRUNDSBERG" DIV.

Zetten

MARSH

Homoet

THOMAS'
43RD WESSEX DIV.
ATTACK HELD UP

Elst   KNAUST'S
"TIGER" TANKS
BLOCK HIGHWAY

GUARDS
STOPPED
SEPT. 22

MARSH

Ressen   Bemmel

SEPT. 22
Oosterhout

WAAL R.

WAAL R.

Lent   GEN. HARMEL FAILS
TO DESTROY BRIDGE

82 ND AIRBORNE
MAKES HEROIC ASSAULT
ACROSS WAAL
TO CAPTURE NORTHERN END
OF NIJMEGEN BRIDGE

GUARDS ARMORED
CROSSES BRIDGE
SEPT. 20

NIJMEGEN

EFFORTS TO RESCUE
BRITISH 1st AIRBORNE
DIVISION

GUARDS ARMORED DIV. &
U.S. 82ND AIRBORNE DIV.
TAKE NIJMEGEN

MAAS-WAAL CANAL

0   Miles   3

palacios

were on the way. Tilly's instructions were clear. Briefed personally by his brigade commander, Brigadier Ben Walton, Tilly was told to "broaden the base of the perimeter." The crossing was to be made at the old ferry site, about a mile west of Oosterbeek. Once across, the Dorsets were "to hang on until reinforced." They would travel light, carrying only enough food and ammunition to last three or four days. As the thirty-five-year-old Tilly saw it, his men "were a task force leading the way for the whole of Dempsey's Second Army." He was acutely conscious of the urgent necessity of reaching Urquhart's men quickly. From all he had learned, the division was dying by the hour.

On Sunday Tilly had climbed to the spire of a damaged Driel church three times to observe the area where his troops would land on the Rhine's northern bank. As the afternoon wore on, at his orchard headquarters south of Driel, he impatiently awaited the full arrival of his battalion from the village of Homoet, a few miles southwest of Driel, and the assault boats being brought up from the corridor.

Shortly after 6 P.M. Brigadier Ben Walton sent for Tilly. At Walton's headquarters in a house south of Driel, Tilly expected the brigade commander to review once more the details of the night's operation. Instead, Walton told him there had been a change in plan. Word had been received, Walton said, that "the whole operation—the large-scale crossing—was off." Tilly's battalion would still cross, but for a different purpose. Tilly listened with increasing dismay. His men were to hold the base of the perimeter while Urquhart's 1st Airborne Division was withdrawn! He was to take as few men as possible—"only enough to do the job"; approximately 400 infantry and 20 officers. Tilly did not need to go; he could detail his second in command, Major James Grafton, to take his place. Although Tilly replied that he would "think about it," he had already decided to lead his men over. As he left Walton's headquarters, Tilly felt that his men were being sacrificed. Walton had said nothing about getting them back. Yet he knew that Walton too was helpless to alter the situation. What puzzled him was what had happened; why had the plan been changed?

The decision to withdraw Urquhart's force—subject to confirmation by Montgomery, who was not to finally approve the order until 9:30 A.M. Monday, September 25—was reached by

General Dempsey at the St. Oedenrode conference with Horrocks and General Browning on Sunday afternoon. After considering his Corps commander's plan for a full-scale crossing of the Rhine, Dempsey turned it down. Unlike Horrocks, Dempsey did not believe the assault could succeed. "No," he said to Horrocks. "Get them out." Turning to Browning, Dempsey asked, "Is that all right with you?" Silent and subdued, Browning nodded. Immediately Dempsey notified General Thomas in Driel. Even as the St. Oedenrode conference was taking place, the Germans, once again, severed the corridor north of Veghel. Cut off, Horrocks used an armored carrier and broke through the German lines to return to his headquarters at Nijmegen. Field Marshal Model's latest attacks would keep the corridor closed for more than forty hours.

In Driel, most of Lieutenant Colonel Tilly's battalion had now arrived. He walked among his troops picking the men he would take. Tapping soldiers on the shoulder, Tilly said, "You go" . . . "You're not going." The real purpose of the assault was secret. He could not tell protesting men why they were being left behind. Tilly "picked those veterans who were absolutely sure—essential—leaving the others behind."

The decision was bitter. Looking at the officers and men who, he believed, "were going to certain death," Tilly called over Major Grafton. "Jimmy," Grafton remembers Tilly saying, "I've got to tell you something, because someone other than me has to know the real purpose of the crossing." Outlining the change in plan, Tilly added quietly, "I'm afraid we're being chucked away."

Stunned, Grafton stared at Tilly. It was vital, Tilly added, that no one else have the information. "It would be too risky," he explained.

Grafton knew what Tilly meant. It would be a terrible blow to morale if the truth was known. As Grafton prepared to leave, Tilly said, "Jimmy, I hope you can swim." Grafton smiled. "I hope so, too," he said.

By 9:30 P.M., as Tilly's men moved down to the river, there was still no sign of the assault craft. "How the hell do they expect me to cross without boats?" Tilly asked his engineering officer, Lieutenant Colonel Charles Henniker. Rations for his men had not arrived either. Testy and burdened by his knowledge of the true reason for the mission, Tilly spoke with Lieutenant Colonel Aubrey Coad, commander of the 5th Dorsets. "Nothing's right," Tilly told him. "The boats haven't come and we haven't been issued rations. If something isn't done soon, I'm not prepared to go." Coad ordered his battalion to turn over rations to Tilly's men.

For three long hours, in a cold, drizzling rain, Tilly's force waited for the assault craft. At midnight word arrived that the boats were now in Driel. But only nine had come through. In the darkness, some trucks had taken a wrong turn and driven into enemy lines; two others, skidding off a muddy dike road, had been lost. At the rendezvous point the boats were carried on the shoulders of the infantry for 600 yards through a swampy marsh to the launching point. Stumbling and slithering over the mud of the polder, the men took more than an hour to wrestle the boats to the river. Not until after 2 A.M. on Monday, September 25, was the assembly complete.

As the men prepared to launch, Tilly handed Major Grafton two messages for General Urquhart: one was a letter from General Browning; the other, a coded message from General Thomas outlining the withdrawal plan. There were two sets of these letters. Lieutenant Colonel Eddie Myers, Urquhart's engineering officer, had returned from Nijmegen and his meeting with Browning. Now Myers, bearing the same letters, was waiting to cross. "Your job," Tilly told Grafton, "is to get through to Urquhart with these messages in case the engineering officer doesn't make it." The paper containing the withdrawal plan was "absolutely vital," Tilly stressed.

At the river it was clear that the Germans were completely prepared for another crossing. Only some fifteen British assault craft—including three DUKWs and the remnants of the little fleet used on the previous night—remained. At the very last minute, because of the boat shortage, it was decided to halt a diversionary crossing scheduled by the Poles to the east of the Dorsets' launching area—and put Tilly's men over in five three-boat waves. As the preparations went on, mortar shells exploded on the southern bank, and heavy machine guns, apparently now carefully lined up along both edges of the perimeter base, swept the water. Lieutenant Colonel Tilly stepped into a boat. The first wave began to cross.

Although every available British gun on the southern side hammered away, sending a canopy of shells above the Dorsets, the crossing was brutally assaulted. The canvas-and-plywood craft were raked, holed and swept away. Some, like Major Grafton's, caught fire before leaving the south bank. Quickly Grafton set out in another. Halfway over he discovered his was the only remaining boat in the wave. In fifteen minutes, feeling "lucky to be alive," Grafton was across.

In the rain and darkness, hemmed in by well-sited machine-gun fire, each of the five waves sustained heavy losses. But the worst enemy by far was the current. Unused to the boats and the unexpected current, which increased in speed after midnight, the helpless Dorsets were swept past the perimeter base and into the hands of the enemy. Scattered for miles, those who survived were quickly cut off and surrounded. Of the 420 officers and men who set out for the perimeter, only 239 reached the northern bank. Lieutenant Colonel Tilly, who upon landing was met by an avalanche of grenades rolled like bowling balls down a hill, was heard leading his men out of the inferno, yelling "Get them with the bayonet!"*

The Dorsets were unable to link up as an effective unit with Urquhart's men. Only a few reached the Hartenstein perimeter, among them Major Grafton, who, with the withdrawal plan intact, came in through Major Dickie Lonsdale's positions near the lower Oosterbeek church. Lieutenant Colonel Myers had already arrived at Urquhart's headquarters with the documents he was carrying. Neither man knew the contents of Thomas' coded message, or its cruelly ironic name. When Montgomery had originally pressed Eisenhower for "a powerful and full-blooded thrust toward Berlin . . . to thus end the war," his single-thrust suggestion had been turned down. "Operation Market-Garden" had been the compromise. Now the withdrawal plan for Urquhart's bloodied men had been officially designated. The remnants of the British 1st Airborne Division were to be evacuated under the code name "Operation Berlin."

---

*One of the bouncing grenades actually hit Tilly's head and exploded. Incredibly he was only slightly wounded and survived as a prisoner of war until the end of hostilities.

4

NOW MARKET-GARDEN, the operation Montgomery hoped would end the war quickly, proceeded inexorably toward its doom. For sixty terrible miles men hung on to bridges and fought for a single road, the corridor. In General Maxwell Taylor's sector north of Eindhoven, troopers bolstered by British armor and infantry repelled one fierce attack after another while trying to reopen the empty stretch of highway severed at Uden; in General Gavin's 82nd area the great Waal bridge was under constant bombardment and the enemy continued to press in from the Reichswald in steadily growing strength. Gone was the attitude of a week before, that the war was almost over. Enemy units were being encountered that had long been written off. The Nazi war machine, thought to be reeling and on the verge of collapse in the first week of September, had miraculously produced sixty Tiger tanks, which were delivered to Model on the morning of September 24.* Market-Garden was strangling, and now the principal objective of the plan, the foothold across the Rhine, the springboard to the Ruhr, was to be abandoned. At 6:05 A.M., Monday, September 25, General Urquhart received the order to withdraw.

In the planning of the Arnhem operation Urquhart had been promised relief within forty-eight hours. General Browning had expected the 1st Airborne Division to hold out alone for no longer than four days at maximum. In an unprecedented feat of arms for an airborne division, outnumbered and outgunned, Urquhart's men had hung on for more than twice that long. To the courageous Scot, commanding an airborne division for the first time, withdrawal was bitter; yet Urquhart knew it was the only course. By now his strength was fewer than 2,500 men, and he could ask no more of these uncompromising troopers. Galling as it was to know that relieving British forces sat barely one mile away, separated from the division only by the width of the Rhine, Urquhart reluctantly agreed

---

* "The tanks arrived in the early hours of the morning," notes General Harmel in Annex No. 6 of his war diary, September 24th, adding that "II Panzer Corps headquarters allocated the bulk of this detachment, 45 tiger tanks, to the 10th SS Frundsberg Division."

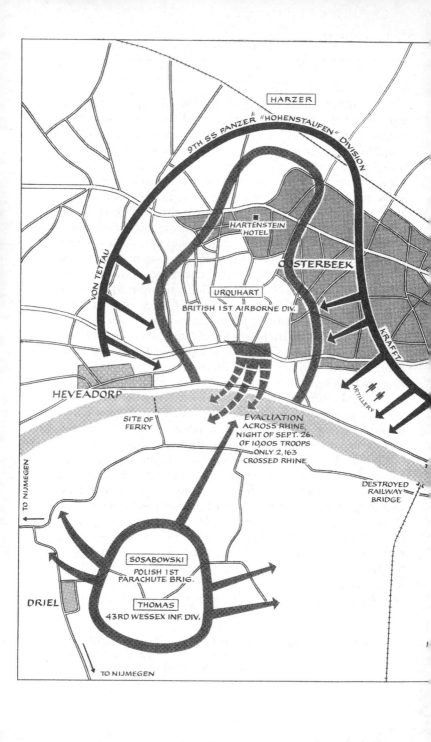

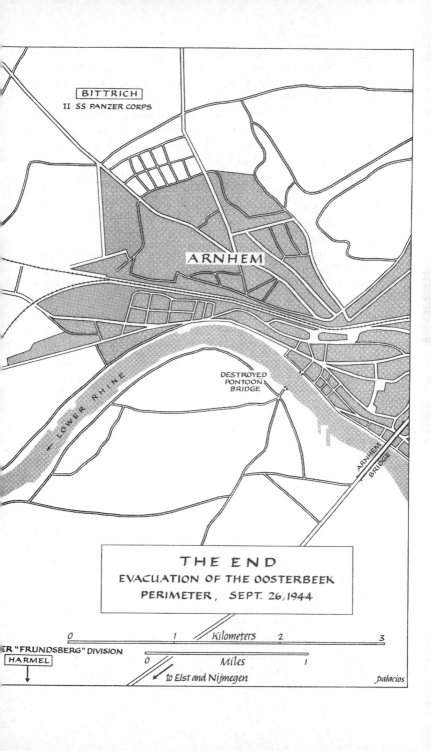

BITTRICH
II SS PANZER CORPS

ARNHEM

LOWER RHINE

DESTROYED
PONTOON
BRIDGE

ARNHEM BRIDGE

THE END
EVACUATION OF THE OOSTERBEEK
PERIMETER, SEPT. 26,1944

0   1   Kilometers   2   3

0   Miles   1

ER "FRUNDSBERG" DIVISION
HARMEL

to Elst and Nijmegen

palacios

with his superiors' decision. The time had come to get the valiant men of Arnhem out.

At the Hartenstein, a weary Lieutenant Colonel Eddie Myers delivered the two letters—Browning's and the withdrawal order from General Thomas—to Urquhart. Browning's congratulatory and encouraging message, written more than twenty-four hours earlier, was outdated. In part it read, ". . . the army is pouring to your assistance, but . . . very late in the day," and "I naturally feel, not so tired and frustrated as you do, but probably almost worse about the whole thing than you do . . ."

The withdrawal order—especially coming from Thomas, whose slowness Urquhart, like Browning, could not forgive —was by far the more depressing. The 43rd Wessex was now beginning to feel the weight of increasing German pressure, Thomas' message said. All hope of developing a major bridgehead across the Rhine must be abandoned; and the withdrawal of the 1st Airborne would take place, by mutual agreement between Urquhart and Thomas, at a designated date and time.

Urquhart pondered his decision. As he listened to the continuing mortar and artillery bombardment outside, he had no doubts about the date and time. If any of his men were to survive, the withdrawal would have to be soon and, obviously, under cover of darkness. At 8:08 A.M. Urquhart contacted General Thomas by radio: "Operation Berlin," he told him, "must be tonight."

Some twenty minutes later Urquhart released the message prepared for Browning that he had given Lieutenant Neville Hay to encode the night before. It was still pertinent, particularly the warning sentence, "Even slight enemy offensive action may cause complete disintegration." For at this moment Urquhart's situation was so desperate that he did not know whether his men could hold until darkness. Then the agonized general began to plan the most difficult maneuver of all: the withdrawal. There was only one way out—across the terrible 400 yards of the Rhine to Driel.

Urquhart's plan was designed along the lines of another classic British withdrawal—Gallipoli, in 1916. There, after months of fighting, troops had finally been pulled out under deceptive cover. Thinned-out lines cloaking the retreat had continued to fire as the main bulk of the force was safely withdrawn. Urquhart planned a similar maneuver. Along the perimeter small groups of men would keep up a fusillade to deceive the enemy while the larger body of troops slipped away. Gradually units along the northern face of the perimeter would move down along its sides to the river, to be evacuated. Then the last forces, closest to the Rhine, would follow. "In effect," Urquhart said later, "I planned the withdrawal like the collapse of a paper bag. I wanted small parties stationed at strategic places to give the impression we were still there, all the while pulling downward and along each flank."

Urquhart hoped to contrive other indications of "normality"—the usual pattern of radio transmissions would continue; Sheriff Thompson's artillery was to fire to the last; and military police in and about the German prisoner-of-war compound on the Hartenstein's tennis courts were to continue their patrols. They would be among the very last to leave. Obviously, besides a rear guard, other men would have to stay behind—doctors, medical orderlies and serious casualties. Wounded men unable to walk but capable of occupying defensive positions would stay and continue firing.

To reach the river, Urquhart's men would follow one route down each side of the perimeter. Glider pilots, acting as guides, would steer them along the escape path, marked in some areas with white tape. Troopers, their boots muffled by strips of cloth, were to make their way to the water's edge. There, beachmasters would load them into a small evacuation fleet: fourteen powered storm boats—managed by two companies of Canadian engineers—each capable of carrying fourteen men, and a variety of smaller craft. Their number was indeterminate. No one, including the beachmasters, would remember how many, but among them were several DUKWs and a few canvas-and-plywood assault craft remaining from previous crossings.

Urquhart was gambling that the Germans observing the boat traffic would assume men were trying to move into the perimeter rather than out of it. Apart from the dreadful possibility of his troops being detected other hazardous difficulties could occur as more than two thousand men tried to escape. If a rigid time schedule was not maintained, Urquhart could foresee, an appalling bottleneck would develop at the narrow base of the perimeter, now barely 650 yards wide. If they were jammed into the embarkation area, his men might be mercilessly annihilated. After the futile experience of the Poles and the Dorsets in trying to enter the perimeter, Urquhart did not expect the evacuation to go unchallenged. Although every gun that XXX Corps could bring to bear would be in action to protect his men, Urquhart still expected the Germans to inflict heavy casualties. Time was an enemy, for it would take hours to complete the evacuation. There was also the problem of keeping the plan secret. Because men might be captured and interrogated during the day, no one, apart from senior officers and those given specific tasks, was to be told of the evacuation until the last minute.

After conferring with General Thomas by radio and obtaining agreement on the major points in his withdrawal plan, Urquhart called a meeting of the few senior officers left: Brigadier Pip Hicks; Lieutenant Colonel Iain Murray of the Glider Pilot Regiment, now in charge of the wounded Hackett's command; Lieutenant Colonel R. G. Loder-Symonds, the division's artillery chief; Colonel Mackenzie, the chief of staff; and Lieutenant Colonel Eddie Myers, the engineering officer who would be in charge of the evacuation. Just before the conference began, Colonel Graeme Warrack, the chief medical officer, arrived to see Urquhart and became the first man to learn of the plan. Warrack was "downcast and unhappy. Not because I had to stay—I had an obligation to the wounded—but because up to this moment I had expected the division to be relieved in a very short time."

In the Hartenstein cellar, surrounded by his officers, Urquhart broke the news. "We're getting out tonight," he told them. Step by step he outlined his plan. The success of the withdrawal would depend on meticulous timing. Any concentration of troops or traffic jams could cause disaster. Men were to be kept moving, without stopping to fight. "While they should take evasive action if fired upon, they should only fire back if it is a matter of life or death." As his despondent officers prepared to leave, Urquhart cautioned them that the evacuation must be kept secret as long as possible. Only those with a need to know were to be told.

The news carried little surprise for Urquhart's senior officers. For hours it had been obvious that the position was hopeless. Still, like Warrack, they were bitter that relief had never arrived. In their minds, too, was the fear that their men might endure an even greater ordeal during the withdrawal than they had in the perimeter. By accident Signalman James Cockrill, attached to division headquarters, heard the terse message: "Operation Berlin is tonight." He puzzled over its meaning. Withdrawal did not even occur to him. Cockrill believed the division "would fight to the last man and the last bullet." He thought that "Operation Berlin" might mean an all-out attempt to break through for the Arnhem bridge "in some kind of heroic 'Charge of the Light Brigade' or something." Another man knew all too clearly what it meant. At the headquarters of the 1st Airlanding Brigade, Colonel Payton-Reid of the KOSB's, helping to arrange details of the evacuation of the western edge of the perimeter, heard Brigadier Pip Hicks mutter something about "another Dunkirk."

All through this day, in a frenzy of attacks, the Germans tried to overrun positions, but still the Red Devils held. Then, men would recall, shortly after 8 P.M. the news of the withdrawal began filtering down. To Major George Powell of Hackett's 156th Battalion, at the top of the perimeter, the news was "an appalling blow. I thought of all the men who had died, and then I thought the whole effort had been a waste." Because his men were among those who had the farthest to come, Powell started them off in single file at 8:15 P.M.

Private Robert Downing of the 10th Parachute Battalion was told to leave his slit trench and go to the Hartenstein Hotel. There, he was met by a sergeant. "There's an old plastic razor over there," the sergeant told him. "You get yourself a dry shave." Downing stared at him. "Hurry up," the sergeant told him. "We're crossing the river and by God we're going back looking like British soldiers."

In a cellar near his position Major Robert Cain borrowed another razor. Someone had found water, and Cain scraped the razor over a week's growth of beard and then dried his face carefully on the inside of his smoke-blackened, bloodstained smock. Coming out he stood for a minute in lashing rain looking at the church in lower Oosterbeek. There was a gold cock on the weather vane. Cain had checked it at intervals during the battle. For him, it was a good luck symbol. As long as the gold cock remained, so would the division. He felt an over-powering sadness. He wondered if the weather vane would still be there tomorrow.

Like other men, Major Thomas Toler of the Glider Pilot Regiment had been told by Colonel Iain Murray to clean up a little. Toler couldn't have cared less. He was so tired that just "thinking about cleaning up was an effort." Murray handed over his own razor. "We're getting out. We don't want the army to think we're a bunch of tramps." With a small dab of lather that Murray had left, Toler too shaved his beard. "It was amazing how much better I felt, mentally and physically," he recalls. In Murray's command post was the Pegasus flag Hackett's men had planned to fly as the Second Army arrived. Toler stared at it for a moment. Then he carefully rolled it up and put it away.

In artillery positions where troopers now would fire at will to help disguise the evacuation, Gunner Robert Christie listened as the troop's signalman, Willie Speedie, called in to the battery. Speedie gave a new station as control and then said simply, "I am closing down now. Out."

Sergeant Stanley Sullivan, one of the pathfinders who had led the way nine days before, was furious when the news reached him. "I had already figured we'd had it anyway and we might as well go down fighting." Sullivan's outpost was in a school "where youngsters had been trying to learn. I was afraid for all those children if we pulled out. I had to let them know, and the Germans too, just how we felt." On the blackboard in the room he had been defending, Sullivan printed large block letters and underlined them several times. The message read: "We'll Be Back!!!"*

At precisely 9 P.M., the night sky was ripped by the flash of XXX Corps's massed guns, and fires broke out all along the edge of the perimeter as a torrent of shells rained down on the

---

*The children would never see it. On September 27, in a brutal reprisal against the Dutch, the Germans ordered the entire Arnhem area evacuated. Arnhem and the surrounding villages were to remain uninhabited until the very last days of the war, when Canadian troops arrived on April 14, 1945.

German positions. Forty-five minutes later, Urquhart's men started to pull out. The bad weather that had prevented the prompt arrival of troops and supplies during the week now worked for the Red Devils; the withdrawal began in near-gale-like conditions which—with the din of the bombardment—helped cover up the British escape.

In driving wind and rain the 1st Airborne survivors, faces blackened, equipment tied down and boots muffled against sound, climbed stiffly out of positions and lined up for the dangerous trek down to the river. The darkness and the weather made it impossible for men to see more than a few feet in front of them. The troopers formed a living chain, holding hands or clinging to the camouflage smock of the man ahead.

Sergeant William Tompson, a glider pilot, hunched his body against the pouring rain. Charged with helping to direct troopers to the riverbank, he was prepared for a long wet night. As he watched men file past he was struck by the fact that "few men but us had ever known what it was like to live in a mile-square abattoir."

To Signalman James Cockrill the meaning of "Operation Berlin" was now only too clear. He had been detailed to stay behind and operate his set as the troops withdrew. His instructions were "to stay on the air and keep the set functioning to make the Germans think everything is normal." Cockrill sat alone in darkness under the veranda of the Hartenstein, "bashing away on the key. I could hear a lot of movement around me, but I had no other instructions than to keep the set on the air." Cockrill was certain that he would be a prisoner before morning. His rifle was propped up beside him, but it was useless. One bullet was a dummy, containing the cypher code used to contact Second Army. It was the only one he had left.

On the Rhine's southern bank, doctors, medical orderlies and Dutch Red Cross nursing personnel stood ready in reception areas and at the collection point. In Driel convoys of ambulances and vehicles waited to move Urquhart's survivors back to Nijmegen. Although preparations for the arrival of the men were going on all about her, Cora Baltussen, after three days and nights tending the wounded, was so exhausted she thought the bombardment and the activities on the southern bank marked the prelude to yet another crossing attempt. In the concentrated shelling of Driel, Cora had been wounded by shrapnel in the head, left shoulder and side. Although the injuries were painful, Cora considered them superficial. She was more concerned about her bloody dress. She cycled home to change before returning to help tend the fresh flow of casualties she was certain would shortly arrive. On the way Cora rode into enemy shellfire. Thrown from her bicycle, she lay unhurt for some time in a muddy ditch, then she set off again. At home exhaustion overcame her. In the cellar she lay down for a short nap. She slept all through the night, unaware that "Operation Berlin" was taking place.

Along the river at the base of the perimeter the evacuation fleet, manned by Canadian and British engineers, lay waiting. So far the enemy's suspicions had not been aroused. In fact, it was clear that the Germans did not know what was happening. Their guns were firing at the remaining Dorsets, who had begun a diversionary attack west of the perimeter. Still farther west, Germans were firing as British artillery laid down a barrage to give the appearance of a river assault in that area. Urquhart's deception plan appeared to be working.

In the drenching rain, lines of men snaked slowly down both sides of the perimeter to the river. Some men were so exhausted that they lost their way and fell into enemy hands; others, unable to go on by themselves, had to be helped. In the inky darkness nobody stopped. To halt invited noise, confusion —and death.

In the ruddy glow of fires and burning buildings, Sergeant Ron Kent, of Major Boy Wilson's pathfinder group, led his platoon to a cabbage patch designated as the company rendezvous point. There they waited until the remainder of the company assembled before moving toward the river. "Although we knew the Rhine lay due south," Kent says, "we didn't know what point they were evacuating us from." Suddenly the men spotted lines of red tracers coming from the south and taking these as a guide, they moved on. Soon they came to white tape and the shadowy figures of glider pilots who directed them along. Kent's group heard machine-gun fire and grenade explosions off to their left. Major Wilson and another group of men had run into Germans. In the fierce skirmish that followed, with safety only a mile away, two soldiers were killed.

Men were to remember the evacuation by small details—poignant, frightening and sometimes humorous. As Private Henry Blyton of the 1st Battalion moved down to the river, he heard someone crying. Ahead, the line stopped. Troopers made for the side of the path. There, lying on the sodden ground, was a wounded soldier crying for his mother. The men were ordered to keep on moving. No one was to stop for the wounded. Yet many did. Before troopers in Major Dickie Lonsdale's force left their positions, they went to the Ter Horst house and took as many of the walking wounded as they could.

Lance Corporal Sydney Nunn, who with a glider pilot had knocked out a Tiger tank earlier in the week, thought he would never make it to the river. By the church where artillery positions had been overrun during the day, Nunn and a group of KOSB's had a sharp, brief skirmish with the Germans. In the rain and darkness most of the men got away. Lying on the ground Nunn received the first injury he had had in nine days of fighting. Shrapnel hit some stones and one of Nunn's front teeth was chipped by a pebble.

Sergeant Thomas Bentley of the 10th Battalion was following the Phantom operator, Lieutenant Neville Hay. "We were sniped at continually," he remembers. "I saw two glider pilots walk out from the shadows and deliberately draw the German fire, apparently so we could see where it was coming from." Both guides were killed.

In the Hartenstein, General Urquhart and his staff prepared to leave. The war diary was closed; papers were burned and then Hancock, the General's batman, wrapped Urquhart's boots with strips of curtain. Everybody knelt as a chaplain said the Lord's Prayer. Urquhart remembered the bottle of whiskey his batman had put in his pack on D Day. "I handed it around," Urquhart says, "and everyone had a nip." Finally Urquhart went down to the cellars to see the wounded "in their bloody bandages and crude splints" and said goodbye to those aware of what was happening. Others, drowsy with morphia, were mercifully unaware of the withdrawal. One haggard soldier, propping himself up against the cellar wall, told Urquhart, "I hope you make it, sir."

Lieutenant Commander Arnoldus Wolters, the Dutch liaison officer at Division headquarters, moving behind the General's

Shoot 14

Place	Date	Hour	Summary of Events and Information	References to Appendices
ARNHEM	25 Sep	0940	Maint Sitrep to Airtps Rear. No resup 24 Sep. Understand med stores, rations, some amn sent over river bu ducks, but unable distribute owing to enemy action and lack of transport. No sups now for 3 days. Water still scarce. Gun amn now very low. Div effective strength approx 2500 excl Poles 120. Resup required 25 Sep as for 23 Sep.	
		1030	Div Comd held conference of all Comds and gave out his orders for 'BERLIN'.	
		1800	A quieter day than yesterday, despite several local attacks, one of which drove in 156 Bn. Infiltration, however, went on steadily and by evening the enemy was firmly established in wood 795777 and at other points inside the perimeter. Most units were therefore to some extent encircled and cut off from their neighbours.	
		2145	First units to withdraw crossed starting line on rd junc 792774 and CHURCH 796774.	
		2200	Crossing over river started, covered by very heavy pre-arranged arty concentration.	
		2230	Last tps of Div H.Q. moved out. Wounded under the care of Lt. RANDALL, RAMC, MO to H.Q., R.A., were left in the cellar of Div H.Q. A.D.M.S., other M.Os. and Senior Chaplain remained with wounded in the M.D.S.	
	26 Sep	0130	Guards of P.W. cage withdrew.	
		0550	Ferrying across river ends. Approx 300 personnel left on North bank. Arranged that boats should return the following evening for any survivors.	
NIJMEGEN		1200	Evacuation of Div H.Q. to NIJMEGEN completed from R.V. at DRIEL, where 130 Bde issued tea and rum, food and one blanket per man.	
		1430	G.O.C. held conference and issued orders re checking of personnel present, billetting, re-organizing and issue of clothing. Units ordered to make contact with seaborne lift, which had already arrived in NIJMEGEN.	

group, observed absolute silence. "With my accent had I opened my mouth I might have been taken for a German," he says. At some point Wolters lost his grip on the man in front of him. "I didn't know what to do. I simply kept going, praying that I was heading in the right direction." Wolters felt particularly depressed. He kept thinking of his wife and the daughter he had never seen. He had not been able to phone them even though his family lived only a few miles from the Hartenstein. The watch he had bought for his wife in England was still in his pocket; the Teddy bear he had planned to give his daughter was somewhere in a wrecked glider. If he was lucky enough to make it back to the river, Wolters would be leaving, probably for England, once more.

At the river the crossings had begun. Lieutenant Colonel Myers and his beachmasters packed men into the boats as fast as they arrived. But now the Germans, though still not aware that a withdrawal was taking place, could see the ferrying operations by the light of flares. Mortars and artillery began ranging in. Boats were holed and capsized. Men struggling in the water screamed for help. Others, already dead, were swept away. Wounded men clung to wreckage and tried to swim to the southern bank. Within one hour half the evacuation fleet was destroyed, but still the ferrying went on.

By the time Major George Powell's men reached the river from their long trek down the eastern side of the perimeter, Powell believed that the evacuation was over. A boat was bobbing up and down in the water, sinking lower as waves hit against it. Powell waded out. The boat was full of holes and the sappers in it were all dead. As some of his men struck out swimming, a boat suddenly appeared out of the dark. Powell hastily organized his men and got some of them aboard. He and the remaining troopers waited until the craft returned. On the high embankment south of the Rhine, Powell stood for a moment looking back north. "All at once I realized I was across. I simply could not believe I had gotten out alive." Turning to his fifteen bedraggled men, Powell said, "Form up in threes." He marched them to the reception center. Outside the building, Powell shouted, "156th Battalion, halt! Right turn! Fall out!" Standing in the rain he watched them head for shelter. "It was all over, but by God we had come out as we had gone in. Proud."

As General Urquhart's crowded boat prepared to leave, it got caught in the mud. Hancock, his batman, jumped out and pushed them off. "He got us clear," Urquhart says, "but as he struggled to get back aboard someone shouted, 'Let go! It's overcrowded already!'" Irked by this ingratitude "Hancock ignored the remark and, with his last reserves, pulled himself into the boat."

Under machine-gun fire Urquhart's boat was halfway across when the engine suddenly stuttered and stopped. The boat began to drift with the current; to Urquhart "it seemed an absolute age before the engine came to life again." Minutes later they reached the southern bank. Looking back Urquhart saw flashes of fire as the Germans raked the river. "I don't think," he says, "they knew what they were firing at."

All along the bank of the Rhine and in the meadows and woods behind, hundreds of men waited. But now with only half the fleet still operable and under heavy machine-gun fire, the bottleneck that Urquhart had feared occurred. Confusion developed in the crowded lines, and although there was no panic, many men tried to push forward, and their officers and sergeants tried to hold them in check. Lance Corporal Thomas Harris of the 1st Battalion remembers "hundreds and hundreds waiting to get across. Boats were being swamped by the weight of the numbers of men trying to board." And mortars were now falling in the embarkation area as the Germans got the range. Harris, like many other men, decided to swim. Taking off his battle dress and boots, he dived in and, to his surprise, made it over.

Others were not so lucky. By the time Gunner Charles Pavey got down to the river, the embarkation area was also under machine-gun fire. As the men huddled on the bank a man came swimming toward the place where Pavey lay. Ignoring the bullets peppering the shore he hauled himself out of the water and, gasping for breath, said, "Thank God, I'm over." Pavey heard someone say, "Bloody fool. You're still on the same side."

Sergeant Alf Roullier, who had managed to cook and serve a stew on Sunday, now attempted to swim the river. As he floundered in the water a boat drew alongside and someone grabbed his collar. He heard a man shout, "It's O.K., mate. Keep going. Keep going." Roullier was totally disoriented. He believed he was drowning. Then he heard the same voice say, "Bloody good, old boy," and a Canadian engineer lifted him into the boat. "Where the hell am I?" the dazed Roullier mumbled. The Canadian grinned. "You're almost home," he said.

It was nearing daybreak when Signalman James Cockrill, still at his set under the veranda of the Hartenstein, heard a fierce whisper. "Come on, Chick," a voice said, "let's go." As the men headed for the river, there was a sudden sharp burst of noise. Cockrill felt a tug on his neck and shoulders. His Sten gun, slung over his back, had been split wide open by shrapnel. Nearing the bank, Cockrill's group came across a few glider pilots standing in the bushes. "Don't go until we tell you," one of the pilots said. "The Germans have got a gun fixed on this area, a Spandau firing about waist high." Coached by the pilots, the men sprinted forward one at a time. When Cockrill's turn came he crouched down and began to run. Seconds later he fell over a pile of bodies. "There must have been twenty or thirty," he remembers. "I heard men shouting for their mothers and others begging us not to leave them there. We couldn't stop." At the river's edge a flare exploded and machine guns began to chatter. Cockrill heard someone shout for those who could to swim. He went into the chilly water, striking out past panic-stricken men who appeared to be floundering all about him.

Suddenly Cockrill heard a voice say, "All right, buddy, don't worry. I've got you." A Canadian hauled him into a boat and seconds later Cockrill heard the boat ground on shore. "I nearly cried when I found I was back where I started," he says. The boat had gone on in to pick up wounded. As men all around helped with the loading, the craft started off again and Cockrill remembers a rush as men climbed in from all sides. Although their boat was weighted down and under fire, the Canadians made it to the far shore. After hours under the veranda and his nightmarish trip across the water, Cockrill was dazed. "The next thing I knew I was in a barn and someone gave me a cigarette." Then Cockrill remembered one thing. Frantically he searched his pockets and brought out his single piece of ammunition: the .303 dummy bullet with his cypher code inside.

Shortly before 2 A.M. what remained of the 1st Airborne's ammunition was blown up. Sheriff Thompson's gunners fired the last remaining shells and artillerymen removed the breech blocks. Lance Bombardier Percy Parkes and the remainder of his crew were told to pull back. Parkes was surprised. He had not thought about the withdrawal. He had expected to stay until his post was overrun by the Germans. He was even more amazed when he reached the river. The area was jammed with hundreds of men and someone said that all the boats had been sunk. A man near Parkes took a deep breath. "It looks like we swim," he said. Parkes stared at the river. "It was very wide. In full flood the current looked to be about nine knots. I didn't think I could make it. I saw men jumping in fully dressed and being swept downstream. Others made it across only to be shot scrambling out of the water. I saw one chap paddle across on a plank, still carrying his pack. If he could do it, I could."

Parkes stripped to his shorts, throwing away everything including his gold pocket watch. In the swift current his shorts slipped down and Parkes kicked them off. He made it over and, hiding by bushes and in ditches, eventually reached a small deserted farm cottage. Parkes went in to find some clothing. Emerging a few minutes later, he encountered a private from the Dorsets, who directed him to a collection point, where he was given a mug of hot tea and some cigarettes. It took the exhausted Parkes some time to understand why everyone was staring at him. He was dressed in a man's colored sports shirt and wore a pair of ladies' linen bloomers tied at the knee.

Private Alfred Dullforce of the 10th Battalion swam to the south bank nude but still carrying a .38. To his embarrassment two women were standing with the soldiers on the bank. Dullforce "felt like diving straight back into the water." One of the women called to him and held out a skirt. "She didn't bat an eyelash at my nakedness," he remembers. "She told me not to worry, because they were there to help the men coming across." In a multicolored skirt that reached to his knees and wearing a pair of clogs, Dullforce was taken to a British truck driving the survivors back to Nijmegen.

By now the Germans were flaying the embarkation area and

mortar shells were screaming in. As Lieutenant Commander Arnoldus Wolters ran behind a line of men for a boat, there was an explosion among the group. "I was absolutely unharmed," Wolters recalls. "But around me lay eight dead men and one severely wounded." He gave the man a shot of morphia and carried him to the boat. In the already overloaded craft there was no place for Wolters. He waded into the water and, hanging onto the side of the boat, was pulled across the river. He staggered onto the southern bank and collapsed.

As dawn came, the evacuation fleet had been almost destroyed, yet the Canadian and British engineers, braving mortar, artillery and heavy machine-gun fire, continued to ferry the men across in the boats that remained. Private Arthur Shearwood of the 11th Battalion found Canadian engineers loading some wounded into a small boat. One of the Canadians motioned for Shearwood to get aboard. The outboard motor could not be restarted, and the Canadians asked all soldiers still carrying rifles to start paddling. Shearwood tapped the man in front of him. "Let's go," he said. "Start paddling." The man looked at Shearwood without expression. "I can't," he said, pointing to his bandaged shoulder. "I've lost an arm."

Major Robert Cain had put all his men across by dawn. With Sergeant Major "Robbo" Robinson, he waited on the bank so he could follow, but no more boats appeared to be heading in. In a group of other men someone pointed to a slightly holed assault craft bobbing on the water and a trooper swam out to bring it back. Using rifle butts, Cain and Robinson began rowing, while troopers who still had helmets bailed. On the south bank a military policeman directed them to a barn. Inside, one of the first men Cain recognized was Brigadier Hicks. The brigadier came over quickly. "Well," he said, "here's one officer, at least, who's shaved." Cain grinned tiredly. "I was well brought up, sir," he said.

On the perimeter's edge scores of men still huddled in the rain under German fire. Although one or two boats attempted to cross under cover of a smoke screen, it was now, in daylight, impossible for the evacuation to continue. Some men who tried to swim for it were caught by the swift current or by machine-gun fire. Others made it. Still others, so badly wounded they could do nothing, sat helplessly in the pounding rain or set out north—back to the hospitals in the perimeter. Many decided to hide out and wait until darkness again before trying to reach the opposite shore. Eventually scores succeeded in making their escape this way.

On the southern bank and in Driel, exhausted, grimy men searched for their units—or what remained of them. Sergeant Stanley Sullivan of the pathfinders, who had printed his defiant message on the school blackboard, remembers someone asking, "Where's the 1st Battalion?" A corporal immediately stood up. "This is it, sir," he said. Beside him a handful of bedraggled men pulled themselves painfully erect. Gunner Robert Christie roamed through crowds of men searching for troopers of his battery. No one looked familiar. Christie suddenly felt tears sting his eyes. He had no idea whether anyone but him was left from Number 2 Battery.

On the road to Driel, General Urquhart came to General Thomas' headquarters. Refusing to go in, he waited outside in the rain as his aide arranged for transportation. It was not necessary. As Urquhart stood outside, a jeep arrived from General Browning's headquarters and an officer escorted Urquhart back to Corps. He and his group were taken to a house on the southern outskirts of Nijmegen. "Browning's aide, Major Harry Cator, showed us into a room and suggested we take off our wet clothes," Urquhart says. The proud Scot refused. "Perversely, I wanted Browning to see us as we were—as we had been." After a long wait Browning appeared, "as immaculate as ever." He looked, Urquhart thought, as if "he had just come off parade, rather than from his bed in the middle of a battle." To the Corps commander Urquhart said simply, "I'm sorry things did not turn out as well as I had hoped." Browning, offering Urquhart a drink, replied, "You did all you could." Later, in the bedroom that he had been given, Urquhart found that the sleep he had yearned for so long was impossible. "There were too many things," he said, "on my mind and my conscience."

There was indeed much to think about. The 1st Airborne Division had been sacrificed and slaughtered. Of Urquhart's original 10,005-man force only 2,163 troopers, along with 160 Poles and 75 Dorsets, came back across the Rhine. After nine days, the division had approximately 1,200 dead and 6,642 missing, wounded or captured. The Germans, it later turned out, had suffered brutally, too: 3,300 casualties, including 1,100 dead.

The Arnhem adventure was over and with it Market-Garden. There was little left to do now but pull back and consolidate. The war would go on until May, 1945. "Thus ended in failure the greatest airborne operation of the war," one American historian later wrote. "Although Montgomery asserted that it had been 90 percent successful, his statement was merely a consoling figure of speech. All objectives save Arnhem had been won, but without Arnhem the rest were as nothing. In return for so much courage and sacrifice, the Allies had won a 50-mile salient—leading nowhere."*

Perhaps because so few were expected to escape, there was not enough transport for the exhausted survivors. Many men, having endured so much else, now had to march back to Nijmegen. On the road Captain Roland Langton of the Irish Guards stood in the cold rain watching the 1st Airborne come back. As tired, filthy men stumbled along, Langton stepped back. He knew his squadron had done its best to drive up the elevated highway from Nijmegen to Arnhem, yet he felt uneasy, "almost embarrassed to speak to them." As one of the men drew abreast of another Guardsman standing silently beside the road, the trooper shouted, "Where the hell have you been, mate?" The Guardsman answered quietly, "We've been fighting for five months." Corporal William Chennell of the Guards heard one of the airborne men say, "Oh? Did you have a nice drive up?"

As the men streamed back one officer, who had stood in the rain for hours, searched every face. Captain Eric Mackay, whose little band of stragglers had held out so gallantly in the schoolhouse near the Arnhem bridge, had escaped and reached Nijmegen. Now he looked for members of his squadron. Most of them had not made it to the Arnhem bridge; but Mackay, with stubborn hope, looked for them in the airborne lines coming out of Oosterbeek. "The worst thing of all was their faces," he says of the troopers. "They all looked unbelievably drawn and

* Dr. John C. Warren, *Airborne Operations in World War II, European Theater*, p. 146.

tired. Here and there you could pick out a veteran—a face with an unmistakable I-don't-give-a-damn look, as if he could never be beaten." All that night and into the dawn Mackay stayed by the road. "I didn't see one face I knew. As I continued to watch I hated everyone. I hated whoever was responsible for this and I hated the army for its indecision and I thought of the waste of life and of a fine division dumped down the drain. And for what?" It was full light when Mackay went back to Nijmegen. There he began to check collecting points and billets, determined to find his men. Of the 200 engineers in his squadron, five, including Mackay, had come back.

On the other side of the river remained the soldiers and civilians whose jobs and injuries demanded that they be left behind. Small bands of men too late to make the trip stayed too, crouched down in the now-unmanned trenches and gun pits. For these survivors there was no longer any hope. In the blackened perimeter they awaited their fate.

Medic Taffy Brace had brought the last of his walking wounded down to the river, only to find the banks now empty. Huddling with them, Brace saw a captain coming forward. "What are we going to do?" the officer asked Brace. "There won't be any more boats." Brace looked at the injured men. "I guess we'll have to stay then," he said. "I can't leave them." The captain shook hands. "Good luck," he told them all. "I'm going to try to swim across." Brace last saw the officer wading out into the water. "Good luck yourself," Brace called. "Goodbye."

For Major Guy Rigby-Jones, a physician at the Tafelberg, "the division's leaving was a bitter pill to swallow," but he carried on his work. With teams of medics Rigby-Jones scoured the houses in the area of the hotel, bringing in wounded men. Often hand-carrying the casualties to collection points, the medics loaded them into German trucks, ambulances and jeeps and then climbed on themselves, heading into captivity.

Padre Pare had slept the whole night through at the Schoonoord. He awoke with a start, sure that something was terribly wrong. Then he realized that it was unnaturally quiet. Hurrying out into a room, he saw a medic standing at a window, in full view of anyone outside. As Pare came up the medic turned around. "The division's gone," he said. Pare, who had not been told about the evacuation, stared at him. "You're mad, man." The medic shook his head. "Look for yourself, sir. We really are prisoners now. Our chaps have had to retreat." Pare couldn't believe it. "Sir," the medic said, "you'll have to break the news to the patients. I haven't got the nerve to tell them." Pare made the rounds of the hotel. "Everyone tried to take it in good heart," he recalls, "but we were all in a fit of deep depression." Then in the large room where most of the wounded still sheltered a soldier sat down at a piano and began to play a medley of popular songs. Men started to sing and Pare found himself joining in.

"It was queer after the hell of the last few days," Pare says. "The Germans could not understand it, but it was easy enough to explain. The suspense, the sense of being left behind produced a tremendous reaction. There was nothing left to do but sing." Later as Hendrika van der Vlist and other Dutch civilians prepared to leave to help the wounded in German hospitals, Pare waved goodbye regretfully. "They had suffered with us, gone hungry and thirsty, and yet they had no thought for themselves." As the last ambulances disappeared, Pare and the medical staff loaded their meager belongings onto a German truck. "The Germans helped us," he recalls. "There was a curious lack of animosity. None of us had anything to say." As the truck drove off, Pare stared moodily at the blackened wreckage of the Schoonoord, "where absolute miracles had been worked." He was "firmly convinced that it was only a matter of a day or two, possibly this coming night, before the Second Army crossed the Rhine and took the area back again."

Across the street from the church, Kate ter Horst had said goodbye to the wounded, all now prisoners. Pulling a hand cart and accompanied by her five children, she set out to walk to Apeldoorn. A short distance away she stopped and looked back at the ancient vicarage that had been her home. "A ray of sunshine strikes a bright yellow parachute hanging from the roof," she wrote. "Bright yellow . . . A greeting from the Airborne . . . Farewell, friends . . . God bless you."

Young Anje van Maanen, also on the road to Apeldoorn, kept looking for her father as the Red Cross cars and ambulances passed, bringing the wounded from the Tafelberg. With her aunt and her brother, Anje stared at the familiar faces she had come to know throughout the week. Then, as a truck passed by, Anje saw her father, riding in it. She screamed to him and began to run. The truck stopped and Dr. van Maanen climbed down to greet his family. Hugging them all, he said, "We have never been so poor and never so rich. We have lost our village, our home and our possessions. But we have each other and we are alive." As Dr. van Maanen got back on the truck to care for the wounded, he arranged for the family to meet in Apeldoorn. As they walked among hundreds of other refugees, Anje turned to look back. "The sky was colored scarlet," she wrote, "like the blood of the airborne who gave their lives for us. We four all are alive, but at the end of this hopeless war week the battle has made an impression on my soul. Glory to all our dear, brave Tommies and to all the people who gave their lives to help and save others."

In Driel, Cora Baltussen awoke to a strange silence. It was midmorning Tuesday, September 26. Painfully stiff from her wounds and puzzled by the silence, Cora limped outside. Smoke billowed up from the center of the town and from Oosterbeek across the river. But the sounds of battle were gone. Getting her bicycle, Cora pedaled slowly toward town. The streets were deserted; the troops had gone. In the distance she saw the last vehicles in a convoy heading south for Nijmegen. Near one of Driel's ruined churches only a few soldiers lingered by some jeeps. Suddenly Cora realized that the British and Poles were withdrawing. The fight was over; the Germans would soon return. As she walked over to the small group of soldiers, the bell in the damaged church steeple began to toll. Cora looked up. Sitting in the belfry was an airborne trooper, a bandage around his head. "What happened?" Cora called out. "It's all over," the trooper shouted. "All over. We pulled out. We're the last lot." Cora stared up at him. "Why are you ringing the bell?" The trooper kicked at it once more. The sound echoed over the thousand-year-old Dutch village of Driel and died away. The trooper looked down at Cora. "It seemed like the right thing to do," he said.

"In my—prejudiced—view, if the operation had been properly backed from its inception, and given the aircraft, ground forces, and administrative resources necessary for the job—it would have succeeded in spite of my mistakes, or the adverse weather, or the presence of the 2nd SS Panzer Corps in the Arnhem area. I remain MARKET-GARDEN'S unrepentant advocate."
—FIELD MARSHAL SIR BERNARD MONTGOMERY,
Memoirs: Montgomery of Alamein, p. 267

"My country can never again afford the luxury of another Montgomery success."
—BERNHARD, THE PRINCE OF THE NETHERLANDS,
to the author.

A NOTE ON CASUALTIES

Allied forces suffered more casualties in Market-Garden than in the mammoth invasion of Normandy. Most historians agree that in the twenty-four-hour period of D Day, June 6, 1944, total Allied losses reached an estimated 10,000–12,000. In the nine days of Market-Garden combined losses—airborne and ground forces— in killed, wounded and missing amounted to more than 17,000.

British casualties were the highest: 13,226. Urquhart's division was almost completely destroyed. In the 10,005 Arnhem force, which includes the Poles and glider pilots, casualties totaled 7,578. In addition to this figure RAF pilot and crew losses came to another 294, making a total in wounded, dead and missing of 7,872. Horrocks' XXX Corps lost 1,480 and the British 8th and 12th Corps another 3,874.

American losses, including glider pilots and IX Troop Carrier Command, are put at 3,974. General Gavin's 82nd Airborne Division had 1,432; General Taylor's 101st, 2,118; and air crew losses 424.

Complete German figures remain unknown but in Arnhem and Oosterbeek admitted casualties came to 3,300 including 1,300 dead. However, in the entire Market-Garden battle area, Model's losses were much higher. While no figure breakdown is available for the number of enemy killed, wounded and missing, from the breakout at Neerpelt, then along the corridor in battles at Nijmegen, Grave, Veghel, Best and Eindhoven, after interviewing German commanders I would conservatively estimate that Army Group B lost at least another 7,500–10,000 men, of which perhaps a quarter were killed.

What were Dutch civilian casualties? No one can say. Deaths in Arnhem and Oosterbeek are said to have been low, less than 500, but no one knows with any certainty. I have heard casualty figures —that is, dead, wounded or missing—given as high as 10,000 in the entire Operation Market-Garden campaign and as a result of the forcible evacuation of the Arnhem sector together with deprivation and starvation in the terrible winter that followed the attack.

THE SOLDIERS AND CIVILIANS OF "A BRIDGE TOO FAR"

What They Do Today

Following is a list of all those who out of their firsthand recollections contributed information to "A Bridge Too Far." First, the men of the Allied armies; then the Dutch who lived in the area during the battle; and finally the German military who fought there. Occupations may have changed since this book went to press, and where an asterisk follows a name it indicates that the contributor has died since these lists were compiled. All ranks given are as of September, 1944.

AMERICAN

Eisenhower, Dwight David,* Gen., Supreme Comdr. [SHAEF]. Gen. of the Army, Comdr. in Chief, President of the United States.

Bradley, Omar Nelson, Gen. [12th Army Group]. Gen. of the Army; *Company director, Beverly Hills, Calif.*

Abel, Leonard Edw., 2nd Lt. [82nd Airborne]. *Attorney, Bay Harbor Islands, Fla.*

Addison, William A. B., Major [82nd Airborne]. *V.-P. and trust officer, South Carolina National Bank, Columbia, S.C.*

Albritton, Earl M., Cpl. [101st Airborne]. *Rural mail carrier, Winnsboro, La.*

Alexander, Mark J., Lt. Col. [82nd Airborne]. *Real-estate broker, Campbell, Calif.*

Alhart, John Lamar, Capt. [82nd Airborne]. *Dentist, Rochester, N.Y.*

Allardyce, James R., P.F.C. [82nd Airborne]. *Engineer, Frankenmuth, Mich.*

Allen, James Mann, Lt. [101st Airborne]. *President, Allen Paint Supply Co., Denver, Colo.*

Allen, John Henry, P.F.C. [82nd Airborne]. *Upholsterer, Levittown, N.Y.*

Allen, Ray Carroll, Lt. Col. [101st Airborne] *Black Angus cattle rancher, Marshall, Tex.*

Altomare, John G., Cpl. [101st Airborne]. *X-ray worker for Westinghouse, Baltimore, Md.*

Anderson, Fred, Jr., Capt. [101st Airborne]. *V.-P. (Sales), International Corporation, Charlotte, N.C.*

Ankenbrandt, Louis E., P.F.C. [82nd Airborne]. *Ammunition plant mechanic, Baraboo, Wis.*

Antonion, Anthony J., P.F.C. [82nd Airborne]. *Shoe corrections, Long Island City, N.Y.*

Appleby, Sam, S/Sgt. [82nd Airborne]. *Attorney, Ozark, Mo.*

Arnold, George Wm., Sgt. [82nd Airborne]. *District manager, Detroit* News, *Birmingham, Mich.*

Asay, Charles Verne, Sgt. [101st Airborne]. *Linotype operator, Sacramento, Calif.*

Atkins, Lynn Cecil, Lt. [82nd Airborne]. *Asst. principal, Roosevelt Elementary School, El Paso, Tex.*

Badeaux, Nelson John, T/5 [82nd Airborne]. *Pipeline maintenance man, Tennessee Gas Pipeline Co., New Iberia, La.*

Bailey, Edward N., Cpl. [82nd Airborne]. *Claims counselor, veterans service, College Park, Ga.*

Bailey, Sam H., Jr., Lt. [82nd Airborne]. *Executive, Connecticut Mutual Life Insurance Co., Miami, Fla.*

Baldinger, Irving M., T/5 [101st Airborne]. *President, Legion-Olmer Bakery Co., New Haven, Conn.*

Baldino, Fred James, Cpl. [82nd Airborne]. *Postman, Burbank, Calif.*

Ballard, Robert Aye, Lt. Col. [101st Airborne]. *Grove owner and operator and Postmaster, Goulds, Fla.*

Barickman, John Hamilton, Sec. Sgt. [101st Airborne]. *Steelworker, Streator, Ill.*

Baugh, James Emory, Lt. [82nd Airborne]. *Medical doctor, Milledgeville, Ga.*

Baxley, George C., Pvt. [101st Airborne]. *Special representative, Southwestern Bell Telephone Co., Hewitt, Tex.*

Beach, Maurice M., Col. [9th Troop Carrier Command]. *Brig. Gen. (Retired), U.S. Air Force; consulting engineer, Garden Grove, Calif.*

Beaudin, Briand N., Capt. [82nd Airborne]. *Pediatrician, West Warwick, R.I.*

Beaver, Neal W., Lt. [82nd Airborne]. *Factory manager, Ottawa Rubber Company of Bradner, O., Wayne, O.*

Bedell, Edwin Allen, Major [82nd Airborne]. *Col. (Retired), U.S. Army; superintendent, Scientists' Cliffs Service Co., Inc., Port Republic, Md.*

Bennett, William A., Sgt. [82nd Airborne]. *Printer, Columbia, Pa.*

Bernardoni, August, P.F.C. [101st Airborne]. *Golf professional, Deerfield, Ill.*

Best, William Grew, Capt. [101st Airborne]. *Pathologist, Glen Mills, Pa.*

Besterbreurtje, Arie D., Capt. [82nd Airborne]. *Clergyman, Charlottesville, Va.*

Biekes, Tillman Edward, Cpl. [82nd Airborne]. *Packinghouse worker, Indianapolis, Ind.*

Bills, Lloyd Elvin, P.F.C. [82nd Airborne]. *Maintenance man, Capital City Telephone Company, Holts Summit, Mo.*

Birtwistle, Owen G., Col. [9th Troop Carrier Command]. *Col. (Retired), U.S. Air Force; Commandant, Extension Course Institute, Air University, Gunter A.F.B., Ala.*

Blackmon, Sumpter, Lt. [101st Airborne]. *Principal, Rigdon Road School, Columbus, Ga.*

Blanchard, Ernest Riley, P.F.C. [82nd Airborne]. *Machinist, Bristol, Conn.*

Blank, William Leonard, S/Sgt. [82nd Airborne]. *Management analyst, Veterans Administration Hospital, Richmond, Va.*

Blatt, A. Ebner, Capt. [101st Airborne]. *Physician, Indianapolis, Ind.*

Blau, Vincent Francis, Cpl. [101st Airborne]. *Electric-meter mechanic, Northern States Power Co., Minneapolis, Minn.*

Blue, James R., Cpl. [82nd Airborne]. *Retired, Dunn, N.C.*

Boling, Earl W., Cpl. [82nd Airborne]. *Security policeman, Security Dept., Veterans Administration Hospital, Akron, O.*

Bommer, Jack Louis, Cpl. [82nd Airborne]. *Salesman, Columbus Sign Co., Columbus, O.*

Borrelli, Anthony N., 2nd Lt. [101st Airborne]. *Customer service man, Peoples Natural Gas Co., Glassport, Pa.*

Bowman, Bernard George, P.F.C. [82nd Airborne]. *Coal miner, Van, W.Va.*

Boyce, Robert Ignatius, Pvt. [101st Airborne]. *Postal clerk, Springfield, Mass.*

Brakken, Joyce Pershing, Pvt. [82nd Airborne]. *Carpenter, Minneapolis, Minn.*

Brandt, John Rudolph, Sgt. [101st Airborne]. *Warehouse foreman, Colma, Calif.*

Brennan, George F., 2nd Lt. [9th Troop Carrier Command]. *Director of Civilian Personnel, U.S. Dept. of Defense, Alexandria, Va.*

Brierre, Eugene Donnaud, Lt. [101st Airborne]. *Attorney, New Orleans, La.*

Brilla, Michael A., Pvt. [82nd Airborne]. *Parts manager, Grabski Ford, Inc., Garfield Hts., O.*

Brockley, Harold Raymond, Cpl. [82nd Airborne]. *Postal clerk, Connersville, Ind.*

Brown, Earl J., P.F.C. [82nd Airborne]. *High-school principal, Wilburton, Okla.*

Brownlee, Richard Harold, 2nd Lt. [82nd Airborne]. *Druggist, Yuma, Colo.*

Brunson, Ernest Merkle, Pvt. [82nd Airborne]. *Screen-room-department operator, Union Camp Paper Corp., Savannah, Ga.*

Bryant, Nelson, Pvt. [82nd Airborne]. *Outdoors writer,* New York Times, *Martha's Vineyard, Mass.*

Buck, Rex Douglas, Cpl. [82nd Airborne]. *Sales and service man, Jamestown Container Corp., Jamestown, N.Y.*

Buffone, Harry Joseph, Cpl. [82nd Airborne]. *Carpenter, Jacksonville, Fla.*

Burns, Robert G., Lt. [101st Airborne]. *College football coach, University of So. Dakota, Sioux Falls, S.D.*

Burriss, Thomas Moffatt, Capt. [82nd Airborne]. *General contractor, Columbia, S.C.*

Busson, Ralph Joseph, S/Sgt. [82nd Airborne]. *Farmer, Doylestown, O.*

Cadden, James Joseph, Pvt. [101st Airborne]. *Detective Lieutenant, Homicide, Baltimore City Police Dept., Cockeysville, Md.*

Campana, Victor Woodrow, Capt. [82nd Airborne]. *Schoolteacher, Lexington, Mass.*

Campbell, Richard Angel, Lt. [101st Airborne]. *Real-estate broker, Palo Alto, Calif.*

Cannon, Harold Felton, Lt. [82nd Airborne]. *Schoolteacher, Lakeside Junior High School, Anderson, S.C.*

Cannon, Howard W., Lt. Col. [9th Troop Carrier Command]. *U.S. Senator from Nevada, Washington, D.C.*

Carmichael, Virgil F., Lt. [82nd Airborne]. *Circuit judge, Cleveland, Tenn.*

Carp, Samuel M., Lt. [101st Airborne]. *Salesman, Rockford Standard Furniture Co., Rockford, Ill.*

Carpenter, Frank J., Sgt. [101st Airborne]. *Pharmaceutical representative, Upland, Calif.*

Carpenter, Lowell Keith, Sgt. [101st Airborne]. *Sales manager, Bend, Ore.*

Carroll, Jack Paul, 2nd Lt. [82nd Airborne]. *Appraiser, Riverside County Assessors Office, Riverside, Calif.*

Carter, Winston Owen, Lt. [82nd Airborne]. *Farmer, Helena, Ark.*

Cartwright, Marvin D., Pvt. [101st Airborne]. *Rural mail carrier, Elk Mound, Wis.*

Cartwright, Robert Stanley, Pvt. [82nd Airborne]. *Maintenance Dept., Detroit Metropolitan Airport, Detroit, Mich.*

Castiglione, Frank B., P.F.C. [101st Airborne]. *Hobbyshop owner, Orange, Conn.*

Cavanagh, Eugene, Pvt. [101st Airborne]. *Brakeman, Penn Central R.R., Croton-on-Hudson, N.Y.*

Chappell, Julian M., Col. [9th Troop Carrier Command]. *Retired, Americus, Ga.*

Chase, Charles Henry, Lt. Col. [101st Airborne]. *Maj. Gen., U.S. Army, Chief of Staff, Heidelberg, Germany.*

Cholmondeley, Jack A.,* M/Sgt. [82nd Airborne]. *Secretary, Kenwood Savings & Loan Assn., Cincinnati, O.*

Cipolla, John J., P.F.C. [101st Airborne]. *Finishing superintendent, Sargent & Greenleaf Inc., Rochester, N.Y.*

Clark, Harold L., Brig. Gen. [9th Troop Carrier Command]. *Brig. Gen. (Retired), U.S. Air Force; company director, Daedalian Foundation, San Antonio, Tex.*

Clarke, Richard Robert, Sgt. [101st Airborne]. *Deputy Information Officer, Office of the Information Officer, Hq., U.S. Air Force Southern Command, Curundu Heights, C.Z.*

Clemons, George W., Sgt. [101st Airborne]. *School principal, Fresno, Calif.*

Cockrell, James Knox, Capt. [82nd Airborne]. *Research engineer, Falls Church, Va.*

Colombi, Gerald, Sgt. [82nd Airborne]. *Real-estate broker and developer, Belmont, Calif.*

Connelly, John J., Pvt. [82nd Airborne]. *Construction electrician, East Islip, N.Y.*

Connelly, John W., Capt. [82nd Airborne]. *County extension agent, Richmond, Ind.*

Cook, Edgar L., 2nd Lt. [82nd Airborne]. *Copy editor, Northfield, Conn.*

Cook, Julian A., Maj. [82nd Airborne]. *Col., U.S. Army, Columbia, S.C.*

Copas, Marshall, T/Sgt. [101st Airborne]. *Sgt. Major, U.S. Army, A.P.O. San Francisco, Calif.*

Corcoran, James S., Sgt. [101st Airborne]. *Sales representative and group consultant, Hospital Service Corp., Chicago, Ill.*

Cox, X. B., Jr., Lt. Col. [101st Airborne]. *Rancher, San Angelo, Tex.*

Coyle, James J., Lt. [82nd Airborne]. *Accountant, American Tobacco Co., Hicksville, N.Y.*

Crabtree, Bernard Gilbert, T/5 [82nd Airborne]. *Teacher, Kissimmee, Fla.*

Craig, William H., Lt. [101st Airborne]. *Sales representative, Sentry Insurance, Pasadena, Tex.*

Cready, Raymond D., P.F.C. [101st Airborne]. *Masonry contractor, North Miami, Fla.*

Cronkite, Walter, News Correspondent. *CBS commentator, New York, N.Y.*

Dahlin, John F., Capt. [101st Airborne]. *Aircraft engineer, North Hollywood, Calif.*

Damianov, George John, T/Sgt. [82nd Airborne]. *Plasterer, King of Prussia, Pa.*

Davidson, Lawrence H., P.F.C. [101st Airborne]. *Owner, Davidson Meat Market, Franklin, Ky.*

Davis, Andrew James, Pvt. [82nd Airborne]. *Heavy equipment operator, Sun Valley, Calif.*

Davis, Robert, Pvt. [82nd Airborne]. *Assistant sales manager, Westport, Conn.*

Dawson, Buck, 2nd Lt. [82nd Airborne]. *International Swimming Hall of Fame, Ft. Lauderdale, Fla.*

De Paul, Leo J., Sgt. [101st Airborne]. *Salesman, Cleveland, O.*

Defer, Raymond Pierre, T/5 [101st Airborne]. *Owner, home appliance sales & service store, Warrenville, Ill.*

Demetras, A. D., Wire Chief [82nd Airborne]. *Attorney at law, Reno, Nev.*

De Vasto, Francis Alphonse, P.F.C. [101st Airborne]. *Contracts Administration, U.S. Government, Burlington, Mass.*

Dickson, Robert S., III, Lt. [101st Airborne]. *Col., U.S. Army, Defense Attaché, Teheran, Iran.*

Dietrich, Frank Leslie, T/Sgt. [82nd Airborne]. *Lt. Col., U.S. Army, Silver Springs, Md.*

Dispenza, Peter, Sgt. [82nd Airborne]. *Police officer, N.Y.C.P.D., Woodside, N.Y.*

Dix, Shirley H., Capt. [82nd Airborne]. *Dentist, Miami, Fla.*

Dobberstein, Hugo Paul, P.F.C. [101st Airborne]. *Laboratory technician, Kimberly-Clark Corp., Appleton, Wis.*

Dodd, Edgar Frank, Cpl. [101st Airborne]. *Minister, Crockett, Tex.*

Dohun, Charles J., S/Sgt [101st Airborne]. *Manager of resort motel, Topsail Beach, N.C.*

Donalson, John M., Col. [9th Troop Carrier Command]. *President, Tennessee Forging Steel Corp., Rockwood, Tenn.*

Donnewirth, George Adam, T/5 [101st Airborne]. *Carpenter, Clyde, O.*

Doxzen, George D., P.F.C. [101st Airborne]. *Installation supervisor, Western Electric Co., Baltimore, Md.*

Druback, William A., Pvt. [101st Airborne]. *Elevator constructor, Otis Elevator Co., Bayonne, N.J.*

Druener, Hanz Karl, 2nd Lt. [82nd Airborne]. *Lt. Col., U.S. Army, Carlisle Barracks, Pa.*

Duke, James Edward, Col. [9th Troop Carrier Command]. *V.-P., Electro-Medics Devices Co., Pacific Palisades, Calif.*

Duncan, John Richard, Sgt. [82nd Airborne]. *Schoolteacher, Quincy, Ill.*

Duva, August John, P.F.C. [82nd Airborne]. *Capt., Jersey City Fire Dept., Jersey City, N.J.*

Dwyer, Francis Patrick Thomas, Sgt. [82nd Airborne]. *Program director, Island Trees, N.Y.*

Dwyer, Robert Joseph, Lt. [82nd Airborne]. *Associate professor of sociology, University of Lethbridge, Alberta, Canada, Missoula, Mont.*

Eason, Bert C., Cpl. [82nd Airborne]. *House painter, Phenix City, Ala.*

Eatman, Harold Lee, Sgt. [82nd Airborne]. *Customer Services, Eastern Air Lines, Charlotte, N.C.*

Eisner, Julius, P.F.C. [82nd Airborne]. *Civil Service, U.S. Government, Miami, Fla.*

Elliott, Chester Harding, Pvt. [101st Airborne]. *Timber worker, Thomasville, Mo.*

Eubanks, Henry Edward, P.F.C. [82nd Airborne]. *Employee, Blue Bell Packing Co., DuQuoin, Ill.*

Felt, Robert H., T/4 [101st Airborne]. *Asst. train dispatcher, N.Y.C. Transit Authority, West Hempstead, N.Y.*

Fergie, Charles, Cpl. [82nd Airborne]. U.S. Army (*Retired*), *Kearney, N.J.*

Ferguson, Arthur William, Capt. [82nd Airborne]. *Senior public health engineer, Warner Robins, Ga.*

Fielder, Robert Abbott, Lt. [82nd Airborne]. *Lt. Col. (Retired), U.S. Army, San Pedro, Calif.*

Finkbeiner, Theodore, Jr., Sgt. [82nd Airborne]. *Capt., Fire Dept., Monroe, La.*

Fischer, Russell W., P.F.C. [82nd Airborne]. *Senior instrumentation tech., Shell Development Corp., Lafayette, Calif.*

Fitzgerald, John E., P.F.C. [101st Airborne]. *Data-processing supervisor, Staten Island Community College, Staten Island, N.Y.*

Foley, John Paul, Lt. [82nd Airborne]. *Owner, picture-frame studio, Durham, N.C.*

Fosburgh, James Whitney, 2nd Lt. [9th Troop Carrier Command]. *Painter, New York, N.Y.*

Fox, James D., 2nd Lt. [9th Troop Carrier Command]. *Ass't. to V.-P., Pan American World Airways, Darien, Conn.*

Franco, Robert, Capt. [82nd Airborne]. *Surgeon, Richland, Wash.*

Franks, Darrell James, Cpl. [82nd Airborne]. *Construction engineer, Asheville, N.C.*

Fransosi, Arthur Arnold, Cpl. [82nd Airborne]. *Postal employee, Cranston, R.I.*

French, Donald J., Lt. Col. [82nd Airborne]. *Col. (Retired), U.S. Air Force; trucking and storage manager, Allied Van Lines, Vacaville, Calif.*

Fuller, Clark H., S/Sgt. [82nd Airborne]. *Cook, Jamaica, N.Y.*

Furey, Thomas Patrick, Lt. [82nd Airborne]. *Col., U.S. Army, Ryukyu Islands, A.P.O. San Francisco, Calif.*

Galvin, Wayne William, Pvt. [82nd Airborne]. *Journeyman painter, Fairview, Ore.*

Garber, Dean Landis, Lt. [82nd Airborne]. *Manager, Personnel & Labor Relations, Jeffrey Mfg. Co., Canal Winchester, O.*

Gariano, Vincent Paul, Pvt. [82nd Airborne]. *Bus driver, Englewood Cliffs, N.J.*

Garofano, Frank P., P.F.C. [101st Airborne]. *Investigator, Commonwealth of Massachusetts, Alcoholic Beverages Control Comm., Medford, Mass.*

Garzia, John, Pvt. [82nd Airborne]. *Owner, TV- and air-conditioning-service business, Hialeah, Fla.*

Gatlin, Hershel L., Sgt. [82nd Airborne]. *Farmer, Colfax, La.*

Gavin, James M., Gen. [82nd Airborne]. *Lt. Gen. (Retired), U.S. Army, Cambridge, Mass.*

Gelber, Aaron, Sgt. [82nd Airborne]. *Sgt. Major (Retired), U.S. Army insurance agent, Fayetteville, N.C.*

Gensemer, Harold Lester, Lt. [82nd Airborne]. *Sgt. Major, U.S. Army, Fort Hood, Tex.*

Gilbertson, Elmer, Sgt. [101st Airborne]. *Salesman, Wausau, Wis.*

Gilliam, Frederick Keene, Flt. Off. [9th Troop Carrier Command]. *C.P.A., Burlington, N.C.*

Goethe, James H., Lt. [82nd Airborne]. *Dentist, St. George, S.C.*

Gore, Tommy B., Sgt. [82nd Airborne]. *Retired, U.S. Army, Tahoe Vista, Calif.*

Gougler, Frederick W., S/Sgt. [82nd Airborne]. *Railroad conductor, Reading Railroad Freight Service, Clifton Heights, Pa.*

Grace, Jack, Pvt. [101st Airborne]. *High-school art teacher, Bartlesville, Okla.*

Graham, Thomas W., Lt. [82nd Airborne]. *Farmer, Bluffton, Ind.*

Gray, William Joseph, Pvt. [82nd Airborne]. *Bus operator, Vincentown, N.J.*

Grey, Thomas Charles, Jr., Sgt. [101st Airborne]. *Rural mail carrier, Macon, Ga.*

Hall, Raymond S., Capt. [101st Airborne]. *Retired minister, Falmouth, Me.*

Haller, Joseph, Jr., Cpl. [101st Airborne]. *Lithographing pressman, Detroit, Mich.*

Handelsman, Oliver, Major [101st Airborne]. *Physician, Pittsburgh, Pa.*

Hanlon, John Douglas, Major [101st Airborne]. *Newspaper columnist, Providence* Evening Bulletin, *Rumford, R.I.*

Hanna, Roy M., Lt. [82nd Airborne]. *Salesman, Berkeley Heights, N.J.*

Hannah, Harold W., Lt. Col. [101st Airborne]. *Law teacher, writer and researcher, Texico, Ill.*

Harmon, George E., T/5 [82nd Airborne]. *Shipping clerk, Wrightsville, Pa.*

Harrell, John Daniel, Capt. [101st Airborne]. *Druggist, Pensacola, Fla.*

Hart, Augustin S., Major [82nd Airborne]. *Exec. V.-P., Quaker Oats Company, Lake Forest, Ill.*

Hart, Leo Michael, Pvt. [82nd Airborne]. *Manufacturer's representative, North Miami, Fla.*

Hauptfleisch, Louis A., Capt. [82nd Airborne]. *V.-P., Halsey, Stuart, and Co., Summit, N.J.*

Heath, Stanley H., Lt. [82nd Airborne]. *Secretary, Masonic bodies, Fargo, N. Dak.*

Helton, Roy Francis, Sgt. [101st Airborne]. *President, J. D. Helton Roofing Co., Chattanooga, Tenn.*

Hennessey, Joseph S., Pvt. [101st Airborne]. *Millwright, Farrell Corp., Beacon Falls, Conn.*

Herkness, Frank G., Lt. [82nd Airborne]. *Supervisor, electrical installations, Railway Division, Budd Co., Philadelphia, Pa.*

Hogenmiller, Joseph James, Cpl. [101st Airborne]. *Glassworker, Crystal City, Mo.*

Holabird, John Augur, Jr., 2nd Lt. [82nd Airborne]. *Architect, Chicago, Ill.*

Hopkins, James Bernard, Flt. Off. [9th Troop Carrier Command]. *Ass't. Director, County Health Dept., St. Petersburg, Fla.*

Horne, Thomas A., P.F.C. [82nd Airborne]. *Pipe fitter, Newport, Division of Tenneco Chemicals, Inc., Oakdale, La.*

Howell, James K., Pvt. [101st Airborne]. *F.B.I., Woodbridge, Va.*

Huebschen, Herbert E., S/Sgt. [82nd Airborne]. *Accountant, assistant office manager, Beatrice Foods Co., Wright & Wagner Dairy Division, Beloit, Wis.*

Hughart, Robert Ralph, P.F.C. [82nd Airborne]. *Steelworker, Kaiser Steel Mill, Fontana, Calif.*

Hull, Logan Ben, Capt. [101st Airborne]. *Obstetrician and gynecologist, Altoona, Pa.*

Hunt, Harold Lawrence, S/Sgt. [101st Airborne]. *U.S. Civil Service, household-goods inspector, Petaluma, Calif.*

Hurtack George J., P.F.C. [101st Airborne]. *Painting contractor, Plainfield, N.J.*

Igoe, Charles M., P.F.C. [82nd Airborne]. *Prop man, U.S. Army film production, Long Branch, N.J.*

Ihlenfeld, Edward W., T/4 [101st Airborne]. *Lieutenant, Milwaukee Police Department, Milwaukee, Wis.*

Ingalls, Wilbur Royce, Cpl. [101st Airborne]. *Signalman, Erie-Lackawanna Railroad, Wellsville, N.Y.*

Ireland, Alfred Warfield, Jr., Major [82nd Airborne]. *Sales executive, Woodland Hills, Calif.*

Irvin, James Morris, Lt. [82nd Airborne]. *District manager, Pendleton Tool Ind., Inc., Greensboro, N.C.*

Isaacs, Jack Roger, Capt. [82nd Airborne]. *Druggist, Coffeyville, Kan.*

Isenekev, Melvin Wm., Pvt. [101st Airborne]. *Rural mail carrier, Boonville, N.Y.*

Jackson, Schuyler W., P.F.C. [101st Airborne]. *Trucker, Bethesda, Md.*

Jacobs, Herbert, Capt. [101st Airborne]. *Physician, Glendora, Calif.*

Jakeway, Donald I., S/Sgt. [82nd Airborne]. *Manager, Export Orders, Ebco Mfg. Co., Johnstown, O.*

James, Lawrence F., Sgt. [82nd Airborne]. *Motorman, N.Y.C. Transit Authority, Brooklyn, N.Y.*

Jedrziewski, Anthony A., Capt. [82nd Airborne]. *Electrical engineer, Belle Vernon, Pa.*

Johnson, Harry F., P.F.C. [101st Airborne]. *Farmer, Arbuckle, Calif.*

Johnson, Joseph Bernard, Jr., Capt. [101st Airborne]. *Lawyer, Duluth, Minn.*

Johnson, LeGrand K., Capt. [101st Airborne]. *Regional manager, Central Region, Ryder Truck Lines, Atlanta, Ga.*

Johnson, Paul B., P.F.C. [101st Airborne]. *V.-P., insurance company, Ridgefield, Conn.*

Johnson, Wilton Harold, Cpl. [82nd Airborne]. *Mail carrier, Palo Alto, Calif.*

Jones, Alvin, Major [101st Airborne]. *Executive, Jones Motor Co., Inc., Allentown, Pa.*

Jones, Delbert Francis, Pvt. [101st Airborne]. *Mushroom grower, Avondale, Pa.*

Jones, Desmond D., Sgt. [101st Airborne]. *Inspector, Sun Oil Co., Brookhaven, Pa.*

Jones, Glynne M., Col. [9th Troop Carrier Command]. *Brig. Gen. (Retired), U.S. Air Force; Director of Aviation, airport manager, New Orleans, La.*

Jones, James Elmo, S/Sgt. [82nd Airborne]. *President, Industrial Plastics, Inc., and Industrial Fabricators, Inc., Greensboro, N.C.*

Jones, Robert Ellis, Capt. [101st Airborne]. *Col., U.S. Army, Bad Toelz, Germany.*

Jones, William I., Lt. [101st Airborne]. *Physician, Charlotte, N.C.*

Joyner, Jonathan S., Sgt. [101st Airborne]. *Civil Service employee, Lawton, Okla.*

Kaiser, James L., Major [82nd Airborne]. *Col., U.S. Army, Washington, D.C.*

Kane, Maurice T., Sgt. [101st Airborne]. *Police officer, Buffalo, N.Y.*

Kantala, Matthew W., Jr., P.F.C. [82nd Airborne]. *Quarry owner, Elberton, Ga.*

Kappel, Carl Wm., Capt. [82nd Airborne]. *Col., U.S. Army, Springfield, Va.*

Kartus, Charles Leroy, S/Sgt. [101st Airborne]. *Merchant, Rock Hill, S.C.*

Keefe, Jack Edward III, Lt. [82nd Airborne]. *Physician, Miami Shores, Fla.*

Keenan, James E., P.F.C. [82nd Airborne]. *Ass't. V.-P., Chemical Bank, Hicksville, N.Y.*

Keep, Henry, Capt. [82nd Airborne]. *Hospital administrator, Villanova, Pa.*

Keith, Herbert Paul, P.F.C. [82nd Airborne]. *Tavern owner, Newcomerstown, O.*

Keith, John Marvin, T/Sgt. [101st Airborne]. *Repairman and installer, Mountain States Tel. & Tel. Co., Stevensville, Mont.*

Keller, John William, P.F.C. [82nd Airborne]. *Toolmaker, Sea Cliff, N.Y.*

Kinnard, Harry William Osburn, Lt. Col. [101st Airborne]. *Lt. Gen., U.S. Army, Ft. Belvoir, Va.*

Kirkwood, Robert S., Capt. [82nd Airborne]. *Lt. Col. (Retired), U.S. Army; senior auditor, N.Y. Telephone Co., New York, N.Y.*

Kissane, Joseph M., Sgt. [82nd Airborne]. *Public accountant, Greenlawn, N.Y.*

Kjell, Clifford George, Capt. [101st Airborne]. *Letter carrier, Rockford, Ill.*

Klein, Richard Lionel, Cpl. [101st Airborne]. *High-school teacher, Huron, O.*

Knox, Clyde F., P.F.C. [82nd Airborne]. *Sgt. Major, U.S. Army, Fayetteville, N.C.*

Koch, Stuart H., T/Sgt. [82nd Airborne]. *General agent, Northwestern Mutual Life Insurance Co., Appleton, Wis.*

Kogut, Michael J., 1st Sgt. [82nd Airborne]. *V.-P., International Molders and Allied Workers Union, AFL-CIO-CLC, Ludlow, Mass.*

Komosa, Adam A, Capt. [82nd Airborne]. *Lt. Col. (Retired), U.S. Army; professor, North Michigan Univ., Jeffersonville, Ind.*

Kos, Rudolph, P.F.C. [82nd Airborne]. *Antique dealer, Deerfield, Ill.*

Kotary, William E., Lt. [82nd Airborne]. *Agency Dept., Philadelphia Life Insurance Co., Wayne, Pa.*

Kough, Frank L., Cpl. [101st Airborne]. *Correctional officer, Western Penitentiary, Pittsburgh, Pa.*

Krantz, Eugene A., P.F.C. [101st Airborne]. *Works supervisor, Chicago, Ill.*

Krebs, Frank X., Lt. Col. [9th Troop Carrier Command]. *Legislative ass't to Senator Cannon, Falls Church, Va.*

Kremer, Jean Harry, Sgt. [101st Airborne]. *Salesman, Westbury, N.Y.*

Kroener, Walter B., Lt. [82nd Airborne]. *Battalion chief, Huntington Park Fire Dept. and Asst. Civil Defense Director, Huntington Park, Calif.*

Kuehl, Delbert A., Capt. [82nd Airborne]. *Executive Asst. Director, Foreign Missions, Elmhurst, Ill.*

Kumler, Lyle Kay, Sgt. [82nd Airborne]. *Insurance business, Gibson City, Ill.*

Lachkovic, John Paul, P.F.C. [101st Airborne]. *Truck driver, Hagerstown, Md.*

La Magdeleine, Leslie Leo, Pvt. [101st Airborne]. *Die setter, Mundelein, Ill.*

Lange, William A., Sgt. [101st Airborne]. *Tenant farmer, Pleasant Plains, Ill.*

Langston, Ledford M., P.F.C. [101st Airborne]. *Industrial employee, Red Banks, Miss.*

Lappegaard, Ray Lenard, Cpl. [101st Airborne]. *Director of organization and Personnel, Toro Manufacturing Corp., St. Paul, Minn.*

La Riviere, Richard G., Lt. [82nd Airborne]. *Construction superintendent, Chicopee Falls, Mass.*

Larkin, Bernard L., Pvt. [101st Airborne]. *Beer distributor, Levittown, Pa.*

Lassen, Donald Douglas, Pvt. [82nd Airborne]. *Plant mgr., Henderson Portion Pak., Miami, Fla.*

Lazenby, Harvill W., Sgt. [82nd Airborne]. *V.A. Hospital staff, Nashville, Tenn.*

Lee, John C. H., Jr., Capt. [82nd Airborne]. *Director, Office of Appalachian Studies, Cincinnati, O.*

Leebrick, Frank Lee, Jr., Cpl. [101st Airborne]. *Letter carrier, Silver Spring, Md.*

Lewis, Mike, T/4 [101st Airborne]. *Services machine tools for the Bendix Corp., North Hollywood, Calif.*

Lillyman, Frank Lewis, Capt. [101st Airborne]. *Deputy Operations Officer, U.S. Army Infantry School, Fort Benning, Ga.*

Lindberg, John Albert, Pvt. [101st Airborne]. *Sales representative, Oklahoma City, Okla.*

Looney, Frank J., T/4 [101st Airborne]. *Tavern owner, Albany, N.Y.*

Loveland, Glenn E., S/Sgt. [82nd Airborne]. *Employee, Board of Education, Shelby, O.*

Luiz, Charles, Cpl. [82nd Airborne]. *Engineering technician, Federal Aviation Administration, Manchester, N.H.*

Macchia, Rocco L., Lt. [82nd Airborne]. *Real estate, Ozone Park, N.Y.*

Machol, Robert Leonard, T/5 [82nd Airborne]. *Electrical foreman for Mafco Electric Co. of West Hartford, Simsbury, Conn.*

Mackey, Leonard Snow, Cpl. [101st Airborne]. *Runs mineral and lapidary shop, Colton, N.Y.*

MacLeod, Tom, Lt. [82nd Airborne]. *Postmaster, Columbia, S.C.*

MacNees, Frank J., Col. [9th Troop Carrier Command]. *Col. (Retired), U.S. Air Force; rancher, Travelers Rest, S.C.*

Maltese, Edward Vincent, Lt. [82nd Airborne]. *Col., U.S. Army, Washington, D.C.*

Mansolillo, Nicholas W., Pvt. [82nd Airborne]. *Works employee, Providence, R.I.*

Marohn, Robert E., P.F.C. [101st Airborne]. *Detective Lieutenant, Tonawanda Police Dept., Tonawanda, N.Y.*

Martin, J. Roy, Jr., Capt. [101st Airborne]. *Roofing contractor, Anderson, S.C.*

Martin, Orville S., P.F.C. [82nd Airborne]. *Laborer, Methyl Ware Corp., Two Rivers, Wis.*

Mason, Charles W., M/Sgt. [82nd Airborne]. *Airborne Historian, Fort Bragg, Fayetteville, N.C.*

Massei, Ernest Lawrence, Jr., Sgt. [82nd Airborne]. *President, Cape Fear Car Service Co., Fayetteville, N.C.*

Mastrangelo, William, Lt. [82nd Airborne]. *Tavern owner, Philadelphia, Pa.*

McCarthy, John T., M/Sgt. [101st Airborne]. *Employee of photoengraving plant, purchasing, estimating and billing, Chicago, Ill.*

McClain, Allen French, III, Lt. [82nd Airborne]. *City fireman, Coral Gables, Fla.*

McDavid, James Earl, P.F.C. [82nd Airborne]. *Construction superintendent, Hayward, Calif.*

McElfresh, John F., P.F.C. [101st Airborne]. *Clerk of Circuit Court, Deeds, Knox County, Edina, Mo.*

McFadden, Frank J., Lt. [101st Airborne]. *Lt. Col. (Retired), U.S. Army; Deputy Director, Tattnall County Civil Defense Unit, Reidsville, Ga.*

McGilvra, LaVerne Russell, P.F.C. [82nd Airborne]. *Beekeeper, Baraboo, Wis.*

McGinnis, Arthur J., P.F.C. [101st Airborne]. *Probation officer and real-estate broker, Elkridge, Md.*

McIlvoy, Daniel B., Major [82nd Airborne]. *Medical doctor, pediatrician, Bowling Green, Ky.*

McIntosh, Ben Charles, Pvt. [101st Airborne]. *Utility man for Board of Education, Bartlesville, Okla.*

McKeage, Donald Wm., Pvt. [82nd Airborne]. *Construction superintendent, Hemlock, Mich.*

McKearney, Bernard J., Lt. [101st Airborne]. *Ass't. Supt. of Schools, Hingham, Mass.*

McMandon, William T., Pvt. [82nd Airborne]. *Branch manager, Singer Company, Miami, Fla.*

McNiece, Jake, Sgt. [101st Airborne]. *Post office clerk, Ponca City, Okla.*

Meddaugh, William J., Lt. [82nd Airborne]. *Personnel specialist, I.B.M. Corp., Hyde Park, N.Y.*

Megellas, James, Lt. [82nd Airborne]. *D.S.C., Director, U.S.A.I.D. mission to Panama, Balboa, C.Z.*

Merlano, Louis P., Sgt. [101st Airborne]. *District sales manager, Hermes Business Machines Paillard Inc., Levittown, Pa.*

Meyer, Ralph F., Pvt. [101st Airborne]. *Union official and salesman, San Francisco, Calif.*

Meyers, James Joseph, Lt. [82nd Airborne]. *Col., U.S. Army, Columbia, S.C.*

Miller, Michael G., Sgt. [101st Airborne]. *Mailman, Edison, N.J.*

Miller, Walter Leroy, Jr., Capt. [101st Airborne]. *National Secretary-Treasurer, 101st Airborne Div. Ass'n., Greenville, Tex.*

Millsaps, Woodrow Wilson, Lt. [82nd Airborne]. *Lt. Col. (Retired), U.S. Army; Civil Service, Columbus, Ga.*

Mitchell, Charles A., S/Sgt. [101st Airborne]. *Insurance consultant, sales director, Talladega, Ala.*

Mitchell, Edward J., Cpl. [101st Airborne]. *Air-mail dispatcher, Oshkosh, Wis.*

Moe, Glenn Allen, Pvt. [101st Airborne]. *Sheet-metal mechanic, Toppenish, Wash.*

Morrison, Thomas J., Pvt. [101st Airborne]. *Advertising-specialty business operator, Ambler, Pa.*

Mulloy, Patrick J., Lt. [82nd Airborne]. *Employment counselor, Gary, Ind.*

Mulvey, Thomas Paris, Capt. [101st Airborne]. *Real-estate broker, stocks and bonds, Clarksville, Tenn.*

Murphy, Ernest P., 2nd Lt. [82nd Airborne]. *Law-enforcement officer, Kissimmee, Fla.*

Murphy, James J., Cpl. [82nd Airborne]. *Salesman, Indianapolis, Ind.*

Nadler, Philip H., Pvt. [82nd Airborne]. *Supervisor, Reichbold Chemicals, Inc., Westwood, N.J.*

Neill, Robert W., 2nd Lt. [101st Airborne]. *Retail-furniture dealer, Pullman, Wash.*

Nichols, Mickey, Sgt. [82nd Airborne]. *Insurance agent, Philadelphia, Pa.*

Nickrent, Roy Walter, S/Sgt. [101st Airborne]. *Town marshal and waterworks Supt. for village, Saybrook, Ill.*

Nicoll, Kenneth S., S/Sgt. [82nd Airborne]. *Ironworker, Montgomery, Tex.*

Norris, James Sherley, Pvt. [101st Airborne]. *Welder, Roanoke, Va.*

Nunan, Paul D., S/Sgt. [82nd Airborne]. *Sgt. Major, U.S. Army, Syracuse, N.Y.*

Oakley, Herbert L., P.F.C. [101st Airborne]. *Dry cleaner, Columbus, O.*

Oatman, William John, Pvt. [101st Airborne]. *Truck driver, Lancaster, Pa.*

O'Connell, Robert Philip, 2nd Lt. [101st Airborne]. *National accounts manager, Group Hospitalization, Inc., Bowie, Md.*

O'Hagan, Patrick J., Pvt. [82nd Airborne]. *Civil Service, N.Y.C. Transit Authority, Brooklyn, N.Y.*

Oldfather, Earl Shively, Cpl. [82nd Airborne]. *Banking officer, Toledo Trust Company, Toledo, O.*

Olsen, William S., Lt. [101st Airborne]. *Asst. to the President, Florida Mobile Home Assoc., Madeira Beach, Fla.*

Olson, Charles Ray, S/Sgt. [101st Airborne]. *Asst. superintendent of the composing room of the Jamestown (N.Y.) Post-Journal, Lakewood, N.Y.*

Olson, Hugo, Lt. [82nd Airborne]. *Attorney, Moorhead, Minn.*

O'Neal, Russell Roy, S/Sgt. [82nd Airborne]. *Restaurant owner, San Anselmo, Calif.*

Osborne, Ernest William, Sgt. [82nd Airborne]. *Material expediter, Union Carbide, Charleston, W. Va.*

Parker, Arthur, Sgt. [101st Airborne]. *Retired fire fighter; television technician, St. Petersburg, Fla.*

Paterson, Charles, Lt. [82nd Airborne]. *Safety supervisor, Armour Agricultural Chemical Co., Winter Haven, Fla.*

Patton, Donald Vickrey, Acting Sgt. [101st Airborne]. *Architect, Allen, Patton & Associates, Rockford, Ill.*

Pearson, Donald T., S/Sgt. [101st Airborne]. *Supervisory Plant Quarantine Inspector, U.S. Dept of Agriculture, Bayside, N.Y.*

Peterson, Theodore L., Lt. [82nd Airborne]. *Manufacturers' representative, Bloomfield Hills, Mich.*

Phillips, Robert Hamilton, Capt. [101st Airborne]. *V.-P., Trust Company of Georgia, Atlanta, Ga.*

Pickens, Oren Clinton, Sgt. [82nd Airborne]. *Postal employee, Homestead, Fla.*

Piper, Robert M., Capt. [82nd Airborne]. *Col., U.S. Army, A.P.O. San Francisco, Calif.*

Prescott, William L., Sgt. [82nd Airborne]. *Artist, San Miguel de Allende, G.T.O., Mexico.*

Pritikin, Marvin E., Sgt. [82nd Airborne]. *President, Illinois Mutual Fire Insurance Co., Chicago, Ill.*

Prow, Robert F., T/Sgt. [101st Airborne]. *Manager of a Pennsylvania state liquor store, Ambler, Pa.*

Purcell, Warren Carver, P.F.C. [101st Airborne]. *Farmer; Deputy Commissioner of Revenue, Petersburg, Va.*

Quirici, Oreste, Pvt. [101st Airborne]. *Manager, Physical Testing Laboratory, Kaiser Steel, Rutherford, Calif.*

Ragland, Robert Eugene, Lt. [82nd Airborne]. *Western regional sales manager, Baldwin, Ehret, Hill Inc., Los Angeles, Calif.*

Randall, Charles H., Jr., Pvt. [101st Airborne]. *Highway engineering technician, Los Altos, Calif.*

Rankin, William J., S/Sgt. [82nd Airborne]. *Carpenter, Kingman, Ariz.*

Richards, Theodore S., Lt. [101st Airborne]. *Sgt. Major, USARSO, Canal Zone, Ft. Amador, C.Z.*

Richardson, William King, Lt. [82nd Airborne]. *Employee, Veterans Administration, Columbia, S.C.*

Richmond, William K., Flt. Off. [9th Troop Carrier Command]. *Building-maintenance employee, Hicksville, N.Y.*

Ridgeway, Matthew B., Maj. Gen. [XVIII Corps]. *General (Retired), U.S. Army, Pittsburgh, Pa.*

Rippel, John Kenneth, P.F.C. [101st Airborne]. *Director, Electronics Mfg., Baltimore, Md.*

Roberts, James J., Col. [9th Troop Carrier Command]. *Col. (Retired), U.S. Air Force, Santa Barbara, Calif.*

Rocca, Francis A., P.F.C. [101st Airborne]. *Machine operator, Pittsfield, Mass.*

Rohr, Willis F., P.F.C. [101st Airborne]. *Carpenter, Hinsdale, Ill.*

Rosemond, St. Julien P., Capt. [101st Airborne]. *First Asst. County Attorney, Miami, Fla.*

Rosenthal, Hillel Z., P.F.C. [101st Airborne]. *Salesman, St. Louis, Mo.*

Rosinski, Harry F., P.F.C. [101st Airborne]. *Auto mechanic, Garfield Heights, O.*

Ruppe, Frank, Cpl. [82nd Airborne]. *Dental laboratory technician, Maspeth, N.Y.*

Ryals, Robert Wilson, Sgt. [101st Airborne]. *Sgt. Major, U.S. Army, Trenton, N.J.*

Sampson, Francis Leon, Capt. (Chaplain) [101st Airborne]. *Brig. Gen., Deputy Chief of Chaplains, U.S. Army, Arlington, Va.*

Sampson, Otis Little, S/Sgt. [82nd Airborne]. *Water company employee, Palm Springs, Calif.*

Sanders, Gus L., Lt. [82nd Airborne]. *Retired postmaster, Springdale, Ark.*

Santarsiero, Charles J., Lt. [101st Airborne]. *Pennsylvania Power & Light Co., Scranton, Pa.*

Scanlon, Wilbur J., 1st Sgt. [82nd Airborne]. *Customer-service manager, General Electric Supply Co., Baton Rouge, La.*

Scheaffer, John E., 2nd Lt. [82nd Airborne]. *Dairy sales manager, Camp Hill, Pa.*

Schmalz, Charles Edward, T/5 [82nd Airborne]. *Laborer, Wheeling Steel, Steubenville, O.*

Schmidt, Nicholas, T/4 [101st Airborne]. *Teacher of English and journalism, Twinsburg, O.*

Schneider, Frank, P.F.C. [82nd Airborne]. *Machine operator, Downers Grove, Ill.*

Schrader, Clifford W., Sgt. [82nd Airborne]. *Construction foreman, Hoffman Estates, Ill.*

Schultz, Arthur B., Pvt. [82nd Airborne]. *Counselor-therapist, San Diego, Calif.*

Schwaber, Sanford, P.F.C. [101st Airborne]. *President, S. & M. Quality Foods and Tasty Mix Products, Brooklyn, N.Y.*

Schwartz, John J., P.F.C. [82nd Airborne]. *Fireman, Rochester, N.Y.*

Schweiter, Leo Henry, Capt. [101st Airborne]. *Brig. Gen., C.O., 173rd Airborne, A.P.O. San Francisco, Calif.*

Schwerin, William Fred, Jr., T/5 [101st Airborne]. *Medical doctor, Pittsburgh, Pa.*

Searrin, William D., Pvt. [82nd Airborne]. *Bell Flower, Calif.*

Sefakis, Manuel John, Pvt. [101st Airborne]. *Worcester, Mass.*

Sessions, Myron Guy, Sgt. [101st Airborne]. *College instructor, Spokane, Wash.*

Shapiro, Hyman D., Lt. [82nd Airborne]. *Ear, nose and throat specialist, East Lansing, Mich.*

Shennum, Merlin J., Cpl. [101st Airborne]. *Farmer, Brockway, Mont.*

Shepard, Robert B., Capt. [101st Airborne]. *Honda motorcycles, Memphis, Tenn.*

Shoemaker, Charles Harry, Sgt. [101st Airborne]. *Maintenance section of National Park Service, Boulder City, Nev.*

Shutt, Harry G., Jr., M/Sgt. [101st Airborne]. *Construction superintendent, Shreveport, La.*

Siegmann, George A., 1st Sgt. [82nd Airborne]. *District sales manager, Temple Terrace, Fla.*

Simmons, Cecil Lee, Capt. [101st Airborne]. *Traffic engineer for City of Grand Rapids and Commanding General of Michigan National Guard, Grand Rapids, Mich.*

Smith, Ralph R., Pvt. [101st Airborne]. *Post-office clerk, St. Petersburg, Fla.*

Smith, Raymond, Pvt. [101st Airborne]. *Owner and president of Smith-Elkhorn Coal Co., Thornton, Ky.*

Smith, William F., P.F.C. [82nd Airborne]. *Gas & Electric Utilities, New Castle, Del.*

Soper, Erwin J., Jr., P.F.C. [307th Engineers]. *Erection superintendent, Haarmann Steel Co., Feeding Hills, Mass.*

Speck, Roger Donald, Pvt. [82nd Airborne]. *Southern Bell Telephone Co. and V.-P. of Local 3204, Communication Workers of America, Atlanta, Ga.*

Stach, Stanfield August, Capt. [101st Airborne]. *U.S. Army (Retired), disability, Houston, Tex.*

Stallbories, Robert Henry, Chief Warrant Officer [82nd Airborne]. *Life insurance agent, Equitable Life Assurance Society, Tulsa, Okla.*

Steed, James Thomas, Sgt. [82nd Airborne]. *Marketing manager, Southern Bell Telephone & Telegraph Co., Ft. Lauderdale, Fla.*

Steele, John M.,* S/Sgt. [82nd Airborne]. *U.S. Army (Retired), Wilmington, N.C.*

Stein, Lester, Capt. [82nd Airborne]. *Eye surgeon, Steubenville, O.*

Steinfield, Manfred, S/Sgt. [82nd Airborne]. *Furniture manufacturer, Skokie, Ill.*

Strayer, Robert L., Lt. Col. [101st Airborne]. *Insurance executive, Springfield, Delaware County, Pa.*

Strieter, William L., Sgt. [82nd Airborne]. *Real-estate broker, Arlington, Va.*

Strunk, Willard M., P.F.C. [82nd Airborne]. *Carpet-store owner, Wheat Ridge, Colo.*

Sult, Vernon Ralph, S/Sgt. [82nd Airborne]. *Liquor salesman, Granada Hills, Calif.*

Swanson, James A., Flt. Off. [9th Troop Carrier Command]. *Material-control manager, Industrial Corporation, Park Forest, Ill.*

Swanson, Wallace Albert, Capt. [101st Airborne]. *Geologist; general foreman & supervisor with W. S. Dickey Clay Mfg. Co., Fairfield, Ala.*

Sweeney, Neil J., Capt. [101st Airborne]. *Civil Service, Villa Park, Ill.*

Sweeney, Patrick J., S/4 [101st Airborne]. *Public-relations coordinator, Wappinger Falls, N.Y.*

Taft, Chester Weldon, P.F.C. [82nd Airborne]. *Millwright-machinist, Seneca Army Depot, Clyde, N.Y.*

Tallerday, Jack, Lt. [82nd Airborne]. *Col., U.S. Army, Fort Bragg, N.C.*

Tallon, Robert M., Sr., S/Sgt. [82nd Airborne]. *Department-store owner-manager, Dillon, S.C.*

Tarbell, Albert A., Sgt. [82nd Airborne]. *Ironworks employee, Nedrow, N.Y.*

Taylor, Frank Curtis, Sgt. [82nd Airborne]. *Retired, Albuquerque, N.M.*

Taylor, John H., Sgt. [101st Airborne]. *Paint and floor-covering contractor and retail-store owner, Lufkin, Tex.*

Taylor, Maxwell D., Maj. Gen. [C.O., 101st Airborne]. *General, Chief of Staff (Retired), U.S. Army.*

Taylor, Ray Edward, S/Sgt. [101st Airborne]. *Plasterer, Ashtabula, O.*

Thain, Carl Ernest, Capt. [82nd Airborne]. *Contractor, McAlester, Okla.*

Tisdale, Paul Arthur, Lt. [9th Troop Carrier Command]. *Col., U.S. Army, Arlington, Va.*

Tomardy, Bernard Joseph, Sgt. [82nd Airborne]. *Washington Gas & Light Co., Vienna, Va.*

Travers, Thomas R., 2nd Lt. [9th Troop Carrier Command]. *Operator, van and storage company, Berkeley, Calif.*

Tremble, Leonard G., P.F.C. [82nd Airborne]. *Staff assistant, petroleum company, Fort Worth, Tex.*

Tribe, Robert Wayne, Lt. [82nd Airborne]. *Specialist, U.S. Bureau of Reclamation, Sacramento, Calif.*

Truax, Kenneth W., P.F.C. [82nd Airborne]. *Agency manager, rural insurance companies, Wisconsin Farm Bureau affiliate, Ettrick, Wis.*

Tucker, Reuben H.,* Col. [82nd Airborne]. *Administrative department of The Citadel, Charleston, S.C.*

Tucker, William Humphrey, Jr., Sgt. [82nd Airborne]. *Attorney; formerly Chairman, U.S. Interstate Commerce Commission, Washington, D.C.*

Tyler, John Norman, Major [101st Airborne]. U.S. Army *(Retired), Cleveland, Tenn.*

Vandervoort, Benjamin Hays, Lt. Col. [82nd Airborne]. *Col. (Retired), U.S. Army, Hilton Head Island, S.C.*

Van Duzer, Franklin Kenneth, S/Sgt. [101st Airborne]. *Owner of Ris-Van Realty Co.; V.-P., Community National Bank; director, Guardsman Life Insurance Co., Clear Lake, Iowa.*

Van Ort, Richard M., Cpl. [82nd Airborne]. *Truck driver, Summit, Ill.*

Vanpoyck, Walter S., Capt. [82nd Airborne]. *Administrative officer, Eastern Air Lines, Miami, Fla.*

Vantrease, Glen Wilson, Sgt. [82nd Airborne]. *C.P.A., Gary, Ind.*

Veach, Donald, P.F.C. [82nd Airborne]. *Farmer, Manila, Ark.*

Vest, Hansford C., Sr., Cpl. [101st Airborne]. *Machinist, Boeing Co., Renton, Wash.*

Vuletich, Michael, S/Sgt. [82nd Airborne]. *Steelworker, South Holland, Ill.*

Wade, James Melvin, 2nd Lt. [82nd Airborne]. *Lt. Col., U.S. Army, Fort Bragg, N.C.*

Wagner, Richard Paul, S/Sgt. [82nd Airborne]. *Electric welder, Baraboo, Wis.*

Waldt, Anthony M., P.F.C. [101st Airborne]. *Clerk, Aberdeen, S.D.*

Webster, Leonard J., P.F.C. [82nd Airborne]. *Heating & air-conditioning engineer, Milwaukee, Wis.*

Weil, Bernard L., Lt. [82nd Airborne]. *Manager, furniture store, Norfolk, Va.*

Weinberg, Stanley, 2nd Lt. [82nd Airborne]. *Haberdasher, Jersey City, N.J.*

Wellems, Edward N., Major [82nd Airborne]. *Col., U.S. Army, Ft. Lewis, Wash.*

Welshons, Don R., Sgt. [101st Airborne]. *Minister, Sunland, Los Angeles, Calif.*

Wetsig, Chester J., S/Sgt. [101st Airborne]. *Micro-electronic engineering at General Electric Co., Marcy, N.Y.*

Whitacre, William B., Col. [9th Troop Carrier Command]. *Retired V.-P., American Airlines, Hot Springs, Ark.*

White, Myron A., P.F.C. [82nd Airborne]. *Farmer, Grinnell, Iowa*

Wienecke, Robert H., Lt. Col. [82nd Airborne]. *Major Gen. (Retired), U.S. Army; consultant and director of insurance company, Ventura, Calif.*

Wierzbowski, Edmund L., Lt. [101st Airborne]. *Special representative, insurance sales, Chicago, Ill. (NOTE: Uses name Edmund L. Weir for business.)*

Wilder, Thomas Patten, Capt. [101st Airborne]. *Yacht consultant, Balboa, Calif.*

Williams, Adriel N., Col. [9th Troop Carrier Command]. *Brig. Gen., U.S. Air Force, Washington, D.C.*

Williams, John Henry, Pvt. [101st Airborne]. *Instructor in R.O.T.C. program at Central High School, Chattanooga, Tenn.*

Williams, Warren R., Jr., Lt. Col. [82nd Airborne]. *Director, U.S. Army Board for Aviation Accident Research, Fort Rucker, Ala.*

Winton, Walter Farrell, Jr., Lt. Col. [82nd Airborne]. *Brig. Gen., U.S. Army, Annandale, Va.*

Woll, Shepherd, P.F.C. [101st Airborne]. *Owner, Wholesale Drug Sundries, Rockville Centre, N.Y.*

Womack, Waymon W., Pvt. [101st Airborne]. *Dow Chemical, Freeport, Tex.*

Wood, Rev. George B., D.D., Capt. [82nd Airborne]. *Rector of Trinity Episcopal Church, Fort Wayne, Ind.*

Wood, Leslie Earl, 1st Sgt. [82nd Airborne]. *Laboratory technician, Wunda Weve Carpet Co., Travelers Rest, S.C.*

Wurst, Spencer F., Sgt. [82nd Airborne]. *Laboratory technician, General Electric Co., and Lt. Col., National Guard, Erie, Pa.*

Wyngaert, Julius A., P.F.C. [82nd Airborne]. *U.S. Army, 3rd Special Forces, Fayetteville, N.C.*

Yates, Gorden Wyatt, S/Sgt. [101st Airborne]. *Assistant produce manager in a supermarket. Attends college nights, Phoenix, Ariz.*

Yedenock, William, Jr., S/Sgt. [82nd Airborne]. *Insurance broker, Berwyn, Pa.*

Yeiter, Robert D., P.F.C. [82nd Airborne]. *Restaurateur, Traverse City, Mich.*

Young, Charles H., Lt. Col. [9th Troop Carrier Command]. *Commercial airlines captain, Grapevine, Tex.*

Zagol, Walter Frank, P.F.C. [101st Airborne]. *State instructor, savings-bank life insurance, Taunton, Mass.*

Zakby, Abdallah K., Major [82nd Airborne]. *Middle East representative, tractor company, A.P.O. New York 09694.*

Zapalski, Daniel J., 1st Sgt. [101st Airborne]. *Retired Army officer; field representative for Prudential Savings & Loan Association, Rosemead, Calif.*

Ziegler, Roland C., 1st Sgt. [82nd Airborne]. *Electrician, Baraboo, Wis.*

BRITISH

Montgomery, Sir Bernard Law, Field Marshal [21st Army Group]. *Viscount Montgomery of Alamein, K.G., retired, Hampshire.*

Adair, Allan, Maj. Gen. [Guards Armoured]. C.V.O., C.B., D.S.O., M.C., *General, British Army, retired, London.*

Allsop, D. Capt. [1st Airborne]. *Transport & dairy manager, Pontesbury, nr. Shrewsbury.*

Anson, Geoffrey F., Capt. [Guards Armoured]. M.C., *Area manager, Ford Motor Credit Co., Ltd., London.*

Ashington, George, Pvt. [1st Airborne]. *Tool setter operator, Birmingham.*

Ashley, Neville L., Sgt. [1st Airborne]. *Teacher, Cheshire.*

Ashworth, Walton, S/Sgt. [Glider Pilot Regt.]. *Watchmaker, Essex.*

Atwell, Douglas, S/Sgt. [Glider Pilot Regt.]. *Valuer, Somersetshire.*

Austin, John Edward, Pvt. [1st Airborne]. *Civil servant, Surrey.*

Axford, James Alfred, L/Cpl. [1st Airborne]. *Postman, Kent.*

Back, Harold E., L/Cpl. [1st Airborne]. *Post-office clerk, London.*

Bagguley, Reginald, Pvt. [1st Airborne]. *Snack-bar proprietor, Staffordshire.*

Ball, Donald, Pvt. [1st Airborne]. *Ambulance driver, Yorkshire.*

Barclay, W. J. J., Pvt. [Pathfinder, 1st Airborne]. M.M., *Major, Ndola, Zambia.*

Barnes, Frank, Sgt. [Guards Armoured]. *Hospital clerk, Belfast.*

Barnett, J. Patrick, Lt. [1st Airborne]. *Golf club secretary, Kent.*

Barry, Peter, Lt. [1st Airborne]. *Medical doctor, Somerset.*

Basnett, Edward F., Sgt. Pilot [Glider Pilot Regt.]. *Housemaster, Home Office Boys School, Salop.*

Baylis, George Sidney, S/Sgt. [Glider Pilot Regt.]. *Cargo superintendent, Kent.*

Beckett, Sir Martyn, Capt. [Welsh Guards]. *Architect, London.*

Bedford, Ronald G., F/Sgt. [R.A.F.]. *Salesman, Torquay, Devonshire.*

Beech, James W. A., Pvt. [1st Airborne]. *Agricultural store manager, Spalding, Lincolnshire.*

Bennett, Clifford J., Guardsman [Guards Armoured]. *Grocery manager, Rugby.*

Bennett, Frederick C., Pvt. [1st Airborne]. *Stock audit, Redditch, Worcestershire.*

Bennett, Henry, Pvt. [1st Airborne]. *Stockbroker's messenger, London.*

Bentley, Thomas C., Sgt. [1st Airborne]. *Warrant Officer, British Army Recruiting, Nottingham.*

Binick, Norman, Sgt. [Pathfinder, 1st Airborne]. *Entertainer, London, S.W. 14.*

Blunt, John Graham, Lt. [1st Airborne]. *Major, Zambia Regiment, Ndola, Zambia.*

Blyton, Henry, Pvt. [1st Airborne]. *Plant operator, Lancashire.*

Boldock, Walter, J. P., Pvt. [1st Airborne]. *Rodent operator, Lincolnshire.*

Boulding, George H. W., Sgt. [1st Airborne]. *Printing-machine minder, Kent.*

Bowden, T. D. L., Trooper Signalman [1st Airborne]. *Manager, the National Kenya Sweepstake, Nairobi, Kenya.*

Bowers, Reverend Raymond E., Chaplain [1st Airborne]. *Parish priest, Richmond Place, Bath.*

Bowles, Dennis A., Signaller [1st Airborne]. *Analytical chemist, Tewkesbury, Gloucestershire.*

Brace, Terry, Cpl./Medic [1st Airborne]. *Storekeeper, Kent.*

Breese, C. F. O., Major [1st Airborne]. *Brigadier, retired; Company director, Yorkshire.*

Breitmeyer, Alan N., Lt. [Grenadier Guards]. *Colonel, commander, Grenadier Guards, London, S.W. 1.*

Bridgewater, William George, Sgt. Major [Glider Pilot Regt.]. *Petworth, Sussex.*

Briggs, Bernard W., Capt. [1st Airborne]. *Lt. Col., British Army (Retired), Dortmund Station, B.F.P.O. 20.*

Brook, Henry, L/Cpl. [1st Airborne]. *Bank messenger, nr. Manchester.*

Brown, Francis Edward, Sgt. [1st Airborne]. *Porter, British Railways, Yorkshire.*

Bruce, David, Capt. [Guards Armoured]. *Stock jobber, London, S.W. 10.*

Bruce, Joseph Morrison, Sgt. [Irish Guards]. *Retired, Belfast 13.*

Bryant, Reginald, Pvt. [1st Airborne]. *Printing engineer, Bristol 5.*

Buchanan-Jardine, Rupert, Lt. [Guards Armoured]. M.C., *Farmer, Dumfriesshire.*

Burton, Arthur Edwin, Cpl. [1st Airborne]. *Assistant superannuation officer, Leicestershire.*

Butcher, John M., W/Sgt. [1st Airborne]. *Works manager, Manchester.*

Cain, Robert,* Major C.O. [1st Airborne]. *V. C., Retired, Oxted, Surrey.*

Callaghan, Harry, Sgt. Major [1st Airborne]. O. B. L., *Civil servant, Aldershot, Hampshire.*

Campbell, Alexander Wm., Cpl. [1st Airborne]. *Patrolman, County Durham.*

Campbell, Gordon, S/Sgt. [Glider Pilot Regt.]. *Order clerk, Workington, Cumberland.*

Campbell, P., Sgt. [1st Airborne]. *Motor parts manager, Johannesburg, South Africa.*

Cannon, Brian Frank, Pvt. [1st Airborne]. *Engineering foreman, Luton, Bedfordshire.*

Carr, B. D., Lt. [1st Airborne]. *Supervisor, trust company, Vancouver, British Columbia.*

Cassie, James, Signalman [1st Airborne]. *Bookbinder, Edinburgh 11, Scotland.*

Cawrey, Victor F., Pvt. [Pathfinder, 1st Airborne]. *Haulage contractor, Leicestershire.*

Chandler, William F., Trooper [1st Airborne]. *Instrument maker, London, S.E., 24.*

Chapman, Harry A., W/S/Sgt. [Glider Pilot Regt.]. *Electrical contracts manager, Cyncoed, Cardiff, Wales.*

Chatterton, George S., Col. [Glider Pilot Regt.]. *Retired brigadier, London, N.W. 8.*

Chennell, William, Cpl. [Guards Armoured]. *Carpenter, London, S.E. 4.*

Christie, Gordon, Sapper [1st Airborne]. *Bricklayer, nr. Spalding, Lincolnshire.*

Christie, Robert K., Gunner [1st Airborne]. *Life-insurance agency superintendent, Surrey.*

Christie, Valentine Brock, Flying Officer [Royal Canadian Air Force]. *Grain farmer, Alberta, Canada.*

Clark, R. J., Capt. [1st Airborne]. *Bank economic adviser, Hertfordshire.*

Clegg, Benjamin B., Capt. [1st Airborne]. *Managing director, Sheffield.*

Clegg, Eric, Gunner [1st Airborne]. *Universal miller, engineering workshop, Lancashire.*

Cleminson, James A. S., Lt. [1st Airborne]. *Company director, Norfolk.*

Cockrill, James D., Signalman [1st Airborne]. *Police sergeant, Norfolk.*

Cole, C. V., Pvt. [1st Airborne]. *Carpenter, North Queensland, Australia.*

Coles, C. J., Cpl. [Guards Armoured]. *Major, Royal Guards, Windsor, Berkshire.*

Consett, William L., Major [Guards Armoured]. *Retired, London.*

Conway, James J., L/Cpl. [1st Airborne]. *Driver, Ministry of Aviation, Camberley, Surrey.*

Cook, Ralph, Gunner [1st Airborne]. *Chemical operator, Grimsby, Lincolnshire.*

Cooper, Derek G. D., Capt. Major [Guards Armoured]. *County Donegal, Ireland.*

Cooper, Frederick S., Pvt. [1st Airborne]. *Driver, Hornsy Rise, London N. 19.*

Copley, Stanley G., Signalman [1st Airborne]. *Public-relations executive, Henley-in-Arden, Warwickshire.*

Corrie, Michael T., Capt. [R.A.F. Glider Pilot]. *Produce broker, London, S.W. 1.*

Cosadinos, George, Cpl. [1st Airborne]. *Barber, Stockport, Cheshire.*

Cosgrove, David Thomas, Pvt. [1st Airborne]. *Trimmer, motor works, Luton, Bedfordshire.*

Cox, Alan Harvey, Lt. [1st Airborne]. *Lt. Col., British Army, Warrington, Lancashire.*

Cox, David, Pvt. [1st Airborne]. *Machine-shop inspector, Hemel Hempstead, Hertfordshire.*

Cox, Ronald Charles Percy, Pvt. [1st Airborne]. *G.P.O. engineer, Hemel Hempstead, Hertfordshire.*

Crawley, Douglas E., Major [1st Airborne]. *Lt. Col., NATO, Kolsås, Norway.*

Creswell, J. N., Lt. [Guards Armoured]. *Lloyd's underwriter, nr. Polegate, Sussex.*

Cronk, Frederick J., W/O Pilot [R.A.F.]. *Coach works director, Nottinghamshire.*

Crook, John W., L/Bombardier [1st Airborne]. *Police sergeant, Shipley, Yorkshire.*

Dakin, John Leslie, Pvt. [1st Airborne]. *Telephone engineer, Spalding, Lincolnshire.*

Dalton, Austin D., F/Sgt. [R.A.F.]. *Compositor, Linotype operator, Belfast.*

Daniells, Frederick T., Pvt. [1st Airborne]. *Engineer, Dunstable, Bedfordshire.*

Dauncey, Michael D. K., Lt. [Glider Pilot Regt.]. *Lt. Col., British Army, Latimer, Chesham, Buckinghamshire.*

Davey, Harold Leonard, C.Q.M.S. [1st Airborne]. *Shopkeeper, nr. Selby, Yorkshire.*

Davis, George E., S/Sgt. [1st Airborne]. *Marketing (sales promotion), N.S.W., Australia.*

Dawson, Alan, Pvt. [Pathfinders, 1st Airborne]. *Company director, Wrington, nr. Bristol.*

Dawson, John Harold, Pvt. [1st Airborne]. *Tool setter, Wolverhampton, Staffordshire.*

Deane-Drummond, Anthony, Major [1st Airborne]. D.S.O., M.C., *Maj. Gen., Commander, 3rd Infantry Division, Tidworth, Hampshire.*

Demetriadi, Springet, Capt. [Phantom Net]. *Member, London Stock Exchange, London, E.C. 2.*

Dent, Ralph, Pvt. [1st Airborne]. *Police sergeant, Scarborough, Yorkshire.*

Dixon, George, Cpl. [1st Airborne]. *Production engineer, Crawley, Sussex.*

Doggart, James, L/Cpl. [Guards Armoured]. *R.Q.M.S. of Irish Guards, Birdcage Walk, London, S.W. 1.*

Downing, Robert W., Pvt. [1st Airborne]. *High-voltage cable jointer, Northampton.*

Drew, James R., Sgt. [1st Airborne]. *Engineer, Stafford, Staffordshire.*

Driver, John, Pvt. [1st Airborne]. *Catering officer, Ashton-under-Lyne.*

Dullforce, Alfred J., Pvt. [1st Airborne]. *Stockroom manager, London.*

Dunn, Pat., Pvt. [1st Airborne]. *Coal merchant, Leicestershire.*

Eagger, Dr. A. Austin, A.D.M.S. [1st Airborne]. *Retired medical doctor, Exeter, Devonshire.*

Edwards, Jimmy, F.O. [R.A.F.]. *Entertainer, Uckfield, Sussex.*

Edwards, Robert C. S., Pvt. [1st Airborne]. *Heavy-goods driver, nr. Coventry.*

Edwards, Roy Norris, Pvt. [1st Airborne]. *Electrician's mate, Barry, Glamorganshire, Wales.*

Egan, Rev. Fr. Bernard M., Chaplain [1st Airborne]. *Headmaster, Wimbledon College Preparatory School, London.*

Ellwood, Richard A., Sgt. [1st Airborne]. *Gas board staff officer, Hammersmith, London.*

Emery, Ronald T., Sapper [1st Airborne]. *Decorator, London.*

Essame, Hubert, Brigadier [43rd Infantry Div.]. C.B.E., D.S.O., M.C., *Retired Major General, N. Chichester.*

Fairclough, Thomas, Sgt. [1st Airborne]. *Civil servant, Lancashire.*

Falconer, Edward, Guardsman [Guards Armoured]. *Laborer, Montrose, Angus, Scotland.*

Faulkner, Maurice A., Pvt. [1st Airborne]. *Gear cutter, Tamworth, Staffordshire.*

Fenge, William J., Sgt. [Glider Pilot Regt.]. *Builder, London, S.W. 17.*

Fieldhouse, Stanley, Gunner [1st Airborne]. *Tailor's cutter, Leeds 16, Yorkshire.*

Firkins, Harold J., Sgt. [1st Airborne]. *Director, insurance brokers, Kings Heath, Birmingham 14.*

FitzGerald, Desmond R. S., Major [Guards Armoured]. *Merchant banker, London.*

Fitzpatrick, Francis "Pat," Sgt. [1st Airborne]. *Office manager, Coulsdon, Surrey.*

Formoy, Leonard, Cpl. [1st Airborne]. *Depot manager for sports manufacturer, London, S.E. 11.*

Foster, Raymond H., Sapper [1st Airborne]. *Shoe repairman, Farnham, Surrey.*

Frater, Les J., S/Sgt. [Glider Pilot Regt.]. *Civil servant, Weston-super-Mare, Somersetshire.*

Freemantle, Albert, Pvt. [1st Airborne]. *Superintendent, British South Africa Police, Rhodesia.*

Frost, John D., Lt. Col. [1st Airborne]. *Retired Major General, Oxshott, Surrey.*

Gammon, Peter John F., Sgt. [Glider Pilot Regt.]. *Chartered surveyor, Woking, Surrey.*

Garfield, Frank, Pvt. [1st Airborne]. *Transport driver, Birmingham.*

Gatland, George, Sgt. Major [1st Airborne]. *Technical assistant, London Street Lighting, Wembley, Middlesex.*

Gay, Robert D., Sgt. Major [1st Airborne]. *Construction manager, Burgh Heath, Surrey.*

George, J. H., Cpl. [1st Airborne]. *Metal engineer, Australia.*

Gibbons, Eric R., Cpl. [1st Airborne]. *Off-license manager, London, N. 7.*

Gibbons, Harry A., S/Sgt. [Glider Pilot Regt.]. *Stock controller, Chippenham, Wiltshire.*

Gibbons, Leslie N., S/Sgt. [Glider Pilot Regt.]. *Sales representative, B.E.A. Airways, Warwickshire.*

Gillie, Thomas, Sgt. [1st Airborne]. *Building foreman, Darlington, County Durham.*

Glover, J. W., Lt/QM [1st Airborne]. *Retired Lt. Col., British Army Administration, York, Yorkshire.*

Glover, Richard, Cpl. [1st Airborne]. *Company representative, Driffield, Yorkshire.*

Goldthorpe, Lawrence, Sgt. [Glider Pilot Regt.]. *Government service, Surrey.*

Gordon-Watson, Michael, Major [Guards Armoured]. O.B.E., M.C., *Stud manager, farmer, Dorsetshire.*

Gorman, John, Lt. [Guards Armoured]. C.V.O., M.B.E., M.C., *Personnel director, B.O.A.C., Sussex.*

Gough, C. F. H., Major [1st Airborne]. *Insurance broker and company director, Lodsworth, Sussex.*

Goulburn, Edward H., Lt. Col. [Guards Armoured]. *Retired Major General, Surrey.*

Grafton, James, Major [43rd Division]. *TV script writer, company director, Strutton Ground, London.*

Grainger, Robert E., Co. Sgt. Major [1st Airborne]. M.B.E., *Racing manager, Greyhound Stadium, nr. Stroud, Gloucestershire.*

Gray, Donald James, Signalman [1st Airborne]. *Builder, Cleethorpes, Lancashire.*

Green, P. J., Pvt. [1st Airborne]. *Slatter, Morayshire, Scotland.*

Green, Thomas C., S/Sgt. [1st Airborne]. *Head remedial gymnast, Marston Green, Birmingham.*

Grieve, Duncan G., Signalman [1st Airborne]. *Rotary-press assistant, Grimsby, Lincolnshire.*

Griffiths, Frederick F., L/Sgt. [Guards Armoured]. *Miner, New Tupton, Chesterfield.*

Growe, Michael G., Pvt. [1st Airborne]. *Inspector of motor components, Sheldon, Birmingham.*

Hackett, John, Brigadier [1st Airborne]. D.S.O., M.B.E., M.C., *Retired Commander in Chief, British Army of the Rhine.*

Hall, Eric, Sgt. [1st Airborne]. *Sales manager, Schweppes, London.*

Hall, J. A., L/Cpl. [1st Airborne]. *Clerk, British Embassy, Louvain, Belgium.*

Halliwell, Stanley, L/Sgt. [1st Airborne]. *Builder, Cheshire.*

Hands, Lewis, Sgt. [1st Airborne]. *Company director, Nottingham.*

Hardman, Donald A., Pvt. [1st Airborne]. *Fireman, Northants.*

Harker, M., Capt. [Phantom Net]. *Director, wine & spirits merchants, London.*

Harris, Thomas H., L/Cpl. [1st Airborne]. *Grinder, Warwickshire.*

Harrison, Charles A., Capt. [1st Airborne]. *Stockbroker, London.*

Harvey, Bernard H., Warrant Off. [R.A.F.]. D.F.C., *Civil servant, Guildford, Surrey.*

Harvey-Kelly, C. William, Lt. [Guards Armoured]. *Colonel, British Army, London.*

Hatch, Roy Ernest, Sgt. [Glider Pilot Regt.]. *Motorcycle dealer, Caterham, Surrey.*

Hawkings, Angela [Red Cross]. *Buyer, New York, N.Y.*

Hay, Neville, Lt. [Phantom Net]. *General manager to a security organization, London.*

Haysom, James N., Signalman [1st Airborne]. *Engineer, Cardiff, Wales.*

Haywood, Bernard, Cpl. [1st Airborne]. *Legal executive, Cheshire.*

Haywood, Leslie N., F/Sgt. [R.A.F.]. *Retired police sergeant, E. Yorkshire.*

Hendy, Arthur S., L/Cpl. [1st Airborne]. *Bus driver, London Transportation, Kent.*

Hennon, Wilfred, Warrant Off. II [1st Airborne]. C.S.M., *Civil servant, Farnborough, Hampshire.*

Herman, Jack, Flying Officer [R.A.F.]. *Investment consultant, London.*

Hewitt, Jack, Signalman [1st Airborne]. *Assistant head postmaster, Yorkshire.*

Heyes, Stanley, Signalman [1st Airborne]. *Sub officer, fire brigade, Cheshire.*

Heywood, A. G., Capt. [Guards Armoured]. C.B.E., M.E., *Colonel, British Army, Wiltshire.*

Hicks, Philip H. W., Brigadier [1st Airborne]. *Retired Major General, Hampshire.*

Hicks, Thomas, Sapper [1st Airborne]. *Locomotive driver, British Railways, Yorkshire.*

Hill, Joseph J., W/Sgt. [Glider Pilot Regt.]. *Personnel officer, Staffordshire.*

Hogan, Patrick, Guardsman [Guards Armoured]. *Postman, Middlesex.*

Holburn, A. R., Pvt. [1st Airborne]. *Lt. Col., Zambia Army, Lusaka, Zambia.*

Hollis, Frank, Pvt. [1st Airborne]. *Oil company driver, Essex.*

Hollobone, Bernard, Sgt. [1st Airborne]. *Shop owner, Leicester.*

Holloway, John J., Signalman [1st Airborne]. *Engineer, Kennington, Oxfordshire.*

Holt, B. R., S/Sgt. [Glider Pilot Regt.]. *Engineering planning manager, Leeds 16, Yorkshire.*

Holt, Ronald C., Pvt. [1st Airborne]. *Managing director, flooring contractor, Saltney, Cheshire.*

Homfray, Frank R., Lt. [Guards Armoured]. *Farmer, Newbury, Berkshire.*

Hopkins, George, Cpl. [1st Airborne]. *Joiner, Tamworth, Staffordshire.*

Hopkinson, H. S., Lt. [Guards Armoured]. *Colonel, commanding Household Cavalry, East Hagbourne, Berkshire.*

Horsefield, James, Pvt. [1st Airborne]. *Planer, Whickham, Newcastle-on-Tyne.*

Hoskins, James, Sgt. [1st Airborne]. *Police constable, Manchester.*

Houghton, H. R., W/Sgt. [1st Airborne]. *Plasterer, Liverpool 7.*

Houston, Francis Wesley, Pvt. [1st Airborne]. *Clerk, Newcastle-upon-Tyne 3.*

Howson, Victor, Pvt. [1st Airborne]. *Heat and frost insulator, London, E. 17.*

Hudson, Frank, L/Cpl. [1st Airborne]. *Lodgeman, Stoke-on-Trent, Staffordshire.*

Humphries, Alan Peter, Lt. [1st Airborne]. *Partner in accounting firm, Esher, Surrey.*

Hunt, Stanley J., Flight Lt. [R.A.F.]. *Education officer, R.A.F. Squadron Leader, Aylesbury, Buckinghamshire.*

Hurst, William, W/Sgt. [1st Airborne]. *Foreman, nr. Bolton, Lancashire.*

Huth, William J., Sgt. [1st Airborne]. *Manager of jewelry shop, Morden, Surrey.*

Inglis, Walter, Sgt. [1st Airborne]. *Hall porter, St. Albans, Hertfordshire.*

Isherwood, Reginald, Sgt. [1st Airborne]. *Managing director, Brentwood, Essex.*

Isitt, Bernard C., Lt. [Guards Armoured]. *Insurance adjuster, Paris, France.*

Jeavons, Sidney T., Pvt. [1st Airborne]. *Machinist, Sheffield, Yorkshire.*

Jenkins, Walter, Pvt. [1st Airborne]. *Nurse, Derbyshire.*

Jennings, Robert, Pvt. [1st Airborne]. *Diesel-plant fitter, Farnborough, Hampshire.*

Johnson, Ronald O., Lt. [Glider Pilot Regt.]. *General manager, Hoover Co., Wien 19, Austria.*

Jones, A. G. C., Lt. [Guards Armoured]. *Lt. Col., British Army, London W. 8.*

Jones, Alfred, Pvt. [Pathfinder, 1st Airborne]. *Civil servant, British Army, Germany.*

Jones, C. P., Lt. Col. [Guards Armoured]. G.C.B., C.B.E., MC., *Retired Army General, Rye, Sussex.*

Jones, Eric, Signalman [1st Airborne]. *Paper converter, Widnes, Lancashire.*

Jones, James F., L/Bombardier [1st Airborne]. *Detective inspector of police, Witney, Oxfordshire.*

Jones, James Henry, Pvt. [1st Airborne]. *Bus driver, Speke, Liverpool.*

Jones, Robert H., Sgt. [1st Airborne]. *Managing director, Transport & General Contractors, Kitwe, Zambia.*

Jones, William, Pvt. [1st Airborne]. *Electrician, Dudley, Worcestershire.*

Jordan, Ronald G., Arm/Cfn. [1st Airborne]. *Sales-office manager, nr. Birmingham.*

Jukes, G. W., Pvt. [1st Airborne]. *Telephone installer, Vancouver, British Columbia.*

Kane, John P., Pvt. [1st Airborne]. *Works foreman, Yorkshire.*

Keenan, James M., Pvt. [1st Airborne]. *Engineer, New Parks, Leicestershire.*

Kelly, Donald, L/Sgt. [1st Airborne]. *Hospital canteen manager, Bishopton, Renfrewshire.*

Kent, Ronald, Sgt. [Pathfinder, 1st Airborne]. *Solicitor, Cape Province, South Africa.*

Kibble, William H., Reg. Sgt. Major [1st Airborne]. *Caretaker, Twerton, Bath.*

Killick, J. E., Capt. [1st Airborne]. *Counselor in H. M. Foreign Service, Washington, D.C.*

King, Charles D., L/Cpl. [1st Airborne]. *Tannery foreman, Little Borough, Lancashire.*

King, Frank D., Capt. [1st Airborne]. *Major General, M.B.E., Whitehall, London, S.W. 1.*

King, Henry A., Flying Officer/Navigator [R.A.F.]. *Queen's Messenger Escort, London, N. 12.*

King, Leonard, S/Sgt. [Glider Pilot Regt.]. *Police sergeant, Barnet, Hertfordshire.*

Kitchener, Joseph H., S/Sgt. [Glider Pilot Regt.]. *Postal and telegraph officer, Lewes, Sussex.*

Knee, Frank, L/Cpl. [1st Airborne]. *Linotype operator, Coventry.*

Langford, Thomas, Pvt. [1st Airborne]. *Industrial buyer, Blaydon-on-Tyne, County Durham.*

Langton, Roland S., Capt. [Irish Guards]. M.V.O., M.C., *Colonel, British Army, Oxfordshire.*

Lankstead, William A., Pvt. [1st Airborne]. *Motor mechanic, Northwich, Cheshire.*

Lathbury, Gerald, Brig. [1st Airborne]. G.C.B., D.S.O., M.B.E., *Gerald, Sir, Governor and Commander in Chief of Gibraltar.*

Lewis, Edward, Cpl. [Guards Armoured]. *Tool setter, Cheltenham, Gloucestershire.*

Lewis, Richard P. C., Major [1st Airborne]. *Corn merchant, Alton, Hampshire.*

Lindley, Francis William, Major [1st Airborne]. *Sub postmaster, Retford, Nottinghamshire.*

Line, Cyril, S/Sgt. [Glider Pilot Regt.]. *Surveyor, Wedmore, Somersetshire.*

Lister, Eric C., Sgt. [Guards Armoured]. *Fish merchant, Strood, Kent.*

Little, Kenneth E., Signalman [1st Airborne]. *Works employee, Bristol 4.*

Loney, Patrick A., Trooper [1st Airborne]. *Lorry driver, London, E. 6.*

Long, Michael W., Lt. [Glider Pilot Regt.]. *Manager, Technical Publications, Stratford-on-Avon, Warwickshire.*

Long, Richard C., S/Sgt. [Glider Pilot Regt.]. *Technical representative, Romford, Essex.*

Longland, Cedric James, Major [1st Airborne]. *Surgeon, Dumbartonshire, Scotland.*

Lonsdale, Richard, Major [1st Airborne]. *Private means, Jersey, Channel Islands.*

Lord, John C.,* Reg. Sgt. Major [1st Airborne]. M.V.O., M.B.E.

Love, Donald, Flight Lt. [Guards Armoured]. *Insurance agency superintendent, Eastbourne, Sussex.*

Luckhurst, Frederick A., Sapper [1st Airborne]. *Aircraft worker, Wooten Bassett, Wiltshire.*

Lumb, D., Cpl. [1st Airborne]. *Toolmaker, Rochdale, Lancashire.*

Lumb, Vernon, Sgt. [1st Airborne]. *Sales manager, Rotherham, Sheffield.*

Mackay, Eric M., Capt. [1st Airborne]. M.B.E., D.S.C., *British Army Colonel, The Maultway, Camerley, Surrey.*

Mackenzie, Charles B., Lt. Col. [1st Airborne]. *Secretary, T. & A.F.A., Glasgow, Scotland.*

Mahaffey, Rupert, Lt. [Guards Armoured]. *Bank director, London, S.W. 3.*

Major, Sidney Francis, L/Sgt. [1st Airborne]. *Sales representative, Hatfield, Hertfordshire.*

Malley, Joe, Cpl. [1st Airborne]. *British Army, Hull, Yorkshire.*

Marples, Graham, Signalman [1st Airborne]. *Land investigator, Penistone, Yorkshire.*

Mason, Valery E. C., Sgt. [Glider Pilot Regt.]. *Official, Zambia government, Ndola, Zambia.*

Mayne, William Victor, Guardsman [Guards Armoured]. *Lorry driver, Newtonabbey, County Antrim, Northern Ireland.*

McBain, Ronald C., Sgt. [1st Airborne]. *Fish merchant, Whitehaven, Cumberland.*

McCardie, W. D. H., Lt. Col. [1st Airborne]. *Company director, Cheltenham, Gloucestershire.*

McClory, Owen D., Pvt. [1st Airborne]. *Records clerk, Billingham-on-Tees, County Durham.*

McGuinness, Hugh, Pvt. [1st Airborne]. *Docker, Whitehaven, Cumberland.*

McMahon, Thomas, Pvt. [Pathfinder, 1st Airborne]. *Turf accountant, Twickenham, Middlesex.*

McNeill, David W., S/Sgt. [Glider Pilot Regt.]. *Company director, Stirlingshire, Scotland.*

Milbourne, Andrew, Pvt. [1st Airborne]. *Civil servant, Newcastle-upon-Tyne.*

Miller, Claire [Civilian]. M.B.E., B.E.M., *Company director, Rickmansworth, Hertfordshire.*

Miller, Victor D., S/Sgt. [Glider Pilot Regt.]. *Technical representative, Walingham, Surrey.*

Mills, John C., Cpl. [1st Airborne]. *Auto association patrol, Scarborough, Yorkshire.*

Mitchell, Edward, Sgt. [Glider Pilot Regt.]. *Maintenance dept., Ford Motor Co., Liverpool 19.*

Mitchell, Gordon L., Pvt. [1st Airborne]. *Process engineer, Heanor, Nottinghamshire.*

Moberly, Richard J., Col. [1st Airborne]. *Retired Major General, British Army, Salisbury, Wiltshire.*

Mole, Joseph D., L/Cpl. [1st Airborne]. *Plasterer, Stepney, London, E. 1.*

Moncur, Francis W., Pvt. [1st Airborne]. *Educational adviser, publishing firm, Wellington, New Zealand.*

Montgomery, Hector, Capt. [1st Airborne]. *Sales manager, Woking, Surrey.*

Moore, Rodney, Lt. Col. [Guards Armoured]. G.C.M.G., K.C.B., C.B.E., D.S.O., *Gen. Sir. (Retired), Ascot, Berkshire.*

Moorwood, S. James D., Lt. [Glider Pilot Regt.]. *Solicitor, Shamley Green, Surrey.*

Morgans, Daniel T., Cpl. [1st Airborne]. *Storeman, Rhondda, Glamorganshire, Wales.*

Morris, Dave, R.Q.M.S. [1st Airborne]. *Security officer, Luton, Bedfordshire.*

Munford, Dennis, Major [1st Airborne]. *Retired Colonial Service official, Southwold, Suffolk.*

Murray, Iain, Lt. Col. [Glider Pilot Regt.]. *Retired, London.*

Nattrass, George, Sgt. [1st Airborne]. *Hotel manager, nr. Middlesbrough, Yorkshire.*

Nayler, Anthony E., Pvt. [1st Airborne]. *Lorry driver, Melton Mowbray, Leicestershire.*

Newbury, Edwin, Capt. [1st Airborne]. *Chief officer of Licensing Dept., London.*

Noble, Jeffrey F., Lt. [1st Airborne]. *Personnel director, Sussex.*

Nunn, Sydney R. G., L/Cpl. [1st Airborne]. *Photographer, Stevenage, Hertfordshire.*

Oakes, William, Sgt. [Glider Pilot Regt.]. *Civil servant, High Barnet, Hertfordshire.*

O'Brien, William A., Pvt. [1st Airborne]. *Salesman, Waltham Cross, Hertfordshire.*

O'Leary, Peter, L/Sgt. [1st Airborne]. *Sales-office manager, Goffs Oak, Hertfordshire.*

Overton, Leonard M., Sgt. [Glider Pilot Regt.]. *Police inspector, West Derby, Liverpool.*

Pare, G. A., Chaplain [Glider Pilot Regt.]. *Vicar, St. James Church, Warrington, Lancashire.*

Paris, Edward P., L/Cpl. [1st Airborne]. *Painter, decorator, Blackheath.*

Parkes, Percy, L/Bombardier [1st Airborne]. *Police superintendent, Derbyshire.*

Partridge, Felix F., Sapper [1st Airborne]. *Carpenter, Sudbury, Suffolk.*

Paterson, William, Signalman [1st Airborne]. *Managing director, Southport, Lancashire.*

Pavey, Charles, Gunner [1st Airborne]. *Painter and decorator, Crawley, Sussex.*

Pawsey, Jack, L/Cpl. [1st Airborne]. *Printer, London.*

Pearce, Kenneth J., Signalman [1st Airborne]. *Head of Science Dept., Longford School, Twickenham, Middlesex.*

Pearce, Thomas W., Sgt. [Glider Pilot Regt.]. *Driver, delivery man, Croydon, Surrey.*

Pearson, Dudley R., S/Sgt. [1st Airborne]. *Auctioneer and estate agent, Weston Favel, Northampton.*

Peatling, Robert, Pvt. [1st Airborne]. *Compositor, London.*

Phillips, Bernard, L/Cpl. [1st Airborne]. *Sales manager, Manchester.*

Phillips, Edward L., C.F. [1st Airborne]. *Vicar, Lewes, Sussex.*

Potter, George H., Cpl. [1st Airborne]. *Decorating contractor, Wednesfield, Staffordshire.*

Powell, George S., Major [1st Airborne]. *Civil servant, London.*

Preston, Henry G. C., Cpl. [1st Airborne]. *Works employee, Syston, Leicestershire.*

Pritchard, Thomas, Pvt. [1st Airborne]. *Prison officer, Edinburgh, Scotland.*

Prosser, John E., Pvt. [1st Airborne]. *Security officer, Reading, Berkshire.*

Pyne, Gordon, Sgt. [Glider Pilot Regt.]. *Company secretary/accountant, Clophill, Bedfordshire.*

Quinan, B. P., Lt. [Guards Armoured]. *Oil company official, Baghdad, Iraq.*

Ralph, Edward E. S., S/Sgt. [Glider Pilot Regt.]. *Planning engineer, Eastleigh, Hampshire.*

Rate, John, Sgt. [1st Airborne]. *Coach driver/courier, Wigston Fields, Leicester.*

Rathband, Harry, Sgt. [Glider Pilot Regt.]. *Oil company service engineer, Oxford.*

Read, Victor H., Signalman [1st Airborne]. *Electrical contractor, Basingstoke, Hampshire.*

Reynolds, Alfred S., Sgt. [1st Airborne]. *Works foreman, nr. Dartford, Kent.*

Richards, John T., Sgt. [1st Airborne]. *Representative, Wilford, Nottinghamshire.*

Rigby-Jones, Guy, Major [1st Airborne]. M.C., T.D., *Orthopedic surgeon, London.*

Robb, Richard, L/Cpl. [1st Airborne]. *Lecturer in surveying, Nottingham.*

Robinson, Peter T., Sgt. [Guards Armoured]. *Excavator driver, Southend, Essex.*

Robinson, Wilfred H., Capt. [1st Airborne]. *Schoolmaster, Kenilworth Cape, South Africa.*

Rose, John William, Pvt. [1st Airborne]. *Postman, South Harrow, Middlesex.*

Roullier, Alfred W., W/Bombardier [1st Airborne]. *Restaurant manager, Egham, Surrey.*

Russell, Cyril, Lt. [Guards Armoured]. *Solicitor, London.*

St. Aubyn, Piers, Lt. [1st Airborne]. M.C., *Stockbroker, Ringmer, Sussex.*

Salt, Wilfred D., Pvt. [1st Airborne]. *Postman, Willenhall, Staffordshire.*

Savage, Gordon, Gunner [1st Airborne]. *Bus driver, Arrowthwaite, Whitehaven, Cumberland.*

Schofield, Allan, Warrant Off. [R.A.F.]. *Nurse, Dawlish, Devonshire.*

Scott-Barrett, David, Lt. [Guards Armoured]. M.B.E., M.C., *Colonel, British Army, British Forces Post Office 15.*

Seaford, Raymond G., Pvt. [1st Airborne]. *Executive director, Luton, Bedfordshire.*

Seccombe, Ernest, Capt. [1st Airborne]. *Senior tutor, Hospital Administrative Staff College, London.*

Seeckts, James, Co. Sgt. Major [1st Airborne]. *Machine operator, Skelmersdale, Lancashire.*

Shackelton, Ralph, Pvt. [1st Airborne]. *Wool broker, Shipley, Yorkshire.*

Shearwood, Arthur, Pvt. [1st Airborne]. *Docker, London.*

Sheath, Alfred H., S/Sgt. [Glider Pilot Regt.]. *Fishmonger, Kent.*

Sheriff, Gordon, Cpl. [1st Airborne]. *Telephonist, Gloucester.*

Short, Edward R., Pvt. [1st Airborne]. *Government housing employee, Westoning, Bedfordshire.*

Simpson, Walter T., Sgt. [R.A.F.]. *Engineering inspector, Cheylesmore, Coventry.*

Sims, James W., Pvt. [1st Airborne]. *Radio clerk, Brighton 6, Sussex.*

Small, Albert E., Pvt. [1st Airborne]. *Vehicle mechanic, Normanton, Yorkshire.*

Smart, Roy J., Pvt. [1st Airborne]. *Racehorse trainer, Johannesburg, South Africa.*

Smith, Arthur J., Sgt. [Guards Armoured]. *Charge Hand, Birmingham 31.*

Smith, Eric, Guardsman [Guards Armoured]. *Police officer, Coventry.*

Smith, Frederick J., Guardsman [Guards Armoured]. *Detective inspector, Bradford 2, Yorkshire.*

Smith, Frederick P., Pvt. [1st Airborne]. *Casualty orderly, London.*

Smith, Henry, Lt. Col. [Guards Armoured]. K.C.M.G., K.C.V.O., D.S.O., *Retired, Windsor, Berkshire.*

Smith, John S., L/Cpl. [1st Airborne]. *Communications engineer, Wolverhampton, Staffordshire.*

Smith, Thomas, Guardsman [Guards Armoured]. *Building foreman, Coventry.*

Southall, William J., Cpl. [1st Airborne]. *Recreational supervisor, Coventry.*

Spelman, Dennis G., S/Sgt. [Glider Pilot Regt.]. *Sales manager, Bromley, Kent.*

Spencer, Harold W., Pvt. [1st Airborne]. *Baker, Grimsby, Lincolnshire.*

Spicer, Gordon F., L/Cpl. [1st Airborne]. *Machine-tool worker, Portslade, Sussex.*

Spivey, Horace, Sgt. [1st Airborne]. *Textile executive, Dewsbury, Yorkshire.*

Stainforth, Peter, Lt. [1st Airborne]. *Chemical engineer, Knebworth, Hertfordshire.*

Standish, Harold, C/Sgt. [1st Airborne]. *Sgt. Major in S.A.S. Regt., Salisbury, Southern Rhodesia.*

Stanley-Clarke, J. Q., Capt. [Guards Armoured]. *Draper's assistant, Shepton-Mallet, Somerset.*

Stanners, Geoffrey, Cpl. [1st Airborne]. *Company director, Great Kingshill, nr. Wycombe, Buckinghamshire.*

Steele, Robert R., Capt. [Guards Armoured]. M.B.E., *Company director, Beaulieu, Hampshire.*

Stewart, Richard, Major [1st Airborne]. M.C., *Solicitor, Scotby, Carlisle.*

Storey, Charles, Sgt. [1st Airborne]. *Captain, Quartermaster, British Army, Bahrain Garrison, B.F.P.O. 63.*

Stretton, Arthur H., Cpl. [1st Airborne]. *Stamford jointer, Tamworth, Staffordshire.*

Sturges, Sidney A., Cpl. [1st Airborne]. *TV representative, Erdington, Birmingham.*

Sullivan, Thomas Stanley, Sgt. [1st Airborne]. *Managing director, Stockport, Derbyshire.*

Sunley, Ralph ("Joe"), Sgt. [1st Airborne]. *Head gardener, Farnham, Surrey.*

Swift, Norman, Sgt. [1st Airborne]. *Police sergeant, Maidstone, Kent.*

Swinfield, William A., Pvt. [1st Airborne]. *Butcher, Burton-on-Trent, Staffordshire.*

Taylor, Arthur Reginald, Sgt. [Guards Armoured]. M.M., *Police inspector, Ipswich, Suffolk.*

Taylor, George, Lt. Col. [43rd Wessex]. C.B.E., D.S.O., *Brigadier (Retired)*, *British Army, Tilford, Surrey.*

Taylor, W. A., T/Capt. [1st Airborne]. *Lt. Col., British Army, Bournemouth, Hampshire.*

Tedman, Francis R., Sgt. [1st Airborne]. D.S.M., M.M., *Panel beater, Tadworth, Surrey.*

Thomas, D., Cpl. [1st Airborne]. *Foreman, TV cabinet firm, Croydon, Surrey.*

Thomas, Sir G. Ivor, Maj. Gen. [43rd Wessex]. G.C.B., K.B.E., D.S.O., M.C., *General (Retired), British Army, Salisbury, Rhodesia.*

Thomas, Thomas, C.Q.M.S. [1st Airborne]. M.B.E., *Major, British Army, Deringlines, Brecon, Wales.*

Thompson, William F. K., Lt. Col. [1st Airborne]. *Brigadier (Retired), British Army; military editor,* Daily Telegraph, *London.*

Thompson, William Peter, Sgt. Pilot [Glider Pilot Regt.]. *Company director, Gateshead, County Durham.*

Thorley, John Henry, Signalman [1st Airborne]. *Businessman, Barnstaple, Devonshire.*

Tilly, Gerald, Lt. Col. [XXX Corps]. D.S.O., T.D., *Board chairman, Coulsdon, Surrey.*

Tims, Eric Lawson, Sgt. [1st Airborne]. *Constable, Eccles, Lancashire.*

Toler, Thomas Ian Jodrell, Major [Glider Pilot Regt.]. *General manager, chemical company, Alvanley, Cheshire.*

Tomblin, Bryan Alan, Sgt. Plt. [Glider Pilot Regt.]. *Police superintendent, Duston, Northamptonshire.*

Tomlin, Edw. Geo., Pvt. [1st Airborne]. B.E.M., *Security officer, Acton, London, W. 3.*

Tompson, William Claude, F/Sgt. [R.A.F.]. *Shopkeeper, London.*

Travis-Davison, Kenneth, Sgt. Plt. [Glider Pilot Regt.]. *Company director, Leeds.*

Turnau, Godfrey Joseph, F/Lt. [R.A.F.]. D.F.C., M.S.C., *Civil servant, Salisbury, Rhodesia.*

Turner, Arthur J. B., L/Cpl. [1st Airborne]. *Chauffeur, Oxford.*

Turner, Desmond N. S., Lt. [Glider Pilot Regt.]. *Probation officer, nr. Bury, Lancashire.*

Turner, John, Pvt. [1st Airborne]. *Social-security administrator, Coventry.*

Tyler, E. G., Major [Guards Armoured]. M.C., Bar, *Company director, Wooburn Green, Buckinghamshire.*

Udal, E. R., Capt. [Guards Armoured]. *Legal adviser, banking group, Hong Kong.*

Umpleby, Kenneth, Guardsman [Guards Armoured]. *Textile foreman, Keighley, Yorkshire.*

Urquhart, Brian, Major [1st Airborne]. *United Nations, New York.*

Urquhart, Robert Elliott (Roy), Maj. Gen. [1st Airborne]. C.B., D.S.O., *Company director, Glasgow, Scotland.*

Vandeleur, Giles A. M., Lt. Col. [Guards Armoured]. D.S.O., *Privately employed, London.*

Vandeleur, J. O. E., Lt. Col. [Guards Armoured]. *Brigadier (Retired), British Army, Maidenhead, Berkshire.*

Van Zoelen, F. W. E. Groeninx, 1st Lt. [Guards Armoured]. *Investment consultant, Madrid, Spain.*

Vincent, Raymond, L/Cpl. [1st Airborne]. *Aeronautical worker, Little Stoke, Bristol.*

Vlasto, Robert A., Lt. [1st Airborne]. *Stockbroker, Worplesdon, Surrey.*

Waddy, John L., Major [1st Airborne]. O.B.E., *Colonel, British Army, Chelsea.*

Walch, A. G., Brig. Gen. [1st Airborne]. O.B.E., *Brigadier (Retired), British Army, Marlborough, Wiltshire.*

Walchli, Robin O., Capt. [R.A.F.]. *Chartered quantity surveyor, Sarratt, Hertfordshire.*

Walton, James, Sgt. [1st Airborne]. *Clerk, Bootle, Lancashire.*

Ward, George William, L/Cpl. [1st Airborne]. *Postman, Reading, Berkshire.*

Ware, Denis J., S/Sgt. [Glider Pilot Regt.]. *Headmaster, Huntingfield School, Mitcham, Surrey.*

Warnock, Geoffrey James, Lt. [Guards Armoured]. *Fellow of Magdalen College; tutor in philosophy, Oxford.*

Warrack, Graeme, Col. [1st Airborne]. *Dentist, Edinburgh, Scotland.*

Warrender, Alfred George, Pvt. [1st Airborne]. *Polishing ship inspector, Wolverhampton, Staffordshire.*

Watson, Arthur A., Pvt. [1st Airborne]. *Printer, London.*

Watson, Arthur E., L/Cpl. [Guards Armoured]. *Lorry driver, Sussex.*

Weallens, Arthur Edward, Sgt. [1st Airborne]. *Post-office employee, Northumberland.*

Wellard, Leonard Edward, Sgt. [Glider Pilot Regt.]. *Bank manager, London.*

Wells, William James, S/Sgt. [Glider Pilot Regt.]. *Administrator, London Electrical Board, London.*

Welsby, Cyril, Pvt. [Guards Armoured]. *Glazier, Manchester.*

Westbury, James Ernest, Pvt. [1st Airborne]. *Postman, Nottingham.*

Wheeler, Jack, Pvt. [1st Airborne]. *Retail grocer, Warwick.*

White, George, W.O.I. [1st Airborne]. *Verger and parish clerk, Bridlington, Yorkshire.*

Whitehead, James, S/Sgt. [Glider Pilot Regt.]. *Relay adjuster, Warwick.*

Wickham, John Thomas, Sapper [1st Airborne]. *Clerk, Leicester.*

Widdowson, G., Major [1st Airborne]. C.B.E., T.D., *Colonel (Retired), British Army; bank manager, Birmingham.*

Wilcox, Geoffrey, Sgt. [Guards Armoured]. D.C.M., *Works manager, Berkshire.*

Wilcox, Ivor, Sgt. [Guards Armoured]. *Welder, Bedfordshire.*

Williams, Cyril, Sgt. [Glider Pilot Regt.]. *Headmaster, School for Handicapped, Bristol.*

Williams, Gwyn, Sgt. [1st Airborne]. *Innkeeper, Cheshire.*

Williams, John James, Pvt. [1st Airborne]. *Steelworks mason, Tredegar, Monmouthshire.*

Willoughby, Michael, Capt. [Guards Armoured]. *Landowner, Yorkshire.*

Wilson, Norman Edward, Pvt. [1st Airborne]. *Works employee, Staffordshire.*
Winterbottom, Lord Ian, 2nd Lt. [Guards Armoured]. *Parliamentary secretary, Public Buildings & Works Ministry, Northamptonshire.*
Wood, Jack, Pvt. [1st Airborne]. *Laboratory assistant, Staffordshire.*
Wordsworth, Ferrers Robin, Lt. [Guards Armoured]. *Company secretary, Welwyn, Hertfordshire.*
Wright, Harry, Pvt. [1st Airborne]. *Structural-design draftsman, Transvaal, South Africa.*
Wright, Leonard, S/Sgt. [Glider Pilot Regt.]. D.F.M., *Schoolteacher, Whitehaven, Cumberland.*
Wright, William Charles, Sgt. Pilot [Glider Pilot Regt.]. *Sales representative, Bristol.*
Wrottesley, Lord Richard John, Capt. [Guards Armoured]. *Private means, Salisbury, Rhodesia.*
Wyllie, George, L/Cpl. [1st Airborne]. *Greengrocer, Warwickshire.*
Yerburgh, J. M. A., Lt. [Guards Armoured]. *Company director, Kirkcudbrightshire.*
York, Harold, L/Sgt. [Guards Armoured]. M.M., *Postman, London.*
Young, Arthur Vincent, Lt. [Guards Armoured]. M.C., *Company director, nr. Stourbridge, Worcestershire.*

DUTCH

Bernhard, The Prince of the Netherlands.
Aa, Rudolph van der [Ede]. *Photographer, Ede.*
Aeyelts, Lauren Daniel [Helmond]. *Staff employee, Royal Zwanenburg factories, Oss.*
Agt, Antonius L.G.M. van [Gemert, Eindhoven]. *Archivist, Eindhoven.*
Aken, Pieter van [Wolfheze]. *Dermatologist, Ede.*
Alsche-deKat, Hermina Jacoba [Elst]. *Housewife, Elst.*
Andriesse, Maurits [Dinther]. *Retired, Veghel.*
Ariëns, Theodorus Antonius [Arnhem]. *Retired cleric, Arnhem.*
Aspert-Doornakkers, Anna Maria van [Zeelst]. *Housewife, Zeelst.*
Assendelft, Leendert van [Huissen]. *Chemical engineer, Arnhem.*
Baak, Norbertus H. J. [Son]. *State policeman, St. Oedenrode.*
Backus, Johannes H.H.E. [Arnhem]. *Personnel manager, Nijmegen.*
Baltussen, Arnoldus J. A. [Driel]. *Burgomaster, Groesbeek.*
Baltussen, Cora [Driel]. *Teacher, Driel.*
Baltussen, Josephus Frans [Driel]. *Company director, Driel.*
Bartels, Willem F. H. [Nijmegen]. *Public prosecutor, St. Odilienberg.*
Barten, Johannes A. [Grave]. *Tailor, Grave.*
Bech, Niels [Wolfheze]. *Works inspector, Oss.*
Beek, Dirk van [Oosterbeek]. *Bakery salesman, Oosterbeek.*
Beek, Marius van der [Wolfheze]. *Psychiatrist, Bergen op Zoom.*
Beekmeyer, Adriaan J. P., Cpl. [British 1st Airborne, England/Arnhem]. *Veterinary-pharmaceutical firm employee, Amsterdam.*

Beermann, Victor Antonius M. [Nijmegen]. *U. N. Representative, Australia.*
Bemen, Bob W. van [Lent]. *Construction mason, Miami, Fla., U.S.A.*
Bergh-Braam, Anna H. M. van den [Gent]. *Housewife, Nijmegen.*
Bergh, Johannes G. van den, Commando [U.S. 82nd Airborne, England]. *Director, Students Housing Foundation, 's Hertogenbosch.*
Bernebeek, Franciscus J. H. van [Groesbeek]. *Printer, Groesbeek.*
Beyerbergen van Heneqouwen, Augustinus N. G. [Oosterbeek]. *Teacher, Amersfoort.*
Bijlsma-Lusschen, Maria [Oosterbeek]. *Oosterbeek.*
Bisterbosch, Heimrich [Arnhem]. *Alderman, Arnhem.*
Bitters, Jacob Johan [Nijmegen]. *Mechanic, Nijmegen.*
Bitters, Janna [Nijmegen]. *Housewife, Nijmegen.*
Blaauw-Baghuis, Fie [Eindhoven]. *Housewife, Arnhem.*
Blokland, Jan Jacob G. B. van Brig. Major [Princess Irene Brigade]. *Colonel (Retired), Dutch Cavalry, Oosterbeek.*
Bode, Nicolaas T. de [Arnhem]. *Supervisor, Netherlands Radio Union, Hilversum.*
Boekraad-Otto, Maria O. [Nijmegen]. *Housewife, Nijmegen.*
Bolderman, Cornelis [Arnhem]. *Sgt. Major, Netherlands Defense Forces, Arnhem.*
Bolle-deWijk, Jutta [Renkum]. *Housewife, Munich.*
Bossert, Gijsbert [Veghel]. *Translator and bank official, Amsterdam.*
Boyens, Jan Peter [Eindhoven]. *Teacher, Eindhoven.*
Brachten, Everardus [Driel]. *Retired, Driel.*
Bremen, Bertha [Oosterbeek]. *Housewife, Oosterbeek.*
Brevet, William Karel [Arnhem]. *Radiologist, Arnhem.*
Broekkamp, Elias Henricus [Nijmegen]. *Wine importer, Nijmegen.*
Brom, Johannes Hendricus [Valkenswaard]. *Caretaker, Town Hall, Valkenswaard.*
Brouwer, Jacobus G. [Nijmegen]. *Major, Royal Land Forces, Deventer.*
Brouwer, Jacobus, G. L. [Oosterbeek]. *Retired, The Hague.*
Brummelkamp-van Maanen, Anje [Oosterbeek]. *Housewife, Middelburg.*
Bruschetto, Peter John [Nijmegen]. *Security police officer, Ontario, Canada.*
Busch, Johannus J. T. [Driel]. *Hotel manager, Driel.*
Bÿen-van de Weerd, Jennie [Bennekom]. *Housewife, Richmond, Calif., U.S.A.*
Claassen, A. [Bladel]. *Teacher, Waalwijk.*
Clous-Veen, Ida Egbertina [Oosterbeek]. *Housewife, Oosterbeek.*
Companjen, Albert G. [Berg en Dal]. *Bookkeeper, Groesbeek.*
Coninx, Guillaume [Lommel, Belgium]. *Superintendent of Police, Lommel, Belgium.*
Deinum, Martijn Louis [Nijmegen]. *Director, Orpheus Theater, Apeldoorn.*
Derksen, Antoon [Arnhem]. *Retired, Arnhem.*
Derksen, Theodorus F. R. [Nijmegen]. *Headwaiter, Amsterdam.*
Deure, Jacob van der [Bennekom]. *Attorney, Ede.*
Deuss, Albertus J. P. [Arnhem]. *Liaison officer, A.K.U. (International), Arnhem.*

Dijk, Sister Christine M. van [Arnhem]. *Retired, Arnhem.*

Dijk, Frans van [Waalre]. *Company director, Waalre.*

Dijker, Reinold F. [Oosterbeek]. *Catholic priest, Sintang Kalbar, Indonesia.*

Does, Jacob van der [Arnhem]. *Retired surgeon, Arnhem.*

Donderwinkel, Jan Willem [Oosterbeek]. *Retired, Oosterbeek.*

Doorne, Herman van [Wolfheze]. *Retired, Wolfheze.*

Driessen, Jan, interpreter [30th Infantry Div.]. *Factory director, Veghel.*

Drost, Johannes C. [Arnhem]. *Physician, Arnhem.*

Edwards, Eric Stuart [Eindhoven]. *Painter, Eindhoven.*

Eerd, Johannes W. A. van [Veghel]. *Photographer, Veghel.*

Eijkelhoff, Jan Adriaan [Oosterbeek]. *Bank clerk, Oosterbeek.*

Eijnden, Lambertus H. van der [Eindhoven]. *Wage administrator, N. V. Philips, Eindhoven.*

Einthoven, Louis [Utrecht]. *Archivist, Lunteren.*

Elst, Evert Jan van den [Nijmegen]. *Retired, Nijmegen.*

Fabius, Kaeso [Doetinchem]. *Burgomaster, Bilthoven.*

Feenstra, Robijn [Kesteren]. *Fruit grower, Kesteren.*

Fischer, Wilhelmus Antonius [Berg en Dal]. *Company director, Bloemendaal.*

Fleskens, Leonardus Johannes J. [Aalst]. *Bank director, Geldrop.*

Gall-van der Heijden, Ida [Acht]. *Housewife, Eindhoven.*

Gelderblom, Jan [Oosterbeek]. *Head surveyor, Oosterbeek Gas Works, Oosterbeek.*

Gent, Jacob van [Nijmegen]. *Company director, Amsterdam.*

Giebing, Willem H. [Oosterbeek]. *Café owner, Doorwerth.*

Giebing-van Kolfschoten, Geertruida W. [Oosterbeek]. *Housewife, Heelsum.*

Gier, Dr. Johannes de [Eindhoven]. *Retired physicist, Eindhoven.*

Goossens, Adrianus [Bladel]. *Teacher at University, Bladel, Den Bosch.*

Goyaerts, Marinus Petrus J. [Veghel]. *Contractor firm employee, Rosmalen.*

Graaf, Kas de, Maj. [Netherlands Forces]. *Managing director, Netherland Shipping Council, Den Haag.*

Graaff, Pieter de [Arnhem]. *Surgeon, Arnhem.*

Gras, Jan Dirk [Princess Irene Brigade, Belgium]. *Captain, Artillery, Breda.*

Groot, Johannes A. de [Uden]. *Farmer, Uden.*

Groot, Johannes T. de [Uden]. *Retired, Rotterdam.*

Gysbers, Gerhardus Wilhelmus [Arnhem]. *Rare-book dealer, Arnhem.*

Haas, Henri Leonard de [Arnhem]. *Oculist, Arnhem.*

Hagens, Herman G. [Wageningen]. *Telephone company employee, Arnhem.*

Hak, Henri Johan [Arnhem]. *Retired minister, Dutch Reformed Church, Arnhem.*

Ham, Gijsbertus J. [Arnhem]. *Arnhem.*

Hapert-Lathouwers, Johanna Theodora M. van [Eindhoven]. *Housewife, Eindhoven.*

Harmsen, Gerrit-Jan [Ellecom]. *Company director, Ellecom.*

Harmsen-Gerritsen, Agnita G. M. [Ellecom]. *Housewife, Ellecom.*

Have, Frans van der [Wageningen]. *School headmaster, Wageningen.*

Heckman, Jacobus A. [Rotterdam]. *Medical doctor, Hilversum.*

Heestermans-Hendriks, Cornelia [Bergeijk]. *Housewife, Valkenswaard.*

Heijden, Jan van der [Netersel]. *Agricultural worker, Netersel.*

Heijden, Johannes A. van der, Sgt. [Netherlands Jendarmerie, Lent]. *Retired, Lent.*

Heijden-Otto, Magtilda J. M. van der [Nijmegen]. *Housewife, Nijmegen.*

Hendriks, Paulus Hendricus [Nijmegen]. *Director-owner, ironworks, Nijmegen.*

Henneman, Dr. Adrianus J. [Groesbeek]. *Retired medical doctor, Groesbeek.*

Henriette, Sister [Schijndel]. *Principal, St. Lidwina Hospital, Schijndel.*

Herbrink, Antonius M., 1st Lt. [Princess Irene Brigade]. *Colonel, Dutch Army, Eindhoven.*

Hezemans, Johannes W. [Aalst]. *Broker, Aalst.*

Hiddink, Dirk Jan F. [Arnhem]. *Photo-typist, Arnhem.*

Hielkema, Hielkem Johannus F., Sgt. [Princess Irene Brigade]. *Captain, Royal Army, The Hague.*

Hoefnagels, Hendrik W. [Arnhem]. *Medical doctor, Arnhem.*

Hoefsloot, Piet [Arnhem]. *Furniture-store owner, Arnhem.*

Hoek, Herman Lodewijk M. [Groesbeek]. *Retired Roman Catholic priest, Groesbeek.*

Hoof, Maria Cornelia van [Hoogeloon]. *Teacher, Hoogeloon.*

Hooff, Antoon Jacques J. M. van [Arnhem]. *Director of Zoo, Arnhem.*

Hooff, Johannes Antonius R.A.M. van [Arnhem]. *Scientific official, Utrecht State University, Bilthoven.*

Hooff, Johannes G. J. van [Veghel]. *Executive chef, Yonkers, N.Y., U.S.A.*

Horst, Jan ter [Oosterbeek]. *Lawyer, Oosterbeek.*

Horst, Kate ter [Oosterbeek]. *Housewife, Oosterbeek.*

Horstman, Albert Jan Carolinus [Arnhem]. *Architect, Amsterdam.*

Houtsma, Johannus H. [Achterhoek]. *Tax adviser, Haarlem.*

Hudd-van Bork, Hendrika [Heelsum]. *Velp.*

Huisson, Abraham [Arnhem]. *Captain (Retired), Royal Army, Utrecht.*

Hulleman, Coenraad [Arnhem]. *Bank director, Rotterdam.*

Hulsen, Johannes M. [St. Oedenrode]. *Bricklayer, St. Oedenrode.*

Hurkx, Joannes Aloisius [St. Oedenrode]. *Retired, St. Oedenrode.*

Hustinx, Charles [Beek en Donk]. *Retired, former Mayor of Nijmegen, Nijmegen.*

Huygen, Frans Josef Aloisius [Lent]. *Medical doctor, Lent.*

Italisander, Arie M. T., Cpl. [British 1st Airborne]. *Engineer, Bilthoven.*

Jans, Leonard [Venlo]. *Provincial commander, civil defense, Bunde.*

Jansen, Benjamin [Driel]. *Florist, Driel.*

Jonkers, Gerardus [Eindhoven]. *Office clerk, Eindhoven.*

Jonkers-Krimpenfort, Therese [Arnhem]. *Housewife, Eindhoven.*

Kaathoven, Franciscus van [St. Oedenrode]. *Retired, St. Oedenrode.*

Karel, Hendrik [Arnhem]. *Streetcar driver, Arnhem.*

Kelderman, Aart C. [Wolfheze]. *Mechanic, Wolfheze.*

Kerssemakers-Asselbergs, Johanna P. M. [Veghel]. *Housewife, Vught.*

Kersten, Jan Henri J. ['s Hertogenbosch]. *Foundation director, Naarden.*

Kip, Louis F. C. van Erp Taalman [Arnhem]. *Neurologist, Arnhem.*

Kippersluijs, Johan [Groesbeek]. *Medical doctor, Groesbeek.*

Kirchner, Gerardina Alexandrina [Arnhem]. *Bookseller, Arnhem.*

Knap, Henri A. A. R. [Arnhem]. *Newspaper columnist, Amsteveleen.*

Knopper-van Dijk, Maria Anna E. [Eindhoven]. *Housewife, Eindhoven.*

Knottenbelt, Maarten Jan [Arnhem]. *Writer, Australia.*

Knuvelder, Gerardus [Eindhoven]. *College president, Eindhoven.*

Kooijk, Johannes van [Eindhoven]. *Merchant, Eindhoven.*

Kooten, Bartholomeus J. C. van [Heerlen]. *Company director, Bussum.*

Kortie, Frans [Eindhoven]. *Municipal Information Dept., Eindhoven.*

Kraats, Wouter van de [Oosterbeek]. *Radio-TV shop owner, Oosterbeek.*

Krap, Charles Douw van der [Oosterbeek]. *Captain (Retired), Dutch Navy, The Hague.*

Kuijk, Joannes van [Arnhem]. *Squadron Sgt. Major, Govt. Police Staff Territorial Inspection, Arnhem, Velp.*

Kuijpers, Theodorus Albertus [Veghel]. *Parish priest, Vught.*

Kuyper, Anthonius [Veghel]. *Cycle dealer, Veghel.*

Labouchère, Charles B. [Velp-Arnhem]. *Retired, Wassenaar.*

Lamberts, Jeanne W. P. C. [Arnhem]. *Arnhem.*

Lamers, Gerardus Johannes [Gennep]. *Archivist, Veldhoven.*

Laterveer, Anton Marie [Arnhem]. *Medical doctor, anesthesiologist, Arnhem.*

Lathouwers, Allegonda L. J. [Eindhoven]. *Teacher, nurse, Enshede.*

Ledoux, Lambert [Heelsum]. *Instrument engineer, South Africa.*

Leegsma, Agardus Marinus [Nijmegen]. *Bookkeeper, Arnhem.*

Leemans, Johannus A. J. [Lith]. *Dentist, Heesch.*

Leeuwen, Johannes C. van [Eindhoven]. *Company director, Sassenheim.*

Legius, Gerardus Laurentius [Eindhoven]. *Town Hall clerk, Eindhoven.*

Lenssen, Jan [Son]. *Miller, Son en Breugel.*

Los, Cornelis Bastiaan [Aalst]. *Engineer, Aalst.*

Luijben, Thomas Arnold J. [Oosteind]. *Municipal Tax Collector, Groesbeek.*

Luiten, Cornelis Hendrikus [Eindhoven]. *Company director, Nijmegen.*

Maanen, Hanno Paul van [Oosterbeek]. *Medical doctor, Heinkenszand.*

Maat, Franciscus van der [St. Oedenrode]. *Factory worker, St. Michielsgestel.*

Maria Veronica, Sister [Schijndel]. *Mother Superior, Schijndel.*

Marinus, Adrianus L. [Eerde]. *Asst. company director, Middlebeers.*

Marinus, Albertus A. J. [Eerde]. *Blacksmith, Veghel.*

Martens, Antonius Hendrik [Nijmegen]. *Retired, Nijmegen.*

Mason-Bremen, Johanna Dina [Nijmegen]. *Housewife, Fayetteville, N.C., U.S.A.*

Mast, Willem van der [Groningen]. *Medical doctor, Haren.*

Meddens, Joseph Ignatius M. [Nijmegen]. *Town Clerk, Nijmegen.*

Meer, Frits Gerben Louis van der [Lent]. *Roman Catholic priest; college professor, Lent.*

Memelink, Garrit [Arnhem]. *Chief Inspector, Royal Netherlands Heath Society, Arnhem.*

Meyjes, Lucretia [Velp]. *Velp.*

Mijnhart, Jan [Arnhem]. *Mortician, Oosterbeek.*

Minderhoud, Christiaan [Arnhem]. *Central Library chief, Eindhoven.*

Montfroy, Harry [Arnhem]. *Member, Arnhem City Council, Arnhem.*

Mortanges, Charles Ferdinand P. de, Lt. Col. [Princess Irene Brigade, Grave]. *General (Retired), Netherlands Defense Forces, Scheveningen.*

Muselaars, Joop [Eindhoven]. *Insurance company employee, 's Hertogenbosch.*

Nefkins, Petrus Antonius [Grave]. *Retired, Grave.*

Niesen-Otto, Elisabeth J. M. [Nijmegen]. *Housewife, Maastricht.*

Nijhoff, Gerrit Jan [Ede]. *Labor cooperator, Ede.*

Nijhoff-van der Meer, Dieuwke [Ede]. *Housewife, Ede.*

Nijholt, Gerrit [Oosterbeek]. *Painter, Oosterbeek.*

Noordermeer, Tiburtius Carolus [Oss]. *Rector, Oyen, N.B.*

Nooy, Cornelia de [Ede]. *Retired, Ede.*

Nooy, Menno Antonie de [Ede]. *Paint manufacturer, Ede.*

Nooy, Willemina de* [Ede]. *Housewife, Ede.*

Numan, Gijsbert Jan [Arnhem]. *Burgomaster, Harderwijk.*

Olivier, Agathes Willem [Eindhoven]. *Official (Retired), Netherlands Railways, Groenekan.*

Ommen, Gerrit Hendrik van [Delden]. *Warehouseman, Delden.*

Onck, Willem [Arnhem]. *Plumber, Arnhem.*

Onstein, Maria Josef F. L. van Grotenhuis van [Groesbeek]. *Retired, Nijmegen.*

Oorschot, Matheas C. van [Schijndel]. *Mineworker, Brunssum.*

Osterom-Janssen, Johanna C. van [Nijmegen]. *Housewife, Nijmegen.*

Oteen, Theodore [Erp]. *Heesch.*

Otten, Antoinette [Erp]. *School principal, Erp.*

Otten, Gerardus [Erp]. *Soest.*

Otten, Harry [Erp]. *Erp.*

Ouweneel-Coppens, Wilhelmina Bartholomea C. [St. Oedenrode]. *Housewife, Eindhoven.*

Oxener, Cornelis Gerard [Oosterbeek]. *P.T.T. official, Terborg.*

Passier, Johannes M. [Son]. *Retired teacher, Son.*

Peassens, Anne, Maj. [Princess Irene Brigade]. *Ministry of Foreign Affairs, The Hague.*

Peelen, Jan [Renkum]. *Chief of expedition, Krommenie.*

Peijnenburg, Henri Joan M. [Nijmegen]. *State Secretary of Defense, Royal Army, Wassenaar.*

Pennings, Jan [Renkum]. *Farmer, Renkum.*

Penseel, Johannes [Arnhem]. *Retired, Arnhem.*

Peterse, Wilhelmus Jozephus [Nijmegen]. *Curate, Rossum.*

Pieper, Jan Willem [Dodewaart]. *Headmaster, boarding school, Harderwijk.*

Pit, Hugo Frans [Oosterbeek]. *Engineer, Sterksel.*

Pol, Hendrikus van de [Ede-Bennekom]. *Deputy director of company, Ede.*

Pol, Leonardus Johannes van de [Son]. *Retired medical doctor, Enschede.*

Ponsioen, Jacobus [Nijmegen]. *Hospital director, Winschoten.*

Post, Hendrikus Jacobus [Arnhem]. *Station chief, central station, Rotterdam.*

Post, Tjerk, Lt. [Princess Irene Brigade]. *Lt. Col. (Retired), Royal Army, Diepenveen.*

Postulart, Johan Wilhelmus [Nijmegen]. *Garage owner, Nijmegen.*
Posthuma, Jan Pieter [The Hague]. *Director, telephone company, Leeuwarden.*
Praag, Simon van [Nijmegen]. *Retired, Nijmegen.*
Presser, Samuel [Arnhem]. *Photographer, Amsterdam.*
Putten, Theo van der* [Eindhoven]. *Municipal official, Eindhoven.*
Ravensbergen, Johannes [Arnhem]. *Retired, Bennekom.*
Remmerde, Dirk [Ittersum]. *P.T.T., Rijswijk.*
Reneman, Nico [Arnhem]. *Oosterbeek.*
Ridder, Tony de [Oosterbeek]. *Housewife, Oosterbeek.*
Rietveld, Jan [Ede]. *Surveyor, Bennebroek.*
Ringelenstein-van Stuyvenberg, Cornelia Elisabeth van [Arnhem]. *Tiel.*
Roefs, Martinus [Son en Breugel]. *Retired official, Son.*
Roelofs, Theodorus [Overasselt]. *Office manager, Eindhoven.*
Rooijens, Cornelis Joannes [Nijmegen]. *Municipal health clerk, Nijmegen.*
Roosendall, Rudolf Bartholomeus E. [Randwijk]. *Psychologist, Arnhem.*
Rooy, Petrus H. van [St. Oedenrode]. *School principal, St. Oedenrode.*
Sabel, Henricus H. G. [Eindhoven]. *School clerk, Eindhoven.*
Sanden, Johannes van der [Veghel]. *Veghel.*
Sanders, Petrus Antonius M. [Ledeacker]. *Civil servant, Eindhoven.*
Schaap, Lambert [Arnhem]. *Retired, Arnhem.*
Schalm, Leendert [Arnhem]. *Medical doctor, Arnhem.*
Schermer, Arjen [Arnhem]. *Retired, Arnhem.*
Schilfgaarde, Anton B. van [Arnhem]. *Retired archivist, Arnhem.*
Schmidt, Willem [Kesteren]. *Schoolteacher, Arnhem.*
Schoenmakers, Anna Maria P. [Groesbeek]. *Housewife, Groesbeek.*
Schol, Annie J. [Hoenderlo]. *Hoenderlo.*
Schouten, Antonius C. [Nijmegen]. *Retired, Nijmegen.*
Schrijvers, Leon [Veghel]. *Heart specialist, Eindhoven.*
Schulte, Marinus Jacobus [Arnhem]. *Doctor (retired), Arnhem.*
Schut, Jacoba Adriana [Oosterbeek]. *Housewife, Doorwerth.*
Schutter, Marinus [Elst]. *Retired, Elst.*
Schuurs, Wilhelmus Antonius [Tilburg]. *Bank manager, Wijchen.*
Six, Pieter Jacob [Amsterdam]. *Chairman, Combined Military Funds, 's Grav-elande.*
Slingerland, Johannus C. [Deurne]. *Inspector of the P.T.T., Leidschendam.*
Smeenk, Bernard Daniel [Renkum]. *Protestant minister, Jerusalem.*
Smeets, Henricus Johannes J. [Roermond]. *Notary, Oss.*
Smulders, Robert M. [Utrecht, Nijmegen]. *Company director, Soest.*
Snoek, Johannes M. [Renkum]. *Minister, Israel.*
Snoek, Maria [Renkum]. *Church social worker, Schiedam.*
Soet, Frans de [Oosterbeek]. *Chief agricultural engineer, State Forest Administration, Zeist.*
Spaander, Jan [Amsterdam]. *General Director, Public Health, Ministry of Social Affairs and Public Health, Bilthoven.*
Spoormans-van Berendonk, Maria Josepha [Westerhoven]. *Housewife, Veldhoven.*

Sprangers, Waltherus [Nijmegen]. *Retired, Nijmegen.*

Steinfort, Johannes Bertus [Arnhem]. *Works employee, Den Haag.*

Stibbe-van Adelsberg, Elma Sara [Renkum]. *Psychiatric social worker, Israel.*

Stranzky, Antonia Maria [Arnhem]. *Nursing sister, Arnhem.*

Striker, Jan [Oosterbeek]. *Plumber, Oosterbeek.*

Struik Dalm-van der Stad, Maria Christina [Nijmegen]. *Housewife, Nijmegen.*

Symons, Sister M. Dosithèe [Nijmegen]. *Buyer of hospital supplies, Nijmegen.*

Tempel, Johannes W. [Nijmegen]. *Municipal employee, Town Hall, Nijmegen.*

Teunissen, Waandert [Velp]. *Coppersmith, plumber, Velp.*

Thomas, Carl Paulus Nicolaas ['s Hertogenbosch]. *Enterprise director, Switzerland.*

Thuys-Damon, Bernardina [Arnhem]. *Retired, Arnhem.*

Thyssen, Augustinus A. J. W. [Beuningen]. *Company director, Nijmegen.*

Tiburtius, Father Bernardus C. N. [Oss]. *Rector, St. Joseph Monastery, Oyen.*

Tiemans, Cornelis Lieuwe [Oosterbeek]. *Director, Conference Center, St. Michielsgestel.*

Tiemans, Willem Hendrik [Arnhem]. *Architect, Oosterbeek.*

Tigler Wybrandi, Adrianus, Lt. [U.S. 101st Airborne Div.]. *Company director, The Hague.*

Top, Gerrit van den [Ede]. *Retired, Ede.*

Uijen, Albertus Franciscus [Nijmegen]. *Municipal employee; head of Dept. of Information and Cultural Affairs, Nijmegen.*

Unck, Nicolaas [Arnhem]. *Schiedam municipality worker, Schiedam.*

Valk, Hendrik [Arnhem]. *Artist, Arnhem.*

Ven, Henricus Cornelis van de [Dinther]. *Company director, Dinther.*

Venderbosch, Anna Berendina [Oosterbeek]. *Social worker, Oosterbeek.*

Verhamme, Gerardus H. A. [Ravestein]. *Town official, Berghem.*

Verwegen, Wilhelmus J. [Vinkel]. *Works employee, Veghel.*

Visser, Cornelis Marinus de [Veghel]. *Elementary-school teacher, Loosbroek.*

Visser, Maria D. de [Veghel]. *Export manager, Den Bosch.*

Vliet, Leendert R. van, Sgt. [Princess Irene Brigade]. *Warrant officer, Netherlands Defense Forces, The Hague.*

Vlist, Hendrika van der [Oosterbeek]. *English teacher, Oosterbeek.*

Voskuil, Bertha [Oosterbeek]. *Housewife, Oosterbeek.*

Voskuil, Jan [Oosterbeek]. *Chemical engineer, Oosterbeek.*

Vries, Izak de [Oosterbeek]. *Librarian, Israel.*

Vroemen, Lucianus Paulus J. [Arnhem]. *Sales representative, Amsterdam.*

Vromen, Abraham [Arnhem]. *Company director, Doetinchem.*

Waard, Willem de [Vlaardingen]. *Office clerk, Voorburg.*

Wachters, Johannes Bernardus H. [Aalst]. *Insurance physician, Berg en Dal.*

Weerd, Nicolaas van de [Bennekom]. *Banking officer, Bennekom.*

Wely, Paul Agatho van [Zetten]. *Medical doctor, Son.*

Werz, Petrus Franciscus A. [Eindhoven]. *Entrepreneur, Roosendaal.*

Westerveld, Carel Christiaan [Amsterdam]. *State official, Rijswijk.*

Wiessing, George Efraim J. [Arnhem]. *Retired, Arnhem.*

Wijburg, Hendrik [Wolfheze]. *Retired, Ede.*

Wijdeven, Marinus Antonius van de [Mariahout]. *Contractor, Mariahout.*

Wijgerden, Antonie van [Geldrop]. *Information official, N.V. Philips, Eindhoven.*

Wijnbergen, Selma [Breugel]. *Textile worker, Eindhoven.*

Wijnen, Alphonse, 1st Lt. [Princess Irene Brigade]. *Lt. Col., commander of infantry, Garrison, Eindhoven.*

Wijt, Adriaan [Arnhem]. *Retired, Hoenderlo.*

Wit, Adrianus de, Sgt. [Princess Irene Brigade]. *Warrant officer, Royal Constabulary, Breda.*

Wit, Gerardus Johannes de [Zeelst]. *Retired, Zeelst.*

Wit, Karel de [Oosterbeek]. *Druggist, Oosterbeek.*

Woensel, Cornelis H. van [Eindhoven]. *Controller, Eindhoven.*

Woestenburg, Frederik J. [Schijndel]. *Roman Catholic priest, Leende.*

Woezik, Johanna Maria van [Eindhoven]. *Hotelkeeper, Eindhoven.*

Wolffensperger-van der Wegen, Helena Elizabeth [Vlokhoven-Woensel]. *Housewife, Heusden aan de Maas.*

Wolters, Arnoldus, Lt. Comdr. [Royal Netherlands Navy]. *Head Commissioner, Rotterdam Municipal Police, Rotterdam.*

Zanten, Wilhelmus Johannes van [Arnhem]. *Section official, electric company, Arnhem.*

Zweden-Rÿser, Suze van [Arnhem], *Mathematics teacher, Arnhem.*

POLISH

Sosabowski, Stanislaw,* Maj. Gen. [C.O., 1st Polish Airborne Brigade].

Chwastek, Mieczyslaw, Pvt. [3rd Battalion]. *Turner, Manchester, England.*

Juhas, Woll W., S/Sgt. [Engineers]. *Slinger, Derbyshire, England.*

Kaczmarek, Stefan, 1st Lt. [Supplies]. *Bank clerk, Sydenham, England.*

Kochalski, Alexander, Cpl. [Engineers]. *Motor mechanic, Surrey, England.* (*Now known as Michael Alexander.*)

Korob, Wladijslaw, Cpl. [Brigade Hq. Co.]. *Car mechanic, Rotterdam, Holland.*

Lesniak, Jerzy, Lt. [1st Battalion]. *Goldsmith, London, England.*

Niebieszczanski, Adam, Cadet [Signal Co.]. *Office manager, Westbury, N.Y.*

Prochowski, Robert L., 1st Lt. [3rd Battalion]. *Senior control buyer, Chicago, Ill.*

Smaczny, Albert T., Lt. [3rd Battalion]. *Foreman, Cambridge, England.*

Szczygiel, Wieslaw, Lt. [Engineers]. *Photographer, Leven, Fife, Scotland.* (*Now known as George W. Harvey.*)

Wojewodka, Boleslaw S., Cpl. [1st Battalion]. *Underwriter for insurance company, Island Park, N.Y.*

GERMAN

Bittrich, Wilhelm, SS Lt. Gen. [II SS Panzer Corps]. *Retired.*

Rundstedt, Gerd von,* Field Marshal, Commander in Chief [OB West, Oberbefehlshaber West].

Student, Kurt, Col. Gen., C.O. [1st Parachute Army]. *Retired.*

Bang, Helmut, Pvt. [Ind. Eng. Battalion]. *Locksmith.*

Becker, Otto, Pvt. [2nd SS Panzer Antitank Regt.]. *Salesman.*

Berthold, Günter, Cpl. [Luftwaffe Flak Battery 591]. *Commercial traveler.*

Blumentritt, Gunther,* Maj. Gen. [OB West; Von Rundstedt's chief of staff].

Borkenhagen, Hans, Lt. [Infantry, Reg. 1036]. *Civil servant.*

Brandt, Georg, Cpl. [Luftwaffe RR Flak Unit]. *Civil servant.*

Brandt, Theo, Pvt. [Grenadier Battalion]. *University purchasing manager.*

Burg, Wilhelm von der, Cpl. [Luftwaffe Flak Antiaircraft Unit]. *Merchant.*

Busch, Karl Martin, Pvt. [Kampfgruppe Knaust]. *Operates commercial-inquiry office.*

Dessloch, Otto, Col. Gen., C.O. [3rd Luftwaffe Air Fleet]. *Retired.*

Fiebig, Werner, Pvt. [SS Panzer Grenadiers Depot Battalion 16]. *Unknown.*

Fromm, Wolgang, Ordnance Officer [59th Infantry Div.]. *Horticultural business owner.*

Gehrhardt, Erwin, Sgt. [Artillery Regt.]. *Civil servant.*

Glücks, Paul, Sgt. [Regiment Jungwirt]. *Member of West-German Broadcasting Company.*

Haberman, Heinz, Sgt. [Luftnachrichteneinheit]. *Civil servant.*

Harmel, Heinz, Maj. Gen., C.O. [10th SS Panzer Div.]. *Manufacturers' representative.*

Harzer, Walter, Lt. Col., C.O. [9th SS Panzer Div.]. *Consulting engineer.*

Heck, Erwin, Liaison Officer [SS Training Battalion, Arnhem]. *Salesman.*

Heydte, Friedrich von der, Lt. Col., C.O. [6th Parachute Regt.]. *Professor, international law.*

Hilberg, Jürgen, Cpl. [Luftwaffe Comm. Battalion]. *Civil servant.*

Hoffman, Heinz-Jürgen, Gunner [15th Army Artillery Battalion]. *Dairy manager.*

Huck, Werner, Col. [Flakbrigade 19]. *Retired.*

Jansen, Georg, Pvt. [Engineers]. *Farmer.*

Jupe, Horst, Cpl. [9th SS Panzer Div.]. *Accountant.*

Knaust, Hans Peter, Maj., C.O. [Kampfgruppe Knaust, with 10th SS Panzer Div.]. *Retired.*

Krafft, Sepp, Major, C.O. [Panzer Grenadiers Training and Reserve Battalion 16]. *Police official.*

Lange, Hans, Maj. [Flak Unit]. *Retired.*

Laurenz, Josef, Pvt. [II Paratroop Replacement & Training Regt., Hermann Göring Panzer Div.]. *Store owner.*

Liermann, Werner, Sgt. [10th SS Panzer Div.]. *Painter.*

Linnenbrügger, Erwin, Pvt. [Infantry Regt. 364]. *Publishers' representative.*

Liss, Gerhard, Pvt. [II Paratroop Replacement & Training Regt., Hermann Göring Panzer Div.]. *Salesman.*

Majewski, Alfred, Maj. [Antiaircraft Unit 591]. *Office clerk.*

Moll, Jakob, Sgt. [Grenadier Regt. 520]. *Police official.*

Moll, Luise [Civilian]. *Housewife.*

Münks, Karl, Pvt. [84th Infantry Div.]. *Farmer.*

Nedel, Gerhard, 1st Lt. [Supply Battalion 801]. *Retired.*

Niemann, Charlotte, Red Cross nurse [Apeldoorn]. *Medical statistician.*

Pemsel, Max, Maj. Gen. [Chief of Staff, Seventh Army]. *Lt. Gen. (Retired), German Army.*

Petersen, Emil, M/Sgt. [Reich Work Service]. *Electrical engineer.*

Poppe, Walter, Lt. Gen., C.O. [59th Infantry Div.]. *Retired.*

Prümen, Josef, Pvt. [Reich Work Service]. *Insurance broker.*

Reichardt, Hans-Joachim, 1st Lt. [Luftwaffe]. *Captain.*

Ringsdorf, Alfred, Pvt. [10th SS Panzer Div.]. *Sales representative.*

Robeus, Hermann, Pvt. [Luftwaffe Paratroop Regt.]. *Tax consultant.*

Rohrbach, Wilhelm, Cpl. [Self-propelled Gun Brigade 280]. *Delicatessen owner.*

Rose, Heinz, Sgt. [Kampfgruppe Harskamp]. *Construction engineer.*

Savelsbergh, Matthias, Pvt. [Engineers]. *Retired.*

Schepers, Bernhard, Pvt. [5th Co.]. *Retired.*

Schmidt, Heinz, Cpl. [Luftwaffe Regt. 201]. *Telephone engineer.*

Sedelhauser, Gustav, 1st Lt. [Model's Hq., Transportation Chief]. *Brewer.*

Seesemann, Hans, Sgt. [Military Police]. *Printer.*

Sick, Josef, Cpl. [9th SS Panzer Div.]. *Truck driver.*

Skalka, Dr. Egon, Maj. [9th SS Panzer Div.]. *Physician.*

Stelzenmüller, Herbert, Cadet [German Naval Hospital, Cleves]. *Metallurgist.*

Strobel, Walter, Sgt. [Antiaircraft Unit]. *Retired.*

Tempelhof, Hans von, Col. [Model's Hq.]. *Retired.*

Tersteegen, Peter, Pvt. [Infantry Reserves Battalion—Wehrkreis—IV]. *Telephone engineer.*

Ullmann, Harry, Cpl. [10th SS Panzer Div.]. *Plant superintendent.*

Weber, Horst, Pvt. [10th SS Panzer Div.]. *Manufacturer.*

Weber, Max, Cpl. [15th Paratroopers Regt.]. *Physician.*

Wienand, Wolfgang, Pvt. [Antiaircraft Unit 591]. *Salesman.*

ACKNOWLEDGMENTS

At this writing almost thirty years have passed since World War II and, in spite of voluminous Allied and German records, the trail is growing cold for the contemporary historian in search of survivors. Many leading personalities are dead, and gone with them are the answers to many baffling questions. Of all the major plans and campaigns following the invasion of Normandy none was more significant than Operation Market-Garden. Yet—apart from some personal memoirs and a few chapters in official and semiofficial histories—the tragic story is virtually unknown in the United States. The successful role of the 82nd and 101st Airborne in the battle—in particular, the crossing of the Waal by Gavin's troops—rarely merits more than a paragraph or two in British accounts.

The stand of the British 1st Airborne Division at Arnhem remains one of the greatest feats of arms in World War II military history. But it was also a major defeat—Britain's second Dunkirk. Thus, as bureaucracies often tend to hide their failures, documentation in both American and British archives is all too frequently scanty and hard to come by. To unscramble some of the riddles and to present what I believe is the first complete version of the combined airborne-ground-attack invasion from the standpoint of all participants— Allied, German, Dutch underground and civilian—has taken me the best part of seven years. There were times during that period, especially when I fell seriously ill, that I despaired of the book's ever reaching publication.

As in my previous works on World War II—*The Longest Day* (1959) and *The Last Battle* (1966)—the backbone of information came from the participants: the men of the Allied Forces, the Germans they fought and the courageous Dutch civilians. In all, some twelve hundred people contributed to the making of *A Bridge Too Far*. Unselfishly and without stint these military personnel, ex-soldiers, and civilians gave freely of their time in interviews, showed me over the battlefield and supplied documentation and details from diaries, letters, military monographs, telephone logs, carefully preserved after-action reports, maps and photographs. Without the help of such contributors (whose names are listed on preceding pages under the heading "What They Do Today") the book could not have been written.

For a variety of reasons—among them duplication, lack of corroboration and sheer bulk—not every personal story or experience could be included. Of the twelve hundred contributors, more than half were interviewed and about four hundred of these accounts were used. But after thirty years memory is not infallible. Certain strict guidelines, similar to research procedures used in my previous books, had to be followed. Every statement or quote in the book is reinforced by documentary evidence or by the corroboration of others who heard or witnessed the event described. Hearsay, rumor or third-party accounts could not be included. My files contain hundreds of stories that may be entirely accurate but cannot be supported by other participants. For reasons of historical truth, they were not used. I hope the many contributors will understand.

So many individuals helped me in reconstructing the nine terrible days of Market-Garden that it is difficult to know where to begin in naming them. At the onset, however, I want especially to thank His Royal Highness, Prince Bernhard for his time and aid in locating and suggesting people to be interviewed and for providing me access to both Dutch and British archives. My warm thanks goes also to De Witt and Lila Wallace of the *Reader's Digest*. They not only underwrote much of the cost of this history but made their reporters and researchers in bureaus both in America and Europe available to me. Among these I wish particularly to thank the following: Heather Chapman, of New York; Julia Morgan, of Washington, D.C.; Michael Randolph, of London; John D. Panitza, John Flint, Ursula Naccache and Giselle Kayser, of Paris; the late Arno Alexi, of Stuttgart; Aad van Leeuwen, Jan Heijn, Liesbeth Stheeman and Jan van Os, of Amsterdam.

A special paragraph must be devoted to the tireless, painstaking work of Frederic Kelly, who for two years acted as my assistant. His research, interviews and fine journalistic procedures in England, Holland and the United States proved invaluable, as did his photographs of the participants as they are today.

Thanks must also be expressed to the U.S. Defense Department's Office of the Chief of Military History under command of Brigadier General Hal C. Pattison (at the time of researching) and the assistants who aided me in developing the military framework—in particular, Ditmar M. Finke and Hannah Zeidlik. Another whose help and encouragement must be mentioned is Charles B. MacDonald of O.C.M.H., whose detailed *The Siegfried Line Campaign* contains a fine and accurate version of Market-Garden. I also depended greatly on *Breakout and Pursuit* by Martin Blumenson, whose work appears in the official O.C.M.H. historical series. And I express my thanks, once again, to Dr. Forrest C. Pogue for his detailed command structure in O.C.M.H.'s *The Supreme Command*.

For their help in locating veterans and arranging interviews throughout the United States and Europe, acknowledgment must go to the officers of the U.S. Defense Department's Magazine and Book Division—Colonel Grover G. Heiman, Jr., U.S.A.F. (Ret.), Chief of Division; Lieutenant Colonel Charles W. Burtyk, Jr., U.S.A. (Deputy); Lieutenant Colonel Robert A. Webb, U.S.A.F.; Miss Anna C. Urband; and, in the Office of the Adjutant General, Seymour J. Pomrenze.

For the German research I am indebted to the following in the U.S. Defense Department's World War II Records Division: Dr. Robert W. Krauskopf, Director; Herman G. Goldbeck, Thomas E. Hohmann, Lois C. Aldridge, Joseph A. Avery, Hazel E. Ward, Caroline V. Moore, and Hildred F. Livingston. Without a complete understanding of the German war diaries and monographs provided, it would have been almost impossible for me to accurately interview the German participants, particularly the SS commanders—Lieutenant General Wilhelm Bittrich, Major General Heinz Harmel and Lieutenant Colonel

Walter Harzer—who for the first time told their version of Market-Garden to an American.

In the Netherlands my assistants and I received the most gracious cooperation from the Dutch archive authorities. I am most grateful to Professor Dr. Louis de Jong, Director of the State Institute for War Documentation; Jacob Zwaan, archivist; the curator of the Arnhem Airborne Museum, Mr. B. G. J. de Vries; and Dr. Eduard and Mrs. Emmie Groeneveld. In the Military History section of the Royal Army of the Netherlands pertinent research was made available to my assistants by many people, among them Lieutenant Colonel Gerrit van Oyen; Lieutenant Colonel August Kneepkens; Captain Gilbert Frackers; Captain Hendrik Hielkema. So detailed was the Dutch help that I was even provided with scale maps, drawings and photographs of the various Market-Garden bridges. Of particular help was Louis Einthoven, postwar Dutch security and intelligence chief, for his assistance in unraveling the story of Cornelius "King Kong" Lindemans, the Dutch spy.

Of vital importance were the municipal archives in Arnhem, Nijmegen, Veghel and Eindhoven, where an abundant amount of background material was located and examined. I am deeply indebted to the following in these centers: Klaas Schaap, Anton Stempher, Dr. Pieter van Iddekinge (Arnhem); Albertus Uijen and Petrus Sliepenbeek (Nijmegen); Jan Jongeneel (Veghel); Frans Kortie (Eindhoven).

Among the many contributors in Holland who deserve special mention are Jan and Kate ter Horst and Jan and Bertha Voskuil of Oosterbeek, who spent hours with me going over every detail of the last days of the 1st Airborne's ordeal in their village. Jan Voskuil took me over the battlefields, and Mr. and Mrs. Ter Horst unraveled the mystery surrounding the Driel ferry for the first time. In Driel the Baltussen family gave me hours of detailed interviews which proved invaluable. And for checking and reading Dutch interviews I must also express my appreciation to a magnificent journalist, A. Hugenot van der Linden, of the Amsterdam *Telegraaf*. Without his watchful eye I would most certainly have made many a mistake. So, too, for Lieutenant Commander Arnoldus Wolters, now Rotterdam's Commissioner of Police, who provided me with an almost minute-by-minute account of the happenings at General Urquhart's headquarters. In Oosterbeek the Maanen family provided extraordinary diaries and interviews, as did Hendrika van der Vlist, whose meticulous notes, like those of the Maanens, gave a clear picture of the situation in the casualty stations. Their vivid records and extraordinary help enabled me to re-create the atmosphere. I am deeply grateful to all of them.

Among the many military contributors who must be singled out for special thanks are General James M. Gavin, General Maxwell D. Taylor, General Roy Urquhart and Colonel Charles Mackenzie—all of whom sat patiently through countless interviews. Others who were most helpful were Major General John D. Frost; Colonel Eric M. Mackay; Major General Philip H. W. Hicks; General John Hackett; Brigadier George S. Chatterton; Brigadier Gordon Walch; Mr. Brian Urquhart; the late Major General Stanislaw Sosabowski; and Chaplain

G. A. Pare, whose notes constitute an unforgettable, poignant document. Lady Browning (Daphne du Maurier) with her wit and common sense proved a delightful correspondent and set straight some of the myths of Arnhem.

In Germany I was assisted greatly in tracing survivors and locating background material, monographs and war diaries by Dr. Bliesener of Bonn's Press and Information Service; Lieutenant Colonel Siegel of the Ministry of Defense; Dr. Wolfgang von Groote and Major Forwick of the Military History Research Department; and Lieutenant Colonel Dr. Stahl of the Federal Archives.

There are many, many others whose support and assistance made this book possible. I must again thank my wife, Kathryn, a writer herself, who organized and collated research, edited and watched for my dangling participles. Also, when I was most seriously ill, I thank with all my heart the ministrations of my good friend, Dr. Patrick Neligan, together with Dr. Willet Whitmore, who in some miraculous way pulled me through and kept me going. Again, also my thanks to Jerry Korn, my chief "nitpicker"; Suzanne Gleaves and John Tower, who read the manuscript so carefully; Anne Bardenhagen, my valued friend and assistant; Judi Muse and Polly Jackson, who, at various times, worked as secretaries. My thanks also go to Paul Gitlin, my agent; Peter Schwed and Michael Korda of Simon and Schuster for their suggestions; and Hobart Lewis, President of the *Reader's Digest*, who waited patiently through all the travail.

BIBLIOGRAPHY

Airborne Assault on Holland. Washington: U.S.A.F., Office of the Assistant Chief of Air Staff, 1945.

Allied documents from U.S., British and Dutch historical sources unpublished: plans, operational orders, logs, telephone and teletype messages, intelligence estimates, war diaries, commanders' reviews and after-action reports from *First Allied Airborne Headquarters; First British Airborne Corps; 1st British Airborne Division; 101st U.S. Airborne Division; 82nd U.S. Airborne Division*; Dutch underground messages, staff college studies, monographs and maps on "Operation Market-Garden"; *82nd and 101st Airborne Divisions* combat interviews.

Ambrose, Stephen E., *The Supreme Commander: The War Years of General Dwight D. Eisenhower.* New York: Doubleday, 1970.

Bauer, Cornelius, *The Battle of Arnhem* (on information supplied by Lieut. Col. Theodor A. Boeree). London: Hodder and Stoughton, 1966.

Bekker, Cajus, *The Luftwaffe War Diaries.* New York: Doubleday, 1968.

Bird, Will R., *No Retreating Footsteps: The Story of the North Nova Scotia Highlanders.* Nova Scotia: Kentville Publishing, 1947.

Blake, George, *Mountain and Flood: The History of the 52nd (Lowland) Division, 1939–46.* Glasgow: Jackson, Son, 1950.

Blumenson, Martin, *U.S. Army in World War II: Breakout and Pursuit.* Washington, D.C.: Office of the Chief of Military History, Dept. of Army, 1961.

Bradley, General Omar N., *A Soldier's Story.* New York: Henry Holt, 1951.

Brammall, R., *The Tenth.* Ipswich: Eastgate Publications, 1965.

Bredin, Lt. Col. A. E. C., *Three Assault Landings.* London: Gale & Polden, 1946.

Brereton, Lt. Gen. Lewis H., *The Brereton Diaries.* New York: William Morrow, 1946.

Bryant, Sir Arthur, *Triumph in the West: The War Diaries of Field Marshal Viscount Alan Brooke.* London: Collins, 1959.

Bullock, Allan, *Hitler: A Study in Tyranny.* London: Odhams Press, 1952.

Butcher, Captain Harry C., *My Three Years with Eisenhower.* New York: Simon and Schuster, 1946.

By Air to Battle: Official Account of the British Airborne Divisions. London: H. M. Stationery Office, 1945.

Carter, Ross, *Those Devils in Baggy Pants.* New York: Appleton-Century-Crofts, 1951.

Chatterton, George S., *The Wings of Pegasus.* London: MacDonald, 1962.

Churchill, Winston S., *The Second World War* (Vols. 1–6). London: Cassell, 1955.

Clay, Maj. Ewart W., M.B.E., *The Path of the 50th: The Story of the 50th (Northumbrian) Division in the Second World War 1939–1945.* Aldershot: Gale & Polden, 1950.

Cole, Lieut. Col. Howard N., *On Wings of Healing*. London: William Blackwood & Sons, 1963.

Collis, Robert, and Hogerziel, Hans, *Straight On*. London: Methuen, 1947.

Covington, Henry L., *A Fighting Heart: An Unofficial Story of the 82nd Airborne*. Fayetteville, N.C.: Privately published, 1949.

Craig, Gordon A., *The Politics of the Prussian Army 1640–1945*. London: Oxford University Press, 1955.

Critchell, Laurence, *Four Stars of Hell*. New York: Macmillan, 1947.

Crosthwait, Maj. A. E. L., *Bridging Normandy to Berlin*. Hanover: British Army of the Rhine, 1945.

Cumberlege, G., editor, *BBC War Report, 6th June 1944–5th May 1945*. Oxford: Oxford University Press, 1946.

D'Arcy-Dawson, John, *European Victory*. London: MacDonald, 1946.

Davis, Kenneth S., *Experience of War*. New York: Doubleday, 1965.

Dawson, W. Forrest, *Saga of the All-American* [82nd Airborne Div.]. Privately printed.

Deane-Drummond, Anthony, *Return Ticket*. London: Collins, 1967.

Dempsey, Gen. Sir Miles, *Operations of the 2nd Army in Europe*. London: War Office, 1947.

Ehrman, John, *History of the Second World War: Grand Strategy* (Vols. V and VI). London: H. M. Stationery Office, 1956.

Eisenhower, Dwight D., *Crusade in Europe*. New York: Doubleday, 1948.

Eisenhower, John S. D., *The Bitter Woods*. New York: G. P. Putnam's Sons, 1969.

Ellis, Maj. L. F., *Welsh Guards at War*. Aldershot: Gale & Polden, 1946.

Essame, Maj. Gen. Hubert, *The Battle for Germany*. New York: Charles Scribner's Sons, 1969.

———, *The 43rd Wessex Division at War*. London: William Clowes & Sons, 1952.

Falls, Cyril, *The Second World War*. London: Methuen, 1948.

Farago, Ladislas, *Patton*. New York: Ivan Obolensky, 1963.

First Infantry Division: Danger Forward, with introduction by Hanson Baldwin: H. R. Knickerbocker, Jack Thompson, Jack Belden, Don Whitehead, A. J. Liebling, Mark Watson, Cy Peterman, Iris Carpenter, Col. R. Ernest Dupuy, Drew Middleton and former officers. Atlanta: Albert Love Enterprises, 1947.

Fitzgerald, Maj. D. J. L., *History of the Irish Guards in the Second World War*. Aldershot: Gale & Polden, 1949.

Flower, Desmond, and Reeves, James, editors, *The War, 1939–45*. London: Cassell, 1960.

Foot, M. R. D., *Special Operations Executive*. London: H. M. Stationery Office, 1967.

Freiden & Richardson, editors, *The Fatal Decisions*. London: Michael Joseph, 1956.

Fuller, Maj. Gen. J. F. C., *The Second World War*. New York: Duell, Sloan and Pearce, 1949.

————, *The Conduct of War, 1789–1961*. London: Eyre & Spottiswoode, 1961.

Gavin, Lt. Gen. James M., *Airborne Warfare*. Washington, D.C.: Infantry Journal Press, 1947.

————, *War and Peace in the Space Age*. New York: Harper & Bros., 1958.

Gibson, Ronald, *Nine Days*. Devon: Arthur H. Stockwell, 1956.

Gilbert, Felix, editor, *Hitler Directs His War*. New York: Oxford University Press, 1950.

Gill, R., and Groves, J., *Club Route in Europe*. Hanover: British Army of the Rhine, 1946.

Godfrey, Maj. E. G., and Goldsmith, Maj. Gen. R. F. K., *History of the Duke of Cornwall's Light Infantry, 1939–1945*. Aldershot: The Regimental History Committee, 1966.

Goerlitz, Walter, *History of the German General Staff*. New York: Frederick A. Praeger, 1953.

Guingand, Maj. Gen. Sir Francis de, *Generals at War*. London: Hodder & Stoughton, 1964.

————, *Operation Victory*. London: Hodder & Stoughton, 1947.

Gunning, Capt. Hugh, *Borderers in Battle*. Berwick-on-Tweed, Scotland: Martin's Printing Works, 1948.

Hagen, Louis, *Arnhem Lift*. London: Pilot Press, 1945.

Hausser, Paul, *Waffen SS in Einsatz*. Göttingen: Plesse, 1953.

Heaps, Capt. Leo, *Escape from Arnhem*. Toronto: Macmillan, 1945.

Heijbroek, M., *The Battle Around the Bridge at Arnhem*. Oosterbeek: The Airborne Museum Collection at Kasteel De Doorwerth, Oosterbeek, 1947.

Heydte, Baron von der, *Daedalus Returned: Crete 1941*. London: Hutchinson, 1958.

Hibbert, Christopher, *The Battle of Arnhem*. London: B. T. Batsford, 1962.

History of the 2nd Battalion, The Parachute Regiment. Aldershot: Gale & Polden, 1946.

Höhne, Heinz, *The Order of the Death's Head*. New York: Coward-McCann, 1970.

Hollister, Paul, and Strunsky, Robert, editors, *D-Day Through Victory in Europe*. New York: Columbia Broadcasting System, 1945.

Horrocks, Lt. Gen. Sir Brian, *A Full Life*. London: Collins, 1960.

Horst, H. B. van der, *Paratroopers Jump*. Privately published, n.d.

Horst, Kate A. ter, *Cloud Over Arnhem*. London: Allan Wingate, 1959.

Howard, Michael, and Sparrow, John, *The Coldstream Guards 1920–1946*. London: Oxford University Press, 1951.

Ingersoll, Ralph, *Top Secret*. New York: Harcourt, Brace, 1946.

Ismay, Gen. Lord, *Memoirs*. New York: Viking Press, 1960.

Jackson, Lt. Col. G. S., *Operations of the VIII Corps*. London: St. Clements Press, 1948.

Joslen, Lt. Col. H. F., *Orders of Battle, Second World War, 1939–45*. London: H. M. Stationery Office, 1960.

Kahn, David, *The Code Breakers*. New York: Macmillan, 1967.

Keitel, Wilhelm, Field Marshal, *The Memoirs of Field Marshal Keitel*; Walter Görlitz, editor. New York: Stein & Day, 1965.

Lederrey, Col. Ernest, *Germany's Defeat in the East—1941–45*. Charles Lavauzelle, France, 1951.

Lewin, Ronald, editor, *The British Army in World War II: The War on Land*. New York: William Morrow, 1970.

Liddell Hart, B. H., *History of the Second World War*. New York: Putnam's Sons, 1971.

———, *The Other Side of the Hill*. London: Cassell, 1948.

Liberation of Eindhoven, The. Eindhoven: The Municipality of Eindhoven, September, 1964.

Life, editors of, *Life's Picture History of World War II*. New York: Time, Inc., 1950.

Lord, W. G., II, *History of the 508th Parachute Infantry*. Privately printed, n.d.

MacDonald, Charles B., *Command Decisions*; Kent Greenfield, editor. London: Methuen, 1960.

———, *The Mighty Endeavor*. New York: Oxford University Press, 1969.

———, *U.S. Army in World War II: The Siegfried Line Campaign*. Washington, D.C.: Office of the Chief of Military History, Dept. of the Army, 1963.

Mackenzie, Brig. C. D., *It Was Like This!* Oosterbeek: Adremo C. V., 1956.

Marshall, S. L. A., *Battalion & Small Unit Study No. 1: Kinnard's Operation in Holland*. Washington, D.C.: Office of the Chief of Military History, Dept. of the Army, 1945.

———, *Battle at Best*. New York: William Morrow, 1963.

———, *Men Against Fire*. New York: William Morrow, 1947.

———, Westover, John G., O'Sullivan, Jeremiah, and Corcoran, George, *The American Divisions in Operation Market*; unpublished monograph, Washington, D.C.: Office of the Chief of Military History, Dept. of the Army, 1945.

Martens, Allard, *The Silent War*. London: Hodder & Stoughton, 1961.

Matloff, Maurice, *Strategic Planning for Coalition Warfare, 1941–2, 43–4*. Washington, D.C.: Office of the Chief of Military History, Dept. of the Army, 1953–59.

Milbourne, Andrew, *Lease of Life*. London: Museum Press, 1952.

Millar, Ian A. L., *The Story of the Royal Canadian Corps*. Privately printed, n.d.

Millis, Walter, *The Last Phase*. Boston: Houghton Mifflin, 1946.

Montgomery, Field Marshal Sir Bernard, *Despatch of Field Marshal The Viscount Montgomery of Alamein*. New York: British Information Services, 1946.

———, *The Memoirs of Field Marshal The Viscount Montgomery of Alamein, K.G.* London: Collins, 1958.

———, *Normandy to the Baltic*. Privately published by Printing & Stationery Service, British Army of the Rhine, 1946.

Moorehead, Alan, *Eclipse*. New York: Coward-McCann, 1945.

———, *Montgomery*. London: Hamish Hamilton, 1946.

Morgan, Gen. Sir Frederick, *Peace and War: A Soldier's Life*. London: Hodder and Stoughton, 1961.

Morison, Samuel Eliot, *The Invasion of France and Germany, 1944–45.* Boston: Little, Brown, 1959.

Nalder, Maj. Gen. R. F. H., *The History of British Army Signals in the Second World War.* Aldershot: Royal Signals Institution, 1953.

Newnham, Group Capt. Maurice, *Prelude to Glory: The Story of the Creation of Britain's Parachute Army.* London: Sampson Low, Marston, 1947.

Nicolson, Captain Nigel, and Forbes, Patrick, *The Grenadier Guards in the War of 1939–1945* (Vol. I). Aldershot: Gale & Polden, 1949.

IX Troop Carrier Command in World War II. Washington, D.C.: U.S. Air Force, Historical Division, n.d.

Nobécourt, Jacques, *Hitler's Last Gamble: The Battle of The Bulge.* New York: Schocken Books, 1967.

North, John, *North-West Europe 1944–5. The Achievement of the 21st Army Group.* London: H. M. Stationery Office, 1953.

Not in Vain, Compilation by the People of Oosterbeek. Arnhem, Holland: Van Lochum Slaterus, 1946.

Orde, Roden, *The Household Cavalry at War: Second Household Cavalry Regiment.* Aldershot: Gale & Polden, 1953.

Otway, Col. Terence, *The Second World War 1939–45: Airborne Forces.* London: War Office, 1946.

Packe, M. *First Airborne.* London: Secker & Warburg, 1948.

Pakenham-Walsh, Maj. Gen. R. P., *History of the Corps of Royal Engineers.* Volume IX, *1938–1948.* Chatham: Institution of Royal Engineers, 1958.

Patton, Gen. George S., Jr., *War as I Knew It.* Boston: Houghton Mifflin, 1947.

Paul, Daniel, with St. John, John, *Surgeon at Arms.* London: William Heinemann, 1958.

Phillips, Norman C., *Holland and the Canadians.* Holland: Contact Publishing Co., 1946.

Pictorial Biography of the U.S. 101st Airborne Division, A, Compiled by the 101st's Public-Relations Unit, Auxerre, France, 1954.

Pinto, Lt. Col. Oreste, *Spy-Catcher.* New York: Harper, 1952.

Pogue, Forrest C., *The Supreme Command.* Washington, D.C.: Office of the Chief of Military History, Department of the Army, 1954.

Rapport, Leonard, and Northwood, Arthur, Jr., *Rendezvous with Destiny: A History of the 101st Airborne Division.* Washington, D.C.: Washington Infantry Journal Press, 1948.

Reader's Digest, *Illustrated Story of World War II.* Pleasantville, N.Y.: The Reader's Digest Association, 1969.

Ridgway, Matthew B., *Soldier: The Memoirs of Matthew B. Ridgway.* New York: Harper & Bros., 1956.

Rosse, Captain the Earl of, and Hill, Col. E. R., *The Story of the Guards Armoured Division.* London: Geoffrey Bles, 1956.

Sampson, Francis, *Paratrooper Padre.* Washington, D.C.: Catholic University of America Press, 1948.

Saunders, Hilary St. George, *The Fight Is Won: Official History Royal Air Force, 1939–1945* (Vol. III). London: H. M. Stationery Office, 1954.

————, *The Red Beret*. London: Michael Joseph, Ltd., 1950.

Seth, Ronald, *Lion With Blue Wings*. London: Victor Gollancz, Ltd., 1955.

Shirer, William L., *The Rise and Fall of the Third Reich: A History of Nazi Germany*. New York: Simon and Schuster, 1960.

Shulman, Milton, *Defeat in the West*. London: Secker and Warburg, 1947.

Smith, Gen. Walter Bedell (with Stewart Beach), *Eisenhower's Six Great Decisions*. New York: Longmans, Green, 1956.

Smyth, Jack, *Five Days in Hell*. London: William Kimber, 1956.

Snyder, Louis L., *The War: A Concise History, 1939–1945*. London: Robert Hale, 1960.

Sosabowski, Maj. Gen. Stanislaw, *Freely I Served*. London: William Kimber, 1960.

Stacey, Col. C. P., *The Canadian Army: 1939–45*. Ottawa: King Printers, 1948.

Stainforth, Peter, *Wings of the Wind*. London: Falcon Press, 1952.

Stein, George H., *The Waffen SS 1939–45*. Ithaca, N.Y.: Cornell University Press, 1966.

Sulzberger, C. L., *The American Heritage Picture History of World War II*. New York: American Heritage Publishing, 1966.

Swiecicki, Marek, *With the Red Devils at Arnhem*. London: Max Love Publishing, 1945.

Tedder, Lord, *With Prejudice: The Memoirs of Marshal of the Royal Air Force Lord Tedder*. London: Cassell, 1966.

Thompson, R. W., *The 85 Days*. New York: Ballantine Books, 1957.

Toland, John, *Battle*. New York: Random House, 1959.

————, *The Last 100 Days*. New York: Random House, 1965.

Trevor-Roper, H. R., editor, *Hitler's War Directives 1939–1945*. London: Sidgwick and Jackson, 1964.

Trials of German Major War Criminals, The (Vols. 1–26). London: H. M. Stationery Office, 1948.

Urquhart, Maj. Gen. R. E., *Arnhem*. New York: W. W. Norton, 1958.

Vandeleur, Brig. J. O. E., *A Soldier's Story*. Aldershot: Gale & Polden, 1967.

Verney, Maj. Gen. G. L., *The Guards Armoured Division*. London: Hutchinson, 1955.

Warlimont, Walter, *Inside Hitler's Headquarters 1939–1945*. London: Weidenfeld & Nicolson, 1964.

Warrack, Graeme, *Travel by Dark: After Arnhem*. London: Harvill Press, 1963.

Warren, Dr. John C., *Airborne Operations in World War II, European Theatre*. Washington, D.C.: U.S. Air Force, Historical Division, 1956.

Watkins, G. J. B., *From Normandy to the Weser: The War History of the Fourth Battalion, the Dorset Regiment*. Dorchester: The Dorset Press, 1952.

Websters, Sir Charles, and Frankland, Noble, *The Strategic Air Offensive Against Germany, 1939–45* (Vols. 1–4). London: H. M. Stationery Office, 1961.

Weller, George, *The Story of the Paratroops*. New York: Random House, 1958.

Wheeler-Bennett, John, *The Nemesis of Power*. New York: St. Martin's Press, 1954.

Wilmot, Chester, *The Struggle for Europe*. New York: Harper & Bros., 1952.

SELECTED ARTICLES

"Arnhem Diary," *Reconnaissance Journal*, Vol. 4, No. 1 (Autumn, 1947).

"Arnhem Was Their Finest Hour," *Soldier*, Vol. 13 (September, 1957).

"Battle of Desperation, The," *Time* Magazine, October 2, 1944.

Best, C. E., M.M., "The Mediums at Arnhem," *Gunner*, Vol. 33, No. 1 (January, 1951).

Bestebreurtje, Maj. A. D., "The Airborne Operations in the Netherlands in Autumn 1944," *Allegemeine Schweizerische Militärzeitschrift*, Vol. 92, No. 6 (1946).

Breese, Maj. C. F. O., "The Airborne Operations in Holland, Sept. 1944," *The Border Magazine*, September, 1948 (Part I), and March, 1949 (Part II).

Burne, Alfred H., "Arnhem," *The Fighting Forces*, 1944.

Chatterton, Brig. G. J. S., "The Glider Pilot Regiment at Arnhem," *The Eagle*, Summer, 1954.

Colman, D. E., "The Phantom Legion," *The Army Quarterly*, April, 1962.

Courtney, W. B., "Army in the Sky," *Collier's*, November, 1944.

Cousens, Maj. H. S., "Arnhem 17th–26th September, 1944," from *The Spring of Shillelagh*, Vol. 28, No. 322 (Spring-Summer, 1948).

Exton, Hugh M., "The Guards Armoured Division in Operation Market-Garden," *Armoured Cavalry Journal*, 1948.

Falls, Cyril, "Arnhem—A Stage in Airborne Tactics," *Illustrated London News*, October, 1945.

Fijalski, Stanley, "Echoes of Arnhem," *Stand-to*, 1950.

Gellhorn, Martha, "Death of a Dutch Town," *Collier's*, December, 1944.

Greelen, Lothar van, "The Puzzle of Arnhem Solved," *Deutsche Wochen Zeitung*, 1964.

Herford, M. E. M., "All in the Day's Work" (Parts 1 and 2), *The Journal of the Royal Army Medical Corps*, 1952.

"How the Supplies Reached Arnhem," *Journal of the Royal Army Service Corps*, Vol. 69, No. 2 (November, 1944).

Intelligence Corps, "With the Airborne at Arnhem," *Notes of Interest*, Vol. 8 (1945).

Lister, Evelyn, "An Echo of Arnhem," *British Legion Journal*, September, 1950.

McCulloch, C. A., "The Epic of Arnhem," *Springbok*, September, 1955.

Mackay, Maj. E. M., "The Battle of Arnhem Bridge," *Blackwood's Magazine*, October, 1945.

Montgomery, Field Marshal Sir Bernard L., "21st [British] Army Group in the Campaign in North-West Europe, 1944–45," *The Journal of the Royal United Service Institution*, Vol. 90, No. 560 (November, 1945).

Packe, Michael St. J., "The Royal Army Service Corps at Arnhem," *The Journal of the R.A.S.C.*, November, 1945.

St. Aubyn, Lt. The Hon. Piers, "Arnhem," *The King's Royal Rifle Corps Chronicle*, 1946.

Smith, Robert, "With the R.A.M.C. at Arnhem," *Stand-to*, Vol. 1, No. 8 (October-November, 1950).

Stevenson, Lt. J., "Arnhem Diary," *Reconnaissance Journal*, Vol. 4, No. 1 (Autumn, 1947).

Tatham-Warter, Maj. A. D., D.S.O., "Escape from Arnhem," *The Oxfordshire and Buckinghamshire Light Infantry Chronicle*, Vol. 48 (1946).

Taylor, Lt. Col. George, D.S.O., "With 30 Corps to Arnhem," *Ça Ira*, Vol. 8, No. 2 (June, 1949).

Tompkins, Col. Rathvon McC., "The Bridge," *Marine Corps Gazette*, April, 1951, and May, 1951.

Tooley, Lt. Col. I. P., "Artillery Support at Arnhem," *The Field Artillery Journal*, April, 1945.

Watkins, Maj. Ernest, "Arnhem, the Landing and the Bridge," *British Army Bureau of Current Affairs*, No. 83 (1944).

Williams, F. Lt. A. A., "I Was at Arnhem," *The Royal Air Force Journal*, December, 1944.

Wilmot, Chester, "What Really Happened at Arnhem," *Stand-to*, Vol. 1, No. 8 (1950).

Winder, Sgt. F., "Postscript" in "Arnhem Diary," *Reconnaissance Journal*, Vol. 4, No. 1 (Autumn, 1947).

Wood, Alan, "How Arnhem Was Reported," *Pegasus*, July and October, 1946.

———, "News from Arnhem," *Pegasus*, October, 1949.

Wooding, F. B., "The Airborne Pioneers," *The Royal Pioneer*, Vol. 7, No. 30 (March, 1952).

GERMAN MANUSCRIPTS, MILITARY STUDIES AND CAPTURED DOCUMENTS

Bittrich, SS General Wilhelm, CO II SS Panzer Corps, H.Q. Battle Orders; *Report on the Activities of the II SS Panzer Corps., Aug.–Nov. 1944*, together with maps; Bittrich's account of Arnhem Battle, September 17–26, 1944; Incoming reports from Commanders of 9th and 10th SS PZ Divisions; Personal papers, diaries and maps—as given to the author.

Blumentritt, General Gunther, *OB West, A Study in Command, Atlantic Wall to Siegfried Line*, Office of the Chief of Military History (hereafter referred to as O.C.M.H.), Department of Army, U.S.A., MS. B-344; Manuscripts, notes and maps as given to the author.

Buttlar, Major General Horst von, *OB West, A Study in Command, Atlantic Wall to Siegfried Line*, O.C.M.H., MS. B-672.

Christiansen, General Friederich, CO Luftwaffe, German Armed Forces in the Netherlands, Interrogation of, File No. 67, Nijmegen Archives; Testimony and trial proceedings, Dutch Ministry of Justice, July-August, 1948.

Feldt, General Kurt, *Corps. H. Q. Feldt and 406th Division from 17–21 September 1944*. O.C.M.H., MS. C-085.

Fullriede, SS Col. F. W. H., C.O. Replacement & Training Para. Brigade Hermann Göring. Utrecht. Personal Diary, September 1–October 5, 1944. Translated by Peter Ranger. Interrogation of, April 8, 1948, Nijmegen Archives, File 83.

Harmel, SS Major General Heinz, C.O. 10th SS PZ Division Frundsberg. Personal diary; maps, Orders of Battle; Operational Orders and pertinent sections of Official War Diary. All called the "Harmel Papers," as given to the author.

Harzer, SS Lt. Col. Walter, C.O., 9th SS PZ Division Hohenstaufen, H.Q. War Diaries, Operation Reports and Interrogations, all under "Harzer Papers." File #74; H.Q. Daily Reports, Document #78013/19. U.S., British and Dutch Archives.

Heichler, Lucien, *The Germans Opposite 30th Corps*, an account of the First Parachute Army on the Albert Canal. Research monograph. Washington, D.C.: O.C.M.H., Dept. of the Army, 1962.

Heydte, Lt. Col. Frederick von der, C.O., 6th Para. Regiment. *6 FS Jaeger Regiment in Action Against U.S. Paratroopers in the Netherlands*, September 1944; maps and overlays. O.C.M.H., MS. C-001.

Krafft, SS Major Sepp, C.O., Panzer Grenadier Depot Battalion 16 Netherlands, correspondence between Krafft and Heinrich Himmler; Krafft "War Diary"; "The Battle of Arnhem" as presented to Heinrich Himmler; British Intelligence Corps translation of Krafft Diary, with commentary.

Mattenklott, Lt. Gen. Frans, Report on Military Area 6 and The Rhineland, 15 September, 1944–21 March, 1945. O.C.M.H., MS. B-044.

Meindl, General Eugen, C.O., II Para. Corps. *The II Para. Corps, 15 September, 1944–21 March, 1945*. Document Nos. III H 15450 and 75145/5.

Model, Field Marshal Walter, OKW—AGpB War Diary, Operational Daily Reports, 1 September–15 October 1944. Document No. III H 15452/2; OKW—AGpB War Diary; Operations and Orders, September 1–September 30, 1944. Document No. III H 15453/2; AGpB—Situation and Weekly Reports; Telephone Log and Teletype Message Files, Proclamations for September, 1944. Document Nos. III H 15450 and 75145/5.

190th Infantry Division, Report of, Commitment 17 September, 1944–16 April, 1945. O.C.M.H., MS. B-195.

Poppe, Major General Walter, C.O., 59th Infantry Division. *2nd Commitment of the 59th Infantry Division in Holland, 18 September–25 November, 1944.* O.C.M.H., MS. B-149; War Diary and Operational Orders as given to the author.

Rauter, SS Lt. Gen. Hans Albin, Trial proceedings, Dutch Ministry of Justice, 1952; Interrogations of and testimony in Dutch Historical Archives and in *The Netherlands in Wartime*, Vol. 4, No. 1 (March, 1949). Rauter's Proclamations, Nijmegen Archives.

Reinhard, Gen. Hans W., C.O. 88 Corps., *Report of the Commander 6 June–21 December 1944*, O.C.M.H., MS. B-343 and MS. B-156.

Reinhardt, Maj. Gen. Hellmuth, C. of S. Wehrmacht Commander in Chief in Denmark, *Commitment of the 406th Division Against the Allied Airborne Assault at Nijmegen, September 17, 1944.* O.C.M.H., MS. C-085; Supplement to the Report, O.C.M.H., MS. C-085A.

Rundstedt, Field Marshal Gerd von, *OB West, Daily Reports of Commander in Chief West, September 2–30, 1944.* Document No. 34002; *OKW—OB West*

War Diary, September–October, 1944, including Annex 2224-2476. British and Dutch archives; *OB West, A Study in Command, Atlantic Wall to Siegfried Line*, Vols. I, II, III, O.C.M.H., MS. B-633.

Scheidt, Wilhelm, *Hitler's Conduct of the War*, O.C.M.H., MS. ML-864.

Schramm, Major Percy E., *The West (1 April 1944–16 December 1944)*, MS. B-034; *Notes on the Execution of War Diaries*, O.C.M.H., MS. A-860.

Skalka, SS Major Egon, Divisional Doctor, 9th SS Panzer Hohenstaufen, Official Headquarters Reports; Medical Estimate of the Arnhem Battle; Interrogation Reports. British and Dutch Archives. Diary, notes as given to the author.

Speidel, Lt. Gen. Dr. Hans, *OB West, A Study in Command, Atlantic Wall to Siegfried Line*, Vols. I, II, III, O.C.M.H., MS. B-718.

Student, Col. Gen. Kurt, C.O. 1st Para. Army, *Battles of the 1st Parachute Army on the Albert Canal*; and *Allied Airborne Operations on 17 September, 1944*, O.C.M.H., MS. B-717. Manuscripts, notes and maps as given to the author. Statement in Nijmegen Archives, File 35.

——, "Arnhem—The Last German Victory," from *The Soldier Speaks*, No. 5, 1952.

Tettau, Lt. Gen. Hans von, *Combat Reports 17 September–26 September, 1944 of Units Committed in the Netherlands*, Document No. 40649H. Dutch Archives.

Warlimont, General Walter, *From the Invasion to the Siegfried Line, 1939–1945*. London: Weidenfeld & Nicolson, 1962.

Zangen, General Gustav von, *Battles of the Fifteenth Army Between the Meuse-Schelde Canal and the Lower Meuse, 15 September–10 November, 1944*, O.C.M.H., MS. B-475.

Zimmerman, Lt. Gen. Bodo, *OB West, A Study in Command, Atlantic Wall to Siegfried Line*, Vols. I, II, III, O.C.M.H., MS. B-308.

OTHER WORLD WAR II
WRITINGS

SELECTED DISPATCHES FOR
The Daily Telegraph
1944–45

OUT WITH THE MARAUDERS OVER FRANCE

4-SPAN BRIDGE HIT

AT A UNITED STATES NINTH AIR FORCE BASE, Sunday.

Queen Anne the Second this morning completed her 75th mission. She is a heavily armoured Marauder, and this morning she dropped more than two tons of bombs on the target area, a four-span bridge not more than 20 feet wide.

I flew with her. At 8.45 a.m. we synchronised our watches in the briefing-room, and the briefing had begun.

A large map covered the whole of one wall and a red streamer ran from our position at the base here to the target.

"That," said Col. Nye, the commanding officer of the group, pointing to the target, "is a four-span bridge about 120ft long, and, gentlemen, your target is small. It must be destroyed."

The route was traced inch by inch across the map; everything was meticulously explained; nothing was left to chance. The lights were extinguished in the briefing room, which rather resembled a theatre, a screen was lowered, and a photograph of the actual target was projected on to it.

There everything was shown in exact detail. So striking was this method, and so lucid were the explanations, that even I had no trouble many hours later in recognising the target.

Intelligence, navigational, meteorological and bombardiering officers followed one another in succession on to the rostrum before the wall map and explained the various problems one by one.

We were finally addressed once more by Col. Nye, who impressed upon the crews the importance of hitting the target only, thus avoiding any loss of life among the French population.

"Nye's Annihilators," as the airmen at this station call themselves, were ready for another attack on occupied France.

I was introduced to the pilot and crew I was to accompany on the mission; then I went with an intelligence officer to the parachute room to pick up my equipment. Here I was fitted with a harness and parachute and a "Mae West" life preserver.

CHOCOLATE RATION

My next step was to hand in all personal papers, letters and other documents which might divulge information to the enemy in the event of the plane I was in being shot down. My papers were taken and secured in a canvas bag, and in return I received a ration of chocolate and chewing gum.

My guide then took me to another supply store, where I was issued with a flying helmet, flying suit, shrapnel helmet and a pair of high-power binoculars. We then left for Queen Anne II.

A few minutes later we were in the air and joining our formation. One flight had already taken off, and we were the second, and followed some miles behind. We flew on the left, or port, side of our leader, whose plane bore the name of Annie Laurie, and on his starboard side flew the plane "Idiot's Delight."

Our crew consisted of pilot, co-pilot, bombardier-navigator, radio-gunner, engineer-gunner, turret-gunner, and myself, making a total of seven.

Each of us wore a throat microphone and headphones, and in this manner spoke and heard one another through the plane inter-communication system.

The pilot, Lt. P. Godwin, showed me over the plane and its armaments.

It has two machine-guns in the front turret, two on each side of the pilot's cockpit, fired by the pilot, a powered twin-gun top turret, a twin-gun tail turret, and two heavy machine-guns firing downwards from the waist. There are so many guns on a B.26 Marauder that space is greatly restricted.

FLEW OVER LONDON

We flew over London, and gradually the quiet folds of the English countryside receded and we were over the Channel. Below us the water was perfectly calm and I could see the white wash of several small ships, which through my glasses looked like corvettes.

Then above us for the first time I noticed our Spitfire escorts weaving back and forth, like sheepdogs watching their flock.

We gradually neared the French coast, and through the intercom came the order to "Don flak suits" and helmets. The "flak" suits and helmets are so heavy and bulky that I could barely move about the plane's interior.

Then we arrived over the French coast. Here we nearly had to queue up to get in. Spitfires, Thunderbolts, Havocs and Marauders were coming and going with impunity.

I examined many miles of the French coastline through my glasses. No sign of life was apparent; everything seemed completely desolate and deserted.

Away in the distance a vast column of smoke swept for many miles into the sky. Through my glasses it looked like a forest on fire—probably from previous bombing raids. Down below I suddenly saw Spitfires escorting to safety two Havoc light bombers returning on one engine each.

"FLAK IN FRONT"

"Flak in front," said the co-pilot. I looked ahead. The German ack-ack batteries had opened up on our first flight. Then they opened up on us. "Flak behind," said the tail gunner.

For a few brief moments, which to me seemed like hours, I saw the black ugly puffs of death-dealing flak coming too close for comfort. Nothing hit us; so far we were safe—but we had a long way to go.

Below us a river twisted backwards and forwards, and to the left I noticed another vast column of smoke circling to the sky. Then we passed over a French town; the pilot reported some movement of people, but our speed made it impossible for me to examine it through my glasses.

Then directly ahead I saw the target. From our height it was just a mere speck. Gradually it became clearer. Through my binoculars I could see it plainly. In the middle of this stretch of the river small islands dotted the river. At the end of these was this graceful four-span bridge.

The first flight of bombers went in. Down went their bombs, spiraling slowly. Then after what seemed an incredibly long time they exploded, and the target area was filled with clouds of smoke as debris shot high in the air.

WATCHED BOMBS FALL

Then we began our bombing run. I stood at the open door which divides the bomb bay from the wireless cabin. The bomb doors opened. Suddenly, with a click no louder than that of an electric light switch, our two tons of destruction had gone.

I watched them as they sailed into space rapidly becoming smaller. Then the bomb bay doors silently closed. We had hit the target area. We turned for home.

I looked back and the whole of the target area was one mass of smoke. We quickly passed over the brown and green mosaic of the French countryside without seeing any further flak, and soon we approached the Channel.

Throughout the whole of the mission we had not seen one enemy fighter. We crossed the Channel, and soon the English coast appeared. To me it was a very wonderful sight.

We removed our heavy equipment and ate our chocolate ration. The radio operator switched us on to the Forces' programme.

We landed shortly before 3 p.m. and were interrogated with the other crews.

As we left the briefing-room I noticed a sign outside which said: "There are only two kinds of combat forces—mobile or defeated." I understand this now, because less than two hours later the crews were being briefed again for another mission.

Monday, May 29, 1944

WATCHED NAVY POUND FRENCH COAST

NO NAZI FIGHTERS OR HEAVY FLAK

AT A UNITED STATES 9TH AIR FORCE MARAUDER BASE, Tuesday.

I was the last correspondent to fly over the Allied beachhead this evening. We took off from this base to bomb gun emplacements on the French coast. The attack was led by the Commanding Officer of this base, Col. Joe W. Kelly.

It was my second attempt in eight hours to fly over the Allied beachhead. My first proved abortive because our plane had to return when we were about five miles off the French coast because of a mechanical failure.

After entering formation over the field here this evening we flew towards the English coast, and set our course for the Allied bridgehead.

Unlike the earlier missions, we had excellent visibility and could see up and down the Channel for many miles. After we had left the coast I suddenly became aware of hundreds of aircraft which thundered over us, forming the area fighter cover.

MASS OF AIRCRAFT

The whole sky as far as one could see in any direction was just one mass of aircraft of every type. Below us, their wings glinting in the sunlight, I could see fighters only a few feet from the water returning to England.

Down below, the Channel looked cold and choppy. Away to the west I saw a sight I shall never forget. Hundreds of craft of every kind were moving towards France. From our height they were only distinguishable by the white wash which churned from their sterns. They looked as if they were strung together by some invisible chain.

Away on the horizon another fleet of vessels moved forward. They were all headed the same way—towards the Allied beachhead.

After some time I could just make out in the distance the coast line between Le Havre and the tip of the Cherbourg Peninsula.

Suddenly below us I saw what appeared to be heavy cruisers. They followed each other in circles, and as each came abreast of the French coast it fired a broadside.

It was a fascinating sight. As they fired their guns a black plume of smoke smudged with crimson flame rolled forward across the water for perhaps 30 to 40 yards.

No sooner had the smoke disappeared from one cruiser than another was firing. We saw them firing as we went in to bomb our target. They were still firing relentlessly when we came out.

Then we saw what must have been thousands of landing craft and shipping of all types dotting the shores and lying off the beach. They stretched for miles from a point low down on the Cherbourg Peninsula.

WHITE PUFFS OF SMOKE

In the distance I could just make out a small town. Two columns of black smoke drifted up. The whole area here was covered with white puffs of smoke like balls of cotton wool. A little past this area another great column of smoke rose to the sky.

Our gunners were tense. We expected that by now the Germans would have thrown in heavy fighter forces—but we need not have worried.

Throughout the whole of the mission and our subsequent return not one member of the formation reported having even seen a German plane. Neither were we bothered with heavy flak. All they could muster was 20mm. Light ack-ack fire.

Our target lay just two miles past a town. It was situated between the beach and a coastal road. I could see the target clearly as we made our bombing run.

This section of the beach was entirely deserted. As the plane levelled off I saw our bombs go pirouetting down to explode with a lurid flash of red flame followed by dense smoke.

SPARKLED WITH FLAME

One by one the other formations, who by now had broken into flights of six, dropped their bombs. The target area sparkled with flame. Then we were in white cloud and the beach was temporarily obscured.

When we came out of this cloud we were some miles from the French coast. Below us the cruisers were still firing. Above us the fighters still patrolled and away to our left streams of shipping continued to flow towards the Allied beachhead.

As far as I could see on the actual beachhead itself everything seemed calm, and but for the towering pillars of smoke it would be difficult to imagine that anything out of the ordinary was taking place.

Our pilot, Lt. John Lytle, set course for England and once again we passed over innumerable convoys of shipping before we finally reached the English coast. We landed here shortly after 8.30 p.m.

Wednesday, June 7, 1944

FLIGHT TO SMASH FRENCH RAIL YARDS

LOW-LEVEL ATTACK

At a Marauder Base, Wednesday.

I have just returned from a low-level bombing attack on a target lying beyond the Allied lines in France. As I write, between 40 and 60 railway trucks and box cars, with their contents, are lying strewn and burning over a large area in what was a railway marshalling yard.

Just after one o'clock to-day the loud-speakers at this station summoned all flying personnel to an urgent briefing. It was short and to the point.

We were addressed by the commanding officer, Col. J. W. Kelly, and Lt.-Col. H. Hankey. "The Germans are trying to move up panzer divisions into the battle area," said Col. Kelly. "This is a crucial point of the invasion. We have got to destroy marshalling yards and everything in them. Go in as low as you dare, but get the target."

IN LEADING PLANE

We took off a little before 2 o'clock. I flew with the leading plane of the formation piloted by Lt.-Col. Hankey. We picked up the remainder of our group, and in a tightly-packed formation headed to the English coast and for the Allied beachhead.

Over the Channel there were still huge convoys of shipping. Hundreds of landing barges and ships of every description were moving in stately line with their fighter escorts weaving just above them.

At one point directly below us I saw a fleet of empty landing craft in line ahead, the white foam from their stern apparently tying them to one another, returning to England. Above them Spitfires frolicked back and forth. They cannot have been more than a few hundred feet above the water.

Above these flew a formation of Lightning fighters weaving in circles. All about us, no matter what way I looked, fighters and bombers thronged the sky.

SUPPLIES STILL ARRIVING

Just before 3 o'clock we crossed the French coast at a point where Allied troops first landed. Here hundreds of ships and landing barges lay off the shore. Supplies were still being unloaded.

Then ahead and below I saw a formation of Spitfires in the distance peeling out of formation to strafe what appeared to be moving vehicles along a road.

One by one they broke formation, rolled over on their sides and dived towards the road. White puffs suddenly appeared from their target on the road, but we had passed and were too far away for me to distinguish what it was.

I followed the white streak of the road for many miles, but nothing moved. We were flying at a very low altitude, and a town lay on our left side. It was a ghastly sight.

Columns of white smoke from burning buildings towered high to the clouds. Below a red glow occasionally burst from burning buildings.

Then against the skyline I could see the towns of what appeared to be Vire, Fler and Vassy. From each of these huge columns of smoke ascended. It was the most awful and fascinating sight I have ever seen.

Suddenly our waist guns opened up and down below on a road I saw a small column of slow-moving tanks or armoured cars. One of these was on fire. Lt.-Col. Hankey immediately called in fighters, and just in front I saw a flight of Thunderbolts which were apparently about to attack the convoy.

Once again our guns opened up. We were firing at more armoured vehicles. The plane vibrated with each burst of machine-gun fire. This was followed by the clang of empty shells striking the floor of the plane. Then we were past and on our way to our target.

SQUARELY ON TARGET

Ahead of us lay the marshalling yard. Our height was just a little over 2,000ft when we began our bombing run. When we reached the target area another flight of Marauders appeared across and dead ahead of us and dropped their bombs squarely on the target.

We had to go below them to avoid collision. We turned and made a second run. I could plainly see about 50 to 60 trucks in two lines in the siding.

Our bombs went down and the area was covered in smoke. We turned and headed for home.

Other formations following behind dropped their bombs in succession until the target was completely obscured by debris and smoke. Throughout the whole of the flight we had seen neither fighters nor anti-aircraft activity.

We reached the French coast and the vast convoy of Allied shipping which lay off the coast had thousands of tiny barrage balloons flying just above them. Continuing across the Channel our waist gunner suddenly reported a dinghy below us.

I looked down and saw the yellow circle of the dinghy. The radio operator immediately called Air Sea Rescue. Then we were heading for our base.

Thursday, June 8, 1944

IN FLAK-SWEPT PLANE TO BOMB RENNES

AIR MASTER-PLAN TO HOLD UP NAZI REINFORCEMENTS

A U.S. NINTH AIR FORCE MARAUDER BASE, Monday.

Marauders of this group this morning blasted a heavily defended marshalling yard at Rennes. The bombers took off from here less than 45 minutes after they had received instructions from United States Ninth Bomber Command.

The briefing was one of the shortest on record for bombers.

It lasted only eight minutes. I flew in the high flight with Major E. A. Rodgers.

We gathered formation over the field and crossed the Allied beachhead in Northern France shortly after noon. Here we picked up our fighter escort of twin-boomed Lightnings. They circled above and on either side of us.

A few miles south of Forges, along a low road which led into the centre of the town, I could see a long convoy of Army vehicles. They included what, from our height, appeared to be armoured cars and tanks.

We were flying at this time at about 11,000 feet when my attention was drawn to the black clouds of anti-aircraft fire which were bursting about 1,000 feet beneath us. Gradually their aim improved and the bursts became higher.

Then the first flight some miles ahead of us was enveloped on either side by flak bursts. Each burst was evenly placed along each side of the flight. We knew that in a few minutes we should have to pass over the same area.

Ahead of us in the distance lay the town of Rennes. At the briefing we had been told that one flight would make for the marshalling yard and a second flight would have as a target a siding some distance to the left of it. Our flight was bombing this siding.

Ahead of us the first flight, still with masses of flak bursting all around it, loosed their bombs, and I watched them as they fell far below on to the long lines of railway trucks and exploded in their midst.

We had turned. We were making our run on our target, the siding. Then suddenly we were in the thick of it.

Flak opened up directly on to our flight. I lay between the waist guns and on each side of our plane through the gun apertures I could see these bursts sailing past.

Tiny fragments of shrapnel rattled all along the plane's fuselage. After every burst the concussion vibrated the whole plane.

PROPELLER HIT

Then there was a sudden bang as one exploded directly beneath us. This was followed by a harsh grating noise and the sound of metal against metal. A piece of shrapnel had gone right through the blade of one of our propellers.

The intensity of the bombardment became worse. Suddenly through the "inter-com" I heard Maj. Rodgers say that his windscreen had been shattered. Then something hit the armoured plate beneath me, and a wisp of black smoke curled into the waist-gun aperture.

The blow was so severe that particles of dirt and cartridge cases lying on the floor of the plane were thrown up.

Then we came into range of the A.A. guns in the marshalling yard, which had turned their attention to us. The bursts were so close that we could actually smell the pungent flak smoke.

The whole formation, covered on either side by flak bursts and bucketing in evasive action, headed for the target. It lay ahead of us, long lines of railway trucks packed closely together.

Then we were over it. I heard the bombardier say: "Bombs away." I looked back. Three huge columns of smoke were rising from both the marshalling yard and the siding.

Once again we were in the midst of flak bursts as we turned from the target. Then we headed for the Allied beachhead.

On our return here we found that our plane had been hit in many places.

Planes examined after the raid showed that a large number had been hit by flak. The C.O., who led the formation, had 116 holes throughout his plane.

With maintenance, armament and radio crews working at full pressure to patch the flak holes, another urgent briefing was called within an hour of the bombers' return. They took off again to bomb marshalling yards at Boetigny, lying south of Paris.

VAST FORCES SEEN

Their mission was a part of the master plan to prevent further reinforcements reaching the Germans. They returned here tonight a little after dusk and reported that the target had been "thoroughly saturated." Smoke was observed rising to a height of nearly 10,000 feet.

Vast numbers of troops and equipment were observed. All along the Seine bridges have been destroyed, and within the last few days the Germans have been throwing across pontoon bridges.

Because of our air superiority over France it is unlikely

that the Germans will be able to move sufficient troops and equipment over the Seine. It is therefore probable that von Rundstedt will have to call on reinforcements from other concentrations coming by rail from Northern France.

It is on this probability that the air forces are continually bombing marshalling yards and railway sidings.

Tuesday, June 13, 1944

NAZI TRAFFIC CENTRE IN UTTER RUIN

BOMBING FLIGHT OVER ST. LO

A U.S. NINTH AIR FORCE MARAUDER BASE, Tuesday.

At 7.15 this morning, from the nose of a B26 Marauder, I saw a shambles that was a town: the town of St. Lo.

The Germans' biggest communication centre in the narrow neck of the Cherbourg peninsula lay below me in utter ruin. Gaunt roofless walls and pitted roads were all that remained after the Allies' ceaseless bombardment and concentrated pattern bombing.

Everything was silent; nothing moved. It was a scene of utter desolation.

The long straight road which runs from Balleroy through the centre of the town was nearly unrecognisable from shell bursts and the flowering circles where bombs had fallen. The only sign of German occupation was a solitary tank, standing in the middle of the town amid the smoking debris.

The Germans still held the town, and this group had orders to bomb the telephone exchange and communication centre lying in a park to the north of it.

CONVOYS FROM COAST

We took off a little after daybreak and crossed the Allied beachhead just after 7 a.m. Despite the early hour, supplies were still being unloaded, and long convoys ran from the coast to the forward positions.

A slight haze hung over the whole area. Away to the right meandered the Vire River, passing just north of St. Lo, and to our left ran the road from Balleroy.

On either side of this road the fields had been so badly bombed that they were just masses of brown earth, no longer covered in green.

On one side a small village was on fire. Apparently it was being shelled. Then ahead of us lay St. Lo. It was easy to recognise it because of the long white road which cuts it practically in half.

In the distance I could see masses of fighter aircraft low over the countryside and above them bombers coming and going over the whole battle area.

MAKING THE RUN

Ahead of us our first formation was already making its bombing run. I saw its bombs fall and explode among the debris below.

A complete pattern fell across the whole area. Then we were over the town and releasing our bombs.

They exploded far beneath us on the target, and we had turned and were leaving the lines behind.

Below us, about three miles inland from the coast, I noticed two airfields already under construction. Each had a runway completed, and below I could see heavy motorised machinery such as bulldozers at work.

Then ahead lay the beachhead armada, with its tiny barrage balloons floating high above, and we were over the coast leaving the smoking ruins of St. Lo far behind.

We had encountered neither A.A. fire nor fighters throughout our six-minute trip over the enemy line.

Wednesday, June 14, 1944

EARLY CAPTURE OF ST. LO EXPECTED

U.S. TROOPS REACH KEY HEIGHTS

WITH THE AMERICAN FORCES IN FRANCE, Sunday.

The fall of St. Lo is not far off. American First Army troops, driving relentlessly forward, have occupied the strategic high ground overlooking the town.

Prisoners are beginning to come in. During the last 24

hours in one sector alone we have taken about 100. Most of these have been in a pitiful condition.

Completely shaken they have complained bitterly of our tremendous artillery barrages, which have been pounding their positions for the past few days.

We now hold all the high ground north and east of St. Lo, and we are, in fact, looking down into the throat of the town. Our line could now be compared to a giant question mark, the tail running parallel to the Periers–St. Lo road.

On this sector to the west, the Germans hold the high ground overlooking this main road. It will be necessary for us to take these heights to gain complete mastery of the area.

The push is being made in the loop of the question mark, which has as its extreme point the salient which has been run down to the little village of La Boulaye.

ONE MILE AWAY

After taking the village of La Luzerne, north-east of the town, troops in this sector have pressed on to within a mile of St. Lo, which lies in a cup with heights on either side ranging to about 500ft above sea-level. While we hold the heights on one side, the Germans hold them on the other.

Their artillery, which since the invasion has been playing a secondary rôle, for the first time started to shell our positions intensively three days ago, but to-day the shelling subsided.

Troops slowly converging on the town met the outposts of a heavily-defended defence line. Our advance has been mainly limited to local actions.

At no time have we thrown in a full and co-ordinated attack, so that this German defence line cannot be compared with previous German defence lines seen in other theatres.

However, it has been and continues to be the strongest the Germans have held since the invasion.

The line is manned by second-line troops reinforced by some sections of crack formations. Among those so far identified are paratroop units, fanatical and ruthless fighters, who do not give in easily.

One group, finding themselves cut off by our advance, fought their way back through our lines. They are well-built and muscular and are certainly the opposite to the second-class troops, who are puny and emaciated.

Among recent prisoners were a number of Alsatians. They said that some of their number had deserted. Those recaptured were immediately sent to the Russian front. They complain of a shortage of food and supplies.

At the other end of the American front in the Lessay area troops advanced a mile, and the town is practically in our grasp.

Monday, July 17, 1944

TANKS POUR INTO THE GAP

MARIGNY, Thursday.

Rapidly advancing American troops and armour to-day achieved the deepest penetration yet made in France.

Gen. Bradley, taking full advantage of the break-through, has been pouring men and tanks through the long funnel which now stretches down from the main Periers-St. Lo road.

There is still some resistance inside this area—but only by small pockets of paratroopers fighting it out to a finish. Our troops advanced so rapidly that they by-passed and outflanked these strongpoints of the Germans' defence.

For the most part these consist of gun nests, which are being wiped out by concentrated artillery fire and fighter-bombers.

The whole area here to-day is a mass of screaming, slithering shells as these points are annihilated one by one.

But the paratroopers are the cream of the German Army. They are not easily frightened, and are returning fire from heavy machine-guns and mortars.

They hold doggedly to their foxholes until they see our infantry with bayonets. Then they give up. They cannot stand cold steel.

This morning I drove down the main Marigny road. Over the same road our armour had moved in a sudden powerful thrust only a few hours before.

Within a few minutes we were in a dirt and dust storm caused by hundreds of vehicles as they thundered along full of armed men.

There were tanks, jeeps, weapon-carriers, half-tracks, armoured tank destroyers, self-propelled guns, again tanks and the inevitable armoured bulldozers.

All the impedimenta of the armoured vehicles of war clattered to the front outside Marigny.

The road was still under small-arms and mortar fire as we passed through the Lozon sector.

The whole area seemed covered by shattering machine gun fire and the whistle of mortars as we rushed along the road.

We were in convoy of armour—and on this front it has priority of movement.

GRAVEYARD OF TANKS
WRECKED GUNS IN FIELDS

This road was a graveyard of German equipment and German paratroopers. Nazi tanks—Mark IV.s and Mark V.s—lay black and smouldering by the sides of the road. Machine-guns and 88s, wrecked and in pieces, lay scattered over the adjoining fields.

Everywhere were grey uniformed German soldiers lying dead by the side of the road.

Examining the German foxholes one understands why the German soldier seems to withstand so well bombing, artillery and mortar fire.

These foxholes are dug very deep and then covered with heavy logs, which are beaten down into the earth.

In one field along the side of the road I saw these holes dug in every 10 yards.

The heavy bombing and artillery fire of the last two days had so churned up this area that as we moved down the road on each side and on the road itself there were huge craters every few yards.

ENTRY INTO MARIGNY
BATTLE ON OUTSKIRTS

Then we had to abandon the jeep as we were nearing Marigny. We moved on foot to the dip, which runs into the town.

Here our troops were entrenched in foxholes overlooking the German defences.

Our machine-guns suddenly opened fire as a German position was observed, and sheets of tracer bullets flashed across the sky.

Then our troops started to move forward. We followed them until we reached the first buildings of the town, but the

Germans put up a powerful barrage of small arms fire and we were unable to reach the centre.

The battle went on here for more than half an hour. Then the company was withdrawn while artillery and fighter-bombers went in to blast the enemy position.

Though we are now well beyond the town German pockets of resistance are still presenting a problem.

Through all this firing ambulances and open jeeps with stretchers strapped across them rushed along the roads coming from the front with our wounded.

ATTACK ON RIDGE
SMOKE SCREEN FOR INFANTRY

Then our artillery began firing against German positions on a ridge outside the town. After a while the guns put down a barrage of fire smoke bombs so that the infantry could advance.

It was remarkable to see flaming tracer bullets passing by the church steeple in the town without apparently even touching it.

Marigny itself does not appear to be much damaged except in the outskirts, where the artillery from both sides has damaged houses.

The town lies in a dip between two ridges. A party of some 50 Germans was still holding out in well-emplaced positions south-east of the town to-night, but our armour was still going through and past to the front.

Some French refugees remained despite the intense battle that had been going on in this area in the last few days.

Friday, July 28, 1944

ROADS TO PARIS BLACK
WITH ALLIED COLUMNS

TANKS MOP UP IN WAKE OF AMERICAN ADVANCE

With Advancing American Armour, Beyond Chartres, Friday.

This is being written by the roadside less than 40 miles from Paris. Allied columns are roaring along the roads to the French capital. There is nothing that can stop them—there is nothing available to the enemy to stop them with.

Officially it is our most forward position, but Allied columns are flying past. Before I have finished they will be many miles ahead. Forward elements are out of touch except by radio with their headquarters, and they are moving so fast that their headquarters are practically unable to keep abreast with the situation.

Since dawn this morning I have travelled 200 miles by car and completed the journey to this point by Piper Cub observation plane. Twice we had to land by the roadside for petrol.

At less than 200 feet from the ground we flew to and fro across the main roads which carry our troops. It was an amazing spectacle.

ROADS BLACK WITH TROOPS

The roads from Argentan to Angers were black with the columns of Gen. Patton's Third Army. The horizon was washed with the smoke of our guns. Fires flickered in the distance, and below the French waved to us as we passed.

We flew just above the dust of the moving vehicles. Tanks, half tracks, self-propelled guns, tank conveyors, tank retrievers, supply trucks, ammunition carriers, infantry trucks, command cars, jeeps, reconnaissance cars, armoured cars, towed artillery and anti-aircraft guns—all the impedimenta of an army hard on the heels of the Germans.

Here and there a few Allied tanks would stop and turn from the road across the open fields with their guns blazing. But the column kept moving.

A few minutes later I could see the blazing hulks of German trucks in the hedges and their crews walking towards the tanks with their hands in the air.

TANKS' PRISONERS

Running before the tanks with their hands in the air, they reached the road. Then they began the long march back to captivity. They went unguarded because nobody had the time to stop and pick them up. The tanks returned to the roadway and continued their advance.

The rolling countryside of shaded browns and greens was alive with Allied troops as we reached the high ground behind Chartres. Suddenly we turned and flew along the edge of a forest.

In a shell-hole a hundred yards ahead of it the pilot had seen something move. We circled the spot while we examined it through glasses. There were five Germans without arms lying in the shell-hole.

The pilot dived down on to it and the Germans at once began to wave white handkerchiefs. We pulled out of the dive and circled them again.

They climbed out of the shell hole and with their hands in the air walked towards the road. We had "captured" five Germans and between us we only had one loaded revolver.

Flying less than 50ft over them we followed them until we saw them reach the road. Then we continued our patrol.

Smoke was pouring from Chartres, which lay to our right. As we flew along the outskirts Allied columns were moving through the town, but fighting was taking place.

The twin spires of the cathedral stood up starkly against the smoke and dust of battle. The crimson streaks of tracer bullets leapt from the half-tracks and armoured cars as they moved through the streets. Parts of the town were ablaze.

Allied infantry, jumping down from their vehicles, were entering the narrow streets.

White bursts of smoke plumed suddenly from buildings as shells exploded. In the midst of the smoke the dust and the orange flashes of Allied guns, a Frenchman, standing in one of the streets, waved a large Tricolor above his head to us.

TOWNSFOLK IGNORED BATTLE

He was not the only one. Hundreds of French people stood openly in the streets at the height of this battle waving to Allied vehicles as they passed through.

We turned in the direction of Dreux with the columns still rolling beneath us. We were running short of petrol, and as the pilot had instructions to find the front line he decided to land and refuel. We circled the small town of Nogent le Roi and then landed just outside the town by the side of the road.

As the plane stopped a jeep pulled up and a colonel came running towards us. He introduced himself and then told us that this was the first Piper Cub observation plane to have reached so far forward. He was an excited and a happy man.

"I have never seen anything like it," he said. "We have been moving all day and the only resistance we have had has been sporadic sniper and machine-gun fire."

"We met several German self-propelled guns this morning all heading towards Alencon. We knocked them out in a matter of minutes. I have not had one casualty since the attack began."

He asked the pilot if he would fly over a road lying towards Chartres. "I think there are Germans trying to escape on bicycles over there—would you have a look?" he said.

The pilot stopped a petrol truck and refuelled his plane and took off to reconnoitre the road.

CHARTRES SURRENDER
BELLS TOLLED SIGNAL

Chartres was set free on Wednesday.

A fusilade of shots died away. In a sudden silence the chimes in the spires of Chartres Cathedral rang out. It was the surrender signal from the four German snipers who all day had held on grimly in the towering steeple.

The tolling of the bells, the cheers of the people and the roar of Allied armour as it careered through the streets proclaimed that resistance had ceased. Chartres was in Allied hands and only 50 minutes away by electric railway lay Paris.

Throughout the campaign in France the Germans, though officially retiring from a town with all their main troops, still leave snipers as rearguards to hold up the Allied advance.

All day on Wednesday these "forgotten men" fought with hand grenades and automatic rifles from the Cathedral. When Allied troops tried to climb the narrow spiral stairs within the spires they were met by hand grenades bowling down the stairs.

One by one these snipers were liquidated by rifle and machine-gun fire from the streets and the remainder surrendered.

Three flags now fly from the top of the tallest spire—the Union Jack, the Stars and Stripes and the French Tricolor.

The city itself has suffered little damage. In the outskirts, where the fighting largely took place, some houses were demolished.

The cathedral, apart from bullet holes, remains untouched.

While the fight was taking place with the snipers in the steeple a priest was asked what his reaction would be if they were forced to use artillery to clear the Germans.

His reply was typically French. He said, "If our men are saved, what difference does it make if all the cathedrals of France are destroyed."

Saturday, August 19, 1944

GERMANS WOULD NOT FIGHT UNDER THE S.S.

FOUND SKULKING IN WOODS

WITH THE ADVANCED U.S. FORCES, ST. QUENTIN, Sunday (delayed).

Fighting in woods in which parties of skulking Germans, long since lost to any unified command, try to hide, the division I am with has a tricky and sometimes dangerous task.

Prisoners come in at the rate of hundreds a day, piled 50 or 60 in lorries. Some of them have made the illuminating remark that they were "not going to fight under the S.S."

The Germans attempt to avoid contact with Allied troops whenever possible as they make their way to the east. When they fight they fight stubbornly, adhering to the text-book rearguard action and fighting until they have no more ammunition.

While they have ammunition they are always dangerous, and when they give themselves up there are always those seconds of doubt as to whether they are "foxing" and may open fire.

Two of our columns of armour and motorised infantry working between Noyon and La Fere have made capital progress. The one to the east, which reached Le Cateau, met stiff resistance, especially in the Busigny woods.

BRIDGES BLOWN UP

All the bridges across the Oise canal or the river had been blown up, but the engineers repaired them swiftly, either with pontoons or treadway.

Whenever the enemy has attempted to check the advance the Allies have side-tracked him. The whole operation can be pictured as a series of "looping" of enemy positions.

During the night tanks crossed the Oise by the determined expedient of turning hands to work and collecting stones, bricks and any other material they could find to construct a ford.

On the slopes by St. Quentin troops are digging themselves in for the night. Each man has his foxhole, into which delighted children are jumping. Little groups are busy cooking in mess tins, which folding handles turn into capital frying-pans.

A little "scrounged" petrol and a few sticks make a hot fire, and a savoury smell pervades this scene of animation.

Unfailingly cheerful, these Americans are full of wise-cracks, but I do wish they had a cup of tea to offer instead of the bumpers of coffee.

Yet within easy reach of all this are still Germans, and it is not to be forgotten. As I came to my bivouac in a wood of tall trees I paused at a fork in the road to ask the way, and a skulker made me jump with a burst of machine-gun fire.

Tuesday, September 5, 1944

MOSELLE LINE BROKEN IN SEVEN PLACES

NAZIS MAY FALL BACK ON SAAR

INSIDE THE SIEGFRIED LINE, Friday.

The Moselle Line has been holed in no fewer than seven places and some of our units are already 15 miles from the Moselle, but the main triumph of the day is the fall of Nancy.

For the past week the 19th Tactical Air Force has been pounding the roads and approaches to the town which Hitler had decreed should be held at all costs, but this morning at 11 o'clock it fell without a shot being fired.

It is probable that the whole line of the Moselle will now swing back to the Saar Valley, leaving France free and Gen. Patton's Army ready to strike through the Siegfried Line and into Germany.

On a heather-covered hillside I stood inside the boundaries of Hitler's Reich. Below was a small bridge over the River Ourthe, the frontier between Luxembourg and Germany.

Above, hidden in mist at the top of the hills, were the outer defences of the Siegfried Line into which American troops had penetrated.

It was the front line down below. We could barely make out a small white postcard village which nestled at the foot of the hill. It was deserted. Its people had fled to outlying farms when the Americans advanced into the Fatherland.

Around us in fields and forests in driving rain were Allied troops beside their guns. Others in more forward positions were lying in foxholes.

SHELLED FROM FORTS

Overhead screamed shells from forts which were plainly visible to the eye across the valley, shells fired by the Germans as our troops in two wet lines began to move up the hill and down the valley on the far side.

Four times in less than 10 minutes I spreadeagled myself in thick mud at the side of the road as these shells burst near. This then was the manner in which we entered Germany—in rain, mud and under shell fire.

Corn and wheat lay stacked. Farmers were working in the fields. Peasants walked or cycled along the roads. All the time there was the sound of shells and mortars.

Apart from the shelling there was silence over the country-side.

The country here was simply a series of heights rising sharply ahead. In between were deep wooded valleys with the white streak of the River Ourthe weaving a line along the boundary.

On top of these heights were a series of forts which, unlike the Maginot Line, were not linked together.

In fact officers commented to me to-day that they could find no communication whatsoever between these forts.

They were built into the side of the mountain. Made of solid concrete, they were camouflaged so well that I was beside one before I realised what it was.

The walls were eight feet thick with a roof of the same thickness. Divided in half by steel doors, they housed six men. But despite the size of these forts they had only one gun. And that was a 30mm machine-gun which seemed hopelessly inadequate considering the strength of the emplacement.

Each fort, in theory, was supposed to cover the next with forward fire. But our infantry fought them one by one up these slopes and even climbed on top of the roof and called through the ventilator to the Germans inside: "Come out and surrender."

Looking at these vast concrete forts and then observing in a narrow slit one small, insignificant machine-gun, I was not surprised that the Germans manning them surrendered.

Saturday, September 16, 1944

'FIGHT ON' CALL BY WOUNDED AT BASTOGNE

EPIC 8-DAY STAND

BASTOGNE, Friday.

Yesterday morning I stood in the wrecked town of Bastogne. Houses were still burning, shells were still landing, and the eerie whistle of mortars sounded in the distance.

But armoured columns were moving through and the pavements were full of pale, sleepy people who had withstood the ordeal of siege and assault without flinching.

The story of Bastogne is so fine that I did not quite know where to start.

Every dirty, bearded soldier, every officer, orderly or cook had a tale of gallantry and heroism. They had gone without food, without medical attention, without sleep, for days on end.

Every one of them, from the commander downwards, lived a life of hell for eight days and nine nights, but not one of them complained. Even the wounded, lying in makeshift hospitals without proper attention, begged the commander not to surrender on their account.

The Bastogne pocket can be likened to an oval five miles long and two and a half miles in width at its narrowest, southern end. The whole perimeter of the line actually covered a distance of 14 miles, with Bastogne lying in the southern end.

When the Germans broke through and began to fan out in all directions, particularly towards Bastogne, this division was ordered to proceed there and to form a line of defence east of the town.

THROUGH BLINDING SNOW

This division received the order to move on Monday, Dec. 18. They were packed into every vehicle that could move. Sometimes as many as 50 men rode in one 2½-ton truck.

Through that day and on through the night, in a blinding snowstorm, this column, miles in length, headed towards Bastogne.

The following morning they reached the area of Bastogne, and the commander, making a swift reconnaissance, bivouacked his units in a fanwise line running east of the town.

Hardly had the whole division taken up position than contact was made with German armoured elements. Moving in columns, they attacked the forward elements of the American division, and for a time succeeded in pushing them farther back towards Bastogne.

For the next 48 hours the situation was confused, to say the least. German columns were reported from all points of the compass.

It was not until midnight on Christmas Eve that the exact position of the Germans about the pocket was established, and at that time it was officially reported Bastogne was completely surrounded.

Fortunately, the telephone wires were still open between the division and corps headquarters. A message from corp headquarters asked the divisional commander for news of the situation.

He replied that he could not give any answer because his lines might be tapped, but said that his position could be likened to "the hole in a doughnut."

In Bastogne the American casualties were being tended by three doctors. They worked day and night.

They had plenty of bandages and other equipment, but they lacked drugs.

The men in the outer defences manning tanks and half-tracks were living in the open in bitterly cold weather, eating only cold rations, but their morale was high. They were killing Germans by the hundreds, and every man held his position until he was knocked out or had knocked out his opponent.

The half-tracks alone perhaps knocked out more tanks than any other weapon. Altogether in the eight days of the siege half-tracks, artillery and the infantry bazooka destroyed 148 tanks and 28 half-tracks. This figure does not include the number accounted for by the air.

AIRMEN TO RESCUE

Then the weather improved, and the sky, which for days had been empty of planes, suddenly filled with fighters and fighter-bombers on Christmas Day.

German tank columns, gun positions, and command posts were wiped out and the shelling of the town temporarily eased.

Then on Tuesday evening at 5.25 the first tanks of relieving armour came to a stop at the shattered town.

Saturday, December 30, 1944

TWO COLUMNS CLOSING ON TRIER

SAARBURG BRIDGEHEAD, Wednesday.

Trier, lying in the valley of the Moselle and reputed the oldest city in Germany, is to-night being shelled as American Third Army infantry and armour draw closer from north and south-west.

The Germans are making frantic preparations to defend it. Fortifications are being dug all about the city's boundaries, and the streets are being barricaded.

Armoured elements which have advanced from the Saarburg bridgehead due north are within 5½ miles of the city. On the other side infantry have drawn in from the south-west to points seven miles from it.

Trier had a peace-time population of nearly 90,000. According to reliable sources orders to evacuate the city were given by Nazi party officials several days ago—but the majority of the population refused to leave.

It is known that the party officials have already fled after proclaiming the city a "fortress to be defended to the last."

The straits to which the Germans have been driven in their search for man-power was illustrated by a group of 400 prisoners whom I saw to-day.

They came from every branch of the German army. Some had been sent to the front line for the first time in five years of war.

There were S.S. men, pay clerks, cooks, Volkssturm, quartermaster and administration units, marines, gunners, medical corps men, supply troops, odd soldiers from mountain brigades—in fact every type from well nigh every unit we have so far encountered.

MOTLEY UNIFORMS

They wore a wide assortment of clothing and badges. Some wore fur caps and sheepskin clothing, others winter German field uniform.

Many, especially the S.S. men, wore the Iron Cross, second class. One youth of 19 with one eye missing had the night before been sent out on a reconnaissance patrol.

He said that his whole battalion had decided that they would not fight the Americans as they had been placed in a position that could not be defended.

The Siegfried defences, built in depth in this area, have literally crumbled. In 24 hours 61 pillboxes and bunkers were captured.

These pillboxes are very much superior to those encountered farther north. Some have electric mortar-throwers, with ammunition fed automatically. The pressing of a button sets the weapon working.

On the whole Third Army front to-day gains of up to one and a half miles were made along a 55-mile front. Our troops captured 15 towns or villages, cleared the important road centre of Bitburg, now a heap of rubble, and entered another small German town.

Tanks and infantry closed up along the Kyll River near Bitburg.

Thursday, March 1, 1945

TRIER BRIDGE WAS CAPTURED INTACT

TRIER, Friday.

American tanks have been roaming through the shattered, desolate streets of Trier for the past 24 hours. All resistance collapsed to-day, and by this evening the city had been captured.

So sudden was this collapse that the main bridge to the south of the city was not destroyed by the enemy.

By mid-day our tanks were roaring across to continue mopping up in that part of the city on the northern bank of the Moselle.

A second bridge farther up the river was destroyed by well-placed explosives, but this operation was nullified by the first bridge being captured intact.

The task force I travelled with was the second one to enter the city since dawn, and we met little trouble. That was not the case with the first force.

On one road leading into the city there is grim evidence of how effective artillery fire can be. After crawling over fields and along the fringes of woods, we slowly began to approach Trier. As we entered the outskirts the scene was one of complete destruction.

Tanks rumbled by in a haze of dust. Solitary civilians standing at the doorways of their wrecked houses looked on in a dazed, bewildered fashion.

Sheets and towels hung from windows and doorways in mute surrender, but in most cases the occupants of the houses had long since fled.

As we drove along the road running by the river American infantrymen marched by leading perhaps 300 German prisoners, while on the bridge hundreds more were lined up to be marched away. Long columns of prisoners were coming from all directions.

A door opened and out walked a member of the Volkssturm with his revolver in one hand and the other raised high in the air. Without a word he walked across the road, handed over his revolver and climbed on a jeep in front of us.

At the Porta Nigra Hotel, near the Roman-built Porta Nigra Arch, an American soldier climbed to set the American flag flying from a flagpole. As he did so two Germans walked out of a house next door beneath a white flag and surrendered to soldiers outside the hotel.

Trier Cathedral, one of the oldest in the world, lies in ruins, while the Basilica nearby has also suffered.

The Roman Amphitheatre and Roman baths have also been greatly damaged. Practically two-thirds of the city has been completely wiped out.

Saturday, March 3, 1945

RHINE VILLAGERS HAVE LOST THEIR TASTE FOR WAR

WITH THE UNITED STATES THIRD ARMY. A Village Near the Rhine.

From the top of a tall flagpole just outside this village there hangs a new German flag. It is the white flag of surrender and it flutters all the way back to the Kyll river, from every village, house, cottage or barn that still stands.

There are not many villages still standing along the path that Gen. Patton's tanks took when they made their spectacular dash for the Rhine a week ago. There are few like this one which has not suffered a bullet hole.

Before the tanks came rumbling along the roads like dinosaurs to bring war and all its miseries to the people of the Eifel country, the swastika, garish and ugly, flew over their villages from specially erected flagpoles. Now this symbol of a catastrophic regime has gone and it will never fly from these proud poles again. Yet it will be long remembered by these people who wander back now, along roads and through fields, looking for a place to live, a place where they can begin to readjust their lives. Typifying Hitler and the New Order it will be remembered not for the glories of the past but for the miseries which followed.

For war has been brought to these bewildered and disillusioned people in a fashion so terrible that they still cannot believe it and, though they fail to realise that they are lucky to be alive, they know that there is absolutely nothing to look forward to but many years of military occupation.

TRIED TO RACE THE TANKS

The civilians that tread the roads back from the Rhine are those that tried to race the advancing Americans and cross to the safety of the eastern bank. But the tanks moved faster than they did and they were cut off between their torn villages and the long armoured arm that shot out suddenly in a semicircle in front of them.

Some of them reached places like Andernach, which lies just above Coblenz, from villages lying close to the Rhine like Polch or Kehrig; but they found that the solitary ferry operating between the two banks was for German military personnel only.

Then Andernach was captured and these confused people turned west again, with their dog-drawn carts, farm carts, bicycles, and wheelbarrows piled high with their belongings, and began the long trek back.

They know that they cannot expect help from their conquerors, though some of the more courageous try to win over American soldiers by being friendly. Some of these beg for lifts in passing jeeps or trucks, offering schnapps or some other gifts. They smile and those that speak English will invariably tell you that they hate Hitler and that it was all a terrible mistake. German women especially are more adept than men in this form of fraternisation. They will tell you that they had no part in this at all and that they do not hate Americans.

NO "FRATERNISATION"

When the American soldiers refuse to converse with them or accept their proffered gifts, and abruptly tell them to keep moving, their attitude changes. Then Americans are not "gentlemen" any more, they are "evil people."

One woman, in a towering rage, said: "I am shocked at the attitude of the Americans; we had no idea that you would act like this." The men are different. They are sullen and beaten and prepared to accept the overrunning of their country. They will tell you that Germany has lost the war and that it must end in a few weeks or perhaps months; that Germany cannot hold out much longer; that they knew it would end in disaster for Germany; that they have always liked Americans; and that Hitler is the cause of it all.

It is difficult for the American soldier to believe this because he knows that his friends have been killed or wounded, perhaps a few days before, by soldiers who, when captured, have made the same statements. Though the American soldier is a very good-natured and good-humoured individual, I find that he is intensely bitter towards German civilians and wants to have nothing to do with them. From what I have seen I do not think that there need be an enforcement of the non-fraternisation order during war-time if the Americans continue to treat the German civilians in the same manner as now.

In villages left intact—and in a circuitous route of nearly 90 miles I only saw half a dozen—the German people are beginning to understand just how difficult war can be when an army moves in on them. All the houses required are taken over in a few hours and the occupants told to move on. They protest, but it is of no avail, and if they do not leave the order is enforced in no light-handed manner.

OUT THEY MUST GO

In villages in the forward area civilians are moved out altogether. Further back, churches, schools, town halls and theatres have become communal centres for the homeless. Hundreds of German people are crammed into these places and there they exist as best they can. They receive nothing from the military authorities except medical aid and they fend for themselves.

In a region such as the Eifel mountains this is not difficult as it is mainly an agricultural area and the majority of these people, when forced to leave their homes, bring with them large quantities of food. Those whose homes have been completely destroyed and who have nothing left are helped by their friends or relatives.

Their attitude on the whole is one of pained surprise that this should happen to them. They do not like being turned out of their villages even though they have been partially destroyed, but particularly if their village has been unscathed they object very strongly.

One little example will perhaps show just how firm Americans are being with people who object to such orders. It occurred in a village near the front which had not been touched.

An American officer gave the occupants of one house one hour to leave and the daughter, who spoke excellent English, objected very strongly. The officer, repeating the order, said, looking at his watch, "You will have one hour to leave from now." The German girl stood before him and said: "Sir, you are no gentleman." The officer glanced once again at his watch and said: "I will now give you exactly five minutes to get out." They had left by the end of five minutes.

Wednesday, March 14, 1945

WHOLESALE MURDERS IN NAZI PRISON CAMP

U.S. TROOPS SHOW GERMANS S.S. MEN'S HANDIWORK

WITH U.S. THIRD ARMY, CENTRAL GERMANY, Sunday.

The partly-clad bodies of 31 men lying huddled grotesquely together where they had been killed by S.S. guards because they were too ill to be moved have been discovered in a bleak prisoner-of-war enclosure near the village of Ohrdruf, about 10 miles south of Gotha, in Thuringia.

In an unpainted wooden shed nearby men of the Fourth Armoured Division found 50 more bodies. They had been sprinkled with quicklime.

Those in the hut had died either from starvation, torture or disease, or they had been beaten to death. Those in the small group before the hut had been shot in the back of the head, with the exception of one American, who had been shot in the throat.

The American authorities ordered a party of prominent people in Ohrdruf to come to the murder camp and there witness the horrors that had been performed by the S.S. men.

They were taken to the camp in trucks. Included in the party as a result of a mistake by the burgomaster were three women. On their arrival the American officer in charge said: "Even Americans would not show such a terrible sight to German women."

"ALWAYS ENEMIES"
COLONEL'S STATEMENT

The men were grouped around the place, where bodies lay shot in the head and throat. Then Col. Hayden Sears, of Boston, said out loud:

"Now you know why we will never be your friends; why we will always hate you; why we will always be your enemies."

The Burgomaster and his wife were not present. They saw the sight the day before. This morning they were both found hanging by the neck, their wrists slashed.

It is thought that both committed suicide because they were afraid to be present with the townsfolk during the conducted tour of the murder camp.

The names of the 28 people who attended were taken and they were told that they would be witnesses at the trial of the S.S. men when they were arrested and charged as war criminals.

Many of them said that they did not know what had been going on. They said that it was the work of a small minority and did not indicate the real feelings of the German people.

They were told that this was the work of men that the German people put in power and that we hold the German people responsible.

HELD 2,000 PRISONERS
GUARD OF 150 S.S. MEN

This camp, known as "Concentration Lager North S.3," had held 2,000 prisoners, Germans, Czechs, Serbs, Slavs, Russians, French, Bulgars and Belgians under the guard of 150 of Hitler's murderous S.S. men.

One of the prisoners was an American soldier. He is reported to have been a paratrooper, though there was no identification tags on his body when examined.

The S.S. guards became uneasy and marched away those who could walk and ruthlessly murdered those who were ill or wounded or who could not walk.

According to one who hid, some 2,000 others died and were piled in a hut and then taken in trucks to a pit in the woods about two miles away, where they were burned.

When the Americans were but five miles away from the camp the last of the prisoners were marched off and those who could not march were ordered out of their huts and told to stand to attention.

Some 53 other prisoners had been ordered to remain behind and their first task was to fill in the pit and to act as burial party for the 31 bodies lying before the hut.

But the tanks of the Fourth Armoured Division were drawing closer and the S.S. men left hurriedly and the majority of the burial party fled to the woods or hid beneath beds.

PRISONERS RETURN
STORIES OF TORTURE

When prisoners of the burial party told their story to a German interpreter the Americans hesitated to believe it and immediately sent out a squad of men under the command of Army Surgeon Maj. John R. Scotti, of Brooklyn. They found that the horrible story was true.

"I could not believe it even when I saw it," said Maj. Scotti. "I could not believe that I was there looking at such things."

Other prisoners who escaped have drifted back and they tell stories of how prisoners have been flogged to death, shot, tortured, and maltreated. There were so many cases that they are unable to remember the number.

They said that the S.S. man in command had many different methods of torture, his most popular one being to make a prisoner stand stiffly to attention until he collapsed then revive him and make him stand upright again. This often lasted 24 hours or more.

On several occasions small groups of men were required for mysterious missions described as "labour in underground shelters."

All the inmates of the camp would be lined up and the Commandant would walk down the lines of the prisoners smoking a cigar. Then he would stop before a group of men, remove the cigar from his mouth, and, with a contemptuous flick of the cigar, would indicate the group he wanted. Those that left for "labour in underground shelters" were never seen again.

The camp lies in a small valley, and on one side are modern military barracks. On the far side is situated this collection of huts. They are without windows and without heat. The whole camp is surrounded by a high double fence of rusted barbed wire with high wooden towers from which S.S. guards watched the prisoners.

There are 80 prisoners who escaped living in the camp now, and because of its filthy condition it has been placed out of bounds for American troops.

Former prisoners are being held there in temporary quarantine until the authorities can decide what to do with them.

Monday, April 9, 1945

GENERAL SHOT HIMSELF AT SURRENDER

PILSEN FREED

PILSEN, Monday.

Pilsen, the first Czech city to be captured by the United States Third Army, was the scene of the biggest demonstrations the American troops had seen since the liberation of Paris.

The city was surrendered by Maj.-Gen. George Majewiski, the garrison commander, who shot himself before his own staff and the American officer of the 16th Armoured Division to whom he surrendered.

He had promised the city's authorities that he would surrender the city when the tanks came near. He kept his word. After taking the surrender of the city the American officer stepped out of the room for a moment.

On his return he heard Gen. Majewiski's wife and staff begging him not to commit suicide. But it was of no avail. Before the American officer realised what was going to happen the general raised a revolver to his head and pulled the trigger.

His wife stepped forward and wiped the blood from the General's face. She did this, according to witnesses, without the slightest emotion.

CITY EN FETE

Outside the building the citizens were cheering and singing. The whole city was en fete.

When the general commanding the 16th Armoured Division appeared at an upper window of the town hall, the square in front was filled to overflowing with thousands of people who burst into song, repeating over and over again the National Anthem of Czechoslovakia.

From every window and tower Czech flags were flying.

After six years the people of Pilsen were freed and they showed their thanks by mobbing every American soldier. It was the same in all the small Czech towns the tanks passed through. In one the people immediately renamed the main square "Roosevelt Square."

Tuesday, May 8, 1945

TOJO SHOT HIMSELF TO ESCAPE TRIAL

EYE-WITNESS TELLS OF SUICIDE ATTEMPT

MACARTHUR ROUNDING UP WAR CRIMINALS

"PEARL HARBOUR" CABINET TO BE ARRESTED

Gen. MacArthur, Allied Supreme Commander, last night ordered the arrest of 39 Japanese and quisling war criminals, including the members of the Tokyo Cabinet that was in office at the time of the attack on Pearl Harbour in December, 1941.

The announcement followed swiftly on the news that Gen. Tojo, one of the men due to be arrested, had attempted suicide by shooting himself with a revolver just below the heart. He was Japanese Prime Minister at the time of Pearl Harbour and until July, 1944. He is 64.

It was stated last night that Tojo might live. He was kept alive with injections of American blood plasma.

In an eye-witness account, our correspondent states that Tojo's act was an attempt to avoid arrest and trial. "I would not like to be judged by a conqueror's court," he said.

Among Tojo's accomplices to be arrested are Togo, who, as Foreign Minister, was conducting negotiations with the United States when the Japanese attacked Pearl Harbour; and Lt.-Gen. Masahara Homma, responsible for the Bataan "death march."

DRAMA IN TOJO'S ROOM
From CORNELIUS RYAN,
Daily Telegraph Special Correspondent

BY TOJO'S BEDSIDE, YOGA SUBURB, TOKYO, Tuesday.

Here in the study of this typical wooden Japanese house Tojo, former Prime Minister of Japan—nicknamed "The Razor" because of his pointed features—the man primarily responsible for plunging Japan into war, lies seriously wounded, perhaps mortally.

He shot himself in an effort to evade arrest by American Counter-Intelligence officers following out an order by Gen. MacArthur issued this morning to take him into custody as the first war criminal to be arrested by the Occupation Forces.

The shot entered his chest just below the heart and the bullet came out through his back. It happened at 4.18 Tokyo time [8.18 a.m. B.S.T.] to-day.

I was outside the window, within two yards of him, when he pulled the trigger.

At 4.10 the officers entered the open door of Tojo's house, which is situated in one of the most exclusive parts of Tokyo, and asked to see the former Prime Minister, who was virtually dictator up to the time Japan began to suffer reverses two years ago.

They were met in the hall by bland, smiling Shigetohatake, his secretary, who said he would inform his master. He came out of the sitting room a moment later and said that Tojo would see them if they would first state "their mission," and asked if they had come to arrest him.

CRACK OF SHOT
OFFICERS KEPT WAITING

At that moment Tojo came to a window and saw half a dozen correspondents who had accompanied the intelligence officers. He stood there a moment and a photographer took a picture.

Tojo promptly closed the window. Intelligence officers, meanwhile, were producing their authority to arrest him. There was the sudden crack of a shot.

He had decided to commit suicide rather than be arrested. His secretary had deliberately held up the officers to give his master time.

Somebody shouted, "He's beaten us to it." Expecting that the gendarmerie, who were all over the gardens and the house, might take the shot as a signal to start shooting at us, everybody, including the correspondents, drew automatics and charged into the house.

The door to the study was locked. The intelligence officers and correspondents shouldered the door and burst it off its hinges.

SMILED AT OFFICERS
TOLD TO DROP REVOLVER

Lying in an armchair in the middle of the room lay Tojo, smiling quietly at us. He still held a Colt automatic in his right hand. An American officer shouted: "Drop that gun."

Tojo dropped the gun limply. The officer promptly stepped into the room and picked up the weapon.

The Japanese leaned back. Blood began to squirt from his chest. He closed his eyes. A fly which had been buzzing over his head settled on his sweating brow. He was wearing a white shirt, grey-blue military riding breeches and brown riding-boots.

Behind him was a divan. Above it hung a painting eight feet by six, depicting Tojo on horseback standing on a bluff, and behind him members of his staff, also mounted, reviewing a stream of armoured cars and tanks moving along a road.

In the foreground of the picture lay a Chinese flag, still on its short mast. It was crumpled and dirty. The artist had painted upon it the marks of the vehicles which had passed over it.

At Tojo's right foot was a box of matches. On a small circular table by his right hand stood an ash tray, with several cigarette ends and a tin of Japanese cigarettes called "Hope," with the words "finest Virginian" underneath.

On a window-sill was a glass with a Japanese design in purple. At the bottom of the glass was sediment, and it appeared that Tojo had taken something to give him the strength to perform the act.

Beside the glass was a silk bag, gold and purple with a golden tassel. It was the bag which contains the ceremonial hara-kiri knife, but the knife was not there.

In one corner of the room stood a tall hat-rack. In another corner was a cedar-wood cupboard. In this cupboard were several Japanese books, automatic revolvers, German, American and Japanese, and ammunition to fit.

There were also several sheets of paper, being the history of Tojo's family.

On the other side of the room, by the door, hung tapestry, the red, white and purple ceremonial Japanese dragon, with fire shooting from its mouth.

There in the simplicity of this room lay the wounded man. He was slowly bleeding to death before our eyes.

Blood seeped across his shirt to his breeches. It seeped through the upholstery of the chair in which he was slumped and was gathering underneath in a large, spreading pool.

Tojo groaned. He clenched and unclenched his hands in a

spasm of agony. He writhed in the chair and bent his knees, with his hands and face twitching.

His secretary, who had been trying to push through the crowd of officers and correspondents, reached his master and with his hands joined began crying bitterly. He placed his arms around Tojo's head and held it lovingly, moving it gently back and forth to the accompaniment of his bitter wailing.

At this point Tojo sank rapidly as if he was prepared to die. But in a few moments he rallied.

"I will become a god to protect our land after my death," he said. Again he paused.

By this time his shirt and trousers were saturated with blood and a small, neat hole in his chest was turning blue around the edges. I felt his pulse. It was hardly perceptible, slow and irregular.

Then, this bald, evil-faced man calmly opened his eyes. Turning to one of his servants, he said: "Give me a cup of water, Hatakiyama." Then he closed his eyes again.

CORPSE FOR MACARTHUR
TOJO'S DEFIANCE

He began to groan and mutter something unintelligible. The servant returned with water and a white cloth. He was followed by another servant, also carrying a glass of water and a white cloth.

Tojo drank some water and the servant wiped his master's sweating head.

Then Tojo began again. "If by mistake I am still alive I know the way to commit hara-kiri. I have ended my responsibility."

Then, in voice stronger than before he said, "Let MacArthur have my corpse. For my corpse I do not care. I told my family all about it. But tell MacArthur that I am not to be shown in public."

That was the finish of his speech. A few moments afterwards he lapsed into unconsciousness.

The chief of Tojo's house guards entered the room, bowed, smiled and begged permission to move him to the bedroom. This request was refused, as the officers did not wish to move him until the arrival of the doctor. He withdrew.

A doctor had been sent for, but up to this time, now nearly

4.40, he had not appeared. Minute by minute blood was flowing faster. At precisely 4.40 the Japanese opened his eyes and began to speak in a voice hardly audible.

Somehow he gathered strength, and between pauses and lapses into unconsciousness made the statement, which was taken down by my interpreter.

TOJO'S STATEMENT
"TAKING SO LONG TO DIE"

He said: "I wished to die by one shot. I am dry. I am sorry it is taking so long to die. The Greater Asiatic War was a just and righteous one, but I am very sorry for the Asiatic nations and all other races for having lost the war."

He stopped for a moment. The strain was too much. He twisted his chair.

Then he began again. He said: "I would not like to be judged before a conqueror's court. I wait for the righteous judgment of history.

"I wanted to commit hara-kiri but sometimes that fails. I wish to die . . . to die . . ."

His voice trailed away, then suddenly came back. ". . . to die by one shot, and please do not make me breathe or care again, because I am happy if I can go to the Land of the Emperors under the spiritual protection of his Majesty the Emperor. By that I wish to help the healthy progress of our nation.

"There are many ways to act as a man of responsibilities, but I did not wish to be judged by conquerors." His lips twisted into a grim smile.

"The conqueror makes his own judgment," he said. "As to my family, I have asked Count Hiroishi to look after them. Banzai to my family and the Emperor."

JAPANESE DOCTOR
WOULD NOT TRY TO SAVE TOJO

At 5.8 a Japanese doctor with a nurse arrived.

The doctor first surveyed the wounded man casually, in a resigned way, and then requested that the divan be moved close to the window. Four of us did so.

Tojo, who was apparently conscious that somebody was

removing his shirt and cleaning blood from his body, opened his eyes and looking at the doctor said: "Don't plug the holes; this body is my own."

The doctor answered: "I must clean the wound and body, at least."

One American officer, Lt. Wilpers, after hearing this from the interpreter, said to the doctor: "You do everything in your power to help him." The doctor refused point blank.

He was fully aware that Tojo wanted to die, and he did not care to treat him because he had been ordered by Tojo not to do so.

Lt. Wilpers repeated sternly the order, and at 5.51, nearly one hour after his arrival, the doctor began trying to plug the wounds.

Tojo was gradually fading. But he rallied once again to say to the doctor: "I did not shoot myself in the head so that people could recognise me."

In a haphazard manner the doctor tried to plug the wounds and the whole time Tojo, with what little strength remained, tried to fight him, refusing to help when the doctor tried to turn him over to get at the wound in his back.

Eventually Tojo collapsed from loss of blood, and lay there groaning and with his legs twitching. All this time photographers were taking pictures from every angle. Correspondents were sitting, notebooks ready, waiting for him to die.

At six o'clock the doctor reported that Tojo "shot himself directly through the heart." There was no hope for him. Already his pulse was failing rapidly.

FIGHT FOR LIFE
ARMY DOCTORS ACT QUICKLY

But 24 minutes later an American ambulance, containing two Army doctors and a man of the Medical Corps, arrived at the house. They rushed into the room and were followed by military police who cleared the room, leaving the officers and correspondents at the doors.

Then began a fight for Tojo's life. Here was a strange twist of fate. American doctors, who probably hated Tojo, were fighting for his life, because he was a human being.

The Japanese doctor was ordered to one side. Lt. Aguino, of Los Angeles, deftly and swiftly began to treat the wounded man.

Capt. Johnson promptly ordered a plasma injection and the hat-rack was hauled to the bedside and acted as a stand for the plasma bottle.

After cleaning the wound in the chest, Capt. Johnson, without giving Tojo an anaesthetic, began to sew the wound, which was immediately padded and strapped with pieces of adhesive tape.

Then Tojo was turned over and the same operation was performed on his back. Capt. Johnson asked the Japanese doctor how much morphine he had given Tojo. The Japanese said "None." Capt. Johnson was obviously annoyed by the lack of medical care, and immediately ordered an injection.

Capt. Johnson was working rapidly in a manner which made the Japanese doctor look on in wonderment. The blood which had flowed for more than two hours and a half was staunched. The room was simply a mass of blood, and, looking at it, I could not help but wonder how Tojo could still be alive. Yet he was and the plasma bottle was slowly dripping blood— American blood which had arrived in Japan only a few days ago—into his veins.

A BARE CHANCE
BULLET NICKED HEART

Capt. Johnson stated after the operation that he was unable to state whether Tojo would live, but "there is a bare chance that the blood plasma may save him.

"The bullet nicked the bottom of the heart. Passing through the sixth and seventh ribs it left the chest. There is just a chance that we may have cheated Tojo's easy way out."

Shortly afterwards Tojo was removed to the 1st Medical Squadron of the 1st Cavalry Regiment at Meiji Park, near the Meiji Shrine, where he was given more blood.

Later he was moved to the 98th Evacuation Hospital, in the Ohtori elementary school at Yokohama.

At the hospital he was immediately taken to the operating theatre and given another blood transfusion. In all, Tojo received 1,100cc. of blood.

On the operating table he came to and asked for a glass of water, and later another. Both were given him. Later Gen. Eichelberger entered.

Tojo, who had regained consciousness, said to Gen. Eichelberger's interpreter: "I am going to die anyway, so don't go to any trouble over me."

Photographers were allowed to enter the operation theatre and doctors removed their face masks so that they could be photographed. Doctors and attendants dipped pieces of cotton wool into Tojo's blood for souvenirs.

Tojo was taken upstairs to the room where he now lies, with nine armed guards in the room and outside.

A midnight report from Gen. Rice, an Eighth Army surgeon, superintending three senior doctors who worked on Tojo, said to-night that Tojo's condition was fair and the prognosis was fair. It was also stated by Col. Shaw that "for a man of his age he has a very good chance." Tojo is 64.

Wednesday, September 12, 1945

The Major of St. Lô

Normandy, June

In the little French town of St. Lô, the elders often gather on the bridge over the river Vire to talk about that which elders know most about—the past. And at this time of the year, now that the apple orchards are in blossom once again and the sun drenches the countryside, there is much to remember. Was it not another time like this, back in 1944, when the invasion began across the beaches only a few miles away? How many brave men died in the hedgerows? And who would believe now that twelve years ago all that remained of St. Lô was a pile of rubble—the aftermath of the invasion's greatest battle? So it goes. But as always, when they talk of the war, the conversation soon turns to the day the town was liberated after 43 days of battle, and to the story of their own personal hero, the American soldier they call the "Major of St. Lô" —a man they never knew.

And if in the telling there is much brandishing of canes and much quivering of down-swooping Norman mustaches, it is only because some point has not been emphasized enough or some detail has been momentarily forgotten. For it is the story of the "Major of St. Lô" that the elders love best—and here on the bridge that saga has been interwoven with legend and the legend has become inseparable from history.

The kerosene lamp hissed quietly. In his battalion command post Major Thomas D. Howie eased his stocky frame into a more comfortable position against the earthen wall. Outside it was dark, but war has no real night. Along the 40-mile American beachhead heavy guns flashed intermittently; streams of tracer bullets waved up into the clouds; and flares hung here and there in the sky.

In the command post—an oversized foxhole with the remains of a barn over it as a roof—the major and his company commanders sat watching Captain William Puntenney, of Phoenix, Arizona, Howie's executive officer, mark up the battalion situation map. Working on the map's plastic overlay with a grease pencil, Puntenney quickly sketched in the 29th Division's latest positions. "That's the picture, Major," he said.

The front lines remained much the same—Howie could see that at a glance. Here a field had been taken or lost; there a ditch or sunken road had been captured or recaptured. But the advance of the 29th, "the Blue and the Gray" Division, through the bloody hedgerows of Normandy could be measured in yards. Major Howie's unit—the 116th Infantry's 3d Battalion—had gained less than 100 yards in 24 hours. But it was within three miles of the division objective—St. Lô.

Howie ached to take St. Lô, as did every battle-weary soldier in the division, right up to Major General Charles H. Gerhardt, the commanding general. Once the town with its vital network of roads fell, the full force of American armor could begin to maneuver and the longed-for breakout might be achieved. For beyond the pile of rubble that had once been a town the hedgerows ended and the plains began.

The Germans appreciated what St. Lô's loss would mean. Until their front could be reinforced, the Allied forces had to be contained in their shallow bridgehead, their backs to the sea. And what better place to fight for time than in these natural trenches of Normandy, where mounds of earth topped by a jungle of bushes surrounded every field? The German high command had issued the order: "*Starre Verteidigung*." ("Stand fast.")

But to Tom Howie the capture of St. Lô had become a personal matter. The men of the 3d Battalion had fought almost continuously for 41 days without rest—from the moment they hit Omaha Beach on the misty morning of June 6th. That morning the thirty-six-year-old major (a former English literature teacher and athletic director at Staunton, Virginia, Military Academy) had captured a machine-gun post, single-handed. Howie felt that casualties alone had earned his men the right to be first into St. Lô. And when they took it, maybe the whole battered division would be relieved.

Tonight in the smoky closeness of his command post the major had little time to think about relief. His foot soldiers were dug in near Martinville, a hamlet straddling a dirt road leading into St. Lô. And the fighting had been toe to toe all day. The 3d Battalion and the Germans laced one another's hedgerow positions with machine-gun fire, tossed hand grenades across the narrow fields, fired rifles at one another at almost point-blank range.

But a mile to the south, on the outskirts of La Madeleine, a small village near St. Lô, Major Sidney Bingham's 2d Battalion was in much greater trouble. The Second had been hit with everything the Germans could throw at them—from artillery bombardment to tank assault. Now they were surrounded and cut off. Out of food, short of ammunition and with casualties mounting, their situation was hourly becoming more desperate.

Major Howie studied the new attack order before him. He had many vital decisions to make within the next few hours. The Third had been ordered to attack directly through the Germans' tough Martinville line. Howie was going to the rescue of Bingham's lost battalion.

While other units of the division were to attack on either side of his battalion, Howie's men had been given the toughest assignment. The Martinville line had held them up for days; now they were being asked to drive through it fast and advance more than a mile. Although all the other officers present knew how Major Howie itched to capture St. Lô, none saw the bitter disappointment for him in the attack order. After relieving the lost battalion, Howie's unit was ordered to stand fast and hold the La Madeleine positions. *Bingham's men were to push on to St. Lô.*

Howie outlined his plan: the battalion would make a silent attack, using bayonets and hand grenades—nothing else. "We're going to give the jerries a touch of steel," he said quietly.

At the end of the briefing, Howie asked his executive officer, Puntenney, to stay behind. When the two were alone, the major spoke: "Bill, take a look at these boots. I've had the same shoes since I left the States. Look at 'em! I've marched and fought in 'em for days. But I'll be damned if I'll make one more attack without a new pair."

"Where in the world am I going to get you a new pair now?" said the surprised exec.

"Bill—I don't care where you get 'em, but get 'em," the CO barked.

Puntenney left the dugout to carry out the order.

In the dank blackness of their foxholes, Howie's men quietly sharpened their bayonets and sweated out the dawn. In his own lighted dugout Tom Howie read his Bible, as he did every night, and wrote a letter home. Earlier he had written his wife, Elizabeth, and their six-year-old daughter at Staunton: "I have no physical reason for thinking so, but I've always felt that your prayers would be answered and that we'd have a grand reunion some fine day." Now, he wrote to another member of his family: "There is no need to worry about me. . . ." He did not mention the impending attack.

It began at 4:30 A.M. A thick early-morning fog carpeted the area when Howie—in a new pair of boots—and his veterans fixed bayonets and rose quietly out of their foxholes. Ahead of them the German hedgerows lay quiet, as though anesthetized. In silence the helmeted figures slipped quickly from their hedgerow positions and disappeared into the fog.

They raced across the cut-up fields, soft earth deadening their footsteps. Nobody spoke. They darted into the hedgerows. Bushes rustled. Twigs cracked sharply. There was a startled shout. Suddenly all along the German line there were quick shouts, muffled screams, the compressed blast of grenades, the abrupt stuttering of Schmeisser "burp" guns—the awful commotion that soldiers make when they are surprised into death.

The first German positions fell fast. Howie's men were through and beyond before the enemy knew what had happened. Deftly, quickly, the men of the Third hit the next line of outposts, and the next. In this way, with surgical preciseness, the major's battalion cut through the Martinville line in less than an hour. Shortly before 6:00 A.M. Howie's men made contact with Major Bingham's 2d Battalion east of La Madeleine.

Down the road, not more than a mile away, lay bombed and shelled St. Lô, the shattered spires of the Cathedral of Notre Dame reaching defiantly out of the heaping ruins. To Howie's cocky infantrymen, huddling in their foxholes, St. Lô seemed only a bus stop away.

The staffs of the two battalions immediately conferred. The linkup, at best, was only temporary. Although the 29th

Division's dawn attack along the St. Lô front had been successful, with troops now almost astraddle the heights overlooking the town, it would be some time before supply lines could be opened. Howie's men had brought communications, ammunition, medical supplies, rations and—more important —themselves. La Madeleine could be held, but it was obvious that the relieved 2d Battalion was exhausted. After three days of almost continuous assault its ranks had been decimated. Bingham's men could not push on to St. Lô. The job was up to Howie—if regimental headquarters agreed.

Howie waited impatiently for his communications to be set up. Speed mattered now. If the Third pressed on before the Germans fully recovered from the attack, Howie felt sure his men could make St. Lô. But the Germans wouldn't sit still for long, especially with a strong force sitting on their doorstep. Both Howie and Bingham knew better.

So did Major General Gerhardt back at division headquarters.

All night Gerhardt had sweated out the advance of his men. Previously he had told his assistant division commander, Brigadier General Norman (Dutch) Cota, to assemble an armored task force and hold it in readiness to dash into St. Lô from the north. Now, as he stood before his big war map with Cota, he thought about this powerful trump card. Had the time come up to send Task Force "C" storming into St. Lô?

"You better get ready, Dutch," he said. "Sometime within the next twenty-four hours, you'll be on your way. It's near the end, but it isn't over yet. Jerry's going to counterattack hard wherever he can." He tapped the map with a forefinger. "And particularly here. They'll throw everything they've got at La Madeleine."

At La Madeleine the lull had already ended.

Far away, the trained ears of the infantrymen heard the shrill birth of the first barrage of mortar shells. They held their breath, listening in the strange hypnotic way that soldiers listen to determine direction by sound. Down they crouched in their foxholes. The barrage screamed toward them like a hundred express trains all converging on a lonely station. The earth shuddered. Bursting shells fine-combed the ground above them. Then it was over and the next shelling began.

Howie crawled from foxhole to foxhole. "Keep down!" he

yelled at his men. "Keep down. We're getting out of here soon. We'll get to St. Lô yet."

Doubled up, dodging from foxhole to foxhole in between shell bursts, he returned to his command post. His company commanders were waiting for him.

"Have you got regiment?" he demanded.

Somebody handed him a phone. Above the noise Howie tried to explain the position quickly.

"The Second can't make it," he yelled into the phone. "They're too cut up. They're exhausted. Yes—we can do it. We're in better shape. Yes—if we jump off now. Okay." A big smile crossed his face.

"See you in St. Lô," he said.

He slammed the phone down and, still smiling, turned to his company commanders. "Well, you heard it," he said. "We're going in. Where's the map?"

Almost deafened by the incessant mortar shelling, Howie's officers gathered around as the major gave the order for the attack on St. Lô. None of them heard the incoming whine of the mortar shell that ended the conference.

The shell burst a few yards away. In that millisecond of destruction, most of the officers were picked up by the blast and slammed to the ground unhurt. Captain Puntenney, standing on the dugout step, was hurled bodily into a hedgerow. Dazed and shaken, he extricated himself from the bushes and saw Howie standing upright a few yards away. The major had his arms in front of him, holding his body. Puntenney rushed over. "My God, Bill, I'm hit," Howie said.

Puntenney carried him to the bottom of the dugout and held him for a few minutes in his arms. He didn't get much wear out of these boots, thought Puntenney as he lowered the body of his CO into the dust.

Several hours later, at division headquarters, the operations officer, Lieutenant Colonel William J. Witte, gave the news to General Gerhardt. "General," he said, "Tom Howie is dead. The Third Battalion attack never really got going."

Gerhardt said nothing. He was sad and terribly angry—sad, because of his fondness for Tom Howie and angry because of the awful casualties his division was suffering. His silent anger infected everybody in the headquarters. Somehow Tom

Howie's death crystallized all the courage and all the heart-break spilled over in the battle of St. Lô.

Gerhardt called General Cota. "Dutch," he said, "one of the last things Tom Howie said was, 'I'll see you in St. Lô.' We're going to fulfill that promise. Take Tom Howie with the task force—he's going to lead the Twenty-ninth into St. Lô."

The next day in St. Lô the townspeople heard a rumor. A powerful column of American tanks, it was said, was heading for the town.

At first they did not believe the story, for there had been many such rumors since the invasion began. But this time it was true. Far off, along the road leading into St. Lô from St. Clair, they heard the rumble and clank of tanks mixed in with the thunder of the enemy's exploding shells. And so in the cellars, in the crypt beneath the church, in all those places where families had survived the bombs and the shells the news spread swiftly. People spoke in whispers, in fear perhaps that they still might be wrong. "They are coming," they said. "Today is the day."

The sounds of the tanks and the exploding shells grew closer. Now, in ones and twos the townspeople left their shelters; they climbed the walls of rubble, stood behind shuttered windows or crouched in doorways oblivious of the dangers. They had waited too long to miss this moment.

The approaching column was clearly marked by a great cloud of dust which bowled along, reaching above the trees lining the road. Here and there black smoke tinged with flame spiraled up through the dust from burning and exploding vehicles. Overhead, clusters of shells whistled toward the road as the Germans stepped up the tempo of their artillery barrage. But under the rain of bursting shells the great cloud of dust came rolling steadily forward and suddenly it rolled into the outskirts of St. Lô. The Americans had arrived.

General Cota's task force poured into the town in an apparently endless column. Prowling tanks swarmed through the streets overrunning the German rearguard antitank positions; self-propelled guns swung into position and began answering the incoming artillery fire; infantrymen climbing through the rubble routed out the last snipers; and the townspeople threw flowers and from hiding places produced bottles of wine which they had saved for this great day.

In their happiness some cried and others remained dazed, unable to believe that the town had been liberated. But in the midst of it all, as the townspeople watched they saw a strange procession threading through the town.

Slowly down the main street rolled an olive-drab ambulance surrounded by an honor guard of armored cars. The column drove through the debris, passing the men and machines who had captured the town, passing under the limp blue and gray flag of the 29th Division now hanging in victory from a second-story window. And as the townspeople watched, hushed and incredulous, the little procession turned into the shell-pocked main square and came quietly to a stop before the shattered Cathedral of Notre Dame.

The ambulance doors opened and a detail of men carefully lifted down a stretcher. Struggling upward, they climbed to the top of a great mound of brick and stone before the ruins of the cathedral. And there, to lie in state on this altar of rubble, they placed the bier with the flag-covered body of Major Thomas D. Howie.

Standing today on a pedestal of concrete, near the bridge over the river Vire, there is a bronze bust of Major Thomas D. Howie. It was erected by the townspeople of St. Lô, and at this time of the year the base of the statue is covered with flowers. The townspeople honor not only the memory of Major Howie, but also the 7,000 men—almost half the 29th Division's fighting strength—who were killed or wounded in the battle for the town.

The elders shrug their shoulders and try to explain the sentiments of the townspeople this way: "L'homme n'est rien, l'oeuvre est tout." ("The man is nothing, the work is everything.") But they look admiringly at the statue and in the same breath they say wonderingly: "Such determination this man had—surely there was some French blood in his veins."

One Minute to Ditch!, 1957

The Longest Day

*T*housands *of people all over the world—some of them D-day
veterans or families of these men—have written me since my
book,* The Longest Day, *was published, supplying new information and posing questions which at the time of the book's writing
could not have been answered. So much new material has reached
me that it would easily fill another book of equal size.*

*One day, perhaps, I will write a companion volume, but in the
meantime here is "More Of The Longest Day"—unknown facts,
stories and vignettes, which either could not be accommodated in
my book or came to me only after its publication.*

The late Admiral Alan G. Kirk, who was to command the
Omaha and Utah Beaches naval task force on D-day, told me
this story: "Churchill called a meeting early in '44 to discuss
the jump-off date and all of us—Eisenhower, Montgomery,
Bradley and Leigh-Mallory—journeyed down to the Prime
Minister's country house, 'Chequers,' in Buckinghamshire."
Everyone was "briefed to the ears," Kirk recalled, on the
weather problem and the demands of each of the services. The
paratroopers wanted a late-rising moon, darkness when they
landed and then moonlight to see by; seaborne troops needed
a low tide; the Air Forces and Navies demanded low ground
winds and good visibility. The possibility that perfect conditions would occur on any single given day in Normandy was
considered highly remote.

Eisenhower and his commanders had gone over the meteorological aspects so many times that as Kirk put it: "We all
sounded like a group of bookies—for we knew the number
of perfect days that Normandy had enjoyed over a period of
a century, and the odds against good weather in any given
month."

Thus prepared, the D-day commanders dined with Churchill. "It was an excellent meal," Kirk remembered, "and the
Prime Minister did not utter a single word about the invasion
date as we ate." After dinner, the discussion began.

General Eisenhower outlined the preparation and build-up

of supplies. Other commanders added information—and Churchill sat deep in his chair and sipped brandy. After a while he leaned up and said: "Gentlemen, when do we go?"

The whole weather question, according to Admiral Kirk, "was then thrashed out." It was generally accepted that the attack would have to take place in the late spring or early summer, but as to the exact date, Churchill was told that, because of the weather problem, it had not yet been fixed. Churchill then leaned forward—to Kirk he looked like "a mild, but somewhat exasperated bulldog"—and looking at the commanders thoughtfully, he rumbled: "Pray, tell me, gentlemen —when did William go?"

There was a long silence. "We looked at each other," Kirk told me, "each hoping that the other knew. Here we sat, the D-day generals and admirals of the U.S. and Great Britain— the products of our respective nations' proud naval and military academies—and not one of us knew the exact date that William the Conqueror, sailing from Normandy, had landed in England."

When *had* William landed? He launched his attack not in the spring or summer, but in the autumn. He came ashore at the little fishing village of Pevensey, near Eastbourne in Sussex, on September 28, 1066. There was another intriguing fact—one that had not escaped the historically minded Prime Minister. *William the First had assembled his ships at Dives, and sailed, the first time, from the Bay of the Seine, although his second and successful departure was from a spot farther north. The Bay of the Seine was the precise area where the Allied armies were to invade almost 900 years later on June 6, 1944.*

Of the many stories that have come to light since my book was written, one unique—and embarrassing—incident stands out. Of the gigantic 5,000-vessel fleet operation, all crossed the Channel and berthed off the beaches—all, that is, but one. The old Indian liner *Neutralia*, loaded with British troops, was forgotten and left behind.

On the evening of June 5, anchored at Spithead, the *Neutralia*'s captain watched ship after ship join convoys and set sail. On her decks, troops of the British 7th Armored Division cheered and waved to their comrades on other ships. But gradually the cheering turned to anger. Officers protested to the captain that something was wrong, that somehow the *Neutralia* seemed to have been forgotten. But the *Neutralia*'s skipper had received no orders and could not move. What had happened?

Through an incredible oversight, the War Office had neglected to notify the responsible authorities about the *Neutralia* and thus orders were never issued. *In fact, the absence of the* Neutralia *and its troops was not even noticed until five days after the invasion. A search was made for the "lost" troop transport and the* Neutralia *was discovered at Spithead, with its cargo of exasperated troops. D-day naval records rather icily note that "the 2nd British Army, for some extraordinary reason, failed to notice that these important troops were even missing."*

Who can adequately write of the sight of the Allied armada, lined up across the horizon, and pounding the coastline as dawn broke on D-day? It was terrifying in its power, majestic in its size, and seems almost to haunt those who saw it.

Some naval officers on nearby ships recall an ancient British gunboat which, just before the dawn bombardment, broke open her colors. Training their binoculars on the rash of snapping flags, these officers read Nelson's famous message to the fleet at Trafalgar: "England Expects Every Man Will Do His Duty." Then the gunboat *which had been towed across the Channel* opened fire with her massive World War I front turret guns. She fired once, magnificently—and then her guns refused to retract. Her flags still valiantly high, she was towed out of the firing line to the cheers of the men on her sister ships close by.

From the German point of view the fleet was staggering in size. They seemed unable to grasp its magnitude—or to understand how it had reached Normandy without being observed. Lieutenant Colonel Friedrich Freiherr von der Heydte, commander of the tough German 6th Parachute Regiment, was given so many varying reports of the attack that he did not know what to believe. He ordered his regiment north from its encampment at Carentan towards Ste. Mère Église and the beaches. He had no communications, for the Resistance had destroyed telephone lines. When he was finally able to call headquarters he learned little. They, too, were confused. They knew that paratroopers had dropped east of Caen and in the Ste. Mère Église area. They were also aware that landings had been made, but only in the Vierville-Colleville area (Omaha Beach) and in the vicinity of Lion-sur-Mer, north of Caen. At 10 a.m. on D-day, headquarters still had no idea that troops had also come ashore around La Madeleine (Utah Beach).

Von der Heydte marched his troops north from Carentan to St. Côme-du-Mont. There he decided to climb the church steeple to see if he could observe anything. "When I got to the top of the tower, I frankly could not believe my eyes," he recalls. "Before me lay the coast and the sea. The battle was in progress. The horizon was strewn with hundreds of ships of all kinds, countless landing boats and barges moving back and forth, bringing troops, tanks and supplies ashore, apparently without any problems. From where I was it seemed almost peaceful. It reminded me of a summer day on the Wannsee."

On the other side of the bay, overlooking the British and Canadian beaches, Major Bruno Müller-Linow, in civilian life a well-known German artist, was overcome by the size of the armada and the immensity of the battle. He quickly got his paints and canvas, set his easel up on a hill and feverishly began to paint. Several times low-flying strafing planes came in over him and seemed undecided what to do. Seeing an artist at work on the very edge of the battlefield was such a shock that they veered off—at least that's what Müller-Linow thinks. "They must have thought I was crazy," he recalls. His painting hangs today in the U.S. Military Academy at West Point.

From their distant vantage points, both men had the feeling that they were looking at something unreal. But for the shocked, sea-sick infantry, desperately trying to get ashore, there was nothing but cold, bloody reality and sudden death.

Most people, when they think about D-day, have a kind of vision of hundreds of thousands of men all swarming ashore at the same time. It was not like that. In the first wave on Omaha Beach there were less than 1,800 men spread over about two to three miles. I doubt that along the 50 miles of beaches the total of all troops in the first wave reached more than 8,000.

The terror and confusion began when the second, third, fourth and subsequent waves piled up behind the first. It is not surprising, therefore, that for a time the Germans actually thought they had stopped the invasion.

There was horror, heroism and extraordinary humor on the beaches. General Harold Blakeley of the U.S. 4th Division will always remember the coolness of his British liaison officer. As they waded through the water Blakeley said: "How many beaches will this one make for you?" A shell burst in the water nearby. The Britisher, without even pausing in his stride, said: "Seven, sir—that is, if you allow me to count Dunkirk."

Sergeant Ernest Haynie, firing his Browning Automatic Rifle from the hip, managed to get himself and his squad up to the cliffs back of Omaha Beach. There he saw a GI who had been hit with a grenade. Blood was pouring from his shoulders, face and mouth. He was "mad, angry and wanted to take on the whole German army," Haynie says. The Sergeant saw the wounded infantryman grab two grenades and begin to climb the bluff all by himself yelling that he was "going to get the son-of-a—."

There was one sight that a score of men remember and still reminisce about, for it was gallantry at its best. At the very height of the battle, a Frenchman and his son appeared on Omaha Beach. "The man was in his late forties, and he and his son had enough courage for fifty of us," recalls Major Elmore Swenson. "They had a boat and as we lay pinned down on the beach we saw them, peppered by small-arms fire, calmly rowing back and forth picking up the dead and wounded." Men yelled to them to "take cover," that this was "no place for civilians." They were deaf to all entreaties. "Who they were," says Swenson, "or where they came from, we never found out."

Some men who climbed Pointe du Hoc swear that this is true. As fast as grappling irons were fired up the sides of the steep cliff Rangers grabbed the ropes and began climbing. Again and again the Germans fought them off. Finally Rangers got to the top. No one knows who was up first, but everyone would like to find him. Several Rangers, reaching the summit, saw scrawled in chalk on a rock: "Kilroy was here."

When 1st Lieutenant Harrison Holland of the 29th Division jumped off his landing craft and ran up Omaha Beach he was so scared that he was "convinced every German in the vicinity was firing at me personally." Men fell all around as he ran and he was quite sure that he would never survive. Ahead he saw a burning tank. He threw himself behind it, and lay there sweating, "thanking God that He had let me live this far." Then there was a sudden lull in the firing and from the other side of the tank, to Harrison's amazement, he heard two soldiers quietly talking. One said to the other: "You wear it on the right side—I know damn well you do." Exasperated, the second soldier replied: "Look, Mac, for the last time, in this here man's army the canteen goes on the left hip—not the right."

All over Sword Beach, British casualties had been heavy. Captain Basil Spence, a noted architect in civilian life, remembers that he approached a German pillbox which had been taken only a short time before. "The bodies were stacked one upon the other," he said, "all around the position. I felt no horror or nausea at the sight of all these young men dead—simply a feeling of awe and overwhelming wonder at the bravery of it all."

What more is there to say than that—the "awe and overwhelming wonder" of the bravery of the men of D-day? Wherever men gather to talk about courage on that day they will also say, as one sergeant told his frightened squad: "O.K., if you get it—the remainder of us will say: it was a good way to die, on the beaches of Normandy."

This Week Magazine, June 6, 1965

Untold Stories from The Longest Day

W HEN I completed *The Longest Day* in 1959, I thought I had little more to say. To detail the awesome 24 hours of that historic invasion of a coastline Hitler claimed to be impregnable, I had leafed through volumes of research, read everything I could unearth on the subject and, with *Reader's Digest* editors and researchers, contacted or interviewed German and Allied D-Day veterans all over the world. But I soon discovered that there was no end to the longest day. The book triggered an avalanche of mail—some 20,000 letters over the years—which has not ceased even now.

Written in various languages, many of the letters are anguished or pathetic. In particular, there are those from German families seeking information on the fate of a son, husband or other relative. The sister of Lt. Col. Hellmuth Meyer, the German intelligence officer who discovered the invasion date by deciphering a message intended for the French resistance, learned from *The Longest Day* that he was alive, and brother and sister were eventually reunited.

One soldier had seemingly no desire to return to the bosom of his household. A wrathful British woman wrote: "I read with amazement your interview with Sgt. ———— in your book. Where is he? I am his wife and have not seen him since before the invasion. You tell him if he doesn't respond, I'll track him down like the rabbit he is. Brave, was he? Well, I'll 'brave' him. You just tell him since his memory's so good, does he happen to remember he's got a wife?"

Perhaps the most heartwarming letter I ever received came from the daughter of a D-Day casualty. In 1970, she wrote: "I am 27, and I never knew my father. He was killed on Omaha Beach. For years I hated him because I was tired of Mother talking about what the war was like and what a big hero my father was." Then, reading about Omaha Beach, she found that her attitude changed. "My father became real to me," she continued. "I cried because I love him, and he might have loved me. I cried, too, because his life was over before mine ever really began, yet he gave me my life. Thank you for giving me my father after all these years." That letter alone made the ten years of work on *The Longest Day* totally worthwhile.

History Lesson. One of the more intriguing aspects of the mail I receive is the revelation of material I did not have when I was writing the book. My favorite "new" fact deals with the historically minded Winston Churchill. Early in 1944, he called a meeting of the Supreme Commander, Gen. Dwight D. Eisenhower, and his D-Day officers to discuss the date of the attack. After dinner at the prime minister's country house, Chequers, in Buckinghamshire, Churchill sipped at a brandy. Leaning forward, he asked, "Gentlemen, when do we go?"

The importance of weather was explained to Churchill, and he was assured that the invasion would take place toward the end of spring or in early summer. The late Rear Adm. Alan G. Kirk, who was to command the Omaha and Utah beaches naval task forces, was struck at that moment by the prime minister's expression. He looked, Kirk thought, like "a mild but somewhat exasperated bulldog." Gazing thoughtfully at each of the D-Day commanders, Churchill rumbled: "Pray tell me, gentlemen, when did William go?"

There was a long, embarrassed silence. Recalled Kirk: "Here we sat, the D-Day generals and admirals of the United States and Great Britain, the products of our respective nations' proud naval and military academies, men who had studied every conceivable problem of the invasion, and not one of us remembered what time of year William the Conqueror, sailing from Normandy, had landed in England."

When *had* William landed? Churchill knew that it was not in the spring or summer, but in the autumn—after the harvest was in. He came ashore at the little fishing village of Pevensey, Sussex, on September 28, 1066. Another intriguing fact of William's conquest had not escaped Churchill. He explained that William had assembled his ships at the mouth of the Dives and sailed from the Bay of the Seine—the precise area where the Allied armies were to invade almost 900 years later. Had the Germans thought of this historical coincidence? Luckily not.

*

What was the German Supreme Commander, Field Marshal Gerd von Rundstedt, doing on the morning of D Day? The gardener employed at the villa next to Von Rundstedt's supplied the information in a letter: Von Rundstedt was working in his rose garden. By coincidence, so was the D-Day Allied commander, British Field Marshal Bernard Law Montgomery. "There was nothing else for me to do," Montgomery explained, "but wait for news of the landings."

Invasion Torchbearers. As midnight of June 5 approached, great trains of paratroop aircraft and infantry-filled gliders towed by DC-3s approached the Normandy coast. What do men think and talk about as they ready themselves for battle? Pvt. Carl Beck of the 82nd Airborne recalls that "Tommy Burke was singing an Irish rebellion song and everyone joined in. Then at times the guys were so quiet you could hear them praying over the roar of the plane's motors." Sgt. Ernest L. Gee remembers that the tension on his plane was broken by a certain Private Huth who, as German anti-aircraft shells started bursting around them, began an uncanny imitation of President Roosevelt's patrician tones: "My friends, I say to you again and again that your sons and my sons will never fight on foreign soil."

Elsewhere men worried about the rumors they had heard. Capt. St. Julien P. Rosemond of the 101st Airborne Division was thinking about the propaganda broadcasts of "Axis Sally" —"The Berlin Bitch," as the troops called her. She had boasted that the Germans were waiting "for you boys to land along the coast"; that all the "church bells will ring" and within minutes "you will be either captured or dead." Standing in the door of his plane as it passed low over the small French village of Ste. Mère Église, Rosemond distinctly heard a church bell tolling in the night. By coincidence, at that moment the villagers were responding to the bell's signal to put out a fire. A few hundred feet above, Captain Rosemond began to think that maybe "The Berlin Bitch" might be telling the truth after all!

Courage and fear rode in every plane. Some paratroopers— like Pvt. Bill Dunnett of the 1st Canadian Parachute Battalion —were so calm that they fell asleep almost before their planes left the ground. Dunnett remembered nothing until he was awakened by the man next to him and, seconds later, was out the door and floating down on Normandy. He thought it was "a hell of a way to wake up—without even a cup of tea."

Sgt. John McCallion May of the British 6th Airborne remembered the pilot's remarks about his plane before they left the ground. "She's rather delicate, so don't move about too much." May spent the entire trip worrying about the plane. And Pvt. Stanley Fortnam fretted about what it would be like to force-land in the English Channel.

Nearing their drop zones, everyone from generals to privates seems to have been fascinated by the peaceful-looking, moonlit landscape over Normandy. Gen. James M. Gavin of the 82nd Airborne mentally noted that "there was no evidence of human habitation . . . no people or vehicles . . . brown-red countryside traced through by neat white roads . . . off to the right, large amounts of flak . . . quite beautiful as it arched up in high and low bursts."

As the first soldiers jumped into the night sky, their parachutes blossoming above them, there was little time to speculate on what lay ahead. As Sergeant May put it: "Everyone was afraid of appearing afraid, and I guess that's what courage really is—not letting the other fellow know how scared you really are."

As one officer stood by the door of his plane ready to jump, he issued a final order that Sgt. John Faor remembers only too well. "Now listen," the officer yelled. "Anyone—and I mean anyone—who breaks a leg on this darn jump gets a court-martial! Got it? Okay, let's go." Minutes later, Faor was lying in an apple orchard—with a broken leg. The officer, who landed nearby, was "cursing his head off." *He* had broken an ankle!

The Greatest Armada. As paratroopers fought in the darkness of the Normandy hedgerows, the great D-Day armada steamed across the Channel. Convoy after convoy—from motor-torpedo boats to supply-laden tramp steamers to troop transports to battleships—plowed through the wind-chopped seas in what must surely go down in naval history as the greatest logistical shipping movement ever attempted. The output of naval orders alone called for several thousand workers. Each vessel was given a numbered position in its convoy, traveled at a certain speed, and upon arrival in the Bay of the Seine rode at anchor according to a master plan—all without breaking radio silence. The wonder is that there were no collisions and that the huge fleet was not detected.

Of the many stories that have come to light since *The Longest Day* was written, a unique incident stands out. In the gigantic 5000-vessel fleet operation, all but one ship crossed the Channel. Anchored off Spithead, the old Indian liner *Neutralia* should have sailed on the evening of June 5. British 7th Armored Division troops on her decks cheered and waved as other ships moved out. Gradually, as the hours passed, the cheering ceased. Army officers aboard protested to the *Neutralia*'s skipper that something had gone wrong—but he had received no orders and could not move without them.

What had happened? Through an oversight, naval orders for the *Neutralia* were never issued. In fact, the absence of the *Neutralia*'s troops was not even noticed until five days after D Day. A search was made for the "lost" transport, and she was discovered still at anchor—along with her cargo of frustrated, angry troops.

As dawn broke on D Day, the majestic Allied armada lined up across the horizon was an unforgettable sight. On the bridge of the *USS Bayfield*, flagship for all the naval forces off Utah Beach, Cmdr. John A. Moreno, assistant planning officer, gazed through his binoculars. One ship in particular intrigued him. Her name remains a mystery but, says Moreno, "she had been built solely to bombard German shore installations in the First World War but was never used."

As the *Bayfield* moved slowly by, Moreno saw the British gunboat break open her colors. "A storm of bunting appeared," Moreno recalls, "spelling out Nelson's famous message to the fleet at Trafalgar: 'England expects every man to do his duty.'" Then with a thunderous roar, the gunboat's two massive 15-inchers opened fire, but only once. They failed to retract, and she couldn't fire again. As she was towed slowly out of the firing line, men lined the rails of other ships to cheer her. Her moment of destiny had come and gone—but it was not forgotten.

The ships poured millions of pounds of high explosives into the German coastal defenses. The U.S. destroyer *Satterlee* lay so close off rocky Pointe du Hoc that many thought she would founder. She moved back and forth all morning, guns firing point-blank to aid U.S. Rangers as they fought up the nine-story-high cliffs to silence guns that they soon discovered had never been installed.

The crew of the destroyer *USS Carmick* fought like men possessed. Just before dawn, her commander, Robert O. Beer, had run up the "biggest U.S. flag in the entire fleet," recalls Watertender First Class Louis A. Busby. "The old man said, 'That flag is just about big enough for the Jerries to see and, after all, we've got to give them something to shoot at.'"

The immensity of the fleet awed the Germans. Maj. Bruno Müller-Linow, a prominent artist in civilian life, was so dazed by the sight that he quickly set up his easel on a hill and began feverishly to paint. Several times low-flying fighters roared in over him. But seeing an artist working on the battlefield's edge was apparently such a surprise that the planes veered off.

On the Beaches. As troops began to wade ashore beneath the bombardment's umbrella, there were incidents of horror, heroism—and even humor. On Omaha Beach, where 2000 Americans became casualties in just three hours, Gen. Harold Blakeley of the U.S. 4th Division was struck by the coolness of his British liaison officer. As they sloshed ashore, Blakeley asked, "How many beaches will this make for you?" A shell burst nearby. Without pausing, the Britisher said, "Seven landings, sir—that is, if you allow me to count Dunkirk." Off Utah Beach, Pvt. K. D. Sulkis, lying in the water, heard a G.I. say anxiously, "You know, you really can't dig a foxhole in the water." (What was the water temperature off the invasion beaches? Best guess now: about 42 degrees.)

Scores of men remember one particular sight. At the height of the battle on Omaha Beach, a middle-aged French civilian appeared with his son. "They had enough courage for 50 of us," recalls Maj. Elmore Swenson. "As we lay pinned down, we saw them, surrounded by small-arms fire, calmly rowing a boat back and forth picking up the dead, dying and wounded from the water. Who they were or where they came from we never found out."

Some wounded men on Omaha Beach thought that they were delirious when in the water off Pointe du Hoc they spotted what appeared to be red fire ladders waving high in the air. They *were* fire ladders. Borrowed from the London Fire

Brigade, they had been mounted in landing craft and from their 100-foot-high tops U.S. Rangers were pouring machine-gun fire at Germans up on the cliffs.

Odd and incongruous incidents remained in the minds of the men of D Day. When 1st Lt. Harrison Holland of the 29th Division ran toward Omaha Beach he was "convinced every German was firing at me personally" and certain he would not survive. With men falling all around him, Holland threw himself down behind a burning tank. There was a sudden lull in the firing and, as Holland gasped for breath, he heard one soldier from the other side of the tank quietly say, "You wear it on the right side. I know damn well you do." A second soldier answered, exasperated: "Look, Mac, for the last time, in this man's army the water bottle goes on the left hip—not the right."

Each beach had its own share of stories. One of the more poignant occurred on Sword Beach. As Cmdr. Philippe Kieffer led his French commandos ashore under a storm of fire, a commando fell fatally wounded next to Kieffer. Dragging the man onto the beach, Kieffer saw that he wore an old World War I French helmet. "It was my father's," the soldier said. "He wore it at Verdun." As Kieffer lowered the man to the beach, the commando spoke once more: "One favor. Before you go, turn my head toward Paris."

Year after year, new information reaches me about D Day. From all sources one belief is expressed again and again: people everywhere identify with and believe in the overwhelming courage shown that day. Many of them have quoted the words of the sergeant who told his frightened squad before the invasion: "Remember this. If you get it, the remainder of us will say of you, it was a good way to die, on the beaches of Normandy."

The Reader's Digest, June 1974

To William Buckley

From: Cornelius Ryan,
230 East 48th St,
New York, N.Y.
Plaza 5-7937

Wm Buckley, Esq.,
Henry Holt & Co, Inc.,
383 Madison Ave,
New York

November 19th, 1957

My dear Bill:

Thanks for seeing me the other day and also for the good advice. I spoke to Phyllis on the phone and we're lunching Monday to review my affairs. She's a good gal. I've known her and her husband for a number of years—anyway if you recommend her that's enough for me. I was thinking of Matson, but Phyllis and MCA are probably better for all my involvements. Anyway I'll talk it over with her and see what we come up with.

Now about the D-day idea. First of all the anniversary of the event is June 6th, 1959—it will be exactly 15 years since that day —the day we held our breaths. Stepping over to the other side of the desk—as an editor now, not a writer—I know damned well that if I was with a magazine, in January or February of 1959 I would begin thinking about an anniversary piece. So that the timing with this book idea is important. I think that it calls for a Spring 1959 effort, but that magazine syndication should be effected in the early fall of 1958—that is, of course, if somebody like *McCalls*, *Life* or whoever, isn't in the act beforehand (like *Day of Infamy*) to shoulder some of the expense in research.

So much for the timing. I mention it first because of its importance and so that all concerned can see how best to get speed out of the entire effort.

Here's the whole idea for the book:

Too many books have been written about the war in which D-day was documented only through the general's eyes. Sure, there have been single incidents written about and so on. One

889

of the reasons why D-day has been brushed off—if that's the
word to use—is because the entire canvas appears to be too
crowded; and what writer can afford to underwrite the major
research involved?

Well my idea is not to try and tell the whole involved story
of some 70,000 odd men landing on that first day (incidentally
one always gets the impression that several million landed!) I
am interested only in taking say, the first two or three hours,
when only a few thousand men with the courage of ignorance
hit those bloody beaches. And I'm interested in finding out
not only what our fellows were doing, but also what Pvt Hans
Schmidt from Darmstadt was doing and how he felt when he
looked out of his pillbox and saw the invasion fleet offshore;
and also what Pierre Doucher, the farmer, his wife and children felt, when paratroopers landed suddenly in their backyard
during the night. In other words Bill, I see this as a carefully
documented human narrative concerned only with ordinary
people caught up in fear and crisis. As you know this is my
forte. The little Ballantine book *One Minute to Ditch!* which I
wrote, contains five of my pieces which are the best examples
of my style—it also contains the two pieces for which I won
this year's Benjamin Franklin and Overseas Press Club Awards.
So that I believe if I wrote this book in the same simple, human
and intimate terms we might have a helluva wallop in its pages.
For example: there's the story of the young-faced soldier, his
M1 under one arm and his pooch under the other. He didn't
know what to expect when he hit those beaches. He waded
ashore holding his gun and dog over his head. He reached the
sands and before he ever learned what it was all about he was
dead, lying there in his own blood. The pooch didn't know
what it was all about either. He just stayed beside the body for
there was no where else for him to go.

There's another example: the story of the Howitzer Company. They had ten howitzers—each one loaded in a landing
barge. Nine of the barges either sank under the weight of their
load or were hit by shells. One remained, water-logged and
sinking. The soldiers were ordered out of it, but one spunky
character got mad: he wouldn't leave, he was determined to
land the gun. So single-handedly he maneuvered the landing barge up and down the beach, but nobody had a crane or

ramps to help him get the gun onto the beaches. He was under constant shelling, lobsided because he was gradually sinking. But he wouldn't give up. Finally after several hours, he ran the barge along a makeshift pier made up of landing barges which had sunk. He ran along this "pier" begging people to help him. But everybody was too busy fighting, trying to save their own lives. In the end he persuaded the crew of a tank with a small crane on top to help him. They stopped firing long enough to back the tank into the water, swing the crane around behind it, over the water, and lift off the gun. The gun was hauled ashore and it was the only howitzer that got into action that day. But the tankers who had helped the GI with his gun never got back onto the beach. Immediately after they had landed the howitzer their tank got a direct hit. They died screaming, roasted alive by their own exploding ammunition.

Another: there was the young German soldier who came face to face with a GI. Both of them had bayonets on their rifles. How long did they look at each other in those terrible moments? Both men were found in a horribly strange death tableau—each of them had been killed by the other's bayonet.

And so on. Now there must be thousands of stories like that on the American, British, French and German sides—think of the book it would make? I want to do a big research job, cull the best out and write a really fine human document. Really if my ego is showing forgive me, there are easier books to write, but this is one I want to write. Maybe it will deal only with the first hour or the first 24 hours—I don't know at this moment, but I know that the story and a great one, is there.

I would first get in touch with each U.S. division and go through their histories then write to various individuals whose names could be found in this research. That by itself would be a long job. At the same time I would get in touch with the Germans and find out what units they had in Normandy. Also the French Government, I know, would help through the Mayors of the various Normandy towns to help place the various families who were in the vicinity that day, or had been moved back say, to some of the large towns. (Towns such as Carentan, Ste Mere Eglise, Nehou and so on just back of the beaches or on the peninsula could produce stories in the paratroop drop during the night of June 5–6.)

Having developed this basic research (plus reading every damn thing that has so far been written about D-day) I would have to spend several months or employ researchers in Germany, Britain and France.

I realize that it is a monumental job that would take a full year, but I think that it could be done.

Now as I told you *McCalls* (Henry Ehrlich) thought the idea was great—even though I only casually mentioned it to Ehrlich. He wants me to sit down and talk it over with Otis Weiss. So I think you might conceivably get them on the hook to foot part of the bill. (I was somewhat surprised at the reaction of Ehrlich, because I didn't think *McCalls* would go for such a thing. But he said—and it's worth remembering: "For God's sake, of course we'd be interested—think of all the mothers, wives and sweethearts who lost men on D-day!")

Also I know that the *Digest* has been looking for a D-day book. As I mentioned to you, one day at lunch they told me about the Landmark book on D-day (Bruce Bliven jnr) and that they would have taken it, but that it was so bad.

Seems to me Bill, that we'd have to develop some sort of a Lord-Life deal, because there's a year's concentrated work in this idea and I'd have to live during that time, do quite a lot of travelling and pay for a helluva lot of research. But I honestly believe there's a package here and a good one.

My best to you,

To Peter Schwed

February 24, 1959

Mr. Peter Schwed
Simon & Shuster
630 Fifth Avenue
New York

Dear Peter:

The second part is rolling along smoothly. Quite honestly there is such an enormous amount of material that I am knee-deep in paper and the problem now is to maintain the suspense and keep myself on a very tight leash.

You will be pleased to know that Gen. James Gavin who promised to read the first half for military inaccuracies has just been on the phone. I don't mind admitting that I darned near burst into tears (as we emotional Irish are prone to do) when he told me that it was "the best work on D-Day that has yet been written." Forgive me if this reads a little egotistical, but those words from Gavin mean a lot to me. The manuscript is also in the hands of Eisenhower and my good friend, Gen. Maxwell D. Taylor, the Chief of Staff. I owe Taylor a lot—it was he who got me permission to get at the German war diaries which, as you know, up to now have been classified. Gavin, by the way, says that the revelations are going to make headline news. I hope he's right.

The extraordinary thing is that the second half has much more exciting material than the first. I suppose the truth is that after all these years of work I am so close to it now that I cannot evaluate the impact anymore. But the reaction to the first half is exactly as predicted by Teddy White. All along he has been saying that the first half would be as exciting as the actual battle.

You asked me to give you a few details on the research. Here they are:

I first began thinking about the book back in 1948. The idea was a simple one: to talk to the men on all sides and get their stories of D-Day. At that time, however, I just began a course of reading. In the next three years, I read about 280 works on the subject. Some books had just a chapter or two on D-Day, others were dull military tomes designed more to prove a course of action rather than to tell a story. I cannot even begin to tell you here the inaccuracies which I ran across.

But the biggest job was to find the men who were there on D-Day—particularly the Germans. Over the years I was able to run down almost 3,000. The breakdown is as follows: U.S. 1,080; Canadians 450; British 680; French 300; and about 400 Germans. Working with the *Digest*'s research department, we sent out questionnaires or wrote letters to them and the returns were as follows: U.S. 698; Canadian 174; British 141; French 70; German 68. But, many of these men automatically had to be eliminated simply because they *thought* they landed or fought on D-Day whereas the records showed that they could not possibly have been there that day. The collation and checking of all these questionnaires and letters took almost six months. Finally however, I settled on approximately 450 German and Allied veterans for interview. And the book is based on their accounts.

The breakthrough as far as I'm concerned occurred when Gen. Taylor had declassified for me the German war diaries. These accounts had not even been translated from the German. The result of this has been that mistakes have passed on from book to book over the years, including the official war histories!

Among the many extraordinary revelations in the war diaries was the chilling fact that the Germans had intercepted the underground messages, and knew the invasion was coming. I need hardly tell you my surprise when I discovered this. I would never have known about it but for a letter from a former German Intelligence Officer who wrote begging to talk with me. I did and he turned out to be the Lt. Col. Meyer who is mentioned in the book. On the basis of his information I had the 15th German Army's war diary translated and sure enough there were the full details of the invasion messages which they had decoded.

The German war diaries, plus the U.S. and British after action reports (down to companies) gave me the book's skeleton and the men's own stories and interviews provided the life. No event or quote has been used unless it stood the test of corroboration. In a way this has been tough for many a man's story has had to go by the board simply for lack of verification. But the line had to be drawn somewhere.

So much tripe has appeared on the subject of D-Day that all along I have been ruthless in sticking to what actually happened *rather than what generals or others thought happened*. Something else: you'll find no mention here of "Mama's blueberry pie" or the term "GI."

I'm doing my best to abide by a single rule of thumb: accuracy. Really, if nothing else I hope *The Longest Day* will set the record straight. It may sound corny but I think the men who died on both sides on D-Day deserve that much.

Cordially,
Cornelius Ryan

Your name _____

Did you by any chance keep a diary of what happened to you that day?

no

Were any of your friends killed or wounded either during the landing or
during the day?

Hundreds

Do you remember any conversations you had with them before they became
casualties?

I remember talking to a Platoon
leader, Lt Shaunnesey, concerning
saving his MG ammo about
two minutes before he was
ambushed and killed.

Were you wounded? yes

Do you remember what it was like--that is, do you remember whether you
felt any pain or were you so surprised that you felt nothing?

During the war I was wounded
3 times — each time it was initially
no more painful than a blow from
some ones fist.

Do you remember seeing or hearing anything that seems funny now, even
though it did not, of course, seem amusing at the time?

I actually thought it was
pathetic that we captured
a church steeple in Colliville
Sur Mere that gave us good
observation of the enemy only
to have it shot down by the US Navy

Do you recall any incident, sad or heroic, or simply memorable, which struck
you more than anything else?

The death of Lt Duckworth,
from rifle fire. He had
married a young English girl
about 5 days earlier.

Sample Response to Questionnaire *for* The Longest Day

For Cornelius Ryan
Book about D-Day

THOUSANDS OF MEN, ON LAND AND SEA AND IN THE AIR, PAR-
TICIPATED IN THE INVASION OF NORMANDY BETWEEN MID-
NIGHT JUNE 5, 1944 AND MIDNIGHT JUNE 6, 1944. IF YOU WERE
ONE OF THEM, PLEASE ANSWER THE FOLLOWING QUESTIONS.

What is your full name?
William Rhinehart Washington

What was your unit and division?
2d Bn. 16th Inf. 1st Inf. Div.

Where did you arrive in Normandy, and at what time?
EASY RED Beach H-Hour plus 30 minutes

What was your rank on June 6, 1944?
Major, AUS

What was your age on June 6, 1944?
25 years

Were you married at that time?
yes

What is your wife's name?
Margaret M. Washington

Did you have any children at that time?
no

897

What do you do now?

Lt Col Regular Army

When did you know that you were going to be part of the invasion?

Fairly strong idea when we left Sicily in Oct 1943. Definite about 5 days before invasion

What was the trip like during the crossing of the Channel? Do you remember, for example, any conversations you had or how you passed the time?

Channel crossing was choppy due to sea conditions. We actually suffered an over confidence, in the ability of the Air Force and Navy to "soften" the beach Defenses.

What were the rumors on board the boat, ship or plane in which you made the crossing? (Some people remember scuttlebutt to the effect that the Germans had poured gasoline on the water and planned to set it afire when the troops came in.)

Troops were thoroughly briefed before we actually cleared sight of land. No basis for rumor—they had the facts.

Did you by any chance keep a diary of what happened to you that day?

no

Were any of your friends killed or wounded either during the landing or during the day?

Hundreds

Do you remember any conversations you had with them before they became casualties?

I remember talking to a Platoon leader, Lt Shaughnesy, concerning saving his MG ammo about two minutes before he was ambushed and killed.

Were you wounded?

yes

Do you remember what it was like—that is, do you remember whether you felt any pain or were you so surprised that you felt nothing?

During the war I was wounded 3 times—each time it was initially no more painful than a blow from some ones fist.

Do you remember seeing or hearing anything that seems funny now, even though it did not, of course, seem amusing at the time?

I actually thought it was pathetic that we captured a church steeple in Colliville Sur Mere that gave us good observation of the enemy only to have it shot down by the US Navy.

Do you recall any incident, sad or heroic, or simply memorable, which struck you more than anything else?

The death of Lt Duckworth, from rifle fire. He had married a young English girl about 5 days earlier.

In times of great crisis, people generally show either great ingenuity or self-reliance; others do incredibly stupid things. Do you remember any examples of either?

Yes but too detailed to relate here

Where were you at midnight on June 5, 1944?

Aboard ship in Falmouth harbor off Portland Harb

Where were you at midnight on June 6, 1944?

One hour short of our "Anchor Position" off EASY RED Beach

Do you know of anybody else who landed within those 24 hours (midnight June 5 to midnight June 6) as infantry, glider or airborne troops, or who took part in the air and sea operations, whom we should write to?

I can relate the names of at least 100 officers and men of the 16th Infantry living today but can probably give address of no more than 20

I would be glad to give any amount of specific info concerning the operation of 2d Bn 16th Inf

PLEASE LET US HAVE THIS QUESTIONNAIRE AS SOON AS POS-
SIBLE, SO THAT WE CAN INCLUDE YOUR EXPERIENCES IN THE
BOOK. WE HOPE THAT YOU WILL CONTINUE YOUR STORY ON
SEPARATE SHEETS IF WE HAVE NOT LEFT SUFFICIENT ROOM.
FULL ACKNOWLEDGEMENT WILL BE GIVEN IN A CHAPTER
CALLED "WHERE THEY ARE NOW"; YOUR NAME AND VOCATION
OR OCCUPATION WILL BE LISTED.

THANK YOU FOR YOUR HELP.

I expect to depart Korea in Dec 58. I would welcome the
chance of interview or any other contribution that I could
make WRW

Cornelius Ryan
Frances Ward
Research, *The Reader's Digest*

Sample Response to Questionnaire
for A Bridge Too Far

The Reader's Digest Association Limited
25 Berkeley Square London W1
Telephone Mayfair 8144
Cables Readigest London W1

20th April, 1967.

J. T. Richards, Esq.,
35, Westerfield Way,
Wilford,
Notts.

Dear Mr. Richards,

Your name appears in the records of those who may have taken part in the airborne assault on Holland in September, 1944. I am therefore writing to ask for your help with some research that we are doing on behalf of Mr. Cornelius Ryan, author of *The Longest Day* and, more recently, *The Last Battle*.

Would you be kind enough to answer the following questions in the spaces provided. Please return this letter to me as soon as possible so that Mr. Ryan may include your experiences in the account of the airborne invasion of Holland which he is planning to write. The book will include a chapter entitled "Where They Are Today", in which your name and occupation will be listed with full acknowledgment. Your assistance will be very much appreciated.

Yours sincerely,

Michael Randolph
Editor, British Editions

1) Are your name and address correct on this letter? If not, please amend them.
CORRECT.

TWO

8) What previous action had you seen? *NORTH AFRICA. 1ST ARMY.*
PRIMASOLA BRIDGE SICILY.
TARANTO LANDINGS ITALY.

9) When did you learn that you were going to take part in the operation in Holland? *THURSDAY 14TH SEPT 1944*

10) What was your reaction? Were you, for example, anxious, resigned or relieved to be going into action?

AS A SEASONED CAMPAINER., IT WAS JUST ROUTINE

11) What was the trip like into Holland? Did you see anything unusual? Do you remember any conversations you had, or how you passed the time on the journey?
THIS TRIP WAS GOOD. MY PLATOON. WERE EXCELLENT SOLDIERS HAVING BEEN IN A LOT OF ACTION. WE WERE ALL MORE CONCERNED WHETHER THE AMERICANS WOULD DROP US ON THE PROPER D.Z. AFTER SICILY EXPERIENCE

12) How did you feel about a daylight operation? Do you recall any conversations with your friends about it? What was said?
WE WERE RATHER CONCERNED ABOUT FLAK GOING INTO BELGIUM COAST. WE HAD EXCELLENT FIGHTER COVER

13) What were the rumours? Had you heard, for example, that if the invasion of Holland was successful, the war would be over by the coming winter?
THE RUMOURS WERE PLENTY ARNHEM WAS SUPPOSED TO HAVE BEEN GUARDED BY A BRIGADE OF EQUIVALANT TO OUR OWN HOME GUARD. THE WAR WOULD HAVE BEEN OVER BY XMAS ACCORDING TO THE EXPERTS IF THE OPERATION WAS SUCCESSFUL

14) Did you keep a diary or notebook of what happened to you during any part of September, 1944? Do you still have it?

No. THE TIME AROUND ARNHEM WAS SPENT FIGHTING NOT WRITING.

15) Were any of your friends killed or wounded on the day of the drop or on subsequent days? *THIS RECORD CONCERNS 11 PLATOON T. COY. 1ST BATT. PARACHUTE REGT*
SUNDAY 17TH 1944   NO CASUALTIES
MONDAY 18 - "   8. WOUNDED INCLUDING; PLT CMDR. LT HELINGOE;
TUESDAY 19 - "   2 KILLED 3. WOUNDED.
TUESDAY EVENING   I AS PLT SGT HAD UNDER MY COMMAND 8. MEN. REMAINDER WERE KILLED; WOUNDED, OR LOST CONTACT WE WERE STILL GOING TOWARDS THE BRIDGE

2) If you can be reached by telephone, please give your number.
NOTTINGHAM 85034

3) What is your present occupation?
REPRESENTATIVE

4) What was your rank and unit in September 1944?
SGT. RICHARDS J. T. 4195046
1ST. BATT PARACHUTE REGT. 1ST BRIGADE

5) What was your age in September 1944?
25.

6) Were you engaged or married then? To whom? If married, did you have any children at that time?
NO.

7) Where were you born?
GROFFTYDD FARM
CARNO
MONTGOMERYSHIRE
WALES

8) What previous action had you seen?
"NORTH AFRICA. 1ST ARMY"
"PRIMASOLA BRIDGE SCICILY."
TARANTO LANDINGS ITALY.

9) When did you learn that you were going to take part in the operation in Holland?
THURSDAY 14TH SEPT 1944

10) What was your reaction? Were you, for example, anxious, resigned or relieved to be going into action?
AS A SEASONED CAMPAIGNER, IT WAS JUST ROUTINE

11) What was the trip like into Holland? Did you see anything unusual? Do you remember any conversations you had, or how you passed the time on the journey?

THIS TRIP WAS GOOD. MY PLATOON WERE EXCELLENT SOLDIERS HAVING BEEN IN A LOT OF ACTION. WE WERE ALL MORE CONCERNED WHETHER THE AMERICANS WOULD DROP US ON THE PROPER D.Z. AFTER SCICILY EXPERIENCE

12) How did you feel about a daylight operation? Do you recall any conversations with your friends about it? What was said?

WE WERE RATHER CONCERNED ABOUT FLAK GOING INTO BELGIUM COAST. WE HAD EXCELLENT FIGHTER COVER

13) What were the rumours? Had you heard, for example, that if the invasion of Holland was successful, the war would be over by the coming winter?

THE RUMOURS WERE PLENTY ARNHEM WAS SUPPOSED TO HAVE BEEN GUARDED BY A BRIGADE OF EQUIVALENT TO OUR OWN HOME GUARD. THE WAR WOULD HAVE BEEN OVER BY XMAS ACCORDING TO THE EXPERTS IF THE OPERATION WAS SUCCESSFUL.

14) Did you keep a diary or notebook of what happened to you during any part of September, 1944? Do you still have it?

NO. THE TIME AROUND ARNHEM WAS SPENT FIGHTING NOT WRITING.

15) Were any of your friends killed or wounded the day of the drop or on subsequent days?

THIS RECORD CONCERNS 11. PLATOON T. COY. 1ST BATT PARACHUTE REGT

SUNDAY 17TH 1944	NO CASUALTIES
MONDAY 18TH	8 WOUNDED INCLUDING PLT CMDR. LT. HELINGOE.
TUESDAY 19-	2 KILLED 3 WOUNDED

Tuesday evening I as Plt. Sgt. had under my command 8 men. Remainder were killed, wounded, or lost contact we were still going towards the bridge

16) Do you remember any conversations you had with them before they became casualties?

No conversations only battle orders

17) Were you wounded or captured during this period? Can you give details?

I along with 3 more of the Plt were captured. Wed 20th 11 OClock in a Dutch family house. The Germans had a mounted machine gun on the balcony all morning. We didnt give much for our chances of survival here. Fortunately the Germans were as scared as we were when they discovered us.

Stalag 8C Sagan

18) Do you remember any significant dealings you may have had with Dutch civilians or members of the Dutch underground? Please explain.

The civilians were very helpful in all ways

19) What do you recall most vividly about the country of Holland?

Very flat. And dykes

20) Do you recall any incidents with the Germans—fights, surrenders, truces or conversations you may have had with them afterwards?

Plenty in camp. I had my teeth knocked out with a rifle butt for reasons better not printed we used to have good sing-songs and in general play hell with the gerry guards

21) Do you know of others who took part in the operation, to whom we might write? Please give their names and last-known addresses.

G. Potter
2 Bradburn Rd
Long Knowle
Wednesfield Staffs

22) Do you recall seeing or hearing anything that seems humorous now, even though it may not have seemed so at the time?

23) Do you recall any incident, sad or heroic or simply memorable, which struck you more than anything else?

24) In times of crisis, people generally show great ingenuity or self-reliance; others sometimes do stupid things. Do you recall any examples of either?

If you need extra space for your answers to any questions, please write below. When you have completed this Questionnaire, we would appreciate your returning it in the enclosed reply-paid envelope. We shall, of course, acknowledge it. Thank you very much for your help.

This might be a point of interest I was awarded the Military Medal Field Marshal Lord Montgomery. Certificate For Gallantry also a Certificate of Gallantry from our own Brigade Commander Brigadier Lathbury.

Chronology

1920   Born Cornelius John Ryan on June 5 in Dublin, Ireland, first child of John Joseph Ryan and Ellen Amelia Clohisey. (Father, born 1895, enlisted in British army in September 1916 and served in France with several motor transport companies that supplied ammunition to heavy artillery units. Discharged in February 1919, he returned to Dublin and found work as a clerk at the successful Johnston, Mooney & O'Brien bakery. Mother, born in 1897, was a member of the Irish Republican women's organization Cumann na mBan. Parents were married on September 8, 1919.) Family lives in house at 33 Heytesbury Street that is also home to uncle John Clohisey. Younger siblings are Joseph, born 1922, Gerald, born 1928, Mary Catherine (Kathleen), born 1931, David, born 1934, and John, born 1936.

1922   Irish Free State established.

1932–36   Attends Christian Brothers school on Synge Street.

1936–40   Takes courses at secretarial college on Harcourt Street and night classes in violin at the Royal Irish Academy of Music. Works for insurance firm and then at the newly opened Dublin Airport, where air traffic declines after outbreak of World War II in September 1939. Travels to London in late 1940 to take junior managerial position in a biscuit factory owned by Canadian businessman Garfield Weston.

1941   Works as copyboy in the London office of Reuters news agency.

1943   Joins staff of *The Daily Telegraph*, national broadsheet newspaper published in London. Sends money home to family in Dublin (will continue to help pay for the schooling of his younger siblings).

1944   Reports from Dublin in early May on Irish general election. Assigned to U.S. Ninth Air Force as war correspondent. Flies on eleven bombing missions over France, May 28–June 25; views Normandy invasion fleet from the air on D-Day, June 6. Reports from Normandy in July on battle for St. Lô. Assigned in August to newly activated Third

909

U.S. Army, commanded by Lieutenant General George S. Patton, and writes about its advance into Brittany and across France. (Ryan will recall in 1970 that "among those brash, irreverent, confident soldiers I found my spiritual home," and that he had learned more from the best American correspondents "than any school could ever have taught me.") Covers the Third Army's fall campaign in Lorraine and its counteroffensive in the Ardennes during the Battle of the Bulge. Visits Bastogne on December 28, two days after the siege of the town is broken.

1945　Reports on the Ardennes and the Third Army's offensive in the Saar-Palatinate. Covers liberation of Ohrdruf concentration camp in April and Third Army advance into Czechoslovakia in early May; all told, Ryan publishes more than 160 bylined articles in the *Daily Telegraph* between D-Day and the German surrender. Writes dispatches from Austria, Czechoslovakia, and Germany until mid-June. Arrives in New York City on August 2 on his way to cover war in the Pacific. Reaches Japan on September 9, one week after the formal Japanese surrender. Witnesses failed suicide attempt on September 11 of General Tojo Hideki, the former prime minister of Japan, 1941–44. (Tojo is convicted of war crimes and hanged in 1948.) Reports on Allied occupation of Japan and aftermath of atomic bombing of Hiroshima.

1946　Leaves Japan on January 26 and sails to California. Reports from San Francisco on failed escape attempt at Alcatraz Federal Penitentiary in early May in which five men are killed. Sails in June to the central Pacific to cover U.S. nuclear tests at Bikini Atoll. Witnesses detonation of bomb dropped from aircraft, July 1, and underwater explosion of bomb, July 25 (tests are fourth and fifth atomic explosions in history). Reports from Palestine, September–December, for the *Telegraph* and as stringer for *Time*. Covers attempts by Jewish refugees to run the British blockade and attacks on British forces by the Jewish underground organizations Irgun Zvai Leumi and Lehi ("Stern Gang"). Takes photograph of two Jewish child refugees from Poland that appears in *Life* on December 30 and attracts wide attention.

1947　Leaves *Telegraph* and joins staff of Time & Life in New York City. *Star-Spangled Mikado*, book on American occupation

of Japan cowritten with Frank Kelley, former Tokyo corre-
spondent for the *New York Herald Tribune*, published on
May 29 by Robert M. McBride & Company. "Beautiful
Murder," report by Ryan on the Trujillo dictatorship in the
Dominican Republic, published in *Life* on June 2. Moves
to New York City.

1948–49   Enjoys working for *Life* but dislikes *Time*. Visits Normandy in June 1949 for the fifth anniversary of D-Day.
Considers writing a book on the invasion and begins reading existing published accounts. Leaves Time & Life and
joins *Newsweek*, where he works on a television news program affiliated with the magazine.

1950   Marries Kathryn Ann Morgan on May 27 at the Church
of St. Ignatius Loyola in New York City. (Morgan, born in
Rose Hill, Iowa, in 1925, is a graduate of the University of
Missouri School of Journalism and an editor at *House and
Garden*.) Becomes a naturalized U.S. citizen in June. Joins
Collier's, a popular weekly magazine published in New
York City, as associate editor. *MacArthur: Man of Action*,
cowritten with Frank Kelley, published on October 19 by
Doubleday. Begins research for book on D-Day.

1951   Publishes "Ireland Today: From Great Famine to Great
Future" in *Collier's*, March 17, defending policies of Prime
Minister John Costello against criticism by Irish Americans ("stage-Irish") opposed to any rapprochement with
Great Britain. Spends most of the year editing "Preview
of the War We Do Not Want," a fictional history of a
war between the United States and the Soviet Union,
1952–55, and the subsequent occupation of Russia by the
United Nations, 1955–60; the "Preview" takes up the entire October 27 issue, and includes contributions by Robert E. Sherwood, Allan Nevins, Edward R. Murrow, Bill
Mauldin, Red Smith, Marguerite Higgins, and Kathryn
Morgan Ryan. Sent by *Collier's* to attend symposium on
"Physics and Medicine of the Upper Atmosphere" held
in San Antonio, Texas, November 6–9, where he meets
physicist Joseph Kaplan, astronomer Fred Whipple, and
rocket engineer Wernher von Braun. (The technical director of the Nazi V-2 missile program, von Braun is now
head of a team of German engineers working on missiles
for the U.S. Army in Alabama.) Initially skeptical, Ryan
becomes convinced of the potential of human spaceflight.

1952   Begins editing series of articles on spaceflight for *Collier's*.
            "Man Will Conquer Space Soon" appears in March 22
            issue, with contributions by von Braun, Whipple, Kap-
            lan, Willy Ley, Heinz Haber, and Oscar Schachter, and
            illustrations by Chesley Bonestell, Fred Freeman, and
            Rolf Klep. (Ryan and Ley do extensive rewriting of draft
            articles.) Father dies in Ireland on September 20. *Across
            the Space Frontier*, expanded version of *Collier's* space
            symposium, published by Viking on September 26 with
            Ryan credited as editor. Space series continues with "Man
            on the Moon" (October 18–25), featuring contributions
            by von Braun and Ley (Ryan continues to serve as von
            Braun's ghostwriter).

1953   Using reports from a panel of consultants, Ryan writes
            "Man's Survival in Space" (February 28–March 14), a
            three-part article on selection and training of future space
            travelers. Series continues with "The Baby Space Station:
            First Step in the Conquest of Space" (June 27), credited
            to von Braun and Ryan. During the year Ryan also writes
            articles for *Collier's* on midget submarines (August 21)
            and sarin nerve gas (November 27). Son Geoffrey John
            Morgan Ryan born August 2. *Collier's* becomes biweekly
            magazine in August as advertising revenues decline. *Con-
            quest of the Moon* published by the Viking Press on Oc-
            tober 19 with Ley, von Braun, and Whipple credited as
            authors and Ryan as editor.

1954   Spaceflight series ends with "Can We Get to Mars?" (April
            30), credited to von Braun and Ryan. Writes articles for
            Collier's about vertical take-off and landing aircraft (April
            2) and advances in solid-state electronics (September 3).

1955   Publishes articles in *Collier's* on the U.S.S. *Albacore* ("I
            Rode the World's Fastest Sub," April 1) and experimental
            single-pilot flying platforms ("The Navy Comes Up with
            a Real 'Flying Saucer'," cowritten with James J. Haggerty
            Jr., April 29).

1956   Writes several articles for *Collier's*: "NATO's Navy" (Jan-
            uary 20); "What Made Vuky Race?" (May 25); about Bill
            Vukovich, champion race car driver killed in the 1955 Indy
            500; and "The Major of St. Lô" (June 8), about an Amer-
            ican infantry officer killed in Normandy in July 1944.
            (Television adaptation of "The Major of St. Lô" starring
            Peter Graves is broadcast on ABC on June 5 as episode

of the *Cavalcade of America* series.) Daughter Victoria Ann Ryan born September 26. Publishes "Five Desperate Hours in Cabin 56" (September 28), account of the July 26 sinking of the Italian ocean liner *Andrea Doria*. (Story is dramatized as "SOS from the Andrea Doria" on NBC, October 16, as part of the Armstrong Circle Theatre.) "One Minute to Ditch!," about emergency water landing of a Pan Am airliner in the Pacific on October 16, 1956, appears in the December 21 issue. Story is on newsstands when it is announced on December 14 that *Collier's* will cease publication.

1957   Continues researching D-Day book as Kathryn, now an associate editor at *House & Home*, supports family. (Kathryn will also help research and edit all three of Ryan's World War II books.) Stories about the *Andrea Doria* and the Pan Am airliner win Benjamin Franklin Magazine Award and receive Overseas Press Club citation. Television adaptation of "One Minute to Ditch!" is broadcast on NBC on March 25 as part of the *Robert Montgomery Presents* program. *One Minute to Ditch!*, collection of five stories written for *Collier's*, published as paperback by Ballantine Books on September 23. Writes articles on the ocean liner *United States* for the *Saturday Evening Post* and on Shannon Airport in Ireland for *Holiday*.

1958   *Reader's Digest* agrees to assist with research for *The Longest Day* in return for rights to condensed version of the book. Publishes articles in *Field & Stream* on fishing in Ireland and deer hunting in Scotland. Sister Kathleen, a chief flight attendant for Pan American Airlines, drowns on June 2 while swimming off coast of Ghana. Ryan flies to Accra and arranges for her body to be flown to Dublin for burial. Signs contract with Simon and Schuster for publication of *The Longest Day* and receives $7,500 advance.

1959   *The Longest Day: June 6, 1944* is published on November 23 by Simon and Schuster and spends twenty-two weeks on *The New York Times* bestseller list. French film producer Raoul Levy buys film rights for $100,000 and hires Ryan to write screenplay for $35,000. (Ryan later recalls being $60,000 in debt at the time of the book's publication.)

1960   Works on screenplay. Family moves from apartment in New York City to modern fifteen-room house on Old Branchville Road in Ridgefield, Connecticut. Reads accounts of the fall of Berlin in 1945, which he is considering making the subject of his next book. Spends election night at the Kennedy family compound in Hyannis Port, Massachusetts, assisting campaign press secretary Pierre Salinger, a former contributing editor at *Collier's*. Hollywood producer Darryl F. Zanuck buys rights to *The Longest Day* from Levy and hires Ryan to write screenplay.

1961   Travels to Paris to work on screenplay with Zanuck. Insists that film be historically accurate and disapproves of Zanuck's willingness to use dramatic license. Submits finished screenplay on April 5, which is then rewritten by Zanuck and associate producer Elmo Williams; Zanuck also hires Romain Gary, James Jones, David Pursall, and Jack Seddon to write additional material. Ryan serves as on-set technical advisor during filming in France of sequences involving American forces. Meets with Soviet officials in Paris about gaining Soviet cooperation for his research on Berlin. Returns to the United States in early September. Relations with Zanuck become increasingly strained.

1962   Reviews *Ploesti* by James Dugan and Carroll Stewart for *The New York Times Book Review* (will review another six books on World War II for the *Book Review* from 1965 to 1972). With assistance from *Reader's Digest*, begins conducting interviews of German and Allied participants in the battle of Berlin. Receives sole credit for screenplay of *The Longest Day* after requesting arbitration by the Writers Guild (Gary, Jones, Pursall, and Seddon receive credit for writing "additional episodes"). *The Longest Day*, directed by Ken Annakin, Andrew Marton, Bernhard Wicki, and an uncredited Zanuck, and featuring an all-star cast that includes John Wayne, Henry Fonda, and Robert Mitchum, is released in the United States on October 4 and becomes a box office success. Despite tensions with Zanuck, Ryan praises film as "probably the most accurate wartime movie ever made."

1963   Receives permission to visit Moscow. On the advice of a Soviet historian, hires John Erickson of the University of Manchester as his Russian translator and research associate. (Erickson, an expert on the Soviet military, later becomes an acclaimed historian of the Soviet-German war.) Discusses trip with President John F. Kennedy, who advises Ryan to be "blunt" in his conversations with the

Soviets. Travels to Moscow in April for three-week visit, during which he is granted access to hitherto restricted documents and allowed to interview prominent wartime commanders Vasily Chuikov, Ivan Konev, Konstantin Rokossovsky, and Vasily Sokolovsky, although he is unable to see Georgy Zhukov, who is in political disfavor.

1964–65   Travels to Normandy with former correspondents for twentieth anniversary of D-Day in 1964 (will make similar trip in 1969). Continues work on Berlin book, conducting interviews with or soliciting written accounts from 700 participants.

1966   *The Last Battle*, published by Simon and Schuster on March 28, spends thirty weeks on *The New York Times* best seller list. Works on screenplay of film version for Metro-Goldwyn-Mayer.

1967–68   With assistance from *Reader's Digest*, Ryan begins research on Operation Market Garden, the failed Allied offensive in Holland in September 1944. Completes screenplay for *The Last Battle*. MGM hires Ryan to write a screen adaptation of *Armageddon*, a novel by Leon Uris set in Berlin during the postwar occupation, which the studio proposes to produce at the same time as *The Last Battle*.

1969   Watches launch of Apollo 11 moon mission with Wernher von Braun at Cape Kennedy, Florida, on July 16. (Von Braun directed the engineering team that designed and built the Saturn rockets used in the Apollo program.) Writes about the launch in "One Small Step—One Giant Leap: The Voyage of Apollo 11," published in October *Reader's Digest*. MGM cancels plans to film *The Last Battle*.

1970   Begins suffering from symptoms of severe prostatitis in April. Receives diagnosis of prostate cancer on July 24. Makes first in a series of secret tape recordings and notebook entries on his illness the next day. Learns in October that cancer has spread to his lymph nodes. Enters Memorial Sloan Kettering Cancer Center in New York City, where he has several dozen radioactive iodine seeds surgically implanted in his prostate.

1971   Works on *A Bridge Too Far*, book on Operation Market Garden, during spring and summer, but completes only forty-seven pages by late August.

1972   Begins estrogen therapy in late spring after scan shows
            that cancer has spread to his bones. Completes Part Two
            of *A Bridge Too Far* on September 29. Kathryn publishes
            novel *The Betty Tree* on November 14.

1973   Discontinues estrogen therapy in February and begins
            taking steroids as cancer continues to spread through his
            bones. Records on February 24 that "*Bridge* has got to
            be what I am not: a testament to the endurance of man."
            Starts chemotherapy treatments in late April while hos-
            pitalized at Memorial Sloan Kettering. Returns home in
            mid-May. Limits use of pain medication in order to write,
            and completes 310 pages of manuscript by the end of
            May. Awarded distinction of the Legion of Honor by the
            French government and is presented with the decoration
            by Jacques Kosciusko-Morizet, the French ambassador to
            the United States, in ceremony held at Ridgefield home
            on July 8. Learns on September 30 of his mother's death
            in Ireland. Completes manuscript of *A Bridge Too Far* on
            October 27. Travels to Holland, Belgium, France, and
            Britain with Kathryn and daughter Victoria in November
            to meet with European publishers.

1974   Receives honorary degree from Ohio University on Janu-
            ary 22 and speaks at its school of communications. Elected
            Fellow of the Society of American Historians (an honor
            Ryan had long hoped for). Travels to Holland, France,
            and Great Britain in June. *A Bridge Too Far* is published
            on September 16 by Simon and Schuster and spends nine-
            teen weeks on *The New York Times* bestseller list. (A film
            adaptation is released in 1977, written by William Gold-
            man, directed by Richard Attenborough, and featuring an
            all-star cast that includes Sean Connery, Michael Caine,
            Ryan O'Neal, and Robert Redford.) Attends events held
            in Holland to commemorate thirtieth anniversary of Op-
            eration Market Garden. Returns to the United States on
            September 23 and moves with Kathryn into apartment at
            the Sherry-Netherland Hotel in New York City. Promotes
            A Bridge Too Far in series of television, radio, and print
            interviews. Begins radiation therapy for hip pain on Octo-
            ber 15. Makes last entry in his "cancer diary" on October
            19. (His tapes and notebooks are found in his home office
            after his death, and form the basis, along with Kathryn's
            diary, for *A Private Battle* by Cornelius Ryan and Kathryn
            Morgan Ryan, published by Simon and Schuster in 1979.

A television adaptation, written by John Gay, directed by Robert Michael Lewis, and starring Jack Warden and Anne Jackson, is shown on CBS in 1980.) Admitted to Memorial Sloan Kettering, October 22. Develops symptoms of pneumonia in November. Dies in hospital on evening of November 23. After an ecumenical service held at St. Mary Parish in Ridgefield on November 26, Ryan is buried in Ridgebury Cemetery.

Note on the Texts

This volume contains two books about World War II by Cornelius Ryan, *The Longest Day: June 6, 1944* (1959) and *A Bridge Too Far* (1974), as well as a section titled "Other World War II Writings" that includes seventeen dispatches that appeared in *The Daily Telegraph* of London from 1944 to 1945; "The Major of St. Lô," an article about the fighting in Normandy that was first published in *Collier's* in 1956; two magazine pieces that followed up on *The Longest Day*, "The Longest Day," published in *This Week* in 1965, and "Untold Stories from The Longest Day," which appeared in *Reader's Digest* in 1974; two letters to publishers about *The Longest Day*, written in 1957 and 1959; and filled-out samples of the questionnaires that Ryan used to research *The Longest Day* and *A Bridge Too Far*.

Ryan flew over the invasion fleet in an American bomber on June 6, 1944, as a reporter for *The Daily Telegraph* and later covered the campaign in Normandy for that newspaper. He returned to France in 1949 for the fifth anniversary of D-Day with a group of former war correspondents. In a 1969 interview Ryan recalled how he had walked along one of the invasion beaches and "began to look at the flotsam and jetsam of war still there: burned-out vehicles, weapons." The experience made him consider writing a book on D-Day, and he began his research by reading more than two hundred published accounts of the invasion. He continued to work on the book while employed as an editor at *Collier's* and turned to it full-time after the magazine ceased publication in December 1956. With financial and research assistance from *Reader's Digest*, Ryan sent out thousands of questionnaires to D-Day veterans and conducted, either in person or through his assistants, several hundred interviews. Simon and Schuster agreed to publish the book and in January 1959 announced that it would be published in June with the title *The Longest Day in History: June 6, 1944*. The publication date was moved back, and the title changed, before excerpts appeared in the June and July 1959 numbers of *Reader's Digest*.

The Longest Day: June 6, 1944 was published by Simon and Schuster on November 23, 1959, in a first printing of 85,000 copies, and became an immediate best seller. A British edition was published by Victor Gollancz on April 4, 1960. Ryan made no changes to the text. (In an interview published in 1969, Ryan said he had learned that the list of D-Day veterans in an appendix to *The Longest Day* contained the names of nine "ringers" who had not landed in Normandy on June 6, 1944, but that he had chosen not to remove them in order to save the men from embarrassment.) This volume prints the text of the 1959 Simon and Schuster edition, and reproduces the photographs and captions included in that edition. The maps printed on the end-papers of the 1959 Simon and Schuster edition are reproduced on the endpapers of this volume.

In 1966 Ryan published *The Last Battle*, an account of the fall of Berlin in 1945, and then began research on Operation Market Garden, the failed Allied attempt to cross the Rhine in Holland in September 1944. This new work, provisionally titled *The Big Drop*, was meant to be the middle book in a planned five-volume history of the European theater in 1944–45 that would begin with *The Longest Day* and end with *The Last Battle*. (It is not known which events Ryan intended to write about in the other two volumes, although he did say they would take place chronologically "on either side" of Operation Market Garden.) He again drew upon the staff of *Reader's Digest* for assistance in locating veterans, sending out questionnaires, and conducting interviews. By the end of 1969 the research was essentially complete, but Ryan found it unusually difficult to begin writing.

Ryan was diagnosed with prostate cancer in July 1970, and for the next year he made little progress on the book, now titled *A Bridge Too Far*, completing only forty-seven pages of finished manuscript by August 1971. Despite his illness he continued to work on the manuscript, assisted by his wife, Kathryn Morgan Ryan, a novelist and former magazine editor, who had helped organize research for and edit *The Longest Day* and *The Last Battle*. Kathryn performed similar work on *A Bridge Too Far* and, in some cases, drafted passages for Ryan to revise. Ryan completed work on the manuscript on October 27, 1973. Simon and Schuster published *A Bridge Too Far* on September 16, 1974, in a first printing of 100,000 copies. A British edition was published the same day by Hamish Hamilton, and the book was excerpted in *Reader's Digest*, October–November 1974. Ryan fell ill in October while promoting *A Bridge Too Far* and died on November 23, 1974. This volume prints the text of the 1974 Simon and Schuster edition and reproduces the maps included in that edition. The photographs and captions are taken from the 1974 Simon and Schuster edition, with one exception. In the 1995 Simon and Schuster trade paperback edition of *A Bridge Too Far*, a new photograph and caption were printed on the bottom of the sixth page of the second photo insert, replacing the photograph and caption that appeared in the 1974 Simon and Schuster edition. This volume accepts the substitution.

The seventeen newspaper dispatches presented in the "Other World War II Writings" section of this volume appeared in *The Daily*

Telegraph of London from May 29, 1944, to September 12, 1945. This volume prints the texts that appeared in the newspaper as follows:

Out with the Marauders over France: *The Daily Telegraph*, May 29, 1944.

Watch Navy Pound French Coast: *The Daily Telegraph*, June 7, 1944.

Flight to Smash French Rail Yards: *The Daily Telegraph*, June 8, 1944.

In Flak-Swept Plane to Bomb Rennes: *The Daily Telegraph*, June 13, 1944.

Nazi Traffic Center in Utter Ruin: *The Daily Telegraph*, June 14, 1944.

Early Capture of St. Lo Expected: *The Daily Telegraph*, July 17, 1944.

Tanks Pour into the Gap: *The Daily Telegraph*, July 28, 1944.

Road to Paris Black with Allied Columns: *The Daily Telegraph*, August 19, 1944.

Germans Would Not Fight Under the S.S.: *The Daily Telegraph*, September 5, 1944.

Moselle Line Broken in Seven Places: *The Daily Telegraph*, September 16, 1944.

Fight On Call by Wounded at Bastogne: *The Daily Telegraph*, December 30, 1944.

Two Columns Closing on Trier: *The Daily Telegraph*, March 1, 1945.

Trier Bridge Was Captured Intact: *The Daily Telegraph*, March 3, 1945.

Rhine Villagers Have Lost Their Taste for War: *The Daily Telegraph*, March 14, 1945.

Wholesale Murders in Nazi Prison Camp: *The Daily Telegraph*, April 9, 1945.

General Shot Himself at Surrender: *The Daily Telegraph*, May 8, 1945.

Tojo Shot Himself to Escape Trial: *The Daily Telegraph*, September 12, 1945.

Copyright © Telegraph Media Group Limited. Reprinted with permission of McIntosh & Otis, Inc.

Ryan published "The Major of St. Lô," about a battle fought in Normandy in July 1944 by one of the American divisions that landed on D-Day, in the June 8, 1956, number of *Collier's*. It was printed in a slightly different form in *One Minute to Ditch!*, a collection of five stories Ryan wrote for *Collier's* published as a mass market paperback by Ballantine Books on September 23, 1957. This volume prints the text that appeared in the 1957 Ballantine Books edition and presents in its notes the endnote to "The Major of St. Lô" Ryan wrote for *One Minute to Ditch!* "The Major of St. Lô" copyright © 1956, 1957 by Cornelius Ryan. Reprinted with permission of McIntosh & Otis, Inc.

In the years following the publication of *The Longest Day* Ryan continued to collect new information about the invasion and received numerous letters from D-Day veterans and their families. He drew upon this material, as well as anecdotes he had not included in his book, in writing "The Longest Day," an article that appeared in *This Week*, a syndicated Sunday newspaper supplement, on June 6, 1965. This volume prints the text that appeared in *This Week*. Ryan later wrote another follow-up article, "Untold Stories from The Longest Day," that appeared in the June 1974 number of *Reader's Digest*. The text printed here is taken from *Reader's Digest*. Both articles are reprinted with permission of McIntosh & Otis, Inc.

Ryan outlined his plans for *The Longest Day* in a letter he wrote to William E. Buckley, vice president of Henry Holt, on November 19, 1957, and discussed his research for the book in a letter sent to Peter Schwed, executive editor of Simon and Schuster, on February 24, 1959. The texts of the letters printed here are taken from the carbon typescript copies in the Cornelius Ryan Collection of World War II Papers, MSS20, Ohio University Libraries, Athens, Ohio. Copyright © 2019 by Victoria Ryan Bida and Chayne Ryan. Reprinted with permission of McIntosh & Otis, Inc.

More than 2,200 questionnaires were sent out by Ryan and his associates as part of the research for *The Longest Day*, and more than 1,100 were returned. The sample questionnaire for *The Longest Day* included in this volume was returned by William Rhinehart Washington, who landed on Omaha Beach with the U.S. 1st Infantry Division. Ryan and his researchers also received more than 1,000 filled-out questionnaires for *A Bridge Too Far*. This volume includes as a sample the response sent by J. T. Richards, who fought at Arnhem with the British 1st Airborne Division. The texts of the questionnaires printed here are taken from the partially printed and partially holograph originals in the Cornelius Ryan Collection of World War II Papers, MSS20, Ohio University Libraries, Athens, Ohio. Copyright © 2019 by Victoria Ryan Bida and Chayne Ryan. Reprinted with permission of McIntosh & Otis, Inc.

Eight errors in the holograph responses to the questionnaires are treated as slips of the pen and corrected in this volume: at 898.28, "Shaunnesey" becomes "Shaughnessy"; at 899.9, "patehetic" becomes "pathetic"; at 899.21, "Aborad" becomes "Aboard" and "Portland Hard" becomes "Portland Harb"; at 903.5, "REPRESTATIVE" becomes "REPRESENTATIVE"; at 903.28, "CAMPAINER" becomes "CAMPAIGNER"; at 906.22, "INTERS" becomes "INTEREST"; at 906.23, "MONGOMERY" becomes "MONTGOMERY." Fifteen typesetting errors that appeared in the printed source texts are also corrected in this volume: at 228.2, "*Minn.*" becomes "*Wis.*"; at 236.24, "Div." becomes "Bn."; at 237.14, "Div." becomes "Bn."; at 264.22, "1946" becomes "1954"; at 266.13, "*the Normandy*" becomes

"*Normandy*"; at 410.30, 591.14, and 622.24, "Hilary" becomes "Hilario"; at 712.30, "Smythe" becomes "Smyth"; at 815.37, "1945" becomes "1959"; at 817.34, "1946" becomes "1954"; at 818.8, "Smythe" becomes "Smyth"; at 818.45, "*Nemesis*" becomes "*The Nemesis*"; at 821.21–22, "*15 September*, tember, 1944" becomes "*15 September, 1944–21 March, 1945*"; and at 866.1, "Aguing" becomes "Aquino." Three errors in photograph captions are corrected as well: on the seventh page of the first photo insert in *The Longest Day*, "LCTs" becomes "LSTs"; on the fourth page of the first insert in *A Bridge Too Far*, "the 19th" becomes "the 20th"; and on the twenty-fourth page of the second insert in *A Bridge Too Far*, "are going" becomes "were going."

This volume presents the texts of the printings, typescripts, and manuscripts chosen as sources here but does not attempt to reproduce features of their design. Errors in alphabetization in the "D-Day Veterans: What They Do Today" appendix and bibliography in the first edition of *The Longest Day*, and in "The Soldiers and Civilians of 'A Bridge Too Far': What They Do Today" appendix in the first edition of *A Bridge Too Far*, have been corrected. The texts are printed without alteration except for the changes previously discussed and for the correction of typographical errors. Spelling, punctuation, and capitalization are often expressive features, and they are not altered, even when inconsistent or irregular. The following is a list of typographical errors corrected, cited by page and line number: 37.21, surprise; 37.38, M.I.5; 76.25, Symond's; 114.38, MI; 135.13, by a; 151.38, 38-millimeter; 170.10, DUKWS; 180.19, Aircraftsman; 187.3, hour's; 221.37, Lebissey.; 229.3, Proctor; 229.6, Pocahoutas; 229.6, *Pocahoutas*; 229.20, Seamen; 231.45, (L) go; 239.15, Ranger.; 242.8, *Oddessa*,; 245.21, *Picaqune*,; 248.12, *Anna*,; 249.7, *Enginering*; 251.12, Aircraftsman; 252.29, *occupation*; 253.43, #101; 259.7–8, Ranger's; 262.28, Royald; 262.30, *Sage*; 263.44, Marrow,; 265.23, Hauser,; 284.38, get get; 303.19, Blaskowitz'; 380.4, Eric; 449.37, 17-pound; 551.40, *Theater.*"; 644.20, is possible.; 680.32, Uruquhart; 723.23–24, Arrnoldus; 723.35, *Hexenkessel.*; 727.26, revealed,; 778.42, *Moorehead*,; 780.25, *Esstates*,; 781.30, *Wheatridge*; 783.32, *3D Special*; 790.31, Bombadier; 791.22, *Gibralter.*; 792.43, G.C.V.G., K.C.R.,; 795.34, *Bahrein*; 800.9, *Eidnhoven*; 802.38, Nigmegen; 803.20, Grosebeek; 807.14, Ordinance; 809.3, voluminuous; 815.9, 1945.; 815.37, Alan; 816.15, *Decision*; 816.31, *Plan*; 821.21, Meindle; 830.25, light; 840.4, Luzon; 845.11, unfied; 845.14, have have; 848.5, machine-guns,; 848.29, and half; 856.33, Haydon; 860.38, at the first; 866.1, Aguing,; 873.29, casualities; 889.14, know; 890.12, Dormstadt; 890.19, *One Minute to Ditch*; 891.6, was to; 891.38, Carenton,; 892.10–11, hook the foot; 892.15, D-day!); 892.19, bad.); 893.15, pront; 898.15, scuttlebut.

Notes

In the notes below, the reference numbers denote page and line of this volume (the line count includes headings). No note is made for material included in the eleventh edition of *Merriam-Webster's Collegiate Dictionary*. Biblical quotations are keyed to the King James Version. Quotations from Shakespeare are keyed to *The Riverside Shakespeare*, ed. G. Blakemore Evans (Boston: Houghton Mifflin, 1974). For further biographical background, see Cornelius Ryan and Kathryn Morgan Ryan, *A Private Battle* (New York: Simon and Schuster, 1979) and Dominic Phelan, *Cornelius Ryan: D-Day Reporter* (Scotts Valley, CA: CreateSpace Independent Publishing, 2014). For further historical background and references to other studies more recent than those cited in *The Longest Day* and *A Bridge Too Far*, see Rick Atkinson, *The Guns at Last Light: The War in Western Europe, 1944–1945* (New York: Henry Holt, 2013).

THE LONGEST DAY: JUNE 6, 1944

10.27–28   Gobelin tapestry] A tapestry made at the Manufacture des Gobelins, a factory established in Paris in 1601 and purchased by Louis XIV in 1662.

10.29   La Rochefoucauld . . . maxims] La Rochefoucauld (1613–1680) published his *Réflexions ou sentences et maximes morales* in Paris in 1665.

10.37   great victories . . . North African deserts] Rommel commanded the German troops sent to Libya in February 1941 after Italian forces suffered a series of defeats at the hands of the British. Beginning in March 1941, Rommel won a series of victories in eastern Libya and western Egypt that ended in July 1942 when his advance on Alexandria was halted in western Egypt at the first battle of El Alamein.

13.13   *Oberbefehlshaber West*] Commander-in-chief West.

15.7–8   Major General Rudolf Schmundt] Schmundt (1896–1944) was badly wounded by the bomb planted in Hitler's headquarters in East Prussia by Colonel Claus von Stauffenberg on July 20, 1944, and died on October 1.

17.1   Wilhelm Keitel] Keitel (1882–1946) served as chief of OKW from 1938 to 1945. He was convicted of committing crimes against peace, war crimes, and crimes against humanity by the Nuremberg tribunal and hanged.

17.16–18   his crushing defeat . . . the year before] The British Eighth Army under Lieutenant General Bernard Montgomery (1887–1976) decisively defeated German and Italian forces in the second battle of El Alamein,

October 23–November 4, 1942, forcing Rommel to retreat across Libya to Tunisia. Montgomery launched his offensive at El Alamein only after gaining numerical superiority in men, aircraft, tanks, and artillery.

17.30–31 Denmark fell . . . six weeks.] The Germans occupied Denmark on April 9, 1940, and invaded Norway the same day. Fighting continued in Norway until June 10, when Norwegian forces inside the country capitulated on the orders of their government-in-exile. The initial sea and air attacks against Norwegian ports and airfields achieved surprise and caused confusion among the defenders, leading many contemporary press reports to attribute German successes to "fifth column" actions by Nazi collaborator Vidkun Quisling (1887–1945) and his small group of followers.

18.20 Franz Halder] Halder (1884–1972) was chief of the army general staff from September 1938 to September 1942, when he was relieved by Hitler.

18.40 Canadians landed at Dieppe.] The Allies raided Dieppe on August 19, 1942, with a force mostly made up of Canadian troops.

19.26–27 Italy . . . invasion of Sicily] Allied troops invaded Sicily on July 10, 1943, beginning a campaign that lasted until the capture of Messina on August 17. Benito Mussolini was overthrown by a coup in Rome on July 25, and the new Italian government began secret talks that led to the surrender of Italy on September 8.

24.36 Admiral Wilhelm Canaris] Canaris (1887–1945) was chief of the Abwehr, the German military intelligence service, from 1935 until his dismissal on February 12, 1944. He was hanged by the SS on April 9, 1945, for plotting to overthrow Hitler.

26.24 Alfred Jodl] Jodl (1890–1946) served as chief of operations for OKW from 1939 to 1945. He was convicted of committing crimes against peace, war crimes, and crimes against humanity by the Nuremberg tribunal and hanged.

31.30 "Axis Sally"] Born in Portland, Maine, Mildred Gillars (1900–1988) moved to Germany in 1934 and began working as an announcer for the overseas service of Reichsradio in 1940. From December 1942 to April 1945 she broadcast propaganda aimed at American servicemen and became widely known as "Axis Sally," although she used the name "Midge" in her broadcasts. Gillars was convicted of treason in federal court in 1949 and served twelve years in prison before being paroled in 1961.

31.39 "I Double Dare You."] Song (1937) by Jimmy Eaton (1906–1979) and Terry Shand (1904–1977) that was recorded by a number of singers, including Louis Armstrong.

32.6–15 "*I double dare . . . dare you.*"] The original lyrics to the song were: "I double dare you to sit over here, / I double dare you to lend me your ear. / Take off your high hat and let's get friendly / Don't be a 'scare-cat,' say what do you care? / Can't you take a dare? / I double dare you to kiss me and then, / I double dare you to kiss me again. / And if that look in your eyes means what I'm thinking of, / I double dare you to fall in love with me, / I double dare you, dare you."

32.23   Wrens] Members of the Women's Royal Naval Service (WRNS).

34.7–8   338,000 British troops . . . Dunkirk] Approximately 225,000 British and 110,000 French troops were evacuated from Dunkirk, May 27–June 4, 1940. Almost all of the French soldiers returned to France before the armistice with Germany was signed on June 22.

35.16–17   white Navy "battle duster."] The white ensign, which was adopted as the sole standard of the Royal Navy in 1864.

37.8–9   Scotland Yard . . . M.I.5] The Security Service, also known as M.I.5, was (and is) not a department of the Metropolitan Police (Scotland Yard). Founded in 1909 as part of the War Office, M.I.5 operated as an interdepartmental intelligence service from 1931 until 1952, when it was placed under the Home Secretary.

38.34   the *Abwehr*] The German military intelligence service established under the Weimar Republic. In February 1944 the organization was placed under the authority of the foreign intelligence branch of the SD, the SS Security Service.

38.36–37   Diello . . . "Cicero"] While working as his valet, Elyesa Bazna (1904–1970) gained access to the safe used by Sir Hughe Knatchbull-Hugessen, the British ambassador to Turkey. In October 1943 Bazna began selling secret information to the SD (SS Security Service) and eventually received a total of £300,000. Fearing exposure, Bazna left his valet's position in April 1944; he later discovered that the SD had used forged British banknotes to pay him. The presence of a German spy within the British embassy in Ankara first became public knowledge in 1950 with the publication of *Operation Cicero* by L. C. Moyzisch, a former SD officer involved in the case. Moyzisch referred to Bazna only by his codename "Cicero," while Franz von Papen, the wartime German ambassador to Turkey, used the name "Diello" in his *Memoirs* (1952). His actual identity became known in 1962, after *The Longest Day* came out, when Bazna published his memoir *I Was Cicero*.

39.5–6   agents . . . British Isles] In 1972 the publication of *The Double-Cross System in the War of 1939–45* by Sir John Masterman revealed that, beginning in 1940, M.I.5 had succeeded in gaining control over the German espionage system in the United Kingdom, and in 1944 used its double agents as part of the deception campaign designed to make the Germans believe the Allies would land in the Pas de Calais.

39.8   the General] Major General Henry Miller (1890–1949), chief of the Ninth Air Force Service Command.

41.2–3   eccentric headgear . . . decorations] Bernard Montgomery (1887–1976) began wearing the black beret of the Royal Tank Regiment in place of the standard British officer's cap shortly after taking command of the Eighth

Army in Egypt in August 1942. George S. Patton (1885–1945) often wore his dress uniform and full decorations on occasions when other senior American commanders appeared in field uniform.

41.16   Walter Bedell Smith] Smith (1895–1961) later served as the U.S. ambassador to the Soviet Union, 1946–49, as director of the Central Intelligence Agency, 1950–53, and as undersecretary of state, 1953–54.

41.40   Heinrich Himmler's] Heinrich Himmler (1900–1945) became head of the SS (Protection Detachment) in 1929. Originally Hitler's Nazi Party bodyguard, under Himmler the SS became the main instrument of state terror and genocide in the Third Reich, gaining control over the police, the secret police, and the concentration camps, and forming its own military force, known after 1940 as the Waffen (Armed) SS. Himmler committed suicide in British custody on May 23, 1945.

44.9   Liberty ships] Oceangoing vessels designed for mass production, Liberty ships measured 441 feet in length and could carry almost 11,000 tons of cargo. More than 2,700 were launched in American shipyards from 1941 to 1945.

48.7–8   Air Chief Marshal Tedder] Sir Arthur Tedder (1890–1967) had served as the R.A.F. commander in the Middle East, 1941–43, and as commander of the Allied air forces in the Mediterranean, 1943–44.

48.9   Admiral Ramsay] Sir Bertram Ramsay (1883–1945) had commanded the evacuation of Dunkirk in 1940 and led the naval forces in the invasion of Sicily in 1943. Ramsay was killed when his transport aircraft crashed near Paris on January 2, 1945.

48.10   Air Chief Marshal Leigh-Mallory] Sir Trafford Leigh-Mallory (1892–1944) had commanded No. 12 Group in R.A.F. Fighter Command during the Battle of Britain. He was killed on November 12, 1944, when his transport aircraft crashed in the French Alps. (Trafford Leigh-Mallory was the younger brother of the mountain climber George Leigh Mallory, who died on Mount Everest in 1924.)

48.11   Montgomery . . . D-Day assault] Montgomery commanded the Allied ground forces on D-Day.

50.22   Arthur B. "Dutch" Schultz] Schultz's nickname was possibly inspired by the notorious New York gangster Dutch Schultz (born Arthur Flegenheimer, 1902–1935).

53.38   Sten gun] A British submachine gun that fired 9 mm ammunition, had a 32-round magazine, weighed seven pounds, and had an effective range of 100 yards.

54.6   Hamble River] A river in Hampshire that flows into Southampton Water.

55.8   invasion of North Africa] Allied forces landed in Morocco and Algeria, then under the control of Vichy France, on November 8, 1942.

56.10   LCT] Land Craft, Tank, a seagoing vessel that could land four to five tanks or nine trucks directly onto a beach.

56.19   LST] Landing Ship, Tank, a seagoing vessel capable of landing 18 tanks, 160 troops, or 500 tons of cargo directly onto a beach.

57.9   LCI] Landing Craft, Infantry, a seagoing vessel that could land 200 men directly onto a beach.

57.15–16   bluebird shit . . . Dover."] Cf. "(There'll Be Bluebirds Over) The White Cliffs of Dover" (1941), a popular wartime song composed by Walter Kent (1911–1994) with lyrics by Nat Burton (1901–1945).

60.16   "Colonel Britain"—Douglas Ritchie] Ritchie (1905–1967), the assistant director of European broadcasts for the BBC, used the pseudonym "Colonel Britton" in his wartime broadcasts to occupied Europe.

64.40   Ernst Junger] A prolific novelist and essayist, Jünger (1895–1998) first became known for *Storm of Steel* (1920, revised 1924), a memoir of his experiences fighting on the Western Front in World War I.

65.15–16   Erich Marcks . . . June 6] Marcks (1891–1944) was killed by an Allied air attack on June 12, 1944.

65.23   General Eugen Meindl] Mendl (1892–1951) commanded the II Parachute Corps, 1943–45.

66.17   91st Air Landing Division] Organized in January 1944, the division was originally intended to be transported by air, but was then sent to France to serve as a regular infantry formation.

73.32–74.1   Philip Vian . . . battleship *Bismarck*] The *Bismarck* sailed from Norway into the North Atlantic on May 21, 1941, and sank the British battlecruiser H.M.S. *Hood* on May 24. Vian (1894–1941) commanded the destroyer flotilla that engaged *Bismarck* on the night of May 26 after an attack by British torpedo bombers jammed its left rudder. The destroyers maintained contact with the battleship until the morning of May 27, when a Royal Navy task force sank the *Bismarck*.

74.3–4   H.M.S. *Ajax* . . . *Graf Spee*] Three British cruisers, *Ajax*, *Exeter*, and *Achilles*, fought the German heavy cruiser *Admiral Graf Spee* in the estuary of the River Plate on December 13, 1939. The badly damaged *Graf Spee* was forced to seek refuge in Montevideo harbor, where it was scuttled on December 17 to avoid internment by the Uruguayan government.

76.14   *Kings Row*] A controversial best-selling novel (1940) by Henry Bellaman (1882–1945) about small-town life in the Midwest in the 1890s.

76.19–20 *A Maid and a Million Men*] Novel (1928) by James G. Dunton (1899–2001) about a young American woman who impersonates her twin brother during World War I and is then sent to fight in France.

76.25 Symonds' *Life of Michelangelo*] *The Life of Michelangelo Buonarroti* (1893) by the English poet and essayist John Addington Symonds (1840–1893).

81.13 NEA's] Newspaper Enterprise Association, a news syndicate founded in 1902. It merged with United Features Syndicate in 1978 to form United Media Enterprises.

87.2 Dakotas] British name for the American C-47 twin-engine transport aircraft, the military version of the DC-3 passenger aircraft.

88.15 *Schmeisser* submachine gun] Allied name for the German MP (Maschinen Pistole) 40. It fired 9 mm ammunition, had a 32-round magazine, weighed about nine pounds, and had an effective range of 100 yards.

90.1 Bren gunner] The Bren was a British light machine gun that fired .303-caliber ammunition, had a top-mounted 30-round magazine, weighed 25 pounds, and had an effective range of 600 yards. Every British and Canadian infantry section (squad) was equipped with a Bren gun as its principal weapon.

95.18 Volkswagen] During World War II the Volkswagen company manufactured military vehicles similar to the American jeep.

98.34 "Red Devils"] Name given to British airborne troops by the Germans during the fighting in Tunisia in 1942–43.

99.16 larger than a DC-3] The DC-3 was 65 feet long and had a wingspan of 95 feet.

104.13 Lancaster bombers] British four-engine heavy bombers.

110.41–42 chaplains . . . captured and executed] Captain Ignatius Maternowski (1912–1944), the Roman Catholic chaplain of the 508th Parachute Infantry Regiment, was shot in the back by a German sniper in Gueutteville, a hamlet about three miles southwest of Ste.-Mère-Église.

114.20–21 airborne assaults in Sicily and Salerno] Units of the 82nd Airborne parachuted behind the German lines in Sicily on the night of July 9, 1943, and into the American beachhead on the night of July 11. During the battle of Salerno in southern Italy they were dropped at night into the American beachhead as emergency reinforcements on September 13 and 14, 1943; another drop was made behind the German lines on September 14.

114.37 M1 rifle] The standard U.S. infantry rifle of World War II, the M-1 was a semiautomatic weapon that fired .30-caliber ammunition, held eight rounds in its magazine, weighed over nine pounds, and had an effective range of 500 yards.

117.13–14 "Never . . . by so many."] Cf. the speech made by Prime Minister Winston Churchill in the House of Commons on August 20, 1940, in which he praised the fighter pilots and bomber aircrew of the R.A.F.: "Never in the field of human conflict was so much owed by so many to so few."

117.23 bazookas] A tube-launched, shoulder-fired rocket launcher designed as a close-range antitank weapon that was also used against fortifications. The launcher was 54 inches long and fired a 3.5-pound projectile 2.36 inches (60 mm) in diameter with an effective range of 100 yards.

124.27–28 battleships *Scharnhorst* . . . in 1942] The battleships *Scharnhorst* and *Gneisenau* and heavy cruiser *Prinz Eugen* left Brest on February 11, 1942, sailed through the English Channel, and reached Helgoland in the North Sea on February 13. *Scharnhorst* was sunk by a Royal Navy task force off the North Cape of Norway on December 26, 1943, while *Gneisenau* was badly damaged in an R.A.F. air raid while in dry dock at Kiel on February 26, 1942, and never returned to service. *Prinz Eugen* survived the war and was used by the U.S. Navy as a target ship in the atomic bomb tests held at Bikini Atoll in the Pacific on July 1 and 25, 1946. (Cornelius Ryan witnessed the Bikini tests as a correspondent for the London *Daily Telegraph*.) After the tests *Prinz Eugen* was towed to Kwajalein Atoll, where it capsized. As of 2018, the wreck remains partially visible and has not been salvaged due to concerns about radioactive contamination.

125.8–9 21st Panzer Division . . . *Afrika Korps*] The 21st Panzer Division fought in North Africa from 1941 to May 1943, when the remnants of the division surrendered in Tunisia. It was reconstituted in France in July 1943 around a cadre of divisional veterans who had been on leave or convalescing at the time of the Tunisian surrender.

131.18 4th and 24th cavalry squadrons] The squadrons were normally used as mechanized reconnaissance troops.

135.29 four guns . . . half the reported size] The battery contained 100 mm Czech guns from World War I that fired 30-pound shells instead of modern 150 mm guns firing 95-pound shells.

138.16 *Panzer Lehr*] Literally, "Panzer Teaching." The division was formed using personnel from the instructional and demonstration units of the panzer training schools, which included many combat veterans from the Eastern Front.

143.32–33 Remember Coventry!] A German air raid on the night of November 14, 1940, killed 568 people in Coventry and destroyed much of the city.

144.28–29 Captain Charles Cawthon] Cawthon (1912–1996) wrote about his experiences on D-Day and in the campaign for St. Lô in *Other Clay: A Remembrance of the World War II Infantry* (1990).

144.29–30 "The Shooting of Dan McGrew"] Poem (1907) by the British Canadian writer Robert W. Service (1874–1958).

144.35–36 "Once more . . . dear friends] *Henry V*, III.i.1–2.

144.40–145.2   "He that . . . is named] *Henry V*, IV.iii.41–42.

145.35   carbine] The U.S. M-I carbine was a semiautomatic weapon that had a 15-round magazine, weighed six pounds, and had an effective range of 200 yards. It fired .30-caliber ammunition that was lighter and less powerful than that used in the M-I rifle.

148.29   *Largs*] H.M.S. *Largs*, a converted French merchant vessel, was the command ship for the Sword Beach landings.

149.6   thirty casualties] Thirty-two Norwegian and one British crew member died in the sinking of the *Svenner*. Launched in 1943 as H.M.S. *Shark*, the destroyer was ceded to the Norwegian navy in March 1944.

149.28   battletested 352nd Division] The division was formed in November 1943 and had yet to see action, although its ranks contained a significant number of combat veterans.

150.22–23   H.M.S. *Ajax* . . . fame] See note 74.3–4.

151.14   Spitfires, Thunderbolts, and Mustangs] The Spitfire was a British single-engine, single-seat fighter aircraft; the P-47 Thunderbolt and P-51 Mustang were American single-engine, single-seat fighter aircraft.

151.18–19   B-26 medium bombers] The B-26 Marauder was an American twin-engine bomber. Ryan flew over Normandy in a B-26 on D-Day (see pp. 829–31 in this volume).

151.21   Fortresses and Liberators] The B-17 Flying Fortress and B-24 Liberator were American four-engine heavy bombers.

151.38   four 380-millimeter rocket tubes] The tubes deployed by the Germans as part of the Omaha Beach defenses fired 320 mm rockets.

152.24   Krupps] Guns made by Krupp, a German steel and armaments manufacturer.

154.32–33   Higgins . . . goddamned boat] New Orleans boatbuilder Andrew J. Higgins (1886–1952) designed and manufactured the LCVP (Landing Craft, Vehicle and Personnel), which could carry 36 troops or a 2.5-ton truck.

155.3   LCA] Landing Craft Assault, the British counterpart to the LCVP.

156.25–26   clip of bullets] The M-I rifle was loaded by inserting an eight-round clip into the weapon's internal magazine.

158.29   Stoney Creek] American forces that had invaded Upper Canada were defeated by the British at Stoney Creek on the night of June 5, 1813, and driven back across the Niagara River.

158.31   Salerno] British and American forces landed at Salerno on September 9, 1943. A series of German counterattacks, September 12–16, threatened the beachhead before they were repulsed.

160.32–39 Dog Green . . . 2nd Ranger Battalion] The assault on the Dog Green sector by Company A of the 116th Infantry Regiment and Company C of the 2nd Ranger Battalion is depicted in fictional form in the opening of the film *Saving Private Ryan* (1998), written by Robert Rodat and directed by Steven Spielberg.

161.13 Tommy gun] The American Thompson submachine gun fired .45-caliber ammunition, had a 20-round magazine, an effective range of 100 yards, and weighed twelve pounds.

165.18 Brigadier General Theodore Roosevelt] Theodore Roosevelt Jr. (1887–1944), the eldest son of President Theodore Roosevelt, had been wounded in France in 1918. He served as the assistant commander of the 1st Infantry Division in Algeria, Tunisia, and Sicily, 1942–43.

168.37 German 88 fire] The high-velocity 88 mm gun was used by the Germans as an antiaircraft, antitank, and field artillery weapon. (Allied troops sometimes identified shell fire from other German antitank and field artillery guns as coming from "88s.")

170.7–8 "potato masher" hand grenades] A German hand grenade with a cylindrical explosive charge attached to a wooden throwing stick.

170.10 DUKWs] A six-wheeled American amphibious truck equipped with a propeller and rudder that could carry 25 men or 5,000 pounds of cargo.

170.14 Browning automatic rifles] American rifle capable of fully automatic fire that used the same .30-caliber ammunition as the M-1 rifle. The BAR was fed from a 20-round magazine, had an effective range of 500 yards, and weighed nineteen pounds.

172.16 Munich] Adolf Hitler, Benito Mussolini, Édouard Daladier, and Neville Chamberlain met at Munich, September 29–30, 1938, and agreed that Czechoslovakia would cede the Sudetenland region to Germany. After Germany occupied the remainder of Czechoslovakia on March 15, 1939, the British and French governments committed themselves to defending Poland against German aggression.

173.6 Teller mines] German antitank mine containing nine to twelve pounds of high explosive.

173.16 Major C. K. "Banger" King] Charles Kenneth King (1904–1945) commanded Company A of the 2nd Battalion East Yorkshire Regiment and later served as the battalion second-in-command. King was killed in northwest Germany on April 17, 1945, when his jeep struck a mine.

173.19–20 "And gentlemen . . . not here] *Henry V*, IV.iii.64–65.

173.36 Bren gun carrier] A British tracked vehicle used to transport men, supplies, mortars, and machine guns. Also known as the Universal Carrier, the vehicle weighed three tons and was frequently armed with a Bren light machine gun.

176.9   Bond Street] A street in the West End of London famous for its luxury shops.

177.16–20   Stanley Hollis . . . kill another ten.] Hollis (1912–1972) would receive the only Victoria Cross awarded for valor on D-Day.

179.10   INS] International News Service, a wire service founded in 1909 that merged with United Press in 1958 to form United Press International.

182.14   Jesse Owens] American athlete Jesse Owens (1913–1980) had won gold medals at the 1936 Berlin Olympics in the 100-meter dash, 200-meter sprint, 4 × 100-meter relay, and the long jump.

184.25   *En Avant*] Forward.

184.36–37   *Reichskanzlei*] Reich Chancellery.

185.6–8   Rome . . . Kesselring's] Allied troops entered Rome, which had been declared an open (undefended) city, on June 4. Kesselring (1885–1960) commanded German forces in Italy, 1943–45.

185.16–17   Jodl's sphere . . . eastern theater] Hitler directed the war on the Eastern Front through the OKH (Army Supreme Command) and on all other fronts through the OKW (Armed Forces Supreme Command).

191.13–14   bazooka man . . . rocket projectile] German troops were equipped with both the *Panzerschreck* ("Panzer Fright"), a reusable rocket launcher similar to the American bazooka, and the more widely used *Panzerfaust* ("Panzer Fist"), a shoulder-launched antitank weapon using a single-shot, disposable firing tube. The *Panzerschreck*, *Panzerfaust*, and bazooka all used specially shaped explosive charges to create a focused jet of heated metal capable of penetrating steel armor.

199.35   JU-88 bombers] The Junkers 88, a twin-engine medium bomber.

200.37   Wodarczyk] Heinz Wodarczyk (1922–1945) was shot down and killed over Holland on January 1, 1945.

204.20   Wing Commander K. T. Lofts] Kenneth Temple Lofts (1918–1951), a Spitfire pilot, was shot down by flak near Bayeux on May 27, 1944. He successfully evaded capture and made contact with Canadian troops on July 19. Lofts was killed in 1951 while flying a Vampire jet fighter in an air race.

208.8–9   forty-six Bedford men . . . only twenty-three] In *Bedford Goes to War: The Heroic Story of a Small Virginia Community in World War II* (3rd edition, 2013), James W. Morrison writes that thirty-eight men from Bedford County were serving with the 116th Regiment on June 6, 1944, and that twenty of them were killed on Omaha Beach, nineteen in Company A and one in Company F. Of the twenty men, six were from the town of Bedford, while the remaining fourteen were from the surrounding county, which was recorded in the 1940 census as having a population of 29,687. Another three men from Bedford County were killed in Normandy and Brittany during the summer of 1944.

208.36–37   Captain Quentin Roosevelt] Quentin Roosevelt II (1919–1948) served as an artillery officer in the 1st Division. He was named after his uncle Quentin Roosevelt (1897–1918), who was killed in World War I while serving as a fighter pilot in France. Quentin Roosevelt II was killed in 1948 when his airliner crashed in Hong Kong.

216.1   "*Bitte! Bitte! Bitte!*"] "Please! Please! Please!"

218.1–2   Lord Lovat . . . Bill Millin] In 1995 Millin (1922–2010) played the bagpipes at the funeral of his former commander, Simon Fraser, Lord Lovat (1911–1995).

221.3   Mark IV tanks] The Mark IV tank weighed 25 tons, had a five-man crew, a maximum speed of 25 mph, armor 80 mm thick at the front and 30 mm thick on the sides, and was armed with a high-velocity 75 mm gun.

222.21–22   "Deutschland über Alles"] The German national anthem, 1922–45. Its lyrics were taken from a patriotic poem (1841) by August Hoffman von Fallersleben (1798–1874) and set to music composed (1796) by Joseph Haydn (1732–1809).

225.22–24   *end of June, Rommel . . . 250,000 men*] In a message sent to Hitler on July 15, 1944, Rommel reported that since the invasion his army group had lost 97,000 men, including 28 generals, 354 commanders, and 2,360 officers, and had received only 6,000 replacements.

227.15   AAA (AW)] Anti-Aircraft Artillery (Automatic Weapons).

227.38   LCI (L)] Landing Craft Infantry (Large).

228.20   Chem. Mortar Bn.] Chemical mortar battalions were equipped with 4.2-inch mortars that fired white phosphorus and high-explosive rounds.

247.12   SC 1332] Submarine Chaser 1332.

248.33   R.N.V.R.] Royal Navy Volunteer Reserve.

248.44   LCS 254] Landing Craft Support 254.

249.31   S.S. Brig.] Special Service Brigade.

250.4   R.A.M.C.] Royal Army Medical Corps.

255.28   2nd T.A.F.] 2nd Tactical Air Force.

258.24   U.S.A.R.] U.S. Army Reserve.

259.41   the Bonn government] The Federal Republic of Germany, which made Bonn its provisional capital from 1949 to 1990.

265.31   Roge, Commander] Commandant Rogé, a French officer.

A BRIDGE TOO FAR

280.2 Wehrmacht] The German armed forces, i.e., the army, navy (Kriegs-marine), and air force (Luftwaffe).

280.3 Waffen SS] The SS military force, which by 1944 had over 500,000 men in its ranks and included seven panzer (armored) divisions.

281.10 Dr. Arthur Seyss-Inquart] Seyss-Inquart (1892–1946) was the Nazi governor of Austria, 1938–39, deputy governor-general of occupied Poland, 1939–40, and commissar of the occupied Netherlands, 1940–45. He was con-victed of war crimes by the Nuremberg international tribunal and hanged on October 16, 1946.

281.11 Anton Mussert] Mussert (1894–1946) was convicted of treason by a Dutch court and shot on May 7, 1946.

282.18–19 Pieter S. Gerbrandy] Gerbrandy (1885–1961) served as prime min-ister of the Netherlands, September 1940–June 1945.

285.36–37 husband, Johan . . . Dachau] Johan van Zweden (1896–1975) was imprisoned in the concentration camp at Vught in Holland from February 1943 to May 1944, when he was sent to Dachau. He was liberated in April 1945.

286.19–20 "Wilhelmus" . . . "Oranje Boven!"] The words to "Wilhelmus van Nassouwe" were written by an unknown author sometime from 1568 to 1572, and were later set to a French melody by Adrianus Valerius (1575–1625). "Wilhelmus" was officially adopted as the Dutch national anthem in 1932. "Oranje Boven!" is a Dutch folk song from the late nineteenth century.

291.29–30 Rommel . . . deserts] See note 10.37.

292.22 Wilhelm Keitel] See note 17.1.

293.1–3 Von Rundstedt . . . attacked Russia] In 1940 von Rundstedt (1875–1953) commanded Army Group A, which included Panzergruppe Kleist, an army-size formation. During the invasion of the Soviet Union in 1941 von Rundstedt commanded Army Group South from the beginning of the cam-paign on June 22 until December 1, when he was dismissed by Hitler.

298.29 Alfred Jodl] See note 26.24.

302.11–12 Some five thousand people lost their lives] About 5,000 people were arrested for suspected involvement in the July 20 assassination plot, and approximately 200 people were executed.

303.6–8 After Rommel . . . replace him.] Von Kluge succeeded Rommel as commander of Army Group B while continuing to serve as OB West. He held both positions until August 17, when he was replaced by Field Marshal Walter Model (1891–1945). Model served as OB West until von Rundstedt's reinstatement on September 4, and as commander of Army Group B until his death. Surrounded by American forces in the Ruhr and facing possible trial by the Soviets for war crimes, Model dissolved his command on April 21, 1945, and then shot himself.

305.24–25   Obergruppenführer] The Waffen SS had its own military ranks, distinct from those used by the German army and Luftwaffe.

306.34   2nd and 116th Panzer units] The 2nd and 116th Panzer Divisions, Wehrmacht formations that had suffered heavy losses in Normandy.

313.7–10   airborne forces . . . been withdrawn] The U.S. 82nd and 101st Airborne Divisions returned to England from Normandy in mid-July 1944, while the British 6th Airborne Division fought on the eastern flank of the Allied beachhead until late August, then advanced to the Seine before returning to England in early September.

321.12–13   ambassador at large, Anthony Biddle] Biddle (1897–1961) had served as the American diplomatic representative to the governments-in-exile of Poland, Belgium, the Netherlands, Norway, Czechoslovakia, Yugoslavia, and Greece from 1941 to 1943. He maintained his contacts with the Dutch government after he joined Eisenhower's staff in January 1944.

333.37   Combined Chiefs of Staff] Created in 1942, the Combined Chiefs of Staff brought together the British Chiefs of Staff and the U.S. Joint Chiefs of Staff to develop and coordinate Allied strategy.

334.9–11   his boyhood . . . lesser schools] Montgomery was the son of a minister in the Church of Ireland who later served as the bishop of Tasmania, and was educated at St. Paul's School in London, founded in 1509.

337.8   Dakotas] British name for the American C-47 twin-engine transport aircraft.

341.28   V-2's] A liquid-fueled guided ballistic missile that traveled at supersonic speeds and carried a 2,000-pound warhead. The V-2 bombardment of London continued until March 27, 1945, and killed more than 2,700 people. V-2s were also used to attack Antwerp from October 1944 to March 1945, killing more than 1,700 soldiers and civilians.

351.36   Hans Krebs] Krebs (1898–1945) later served as chief of staff of the German army from April 1 to May 2, 1945, when he committed suicide in Berlin.

358.13   the Germans did have night fighters] German night fighter units were deployed to defend Germany against R.A.F. bomber raids, and therefore were not in position to intercept the Allied transports that flew over Normandy on the night of June 5–6, 1944.

358.24   self-sealing gas tanks] Airplane fuel tanks with a rubber inner lining that would close up after being punctured, reducing the risk of fire.

364.23–26 intelligence staff . . . Holland to refit."] Ryan completed *A Bridge Too Far* before it became publicly known that the British had succeeded in breaking many high-level German cipher systems during World War II. While Ultra intelligence derived from signals intercepted before the beginning of Market Garden revealed that the 9th and 10th SS Panzer Divisions had been moved to the Arnhem area, the deciphered messages did not contain detailed information about their equipment, personnel strength, or operational readiness.

370.37–38 Urquhart . . . Highland Division] Urquhart (1901–1988) had commanded the 231st Brigade Group, part of the 51st Highland Division, in Tunisia, Sicily and Italy, May–September 1943.

378.15 Tiger tanks] The German Mark VI heavy tank, commonly known as the Tiger, entered service in late 1942. It weighed 60 tons, had a five-man crew, a maximum speed of 25 mph, armor 100 mm thick on the front hull and turret and 50 mm thick on the side, and was armed with a high-velocity 88 mm gun. The Tiger II, commonly known as the Royal Tiger or King Tiger, entered service in the summer of 1944. It weighed 76 tons, had armor 150 mm thick on the front hull, and was armed with a more powerful version of the 88 mm gun. Allied soldiers often identified other German armored vehicles as Tigers, including the more common Mark IV medium tank, whose silhouette closely resembled that of the Tiger I. The Germans deployed fourteen Tiger I tanks to Arnhem and Elst, beginning on September 19, and twenty-eight Tiger II tanks to the Arnhem-Oosterbeek area, beginning on September 24, 1944.

379.24–25 secret German air-force . . . the Russians] The German military maintained a secret aircraft training school in the Soviet Union from 1926 to 1933 in order to circumvent the Treaty of Versailles, which prohibited Germany from having military aircraft.

379.33–34 Bittrich . . . innocent and released] A French military court in Marseilles sentenced Bittrich on June 23, 1953, to five-years imprisonment for his involvement in the hanging of seventeen suspected members of the French Resistance at Nîmes in March 1944. The verdict was later reversed, and Bittrich was released in 1954. After returning to Germany Bittrich became active in the HIAG, a controversial right-wing Waffen SS veteran organization.

380.33–34 "*der alte Frundsberg*"] "Old man Frundsberg."

381.13 Mark V Panther] The Panther medium tank weighed 49 tons, had a five-man crew, a maximum speed of 29 mph, and was armed with a high-velocity 75 mm gun. Its frontal armor, 80 mm thick, was sloped to deflect antitank shells; the side armor was 40 mm thick.

381.15 self-propelled guns] The StuG III, the most common German self-propelled gun, was a turretless tracked armored vehicle built on a tank chassis. It weighed 26 tons, was armed with a casemate-mounted high-velocity 75 mm gun, had a four-man crew, a maximum speed of 25 mph, and frontal armor 80 mm thick.

394.5   Irish Guards Armored Group] The Group was made up of the 3rd Irish Guards, an infantry battalion commanded by J.O.E. Vandeleur (1903–1988), and the 2nd Irish Guards, an armored battalion led by his second cousin, Lieutenant Colonel Giles Vandeleur (1911–1978).

395.32   rocket-firing Typhoons] The Hawker Typhoon, a single-engine, single-seat fighter bomber, was armed with four 20 mm cannon and could be equipped to fire eight unguided air-to-ground rockets with 60-pound warheads.

396.16   famed Guards Armored Division] Formed in 1941, the division went into action for the first time in Normandy in July 1944.

396.30   brigade major] The chief of staff of a British brigade.

398.35–38   Gorman . . . killed its crew] Both crews escaped after Gorman (1923–2014) encountered the German tank, a Tiger II, near Caen on July 18, 1944.

401.6–7   "Praise the Lord . . . Ammunition."] Patriotic song (1942) written by Frank Loesser (1910–1969) that was inspired by a remark reportedly made by a U.S. Navy chaplain during the Japanese attack on Pearl Harbor.

403.36–37   Louis Mendez . . . 508th Regiment] Mendez (1915–2001) commanded the 3rd Battalion of the 508th Parachute Infantry Regiment.

407.27   diameter of three to five miles] This is possibly an editing error, with "diameter" appearing in the place of "radius," i.e. the "22" set had an effective range of three to five miles.

416.20   Halifaxes, Stirlings, and Albemarles] The Halifax and Stirling were four-engine heavy bombers, the Albemarle a twin-engine medium bomber.

416.29–30   Tempests . . . Lightnings] The Tempest was a single-engine, single-seat fighter; the Mosquito, a twin-engine, two-seat light bomber; the Lightning, a twin-engine, twin-boom, single-seat fighter bomber.

428.5–6   Flying Fortresses . . . nightly bombing] The American B-17 Flying Fortress was used for daylight bombing, while the night bombing of Germany was carried out by the R.A.F. using Lancasters, Halifaxes, and Mosquitoes.

442.30   Walter Cronkite] Cronkite (1916–2009) joined CBS in 1950 and was the anchor and managing editor of the CBS Evening News, 1962–1981.

443.25   Unteroffizier] A general term for noncommissioned officers that can also be used specifically for a rank equivalent to a sergeant in the U.S. Army.

448.38   75 mm. howitzer] The 75 mm howitzer used by British and American airborne troops fired a 14.6-pound shell and had a range of 9,760 yards (5.5 miles).

449.36   17-pounder artillery pieces] The 17-pounder was a British antitank gun that fired a high-velocity 76.2 mm projectile weighing seventeen pounds.

455.6–7 rocket-propelled . . . oversized mortar shells] A 320 mm rocket launcher that could fire shells weighing 174 pounds out to a range of 2,400 yards.

455.35 *Nebelwerfer*] "Smoke thrower." The smaller *Nebelwerfer* were multi-barreled rocket launchers that fired 150 mm and 210 mm mortar shells.

460.17 a P-47] A Thunderbolt; see note 151.14.

460.28 a P-51] A Mustang; see note 151.14.

464.28 an 88] See note 168.37.

465.34 Daphne du Maurier] Du Maurier (1907–1989) was the author of *Jamaica Inn* (1936), *Rebecca* (1938), and *Frenchman's Creek* (1941). Her later works included the stories "The Birds" (1952) and "Don't Look Now" (1971).

469.7 Bren gun] See note 90.1.

469.12 Sherman] British name for the American M4 medium tank, which equipped most British armored units in 1944–45. The Sherman weighed 33 tons, had a five-man crew, a maximum speed of 25 mph, armor ranging in thickness from 25 to 75 mm, and was armed with a medium-velocity 75 mm gun. While the Sherman proved to be mechanically reliable and had a faster turret traverse than German tanks, its frontal armor provided inadequate protection against high-velocity German 75 mm and 88 mm armor-piercing shells, while its 75 mm gun proved incapable of penetrating the frontal armor of Panther and Tiger tanks under almost all combat conditions.

470.10 Bren gun carrier] See note 173.36.

471.3 Sten guns] See note 53.38. The British airborne forces at Arnhem used the Mark V Sten, an improved version with a wooden stock, pistol grip, and forward grip, while other troops continued to use the all-metal Mark II.

471.38–39 a 17-pounder Sherman] In 1944 the British began equipping modified Sherman tanks with high-velocity 17-pounder antitank guns (see note 449.36) in order to engage German armor on more equal terms (see note 469.12). In the Guards Armored Division about one in four Shermans carried a 17-pounder. (In order to store the larger ammunition used by the new gun, the crew was reduced from five men to four.)

481.30 Players] A British cigarette company.

483.13 Schmeisser] See note 88.15.

484.38 Vickers machine gun] A water-cooled, tripod-mounted, belt-fed British medium machine gun that fired .303-caliber ammunition.

493.14 Piat] An abbreviation for Projector, Infantry, Anti-Tank.

499.21–22 airborne forces . . . Warsaw, Poland] An uprising by the underground Polish Home Army began in Warsaw on August 1, 1944. The Germans used aircraft, heavy artillery, and tanks against the insurgents while sending special SS units made up of German criminals and Russian deserters into the city. More than 200,000 Poles were killed and most of Warsaw was destroyed before the fighting ended on October 2. During the uprising R.A.F. aircraft based in Italy flew low-level night missions to parachute supplies to the insurgents.

506.18   M-1 rifles] See note 114.37.

506.24   Tommy gun] See note 161.13.

515.37   21st Panzer Grenadier Regiment] The regiment was part of the 10th SS Panzer Division. ("Panzer grenadiers" were motorized infantry transported by truck or in half-tracks; most German infantry units in 1944 still marched on foot and relied upon horse-drawn transport.)

516.1   *Panzerfäuste*] See note 191.13–14.

516.38–39   German version . . . firing a 20-pound projectile] The *Panzer-schreck* (see note 191.13–14) weighed 24 pounds and fired a 7-pound projectile.

522.21   a 6-pounder antitank gun] The 6-pounder antitank gun fired a high-velocity 57 mm projectile weighing six pounds. It was easier to transport and position than the heavier 17-pounder antitank gun, but not as effective when faced by heavy German armor.

538.15   Teller mines] See note 173.6.

542.30   Brigadier Norman Gwatkin, chief of staff] Gwatkin (1899–1971) was commander of the 5th Guards Armored Brigade and J.O.E. Vandeleur's immediate superior; Lieutenant Colonel Patrick Hobart (1917–1986) was GSO 1 (chief of staff) of the Guards Armored Division.

547.7–8   Robert Cole . . . Medal of Honor] Cole (1915–1944) was post-humously awarded the Medal of Honor on October 4, 1944, for leading a bayonet charge on the outskirts of Carentan on June 11, 1944.

549.1   "Dutch" Schultz] See note 50.22.

549.2   Browning automatic gunner] See note 170.14.

551.30   Messerschmitts and FW-190's] The Messerschmitt Bf 109 and Focke-Wulf 190 were both single-engine, single-seat fighters.

554.29   Major J.L. Waddy] John L. Waddy (b. 1920) was not related to Major Peter Waddy (1919–1944), who was killed in Arnhem on September 18 (see p. 532.31–38).

560.30–31   Hackett was a cavalryman] Hackett (1910–1997) was commissioned in the 8th King's Royal Irish Hussars in 1933 and had been wounded in North Africa in 1942 while leading a squadron of Stuart light tanks.

587.16–17   *Nebelwerfer* mortar thrower . . . screaming sound] *Nebelwerfer* rockets were fitted with sirens that wailed in flight in order to increase their psychological impact.

591.20–21   Barlow never reached . . . "He simply vanished"] In *Arnhem 1944: The Airborne Battle, 17–26 September* (1994), Martin Middlebrook quoted from an account by Captain John McCooke of the 2nd South Staffords, who encountered Hilaro Barlow (1906–1944) and his batman, Lance-Corporal Raymond Singer, near the river in Arnhem. As the three men moved toward the front lines a mortar shell killed Singer and disintegrated Barlow's body, leaving his remains in an unidentifiable condition.

591.38   Bailey bridge] A steel bridge assembled from prefabricated sections.

598.14   liberating Warsaw] See note 499.21–22.

616.3   Mark IV's] See note 221.3.

622.4   5 Guards Brigade] One of the two brigades in the Guards Armored Division.

623.21–22   Major Herman Giskes, Nazi spy chief] Giskes (1896–1977) was the Abwehr counterintelligence chief for Holland.

623.29   British intelligence] Nine of the agents captured in Holland worked for the British secret intelligence service (M.I.6), while fifty-one were sent by the Special Operations Executive, a rival organization founded in July 1940 to organize and support resistance networks in occupied Europe that would engage in sabotage, subversion, and guerrilla warfare.

632.1–2   *Kampfgruppe*] Battle Group.

638.27   Anzio] After fighting in Sicily and southern Italy, the 504th Parachute Infantry Regiment landed by sea at Anzio on January 22, 1944, as part of the Allied assault force attempting to outflank the Gustav Line. The 504th fought on the beachhead until March 23, when it was withdrawn after losing nearly 600 men killed, wounded, or missing. It joined the 82nd Airborne Division in England in April, but was prevented by a shortage of replacements from participating in the Normandy invasion.

662.28–29   Brigadier Gwatkin, . . . chief of staff] See note 542.30.

669.20   batteries . . . 64th Medium Regiment] The regiment was equipped with 4.5-inch guns that could fire a 55-pound shell 11.65 miles.

671.2   soldiers from the Glider Pilot Regiment] Members of the Glider Pilot Regiment were trained to fight as infantry.

686.39   "*Sehr warm*"] "Very hot."

687.20   Glenn Miller's "In the Mood"] Song (1938) with music by Joe Garland (1903–1977). Miller recorded a successful instrumental version in 1939, the same year that Andy Razaf (1895–1973) wrote lyrics to the tune.

692.21   DUKWs] See note 170.10.

692.31   Dragoon Guards] The 4th/7th Dragoon Guards, part of the independent 8th Armored Brigade.

706.3 the 32nd Guards Brigade] One of the two brigades in the Guards Armored Division.

708.18 Spandau machine guns] Name used by Allied soldiers for the German MG34 and MG42, air-cooled, belt-fed machine guns that fired 7.92 mm ammunition. Both weapons had a significantly higher rate of fire than Allied machine guns.

712.29–34 Alan Wood . . . all are dead] Alan Wood (1914–1957) continued to report for the *Daily Express* after returning from Arnhem. On March 24, 1945, he parachuted into Germany with the 6th Airborne Division during the Allied assault crossing of the Rhine, and was seriously wounded, losing a leg. Wood wrote several books, including *The Falaise Road* (1944) and biographies of J. Arthur Rank (1952) and Bertrand Russell (1957). He committed suicide in 1957 after being diagnosed with an incurable disease. Stanley Maxted (1897–1963) reported on the Japanese surrender in 1945, worked for the BBC after the war, and became an actor. Maxted died from heart disease in 1963. Guy Byam (1918–1945) flew to Berlin on February 3, 1945, as a correspondent on an American B-17 bomber. His aircraft was damaged by flak and disappeared over the North Sea while returning to England. Jack Smyth (1918–1956) was captured at Arnhem and held in a German P.O.W. camp until April 1945. He later became managing editor of the *Irish Press* and published *Five Days in Hell* (1956), a memoir of Arnhem and his subsequent captivity. Smyth and his wife, Eileen, died three weeks after its publication when he accidentally drove into the River Liffey in Dublin. Marek Święcicki (1915–1994) published *With the Red Devils at Arnhem* (1945) and *Seven Roads to Bologna* (1946), about the final battles of the Polish Corps in Italy. He later worked for Radio Free Europe and for the Polish section of the Voice of America, 1958–91. Święcicki died in Washington, D.C., in 1994 from cancer.

718.10 "British Grenadiers" and "Scotland the Brave"] "British Grenadiers" is a traditional song dating from the early eighteenth century; "Scotland the Brave" was first published in 1911, although it may have been composed in the late nineteenth century.

718.31–33 "Take no thought . . . be clothed."] Cf. Matthew 6:25, 31, 34.

718.34–35 "Abide With Me"] Hymn with words (1847) by Henry Francis Lyte (1793–1847), sung to "Eventide," a tune composed in 1861 by William Henry Monk (1823–1889).

719.35–36 "Thou shalt not . . . by day"] Psalm 91:5.

727.30–31 Both brigadiers . . . hid out.] John (Shan) Hackett (1910–1997) escaped from the hospital in October with help from the underground and hid with a Dutch family until February 1945, when he managed to cross the lines into Allied territory. Hackett wrote about his escape and months in hiding in a memoir, *I Was a Stranger* (1977). He also was the lead author of a collaborative work, the best-selling *The Third World War: August 1985* (1978).

737.2   commander, Brigadier Ben Walton] Bendyshe Brome Walton (1905–1987) commanded the 130th Brigade, 43rd Division.

738.38–39   his engineering officer . . . Henniker] Henniker was the commander, Royal Engineers, for the 43rd Division.

757.22   Major Robert Cain] Cain (1909–1974) was awarded the Victoria Cross for his gallantry at Arnhem.

765.35   *deprivation . . . terrible winter*] The Germans deliberately deprived the Dutch population of food during the "hunger winter" of 1944–45, resulting in an estimated 16,000 to 20,000 civilian deaths.

770.29   C.Z.] Canal Zone, i.e., the Panama Canal Zone.

784.4   M.C.] Military Cross, a decoration for gallantry awarded to officers.

784.18   M.M.] Military Medal, a decoration for gallantry awarded to soldiers and noncommissioned officers.

795.24   *S.A.S. Regt.*] Special Air Service Regiment, a special forces unit.

795.36   M.C., Bar] The "Bar" denotes a second award of the decoration.

OTHER WORLD WAR II WRITINGS

825.8   Marauder] A B-26 twin-engine medium bomber.

825.15   Col. Nye] Glenn C. Nye (1912–1952) commanded the 322nd Bombardment Group (Medium), stationed at Andrews Field near Great Dunmow, Essex, from May 1943 to July 1944. Nye was later killed in Korea while commanding a wing of A-26 Invader light bombers.

827.14   Havocs] American A-20 twin-engine light bombers, also known as "Bostons" (their R.A.F. name.)

829.8   Col. Joe W. Kelly] Kelly (1910–1979) commanded the 386th Bombardment Group (Medium), January–August 1944.

831.24   Lt.-Col. H. Hankey] Harry G. Hankey (1917–1994) was the operations officer of the 386th Bombardment Group.

834.2   Major E.A. Rodgers] Ervin A. Rodgers (1917–1989) was the assistant operations officer of the 386th.

839.9   MARIGNY] A town about seven miles west of St. Lô. On July 25 American troops had succeeded in breaking through the German defenses west of St. Lô.

839.12   Gen. Bradley] Lieutenant General Omar N. Bradley (1893–1981), commander of the U.S. First Army.

840.4   Lozon] A town about three miles north of Marigny.

842.14   Gen. Patton's Third Army] The U.S. Third Army became active on August 1, 1944, the same day that Bradley became commander of the newly activated 12th Army Group.

846.23   19th Tactical Air Force] The XIX Tactical Air Command, part of the U.S. Ninth Air Force, provided fighter and fighter bomber support for the Third Army.

848.11   Yesterday morning] The morning of December 28, 1944, two days after troops from the Third Army broke through the German forces encircling Bastogne.

848.34   this division] The U.S. 101st Airborne.

849.9   the commander] Brigadier General Anthony McAuliffe (1898–1975), acting commander of the 101st Airborne in the absence of Major General Maxwell Taylor, who was attending a conference in the United States when the German offensive in the Ardennes began on December 16.

850.3–4   destroyed 148 tanks and 28 half-tracks] These claims were not confirmed.

851.3   Volksturm] A German militia, organized in September 1944, made up of previously unconscripted males aged sixteen to sixty.

856.12   Ohrdruf] The Ohrdruf camp was a satellite of the Buchenwald concentration camp.

856.33   Col. Hayden Sears] Sears (1899–1984) was the commander of Combat Command A of the 4th Armored Division.

860.5–6   ordered . . . quisling war criminals] The list of men to be arrested included three former members of the Filipino puppet government, as well as American, Australian, and Dutch nationals accused of making propaganda broadcasts for the Japanese.

860.9–10   Gen. Tojo] Hideki Tojo (1884–1948) served as minister of war, July 1940–July 1944, and as prime minister, October 1941–July 1944. Tojo was convicted of waging wars of aggression and war crimes by the Tokyo international military tribunal and hanged on December 23, 1948.

860.19   Togo] Shigenori Tōgō (1882–1950) served as foreign minister, October 1941–September 1942 and April–August 1945. Togo was convicted by the Tokyo tribunal of waging wars of aggression, sentenced to twenty years, and died in prison.

860.22   Masahara Homma] Homma (1887–1946) commanded the Japanese army in the Philippines, 1941–42. He was convicted of war crimes by an American military tribunal in the Philippines and shot on April 3, 1946.

861.3   B.S.T.] British Summer Time.

864.10   Greater Asiatic War] The Pacific War of 1941–45.

867.2–3   Gen. Eichelberger] Lieutenant General Robert L. Eichelberger (1886–1961), commander of the U.S. Eighth Army.

868.1   *The Major of St. Lô*] Ryan first published this story in the June 8, 1956, issue of *Collier's* and then included it in slightly revised form in *One Minute to Ditch!* (1957), a paperback that collected five of his stories for *Collier's*. *One Minute to Ditch!* included this endnote:

> I saw them bring Tom Howie's body into St. Lô and place it in front of the cathedral. The cathedral was on fire and ruined by shelling, but it was fitting to lay him there. I knew one day I would write the story about him. It took me almost twelve years to do it.
>
> During those twelve years I made three trips back to St. Lô, but it wasn't until 1954 that I learned of the crypt beneath the cathedral and of what had happened to the townspeople in St. Lô during the attack. I had known Howie and the Army side of the story. Now I had both sides of the picture. Mrs. Howie sent me the Major's letters and General Gerhardt supplied additional data. In the fall of 1954 I sat down and wrote a rough draft of the story. By April, 1955 I had written the story nine times. Factually it is right, but I am still not entirely satisfied with it. You always think when writing about a man like Howie that you ought to do more.
>
> The story appeared in *Collier's* June, 1956. The same week it was televised on Du Pont's "Cavalcade of America" (ABC-TV). It was re-shown June 4, 1957 on the same network for the same sponsors. I wrote the television treatment.

869.6   "the Blue and the Gray" Division] When the 29th Division was formed in 1917 it was made up of National Guard units from New Jersey, Maryland, and Virginia that traced their lineage back to the Civil War.

869.12   Major General Charles H. Gerhardt] Gerhardt (1895–1976) commanded the 29th Division from July 1943 through the end of the war.

870.5   Sidney Bingham's] Bingham (1915–1993) became commander of the 116th Infantry in December 1944 and led it for the remainder of the war.

872.19–20   Brigadier General Norman (Dutch) Cota] Cota (1893–1971) was the assistant commander of the 29th Division, October 1943–August 1944, and commander of the 28th Division from August 1944 through the end of the war.

873.29   Puntenney] William H. Puntenney (1919–1999) became the commander of the 3rd Battalion, 116th Infantry, after Howie's death and led it for the remainder of the war.

873.34   William J. Witte] Witte (1914–1978) served as operations officer of the 29th Division throughout the 1944–45 campaign.

875.24–26   *the 7,000 . . . battle for the town.*] In 1944 the authorized full strength of an American infantry division was 14,253 men. The 29th Division reported a total of 8,972 battle casualties (1,818 killed, 6,060 wounded, 317 injured, 777 missing) for June and July 1944.

877.36   Spithead] An anchorage between Southampton and the Isle of Wight.

878.18–26   ancient British gunboat . . . refused to retract.] H.M.S. *Erebus*, an 8,000-ton monitor, displayed the signal sent by Admiral Lord Horatio Nelson (1758–1805) at the battle of Trafalgar on October 21, 1805. Commissioned in 1916, *Erebus* had bombarded German positions along the Belgian coast in World War I and participated in the invasion of Sicily in 1943. *Erebus* crossed the Channel under its own power on the night of June 5, 1944, and on D-Day fired a total of forty rounds at several German shore batteries before the premature explosion of a shell inside the barrel of one of its twin 15-inch guns put the ship out of action. After being repaired *Erebus* returned into service, bombarding German positions in Normandy during the summer and shelling Walcheren in November as part of the opening of the Scheldt.

879.16   the Wannsee] A lake in southwest Berlin.

880.6   Harold Blakeley . . . 4th Division] Brigadier General Harold Blakeley (1893–1966) served as the artillery commander of the 4th Division, January–December 1944, and commanded the division from December 1944 through the end of the war.

880.25–26   Major Elmore Swenson] Swenson (1916–1972) commanded the light aircraft used by the 29th Division for artillery observation and reconnaissance.

881.3   "Kilroy was here"] Graffiti message popular among American servicemen during World War II.

881.18   Basil Spence, a noted architect] Spence (1907–1976) served as a camouflage officer with the Royal Artillery. He was best known for his modern design for the rebuilt Coventry Cathedral, completed in 1962.

884.11   DC-3s] See note 87.2.

884.19–22   President Roosevelt's . . . on foreign soil."] Cf. Roosevelt's speech to a campaign rally held in Boston on October 30, 1940: "And while I am talking to you mothers and fathers, I give you one more assurance. I have said this before, but I shall say it again and again and again: Your boys are not going to be sent into any foreign wars. They are going into training to form a force so strong that, by its very existence, it will keep the threat of war far away from our shores. The purpose of our defense is defense."

884.24   Capt. St. Julien P. Rosemond] Rosemond (1912–1985) served with the 377th Parachute Field Artillery Battalion.

887.18–20 Omaha Beach . . . Blakeley] Blakeley (see note 880.6) landed on Utah Beach, not Omaha.

888.24 Verdun] The battle of Verdun, February 21–December 18, 1916, ended in a defensive victory for the French at the cost of 377,000 men killed, wounded, or missing.

889.1 *William Buckley*] William E. Buckley (1913–2008) was vice president of Henry Holt, 1953–58.

889.14–16 Phyllis . . . her husband] Phyllis Jackson (1907–1977), a literary agent with MCA, and Alan R. Jackson (c. 1905–1965), a story editor for Paramount Pictures.

889.17 Matson] Literary agent Harold Matson (1898–1988).

890.19–20 *One Minute to Ditch!* . . . five of my pieces] The paperback, published in 1957, collected five stories Ryan had written for *Collier's* in 1955–56: "One Minute to Ditch!," about the forced landing of an airliner in the Pacific in October 1956; "The Major of St. Lô" (see pp. 868–75 in this volume); "What Made Vuky Race?," about Indy 500 driver Bill Vukovich; "I Rode the World's Fastest Sub," about the U.S.S. *Albacore*; and "Five Desperate Hours in Cabin 56," about the sinking of the ocean liner *Andrea Doria*.

890.22 the two pieces] "One Minute to Ditch!" and "Five Desperate Hours in Cabin 56."

892.7 (Henry Ehrlich)] Ehrlich (1912–1995) was a features editor at *McCall's*.

892.9–10 Otis Weiss] Otis Wiese (1905–1972), the editor and publisher of *McCall's*.

892.18 Landmark book . . . Bruce Bliven jnr] *The Story of D-Day: June 6, 1944* (1956), by Bruce Bliven Jr. (1916–2002), published by Random House in its Landmark Books series for young readers.

892.22 Lord-Life deal] Walter Lord (1917–2002) had been assisted by *Life* magazine in researching *Day of Infamy*, his account of the attack on Pearl Harbor. The book was excerpted by *Life* in December 1956 and then published by Henry Holt in March 1957.

893.1 *Peter Schwed*] Schwed (1911–2003) was executive editor and vice president of Simon and Schuster, 1957–66, and publisher of its trade book division, 1966–72.

893.20 Maxwell D. Taylor, the Chief of Staff.] Taylor (1901–1987) served as chief of staff of the U.S. Army, 1955–59.

893.29 Teddy White] The journalist Theodore H. White (1915–1986), author of *Thunder Out of China* (with Annalee Jacoby, 1946) and *Fire in the Ashes: Europe in Mid Century* (1953), had worked with Ryan at *Collier's* in 1955–56. He would later write the best-selling *The Making of the President, 1960* (1961).

897.12   William Rhinehart Washington] Washington (1918–1987) was the executive officer of the 2nd Battalion, 16th Infantry, on D-Day. He was awarded the Distinguished Service Cross for his actions on June 6.

898.2   Lt Col Regular Army] Washington eventually retired with the rank of colonel.

898.28   Lt Shaughnessy] First Lieutenant John J. Shaughnessy (1917–1944) commanded a machine gun platoon in Company H, 2nd Battalion, 16th Infantry.

899.9–11   church steeple . . . US Navy] The shelling of the church in Colleville-sur-Mer by U.S. destroyers killed or wounded several men from the 16th Infantry.

899.14   Lt Duckworth] First Lieutenant Edmund W. Duckworth (1921–1944), the executive officer of Company E, 2nd Battalion, 16th Infantry, was hit in the head and killed when he looked over the top of the shingle bank he had taken cover behind. His widow, Audrey Travers Duckworth (1927–2001), and their son Patrick (1944–1995) moved to the United States in 1946. Duckworth was awarded the Silver Star twice for valor in Tunisia and in Sicily. See also p. 207.10–15 in this volume.

899.21–24   Where were you . . . EASY RED Beach] Washington apparently misunderstood the questions and reported where he was at midnight on June 4 and 5 instead of June 5 and 6. At midnight on June 6 Washington was inland in the vicinity of Colleville-sur-Mer.

903.20–22   "NORTH AFRICA . . . ITALY."] Richards had fought in 1943 with the 1st Parachute Brigade in Tunisia, where they were used as infantry. The brigade jumped into Sicily on the night of July 13, 1943, with the objective of capturing the Primosole Bridge over the Simeto River, and landed by sea at Taranto in southern Italy on September 9.

904.7–8   THE AMERICANS WOULD DROP . . . PROPER D.Z.] The 1st Parachute Brigade was flown to Sicily by American transport aircraft and ended up widely scattered, with fewer than 300 men out of 1,856 reaching their rendezvous points.

904.20   OUR OWN HOME GUARD] The British Home Guard, formed in 1940, was made up of men from ages seventeen to sixty-five who were not otherwise in military service.

904.35   LT. HELINGOE] Lieutenant John Edward Helingoe (1923–1996) was captured and spent the remainder of the war in a German prisoner-of-war camp.

Index

948

*This book is set in 10 point ITC Galliard Pro, a face
designed for digital composition by Matthew Carter and based
on the sixteenth-century face Granjon. The paper is acid-free
lightweight opaque that will not turn yellow or brittle with age.
The binding is sewn, which allows the book to open easily and lie flat.
The binding board is covered in Brillianta, a woven rayon cloth
made by Van Heek–Scholco Textielfabrieken, Holland.
Composition by Dedicated Book Services.
Printing and binding by LSC Communications.
Designed by Bruce Campbell.*

THE LIBRARY OF AMERICA SERIES

Library of America fosters appreciation of America's literary heritage by publishing, and keeping permanently in print, authoritative editions of America's best and most significant writing. An independent nonprofit organization, it was founded in 1979 with seed funding from the National Endowment for the Humanities and the Ford Foundation.

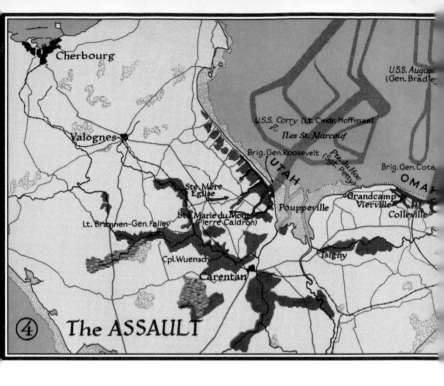

④ The ASSAULT

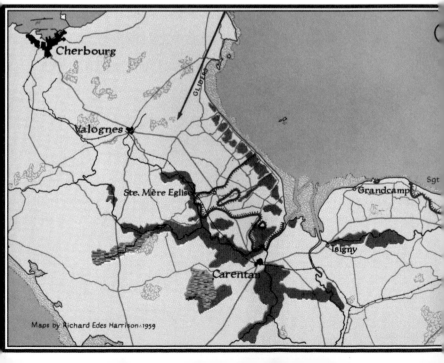

Maps by Richard Edes Harrison · 1959